America's
Top-Rated Cities:
A Statistical Handbook

Volume 2

2007
Fourteenth Edition

America's
Top-Rated Cities:
A Statistical Handbook

Volume 2: Western Region

A UNIVERSAL REFERENCE BOOK

Grey House
Publishing

PUBLISHER:	Leslie Mackenzie
EDITORIAL DIRECTOR:	Laura Mars-Proietti
EDITOR:	David Garoogian
PRODUCTION:	Melissa Davis; Karynn Ketiinq; Jael Powell
MARKETING DIRECTOR:	Jessica Moody

A Universal Reference Book
Grey House Publishing, Inc.
185 Millerton Road
Millerton, NY 12546
Phone: 518.789.8700 Fax: 518.789.0545
www.greyhouse.com
e-mail: books @greyhouse.com

Fourteenth edition
Printed in the USA

Publisher's Cataloging-in-Publication Data
(Prepared by The Donohue Group, Inc.)

America's top-rated cities. Vol. II, Western region : a statistical handbook.. -- 1992 -

  v. : ill. ; cm.
Annual, 1995-
Irregular, 1992-1993
ISSN: 1082-7102

1. Cities and towns--Ratings—Western States--Statistics--Periodicals. 2. Cities and towns—Western States--Statistics--Periodicals. 3. Social indicators—Western States--Periodicals. 4. Quality of life—Western States--Statistics--Periodicals. 5. Western States--Social conditions--Statistics--Periodicals. I. Title: America's top rated cities. II. Title: Western region

HT123.5.S6 A44
307.76/0973/05   95644648

4-Volume Set	ISBN: 978-1-59237-184-6
Volume 1	ISBN: 978-1-59237-185-3
Volume 2	**ISBN: 978-1-59237-186-0**
Volume 3	ISBN: 978-1-59237-187-7
Volume 4	ISBN: 978-1-59237-188-4

Albuquerque, New Mexico

Anchorage, Alaska

Bellevue, Washington

Boise City, Idaho

Boulder, Colorado

Colorado Springs, Colorado

Denver, Colorado

Eugene, Oregon

Fort Collins, Colorado

Honolulu, Hawaii

Irvine, California

Las Vegas, Nevada

Los Angeles, California

Phoenix, Arizona

Portland, Oregon

Provo, Utah

Reno, Nevada

Salt Lake City, Utah

Sacramento, California

San Diego, California

San Francisco, California

San Jose, California

Scottsdale, Arizona

Seattle, Washington

Thousand Oaks, California

Tucson, Arizona

Appendices

Introduction

Welcome to the fourteenth edition of *America's Top-Rated Cities (ATRC)*, a concise, statistical, 4-volume work identifying America's top-rated cities with populations of 100,000 or more. As with previous editions, it covers 100 cities that have received high marks for their business and living environment from both long-running surveys, such as those appearing in *Money, Forbes, Men's Health, Entrepreneur, Conde Nast Traveler,* and *Expansion Management,* as well as first-hand visits, interviews and reports of our editors and research staff.

Each volume covers a different region of the country -- Southern, Western, Central and Eastern. Each includes a detailed Table of Contents, City Chapters, five Appendices and Maps that locate all top-rated cities. Each city chapter incorporates information from hundreds of resources to create three major sections: **Background** – updated with significant news in both business and living environments; **Rankings** – enhanced with survey results from over 200 sources (many more than 2006); and **Statistical Tables** – updated with new data plus many new data points. After the city chapters, **Comparative Statistics** compare the data in 73 tables.

New cities to this edition include Edison NJ, Cary NC and Thousand Oaks CA.

BACKGROUND

Each of the 100 city chapters begins with an informative, Background that combines history with current events. Our revision process updates these narratives to reflect changes that have occurred in the city during the past year. They touch on the city's environment, politics, employment, cultural offerings, climate, and often include interesting trivia. For example (answers at end of Introduction):

1. Where can you watch glacier calving (big chunks of ice crashing into the water)?
2. Which city's name was most likely derived from an error in pronouncing Belle Fleuve (Beautiful River)?
3. Where will you find the World Figure Skating Museum and Hall of Fame?
4. Which city ranks 9th in the world for cities with the most billionaires?
5. What was the original name of Edison, the city where Thomas Edison invented the phonograph and the light bulb?

RANKINGS

Again this year, this section has grown tremendously over previous editions. Many cities have 6 or more pages of Rankings, with data from more than 200 books, articles, and reports – many more than last edition. Again this year we categorized the Rankings into **11 categories** for easy reference: **General; Business/Finance; Health/Environment; Women/Minorities; Seniors/Retirement; Children/Family; Safety; Sports/Recreation; Dating/Romance; Culture/Performing Arts; Miscellaneous.**

The Rankings are still presented in an easy-to-read, bulleted format and includes results from both annual surveys and one-shot studies. You'll recognize many topics from previous editions, such as **Healthiest Cities for People and Pets . . . Most Creative . . . Picture Perfect . . . Most Fun . . . Safest . . . Most Alive . . . Most Wired . . . Best to Save Money . . . Most Polite . . . Top Arts . . . Best to Relocate/Retire . . . Best/Worst for Dating . . . Most Vegetarian-Friendly . . . Least**

Stressful . . . **Best Sleeping** . . . **Low-Carb** and overall **Best Cities** for Black Women, Singles, Men, Lesbians, Children, Sports Fans, Online Shoppers, Tourists, and Job Seekers.

This 2007 edition also includes many new Rankings, such as **Best Drivers . . . Road Rage . . . Sweatiest . . . Brainiest . . . Greenest . . . Dog Friendliest . . . and Most Inventive**

You will also find Rankings that are not that flattering, such **as Fattest . . . Asthma Hot Spots . . . Most Dangerous for Pedestrians . . . Fall/Spring Allergy Capital . . . Most Polluted . . . Meanest Cities**. Top–rated doesn't mean perfect, and *America's Top-Rated Cities* provides an accurate, balanced portrait of featured cities.

Sources for these Rankings include both well-known magazines and other media, including *Forbes, Fortune, Inc. Magazine, Working Mother, Prevention, Business Week, Men's Journal,* and *Travel & Leisure,* as well as resources not as well known, such as *Inside Triathlon, Country Home, The National Coalition for the Homeless, Center for Digital Government, U.S. Conference of Mayors, Partners for Livable Communities,* and *Mercer Human Resources Consulting.*

STATISTICAL TABLES
As with the Rankings, the Statistical Tables have been increased and enhanced over the years so that now, each city chapter in this 2007 edition includes 94 tables – 52 in the BUSINESS section and 42 in the LIVING section. This is 6 more tables than the 2006 edition and more than 50 more than the earliest editions. As for all new editions, at least 75% of all data has been updated and several tables have been significantly enhanced.

Business Environment includes hard facts and figures on 13 topics, including City Finances, Demographics, Income, Employment, Taxes, Real Estate, and Transportation. **Living Environment** also includes 13 topics, such as Housing, Health, Education, Safety, Recreation, Media, and Climate. New topics include **Best High Schools**, **Mortality Rates**, **Health Risk Data**, **Educational Attainment** and **Home Price Valuations.** In addition, you'll find new data on **air quality.**

To compile the Statistical Tables, our editors have again turned to a wide range of sources, some of which are obvious, such as the *U.S. Census Bureau, U.S. Environmental Protection Agency, Centers for Disease Control and Prevention,* and the *Federal Bureau of Investigation,* as well as some more obscure, like *The Tax Foundation, The Council for Community and Economic Research, Claritas,* and *Glenmary Research Center.*

APPENDICES
Appendix A – Historical Metropolitan Area Definitions

Appendix B – Current Metropolitan Area Definitions

Appendix C – Counties

Appendix D – Chambers of Commerce and Economic Development Organizations: Addresses, phone numbers and fax numbers of these additional resources help readers find more detailed information on each city.

Appendix E – State Departments of Labor and Employment: A source for additional, more specific economic and employment data, with address and phone number for easy access.

Appendix F – Comparative Statistics: City-by-city comparison comprised of 73 tables. All volumes include all 100 cities, making for easy comparisons.

As in all previous editions, the material provided by public and private agencies and organizations was supplemented by original research, numerous library sources and Internet sites. *America's Top-Rated Cities, 2007*, is designed for a wide range of readers: private individuals considering relocating a residence or business; professionals considering expanding their businesses or changing careers; corporations considering relocation, opening up additional offices or creating new divisions; government agencies; general and market researchers; real estate consultants; human resource personnel; urban planners; investors; and urban government students.

1. Anchorage
2. Buffalo
3. Colorado Springs
4. Dallas
5. Raritan

Western United States

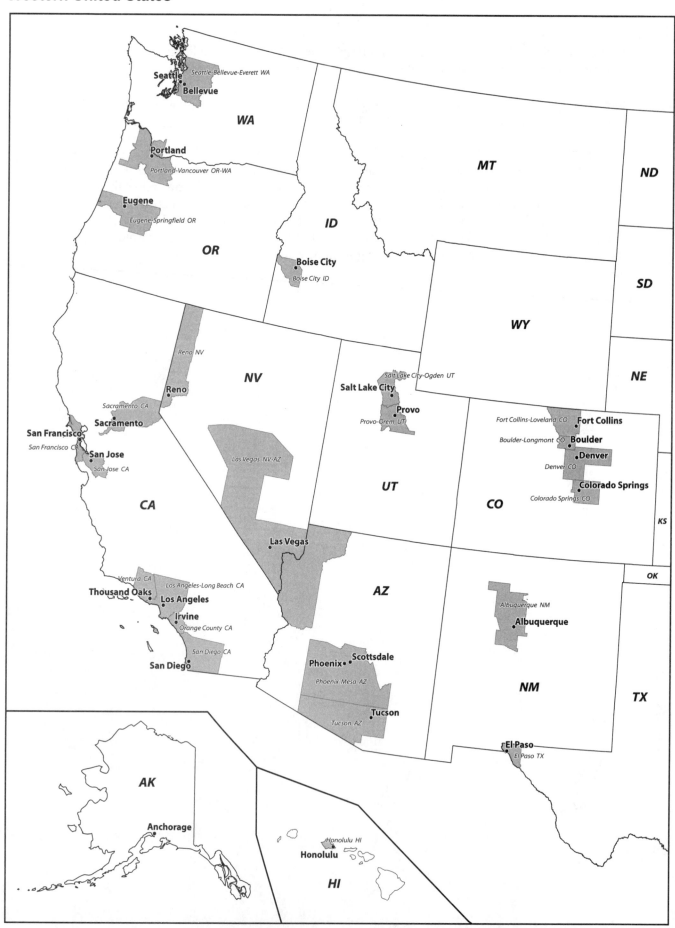

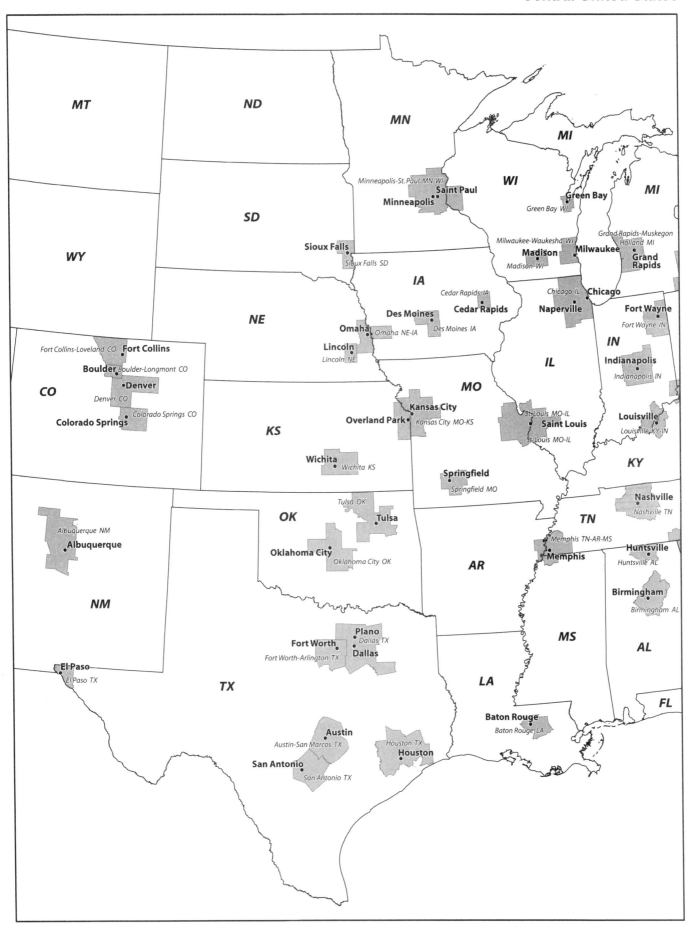

Central United States

Southeastern United States

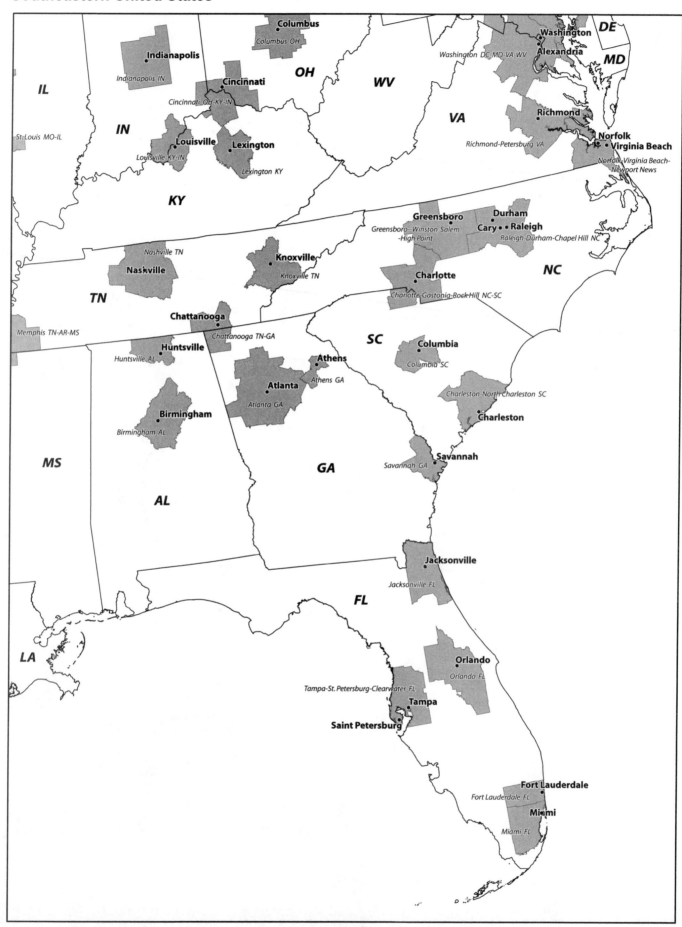

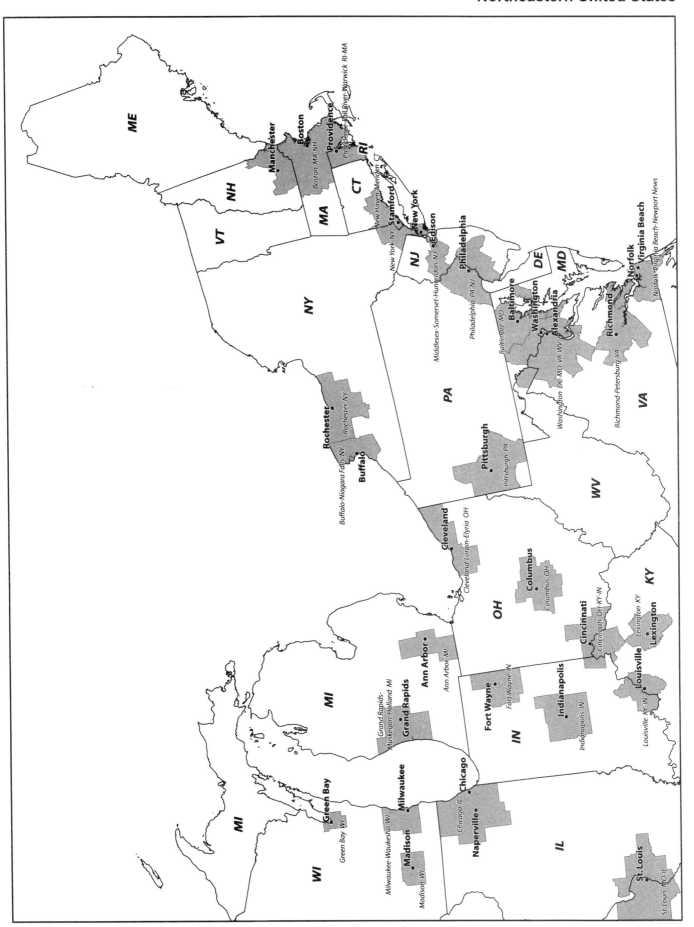

Albuquerque, New Mexico

Background

Pueblo Indians originally inhabited what is now the Albuquerque metropolitan area. In the sixteenth century, Spaniards began pushing up from Mexico in search of riches, but it was not until 1706 that they founded the settlement, naming it after the viceroy of New Spain, San Francisco Xavier de Alburquerque, a duke whose permission was needed to set up the town. Eventually, the city's name would lose a consonant and become Albuquerque. The city earned the sobriquet "Duke City" because of its namesake.

In the early nineteenth century, Mexico secured her independence from Spanish rule and allowed Americans to enter the province of New Mexico to trade. During the Mexican War of the 1840s, Americans under the command of General Stephen Kearny captured the town, and New Mexico was transferred to the United States in the Treaty of Guadalupe Hidalgo, ending the war.

During the Civil War, Confederates held the town for a few weeks, eventually surrendering it to a besieging Union army. After the war, the railroad arrived in 1880, bringing with it people and business. In 1891 the town received a city charter. Albuquerque became an important site for tuberculosis sanatoriums during the next few decades because of the healing nature of the dry desert air.

World War II had a great impact on Albuquerque, as Kirtland Air Force Base became an important site for the making of the atomic bomb. Sandia National Laboratories was founded in the city after the war and played an important role in defense-related research during the Cold War.

Even though the Cold War is now over, the defense industry is still of prime significance to Albuquerque. Institutions once dedicated to defense research are now involved in applying such technology to the private sector, making the city a perfect place for high-tech concerns. In addition to Sandia, the city hosts a branch of the Air Force Research Laboratories and the Los Alamos National Laboratory. Biotechnical and semiconductor industries also have had a positive impact on the city's economy. In addition, in 2007 Tesla Motors began breaking ground on a $35 million 150,000-square-foot electric car plant. By 2009, Tesla plans to roll-out a four-door, five-person sedan, producing at least 10,000 a year from the West Side plant.

Albuquerque and New Mexico have many programs to assist business. The state has property taxes that are among the lowest in the nation.

More traditional forms of making a living are still present, as the city is located in an area where ranchers raise sheep and other livestock.

Albuquerque is also a critical transportation center for the American Southwest, with two major interstates that intersect there. Its airport, Albuquerque International Sunport, supports more than eight major carriers and five commuter airlines. In 2004, Mayor Martin J. Chavez appointed a task force to study expansion of the facility south and west, creating an "aerotropolis" of state-of-the-art manufacturing and shipping facilities and including a free-trade zone. One such expansion, Mesa del Sol, will be a mixed-used development site on 12,000 acres, connected to the airport by light-rail. The city has recently incorporated a commuter rail line that serves the region. The New Mexico Rail Runner Express system began operation in July 2006, and phase two of the project expanding the line to Sante Fe is expected to be completed in 2008. A new 11-mile bus service, Rapid Ride, is proving to be extremely popular with the city's residents, with such significant increases in ridership that the line was extended in 2007.

There are various venues for higher education located in Albuquerque, the most significant of which is the University of New Mexico.

There are festive events scheduled throughout the year. The annual Albuquerque Balloon Fiesta has become an annual "must" for residents and visitors alike. The city is also home to the annual Gathering of Nations Pow-Wow, an international event featuring over 3,000 indigenous Native American dancers and singers representing more than 500 tribes from Canada and the United States.

Albuquerque enjoys a dry, arid climate, with plenty of sunshine, low humidity, and scant rainfall. More than three-fourths of the daylight hours have sunshine, summer and winter. As in all desert climates, temperatures can fluctuate widely between day and night, all year round. Precipitation is meager during the winter, more abundant in summer with afternoon and evening thunderstorms.

Rankings

General Rankings

■ Albuquerque was ranked #45 out of 331 metro areas in *Cities Ranked & Rated*. Criteria: cost of living; climate; crime; transportation; economy and jobs; education; arts and culture; health and healthcare; leisure. *Cities Ranked & Rated, 1st Edition, 2004*

■ The Albuquerque area was selected as one of "60 Cheap Places to Live" in the U.S. The area appeared in the "Telecommuting Heavens" category. *Forbes.com, August 20, 2004*

Business/Finance Rankings

■ Albuquerque was selected as one of the best places to start and grow a company by *Entrepreneur* and the National Policy Research Council. The Albuquerque metro area ranked #14 out of 63 mid-size metro areas. Criteria: business formation and growth (firms started four to 14 years ago that still employ at least 5 people and experienced rapid growth over the last four years). *Entrepreneur/National Policy Research Council, "Hot Cities for Entrepreneurs," September 2006*

■ The Albuquerque metro area was selected as one of "America's 50 Hottest Cities" for business relocations and expansions. Criteria: industry's most prominent site selection consultants were asked to list their top city choices for relocating and expanding manufacturing companies, taking into consideration such factors as the business climate, work force quality, operating costs, incentive programs, and the ease of working with local political and economic development officials. *Expansion Management, January-February 2007*

■ The Albuquerque metro area was selected as one of the "Top 40 Real Estate Markets" for expanding or relocating businesses. The area ranked #22 out of 40. Criteria: rental costs; purchase prices; and vacancy rates of office and warehouse space. *Expansion Management, October 2006*

■ Intel, in partnership with Sperling's BestPlaces, ranked the 80 "Best Cities for Teleworking" in America. The Albuquerque metro area ranked #15 among mid-sized metro areas. The study identifies cities that hold the greatest potential for teleworking based on a host of factors including typical commuting times, fuel prices, availability of broadband Internet access and percentage of the population in telework friendly jobs. The study also factored in extreme climate and natural hazards. *Intel, "Best Cities for Teleworking," March 30, 2006*

■ The Albuquerque metro area was selected as one of the "25 Hottest Housing Markets" in the U.S. The area ranked #15 out of 156 markets with a home price appreciation rate of 7.7%. Criteria: year-over-year change of median sales price of existing single-family homes between the 4th quarter of 2005 and the 4th quarter of 2006. *National Association of Realtors, Median Sales Price of Existing Single-Family Homes for Metropolitan Areas, 4th Quarter 2006*

■ The Albuquerque metro area appeared on the Milken Institute "2005 Best Performing Cities" index. Rank: #43 out of 200 large metro areas. Criteria: job growth; wage and salary growth; high-tech output growth. *Milken Institute, "2005 Best Performing Cities," February 2006*

■ The Albuquerque metro area was selected as one of "The Best Cities for Doing Business in America." *Inc.* magazine measured employment growth in 393 regions using the following criteria: recent growth trend; mid-term growth; long-term trend; and current year growth. The Albuquerque metro area ranked #29 among mid-sized metro areas and #130 overall. *Inc., May 2006*

■ Albuquerque was identified as one of the 100 "Most Unwired Cities" in the U.S. The area ranked #30 out of the 100 largest metro areas in the U.S. Criteria: number of public and commercial wireless access points (hotspots); airports with wireless Internet access; broadband availability; local wireless networks; and wireless email devices. *Intel, "Most Unwired Cities Survey," June 7, 2005*

- *Forbes* ranked the 200 most populous metro areas in the U.S. in terms of the "Best Places for Business and Careers." The Albuquerque metro area was ranked #6. Criteria: business costs (labor, energy, tax and office space expenses); living costs (housing, transportation, food and other household expenditures); education levels of the work force; job growth; income growth; migration trends; crime rates; and culture/leisure. *Forbes, April 23, 2007*

- Albuquerque was identified as one of the top 20 metro areas with the highest rate of home price appreciation in 2006. The area ranked #19 with a one-year price appreciation of 14.5% through the 4th quarter 2006. *Office of Federal Housing Enterprise Oversight, House Price Index, 4th Quarter 2006*

- *Kiplinger's Personal Finance* ranked 101 U.S. cities in terms of their total tax burdens. Albuquerque ranked #36 (#1 had the lowest overall tax burden). Criteria: state income tax; property tax; sales tax; personal property tax; and gasoline tax. *Kiplinger's Personal Finance, July 2004*

- *Fortune* ranked the 100 largest metro areas in the U.S. in terms of projected median home price change in 2006. The Albuquerque metro area ranked #14. *Fortune, "The Top 100: Is the Party Over?" December 26, 2005*

Health/Environment Rankings

- Sanofi-aventis, in partnership with Sperling's BestPlaces, ranked the 50 worst cities for respiratory infections in the U.S. Albuquerque ranked #42. Criteria: prevalence of sinusitis, pharyngitis (sore throat), bronchitis, acute upper respiratory infections, pneumonia, otitis media (middle ear infection), other respiratory tract infections and the common cold; total per capita prescriptions written for oral antibiotics for respiratory tract infections; and prevalence of state level antibiotic resistance. *Sanofi-aventis, "America's Worst Cities for Respiratory Infections," December 6, 2005*

- The Albuquerque metro area appeared in *Country Home's* "2007 Best Green Places Report". The area ranked #128. Criteria included: air and watershed quality; miles of mass transit; green power; number of farmer's markets, organic producers and groceries. *Country Home, "2007 Best Green Places Report," April 2007*

- The American Podiatric Medical Association and *Prevention* magazine ranked America's 100 most populated cities based on fitness-walker friendliness. The best cities have safe streets, beautiful places to walk, mild weather and good air quality. Albuquerque ranked #45. *Prevention, "The Best Walking Cities of 2007," April 2007; American Podiatric Medical Association, "2007 Best Fitness-Walking Cities"*

- Albuquerque was selected as one of the 25 fittest cities in America by *Men's Fitness Online*. It ranked #13 out of America's 50 largest cities. Criteria: gyms/sporting goods; nutrition; exercise/sports; overweight/sedentary; junk food; alcohol; smoking; television; air and water quality; climate; geography; commute time; parks/open space; recreation facilities; health care; motivation; civic legislation and leadership. *Men's Fitness Online, America's Fittest/Fattest Cities 2006*

- Albuquerque was identified as a "2007 Asthma Capital." The area ranked #57 out of the nation's 100 largest metropolitan areas. Twelve factors were used to identify the most challenging places to live for people with asthma: estimated prevalence; self-reported prevalence; crude death rate for asthma; annual pollen score; annual air quality; public smoking laws; number of board-certified asthma specialists; school inhaler access laws; rescue medication use; controller medication use; uninsured rate; poverty rate. *Asthma and Allergy Foundation of America, "2007 Asthma Capitals"*

- Albuquerque was identified as a "Spring Allergy Capital." The area ranked #38 out of 100. Three groups of factors were used to identify the most severe cities for people with allergies during the spring season: annual pollen levels; medicine utilization; access to board-certified allergists. *Asthma and Allergy Foundation of America, "2007 Spring Allergy Capital Rankings"*

■ Albuquerque was identified as a "Fall Allergy Capital." The area ranked #80 out of 100. Three groups of factors were used to identify the most severe cities for people with allergies during the fall season: annual pollen levels; medicine utilization; access to board-certified allergists. *Asthma and Allergy Foundation of America, "2006 Fall Allergy Capital Rankings"*

■ Albuquerque was selected as one of "America's Healthiest Cities" by *Natural Health* magazine. The city was ranked #19 out of the 50 largest urban areas in the U.S. Twenty-six criteria in the following four categories were examined: whether the city boasts natural offerings; how well the city promotes its residents' physical health; whether the city offers a healthy environment; how well the city fosters a sense of community. *Natural Health, April 2003*

■ *Men's Health* ranked the nation's largest 100 cities in terms of the *Best (and Worst) Cities for Men*. Albuquerque was ranked #39. Criteria: 24 statistical parameters of long life in the categories of health, quality of life, and fitness. *Men's Health, January/February 2007*

■ *Men's Health* ranked 100 U.S. cities in terms of the quality of their tap water. Albuquerque was ranked #40 and received a grade of C. Criteria: levels of total coliform bacteria, arsenic, lead, total trihalomethanes (linked to cancer), and halo-acetic acids, plus the number of EPA water-system violations from 1995 to 2005. *Men's Health, March 2007*

■ GlaxoSmithKline, in partnership with Sperling's BestPlaces, analyzed the nation's 100 largest metro areas and identified 25 asthma "hot spots" where high prevalence makes the condition a key issue and environmental triggers and other factors can make living with asthma a particular challenge. The Albuquerque metro area ranked #7 with #1 being the most challenging place to live. Criteria: asthma prevalence; asthma mortality; pollen scores; number of asthma specialists per capita; ratio of prescriptions for rescue medications to prescriptions for controller medications (an indicator of proper asthma treatment); air pollution; smoking laws; climate; and prevalence of tobacco use. *GlaxoSmithKline, "Asthma Hot Spots," October 29, 2002*

■ Ortho-McNeil Neurologics, in partnership with Sperling's BestPlaces, analyzed 110 metro areas and identified those U.S. cities with the highest prevalence of factors that are most commonly associated with migraine headaches. The Albuquerque metro area ranked #83. Criteria: number of migraine-related drug prescriptions per capita; lifestyle factors that can contribute to migraines; environmental factors that can trigger migraines; and consumption of migraine-triggering foods. *Ortho-McNeil Neurologics, "America's Migraine Hot Spots," March 14, 2006*

■ Sperling's BestPlaces ranked 331 metro areas and identified the most and least stressful U.S. cities. The Albuquerque metro area ranked #29 out of the 100 largest metro areas (#1 = most stressful). Criteria: divorce rate; unemployment rate; violent and property crime; suicide rate; commute time; mental health; alcohol consumption; cloudy days. *www.BestPlaces.net, January 9, 2004*

■ Sperling's BestPlaces in partnership with Vistakon ranked the 100 largest metro areas and identified "America's 10 Worst Cities for Comfortable Eyes." The Albuquerque metro area ranked #2. Criteria: altitude; sunny days; wind; extreme temperatures; humidity; pollution; commute time; computer use. *Vistakon, "America's Best and Worst Cities for Comfortable Eyes," June 15, 2004*

■ Albuquerque was highlighted as one of the top 25 cleanest metro areas for long-term particle pollution (PM 2.5) in the U.S. The area ranked #9. *American Lung Association, State of the Air 2006*

Women/Minorities Rankings

■ Albuquerque was ranked #44 out of 100 metro areas in *SELF Magazine's* ranking of "America's Best Places for Women." A panel of experts came up with nearly 40 criteria including: drinking and smoking rates; depression; unemployment; parks; crime; disease; healthcare insurance coverage; air quality; and commute times. *SELF Magazine, "America's Best Places for Women 2006," December 2006*

- *Ladies Home Journal* ranked America's 200 largest cities based on the qualities women surveyed care about most. Albuquerque ranked #47 out of 57 in the big city category (population over 300,000). Criteria: crime; lifestyle; education; jobs; health; child care; politics; and the economy. *Ladies Home Journal Online, "The Best Cities for Women 2002"*

- Albuquerque appeared on a list of the top 10 metro areas with the highest concentration of same-sex households. The area ranked #8. *Urban Institute Press, The Gay and Lesbian Atlas, May 2004*

- Albuquerque was identified as one of the top 25 metropolitan statistical areas ranked by percentage of coupled households that are gay or lesbian." The area ranked #11. *Human Rights Campaign, "Gay and Lesbian Families in the United States: Same-Sex Unmarried Partner Households," August 1, 2001*

- Albuquerque was selected as one of the "Top 10 Cities for Hispanics to Live In." The city was ranked #6. The cities were selected based on data from the following sources: U.S. Census; *Forbes; Fortune; Money*; local newspapers; natives and residents; www.bestplaces.net; www.findyourspot.com. *Hispanic Magazine, July/August 2004*

Seniors/Retirement Rankings

- Albuquerque was profiled in the book *Where to Retire: America's Best and Most Affordable Places*. Cities were selected based on personal visits by the author and interviews with local residents coupled with statistics from various government agencies. *Where to Retire: America's Best and Most Affordable Places, 2006*

- A.G. Edwards ranked America's 500 top-performing communities based on their residents' personal savings and investing behavior. The Albuquerque metro area ranked #422 with an index score of 96.53 (national average = 100.00). A dozen statistical factors were measured including: participation in retirement savings plans; personal debt levels; and home ownership. *A.G. Edwards, "2006 Nest Egg Index", September 6, 2006*

Children/Family Rankings

- The Albuquerque metro area was selected as one of the "Best Cities for Relocating Families" by Worldwide ERC and Primacy Relocation. Criteria: tax rates; average home costs and home appreciation; ability to qualify for in-state tuition; service quality of local utilities; per-capita volunteerism; auto taxes; and quantity of fun, family-friendly events and venues. *Worldwide ERC and Primacy Relocation, "2006 Best Cities for Relocating Families"*

- *Zero Population Growth* ranked 100 cities in terms of children's health, safety, and economic well-being. Albuquerque was ranked #53 out of 80 Large Cities (remainder of the 100 largest cities in the U.S.) and was given a grade of B-. Criteria: total population and population growth; percent of population under 18 years of age; percent of births to teens; infant mortality rate; percent of eligible women not receiving Title X services; contraceptive equity indicator; percent of children without health insurance; percent of city residents over age 25 with a high-school diploma; ration of PopEd (Population Connection's Education Program) teachers trained; sexuality education indicator; proficiency in reading and math; percent of kids living in poverty; percent growth in urbanized land; violent crime rate; recycling. *Population Connection, Kid Friendly Cities: Report Card 2004*

- *Fit Pregnancy* magazine ranked the 50 best U.S. cities in which to have a baby. Albuquerque was ranked #24. Criteria: fertility services; maternal and infant health risk; access to hospitals and doctors; safety; affordability; stroller friendliness; and birthing options. *Fit Pregnancy, February/March, 2006*

- Albuquerque was chosen as one of America's "100 Best Communities for Young People." The winners were selected based upon detailed information provided about each community's efforts to fulfill five essential promises critical to the well-being of young people: caring adults who are actively involved in their lives; safe places in which to learn and grow; a healthy start toward adulthood; an effective education that builds marketable skills; and opportunities to help others. *America's Promise, "100 Best Communities for Young People," September 26, 2005*

SafetyRankings

- Allstate ranked the 200 largest cities in America in terms of driver safety. Albuquerque ranked #78. In addition, drivers were 4.7% more likely to have had an accident compared to the national average. Allstate researchers analyzed internal Property Damage reported claims over a two-year period (from January 2003 to December 2004) to ensure the findings would not be affected by external influences such as weather or road construction. A weighted average of the two-year numbers determined the annual percentages. The report defines an auto crash has any collision resulting in a property damage claim. *Allstate, "Allstate America's Best Drivers Report 2006," May 24, 2006*

- *Ladies Home Journal* ranked America's 200 largest cities in terms of safety. Albuquerque ranked #163 out of 200. Criteria: violent crimes; crimes against property; and rape. *Ladies Home Journal Online, "The Best Cities for Women 2002"*

Sports/Recreation Rankings

- The Albuquerque metro area appeared on *The Sporting News* list of the "Best Sports Cities 2006". The area ranked #89 out of 99 cities in North America. To be included in the rankings, a city must have at least one of the following: NCAA Division I basketball team; Class A minor league baseball team; training camp for a major league or NFL team; NASCAR Nextel Cup race; NCAA Division I-A bowl game; PGA Tour tournament; Triple Crown horse race. Once a city qualifies, a 12-month snapshot is taken of the sports atmosphere, putting a heavy premium on regular-season won-lost records; playoff berths, bowl appearances and tournament bids; championships; applicable power ratings; quality of competition; overall fan fervor; sports atmosphere and fan knowledge; abundance of teams (quality over quantity); stadium/arena quality; ticket availability and prices; franchise ownership; and the marquee appeal of athletes. *SportingNews.com, "Best Sports Cities 2006," August 1, 2006*

- Albuquerque was chosen as one of America's best cities for bicycling. The city ranked #3 in the mid-sized city category (population 200,000 to 500,000). Criteria: cycling-friendly statistics (number of bike lanes and routes, number of bike racks, city bike projects completed and planned; bike culture (number of bike commuters, popular clubs, cool cycling events, renowned bike shops); climate/geography (the quality of roads and trails for riding, and how frequently mother nature lets riders enjoy them). *Bicycling, March 2006*

- *Golf Digest* ranked 330 metro areas in the U.S. in terms of golf. The Albuquerque metro area was ranked #267. Criteria: access to golf; weather; value of golf; and quality of golf. *Golf Digest, "Metro Golf Rankings," August 2005*

Dating/Romance Rankings

- The Albuquerque metro area was selected as one of the "Best Cities for Relocating Singles" by Worldwide ERC and Primacy Relocation. The area ranked #23 out of the 100 largest metro areas in the U.S. Areas were selected based on the following criteria: Population Criteria (local percentage and growth trends of unmarried residents aged 25-34; male-female ratios; the number of newcomers to the area; diversity and density); Economic Criteria (job growth vs. unemployment rates; apartment rental costs; fee and occupancy rates for temporary housing and mini-storage; higher education costs, including in-state and out-of-state tuition requirements; vehicle tax rates and quality of service from utility providers); Quality-of-Life Criteria (level of per capita volunteering; quality and quantity of collegiate and professional sports with fun, fan-friendly venues; number of Starbucks and other coffee shops; quality or popularity of restaurants, nightspots, health clubs, and online dating; moderate climates with sustainable water supplies). *Worldwide ERC and Primacy Relocation, "2006 Best Cities for Relocating Singles," October 11, 2006*

- Sperling's BestPlaces in partnership with AXE Deodorant Bodyspray ranked 80 metro areas and identified "America's Best (and Worst) Cities for Dating." The Albuquerque metro area ranked #65. Criteria: percentage of singles ages 18-24; population density; dating venues per capita. *AXE Deodorant Bodyspray, "America's Best (and Worst) Cities for Dating," May, 2004*

Culture/Performing Arts Rankings

- Albuquerque was selected as one of "America's Top 25 Arts Destinations." The city ranked #2 in the mid-sized city (population 100,000 to 499,999) category. Criteria: readers' top choices for arts travel destinations based on the richness and variety of visual arts sites, activities and events. *American Style, June 2006*

- Scarborough Research, a leading market research firm, identified the top local markets for rock concert attendance. The Albuquerque DMA (Designated Market Area) ranked in the top 25 with 14% of consumers, 18 years old and over, reporting that they have attended a rock concert during the past year. *Scarborough Research, Scarborough USA+ 2003 Release 2*

Miscellaneous Rankings

- Albuquerque was selected as a runner-up in *Dog Fancy's* DogTown USA contest. Criteria: access to top veterinary professionals, dog parks, and canine-friendly businesses; shelter-euthanasia rates; and owner responsibility. *Dog Fancy, "DogTown USA," 2006*

- Albuquerque was determined to be one of America's smartest cities. The city ranked #10 in the large city category (200,000+ adults 25 years and older). Criteria: the editors rated the collective brainpower of U.S communities based on the educational attainment of its residents. *American City Business Journals, www.bizjournals.com, June 12, 2006*

- Albuquerque was identified as one of North America's most accommodating cities for travelers with pets. The city was ranked #4. Criteria: number of AAA Approved and Diamond rated pet-friendly hotels. *AAA, Traveling with your Pet: The AAA PetBook, 2006*

- Albuquerque was selected as one of the "Top 100 Sweatiest Summer Cities". The city was ranked #46. The ranking was based on the average male/female height/weight, average high temperature, and average relative humidity levels for 2002 in each of the cities during June, July and August. The sweat level was analyzed based on the assumption that the individual was walking for one hour. *Procter & Gamble, Old Spice, June 18, 2003*

- Albuquerque appeared on ApartmentRatings.com "Top Cities for Renters List 2006". The area ranked #64 out of 138. Criteria: renter satisfaction; affordability; and vacancy. *ApartmentRatings.com, "Top Cities for Renters List 2006"*

- Sperling's BestPlaces in partnership with Pep Boys ranked 77 metro areas and identified "America's Most Drivable Cities." The Albuquerque metro area ranked #33. Criteria: climate; road roughness; urban mobility; gas prices. *Pep Boys, "America's Most Drivable Cities," April 9, 2003*

- Albuquerque was selected as one of "America's Most Literate Cities." The city ranked #38 out of the 70 largest U.S. cities. Criteria: number of booksellers; library resources; Internet resources; educational attainment; periodical publishing resources; newspaper circulation. *Central Connecticut State University, "America's Most Literate Cities 2006"*

Business Environment

CITY FINANCES

City Government Finances

Component	2003-2004 ($000)	2003-2004 ($ per capita)
Total Revenues	892,128	1,923
Total Expenditures	788,563	1,700
Debt Outstanding	953,936	2,056
Cash and Securities	690,735	1,489

Source: U.S Census Bureau, Government Finances 2003-2004

City Government Revenue by Source

Source	2003-2004 ($000)	2003-2004 ($ per capita)
General Revenue		
From Federal Government	45,237	98
From State Government	196,872	424
From Local Governments	21,431	46
Taxes		
Property	88,250	190
Sales	159,284	343
Personal Income	0	0
License	0	0
Charges	200,215	432
Liquor Store	0	0
Utility	98,069	211
Employee Retirement	0	0
Other	82,770	178

Source: U.S Census Bureau, Government Finances 2003-2004

City Government Expenditures by Function

Function	2003-2004 ($000)	2003-2004 ($ per capita)	2003-2004 (%)
General Expenditures			
Airports	32,396	70	4.1
Corrections	44,003	95	5.6
Education	0	0	0.0
Fire Protection	49,212	106	6.2
Governmental Administration	43,444	94	5.5
Health	17,006	37	2.2
Highways	41,760	90	5.3
Hospitals	0	0	0.0
Housing and Community Development	34,625	75	4.4
Interest on General Debt	30,704	66	3.9
Libraries	12,456	27	1.6
Parking	4,488	10	0.6
Parks and Recreation	89,207	192	11.3
Police Protection	100,788	217	12.8
Public Welfare	8,991	19	1.1
Sewerage	32,921	71	4.2
Solid Waste Management	41,503	89	5.3
Liquor Store	0	0	0.0
Utility	91,445	197	11.6
Employee Retirement	0	0	0.0
Other	113,614	245	14.4

Source: U.S Census Bureau, Government Finances 2003-2004

Municipal Bond Ratings

Area	Moody's
City	Aaa

Source: Mergent Bond Record, January 2007 (unless noted otherwise)

DEMOGRAPHICS

Population Growth

Area	1990 Census	2000 Census	2006 Estimate	2011 Projection	Population Growth (%) 1990-2000	Population Growth (%) 2000-2011
City	388,375	448,607	496,349	538,474	15.5	20.0
MSA[1]	599,416	729,649	801,836	865,893	21.7	18.7
U.S.	248,709,873	281,421,906	298,021,266	312,383,955	13.2	11.0

Note: (1) Metropolitan Statistical Area - see Appendix B for areas included
Source: Claritas, Inc.

Number of Households and Average Household Size

Area	2006 Estimate	2006 Average Household Size
City	204,602	2.43
MSA[1]	312,869	2.56
U.S.	112,267,302	2.65

Note: (1) Metropolitan Statistical Area - see Appendix B for areas included
Source: Claritas, Inc.

Race and Ethnicity

Area	White Alone[2]	Black Alone[2]	Asian Alone[2]	Other Race Alone[2]	Hispanic[3]
City	69.3	3.2	2.4	25.1	42.7
MSA[1]	68.1	2.6	1.7	27.6	43.3
U.S.	73.3	12.4	4.2	10.1	14.5

Note: Figures are 2006 estimates; (1) Metropolitan Statistical Area - see Appendix B for areas included
(2) Alone is defined as not being in combination with one or more other races; (3) May be of any race.
Source: Claritas, Inc.

Segregation

City		MSA[1]	
Index[2]	Rank[3]	Index[2]	Rank[4]
39.5	86	40.0	301

Note: Figures are based on an analysis of Census 2000 data; (1) Metropolitan Statistical Area - see Appendix A for areas included; (2) White/Black Dissimilarity Index—the most commonly used measure of segregation between two groups, reflecting their relative distributions across neighborhoods within a city or metropolitan area. It can range in value from 0, indicating complete integration, to 100, indicating complete segregation; (3) Ranges from 1 (most segregated) to 100 (least segregated) and includes all the cities in this book; (4) Ranges from 1 (most segregated) to 318 (least segregated) and includes 318 metropolitan areas.
Source: www.CensusScope.org

Ancestry

Area	German	Irish[2]	English	American	Italian	Polish	French[3]	Scottish
City	12.6	9.2	9.0	4.1	3.7	1.7	2.6	2.2
MSA[1]	11.8	8.5	8.5	4.3	3.5	1.6	2.4	1.9
U.S.	15.2	10.9	8.7	7.3	5.6	3.2	3.0	1.7

Note: Figures include multiple ancestry (e.g. if a person reported being Irish and Italian, they were included in both columns); (1) Metropolitan Statistical Area - see Appendix A for areas included; (2) Includes Celtic; (3) Includes Alsatian but excludes Basque
Source: Census 2000, Summary File 3

Foreign-Born Population

Area	Any Foreign Country	Europe	Asia	Africa	Oceania[2]	Canada	Mexico	Latin America[3]
	Percent of Population Born in							
City	8.9	1.1	1.6	0.1	0.1	0.3	4.9	0.8
MSA[1]	7.9	1.0	1.2	0.1	0.0	0.3	4.7	0.6
U.S.	11.1	1.7	2.9	0.3	0.1	0.3	3.3	2.5

Note: (1) Metropolitan Statistical Area - see Appendix A for areas included; (2) Includes Australia, New Zealand subregion, Melanesia, Micronesia, Polynesia, and Oceania n.e.c; (3) Includes Central America (excluding Mexico), South America, and the Caribbean.
Source: Census 2000, Summary File 3

Marriage Status

Area	Never Married	Now Married (excluding Separated)	Separated	Widowed	Divorced
City	30.2	48.7	1.7	5.7	13.7
MSA[1]	28.6	51.5	1.6	5.6	12.6
U.S.	27.1	54.4	2.2	6.6	9.7

Note: Figures are percentages and cover the population 15 years of age and older;
(1) Metropolitan Statistical Area - see Appendix A for areas included
Source: Census 2000, Summary File 3

Age Distribution

Area	Percent of Population						
	Under Age 5	Age 5 to 17	Age 18 to 34	Age 35 to 49	Age 50 to 64	Age 65 to 79	80 Years and Over
City	6.9	17.5	25.4	23.9	14.4	8.7	3.2
MSA[1]	7.0	19.2	23.6	24.3	14.6	8.4	2.8
U.S.	6.8	18.9	23.7	23.5	14.8	9.2	3.2

Note: (1) Metropolitan Statistical Area - see Appendix A for areas included
Source: Census 2000, Summary File 3

Male/Female Ratio

Area	Males	Females	Males per 100 Females
City	241,413	254,936	94.7
MSA[1]	393,455	408,381	96.3
U.S.	146,712,712	151,308,554	97.0

Note: Figures are 2006 estimates; (1) Metropolitan Statistical Area -
see Appendix B for areas included
Source: Claritas, Inc.

Religion

Area	Catholic	Southern Baptist	United Methodist	ELCA[1]	LDS[2]	Presbyterian Church USA	Jewish Est.	Muslim Est.
County	34.4	4.0	2.0	1.4	1.5	0.9	1.4	0.3
U.S.	22.0	7.1	3.7	1.8	1.5	1.1	2.2	0.6

Note: Figures are the number of adherents as a percentage of the total population; Adherents are defined as all members, including full members, their children and the estimated number of other participants who are not considered members (e.g. the baptized, those not confirmed, those regularly attending services, etc.);
(1) Evangelical Lutheran Church in America; (2) The Church of Jesus Christ of Latter Day Saints
Source: Reprinted with permission from Religious Congregations and Membership in the United States 2000 (Nashville, Glenmary Research Center, 2002) Copyright Association of Statisticians of American Religious Bodies. All rights reserved.

ECONOMY

Gross Metropolitan Product

Area	2002	2003	2004	2005	2005 Rank[2]
MSA[1]	24.7	27.0	29.9	32.3	65

Note: Figures are in billions of dollars; (1) Albuquerque, NM Metropolitan Statistical Area - see Appendix A for areas included; (2) Rank ranges from 1 to 361
Source: The U.S. Conference of Mayors, "U.S. Metro Economies: GMP - The Engines of America's Growth," January 2007

Economic Growth

Area	1995 GMP	2005 GMP	Average Annual Growth Rate	Growth Rate Rank[2]
MSA[1]	20.4	32.3	4.7	253

Note: Figures are in billions of dollars; GMP = Gross Metropolitan Product; (1) Albuquerque, NM Metropolitan Statistical Area - see Appendix A for areas included; (2) Rank ranges from 1 to 361
Source: The U.S. Conference of Mayors, "U.S. Metro Economies: GMP - The Engines of America's Growth," January 2007

INCOME

Per Capita/Median/Average Income

Area	Per Capita ($)	Median Household ($)	Average Household ($)
City	24,791	45,256	59,413
MSA[1]	24,037	46,123	60,958
U.S.	25,129	48,775	65,849

Note: Figures are 2006 estimates; (1) Metropolitan Statistical Area - see Appendix B for areas included
Source: Claritas, Inc.

Household Income Distribution

Area	Under $15,000	$15,000 -24,999	$25,000 -34,999	$35,000 -49,999	$50,000 -74,999	$75,000 -99,000	$100,000 -149,999	$150,000 and up
City	13.8	12.2	12.5	16.8	19.0	10.9	10.1	4.7
MSA[1]	13.3	12.0	12.2	16.8	19.5	11.0	10.2	5.0
U.S.	13.3	11.0	11.3	15.7	19.5	11.8	11.0	6.4

(Percent of Households Earning)

Note: Figures are 2006 estimates; (1) Metropolitan Statistical Area - see Appendix B for areas included
Source: Claritas, Inc.

Poverty Rates by Age

Area	All Ages	Under 5 Years Old	5 to 17 Years Old	18 to 64 Years Old	65 Years and Over
City	13.5	1.4	3.0	8.2	1.0
MSA[1]	13.8	1.5	3.4	7.9	1.0
U.S.	12.4	1.2	3.0	6.9	1.2

Note: Figures are percent of population with income in 1999 below poverty level and only include population for whom poverty status is determined; (1) Metropolitan Statistical Area - see Appendix A for areas included
Source: Census 2000, Summary File 3

Personal Bankruptcy Filing Rate

Area	2003	2004	2005
Bernalillo County	5.59	5.27	6.71
U.S.	5.57	5.31	6.88

Note: Numbers are per 1,000 population and include Chapter 7 and Chapter 13 filings
Source: Federal Deposit Insurance Corporation (FDIC), Regional Economic Conditions (RECON), 3/24/2006

EMPLOYMENT

Labor Force and Employment

Area	Civilian Labor Force			Workers Employed		
	Dec. 2005	Dec. 2006	% Chg.	Dec. 2005	Dec. 2006	% Chg.
City	263,806	264,742	0.4	253,830	257,181	1.3
MSA[1]	406,138	407,809	0.4	389,781	394,927	1.3
U.S.	149,874,000	152,571,000	1.8	142,918,000	146,081,000	2.2

Note: Data is not seasonally adjusted and covers workers 16 years of age and older;
(1) Metropolitan Statistical Area - see Appendix B for areas included
Source: Bureau of Labor Statistics, http://stats.bls.gov

Unemployment Rate

Area	2006											
	Jan.	Feb.	Mar.	Apr.	May	Jun.	Jul.	Aug.	Sep.	Oct.	Nov.	Dec.
City	4.1	4.1	3.2	3.5	3.4	4.1	4.2	3.7	3.7	3.7	3.5	2.9
MSA[1]	4.6	4.5	3.5	3.8	3.7	4.4	4.6	4.0	4.0	4.0	3.8	3.2
U.S.	5.1	5.1	4.8	4.5	4.4	4.8	5.0	4.6	4.4	4.1	4.3	4.3

Note: Data is not seasonally adjusted and covers workers 16 years of age and older; All figures are percentages; (1) Metropolitan Statistical Area - see Appendix B for areas included
Source: Bureau of Labor Statistics, http://stats.bls.gov

Employment by Occupation

Occupation Classification	City (%)	MSA[1] (%)	U.S. (%)
Sales and Office	29.1	28.1	26.7
Professional and Related	25.1	23.7	20.2
Service	15.8	15.7	14.9
Production, Transportation, and Material Moving	8.7	9.9	14.6
Management, Business, and Financial	13.4	13.1	13.5
Construction, Extraction, and Maintenance	7.8	9.4	9.4
Farming, Forestry, and Fishing	0.1	0.2	0.7

Note: Figures cover employed civilians 16 years of age and older;
(1) Metropolitan Statistical Area - see Appendix A for areas included
Source: Census 2000, Summary File 3

Employment by Industry

Sector	MSA[1] Number of Employees	MSA[1] Percent of Total	U.S. Percent of Total
Government	80,600	20.3	16.3
Education and Health Services	48,600	12.2	13.2
Professional and Business Services	63,900	16.1	12.9
Retail Trade	46,200	11.6	11.5
Manufacturing	24,200	6.1	10.2
Leisure and Hospitality	38,300	9.6	9.5
Financial Activities	19,200	4.8	6.1
Construction	n/a	n/a	5.5
Wholesale Trade	13,500	3.4	4.3
Other Services	12,200	3.1	3.9
Transportation and Utilities	10,700	2.7	3.7
Information	9,300	2.3	2.2
Natural Resources and Mining	n/a	n/a	0.5

Note: Figures cover non-farm employment as of December 2006 and are not seasonally adjusted;
(1) Metropolitan Statistical Area - see Appendix B for areas included; n/a not available
Source: Bureau of Labor Statistics, http://stats.bls.gov

Occupations with Greatest Projected Employment Growth: 2002 - 2012

Occupation[1]	2002 Employment	2012 Projected Employment	Numeric Employment Change	Percent Employment Change
Registered Nurses	12,270	16,810	4,540	37.0
Combined Food Preparation and Serving Workers, Including Fast Food	12,390	16,450	4,060	32.8
Retail Salespersons	25,120	29,180	4,060	16.2
Waiters and Waitresses	14,600	18,350	3,750	25.7
Customer Service Representatives	9,250	12,660	3,410	36.9
General and Operations Managers	16,100	19,460	3,360	20.9
Janitors and Cleaners, Except Maids and Housekeeping Cleaners	13,160	16,220	3,060	23.3
Cashiers	19,230	22,070	2,840	14.8
Security Guards	6,460	9,060	2,600	40.2
Police and Sheriffs Patrol Officers	5,630	7,920	2,290	40.7

Note: Projections cover New Mexico; (1) Sorted by numeric employment change
Source: www.projectionscentral.com, State Occupational Projections, 2002-2012 Long-Term Projections

Fastest Growing Occupations: 2002 - 2012

Occupation[1]	2002 Employment	2012 Projected Employment	Numeric Employment Change	Percent Employment Change
Fitness Trainers and Aerobics Instructors	1,070	1,830	760	71.0
Computer Software Engineers, Systems Software	940	1,600	660	70.2
Medical Assistants	2,320	3,800	1,480	63.8
Medical Records and Health Information Technicians	1,390	2,180	790	56.8
Packaging and Filling Machine Operators and Tenders	1,750	2,730	980	56.0
Social and Human Service Assistants	1,650	2,560	910	55.2
Self-Enrichment Education Teachers	1,030	1,570	540	52.4
Physician Assistants	660	990	330	50.0
Network and Computer Systems Administrators	1,030	1,530	500	48.5
Database Administrators	550	810	260	47.3

Note: Projections cover New Mexico; (1) Sorted by percent employment change and excludes occupations with numeric employment change less than 200
Source: www.projectionscentral.com, State Occupational Projections, 2002-2012 Long-Term Projections

Average Wages

Occupation	$/Hr.	Occupation	$/Hr.
Accountants and Auditors	25.39	Maids and Housekeeping Cleaners	6.95
Automotive Mechanics	16.21	Maintenance and Repair Workers	13.54
Bookkeepers	13.86	Marketing Managers	36.03
Carpenters	13.70	Nuclear Medicine Technologists	n/a
Cashiers	8.30	Nurses, Licensed Practical	18.28
Clerks, General Office	10.55	Nurses, Registered	27.03
Clerks, Receptionists/Information	10.16	Nursing Aides/Orderlies/Attendants	10.13
Clerks, Shipping/Receiving	11.77	Packers and Packagers, Hand	8.70
Computer Programmers	29.67	Physical Therapists	26.91
Computer Support Specialists	18.85	Postal Service Mail Carriers	21.79
Computer Systems Analysts	29.59	Real Estate Brokers	n/a
Cooks, Restaurant	8.50	Retail Salespersons	10.75
Dentists	n/a	Sales Reps., Exc. Tech./Scientific	20.29
Electrical Engineers	38.35	Sales Reps., Tech./Scientific	29.20
Electricians	17.99	Secretaries, Exc. Legal/Med./Exec.	12.62
Financial Managers	35.60	Security Guards	10.57
First-Line Supervisors/Mgrs., Sales	15.57	Surgeons	84.95
Food Preparation Workers	7.74	Teacher Assistants	8.00
General and Operations Managers	42.39	Teachers, Elementary School	17.80
Hairdressers/Cosmetologists	9.43	Teachers, Secondary School	21.10
Internists	86.54	Telemarketers	12.57
Janitors and Cleaners	8.95	Truck Drivers, Heavy/Tractor-Trailer	17.53
Landscaping/Groundskeeping Workers	8.15	Truck Drivers, Light/Delivery Svcs.	12.54
Lawyers	48.70	Waiters and Waitresses	6.66

Note: Wage data is for May 2005 and covers the Albuquerque, NM Metropolitan Statistics Area - see Appendix B for areas included. Hourly wages for elementary/secondary school teachers and teacher assistants were calculated by the editors from annual wage data assuming a 40 hour work week; n/a not available.
Source: Bureau of Labor Statistics, May 2005 Metro Area Occupational Employment and Wage Estimates

RESIDENTIAL REAL ESTATE

Building Permits

Area	Single-Family			Multi-Family			Total		
	2005	2006p	Pct. Chg.	2005	2006p	Pct. Chg.	2005	2006p	Pct. Chg.
City	4,764	3,414	-28.3	314	660	110.2	5,078	4,074	-19.8
U.S.	1,682,000	1,380,000	-18.0	473,300	457,300	-3.4	2,155,300	1,837,300	-14.8

Note: (p) preliminary; figures represent new, privately-owned housing units authorized (unadjusted data); All permit data are based on estimates with imputation; U.S. figures are based on the new 20,000-place series.
Source: U.S. Census Bureau, Manufacturing, Mining, and Construction Statistics

Homeownership and Housing Vacancies

Area	Homeownership Rate[2] (%)			Rental Vacancy Rate[3] (%)			Homeowner Vacancy Rate[4] (%)		
	2004	2005	2006	2004	2005	2006	2004	2005	2006
MSA[1]	n/a	n/a	n/a	n/a	n/a	n/a	n/a	n/a	n/a
U.S.	69.0	68.9	68.8	10.2	9.8	9.7	1.7	1.9	2.4

Note: Comparable 2004 data was not available due to changes in metropolitan area definitions; (1) Metropolitan Statistical Area - see Appendix B for areas included; (2) The proportion of households that are owners; (3) The proportion of the rental inventory that is vacant for rent; (4) The proportion of the homeowner inventory that is vacant for sale; n/a not available
Source: U.S. Census Bureau, Housing Vacancies and Homeownership Annual Statistics: 2006

TAXES

State Corporate Income Tax Rates

State	Rate (%)	Number of Brackets	Low Bracket (Under $)	High Bracket (Over $)
New Mexico	4.8-7.6	3	0	1,000,000

Note: Tax rates as of December 31, 2006; na not applicable
Source: Tax Foundation, www.taxfoundation.org

State Individual Income Tax Rates

State	Federal Deductibility	Marginal Rate (%)	Number of Brackets	Low Bracket (Under $)	High Bracket (Over $)
New Mexico	No	1.7-5.7 (y)	4	0	16,000

Note: Tax rates as of December 31, 2006; Brackets apply to single taxpayers and married people filing separately; na not applicable; (y) Brackets are not double for married taxpayers.
Source: Tax Foundation, www.taxfoundation.org

Various State and Local Tax Rates

State and Local Sales and Use (%)	State Sales and Use (%)	Gasoline ($/gal.)	Cigarette ($/pack)	Spirits ($/gal.)	Table Wine ($/gal.)	Beer ($/gal.)
6.8745	5.0	0.18 (m)	0.91	6.06	1.70	0.41

Note: Tax rates as of December 31, 2006; (m) Additional cents per gallon taxes added this year that were not included in previous years' tables.
Source: Tax Foundation, www.taxfoundation.org; The Sales Tax Clearinghouse, www.thestc.com

State Tax Burdens

Area	Combined State and Local Tax Burden		Combined Federal, State and Local Tax Burden	
	Percent	Rank	Percent	Rank
New Mexico	9.9	36	28.5	45
U.S. Average	10.6	-	31.6	-

Note: Figures are for 2006 and measure taxes as a percentage of income
Source: Tax Foundation, www.taxfoundation.org

Internal Revenue Service Tax Audits

IRS District	Percent of Returns Audited				
	1996	1997	1998	1999	2000
Southwest	0.80	0.81	0.61	0.36	0.29
U.S.	0.66	0.61	0.46	0.31	0.20

Note: Figures cover IRS district audits of federal income tax returns filed by individuals. Geographic data on district audits after the year 2000 are being withheld by the IRS. TRAC is challenging this policy.
Source: Syracuse University, Transactional Records Access Clearinghouse (TRAC), "Odds of IRS District Tax Audit 2000"

COMMERCIAL REAL ESTATE

Office Market

Market Area	Inventory (sq. ft.)	Vacant (sq. ft.)	Vac. Rate (%)	Under Constr. (sq. ft.)	Asking Rent ($/sf)	
					Class A	Class B
Albuquerque	12,662,613	1,693,638	13.4	126,363	19.87	16.20

Source: Grubb & Ellis, Office Markets Trends, 4th Quarter 2006

Industrial Market

Market Area	Inventory (sq. ft.)	Vacant (sq. ft.)	Vac. Rate (%)	Under Constr. (sq. ft.)	Asking Rent ($/sf)	
					WH/Dist	R&D/Flex
Albuquerque	34,027,079	2,201,033	6.5	1,083,941	6.05	9.23

Source: Grubb & Ellis, Industrial Markets Trends, 4th Quarter 2006

COMMERCIAL UTILITIES

Typical Monthly Electric Bills

Area	Commercial Service ($/month)		Industrial Service ($/month)	
	3 kW demand 1,000 kWh	40 kW demand 14,000 kWh	1,000 kW demand 200,000 kWh	50,000 kW demand 15,000,000 kWh
City	n/a	n/a	n/a	n/a
Average[1]	123	1,413	22,000	1,306,315

Note: Based on total rates in effect July 1, 2006; (1) average based on 196 utilities; n/a not available
Source: Edison Electric Institute, Typical Bills and Average Rates Report, Summer 2006

TRANSPORTATION

Means of Transportation to Work

Area	Car/Truck/Van		Public Transportation			Bicycle	Walked	Other Means	Worked at Home
	Drove Alone	Car-pooled	Bus	Subway	Railroad				
City	77.7	12.5	1.6	0.0	0.0	1.1	2.7	0.7	3.6
MSA[1]	77.7	13.3	1.2	0.0	0.0	0.8	2.3	0.9	3.9
U.S.	75.7	12.2	2.5	1.5	0.5	0.4	2.9	1.0	3.3

Note: Figures are percentages and cover workers 16 years of age and older;
(1) Metropolitan Statistical Area - see Appendix A for areas included
Source: Census 2000, Summary File 3

Travel Time to Work

Area	Less Than 15 Minutes	15 to 29 Minutes	30 to 44 Minutes	45 to 59 Minutes	60 Minutes or More
City	29.4	50.5	14.3	2.5	3.3
MSA[1]	26.9	45.1	18.4	5.3	4.3
U.S.	29.4	36.1	19.1	7.4	8.0

Note: Figures are percentages and include workers 16 years old and over; (1) Metropolitan Statistical Area -
see Appendix A for areas included
Source: Census 2000, Summary File 3

Travel Time Index

Area	1982	1993	2002	2003
Urban Area[1]	1.04	1.14	1.17	1.17
Average[2]	1.12	1.28	1.37	1.37

Note: Travel Time Index - The ratio of travel time in the peak period to the travel time at
free-flow conditions. A value of 1.35 indicates a 20-minute free-flow trip takes 27 minutes
in the peak. Free-flow speeds (60 mph on freeways and 35 mph on principal arterials)
are used as the comparison threshold; (1) Covers the Albuquerque, NM urban area;
(2) average of 85 urban areas
Source: Texas Transportation Institute, The 2005 Urban Mobility Report, May 2005

Public Transportation

Agency name:	ABQ Ride
Vehicle type:	Bus
Average fleet age in years:	9.3
No. operated in max. service:	150
Vehicle type:	Demand response
Average fleet age in years:	5.1
No. operated in max. service:	50

Source: Federal Transit Administration, National Transit Database, 2005

Air Transportation

Airport name and code:	Albuquerque International (ABQ)
Domestic service (2006)	
Passenger airlines[1]:	27
Passenger enplanements:	3,172,704
Freight carriers[2]:	17
Freight (lbs.):	102,488,186
International service (2005)	
Passenger airlines[1]:	5
Passenger enplanements:	505
Freight carriers[2]:	0
Freight (lbs.):	0

Note: (1) Includes all major, minor and commuter airlines that carried at least one passenger during the year; (2) Includes all airlines and freight carriers that transported at least one pound of freight during the year
Source: Bureau of Transportation Statistics, The Intermodal Transportation Database, Air Carriers: T-100 International Market, 2004; Bureau of Transportation Statistics, The Intermodal Transportation Database, Air Carriers: T-100 Domestic Market, 2005

Other Transportation Statistics

Interstate highways:	I-25; I-40
Amtrak service:	Yes
Major waterways/ports:	None

Source: Editor & Publisher Market Guide, 2006; Amtrak.com; Rand McNally 2006 Road Atlas

BUSINESSES

Major Business Headquarters

Company Name	2006 Rankings	
	Fortune[1]	Forbes[2]
No companies listed	-	-

Note: (1) Fortune 500 - companies that produce a 10-K are ranked 1 to 500 based on 2005 revenue; (2) Forbes Largest Private Companies - all private companies with at least $1 billion in annual revenue are ranked 1 to 394; companies listed are located in the city; dashes indicate no ranking
Source: Fortune, April 17, 2006; Forbes, November 9, 2006

Best Companies to Work For

UNM Hospitals, headquartered in Albuquerque, is among the "50 Best Employers for Workers Over 50." Criteria: recruiting practices; opportunities for training, education, and career development; workplace accommodations; alternative work options, such as flexible scheduling, job sharing, and phased retirement; employee health and pension benefits; and retiree benefits. Any employer with at least 50 employees based in the U.S. is eligible. This includes for-profit companies, not-for-profit organizations, and government employers. *AARP, "AARP Best Employers for Workers Over 50," 2006*

PNM Resources, headquartered in Albuquerque, is among the "50 Best Companies for Minorities." Criteria: 1,200 of the largest U.S employers were surveyed. Those companies were analyzed on information such as the number of minorities in the workforce and on the board, and the rate at which minority employees are hired (and fired). *Fortune, "50 Best Companies for Minorities," June 28, 2004*

Fast-Growing Businesses

According to *Inc.*, Albuquerque is home to one of America's 500 fastest-growing private companies: **RhinoCorps**. Criteria: must be an independent, privately-held, U.S. corporation, proprietorship or partnership; net sales of at least $600,000 in FY2002; four-year operating/sales history; holding companies, regulated banks, and utilities were excluded. *Inc., "America's 500 Fastest-Growing Private Companies," September 2006*

Women-Owned Businesses: 1997 and 2002

Year	All Firms		Firms with Paid Employees			
	Firms	Sales ($000)	Firms	Sales ($000)	Employees	Payroll ($000)
1997	10,043	1,475,424	1,788	1,311,220	13,241	277,839
2002	11,809	1,432,208	2,019	1,225,503	14,189	322,588

Note: Figures cover firms located in the city; Women-owned business are defined as firms in which women own 51% or more of the stock or equity of the company; (a) Withheld to avoid disclosing data for individual companies; (b) Withheld because estimate did not meet publication standards; n/a not available
Source: 1997 Economic Census, Survey of Minority- and Women-Owned Business Enterprises; 2002 Economic Census, Survey of Business Owners (released February 9, 2006)

Minority Business Opportunity

19 of the 500 largest Hispanic-owned companies in the U.S. are located in Albuquerque. *Hispanic Business, "Hispanic Business 500," June 2006*

Albuquerque is home to two companies which are on the Hispanic Business Fastest-Growing 100 list (greatest sales growth over the past five years): **Networx; Integrated Control Systems**. *Hispanic Business, July/August 2006*

HOTELS

Hotels/Motels

Area	Hotels/Motels	Average Minimum Rates ($)		
		Tourist	First-Class	Deluxe
City	126	54	84	89

Source: OAG Travel Planner Online, Spring 2006

EVENT SITES

Stadiums, Arenas, and Auditoriums

Name	Capacity
Sam Houston Coliseum	11,206
The Summit	17,050
Tingley Coliseum	12,000
University of New Mexico Stadium	30,000

Source: www.officialtravelguide.com; www.eventective.com; original research

Convention Centers

Name	Overall Space (sq. ft.)	Exhibit Space (sq. ft.)	Meeting Space (sq. ft.)	Meeting Rooms
Albuquerque Convention Center	167,000	40,140	166,546	27

Source: www.officialtravelguide.com; www.eventective.com; original research

Hotels/Conference Centers

Name	Guest Rooms	Exhibit Space (sq. ft.)	Meeting Space (sq. ft.)
Crowne Plaza Pyramid at Journal Center	n/a	n/a	n/a
Hyatt Regency Albuquerque	395	n/a	24,000
Radisson Astrodome Hotel & Convention Center	n/a	n/a	n/a
Radisson Hotel & Conference Center	366	7,031	22,000

Note: n/a not available
Source: www.officialtravelguide.com; www.eventective.com; original research

Living Environment

COST OF LIVING

Cost of Living Index

Year	Composite Index	Groceries	Housing	Utilities	Trans- portation	Health Care	Misc. Goods/ Services
2004	103.1	99.7	106.6	120.7	100.4	106.5	97.0
2005	105.5	108.4	114.0	99.8	118.1	100.7	96.2
2006	102.5	105.2	109.7	93.0	103.4	101.1	98.4

Note: U.S. = 100
Source: The Council for Community and Economic Research (formerly ACCRA), Cost of Living Index, 2004, 2005 and 2006 4-Quarter Averages

HOUSING

House Price Index (HPI)

Area	National Ranking[2]	Quarterly Change (%)	One-Year Change (%)	Five-Year Change (%)
MSA[1]	19	1.69	14.46	55.12
U.S.[3]	-	1.12	5.87	55.21

Note: The HPI is a weighted repeat sales index. It measures average price changes in repeat sales or refinancings on the same properties. This information is obtained by reviewing repeat mortgage transactions on single-family properties whose mortgages have been purchased or securitized by Fannie Mae or Freddie Mac in January 1975; (1) Metropolitan Statistical Area - see Appendix B for areas included; (2) Rankings are based on annual percentage change for all metro areas containing at least 15,000 transactions over the last 10 years and ranges from 1 to 282; (3) figures based on a weighted division average; all figures are for the period ending December 31, 2006
Source: Office of Federal Housing Enterprise Oversight, House Price Index, March 1, 2007

House Price Valuations

Area	Q4 1999	Q4 2000	Q4 2001	Q4 2002	Q4 2003	Q4 2004	Q4 2005	Q4 2006
MSA[1]	-4.2	-7.0	-12.4	-8.3	-5.4	-3.5	7.6	11.2

Note: Figures show the percentage of over- or under-valuation of single family homes relative to statistically normal house values (e.g. a value of 23.6 indicates that house values are 23.6% overvalued). Statistically normal house values are based on house prices, interest rates, household incomes, population densities, and any historical premiums or discounts metropolitan areas have exhibited over time; (1) Figures cover the Metropolitan Statistical Area - see Appendix B for areas included
Source: Global Insight/National City Corporation, House Prices in America, March 2007

Median Home Prices

Area	2004	2005	2006[p]	Percent Change 2005 to 2006
Metro Area[1]	145.4	169.2	184.2	8.9
U.S. Average	195.2	219.0	222.0	1.4

Note: Figures are median sales prices of existing single-family homes in thousands of dollars; (p) preliminary; n/a not available; (1) Covers the Albuquerque, NM Metropolitan Statistical Area - see Appendix B for areas included
Source: National Association of Realtors, Metropolitan Area Prices, 4th Quarter 2006

Housing: Year Structure Built

Area	1990 -2000	1980 -1989	1970 -1979	1960 -1969	1950 -1959	1940 -1949	Before 1940	Median Year
City	20.1	18.4	23.5	13.8	14.6	5.9	3.6	1975
MSA[1]	24.3	20.3	22.0	12.5	12.0	5.1	3.7	1978
U.S.	17.0	15.8	18.5	13.7	12.7	7.3	15.0	1971

Note: Figures are percentages; (1) Metropolitan Statistical Area - see Appendix A for areas included
Source: Census 2000, Summary File 3

Average New Home Price

Area	2004	2005	2006
City	268,792	311,601	332,293
U.S.	253,574	275,712	299,269

Note: Figures, in dollars, are based on a new home with 2,400 sq. ft. of living area on an 8,000 sq. ft. lot.
Source: The Council for Community and Economic Research (formerly ACCRA), Cost of Living Index, 2004, 2005 and 2006 4-Quarter Averages

Average Apartment Rent

Area	2004	2005	2006
City	745	764	774
U.S.	716	740	766

Note: Figures, in dollars per month, are based on an unfurnished two bedroom, 1-1/2 or 2 bath apartment, approximately 950 sq. ft. in size, excluding all utilities except water
Source: The Council for Community and Economic Research (formerly ACCRA), Cost of Living Index, 2004, 2005 and 2006 4-Quarter Averages

RESIDENTIAL UTILITIES

Average Residential Utility Costs

Area	All Electric ($/mth)	Part Electric ($/mth)	Other Energy ($/mth)	Phone ($/mth)
City	–	55.76	87.40	25.18
U.S.	136.00	76.53	90.52	25.87

Source: The Council for Community and Economic Research (formerly ACCRA), Cost of Living Index, 2006 4-Quarter Average

HEALTH

Average Health Care Costs

Area	Optometrist ($/visit)	Doctor ($/visit)	Dentist ($/visit)
City	78.56	82.28	66.93
U.S.	76.38	76.10	68.72

Note: Optometrist—based on a full vision eye exam for an established adult patient;
Doctor—based on a general practitioner's routine exam of an established patient;
Dentist—based on adult teeth cleaning and periodic oral exam.
Source: The Council for Community and Economic Research (formerly ACCRA), Cost of Living Index, 2006 4-Quarter Average

Mortality Rates

ICD-10 Sub-Chapter	ICD-10 Code	Age-Adjusted Death Rate per 100,000 population[1]	U.S. Age-Adjusted Death Rate per 100,000 population
Malignant neoplasms	C00-C97	171.2	185.8
Ischaemic heart diseases	I20-I25	115.7	150.2
Other forms of heart disease	I30-I51	40.3	50.8
Cerebrovascular diseases	I60-I69	48.0	50.0
Chronic lower respiratory diseases	J40-J47	43.7	41.1
Diabetes mellitus	E10-E14	23.5	24.5
Other degenerative diseases of the nervous system	G30-G31	21.8	22.3
Other external causes of accidental injury	W00-X59	45.0	21.2
Influenza and pneumonia	J10-J18	17.3	19.8
Hypertensive diseases	I10-I13	16.6	18.1

Note: ICD-10 = International Classification of Diseases 10th Revision; (1) Figures cover Bernalillo County, NM
Source: Centers for Disease Control and Prevention, National Center for Health Statistics. Compressed Mortality File 1999-2004. CDC WONDER On-line Database, compiled from Compressed Mortality File 1999-2004 Series 20 No. 2J, 2007.

Health Risk Data

Item	Area[1] (%)	U.S. (%)
Adults who have been told they have high blood pressure	22.0	25.5
Adults who have been told they have high blood cholesterol	28.0	35.6
Adults who have been told they have diabetes[2]	5.7	7.3
Adults who have been told they have arthritis	22.5	27.0
Adults who have been told they currently have asthma	8.6	8.0
Adults who are current smokers	21.3	20.6

Note: (1) Figures cover the Metropolitan Statistical Area - see Appendix B for areas included; (2) Figures do not include pregnancy-related diabetes, pre-diabetes or borderline diabetes
Source: Centers for Disease Control and Prevention, Behaviorial Risk Factor Surveillance System, SMART: Selected Metropolitan/Micropolitan Area Trends, 2005

Distribution of Office-Based Physicians

Area	Total	Family/ General Practice	Specialties		
			Medical	Surgical	Other
MSA[1] (number)	1,474	207	526	292	449
MSA[1] (rate per 10,000 pop.)	20.4	2.9	7.3	4.0	6.2
Metro Average[2] (rate per 10,000 pop.)	19.4	2.1	7.5	4.5	5.3

Note: Data as of December 31, 2004; (1) Metropolitan Statistical Area - see Appendix A for areas included; (2) Average of the 79 unique MSAs and CMSAs in this book
Source: American Medical Association, Physician Characteristics & Distribution in the U.S., 2006

Hospitals

Albuquerque has the following hospitals: 8 general medical and surgical; 2 psychiatric; 2 rehabilitation; 2 long-term acute care; 1 children's orthopedic.
AHA Guide to the Healthcare Field 2007

According to *U.S. News,* the Albuquerque metro area is home to one of the best hospitals in the U.S.: **University Hospital**; *U.S. News Online, "America's Best Hospitals 2006"*

EDUCATION

Public School District Statistics

District Name	Schls	Pupils	Pupil/ Teacher Ratio	Minority Pupils[1] (%)	Free Lunch Eligible[2] (%)	IEP[3] (%)
Albuquerque Public Schools	157	93,341	15.1	64.8	41.0	19.3

Note: Table includes regular local school districts with 2,000 or more students; (1) Percentage of students that are not white, non-Hispanic; (2) Percentage of students that are eligible for the free lunch program; (3) Percentage of students that have an Individualized Education Program.
Source: U.S. Department of Education, National Center for Education Statistics, Common Core of Data, Local Education Agency (School District) Universe Survey: School Year 2004-2005; U.S. Department of Education, National Center for Education Statistics, Common Core of Data, Public Elementary/Secondary School Universe Survey: School Year 2004-2005

Educational Quality

School District	Education Quotient[1]	Graduate Outcome[2]	Community Index[3]	Resource Index[4]	Rating[5]
Albuquerque Public Schools	56	62	56	4	Green

Note: Scores are national percentile rankings and range from 1 (worst) to 99 (best); (1) Combination of the Graduate Outcome, Community and Resource Indexes weighted to reflect the greater importance of the Graduate Outcome and Resource Index; (2) Based on graduation rates and college board scores (SAT/ACT); (3) Based on the surrounding community's level of affluence and adult education; (4) Based on teacher salaries, per-pupil expenditures and student-teacher ratios; (5) School districts receive one of five rankings: Gold Medal (top 16 percent of districts evaluated); Blue Ribbon (top third); Green Light (average); Yellow Light (bottom 25 percent); Red Light (bottom 10 percent).
Source: Expansion Management, "2007 Education Quotient," January 2007

Highest Level of Education

Area	Less than H.S.	H.S. Diploma	Some College, No Deg.	Associate Degree	Bachelors Degree	Masters Degree	Profess. School Degree	Doctorate Degree
City	13.9	24.1	24.4	6.0	18.4	9.0	2.3	1.9
MSA[1]	15.9	25.9	23.9	6.1	16.5	7.9	2.2	1.6
U.S.	19.4	28.4	21.2	6.4	15.7	5.9	2.0	1.0

Note: Figures are 2006 estimated percentages and cover persons age 25 and over; (1) Metropolitan Statistical Area - see Appendix B for areas included
Source: Claritas, Inc.

Educational Attainment by Race

Area	High School Graduate (%)					Bachelor's Degree (%)				
	Total	White	Black	Asian	Hisp.[2]	Total	White	Black	Asian	Hisp.[2]
City	85.9	88.6	86.3	81.1	72.4	31.8	35.8	23.7	40.3	15.2
MSA[1]	83.9	87.3	85.3	81.1	70.4	28.4	32.8	22.5	39.4	13.2
U.S.	80.4	83.6	72.3	80.4	52.4	24.4	26.1	14.3	44.1	10.4

Note: Figures shown cover persons 25 years old and over; (1) Metropolitan Statistical Area - see Appendix A for areas included; (2) people of Hispanic origin can be of any race
Source: Census 2000, Summary File 3

School Enrollment by Type

Area	Grades KG to 8				Grades 9 to 12			
	Public		Private		Public		Private	
	Enrollment	%	Enrollment	%	Enrollment	%	Enrollment	%
City	47,609	87.4	6,870	12.6	22,015	89.4	2,624	10.6
MSA[1]	84,412	88.0	11,536	12.0	37,748	89.6	4,358	10.4
U.S.	33,526,011	88.7	4,285,121	11.3	14,848,628	90.6	1,532,323	9.4

Note: Figures shown cover persons 3 years old and over; (1) Metropolitan Statistical Area - see Appendix A for areas included
Source: Census 2000, Summary File 3

School Enrollment by Race

Area	Grades KG to 8 (%)				Grades 9 to 12 (%)			
	White	Black	Asian	Hisp.[1]	White	Black	Asian	Hisp.[1]
City	63.7	3.5	1.8	49.7	64.3	3.8	2.0	47.7
MSA[2]	61.5	2.6	1.2	50.4	62.9	2.5	1.5	49.0
U.S.	68.5	15.5	3.3	16.8	68.8	15.5	3.8	15.7

Note: Figures shown cover persons 3 years old and over; (1) people of Hispanic origin can be of any race; (2) Metropolitan Statistical Area - see Appendix A for areas included
Source: Census 2000, Summary File 3

Average Salaries of Public School Teachers

District	2004-05		2005-06		Percent Change 2004-05 to 2005-06
	Dollars	Rank[1]	Dollars	Rank[1]	
NEW MEXICO	39,391	40	41,637	37	5.70
U.S. Average	47,674	-	49,109	-	3.01

Note: (1) State rank ranges from 1 to 51.
Source: National Education Association, Rankings & Estimates: Rankings of the States 2005 and Estimates of School Statistics 2006, November 2006

Higher Education

Four-Year Colleges			Two-Year Colleges			Medical Schools[1]	Law Schools[2]	Voc/ Tech[3]
Public	Private Non-profit	Private For-profit	Public	Private Non-profit	Private For-profit			
1	2	4	2	0	1	1	1	5

Note: Figures cover institutions located within the city limits; (1) includes schools accredited by the Liaison Committee on Medical Education and the American Osteopathic Association; (2) includes American Bar Association-accredited law schools; (3) includes all schools with programs that are less than 2 years Source: National Center for Education Statistics, The Integrated Postsecondary Education System (IPEDS) Peer Analysis System, 2006; www.usnews.com, America's Best Graduate Schools 2008, Medical School Directory; www.usnews.com, America's Best Graduate Schools 2008, Law School Directory

PRESIDENTIAL ELECTION

2004 Presidential Election Results

Area	Bush	Kerry	Nader	Other
Bernalillo County	47.3	51.5	0.6	0.6
U.S.	50.7	48.3	0.4	0.6

Note: Results are percentages and may not add to 100% due to rounding Source: Dave Leip's Atlas of U.S. Presidential Elections, www.uselectionatlas.org

MAJOR EMPLOYERS

Major Employers

Company Name	Industry	Type of Site
AOL	Telephone communication, except radio	Branch
Children Youth Families NM Dept	Administration of social & manpower programs	Branch
City Albuquerque Police Dept	Police protection	Branch
City of Albuquerque	Executive offices	Headquarters
Intel	Semiconductors and related devices	Branch
Kirtland AFB	National security	Branch
Lovelace Health Systems Inc	Offices and clinics of medical doctors	Headquarters
Mediplex	Skilled nursing care facilities	Single
NM Veterans Medical Center	Administration of veterans' affairs	Branch
Presybterian Hospital	General medical and surgical hospitals	Branch
Sandia National Laboratories	Administration of general economic programs	Branch
Sandia National Laboratories	Noncommercial research organizations	Headquarters
T-Mobile USA Inc	Radiotelephone communication	Branch
TVI	Vocational schools, nec	Headquarters
United States Dept of Energy	Administration of general economic programs	Branch
University Hospital	General medical and surgical hospitals	Branch
VA Medical Center	Administration of veterans' affairs	Branch

Note: Companies shown are located within the metropolitan area and have 1,000 or more employees; nec = not elsewhere classified. Source: www.zapdata.com, January 2007

PUBLIC SAFETY

Crime Rate

Area	All Crimes	Violent Crimes				Property Crimes		
		Murder	Forcible Rape	Robbery	Aggrav. Assault	Burglary	Larceny -Theft	Motor Vehicle Theft
City	7,115.9	10.8	58.1	234.4	648.6	1,170.7	4,219.7	773.7
Suburbs[1]	3,533.2	7.0	30.6	62.1	555.3	979.3	1,458.2	440.7
Metro[2]	5,753.3	9.3	47.6	168.9	613.1	1,097.9	3,169.4	647.0
U.S.	3,899.0	5.6	31.7	140.7	291.1	726.7	2,286.3	416.7

Note: Figures are crimes per 100,000 population; (1) All areas within the metro area that are located outside the city limits; (2) Metropolitan Statistical Area - see Appendix B for areas included Source: FBI Uniform Crime Reports, 2005

Hate Crimes

Area	Number of Quarters Reported	Bias Motivation				
		Race	Religion	Sexual Orientation	Ethnicity	Disability
City	4	8	1	1	1	0

Source: Federal Bureau of Investigation, Hate Crime Statistics 2005

RECREATION

Culture

Dance[1]	Theatre[1]	Instrumental Music[1]	Vocal Music[1]	Series/ Festivals	Museums	Zoos
2	4	2	2	2	15	1

Note: (1) number of professional perfoming groups
Source: The Grey House Performing Arts Directory, 2007; Official Museum Directory, 2007

Professional Sports Teams

Major League Baseball	National Basketball Association	National Football League	National Hockey League	Major League Soccer	Women's National Basketball Association
0	0	0	0	0	0

Note: Includes teams located in the Albuquerque metro area.
Source: www.sportsvenues.com, Listing of Venues by State/Province and City, 2006

MEDIA

Newspapers

Name	Target Audience	Frequency	Circulation
Albuquerque Journal	n/a	Daily	110,000
The Albuquerque Tribune	n/a	Daily	14,862
El Hispano News	Hispanic	Non-Daily	10,000
Health City Sun	General	Non-Daily	4,136
Weekly Alibi	Alternative/General	Non-Daily	45,000

Note: Includes newspapers whose offices are located in the city and whose circulations are 1,000 or more; n/a not available
Source: BurrellesLuce, MediaContacts Online, January 2006

Television Stations

Name	Ch.	Network(s)	Type	Ownership
KASA	2	Fox	Commercial	Raycom Media Inc.
KOFT	3	ABC	Commercial	Hearst-Argyle Broadcasting
KOB	4	NBC	Commercial	Hubbard Broadcasting Inc.
KNME	5	PBS	Public	n/a
KOCT	6	ABC	Commercial	Hearst-Argyle Broadcasting
KREZ	6	CBS	Commercial	Lee Enterprises Inc.
KOAT	7	ABC	Commercial	Hearst-Argyle Broadcasting
KOBR	8	NBC	Commercial	Hubbard Broadcasting Inc.
KBIM	10	CBS	Commercial	Emmis Communications
KOVT	10	ABC	Commercial	Hearst-Argyle Broadcasting
KCHF	11	n/a	Commercial	Son Broadcasting
KOBF	12	NBC	Commercial	Hubbard Broadcasting Inc.
KRQE	13	CBS	Commercial	Lee Enterprises Inc.
KWBQ	19	WBN	Commercial	n/a
KNAT	23	n/a	Non-comm.	All American Network
KAZQ	32	n/a	Non-comm.	Alpha Omega Broadcasting of Albuquerque
KLUZ	41	Univision	Commercial	Entravision Communications
KRPV	42	n/a	Non-comm.	Prime Time Christian Broadcasting Inc.
KASY	50	UPN	Commercial	Acme Broadcasting Inc.

Note: Stations included cover the Albuquerque-Santa Fe DMA (Designated Market Area)
BurrellesLuce, MediaContacts Online, January 2006

Major AM Radio Stations

Call Letters	Freq. (kHz)	Station Type	Target Audience	Station Format	Music Format
KLLV	550	Non-Comm	General/Religious	Educational/Music	Gospel
KNML	610	Commercial	General	Sports/Talk	n/a
KTNN	660	Commercial	Gen/Nat Amer/Nat Can	Educational/Music/News	Country
KKOB	770	n/a	General	Music/News	n/a
KSWV	810	Commercial	General/Hispanic	Educational/Music/News	Latin
KHAC	880	Commercial	Gen/Nat Amer/Rel	Educational/Music	Christian
KBIM	910	Commercial	General	News/Sports/Talk	n/a
KIUP	930	Commercial	General	Music/News/Sports/Talk	Oldies
KNFT	950	Commercial	General/Hispanic	Music/Talk	Blues
KNDN	960	Commercial	General/Native Amer	Music/News	World Music
KKIM	1000	Commercial	General/Religious	Talk	n/a
KINF	1020	Commercial	General/Hispanic	Music	Oldies
KYKK	1110	Commercial	General	News/Talk	n/a
KXKS	1190	Commercial	Hispanic	Music/News/Talk	Latin
KVSF	1260	n/a	General	Talk	n/a
KRDD	1320	Commercial	General/Hispanic	Educational/Music	Latin
KGAK	1330	Commercial	General/Native Amer	Music	International
KABQ	1350	Commercial	Hispanic	Music/News/Talk	Latin
KBUY	1360	Commercial	General	Music	Oldies
KENN	1390	Commercial	General	Talk	n/a
KCRX	1430	n/a	General	Music	Classical

Note: Stations included cover the Albuquerque-Santa Fe DMA (Designated Market Area); n/a not available
Source: BurrellesLuce, MediaContacts Online, January 2006

Major FM Radio Stations

Call Letters	Freq. (mHz)	Station Type	Target Audience	Station Format	Music Format
KFLQ	91.5	Non-Comm	General/Religious	Educational/Music/News	Christian
KRST	92.3	Commercial	General	Music/News/Talk	Country
KTZA	92.9	Commercial	General	Music	Contemp. Country
KRWN	92.9	Commercial	General	Music	Modern Rock
KXXI	93.7	Commercial	General	Music	Classic Rock
KZRR	94.1	Commercial	General	Music/News/Talk	Modern Rock
KKOR	94.5	Commercial	General	Music	Top 40
KBOM	94.7	n/a	General	Music/News/Talk	n/a
KBIM	94.9	Commercial	General	Music/News/Sports/Talk	Adult Contemp.
KWYK	94.9	Commercial	General	Music	Adult Contemp.
KWRK	96.1	Commercial	General	Music	Adult Top 40
KDAG	96.9	Commercial	General	Music	Classic Rock
KBCQ	97.1	Commercial	General	Music	Top 40
KKSS	97.3	Commercial	General	Music/News/Talk	Rhythm & Blues
KLVO	97.7	Commercial	General/Hispanic	Music/News/Talk	Latin
KISZ	97.9	Commercial	General	Music	Contemp. Country
KABG	98.5	Commercial	General	Music/News/Talk	Oldies
KRSJ	100.5	Commercial	General	Music	Contemp. Country
KKIT	100.7	Commercial	General	Music/News/Sports/Talk	Modern Rock
KIQX	101.3	Commercial	General	Music	Alternative
KTRA	102.1	n/a	General	Music/News	n/a
KIXN	102.9	Commercial	General	Music	Contemp. Country
KNFT	102.9	Commercial	General	Music	Country
KTZO	103.3	Commercial	General	Music/News/Talk	Alternative
KYVA	103.7	Commercial	General	Music/News	Oldies
KBAC	104.1	Commercial	General	Music	Alternative
KCDY	104.1	Commercial	General	Music	Adult Contemp.
KKFG	104.5	Commercial	General	Music	Oldies
KTEG	104.7	n/a	Asian/Hispanic	Talk	n/a
KMOU	104.7	Commercial	General	Ed/Music/News/Sports/Talk	Country
KYLZ	106.3	Commercial	General	Music/News/Talk	Urban Contemp.
KZNM	106.7	n/a	General	Music/News/Sports	n/a

Note: Stations included cover the Albuquerque-Santa Fe DMA (Designated Market Area); n/a not available
BurrellesLuce, MediaContacts Online, January 2006

CLIMATE

Average and Extreme Temperatures

Temperature	Jan	Feb	Mar	Apr	May	Jun	Jul	Aug	Sep	Oct	Nov	Dec	Yr.
Extreme High (°F)	69	76	85	89	98	105	105	101	100	91	77	72	105
Average High (°F)	47	53	61	71	80	90	92	89	83	72	57	48	70
Average Temp. (°F)	35	40	47	56	65	75	79	76	70	58	45	36	57
Average Low (°F)	23	27	33	41	50	59	65	63	56	44	31	24	43
Extreme Low (°F)	-17	-5	8	19	28	40	52	50	37	21	-7	-7	-17

Note: Figures cover the years 1948-1992
Source: National Climatic Data Center, International Station Meteorological Climate Summary, 9/96

Average Precipitation/Snowfall/Humidity

Precip./Humidity	Jan	Feb	Mar	Apr	May	Jun	Jul	Aug	Sep	Oct	Nov	Dec	Yr.
Avg. Precip. (in.)	0.4	0.4	0.5	0.4	0.5	0.5	1.4	1.5	0.9	0.9	0.4	0.5	8.5
Avg. Snowfall (in.)	3	2	2	1	Tr	0	0	0	Tr	Tr	1	3	11
Avg. Rel. Hum. 5am (%)	68	64	55	48	48	45	60	65	61	60	63	68	59
Avg. Rel. Hum. 5pm (%)	41	33	25	20	19	18	27	30	29	29	35	43	29

Note: Figures cover the years 1948-1992; Tr = Trace amounts (<0.05 in. of rain; <0.5 in. of snow)
Source: National Climatic Data Center, International Station Meteorological Climate Summary, 9/96

Weather Conditions

Temperature			Daytime Sky			Precipitation		
10°F & below	32°F & below	90°F & above	Clear	Partly cloudy	Cloudy	0.01 inch or more precip.	0.1 inch or more snow/ice	Thunder-storms
4	114	65	140	161	64	60	9	38

Note: Figures are average number of days per year and cover the years 1948-1992
Source: National Climatic Data Center, International Station Meteorological Climate Summary, 9/96

HAZARDOUS WASTE

Superfund Sites

Albuquerque has three hazardous waste sites on the EPA's Superfund Final National Priorities List: **AT&SF (Albuquerque)**; **Fruit Avenue Plume**; **South Valley**. *U.S. Environmental Protection Agency, Final National Priorities List, March 20, 2007*

AIR & WATER QUALITY

Air Quality Index

Area	Percent of Days when Air Quality was...[2]				AQI Statistics	
	Good	Moderate	Unhealthy for Sensitive Groups	Unhealthy	Maximum	Median
MSA[1]	32.1	61.9	4.7	1.4	169	59

Note: The Air Quality Index (AQI) is an index for reporting daily air quality. EPA calculates the AQI for five major air pollutants regulated by the Clean Air Act: ground-level ozone, particle pollution (also known as particulate matter), carbon monoxide, sulfur dioxide, and nitrogen dioxide. The AQI runs from 0 to 500. The higher the AQI value, the greater the level of air pollution and the greater the health concern. There are six AQI categories: "Good" The AQI is between 0 and 50. Air quality is considered satisfactory; "Moderate" The AQI is between 51 and 100. Air quality is acceptable; "Unhealthy for Sensitive Groups" When AQI values are between 101 and 150, members of sensitive groups may experience health effects; "Unhealthy" When AQI values are between 151 and 200 everyone may begin to experience health effects; "Very Unhealthy" AQI values between 201 and 300 trigger a health alert; "Hazardous" AQI values over 300 trigger health warnings of emergency conditions; (1) Metropolitan Statistical Area - see Appendix A for areas included; (2) Based on 365 days with AQI data in 2005.
Source: U.S. Environmental Protection Agency, Air Quality Index Report, 2005

Air Quality Index Pollutants

Area	Percent of Days when AQI Pollutant was...[2]					
	Carbon Monoxide	Nitrogen Dioxide	Ozone	Sulfur Dioxide	Particulate Matter 2.5	Particulate Matter 10
MSA[1]	0.0	0.0	12.1	0.0	44.4	43.6

Note: The Air Quality Index (AQI) is an index for reporting daily air quality. EPA calculates the AQI for five major air pollutants regulated by the Clean Air Act: ground-level ozone, particle pollution (also known as particulate matter), carbon monoxide, sulfur dioxide, and nitrogen dioxide. The AQI runs from 0 to 500. The higher the AQI value, the greater the level of air pollution and the greater the health concern; (1) Metropolitan Statistical Area - see Appendix A for areas included; (2) Based on 365 days with AQI data in 2005.
Source: U.S. Environmental Protection Agency, Air Quality Index Report, 2005

Number of Days with Air Quality Index Values Greater than 100

Area	Trend Sites (18)								All Sites (68)
	1998	1999	2000	2001	2002	2003	2004	2005	2005
MSA[1]	0	1	0	1	4	2	2	0	3

Note: An AQI value greater than 100 indicates that air quality would have been in the unhealthful range on that day. Data from exceptional events are not included. These counts are presented in two ways. First, the counts are based on sites having an adequate record of monitoring data during the trend period (trend sites). These counts represent the relative change in the number of days with AQI values greater than 100. In the last column, the counts are based on all sites with data in the most recent year (because it is possible for a site to have data in the most recent year but not enough data to be a trend site); (1) Metropolitan Statistical Area - see Appendix A for areas included; n/a not available.
Source: U.S. Environmental Protection Agency, Air Trends Fact Book 2005

Maximum Pollutant Concentrations

	Particulate Matter 10 (ug/m^3)	Particulate Matter 2.5 (ug/m^3)	Ozone 1-hour (ppm)	Carbon Monoxide (ppm)	Sulfur Dioxide (ppm)	Nitrogen Dioxide (ppm)	Lead (ug/m^3)
MSA[1] Level	162	19	0.093	3	n/a	0.016	n/a
NAAQS[2]	150	65	0.125	9	0.140	0.053	1.50
Met NAAQS[2]	No	Yes	Yes	Yes	n/a	Yes	n/a

Note: Data from exceptional events are not included; (1) Metropolitan Statistical Area - see Appendix A for areas included; (2) National Ambient Air Quality Standards; n/a not available
Units: ppm = parts per million; ug/m^3 = micrograms per cubic meter
Source: U.S. Environmental Protection Agency, Air Trends Fact Book 2005

Watershed Health

The U.S. Environmental Protection Agency monitors the health of the aquatic resources for the nation's 2,000+ watersheds. **The Rio Grande-Albuquerque watershed serves the Albuquerque area and received an overall Index of Watershed Indicators (IWI) score of 3 (less serious problems - low vulnerability).** The IWI score is based on seven condition and nine vulnerability indicators. The overall IWI score ranges from 1 (best health) to 6 (worst health). The Condition Indicators include: designated use attainment, fish and wildlife consumption advisories, source water condition, contaminated sediments, ambient water quality, and wetlands loss index. The Vulnerability Indicators include: aquatic species at risk, conventional and toxic loads over permitted limits, urban and agricultural runoff potential, population change, hydrologic modification, estuarine pollution susceptibility, and air deposition. *Note: The IWI is no longer being updated by the U.S. EPA. Source: U.S. Environmental Protection Agency, Index of Watershed Indicators, October 26, 2001*

Drinking Water

Water System Name	Pop. Served	Primary Water Source Type	Number of Violations in 2006[a]		
			Health Based	Significant Monitoring	Monitoring
Albuquerque Water System	453,000	Ground	None	None	None

Note: (a) Based on violation data from January 1, 2006 to December 31, 2006
Source: U.S. Environmental Protection Agency, Office of Ground Water and Drinking Water, Safe Drinking Water Information System (data extracted April 12, 2007)

Albuquerque tap water is alkaline, hard and fluoridated.
Editor & Publisher Market Guide, 2005

Anchorage, Alaska

Background

Anchorage is Alaska's largest city and a center for the state's communication, transportation, health care, and finance industries. Originally powered by the railroads and the fishing industry, Anchorage's economy has in more recent times been closely tied to petroleum production, which accounts for more than 22 percent of the nation's oil reserves.

Anchorage, in south-central Alaska, is a modern city in a spectacular natural setting, with the Chugach Mountain Range lying across its eastern skyline and the waters of the Cook Inlet to the west. The city can boast all the advantages of a dynamic urban center, while its residents enjoy a natural environment that still teems with bear, moose, caribou, fox, eagles, wolves, dall sheep, orcas, and beluga whales.

The city is young, having been incorporated in 1920, and grew slowly for the next several decades. During World War II, when airfields and roads were constructed to aid in the war effort, the population expanded dramatically; by 1946, Anchorage was home to more than 40,000 people.

In 1964, the region was hit by the strongest earthquake ever to strike North America. There was extensive damage and some loss of life, but the city was quickly rebuilt; in fact, reconstruction was so prompt, efficient, and successful that many look back on the period with considerable civic pride.

In 1951, Anchorage International Airport, which is now Ted Stevens International Airport (ANC), was completed, and the city became vital to the emerging air transport industry as new routes were created. The ANC flies more than 560 transcontinental cargo flights each week. Elmendorf Air Force Base at the northeast end of town, and Anchorage's pioneering development of "bush" aviation, which serves the entire interior of Alaska, further testify to the importance of air travel to the city's development. Also located at the airport are Fort Richardson Army Post and Kulis Air National Guard Base, that together employ 8,500.

Oil in Alaska was first discovered in 1957, and 17 oil companies subsequently set up headquarters in Anchorage, giving the city a tremendous economic boost. In 1968, when the even larger North Slope field was discovered, Anchorage was again a major beneficiary. With the completion of the Trans-Alaskan Pipeline System in 1977, Anchorage entered into its contemporary period of sustained population growth and dynamic economic development.

Alaska's tourism industry accounts for more than 30,000 statewide jobs and an estimated economic impact of nearly $80 million in Anchorage alone.

In 1999, two new fiber-optic cables were installed between Alaska and the continental U.S., increasing capabilities of computer networks statewide.

The city's cultural amenities include the Anchorage Museum of History and Art and the Alaska Aviation Heritage Museum, which chronicles the story of Alaska's early and pioneering air transport system. Near the city is the Potter Section House Railway Museum, which pays homage to the state's vital rail industry. The city also boasts the Alaska Center for the Performing Arts and the Alaska Botanical Gardens. Delaney Park, also known as the Park Strip, is a venerable and valued recreational resource in the city's business district, and its ongoing improvement looks toward a year-round "Central Park" for Anchorage.

Because of its long summer days and relatively mild temperatures, Anchorage is called "The City of Lights and Flowers," and is adorned in summer throughout the municipality with open, grassy expanses and flowers. The season brings out a friendly competition among the city's residents, who plant along streets, in parks, private gardens, window boxes, and lobbies.

The natural environment of Anchorage is spectacular, and at nearby Portage Glacier, one can watch the glacier "calving," as huge blocks of ice crash into the lake below. Anchorage is also located at one end of the famous annual Iditarod Trail Sled Dog Race.

The city is an educational center with two universities and many technical, vocational, and private schools. A campus of the University of Alaska has been in Anchorage since 1954, and the city is also home to Alaska Pacific University.

The weather in Anchorage, contrary to what many believe, is not savagely cold. It is tempered by the city's location on the coast and by the Alaska Mountain Range, which acts as a barrier to very cold air from the north. Snow season lasts from October to May. Summers can bring fog and rain.

Rankings

General Rankings

■ Anchorage was ranked #160 out of 331 metro areas in *Cities Ranked & Rated*. Criteria: cost of living; climate; crime; transportation; economy and jobs; education; arts and culture; health and healthcare; leisure. *Cities Ranked & Rated, 1st Edition, 2004*

■ Anchorage was selected as one of "America's Top 100 Places to Live" by Relocate-America.com. Nominations were accepted throughout the year for cities and towns considered to be "great places to live." The nominations, along with key data regarding education, employment, economy, crime, parks, recreation and housing were reviewed, rated and judged by the Relocate-America.com editorial staff. *Relocate-America.com, "Relocate America's Top 100 Places to Live in 2006"*

Business/Finance Rankings

■ Anchorage was selected as one of the best places to start and grow a company by *Entrepreneur* and the National Policy Research Council. The Anchorage metro area ranked #20 out of 162 small metro areas. Criteria: business formation and growth (firms started four to 14 years ago that still employ at least 5 people and experienced rapid growth over the last four years). *Entrepreneur/National Policy Research Council, "Hot Cities for Entrepreneurs," September 2006*

■ Intel, in partnership with Sperling's BestPlaces, ranked the 80 "Best Cities for Teleworking" in America. The Anchorage metro area ranked #3 among small metro areas. The study identifies cities that hold the greatest potential for teleworking based on a host of factors including typical commuting times, fuel prices, availability of broadband Internet access and percentage of the population in telework friendly jobs. The study also factored in extreme climate and natural hazards. *Intel, "Best Cities for Teleworking," March 30, 2006*

■ The Anchorage metro area appeared on the Milken Institute "2005 Best Performing Cities" index. Rank: #49 out of 200 large metro areas. Criteria: job growth; wage and salary growth; high-tech output growth. *Milken Institute, "2005 Best Performing Cities," February 2006*

■ The Anchorage metro area was selected as one of "The Best Cities for Doing Business in America." *Inc.* magazine measured employment growth in 393 regions using the following criteria: recent growth trend; mid-term growth; long-term trend; and current year growth. The Anchorage metro area ranked #14 among mid-sized metro areas and #63 overall. *Inc., May 2006*

■ *Forbes* ranked the 200 most populous metro areas in the U.S. in terms of the "Best Places for Business and Careers." The Anchorage metro area was ranked #124. Criteria: business costs (labor, energy, tax and office space expenses); living costs (housing, transportation, food and other household expenditures); education levels of the work force; job growth; income growth; migration trends; crime rates; and culture/leisure. *Forbes, April 23, 2007*

■ *Kiplinger's Personal Finance* ranked 101 U.S. cities in terms of their total tax burdens. Anchorage ranked #14 (#1 had the lowest overall tax burden). Criteria: state income tax; property tax; sales tax; personal property tax; and gasoline tax. *Kiplinger's Personal Finance, July 2004*

■ Anchorage was identified as one of the top 10 richest major cities in the U.S. The city ranked #2. Criteria: 2004 median household income. *Forbes, "Richest Cities in the U.S.," October 27, 2005*

Health/Environment Rankings

■ The Anchorage metro area appeared in *Country Home's* "2007 Best Green Places Report". The area ranked #308. Criteria included: air and watershed quality; miles of mass transit; green power; number of farmer's markets, organic producers and groceries. *Country Home, "2007 Best Green Places Report," April 2007*

- The American Podiatric Medical Association and *Prevention* magazine ranked America's 100 most populated cities based on fitness-walker friendliness. The best cities have safe streets, beautiful places to walk, mild weather and good air quality. Anchorage ranked #18. *Prevention, "The Best Walking Cities of 2007," April 2007; American Podiatric Medical Association, "2007 Best Fitness-Walking Cities"*

- *Men's Health* ranked the nation's largest 100 cities in terms of the *Best (and Worst) Cities for Men*. Anchorage was ranked #7. Criteria: 24 statistical parameters of long life in the categories of health, quality of life, and fitness. *Men's Health, January/February 2007*

- *Men's Health* ranked 100 U.S. cities in terms of the quality of their tap water. Anchorage was ranked #71 and received a grade of C. Criteria: levels of total coliform bacteria, arsenic, lead, total trihalomethanes (linked to cancer), and halo-acetic acids, plus the number of EPA water-system violations from 1995 to 2005. *Men's Health, March 2007*

- Sperling's BestPlaces ranked 331 metro areas and identified the most and least stressful U.S. cities. The Anchorage metro area ranked #32 out of 114 mid-size metro areas (#1 = most stressful). Criteria: divorce rate; unemployment rate; violent and property crime; suicide rate; commute time; mental health; alcohol consumption; cloudy days. *www.BestPlaces.net, January 9, 2004*

- Anchorage was highlighted as one of the top 25 cleanest metro areas for long-term particle pollution (PM 2.5) in the U.S. The area ranked #6. *American Lung Association, State of the Air 2006*

Women/Minorities Rankings

- Anchorage was ranked #22 out of 100 metro areas in *SELF Magazine's* ranking of "America's Best Places for Women." A panel of experts came up with nearly 40 criteria including: drinking and smoking rates; depression; unemployment; parks; crime; disease; healthcare insurance coverage; air quality; and commute times. *SELF Magazine, "America's Best Places for Women 2006," December 2006*

- *Ladies Home Journal* ranked America's 200 largest cities based on the qualities women surveyed care about most. Anchorage ranked #42 out of 143 in the smaller city category (population under 300,000). Criteria: crime; lifestyle; education; jobs; health; child care; politics; and the economy. *Ladies Home Journal Online, "The Best Cities for Women 2002"*

Seniors/Retirement Rankings

- A.G. Edwards ranked America's 500 top-performing communities based on their residents' personal savings and investing behavior. The Anchorage metro area ranked #96 with an index score of 107.01 (national average = 100.00). A dozen statistical factors were measured including: participation in retirement savings plans; personal debt levels; and home ownership. *A.G. Edwards, "2006 Nest Egg Index", September 6, 2006*

Children/Family Rankings

- *Zero Population Growth* ranked 100 cities in terms of children's health, safety, and economic well-being. Anchorage was ranked #13 out of 80 Large Cities (remainder of the 100 largest cities in the U.S.) and was given a grade of A-. Criteria: total population and population growth; percent of population under 18 years of age; percent of births to teens; infant mortality rate; percent of eligible women not receiving Title X services; contraceptive equity indicator; percent of children without health insurance; percent of city residents over age 25 with a high-school diploma; ration of PopEd (Population Connection's Education Program) teachers trained; sexuality education indicator; proficiency in reading and math; percent of kids living in poverty; percent growth in urbanized land; violent crime rate; recycling. *Population Connection, Kid Friendly Cities: Report Card 2004*

■ Anchorage was chosen as one of America's "100 Best Communities for Young People." The winners were selected based upon detailed information provided about each community's efforts to fulfill five essential promises critical to the well-being of young people: caring adults who are actively involved in their lives; safe places in which to learn and grow; a healthy start toward adulthood; an effective education that builds marketable skills; and opportunities to help others. *America's Promise, "100 Best Communities for Young People," September 26, 2005*

Safety Rankings

■ Allstate ranked the 200 largest cities in America in terms of driver safety. Anchorage ranked #97. In addition, drivers were 8.4% more likely to have had an accident compared to the national average. Allstate researchers analyzed internal Property Damage reported claims over a two-year period (from January 2003 to December 2004) to ensure the findings would not be affected by external influences such as weather or road construction. A weighted average of the two-year numbers determined the annual percentages. The report defines an auto crash as any collision resulting in a property damage claim. *Allstate, "Allstate America's Best Drivers Report 2006," May 24, 2006*

■ *Men's Health* ranked 101 U.S. cities in terms of the likelihood of being robbed. Anchorage was ranked #5 and received a grade of A+. *Men's Health, June 2005*

■ *Ladies Home Journal* ranked America's 200 largest cities in terms of safety. Anchorage ranked #92 out of 200. Criteria: violent crimes; crimes against property; and rape. *Ladies Home Journal Online, "The Best Cities for Women 2002"*

Sports/Recreation Rankings

■ Anchorage was chosen as one of America's 25 best cities for running. The city was ranked #16. Criteria: number of running clubs per city; amount of land set aside for park usage; air quality; weather; crime rates; and results from a *Runner's World* poll in which readers ranked their favorite running cities. *Runner's World, "The 25 Best Running Cities in America," July 2005*

■ Anchorage was chosen as one of America's best cities for bicycling. The city ranked #0 in the large city category (population 500,000 to 1 million). Criteria: cycling-friendly statistics (number of bike lanes and routes, number of bike racks, city bike projects completed and planned; bike culture (number of bike commuters, popular clubs, cool cycling events, renowned bike shops); climate/geography (the quality of roads and trails for riding, and how frequently mother nature lets riders enjoy them). *Bicycling, March 2006*

■ *Golf Digest* ranked 330 metro areas in the U.S. in terms of golf. The Anchorage metro area was ranked #327. Criteria: access to golf; weather; value of golf; and quality of golf. *Golf Digest, "Metro Golf Rankings," August 2005*

Dating/Romance Rankings

■ The Anchorage metro area was selected as one of the "Top Ten U.S. Cities for Finding a Rich, Single Man" by Teasley, a Manhattan-based marketing consulting firm. The area ranked #2. Criteria: high single-male to single-female ratios and higher income to cost-of-living ratios. *Teasley, February 10, 2004*

Miscellaneous Rankings

■ Anchorage was selected as one of America's "20 Meanest Cities" by the National Coalition for the Homeless and The National Law Center on Homelessness & Poverty. The city was ranked #16. Criteria: the number of anti-homeless laws; the enforcement of those laws and severities of penalties; the general political climate towards homeless people; local advocate support for the meanest designation; the city's history of criminalization measures; and the existence of pending or recently enacted criminalization legislation. *National Coalition for the Homeless and The National Law Center on Homelessness & Poverty, "A Dream Denied: The Criminalization of Homelessness in U.S. Cities," January 2006*

■ Sperling's BestPlaces in partnership with Pep Boys ranked 77 metro areas and identified "America's Most Drivable Cities." The Anchorage metro area ranked #61. Criteria: climate; road roughness; urban mobility; gas prices. *Pep Boys, "America's Most Drivable Cities," April 9, 2003*

■ Anchorage was selected as one of "America's Most Literate Cities." The city ranked #47 out of the 70 largest U.S. cities. Criteria: number of booksellers; library resources; Internet resources; educational attainment; periodical publishing resources; newspaper circulation. *Central Connecticut State University, "America's Most Literate Cities 2006"*

■ A study by Sperling's BestPlaces examined which U.S. metro areas were most affected by the fuel crunch in 2005. The Anchorage metro area was selected as being one of the least impacted areas. The area ranked #1 out of 10. Criteria: average miles driven per day per peak traveler; average gallons of gas used per peak traveler; money spent on gas per driver. *Sperling's BestPlaces, www.bestplaces.net, September 29, 2005*

Business Environment

CITY FINANCES

City Government Finances

Component	2003-2004 ($000)	2003-2004 ($ per capita)
Total Revenues	1,044,097	3,882
Total Expenditures	1,123,377	4,176
Debt Outstanding	1,371,881	5,100
Cash and Securities	775,974	2,885

Source: U.S Census Bureau, Government Finances 2003-2004

City Government Revenue by Source

Source	2003-2004 ($000)	2003-2004 ($ per capita)
General Revenue		
From Federal Government	34,670	129
From State Government	314,994	1,171
From Local Governments	0	0
Taxes		
Property	318,527	1,184
Sales	15,022	56
Personal Income	0	0
License	9,617	36
Charges	93,548	348
Liquor Store	0	0
Utility	122,724	456
Employee Retirement	71,825	267
Other	63,170	235

Source: U.S Census Bureau, Government Finances 2003-2004

City Government Expenditures by Function

Function	2003-2004 ($000)	2003-2004 ($ per capita)	2003-2004 (%)
General Expenditures			
Airports	2,926	11	0.3
Corrections	0	0	0.0
Education	542,080	2,015	48.3
Fire Protection	45,956	171	4.1
Governmental Administration	29,163	108	2.6
Health	29,841	111	2.7
Highways	67,142	250	6.0
Hospitals	0	0	0.0
Housing and Community Development	0	0	0.0
Interest on General Debt	64,741	241	5.8
Libraries	5,852	22	0.5
Parking	3,632	14	0.3
Parks and Recreation	28,513	106	2.5
Police Protection	67,843	252	6.0
Public Welfare	0	0	0.0
Sewerage	26,883	100	2.4
Solid Waste Management	18,440	69	1.6
Liquor Store	0	0	0.0
Utility	136,911	509	12.2
Employee Retirement	21,030	78	1.9
Other	32,424	121	2.9

Source: U.S Census Bureau, Government Finances 2003-2004

Municipal Bond Ratings

Area	Moody's
City	Aaa (1/2006)

Source: Mergent Bond Record, January 2007 (unless noted otherwise)

DEMOGRAPHICS

Population Growth

Area	1990 Census	2000 Census	2006 Estimate	2011 Projection	Population Growth (%) 1990-2000	Population Growth (%) 2000-2011
City	226,338	260,283	280,215	299,649	15.0	15.1
MSA[1]	266,021	319,605	355,824	387,974	20.1	21.4
U.S.	248,709,873	281,421,906	298,021,266	312,383,955	13.2	11.0

Note: (1) Metropolitan Statistical Area - see Appendix B for areas included
Source: Claritas, Inc.

Number of Households and Average Household Size

Area	2006 Estimate	2006 Average Household Size
City	102,096	2.74
MSA[1]	128,706	2.76
U.S.	112,267,302	2.65

Note: (1) Metropolitan Statistical Area - see Appendix B for areas included
Source: Claritas, Inc.

Race and Ethnicity

Area	White Alone[2]	Black Alone[2]	Asian Alone[2]	Other Race Alone[2]	Hispanic[3]
City	69.2	5.9	6.5	18.4	7.2
MSA[1]	72.9	4.9	5.3	16.9	6.3
U.S.	73.3	12.4	4.2	10.1	14.5

Note: Figures are 2006 estimates; (1) Metropolitan Statistical Area - see Appendix B for areas included
(2) Alone is defined as not being in combination with one or more other races; (3) May be of any race.
Source: Claritas, Inc.

Segregation

City Index[2]	City Rank[3]	MSA[1] Index[2]	MSA[1] Rank[4]
41.4	82	41.4	295

Note: Figures are based on an analysis of Census 2000 data; (1) Metropolitan Statistical Area - see Appendix A for areas included; (2) White/Black Dissimilarity Index—the most commonly used measure of segregation between two groups, reflecting their relative distributions across neighborhoods within a city or metropolitan area. It can range in value from 0, indicating complete integration, to 100, indicating complete segregation; (3) Ranges from 1 (most segregated) to 100 (least segregated) and includes all the cities in this book; (4) Ranges from 1 (most segregated) to 318 (least segregated) and includes 318 metropolitan areas.
Source: www.CensusScope.org

Ancestry

Area	German	Irish[2]	English	American	Italian	Polish	French[3]	Scottish
City	17.6	11.6	10.0	6.0	3.2	2.3	3.4	2.7
MSA[1]	17.6	11.6	10.0	6.0	3.2	2.3	3.4	2.7
U.S.	15.2	10.9	8.7	7.3	5.6	3.2	3.0	1.7

Note: Figures include multiple ancestry (e.g. if a person reported being Irish and Italian, they were included in both columns); (1) Metropolitan Statistical Area - see Appendix A for areas included; (2) Includes Celtic; (3) Includes Alsatian but excludes Basque
Source: Census 2000, Summary File 3

Foreign-Born Population

Area	Any Foreign Country	Percent of Population Born in Europe	Asia	Africa	Oceania[2]	Canada	Mexico	Latin America[3]
City	8.2	1.6	4.1	0.1	0.2	0.5	0.6	1.1
MSA[1]	8.2	1.6	4.1	0.1	0.2	0.5	0.6	1.1
U.S.	11.1	1.7	2.9	0.3	0.1	0.3	3.3	2.5

Note: (1) Metropolitan Statistical Area - see Appendix A for areas included; (2) Includes Australia, New Zealand subregion, Melanesia, Micronesia, Polynesia, and Oceania n.e.c; (3) Includes Central America (excluding Mexico), South America, and the Caribbean.
Source: Census 2000, Summary File 3

Marriage Status

Area	Never Married	Now Married (excluding Separated)	Separated	Widowed	Divorced
City	28.4	53.7	2.1	3.2	12.5
MSA[1]	28.4	53.7	2.1	3.2	12.5
U.S.	27.1	54.4	2.2	6.6	9.7

Note: Figures are percentages and cover the population 15 years of age and older;
(1) Metropolitan Statistical Area - see Appendix A for areas included
Source: Census 2000, Summary File 3

Age Distribution

Area	Percent of Population						
	Under Age 5	Age 5 to 17	Age 18 to 34	Age 35 to 49	Age 50 to 64	Age 65 to 79	80 Years and Over
City	7.6	21.5	24.9	27.2	13.5	4.3	1.0
MSA[1]	7.6	21.5	24.9	27.2	13.5	4.3	1.0
U.S.	6.8	18.9	23.7	23.5	14.8	9.2	3.2

Note: (1) Metropolitan Statistical Area - see Appendix A for areas included
Source: Census 2000, Summary File 3

Male/Female Ratio

Area	Males	Females	Males per 100 Females
City	142,084	138,131	102.9
MSA[1]	181,327	174,497	103.9
U.S.	146,712,712	151,308,554	97.0

Note: Figures are 2006 estimates; (1) Metropolitan Statistical Area -
see Appendix B for areas included
Source: Claritas, Inc.

Religion

Area	Catholic	Southern Baptist	United Methodist	ELCA[1]	LDS[2]	Presbyterian Church USA	Jewish Est.	Muslim Est.
County	8.8	4.6	0.9	1.8	3.2	0.8	0.9	0.5
U.S.	22.0	7.1	3.7	1.8	1.5	1.1	2.2	0.6

Note: Figures are the number of adherents as a percentage of the total population; Adherents are defined as all
members, including full members, their children and the estimated number of other participants who are not
considered members (e.g. the baptized, those not confirmed, those regularly attending services, etc.);
(1) Evangelical Lutheran Church in America; (2) The Church of Jesus Christ of Latter Day Saints
Source: Reprinted with permission from Religious Congregations and Membership in the United States 2000
(Nashville, Glenmary Research Center, 2002) Copyright Association of Statisticians of American Religious
Bodies. All rights reserved.

ECONOMY

Gross Metropolitan Product

Area	2002	2003	2004	2005	2005 Rank[2]
MSA[1]	15.3	16.4	18.8	20.5	91

Note: Figures are in billions of dollars; (1) Anchorage, AK Metropolitan Statistical Area - see Appendix A for
areas included; (2) Rank ranges from 1 to 361
Source: The U.S. Conference of Mayors, "U.S. Metro Economies: GMP - The Engines of America's Growth,"
January 2007

Economic Growth

Area	1995 GMP	2005 GMP	Average Annual Growth Rate	Growth Rate Rank[2]
MSA[1]	11.1	20.5	6.4	85

Note: Figures are in billions of dollars; GMP = Gross Metropolitan Product; (1) Anchorage, AK Metropolitan
Statistical Area - see Appendix A for areas included; (2) Rank ranges from 1 to 361
Source: The U.S. Conference of Mayors, "U.S. Metro Economies: GMP - The Engines of America's Growth,"
January 2007

INCOME

Per Capita/Median/Average Income

Area	Per Capita ($)	Median Household ($)	Average Household ($)
City	29,398	64,048	79,341
MSA[1]	28,496	63,018	77,607
U.S.	25,129	48,775	65,849

Note: Figures are 2006 estimates; (1) Metropolitan Statistical Area - see Appendix B for areas included
Source: Claritas, Inc.

Household Income Distribution

Area	Percent of Households Earning							
	Under $15,000	$15,000 -24,999	$25,000 -34,999	$35,000 -49,999	$50,000 -74,999	$75,000 -99,000	$100,000 -149,999	$150,000 and up
City	6.7	7.8	9.6	14.1	21.1	15.2	16.5	9.1
MSA[1]	7.4	8.1	9.5	14.1	21.1	15.2	16.2	8.5
U.S.	13.3	11.0	11.3	15.7	19.5	11.8	11.0	6.4

Note: Figures are 2006 estimates; (1) Metropolitan Statistical Area - see Appendix B for areas included
Source: Claritas, Inc.

Poverty Rates by Age

Area	All Ages	Under 5 Years Old	5 to 17 Years Old	18 to 64 Years Old	65 Years and Over
City	7.3	0.8	1.9	4.3	0.3
MSA[1]	7.3	0.8	1.9	4.3	0.3
U.S.	12.4	1.2	3.0	6.9	1.2

Note: Figures are percent of population with income in 1999 below poverty level and only include population for whom poverty status is determined; (1) Metropolitan Statistical Area - see Appendix A for areas included
Source: Census 2000, Summary File 3

Personal Bankruptcy Filing Rate

Area	2003	2004	2005
Anchorage Borough	2.59	2.88	3.92
U.S.	5.57	5.31	6.88

Note: Numbers are per 1,000 population and include Chapter 7 and Chapter 13 filings
Source: Federal Deposit Insurance Corporation (FDIC), Regional Economic Conditions (RECON), 3/24/2006

EMPLOYMENT

Labor Force and Employment

Area	Civilian Labor Force			Workers Employed		
	Dec. 2005	Dec. 2006	% Chg.	Dec. 2005	Dec. 2006	% Chg.
City	152,431	158,071	3.7	144,666	150,116	3.8
MSA[1]	188,635	195,636	3.7	178,092	184,802	3.8
U.S.	149,874,000	152,571,000	1.8	142,918,000	146,081,000	2.2

Note: Data is not seasonally adjusted and covers workers 16 years of age and older;
(1) Metropolitan Statistical Area - see Appendix B for areas included
Source: Bureau of Labor Statistics, http://stats.bls.gov

Unemployment Rate

Area	2006											
	Jan.	Feb.	Mar.	Apr.	May	Jun.	Jul.	Aug.	Sep.	Oct.	Nov.	Dec.
City	5.8	6.2	5.9	5.9	5.6	5.6	5.4	4.8	5.2	4.5	4.6	5.0
MSA[1]	6.4	6.8	6.5	6.3	5.9	5.8	5.7	5.0	5.4	4.8	5.0	5.5
U.S.	5.1	5.1	4.8	4.5	4.4	4.8	5.0	4.6	4.4	4.1	4.3	4.3

Note: Data is not seasonally adjusted and covers workers 16 years of age and older; All figures are percentages; (1) Metropolitan Statistical Area - see Appendix B for areas included
Source: Bureau of Labor Statistics, http://stats.bls.gov

Employment by Occupation

Occupation Classification	City (%)	MSA[1] (%)	U.S. (%)
Sales and Office	28.5	28.5	26.7
Professional and Related	22.2	22.2	20.2
Service	15.1	15.1	14.9
Production, Transportation, and Material Moving	9.6	9.6	14.6
Management, Business, and Financial	14.6	14.6	13.5
Construction, Extraction, and Maintenance	9.7	9.7	9.4
Farming, Forestry, and Fishing	0.3	0.3	0.7

Note: Figures cover employed civilians 16 years of age and older;
(1) Metropolitan Statistical Area - see Appendix A for areas included
Source: Census 2000, Summary File 3

Employment by Industry

Sector	MSA[1] Number of Employees	MSA[1] Percent of Total	U.S. Percent of Total
Government	34,500	20.7	16.3
Education and Health Services	22,700	13.7	13.2
Professional and Business Services	17,600	10.6	12.9
Retail Trade	21,300	12.8	11.5
Manufacturing	2,000	1.2	10.2
Leisure and Hospitality	17,200	10.3	9.5
Financial Activities	10,200	6.1	6.1
Construction	10,200	6.1	5.5
Wholesale Trade	5,100	3.1	4.3
Other Services	6,300	3.8	3.9
Transportation and Utilities	11,700	7.0	3.7
Information	5,000	3.0	2.2
Natural Resources and Mining	2,500	1.5	0.5

Note: Figures cover non-farm employment as of December 2006 and are not seasonally adjusted;
(1) Metropolitan Statistical Area - see Appendix B for areas included
Source: Bureau of Labor Statistics, http://stats.bls.gov

Occupations with Greatest Projected Employment Growth: 2002 - 2012

Occupation[1]	2002 Employment	2012 Projected Employment	Numeric Employment Change	Percent Employment Change
Retail Salespersons	8,480	11,050	2,570	30.3
Cashiers	6,720	8,570	1,850	27.5
Registered Nurses	5,000	6,670	1,670	33.4
Combined Food Preparation and Serving Workers, Including Fast Food	4,730	6,220	1,490	31.5
General and Operations Managers	7,390	8,680	1,290	17.5
Waiters and Waitresses	4,650	5,820	1,170	25.2
Truck Drivers, Heavy and Tractor-Trailer	2,890	3,800	910	31.5
First-Line Supervisors/Managers of Retail Sales Workers	3,400	4,090	690	20.3
Carpenters	4,760	5,420	660	13.9
Laborers and Freight, Stock, and Material Movers, Hand	4,320	4,950	630	14.6

Note: Projections cover Alaska; (1) Sorted by numeric employment change
Source: www.projectionscentral.com, State Occupational Projections, 2002-2012 Long-Term Projections

Fastest Growing Occupations: 2002 - 2012

Occupation[1]	2002 Employment	2012 Projected Employment	Numeric Employment Change	Percent Employment Change
Pharmacy Technicians	360	570	210	58.3
Medical Records and Health Information Technicians	360	550	190	52.8
Hazardous Materials Removal Workers	300	450	150	50.0
Pharmacists	360	540	180	50.0
Medical Assistants	530	780	250	47.2
Personal and Home Care Aides	1,490	2,110	620	41.6
Home Health Aides	1,170	1,650	480	41.0
Dental Hygienists	440	620	180	40.9
Dental Assistants	700	980	280	40.0
Social and Human Service Assistants	1,120	1,500	380	33.9

Note: Projections cover Alaska; (1) Sorted by percent employment change and excludes occupations with numeric employment change less than 100
Source: www.projectionscentral.com, State Occupational Projections, 2002-2012 Long-Term Projections

Average Wages

Occupation	$/Hr.	Occupation	$/Hr.
Accountants and Auditors	27.26	Maids and Housekeeping Cleaners	10.20
Automotive Mechanics	21.40	Maintenance and Repair Workers	18.73
Bookkeepers	17.65	Marketing Managers	34.48
Carpenters	25.35	Nuclear Medicine Technologists	n/a
Cashiers	10.49	Nurses, Licensed Practical	20.01
Clerks, General Office	14.65	Nurses, Registered	30.34
Clerks, Receptionists/Information	13.25	Nursing Aides/Orderlies/Attendants	n/a
Clerks, Shipping/Receiving	16.57	Packers and Packagers, Hand	11.03
Computer Programmers	29.75	Physical Therapists	36.88
Computer Support Specialists	22.38	Postal Service Mail Carriers	22.55
Computer Systems Analysts	35.30	Real Estate Brokers	n/a
Cooks, Restaurant	13.01	Retail Salespersons	12.86
Dentists	n/a	Sales Reps., Exc. Tech./Scientific	22.63
Electrical Engineers	41.78	Sales Reps., Tech./Scientific	29.37
Electricians	28.36	Secretaries, Exc. Legal/Med./Exec.	16.58
Financial Managers	37.77	Security Guards	12.17
First-Line Supervisors/Mgrs., Sales	17.86	Surgeons	n/a
Food Preparation Workers	10.30	Teacher Assistants	n/a
General and Operations Managers	35.26	Teachers, Elementary School	n/a
Hairdressers/Cosmetologists	12.63	Teachers, Secondary School	n/a
Internists	81.91	Telemarketers	8.33
Janitors and Cleaners	12.34	Truck Drivers, Heavy/Tractor-Trailer	20.61
Landscaping/Groundskeeping Workers	11.89	Truck Drivers, Light/Delivery Svcs.	14.52
Lawyers	47.22	Waiters and Waitresses	10.53

Note: Wage data is for May 2005 and covers the Anchorage, AK Metropolitan Statistics Area - see Appendix B for areas included. Hourly wages for elementary/secondary school teachers and teacher assistants were calculated by the editors from annual wage data assuming a 40 hour work week; n/a not available.
Source: Bureau of Labor Statistics, May 2005 Metro Area Occupational Employment and Wage Estimates

RESIDENTIAL REAL ESTATE

Building Permits

Area	Single-Family			Multi-Family			Total		
	2005	2006p	Pct. Chg.	2005	2006p	Pct. Chg.	2005	2006p	Pct. Chg.
Bor.	668	550	-17.7	998	812	-18.6	1,666	1,362	-18.2
U.S.	1,682,000	1,380,000	-18.0	473,300	457,300	-3.4	2,155,300	1,837,300	-14.8

Note: (p) preliminary; figures cover Anchorage Borough and represent new, privately-owned housing units authorized (unadjusted data); All permit data are based on estimates with imputation; U.S. figures are based on the new 20,000-place series.
Source: U.S. Census Bureau, Manufacturing, Mining, and Construction Statistics

Homeownership and Housing Vacancies

Area	Homeownership Rate[2] (%)			Rental Vacancy Rate[3] (%)			Homeowner Vacancy Rate[4] (%)		
	2004	2005	2006	2004	2005	2006	2004	2005	2006
MSA[1]	n/a	n/a	n/a	n/a	n/a	n/a	n/a	n/a	n/a
U.S.	69.0	68.9	68.8	10.2	9.8	9.7	1.7	1.9	2.4

Note: Comparable 2004 data was not available due to changes in metropolitan area definitions; (1) Metropolitan Statistical Area - see Appendix B for areas included; (2) The proportion of households that are owners; (3) The proportion of the rental inventory that is vacant for rent; (4) The proportion of the homeowner inventory that is vacant for sale; n/a not available
Source: U.S. Census Bureau, Housing Vacancies and Homeownership Annual Statistics: 2006

TAXES

State Corporate Income Tax Rates

State	Rate (%)	Number of Brackets	Low Bracket (Under $)	High Bracket (Over $)
Alaska	1.0-9.4	10	0	90,000

Note: Tax rates as of December 31, 2006; na not applicable
Source: Tax Foundation, www.taxfoundation.org

State Individual Income Tax Rates

State	Federal Deductibility	Marginal Rate (%)	Number of Brackets	Low Bracket (Under $)	High Bracket (Over $)
Alaska	No	None	na	na	na

Note: Tax rates as of December 31, 2006; Brackets apply to single taxpayers and married people filing separately; na not applicable
Source: Tax Foundation, www.taxfoundation.org

Various State and Local Tax Rates

State and Local Sales and Use (%)	State Sales and Use (%)	Gasoline ($/gal.)	Cigarette ($/pack)	Spirits ($/gal.)	Table Wine ($/gal.)	Beer ($/gal.)
0	None	0.08	1.8	12.8	2.50	1.07

Note: Tax rates as of December 31, 2006
Source: Tax Foundation, www.taxfoundation.org; The Sales Tax Clearinghouse, www.thestc.com

State Tax Burdens

Area	Combined State and Local Tax Burden		Combined Federal, State and Local Tax Burden	
	Percent	Rank	Percent	Rank
Alaska	6.6	50	27.9	49
U.S. Average	10.6	-	31.6	-

Note: Figures are for 2006 and measure taxes as a percentage of income
Source: Tax Foundation, www.taxfoundation.org

Internal Revenue Service Tax Audits

IRS District	Percent of Returns Audited				
	1996	1997	1998	1999	2000
Pacific Northwest	0.63	0.51	0.37	0.24	0.15
U.S.	0.66	0.61	0.46	0.31	0.20

Note: Figures cover IRS district audits of federal income tax returns filed by individuals. Geographic data on district audits after the year 2000 are being withheld by the IRS. TRAC is challenging this policy.
Source: Syracuse University, Transactional Records Access Clearinghouse (TRAC), "Odds of IRS District Tax Audit 2000"

COMMERCIAL UTILITIES

Typical Monthly Electric Bills

Area	Commercial Service ($/month)		Industrial Service ($/month)	
	3 kW demand 1,000 kWh	40 kW demand 14,000 kWh	1,000 kW demand 200,000 kWh	50,000 kW demand 15,000,000 kWh
City	n/a	n/a	n/a	n/a
Average[1]	123	1,413	22,000	1,306,315

Note: Based on total rates in effect July 1, 2006; (1) average based on 196 utilities; n/a not available
Source: Edison Electric Institute, Typical Bills and Average Rates Report, Summer 2006

TRANSPORTATION

Means of Transportation to Work

Area	Car/Truck/Van		Public Transportation			Bicycle	Walked	Other Means	Worked at Home
	Drove Alone	Car-pooled	Bus	Subway	Railroad				
City	74.4	14.6	1.8	0.0	0.0	0.5	2.7	2.3	3.7
MSA[1]	74.4	14.6	1.8	0.0	0.0	0.5	2.7	2.3	3.7
U.S.	75.7	12.2	2.5	1.5	0.5	0.4	2.9	1.0	3.3

Note: Figures are percentages and cover workers 16 years of age and older;
(1) Metropolitan Statistical Area - see Appendix A for areas included
Source: Census 2000, Summary File 3

Travel Time to Work

Area	Less Than 15 Minutes	15 to 29 Minutes	30 to 44 Minutes	45 to 59 Minutes	60 Minutes or More
City	36.4	46.7	11.2	2.3	3.4
MSA[1]	36.4	46.7	11.2	2.3	3.4
U.S.	29.4	36.1	19.1	7.4	8.0

Note: Figures are percentages and include workers 16 years old and over; (1) Metropolitan Statistical Area -
see Appendix A for areas included
Source: Census 2000, Summary File 3

Travel Time Index

Area	1982	1993	2002	2003
Urban Area[1]	1.04	1.03	1.05	1.05
Average[2]	1.12	1.28	1.37	1.37

Note: Travel Time Index - The ratio of travel time in the peak period to the travel time at
free-flow conditions. A value of 1.35 indicates a 20-minute free-flow trip takes 27 minutes
in the peak. Free-flow speeds (60 mph on freeways and 35 mph on principal arterials)
are used as the comparison threshold; (1) Covers the Anchorage, AK urban area;
(2) average of 85 urban areas
Source: Texas Transportation Institute, The 2005 Urban Mobility Report, May 2005

Public Transportation

Agency name:	Anchorage Public Transportation Dept. (People Mover)
Vehicle type:	Bus
Average fleet age in years:	7.5
No. operated in max. service:	46
Vehicle type:	Demand response
Average fleet age in years:	3.5
No. operated in max. service:	28
Vehicle type:	Vanpool
Average fleet age in years:	2.7
No. operated in max. service:	19

Source: Federal Transit Administration, National Transit Database, 2005

Air Transportation

Airport name and code:	Anchorage International (ANC)
Domestic service (2006)	
Passenger airlines[1]:	30
Passenger enplanements:	2,165,670
Freight carriers[2]:	43
Freight (lbs.):	1,098,156,038
International service (2005)	
Passenger airlines[1]:	14
Passenger enplanements:	58,078
Freight carriers[2]:	22
Freight (lbs.):	450,056,455

Note: (1) Includes all major, minor and commuter airlines that carried at least one passenger during the year; (2) Includes all airlines and freight carriers that transported at least one pound of freight during the year
Source: Bureau of Transportation Statistics, The Intermodal Transportation Database, Air Carriers: T-100 International Market, 2004; Bureau of Transportation Statistics, The Intermodal Transportation Database, Air Carriers: T-100 Domestic Market, 2005

Other Transportation Statistics

Interstate highways:	None
Amtrak service:	No
Major waterways/ports:	Gulf of Alaska

Source: Editor & Publisher Market Guide, 2006; Amtrak.com; Rand McNally 2006 Road Atlas

BUSINESSES

Major Business Headquarters

Company Name	2006 Rankings	
	Fortune[1]	Forbes[2]
No companies listed	-	-

Note: (1) Fortune 500 - companies that produce a 10-K are ranked 1 to 500 based on 2005 revenue; (2) Forbes Largest Private Companies - all private companies with at least $1 billion in annual revenue are ranked 1 to 394; companies listed are located in the city; dashes indicate no ranking
Source: Fortune, April 17, 2006; Forbes, November 9, 2006

Best Companies to Work For

Providence Alaska Medical Center, headquartered in Anchorage, is among the "100 Best Companies for Working Mothers." Criteria: workforce profile; compensation; child care; flexibility; time off and leaves; family-friendly programs; and company culture. This year *Working Mother* gave particular weight to flex and time off. *Working Mother, "100 Best Companies," October 2006*

Fast-Growing Businesses

According to *Inc.*, Anchorage is home to one of America's 500 fastest-growing private companies: **Immediate-Care**. Criteria: must be an independent, privately-held, U.S. corporation, proprietorship or partnership; net sales of at least $600,000 in FY2002; four-year operating/sales history; holding companies, regulated banks, and utilities were excluded. *Inc., "America's 500 Fastest-Growing Private Companies," September 2006*

Women-Owned Businesses: 1997 and 2002

Year	All Firms		Firms with Paid Employees			
	Firms	Sales ($000)	Firms	Sales ($000)	Employees	Payroll ($000)
1997	7,306	925,803	1,170	789,931	7,736	199,788
2002	7,182	1,293,497	1,312	1,123,777	8,970	264,392

Note: Figures cover firms located in the city; Women-owned business are defined as firms in which women own 51% or more of the stock or equity of the company; (a) Withheld to avoid disclosing data for individual companies; (b) Withheld because estimate did not meet publication standards; n/a not available
Source: 1997 Economic Census, Survey of Minority- and Women-Owned Business Enterprises; 2002 Economic Census, Survey of Business Owners (released February 9, 2006)

HOTELS

Hotels/Motels

Area	Hotels/Motels	Average Minimum Rates ($)		
		Tourist	First-Class	Deluxe
City	73	105	111	130

Source: OAG Travel Planner Online, Spring 2006

EVENT SITES

Stadiums, Arenas, and Auditoriums

Name	Capacity
William A. Egan Civic Center	2,540

Source: www.officialtravelguide.com; www.eventective.com; original research

Hotels/Conference Centers

Name	Guest Rooms	Exhibit Space (sq. ft.)	Meeting Space (sq. ft.)
Anchorage Marriott Downtown	392	n/a	14,000
Hilton Anchorage	605	21,355	21,355
Hotel Captain Cook	547	9,000	19,000
Sheraton Anchorage Hotel	375	10,000	23,000

Note: n/a not available
Source: www.officialtravelguide.com; www.eventective.com; original research

Living Environment

COST OF LIVING

Cost of Living Index

Year	Composite Index	Groceries	Housing	Utilities	Trans-portation	Health Care	Misc. Goods/ Services
2004	125.5	131.7	136.5	87.2	106.5	160.4	124.4
2005	119.4	128.5	128.5	82.4	108.6	132.3	120.4
2006	119.1	125.7	126.0	93.0	102.6	133.5	121.8

Note: U.S. = 100
Source: The Council for Community and Economic Research (formerly ACCRA), Cost of Living Index, 2004, 2005 and 2006 4-Quarter Averages

HOUSING

House Price Index (HPI)

Area	National Ranking[2]	Quarterly Change (%)	One-Year Change (%)	Five-Year Change (%)
MSA[1]	76	0.31	8.15	57.34
U.S.[3]	-	1.12	5.87	55.21

Note: The HPI is a weighted repeat sales index. It measures average price changes in repeat sales or refinancings on the same properties. This information is obtained by reviewing repeat mortgage transactions on single-family properties whose mortgages have been purchased or securitized by Fannie Mae or Freddie Mae in January 1975; (1) Metropolitan Statistical Area - see Appendix B for areas included; (2) Rankings are based on annual percentage change for all metro areas containing at least 15,000 transactions over the last 10 years and ranges from 1 to 282; (3) figures based on a weighted division average; all figures are for the period ending December 31, 2006
Source: Office of Federal Housing Enterprise Oversight, House Price Index, March 1, 2007

House Price Valuations

Area	Q4 1999	Q4 2000	Q4 2001	Q4 2002	Q4 2003	Q4 2004	Q4 2005	Q4 2006
MSA[1]	1.0	-1.5	-6.0	-4.0	3.8	8.9	19.1	20.7

Note: Figures show the percentage of over- or under-valuation of single family homes relative to statistically normal house values (e.g. a value of 23.6 indicates that house values are 23.6% overvalued). Statistically normal house values are based on house prices, interest rates, household incomes, population densities, and any historical premiums or discounts metropolitan areas have exhibited over time; (1) Figures cover the Metropolitan Statistical Area - see Appendix B for areas included
Source: Global Insight/National City Corporation, House Prices in America, March 2007

Median Home Prices

Area	2004	2005	2006p	Percent Change 2005 to 2006
Metro Area[1]	n/a	n/a	n/a	n/a
U.S. Average	195.2	219.0	222.0	1.4

Note: Figures are median sales prices of existing single-family homes in thousands of dollars; (p) preliminary; n/a not available; (1) Covers the Anchorage, AK Metropolitan Statistical Area - see Appendix B for areas included
Source: National Association of Realtors, Metropolitan Area Prices, 4th Quarter 2006

Housing: Year Structure Built

Area	1990 -2000	1980 -1989	1970 -1979	1960 -1969	1950 -1959	1940 -1949	Before 1940	Median Year
City	12.6	28.2	34.7	13.8	7.9	2.1	0.6	1977
MSA[1]	12.6	28.2	34.7	13.8	7.9	2.1	0.6	1977
U.S.	17.0	15.8	18.5	13.7	12.7	7.3	15.0	1971

Note: Figures are percentages; (1) Metropolitan Statistical Area - see Appendix A for areas included
Source: Census 2000, Summary File 3

Average New Home Price

Area	2004	2005	2006
City	346,374	351,399	371,296
U.S.	253,574	275,712	299,269

Note: Figures, in dollars, are based on a new home with 2,400 sq. ft. of living area on an 8,000 sq. ft. lot.
Source: The Council for Community and Economic Research (formerly ACCRA), Cost of Living Index, 2004, 2005 and 2006 4-Quarter Averages

Average Apartment Rent

Area	2004	2005	2006
City	833	933	998
U.S.	716	740	766

Note: Figures, in dollars per month, are based on an unfurnished two bedroom, 1-1/2 or 2 bath apartment, approximately 950 sq. ft. in size, excluding all utilities except water
Source: The Council for Community and Economic Research (formerly ACCRA), Cost of Living Index, 2004, 2005 and 2006 4-Quarter Averages

RESIDENTIAL UTILITIES

Average Residential Utility Costs

Area	All Electric ($/mth)	Part Electric ($/mth)	Other Energy ($/mth)	Phone ($/mth)
City	–	64.53	86.94	23.04
U.S.	136.00	76.53	90.52	25.87

Source: The Council for Community and Economic Research (formerly ACCRA), Cost of Living Index, 2006 4-Quarter Average

HEALTH

Average Health Care Costs

Area	Optometrist ($/visit)	Doctor ($/visit)	Dentist ($/visit)
City	112.10	111.25	108.39
U.S.	76.38	76.10	68.72

Note: Optometrist—based on a full vision eye exam for an established adult patient;
Doctor—based on a general practitioner's routine exam of an established patient;
Dentist—based on adult teeth cleaning and periodic oral exam.
Source: The Council for Community and Economic Research (formerly ACCRA), Cost of Living Index, 2006 4-Quarter Average

Mortality Rates

ICD-10 Sub-Chapter	ICD-10 Code	Age-Adjusted Death Rate per 100,000 population[1]	U.S. Age-Adjusted Death Rate per 100,000 population
Malignant neoplasms	C00-C97	167.5	185.8
Ischaemic heart diseases	I20-I25	90.4	150.2
Other forms of heart disease	I30-I51	37.4	50.8
Cerebrovascular diseases	I60-I69	52.7	50.0
Chronic lower respiratory diseases	J40-J47	37.4	41.1
Diabetes mellitus	E10-E14	21.1	24.5
Other degenerative diseases of the nervous system	G30-G31	18.3	22.3
Other external causes of accidental injury	W00-X59	20.9	21.2
Influenza and pneumonia	J10-J18	8.1 (Unreliable)	19.8
Hypertensive diseases	I10-I13	17.2	18.1

Note: ICD-10 = International Classification of Diseases 10th Revision; (1) Figures cover Anchorage Borough, AK
Source: Centers for Disease Control and Prevention, National Center for Health Statistics. Compressed Mortality File 1999-2004. CDC WONDER On-line Database, compiled from Compressed Mortality File 1999-2004 Series 20 No. 2J, 2007.

Health Risk Data

Item	Area[1] (%)	U.S. (%)
Adults who have been told they have high blood pressure	20.6	25.5
Adults who have been told they have high blood cholesterol	33.0	35.6
Adults who have been told they have diabetes[2]	4.0	7.3
Adults who have been told they have arthritis	23.0	27.0
Adults who have been told they currently have asthma	8.7	8.0
Adults who are current smokers	23.8	20.6

Note: (1) Figures cover the Metropolitan Statistical Area - see Appendix B for areas included; (2) Figures do not include pregnancy-related diabetes, pre-diabetes or borderline diabetes
Source: Centers for Disease Control and Prevention, Behaviorial Risk Factor Surveillance System, SMART: Selected Metropolitan/Micropolitan Area Trends, 2005

Distribution of Office-Based Physicians

Area	Total	Family/ General Practice	Specialties		
			Medical	Surgical	Other
MSA[1] (number)	664	117	180	179	188
MSA[1] (rate per 10,000 pop.)	25.0	4.4	6.8	6.7	7.1
Metro Average[2] (rate per 10,000 pop.)	19.4	2.1	7.5	4.5	5.3

Note: Data as of December 31, 2004; (1) Metropolitan Statistical Area - see Appendix A for areas included; (2) Average of the 79 unique MSAs and CMSAs in this book
Source: American Medical Association, Physician Characteristics & Distribution in the U.S., 2006

Hospitals

Anchorage has the following hospitals: 3 general medical and surgical; 2 psychiatric.
AHA Guide to the Healthcare Field 2007

EDUCATION

Public School District Statistics

District Name	Schls	Pupils	Pupil/ Teacher Ratio	Minority Pupils[1] (%)	Free Lunch Eligible[2] (%)	IEP[3] (%)
Anchorage School District	97	49,545	17.5	41.5	13.6	14.1

Note: Table includes regular local school districts with 2,000 or more students; (1) Percentage of students that are not white, non-Hispanic; (2) Percentage of students that are eligible for the free lunch program; (3) Percentage of students that have an Individualized Education Program.
Source: U.S. Department of Education, National Center for Education Statistics, Common Core of Data, Local Education Agency (School District) Universe Survey: School Year 2004-2005; U.S. Department of Education, National Center for Education Statistics, Common Core of Data, Public Elementary/Secondary School Universe Survey: School Year 2004-2005

Educational Quality

School District	Education Quotient[1]	Graduate Outcome[2]	Community Index[3]	Resource Index[4]	Rating[5]
Anchorage	48	52	73	17	Green

Note: Scores are national percentile rankings and range from 1 (worst) to 99 (best); (1) Combination of the Graduate Outcome, Community and Resource Indexes weighted to reflect the greater importance of the Graduate Outcome and Resource Index; (2) Based on graduation rates and college board scores (SAT/ACT); (3) Based on the surrounding community's level of affluence and adult education; (4) Based on teacher salaries, per-pupil expenditures and student-teacher ratios; (5) School districts receive one of five rankings: Gold Medal (top 16 percent of districts evaluated); Blue Ribbon (top third); Green Light (average); Yellow Light (bottom 25 percent); Red Light (bottom 10 percent).
Source: Expansion Management, "2007 Education Quotient," January 2007

Highest Level of Education

Area	Less than H.S.	H.S. Diploma	Some College, No Deg.	Associate Degree	Bachelors Degree	Masters Degree	Profess. School Degree	Doctorate Degree
City	9.6	24.2	29.3	7.9	18.7	7.0	2.3	0.9
MSA[1]	10.1	25.7	29.4	8.1	17.4	6.5	2.0	0.8
U.S.	19.4	28.4	21.2	6.4	15.7	5.9	2.0	1.0

Note: Figures are 2006 estimated percentages and cover persons age 25 and over; (1) Metropolitan Statistical Area - see Appendix B for areas included
Source: Claritas, Inc.

Educational Attainment by Race

Area	High School Graduate (%)					Bachelor's Degree (%)				
	Total	White	Black	Asian	Hisp.[2]	Total	White	Black	Asian	Hisp.[2]
City	90.3	93.6	87.9	73.2	76.4	28.9	32.6	15.5	24.0	16.3
MSA[1]	90.3	93.6	87.9	73.2	76.4	28.9	32.6	15.5	24.0	16.3
U.S.	80.4	83.6	72.3	80.4	52.4	24.4	26.1	14.3	44.1	10.4

Note: Figures shown cover persons 25 years old and over; (1) Metropolitan Statistical Area - see Appendix A for areas included; (2) people of Hispanic origin can be of any race
Source: Census 2000, Summary File 3

School Enrollment by Type

Area	Grades KG to 8				Grades 9 to 12			
	Public		Private		Public		Private	
	Enrollment	%	Enrollment	%	Enrollment	%	Enrollment	%
City	36,289	91.6	3,329	8.4	14,603	93.1	1,075	6.9
MSA[1]	36,289	91.6	3,329	8.4	14,603	93.1	1,075	6.9
U.S.	33,526,011	88.7	4,285,121	11.3	14,848,628	90.6	1,532,323	9.4

Note: Figures shown cover persons 3 years old and over; (1) Metropolitan Statistical Area - see Appendix A for areas included
Source: Census 2000, Summary File 3

School Enrollment by Race

Area	Grades KG to 8 (%)				Grades 9 to 12 (%)			
	White	Black	Asian	Hisp.[1]	White	Black	Asian	Hisp.[1]
City	64.7	6.7	5.2	7.1	65.9	7.7	6.9	7.1
MSA[2]	64.7	6.7	5.2	7.1	65.9	7.7	6.9	7.1
U.S.	68.5	15.5	3.3	16.8	68.8	15.5	3.8	15.7

Note: Figures shown cover persons 3 years old and over; (1) people of Hispanic origin can be of any race; (2) Metropolitan Statistical Area - see Appendix A for areas included
Source: Census 2000, Summary File 3

Average Salaries of Public School Teachers

District	2004-05		2005-06		Percent Change 2004-05 to 2005-06
	Dollars	Rank[1]	Dollars	Rank[1]	
ALASKA	52,424	11	53,553	13	2.15
U.S. Average	47,674	-	49,109	-	3.01

Note: (1) State rank ranges from 1 to 51.
Source: National Education Association, Rankings & Estimates: Rankings of the States 2005 and Estimates of School Statistics 2006, November 2006

Higher Education

Four-Year Colleges			Two-Year Colleges			Medical Schools[1]	Law Schools[2]	Voc/ Tech[3]
Public	Private Non-profit	Private For-profit	Public	Private Non-profit	Private For-profit			
1	1	1	0	0	0	0	0	1

Note: Figures cover institutions located within the city limits; (1) includes schools accredited by the Liaison Committee on Medical Education and the American Osteopathic Association; (2) includes American Bar Association-accredited law schools; (3) includes all schools with programs that are less than 2 years
Source: National Center for Education Statistics, The Integrated Postsecondary Education System (IPEDS) Peer Analysis System, 2006; www.usnews.com, America's Best Graduate Schools 2008, Medical School Directory; www.usnews.com, America's Best Graduate Schools 2008, Law School Directory

PRESIDENTIAL ELECTION

2004 Presidential Election Results

Area	Bush	Kerry	Nader	Other
Anchorage - Region II	62.3	34.7	1.5	1.4
U.S.	50.7	48.3	0.4	0.6

Note: Results are percentages and may not add to 100% due to rounding
Source: Dave Leip's Atlas of U.S. Presidential Elections, www.uselectionatlas.org

MAJOR EMPLOYERS

Major Employers

Company Name	Industry	Type of Site
Alaska Air National Guard 176 Group	National security	Branch
Alaska Airlines	Air transportation, scheduled	Branch
Alaska Native Medical Center	General medical and surgicalhospitals	Branch
Alaska Native Tribal Health	Social services, nec	Headquarters
Alaska Regional Hospital	General medical and surgical hospitals	Headquarters
Alaska State Office	Land, mineral, and wildlife conservation	Branch
B P Exploration (Alaska) Inc	Crude petroleum and natural gas	Headquarters
Doyon Universal Services JV	Amusement and recreation, nec	Single
Fedex	Air transportation scheduled	Branch
Kulis Air National Guard	National security	Branch
L M Berry and Company	Advertising agencies	Branch
MosquitoNet	Telephone communication, except radio	Headquarters
Nabors Alaska Drilling Inc	Drilling oil and gas wells	Single
Providence Hospital	General medical and surgical hospitals	Branch
RD Medical Group	National security	Branch
Swan Employer Services	Help supply services	Single
US Dept of the Air Force	National security	Branch
United States Postal Service	U.S. Postal Service	Branch

Note: Companies shown are located within the metropolitan area and have 600 or more employees; nec = not elsewhere classified.
Source: www.zapdata.com, January 2007

PUBLIC SAFETY

Crime Rate

Area	All Crimes	Violent Crimes				Property Crimes		
		Murder	Forcible Rape	Robbery	Aggrav. Assault	Burglary	Larceny -Theft	Motor Vehicle Theft
City	4,851.7	5.8	81.1	139.1	509.6	645.8	2,987.2	483.1
Suburbs[1]	8,198.5	0.0	25.8	83.8	966.8	638.1	5,910.4	573.6
Metro[2]	5,029.8	5.5	78.2	136.1	533.9	645.4	3,142.7	488.0
U.S.	3,899.0	5.6	31.7	140.7	291.1	726.7	2,286.3	416.7

Note: Figures are crimes per 100,000 population; (1) All areas within the metro area that are located outside the city limits; (2) Metropolitan Statistical Area - see Appendix B for areas included
Source: FBI Uniform Crime Reports, 2005

Hate Crimes

Area	Number of Quarters Reported	Bias Motivation				
		Race	Religion	Sexual Orientation	Ethnicity	Disability
City	4	4	0	0	0	0

Source: Federal Bureau of Investigation, Hate Crime Statistics 2005

RECREATION

Culture

Dance[1]	Theatre[1]	Instrumental Music[1]	Vocal Music[1]	Series/ Festivals	Museums	Zoos
1	4	2	3	2	7	1

Note: (1) number of professional perfoming groups
Source: The Grey House Performing Arts Directory, 2007; Official Museum Directory, 2007

Professional Sports Teams

Major League Baseball	National Basketball Association	National Football League	National Hockey League	Major League Soccer	Women's National Basketball Association
0	0	0	0	0	0

Note: Includes teams located in the Anchorage metro area.
Source: www.sportsvenues.com, Listing of Venues by State/Province and City, 2006

MEDIA

Newspapers

Name	Target Audience	Frequency	Circulation
Anchorage Daily News	n/a	Daily	80,331
The Anchorage Press	General	Non-Daily	19,000
Arctic Sounder	General	Non-Daily	2,537
Petroleum News Alaska	General	Non-Daily	2,100

Note: Includes newspapers whose offices are located in the city and whose circulations are 1,000 or more; n/a not available
Source: BurrellesLuce, MediaContacts Online, January 2006

Television Stations

Name	Ch.	Network(s)	Type	Ownership
KTUU	2	NBC	Commercial	Zaser & Longston Inc.
KTBY	4	n/a	Commercial	Grapevine Broadcasting
KYES	5	UPN	Commercial	Fireweed Communications Corporation
KAKM	7	PBS	Public	Alaska Public Telecommunications Inc.
KTVA	11	CBS	Commercial	Northern Television Inc.
KIMO	13	ABC	Commercial	Smith Broadcasting of Santa Barbara
KDMD	33	Pax	Commercial	Green TV Corporation

Note: Stations included cover the Anchorage DMA (Designated Market Area)
BurrellesLuce, MediaContacts Online, January 2006

Major AM Radio Stations

Call Letters	Freq. (kHz)	Station Type	Target Audience	Station Format	Music Format
KTZN	550	Commercial	General	Sports/Talk	n/a
KHAR	590	n/a	General	Music/News	n/a
KGTL	620	n/a	General	Music/News/Sports	n/a
KENI	650	n/a	General	News/Talk	n/a
KBYR	700	Commercial	General	News	n/a
KFQD	750	n/a	General	News/Talk	n/a
KBBI	890	Public	General	Music/News	World Music
KSRM	920	Commercial	General	Talk	n/a
KSLD	1140	Commercial	General	Music/News/Sports	Classic Rock

Note: Stations included cover the Anchorage DMA (Designated Market Area); n/a not available
Source: BurrellesLuce, MediaContacts Online, January 2006

Major FM Radio Stations

Call Letters	Freq. (mHz)	Station Type	Target Audience	Station Format	Music Format
KZND	87.7	Commercial	General	Music	Alternative
KATB	89.3	Non-Comm	General/Religious	Educational/Music/Talk	Christian
KNBA	90.3	Public	General	Music/News/Sports/Talk	Urban Contemp.
KSKA	91.1	Public	General	Music/News/Talk	Jazz
KDLL	91.9	Public	General	Educational/Music/News	Blues
KQEZ	92.1	n/a	General	Music/News	n/a
KFAT	92.9	n/a	General	Music	n/a
KKIS	96.5	Commercial	General	Music/News	Alternative
KEAG	97.3	Commercial	General	Music/News/Talk	Oldies
KLEF	98.1	Commercial	General	Music	Classical
KYMG	98.9	Commercial	General	Music	Adult Contemp.
KMBQ	99.7	Commercial	General	Music/Sports	Adult Contemp.
KWHQ	100.1	n/a	General	Music/News/Talk	n/a
KBFX	100.5	n/a	General	Music	n/a
KGOT	101.3	Commercial	General	Music/News	Top 40
KPEN	101.7	n/a	General	Music/Talk	n/a
KMXS	103.1	n/a	General	Music/News	n/a
KWVV	103.5	Commercial	General	Music/News/Sports	Adult Contemp.
KBRJ	104.1	Commercial	General	Music	Country
KNIK	105.3	Commercial	General	Music/News/Talk	Jazz
KWHL	106.5	n/a	General	Music	n/a
KASH	107.5	Commercial	General	Music	Country

Note: Stations included cover the Anchorage DMA (Designated Market Area); n/a not available
BurrellesLuce, MediaContacts Online, January 2006

CLIMATE

Average and Extreme Temperatures

Temperature	Jan	Feb	Mar	Apr	May	Jun	Jul	Aug	Sep	Oct	Nov	Dec	Yr.
Extreme High (°F)	50	48	51	65	77	85	82	82	73	61	53	48	85
Average High (°F)	22	25	33	43	55	62	65	63	55	41	28	22	43
Average Temp. (°F)	15	18	25	36	47	55	59	57	48	35	22	16	36
Average Low (°F)	8	11	17	28	39	47	51	49	41	28	15	10	29
Extreme Low (°F)	-34	-26	-24	-4	17	33	36	31	19	-5	-21	-30	-34

Note: Figures cover the years 1953-1995
Source: National Climatic Data Center, International Station Meteorological Climate Summary, 9/96

Average Precipitation/Snowfall/Humidity

Precip./Humidity	Jan	Feb	Mar	Apr	May	Jun	Jul	Aug	Sep	Oct	Nov	Dec	Yr.
Avg. Precip. (in.)	0.8	0.8	0.7	0.6	0.7	1.0	1.9	2.4	2.7	1.9	1.1	1.1	15.7
Avg. Snowfall (in.)	10	12	10	5	Tr	0	0	0	Tr	8	12	15	71
Avg. Rel. Hum. 6am (%)	74	74	72	75	73	74	80	84	84	78	78	78	77
Avg. Rel. Hum. 3pm (%)	73	67	57	54	50	55	62	64	64	67	74	76	64

Note: Figures cover the years 1953-1995; Tr = Trace amounts (<0.05 in. of rain; <0.5 in. of snow)
Source: National Climatic Data Center, International Station Meteorological Climate Summary, 9/96

Weather Conditions

Temperature			Daytime Sky			Precipitation		
0°F & below	32°F & below	65°F & above	Clear	Partly cloudy	Cloudy	0.01 inch or more precip.	0.1 inch or more snow/ice	Thunder-storms
32	194	41	50	115	200	113	49	2

Note: Figures are average number of days per year and cover the years 1953-1995
Source: National Climatic Data Center, International Station Meteorological Climate Summary, 9/96

HAZARDOUS WASTE

Superfund Sites

Anchorage has two hazardous waste sites on the EPA's Superfund Final National Priorities List: **Elmendorf Air Force Base**; **Fort Richardson (USARMY)**. *U.S. Environmental Protection Agency, Final National Priorities List, March 20, 2007*

AIR & WATER QUALITY

Air Quality Index

Area	Percent of Days when Air Quality was...[2]				AQI Statistics	
	Good	Moderate	Unhealthy for Sensitive Groups	Unhealthy	Maximum	Median
MSA[1]	90.4	9.3	0.3	0.0	131	20

Note: The Air Quality Index (AQI) is an index for reporting daily air quality. EPA calculates the AQI for five major air pollutants regulated by the Clean Air Act: ground-level ozone, particle pollution (also known as particulate matter), carbon monoxide, sulfur dioxide, and nitrogen dioxide. The AQI runs from 0 to 500. The higher the AQI value, the greater the level of air pollution and the greater the health concern. There are six AQI categories: "Good" The AQI is between 0 and 50. Air quality is considered satisfactory; "Moderate" The AQI is between 51 and 100. Air quality is acceptable; "Unhealthy for Sensitive Groups" When AQI values are between 101 and 150, members of sensitive groups may experience health effects; "Unhealthy" When AQI values are between 151 and 200 everyone may begin to experience health effects; "Very Unhealthy" AQI values between 201 and 300 trigger a health alert; "Hazardous" AQI values over 300 trigger health warnings of emergency conditions; (1) Metropolitan Statistical Area - see Appendix A for areas included; (2) Based on 302 days with AQI data in 2005.
Source: U.S. Environmental Protection Agency, Air Quality Index Report, 2005

Air Quality Index Pollutants

Area	Percent of Days when AQI Pollutant was...[2]					
	Carbon Monoxide	Nitrogen Dioxide	Ozone	Sulfur Dioxide	Particulate Matter 2.5	Particulate Matter 10
MSA[1]	42.7	0.0	0.0	0.0	20.9	36.4

Note: The Air Quality Index (AQI) is an index for reporting daily air quality. EPA calculates the AQI for five major air pollutants regulated by the Clean Air Act: ground-level ozone, particle pollution (also known as particulate matter), carbon monoxide, sulfur dioxide, and nitrogen dioxide. The AQI runs from 0 to 500. The higher the AQI value, the greater the level of air pollution and the greater the health concern; (1) Metropolitan Statistical Area - see Appendix A for areas included; (2) Based on 302 days with AQI data in 2005.
Source: U.S. Environmental Protection Agency, Air Quality Index Report, 2005

Number of Days with Air Quality Index Values Greater than 100

Area	Trend Sites								All Sites
	1998	1999	2000	2001	2002	2003	2004	2005	2005
MSA[1]	n/a	n/a	n/a	n/a	n/a	n/a	n/a	n/a	n/a

Note: An AQI value greater than 100 indicates that air quality would have been in the unhealthful range on that day. Data from exceptional events are not included. These counts are presented in two ways. First, the counts are based on sites having an adequate record of monitoring data during the trend period (trend sites). These counts represent the relative change in the number of days with AQI values greater than 100. In the last column, the counts are based on all sites with data in the most recent year (because it is possible for a site to have data in the most recent year but not enough data to be a trend site); (1) Metropolitan Statistical Area - see Appendix A for areas included; n/a not available.
Source: U.S. Environmental Protection Agency, Air Trends Fact Book 2005

Maximum Pollutant Concentrations

	Particulate Matter 10 (ug/m^3)	Particulate Matter 2.5 (ug/m^3)	Ozone 1-hour (ppm)	Carbon Monoxide (ppm)	Sulfur Dioxide (ppm)	Nitrogen Dioxide (ppm)	Lead (ug/m^3)
MSA[1] Level	145	18	n/a	5	n/a	n/a	n/a
NAAQS[2]	150	65	0.125	9	0.140	0.053	1.50
Met NAAQS[2]	Yes	Yes	n/a	Yes	n/a	n/a	n/a

Note: Data from exceptional events are not included; (1) Metropolitan Statistical Area - see Appendix A for areas included; (2) National Ambient Air Quality Standards; n/a not available
Units: ppm = parts per million; ug/m^3 = micrograms per cubic meter
Source: U.S. Environmental Protection Agency, Air Trends Fact Book 2005

Watershed Health

The U.S. Environmental Protection Agency monitors the health of the aquatic resources for the nation's 2,000+ watersheds. **The Anchorage watershed serves the Anchorage area and received an overall Index of Watershed Indicators (IWI) score of n/a (insufficient data).** The IWI score is based on seven condition and nine vulnerability indicators. The overall IWI score ranges from 1 (best health) to 6 (worst health). The Condition Indicators include: designated use attainment, fish and wildlife consumption advisories, source water condition, contaminated sediments, ambient water quality, and wetlands loss index. The Vulnerability

Indicators include: aquatic species at risk, conventional and toxic loads over permitted limits, urban and agricultural runoff potential, population change, hydrologic modification, estuarine pollution susceptibility, and air deposition. *Note: The IWI is no longer being updated by the U.S. EPA. Source: U.S. Environmental Protection Agency, Index of Watershed Indicators, October 26, 2001*

Drinking Water

Water System Name	Pop. Served	Primary Water Source Type	Number of Violations in 2006[a]		
			Health Based	Significant Monitoring	Monitoring
MOA Municipality of Anchorage	251,776	Surface	None	None	None

Note: (a) Based on violation data from January 1, 2006 to December 31, 2006
Source: U.S. Environmental Protection Agency, Office of Ground Water and Drinking Water, Safe Drinking Water Information System (data extracted April 12, 2007)

Anchorage tap water is neutral, hard and fluoridated.
Editor & Publisher Market Guide, 2005

Bellevue, Washington

Background

Bellevue, Washington, is situated in a postcard-perfect site between Lake Washington and Lake Sammamish, west of the Cascade Mountains and east of the Olympics. To its south is Mt. Rainier, and to the north, Mt. Baker, marking the Canadian border. Linked by bridges to the charms and resources of Seattle, two miles away, Bellevue is both an elegant suburban community and a thriving high-tech manufacturing site, well known for the production of cutting-edge electronic components and control systems. Bellevue enjoys the benefits of a diversified economy in the region, and is home to a highly trained workforce. It is the second-largest city in King County, and the fourth-largest in the state.

Bellevue was founded in 1869 by William Meydenbauer, but not incorporated as a city until 1953. Growth was slow until 1941, when the Floating Bridge first directly linked Bellevue to Seattle. In 1963, a second bridge to Seattle, the Evergreen Point Floating Bridge, was constructed, and Bellevue took its modern shape.

A thriving community, the city has in recent years experienced considerable economic growth well above the U.S. average. Population and employment are expected to grow at high rates over the next two decades. The city has worked with regional transit authorities to improve transportation in the eastern Puget Sound corridor. Access to Bellevue's downtown has recently improved with the completion of several new ramps including one that provides direct access for buses serving the Bellevue Transit Center. The Rider Services Building, housing customer commuting information and bike racks, opened in April 2006.

The city also prides itself as a leader in urban environmental activism such as its continued investments in threatened chinook salmon habitat improvements, re-vegetation projects, erosion control, and culvert and weir renovation for easier salmon passage.

In addition to the many attractions available in Seattle, Bellevue offers much within its own borders. Bellevue's Meydenbauer Center is the hub of an active and varied arts community. Regarded by many as the most important community-based arts center in the Pacific Northwest, the Meydenbauer annually hosts a wide array of regional, national, and local performing arts groups, including the Bellevue Philharmonic Orchestra, Ballet Bellevue, the Bellevue Chamber Chorus, and the Bellevue Civic Theater. The city is also home to Music Works Northwest and Bellevue Community College's Carlson Theatre.

The Bellevue Arts & Crafts Fair, which takes place at the end of July, is one of the most important festivals in the state, drawing more than 300,000 annually, with 325 artists' booths as well as demonstrations, exhibitions, performing arts, cuisine, and children's activities. The Bellevue Arts Museum, designed by architect Steven Holl, was extensively renovated in 2005 and features works of regional artists. Also in Bellevue are the Rosalie Whyel Museum of Doll Art, many private art galleries, more than 100 publicly sited artworks, and an annual Jazz Festival.

Institutions of higher education in the city and environs include Bellevue Community College, Lake Washington Technical College, the University of Washington at Bothell, and Cascadia Community College.

Bellevue's climate is best described as marine — mild and moist. The Pacific Ocean governs weather year-round, and in addition the city is protected from the extremes of continental weather by the Cascade Mountains to the east. Most rain falls between October and April, but not in the huge amounts for which the Northwest is famous elsewhere. In summer, weather is drier and sunnier, but not hot.

Rankings

General Rankings

- Seattle was ranked #88 out of 331 metro areas in *Cities Ranked & Rated*. Criteria: cost of living; climate; crime; transportation; economy and jobs; education; arts and culture; health and healthcare; leisure. *Cities Ranked & Rated, 1st Edition, 2004*

- The Seattle metro area was selected one of America's "Top 10 Metros Overall" by *Expansion Management* in their 4th annual Mayor's Challenge ranking of metro areas that have achieved solid ratings across the board in numerous *EM* studies during the past 12 months. The area ranked #8. Criteria: education (with emphasis on college board test results and high school graduation rates); availability of quality healthcare services and the cost to employers; quality of life; logistics workforce and companies; transportation infrastructure; quality and quantity of highly educated technical workers; and business climate. *Expansion Management, August 2006*

- The Seattle metro area was selected as one of "America's Best Places to Live and Work" by *Employment Review*. The area ranked #17 out of 20. Criteria: unemployment rate; projected job growth; cost of living; and industry specific data. *Employment Review, www.bestjobsusa.com, 2003*

- Bellevue was selected as one of the "Best Places to Live 2006" by *Money* magazine. The city ranked #21 out of 90 in the small city (under 300,000 population) category. Places were ranked using 38 quality-of-life indicators and six economic opportunity measures in the following categories: ease of living; health; education; crime; park space; arts and leisure. *Money, "Best Places to Live 2006"*

Business/Finance Rankings

- Seattle was selected as one of the best places to start and grow a company by *Entrepreneur* and the National Policy Research Council. The Seattle metro area ranked #31 out of 50 large metro areas. Criteria: business formation and growth (firms started four to 14 years ago that still employ at least 5 people and experienced rapid growth over the last four years). *Entrepreneur/National Policy Research Council, "Hot Cities for Entrepreneurs," September 2006*

- The Seattle metro area was selected as one of "America's 50 Hottest Cities" for business relocations and expansions. Criteria: industry's most prominent site selection consultants were asked to list their top city choices for relocating and expanding manufacturing companies, taking into consideration such factors as the business climate, work force quality, operating costs, incentive programs, and the ease of working with local political and economic development officials. *Expansion Management, January-February 2007*

- Intel, in partnership with Sperling's BestPlaces, ranked the 80 "Best Cities for Teleworking" in America. The Seattle metro area ranked #10 among extra large metro areas. The study identifies cities that hold the greatest potential for teleworking based on a host of factors including typical commuting times, fuel prices, availability of broadband Internet access and percentage of the population in telework friendly jobs. The study also factored in extreme climate and natural hazards. *Intel, "Best Cities for Teleworking," March 30, 2006*

- The Seattle metro area was selected as one of the "25 Hottest Housing Markets" in the U.S. The area ranked #10 out of 156 markets with a home price appreciation rate of 11.3%. Criteria: year-over-year change of median sales price of existing single-family homes between the 4th quarter of 2005 and the 4th quarter of 2006. *National Association of Realtors, Median Sales Price of Existing Single-Family Homes for Metropolitan Areas, 4th Quarter 2006*

- The Seattle metro area appeared on the Milken Institute "2005 Best Performing Cities" index. Rank: #127 out of 200 large metro areas. Criteria: job growth; wage and salary growth; high-tech output growth. *Milken Institute, "2005 Best Performing Cities," February 2006*

■ The Seattle metro area was selected as one of "The Best Cities for Doing Business in America." *Inc.* magazine measured employment growth in 393 regions using the following criteria: recent growth trend; mid-term growth; long-term trend; and current year growth. The Seattle metro area ranked #28 among large metro areas and #179 overall. *Inc., May 2006*

■ The Seattle metro area was selected as one of "The Top 20 Boom Towns in America." *Business 2.0* magazine and econometric research firm Global Insight compared 319 metropolitan areas in the U.S. and ranked the 61 with populations over 1 million. Criteria: a weighted formula that includes forecast growth rates in sectors that contain the economy's 10 most skilled occupational clusters; the prevalence of college degrees in the local workforce; median salary. The area ranked #9 among large metro areas. *Business 2.0 Magazine, March 2004*

■ Seattle was identified as one of the 100 "Most Unwired Cities" in the U.S. The area ranked #1 out of the 100 largest metro areas in the U.S. Criteria: number of public and commercial wireless access points (hotspots); airports with wireless Internet access; broadband availability; local wireless networks; and wireless email devices. *Intel, "Most Unwired Cities Survey," June 7, 2005*

■ Seattle was ranked #5 out of 125 regions worldwide in terms of its "Knowledge Competitiveness Index." The index attempts to measure the knowledge-based development taking place throughout the world and is based on 19 measures of economic performance that indicate a region's ability to translate its knowledge capacity into economic value. *Robert Huggins Associates, World Knowledge Competitiveness Index 2005*

■ *Forbes* ranked the 200 most populous metro areas in the U.S. in terms of the "Best Places for Business and Careers." The Seattle metro area was ranked #62. Criteria: business costs (labor, energy, tax and office space expenses); living costs (housing, transportation, food and other household expenditures); education levels of the work force; job growth; income growth; migration trends; crime rates; and culture/leisure. *Forbes, April 23, 2007*

■ Bellevue was selected as a 2006 Digital Cities Survey winner. The city ranked #9 in the small city (75,000 to 124,999 population) category. The survey examined and assessed how city governments are utilizing information technology to operate and deliver quality service to their customers and citizens. Survey questions focused on implementation and adoption of online service delivery; planning and governance; and the infrastructure and architecture that make the transformation to digital government possible. *Center for Digital Government, "2006 Digital Cities Survey"*

■ Seattle was identified as one of the top 20 metro areas with the highest rate of home price appreciation in 2006. The area ranked #18 with a one-year price appreciation of 14.5% through the 4th quarter 2006. *Office of Federal Housing Enterprise Oversight, House Price Index, 4th Quarter 2006*

■ *Fortune* ranked the 100 largest metro areas in the U.S. in terms of projected median home price change in 2006. The Seattle metro area ranked #65. *Fortune, "The Top 100: Is the Party Over?" December 26, 2005*

■ Seattle was identified as one of the "Most Overpriced Places in the U.S." The area ranked #1 out of the nations 150 largest metro areas. Criteria: job growth; income growth; cost of living; and housing affordability. *Forbes.com, "Most Overpriced Places in the U.S. 2005"*

Health/Environment Rankings

■ *Reader's Digest* ranked the 50 largest metro areas in the U.S. in terms of how "clean" they are. The Seattle metro area ranked #27. Criteria: air quality; water quality; toxic industrial pollution; Superfund sites; and sanitation. *Reader's Digest, "The 50 Cleanest (and Dirtiest) Cities in America," July 2005*

■ *Business Week* identified the 15 metro areas that saw the steepest declines in ground-level ozone pollution between 1990 and 2005. The Seattle metro area ranked #2. *Business Week, "America's Most Cleaned-Up Metro Areas," March 23, 2007*

- The Seattle metro area appeared in *Country Home's* "2007 Best Green Places Report". The area ranked #32. Criteria included: air and watershed quality; miles of mass transit; green power; number of farmer's markets, organic producers and groceries. *Country Home, "2007 Best Green Places Report," April 2007*

- Wyeth Consumer Healthcare, in partnership with Sperling's BestPlaces, ranked the nation's 50 most populous metro areas in terms of five key health factors. The Seattle metro area ranked #4. Criteria: physical activity, health status, nutrition, lifestyle pursuits; and mental wellness. *Wyeth Consumer Healthcare, "Centrum Healthiest Cities Study," April 19, 2005*

- HealthGrades surveyed over 41,000 individuals on doctor satisfaction and ranked the 20 largest metro areas based on the highest "definitely yes" responses to the question "Do you trust the physician to make decisions/recommendations that are in your best interest?" The Seattle metro area ranked #9. *HealthGrades.com, "Top Cities in Doctor-Trust," September 7, 2006*

- Seattle was identified as a "2007 Asthma Capital." The area ranked #100 out of the nation's 100 largest metropolitan areas. Twelve factors were used to identify the most challenging places to live for people with asthma: estimated prevalence; self-reported prevalence; crude death rate for asthma; annual pollen score; annual air quality; public smoking laws; number of board-certified asthma specialists; school inhaler access laws; rescue medication use; controller medication use; uninsured rate; poverty rate. *Asthma and Allergy Foundation of America, "2007 Asthma Capitals"*

- Seattle was identified as a "Spring Allergy Capital." The area ranked #96 out of 100. Three groups of factors were used to identify the most severe cities for people with allergies during the spring season: annual pollen levels; medicine utilization; access to board-certified allergists. *Asthma and Allergy Foundation of America, "2007 Spring Allergy Capital Rankings"*

- Seattle was identified as a "Fall Allergy Capital." The area ranked #94 out of 100. Three groups of factors were used to identify the most severe cities for people with allergies during the fall season: annual pollen levels; medicine utilization; access to board-certified allergists. *Asthma and Allergy Foundation of America, "2006 Fall Allergy Capital Rankings"*

- Ortho-McNeil Neurologics, in partnership with Sperling's BestPlaces, analyzed 110 metro areas and identified those U.S. cities with the highest prevalence of factors that are most commonly associated with migraine headaches. The Seattle metro area ranked #59. Criteria: number of migraine-related drug prescriptions per capita; lifestyle factors that can contribute to migraines; environmental factors that can trigger migraines; and consumption of migraine-triggering foods. *Ortho-McNeil Neurologics, "America's Migraine Hot Spots," March 14, 2006*

- Sperling's BestPlaces ranked 331 metro areas and identified the most and least stressful U.S. cities. The Seattle metro area ranked #11 out of the 100 largest metro areas (#1 = most stressful). Criteria: divorce rate; unemployment rate; violent and property crime; suicide rate; commute time; mental health; alcohol consumption; cloudy days. *www.BestPlaces.net, January 9, 2004*

- Sperling's BestPlaces in partnership with Vistakon ranked the 100 largest metro areas and identified "America's 10 Best Cities for Comfortable Eyes." The Seattle metro area ranked #10. Criteria: altitude; sunny days; wind; extreme temperatures; humidity; pollution; commute time; computer use. *Vistakon, "America's Best and Worst Cities for Comfortable Eyes," June 15, 2004*

- HealthGrades evaluated the performance of America's 25 most populous metropolitan areas by measuring the outcomes of five of the highest volume and most widely studied procedures and diagnoses: coronary artery bypass graft surgery; percutaneus coronary interventions; acute myocardial infarction/heart attack in angioplasty-capable hospitals; congestive heart failure; and community acquired pneumonia. The Seattle metro area ranked #24. *HealthGrades, "HealthGrades Hospital Quality in America Study," October 12, 2004*

■ Seattle was selected as one of "America's Top 10 Low-Carb Cities" by *LowCarbiz Magazine*. Criteria: abundance of low-carb products; restaurants with low-carb menu items; health practitioners supportive of carb-cutting regimens; local culture generally conducive to exercise and health. *LowCarbiz Magazine, April 2004*

■ Seattle was selected as one of "America's Pet Healthiest Cities" by Purina. The city ranked #11 out of 50. Criteria: veterinary services; environment; legislation; preventative care; obesity/body condition. *Purina Pet Institute, "America's Pet Healthiest Cities," May 20, 2003*

Women/Minorities Rankings

■ Seattle was ranked #18 out of 100 metro areas in *SELF Magazine's* ranking of "America's Best Places for Women." A panel of experts came up with nearly 40 criteria including: drinking and smoking rates; depression; unemployment; parks; crime; disease; healthcare insurance coverage; air quality; and commute times. *SELF Magazine, "America's Best Places for Women 2006," December 2006*

■ Seattle appeared on a list of the top 10 metro areas with the highest concentration of same-sex households. The area ranked #3. *Urban Institute Press, The Gay and Lesbian Atlas, May 2004*

■ Seattle appeared on a list of the top 10 metro areas with the highest concentration of gay male couples. The area ranked #4. *Urban Institute Press, The Gay and Lesbian Atlas, May 2004*

■ Seattle appeared on a list of the top 10 metro areas with the highest concentration of African-American same-sex couples among all African-American households. The area ranked #6. *Urban Institute Press, The Gay and Lesbian Atlas, May 2004*

■ Seattle appeared on a list of the top 10 metro areas with the highest concentration of Hispanic same-sex couples among all Hispanic households. The area ranked #5. *Urban Institute Press, The Gay and Lesbian Atlas, May 2004*

■ Seattle was identified as one of the top 25 metropolitan statistical areas ranked by percentage of coupled households that are gay or lesbian." The area ranked #10. *Human Rights Campaign, "Gay and Lesbian Families in the United States: Same-Sex Unmarried Partner Households," August 1, 2001*

Seniors/Retirement Rankings

■ Sperling's Best Places in partnership with Bankers Life & Casualty Company designed a survey to identify the top 50 metro areas in the U.S. that offer the best overall qualities for senior living. The Seattle metro area ranked #2. The following criteria were statistically weighted to reflect the needs of the senior population: health; disease; economics; social; environment; spiritual; transportation; housing; and crime. *Bankers Life & Casualty Company, "Best Cities for Seniors 2005"*

■ A.G. Edwards ranked America's 500 top-performing communities based on their residents' personal savings and investing behavior. The Seattle metro area ranked #73 with an index score of 108.06 (national average = 100.00). A dozen statistical factors were measured including: participation in retirement savings plans; personal debt levels; and home ownership. *A.G. Edwards, "2006 Nest Egg Index", September 6, 2006*

Children/Family Rankings

■ The Seattle metro area was selected as one of the "Best Cities for Relocating Families" by Worldwide ERC and Primacy Relocation. Criteria: tax rates; average home costs and home appreciation; ability to qualify for in-state tuition; service quality of local utilities; per-capita volunteerism; auto taxes; and quantity of fun, family-friendly events and venues. *Worldwide ERC and Primacy Relocation, "2006 Best Cities for Relocating Families"*

■ Bellevue was chosen as one of America's "100 Best Communities for Young People." The winners were selected based upon detailed information provided about each community's efforts to fulfill five essential promises critical to the well-being of young people: caring adults who are actively involved in their lives; safe places in which to learn and grow; a healthy start toward adulthood; an effective education that builds marketable skills; and opportunities to help others. *America's Promise, "100 Best Communities for Young People," September 26, 2005*

Safety Rankings

■ Seattle was identified as one of the most dangerous large metro areas for pedestrians in the U.S. The area ranked #40 out of the nations 50 largest metro areas. Criteria: average yearly pedestrian fatalities per capita (for the years 2002 and 2003) adjusted for the number of walkers. *Surface Transportation Policy Project, "Mean Streets 2004"*

Sports/Recreation Rankings

■ The Seattle metro area appeared on *The Sporting News* list of the "Best Sports Cities 2006". The area ranked #15 out of 99 cities in North America. To be included in the rankings, a city must have at least one of the following: NCAA Division I basketball team; Class A minor league baseball team; training camp for a major league or NFL team; NASCAR Nextel Cup race; NCAA Division I-A bowl game; PGA Tour tournament; Triple Crown horse race. Once a city qualifies, a 12-month snapshot is taken of the sports atmosphere, putting a heavy premium on regular-season won-lost records; playoff berths, bowl appearances and tournament bids; championships; applicable power ratings; quality of competition; overall fan fervor; sports atmosphere and fan knowledge; abundance of teams (quality over quantity); stadium/arena quality; ticket availability and prices; franchise ownership; and the marquee appeal of athletes. *SportingNews.com, "Best Sports Cities 2006," August 1, 2006*

■ The Seattle metro area was selected by *Cranium* as one of the "Top 50 Fun Cities" in America. The area ranked #10. Criteria includes: number of sports teams, restaurants, and dance performances; number of toy stores; city budget spent on recreation. *Cranium, November 4, 2003*

■ *Golf Digest* ranked 330 metro areas in the U.S. in terms of golf. The Seattle metro area was ranked #315. Criteria: access to golf; weather; value of golf; and quality of golf. *Golf Digest, "Metro Golf Rankings," August 2005*

Dating/Romance Rankings

■ The Seattle metro area was selected as one of the "Best Cities for Relocating Singles" by Worldwide ERC and Primacy Relocation. The area ranked #10 out of the 100 largest metro areas in the U.S. Areas were selected based on the following criteria: Population Criteria (local percentage and growth trends of unmarried residents aged 25-34; male-female ratios; the number of newcomers to the area; diversity and density); Economic Criteria (job growth vs. unemployment rates; apartment rental costs; fee and occupancy rates for temporary housing and mini-storage; higher education costs, including in-state and out-of-state tuition requirements; vehicle tax rates and quality of service from utility providers); Quality-of-Life Criteria (level of per capita volunteering; quality and quantity of collegiate and professional sports with fun, fan-friendly venues; number of Starbucks and other coffee shops; quality or popularity of restaurants, nightspots, health clubs, and online dating; moderate climates with sustainable water supplies). *Worldwide ERC and Primacy Relocation, "2006 Best Cities for Relocating Singles," October 11, 2006*

■ *Forbes* ranked the 40 most populous metro areas in the U.S. in terms of the "Best Cities for Singles." The Seattle metro area was ranked #7. Criteria: number of singles; cost of living alone; nightlife; culture; job growth; coolness; and online dating. *Forbes.com, July 25, 2006*

■ Sperling's BestPlaces in partnership with AXE Deodorant Bodyspray ranked 80 metro areas and identified "America's Best (and Worst) Cities for Dating." The Seattle metro area ranked #5. Criteria: percentage of singles ages 18-24; population density; dating venues per capita. *AXE Deodorant Bodyspray, "America's Best (and Worst) Cities for Dating," May, 2004*

Culture/Performing Arts Rankings

■ Scarborough Research, a leading market research firm, identified the top local markets for rock concert attendance. The Seattle DMA (Designated Market Area) ranked in the top 25 with 14% of consumers, 18 years old and over, reporting that they have attended a rock concert during the past year. *Scarborough Research, Scarborough USA+ 2003 Release 2*

Miscellaneous Rankings

■ Avis Rent-A-Car and Motorola, in partnership with Sperling's BestPlaces, ranked the nation's 75 most populous metro areas in terms of how difficult they are to navigate. The Seattle metro area ranked #8 with #1 being the most challenging. Criteria: street layouts; overall design and layout; travel time index; percent of congested freeway and street lane miles; bodies of water; complexity of directions needed to travel from major airports to city center; annual delay per person; days of snow exceeding 1.5 inches; and days of rain exceeding 0.5 inch. *Avis Rent-A-Car and Motorola, "America's Most Challenging Cities to Navigate," August 3, 2004*

■ The Seattle metro area appeared on *Forbes* list of "America's Drunkest Cities". The area ranked #12. Criteria: 35 of the largest continental U.S. metro areas were chosen based on availability of data and geographic diversity. Each metro was ranked in five areas: state laws; drinkers; heavy drinkers; binge drinkers; and alcoholism. *Forbes.com, "America's Drunkest Cities," August 22, 2006*

■ Bellevue appeared on ApartmentRatings.com "Top Cities for Renters List 2006". The area ranked #102 out of 138. Criteria: renter satisfaction; affordability; and vacancy. *ApartmentRatings.com, "Top Cities for Renters List 2006"*

■ Sperling's BestPlaces in partnership with Pep Boys ranked 77 metro areas and identified "America's Most Drivable Cities." The Seattle metro area ranked #69. Criteria: climate; road roughness; urban mobility; gas prices. *Pep Boys, "America's Most Drivable Cities," April 9, 2003*

■ Seattle was ranked #5 out of 268 metro areas in terms of its Creativity Index. The Creativity Index is a mix of four equally weighted factors: the Creative Class (scientists, engineers, architects, designers, writers, artists, musicians, or any profession where creativity is a key factor) share of the workforce; innovation, measured as patents per capita; high-tech industry, using the Milken Institute's Tech Pole Index; and diversity, measured by the Gay Index (a reasonable proxy for an areas' openness to different kinds of people and ideas). *The Rise of the Creative Class, 2002*

■ State Farm Insurance, in partnership with Sperling's BestPlaces, analyzed several key factors that contribute to overall family preparedness. The Seattle metro area ranked #8 out of the nation's 50 most populous metro areas. Criteria: quality of life; life insurance coverage; and investments. *State Farm Life Insurance, "Fiscally Fit Cities Report," July 20, 2004*

■ Scarborough Research, a leading market research firm, identified the top local markets for coffee bar patronage. The Seattle DMA (Designated Market Area) ranked in the top 10 with 23% of adults reporting that they have used any coffee house/bar during the past 30 days. *Scarborough Research, Scarborough USA+ 2004 Release 1*

■ Bellevue was selected as having one of the highest number of Starbucks stores per capita in the U.S. The city appeared in the large city category. Criteria: U.S. cities with populations of 10,000 or more were analyzed with regards to the number of Starbucks stores per capita. Supermarkets and other stores selling coffee beans were not included. *ePodunk.com, "Coffee Quotients," March 2005*

Business Environment

CITY FINANCES

City Government Finances

Component	2003-2004 ($000)	2003-2004 ($ per capita)
Total Revenues	245,032	2,170
Total Expenditures	215,484	1,909
Debt Outstanding	72,601	643
Cash and Securities	134,122	1,188

Source: U.S Census Bureau, Government Finances 2003-2004

City Government Revenue by Source

Source	2003-2004 ($000)	2003-2004 ($ per capita)
General Revenue		
From Federal Government	1,245	11
From State Government	9,792	87
From Local Governments	14,383	127
Taxes		
Property	27,496	244
Sales	68,002	602
Personal Income	0	0
License	0	0
Charges	43,616	386
Liquor Store	0	0
Utility	25,939	230
Employee Retirement	0	0
Other	54,559	483

Source: U.S Census Bureau, Government Finances 2003-2004

City Government Expenditures by Function

Function	2003-2004 ($000)	2003-2004 ($ per capita)	2003-2004 (%)
General Expenditures			
Airports	0	0	0.0
Corrections	2,723	24	1.3
Education	0	0	0.0
Fire Protection	11,948	106	5.5
Governmental Administration	21,467	190	10.0
Health	10,562	94	4.9
Highways	36,542	324	17.0
Hospitals	0	0	0.0
Housing and Community Development	8,941	79	4.1
Interest on General Debt	2,925	26	1.4
Libraries	0	0	0.0
Parking	0	0	0.0
Parks and Recreation	30,304	268	14.1
Police Protection	19,896	176	9.2
Public Welfare	90	1	0.0
Sewerage	22,461	199	10.4
Solid Waste Management	147	1	0.1
Liquor Store	0	0	0.0
Utility	16,294	144	7.6
Employee Retirement	0	0	0.0
Other	31,184	276	14.5

Source: U.S Census Bureau, Government Finances 2003-2004

Municipal Bond Ratings

Area	Moody's
City	Aa1

Source: Mergent Bond Record, January 2007 (unless noted otherwise)

DEMOGRAPHICS

Population Growth

Area	1990 Census	2000 Census	2006 Estimate	2011 Projection	Population Growth (%) 1990-2000	Population Growth (%) 2000-2011
City	99,057	109,569	115,750	121,418	10.6	10.8
MSA[1]	2,559,164	3,043,878	3,226,674	3,397,122	18.9	11.6
U.S.	248,709,873	281,421,906	298,021,266	312,383,955	13.2	11.0

Note: (1) Metropolitan Statistical Area - see Appendix B for areas included
Source: Claritas, Inc.

Number of Households and Average Household Size

Area	2006 Estimate	2006 Average Household Size
City	49,309	2.35
MSA[1]	1,270,402	2.54
U.S.	112,267,302	2.65

Note: (1) Metropolitan Statistical Area - see Appendix B for areas included
Source: Claritas, Inc.

Race and Ethnicity

Area	White Alone[2]	Black Alone[2]	Asian Alone[2]	Other Race Alone[2]	Hispanic[3]
City	69.0	2.0	21.7	7.3	6.7
MSA[1]	75.5	5.2	10.0	9.3	6.6
U.S.	73.3	12.4	4.2	10.1	14.5

Note: Figures are 2006 estimates; (1) Metropolitan Statistical Area - see Appendix B for areas included
(2) Alone is defined as not being in combination with one or more other races; (3) May be of any race.
Source: Claritas, Inc.

Segregation

City Index[2]	City Rank[3]	MSA[1] Index[2]	MSA[1] Rank[4]
33.5	95	57.9	172

Note: Figures are based on an analysis of Census 2000 data; (1) Metropolitan Statistical Area - see Appendix A for areas included; (2) White/Black Dissimilarity Index—the most commonly used measure of segregation between two groups, reflecting their relative distributions across neighborhoods within a city or metropolitan area. It can range in value from 0, indicating complete integration, to 100, indicating complete segregation; (3) Ranges from 1 (most segregated) to 100 (least segregated) and includes all the cities in this book; (4) Ranges from 1 (most segregated) to 318 (least segregated) and includes 318 metropolitan areas.
Source: www.CensusScope.org

Ancestry

Area	German	Irish[2]	English	American	Italian	Polish	French[3]	Scottish
City	15.8	10.3	12.8	3.4	3.3	2.1	3.5	3.1
MSA[1]	17.6	11.5	12.3	4.3	3.6	2.0	3.6	3.3
U.S.	15.2	10.9	8.7	7.3	5.6	3.2	3.0	1.7

Note: Figures include multiple ancestry (e.g. if a person reported being Irish and Italian, they were included in both columns); (1) Metropolitan Statistical Area - see Appendix A for areas included; (2) Includes Celtic; (3) Includes Alsatian but excludes Basque
Source: Census 2000, Summary File 3

Foreign-Born Population

Area	Any Foreign Country	Percent of Population Born in Europe	Asia	Africa	Oceania[2]	Canada	Mexico	Latin America[3]
City	24.5	5.3	13.6	0.6	0.3	1.6	2.2	0.9
MSA[1]	13.8	2.8	6.9	0.7	0.2	1.0	1.5	0.6
U.S.	11.1	1.7	2.9	0.3	0.1	0.3	3.3	2.5

Note: (1) Metropolitan Statistical Area - see Appendix A for areas included; (2) Includes Australia, New Zealand subregion, Melanesia, Micronesia, Polynesia, and Oceania n.e.c; (3) Includes Central America (excluding Mexico), South America, and the Caribbean.
Source: Census 2000, Summary File 3

Marriage Status

Area	Never Married	Now Married (excluding Separated)	Separated	Widowed	Divorced
City	25.3	58.5	1.0	5.1	10.1
MSA[1]	29.2	53.2	1.5	4.8	11.3
U.S.	27.1	54.4	2.2	6.6	9.7

Note: Figures are percentages and cover the population 15 years of age and older;
(1) Metropolitan Statistical Area - see Appendix A for areas included
Source: Census 2000, Summary File 3

Age Distribution

Area	Percent of Population						
	Under Age 5	Age 5 to 17	Age 18 to 34	Age 35 to 49	Age 50 to 64	Age 65 to 79	80 Years and Over
City	5.6	15.5	23.4	24.6	17.4	10.2	3.3
MSA[1]	6.3	17.4	25.2	26.1	14.7	7.4	2.9
U.S.	6.8	18.9	23.7	23.5	14.8	9.2	3.2

Note: (1) Metropolitan Statistical Area - see Appendix A for areas included
Source: Census 2000, Summary File 3

Male/Female Ratio

Area	Males	Females	Males per 100 Females
City	57,289	58,461	98.0
MSA[1]	1,609,994	1,616,680	99.6
U.S.	146,712,712	151,308,554	97.0

Note: Figures are 2006 estimates; (1) Metropolitan Statistical Area -
see Appendix B for areas included
Source: Claritas, Inc.

Religion

Area	Catholic	Southern Baptist	United Methodist	ELCA[1]	LDS[2]	Presbyterian Church USA	Jewish Est.	Muslim Est.
County	16.2	0.7	1.1	2.0	2.3	1.6	1.9	0.5
U.S.	22.0	7.1	3.7	1.8	1.5	1.1	2.2	0.6

Note: Figures are the number of adherents as a percentage of the total population; Adherents are defined as all members, including full members, their children and the estimated number of other participants who are not considered members (e.g. the baptized, those not confirmed, those regularly attending services, etc.);
(1) Evangelical Lutheran Church in America; (2) The Church of Jesus Christ of Latter Day Saints
Source: Reprinted with permission from Religious Congregations and Membership in the United States 2000 (Nashville, Glenmary Research Center, 2002) Copyright Association of Statisticians of American Religious Bodies. All rights reserved.

ECONOMY

Gross Metropolitan Product

Area	2002	2003	2004	2005	2005 Rank[2]
MSA[1]	138.9	142.3	149.0	158.0	13

Note: Figures are in billions of dollars; (1) Seattle-Tacoma-Bellevue, WA Metropolitan Statistical Area - see Appendix A for areas included; (2) Rank ranges from 1 to 361
Source: The U.S. Conference of Mayors, "U.S. Metro Economies: GMP - The Engines of America's Growth," January 2007

Economic Growth

Area	1995 GMP	2005 GMP	Average Annual Growth Rate	Growth Rate Rank[2]
MSA[1]	90.9	158.0	5.7	144

Note: Figures are in billions of dollars; GMP = Gross Metropolitan Product; (1) Seattle-Tacoma-Bellevue, WA Metropolitan Statistical Area - see Appendix A for areas included; (2) Rank ranges from 1 to 361
Source: The U.S. Conference of Mayors, "U.S. Metro Economies: GMP - The Engines of America's Growth," January 2007

INCOME

Per Capita/Median/Average Income

Area	Per Capita ($)	Median Household ($)	Average Household ($)
City	39,205	68,015	91,588
MSA[1]	29,569	58,417	74,194
U.S.	25,129	48,775	65,849

Note: Figures are 2006 estimates; (1) Metropolitan Statistical Area - see Appendix B for areas included
Source: Claritas, Inc.

Household Income Distribution

Area	Percent of Households Earning							
	Under $15,000	$15,000 -24,999	$25,000 -34,999	$35,000 -49,999	$50,000 -74,999	$75,000 -99,000	$100,000 -149,999	$150,000 and up
City	7.1	6.4	8.0	13.9	20.2	14.6	16.4	13.4
MSA[1]	9.3	8.4	9.9	15.2	21.1	14.4	14.0	7.6
U.S.	13.3	11.0	11.3	15.7	19.5	11.8	11.0	6.4

Note: Figures are 2006 estimates; (1) Metropolitan Statistical Area - see Appendix B for areas included
Source: Claritas, Inc.

Poverty Rates by Age

Area	All Ages	Under 5 Years Old	5 to 17 Years Old	18 to 64 Years Old	65 Years and Over
City	5.7	0.3	1.0	3.6	0.8
MSA[1]	7.9	0.6	1.6	5.0	0.7
U.S.	12.4	1.2	3.0	6.9	1.2

Note: Figures are percent of population with income in 1999 below poverty level and only include population for whom poverty status is determined; (1) Metropolitan Statistical Area - see Appendix A for areas included
Source: Census 2000, Summary File 3

Personal Bankruptcy Filing Rate

Area	2003	2004	2005
King County	4.88	4.69	6.13
U.S.	5.57	5.31	6.88

Note: Numbers are per 1,000 population and include Chapter 7 and Chapter 13 filings
Source: Federal Deposit Insurance Corporation (FDIC), Regional Economic Conditions (RECON), 3/24/2006

EMPLOYMENT

Labor Force and Employment

Area	Civilian Labor Force			Workers Employed		
	Dec. 2005	Dec. 2006	% Chg.	Dec. 2005	Dec. 2006	% Chg.
City	65,962	67,287	2.0	63,594	65,143	2.4
MD[1]	1,384,455	1,408,918	1.8	1,323,572	1,350,252	2.0
U.S.	149,874,000	152,571,000	1.8	142,918,000	146,081,000	2.2

Note: Data is not seasonally adjusted and covers workers 16 years of age and older;
(1) Metropolitan Division - see Appendix B for areas included
Source: Bureau of Labor Statistics, http://stats.bls.gov

Unemployment Rate

Area	2006											
	Jan.	Feb.	Mar.	Apr.	May	Jun.	Jul.	Aug.	Sep.	Oct.	Nov.	Dec.
City	3.4	3.8	3.4	3.2	3.8	3.7	3.4	3.3	3.8	3.4	3.7	3.2
MD[1]	4.3	4.7	4.5	4.0	4.4	4.4	4.1	4.0	4.4	4.1	4.5	4.2
U.S.	5.1	5.1	4.8	4.5	4.4	4.8	5.0	4.6	4.4	4.1	4.3	4.3

Note: Data is not seasonally adjusted and covers workers 16 years of age and older; All figures are percentages; (1) Metropolitan Division - see Appendix B for areas included
Source: Bureau of Labor Statistics, http://stats.bls.gov

Employment by Occupation

Occupation Classification	City (%)	MSA[1] (%)	U.S. (%)
Sales and Office	26.4	26.4	26.7
Professional and Related	31.6	24.3	20.2
Service	10.1	13.1	14.9
Production, Transportation, and Material Moving	6.2	10.9	14.6
Management, Business, and Financial	21.5	16.6	13.5
Construction, Extraction, and Maintenance	4.1	8.3	9.4
Farming, Forestry, and Fishing	0.1	0.3	0.7

Note: Figures cover employed civilians 16 years of age and older;
(1) Metropolitan Statistical Area - see Appendix A for areas included
Source: Census 2000, Summary File 3

Employment by Industry

| Sector | MSA[1] | | U.S. |
	Number of Employees	Percent of Total	Percent of Total
Government	200,700	13.9	16.3
Education and Health Services	149,900	10.4	13.2
Professional and Business Services	208,500	14.4	12.9
Retail Trade	152,900	10.6	11.5
Manufacturing	163,800	11.3	10.2
Leisure and Hospitality	131,200	9.1	9.5
Financial Activities	90,000	6.2	6.1
Construction	93,000	6.4	5.5
Wholesale Trade	71,900	5.0	4.3
Other Services	50,300	3.5	3.9
Transportation and Utilities	51,600	3.6	3.7
Information	81,100	5.6	2.2
Natural Resources and Mining	1,100	0.1	0.5

Note: Figures cover non-farm employment as of December 2006 and are not seasonally adjusted;
(1) Metropolitan Statistical Area - see Appendix B for areas included
Source: Bureau of Labor Statistics, http://stats.bls.gov

Occupations with Greatest Projected Employment Growth: 2002 - 2012

Occupation[1]	2002 Employment	2012 Projected Employment	Numeric Employment Change	Percent Employment Change
Maids and Housekeeping Cleaners	42,770	57,330	14,560	34.0
Child Care Workers	42,180	56,290	14,110	33.5
Retail Salespersons	78,000	89,630	11,630	14.9
Cashiers	63,700	73,900	10,200	16.0
Janitors and Cleaners, Except Maids and Housekeeping Cleaners	44,260	54,430	10,170	23.0
Office Clerks, General	53,850	63,570	9,720	18.1
Registered Nurses	45,930	55,260	9,330	20.3
Combined Food Preparation and Serving Workers, Including Fast Food	48,250	56,000	7,750	16.1
Teacher Assistants	33,570	40,890	7,320	21.8
Waiters and Waitresses	42,670	49,900	7,230	16.9

Note: Projections cover Washington; (1) Sorted by numeric employment change
Source: www.projectionscentral.com, State Occupational Projections, 2002-2012 Long-Term Projections

Fastest Growing Occupations: 2002 - 2012

Occupation[1]	2002 Employment	2012 Projected Employment	Numeric Employment Change	Percent Employment Change
Veterinary Assistants and Laboratory Animal Caretakers	1,140	1,570	430	37.7
Medical Scientists, Except Epidemiologists	930	1,270	340	36.6
Veterinary Technologists and Technicians	930	1,270	340	36.6
Dental Laboratory Technicians	870	1,180	310	35.6
Veterinarians	1,210	1,640	430	35.5
Maids and Housekeeping Cleaners	42,770	57,330	14,560	34.0
Computer Software Engineers, Applications	15,890	21,220	5,330	33.5
Child Care Workers	42,180	56,290	14,110	33.5
Technical Writers	3,030	3,990	960	31.7
Computer Software Engineers, Systems Software	12,970	16,900	3,930	30.3

Note: Projections cover Washington; (1) Sorted by percent employment change and excludes occupations with numeric employment change less than 300
Source: www.projectionscentral.com, State Occupational Projections, 2002-2012 Long-Term Projections

Average Wages

Occupation	$/Hr.	Occupation	$/Hr.
Accountants and Auditors	29.34	Maids and Housekeeping Cleaners	9.81
Automotive Mechanics	21.00	Maintenance and Repair Workers	18.74
Bookkeepers	16.35	Marketing Managers	60.40
Carpenters	23.96	Nuclear Medicine Technologists	33.41
Cashiers	11.43	Nurses, Licensed Practical	20.88
Clerks, General Office	13.73	Nurses, Registered	32.89
Clerks, Receptionists/Information	12.41	Nursing Aides/Orderlies/Attendants	12.72
Clerks, Shipping/Receiving	14.80	Packers and Packagers, Hand	10.08
Computer Programmers	n/a	Physical Therapists	30.00
Computer Support Specialists	26.04	Postal Service Mail Carriers	21.85
Computer Systems Analysts	37.06	Real Estate Brokers	38.04
Cooks, Restaurant	11.70	Retail Salespersons	13.05
Dentists	n/a	Sales Reps., Exc. Tech./Scientific	29.26
Electrical Engineers	36.09	Sales Reps., Tech./Scientific	35.04
Electricians	26.68	Secretaries, Exc. Legal/Med./Exec.	16.18
Financial Managers	50.99	Security Guards	13.55
First-Line Supervisors/Mgrs., Sales	22.77	Surgeons	87.88
Food Preparation Workers	10.71	Teacher Assistants	12.60
General and Operations Managers	62.86	Teachers, Elementary School	21.70
Hairdressers/Cosmetologists	13.61	Teachers, Secondary School	22.50
Internists	78.35	Telemarketers	13.95
Janitors and Cleaners	12.44	Truck Drivers, Heavy/Tractor-Trailer	18.91
Landscaping/Groundskeeping Workers	13.27	Truck Drivers, Light/Delivery Svcs.	14.32
Lawyers	48.51	Waiters and Waitresses	10.78

Note: Wage data is for May 2005 and covers the Seattle-Bellevue-Everett, WA Metropolitan Division - see Appendix B for areas included. Hourly wages for elementary/secondary school teachers and teacher assistants were calculated by the editors from annual wage data assuming a 40 hour work week; n/a not available.
Source: Bureau of Labor Statistics, May 2005 Metro Area Occupational Employment and Wage Estimates

RESIDENTIAL REAL ESTATE

Building Permits

Area	Single-Family			Multi-Family			Total		
	2005	2006p	Pct. Chg.	2005	2006p	Pct. Chg.	2005	2006p	Pct. Chg.
City	171	238	39.2	367	805	119.3	538	1,043	93.9
U.S.	1,682,000	1,380,000	-18.0	473,300	457,300	-3.4	2,155,300	1,837,300	-14.8

Note: (p) preliminary; figures represent new, privately-owned housing units authorized (unadjusted data); All permit data are based on estimates with imputation; U.S. figures are based on the new 20,000-place series.
Source: U.S. Census Bureau, Manufacturing, Mining, and Construction Statistics

Homeownership and Housing Vacancies

Area	Homeownership Rate[2] (%)			Rental Vacancy Rate[3] (%)			Homeowner Vacancy Rate[4] (%)		
	2004	2005	2006	2004	2005	2006	2004	2005	2006
MSA[1]	n/a	64.5	63.7	n/a	6.9	5.6	n/a	1.0	0.9
U.S.	69.0	68.9	68.8	10.2	9.8	9.7	1.7	1.9	2.4

Note: Comparable 2004 data was not available due to changes in metropolitan area definitions; (1) Metropolitan Statistical Area - see Appendix B for areas included; (2) The proportion of households that are owners; (3) The proportion of the rental inventory that is vacant for rent; (4) The proportion of the homeowner inventory that is vacant for sale; n/a not available
Source: U.S. Census Bureau, Housing Vacancies and Homeownership Annual Statistics: 2006

TAXES

State Corporate Income Tax Rates

State	Rate (%)	Number of Brackets	Low Bracket (Under $)	High Bracket (Over $)
Washington	None	na	na	na

Note: Tax rates as of December 31, 2006; na not applicable; Gross receipts tax called Business & Operations (B&O) Tax.
Source: Tax Foundation, www.taxfoundation.org

State Individual Income Tax Rates

State	Federal Deductibility	Marginal Rate (%)	Number of Brackets	Low Bracket (Under $)	High Bracket (Over $)
Washington	No	None	na	na	na

Note: Tax rates as of December 31, 2006; Brackets apply to single taxpayers and married people filing separately; na not applicable
Source: Tax Foundation, www.taxfoundation.org

Various State and Local Tax Rates

State and Local Sales and Use (%)	State Sales and Use (%)	Gasoline ($/gal.)	Cigarette ($/pack)	Spirits ($/gal.)	Table Wine ($/gal.)	Beer ($/gal.)
8.9	6.5	0.34 (p)	2.03	21.30 (b)	0.88	0.26

Note: Tax rates as of December 31, 2006; (b) States where the state government controls all sales. Excise tax rate is calculated using methodology designed by the Distilled Spirits Council of the United States (DISCUS); (p) Was $.28 per gallon. Will increase to $.36 per gallon July 1, 2007, $.375 July 1, 2008.
Source: Tax Foundation, www.taxfoundation.org; The Sales Tax Clearinghouse, www.thestc.com

State Tax Burdens

Area	Combined State and Local Tax Burden		Combined Federal, State and Local Tax Burden	
	Percent	Rank	Percent	Rank
Washington	10.9	13	33.7	4
U.S. Average	10.6	-	31.6	-

Note: Figures are for 2006 and measure taxes as a percentage of income
Source: Tax Foundation, www.taxfoundation.org

Internal Revenue Service Tax Audits

IRS District	Percent of Returns Audited				
	1996	1997	1998	1999	2000
Pacific Northwest	0.63	0.51	0.37	0.24	0.15
U.S.	0.66	0.61	0.46	0.31	0.20

Note: Figures cover IRS district audits of federal income tax returns filed by individuals. Geographic data on district audits after the year 2000 are being withheld by the IRS. TRAC is challenging this policy.
Source: Syracuse University, Transactional Records Access Clearinghouse (TRAC), "Odds of IRS District Tax Audit 2000"

COMMERCIAL REAL ESTATE

Office Market

Market Area	Inventory (sq. ft.)	Vacant (sq. ft.)	Vac. Rate (%)	Under Constr. (sq. ft.)	Asking Rent ($/sf)	
					Class A	Class B
Seattle	83,070,751	8,341,020	10.0	3,027,368	28.50	21.81

Source: Grubb & Ellis, Office Markets Trends, 4th Quarter 2006

Industrial Market

Market Area	Inventory (sq. ft.)	Vacant (sq. ft.)	Vac. Rate (%)	Under Constr. (sq. ft.)	Asking Rent ($/sf)	
					WH/Dist	R&D/Flex
Seattle	155,456,409	10,373,348	6.7	4,546,453	5.76	11.88

Source: Grubb & Ellis, Industrial Markets Trends, 4th Quarter 2006

COMMERCIAL UTILITIES

Typical Monthly Electric Bills

Area	Commercial Service ($/month)		Industrial Service ($/month)	
	3 kW demand 1,000 kWh	40 kW demand 14,000 kWh	1,000 kW demand 200,000 kWh	50,000 kW demand 15,000,000 kWh
City	89	1,114	17,329	950,183
Average[1]	123	1,413	22,000	1,306,315

Note: Based on total rates in effect July 1, 2006; (1) average based on 196 utilities
Source: Edison Electric Institute, Typical Bills and Average Rates Report, Summer 2006

TRANSPORTATION

Means of Transportation to Work

Area	Car/Truck/Van		Public Transportation			Bicycle	Walked	Other Means	Worked at Home
	Drove Alone	Car-pooled	Bus	Subway	Railroad				
City	74.0	10.6	6.6	0.0	0.0	0.4	2.6	0.6	5.1
MSA[1]	70.4	12.6	7.8	0.0	0.0	0.7	3.2	0.9	4.4
U.S.	75.7	12.2	2.5	1.5	0.5	0.4	2.9	1.0	3.3

Note: Figures are percentages and cover workers 16 years of age and older;
(1) Metropolitan Statistical Area - see Appendix A for areas included
Source: Census 2000, Summary File 3

Travel Time to Work

Area	Less Than 15 Minutes	15 to 29 Minutes	30 to 44 Minutes	45 to 59 Minutes	60 Minutes or More
City	28.8	44.5	20.2	3.8	2.7
MSA[1]	22.1	36.9	23.9	9.2	7.9
U.S.	29.4	36.1	19.1	7.4	8.0

Note: Figures are percentages and include workers 16 years old and over; (1) Metropolitan Statistical Area -
see Appendix A for areas included
Source: Census 2000, Summary File 3

Public Transportation

Agency name:	King County Department of Transportation (KC Metro)
Vehicle type:	Bus
Average fleet age in years:	5.6
No. operated in max. service:	1,176
Vehicle type:	Trolleybus
Average fleet age in years:	8.2
No. operated in max. service:	159
Vehicle type:	Demand response
Average fleet age in years:	4.8
No. operated in max. service:	471
Vehicle type:	Vanpool
Average fleet age in years:	3.4
No. operated in max. service:	746
Vehicle type:	Light rail
Average fleet age in years:	0.0
No. operated in max. service:	3

Source: Federal Transit Administration, National Transit Database, 2005

Air Transportation

Airport name and code:	Seattle-Tacoma International (SEA)
Domestic service (2006)	
Passenger airlines[1]:	31
Passenger enplanements:	13,560,817
Freight carriers[2]:	30
Freight (lbs.):	238,810,454
International service (2005)	
Passenger airlines[1]:	22
Passenger enplanements:	1,113,722
Freight carriers[2]:	22
Freight (lbs.):	88,323,996

*Note: (1) Includes all major, minor and commuter airlines that carried at least one passenger during the year;
(2) Includes all airlines and freight carriers that transported at least one pound of freight during the year
Source: Bureau of Transportation Statistics, The Intermodal Transportation Database, Air Carriers: T-100
International Market, 2004; Bureau of Transportation Statistics, The Intermodal Transportation Database, Air
Carriers: T-100 Domestic Market, 2005*

Other Transportation Statistics

Interstate highways:	I-50; I-90
Amtrak service:	No
Major waterways/ports:	Lake Washington; Near Puget Sound (8 miles)

Source: Editor & Publisher Market Guide, 2006; Amtrak.com; Rand McNally 2006 Road Atlas

BUSINESSES

Major Business Headquarters

Company Name	2006 Rankings	
	Fortune[1]	Forbes[2]
Paccar	157	-

*Note: (1) Fortune 500 - companies that produce a 10-K are ranked 1 to 500 based on 2005 revenue; (2) Forbes
Largest Private Companies - all private companies with at least $1 billion in annual revenue are ranked 1 to
394; companies listed are located in the city; dashes indicate no ranking
Source: Fortune, April 17, 2006; Forbes, November 9, 2006*

Fast-Growing Businesses

According to *Inc.*, Bellevue is home to four of America's 500 fastest-growing private
companies: **Ascentium; Smooth Corp; Techlink Northwest; eNom**. Criteria: must be an
independent, privately-held, U.S. corporation, proprietorship or partnership; net sales of at
least $600,000 in FY2002; four-year operating/sales history; holding companies, regulated
banks, and utilities were excluded. *Inc., "America's 500 Fastest-Growing Private
Companies,"September 2006*

According to *Business 2.0*, Bellevue is home to one of America's 100 fastest-growing
technology companies: **Esterline Technologies**. The 100 Fastest-Growing Technology
Companies (B2 100) is a yearly ranking published by Business 2.0 magazine of businesses

whose inventiveness and quick reflexes are helping them to set the pace for the economy. To find the B2 100, Zacks Investment Research of Chicago ranked 2,000 publicly traded companies using a rigorous combination of four financial criteria: growth in revenue, profit, and operating cash flow during the past three years; and the 12-month stock market return as of March 31, 2006. *Business 2.0, "100 Fastest-Growing Tech Companies 2006," June 2006*

According to Deloitte & Touche LLP, Bellevue is home to one of North America's 500 fastest-growing high-technology companies: **Coinstar**. Companies are ranked by percentage growth in revenue over a five-year period. Criteria for inclusion: company must be headquartered within North America; company must own proprietary intellectual property or proprietary technology that contributes to a significant portion of the company's operating revenue or devotes a significant proportion of revenues to research and development of technology; company must have been in business for a minumum of five years with 2001 operating revenues of at least $50,000 USD or $75,000 CD and 2005 operating revenues of at least $5 million USD/CD. *Deloitte & Touche LLP, 2006 Technology Fast 500*

Women-Owned Businesses: 1997 and 2002

Year	All Firms		Firms with Paid Employees			
	Firms	Sales ($000)	Firms	Sales ($000)	Employees	Payroll ($000)
1997	3,490	1,047,625	855	941,974	4,499	131,977
2002	3,881	1,024,886	946	951,617	7,191	264,561

Note: Figures cover firms located in the city; Women-owned business are defined as firms in which women own 51% or more of the stock or equity of the company; (a) Withheld to avoid disclosing data for individual companies; (b) Withheld because estimate did not meet publication standards; n/a not available
Source: 1997 Economic Census, Survey of Minority- and Women-Owned Business Enterprises; 2002 Economic Census, Survey of Business Owners (released February 9, 2006)

HOTELS

Hotels/Motels

Area	Hotels/Motels	Average Minimum Rates ($)		
		Tourist	First-Class	Deluxe
City	21	62	94	165

Source: OAG Travel Planner Online, Spring 2006

The Seattle metro area is home to four of the top 187 hotels in the U.S. according to *Travel & Leisure*: **Inn at the Market** (#51); **Bellevue Club Hotel** (#67); **Fairmont Olympic Hotel** (#150); **Alexis Hotel** (#179). Criteria: service; location; rooms; food; and value. *Travel & Leisure, "The T+L 500, 2007"*

EVENT SITES

Stadiums, Arenas, and Auditoriums

Name	Capacity
Meydenbauer Center	3,500

Source: www.officialtravelguide.com; www.eventective.com; original research

Hotels/Conference Centers

Name	Guest Rooms	Exhibit Space (sq. ft.)	Meeting Space (sq. ft.)
Bellevue Conference Center	n/a	n/a	n/a
Doubletree Hotel Bellevue	353	35,000	17,000
Hyatt Regency Bellevue	382	n/a	17,390

Note: n/a not available
Source: www.officialtravelguide.com; www.eventective.com; original research

Living Environment

COST OF LIVING

Cost of Living Index

Year	Composite Index	Groceries	Housing	Utilities	Trans-portation	Health Care	Misc. Goods/Services
2004	120.6	112.4	132.2	110.7	115.6	144.2	114.7
2005	117.0	110.0	132.7	105.3	110.4	121.6	111.2
2006	115.8	109.6	135.0	99.7	109.2	120.2	108.8

Note: U.S. = 100; Figures are for Seattle (data for Bellevue was not available)
Source: The Council for Community and Economic Research (formerly ACCRA), Cost of Living Index, 2004, 2005 and 2006 4-Quarter Averages

HOUSING

House Price Index (HPI)

Area	National Ranking[2]	Quarterly Change (%)	One-Year Change (%)	Five-Year Change (%)
MD[1]	18	1.52	14.50	64.62
U.S.[3]	-	1.12	5.87	55.21

Note: The HPI is a weighted repeat sales index. It measures average price changes in repeat sales or refinancings on the same properties. This information is obtained by reviewing repeat mortgage transactions on single-family properties whose mortgages have been purchased or securitized by Fannie Mae or Freddie Mac in January 1975; (1) Metropolitan Division - see Appendix B for areas included; (2) Rankings are based on annual percentage change for all metro areas containing at least 15,000 transactions over the last 10 years and ranges from 1 to 282; (3) figures based on a weighted division average; all figures are for the period ending December 31, 2006
Source: Office of Federal Housing Enterprise Oversight, House Price Index, March 1, 2007

House Price Valuations

Area	Q4 1999	Q4 2000	Q4 2001	Q4 2002	Q4 2003	Q4 2004	Q4 2005	Q4 2006
MSA[1]	-9.6	-2.7	2.0	6.2	10.0	-6.9	25.5	31.7

Note: Figures show the percentage of over- or under-valuation of single family homes relative to statistically normal house values (e.g. a value of 23.6 indicates that house values are 23.6% overvalued). Statistically normal house values are based on house prices, interest rates, household incomes, population densities, and any historical premiums or discounts metropolitan areas have exhibited over time; (1) Figures cover the Metropolitan Statistical Area - see Appendix B for areas included
Source: Global Insight/National City Corporation, House Prices in America, March 2007

Median Home Prices

Area	2004	2005	2006P	Percent Change 2005 to 2006
Metro Area[1]	284.6	316.8	361.2	14.0
U.S. Average	195.2	219.0	222.0	1.4

Note: Figures are median sales prices of existing single-family homes in thousands of dollars; (p) preliminary; n/a not available; (1) Covers the Seattle-Tacoma-Bellevue, WA Metropolitan Statistical Area - see Appendix B for areas included
Source: National Association of Realtors, Metropolitan Area Prices, 4th Quarter 2006

Housing: Year Structure Built

Area	1990 -2000	1980 -1989	1970 -1979	1960 -1969	1950 -1959	1940 -1949	Before 1940	Median Year
City	17.2	18.9	25.7	23.6	11.8	1.5	1.2	1975
MSA[1]	19.8	18.4	17.7	14.7	10.3	6.4	12.5	1973
U.S.	17.0	15.8	18.5	13.7	12.7	7.3	15.0	1971

Note: Figures are percentages; (1) Metropolitan Statistical Area - see Appendix A for areas included
Source: Census 2000, Summary File 3

Average New Home Price

Area	2004	2005	2006
City[1]	328,253	366,755	407,594
U.S.	253,574	275,712	299,269

*Note: Figures, in dollars, are based on a new home with 2,400 sq. ft. of living area on an 8,000 sq. ft. lot;
(1) Seattle (data for Bellevue was not available)
Source: The Council for Community and Economic Research (formerly ACCRA), Cost of Living Index, 2004,
2005 and 2006 4-Quarter Averages*

Average Apartment Rent

Area	2004	2005	2006
City[1]	1,054	1,062	1,055
U.S.	716	740	766

*Note: Figures, in dollars per month, are based on an unfurnished two bedroom, 1-1/2 or 2 bath apartment,
approximately 950 sq. ft. in size, excluding all utilities except water; (1) Seattle (data for Bellevue was not
available)
Source: The Council for Community and Economic Research (formerly ACCRA), Cost of Living Index, 2004,
2005 and 2006 4-Quarter Averages*

**RESIDENTIAL
UTILITIES**

Average Residential Utility Costs

Area	All Electric ($/mth)	Part Electric ($/mth)	Other Energy ($/mth)	Phone ($/mth)
City[1]	156.49	–	–	26.48
U.S.	136.00	76.53	90.52	25.87

*Note: (1) Seattle (data for Bellevue was not available)
Source: The Council for Community and Economic Research (formerly ACCRA), Cost of Living Index, 2006
4-Quarter Average*

HEALTH

Average Health Care Costs

Area	Optometrist ($/visit)	Doctor ($/visit)	Dentist ($/visit)
City[1]	104.93	91.36	93.85
U.S.	76.38	76.10	68.72

*Note: Optometrist—based on a full vision eye exam for an established adult patient;
Doctor—based on a general practitioner's routine exam of an established patient;
Dentist—based on adult teeth cleaning and periodic oral exam;
(1) Seattle (data for Bellevue was not available)
Source: The Council for Community and Economic Research (formerly ACCRA), Cost of Living Index, 2006
4-Quarter Average*

Mortality Rates

ICD-10 Sub-Chapter	ICD-10 Code	Age-Adjusted Death Rate per 100,000 population[1]	U.S. Age-Adjusted Death Rate per 100,000 population
Malignant neoplasms	C00-C97	165.4	185.8
Ischaemic heart diseases	I20-I25	108.9	150.2
Other forms of heart disease	I30-I51	31.7	50.8
Cerebrovascular diseases	I60-I69	50.7	50.0
Chronic lower respiratory diseases	J40-J47	32.1	41.1
Diabetes mellitus	E10-E14	20.3	24.5
Other degenerative diseases of the nervous system	G30-G31	34.2	22.3
Other external causes of accidental injury	W00-X59	22.9	21.2
Influenza and pneumonia	J10-J18	12.1	19.8
Hypertensive diseases	I10-I13	15.1	18.1

*Note: ICD-10 = International Classification of Diseases 10th Revision; (1) Figures cover King County, WA
Source: Centers for Disease Control and Prevention, National Center for Health Statistics. Compressed
Mortality File 1999-2004. CDC WONDER On-line Database, compiled from Compressed Mortality File
1999-2004 Series 20 No. 2J, 2007.*

Health Risk Data

Item	Area[1] (%)	U.S. (%)
Adults who have been told they have high blood pressure	22.3	25.5
Adults who have been told they have high blood cholesterol	35.5	35.6
Adults who have been told they have diabetes[2]	6.3	7.3
Adults who have been told they have arthritis	23.3	27.0
Adults who have been told they currently have asthma	8.0	8.0
Adults who are current smokers	14.7	20.6

Note: (1) Figures cover the Metropolitan Division - see Appendix B for areas included; (2) Figures do not include pregnancy-related diabetes, pre-diabetes or borderline diabetes
Source: Centers for Disease Control and Prevention, Behaviorial Risk Factor Surveillance System, SMART: Selected Metropolitan/Micropolitan Area Trends, 2005

Distribution of Office-Based Physicians

Area	Total	Family/General Practice	Specialties		
			Medical	Surgical	Other
CMSA[1] (number)	7,788	1,393	2,530	1,614	2,251
CMSA[1] (rate per 10,000 pop.)	21.6	3.9	7.0	4.5	6.2
Metro Average[2] (rate per 10,000 pop.)	19.4	2.1	7.5	4.5	5.3

Note: Data as of December 31, 2004; (1) Seattle-Tacoma-Bremerton, WA Consolidated Metropolitan Statistical Area includes the following counties: Island; King; Kitsap; Pierce; Snohomish; Thurston;
(2) Average of the 79 unique MSAs and CMSAs in this book
Source: American Medical Association, Physician Characteristics & Distribution in the U.S., 2006

Hospitals

Bellevue has the following hospitals: 1 general medical and surgical.
AHA Guide to the Healthcare Field 2007

According to *U.S. News,* the Seattle metro area is home to four of the best hospitals in the U.S.: **Children's Hospital and Regional Medical Center**; **Harborview Medical Center**; **University of Washington Medical Center**; **Virginia Mason Medical Center**; *U.S. News Online, "America's Best Hospitals 2006"*

EDUCATION

Public School District Statistics

District Name	Schls	Pupils	Pupil/Teacher Ratio	Minority Pupils[1] (%)	Free Lunch Eligible[2] (%)	IEP[3] (%)
Bellevue School Dist 405	31	15,848	17.8	41.1	13.4	10.4

Note: Table includes regular local school districts with 2,000 or more students; (1) Percentage of students that are not white, non-Hispanic; (2) Percentage of students that are eligible for the free lunch program;
(3) Percentage of students that have an Individualized Education Program.
Source: U.S. Department of Education, National Center for Education Statistics, Common Core of Data, Local Education Agency (School District) Universe Survey: School Year 2004-2005; U.S. Department of Education, National Center for Education Statistics, Common Core of Data, Public Elementary/Secondary School Universe Survey: School Year 2004-2005

Top Public High Schools

High School Name	Index[1]	Rank[1]	Subsidized Lunch (%)[2]	E&E (%)[3]
Bellevue	3.887	49	10.0	61.9
Interlake	3.980	44	30.0	44.3**
International School	3.741	57	4.5	34.5
Newport	4.067	37	7.3	n/a
Sammamish	2.516	193	28.0	15.0

Note: (1) Public schools are ranked according to a ratio that is the number of Advanced Placement and/or International Baccalaureate tests taken by all students at a school in 2005 divided by the number of graduating seniors. All of the schools on the list have an index of at least 1.000; they are in the top five percent of public schools measured this way. The rankings range from 1 to 1,236; (2) Percentage of students receiving federally subsidized meals; (3) E & E stands for equity and excellence percentage: the portion of all graduating seniors at a school that had at least one passing grade on one AP or IB test; (*) Gave just IB tests; (**) Gave both IB and AP tests. AP and IB participation are indicators of a school's efforts to get students to excel and prepare for college; n/a not available
Source: Newsweek Online, May 23, 2006

Educational Quality

School District	Education Quotient[1]	Graduate Outcome[2]	Community Index[3]	Resource Index[4]	Rating[5]
Bellevue SD 405	81	81	91	49	Blue

Note: Scores are national percentile rankings and range from 1 (worst) to 99 (best); (1) Combination of the Graduate Outcome, Community and Resource Indexes weighted to reflect the greater importance of the Graduate Outcome and Resource Index; (2) Based on graduation rates and college board scores (SAT/ACT); (3) Based on the surrounding community's level of affluence and adult education; (4) Based on teacher salaries, per-pupil expenditures and student-teacher ratios; (5) School districts receive one of five rankings: Gold Medal (top 16 percent of districts evaluated); Blue Ribbon (top third); Green Light (average); Yellow Light (bottom 25 percent); Red Light (bottom 10 percent).
Source: Expansion Management, "2007 Education Quotient," January 2007

Highest Level of Education

Area	Less than H.S.	H.S. Diploma	Some College, No Deg.	Associate Degree	Bachelors Degree	Masters Degree	Profess. School Degree	Doctorate Degree
City	5.7	12.7	20.7	6.9	34.6	13.2	3.8	2.4
MSA[1]	10.8	22.9	25.9	8.0	21.9	7.1	2.3	1.2
U.S.	19.4	28.4	21.2	6.4	15.7	5.9	2.0	1.0

Note: Figures are 2006 estimated percentages and cover persons age 25 and over; (1) Metropolitan Statistical Area - see Appendix B for areas included
Source: Claritas, Inc.

Educational Attainment by Race

Area	High School Graduate (%)					Bachelor's Degree (%)				
	Total	White	Black	Asian	Hisp.[2]	Total	White	Black	Asian	Hisp.[2]
City	94.3	95.9	93.4	92.8	65.9	54.1	54.2	39.1	63.0	28.7
MSA[1]	90.1	92.3	82.4	82.2	67.8	35.9	37.0	21.1	40.9	19.0
U.S.	80.4	83.6	72.3	80.4	52.4	24.4	26.1	14.3	44.1	10.4

Note: Figures shown cover persons 25 years old and over; (1) Metropolitan Statistical Area - see Appendix A for areas included; (2) people of Hispanic origin can be of any race
Source: Census 2000, Summary File 3

School Enrollment by Type

Area	Grades KG to 8				Grades 9 to 12			
	Public		Private		Public		Private	
	Enrollment	%	Enrollment	%	Enrollment	%	Enrollment	%
City	10,116	86.7	1,558	13.3	4,678	90.8	473	9.2
MSA[1]	260,622	88.3	34,672	11.7	116,866	91.1	11,446	8.9
U.S.	33,526,011	88.7	4,285,121	11.3	14,848,628	90.6	1,532,323	9.4

Note: Figures shown cover persons 3 years old and over; (1) Metropolitan Statistical Area - see Appendix A for areas included
Source: Census 2000, Summary File 3

School Enrollment by Race

Area	Grades KG to 8 (%)				Grades 9 to 12 (%)			
	White	Black	Asian	Hisp.[1]	White	Black	Asian	Hisp.[1]
City	67.4	2.5	17.8	6.3	65.5	2.3	20.8	6.6
MSA[2]	73.2	5.5	9.2	6.6	73.1	5.4	10.5	5.8
U.S.	68.5	15.5	3.3	16.8	68.8	15.5	3.8	15.7

Note: Figures shown cover persons 3 years old and over; (1) people of Hispanic origin can be of any race; (2) Metropolitan Statistical Area - see Appendix A for areas included
Source: Census 2000, Summary File 3

Average Salaries of Public School Teachers

District	2004-05		2005-06		Percent Change 2004-05 to 2005-06
	Dollars	Rank[1]	Dollars	Rank[1]	
WASHINGTON	45,718	20	46,326	22	1.33
U.S. Average	47,674	-	49,109	-	3.01

Note: (1) State rank ranges from 1 to 51.
Source: National Education Association, Rankings & Estimates: Rankings of the States 2005 and Estimates of School Statistics 2006, November 2006

Higher Education

Four-Year Colleges			Two-Year Colleges			Medical Schools[1]	Law Schools[2]	Voc/ Tech[3]
Public	Private Non-profit	Private For-profit	Public	Private Non-profit	Private For-profit			
0	1	0	1	0	1	0	0	1

Note: Figures cover institutions located within the city limits; (1) includes schools accredited by the Liaison Committee on Medical Education and the American Osteopathic Association; (2) includes American Bar Association-accredited law schools; (3) includes all schools with programs that are less than 2 years
Source: National Center for Education Statistics, The Integrated Postsecondary Education System (IPEDS) Peer Analysis System, 2006; www.usnews.com, America's Best Graduate Schools 2008, Medical School Directory; www.usnews.com, America's Best Graduate Schools 2008, Law School Directory

PRESIDENTIAL ELECTION

2004 Presidential Election Results

Area	Bush	Kerry	Nader	Other
King County	33.6	64.9	0.7	0.8
U.S.	50.7	48.3	0.4	0.6

Note: Results are percentages and may not add to 100% due to rounding
Source: Dave Leip's Atlas of U.S. Presidential Elections, www.uselectionatlas.org

MAJOR EMPLOYERS

Major Employers

Company Name	Industry	Type of Site
Alaska Airlines	General warehousing and storage	Branch
Bailey-Boushay House	Offices and clinics of medical doctors	Headquarters
Childrens Health Care System	Specialty hospitals, except psychiatric	Single
Harborview Medical Center	General medical and surgical hospitals	Single
Microsoft	Prepackaged software	Headquarters
Neurological Surgery	Colleges and universities	Branch
R U I One Corp	Eating places	Single
SNC Lavalin Thermal Power	Heavy construction, nec	Headquarters
Swedish Med Center/First Hl	General medical and surgical hospitals	Headquarters
TCI West Inc	Cable and other pay television services	Single
UPS	Air courier services	Branch
University of Washington Press	Colleges and universities	Headquarters
Washington University of Inc	Colleges and universities	Branch
Weyerhaeuser Company	General warehousing and storage	Branch
Weyerhaeuser Company	Lumber, plywood, and millwork	Branch

Note: Companies shown are located within the metropolitan area and have 2,700 or more employees; nec = not elsewhere classified.
Source: www.zapdata.com, January 2007

PUBLIC SAFETY

Crime Rate

Area	All Crimes	Violent Crimes				Property Crimes		
		Murder	Forcible Rape	Robbery	Aggrav. Assault	Burglary	Larceny -Theft	Motor Vehicle Theft
City	4,082.0	1.7	24.5	41.4	77.6	502.1	2,956.2	478.5
Suburbs[1]	5,817.6	3.1	39.3	135.0	238.0	975.3	3,287.5	1,139.3
Metro[2]	5,753.5	3.1	38.8	131.5	232.0	957.8	3,275.3	1,114.9
U.S.	3,899.0	5.6	31.7	140.7	291.1	726.7	2,286.3	416.7

Note: Figures are crimes per 100,000 population; (1) All areas within the metro area that are located outside the city limits; (2) Metropolitan Statistical Area - see Appendix B for areas included
Source: FBI Uniform Crime Reports, 2005

Hate Crimes

Area	Number of Quarters Reported	Bias Motivation				
		Race	Religion	Sexual Orientation	Ethnicity	Disability
City	4	0	1	0	0	0

Source: Federal Bureau of Investigation, Hate Crime Statistics 2005

RECREATION

Culture

Dance[1]	Theatre[1]	Instrumental Music[1]	Vocal Music[1]	Series/ Festivals	Museums	Zoos
0	0	1	0	0	4	0

Note: (1) number of professional perfoming groups
Source: The Grey House Performing Arts Directory, 2007; Official Museum Directory, 2007

Professional Sports Teams

Major League Baseball	National Basketball Association	National Football League	National Hockey League	Major League Soccer	Women's National Basketball Association
1	1	1	0	0	1

Note: Includes teams located in the Seattle-Bellevue metro area.
Source: www.sportsvenues.com, Listing of Venues by State/Province and City, 2006

MEDIA

Newspapers

Name	Target Audience	Frequency	Circulation
Eastside Journal	n/a	Daily	26,581

Note: Includes newspapers whose offices are located in the city and whose circulations are 500 or more; n/a not available
Source: BurrellesLuce, MediaContacts Online, January 2006

Television Stations

Name	Ch.	Network(s)	Type	Ownership
KOMO	4	ABC	Commercial	Fisher Broadcasting Inc.
KING	5	NBC	Commercial	Belo Corporation
KIRO	7	CBS	Commercial	Cox Enterprises Inc.
KCTS	9	PBS	Public	KCTS
KSTW	11	UPN	Commercial	Paramount Communications Inc.
KBTC	12	PBS	Public	State Board for Community and Technical Colleges
KVOS	12	n/a	Commercial	Clear Channel Communications Inc.
KCPQ	13	Fox	Commercial	Tribune Broadcasting Company
KONG	16	n/a	Commercial	Zeus Corporation
KTBW	20	n/a	Non-comm.	Trinity Broadcasting Network
KTWB	22	WBN	Commercial	Dudley Broadcast Management
KBCB	24	n/a	Commercial	World Television of Washington
KCKA	28	PBS	Public	State Board for Community and Technical Colleges
KWPX	33	Pax	Commercial	Paxson Communications Corporation

Note: Stations included cover the Seattle-Tacoma DMA (Designated Market Area)
BurrellesLuce, MediaContacts Online, January 2006

Major AM Radio Stations

Call Letters	Freq. (kHz)	Station Type	Target Audience	Station Format	Music Format
KARI	550	n/a	Religious	News/Sports/Talk	n/a
KPQ	560	Commercial	General	News/Talk	n/a
KVI	570	Commercial	General	Talk	n/a
KAPS	660	n/a	General	Music/News	n/a
KIRO	710	Commercial	General	News/Talk	n/a
KNWX	770	n/a	General	News/Talk	n/a
KGMI	790	Commercial	General	News/Talk	n/a
KGNW	820	Commercial	General/Religious	News/Talk	n/a
KMTT	850	Commercial	General	Music	A.O. Rock
KHHO	850	n/a	General/Men	Music/News/Sports/Talk	n/a
KIXI	880	n/a	General	Music/News	n/a
KJR	950	n/a	General	Music/Sports/Talk	n/a
KOMO	1000	Commercial	General	News/Talk	n/a
KMAS	1030	Commercial	General	Music/News	Adult Contemp.
KYCW	1090	n/a	General	Music	n/a
KKNW	1150	n/a	General	News/Sports	n/a
KPUG	1170	Commercial	General	Sports/Talk	n/a
KLAY	1180	Commercial	General	News/Sports/Talk	n/a
KBSG	1210	Commercial	General	Music	Oldies
KKDZ	1250	n/a	Children	Music	n/a
KKOL	1300	Commercial	General	News/Talk	n/a
KMPS	1300	Commercial	General	Music/News/Sports	Country
KXRO	1320	Commercial	General	Talk	n/a
KKMO	1360	Commercial	General/Hispanic	Music/Talk	Latin
KRKO	1380	n/a	General	News/Sports/Talk	n/a
KITI	1420	Commercial	General	Music/News	Oldies
KBRC	1430	n/a	General	Music/News	n/a
KELA	1470	Commercial	General	News/Sports/Talk	n/a
KXPA	1540	n/a	Ethnic/Hispanic	Ed/Music/News/Talk	n/a
KRPI	1550	n/a	Religious	Educational/Music/News	n/a
KZIZ	1560	Commercial	General	Music	Urban Contemp.
KLFE	1590	Commercial	General/Religious	Music/Talk	Gospel
KYIZ	1620	Commercial	General	Music	Urban Contemp.

Note: Stations included cover the Seattle-Tacoma DMA (Designated Market Area); n/a not available
Source: BurrellesLuce, MediaContacts Online, January 2006

Major FM Radio Stations

Call Letters	Freq. (mHz)	Station Type	Target Audience	Station Format	Music Format
KPLU	88.5	College	General	Music/News	n/a
KVTI	90.9	College	Young Adult	Music/News/Sports	n/a
KLSY	92.5	n/a	General	Music/News	n/a
KISM	92.9	Commercial	General	Music/News	Classic Rock
KUBE	93.3	n/a	General	Music/Talk	n/a
KMPS	94.1	n/a	General	Music	n/a
KUOW	94.9	College	General	Educational/News	n/a
KJR	95.7	n/a	General	n/a	n/a
KXXO	96.1	n/a	General	Music/News	n/a
KBSG	97.3	n/a	General	Music/News	n/a
KING	98.1	Commercial	General	Music	Classical
KISW	99.9	Commercial	General	Music/News/Talk	Classic Rock
KQBZ	100.7	Commercial	General	Talk	n/a
KPLZ	101.5	n/a	General	Music/News	n/a
KMNT	102.9	Commercial	General	Music/News/Sports	Country
KMTT	103.7	n/a	General	Music	n/a
KAFE	104.3	Commercial	General	Music/News	Soft Rock
KCMS	105.3	Commercial	General/Religious	Music	Christian
KBKS	106.1	n/a	General/Women	Music/News/Talk	n/a
KWPZ	106.5	n/a	Religious	Music/Talk	n/a
KRWM	106.9	n/a	General	Music	n/a
KNDD	107.7	Commercial	General	Music/News/Talk	Modern Rock

Note: Stations included cover the Seattle-Tacoma DMA (Designated Market Area); n/a not available
BurrellesLuce, MediaContacts Online, January 2006

CLIMATE

Average and Extreme Temperatures

Temperature	Jan	Feb	Mar	Apr	May	Jun	Jul	Aug	Sep	Oct	Nov	Dec	Yr.
Extreme High (°F)	64	70	75	85	93	96	98	99	98	89	74	63	99
Average High (°F)	44	48	52	57	64	69	75	74	69	59	50	45	59
Average Temp. (°F)	39	43	45	49	55	61	65	65	60	52	45	41	52
Average Low (°F)	34	36	38	41	46	51	54	55	51	45	39	36	44
Extreme Low (°F)	0	1	11	29	28	38	43	44	35	28	6	6	0

Note: Figures cover the years 1948-1990
Source: National Climatic Data Center, International Station Meteorological Climate Summary, 9/96

Average Precipitation/Snowfall/Humidity

Precip./Humidity	Jan	Feb	Mar	Apr	May	Jun	Jul	Aug	Sep	Oct	Nov	Dec	Yr.
Avg. Precip. (in.)	5.7	4.2	3.7	2.4	1.7	1.4	0.8	1.1	1.9	3.5	5.9	5.9	38.4
Avg. Snowfall (in.)	5	2	1	Tr	Tr	0	0	0	0	Tr	1	3	13
Avg. Rel. Hum. 7am (%)	83	83	84	83	80	79	79	84	87	88	85	85	83
Avg. Rel. Hum. 4pm (%)	76	69	63	57	54	54	49	51	57	68	76	79	63

Note: Figures cover the years 1948-1990; Tr = Trace amounts (<0.05 in. of rain; <0.5 in. of snow)
Source: National Climatic Data Center, International Station Meteorological Climate Summary, 9/96

Weather Conditions

Temperature			Daytime Sky			Precipitation		
5°F & below	32°F & below	90°F & above	Clear	Partly cloudy	Cloudy	0.01 inch or more precip.	0.1 inch or more snow/ice	Thunder-storms
< 1	38	3	57	121	187	157	8	8

Note: Figures are average number of days per year and cover the years 1948-1990
Source: National Climatic Data Center, International Station Meteorological Climate Summary, 9/96

HAZARDOUS WASTE

Superfund Sites

Bellevue has no sites on the EPA's Superfund Final National Priorities List.
U.S. Environmental Protection Agency, Final National Priorities List, March 20, 2007

**AIR & WATER
QUALITY**

Air Quality Index

Area	Percent of Days when Air Quality was...[2]				AQI Statistics	
	Good	Moderate	Unhealthy for Sensitive Groups	Unhealthy	Maximum	Median
MSA[1]	67.9	30.1	1.9	0.0	144	40

Note: The Air Quality Index (AQI) is an index for reporting daily air quality. EPA calculates the AQI for five major air pollutants regulated by the Clean Air Act: ground-level ozone, particle pollution (also known as particulate matter), carbon monoxide, sulfur dioxide, and nitrogen dioxide. The AQI runs from 0 to 500. The higher the AQI value, the greater the level of air pollution and the greater the health concern. There are six AQI categories: "Good" The AQI is between 0 and 50. Air quality is considered satisfactory; "Moderate" The AQI is between 51 and 100. Air quality is acceptable; "Unhealthy for Sensitive Groups" When AQI values are between 101 and 150, members of sensitive groups may experience health effects; "Unhealthy" When AQI values are between 151 and 200 everyone may begin to experience health effects; "Very Unhealthy" AQI values between 201 and 300 trigger a health alert; "Hazardous" AQI values over 300 trigger health warnings of emergency conditions; (1) Metropolitan Statistical Area - see Appendix A for areas included; (2) Based on 365 days with AQI data in 2005.
Source: U.S. Environmental Protection Agency, Air Quality Index Report, 2005

Air Quality Index Pollutants

Area	Percent of Days when AQI Pollutant was...[2]					
	Carbon Monoxide	Nitrogen Dioxide	Ozone	Sulfur Dioxide	Particulate Matter 2.5	Particulate Matter 10
MSA[1]	0.3	0.0	9.9	0.0	89.6	0.3

Note: The Air Quality Index (AQI) is an index for reporting daily air quality. EPA calculates the AQI for five major air pollutants regulated by the Clean Air Act: ground-level ozone, particle pollution (also known as particulate matter), carbon monoxide, sulfur dioxide, and nitrogen dioxide. The AQI runs from 0 to 500. The higher the AQI value, the greater the level of air pollution and the greater the health concern; (1) Metropolitan Statistical Area - see Appendix A for areas included; (2) Based on 365 days with AQI data in 2005.
Source: U.S. Environmental Protection Agency, Air Quality Index Report, 2005

Number of Days with Air Quality Index Values Greater than 100

Area	Trend Sites (9)								All Sites (63)
	1998	1999	2000	2001	2002	2003	2004	2005	2005
MSA[1]	3	6	7	6	6	2	1	1	1

Note: An AQI value greater than 100 indicates that air quality would have been in the unhealthful range on that day. Data from exceptional events are not included. These counts are presented in two ways. First, the counts are based on sites having an adequate record of monitoring data during the trend period (trend sites). These counts represent the relative change in the number of days with AQI values greater than 100. In the last column, the counts are based on all sites with data in the most recent year (because it is possible for a site to have data in the most recent year but not enough data to be a trend site); (1) Metropolitan Statistical Area - see Appendix A for areas included; n/a not available.
Source: U.S. Environmental Protection Agency, Air Trends Fact Book 2005

Maximum Pollutant Concentrations

	Particulate Matter 10 (ug/m^3)	Particulate Matter 2.5 (ug/m^3)	Ozone 1-hour (ppm)	Carbon Monoxide (ppm)	Sulfur Dioxide (ppm)	Nitrogen Dioxide (ppm)	Lead (ug/m^3)
MSA[1] Level	70	37	0.085	4	0.012	n/a	n/a
NAAQS[2]	150	65	0.125	9	0.140	0.053	1.50
Met NAAQS[2]	Yes	Yes	Yes	Yes	Yes	n/a	n/a

Note: Data from exceptional events are not included; (1) Metropolitan Statistical Area - see Appendix A for areas included; (2) National Ambient Air Quality Standards; n/a not available
Units: ppm = parts per million; ug/m^3 = micrograms per cubic meter
Source: U.S. Environmental Protection Agency, Air Trends Fact Book 2005

Watershed Health

The U.S. Environmental Protection Agency monitors the health of the aquatic resources for the nation's 2,000+ watersheds. **The Puget Sound watershed serves the Bellevue area and received an overall Index of Watershed Indicators (IWI) score of 5 (more serious problems - low vulnerability)**. The IWI score is based on seven condition and nine vulnerability indicators. The overall IWI score ranges from 1 (best health) to 6 (worst health). The Condition Indicators include: designated use attainment, fish and wildlife consumption advisories, source water condition, contaminated sediments, ambient water quality, and wetlands loss index. The Vulnerability Indicators include: aquatic species at risk, conventional and toxic loads over permitted limits, urban and agricultural runoff potential, population change, hydrologic modification, estuarine pollution susceptibility, and air deposition. *Note: The IWI is no longer being updated by the U.S. EPA. Source: U.S. Environmental Protection Agency, Index of Watershed Indicators, October 26, 2001*

Drinking Water

Water System Name	Pop. Served	Primary Water Source Type	Number of Violations in 2006[a]		
			Health Based	Significant Monitoring	Monitoring
City of Bellevue	132,000	Purchased surface	None	None	None

Note: (a) Based on violation data from January 1, 2006 to December 31, 2006
Source: U.S. Environmental Protection Agency, Office of Ground Water and Drinking Water, Safe Drinking Water Information System (data extracted April 12, 2007)

Bellevue tap water is soft.
Editor & Publisher Market Guide, 2005

Boise City, Idaho

Background

Boise (pronounced boy-see, not boy-zee)is the capital and largest city in Idaho, lying along the Boise River adjacent to the foothills of the Rocky Mountains. The city is located south and west of the western slopes of the Rockies, and is the site of a great system of natural warm water springs.

Boise's spectacular natural location is its first and most obvious attraction, and this, coupled with its dynamic economic growth in recent decades, makes Boise an altogether remarkable city. The splendor of its surroundings, together with an average 18-minute drive to work, has allowed the city to combine pleasure and efficiency in an enviable mix.

French-Canadian trappers were familiar with Boise and its environs by 1811, and the name of the city is an Anglicization of the French Les Bois — the trees. The first substantial European settlement dates to 1863 when, in the spring of that year, I.M. Coston built from pegged driftwood a great house that served as a hub for the activities of prospectors, traders, and Native Americans. In the same year, the U.S. Army built Fort Boise, and considerable deposits of gold and silver were discovered in the area. The U.S. Assay Office in Boise, in 1870-71 alone, is said to have valuated more than $75 million in precious metals.

The area is rich in gold rush lore, and six miles above Boise, on the south side of the river, there may even be buried treasure from that era. The eastbound stagecoach from Boise was said to have been waylaid by a robber who, though wounded in the attack by a resourceful passenger, managed to drag off a strongbox filled with $50,000 in gold. The robber died of his wounds and was discovered the next day, but he had apparently buried his loot. No one has ever located it.

The Boise area was subsequently developed for farming, as crops of grains, vegetables, and fruits, replaced the mines as its source of wealth. It became the territorial capital of Idaho in 1864 and the state capital in 1890. Education was served with the opening of a university in 1932, which became Boise State University in 1974 and now enrolls 15,000 students.

The city's natural setting offers a great range of outdoor activities that are pursued energetically by its citizens. Its rivers, mountains, deserts, and lakes offer world-class skiing, hiking, camping, kayaking, river rafting, hunting, and fishing.

Many large regional, national, and international companies are headquartered there, including Washington Group International (involved in reconstruction in Iraq and Afghanistan), Boise Cascade, Micron Technology, Simplot, and Hewlett-Packard's printer division.

The city produces high- and low-tech products and everything in between: software, computer components, steel and sheet metal products, mobile homes, lumber products, farm machinery, packed meats, and processed foods. Increasingly an advanced technological center, it continues to serve as a trading center for the greater agricultural region.

By virtue of its history and geographical character, the city can be considered a presence on the Pacific Rim. In a more tangible vein, Boise, with seven airlines operating at its airport, is conveniently tied to the wider world.

Boise's Basque community, numbering about 15,000, is the largest in the United States and the third largest in the world outside Argentina and the Basque Country in Spain and France. A large Basque festival known as Jaialdi is held once every five years, the next to be held in 2010. Boise (along with Valley and Boise Counties) will host the Winter 2009 Special Olympics World Games. More than 2,500 athletes from over 85 countries will participate.

The city is protected by the mountains to the north in such a way that it is largely unbothered by the extreme blizzards that affect eastern Idaho and parts of neighboring states. Boise, and this section of western Idaho generally, is affected by climatic influences from the Pacific Ocean and exhibits an unusually mild climate for this latitude. Summers can be hot, but nights are almost always cool, and sunshine generally prevails.

Rankings

General Rankings

■ Boise City was ranked #68 out of 331 metro areas in *Cities Ranked & Rated*. Criteria: cost of living; climate; crime; transportation; economy and jobs; education; arts and culture; health and healthcare; leisure. *Cities Ranked & Rated, 1st Edition, 2004*

■ The Boise City metro area was selected as one of America's "Best Places to Live and Work" by *Expansion Management* and rated as a "5-Star Community" (a distinction the magazine awards to the top 20 percent of metro areas studied). The annual "Quality of Life Quotient" measures 49 indicators and compares them among the 362 metropolitan statistical areas in the United States. *Expansion Management, June 2006*

■ Boise City was selected as one of the "Best Places to Live 2006" by *Money* magazine. The city ranked #8 out of 90 in the small city (under 300,000 population) category. Places were ranked using 38 quality-of-life indicators and six economic opportunity measures in the following categories: ease of living; health; education; crime; park space; arts and leisure. *Money, "Best Places to Live 2006"*

■ Boise City was selected as one of "8 Cheap Places You'd Want to Live." Criteria: relatively inexpensive housing; affordable cost of living; and a strong local economy. *BestPlaces.net and msn.com, "8 Cheap Places You'd Want to Live," July 2006*

■ Boise City was selected as one of "60 Cheap Places to Live" in the U.S. The city appeared in the "Porch-Swing Communities" (best family-friendly cities) category. *Forbes.com, August 20, 2004*

Business/Finance Rankings

■ Boise City was selected as one of the best places to start and grow a company by *Entrepreneur* and the National Policy Research Council. The Boise City metro area ranked #30 out of 63 mid-size metro areas. Criteria: business formation and growth (firms started four to 14 years ago that still employ at least 5 people and experienced rapid growth over the last four years). *Entrepreneur/National Policy Research Council, "Hot Cities for Entrepreneurs," September 2006*

■ Boise City was identified as one of "The Most Inventive Towns in America". The city ranked #8. Criteria: places with the most patents overall, combining those of large companies and individual inventors. *The Wall Street Journal, July 22-23, 2006*

■ The Boise City metro area appeared on the Milken Institute "2005 Best Performing Cities" index. Rank: #32 out of 200 large metro areas. Criteria: job growth; wage and salary growth; high-tech output growth. *Milken Institute, "2005 Best Performing Cities," February 2006*

■ The Boise City metro area was selected as one of "The Best Cities for Doing Business in America." *Inc.* magazine measured employment growth in 393 regions using the following criteria: recent growth trend; mid-term growth; long-term trend; and current year growth. The Boise City metro area ranked #11 among mid-sized metro areas and #48 overall. *Inc., May 2006*

■ The Boise City metro area was selected as one of "The Top 10 Boom Villages in America." *Business 2.0* magazine and econometric research firm Global Insight compared 319 metropolitan areas in the U.S. Criteria: a weighted formula that includes forecast growth rates in sectors that contain the economy's 10 most skilled occupational clusters; the prevalence of college degrees in the local workforce; median salary. The area ranked #5 among small metro areas. *Business 2.0 Magazine, March 2004*

■ *Forbes* ranked the 200 most populous metro areas in the U.S. in terms of the "Best Places for Business and Careers." The Boise City metro area was ranked #3. Criteria: business costs (labor, energy, tax and office space expenses); living costs (housing, transportation, food and other household expenditures); education levels of the work force; job growth; income growth; migration trends; crime rates; and culture/leisure. *Forbes, April 23, 2007*

- Boise City was identified as one of the top 20 metro areas with the highest rate of home price appreciation in 2006. The area ranked #5 with a one-year price appreciation of 17.9% through the 4th quarter 2006. *Office of Federal Housing Enterprise Oversight, House Price Index, 4th Quarter 2006*

- *Kiplinger's Personal Finance* ranked 101 U.S. cities in terms of their total tax burdens. Boise City ranked #48 (#1 had the lowest overall tax burden). Criteria: state income tax; property tax; sales tax; personal property tax; and gasoline tax. *Kiplinger's Personal Finance, July 2004*

Health/Environment Rankings

- The Boise City metro area appeared in *Country Home's* "2007 Best Green Places Report". The area ranked #168. Criteria included: air and watershed quality; miles of mass transit; green power; number of farmer's markets, organic producers and groceries. *Country Home, "2007 Best Green Places Report," April 2007*

- The American Podiatric Medical Association and *Prevention* magazine ranked America's 100 most populated cities based on fitness-walker friendliness. The best cities have safe streets, beautiful places to walk, mild weather and good air quality. Boise City ranked #17. *Prevention, "The Best Walking Cities of 2007," April 2007; American Podiatric Medical Association, "2007 Best Fitness-Walking Cities"*

- Boise City was identified as a "2007 Asthma Capital." The area ranked #88 out of the nation's 100 largest metropolitan areas. Twelve factors were used to identify the most challenging places to live for people with asthma: estimated prevalence; self-reported prevalence; crude death rate for asthma; annual pollen score; annual air quality; public smoking laws; number of board-certified asthma specialists; school inhaler access laws; rescue medication use; controller medication use; uninsured rate; poverty rate. *Asthma and Allergy Foundation of America, "2007 Asthma Capitals"*

- Boise City was identified as a "Spring Allergy Capital." The area ranked #86 out of 100. Three groups of factors were used to identify the most severe cities for people with allergies during the spring season: annual pollen levels; medicine utilization; access to board-certified allergists. *Asthma and Allergy Foundation of America, "2007 Spring Allergy Capital Rankings"*

- Boise City was identified as a "Fall Allergy Capital." The area ranked #62 out of 100. Three groups of factors were used to identify the most severe cities for people with allergies during the fall season: annual pollen levels; medicine utilization; access to board-certified allergists. *Asthma and Allergy Foundation of America, "2006 Fall Allergy Capital Rankings"*

- *Men's Health* ranked the nation's largest 100 cities in terms of the *Best (and Worst) Cities for Men.* Boise City was ranked #18. Criteria: 24 statistical parameters of long life in the categories of health, quality of life, and fitness. *Men's Health, January/February 2007*

- Ortho-McNeil Neurologics, in partnership with Sperling's BestPlaces, analyzed 110 metro areas and identified those U.S. cities with the highest prevalence of factors that are most commonly associated with migraine headaches. The Boise City metro area ranked #41. Criteria: number of migraine-related drug prescriptions per capita; lifestyle factors that can contribute to migraines; environmental factors that can trigger migraines; and consumption of migraine-triggering foods. *Ortho-McNeil Neurologics, "America's Migraine Hot Spots," March 14, 2006*

- Sperling's BestPlaces ranked 331 metro areas and identified the most and least stressful U.S. cities. The Boise City metro area ranked #60 out of 114 mid-size metro areas (#1 = most stressful). Criteria: divorce rate; unemployment rate; violent and property crime; suicide rate; commute time; mental health; alcohol consumption; cloudy days. *www.BestPlaces.net, January 9, 2004*

Women/MinoritiesRankings

■ Boise City was ranked #39 out of 100 metro areas in *SELF Magazine's* ranking of "America's Best Places for Women." A panel of experts came up with nearly 40 criteria including: drinking and smoking rates; depression; unemployment; parks; crime; disease; healthcare insurance coverage; air quality; and commute times. *SELF Magazine, "America's Best Places for Women 2006," December 2006*

■ *Ladies Home Journal* ranked America's 200 largest cities based on the qualities women surveyed care about most. Boise City ranked #28 out of 143 in the smaller city category (population under 300,000). Criteria: crime; lifestyle; education; jobs; health; child care; politics; and the economy. *Ladies Home Journal Online, "The Best Cities for Women 2002"*

Seniors/Retirement Rankings

■ Boise City was profiled in the book *Where to Retire: America's Best and Most Affordable Places*. Cities were selected based on personal visits by the author and interviews with local residents coupled with statistics from various government agencies. *Where to Retire: America's Best and Most Affordable Places, 2006*

■ Boise City was identified as one of the "100 Most Popular Places to Retire" by *Where to Retire* magazine. The city ranked #93. Criteria: net retirees received from 1995-2000 (derived by subtracting all outbound retirees from inbound retirees for the county or county group - includes interstate moves only). *Where to Retire, "100 Most Popular Places to Retire," January/February 2007*

■ A.G. Edwards ranked America's 500 top-performing communities based on their residents' personal savings and investing behavior. The Boise City metro area ranked #243 with an index score of 102.05 (national average = 100.00). A dozen statistical factors were measured including: participation in retirement savings plans; personal debt levels; and home ownership. *A.G. Edwards, "2006 Nest Egg Index", September 6, 2006*

Children/Family Rankings

■ The Boise City metro area was selected as one of the "Best Cities for Relocating Families" by Worldwide ERC and Primacy Relocation. Criteria: tax rates; average home costs and home appreciation; ability to qualify for in-state tuition; service quality of local utilities; per-capita volunteerism; auto taxes; and quantity of fun, family-friendly events and venues. *Worldwide ERC and Primacy Relocation, "2006 Best Cities for Relocating Families"*

Safety Rankings

■ Farmers Insurance Group of Companies, in partnership with Sperling's BestPlaces, ranked 331 metro areas and identified the "Most Secure U.S. Place to Live." The Boise City metro area ranked #4 out of the top 20 in the mid-size city category (150,000 to 500,000 residents). Criteria: crime rates; risk of natural disasters; and job loss numbers. *Farmers Insurance Group, "25 Most Secure U.S. Place to Live," June 6, 2005*

■ Allstate ranked the 200 largest cities in America in terms of driver safety. Boise City ranked #18. In addition, drivers were 14.1% less likely to have had an accident compared to the national average. Allstate researchers analyzed internal Property Damage reported claims over a two-year period (from January 2003 to December 2004) to ensure the findings would not be affected by external influences such as weather or road construction. A weighted average of the two-year numbers determined the annual percentages. The report defines an auto crash as any collision resulting in a property damage claim. *Allstate, "Allstate America's Best Drivers Report 2006," May 24, 2006*

■ Boise City was identified as one of the safest places in the U.S. in terms of its vulnerability to natural disasters and weather extremes. The city ranked #2 out of 10. Sperling's BestPlaces analyzed data to show a metro areas' relative tendency to experience natural disasters (hail, tornados, high winds, hurricanes, earthquakes, and brush fires) or extreme weather (abundant rain or snowfall or days that are below freezing or above 90 degrees Fahrenheit). *Forbes, "Safest and Least Safe Places in the U.S.," August 30, 2005*

■ *Ladies Home Journal* ranked America's 200 largest cities in terms of safety. Boise City ranked #46 out of 200. Criteria: violent crimes; crimes against property; and rape. *Ladies Home Journal Online, "The Best Cities for Women 2002"*

Sports/Recreation Rankings

■ The Boise City metro area appeared on *The Sporting News* list of the "Best Sports Cities 2006". The area ranked #96 out of 99 cities in North America. To be included in the rankings, a city must have at least one of the following: NCAA Division I basketball team; Class A minor league baseball team; training camp for a major league or NFL team; NASCAR Nextel Cup race; NCAA Division I-A bowl game; PGA Tour tournament; Triple Crown horse race. Once a city qualifies, a 12-month snapshot is taken of the sports atmosphere, putting a heavy premium on regular-season won-lost records; playoff berths, bowl appearances and tournament bids; championships; applicable power ratings; quality of competition; overall fan fervor; sports atmosphere and fan knowledge; abundance of teams (quality over quantity); stadium/arena quality; ticket availability and prices; franchise ownership; and the marquee appeal of athletes. *SportingNews.com, "Best Sports Cities 2006," August 1, 2006*

■ Boise City was chosen as one of "The 10 Best Cities for Mountain Bikers." The city was ranked #1. The criteria for making the list was two-fold: 1) great trails within or very close to the city; 2) the city had to be a place where people could actually live—with good jobs, decent schools, affordable housing, arts and sports, and a sense of community. *Mountain Bike, June 2001*

■ *Golf Digest* ranked 330 metro areas in the U.S. in terms of golf. The Boise City metro area was ranked #135. Criteria: access to golf; weather; value of golf; and quality of golf. *Golf Digest, "Metro Golf Rankings," August 2005*

Miscellaneous Rankings

■ Boise City was determined to be one of America's smartest cities. The city ranked #10 in the mid-sized city category (100,000 to 200,000 adults 25 years and older). Criteria: the editors rated the collective brainpower of U.S communities based on the educational attainment of its residents. *American City Business Journals, www.bizjournals.com, June 12, 2006*

Business Environment

CITY FINANCES

City Government Finances

Component	2003-2004 ($000)	2003-2004 ($ per capita)
Total Revenues	207,560	1,093
Total Expenditures	219,013	1,154
Debt Outstanding	208,625	1,099
Cash and Securities	94,625	498

Source: U.S Census Bureau, Government Finances 2003-2004

City Government Revenue by Source

Source	2003-2004 ($000)	2003-2004 ($ per capita)
General Revenue		
From Federal Government	31,486	166
From State Government	13,197	70
From Local Governments	0	0
Taxes		
Property	71,382	376
Sales	5,031	27
Personal Income	0	0
License	0	0
Charges	72,000	379
Liquor Store	0	0
Utility	929	5
Employee Retirement	0	0
Other	13,535	71

Source: U.S Census Bureau, Government Finances 2003-2004

City Government Expenditures by Function

Function	2003-2004 ($000)	2003-2004 ($ per capita)	2003-2004 (%)
General Expenditures			
Airports	49,043	258	22.4
Corrections	0	0	0.0
Education	0	0	0.0
Fire Protection	22,173	117	10.1
Governmental Administration	14,351	76	6.6
Health	654	3	0.3
Highways	2,185	12	1.0
Hospitals	0	0	0.0
Housing and Community Development	3,932	21	1.8
Interest on General Debt	12,764	67	5.8
Libraries	5,005	26	2.3
Parking	1,093	6	0.5
Parks and Recreation	12,417	65	5.7
Police Protection	27,730	146	12.7
Public Welfare	0	0	0.0
Sewerage	22,076	116	10.1
Solid Waste Management	13,913	73	6.4
Liquor Store	0	0	0.0
Utility	3,359	18	1.5
Employee Retirement	0	0	0.0
Other	28,318	149	12.9

Source: U.S Census Bureau, Government Finances 2003-2004

Municipal Bond Ratings

Area	Moody's
City	Aaa

Source: Mergent Bond Record, January 2007 (unless noted otherwise)

DEMOGRAPHICS

Population Growth

Area	1990 Census	2000 Census	2006 Estimate	2011 Projection	Population Growth (%) 1990-2000	Population Growth (%) 2000-2011
City	144,317	185,787	190,621	196,868	28.7	6.0
MSA[1]	319,596	464,840	544,754	612,275	45.4	31.7
U.S.	248,709,873	281,421,906	298,021,266	312,383,955	13.2	11.0

Note: (1) Metropolitan Statistical Area - see Appendix B for areas included
Source: Claritas, Inc.

Number of Households and Average Household Size

Area	2006 Estimate	2006 Average Household Size
City	77,356	2.46
MSA[1]	198,867	2.74
U.S.	112,267,302	2.65

Note: (1) Metropolitan Statistical Area - see Appendix B for areas included
Source: Claritas, Inc.

Race and Ethnicity

Area	White Alone[2]	Black Alone[2]	Asian Alone[2]	Other Race Alone[2]	Hispanic[3]
City	90.5	1.0	2.4	6.1	5.7
MSA[1]	88.4	0.7	1.4	9.5	10.5
U.S.	73.3	12.4	4.2	10.1	14.5

Note: Figures are 2006 estimates; (1) Metropolitan Statistical Area - see Appendix B for areas included
(2) Alone is defined as not being in combination with one or more other races; (3) May be of any race.
Source: Claritas, Inc.

Segregation

City Index[2]	City Rank[3]	MSA[1] Index[2]	MSA[1] Rank[4]
32.9	96	37.1	310

Note: Figures are based on an analysis of Census 2000 data; (1) Metropolitan Statistical Area - see Appendix A for areas included; (2) White/Black Dissimilarity Index—the most commonly used measure of segregation between two groups, reflecting their relative distributions across neighborhoods within a city or metropolitan area. It can range in value from 0, indicating complete integration, to 100, indicating complete segregation; (3) Ranges from 1 (most segregated) to 100 (least segregated) and includes all the cities in this book; (4) Ranges from 1 (most segregated) to 318 (least segregated) and includes 318 metropolitan areas.
Source: www.CensusScope.org

Ancestry

Area	German	Irish[2]	English	American	Italian	Polish	French[3]	Scottish
City	20.6	12.5	17.2	7.1	3.1	1.5	3.6	3.9
MSA[1]	19.3	11.1	16.0	7.7	2.8	1.2	3.1	3.4
U.S.	15.2	10.9	8.7	7.3	5.6	3.2	3.0	1.7

Note: Figures include multiple ancestry (e.g. if a person reported being Irish and Italian, they were included in both columns); (1) Metropolitan Statistical Area - see Appendix A for areas included; (2) Includes Celtic; (3) Includes Alsatian but excludes Basque
Source: Census 2000, Summary File 3

Foreign-Born Population

Area	Any Foreign Country	Percent of Population Born in Europe	Asia	Africa	Oceania[2]	Canada	Mexico	Latin America[3]
City	4.8	2.0	1.4	0.1	0.0	0.3	0.7	0.2
MSA[1]	5.6	1.3	1.0	0.1	0.0	0.3	2.6	0.3
U.S.	11.1	1.7	2.9	0.3	0.1	0.3	3.3	2.5

Note: (1) Metropolitan Statistical Area - see Appendix A for areas included; (2) Includes Australia, New Zealand subregion, Melanesia, Micronesia, Polynesia, and Oceania n.e.c; (3) Includes Central America (excluding Mexico), South America, and the Caribbean.
Source: Census 2000, Summary File 3

Marriage Status

Area	Never Married	Now Married (excluding Separated)	Separated	Widowed	Divorced
City	27.0	53.3	1.1	4.9	13.6
MSA[1]	23.4	58.9	1.2	4.7	11.7
U.S.	27.1	54.4	2.2	6.6	9.7

Note: Figures are percentages and cover the population 15 years of age and older;
(1) Metropolitan Statistical Area - see Appendix A for areas included
Source: Census 2000, Summary File 3

Age Distribution

Area	Percent of Population						
	Under Age 5	Age 5 to 17	Age 18 to 34	Age 35 to 49	Age 50 to 64	Age 65 to 79	80 Years and Over
City	7.0	18.2	27.8	23.9	13.0	6.9	3.2
MSA[1]	8.1	20.2	25.8	23.1	13.1	6.9	2.8
U.S.	6.8	18.9	23.7	23.5	14.8	9.2	3.2

Note: (1) Metropolitan Statistical Area - see Appendix A for areas included
Source: Census 2000, Summary File 3

Male/Female Ratio

Area	Males	Females	Males per 100 Females
City	94,960	95,661	99.3
MSA[1]	273,723	271,031	101.0
U.S.	146,712,712	151,308,554	97.0

Note: Figures are 2006 estimates; (1) Metropolitan Statistical Area -
see Appendix B for areas included
Source: Claritas, Inc.

Religion

Area	Catholic	Southern Baptist	United Methodist	ELCA[1]	LDS[2]	Presbyterian Church USA	Jewish Est.	Muslim Est.
County	12.3	1.0	2.0	1.0	15.2	0.7	0.3	0.1
U.S.	22.0	7.1	3.7	1.8	1.5	1.1	2.2	0.6

Note: Figures are the number of adherents as a percentage of the total population; Adherents are defined as all
members, including full members, their children and the estimated number of other participants who are not
considered members (e.g. the baptized, those not confirmed, those regularly attending services, etc.);
(1) Evangelical Lutheran Church in America; (2) The Church of Jesus Christ of Latter Day Saints
Source: Reprinted with permission from Religious Congregations and Membership in the United States 2000
(Nashville, Glenmary Research Center, 2002) Copyright Association of Statisticians of American Religious
Bodies. All rights reserved.

ECONOMY

Gross Metropolitan Product

Area	2002	2003	2004	2005	2005 Rank[2]
MSA[1]	14.5	15.3	17.3	19.2	97

Note: Figures are in billions of dollars; (1) Boise City-Nampa, ID Metropolitan Statistical Area - see Appendix
A for areas included; (2) Rank ranges from 1 to 361
Source: The U.S. Conference of Mayors, "U.S. Metro Economies: GMP - The Engines of America's Growth,"
January 2007

Economic Growth

Area	1995 GMP	2005 GMP	Average Annual Growth Rate	Growth Rate Rank[2]
MSA[1]	9.9	19.2	6.9	50

Note: Figures are in billions of dollars; GMP = Gross Metropolitan Product; (1) Boise City-Nampa, ID
Metropolitan Statistical Area - see Appendix A for areas included; (2) Rank ranges from 1 to 361
Source: The U.S. Conference of Mayors, "U.S. Metro Economies: GMP - The Engines of America's Growth,"
January 2007

INCOME

Per Capita/Median/Average Income

Area	Per Capita ($)	Median Household ($)	Average Household ($)
City	26,058	48,200	63,296
MSA[1]	23,024	48,281	62,235
U.S.	25,129	48,775	65,849

Note: Figures are 2006 estimates; (1) Metropolitan Statistical Area - see Appendix B for areas included
Source: Claritas, Inc.

Household Income Distribution

Area	Under $15,000	$15,000 -24,999	$25,000 -34,999	$35,000 -49,999	$50,000 -74,999	$75,000 -99,000	$100,000 -149,999	$150,000 and up
City	10.3	11.9	12.3	17.6	20.7	11.9	10.0	5.3
MSA[1]	10.4	11.4	12.5	17.6	21.0	12.1	10.1	4.7
U.S.	13.3	11.0	11.3	15.7	19.5	11.8	11.0	6.4

Note: Figures are 2006 estimates; (1) Metropolitan Statistical Area - see Appendix B for areas included
Source: Claritas, Inc.

Poverty Rates by Age

Area	All Ages	Under 5 Years Old	5 to 17 Years Old	18 to 64 Years Old	65 Years and Over
City	8.4	0.9	1.7	5.3	0.6
MSA[1]	9.0	1.1	2.2	5.0	0.7
U.S.	12.4	1.2	3.0	6.9	1.2

Note: Figures are percent of population with income in 1999 below poverty level and only include population for whom poverty status is determined; (1) Metropolitan Statistical Area - see Appendix A for areas included
Source: Census 2000, Summary File 3

Personal Bankruptcy Filing Rate

Area	2003	2004	2005
Ada County	7.51	7.18	8.93
U.S.	5.57	5.31	6.88

Note: Numbers are per 1,000 population and include Chapter 7 and Chapter 13 filings
Source: Federal Deposit Insurance Corporation (FDIC), Regional Economic Conditions (RECON), 3/24/2006

EMPLOYMENT

Labor Force and Employment

Area	Civilian Labor Force			Workers Employed		
	Dec. 2005	Dec. 2006	% Chg.	Dec. 2005	Dec. 2006	% Chg.
City	122,534	125,796	2.7	119,395	122,691	2.8
MSA[1]	289,945	297,751	2.7	282,087	289,875	2.8
U.S.	149,874,000	152,571,000	1.8	142,918,000	146,081,000	2.2

Note: Data is not seasonally adjusted and covers workers 16 years of age and older;
(1) Metropolitan Statistical Area - see Appendix B for areas included
Source: Bureau of Labor Statistics, http://stats.bls.gov

Unemployment Rate

Area	2006											
	Jan.	Feb.	Mar.	Apr.	May	Jun.	Jul.	Aug.	Sep.	Oct.	Nov.	Dec.
City	3.4	3.3	3.2	3.0	2.7	3.0	2.9	2.7	2.6	2.4	2.7	2.5
MSA[1]	3.6	3.5	3.3	3.0	2.6	2.9	2.9	2.6	2.5	2.3	2.8	2.6
U.S.	5.1	5.1	4.8	4.5	4.4	4.8	5.0	4.6	4.4	4.1	4.3	4.3

Note: Data is not seasonally adjusted and covers workers 16 years of age and older; All figures are percentages; (1) Metropolitan Statistical Area - see Appendix B for areas included
Source: Bureau of Labor Statistics, http://stats.bls.gov

Employment by Occupation

Occupation Classification	City (%)	MSA[1] (%)	U.S. (%)
Sales and Office	28.0	26.9	26.7
Professional and Related	23.2	20.4	20.2
Service	14.9	14.5	14.9
Production, Transportation, and Material Moving	9.9	12.6	14.6
Management, Business, and Financial	15.6	14.5	13.5
Construction, Extraction, and Maintenance	8.0	10.0	9.4
Farming, Forestry, and Fishing	0.3	1.1	0.7

Note: Figures cover employed civilians 16 years of age and older;
(1) Metropolitan Statistical Area - see Appendix A for areas included
Source: Census 2000, Summary File 3

Employment by Industry

Sector	MSA[1] Number of Employees	MSA[1] Percent of Total	U.S. Percent of Total
Government	42,600	15.3	16.3
Education and Health Services	32,400	11.6	13.2
Professional and Business Services	40,000	14.3	12.9
Retail Trade	35,500	12.7	11.5
Manufacturing	32,200	11.5	10.2
Leisure and Hospitality	23,900	8.6	9.5
Financial Activities	15,200	5.4	6.1
Construction	n/a	n/a	5.5
Wholesale Trade	12,100	4.3	4.3
Other Services	7,700	2.8	3.9
Transportation and Utilities	7,800	2.8	3.7
Information	4,600	1.6	2.2
Natural Resources and Mining	n/a	n/a	0.5

Note: Figures cover non-farm employment as of December 2006 and are not seasonally adjusted;
(1) Metropolitan Statistical Area - see Appendix B for areas included; n/a not available
Source: Bureau of Labor Statistics, http://stats.bls.gov

Occupations with Greatest Projected Employment Growth: 2002 - 2012

Occupation[1]	2002 Employment	2012 Projected Employment	Numeric Employment Change	Percent Employment Change
Registered Nurses	9,890	14,630	4,740	47.9
Retail Salespersons	18,120	21,950	3,830	21.1
Customer Service Representatives	7,250	10,350	3,100	42.8
Nursing Aides, Orderlies, and Attendants	6,870	9,970	3,100	45.1
Janitors and Cleaners, Except Maids and Housekeeping Cleaners	10,400	13,500	3,100	29.8
General and Operations Managers	11,880	14,970	3,090	26.0
Combined Food Preparation and Serving Workers, Including Fast Food	9,450	12,450	3,000	31.7
Waiters and Waitresses	9,930	12,560	2,630	26.5
Cashiers	15,310	17,850	2,540	16.6
Carpenters	6,920	9,340	2,420	35.0

Note: Projections cover Idaho; (1) Sorted by numeric employment change
Source: www.projectionscentral.com, State Occupational Projections, 2002-2012 Long-Term Projections

Fastest Growing Occupations: 2002 - 2012

Occupation[1]	2002 Employment	2012 Projected Employment	Numeric Employment Change	Percent Employment Change
Medical Assistants	950	1,730	780	82.1
Social and Human Service Assistants	2,390	4,220	1,830	76.6
Network Systems and Data Communications Analysts	470	820	350	74.5
Roofers	1,510	2,600	1,090	72.2
Medical Records and Health Information Technicians	640	1,050	410	64.1
Home Health Aides	2,270	3,700	1,430	63.0
Cement Masons and Concrete Finishers	1,030	1,670	640	62.1
Heating, Air Conditioning, and Refrigeration Mechanics and Installers	1,130	1,830	700	61.9
Personal and Home Care Aides	1,150	1,860	710	61.7
Tile and Marble Setters	390	630	240	61.5

Note: Projections cover Idaho; (1) Sorted by percent employment change and excludes occupations with numeric employment change less than 200
Source: www.projectionscentral.com, State Occupational Projections, 2002-2012 Long-Term Projections

Average Wages

Occupation	$/Hr.	Occupation	$/Hr.
Accountants and Auditors	21.05	Maids and Housekeeping Cleaners	7.54
Automotive Mechanics	16.24	Maintenance and Repair Workers	14.40
Bookkeepers	13.06	Marketing Managers	41.32
Carpenters	14.41	Nuclear Medicine Technologists	22.45
Cashiers	8.52	Nurses, Licensed Practical	16.57
Clerks, General Office	11.32	Nurses, Registered	24.38
Clerks, Receptionists/Information	10.63	Nursing Aides/Orderlies/Attendants	9.34
Clerks, Shipping/Receiving	11.74	Packers and Packagers, Hand	8.04
Computer Programmers	28.22	Physical Therapists	32.16
Computer Support Specialists	19.12	Postal Service Mail Carriers	20.96
Computer Systems Analysts	30.18	Real Estate Brokers	n/a
Cooks, Restaurant	8.79	Retail Salespersons	11.68
Dentists	n/a	Sales Reps., Exc. Tech./Scientific	20.33
Electrical Engineers	n/a	Sales Reps., Tech./Scientific	22.88
Electricians	19.66	Secretaries, Exc. Legal/Med./Exec.	10.70
Financial Managers	33.51	Security Guards	10.77
First-Line Supervisors/Mgrs., Sales	18.16	Surgeons	93.76
Food Preparation Workers	8.22	Teacher Assistants	7.90
General and Operations Managers	29.85	Teachers, Elementary School	n/a
Hairdressers/Cosmetologists	9.05	Teachers, Secondary School	n/a
Internists	n/a	Telemarketers	9.42
Janitors and Cleaners	9.36	Truck Drivers, Heavy/Tractor-Trailer	14.22
Landscaping/Groundskeeping Workers	10.69	Truck Drivers, Light/Delivery Svcs.	11.02
Lawyers	48.19	Waiters and Waitresses	6.57

Note: Wage data is for May 2005 and covers the Boise City-Nampa, ID Metropolitan Statistics Area - see Appendix B for areas included. Hourly wages for elementary/secondary school teachers and teacher assistants were calculated by the editors from annual wage data assuming a 40 hour work week; n/a not available.
Source: Bureau of Labor Statistics, May 2005 Metro Area Occupational Employment and Wage Estimates

RESIDENTIAL
REAL ESTATE

Building Permits

Area	Single-Family			Multi-Family			Total		
	2005	2006p	Pct. Chg.	2005	2006p	Pct. Chg.	2005	2006p	Pct. Chg.
City	955	588	-38.4	354	584	65.0	1,309	1,172	-10.5
U.S.	1,682,000	1,380,000	-18.0	473,300	457,300	-3.4	2,155,300	1,837,300	-14.8

Note: (p) preliminary; figures represent new, privately-owned housing units authorized (unadjusted data); All permit data are based on estimates with imputation; U.S. figures are based on the new 20,000-place series.
Source: U.S. Census Bureau, Manufacturing, Mining, and Construction Statistics

Homeownership and Housing Vacancies

Area	Homeownership Rate[2] (%)			Rental Vacancy Rate[3] (%)			Homeowner Vacancy Rate[4] (%)		
	2004	2005	2006	2004	2005	2006	2004	2005	2006
MSA[1]	n/a	n/a	n/a	n/a	n/a	n/a	n/a	n/a	n/a
U.S.	69.0	68.9	68.8	10.2	9.8	9.7	1.7	1.9	2.4

Note: Comparable 2004 data was not available due to changes in metropolitan area definitions; (1) Metropolitan Statistical Area - see Appendix B for areas included; (2) The proportion of households that are owners; (3) The proportion of the rental inventory that is vacant for rent; (4) The proportion of the homeowner inventory that is vacant for sale; n/a not available
Source: U.S. Census Bureau, Housing Vacancies and Homeownership Annual Statistics: 2006

TAXES

State Corporate Income Tax Rates

State	Rate (%)	Number of Brackets	Low Bracket (Under $)	High Bracket (Over $)
Idaho	7.6	1	na	na

Note: Tax rates as of December 31, 2006; na not applicable; Minimum tax is $20.
Source: Tax Foundation, www.taxfoundation.org

State Individual Income Tax Rates

State	Federal Deductibility	Marginal Rate (%)	Number of Brackets	Low Bracket (Under $)	High Bracket (Over $)
Idaho	No	1.6-7.8 (r)	8	0	23,963

Note: Tax rates as of December 31, 2006; Brackets apply to single taxpayers and married people filing separately; na not applicable; (r) Indexed for Inflation.
Source: Tax Foundation, www.taxfoundation.org

Various State and Local Tax Rates

State and Local Sales and Use (%)	State Sales and Use (%)	Gasoline ($/gal.)	Cigarette ($/pack)	Spirits ($/gal.)	Table Wine ($/gal.)	Beer ($/gal.)
6.0	6.0	0.25	0.57	8.86 (b)	0.45	0.15

Note: Tax rates as of December 31, 2006; (b) States where the state government controls all sales. Excise tax rate is calculated using methodology designed by the Distilled Spirits Council of the United States (DISCUS).
Source: Tax Foundation, www.taxfoundation.org; The Sales Tax Clearinghouse, www.thestc.com

State Tax Burdens

Area	Combined State and Local Tax Burden		Combined Federal, State and Local Tax Burden	
	Percent	Rank	Percent	Rank
Idaho	10.2	31	29.0	42
U.S. Average	10.6	-	31.6	-

Note: Figures are for 2006 and measure taxes as a percentage of income
Source: Tax Foundation, www.taxfoundation.org

Internal Revenue Service Tax Audits

IRS District	Percent of Returns Audited				
	1996	1997	1998	1999	2000
Rocky Mountain	0.73	0.67	0.49	0.28	0.20
U.S.	0.66	0.61	0.46	0.31	0.20

Note: Figures cover IRS district audits of federal income tax returns filed by individuals. Geographic data on district audits after the year 2000 are being withheld by the IRS. TRAC is challenging this policy.
Source: Syracuse University, Transactional Records Access Clearinghouse (TRAC), "Odds of IRS District Tax Audit 2000"

**COMMERCIAL
REAL ESTATE**

Office Market

Market Area	Inventory (sq. ft.)	Vacant (sq. ft.)	Vac. Rate (%)	Under Constr. (sq. ft.)	Asking Rent ($/sf)	
					Class A	Class B
Boise City	11,877,044	1,322,594	11.1	675,667	17.16	16.20

Source: Grubb & Ellis, Office Markets Trends, 4th Quarter 2006

Industrial Market

Market Area	Inventory (sq. ft.)	Vacant (sq. ft.)	Vac. Rate (%)	Under Constr. (sq. ft.)	Asking Rent ($/sf)	
					WH/Dist	R&D/Flex
Boise City	23,290,069	1,911,749	8.2	315,500	4.88	6.52

Source: Grubb & Ellis, Industrial Markets Trends, 4th Quarter 2006

**COMMERCIAL
UTILITIES**

Typical Monthly Electric Bills

Area	Commercial Service ($/month)		Industrial Service ($/month)	
	3 kW demand 1,000 kWh	40 kW demand 14,000 kWh	1,000 kW demand 200,000 kWh	50,000 kW demand 15,000,000 kWh
City	72	540	8,303	n/a
Average[1]	123	1,413	22,000	1,306,315

Note: Based on total rates in effect July 1, 2006; (1) average based on 196 utilities; n/a not available
Source: Edison Electric Institute, Typical Bills and Average Rates Report, Summer 2006

TRANSPORTATION

Means of Transportation to Work

Area	Car/Truck/Van		Public Transportation			Bicycle	Walked	Other Means	Worked at Home
	Drove Alone	Car-pooled	Bus	Subway	Railroad				
City	79.9	10.3	1.1	0.0	0.0	1.7	2.3	0.8	4.0
MSA[1]	79.9	11.4	0.6	0.0	0.0	1.0	2.2	0.8	4.1
U.S.	75.7	12.2	2.5	1.5	0.5	0.4	2.9	1.0	3.3

Note: Figures are percentages and cover workers 16 years of age and older;
(1) Metropolitan Statistical Area - see Appendix A for areas included
Source: Census 2000, Summary File 3

Travel Time to Work

Area	Less Than 15 Minutes	15 to 29 Minutes	30 to 44 Minutes	45 to 59 Minutes	60 Minutes or More
City	38.4	48.2	9.3	1.6	2.4
MSA[1]	33.1	45.9	15.3	3.1	2.7
U.S.	29.4	36.1	19.1	7.4	8.0

Note: Figures are percentages and include workers 16 years old and over; (1) Metropolitan Statistical Area -
see Appendix A for areas included
Source: Census 2000, Summary File 3

Public Transportation

Agency name:	ValleyRide
Vehicle type:	Bus
Average fleet age in years:	5.7
No. operated in max. service:	40
Vehicle type:	Demand response
Average fleet age in years:	1.7
No. operated in max. service:	8

Source: Federal Transit Administration, National Transit Database, 2005

Air Transportation

Airport name and code:	Boise Air Terminal-Gowen Field (BOI)
Domestic service (2006)	
Passenger airlines[1]:	24
Passenger enplanements:	1,654,293
Freight carriers[2]:	15
Freight (lbs.):	45,081,351
International service (2005)	
Passenger airlines[1]:	6
Passenger enplanements:	524
Freight carriers[2]:	0
Freight (lbs.):	0

*Note: (1) Includes all major, minor and commuter airlines that carried at least one passenger during the year;
(2) Includes all airlines and freight carriers that transported at least one pound of freight during the year
Source: Bureau of Transportation Statistics, The Intermodal Transportation Database, Air Carriers: T-100
International Market, 2004; Bureau of Transportation Statistics, The Intermodal Transportation Database, Air
Carriers: T-100 Domestic Market, 2005*

Other Transportation Statistics

Interstate highways:	I-84
Amtrak service:	Bus connection
Major waterways/ports:	None

Source: Editor & Publisher Market Guide, 2006; Amtrak.com; Rand McNally 2006 Road Atlas

BUSINESSES

Major Business Headquarters

Company Name	2006 Rankings	
	Fortune[1]	Forbes[2]
Albertson's	47	-
Boise Cascade	-	36
JR Simplot	-	85
Micron Technology	438	-
WinCo Foods	-	105

*Note: (1) Fortune 500 - companies that produce a 10-K are ranked 1 to 500 based on 2005 revenue; (2) Forbes
Largest Private Companies - all private companies with at least $1 billion in annual revenue are ranked 1 to
394; companies listed are located in the city; dashes indicate no ranking
Source: Fortune, April 17, 2006; Forbes, November 9, 2006*

Women-Owned Businesses: 1997 and 2002

Year	All Firms		Firms with Paid Employees			
	Firms	Sales ($000)	Firms	Sales ($000)	Employees	Payroll ($000)
1997	4,276	538,132	713	446,739	5,305	112,476
2002	5,252	925,417	969	833,916	7,401	171,067

*Note: Figures cover firms located in the city; Women-owned business are defined as firms in which women own
51% or more of the stock or equity of the company; (a) Withheld to avoid disclosing data for individual
companies; (b) Withheld because estimate did not meet publication standards; n/a not available
Source: 1997 Economic Census, Survey of Minority- and Women-Owned Business Enterprises; 2002 Economic
Census, Survey of Business Owners (released February 9, 2006)*

HOTELS

Hotels/Motels

Area	Hotels/Motels	Average Minimum Rates ($)		
		Tourist	First-Class	Deluxe
City	45	58	75	n/a

*Note: n/a not available
Source: OAG Travel Planner Online, Spring 2006*

EVENT SITES

Stadiums, Arenas, and Auditoriums

Name	Capacity
Boise State University, Bronco Stadium	30,000
Boise State University, Taco Bell Arena	12,380

Source: www.officialtravelguide.com; www.eventective.com; original research

Convention Centers

Name	Overall Space (sq. ft.)	Exhibit Space (sq. ft.)	Meeting Space (sq. ft.)	Meeting Rooms
Boise Centre on the Grove	n/a	n/a	75,614	20

Note: n/a not available
Source: www.officialtravelguide.com; www.eventective.com; original research

Hotels/Conference Centers

Name	Guest Rooms	Exhibit Space (sq. ft.)	Meeting Space (sq. ft.)
Holiday Inn Boise-Airport	265	6,400	12,000
Red Lion Hotel Boise Downtowner	182	3,654	8,270
The Grove Hotel	254	n/a	36,000
The Grove Hotel	254	23,000	16,000

Note: n/a not available
Source: www.officialtravelguide.com; www.eventective.com; original research

Living Environment

COST OF LIVING

Cost of Living Index

Year	Composite Index	Groceries	Housing	Utilities	Trans-portation	Health Care	Misc. Goods/ Services
2004	97.2	87.8	93.6	95.5	103.6	110.3	101.1
2005	95.8	87.3	90.5	91.7	102.2	102.6	102.0
2006	97.3	93.8	88.2	93.8	99.8	101.3	105.8

Note: U.S. = 100
Source: The Council for Community and Economic Research (formerly ACCRA), Cost of Living Index, 2004, 2005 and 2006 4-Quarter Averages

HOUSING

House Price Index (HPI)

Area	National Ranking[2]	Quarterly Change (%)	One-Year Change (%)	Five-Year Change (%)
MSA[1]	5	1.02	17.94	67.66
U.S.[3]	-	1.12	5.87	55.21

Note: The HPI is a weighted repeat sales index. It measures average price changes in repeat sales or refinancings on the same properties. This information is obtained by reviewing repeat mortgage transactions on single-family properties whose mortgages have been purchased or securitized by Fannie Mae or Freddie Mac in January 1975; (1) Metropolitan Statistical Area - see Appendix B for areas included; (2) Rankings are based on annual percentage change for all metro areas containing at least 15,000 transactions over the last 10 years and ranges from 1 to 282; (3) figures based on a weighted division average; all figures are for the period ending December 31, 2006
Source: Office of Federal Housing Enterprise Oversight, House Price Index, March 1, 2007

House Price Valuations

Area	Q4 1999	Q4 2000	Q4 2001	Q4 2002	Q4 2003	Q4 2004	Q4 2005	Q4 2006
MSA[1]	-8.7	-8.8	-5.6	-2.5	4.0	3.4	20.3	30.0

Note: Figures show the percentage of over- or under-valuation of single family homes relative to statistically normal house values (e.g. a value of 23.6 indicates that house values are 23.6% overvalued). Statistically normal house values are based on house prices, interest rates, household incomes, population densities, and any historical premiums or discounts metropolitan areas have exhibited over time; (1) Figures cover the Metropolitan Statistical Area - see Appendix B for areas included
Source: Global Insight/National City Corporation, House Prices in America, March 2007

Median Home Prices

Area	2004	2005	2006p	Percent Change 2005 to 2006
Metro Area[1]	135.9	147.0	n/a	n/a
U.S. Average	195.2	219.0	222.0	1.4

Note: Figures are median sales prices of existing single-family homes in thousands of dollars; (p) preliminary; n/a not available; (1) Covers the Boise City-Nampa, ID Metropolitan Statistical Area - see Appendix B for areas included
Source: National Association of Realtors, Metropolitan Area Prices, 4th Quarter 2006

Housing: Year Structure Built

Area	1990 -2000	1980 -1989	1970 -1979	1960 -1969	1950 -1959	1940 -1949	Before 1940	Median Year
City	26.6	15.4	23.8	10.0	10.3	5.9	8.0	1977
MSA[1]	33.8	12.7	24.4	8.3	8.1	5.2	7.4	1979
U.S.	17.0	15.8	18.5	13.7	12.7	7.3	15.0	1971

Note: Figures are percentages; (1) Metropolitan Statistical Area - see Appendix A for areas included
Source: Census 2000, Summary File 3

Average New Home Price

Area	2004	2005	2006
City	230,947	242,448	257,334
U.S.	253,574	275,712	299,269

Note: Figures, in dollars, are based on a new home with 2,400 sq. ft. of living area on an 8,000 sq. ft. lot.
Source: The Council for Community and Economic Research (formerly ACCRA), Cost of Living Index, 2004, 2005 and 2006 4-Quarter Averages

Average Apartment Rent

Area	2004	2005	2006
City	744	753	764
U.S.	716	740	766

Note: Figures, in dollars per month, are based on an unfurnished two bedroom, 1-1/2 or 2 bath apartment, approximately 950 sq. ft. in size, excluding all utilities except water
Source: The Council for Community and Economic Research (formerly ACCRA), Cost of Living Index, 2004, 2005 and 2006 4-Quarter Averages

RESIDENTIAL UTILITIES

Average Residential Utility Costs

Area	All Electric ($/mth)	Part Electric ($/mth)	Other Energy ($/mth)	Phone ($/mth)
City	–	48.10	89.77	27.01
U.S.	136.00	76.53	90.52	25.87

Source: The Council for Community and Economic Research (formerly ACCRA), Cost of Living Index, 2006 4-Quarter Average

HEALTH

Average Health Care Costs

Area	Optometrist ($/visit)	Doctor ($/visit)	Dentist ($/visit)
City	76.32	78.34	72.63
U.S.	76.38	76.10	68.72

Note: Optometrist—based on a full vision eye exam for an established adult patient;
Doctor—based on a general practitioner's routine exam of an established patient;
Dentist—based on adult teeth cleaning and periodic oral exam.
Source: The Council for Community and Economic Research (formerly ACCRA), Cost of Living Index, 2006 4-Quarter Average

Mortality Rates

ICD-10 Sub-Chapter	ICD-10 Code	Age-Adjusted Death Rate per 100,000 population[1]	U.S. Age-Adjusted Death Rate per 100,000 population
Malignant neoplasms	C00-C97	173.8	185.8
Ischaemic heart diseases	I20-I25	104.9	150.2
Other forms of heart disease	I30-I51	43.9	50.8
Cerebrovascular diseases	I60-I69	49.7	50.0
Chronic lower respiratory diseases	J40-J47	44.1	41.1
Diabetes mellitus	E10-E14	23.2	24.5
Other degenerative diseases of the nervous system	G30-G31	35.7	22.3
Other external causes of accidental injury	W00-X59	17.3	21.2
Influenza and pneumonia	J10-J18	10.8	19.8
Hypertensive diseases	I10-I13	15.5	18.1

Note: ICD-10 = International Classification of Diseases 10th Revision; (1) Figures cover Ada County, ID
Source: Centers for Disease Control and Prevention, National Center for Health Statistics. Compressed Mortality File 1999-2004. CDC WONDER On-line Database, compiled from Compressed Mortality File 1999-2004 Series 20 No. 2J, 2007.

Health Risk Data

Item	Area[1] (%)	U.S. (%)
Adults who have been told they have high blood pressure	23.5	25.5
Adults who have been told they have high blood cholesterol	35.2	35.6
Adults who have been told they have diabetes[2]	7.3	7.3
Adults who have been told they have arthritis	24.0	27.0
Adults who have been told they currently have asthma	6.7	8.0
Adults who are current smokers	17.8	20.6

Note: (1) Figures cover the Metropolitan Statistical Area - see Appendix B for areas included; (2) Figures do not include pregnancy-related diabetes, pre-diabetes or borderline diabetes
Source: Centers for Disease Control and Prevention, Behaviorial Risk Factor Surveillance System, SMART: Selected Metropolitan/Micropolitan Area Trends, 2005

Distribution of Office-Based Physicians

Area	Total	Family/ General Practice	Specialties		
			Medical	Surgical	Other
MSA[1] (number)	874	162	237	261	214
MSA[1] (rate per 10,000 pop.)	19.2	3.6	5.2	5.7	4.7
Metro Average[2] (rate per 10,000 pop.)	19.4	2.1	7.5	4.5	5.3

Note: Data as of December 31, 2004; (1) Metropolitan Statistical Area - see Appendix A for areas included; (2) Average of the 79 unique MSAs and CMSAs in this book
Source: American Medical Association, Physician Characteristics & Distribution in the U.S., 2006

Hospitals

Boise City has the following hospitals: 3 general medical and surgical; 1 psychiatric; 1 rehabilitation; 1 surgical.
AHA Guide to the Healthcare Field 2007

According to *U.S. News*, the Boise City metro area is home to one of the best hospitals in the U.S.: **Saint Luke's Regional Medical Center**; *U.S. News Online, "America's Best Hospitals 2006"*

EDUCATION

Public School District Statistics

District Name	Schls	Pupils	Pupil/ Teacher Ratio	Minority Pupils[1] (%)	Free Lunch Eligible[2] (%)	IEP[3] (%)
Boise Independent District	55	26,268	17.4	13.6	23.4	11.4

Note: Table includes regular local school districts with 2,000 or more students; (1) Percentage of students that are not white, non-Hispanic; (2) Percentage of students that are eligible for the free lunch program; (3) Percentage of students that have an Individualized Education Program.
Source: U.S. Department of Education, National Center for Education Statistics, Common Core of Data, Local Education Agency (School District) Universe Survey: School Year 2004-2005; U.S. Department of Education, National Center for Education Statistics, Common Core of Data, Public Elementary/Secondary School Universe Survey: School Year 2004-2005

Top Public High Schools

High School Name	Index[1]	Rank[1]	Subsidized Lunch (%)[2]	E&E (%)[3]
Boise	1.745	503	39.0	37.3

Note: (1) Public schools are ranked according to a ratio that is the number of Advanced Placement and/or International Baccalaureate tests taken by all students at a school in 2005 divided by the number of graduating seniors. All of the schools on the list have an index of at least 1.000; they are in the top five percent of public schools measured this way. The rankings range from 1 to 1,236; (2) Percentage of students receiving federally subsidized meals; (3) E & E stands for equity and excellence percentage: the portion of all graduating seniors at a school that had at least one passing grade on one AP or IB test; (*) Gave just IB tests; (**) Gave both IB and AP tests. AP and IB participation are indicators of a school's efforts to get students to excel and prepare for college.
Source: Newsweek Online, May 23, 2006

Educational Quality

School District	Education Quotient[1]	Graduate Outcome[2]	Community Index[3]	Resource Index[4]	Rating[5]
Boise Independent	64	67	68	32	Green

Note: Scores are national percentile rankings and range from 1 (worst) to 99 (best); (1) Combination of the Graduate Outcome, Community and Resource Indexes weighted to reflect the greater importance of the Graduate Outcome and Resource Index; (2) Based on graduation rates and college board scores (SAT/ACT); (3) Based on the surrounding community's level of affluence and adult education; (4) Based on teacher salaries, per-pupil expenditures and student-teacher ratios; (5) School districts receive one of five rankings: Gold Medal (top 16 percent of districts evaluated); Blue Ribbon (top third); Green Light (average); Yellow Light (bottom 25 percent); Red Light (bottom 10 percent).
Source: Expansion Management, "2007 Education Quotient," January 2007

Highest Level of Education

Area	Less than H.S.	H.S. Diploma	Some College, No Deg.	Associate Degree	Bachelors Degree	Masters Degree	Profess. School Degree	Doctorate Degree
City	8.8	21.1	29.1	7.2	23.1	7.4	2.3	1.0
MSA[1]	13.9	26.0	27.8	6.9	17.7	5.3	1.7	0.7
U.S.	19.4	28.4	21.2	6.4	15.7	5.9	2.0	1.0

Note: Figures are 2006 estimated percentages and cover persons age 25 and over; (1) Metropolitan Statistical Area - see Appendix B for areas included
Source: Claritas, Inc.

Educational Attainment by Race

Area	High School Graduate (%)					Bachelor's Degree (%)				
	Total	White	Black	Asian	Hisp.[2]	Total	White	Black	Asian	Hisp.[2]
City	91.1	91.8	85.4	81.8	76.5	33.6	33.9	30.8	45.2	18.2
MSA[1]	86.5	88.6	80.5	80.6	50.0	26.5	27.3	26.3	38.7	8.8
U.S.	80.4	83.6	72.3	80.4	52.4	24.4	26.1	14.3	44.1	10.4

Note: Figures shown cover persons 25 years old and over; (1) Metropolitan Statistical Area - see Appendix A for areas included; (2) people of Hispanic origin can be of any race
Source: Census 2000, Summary File 3

School Enrollment by Type

Area	Grades KG to 8				Grades 9 to 12			
	Public		Private		Public		Private	
	Enrollment	%	Enrollment	%	Enrollment	%	Enrollment	%
City	21,529	90.8	2,176	9.2	9,656	92.2	819	7.8
MSA[1]	55,566	91.3	5,311	8.7	24,072	92.7	1,882	7.3
U.S.	33,526,011	88.7	4,285,121	11.3	14,848,628	90.6	1,532,323	9.4

Note: Figures shown cover persons 3 years old and over; (1) Metropolitan Statistical Area - see Appendix A for areas included
Source: Census 2000, Summary File 3

School Enrollment by Race

Area	Grades KG to 8 (%)				Grades 9 to 12 (%)			
	White	Black	Asian	Hisp.[1]	White	Black	Asian	Hisp.[1]
City	90.6	0.9	1.4	6.0	90.5	1.2	1.8	4.3
MSA[2]	87.2	0.6	0.9	12.0	87.9	0.8	1.2	10.6
U.S.	68.5	15.5	3.3	16.8	68.8	15.5	3.8	15.7

Note: Figures shown cover persons 3 years old and over; (1) people of Hispanic origin can be of any race; (2) Metropolitan Statistical Area - see Appendix A for areas included
Source: Census 2000, Summary File 3

Average Salaries of Public School Teachers

District	2004-05		2005-06		Percent Change 2004-05 to 2005-06
	Dollars	Rank[1]	Dollars	Rank[1]	
IDAHO	42,122	30	43,390	29	3.01
U.S. Average	47,674	-	49,109	-	3.01

Note: (1) State rank ranges from 1 to 51.
Source: National Education Association, Rankings & Estimates: Rankings of the States 2005 and Estimates of School Statistics 2006, November 2006

Higher Education

Four-Year Colleges			Two-Year Colleges			Medical Schools[1]	Law Schools[2]	Voc/ Tech[3]
Public	Private Non-profit	Private For-profit	Public	Private Non-profit	Private For-profit			
1	1	1	0	0	3	0	0	1

Note: Figures cover institutions located within the city limits; (1) includes schools accredited by the Liaison Committee on Medical Education and the American Osteopathic Association; (2) includes American Bar Association-accredited law schools; (3) includes all schools with programs that are less than 2 years
Source: National Center for Education Statistics, The Integrated Postsecondary Education System (IPEDS) Peer Analysis System, 2006; www.usnews.com, America's Best Graduate Schools 2008, Medical School Directory; www.usnews.com, America's Best Graduate Schools 2008, Law School Directory

PRESIDENTIAL ELECTION

2004 Presidential Election Results

Area	Bush	Kerry	Nader	Other
Ada County	61.0	37.7	0.2	1.0
U.S.	50.7	48.3	0.4	0.6

Note: Results are percentages and may not add to 100% due to rounding
Source: Dave Leip's Atlas of U.S. Presidential Elections, www.uselectionatlas.org

MAJOR EMPLOYERS

Major Employers

Company Name	Industry	Type of Site
Albertsons	Grocery stores	Headquarters
Boise State University	Colleges and universities	Headquarters
Call Saint Lukes	General medical and surgical hospitals	Headquarters
Down Town YS Kids	Child day care services	Branch
HP	Computers, peripherals, and software	Branch
Idaho Press-Tribune	Newspapers	Single
Micron Technology Inc	Semiconductors and related devices	Headquarters
St Alphonsus Regional Med Ctr	General medical and surgical hospitals	Headquarters
Washington Closure Company LLC	Sanitary services, nec	Single
Washington Group	Equipment rental and leasing, nec	Single

Note: Companies shown are located within the metropolitan area and have 750 or more employees; nec = not elsewhere classified.
Source: www.zapdata.com, January 2007

PUBLIC SAFETY

Crime Rate

Area	All Crimes	Violent Crimes				Property Crimes		
		Murder	Forcible Rape	Robbery	Aggrav. Assault	Burglary	Larceny -Theft	Motor Vehicle Theft
City	4,221.3	2.6	61.5	44.1	275.4	696.4	2,885.5	255.9
Suburbs[1]	n/a	n/a	n/a	n/a	n/a	n/a	n/a	n/a
Metro[2]	n/a	n/a	n/a	n/a	n/a	n/a	n/a	n/a
U.S.	3,899.0	5.6	31.7	140.7	291.1	726.7	2,286.3	416.7

Note: Figures are crimes per 100,000 population; (1) All areas within the metro area that are located outside the city limits; (2) Metropolitan Statistical Area - see Appendix B for areas included; n/a not available
Source: FBI Uniform Crime Reports, 2005

Hate Crimes

Area	Number of Quarters Reported	Bias Motivation				
		Race	Religion	Sexual Orientation	Ethnicity	Disability
Area[2]	4	5	2	2	2	0

Note: (2) Figures cover Boise.
Source: Federal Bureau of Investigation, Hate Crime Statistics 2005

RECREATION

Culture

Dance[1]	Theatre[1]	Instrumental Music[1]	Vocal Music[1]	Series/ Festivals	Museums	Zoos
2	1	3	3	3	7	1

Note: (1) number of professional perfoming groups
Source: The Grey House Performing Arts Directory, 2007; Official Museum Directory, 2007

Professional Sports Teams

Major League Baseball	National Basketball Association	National Football League	National Hockey League	Major League Soccer	Women's National Basketball Association
0	0	0	0	0	0

Note: Includes teams located in the Boise City metro area.
Source: www.sportsvenues.com, Listing of Venues by State/Province and City, 2006

MEDIA

Newspapers

Name	Target Audience	Frequency	Circulation
Boise Weekly	Alternative/General	Non-Daily	25,000
Idaho Catholic Register	Catholic/Religious	Non-Daily	16,400
The Idaho Statesman	n/a	Daily	66,555
Treasure Valley Christian News	Christian	Non-Daily	30,000

Note: Includes newspapers whose offices are located in the city and whose circulations are 500 or more; n/a not available
Source: BurrellesLuce, MediaContacts Online, January 2006

Television Stations

Name	Ch.	Network(s)	Type	Ownership
KBCI	2	CBS	Commercial	Fisher Broadcasting Inc.
KAID	4	PBS	Public	Idaho State Board of Education
KIVI	6	ABC	Commercial	Journal Broadcast Group
KTVB	7	NBC	Commercial	Belo Corporation
KTRV	12	Fox	Commercial	Idaho Independent Television
KIPT	13	PBS	Public	Idaho State Board of Education

Note: Stations included cover the Boise DMA (Designated Market Area)
BurrellesLuce, MediaContacts Online, January 2006

Major AM Radio Stations

Call Letters	Freq. (kHz)	Station Type	Target Audience	Station Format	Music Format
KFXD	580	Commercial	General	Music/News	Country
KIDO	630	Commercial	General	Talk	n/a
KBOI	670	Commercial	General	News/Talk	n/a
KBSU	730	College	General/Hispanic	Educational/Music	Blues
KSPD	790	Commercial	General/Religious	Music/Talk	Christian
KNJY	950	n/a	Religious	Educational/Music/Talk	n/a
KBGN	1060	Commercial	Christian/General	Ed/Music/News/Talk	Gospel
KGEM	1140	n/a	General	Music	n/a
KMHI	1240	Commercial	General	Ed/Music/News/Sports	Country
KTIK	1350	n/a	Men	Sports	n/a
KSRV	1380	Commercial	General	News/Sports/Talk	n/a
KJDY	1400	n/a	General	Music/Talk	n/a
KCID	1490	Commercial	General	Music	Oldies

Note: Stations included cover the Boise DMA (Designated Market Area); n/a not available
Source: BurrellesLuce, MediaContacts Online, January 2006

Major FM Radio Stations

Call Letters	Freq. (mHz)	Station Type	Target Audience	Station Format	Music Format
KTSY	89.5	Public	General/Religious	Educational/Music/News	Christian
KBSU	90.3	College	General	Music/Talk	Jazz
KBSX	91.5	Public	General	Educational/Talk	n/a
KBSW	91.7	Public	General	Ed/Music/News/Talk	Classical
KIZN	92.3	Commercial	General	Music/News	Country
KBXL	94.1	Commercial	General/Religious	Music/Talk	Christian
KSRV	96.1	Commercial	General	Music/News	Country
KKGL	96.9	Commercial	General	Music/News	Classic Rock
KQFC	97.9	Commercial	General	Music/News/Talk	Country
KWEI	99.5	Commercial	General/Hispanic	Music/News	Latin
KQXR	100.3	Commercial	Young Adult	Music/News/Talk	A.O. Rock
KMCL	101.1	Commercial	General	Music	Adult Contemp.
KJHY	101.9	n/a	Hispanic	Music	n/a
KSAS	103.3	Commercial	General	Music/News	Urban Contemp.
KLTB	104.3	Commercial	General	Music/News	Oldies
KJOT	105.1	Commercial	General	Music/News	Classic Rock
KCIX	105.9	Commercial	General	Music	Adult Top 40
KXLT	107.9	Commercial	General	Music	Adult Contemp.

Note: Stations included cover the Boise DMA (Designated Market Area); n/a not available
BurrellesLuce, MediaContacts Online, January 2006

CLIMATE

Average and Extreme Temperatures

Temperature	Jan	Feb	Mar	Apr	May	Jun	Jul	Aug	Sep	Oct	Nov	Dec	Yr.
Extreme High (°F)	63	70	81	92	98	105	111	110	101	94	74	65	111
Average High (°F)	36	44	53	62	71	80	90	88	78	65	48	38	63
Average Temp. (°F)	29	36	42	49	58	66	74	73	63	52	40	31	51
Average Low (°F)	22	27	31	37	44	52	58	57	48	39	30	23	39
Extreme Low (°F)	-17	-15	6	19	22	31	35	34	23	11	-3	-25	-25

Note: Figures cover the years 1948-1995
Source: National Climatic Data Center, International Station Meteorological Climate Summary, 9/96

Average Precipitation/Snowfall/Humidity

Precip./Humidity	Jan	Feb	Mar	Apr	May	Jun	Jul	Aug	Sep	Oct	Nov	Dec	Yr.
Avg. Precip. (in.)	1.4	1.1	1.2	1.2	1.2	0.9	0.3	0.3	0.6	0.7	1.4	1.4	11.8
Avg. Snowfall (in.)	7	4	2	1	Tr	Tr	0	0	0	Tr	2	6	22
Avg. Rel. Hum. 7am (%)	81	80	75	69	65	59	48	50	58	67	77	81	68
Avg. Rel. Hum. 4pm (%)	68	58	45	35	34	29	22	23	28	36	55	67	42

Note: Figures cover the years 1948-1995; Tr = Trace amounts (<0.05 in. of rain; <0.5 in. of snow)
Source: National Climatic Data Center, International Station Meteorological Climate Summary, 9/96

Weather Conditions

	Temperature			Daytime Sky			Precipitation	
5°F & below	32°F & below	90°F & above	Clear	Partly cloudy	Cloudy	0.01 inch or more precip.	0.1 inch or more snow/ice	Thunder-storms
6	124	45	106	133	126	91	22	14

Note: Figures are average number of days per year and cover the years 1948-1995
Source: National Climatic Data Center, International Station Meteorological Climate Summary, 9/96

HAZARDOUS WASTE

Superfund Sites

Boise City has no sites on the EPA's Superfund Final National Priorities List.
U.S. Environmental Protection Agency, Final National Priorities List, March 20, 2007

AIR & WATER QUALITY

Air Quality Index

Area	Percent of Days when Air Quality was...[2]				AQI Statistics	
	Good	Moderate	Unhealthy for Sensitive Groups	Unhealthy	Maximum	Median
MSA[1]	76.7	21.4	1.9	0.0	138	38

Note: The Air Quality Index (AQI) is an index for reporting daily air quality. EPA calculates the AQI for five major air pollutants regulated by the Clean Air Act: ground-level ozone, particle pollution (also known as particulate matter), carbon monoxide, sulfur dioxide, and nitrogen dioxide. The AQI runs from 0 to 500. The higher the AQI value, the greater the level of air pollution and the greater the health concern. There are six AQI categories: "Good" The AQI is between 0 and 50. Air quality is considered satisfactory; "Moderate" The AQI is between 51 and 100. Air quality is acceptable; "Unhealthy for Sensitive Groups" When AQI values are between 101 and 150, members of sensitive groups may experience health effects; "Unhealthy" When AQI values are between 151 and 200 everyone may begin to experience health effects; "Very Unhealthy" AQI values between 201 and 300 trigger a health alert; "Hazardous" AQI values over 300 trigger health warnings of emergency conditions; (1) Metropolitan Statistical Area - see Appendix A for areas included; (2) Based on 365 days with AQI data in 2005.
Source: U.S. Environmental Protection Agency, Air Quality Index Report, 2005

Air Quality Index Pollutants

Area	Percent of Days when AQI Pollutant was...[2]					
	Carbon Monoxide	Nitrogen Dioxide	Ozone	Sulfur Dioxide	Particulate Matter 2.5	Particulate Matter 10
MSA[1]	4.1	0.0	33.4	0.0	52.3	10.1

Note: The Air Quality Index (AQI) is an index for reporting daily air quality. EPA calculates the AQI for five major air pollutants regulated by the Clean Air Act: ground-level ozone, particle pollution (also known as particulate matter), carbon monoxide, sulfur dioxide, and nitrogen dioxide. The AQI runs from 0 to 500. The higher the AQI value, the greater the level of air pollution and the greater the health concern; (1) Metropolitan Statistical Area - see Appendix A for areas included; (2) Based on 365 days with AQI data in 2005.
Source: U.S. Environmental Protection Agency, Air Quality Index Report, 2005

Number of Days with Air Quality Index Values Greater than 100

Area	Trend Sites								All Sites
	1998	1999	2000	2001	2002	2003	2004	2005	2005
MSA[1]	n/a	n/a	n/a	n/a	n/a	n/a	n/a	n/a	n/a

Note: An AQI value greater than 100 indicates that air quality would have been in the unhealthful range on that day. Data from exceptional events are not included. These counts are presented in two ways. First, the counts are based on sites having an adequate record of monitoring data during the trend period (trend sites). These counts represent the relative change in the number of days with AQI values greater than 100. In the last column, the counts are based on all sites with data in the most recent year (because it is possible for a site to have data in the most recent year but not enough data to be a trend site); (1) Metropolitan Statistical Area - see Appendix A for areas included; n/a not available.
Source: U.S. Environmental Protection Agency, Air Trends Fact Book 2005

Maximum Pollutant Concentrations

	Particulate Matter 10 (ug/m^3)	Particulate Matter 2.5 (ug/m^3)	Ozone 1-hour (ppm)	Carbon Monoxide (ppm)	Sulfur Dioxide (ppm)	Nitrogen Dioxide (ppm)	Lead (ug/m^3)
MSA[1] Level	94	44	0.099	3	n/a	n/a	n/a
NAAQS[2]	150	65	0.125	9	0.140	0.053	1.50
Met NAAQS[2]	Yes	Yes	Yes	Yes	n/a	n/a	n/a

Note: Data from exceptional events are not included; (1) Metropolitan Statistical Area - see Appendix A for areas included; (2) National Ambient Air Quality Standards; n/a not available
Units: ppm = parts per million; ug/m^3 = micrograms per cubic meter
Source: U.S. Environmental Protection Agency, Air Trends Fact Book 2005

Watershed Health

The U.S. Environmental Protection Agency monitors the health of the aquatic resources for the nation's 2,000+ watersheds. **The Lower Boise watershed serves the Boise City area and received an overall Index of Watershed Indicators (IWI) score of 5 (more serious problems - low vulnerability).** The IWI score is based on seven condition and nine vulnerability indicators. The overall IWI score ranges from 1 (best health) to 6 (worst health). The Condition Indicators include: designated use attainment, fish and wildlife consumption advisories, source water condition, contaminated sediments, ambient water quality, and wetlands loss index. The Vulnerability Indicators include: aquatic species at risk, conventional and toxic loads over permitted limits, urban and agricultural runoff potential, population change, hydrologic modification, estuarine pollution susceptibility, and air deposition. *Note: The IWI is no longer being updated by the U.S. EPA. Source: U.S. Environmental Protection Agency, Index of Watershed Indicators, October 26, 2001*

Drinking Water

Water System Name	Pop. Served	Primary Water Source Type	Number of Violations in 2006[a]		
			Health Based	Significant Monitoring	Monitoring
United Water Idaho	186,000	Ground	None	None	None

Note: (a) Based on violation data from January 1, 2006 to December 31, 2006
Source: U.S. Environmental Protection Agency, Office of Ground Water and Drinking Water, Safe Drinking Water Information System (data extracted April 12, 2007)

Boise City tap water is alkaline, soft.
Editor & Publisher Market Guide, 2005

Boulder, Colorado

Background

Boulder, Colorado, lies at the foot of the Rocky Mountains in Boulder County. It is the eighth largest city in Colorado, with 27.8 square miles. Tourism is a major industry in Boulder, which offers spectacular views from its elevation of 5,430 feet and many outdoor recreation opportunities in over 31,000 acres of open space.

Boulder Valley originally was home to the Southern Arapahoe tribe. The first white settlement was established by gold miners in 1858 near the entrance to Boulder Canyon at Red Rocks. In 1859, the Boulder City Town Company was formed. The town's first schoolhouse was built in 1860, and in 1874, the University of Colorado opened.

Boulder was incorporated as a town in 1871 and as a city in 1882. By 1890, the railroad provided service from Boulder to Golden, Denver, and the western mining camps. In 1905, amidst a weakening economy, Boulder began promoting tourism to boost its finances. The city raised money to construct a first-class hotel, which was completed in 1908 and named Hotel Boulderado.

Although tourism remained strong until the late 1930s, it had begun to decline by World War II. However, the U.S. Navy's Japanese language school, housed at the city's University of Colorado, proved to be an impressive introduction to the area, and many people later returned to Boulder as students, professionals, and veterans attending the university on the GI Bill. Consequently, Boulder's population grew from 12,958 in 1940 to 20,000 in 1950. To accommodate this huge increase, new public buildings, highways, residential areas, and shopping centers developed, spurring further economic expansion.

Major employers in the Boulder area include IBM, Ball Aerospace, Tyco Healthcare, and Level 3 Communications, one of the largest communications and Internet backbones in the world. NOAA, the National Oceanic and Atmospheric Administration, also operates here.

Boulder is home to the University of Colorado, which houses a research park that includes corporate tenants such as Qwest. Cultural venues in the city include the Boulder Dushanbe Teahouse, a gift to the city from its sister city of Dushanbe in Tajikistan, and the Pearl Street Mall, an open-air walkway that was the city's original downtown and is today rich with restaurants, cafes, bookstores, and street entertainers. Boulder offers many scenic opportunities for outdoor activities, with parks, recreation areas, and hiking trails.

Annual attractions include the Creek Festival in May, Art Fair in July, Fall Festival, and Lights of December Parade. Each Memorial Day, over 40,000 runners participate in the "Bolder Boulder," a popular race that lures 80,000 spectators.

Like the rest of Colorado, Boulder enjoys a cool, dry highland continental climate. In winter, the mountains to the west shield the city from the coldest temperatures. Humidity is generally low. Winter storms moving east from the Pacific drop most of their moisture on the mountains to the west, while summer precipitation comes from scattered thunderstorms.

Rankings

General Rankings

- Boulder was ranked #142 out of 331 metro areas in *Cities Ranked & Rated*. Criteria: cost of living; climate; crime; transportation; economy and jobs; education; arts and culture; health and healthcare; leisure. *Cities Ranked & Rated, 1st Edition, 2004*

- Boulder was selected as one of "America's Top 10 Places to Live" by Relocate-America.com. Nominations were accepted throughout the year for cities and towns considered to be "great places to live." The nominations, along with key data regarding education, employment, economy, crime, parks, recreation and housing were reviewed, rated and judged by the Relocate-America.com editorial staff. *Relocate-America.com, "Relocate America's Top 10 Places to Live in 2006"*

- The Boulder metro area was selected as one of "America's Best Places to Live and Work" by *Employment Review*. The area ranked #20 out of 20. Criteria: unemployment rate; projected job growth; cost of living; and industry specific data. *Employment Review, www.bestjobsusa.com, 2003*

- Boulder was selected as one of "America's Best Places to Live" by monstermoving.com. The top 10 cities were selected based on the fact that they appear repeatedly on other publications' "Top Cities" lists. *www.monstermoving.com, February 26, 2004*

- Boulder was selected as one of the "50 Best Places to Live" by *Men's Journal*. The city ranked #4 in the "Healthiest Places" category. Criteria: illness rates; eating habits; medical resources available. *Men's Journal, April 2007*

- The Boulder area was selected as one of "60 Cheap Places to Live" in the U.S. The area appeared in the "IQ Campuses" (emerging centers of biotech and infotech) category. *Forbes.com, August 20, 2004*

- Boulder was selected as one of the "Best Places to Live" by MSN House & Home. The city appeared in the best small city category. Criteria: lively economy; diverse cultural amenities; and abundant recreational activities. *Houseandhome.msn.com, "Best Places to Live," September 2003*

Business/Finance Rankings

- Boulder was selected as one of the best places to start and grow a company by *Entrepreneur* and the National Policy Research Council. The Boulder metro area ranked #19 out of 50 large metro areas. Criteria: business formation and growth (firms started four to 14 years ago that still employ at least 5 people and experienced rapid growth over the last four years). *Entrepreneur/National Policy Research Council, "Hot Cities for Entrepreneurs," September 2006*

- The Boulder metro area was selected one of America's "Top 10 Knowledge Worker Metros." The area ranked #2. Criteria: degree holders (bachelors, masters, professional, and Ph.D.) as a percent of the workforce; science and engineering workers as a percent of the workforce; number of patents issued; number and type of colleges in each metro area. *Expansion Management, April 2006*

- Intel, in partnership with Sperling's BestPlaces, ranked the 80 "Best Cities for Teleworking" in America. The Boulder metro area ranked #1 among small metro areas. The study identifies cities that hold the greatest potential for teleworking based on a host of factors including typical commuting times, fuel prices, availability of broadband Internet access and percentage of the population in telework friendly jobs. The study also factored in extreme climate and natural hazards. *Intel, "Best Cities for Teleworking," March 30, 2006*

- Boulder was selected as one of 20 cities in North America that is doing its part to host green conventions by providing renewable energy, intelligent recycling programs, transportation that minimizes usage of fossil fuels, and plenty of parkland. The city was ranked #9. *Meetings and Conventions, "Natural Choices," August 2006*

- The Boulder metro area appeared on the Milken Institute "2005 Best Performing Cities" index. Rank: #92 out of 200 large metro areas. Criteria: job growth; wage and salary growth; high-tech output growth. *Milken Institute, "2005 Best Performing Cities," February 2006*

- The Boulder metro area was selected as one of "The Best Cities for Doing Business in America." *Inc.* magazine measured employment growth in 393 regions using the following criteria: recent growth trend; mid-term growth; long-term trend; and current year growth. The Boulder metro area ranked #37 among mid-sized metro areas and #162 overall. *Inc., May 2006*

- The Boulder metro area was selected as one of "The Top 10 Boom Villages in America." *Business 2.0* magazine and econometric research firm Global Insight compared 319 metropolitan areas in the U.S. Criteria: a weighted formula that includes forecast growth rates in sectors that contain the economy's 10 most skilled occupational clusters; the prevalence of college degrees in the local workforce; median salary. The area ranked #1 among small metro areas. *Business 2.0 Magazine, March 2004*

- *Forbes* ranked the 200 most populous metro areas in the U.S. in terms of the "Best Places for Business and Careers." The Boulder metro area was ranked #145. Criteria: business costs (labor, energy, tax and office space expenses); living costs (housing, transportation, food and other household expenditures); education levels of the work force; job growth; income growth; migration trends; crime rates; and culture/leisure. *Forbes, April 23, 2007*

- Boulder was selected as a 2006 Digital Cities Survey winner. The city ranked #7 in the small city (75,000 to 124,999 population) category. The survey examined and assessed how city governments are utilizing information technology to operate and deliver quality service to their customers and citizens. Survey questions focused on implementation and adoption of online service delivery; planning and governance; and the infrastructure and architecture that make the transformation to digital government possible. *Center for Digital Government, "2006 Digital Cities Survey"*

Health/Environment Rankings

- Boulder was named the "Top Triathlon Town" by *Inside Triathlon* magazine. With miles of high-altitude running trails and cycling routes, Boulder has been a choice locale for endurance training since the 1960's and now boasts one of the largest and most elite sets of professional single-sport and multisport athletes in the world. *Inside Triathlon, April 2007*

- The Boulder metro area appeared in *Country Home's* "2007 Best Green Places Report". The area ranked #7. Criteria included: air and watershed quality; miles of mass transit; green power; number of farmer's markets, organic producers and groceries. *Country Home, "2007 Best Green Places Report," April 2007*

- Boulder was identified as one of "America's Heart-Healthiest Cities" by *Men's Journal.* The city ranked #4 out of 8. Criteria: easy access to the outdoors; strong park and trail system; clear culture of activity (i.e. outdoor festivals, street fairs, bike racks and local distance races); city should be dense (good walkability), but not big (too stressful). *Men's Journal, "Where You Live is Key," August 2006*

- Boulder was selected as one of "The Top 10 Greenest Cities" in the U.S." Criteria: cities that are obsessed with clean air and clean water, renewable energy, reliable city buses, trams, streetcars and subways, a growing number of parks, greenbelts, farmer's markets, and opportunities for community involvement. *Homestore.com, "The Top 10 Greenest Cities," April 2006*

- Boulder was selected as one of "greenest" cities in the U.S. Criteria: good water- and air-quality; efficient use of resources; renewable energy leadership; accessible and reliable public transportation; green building practices; number of parks and greenbelts; access to locally-grown fresh food through farmers' markets and community supported agriculture groups; and affordability. *The Green Guide Institute, "The Top 10 Green Cities in the U.S.: 2005," April 19, 2005*

- Ortho-McNeil Neurologics, in partnership with Sperling's BestPlaces, analyzed 110 metro areas and identified those U.S. cities with the highest prevalence of factors that are most commonly associated with migraine headaches. The Boulder metro area ranked #63. Criteria: number of migraine-related drug prescriptions per capita; lifestyle factors that can contribute to migraines; environmental factors that can trigger migraines; and consumption of migraine-triggering foods. *Ortho-McNeil Neurologics, "America's Migraine Hot Spots," March 14, 2006*

- Sperling's BestPlaces ranked 331 metro areas and identified the most and least stressful U.S. cities. The Boulder metro area ranked #63 out of 114 mid-size metro areas (#1 = most stressful). Criteria: divorce rate; unemployment rate; violent and property crime; suicide rate; commute time; mental health; alcohol consumption; cloudy days. *www.BestPlaces.net, January 9, 2004*

Women/Minorities Rankings

- Boulder was profiled in the book *50 Fabulous Gay-Friendly Places to Live*. Criteria: an active gay community; positive gay health programs; youth outreach; gay-friendly politics; gay-owned and gay-friendly businesses; employment opportunities; fun nightlife; cultural opportunities; recreational opportunities; housing options. *50 Fabulous Gay-Friendly Places to Live, 2005*

- Boulder was identified as one of the top 25 metropolitan statistical areas ranked by percentage of coupled households that are gay or lesbian." The area ranked #24. *Human Rights Campaign, "Gay and Lesbian Families in the United States: Same-Sex Unmarried Partner Households," August 1, 2001*

Seniors/Retirement Rankings

- Boulder was profiled in the book *Where to Retire: America's Best and Most Affordable Places*. Cities were selected based on personal visits by the author and interviews with local residents coupled with statistics from various government agencies. *Where to Retire: America's Best and Most Affordable Places, 2006*

- Boulder was profiled in the book *Retire in Style: 60 Outstanding Places Across the USA and Canada*. Criteria: landscape; climate; quality of life; cost of living; transportation; retail services; health care; community services; cultural and educational activities; recreational activities; work and volunteer activities; crime rates and public safety. *Retire in Style: 60 Outstanding Places Across the USA and Canada, 2005*

- Boulder was selected as one of the best places to retire by *Fortune*. *Fortune, "Best Places to Retire," June 2006*

- A.G. Edwards ranked America's 500 top-performing communities based on their residents' personal savings and investing behavior. The Boulder metro area ranked #23 with an index score of 113.58 (national average = 100.00). A dozen statistical factors were measured including: participation in retirement savings plans; personal debt levels; and home ownership. *A.G. Edwards, "2006 Nest Egg Index", September 6, 2006*

Children/Family Rankings

- The Boulder metro area was selected as one of the "Best Cities for Relocating Families" by Worldwide ERC and Primacy Relocation. Criteria: tax rates; average home costs and home appreciation; ability to qualify for in-state tuition; service quality of local utilities; per-capita volunteerism; auto taxes; and quantity of fun, family-friendly events and venues. *Worldwide ERC and Primacy Relocation, "2006 Best Cities for Relocating Families"*

Safety Rankings

- Boulder was identified as one of the most dangerous large metro areas for pedestrians in the U.S. The area ranked #29 out of the nations 50 largest metro areas. Criteria: average yearly pedestrian fatalities per capita (for the years 2002 and 2003) adjusted for the number of walkers. *Surface Transportation Policy Project, "Mean Streets 2004"*

Sports/Recreation Rankings

■ Boulder was selected as the "city you dream of living in" by readers of *Backpacker* magazine. *Backpacker, "2nd Annual Readers' Choice Awards," February 2006*

■ Boulder was chosen as one of America's 25 best cities for running. The city was ranked #7. Criteria: number of running clubs per city; amount of land set aside for park usage; air quality; weather; crime rates; and results from a *Runner's World* poll in which readers ranked their favorite running cities. *Runner's World, "The 25 Best Running Cities in America," July 2005*

■ Boulder was selected as one of the "Best Outside Towns." Editors at *Outside Magazine* asked the best adventure athletes in America where they live and why. *Outside Magazine, August 2006*

■ Boulder was selected as one of "10 Great Biking Cities." Editors at the Washington Post asked Adventure Cycling Association, a non-profit bike organization in Montana, and *Bicycling* magazine for their suggestions on the most bike-friendly cities in the country. *Washington Post, October 1, 2006*

■ Boulder was chosen as one of America's best cities for bicycling. The city ranked #1 in the small city category (population 75,000 to 200,000). Criteria: cycling-friendly statistics (number of bike lanes and routes, number of bike racks, city bike projects completed and planned; bike culture (number of bike commuters, popular clubs, cool cycling events, renowned bike shops); climate/geography (the quality of roads and trails for riding, and how frequently mother nature lets riders enjoy them). *Bicycling, March 2006*

■ *Golf Digest* ranked 330 metro areas in the U.S. in terms of golf. The Boulder metro area was ranked #312. Criteria: access to golf; weather; value of golf; and quality of golf. *Golf Digest, "Metro Golf Rankings," August 2005*

Dating/Romance Rankings

■ *Forbes* ranked the 40 most populous metro areas in the U.S. in terms of the "Best Cities for Singles." The Boulder metro area was ranked #1. Criteria: number of singles; cost of living alone; nightlife; culture; job growth; coolness; and online dating. *Forbes.com, July 25, 2006*

Culture/Performing Arts Rankings

■ Boulder was selected as one of America's 10 best large (population 30,000 - 100,000) art towns. The city ranked #6. Criteria: number of art galleries; affordability; natural beauty; local support for the arts; availability of suitable studio and rehearsal space; frequency and impact of art festivals; cohesiveness of the local arts community; diversity of creative statements being made by local visual and performing artists; number of theaters, art schools, art museums, and alternative exhibition and performance venues. *The 100 Best Art Towns in America: A Guide to Galleries, Museums, Festivals, Lodging, and Dining, 4th Edition, 2005*

■ Boulder was selected as one of "America's Top 25 Arts Destinations." The city ranked #10 in the small city (population under 100,000) category. Criteria: readers' top choices for arts travel destinations based on the richness and variety of visual arts sites, activities and events. *American Style, June 2006*

Miscellaneous Rankings

■ Boulder was determined to be one of America's smartest cities. The city ranked #3 in the small city category (50,000 to 100,000 adults 25 years and older). Criteria: the editors rated the collective brainpower of U.S communities based on the educational attainment of its residents. *American City Business Journals, www.bizjournals.com, June 12, 2006*

■ The Boulder metro area appeared on *Forbes* list of "America's Drunkest Cities". The area ranked #15. Criteria: 35 of the largest continental U.S. metro areas were chosen based on availability of data and geographic diversity. Each metro was ranked in five areas: state laws; drinkers; heavy drinkers; binge drinkers; and alcoholism. *Forbes.com, "America's Drunkest Cities," August 22, 2006*

- The Boulder metro area was identified one of "America's Smartest Cities" by *Forbes*. The area ranked #1. Criteria: 200 of the largest U.S. metro areas were ranked based on the percentage of the population age 25 and over with at least a bachelor's degree. *Forbes.com, "America's Smartest Cities," December 15, 2006*

- Boulder appeared on ApartmentRatings.com "Top Cities for Renters List 2006". The area ranked #14 out of 138. Criteria: renter satisfaction; affordability; and vacancy. *ApartmentRatings.com, "Top Cities for Renters List 2006"*

- Boulder was selected as one of "America's Best Vegetarian-Friendly Small Cities." The city was ranked #7. *www.peta.org, April 2006*

- Sperling's BestPlaces in partnership with Pep Boys ranked 77 metro areas and identified "America's Most Drivable Cities." The Boulder metro area ranked #46. Criteria: climate; road roughness; urban mobility; gas prices. *Pep Boys, "America's Most Drivable Cities," April 9, 2003*

- Boulder was selected as a "Great College Town" by ePodunk. The city ranked #4 in the small city category. ePodunk.com looked at communities with four-year colleges and a total student enrollment of at least 1,500. Communities where the student ratio was too low or too high were ruled out, as were small cities with low rates of owner-occupied housing. Fifteen variables were then applied to assess arts and culture, recreation, intellectual activity, historic preservation, and cost of living. *www.ePodunk.com, April, 2002*

Business Environment

CITY FINANCES

City Government Finances

Component	2003-2004 ($000)	2003-2004 ($ per capita)
Total Revenues	195,294	2,074
Total Expenditures	201,964	2,145
Debt Outstanding	199,956	2,123
Cash and Securities	155,962	1,656

Source: U.S Census Bureau, Government Finances 2003-2004

City Government Revenue by Source

Source	2003-2004 ($000)	2003-2004 ($ per capita)
General Revenue		
From Federal Government	0	0
From State Government	22,008	234
From Local Governments	0	0
Taxes		
Property	19,195	204
Sales	81,120	861
Personal Income	0	0
License	0	0
Charges	26,636	283
Liquor Store	0	0
Utility	20,040	213
Employee Retirement	5,730	61
Other	20,565	218

Source: U.S Census Bureau, Government Finances 2003-2004

City Government Expenditures by Function

Function	2003-2004 ($000)	2003-2004 ($ per capita)	2003-2004 (%)
General Expenditures			
Airports	661	7	0.3
Corrections	0	0	0.0
Education	0	0	0.0
Fire Protection	11,149	118	5.5
Governmental Administration	12,997	138	6.4
Health	0	0	0.0
Highways	24,612	261	12.2
Hospitals	0	0	0.0
Housing and Community Development	13,587	144	6.7
Interest on General Debt	8,727	93	4.3
Libraries	6,937	74	3.4
Parking	10,007	106	5.0
Parks and Recreation	22,656	241	11.2
Police Protection	22,635	240	11.2
Public Welfare	0	0	0.0
Sewerage	7,702	82	3.8
Solid Waste Management	0	0	0.0
Liquor Store	0	0	0.0
Utility	27,556	293	13.6
Employee Retirement	3,652	39	1.8
Other	29,086	309	14.4

Source: U.S Census Bureau, Government Finances 2003-2004

Municipal Bond Ratings

Area	Moody's
City	Aaa

Source: Mergent Bond Record, January 2007 (unless noted otherwise)

DEMOGRAPHICS

Population Growth

Area	1990 Census	2000 Census	2006 Estimate	2011 Projection	Population Growth (%) 1990-2000	2000-2011
City	87,737	94,673	92,593	91,744	7.9	-3.1
MSA[1]	208,898	269,758	282,726	294,207	29.1	9.1
U.S.	248,709,873	281,421,906	298,021,266	312,383,955	13.2	11.0

Note: (1) Metropolitan Statistical Area - see Appendix B for areas included
Source: Claritas, Inc.

Number of Households and Average Household Size

Area	2006 Estimate	2006 Average Household Size
City	38,924	2.38
MSA[1]	111,423	2.54
U.S.	112,267,302	2.65

Note: (1) Metropolitan Statistical Area - see Appendix B for areas included
Source: Claritas, Inc.

Race and Ethnicity

Area	White Alone[2]	Black Alone[2]	Asian Alone[2]	Other Race Alone[2]	Hispanic[3]
City	86.6	1.3	4.5	7.5	10.2
MSA[1]	86.2	1.0	3.8	9.1	12.9
U.S.	73.3	12.4	4.2	10.1	14.5

Note: Figures are 2006 estimates; (1) Metropolitan Statistical Area - see Appendix B for areas included
(2) Alone is defined as not being in combination with one or more other races; (3) May be of any race.
Source: Claritas, Inc.

Segregation

City		MSA[1]	
Index[2]	Rank[3]	Index[2]	Rank[4]
34.2	94	36.7	312

Note: Figures are based on an analysis of Census 2000 data; (1) Metropolitan Statistical Area - see Appendix A for areas included; (2) White/Black Dissimilarity Index—the most commonly used measure of segregation between two groups, reflecting their relative distributions across neighborhoods within a city or metropolitan area. It can range in value from 0, indicating complete integration, to 100, indicating complete segregation; (3) Ranges from 1 (most segregated) to 100 (least segregated) and includes all the cities in this book; (4) Ranges from 1 (most segregated) to 318 (least segregated) and includes 318 metropolitan areas.
Source: www.CensusScope.org

Ancestry

Area	German	Irish[2]	English	American	Italian	Polish	French[3]	Scottish
City	20.9	13.9	15.1	2.9	5.6	3.7	3.3	4.2
MSA[1]	24.1	13.9	14.9	4.0	5.3	3.4	3.5	3.9
U.S.	15.2	10.9	8.7	7.3	5.6	3.2	3.0	1.7

Note: Figures include multiple ancestry (e.g. if a person reported being Irish and Italian, they were included in both columns); (1) Metropolitan Statistical Area - see Appendix A for areas included; (2) Includes Celtic; (3) Includes Alsatian but excludes Basque
Source: Census 2000, Summary File 3

Foreign-Born Population

Area	Any Foreign Country	Percent of Population Born in Europe	Asia	Africa	Oceania[2]	Canada	Mexico	Latin America[3]
City	11.5	2.8	3.3	0.4	0.2	0.6	3.5	0.7
MSA[1]	9.4	2.1	2.5	0.2	0.1	0.5	3.5	0.5
U.S.	11.1	1.7	2.9	0.3	0.1	0.3	3.3	2.5

Note: (1) Metropolitan Statistical Area - see Appendix A for areas included; (2) Includes Australia, New Zealand subregion, Melanesia, Micronesia, Polynesia, and Oceania n.e.c; (3) Includes Central America (excluding Mexico), South America, and the Caribbean.
Source: Census 2000, Summary File 3

Marriage Status

Area	Never Married	Now Married (excluding Separated)	Separated	Widowed	Divorced
City	49.1	37.5	1.1	3.5	8.8
MSA[1]	32.9	52.1	1.2	3.7	10.1
U.S.	27.1	54.4	2.2	6.6	9.7

Note: Figures are percentages and cover the population 15 years of age and older;
(1) Metropolitan Statistical Area - see Appendix A for areas included
Source: Census 2000, Summary File 3

Age Distribution

Area	Under Age 5	Age 5 to 17	Age 18 to 34	Age 35 to 49	Age 50 to 64	Age 65 to 79	80 Years and Over
City	3.9	10.7	45.5	20.4	11.5	5.3	2.6
MSA[1]	6.0	16.8	29.5	26.0	13.8	5.7	2.1
U.S.	6.8	18.9	23.7	23.5	14.8	9.2	3.2

Note: (1) Metropolitan Statistical Area - see Appendix A for areas included
Source: Census 2000, Summary File 3

Male/Female Ratio

Area	Males	Females	Males per 100 Females
City	47,872	44,721	107.0
MSA[1]	142,943	139,783	102.3
U.S.	146,712,712	151,308,554	97.0

Note: Figures are 2006 estimates; (1) Metropolitan Statistical Area -
see Appendix B for areas included
Source: Claritas, Inc.

Religion

Area	Catholic	Southern Baptist	United Methodist	ELCA[1]	LDS[2]	Presbyterian Church USA	Jewish Est.	Muslim Est.
County	20.2	1.0	1.8	3.0	1.6	1.8	4.5	1.4
U.S.	22.0	7.1	3.7	1.8	1.5	1.1	2.2	0.6

Note: Figures are the number of adherents as a percentage of the total population; Adherents are defined as all
members, including full members, their children and the estimated number of other participants who are not
considered members (e.g. the baptized, those not confirmed, those regularly attending services, etc.);
(1) Evangelical Lutheran Church in America; (2) The Church of Jesus Christ of Latter Day Saints
Source: Reprinted with permission from Religious Congregations and Membership in the United States 2000
(Nashville, Glenmary Research Center, 2002) Copyright Association of Statisticians of American Religious
Bodies. All rights reserved.

ECONOMY

Gross Metropolitan Product

Area	2002	2003	2004	2005	2005 Rank[2]
MSA[1]	13.3	13.5	14.2	15.2	122

Note: Figures are in billions of dollars; (1) Boulder, CO Metropolitan Statistical Area - see Appendix A for
areas included; (2) Rank ranges from 1 to 361
Source: The U.S. Conference of Mayors, "U.S. Metro Economies: GMP - The Engines of America's Growth,"
January 2007

Economic Growth

Area	1995 GMP	2005 GMP	Average Annual Growth Rate	Growth Rate Rank[2]
MSA[1]	8.0	15.2	6.7	58

Note: Figures are in billions of dollars; GMP = Gross Metropolitan Product; (1) Boulder, CO Metropolitan
Statistical Area - see Appendix A for areas included; (2) Rank ranges from 1 to 361
Source: The U.S. Conference of Mayors, "U.S. Metro Economies: GMP - The Engines of America's Growth,"
January 2007

INCOME

Per Capita/Median/Average Income

Area	Per Capita ($)	Median Household ($)	Average Household ($)
City	30,468	49,778	70,967
MSA[1]	34,342	65,719	86,342
U.S.	25,129	48,775	65,849

Note: Figures are 2006 estimates; (1) Metropolitan Statistical Area - see Appendix B for areas included
Source: Claritas, Inc.

Household Income Distribution

Area	Percent of Households Earning							
	Under $15,000	$15,000 -24,999	$25,000 -34,999	$35,000 -49,999	$50,000 -74,999	$75,000 -99,000	$100,000 -149,999	$150,000 and up
City	14.8	10.5	10.6	14.3	17.0	11.0	12.9	8.9
MSA[1]	9.2	7.5	8.4	13.2	18.6	13.8	16.8	12.4
U.S.	13.3	11.0	11.3	15.7	19.5	11.8	11.0	6.4

Note: Figures are 2006 estimates; (1) Metropolitan Statistical Area - see Appendix B for areas included
Source: Claritas, Inc.

Poverty Rates by Age

Area	All Ages	Under 5 Years Old	5 to 17 Years Old	18 to 64 Years Old	65 Years and Over
City	17.4	0.6	1.2	15.1	0.5
MSA[1]	9.5	0.6	1.3	7.1	0.5
U.S.	12.4	1.2	3.0	6.9	1.2

Note: Figures are percent of population with income in 1999 below poverty level and only include population for whom poverty status is determined; (1) Metropolitan Statistical Area - see Appendix A for areas included
Source: Census 2000, Summary File 3

Personal Bankruptcy Filing Rate

Area	2003	2004	2005
Boulder County	3.66	3.92	6.09
U.S.	5.57	5.31	6.88

Note: Numbers are per 1,000 population and include Chapter 7 and Chapter 13 filings
Source: Federal Deposit Insurance Corporation (FDIC), Regional Economic Conditions (RECON), 3/24/2006

EMPLOYMENT

Labor Force and Employment

Area	Civilian Labor Force			Workers Employed		
	Dec. 2005	Dec. 2006	% Chg.	Dec. 2005	Dec. 2006	% Chg.
City	55,968	57,954	3.5	53,520	55,784	4.2
MSA[1]	168,778	174,907	3.6	162,302	169,166	4.2
U.S.	149,874,000	152,571,000	1.8	142,918,000	146,081,000	2.2

Note: Data is not seasonally adjusted and covers workers 16 years of age and older;
(1) Metropolitan Statistical Area - see Appendix B for areas included
Source: Bureau of Labor Statistics, http://stats.bls.gov

Unemployment Rate

Area	2006											
	Jan.	Feb.	Mar.	Apr.	May	Jun.	Jul.	Aug.	Sep.	Oct.	Nov.	Dec.
City	5.1	4.5	4.5	4.1	4.2	4.7	4.7	4.7	4.2	4.1	3.9	3.7
MSA[1]	4.4	4.0	4.0	3.6	3.7	4.2	4.1	4.1	3.7	3.6	3.4	3.3
U.S.	5.1	5.1	4.8	4.5	4.4	4.8	5.0	4.6	4.4	4.1	4.3	4.3

Note: Data is not seasonally adjusted and covers workers 16 years of age and older; All figures are percentages; (1) Metropolitan Statistical Area - see Appendix B for areas included
Source: Bureau of Labor Statistics, http://stats.bls.gov

Employment by Occupation

Occupation Classification	City (%)	MSA[1] (%)	U.S. (%)
Sales and Office	22.6	23.7	26.7
Professional and Related	38.3	32.3	20.2
Service	14.4	12.1	14.9
Production, Transportation, and Material Moving	5.2	7.6	14.6
Management, Business, and Financial	15.3	17.9	13.5
Construction, Extraction, and Maintenance	4.2	6.3	9.4
Farming, Forestry, and Fishing	0.1	0.2	0.7

Note: Figures cover employed civilians 16 years of age and older;
(1) Metropolitan Statistical Area - see Appendix A for areas included
Source: Census 2000, Summary File 3

Employment by Industry

Sector	MSA[1] Number of Employees	MSA[1] Percent of Total	U.S. Percent of Total
Government	30,900	18.4	16.3
Education and Health Services	18,700	11.1	13.2
Professional and Business Services	30,400	18.1	12.9
Retail Trade	17,600	10.5	11.5
Manufacturing	18,600	11.1	10.2
Leisure and Hospitality	16,800	10.0	9.5
Financial Activities	7,500	4.5	6.1
Construction	n/a	n/a	5.5
Wholesale Trade	5,700	3.4	4.3
Other Services	5,100	3.0	3.9
Transportation and Utilities	1,600	1.0	3.7
Information	9,000	5.3	2.2
Natural Resources and Mining	n/a	n/a	0.5

Note: Figures cover non-farm employment as of December 2006 and are not seasonally adjusted;
(1) Metropolitan Statistical Area - see Appendix B for areas included; n/a not available
Source: Bureau of Labor Statistics, http://stats.bls.gov

Occupations with Greatest Projected Employment Growth: 2002 - 2012

Occupation[1]	2002 Employment	2012 Projected Employment	Numeric Employment Change	Percent Employment Change
Retail Salespersons	84,250	100,890	16,640	19.8
Registered Nurses	30,350	43,380	13,030	42.9
Waiters and Waitresses	45,780	58,380	12,600	27.5
Customer Service Representatives	36,940	48,920	11,980	32.4
Combined Food Preparation and Serving Workers, Including Fast Food	38,320	50,090	11,770	30.7
Cashiers	53,660	64,910	11,250	21.0
Janitors and Cleaners, Except Maids and Housekeeping Cleaners	34,580	45,460	10,880	31.5
Postsecondary Teachers	19,560	29,660	10,100	51.6
Office Clerks, General	60,720	69,590	8,870	14.6
General and Operations Managers	32,920	40,890	7,970	24.2

Note: Projections cover Colorado; (1) Sorted by numeric employment change
Source: www.projectionscentral.com, State Occupational Projections, 2002-2012 Long-Term Projections

Fastest Growing Occupations: 2002 - 2012

Occupation[1]	2002 Employment	2012 Projected Employment	Numeric Employment Change	Percent Employment Change
Network Systems and Data Communications Analysts	4,980	8,280	3,300	66.3
Medical Assistants	5,780	9,440	3,660	63.3
Medical Records and Health Information Technicians	2,250	3,580	1,330	59.1
Pharmacists	3,020	4,780	1,760	58.3
Database Administrators	2,970	4,690	1,720	57.9
Cardiovascular Technologists and Technicians	530	830	300	56.6
Computer Software Engineers, Systems Software	9,470	14,600	5,130	54.2
Environmental Engineers	1,110	1,700	590	53.2
Computer Software Engineers, Applications	14,640	22,270	7,630	52.1
Physician Assistants	1,470	2,230	760	51.7

Note: Projections cover Colorado; (1) Sorted by percent employment change and excludes occupations with numeric employment change less than 250
Source: www.projectionscentral.com, State Occupational Projections, 2002-2012 Long-Term Projections

Average Wages

Occupation	$/Hr.	Occupation	$/Hr.
Accountants and Auditors	29.90	Maids and Housekeeping Cleaners	8.84
Automotive Mechanics	19.91	Maintenance and Repair Workers	16.43
Bookkeepers	16.31	Marketing Managers	48.97
Carpenters	17.87	Nuclear Medicine Technologists	29.91
Cashiers	10.25	Nurses, Licensed Practical	19.29
Clerks, General Office	13.77	Nurses, Registered	27.81
Clerks, Receptionists/Information	12.32	Nursing Aides/Orderlies/Attendants	11.63
Clerks, Shipping/Receiving	13.76	Packers and Packagers, Hand	9.18
Computer Programmers	37.61	Physical Therapists	26.98
Computer Support Specialists	25.72	Postal Service Mail Carriers	21.64
Computer Systems Analysts	n/a	Real Estate Brokers	n/a
Cooks, Restaurant	9.87	Retail Salespersons	12.91
Dentists	n/a	Sales Reps., Exc. Tech./Scientific	31.90
Electrical Engineers	42.90	Sales Reps., Tech./Scientific	43.28
Electricians	22.46	Secretaries, Exc. Legal/Med./Exec.	15.21
Financial Managers	55.55	Security Guards	13.03
First-Line Supervisors/Mgrs., Sales	20.30	Surgeons	n/a
Food Preparation Workers	9.16	Teacher Assistants	11.10
General and Operations Managers	49.90	Teachers, Elementary School	23.40
Hairdressers/Cosmetologists	12.23	Teachers, Secondary School	24.00
Internists	88.90	Telemarketers	13.16
Janitors and Cleaners	11.64	Truck Drivers, Heavy/Tractor-Trailer	16.71
Landscaping/Groundskeeping Workers	11.51	Truck Drivers, Light/Delivery Svcs.	12.99
Lawyers	n/a	Waiters and Waitresses	8.28

Note: Wage data is for May 2005 and covers the Boulder, CO Metropolitan Statistics Area - see Appendix B for areas included. Hourly wages for elementary/secondary school teachers and teacher assistants were calculated by the editors from annual wage data assuming a 40 hour work week; n/a not available.
Source: Bureau of Labor Statistics, May 2005 Metro Area Occupational Employment and Wage Estimates

RESIDENTIAL REAL ESTATE

Building Permits

Area	Single-Family			Multi-Family			Total		
	2005	2006p	Pct. Chg.	2005	2006p	Pct. Chg.	2005	2006p	Pct. Chg.
City	77	55	-28.6	107	124	15.9	184	179	-2.7
U.S.	1,682,000	1,380,000	-18.0	473,300	457,300	-3.4	2,155,300	1,837,300	-14.8

Note: (p) preliminary; figures represent new, privately-owned housing units authorized (unadjusted data); All permit data are based on estimates with imputation; U.S. figures are based on the new 20,000-place series.
Source: U.S. Census Bureau, Manufacturing, Mining, and Construction Statistics

Homeownership and Housing Vacancies

Area	Homeownership Rate[2] (%)			Rental Vacancy Rate[3] (%)			Homeowner Vacancy Rate[4] (%)		
	2004	2005	2006	2004	2005	2006	2004	2005	2006
MSA[1]	n/a	n/a	n/a	n/a	n/a	n/a	n/a	n/a	n/a
U.S.	69.0	68.9	68.8	10.2	9.8	9.7	1.7	1.9	2.4

Note: Comparable 2004 data was not available due to changes in metropolitan area definitions; (1) Metropolitan Statistical Area - see Appendix B for areas included; (2) The proportion of households that are owners; (3) The proportion of the rental inventory that is vacant for rent; (4) The proportion of the homeowner inventory that is vacant for sale; n/a not available
Source: U.S. Census Bureau, Housing Vacancies and Homeownership Annual Statistics: 2006

TAXES

State Corporate Income Tax Rates

State	Rate (%)	Number of Brackets	Low Bracket (Under $)	High Bracket (Over $)
Colorado	4.63	1	na	na

Note: Tax rates as of December 31, 2006; na not applicable
Source: Tax Foundation, www.taxfoundation.org

State Individual Income Tax Rates

State	Federal Deductibility	Marginal Rate (%)	Number of Brackets	Low Bracket (Under $)	High Bracket (Over $)
Colorado	No	4.63 (1)	1	na	na

Note: Tax rates as of December 31, 2006; Brackets apply to single taxpayers and married people filing separately; na not applicable; (1) 4.63% of federal taxable income.
Source: Tax Foundation, www.taxfoundation.org

Various State and Local Tax Rates

State and Local Sales and Use (%)	State Sales and Use (%)	Gasoline ($/gal.)	Cigarette ($/pack)	Spirits ($/gal.)	Table Wine ($/gal.)	Beer ($/gal.)
8.31	2.9	0.22	0.84	2.28	0.32	0.08

Note: Tax rates as of December 31, 2006
Source: Tax Foundation, www.taxfoundation.org; The Sales Tax Clearinghouse, www.thestc.com

State Tax Burdens

Area	Combined State and Local Tax Burden		Combined Federal, State and Local Tax Burden	
	Percent	Rank	Percent	Rank
Colorado	9.8	38	30.7	23
U.S. Average	10.6	-	31.6	-

Note: Figures are for 2006 and measure taxes as a percentage of income
Source: Tax Foundation, www.taxfoundation.org

Internal Revenue Service Tax Audits

IRS District	Percent of Returns Audited				
	1996	1997	1998	1999	2000
Rocky Mountain	0.73	0.67	0.49	0.28	0.20
U.S.	0.66	0.61	0.46	0.31	0.20

Note: Figures cover IRS district audits of federal income tax returns filed by individuals. Geographic data on district audits after the year 2000 are being withheld by the IRS. TRAC is challenging this policy.
Source: Syracuse University, Transactional Records Access Clearinghouse (TRAC), "Odds of IRS District Tax Audit 2000"

COMMERCIAL UTILITIES

Typical Monthly Electric Bills

Area	Commercial Service ($/month)		Industrial Service ($/month)	
	3 kW demand 1,000 kWh	40 kW demand 14,000 kWh	1,000 kW demand 200,000 kWh	50,000 kW demand 15,000,000 kWh
City	87	1,045	19,710	1,131,277
Average[1]	123	1,413	22,000	1,306,315

Note: Based on total rates in effect July 1, 2006; (1) average based on 196 utilities
Source: Edison Electric Institute, Typical Bills and Average Rates Report, Summer 2006

TRANSPORTATION

Means of Transportation to Work

Area	Car/Truck/Van		Public Transportation			Bicycle	Walked	Other Means	Worked at Home
	Drove Alone	Car-pooled	Bus	Subway	Railroad				
City	59.8	8.7	8.3	0.0	0.0	6.9	9.0	0.8	6.5
MSA[1]	70.8	10.4	4.8	0.0	0.0	2.8	4.1	0.7	6.4
U.S.	75.7	12.2	2.5	1.5	0.5	0.4	2.9	1.0	3.3

Note: Figures are percentages and cover workers 16 years of age and older;
(1) Metropolitan Statistical Area - see Appendix A for areas included
Source: Census 2000, Summary File 3

Travel Time to Work

Area	Less Than 15 Minutes	15 to 29 Minutes	30 to 44 Minutes	45 to 59 Minutes	60 Minutes or More
City	45.5	35.1	10.1	4.8	4.5
MSA[1]	34.2	37.9	16.4	6.2	5.2
U.S.	29.4	36.1	19.1	7.4	8.0

Note: Figures are percentages and include workers 16 years old and over; (1) Metropolitan Statistical Area -
see Appendix A for areas included
Source: Census 2000, Summary File 3

Travel Time Index

Area	1982	1993	2002	2003
Urban Area[1]	1.02	1.05	1.09	1.08
Average[2]	1.12	1.28	1.37	1.37

Note: Travel Time Index - The ratio of travel time in the peak period to the travel time at
free-flow conditions. A value of 1.35 indicates a 20-minute free-flow trip takes 27 minutes
in the peak. Free-flow speeds (60 mph on freeways and 35 mph on principal arterials)
are used as the comparison threshold; (1) Covers the Boulder, CO urban area;
(2) average of 85 urban areas
Source: Texas Transportation Institute, The 2005 Urban Mobility Report, May 2005

Public Transportation

Agency name:	Not available

Source: Federal Transit Administration, National Transit Database, 2005

Air Transportation

Airport name and code:	Denver International (40 miles southeast) (DEN)
Domestic service (2006)	
Passenger airlines[1]:	45
Passenger enplanements:	21,864,651
Freight carriers[2]:	30
Freight (lbs.):	259,741,180
International service (2005)	
Passenger airlines[1]:	21
Passenger enplanements:	819,590
Freight carriers[2]:	10
Freight (lbs.):	11,520,105

Note: (1) Includes all major, minor and commuter airlines that carried at least one passenger during the year; (2) Includes all airlines and freight carriers that transported at least one pound of freight during the year
Source: Bureau of Transportation Statistics, The Intermodal Transportation Database, Air Carriers: T-100 International Market, 2004; Bureau of Transportation Statistics, The Intermodal Transportation Database, Air Carriers: T-100 Domestic Market, 2005

Other Transportation Statistics

Interstate highways:	SR-36 connecting to I-25, I-70 and I-76
Amtrak service:	No
Major waterways/ports:	None

Source: Editor & Publisher Market Guide, 2006; Amtrak.com; Rand McNally 2006 Road Atlas

BUSINESSES

Major Business Headquarters

Company Name	2006 Rankings	
	Fortune[1]	Forbes[2]
No companies listed	-	-

Note: (1) Fortune 500 - companies that produce a 10-K are ranked 1 to 500 based on 2005 revenue; (2) Forbes Largest Private Companies - all private companies with at least $1 billion in annual revenue are ranked 1 to 394; companies listed are located in the city; dashes indicate no ranking
Source: Fortune, April 17, 2006; Forbes, November 9, 2006

Best Companies to Work For

Amgen; Qualcomm, headquartered in Boulder, are among the "100 Best Companies to Work For." Criteria: More than 105,000 employees from 446 companies responded to a 57-question survey created by the Great Place to Work Institute. Two-thirds of a company's score is based on the survey, which covers topics such as attitudes towards management, job satisfaction, and camaraderie. The remaining third of the score comes from each company's responses to the Institute's Culture Audit, which includes detailed questions about demographic makeup, pay and benefits programs, and open-ended questions about the company's people-management philosophy, internal communications, opportunities, compensation practices, diversity programs, etc. Any company that is at least seven years old and has a minimum of 1,000 U.S. employees is eligible. The top three U.S. locations are shown for companies with more than one location. *Fortune, "100 Best Companies to Work for 2007," January 22, 2007*

Fast-Growing Businesses

According to *Inc.*, Boulder is home to two of America's 500 fastest-growing private companies: **Booyah Networks; Flatirons Solutions**. Criteria: must be an independent, privately-held, U.S. corporation, proprietorship or partnership; net sales of at least $600,000 in FY2002; four-year operating/sales history; holding companies, regulated banks, and utilities were excluded. *Inc., "America's 500 Fastest-Growing Private Companies," September 2006*

Boulder is home to one of *Business Week's* "Hot Growth Companies:" **Dynamic Materials**. To qualify, a company must have annual sales of more than $50 million and less than $1.5 billion, a current market value greater than $25 million, a current stock price of at least $5, and be actively traded. Banks, insurers, real estate firms, and utilities are excluded. So are companies with declines in current financial results or in stock price, as well as companies where other developments raise questions about future performance. Companies were selected based on three-year results in sales growth, earnings growth, and return on invested capital. *Business Week, June 5, 2006*

According to *Fortune*, Boulder is home to one of America's 100 fastest-growing companies: **Dynamic Materials**. Companies were ranked based on earnings-per-share growth, revenue growth and total return over the previous three years. Criteria for inclusion: public companies with sales of at least $50 million. Companies that lost money in the most recent quarter, or ended in the red for the past four quarters as a whole, were not eligible. Limited partnerships and REITs were also not considered. *Fortune, "America's Fastest-Growing Companies," September 18, 2006*

According to Deloitte & Touche LLP, Boulder is home to one of North America's 500 fastest-growing high-technology companies: **Incentra Solutions**. Companies are ranked by percentage growth in revenue over a five-year period. Criteria for inclusion: company must be headquartered within North America; company must own proprietary intellectual property or proprietary technology that contributes to a significant portion of the company's operating revenue or devotes a significant proportion of revenues to research and development of technology; company must have been in business for a minumum of five years with 2001 operating revenues of at least $50,000 USD or $75,000 CD and 2005 operating revenues of at least $5 million USD/CD. *Deloitte & Touche LLP, 2006 Technology Fast 500*

Women-Owned Businesses: 1997 and 2002

Year	All Firms		Firms with Paid Employees			
	Firms	Sales ($000)	Firms	Sales ($000)	Employees	Payroll ($000)
1997	5,021	504,278	1,100	409,171	6,449	117,084
2002	4,663	486,433	862	376,738	4,772	121,050

Note: Figures cover firms located in the city; Women-owned business are defined as firms in which women own 51% or more of the stock or equity of the company; (a) Withheld to avoid disclosing data for individual companies; (b) Withheld because estimate did not meet publication standards; n/a not available
Source: 1997 Economic Census, Survey of Minority- and Women-Owned Business Enterprises; 2002 Economic Census, Survey of Business Owners (released February 9, 2006)

HOTELS

Hotels/Motels

Area	Hotels/Motels	Average Minimum Rates ($)		
		Tourist	First-Class	Deluxe
City	29	71	90	n/a

Note: n/a not available
Source: OAG Travel Planner Online, Spring 2006

EVENT SITES

Hotels/Conference Centers

Name	Guest Rooms	Exhibit Space (sq. ft.)	Meeting Space (sq. ft.)
Broker Inn	115	4,950	4,950
Hotel Boulderado	160	n/a	8,000
Millenium Harvest House	269	18,150	18,863

Note: n/a not available
Source: www.officialtravelguide.com; www.eventective.com; original research

Living Environment

COST OF LIVING

Cost of Living Index

Year	Composite Index	Groceries	Housing	Utilities	Trans-portation	Health Care	Misc. Goods/ Services
2004	n/a	n/a	n/a	n/a	n/a	n/a	n/a
2005	n/a	n/a	n/a	n/a	n/a	n/a	n/a
2006	n/a	n/a	n/a	n/a	n/a	n/a	n/a

Note: U.S. = 100; n/a not available
Source: The Council for Community and Economic Research (formerly ACCRA), Cost of Living Index, 2004, 2005 and 2006 4-Quarter Averages

HOUSING

House Price Index (HPI)

Area	National Ranking[2]	Quarterly Change (%)	One-Year Change (%)	Five-Year Change (%)
MSA[1]	223	0.14	1.68	15.17
U.S.[3]	-	1.12	5.87	55.21

Note: The HPI is a weighted repeat sales index. It measures average price changes in repeat sales or refinancings on the same properties. This information is obtained by reviewing repeat mortgage transactions on single-family properties whose mortgages have been purchased or securitized by Fannie Mae or Freddie Mac in January 1975; (1) Metropolitan Statistical Area - see Appendix B for areas included; (2) Rankings are based on annual percentage change for all metro areas containing at least 15,000 transactions over the last 10 years and ranges from 1 to 282; (3) figures based on a weighted division average; all figures are for the period ending December 31, 2006
Source: Office of Federal Housing Enterprise Oversight, House Price Index, March 1, 2007

House Price Valuations

Area	Q4 1999	Q4 2000	Q4 2001	Q4 2002	Q4 2003	Q4 2004	Q4 2005	Q4 2006
MSA[1]	-1.7	4.6	13.4	17.3	17.2	13.7	14.6	12.3

Note: Figures show the percentage of over- or under-valuation of single family homes relative to statistically normal house values (e.g. a value of 23.6 indicates that house values are 23.6% overvalued). Statistically normal house values are based on house prices, interest rates, household incomes, population densities, and any historical premiums or discounts metropolitan areas have exhibited over time; (1) Figures cover the Metropolitan Statistical Area - see Appendix B for areas included
Source: Global Insight/National City Corporation, House Prices in America, March 2007

Median Home Prices

Area	2004	2005	2006p	Percent Change 2005 to 2006
Metro Area[1]	325.3	348.4	366.4	5.2
U.S. Average	195.2	219.0	222.0	1.4

Note: Figures are median sales prices of existing single-family homes in thousands of dollars; (p) preliminary; n/a not available; (1) Covers the Boulder, CO Metropolitan Statistical Area - see Appendix B for areas included
Source: National Association of Realtors, Metropolitan Area Prices, 4th Quarter 2006

Housing: Year Structure Built

Area	1990 -2000	1980 -1989	1970 -1979	1960 -1969	1950 -1959	1940 -1949	Before 1940	Median Year
City	12.3	16.9	26.7	21.3	11.7	2.8	8.3	1972
MSA[1]	24.6	17.7	26.4	14.4	7.7	2.5	6.9	1977
U.S.	17.0	15.8	18.5	13.7	12.7	7.3	15.0	1971

Note: Figures are percentages; (1) Metropolitan Statistical Area - see Appendix A for areas included
Source: Census 2000, Summary File 3

Average New Home Price

Area	2004	2005	2006
City	n/a	n/a	n/a
U.S.	253,574	275,712	299,269

Note: n/a not available
Source: The Council for Community and Economic Research (formerly ACCRA), Cost of Living Index, 2004, 2005 and 2006 4-Quarter Averages

Average Apartment Rent

Area	2004	2005	2006
City	n/a	n/a	n/a
U.S.	716	740	766

Note: n/a not available
Source: The Council for Community and Economic Research (formerly ACCRA), Cost of Living Index, 2004, 2005 and 2006 4-Quarter Averages

RESIDENTIAL UTILITIES

Average Residential Utility Costs

Area	All Electric ($/mth)	Part Electric ($/mth)	Other Energy ($/mth)	Phone ($/mth)
City	n/a	n/a	n/a	n/a
U.S.	136.00	76.53	90.52	25.87

Note: n/a not available
Source: The Council for Community and Economic Research (formerly ACCRA), Cost of Living Index, 2006 4-Quarter Average

HEALTH

Average Health Care Costs

Area	Optometrist ($/visit)	Doctor ($/visit)	Dentist ($/visit)
City	n/a	n/a	n/a
U.S.	76.38	76.10	68.72

Note: n/a not available
Source: The Council for Community and Economic Research (formerly ACCRA), Cost of Living Index, 2006 4-Quarter Average

Mortality Rates

ICD-10 Sub-Chapter	ICD-10 Code	Age-Adjusted Death Rate per 100,000 population[1]	U.S. Age-Adjusted Death Rate per 100,000 population
Malignant neoplasms	C00-C97	140.9	185.8
Ischaemic heart diseases	I20-I25	103.7	150.2
Other forms of heart disease	I30-I51	29.1	50.8
Cerebrovascular diseases	I60-I69	46.6	50.0
Chronic lower respiratory diseases	J40-J47	40.9	41.1
Diabetes mellitus	E10-E14	15.9	24.5
Other degenerative diseases of the nervous system	G30-G31	30.1	22.3
Other external causes of accidental injury	W00-X59	34.7	21.2
Influenza and pneumonia	J10-J18	21.7	19.8
Hypertensive diseases	I10-I13	5.6 (Unreliable)	18.1

Note: ICD-10 = International Classification of Diseases 10th Revision; (1) Figures cover Boulder County, CO
Source: Centers for Disease Control and Prevention, National Center for Health Statistics. Compressed Mortality File 1999-2004. CDC WONDER On-line Database, compiled from Compressed Mortality File 1999-2004 Series 20 No. 2J, 2007.

Health Risk Data

Item	Area[1] (%)	U.S. (%)
Adults who have been told they have high blood pressure	n/a	25.5
Adults who have been told they have high blood cholesterol	n/a	35.6
Adults who have been told they have diabetes[2]	n/a	7.3
Adults who have been told they have arthritis	n/a	27.0
Adults who have been told they currently have asthma	n/a	8.0
Adults who are current smokers	n/a	20.6

Note: (1) Figures cover the Metropolitan Statistical Area - see Appendix B for areas included; n/a not available; (2) Figures do not include pregnancy-related diabetes, pre-diabetes or borderline diabetes
Source: Centers for Disease Control and Prevention, Behaviorial Risk Factor Surveillance System, SMART: Selected Metropolitan/Micropolitan Area Trends, 2005

Distribution of Office-Based Physicians

Area	Total	Family/ General Practice	Specialties		
			Medical	Surgical	Other
CMSA[1] (number)	4,996	705	1,775	1,064	1,452
CMSA[1] (rate per 10,000 pop.)	18.7	2.6	6.7	4.0	5.4
Metro Average[2] (rate per 10,000 pop.)	19.4	2.1	7.5	4.5	5.3

Note: Data as of December 31, 2004; (1) Denver-Boulder-Greeley, CO Consolidated Metropolitan Statistical Area includes the following counties: Adams; Arapahoe; Boulder; Denver; Douglas; Jefferson; Weld; (2) Average of the 79 unique MSAs and CMSAs in this book
Source: American Medical Association, Physician Characteristics & Distribution in the U.S., 2006

Hospitals

Boulder has the following hospitals: 1 general medical and surgical.
AHA Guide to the Healthcare Field 2007

EDUCATION

Public School District Statistics

District Name	Schls	Pupils	Pupil/ Teacher Ratio	Minority Pupils[1] (%)	Free Lunch Eligible[2] (%)	IEP[3] (%)
Boulder Valley Re 2	53	27,926	16.7	21.5	11.3	11.8

Note: Table includes regular local school districts with 2,000 or more students; (1) Percentage of students that are not white, non-Hispanic; (2) Percentage of students that are eligible for the free lunch program; (3) Percentage of students that have an Individualized Education Program.
Source: U.S. Department of Education, National Center for Education Statistics, Common Core of Data, Local Education Agency (School District) Universe Survey: School Year 2004-2005; U.S. Department of Education, National Center for Education Statistics, Common Core of Data, Public Elementary/Secondary School Universe Survey: School Year 2004-2005

Top Public High Schools

High School Name	Index[1]	Rank[1]	Subsidized Lunch (%)[2]	E&E (%)[3]
Boulder	2.352	244	6.5	n/a
Fairview	2.355	241	5.0	42.8**

Note: (1) Public schools are ranked according to a ratio that is the number of Advanced Placement and/or International Baccalaureate tests taken by all students at a school in 2005 divided by the number of graduating seniors. All of the schools on the list have an index of at least 1.000; they are in the top five percent of public schools measured this way. The rankings range from 1 to 1,236; (2) Percentage of students receiving federally subsidized meals; (3) E & E stands for equity and excellence percentage: the portion of all graduating seniors at a school that had at least one passing grade on one AP or IB test; (*) Gave just IB tests; (**) Gave both IB and AP tests. AP and IB participation are indicators of a school's efforts to get students to excel and prepare for college; n/a not available
Source: Newsweek Online, May 23, 2006

Educational Quality

School District	Education Quotient[1]	Graduate Outcome[2]	Community Index[3]	Resource Index[4]	Rating[5]
Boulder Valley RE 2	82	79	90	64	Blue

Note: Scores are national percentile rankings and range from 1 (worst) to 99 (best); (1) Combination of the Graduate Outcome, Community and Resource Indexes weighted to reflect the greater importance of the Graduate Outcome and Resource Index; (2) Based on graduation rates and college board scores (SAT/ACT); (3) Based on the surrounding community's level of affluence and adult education; (4) Based on teacher salaries, per-pupil expenditures and student-teacher ratios; (5) School districts receive one of five rankings: Gold Medal (top 16 percent of districts evaluated); Blue Ribbon (top third); Green Light (average); Yellow Light (bottom 25 percent); Red Light (bottom 10 percent).
Source: Expansion Management, "2007 Education Quotient," January 2007

Highest Level of Education

Area	Less than H.S.	H.S. Diploma	Some College, No Deg.	Associate Degree	Bachelors Degree	Masters Degree	Profess. School Degree	Doctorate Degree
City	5.4	8.9	15.5	3.9	36.3	19.4	4.1	6.6
MSA[1]	7.4	14.8	19.4	5.7	31.4	14.2	3.2	4.0
U.S.	19.4	28.4	21.2	6.4	15.7	5.9	2.0	1.0

Note: Figures are 2006 estimated percentages and cover persons age 25 and over; (1) Metropolitan Statistical Area - see Appendix B for areas included
Source: Claritas, Inc.

Educational Attainment by Race

Area	High School Graduate (%)					Bachelor's Degree (%)				
	Total	White	Black	Asian	Hisp.[2]	Total	White	Black	Asian	Hisp.[2]
City	94.7	96.1	92.7	92.1	54.4	66.9	68.1	48.8	78.6	29.3
MSA[1]	92.8	94.6	91.5	90.1	57.6	52.4	53.8	45.0	65.2	18.2
U.S.	80.4	83.6	72.3	80.4	52.4	24.4	26.1	14.3	44.1	10.4

Note: Figures shown cover persons 25 years old and over; (1) Metropolitan Statistical Area - see Appendix A for areas included; (2) people of Hispanic origin can be of any race
Source: Census 2000, Summary File 3

School Enrollment by Type

Area	Grades KG to 8				Grades 9 to 12			
	Public		Private		Public		Private	
	Enrollment	%	Enrollment	%	Enrollment	%	Enrollment	%
City	6,276	88.9	787	11.1	2,815	90.5	296	9.5
MSA[1]	30,621	88.7	3,890	11.3	13,101	92.0	1,146	8.0
U.S.	33,526,011	88.7	4,285,121	11.3	14,848,628	90.6	1,532,323	9.4

Note: Figures shown cover persons 3 years old and over; (1) Metropolitan Statistical Area - see Appendix A for areas included
Source: Census 2000, Summary File 3

School Enrollment by Race

Area	Grades KG to 8 (%)				Grades 9 to 12 (%)			
	White	Black	Asian	Hisp.[1]	White	Black	Asian	Hisp.[1]
City	83.8	1.5	3.1	12.6	85.4	1.5	3.3	10.4
MSA[2]	85.0	0.7	3.0	15.5	87.0	0.8	2.6	12.7
U.S.	68.5	15.5	3.3	16.8	68.8	15.5	3.8	15.7

Note: Figures shown cover persons 3 years old and over; (1) people of Hispanic origin can be of any race; (2) Metropolitan Statistical Area - see Appendix A for areas included
Source: Census 2000, Summary File 3

Average Salaries of Public School Teachers

District	2004-05		2005-06		Percent Change 2004-05 to 2005-06
	Dollars	Rank[1]	Dollars	Rank[1]	
COLORADO	43,949	23	45,616	23	3.79
U.S. Average	47,674	-	49,109	-	3.01

Note: (1) State rank ranges from 1 to 51.
Source: National Education Association, Rankings & Estimates: Rankings of the States 2005 and Estimates of School Statistics 2006, November 2006

Higher Education

Four-Year Colleges			Two-Year Colleges			Medical Schools[1]	Law Schools[2]	Voc/ Tech[3]
Public	Private Non-profit	Private For-profit	Public	Private Non-profit	Private For-profit			
1	2	1	0	1	0	0	1	0

Note: Figures cover institutions located within the city limits; (1) includes schools accredited by the Liaison Committee on Medical Education and the American Osteopathic Association; (2) includes American Bar Association-accredited law schools; (3) includes all schools with programs that are less than 2 years
Source: National Center for Education Statistics, The Integrated Postsecondary Education System (IPEDS) Peer Analysis System, 2006; www.usnews.com, America's Best Graduate Schools 2008, Medical School Directory; www.usnews.com, America's Best Graduate Schools 2008, Law School Directory

PRESIDENTIAL ELECTION

2004 Presidential Election Results

Area	Bush	Kerry	Nader	Other
Boulder County	32.4	66.3	0.6	0.7
U.S.	50.7	48.3	0.4	0.6

Note: Results are percentages and may not add to 100% due to rounding
Source: Dave Leip's Atlas of U.S. Presidential Elections, www.uselectionatlas.org

MAJOR EMPLOYERS

Major Employers

Company Name	Industry	Type of Site
Avista Adventist Hospital	General medical and surgical hospitals	Branch
Ball Corporation	Metal cans	Headquarters
Boulder Community Hospital	Psychiatric hospitals	Headquarters
City Budget Office	Executive offices	Branch
City of Longmont	Executive offices	Headquarters
Corr Logic Inc	Semiconductors and related devices	Single
Design Center	Computer storage devices	Branch
Environmental Research Lab	Administration of general economic programs	Branch
Exempla Good Samaritan Med Ctr	General medical and surgical hospitals	Headquarters
IBM	Computer storage devices	Branch
Key Equipment Finance	Miscellaneous business credit	Single
Longmont United Hospital	General medical and surgical hospitals	Headquarters
Maxtor Corporation (Delaware)	Computer storage devices	Branch
Micro Motion Inc	Fluid meters and counting devices	Headquarters
National Oceanic Atmospheric Admin	Air, water, and solid waste management	Branch
National Telecom Info Admin	Commercial physical research	Branch
Sandoz Inc	Pharmaceutical preparations	Branch
Storagetek	Computer storage devices	Headquarters
Valley Lab	Surgical and medical instruments	Branch
Window Fashions Divisions	Mineral wool	Branch

Note: Companies shown are located within the metropolitan area and have 600 or more employees; nec = not elsewhere classified.
Source: www.zapdata.com, January 2007

PUBLIC SAFETY

Crime Rate

Area	All Crimes	Violent Crimes				Property Crimes		
		Murder	Forcible Rape	Robbery	Aggrav. Assault	Burglary	Larceny -Theft	Motor Vehicle Theft
City	4,108.1	0.0	44.9	36.4	149.8	589.5	3,018.0	269.6
Suburbs[1]	n/a	n/a	n/a	n/a	n/a	n/a	n/a	n/a
Metro[2]	n/a	n/a	n/a	n/a	n/a	n/a	n/a	n/a
U.S.	3,899.0	5.6	31.7	140.7	291.1	726.7	2,286.3	416.7

Note: Figures are crimes per 100,000 population; (1) All areas within the metro area that are located outside the city limits; (2) Metropolitan Statistical Area - see Appendix B for areas included; n/a not available
Source: FBI Uniform Crime Reports, 2005

Hate Crimes

Area	Number of Quarters Reported	Bias Motivation				
		Race	Religion	Sexual Orientation	Ethnicity	Disability
City	4	6	0	4	0	0

Source: Federal Bureau of Investigation, Hate Crime Statistics 2005

RECREATION

Culture

Dance[1]	Theatre[1]	Instrumental Music[1]	Vocal Music[1]	Series/ Festivals	Museums	Zoos
2	3	2	0	9	6	0

Note: (1) number of professional perfoming groups
Source: The Grey House Performing Arts Directory, 2007; Official Museum Directory, 2007

Professional Sports Teams

Major League Baseball	National Basketball Association	National Football League	National Hockey League	Major League Soccer	Women's National Basketball Association
0	0	0	0	0	0

Note: Includes teams located in the Boulder metro area.
Source: www.sportsvenues.com, Listing of Venues by State/Province and City, 2006

MEDIA

Newspapers

Name	Target Audience	Frequency	Circulation
Boulder Weekly	Alternative/General	Non-Daily	25,000
Daily Camera	n/a	Daily	33,249
Dirt	n/a	Daily	10,000

Note: Includes newspapers whose offices are located in the city and whose circulations are 500 or more; n/a not available
Source: BurrellesLuce, MediaContacts Online, January 2006

Television Stations

Name	Ch.	Network(s)	Type	Ownership
KWGN	2	WBN	Commercial	Tribune Broadcasting Company
KCNC	4	CBS	Commercial	CBS Broadcasting Company
KRMA	6	PBS	Public	Rocky Mountain Public Broadcasting Network
KMGH	7	ABC	Commercial	The McGraw-Hill Companies
KACT	8	n/a	Non-comm.	City of Aurora
KUSA	9	NBC	Commercial	Gannett Broadcasting
KBDI	12	PBS	Public	Front Range Educational Media Corp.
KTVJ	14	Univision	Commercial	Roberts Broadcasting Inc.
KTVD	20	UPN	Commercial	Channel 20 TV Company
KDEN	25	n/a	Commercial	Flinn Broadcasting Corporation
KDVR	31	Fox	Commercial	Fox Television Stations Inc.
KRMT	41	n/a	Non-comm.	Word of God Fellowship
KCEC	50	Univision	Commercial	Golden Hills Broadcasting
KWHD	53	n/a	Commercial	LeSea Inc.
KPXC	59	Pax	Commercial	Paxson Communications Corporation
KMAS	63	Telemundo	Commercial	n/a

Note: Stations included cover the Denver DMA (Designated Market Area); n/a not available
BurrellesLuce, MediaContacts Online, January 2006

Major AM Radio Stations

Call Letters	Freq. (kHz)	Station Type	Target Audience	Station Format	Music Format
KLZ	560	n/a	General/Religious	News/Talk	n/a
KIIX	600	Commercial	General	Sports/Talk	n/a
KHOW	630	n/a	General	Music/News/Talk	n/a
KLTT	670	n/a	General/Religious	Talk	n/a
KNUS	710	n/a	General	News/Sports/Talk	n/a
KKZN	760	n/a	General	Sports/Talk	n/a
KOA	850	n/a	General	Music/News/Sports/Talk	n/a
KPOF	910	Non-Comm	General/Religious	Educational/Music	Classical
KLMR	920	n/a	General	Music/News/Sports/Talk	n/a
KOGA	930	n/a	General	n/a	n/a
KKFN	950	n/a	General	Music/Sports/Talk	n/a
KRKS	990	Commercial	General/Religious	News/Talk	n/a
KSIR	1010	Commercial	General	News/Sports/Talk	n/a
KLMO	1060	Commercial	General	Talk	n/a
KMXA	1090	n/a	General/Hispanic	Music/Talk	n/a
KCUV	1150	n/a	General/Hispanic	Sports	n/a
KVCU	1190	College	General	Ed/Music/News/Sports	Urban Contemp.
KLVZ	1220	n/a	General/Religious	Music	n/a
KRAL	1240	Commercial	General	Music/News	Adult Contemp.
KIML	1270	Commercial	General	Music/News/Sports	n/a
KBNO	1280	n/a	Hispanic	Music/News/Talk	n/a
KOWB	1290	n/a	General	News/Talk	n/a
KFKA	1310	Commercial	General	Ed/News/Sports/Talk	n/a
KCOL	1410	Commercial	General	News/Talk	n/a
KRDZ	1440	Commercial	General	Music/News/Sports	Oldies
KADZ	1550	Commercial	Children/Religious	Music/Talk	Adult Contemp.
KCKK	1600	n/a	General	Music	n/a
KBJD	1650	Commercial	General	News/Talk	n/a

Note: Stations included cover the Denver DMA (Designated Market Area); n/a not available
Source: BurrellesLuce, MediaContacts Online, January 2006

Major FM Radio Stations

Call Letters	Freq. (mHz)	Station Type	Target Audience	Station Format	Music Format
KLDV	91.1	Non-Comm	Religious	Music	Christian
KUNC	91.5	n/a	General	Ed/Music/News/Talk	Jazz
KUWR	91.9	College	General	Music/News/Talk	Jazz
KLGT	92.9	n/a	General/Religious	n/a	n/a
KTCL	93.3	n/a	General	Music	n/a
KLMR	93.3	n/a	General	Music/News/Sports	A.O. Rock
KRAI	93.7	Commercial	General	Music/News	Adult Contemp.
KRKS	94.7	Commercial	General/Religious	Music/News/Talk	Christian
KCGY	95.1	n/a	General	Music/Sports	n/a
KFMD	95.7	n/a	General	Music	n/a
KGLL	96.1	Commercial	General	Music	Top 40
KAML	96.9	n/a	General	Music/News/Sports	Classic Rock
KBCO	97.3	Commercial	General	Music/News	Classic Rock
KQSK	97.5	Commercial	General	Music/News	Country
KYGO	98.5	n/a	General	Music	n/a
KSID	98.7	n/a	General	Music/News/Sports	n/a
KUAD	99.1	Commercial	General	Music	Country
KOGA	99.7	n/a	General	Music/News	n/a
KIMN	100.3	n/a	General	n/a	n/a
KGWY	100.7	Commercial	General	Music/News/Sports	Country
KOSI	101.1	n/a	General	Music	n/a
KPNY	102.1	Commercial	General	Music/News	Adult Contemp.
KRFX	103.5	n/a	General	Music/News/Sports	n/a
KJCD	104.3	n/a	General	Music/News/Talk	n/a
KNNG	104.7	Commercial	General	Music/News	Country
KXKL	105.1	n/a	General	Music/News	n/a
KIMX	105.5	n/a	General/Women	Music/News/Sports	n/a
KVAY	105.7	Commercial	General	Music	Oldies
KALC	105.9	Commercial	General	Music	Adult Contemp.
KAAQ	105.9	n/a	General	Music/News/Sports	n/a
KMCX	106.5	Commercial	General	Music/News	Country
KBPI	106.7	n/a	General	Music/News/Talk	n/a
KQKS	107.5	Commercial	General	Music	Urban Contemp.

Note: Stations included cover the Denver DMA (Designated Market Area); n/a not available
BurrellesLuce, MediaContacts Online, January 2006

CLIMATE

Average and Extreme Temperatures

Temperature	Jan	Feb	Mar	Apr	May	Jun	Jul	Aug	Sep	Oct	Nov	Dec	Yr.
Extreme High (°F)	73	76	84	90	93	102	103	100	97	89	79	75	103
Average High (°F)	43	47	52	62	71	81	88	86	77	67	52	45	64
Average Temp. (°F)	30	34	39	48	58	67	73	72	63	52	39	32	51
Average Low (°F)	16	20	25	34	44	53	59	57	48	37	25	18	37
Extreme Low (°F)	-25	-25	-10	-2	22	30	43	41	17	3	-8	-25	-25

Note: Figures cover the years 1948-1992
Source: National Climatic Data Center, International Station Meteorological Climate Summary, 9/96

Average Precipitation/Snowfall/Humidity

Precip./Humidity	Jan	Feb	Mar	Apr	May	Jun	Jul	Aug	Sep	Oct	Nov	Dec	Yr.
Avg. Precip. (in.)	0.6	0.6	1.3	1.7	2.5	1.7	1.9	1.5	1.1	1.0	0.9	0.6	15.5
Avg. Snowfall (in.)	9	7	14	9	2	Tr	0	0	2	4	9	8	63
Avg. Rel. Hum. 5am (%)	62	65	67	66	70	68	67	68	66	63	66	63	66
Avg. Rel. Hum. 5pm (%)	49	44	40	35	38	34	34	34	32	34	47	50	39

Note: Figures cover the years 1948-1992; Tr = Trace amounts (<0.05 in. of rain; <0.5 in. of snow)
Source: National Climatic Data Center, International Station Meteorological Climate Summary, 9/96

Weather Conditions

Temperature			Daytime Sky			Precipitation		
10°F & below	32°F & below	90°F & above	Clear	Partly cloudy	Cloudy	0.01 inch or more precip.	0.1 inch or more snow/ice	Thunder-storms
24	155	33	99	177	89	90	38	39

Note: Figures are average number of days per year and cover the years 1948-1992
Source: National Climatic Data Center, International Station Meteorological Climate Summary, 9/96

HAZARDOUS WASTE

Superfund Sites

Boulder has one hazardous waste site on the EPA's Superfund Final National Priorities List: **Marshall Landfill**. *U.S. Environmental Protection Agency, Final National Priorities List, March 20, 2007*

AIR & WATER QUALITY

Air Quality Index

Area	Percent of Days when Air Quality was...[2]				AQI Statistics	
	Good	Moderate	Unhealthy for Sensitive Groups	Unhealthy	Maximum	Median
MSA[1]	88.8	11.2	0.0	0.0	100	38

Note: The Air Quality Index (AQI) is an index for reporting daily air quality. EPA calculates the AQI for five major air pollutants regulated by the Clean Air Act: ground-level ozone, particle pollution (also known as particulate matter), carbon monoxide, sulfur dioxide, and nitrogen dioxide. The AQI runs from 0 to 500. The higher the AQI value, the greater the level of air pollution and the greater the health concern. There are six AQI categories: "Good" The AQI is between 0 and 50. Air quality is considered satisfactory; "Moderate" The AQI is between 51 and 100. Air quality is acceptable; "Unhealthy for Sensitive Groups" When AQI values are between 101 and 150, members of sensitive groups may experience health effects; "Unhealthy" When AQI values are between 151 and 200 everyone may begin to experience health effects; "Very Unhealthy" AQI values between 201 and 300 trigger a health alert; "Hazardous" AQI values over 300 trigger health warnings of emergency conditions; (1) Metropolitan Statistical Area - see Appendix A for areas included; (2) Based on 365 days with AQI data in 2005.
Source: U.S. Environmental Protection Agency, Air Quality Index Report, 2005

Air Quality Index Pollutants

Area	Percent of Days when AQI Pollutant was...[2]					
	Carbon Monoxide	Nitrogen Dioxide	Ozone	Sulfur Dioxide	Particulate Matter 2.5	Particulate Matter 10
MSA[1]	0.8	0.0	81.6	0.0	17.3	0.3

Note: The Air Quality Index (AQI) is an index for reporting daily air quality. EPA calculates the AQI for five major air pollutants regulated by the Clean Air Act: ground-level ozone, particle pollution (also known as particulate matter), carbon monoxide, sulfur dioxide, and nitrogen dioxide. The AQI runs from 0 to 500. The higher the AQI value, the greater the level of air pollution and the greater the health concern; (1) Metropolitan Statistical Area - see Appendix A for areas included; (2) Based on 365 days with AQI data in 2005.
Source: U.S. Environmental Protection Agency, Air Quality Index Report, 2005

Number of Days with Air Quality Index Values Greater than 100

Area	Trend Sites								All Sites
	1998	1999	2000	2001	2002	2003	2004	2005	2005
MSA[1]	n/a	n/a	n/a	n/a	n/a	n/a	n/a	n/a	n/a

Note: An AQI value greater than 100 indicates that air quality would have been in the unhealthful range on that day. Data from exceptional events are not included. These counts are presented in two ways. First, the counts are based on sites having an adequate record of monitoring data during the trend period (trend sites). These counts represent the relative change in the number of days with AQI values greater than 100. In the last column, the counts are based on all sites with data in the most recent year (because it is possible for a site to have data in the most recent year but not enough data to be a trend site); (1) Metropolitan Statistical Area - see Appendix A for areas included; n/a not available.
Source: U.S. Environmental Protection Agency, Air Trends Fact Book 2005

Maximum Pollutant Concentrations

	Particulate Matter 10 (ug/m^3)	Particulate Matter 2.5 (ug/m^3)	Ozone 1-hour (ppm)	Carbon Monoxide (ppm)	Sulfur Dioxide (ppm)	Nitrogen Dioxide (ppm)	Lead (ug/m^3)
MSA[1] Level	38	18	0.094	2	n/a	n/a	n/a
NAAQS[2]	150	65	0.125	9	0.140	0.053	1.50
Met NAAQS[2]	Yes	Yes	Yes	Yes	n/a	n/a	n/a

Note: Data from exceptional events are not included; (1) Metropolitan Statistical Area - see Appendix A for areas included; (2) National Ambient Air Quality Standards; n/a not available
Units: ppm = parts per million; ug/m^3 = micrograms per cubic meter
Source: U.S. Environmental Protection Agency, Air Trends Fact Book 2005

Watershed Health

The U.S. Environmental Protection Agency monitors the health of the aquatic resources for the nation's 2,000+ watersheds. **The watershed serves the area and received an overall Index of Watershed Indicators (IWI) score of n/a (insufficient data)**. The IWI score is based on seven condition and nine vulnerability indicators. The overall IWI score ranges from 1 (best health) to 6 (worst health). The Condition Indicators include: designated use attainment, fish and wildlife consumption advisories, source water condition, contaminated sediments, ambient water quality, and wetlands loss index. The Vulnerability Indicators include: aquatic species at risk, conventional and toxic loads over permitted limits, urban and agricultural runoff potential, population change, hydrologic modification, estuarine pollution susceptibility, and air deposition. *Note: The IWI is no longer being updated by the U.S. EPA. Source: U.S. Environmental Protection Agency, Index of Watershed Indicators, October 26, 2001*

Drinking Water

Water System Name	Pop. Served	Primary Water Source Type	Number of Violations in 2006[a]		
			Health Based	Significant Monitoring	Monitoring
City of Boulder	168,000	Surface	None	None	None

Note: (a) Based on violation data from January 1, 2006 to December 31, 2006
Source: U.S. Environmental Protection Agency, Office of Ground Water and Drinking Water, Safe Drinking Water Information System (data extracted April 12, 2007)

Boulder tap water is neutral, very soft and fluoridated.
Editor & Publisher Market Guide, 2005

Colorado Springs, Colorado

Background

Colorado Springs is the seat of El Paso County in central Colorado and sits at the foot of Pike's Peak. A dynamic and growing city, its economy is based on high-tech manufacturing, tourism, and sports, with strong employment links to nearby military installations. With such an economic base and gorgeous surroundings, it is no wonder that Colorado Springs ranks as one of the fastest-growing cities in the country.

In 1806, Lieutenant Zebulon Pike visited the site and the mountain that now bears his name, but true settlement did not begin in earnest until gold was discovered in 1859 and miners flooded into the area.

In 1871, General William Jackson Palmer, a railroad tycoon, purchased the site for $10,000 and began promoting the area as a health and recreation resort. Pike's Peak was already well known as a scenic landmark, and very soon the Garden of the Gods, Seven Falls, Cheyenne Mountain, and Manitou Springs were also widely known as spectacular natural sites. The extraordinary nature of the natural environment has long been celebrated, but perhaps the highest testimonial came from Katherine Lee Bates, who, after a trip to Pike's Peak in 1893, wrote "America the Beautiful."

The planned community of Colorado Springs was incorporated in 1876. As a resort, it was wildly successful, hosting the likes of Oscar Wilde and John D. Rockefeller. It became a special favorite of English visitors, one of whom made the claim that there were two "civilized" places between the Atlantic and the Pacific — Chicago and Colorado Springs.

The English were so enamored of the place, in fact, that it came to be called "Little London," as English visitors settled in the area, introducing golf, cricket, polo, and fox hunting; but since there were no local foxes, an artificial scent was spread out for the hounds, or sometimes a coyote was substituted. Several sumptuous hotels were built during this period, as was an elegantly appointed opera house.

In 1891, gold was again discovered, and the city's population tripled to 35,000 in the following decade. Sufficient gold deposits allowed a lucky few to amass considerable fortunes and build huge houses north of the city. However, not all of the newly minted millionaires were inclined toward conspicuous display; Winfield Scott Stratton, "Midas of the Rockies," bruised emerging aesthetic sensibilities by constructing a crude wooden frame house near the business district.

After the 1890s rush ended, Colorado Springs resumed a more measured pace of growth. During and after World War II, though, the town again saw considerable development as Fort Carson and the Peterson Air Force Base were established, followed by the North American Aerospace Defense Command (NORAD) and the U.S. Air Force Academy in the 1950s. Today NORAD is primarily concerned with the tracking of ICBMs, but the military has recently decided to put Cheyenne Mountain's NORAD/NORTHCOM operations on standby and move operations to nearby Peterson Air Force Base. The city's military connection has contributed in large part to the economic base of the area, and to the presence of a highly educated and technically skilled workforce. The city is currently experiencing growth in the service sector and has been identified as one of the nation's top ten fastest growing economies.

The area's major employers include Verizon, Hewlett Packard, Intel, Memorial Hospital, Penrose-St. Francis Health Services, and Carter & Burgess, the consulting company. Military establishments also provide employment.

Colorado Springs is the site of the headquarters of the United States Olympics Committee, which maintains an important Olympic training center there. It is also home to the World Figure Skating Museum and Hall of Fame

The city hosts several institutions of higher learning, including Colorado College (1874), the U.S. Air Force Academy (1954), a campus of the University of Colorado (1965), and Nazarene Bible College (1967). Cultural amenities include the Fine Arts Center and the Colorado Springs Pioneer Museum.

The region enjoys four seasons, with plenty of sunshine — 300 days each year. Rainfall is relatively minimal, but snow can pile up.

Rankings

General Rankings

- Colorado Springs was ranked #18 out of 331 metro areas in *Cities Ranked & Rated*. Criteria: cost of living; climate; crime; transportation; economy and jobs; education; arts and culture; health and healthcare; leisure. *Cities Ranked & Rated, 1st Edition, 2004*

- Colorado Springs was selected as one of "America's Top 100 Places to Live" by Relocate-America.com. Nominations were accepted throughout the year for cities and towns considered to be "great places to live." The nominations, along with key data regarding education, employment, economy, crime, parks, recreation and housing were reviewed, rated and judged by the Relocate-America.com editorial staff. *Relocate-America.com, "Relocate America's Top 100 Places to Live in 2006"*

- Colorado Springs was selected as one of the "Best Places to Live 2006" by *Money* magazine. The city ranked #1 out of 10 in the big city (300,000+ population) category. Places were ranked using 38 quality-of-life indicators and six economic opportunity measures in the following categories: ease of living; health; education; crime; park space; arts and leisure. *Money, "Best Places to Live 2006"*

- The Colorado Springs area was selected as one of "60 Cheap Places to Live" in the U.S. The area appeared in the "Steroid Cities" (fast-growing, business-friendly metro areas) category. *Forbes.com, August 20, 2004*

Business/Finance Rankings

- Colorado Springs was selected as one of the best places to start and grow a company by *Entrepreneur* and the National Policy Research Council. The Colorado Springs metro area ranked #20 out of 63 mid-size metro areas. Criteria: business formation and growth (firms started four to 14 years ago that still employ at least 5 people and experienced rapid growth over the last four years). *Entrepreneur/National Policy Research Council, "Hot Cities for Entrepreneurs," September 2006*

- The Colorado Springs metro area was selected as one of "America's 50 Hottest Cities" for business relocations and expansions. Criteria: industry's most prominent site selection consultants were asked to list their top city choices for relocating and expanding manufacturing companies, taking into consideration such factors as the business climate, work force quality, operating costs, incentive programs, and the ease of working with local political and economic development officials. *Expansion Management, January-February 2007*

- Intel, in partnership with Sperling's BestPlaces, ranked the 80 "Best Cities for Teleworking" in America. The Colorado Springs metro area ranked #2 among small metro areas. The study identifies cities that hold the greatest potential for teleworking based on a host of factors including typical commuting times, fuel prices, availability of broadband Internet access and percentage of the population in telework friendly jobs. The study also factored in extreme climate and natural hazards. *Intel, "Best Cities for Teleworking," March 30, 2006*

- The Colorado Springs metro area appeared on the Milken Institute "2005 Best Performing Cities" index. Rank: #71 out of 200 large metro areas. Criteria: job growth; wage and salary growth; high-tech output growth. *Milken Institute, "2005 Best Performing Cities," February 2006*

- The Colorado Springs metro area was selected as one of "The Best Cities for Doing Business in America." *Inc.* magazine measured employment growth in 393 regions using the following criteria: recent growth trend; mid-term growth; long-term trend; and current year growth. The Colorado Springs metro area ranked #43 among mid-sized metro areas and #187 overall. *Inc., May 2006*

- The Colorado Springs metro area was selected as one of "The Top 10 Boom Villages in America." *Business 2.0* magazine and econometric research firm Global Insight compared 319 metropolitan areas in the U.S. Criteria: a weighted formula that includes forecast growth rates in sectors that contain the economy's 10 most skilled occupational clusters; the prevalence of college degrees in the local workforce; median salary. The area ranked #6 among small metro areas. *Business 2.0 Magazine, March 2004*

- Colorado Springs was identified as one of the 100 "Most Unwired Cities" in the U.S. The area ranked #15 out of the 100 largest metro areas in the U.S. Criteria: number of public and commercial wireless access points (hotspots); airports with wireless Internet access; broadband availability; local wireless networks; and wireless email devices. *Intel, "Most Unwired Cities Survey," June 7, 2005*

- *Forbes* ranked the 200 most populous metro areas in the U.S. in terms of the "Best Places for Business and Careers." The Colorado Springs metro area was ranked #75. Criteria: business costs (labor, energy, tax and office space expenses); living costs (housing, transportation, food and other household expenditures); education levels of the work force; job growth; income growth; migration trends; crime rates; and culture/leisure. *Forbes, April 23, 2007*

- Colorado Springs was selected as a 2006 Digital Cities Survey winner. The city ranked #6 in the large city (250,000 or more population) category. The survey examined and assessed how city governments are utilizing information technology to operate and deliver quality service to their customers and citizens. Survey questions focused on implementation and adoption of online service delivery; planning and governance; and the infrastructure and architecture that make the transformation to digital government possible. *Center for Digital Government, "2006 Digital Cities Survey"*

Health/Environment Rankings

- The Colorado Springs metro area appeared in *Country Home's* "2007 Best Green Places Report". The area ranked #70. Criteria included: air and watershed quality; miles of mass transit; green power; number of farmer's markets, organic producers and groceries. *Country Home, "2007 Best Green Places Report," April 2007*

- The American Podiatric Medical Association and *Prevention* magazine ranked America's 100 most populated cities based on fitness-walker friendliness. The best cities have safe streets, beautiful places to walk, mild weather and good air quality. Colorado Springs ranked #13. *Prevention, "The Best Walking Cities of 2007," April 2007; American Podiatric Medical Association, "2007 Best Fitness-Walking Cities"*

- Colorado Springs was selected as one of the 25 fittest cities in America by *Men's Fitness Online*. It ranked #6 out of America's 50 largest cities. Criteria: gyms/sporting goods; nutrition; exercise/sports; overweight/sedentary; junk food; alcohol; smoking; television; air and water quality; climate; geography; commute time; parks/open space; recreation facilities; health care; motivation; civic legislation and leadership. *Men's Fitness Online, America's Fittest/Fattest Cities 2006*

- Colorado Springs was identified as a "2007 Asthma Capital." The area ranked #95 out of the nation's 100 largest metropolitan areas. Twelve factors were used to identify the most challenging places to live for people with asthma: estimated prevalence; self-reported prevalence; crude death rate for asthma; annual pollen score; annual air quality; public smoking laws; number of board-certified asthma specialists; school inhaler access laws; rescue medication use; controller medication use; uninsured rate; poverty rate. *Asthma and Allergy Foundation of America, "2007 Asthma Capitals"*

- Colorado Springs was identified as a "Spring Allergy Capital." The area ranked #81 out of 100. Three groups of factors were used to identify the most severe cities for people with allergies during the spring season: annual pollen levels; medicine utilization; access to board-certified allergists. *Asthma and Allergy Foundation of America, "2007 Spring Allergy Capital Rankings"*

- Colorado Springs was identified as a "Fall Allergy Capital." The area ranked #92 out of 100. Three groups of factors were used to identify the most severe cities for people with allergies during the fall season: annual pollen levels; medicine utilization; access to board-certified allergists. *Asthma and Allergy Foundation of America, "2006 Fall Allergy Capital Rankings"*

- Colorado Springs was selected as one of "America's Healthiest Cities" by *Natural Health* magazine. The city was ranked #18 out of the 50 largest urban areas in the U.S. Twenty-six criteria in the following four categories were examined: whether the city boasts natural offerings; how well the city promotes its residents' physical health; whether the city offers a healthy environment; how well the city fosters a sense of community. *Natural Health, April 2003*

- *Men's Health* ranked the nation's largest 100 cities in terms of the *Best (and Worst) Cities for Men.* Colorado Springs was ranked #19. Criteria: 24 statistical parameters of long life in the categories of health, quality of life, and fitness. *Men's Health, January/February 2007*

- *Men's Health* ranked 100 U.S. cities in terms of the quality of their tap water. Colorado Springs was ranked #44 and received a grade of C. Criteria: levels of total coliform bacteria, arsenic, lead, total trihalomethanes (linked to cancer), and halo-acetic acids, plus the number of EPA water-system violations from 1995 to 2005. *Men's Health, March 2007*

- Ortho-McNeil Neurologics, in partnership with Sperling's BestPlaces, analyzed 110 metro areas and identified those U.S. cities with the highest prevalence of factors that are most commonly associated with migraine headaches. The Colorado Springs metro area ranked #61. Criteria: number of migraine-related drug prescriptions per capita; lifestyle factors that can contribute to migraines; environmental factors that can trigger migraines; and consumption of migraine-triggering foods. *Ortho-McNeil Neurologics, "America's Migraine Hot Spots," March 14, 2006*

- Sperling's BestPlaces ranked 331 metro areas and identified the most and least stressful U.S. cities. The Colorado Springs metro area ranked #44 out of the 100 largest metro areas (#1 = most stressful). Criteria: divorce rate; unemployment rate; violent and property crime; suicide rate; commute time; mental health; alcohol consumption; cloudy days. *www.BestPlaces.net, January 9, 2004*

- Colorado Springs was highlighted as one of the top 25 cleanest metro areas for long-term particle pollution (PM 2.5) in the U.S. The area ranked #18. *American Lung Association, State of the Air 2006*

- Colorado Springs was highlighted as one of the top 25 cleanest metro areas for ozone air pollution in the U.S. The list represents cities with no monitored ozone air pollution in the unhealthful range. *American Lung Association, State of the Air 2006*

Women/Minorities Rankings

- *Ladies Home Journal* ranked America's 200 largest cities based on the qualities women surveyed care about most. Colorado Springs ranked #8 out of 57 in the big city category (population over 300,000). Criteria: crime; lifestyle; education; jobs; health; child care; politics; and the economy. *Ladies Home Journal Online, "The Best Cities for Women 2002"*

Seniors/Retirement Rankings

- Colorado Springs was profiled in the book *Where to Retire: America's Best and Most Affordable Places.* Cities were selected based on personal visits by the author and interviews with local residents coupled with statistics from various government agencies. *Where to Retire: America's Best and Most Affordable Places, 2006*

- Colorado Springs was profiled in the book *Retire in Style: 60 Outstanding Places Across the USA and Canada.* Criteria: landscape; climate; quality of life; cost of living; transportation; retail services; health care; community services; cultural and educational activities; recreational activities; work and volunteer activities; crime rates and public safety. *Retire in Style: 60 Outstanding Places Across the USA and Canada, 2005*

■ Colorado Springs was selected as one of the best places to retire by *Retirement Places Rated.* Criteria: cost of living; climate; personal safety; services; economy. The city was ranked #47 out of 200. *Retirement Places Rated, 6th Edition, 2004*

■ A.G. Edwards ranked America's 500 top-performing communities based on their residents' personal savings and investing behavior. The Colorado Springs metro area ranked #171 with an index score of 104.26 (national average = 100.00). A dozen statistical factors were measured including: participation in retirement savings plans; personal debt levels; and home ownership. *A.G. Edwards, "2006 Nest Egg Index", September 6, 2006*

Children/Family Rankings

■ The Colorado Springs metro area was selected as one of the "Best Cities for Relocating Families" by Worldwide ERC and Primacy Relocation. Criteria: tax rates; average home costs and home appreciation; ability to qualify for in-state tuition; service quality of local utilities; per-capita volunteerism; auto taxes; and quantity of fun, family-friendly events and venues. *Worldwide ERC and Primacy Relocation, "2006 Best Cities for Relocating Families"*

■ *Zero Population Growth* ranked 100 cities in terms of children's health, safety, and economic well-being. Colorado Springs was ranked #33 out of 80 Large Cities (remainder of the 100 largest cities in the U.S.) and was given a grade of B+. Criteria: total population and population growth; percent of population under 18 years of age; percent of births to teens; infant mortality rate; percent of eligible women not receiving Title X services; contraceptive equity indicator; percent of children without health insurance; percent of city residents over age 25 with a high-school diploma; ration of PopEd (Population Connection's Education Program) teachers trained; sexuality education indicator; proficiency in reading and math; percent of kids living in poverty; percent growth in urbanized land; violent crime rate; recycling. *Population Connection, Kid Friendly Cities: Report Card 2004*

■ *Fit Pregnancy* magazine ranked the 50 best U.S. cities in which to have a baby. Colorado Springs was ranked #9. Criteria: fertility services; maternal and infant health risk; access to hospitals and doctors; safety; affordability; stroller friendliness; and birthing options. *Fit Pregnancy, February/March, 2006*

Safety Rankings

■ Farmers Insurance Group of Companies, in partnership with Sperling's BestPlaces, ranked 331 metro areas and identified the "Most Secure U.S. Place to Live." The Colorado Springs metro area ranked #19 out of the top 20 in the large city category (500,000 or more residents). Criteria: crime rates; risk of natural disasters; and job loss numbers. *Farmers Insurance Group, "25 Most Secure U.S. Place to Live," June 6, 2005*

■ Allstate ranked the 200 largest cities in America in terms of driver safety. Colorado Springs ranked #9. In addition, drivers were 19.0% less likely to have had an accident compared to the national average. Allstate researchers analyzed internal Property Damage reported claims over a two-year period (from January 2003 to December 2004) to ensure the findings would not be affected by external influences such as weather or road construction. A weighted average of the two-year numbers determined the annual percentages. The report defines an auto crash as any collision resulting in a property damage claim. *Allstate, "Allstate America's Best Drivers Report 2006," May 24, 2006*

■ *Ladies Home Journal* ranked America's 200 largest cities in terms of safety. Colorado Springs ranked #81 out of 200. Criteria: violent crimes; crimes against property; and rape. *Ladies Home Journal Online, "The Best Cities for Women 2002"*

Sports/Recreation Rankings

- The Colorado Springs metro area appeared on *The Sporting News* list of the "Best Sports Cities 2006". The area ranked #91 out of 99 cities in North America. To be included in the rankings, a city must have at least one of the following: NCAA Division I basketball team; Class A minor league baseball team; training camp for a major league or NFL team; NASCAR Nextel Cup race; NCAA Division I-A bowl game; PGA Tour tournament; Triple Crown horse race. Once a city qualifies, a 12-month snapshot is taken of the sports atmosphere, putting a heavy premium on regular-season won-lost records; playoff berths, bowl appearances and tournament bids; championships; applicable power ratings; quality of competition; overall fan fervor; sports atmosphere and fan knowledge; abundance of teams (quality over quantity); stadium/arena quality; ticket availability and prices; franchise ownership; and the marquee appeal of athletes. *SportingNews.com, "Best Sports Cities 2006," August 1, 2006*

- Colorado Springs was chosen as one of America's 25 best cities for running. The city was ranked #14. Criteria: number of running clubs per city; amount of land set aside for park usage; air quality; weather; crime rates; and results from a *Runner's World* poll in which readers ranked their favorite running cities. *Runner's World, "The 25 Best Running Cities in America," July 2005*

- *Golf Digest* ranked 330 metro areas in the U.S. in terms of golf. The Colorado Springs metro area was ranked #209. Criteria: access to golf; weather; value of golf; and quality of golf. *Golf Digest, "Metro Golf Rankings," August 2005*

Dating/Romance Rankings

- The Colorado Springs metro area was selected as one of the "Best Cities for Relocating Singles" by Worldwide ERC and Primacy Relocation. The area ranked #73 out of the 100 largest metro areas in the U.S. Areas were selected based on the following criteria: Population Criteria (local percentage and growth trends of unmarried residents aged 25-34; male-female ratios; the number of newcomers to the area; diversity and density); Economic Criteria (job growth vs. unemployment rates; apartment rental costs; fee and occupancy rates for temporary housing and mini-storage; higher education costs, including in-state and out-of-state tuition requirements; vehicle tax rates and quality of service from utility providers); Quality-of-Life Criteria (level of per capita volunteering; quality and quantity of collegiate and professional sports with fun, fan-friendly venues; number of Starbucks and other coffee shops; quality or popularity of restaurants, nightspots, health clubs, and online dating; moderate climates with sustainable water supplies). *Worldwide ERC and Primacy Relocation, "2006 Best Cities for Relocating Singles," October 11, 2006*

- Sperling's BestPlaces in partnership with AXE Deodorant Bodyspray ranked 80 metro areas and identified "America's Best (and Worst) Cities for Dating." The Colorado Springs metro area ranked #2. Criteria: percentage of singles ages 18-24; population density; dating venues per capita. *AXE Deodorant Bodyspray, "America's Best (and Worst) Cities for Dating," May, 2004*

Culture/Performing Arts Rankings

- Colorado Springs was selected as one of "America's Top 25 Arts Destinations." The city ranked #21 in the mid-sized city (population 100,000 to 499,999) category. Criteria: readers' top choices for arts travel destinations based on the richness and variety of visual arts sites, activities and events. *American Style, June 2006*

Miscellaneous Rankings

- Colorado Springs was determined to be one of America's smartest cities. The city ranked #4 in the large city category (200,000+ adults 25 years and older). Criteria: the editors rated the collective brainpower of U.S communities based on the educational attainment of its residents. *American City Business Journals, www.bizjournals.com, June 12, 2006*

- Colorado Springs was selected as one of the "Top 100 Sweatiest Summer Cities". The city was ranked #86. The ranking was based on the average male/female height/weight, average high temperature, and average relative humidity levels for 2002 in each of the cities during June, July and August. The sweat level was analyzed based on the assumption that the individual was walking for one hour. *Procter & Gamble, Old Spice, June 18, 2003*

- Colorado Springs appeared on ApartmentRatings.com "Top Cities for Renters List 2006". The area ranked #16 out of 138. Criteria: renter satisfaction; affordability; and vacancy. *ApartmentRatings.com, "Top Cities for Renters List 2006"*

- Sperling's BestPlaces in partnership with Pep Boys ranked 77 metro areas and identified "America's Most Drivable Cities." The Colorado Springs metro area ranked #43. Criteria: climate; road roughness; urban mobility; gas prices. *Pep Boys, "America's Most Drivable Cities," April 9, 2003*

- Colorado Springs was selected as one of "America's Most Literate Cities." The city ranked #33 out of the 70 largest U.S. cities. Criteria: number of booksellers; library resources; Internet resources; educational attainment; periodical publishing resources; newspaper circulation. *Central Connecticut State University, "America's Most Literate Cities 2006"*

Business Environment

CITY FINANCES

City Government Finances

Component	2003-2004 ($000)	2003-2004 ($ per capita)
Total Revenues	1,207,873	3,254
Total Expenditures	1,323,926	3,567
Debt Outstanding	1,653,281	4,454
Cash and Securities	724,089	1,951

Source: U.S Census Bureau, Government Finances 2003-2004

City Government Revenue by Source

Source	2003-2004 ($000)	2003-2004 ($ per capita)
General Revenue		
From Federal Government	21,365	58
From State Government	18,579	50
From Local Governments	3,013	8
Taxes		
Property	19,982	54
Sales	166,425	448
Personal Income	0	0
License	0	0
Charges	420,668	1,133
Liquor Store	0	0
Utility	471,121	1,269
Employee Retirement	0	0
Other	86,720	234

Source: U.S Census Bureau, Government Finances 2003-2004

City Government Expenditures by Function

Function	2003-2004 ($000)	2003-2004 ($ per capita)	2003-2004 (%)
General Expenditures			
Airports	18,563	50	1.4
Corrections	0	0	0.0
Education	0	0	0.0
Fire Protection	34,797	94	2.6
Governmental Administration	38,678	104	2.9
Health	965	3	0.1
Highways	116,410	314	8.8
Hospitals	360,562	971	27.2
Housing and Community Development	10,612	29	0.8
Interest on General Debt	35,610	96	2.7
Libraries	0	0	0.0
Parking	1,873	5	0.1
Parks and Recreation	21,453	58	1.6
Police Protection	66,431	179	5.0
Public Welfare	0	0	0.0
Sewerage	58,869	159	4.4
Solid Waste Management	0	0	0.0
Liquor Store	0	0	0.0
Utility	513,756	1,384	38.8
Employee Retirement	0	0	0.0
Other	45,347	122	3.4

Source: U.S Census Bureau, Government Finances 2003-2004

Municipal Bond Ratings

Area	Moody's
City	Aaa

Source: Mergent Bond Record, January 2007 (unless noted otherwise)

DEMOGRAPHICS

Population Growth

| Area | 1990 Census | 2000 Census | 2006 Estimate | 2011 Projection | Population Growth (%) | |
					1990-2000	2000-2011
City	283,798	360,890	370,258	378,756	27.2	5.0
MSA[1]	409,482	537,484	584,959	622,060	31.3	15.7
U.S.	248,709,873	281,421,906	298,021,266	312,383,955	13.2	11.0

Note: (1) Metropolitan Statistical Area - see Appendix B for areas included
Source: Claritas, Inc.

Number of Households and Average Household Size

Area	2006 Estimate	2006 Average Household Size
City	145,963	2.54
MSA[1]	218,358	2.68
U.S.	112,267,302	2.65

Note: (1) Metropolitan Statistical Area - see Appendix B for areas included
Source: Claritas, Inc.

Race and Ethnicity

Area	White Alone[2]	Black Alone[2]	Asian Alone[2]	Other Race Alone[2]	Hispanic[3]
City	79.1	6.4	3.1	11.4	13.9
MSA[1]	80.4	6.1	2.6	10.9	12.6
U.S.	73.3	12.4	4.2	10.1	14.5

Note: Figures are 2006 estimates; (1) Metropolitan Statistical Area - see Appendix B for areas included
(2) Alone is defined as not being in combination with one or more other races; (3) May be of any race.
Source: Claritas, Inc.

Segregation

| City | | MSA[1] | |
Index[2]	Rank[3]	Index[2]	Rank[4]
46.1	71	46.5	261

Note: Figures are based on an analysis of Census 2000 data; (1) Metropolitan Statistical Area - see Appendix A for areas included; (2) White/Black Dissimilarity Index—the most commonly used measure of segregation between two groups, reflecting their relative distributions across neighborhoods within a city or metropolitan area. It can range in value from 0, indicating complete integration, to 100, indicating complete segregation; (3) Ranges from 1 (most segregated) to 100 (least segregated) and includes all the cities in this book; (4) Ranges from 1 (most segregated) to 318 (least segregated) and includes 318 metropolitan areas.
Source: www.CensusScope.org

Ancestry

Area	German	Irish[2]	English	American	Italian	Polish	French[3]	Scottish
City	22.0	12.5	12.4	5.5	4.6	2.5	3.4	2.9
MSA[1]	22.4	12.4	12.0	5.9	4.5	2.5	3.4	2.8
U.S.	15.2	10.9	8.7	7.3	5.6	3.2	3.0	1.7

Note: Figures include multiple ancestry (e.g. if a person reported being Irish and Italian, they were included in both columns); (1) Metropolitan Statistical Area - see Appendix A for areas included; (2) Includes Celtic; (3) Includes Alsatian but excludes Basque
Source: Census 2000, Summary File 3

Foreign-Born Population

| Area | Percent of Population Born in | | | | | | | |
	Any Foreign Country	Europe	Asia	Africa	Oceania[2]	Canada	Mexico	Latin America[3]
City	7.0	2.1	2.2	0.1	0.1	0.4	1.5	0.6
MSA[1]	6.4	2.1	2.0	0.1	0.1	0.4	1.3	0.5
U.S.	11.1	1.7	2.9	0.3	0.1	0.3	3.3	2.5

Note: (1) Metropolitan Statistical Area - see Appendix A for areas included; (2) Includes Australia, New Zealand subregion, Melanesia, Micronesia, Polynesia, and Oceania n.e.c; (3) Includes Central America (excluding Mexico), South America, and the Caribbean.
Source: Census 2000, Summary File 3

Marriage Status

Area	Never Married	Now Married (excluding Separated)	Separated	Widowed	Divorced
City	25.0	56.5	1.9	4.9	11.8
MSA[1]	24.6	58.2	1.8	4.4	10.9
U.S.	27.1	54.4	2.2	6.6	9.7

Note: Figures are percentages and cover the population 15 years of age and older;
(1) Metropolitan Statistical Area - see Appendix A for areas included
Source: Census 2000, Summary File 3

Age Distribution

Area	Percent of Population						
	Under Age 5	Age 5 to 17	Age 18 to 34	Age 35 to 49	Age 50 to 64	Age 65 to 79	80 Years and Over
City	7.5	19.0	25.6	24.9	13.5	7.1	2.5
MSA[1]	7.5	19.9	25.5	25.0	13.3	6.6	2.0
U.S.	6.8	18.9	23.7	23.5	14.8	9.2	3.2

Note: (1) Metropolitan Statistical Area - see Appendix A for areas included
Source: Census 2000, Summary File 3

Male/Female Ratio

Area	Males	Females	Males per 100 Females
City	182,715	187,543	97.4
MSA[1]	292,912	292,047	100.3
U.S.	146,712,712	151,308,554	97.0

Note: Figures are 2006 estimates; (1) Metropolitan Statistical Area -
see Appendix B for areas included
Source: Claritas, Inc.

Religion

Area	Catholic	Southern Baptist	United Methodist	ELCA[1]	LDS[2]	Presbyterian Church USA	Jewish Est.	Muslim Est.
County	11.3	4.0	2.0	1.6	2.2	1.7	0.3	0.1
U.S.	22.0	7.1	3.7	1.8	1.5	1.1	2.2	0.6

Note: Figures are the number of adherents as a percentage of the total population; Adherents are defined as all
members, including full members, their children and the estimated number of other participants who are not
considered members (e.g. the baptized, those not confirmed, those regularly attending services, etc.);
(1) Evangelical Lutheran Church in America; (2) The Church of Jesus Christ of Latter Day Saints
Source: Reprinted with permission from Religious Congregations and Membership in the United States 2000
(Nashville, Glenmary Research Center, 2002) Copyright Association of Statisticians of American Religious
Bodies. All rights reserved.

ECONOMY

Gross Metropolitan Product

Area	2002	2003	2004	2005	2005 Rank[2]
MSA[1]	22.0	22.7	24.2	26.1	76

Note: Figures are in billions of dollars; (1) Colorado Springs, CO Metropolitan Statistical Area - see Appendix
A for areas included; (2) Rank ranges from 1 to 361
Source: The U.S. Conference of Mayors, "U.S. Metro Economies: GMP - The Engines of America's Growth,"
January 2007

Economic Growth

Area	1995 GMP	2005 GMP	Average Annual Growth Rate	Growth Rate Rank[2]
MSA[1]	13.4	26.1	6.9	47

Note: Figures are in billions of dollars; GMP = Gross Metropolitan Product; (1) Colorado Springs, CO
Metropolitan Statistical Area - see Appendix A for areas included; (2) Rank ranges from 1 to 361
Source: The U.S. Conference of Mayors, "U.S. Metro Economies: GMP - The Engines of America's Growth,"
January 2007

INCOME

Per Capita/Median/Average Income

Area	Per Capita ($)	Median Household ($)	Average Household ($)
City	26,683	52,833	67,021
MSA[1]	26,471	56,186	69,927
U.S.	25,129	48,775	65,849

Note: Figures are 2006 estimates; (1) Metropolitan Statistical Area - see Appendix B for areas included
Source: Claritas, Inc.

Household Income Distribution

Area	Percent of Households Earning							
	Under $15,000	$15,000 -24,999	$25,000 -34,999	$35,000 -49,999	$50,000 -74,999	$75,000 -99,000	$100,000 -149,999	$150,000 and up
City	9.5	9.9	11.8	16.3	21.7	13.0	11.8	5.9
MSA[1]	8.3	8.9	11.1	16.1	22.5	13.6	13.0	6.4
U.S.	13.3	11.0	11.3	15.7	19.5	11.8	11.0	6.4

Note: Figures are 2006 estimates; (1) Metropolitan Statistical Area - see Appendix B for areas included
Source: Claritas, Inc.

Poverty Rates by Age

Area	All Ages	Under 5 Years Old	5 to 17 Years Old	18 to 64 Years Old	65 Years and Over
City	8.7	0.9	2.1	5.0	0.7
MSA[1]	8.0	0.9	2.0	4.5	0.6
U.S.	12.4	1.2	3.0	6.9	1.2

Note: Figures are percent of population with income in 1999 below poverty level and only include population for whom poverty status is determined; (1) Metropolitan Statistical Area - see Appendix A for areas included
Source: Census 2000, Summary File 3

Personal Bankruptcy Filing Rate

Area	2003	2004	2005
El Paso County	6.63	6.49	9.80
U.S.	5.57	5.31	6.88

Note: Numbers are per 1,000 population and include Chapter 7 and Chapter 13 filings
Source: Federal Deposit Insurance Corporation (FDIC), Regional Economic Conditions (RECON), 3/24/2006

EMPLOYMENT

Labor Force and Employment

Area	Civilian Labor Force			Workers Employed		
	Dec. 2005	Dec. 2006	% Chg.	Dec. 2005	Dec. 2006	% Chg.
City	206,633	213,846	3.5	197,086	204,983	4.0
MSA[1]	300,108	310,498	3.5	285,915	297,371	4.0
U.S.	149,874,000	152,571,000	1.8	142,918,000	146,081,000	2.2

Note: Data is not seasonally adjusted and covers workers 16 years of age and older;
(1) Metropolitan Statistical Area - see Appendix B for areas included
Source: Bureau of Labor Statistics, http://stats.bls.gov

Unemployment Rate

Area	2006											
	Jan.	Feb.	Mar.	Apr.	May	Jun.	Jul.	Aug.	Sep.	Oct.	Nov.	Dec.
City	5.2	4.8	4.8	4.3	4.4	5.0	4.9	5.0	4.5	4.4	4.3	4.1
MSA[1]	5.4	4.9	4.9	4.4	4.5	5.1	5.1	5.1	4.6	4.5	4.3	4.2
U.S.	5.1	5.1	4.8	4.5	4.4	4.8	5.0	4.6	4.4	4.1	4.3	4.3

Note: Data is not seasonally adjusted and covers workers 16 years of age and older; All figures are percentages; (1) Metropolitan Statistical Area - see Appendix B for areas included
Source: Bureau of Labor Statistics, http://stats.bls.gov

Employment by Occupation

Occupation Classification	City (%)	MSA[1] (%)	U.S. (%)
Sales and Office	27.9	27.7	26.7
Professional and Related	24.5	23.4	20.2
Service	14.7	14.5	14.9
Production, Transportation, and Material Moving	10.3	10.7	14.6
Management, Business, and Financial	13.7	13.8	13.5
Construction, Extraction, and Maintenance	8.9	9.8	9.4
Farming, Forestry, and Fishing	0.1	0.1	0.7

Note: Figures cover employed civilians 16 years of age and older;
(1) Metropolitan Statistical Area - see Appendix A for areas included
Source: Census 2000, Summary File 3

Employment by Industry

Sector	MSA[1] Number of Employees	MSA[1] Percent of Total	U.S. Percent of Total
Government	45,100	17.3	16.3
Education and Health Services	26,100	10.0	13.2
Professional and Business Services	40,200	15.4	12.9
Retail Trade	31,000	11.9	11.5
Manufacturing	17,700	6.8	10.2
Leisure and Hospitality	30,600	11.7	9.5
Financial Activities	18,300	7.0	6.1
Construction	n/a	n/a	5.5
Wholesale Trade	5,900	2.3	4.3
Other Services	14,700	5.6	3.9
Transportation and Utilities	5,500	2.1	3.7
Information	8,000	3.1	2.2
Natural Resources and Mining	n/a	n/a	0.5

Note: Figures cover non-farm employment as of December 2006 and are not seasonally adjusted;
(1) Metropolitan Statistical Area - see Appendix B for areas included; n/a not available
Source: Bureau of Labor Statistics, http://stats.bls.gov

Occupations with Greatest Projected Employment Growth: 2002 - 2012

Occupation[1]	2002 Employment	2012 Projected Employment	Numeric Employment Change	Percent Employment Change
Retail Salespersons	84,250	100,890	16,640	19.8
Registered Nurses	30,350	43,380	13,030	42.9
Waiters and Waitresses	45,780	58,380	12,600	27.5
Customer Service Representatives	36,940	48,920	11,980	32.4
Combined Food Preparation and Serving Workers, Including Fast Food	38,320	50,090	11,770	30.7
Cashiers	53,660	64,910	11,250	21.0
Janitors and Cleaners, Except Maids and Housekeeping Cleaners	34,580	45,460	10,880	31.5
Postsecondary Teachers	19,560	29,660	10,100	51.6
Office Clerks, General	60,720	69,590	8,870	14.6
General and Operations Managers	32,920	40,890	7,970	24.2

Note: Projections cover Colorado; (1) Sorted by numeric employment change
Source: www.projectionscentral.com, State Occupational Projections, 2002-2012 Long-Term Projections

Fastest Growing Occupations: 2002 - 2012

Occupation[1]	2002 Employment	2012 Projected Employment	Numeric Employment Change	Percent Employment Change
Network Systems and Data Communications Analysts	4,980	8,280	3,300	66.3
Medical Assistants	5,780	9,440	3,660	63.3
Medical Records and Health Information Technicians	2,250	3,580	1,330	59.1
Pharmacists	3,020	4,780	1,760	58.3
Database Administrators	2,970	4,690	1,720	57.9
Cardiovascular Technologists and Technicians	530	830	300	56.6
Computer Software Engineers, Systems Software	9,470	14,600	5,130	54.2
Environmental Engineers	1,110	1,700	590	53.2
Computer Software Engineers, Applications	14,640	22,270	7,630	52.1
Physician Assistants	1,470	2,230	760	51.7

Note: Projections cover Colorado; (1) Sorted by percent employment change and excludes occupations with numeric employment change less than 250
Source: www.projectionscentral.com, State Occupational Projections, 2002-2012 Long-Term Projections

Average Wages

Occupation	$/Hr.	Occupation	$/Hr.
Accountants and Auditors	25.20	Maids and Housekeeping Cleaners	9.00
Automotive Mechanics	17.11	Maintenance and Repair Workers	15.62
Bookkeepers	14.54	Marketing Managers	45.94
Carpenters	18.25	Nuclear Medicine Technologists	27.79
Cashiers	9.07	Nurses, Licensed Practical	17.32
Clerks, General Office	12.18	Nurses, Registered	25.54
Clerks, Receptionists/Information	11.25	Nursing Aides/Orderlies/Attendants	10.84
Clerks, Shipping/Receiving	12.02	Packers and Packagers, Hand	9.13
Computer Programmers	29.22	Physical Therapists	31.36
Computer Support Specialists	19.84	Postal Service Mail Carriers	21.42
Computer Systems Analysts	33.13	Real Estate Brokers	22.28
Cooks, Restaurant	10.01	Retail Salespersons	12.50
Dentists	n/a	Sales Reps., Exc. Tech./Scientific	23.84
Electrical Engineers	40.00	Sales Reps., Tech./Scientific	34.51
Electricians	20.47	Secretaries, Exc. Legal/Med./Exec.	14.75
Financial Managers	50.19	Security Guards	11.74
First-Line Supervisors/Mgrs., Sales	19.34	Surgeons	91.63
Food Preparation Workers	9.06	Teacher Assistants	10.40
General and Operations Managers	42.69	Teachers, Elementary School	19.30
Hairdressers/Cosmetologists	12.38	Teachers, Secondary School	19.10
Internists	n/a	Telemarketers	n/a
Janitors and Cleaners	11.35	Truck Drivers, Heavy/Tractor-Trailer	17.15
Landscaping/Groundskeeping Workers	10.66	Truck Drivers, Light/Delivery Svcs.	12.61
Lawyers	40.70	Waiters and Waitresses	7.29

Note: Wage data is for May 2005 and covers the Colorado Springs, CO Metropolitan Statistics Area - see Appendix B for areas included. Hourly wages for elementary/secondary school teachers and teacher assistants were calculated by the editors from annual wage data assuming a 40 hour work week; n/a not available.
Source: Bureau of Labor Statistics, May 2005 Metro Area Occupational Employment and Wage Estimates

**RESIDENTIAL
REAL ESTATE**

Building Permits

Area	Single-Family			Multi-Family			Total		
	2005	2006ᵖ	Pct. Chg.	2005	2006ᵖ	Pct. Chg.	2005	2006ᵖ	Pct. Chg.
Co.	6,250	4,129	-33.9	532	295	-44.5	6,782	4,424	-34.8
U.S.	1,682,000	1,380,000	-18.0	473,300	457,300	-3.4	2,155,300	1,837,300	-14.8

Note: (p) preliminary; figures cover El Paso County and represent new, privately-owned housing units authorized (unadjusted data); All permit data are based on estimates with imputation; U.S. figures are based on the new 20,000-place series.
Source: U.S. Census Bureau, Manufacturing, Mining, and Construction Statistics

Homeownership and Housing Vacancies

Area	Homeownership Rate[2] (%)			Rental Vacancy Rate[3] (%)			Homeowner Vacancy Rate[4] (%)		
	2004	2005	2006	2004	2005	2006	2004	2005	2006
MSA[1]	n/a	n/a	n/a	n/a	n/a	n/a	n/a	n/a	n/a
U.S.	69.0	68.9	68.8	10.2	9.8	9.7	1.7	1.9	2.4

Note: Comparable 2004 data was not available due to changes in metropolitan area definitions; (1) Metropolitan Statistical Area - see Appendix B for areas included; (2) The proportion of households that are owners; (3) The proportion of the rental inventory that is vacant for rent; (4) The proportion of the homeowner inventory that is vacant for sale; n/a not available
Source: U.S. Census Bureau, Housing Vacancies and Homeownership Annual Statistics: 2006

TAXES

State Corporate Income Tax Rates

State	Rate (%)	Number of Brackets	Low Bracket (Under $)	High Bracket (Over $)
Colorado	4.63	1	na	na

Note: Tax rates as of December 31, 2006; na not applicable
Source: Tax Foundation, www.taxfoundation.org

State Individual Income Tax Rates

State	Federal Deductibility	Marginal Rate (%)	Number of Brackets	Low Bracket (Under $)	High Bracket (Over $)
Colorado	No	4.63 (1)	1	na	na

Note: Tax rates as of December 31, 2006; Brackets apply to single taxpayers and married people filing separately; na not applicable; (1) 4.63% of federal taxable income.
Source: Tax Foundation, www.taxfoundation.org

Various State and Local Tax Rates

State and Local Sales and Use (%)	State Sales and Use (%)	Gasoline ($/gal.)	Cigarette ($/pack)	Spirits ($/gal.)	Table Wine ($/gal.)	Beer ($/gal.)
7.4	2.9	0.22	0.84	2.28	0.32	0.08

Note: Tax rates as of December 31, 2006
Source: Tax Foundation, www.taxfoundation.org; The Sales Tax Clearinghouse, www.thestc.com

State Tax Burdens

Area	Combined State and Local Tax Burden		Combined Federal, State and Local Tax Burden	
	Percent	Rank	Percent	Rank
Colorado	9.8	38	30.7	23
U.S. Average	10.6	-	31.6	-

Note: Figures are for 2006 and measure taxes as a percentage of income
Source: Tax Foundation, www.taxfoundation.org

Internal Revenue Service Tax Audits

IRS District	Percent of Returns Audited				
	1996	1997	1998	1999	2000
Rocky Mountain	0.73	0.67	0.49	0.28	0.20
U.S.	0.66	0.61	0.46	0.31	0.20

Note: Figures cover IRS district audits of federal income tax returns filed by individuals. Geographic data on district audits after the year 2000 are being withheld by the IRS. TRAC is challenging this policy.
Source: Syracuse University, Transactional Records Access Clearinghouse (TRAC), "Odds of IRS District Tax Audit 2000"

COMMERCIAL UTILITIES

Typical Monthly Electric Bills

Area	Commercial Service ($/month)		Industrial Service ($/month)	
	3 kW demand 1,000 kWh	40 kW demand 14,000 kWh	1,000 kW demand 200,000 kWh	50,000 kW demand 15,000,000 kWh
City	n/a	n/a	n/a	n/a
Average[1]	123	1,413	22,000	1,306,315

Note: Based on total rates in effect July 1, 2006; (1) average based on 196 utilities; n/a not available
Source: Edison Electric Institute, Typical Bills and Average Rates Report, Summer 2006

TRANSPORTATION

Means of Transportation to Work

Area	Car/Truck/Van		Public Transportation			Bicycle	Walked	Other Means	Worked at Home
	Drove Alone	Car-pooled	Bus	Subway	Railroad				
City	79.6	11.7	1.0	0.0	0.0	0.5	2.5	0.9	3.8
MSA[1]	78.0	12.0	0.8	0.0	0.0	0.4	3.7	0.9	4.0
U.S.	75.7	12.2	2.5	1.5	0.5	0.4	2.9	1.0	3.3

Note: Figures are percentages and cover workers 16 years of age and older;
(1) Metropolitan Statistical Area - see Appendix A for areas included
Source: Census 2000, Summary File 3

Travel Time to Work

Area	Less Than 15 Minutes	15 to 29 Minutes	30 to 44 Minutes	45 to 59 Minutes	60 Minutes or More
City	31.4	48.0	13.7	2.8	4.1
MSA[1]	30.4	44.9	16.0	3.9	4.8
U.S.	29.4	36.1	19.1	7.4	8.0

Note: Figures are percentages and include workers 16 years old and over; (1) Metropolitan Statistical Area - see Appendix A for areas included
Source: Census 2000, Summary File 3

Travel Time Index

Area	1982	1993	2002	2003
Urban Area[1]	1.02	1.07	1.21	1.19
Average[2]	1.12	1.28	1.37	1.37

Note: Travel Time Index - The ratio of travel time in the peak period to the travel time at free-flow conditions. A value of 1.35 indicates a 20-minute free-flow trip takes 27 minutes in the peak. Free-flow speeds (60 mph on freeways and 35 mph on principal arterials) are used as the comparison threshold; (1) Covers the Colorado Springs, CO urban area; (2) average of 85 urban areas
Source: Texas Transportation Institute, The 2005 Urban Mobility Report, May 2005

Public Transportation

Agency name:	Colorado Springs Transit System
Vehicle type:	Bus
Average fleet age in years:	7.4
No. operated in max. service:	78
Vehicle type:	Demand response
Average fleet age in years:	1.8
No. operated in max. service:	41

Source: Federal Transit Administration, National Transit Database, 2005

Air Transportation

Airport name and code:	City of Colorado Springs Municipal (COS)
Domestic service (2006)	
Passenger airlines[1]:	25
Passenger enplanements:	993,535
Freight carriers[2]:	14
Freight (lbs.):	11,295,396
International service (2005)	
Passenger airlines[1]:	4
Passenger enplanements:	615
Freight carriers[2]:	1
Freight (lbs.):	251,391

Note: (1) Includes all major, minor and commuter airlines that carried at least one passenger during the year; (2) Includes all airlines and freight carriers that transported at least one pound of freight during the year
Source: Bureau of Transportation Statistics, The Intermodal Transportation Database, Air Carriers: T-100 International Market, 2004; Bureau of Transportation Statistics, The Intermodal Transportation Database, Air Carriers: T-100 Domestic Market, 2005

Other Transportation Statistics

Interstate highways:	I-25
Amtrak service:	Bus connection
Major waterways/ports:	None

Source: Editor & Publisher Market Guide, 2006; Amtrak.com; Rand McNally 2006 Road Atlas

BUSINESSES

Major Business Headquarters

Company Name	2006 Rankings	
	Fortune[1]	Forbes[2]
No companies listed	-	-

Note: (1) Fortune 500 - companies that produce a 10-K are ranked 1 to 500 based on 2005 revenue; (2) Forbes Largest Private Companies - all private companies with at least $1 billion in annual revenue are ranked 1 to 394; companies listed are located in the city; dashes indicate no ranking
Source: Fortune, April 17, 2006; Forbes, November 9, 2006

Best Companies to Work For

Booz Allen Hamilton, headquartered in Colorado Springs, is among the "100 Best Companies to Work For." Criteria: More than 105,000 employees from 446 companies responded to a 57-question survey created by the Great Place to Work Institute. Two-thirds of a company's score is based on the survey, which covers topics such as attitudes towards management, job satisfaction, and camaraderie. The remaining third of the score comes from each company's responses to the Institute's Culture Audit, which includes detailed questions about demographic makeup, pay and benefits programs, and open-ended questions about the company's people-management philosophy, internal communications, opportunities, compensation practices, diversity programs, etc. Any company that is at least seven years old and has a minimum of 1,000 U.S. employees is eligible. The top three U.S. locations are shown for companies with more than one location. *Fortune, "100 Best Companies to Work for 2007," January 22, 2007*

Fast-Growing Businesses

According to *Inc.*, Colorado Springs is home to one of America's 500 fastest-growing private companies: **Intelligent Software Solutions**. Criteria: must be an independent, privately-held, U.S. corporation, proprietorship or partnership; net sales of at least $600,000 in FY2002; four-year operating/sales history; holding companies, regulated banks, and utilities were excluded. *Inc., "America's 500 Fastest-Growing Private Companies," September 2006*

According to Deloitte & Touche LLP, Colorado Springs is home to two of North America's 500 fastest-growing high-technology companies: **Intelligent Software Solutions; Ramtron International Corporation**. Companies are ranked by percentage growth in revenue over a five-year period. Criteria for inclusion: company must be headquartered within North America; company must own proprietary intellectual property or proprietary technology that contributes to a significant portion of the company's operating revenue or devotes a significant proportion of revenues to research and development of technology; company must have been in business for a minumum of five years with 2001 operating revenues of at least $50,000

USD or $75,000 CD and 2005 operating revenues of at least $5 million USD/CD. *Deloitte & Touche LLP, 2006 Technology Fast 500*

Women-Owned Businesses: 1997 and 2002

Year	All Firms		Firms with Paid Employees			
	Firms	Sales ($000)	Firms	Sales ($000)	Employees	Payroll ($000)
1997	9,581	843,782	1,486	704,894	10,633	214,333
2002	10,104	1,182,986	1,804	1,027,877	10,911	264,565

Note: Figures cover firms located in the city; Women-owned business are defined as firms in which women own 51% or more of the stock or equity of the company; (a) Withheld to avoid disclosing data for individual companies; (b) Withheld because estimate did not meet publication standards; n/a not available
Source: 1997 Economic Census, Survey of Minority- and Women-Owned Business Enterprises; 2002 Economic Census, Survey of Business Owners (released February 9, 2006)

Minority Business Opportunity

Three of the 500 largest Hispanic-owned companies in the U.S. are located in Colorado Springs.
Hispanic Business, "Hispanic Business 500," June 2006

Colorado Springs is home to one company which is on the Hispanic Business Fastest-Growing 100 list (greatest sales growth over the past five years): **TORIX General Contractors**. *Hispanic Business, July/August 2006*

HOTELS

Hotels/Motels

Area	Hotels/Motels	Average Minimum Rates ($)		
		Tourist	First-Class	Deluxe
City	90	60	80	325

Source: OAG Travel Planner Online, Spring 2006

The Colorado Springs metro area is home to two of the top 187 hotels in the U.S. according to *Travel & Leisure*: **Cliff House at Pikes Peak** (#19); **The Broadmoor** (#34). Criteria: service; location; rooms; food; and value. *Travel & Leisure, "The T+L 500, 2007"*

EVENT SITES

Hotels/Conference Centers

Name	Guest Rooms	Exhibit Space (sq. ft.)	Meeting Space (sq. ft.)
Antlers Adam's Mark	n/a	n/a	n/a
Doubletree Hotel Colorado Springs	293	10,240	21,000
Sheraton Colorado Springs Hotel	500	42,000	42,000
The Broadmoor	700	33,474	110,000
Wyndham Colorado Springs	311	13,000	13,000

Note: n/a not available
Source: www.officialtravelguide.com; www.eventective.com; original research

Living Environment

COST OF LIVING

Cost of Living Index

Year	Composite Index	Groceries	Housing	Utilities	Trans-portation	Health Care	Misc. Goods/ Services
2004	97.7	104.3	99.6	79.8	103.9	109.5	95.4
2005	95.7	98.4	93.5	91.7	105.3	108.8	93.7
2006	94.6	98.2	87.4	96.6	106.0	107.0	93.8

Note: U.S. = 100
Source: The Council for Community and Economic Research (formerly ACCRA), Cost of Living Index, 2004, 2005 and 2006 4-Quarter Averages

HOUSING

House Price Index (HPI)

Area	National Ranking[2]	Quarterly Change (%)	One-Year Change (%)	Five-Year Change (%)
MSA[1]	153	1.19	4.70	27.95
U.S.[3]	-	1.12	5.87	55.21

Note: The HPI is a weighted repeat sales index. It measures average price changes in repeat sales or refinancings on the same properties. This information is obtained by reviewing repeat mortgage transactions on single-family properties whose mortgages have been purchased or securitized by Fannie Mae or Freddie Mac in January 1975; (1) Metropolitan Statistical Area - see Appendix B for areas included; (2) Rankings are based on annual percentage change for all metro areas containing at least 15,000 transactions over the last 10 years and ranges from 1 to 282; (3) figures based on a weighted division average; all figures are for the period ending December 31, 2006
Source: Office of Federal Housing Enterprise Oversight, House Price Index, March 1, 2007

House Price Valuations

Area	Q4 1999	Q4 2000	Q4 2001	Q4 2002	Q4 2003	Q4 2004	Q4 2005	Q4 2006
MSA[1]	-5.6	-5.2	0.8	5.1	6.9	6.3	10.2	11.0

Note: Figures show the percentage of over- or under-valuation of single family homes relative to statistically normal house values (e.g. a value of 23.6 indicates that house values are 23.6% overvalued). Statistically normal house values are based on house prices, interest rates, household incomes, population densities, and any historical premiums or discounts metropolitan areas have exhibited over time; (1) Figures cover the Metropolitan Statistical Area - see Appendix B for areas included
Source: Global Insight/National City Corporation, House Prices in America, March 2007

Median Home Prices

Area	2004	2005	2006p	Percent Change 2005 to 2006
Metro Area[1]	187.6	205.9	218.2	6.0
U.S. Average	195.2	219.0	222.0	1.4

Note: Figures are median sales prices of existing single-family homes in thousands of dollars; (p) preliminary; n/a not available; (1) Covers the Colorado Springs, CO Metropolitan Statistical Area - see Appendix B for areas included
Source: National Association of Realtors, Metropolitan Area Prices, 4th Quarter 2006

Housing: Year Structure Built

Area	1990 -2000	1980 -1989	1970 -1979	1960 -1969	1950 -1959	1940 -1949	Before 1940	Median Year
City	20.1	22.5	24.3	13.4	9.2	2.8	7.7	1977
MSA[1]	22.0	22.2	23.6	13.1	9.2	2.6	7.2	1978
U.S.	17.0	15.8	18.5	13.7	12.7	7.3	15.0	1971

Note: Figures are percentages; (1) Metropolitan Statistical Area - see Appendix A for areas included
Source: Census 2000, Summary File 3

Average New Home Price

Area	2004	2005	2006
City	250,416	256,129	257,833
U.S.	253,574	275,712	299,269

Note: Figures, in dollars, are based on a new home with 2,400 sq. ft. of living area on an 8,000 sq. ft. lot.
Source: The Council for Community and Economic Research (formerly ACCRA), Cost of Living Index, 2004, 2005 and 2006 4-Quarter Averages

Average Apartment Rent

Area	2004	2005	2006
City	738	726	706
U.S.	716	740	766

Note: Figures, in dollars per month, are based on an unfurnished two bedroom, 1-1/2 or 2 bath apartment, approximately 950 sq. ft. in size, excluding all utilities except water
Source: The Council for Community and Economic Research (formerly ACCRA), Cost of Living Index, 2004, 2005 and 2006 4-Quarter Averages

RESIDENTIAL
UTILITIES

Average Residential Utility Costs

Area	All Electric ($/mth)	Part Electric ($/mth)	Other Energy ($/mth)	Phone ($/mth)
City	–	55.40	80.70	29.35
U.S.	136.00	76.53	90.52	25.87

Source: The Council for Community and Economic Research (formerly ACCRA), Cost of Living Index, 2006 4-Quarter Average

HEALTH

Average Health Care Costs

Area	Optometrist ($/visit)	Doctor ($/visit)	Dentist ($/visit)
City	86.03	83.13	77.98
U.S.	76.38	76.10	68.72

Note: Optometrist—based on a full vision eye exam for an established adult patient;
Doctor—based on a general practitioner's routine exam of an established patient;
Dentist—based on adult teeth cleaning and periodic oral exam.
Source: The Council for Community and Economic Research (formerly ACCRA), Cost of Living Index, 2006 4-Quarter Average

Mortality Rates

ICD-10 Sub-Chapter	ICD-10 Code	Age-Adjusted Death Rate per 100,000 population[1]	U.S. Age-Adjusted Death Rate per 100,000 population
Malignant neoplasms	C00-C97	166.4	185.8
Ischaemic heart diseases	I20-I25	110.3	150.2
Other forms of heart disease	I30-I51	27.4	50.8
Cerebrovascular diseases	I60-I69	57.6	50.0
Chronic lower respiratory diseases	J40-J47	57.6	41.1
Diabetes mellitus	E10-E14	13.2	24.5
Other degenerative diseases of the nervous system	G30-G31	36.1	22.3
Other external causes of accidental injury	W00-X59	19.0	21.2
Influenza and pneumonia	J10-J18	15.4	19.8
Hypertensive diseases	I10-I13	11.3	18.1

Note: ICD-10 = International Classification of Diseases 10th Revision; (1) Figures cover El Paso County, CO
Source: Centers for Disease Control and Prevention, National Center for Health Statistics. Compressed Mortality File 1999-2004. CDC WONDER On-line Database, compiled from Compressed Mortality File 1999-2004 Series 20 No. 2J, 2007.

Health Risk Data

Item	Area[1] (%)	U.S. (%)
Adults who have been told they have high blood pressure	18.5	25.5
Adults who have been told they have high blood cholesterol	31.7	35.6
Adults who have been told they have diabetes[2]	5.6	7.3
Adults who have been told they have arthritis	23.5	27.0
Adults who have been told they currently have asthma	8.8	8.0
Adults who are current smokers	21.2	20.6

Note: (1) Figures cover the Metropolitan Statistical Area - see Appendix B for areas included; (2) Figures do not include pregnancy-related diabetes, pre-diabetes or borderline diabetes
Source: Centers for Disease Control and Prevention, Behaviorial Risk Factor Surveillance System, SMART: Selected Metropolitan/Micropolitan Area Trends, 2005

Distribution of Office-Based Physicians

Area	Total	Family/ General Practice	Specialties		
			Medical	Surgical	Other
MSA[1] (number)	921	108	270	247	296
MSA[1] (rate per 10,000 pop.)	17.1	2.0	5.0	4.6	5.5
Metro Average[2] (rate per 10,000 pop.)	19.4	2.1	7.5	4.5	5.3

Note: Data as of December 31, 2004; (1) Metropolitan Statistical Area - see Appendix A for areas included; (2) Average of the 79 unique MSAs and CMSAs in this book
Source: American Medical Association, Physician Characteristics & Distribution in the U.S., 2006

Hospitals

Colorado Springs has the following hospitals: 2 general medical and surgical; 1 psychiatric; 1 rehabilitation; 1 long-term acute care.
AHA Guide to the Healthcare Field 2007

According to *U.S. News,* the Colorado Springs metro area is home to one of the best hospitals in the U.S.: **Penrose-Saint Francis Health Services**; *U.S. News Online, "America's Best Hospitals 2006"*

EDUCATION

Public School District Statistics

District Name	Schls	Pupils	Pupil/ Teacher Ratio	Minority Pupils[1] (%)	Free Lunch Eligible[2] (%)	IEP[3] (%)
Academy 20	26	19,825	16.5	16.1	3.4	7.6
Cheyenne Mountain 12	9	4,475	18.5	17.6	4.7	4.8
Colorado Springs 11	66	31,420	16.6	34.4	30.1	9.2
Harrison 2	25	10,705	13.9	65.4	48.9	12.5
Widefield 3	17	8,508	17.6	37.9	16.6	13.7

Note: Table includes regular local school districts with 2,000 or more students; (1) Percentage of students that are not white, non-Hispanic; (2) Percentage of students that are eligible for the free lunch program; (3) Percentage of students that have an Individualized Education Program.
Source: U.S. Department of Education, National Center for Education Statistics, Common Core of Data, Local Education Agency (School District) Universe Survey: School Year 2004-2005; U.S. Department of Education, National Center for Education Statistics, Common Core of Data, Public Elementary/Secondary School Universe Survey: School Year 2004-2005

Top Public High Schools

High School Name	Index[1]	Rank[1]	Subsidized Lunch (%)[2]	E&E (%)[3]
Air Academy	1.561	657	3.0	31.9
Cheyenne Mountain	2.155	309	<1.0	35.1
Liberty	1.942	389	n/a	n/a
Rampart	1.676	563	3.7	n/a**

Note: (1) Public schools are ranked according to a ratio that is the number of Advanced Placement and/or International Baccalaureate tests taken by all students at a school in 2005 divided by the number of graduating seniors. All of the schools on the list have an index of at least 1.000; they are in the top five percent of public schools measured this way. The rankings range from 1 to 1,236; (2) Percentage of students receiving federally subsidized meals; (3) E & E stands for equity and excellence percentage: the portion of all graduating seniors at a school that had at least one passing grade on one AP or IB test; (*) Gave just IB tests; (**) Gave both IB and AP tests. AP and IB participation are indicators of a school's efforts to get students to excel and prepare for college; n/a not available
Source: Newsweek Online, May 23, 2006

Educational Quality

School District	Education Quotient[1]	Graduate Outcome[2]	Community Index[3]	Resource Index[4]	Rating[5]
Academy 20	71	68	92	57	Blue

Note: Scores are national percentile rankings and range from 1 (worst) to 99 (best); (1) Combination of the Graduate Outcome, Community and Resource Indexes weighted to reflect the greater importance of the Graduate Outcome and Resource Index; (2) Based on graduation rates and college board scores (SAT/ACT); (3) Based on the surrounding community's level of affluence and adult education; (4) Based on teacher salaries, per-pupil expenditures and student-teacher ratios; (5) School districts receive one of five rankings: Gold Medal (top 16 percent of districts evaluated); Blue Ribbon (top third); Green Light (average); Yellow Light (bottom 25 percent); Red Light (bottom 10 percent).
Source: Expansion Management, "2007 Education Quotient," January 2007

Highest Level of Education

Area	Less than H.S.	H.S. Diploma	Some College, No Deg.	Associate Degree	Bachelors Degree	Masters Degree	Profess. School Degree	Doctorate Degree
City	8.6	21.5	26.3	9.2	21.9	9.5	1.8	1.1
MSA[1]	8.2	22.5	27.4	9.6	20.6	9.1	1.5	1.1
U.S.	19.4	28.4	21.2	6.4	15.7	5.9	2.0	1.0

Note: Figures are 2006 estimated percentages and cover persons age 25 and over; (1) Metropolitan Statistical Area - see Appendix B for areas included
Source: Claritas, Inc.

Educational Attainment by Race

Area	High School Graduate (%)					Bachelor's Degree (%)				
	Total	White	Black	Asian	Hisp.[2]	Total	White	Black	Asian	Hisp.[2]
City	90.9	92.4	90.4	83.2	72.9	33.6	36.0	19.2	38.7	14.1
MSA[1]	91.3	92.5	91.7	82.6	74.5	31.8	34.0	19.0	35.4	14.1
U.S.	80.4	83.6	72.3	80.4	52.4	24.4	26.1	14.3	44.1	10.4

Note: Figures shown cover persons 25 years old and over; (1) Metropolitan Statistical Area - see Appendix A for areas included; (2) people of Hispanic origin can be of any race
Source: Census 2000, Summary File 3

School Enrollment by Type

Area	Grades KG to 8				Grades 9 to 12			
	Public		Private		Public		Private	
	Enrollment	%	Enrollment	%	Enrollment	%	Enrollment	%
City	43,127	89.7	4,978	10.3	18,240	90.6	1,898	9.4
MSA[1]	65,944	90.7	6,787	9.3	27,884	91.4	2,632	8.6
U.S.	33,526,011	88.7	4,285,121	11.3	14,848,628	90.6	1,532,323	9.4

Note: Figures shown cover persons 3 years old and over; (1) Metropolitan Statistical Area - see Appendix A for areas included
Source: Census 2000, Summary File 3

School Enrollment by Race

Area	Grades KG to 8 (%)				Grades 9 to 12 (%)			
	White	Black	Asian	Hisp.[1]	White	Black	Asian	Hisp.[1]
City	76.6	7.4	2.1	14.6	75.7	8.3	3.4	14.1
MSA[2]	77.2	7.0	1.7	14.0	77.5	7.4	2.9	13.4
U.S.	68.5	15.5	3.3	16.8	68.8	15.5	3.8	15.7

*Note: Figures shown cover persons 3 years old and over; (1) people of Hispanic origin can be of any race;
(2) Metropolitan Statistical Area - see Appendix A for areas included
Source: Census 2000, Summary File 3*

Average Salaries of Public School Teachers

District	2004-05		2005-06		Percent Change 2004-05 to 2005-06
	Dollars	Rank[1]	Dollars	Rank[1]	
COLORADO	43,949	23	45,616	23	3.79
U.S. Average	47,674	-	49,109	-	3.01

*Note: (1) State rank ranges from 1 to 51.
Source: National Education Association, Rankings & Estimates: Rankings of the States 2005 and Estimates of
School Statistics 2006, November 2006*

Higher Education

Four-Year Colleges			Two-Year Colleges			Medical Schools[1]	Law Schools[2]	Voc/ Tech[3]
Public	Private Non-profit	Private For-profit	Public	Private Non-profit	Private For-profit			
1	3	6	1	0	5	0	0	2

*Note: Figures cover institutions located within the city limits; (1) includes schools accredited by the Liaison
Committee on Medical Education and the American Osteopathic Association; (2) includes American Bar
Association-accredited law schools; (3) includes all schools with programs that are less than 2 years
Source: National Center for Education Statistics, The Integrated Postsecondary Education System (IPEDS)
Peer Analysis System, 2006; www.usnews.com, America's Best Graduate Schools 2008, Medical School
Directory; www.usnews.com, America's Best Graduate Schools 2008, Law School Directory*

**PRESIDENTIAL
ELECTION**

2004 Presidential Election Results

Area	Bush	Kerry	Nader	Other
El Paso County	66.7	32.1	0.5	0.6
U.S.	50.7	48.3	0.4	0.6

*Note: Results are percentages and may not add to 100% due to rounding
Source: Dave Leip's Atlas of U.S. Presidential Elections, www.uselectionatlas.org*

**MAJOR
EMPLOYERS**

Major Employers

Company Name	Industry	Type of Site
AFMC SSSG/SDCE	National security	Branch
Academy School District 20	Elementary and secondary schools	Headquarters
Agilent Colorado Springs Site	Instruments to measure electricity	Branch
Atmel Corporation	Semiconductors and related devices	Branch
Compassion Int'l	Social services, nec	Single
Current USA Inc	Catalog and mail-order houses	Headquarters
Direct Checks Unlimited Inc	Blankbooks and looseleaf binders	Single
Focus On Family Inc	Individual and family services	Headquarters
HP	Accounting, auditing, and bookkeeping	Branch
HP	Computer rental and leasing	Branch
Ingersoll-Rand	Hardware, nec	Branch
KXRM-TV	Television broadcasting stations	Single
Lockheed Martin	Engineering services	Branch
Memorial Hospital Corporation	General medical and surgical hospitals	Headquarters
Wendys	Eating places	Headquarters

*Note: Companies shown are located within the metropolitan area and have 750 or more employees; nec = not
elsewhere classified.
Source: www.zapdata.com, January 2007*

PUBLIC SAFETY

Crime Rate

Area	All Crimes	Violent Crimes				Property Crimes		
		Murder	Forcible Rape	Robbery	Aggrav. Assault	Burglary	Larceny -Theft	Motor Vehicle Theft
City	5,717.5	3.2	67.0	117.2	291.1	981.6	3,782.3	475.1
Suburbs[1]	2,559.7	2.4	31.5	17.2	424.8	465.3	1,407.8	210.7
Metro[2]	4,583.8	2.9	54.3	81.3	339.1	796.3	2,929.8	380.2
U.S.	3,899.0	5.6	31.7	140.7	291.1	726.7	2,286.3	416.7

Note: Figures are crimes per 100,000 population; (1) All areas within the metro area that are located outside the city limits; (2) Metropolitan Statistical Area - see Appendix B for areas included
Source: FBI Uniform Crime Reports, 2005

Hate Crimes

Area	Number of Quarters Reported	Bias Motivation				
		Race	Religion	Sexual Orientation	Ethnicity	Disability
City	4	7	2	0	1	0

Source: Federal Bureau of Investigation, Hate Crime Statistics 2005

RECREATION

Culture

Dance[1]	Theatre[1]	Instrumental Music[1]	Vocal Music[1]	Series/ Festivals	Museums	Zoos
0	0	1	2	2	11	1

Note: (1) number of professional perfoming groups
Source: The Grey House Performing Arts Directory, 2007; Official Museum Directory, 2007

Professional Sports Teams

Major League Baseball	National Basketball Association	National Football League	National Hockey League	Major League Soccer	Women's National Basketball Association
0	0	0	0	0	0

Note: Includes teams located in the Colorado Springs metro area.
Source: www.sportsvenues.com, Listing of Venues by State/Province and City, 2006

MEDIA

Newspapers

Name	Target Audience	Frequency	Circulation
Black Forest News and Palmer Divide Pioneer	General	Non-Daily	1,000
Colorado Springs Independent	Alternative/General	Non-Daily	30,500
Daily Transcript	n/a	Daily	1,000
The Gazette	n/a	Daily	97,791
Hispania News	Hispanic	Non-Daily	10,000
Mountaineer	General	Non-Daily	15,000
Satellite Flyer	General	Non-Daily	4,500
Space Observer	n/a	Non-Daily	7,500

Note: Includes newspapers whose offices are located in the city and whose circulations are 1,000 or more; n/a not available
Source: BurrellesLuce, MediaContacts Online, January 2006

Television Stations

Name	Ch.	Network(s)	Type	Ownership
KOAA	5	NBC	Commercial	Evening Post Publishing
KTSC	8	PBS	Public	Rocky Mountain Public Broadcasting Network
KKTV	11	CBS	Commercial	Benedek Broadcasting Corporation
KRDO	13	ABC	Commercial	Harry W. Hoth
KXRM	21	Fox/UPN	Commercial	Ray Com Media Inc.

Note: Stations included cover the Colorado Springs-Pueblo DMA (Designated Market Area)
BurrellesLuce, MediaContacts Online, January 2006

Major AM Radio Stations

Call Letters	Freq. (kHz)	Station Type	Target Audience	Station Format	Music Format
KCSJ	590	Commercial	General	News/Sports/Talk	n/a
KRMX	690	n/a	General/Hispanic	Educational/Music/News	n/a
KVOR	740	Commercial	General	News/Talk	n/a
KFEL	970	n/a	Religious	Ed/Music/News/Sports/Talk	n/a
KCBR	1040	n/a	General/Religious	Talk	n/a
KDZA	1080	Commercial	General	Music	Oldies
KRDO	1240	Commercial	General	Talk	n/a
KCRT	1240	Commercial	General	Music	Country
KKML	1300	n/a	General	Music/Sports	n/a
KGHF	1350	Commercial	General	Sports/Talk	n/a
KRLN	1400	Commercial	General	Music/Talk	Oldies
KBLJ	1400	Commercial	General	Music/Sports	Oldies
KKCS	1460	n/a	General	News/Sports/Talk	n/a
KCMN	1530	Commercial	General	Music	Classical
KWYD	1580	n/a	General/Religious	Educational/News/Talk	n/a

Note: Stations included cover the Colorado Springs-Pueblo DMA (Designated Market Area); n/a not available
Source: BurrellesLuce, MediaContacts Online, January 2006

Major FM Radio Stations

Call Letters	Freq. (mHz)	Station Type	Target Audience	Station Format	Music Format
KCME	88.7	Non-Comm	General	Music	Jazz
KTLC	89.1	Non-Comm	General	Educational/Music	Christian
KTSC	89.5	College	General	Music/News/Sports/Talk	A.O. Rock
KEPC	89.7	College	General	Educational/Music	Alternative
KTLF	90.5	Commercial	General/Religious	Educational/Music	Christian
KTHN	92.1	Commercial	General	Music/News/Sports	Country
KCRT	92.5	Commercial	General	Music	Classic Rock
KSPZ	92.9	Commercial	General	Music	Oldies
KILO	93.9	Commercial	General	Music/News	Modern Rock
KRDO	95.1	Commercial	General	Music/News	Adult Contemp.
KCCY	96.9	Commercial	General	Music/News	Country
KKFM	98.1	Commercial	General	Music	Classic Rock
KKMG	98.9	Commercial	General	Music	Top 40
KVUU	99.9	Commercial	General	Music	Adult Contemp.
KGFT	100.7	n/a	General	Educational/Talk	n/a
KKCS	101.9	Commercial	General	Music/News/Talk	Country
KSPK	102.3	n/a	General	Music/Sports	n/a
KSTY	104.5	Commercial	General	Music	Country
KYZX	104.5	Commercial	General	Music/News/Talk	Classic Rock
KSKX	105.5	Commercial	General	Music	Jazz
KNKN	107.1	n/a	General/Hispanic	Music	n/a
KDZA	107.9	Commercial	General	Music/News	Oldies

Note: Stations included cover the Colorado Springs-Pueblo DMA (Designated Market Area); n/a not available
BurrellesLuce, MediaContacts Online, January 2006

CLIMATE

Average and Extreme Temperatures

Temperature	Jan	Feb	Mar	Apr	May	Jun	Jul	Aug	Sep	Oct	Nov	Dec	Yr.
Extreme High (°F)	71	72	78	87	93	99	98	97	94	86	78	75	99
Average High (°F)	41	44	51	61	68	79	85	81	75	63	49	41	62
Average Temp. (°F)	29	32	39	48	55	66	71	69	61	50	37	30	49
Average Low (°F)	17	20	26	34	42	52	57	55	48	36	24	17	36
Extreme Low (°F)	-20	-19	-3	8	22	36	48	39	22	7	-5	-24	-24

Note: Figures cover the years 1948-1993
Source: National Climatic Data Center, International Station Meteorological Climate Summary, 9/96

Average Precipitation/Snowfall/Humidity

Precip./Humidity	Jan	Feb	Mar	Apr	May	Jun	Jul	Aug	Sep	Oct	Nov	Dec	Yr.
Avg. Precip. (in.)	0.3	0.4	1.3	1.3	2.6	2.1	2.6	3.4	1.0	0.9	0.6	0.5	17.0
Avg. Snowfall (in.)	6	6	10	5	2	0	0	0	Tr	3	7	8	48
Avg. Rel. Hum. 5am (%)	57	60	62	62	69	67	66	71	66	59	60	59	63
Avg. Rel. Hum. 5pm (%)	48	43	39	34	39	36	36	43	36	36	45	52	41

Note: Figures cover the years 1948-1993; Tr = Trace amounts (<0.05 in. of rain; <0.5 in. of snow)
Source: National Climatic Data Center, International Station Meteorological Climate Summary, 9/96

Weather Conditions

Temperature			Daytime Sky			Precipitation		
10°F & below	32°F & below	90°F & above	Clear	Partly cloudy	Cloudy	0.01 inch or more precip.	0.1 inch or more snow/ice	Thunder-storms
21	161	18	108	157	100	98	33	49

Note: Figures are average number of days per year and cover the years 1948-1993
Source: National Climatic Data Center, International Station Meteorological Climate Summary, 9/96

HAZARDOUS WASTE

Superfund Sites

Colorado Springs has no sites on the EPA's Superfund Final National Priorities List.
U.S. Environmental Protection Agency, Final National Priorities List, March 20, 2007

AIR & WATER QUALITY

Air Quality Index

Area	Percent of Days when Air Quality was...[2]				AQI Statistics	
	Good	Moderate	Unhealthy for Sensitive Groups	Unhealthy	Maximum	Median
MSA[1]	90.1	9.6	0.3	0.0	104	38

Note: The Air Quality Index (AQI) is an index for reporting daily air quality. EPA calculates the AQI for five major air pollutants regulated by the Clean Air Act: ground-level ozone, particle pollution (also known as particulate matter), carbon monoxide, sulfur dioxide, and nitrogen dioxide. The AQI runs from 0 to 500. The higher the AQI value, the greater the level of air pollution and the greater the health concern. There are six AQI categories: "Good" The AQI is between 0 and 50. Air quality is considered satisfactory; "Moderate" The AQI is between 51 and 100. Air quality is acceptable; "Unhealthy for Sensitive Groups" When AQI values are between 101 and 150, members of sensitive groups may experience health effects; "Unhealthy" When AQI values are between 151 and 200 everyone may begin to experience health effects; "Very Unhealthy" AQI values between 201 and 300 trigger a health alert; "Hazardous" AQI values over 300 trigger health warnings of emergency conditions; (1) Metropolitan Statistical Area - see Appendix A for areas included; (2) Based on 365 days with AQI data in 2005.
Source: U.S. Environmental Protection Agency, Air Quality Index Report, 2005

Air Quality Index Pollutants

Area	Percent of Days when AQI Pollutant was...[2]					
	Carbon Monoxide	Nitrogen Dioxide	Ozone	Sulfur Dioxide	Particulate Matter 2.5	Particulate Matter 10
MSA[1]	1.6	0.0	91.0	0.0	4.7	2.7

Note: The Air Quality Index (AQI) is an index for reporting daily air quality. EPA calculates the AQI for five major air pollutants regulated by the Clean Air Act: ground-level ozone, particle pollution (also known as particulate matter), carbon monoxide, sulfur dioxide, and nitrogen dioxide. The AQI runs from 0 to 500. The higher the AQI value, the greater the level of air pollution and the greater the health concern; (1) Metropolitan Statistical Area - see Appendix A for areas included; (2) Based on 365 days with AQI data in 2005.
Source: U.S. Environmental Protection Agency, Air Quality Index Report, 2005

Number of Days with Air Quality Index Values Greater than 100

Area	Trend Sites								All Sites
	1998	1999	2000	2001	2002	2003	2004	2005	2005
MSA[1]	n/a	n/a	n/a	n/a	n/a	n/a	n/a	n/a	n/a

Note: An AQI value greater than 100 indicates that air quality would have been in the unhealthful range on that day. Data from exceptional events are not included. These counts are presented in two ways. First, the counts are based on sites having an adequate record of monitoring data during the trend period (trend sites). These counts represent the relative change in the number of days with AQI values greater than 100. In the last column, the counts are based on all sites with data in the most recent year (because it is possible for a site to have data in the most recent year but not enough data to be a trend site); (1) Metropolitan Statistical Area - see Appendix A for areas included; n/a not available.
Source: U.S. Environmental Protection Agency, Air Trends Fact Book 2005

Maximum Pollutant Concentrations

	Particulate Matter 10 (ug/m^3)	Particulate Matter 2.5 (ug/m^3)	Ozone 1-hour (ppm)	Carbon Monoxide (ppm)	Sulfur Dioxide (ppm)	Nitrogen Dioxide (ppm)	Lead (ug/m^3)
MSA[1] Level	74	17	0.098	3	n/a	n/a	0.09
NAAQS[2]	150	65	0.125	9	0.140	0.053	1.50
Met NAAQS[2]	Yes	Yes	Yes	Yes	n/a	n/a	Yes

Note: Data from exceptional events are not included; (1) Metropolitan Statistical Area - see Appendix A for areas included; (2) National Ambient Air Quality Standards; n/a not available
Units: ppm = parts per million; ug/m^3 = micrograms per cubic meter
Source: U.S. Environmental Protection Agency, Air Trends Fact Book 2005

Watershed Health

The U.S. Environmental Protection Agency monitors the health of the aquatic resources for the nation's 2,000+ watersheds. **The Fountain watershed serves the Colorado Springs area and received an overall Index of Watershed Indicators (IWI) score of 1 (better quality - low vulnerability).** The IWI score is based on seven condition and nine vulnerability indicators. The overall IWI score ranges from 1 (best health) to 6 (worst health). The Condition Indicators include: designated use attainment, fish and wildlife consumption advisories, source water condition, contaminated sediments, ambient water quality, and wetlands loss index. The Vulnerability Indicators include: aquatic species at risk, conventional and toxic loads over permitted limits, urban and agricultural runoff potential, population change, hydrologic modification, estuarine pollution susceptibility, and air deposition. *Note: The IWI is no longer being updated by the U.S. EPA. Source: U.S. Environmental Protection Agency, Index of Watershed Indicators, October 26, 2001*

Drinking Water

Water System Name	Pop. Served	Primary Water Source Type	Number of Violations in 2006[a]		
			Health Based	Significant Monitoring	Monitoring
Colorado Springs Utilities	422,094	Surface	None	None	1

Note: (a) Based on violation data from January 1, 2006 to December 31, 2006
Source: U.S. Environmental Protection Agency, Office of Ground Water and Drinking Water, Safe Drinking Water Information System (data extracted April 12, 2007)

Colorado Springs tap water is from watershed on Pikes Peak and Continental Divide. It's pure, filtered and fluoridated.
Editor & Publisher Market Guide, 2005

Denver, Colorado

Background

From almost anywhere in Denver, you can command a breathtaking view of the 14,000-foot Rocky Mountains. However, the early settlers of Denver were not attracted to the city because of its vistas; they were there in search of gold.

In 1858, there were rumors that gold had been discovered in Cherry Creek, one of the waterways on which Denver stands. Although prospectors came and went without much luck, later it was discovered that there really was gold, and silver as well. By 1867, Denver had been established.

Today, Denver, with its sparkling, dramatic skyline of glass and steel towers, bears little resemblance to the dusty frontier village of the nineteenth century. With an excellent location, the "Mile High City" has become a manufacturing, distribution, and transportation center that serves not only the western regions of the United States, but the entire nation. Denver is also home to many companies that are engaged in alternative fuel research and development.

The massively renovated Colorado Convention Center — now 584,000 square feet — is a magnet for regional and national conferences and shows, and its attractions are multiplied by the nearby location of a new 1,100 room Hyatt Regency Hotel. A master plan to renovate and expand the historic Denver Union Station is underway, which will operate as a mixed-use retail and multi-modal transportation hub.

The city is also home to a lively cultural, recreational, and educational scene. There are concerts at the Boettcher Concert Hall of the Denver Center for the Performing Arts, seasonal drives through the Denver Mountain Park Circle Drive, and skiing and hiking the Rockies just 90 minutes away. Other area attractions include the Denver Museum of Nature and Science, the Colorado History Museum, and the Denver Art Museum, which increased its exhibition space in 2006 with a dramatic new building designed by Daniel Libeskin. Opposite the museum, a new condominium complex, Museum Residences, also by Libeskind, recently opened it sales office.

Another architecturally interesting building is the terminal at Denver's airport, the largest international hub in the United States. The unique roof is made of heat- and light-reflecting tension fabric. The airport is huge, with 53 square miles and 6 million square feet of public space and more than 100 gates.

The city has developed a 12-year, $4.7 billion public transportation expansion plan for the Denver-Aurora and Boulder Metropolitan Areas, developed by the Regional Transportation District. The plan calls for six light rail and diesel commuter rail lines with a combined length of 119 miles to be opened between 2013 and 2016.

The city also has its share of offbeat, distinctive places to have fun including the hip Capitol Hill district, which offers small music venues and dank bars that appeal to University of Denver students. Sports fans have the Colorado Avalanche hockey team, the Denver Nuggets basketball team, the Colorado Rockies baseball team, and the Denver Broncos football team. The city also has the Six Flags Elitch Gardens amusement park.

The Denver Zoo is open year-round and houses nearly 4,000 animals representing 700 species, including the okapi, red-bellied lemur, Amur leopard, black rhino, and Siberian tiger. In recent years, the zoo has been implementing features of a master modernization plan of habitats. Most recently was the completion of Predator Ridge, home to 14 African species of mammals, birds and reptiles, and an indoor tropical rain forest.

The University of Denver, Community College of Denver, Metropolitan State College, and the University of Colorado at Denver are only a few of the many excellent educational opportunities available in the city.

Denver's invigorating climate matches much of the central Rocky Mountain region, without the frigidly cold mornings of the higher elevations during winter, or the hot afternoons of summer at lower altitudes. Extreme cold and heat are generally short-lived. Low relative humidity, light precipitation, and abundant sunshine characterize Denver's weather. Spring is the cloudiest, wettest, and windiest season, while autumn is the most pleasant. Air pollution, known locally as the "brown cloud," which the city has spent decades combating, continues to be a problem.

Rankings

GeneralRankings

■ Denver was ranked #60 out of 331 metro areas in *Cities Ranked & Rated*. Criteria: cost of living; climate; crime; transportation; economy and jobs; education; arts and culture; health and healthcare; leisure. *Cities Ranked & Rated, 1st Edition, 2004*

■ Denver was selected as one of the top places to live in the U.S. according to Harris Interactive. The city ranked #7 out of 10. Criteria: 3,685 U.S. adults were polled as to where they would choose to live if they could live anywhere in the country. *Harris Interactive, September 6, 2006*

■ Denver was selected as one of "America's Best Places to Live" by monstermoving.com. The top 10 cities were selected based on the fact that they appear repeatedly on other publications' "Top Cities" lists. *www.monstermoving.com, February 26, 2004*

■ Denver was selected as one of the "50 Best Places to Live" by *Men's Journal*. The city ranked #3 in the "Best Downtowns" category. These city centers were selected based on the fact that you can enjoy all the amenities of urban living, find a range of great housing options, and still get your fix of active puruits. *Men's Journal, April 2007*

■ Denver was selected as one of "60 Cheap Places to Live" in the U.S. The city appeared in the "Bohemian Bargains" (lively inner cities) category. *Forbes.com, August 20, 2004*

■ Denver was selected as one of "America's 30 Most Livable Communities" by the non-profit group, Partners for Livable Communities. Criteria: environmental quality; parkland; ability to train new workers; job market; education; and use of the arts for economic development. *Partners for Livable Communities, www.mostlivable.org, April 20, 2004*

Business/Finance Rankings

■ Denver was selected as one of the best places to start and grow a company by *Entrepreneur* and the National Policy Research Council. The Denver metro area ranked #19 out of 50 large metro areas. Criteria: business formation and growth (firms started four to 14 years ago that still employ at least 5 people and experienced rapid growth over the last four years). *Entrepreneur/National Policy Research Council, "Hot Cities for Entrepreneurs," September 2006*

■ The Denver metro area was selected as one of "America's 50 Hottest Cities" for business relocations and expansions. Criteria: industry's most prominent site selection consultants were asked to list their top city choices for relocating and expanding manufacturing companies, taking into consideration such factors as the business climate, work force quality, operating costs, incentive programs, and the ease of working with local political and economic development officials. *Expansion Management, January-February 2007*

■ The Denver metro area was selected as one of the "Top 40 Real Estate Markets" for expanding or relocating businesses. The area ranked #35 out of 40. Criteria: rental costs; purchase prices; and vacancy rates of office and warehouse space. *Expansion Management, October 2006*

■ Intel, in partnership with Sperling's BestPlaces, ranked the 80 "Best Cities for Teleworking" in America. The Denver metro area ranked #3 among large metro areas. The study identifies cities that hold the greatest potential for teleworking based on a host of factors including typical commuting times, fuel prices, availability of broadband Internet access and percentage of the population in telework friendly jobs. The study also factored in extreme climate and natural hazards. *Intel, "Best Cities for Teleworking," March 30, 2006*

■ The Denver metro area appeared on the Milken Institute "2005 Best Performing Cities" index. Rank: #105 out of 200 large metro areas. Criteria: job growth; wage and salary growth; high-tech output growth. *Milken Institute, "2005 Best Performing Cities," February 2006*

■ The Denver metro area was selected as one of "The Best Cities for Doing Business in America." *Inc.* magazine measured employment growth in 393 regions using the following criteria: recent growth trend; mid-term growth; long-term trend; and current year growth. The Denver metro area ranked #37 among large metro areas and #231 overall. *Inc., May 2006*

- The Denver metro area was selected as one of "The Top 20 Boom Towns in America." *Business 2.0* magazine and econometric research firm Global Insight compared 319 metropolitan areas in the U.S. and ranked the 61 with populations over 1 million. Criteria: a weighted formula that includes forecast growth rates in sectors that contain the economy's 10 most skilled occupational clusters; the prevalence of college degrees in the local workforce; median salary. The area ranked #14 among large metro areas. *Business 2.0 Magazine, March 2004*

- Denver was identified as one of the 100 "Most Unwired Cities" in the U.S. The area ranked #7 out of the 100 largest metro areas in the U.S. Criteria: number of public and commercial wireless access points (hotspots); airports with wireless Internet access; broadband availability; local wireless networks; and wireless email devices. *Intel, "Most Unwired Cities Survey," June 7, 2005*

- Denver was ranked #14 out of 125 regions worldwide in terms of its "Knowledge Competitiveness Index." The index attempts to measure the knowledge-based development taking place throughout the world and is based on 19 measures of economic performance that indicate a region's ability to translate its knowledge capacity into economic value. *Robert Huggins Associates, World Knowledge Competitiveness Index 2005*

- *Forbes* ranked the 200 most populous metro areas in the U.S. in terms of the "Best Places for Business and Careers." The Denver metro area was ranked #104. Criteria: business costs (labor, energy, tax and office space expenses); living costs (housing, transportation, food and other household expenditures); education levels of the work force; job growth; income growth; migration trends; crime rates; and culture/leisure. *Forbes, April 23, 2007*

- *Kiplinger's Personal Finance* ranked 101 U.S. cities in terms of their total tax burdens. Denver ranked #26 (#1 had the lowest overall tax burden). Criteria: state income tax; property tax; sales tax; personal property tax; and gasoline tax. *Kiplinger's Personal Finance, July 2004*

- *Fortune* ranked the 100 largest metro areas in the U.S. in terms of projected median home price change in 2006. The Denver metro area ranked #63. *Fortune, "The Top 100: Is the Party Over?" December 26, 2005*

- Denver was identified as one of the "Most Overpriced Places in the U.S." The area ranked #9 out of the nations 150 largest metro areas. Criteria: job growth; income growth; cost of living; and housing affordability. *Forbes.com, "Most Overpriced Places in the U.S. 2005"*

Health/Environment Rankings

- *Reader's Digest* ranked the 50 largest metro areas in the U.S. in terms of how "clean" they are. The Denver metro area ranked #6. Criteria: air quality; water quality; toxic industrial pollution; Superfund sites; and sanitation. *Reader's Digest, "The 50 Cleanest (and Dirtiest) Cities in America," July 2005*

- Sanofi-aventis, in partnership with Sperling's BestPlaces, ranked the 50 worst cities for respiratory infections in the U.S. Denver ranked #33. Criteria: prevalence of sinusitis, pharyngitis (sore throat), bronchitis, acute upper respiratory infections, pneumonia, otitis media (middle ear infection), other respiratory tract infections and the common cold; total per capita prescriptions written for oral antibiotics for respiratory tract infections; and prevalence of state level antibiotic resistance. *Sanofi-aventis, "America's Worst Cities for Respiratory Infections," December 6, 2005*

- The Denver metro area appeared in *Country Home's* "2007 Best Green Places Report". The area ranked #79. Criteria included: air and watershed quality; miles of mass transit; green power; number of farmer's markets, organic producers and groceries. *Country Home, "2007 Best Green Places Report," April 2007*

- Wyeth Consumer Healthcare, in partnership with Sperling's BestPlaces, ranked the nation's 50 most populous metro areas in terms of five key health factors. The Denver metro area ranked #9. Criteria: physical activity, health status, nutrition, lifestyle pursuits; and mental wellness. *Wyeth Consumer Healthcare, "Centrum Healthiest Cities Study," April 19, 2005*

- HealthGrades identified the 10 worst cities for nursing home care in the U.S. Denver ranked #10. Criteria: proportion of facilities that had four or more actual harm violations from health or complaint surveys in the last four years. *www.HealthGrades.com, "Best and Worst Cities for Nursing Home Care," March 16, 2004*

- HealthGrades surveyed over 41,000 individuals on doctor satisfaction and ranked the 20 largest metro areas based on the highest "definitely yes" responses to the question "Do you trust the physician to make decisions/recommendations that are in your best interest?" The Denver metro area ranked #4. *HealthGrades.com, "Top Cities in Doctor-Trust," September 7, 2006*

- The American Podiatric Medical Association and *Prevention* magazine ranked America's 100 most populated cities based on fitness-walker friendliness. The best cities have safe streets, beautiful places to walk, mild weather and good air quality. Denver ranked #22. *Prevention, "The Best Walking Cities of 2007," April 2007; American Podiatric Medical Association, "2007 Best Fitness-Walking Cities"*

- Denver was selected as one of the 25 fittest cities in America by *Men's Fitness Online*. It ranked #20 out of America's 50 largest cities. Criteria: gyms/sporting goods; nutrition; exercise/sports; overweight/sedentary; junk food; alcohol; smoking; television; air and water quality; climate; geography; commute time; parks/open space; recreation facilities; health care; motivation; civic legislation and leadership. *Men's Fitness Online, America's Fittest/Fattest Cities 2006*

- Denver was identified as a "2007 Asthma Capital." The area ranked #78 out of the nation's 100 largest metropolitan areas. Twelve factors were used to identify the most challenging places to live for people with asthma: estimated prevalence; self-reported prevalence; crude death rate for asthma; annual pollen score; annual air quality; public smoking laws; number of board-certified asthma specialists; school inhaler access laws; rescue medication use; controller medication use; uninsured rate; poverty rate. *Asthma and Allergy Foundation of America, "2007 Asthma Capitals"*

- Denver was identified as a "Spring Allergy Capital." The area ranked #55 out of 100. Three groups of factors were used to identify the most severe cities for people with allergies during the spring season: annual pollen levels; medicine utilization; access to board-certified allergists. *Asthma and Allergy Foundation of America, "2007 Spring Allergy Capital Rankings"*

- Denver was identified as a "Fall Allergy Capital." The area ranked #81 out of 100. Three groups of factors were used to identify the most severe cities for people with allergies during the fall season: annual pollen levels; medicine utilization; access to board-certified allergists. *Asthma and Allergy Foundation of America, "2006 Fall Allergy Capital Rankings"*

- Denver was selected as one of "America's Healthiest Cities" by *Natural Health* magazine. The city was ranked #8 out of the 50 largest urban areas in the U.S. Twenty-six criteria in the following four categories were examined: whether the city boasts natural offerings; how well the city promotes its residents' physical health; whether the city offers a healthy environment; how well the city fosters a sense of community. *Natural Health, April 2003*

- *Men's Health* ranked the nation's largest 100 cities in terms of the *Best (and Worst) Cities for Men*. Denver was ranked #24. Criteria: 24 statistical parameters of long life in the categories of health, quality of life, and fitness. *Men's Health, January/February 2007*

- *Men's Health* ranked 100 U.S. cities in terms of the quality of their tap water. Denver was ranked #1 and received a grade of A. Criteria: levels of total coliform bacteria, arsenic, lead, total trihalomethanes (linked to cancer), and halo-acetic acids, plus the number of EPA water-system violations from 1995 to 2005. *Men's Health, March 2007*

- GlaxoSmithKline, in partnership with Sperling's BestPlaces, analyzed the nation's 100 largest metro areas and identified 25 asthma "hot spots" where high prevalence makes the condition a key issue and environmental triggers and other factors can make living with asthma a particular challenge. The Denver metro area ranked #16 with #1 being the most challenging place to live. Criteria: asthma prevalence; asthma mortality; pollen scores; number of asthma specialists per capita; ratio of prescriptions for rescue medications to prescriptions for controller medications (an indicator of proper asthma treatment); air pollution; smoking laws; climate; and prevalence of tobacco use. *GlaxoSmithKline, "Asthma Hot Spots," October 29, 2002*

- Ortho-McNeil Neurologics, in partnership with Sperling's BestPlaces, analyzed 110 metro areas and identified those U.S. cities with the highest prevalence of factors that are most commonly associated with migraine headaches. The Denver metro area ranked #63. Criteria: number of migraine-related drug prescriptions per capita; lifestyle factors that can contribute to migraines; environmental factors that can trigger migraines; and consumption of migraine-triggering foods. *Ortho-McNeil Neurologics, "America's Migraine Hot Spots," March 14, 2006*

- Sperling's BestPlaces ranked 331 metro areas and identified the most and least stressful U.S. cities. The Denver metro area ranked #17 out of the 100 largest metro areas (#1 = most stressful). Criteria: divorce rate; unemployment rate; violent and property crime; suicide rate; commute time; mental health; alcohol consumption; cloudy days. *www.BestPlaces.net, January 9, 2004*

- Sperling's BestPlaces in partnership with Vistakon ranked the 100 largest metro areas and identified "America's 10 Worst Cities for Comfortable Eyes." The Denver metro area ranked #1. Criteria: altitude; sunny days; wind; extreme temperatures; humidity; pollution; commute time; computer use. *Vistakon, "America's Best and Worst Cities for Comfortable Eyes," June 15, 2004*

- HealthGrades evaluated the performance of America's 25 most populous metropolitan areas by measuring the outcomes of five of the highest volume and most widely studied procedures and diagnoses: coronary artery bypass graft surgery; percutaneus coronary interventions; acute myocardial infarction/heart attack in angioplasty-capable hospitals; congestive heart failure; and community acquired pneumonia. The Denver metro area ranked #6. *HealthGrades, "HealthGrades Hospital Quality in America Study," October 12, 2004*

- Denver was selected as one of "America's Pet Healthiest Cities" by Purina. The city ranked #1 out of 50. Criteria: veterinary services; environment; legislation; preventative care; obesity/body condition. *Purina Pet Institute, "America's Pet Healthiest Cities," May 20, 2003*

Women/Minorities Rankings

- Denver was ranked #50 out of 100 metro areas in *SELF Magazine's* ranking of "America's Best Places for Women." A panel of experts came up with nearly 40 criteria including: drinking and smoking rates; depression; unemployment; parks; crime; disease; healthcare insurance coverage; air quality; and commute times. *SELF Magazine, "America's Best Places for Women 2006," December 2006*

- *Ladies Home Journal* ranked America's 200 largest cities based on the qualities women surveyed care about most. Denver ranked #30 out of 57 in the big city category (population over 300,000). Criteria: crime; lifestyle; education; jobs; health; child care; politics; and the economy. *Ladies Home Journal Online, "The Best Cities for Women 2002"*

- Denver was profiled in the book *50 Fabulous Gay-Friendly Places to Live*. Criteria: an active gay community; positive gay health programs; youth outreach; gay-friendly politics; gay-owned and gay-friendly businesses; employment opportunities; fun nightlife; cultural opportunities; recreational opportunities; housing options. *50 Fabulous Gay-Friendly Places to Live, 2005*

- Denver was identified as one of the top 25 metropolitan statistical areas ranked by percentage of coupled households that are gay or lesbian." The area ranked #24. *Human Rights Campaign, "Gay and Lesbian Families in the United States: Same-Sex Unmarried Partner Households," August 1, 2001*

- Denver was selected as one of the "Top 10 Best Lesbian Places to Live" by *Girlfriends* magazine. The city ranked #6. Criteria: crime; unemployment; housing costs; climate; accessibility to lesbian, gay, bisexual, and transgender businesses; and domestic partnership protections. *Girlfriends, "Top 10 Best Lesbian Places to Live for 2002"*

Seniors/Retirement Rankings

- Sperling's BestPlaces in partnership with Bankers Life & Casualty Company designed a survey to identify the top 50 metro areas in the U.S. that offer the best overall qualities for senior living. The Denver metro area ranked #19. The following criteria were statistically weighted to reflect the needs of the senior population: health; disease; economics; social; environment; spiritual; transportation; housing; and crime. *Bankers Life & Casualty Company, "Best Cities for Seniors 2005"*

- A.G. Edwards ranked America's 500 top-performing communities based on their residents' personal savings and investing behavior. The Denver metro area ranked #47 with an index score of 109.91 (national average = 100.00). A dozen statistical factors were measured including: participation in retirement savings plans; personal debt levels; and home ownership. *A.G. Edwards, "2006 Nest Egg Index", September 6, 2006*

Children/Family Rankings

- The Denver metro area was selected as one of the "Best Cities for Relocating Families" by Worldwide ERC and Primacy Relocation. Criteria: tax rates; average home costs and home appreciation; ability to qualify for in-state tuition; service quality of local utilities; per-capita volunteerism; auto taxes; and quantity of fun, family-friendly events and venues. *Worldwide ERC and Primacy Relocation, "2006 Best Cities for Relocating Families"*

- *Zero Population Growth* ranked 100 cities in terms of children's health, safety, and economic well-being. Denver was ranked #7 out of 20 Major Cities (main city in a metro area with population of greater than 2.5 million) and was given a grade of B+. Criteria: total population and population growth; percent of population under 18 years of age; percent of births to teens; infant mortality rate; percent of eligible women not receiving Title X services; contraceptive equity indicator; percent of children without health insurance; percent of city residents over age 25 with a high-school diploma; ration of PopEd (Population Connection's Education Program) teachers trained; sexuality education indicator; proficiency in reading and math; percent of kids living in poverty; percent growth in urbanized land; violent crime rate; recycling. *Population Connection, Kid Friendly Cities: Report Card 2004*

- *Fit Pregnancy* magazine ranked the 50 best U.S. cities in which to have a baby. Denver was ranked #5. Criteria: fertility services; maternal and infant health risk; access to hospitals and doctors; safety; affordability; stroller friendliness; and birthing options. *Fit Pregnancy, February/March, 2006*

Safety Rankings

- Allstate ranked the 200 largest cities in America in terms of driver safety. Denver ranked #39. In addition, drivers were 6.5% less likely to have had an accident compared to the national average. Allstate researchers analyzed internal Property Damage reported claims over a two-year period (from January 2003 to December 2004) to ensure the findings would not be affected by external influences such as weather or road construction. A weighted average of the two-year numbers determined the annual percentages. The report defines an auto crash as any collision resulting in a property damage claim. *Allstate, "Allstate America's Best Drivers Report 2006," May 24, 2006*

- Denver was identified as one of the most dangerous large metro areas for pedestrians in the U.S. The area ranked #29 out of the nations 50 largest metro areas. Criteria: average yearly pedestrian fatalities per capita (for the years 2002 and 2003) adjusted for the number of walkers. *Surface Transportation Policy Project, "Mean Streets 2004"*

- *Ladies Home Journal* ranked America's 200 largest cities in terms of safety. Denver ranked #94 out of 200. Criteria: violent crimes; crimes against property; and rape. *Ladies Home Journal Online, "The Best Cities for Women 2002"*

Sports/Recreation Rankings

■ The Denver metro area appeared on *The Sporting News* list of the "Best Sports Cities 2006". The area ranked #6 out of 99 cities in North America. To be included in the rankings, a city must have at least one of the following: NCAA Division I basketball team; Class A minor league baseball team; training camp for a major league or NFL team; NASCAR Nextel Cup race; NCAA Division I-A bowl game; PGA Tour tournament; Triple Crown horse race. Once a city qualifies, a 12-month snapshot is taken of the sports atmosphere, putting a heavy premium on regular-season won-lost records; playoff berths, bowl appearances and tournament bids; championships; applicable power ratings; quality of competition; overall fan fervor; sports atmosphere and fan knowledge; abundance of teams (quality over quantity); stadium/arena quality; ticket availability and prices; franchise ownership; and the marquee appeal of athletes. *SportingNews.com, "Best Sports Cities 2006," August 1, 2006*

■ Denver was chosen as one of America's 25 best cities for running. The city was ranked #9. Criteria: number of running clubs per city; amount of land set aside for park usage; air quality; weather; crime rates; and results from a *Runner's World* poll in which readers ranked their favorite running cities. *Runner's World, "The 25 Best Running Cities in America," July 2005*

■ Denver was chosen as one of "The 10 Best Cities for Mountain Bikers." The city was ranked #5. The criteria for making the list was two-fold: 1) great trails within or very close to the city; 2) the city had to be a place where people could actually live—with good jobs, decent schools, affordable housing, arts and sports, and a sense of community. *Mountain Bike, June 2001*

■ Denver was chosen as one of America's best cities for bicycling. The city ranked #2 in the large city category (population 500,000 to 1 million). Criteria: cycling-friendly statistics (number of bike lanes and routes, number of bike racks, city bike projects completed and planned; bike culture (number of bike commuters, popular clubs, cool cycling events, renowned bike shops); climate/geography (the quality of roads and trails for riding, and how frequently mother nature lets riders enjoy them). *Bicycling, March 2006*

■ The Denver metro area was selected by *Cranium* as one of the "Top 50 Fun Cities" in America. The area ranked #15. Criteria includes: number of sports teams, restaurants, and dance performances; number of toy stores; city budget spent on recreation. *Cranium, November 4, 2003*

■ *Golf Digest* ranked 330 metro areas in the U.S. in terms of golf. The Denver metro area was ranked #299. Criteria: access to golf; weather; value of golf; and quality of golf. *Golf Digest, "Metro Golf Rankings," August 2005*

Dating/Romance Rankings

■ Denver was selected as one of the "Best Cities for Dating" by Love@AOL. The area ranked #9 out of 10. Criteria: Love@AOL surveyed singles and looked at a wide range of dating characteristics such as: are there lots of places to take a date; how easy is it to find a date; and when you're dating, do you acknowledge Valentine's Day? *Love@AOL, "2006 Dating Trends Survey: Best Cities for Dating"*

■ The Denver metro area was selected as one of the "Best Cities for Relocating Singles" by Worldwide ERC and Primacy Relocation. The area ranked #24 out of the 100 largest metro areas in the U.S. Areas were selected based on the following criteria: Population Criteria (local percentage and growth trends of unmarried residents aged 25-34; male-female ratios; the number of newcomers to the area; diversity and density); Economic Criteria (job growth vs. unemployment rates; apartment rental costs; fee and occupancy rates for temporary housing and mini-storage; higher education costs, including in-state and out-of-state tuition requirements; vehicle tax rates and quality of service from utility providers); Quality-of-Life Criteria (level of per capita volunteering; quality and quantity of collegiate and professional sports with fun, fan-friendly venues; number of Starbucks and other coffee shops; quality or popularity of restaurants, nightspots, health clubs, and online dating; moderate climates with sustainable water supplies). *Worldwide ERC and Primacy Relocation, "2006 Best Cities for Relocating Singles," October 11, 2006*

- *Forbes* ranked the 40 most populous metro areas in the U.S. in terms of the "Best Cities for Singles." The Denver metro area was ranked #1. Criteria: number of singles; cost of living alone; nightlife; culture; job growth; coolness; and online dating. *Forbes.com, July 25, 2006*

- Sperling's BestPlaces in partnership with AXE Deodorant Bodyspray ranked 80 metro areas and identified "America's Best (and Worst) Cities for Dating." The Denver metro area ranked #16. Criteria: percentage of singles ages 18-24; population density; dating venues per capita. *AXE Deodorant Bodyspray, "America's Best (and Worst) Cities for Dating," May, 2004*

Culture/Performing Arts Rankings

- Denver was selected as one of "The Top Ten Cities that Rock." The city was ranked #2. Criteria: overall music scene; retail music stores; live music venues. *Esquire, March 2004*

- Denver was selected as one of "America's Top 25 Arts Destinations." The city ranked #14 in the big city (population 500,000 and over) category. Criteria: readers' top choices for arts travel destinations based on the richness and variety of visual arts sites, activities and events. *American Style, June 2006*

- Scarborough Research, a leading market research firm, identified the top local markets for rock concert attendance. The Denver DMA (Designated Market Area) ranked in the top 25 with 16% of consumers, 18 years old and over, reporting that they have attended a rock concert during the past year. *Scarborough Research, Scarborough USA+ 2003 Release 2*

Miscellaneous Rankings

- Denver was determined to be one of America's smartest cities. The city ranked #14 in the large city category (200,000+ adults 25 years and older). Criteria: the editors rated the collective brainpower of U.S communities based on the educational attainment of its residents. *American City Business Journals, www.bizjournals.com, June 12, 2006*

- Denver was selected as one of the "Top 100 Sweatiest Summer Cities". The city was ranked #71. The ranking was based on the average male/female height/weight, average high temperature, and average relative humidity levels for 2002 in each of the cities during June, July and August. The sweat level was analyzed based on the assumption that the individual was walking for one hour. *Procter & Gamble, Old Spice, June 18, 2003*

- The Denver metro area appeared on *Forbes* list of "America's Drunkest Cities". The area ranked #15. Criteria: 35 of the largest continental U.S. metro areas were chosen based on availability of data and geographic diversity. Each metro was ranked in five areas: state laws; drinkers; heavy drinkers; binge drinkers; and alcoholism. *Forbes.com, "America's Drunkest Cities," August 22, 2006*

- Denver appeared on ApartmentRatings.com "Top Cities for Renters List 2006". The area ranked #40 out of 138. Criteria: renter satisfaction; affordability; and vacancy. *ApartmentRatings.com, "Top Cities for Renters List 2006"*

- Sperling's BestPlaces in partnership with Pep Boys ranked 77 metro areas and identified "America's Most Drivable Cities." The Denver metro area ranked #74. Criteria: climate; road roughness; urban mobility; gas prices. *Pep Boys, "America's Most Drivable Cities," April 9, 2003*

- Denver was selected as a "Great College Town" by ePodunk. The city ranked #3 in the big city category. ePodunk.com looked at communities with four-year colleges and a total student enrollment of at least 1,500. Communities where the student ratio was too low or too high were ruled out, as were small cities with low rates of owner-occupied housing. Fifteen variables were then applied to assess arts and culture, recreation, intellectual activity, historic preservation, and cost of living. *www.ePodunk.com, April, 2002*

- Denver was ranked #14 out of 268 metro areas in terms of its Creativity Index. The Creativity Index is a mix of four equally weighted factors: the Creative Class (scientists, engineers, architects, designers, writers, artists, musicians, or any profession where creativity is a key factor) share of the workforce; innovation, measured as patents per capita; high-tech industry, using the Milken Institute's Tech Pole Index; and diversity, measured by the Gay Index (a reasonable proxy for an areas' openness to different kinds of people and ideas). *The Rise of the Creative Class, 2002*

- Denver was selected as one of "America's Most Literate Cities." The city ranked #8 out of the 70 largest U.S. cities. Criteria: number of booksellers; library resources; Internet resources; educational attainment; periodical publishing resources; newspaper circulation. *Central Connecticut State University, "America's Most Literate Cities 2006"*

- State Farm Insurance, in partnership with Sperling's BestPlaces, analyzed several key factors that contribute to overall family preparedness. The Denver metro area ranked #23 out of the nation's 50 most populous metro areas. Criteria: quality of life; life insurance coverage; and investments. *State Farm Life Insurance, "Fiscally Fit Cities Report," July 20, 2004*

- Scarborough Research, a leading market research firm, identified the top local markets for coffee bar patronage. The Denver DMA (Designated Market Area) ranked in the top 10 with 18% of adults reporting that they have used any coffee house/bar during the past 30 days. *Scarborough Research, Scarborough USA+ 2004 Release 1*

- Denver appeared on *Kiplinger's* list of "Seven Cool Cities," top towns for young professionals. The cities selected all have a healthy head count of people under 30 and a solid or improving job market. In addition, each city's cost of living is at or near the national average for students and young wage earners. *Kiplinger's Personal Finance, "Seven Cool Cities," October 2005*

Business Environment

CITY FINANCES

City Government Finances

Component	2003-2004 ($000)	2003-2004 ($ per capita)
Total Revenues	2,171,834	3,875
Total Expenditures	2,553,658	4,557
Debt Outstanding	5,428,459	9,686
Cash and Securities	3,026,636	5,401

Source: U.S Census Bureau, Government Finances 2003-2004

City Government Revenue by Source

Source	2003-2004 ($000)	2003-2004 ($ per capita)
General Revenue		
From Federal Government	19,357	35
From State Government	233,545	417
From Local Governments	0	0
Taxes		
Property	153,193	273
Sales	453,284	809
Personal Income	0	0
License	1,747	3
Charges	749,696	1,338
Liquor Store	0	0
Utility	138,709	248
Employee Retirement	97,173	173
Other	325,130	580

Source: U.S Census Bureau, Government Finances 2003-2004

City Government Expenditures by Function

Function	2003-2004 ($000)	2003-2004 ($ per capita)	2003-2004 (%)
General Expenditures			
Airports	343,289	613	13.4
Corrections	65,859	118	2.6
Education	0	0	0.0
Fire Protection	74,343	133	2.9
Governmental Administration	150,672	269	5.9
Health	55,470	99	2.2
Highways	82,006	146	3.2
Hospitals	0	0	0.0
Housing and Community Development	63,527	113	2.5
Interest on General Debt	250,274	447	9.8
Libraries	30,872	55	1.2
Parking	0	0	0.0
Parks and Recreation	159,583	285	6.2
Police Protection	153,255	273	6.0
Public Welfare	105,597	188	4.1
Sewerage	69,118	123	2.7
Solid Waste Management	0	0	0.0
Liquor Store	0	0	0.0
Utility	238,680	426	9.3
Employee Retirement	85,528	153	3.3
Other	625,585	1,116	24.5

Source: U.S Census Bureau, Government Finances 2003-2004

Municipal Bond Ratings

Area	Moody's
City	A1

Source: Mergent Bond Record, January 2007 (unless noted otherwise)

DEMOGRAPHICS

Population Growth

Area	1990 Census	2000 Census	2006 Estimate	2011 Projection	Population Growth (%)	
					1990-2000	2000-2011
City	467,153	554,636	559,136	564,246	18.7	1.7
MSA[1]	1,666,935	2,179,296	2,375,424	2,534,563	30.7	16.3
U.S.	248,709,873	281,421,906	298,021,266	312,383,955	13.2	11.0

Note: (1) Metropolitan Statistical Area - see Appendix B for areas included
Source: Claritas, Inc.

Number of Households and Average Household Size

Area	2006 Estimate	2006 Average Household Size
City	236,917	2.36
MSA[1]	919,327	2.58
U.S.	112,267,302	2.65

Note: (1) Metropolitan Statistical Area - see Appendix B for areas included
Source: Claritas, Inc.

Race and Ethnicity

Area	White Alone[2]	Black Alone[2]	Asian Alone[2]	Other Race Alone[2]	Hispanic[3]
City	64.0	10.3	3.1	22.7	35.4
MSA[1]	77.5	5.4	3.3	13.8	21.9
U.S.	73.3	12.4	4.2	10.1	14.5

Note: Figures are 2006 estimates; (1) Metropolitan Statistical Area - see Appendix B for areas included
(2) Alone is defined as not being in combination with one or more other races; (3) May be of any race.
Source: Claritas, Inc.

Segregation

City		MSA[1]	
Index[2]	Rank[3]	Index[2]	Rank[4]
67.4	29	66.2	86

Note: Figures are based on an analysis of Census 2000 data; (1) Metropolitan Statistical Area - see Appendix A for areas included; (2) White/Black Dissimilarity Index—the most commonly used measure of segregation between two groups, reflecting their relative distributions across neighborhoods within a city or metropolitan area. It can range in value from 0, indicating complete integration, to 100, indicating complete segregation; (3) Ranges from 1 (most segregated) to 100 (least segregated) and includes all the cities in this book; (4) Ranges from 1 (most segregated) to 318 (least segregated) and includes 318 metropolitan areas.
Source: www.CensusScope.org

Ancestry

Area	German	Irish[2]	English	American	Italian	Polish	French[3]	Scottish
City	13.8	9.6	8.3	3.4	3.5	2.0	2.5	2.0
MSA[1]	21.3	12.5	11.5	4.5	4.9	2.5	3.4	2.5
U.S.	15.2	10.9	8.7	7.3	5.6	3.2	3.0	1.7

Note: Figures include multiple ancestry (e.g. if a person reported being Irish and Italian, they were included in both columns); (1) Metropolitan Statistical Area - see Appendix A for areas included; (2) Includes Celtic; (3) Includes Alsatian but excludes Basque
Source: Census 2000, Summary File 3

Foreign-Born Population

Area	Percent of Population Born in							
	Any Foreign Country	Europe	Asia	Africa	Oceania[2]	Canada	Mexico	Latin America[3]
City	17.4	1.8	2.3	0.6	0.1	0.3	11.4	0.9
MSA[1]	11.1	1.7	2.3	0.4	0.1	0.4	5.5	0.7
U.S.	11.1	1.7	2.9	0.3	0.1	0.3	3.3	2.5

Note: (1) Metropolitan Statistical Area - see Appendix A for areas included; (2) Includes Australia, New Zealand subregion, Melanesia, Micronesia, Polynesia, and Oceania n.e.c; (3) Includes Central America (excluding Mexico), South America, and the Caribbean.
Source: Census 2000, Summary File 3

Marriage Status

Area	Never Married	Now Married (excluding Separated)	Separated	Widowed	Divorced
City	35.9	43.2	2.3	5.8	12.7
MSA[1]	27.8	54.2	1.7	4.6	11.7
U.S.	27.1	54.4	2.2	6.6	9.7

Note: Figures are percentages and cover the population 15 years of age and older;
(1) Metropolitan Statistical Area - see Appendix A for areas included
Source: Census 2000, Summary File 3

Age Distribution

Area	Percent of Population						
	Under Age 5	Age 5 to 17	Age 18 to 34	Age 35 to 49	Age 50 to 64	Age 65 to 79	80 Years and Over
City	6.7	15.1	31.2	22.9	12.9	8.1	3.2
MSA[1]	7.1	18.6	25.6	25.6	14.1	6.8	2.2
U.S.	6.8	18.9	23.7	23.5	14.8	9.2	3.2

Note: (1) Metropolitan Statistical Area - see Appendix A for areas included
Source: Census 2000, Summary File 3

Male/Female Ratio

Area	Males	Females	Males per 100 Females
City	282,997	276,139	102.5
MSA[1]	1,191,679	1,183,745	100.7
U.S.	146,712,712	151,308,554	97.0

Note: Figures are 2006 estimates; (1) Metropolitan Statistical Area -
see Appendix B for areas included
Source: Claritas, Inc.

Religion

Area	Catholic	Southern Baptist	United Methodist	ELCA[1]	LDS[2]	Presbyterian Church USA	Jewish Est.	Muslim Est.
County	28.7	1.3	1.6	0.9	0.6	1.1	6.9	1.1
U.S.	22.0	7.1	3.7	1.8	1.5	1.1	2.2	0.6

Note: Figures are the number of adherents as a percentage of the total population; Adherents are defined as all
members, including full members, their children and the estimated number of other participants who are not
considered members (e.g. the baptized, those not confirmed, those regularly attending services, etc.);
(1) Evangelical Lutheran Church in America; (2) The Church of Jesus Christ of Latter Day Saints
Source: Reprinted with permission from Religious Congregations and Membership in the United States 2000
(Nashville, Glenmary Research Center, 2002) Copyright Association of Statisticians of American Religious
Bodies. All rights reserved.

ECONOMY

Gross Metropolitan Product

Area	2002	2003	2004	2005	2005 Rank[2]
MSA[1]	98.7	102.4	108.5	116.4	19

Note: Figures are in billions of dollars; (1) Denver-Aurora, CO Metropolitan Statistical Area - see Appendix A
for areas included; (2) Rank ranges from 1 to 361
Source: The U.S. Conference of Mayors, "U.S. Metro Economies: GMP - The Engines of America's Growth,"
January 2007

Economic Growth

Area	1995 GMP	2005 GMP	Average Annual Growth Rate	Growth Rate Rank[2]
MSA[1]	61.5	116.4	6.6	71

Note: Figures are in billions of dollars; GMP = Gross Metropolitan Product; (1) Denver-Aurora, CO
Metropolitan Statistical Area - see Appendix A for areas included; (2) Rank ranges from 1 to 361
Source: The U.S. Conference of Mayors, "U.S. Metro Economies: GMP - The Engines of America's Growth,"
January 2007

INCOME

Per Capita/Median/Average Income

Area	Per Capita ($)	Median Household ($)	Average Household ($)
City	28,939	48,282	67,586
MSA[1]	30,901	61,786	79,304
U.S.	25,129	48,775	65,849

Note: Figures are 2006 estimates; (1) Metropolitan Statistical Area - see Appendix B for areas included
Source: Claritas, Inc.

Household Income Distribution

Area	Percent of Households Earning							
	Under $15,000	$15,000 -24,999	$25,000 -34,999	$35,000 -49,999	$50,000 -74,999	$75,000 -99,000	$100,000 -149,999	$150,000 and up
City	13.1	10.4	11.8	16.6	19.1	11.0	10.8	7.2
MSA[1]	7.9	7.5	9.5	15.1	21.1	14.6	15.2	9.1
U.S.	13.3	11.0	11.3	15.7	19.5	11.8	11.0	6.4

Note: Figures are 2006 estimates; (1) Metropolitan Statistical Area - see Appendix B for areas included
Source: Claritas, Inc.

Poverty Rates by Age

Area	All Ages	Under 5 Years Old	5 to 17 Years Old	18 to 64 Years Old	65 Years and Over
City	14.3	1.4	3.1	8.7	1.1
MSA[1]	8.1	0.8	1.8	4.8	0.6
U.S.	12.4	1.2	3.0	6.9	1.2

Note: Figures are percent of population with income in 1999 below poverty level and only include population for whom poverty status is determined; (1) Metropolitan Statistical Area - see Appendix A for areas included
Source: Census 2000, Summary File 3

Personal Bankruptcy Filing Rate

Area	2003	2004	2005
Denver County	5.52	6.15	9.76
U.S.	5.57	5.31	6.88

Note: Numbers are per 1,000 population and include Chapter 7 and Chapter 13 filings
Source: Federal Deposit Insurance Corporation (FDIC), Regional Economic Conditions (RECON), 3/24/2006

EMPLOYMENT

Labor Force and Employment

Area	Civilian Labor Force			Workers Employed		
	Dec. 2005	Dec. 2006	% Chg.	Dec. 2005	Dec. 2006	% Chg.
City	307,294	315,019	2.5	290,786	300,390	3.3
MSA[1]	1,315,904	1,350,723	2.6	1,255,309	1,296,771	3.3
U.S.	149,874,000	152,571,000	1.8	142,918,000	146,081,000	2.2

Note: Data is not seasonally adjusted and covers workers 16 years of age and older;
(1) Metropolitan Statistical Area - see Appendix B for areas included
Source: Bureau of Labor Statistics, http://stats.bls.gov

Unemployment Rate

Area	2006											
	Jan.	Feb.	Mar.	Apr.	May	Jun.	Jul.	Aug.	Sep.	Oct.	Nov.	Dec.
City	6.2	5.6	5.5	4.9	5.0	5.5	5.5	5.5	5.1	4.9	4.7	4.6
MSA[1]	5.3	4.8	4.8	4.4	4.4	4.9	4.8	4.8	4.4	4.2	4.1	4.0
U.S.	5.1	5.1	4.8	4.5	4.4	4.8	5.0	4.6	4.4	4.1	4.3	4.3

Note: Data is not seasonally adjusted and covers workers 16 years of age and older; All figures are percentages; (1) Metropolitan Statistical Area - see Appendix B for areas included
Source: Bureau of Labor Statistics, http://stats.bls.gov

Employment by Occupation

Occupation Classification	City (%)	MSA[1] (%)	U.S. (%)
Sales and Office	26.3	28.9	26.7
Professional and Related	22.9	21.8	20.2
Service	15.2	12.4	14.9
Production, Transportation, and Material Moving	10.4	10.1	14.6
Management, Business, and Financial	15.0	16.8	13.5
Construction, Extraction, and Maintenance	10.0	9.9	9.4
Farming, Forestry, and Fishing	0.2	0.1	0.7

Note: Figures cover employed civilians 16 years of age and older;
(1) Metropolitan Statistical Area - see Appendix A for areas included
Source: Census 2000, Summary File 3

Employment by Industry

Sector	MSA[1] Number of Employees	MSA[1] Percent of Total	U.S. Percent of Total
Government	169,800	13.8	16.3
Education and Health Services	124,900	10.1	13.2
Professional and Business Services	203,900	16.5	12.9
Retail Trade	131,900	10.7	11.5
Manufacturing	72,400	5.9	10.2
Leisure and Hospitality	125,300	10.2	9.5
Financial Activities	101,600	8.2	6.1
Construction	n/a	n/a	5.5
Wholesale Trade	66,000	5.4	4.3
Other Services	46,800	3.8	3.9
Transportation and Utilities	52,000	4.2	3.7
Information	47,100	3.8	2.2
Natural Resources and Mining	n/a	n/a	0.5

Note: Figures cover non-farm employment as of December 2006 and are not seasonally adjusted;
(1) Metropolitan Statistical Area - see Appendix B for areas included; n/a not available
Source: Bureau of Labor Statistics, http://stats.bls.gov

Occupations with Greatest Projected Employment Growth: 2002 - 2012

Occupation[1]	2002 Employment	2012 Projected Employment	Numeric Employment Change	Percent Employment Change
Retail Salespersons	84,250	100,890	16,640	19.8
Registered Nurses	30,350	43,380	13,030	42.9
Waiters and Waitresses	45,780	58,380	12,600	27.5
Customer Service Representatives	36,940	48,920	11,980	32.4
Combined Food Preparation and Serving Workers, Including Fast Food	38,320	50,090	11,770	30.7
Cashiers	53,660	64,910	11,250	21.0
Janitors and Cleaners, Except Maids and Housekeeping Cleaners	34,580	45,460	10,880	31.5
Postsecondary Teachers	19,560	29,660	10,100	51.6
Office Clerks, General	60,720	69,590	8,870	14.6
General and Operations Managers	32,920	40,890	7,970	24.2

Note: Projections cover Colorado; (1) Sorted by numeric employment change
Source: www.projectionscentral.com, State Occupational Projections, 2002-2012 Long-Term Projections

Fastest Growing Occupations: 2002 - 2012

Occupation[1]	2002 Employment	2012 Projected Employment	Numeric Employment Change	Percent Employment Change
Network Systems and Data Communications Analysts	4,980	8,280	3,300	66.3
Medical Assistants	5,780	9,440	3,660	63.3
Medical Records and Health Information Technicians	2,250	3,580	1,330	59.1
Pharmacists	3,020	4,780	1,760	58.3
Database Administrators	2,970	4,690	1,720	57.9
Cardiovascular Technologists and Technicians	530	830	300	56.6
Computer Software Engineers, Systems Software	9,470	14,600	5,130	54.2
Environmental Engineers	1,110	1,700	590	53.2
Computer Software Engineers, Applications	14,640	22,270	7,630	52.1
Physician Assistants	1,470	2,230	760	51.7

Note: Projections cover Colorado; (1) Sorted by percent employment change and excludes occupations with numeric employment change less than 250
Source: www.projectionscentral.com, State Occupational Projections, 2002-2012 Long-Term Projections

Average Wages

Occupation	$/Hr.	Occupation	$/Hr.
Accountants and Auditors	28.98	Maids and Housekeeping Cleaners	9.17
Automotive Mechanics	18.16	Maintenance and Repair Workers	16.31
Bookkeepers	16.46	Marketing Managers	43.67
Carpenters	18.63	Nuclear Medicine Technologists	28.77
Cashiers	9.85	Nurses, Licensed Practical	19.02
Clerks, General Office	13.86	Nurses, Registered	28.35
Clerks, Receptionists/Information	12.70	Nursing Aides/Orderlies/Attendants	12.63
Clerks, Shipping/Receiving	13.39	Packers and Packagers, Hand	9.08
Computer Programmers	37.26	Physical Therapists	27.64
Computer Support Specialists	24.61	Postal Service Mail Carriers	21.76
Computer Systems Analysts	35.01	Real Estate Brokers	30.46
Cooks, Restaurant	10.00	Retail Salespersons	11.95
Dentists	n/a	Sales Reps., Exc. Tech./Scientific	27.86
Electrical Engineers	36.52	Sales Reps., Tech./Scientific	34.36
Electricians	21.54	Secretaries, Exc. Legal/Med./Exec.	15.11
Financial Managers	48.31	Security Guards	12.32
First-Line Supervisors/Mgrs., Sales	19.82	Surgeons	82.67
Food Preparation Workers	9.18	Teacher Assistants	11.40
General and Operations Managers	51.71	Teachers, Elementary School	22.50
Hairdressers/Cosmetologists	12.84	Teachers, Secondary School	23.30
Internists	81.84	Telemarketers	11.66
Janitors and Cleaners	10.07	Truck Drivers, Heavy/Tractor-Trailer	18.47
Landscaping/Groundskeeping Workers	11.58	Truck Drivers, Light/Delivery Svcs.	14.12
Lawyers	51.51	Waiters and Waitresses	8.32

Note: Wage data is for May 2005 and covers the Denver-Aurora, CO Metropolitan Statistics Area - see Appendix B for areas included. Hourly wages for elementary/secondary school teachers and teacher assistants were calculated by the editors from annual wage data assuming a 40 hour work week; n/a not available.
Source: Bureau of Labor Statistics, May 2005 Metro Area Occupational Employment and Wage Estimates

RESIDENTIAL REAL ESTATE

Building Permits

Area	Single-Family			Multi-Family			Total		
	2005	2006p	Pct. Chg.	2005	2006p	Pct. Chg.	2005	2006p	Pct. Chg.
City	2,029	1,808	-10.9	1,135	1,967	73.3	3,164	3,775	19.3
U.S.	1,682,000	1,380,000	-18.0	473,300	457,300	-3.4	2,155,300	1,837,300	-14.8

Note: (p) preliminary; figures represent new, privately-owned housing units authorized (unadjusted data); All permit data are based on estimates with imputation; U.S. figures are based on the new 20,000-place series.
Source: U.S. Census Bureau, Manufacturing, Mining, and Construction Statistics

Homeownership and Housing Vacancies

Area	Homeownership Rate[2] (%)			Rental Vacancy Rate[3] (%)			Homeowner Vacancy Rate[4] (%)		
	2004	2005	2006	2004	2005	2006	2004	2005	2006
MSA[1]	n/a	70.7	70.0	n/a	12.0	11.1	n/a	2.7	3.7
U.S.	69.0	68.9	68.8	10.2	9.8	9.7	1.7	1.9	2.4

Note: Comparable 2004 data was not available due to changes in metropolitan area definitions; (1) Metropolitan Statistical Area - see Appendix B for areas included; (2) The proportion of households that are owners; (3) The proportion of the rental inventory that is vacant for rent; (4) The proportion of the homeowner inventory that is vacant for sale; n/a not available
Source: U.S. Census Bureau, Housing Vacancies and Homeownership Annual Statistics: 2006

TAXES

State Corporate Income Tax Rates

State	Rate (%)	Number of Brackets	Low Bracket (Under $)	High Bracket (Over $)
Colorado	4.63	1	na	na

Note: Tax rates as of December 31, 2006; na not applicable
Source: Tax Foundation, www.taxfoundation.org

State Individual Income Tax Rates

State	Federal Deductibility	Marginal Rate (%)	Number of Brackets	Low Bracket (Under $)	High Bracket (Over $)
Colorado	No	4.63 (1)	1	na	na

Note: Tax rates as of December 31, 2006; Brackets apply to single taxpayers and married people filing separately; na not applicable; (1) 4.63% of federal taxable income.
Source: Tax Foundation, www.taxfoundation.org

Various State and Local Tax Rates

State and Local Sales and Use (%)	State Sales and Use (%)	Gasoline ($/gal.)	Cigarette ($/pack)	Spirits ($/gal.)	Table Wine ($/gal.)	Beer ($/gal.)
7.72	2.9	0.22	0.84	2.28	0.32	0.08

Note: Tax rates as of December 31, 2006
Source: Tax Foundation, www.taxfoundation.org; The Sales Tax Clearinghouse, www.thestc.com

State Tax Burdens

Area	Combined State and Local Tax Burden		Combined Federal, State and Local Tax Burden	
	Percent	Rank	Percent	Rank
Colorado	9.8	38	30.7	23
U.S. Average	10.6	-	31.6	-

Note: Figures are for 2006 and measure taxes as a percentage of income
Source: Tax Foundation, www.taxfoundation.org

Internal Revenue Service Tax Audits

IRS District	Percent of Returns Audited				
	1996	1997	1998	1999	2000
Rocky Mountain	0.73	0.67	0.49	0.28	0.20
U.S.	0.66	0.61	0.46	0.31	0.20

Note: Figures cover IRS district audits of federal income tax returns filed by individuals. Geographic data on district audits after the year 2000 are being withheld by the IRS. TRAC is challenging this policy.
Source: Syracuse University, Transactional Records Access Clearinghouse (TRAC), "Odds of IRS District Tax Audit 2000"

**COMMERCIAL
REAL ESTATE**

Office Market

Market Area	Inventory (sq. ft.)	Vacant (sq. ft.)	Vac. Rate (%)	Under Constr. (sq. ft.)	Asking Rent ($/sf) Class A	Asking Rent ($/sf) Class B
Denver	94,247,745	14,025,602	14.9	757,227	22.48	18.83

Source: Grubb & Ellis, Office Markets Trends, 4th Quarter 2006

Industrial Market

Market Area	Inventory (sq. ft.)	Vacant (sq. ft.)	Vac. Rate (%)	Under Constr. (sq. ft.)	Asking Rent ($/sf) WH/Dist	Asking Rent ($/sf) R&D/Flex
Denver	209,454,266	17,853,108	8.5	1,503,096	4.35	8.87

Source: Grubb & Ellis, Industrial Markets Trends, 4th Quarter 2006

**COMMERCIAL
UTILITIES**

Typical Monthly Electric Bills

Area	Commercial Service ($/month) 3 kW demand 1,000 kWh	Commercial Service ($/month) 40 kW demand 14,000 kWh	Industrial Service ($/month) 1,000 kW demand 200,000 kWh	Industrial Service ($/month) 50,000 kW demand 15,000,000 kWh
City	87	1,045	19,710	1,131,277
Average[1]	123	1,413	22,000	1,306,315

Note: Based on total rates in effect July 1, 2006; (1) average based on 196 utilities
Source: Edison Electric Institute, Typical Bills and Average Rates Report, Summer 2006

TRANSPORTATION

Means of Transportation to Work

Area	Car/Truck/Van Drove Alone	Car/Truck/Van Car-pooled	Public Transportation Bus	Public Transportation Subway	Public Transportation Railroad	Bicycle	Walked	Other Means	Worked at Home
City	68.3	13.5	8.0	0.1	0.1	1.0	4.3	1.1	3.7
MSA[1]	76.1	11.6	4.4	0.1	0.0	0.4	2.1	0.8	4.5
U.S.	75.7	12.2	2.5	1.5	0.5	0.4	2.9	1.0	3.3

Note: Figures are percentages and cover workers 16 years of age and older;
(1) Metropolitan Statistical Area - see Appendix A for areas included
Source: Census 2000, Summary File 3

Travel Time to Work

Area	Less Than 15 Minutes	15 to 29 Minutes	30 to 44 Minutes	45 to 59 Minutes	60 Minutes or More
City	24.6	41.8	22.0	6.1	5.5
MSA[1]	21.6	38.4	25.3	8.6	6.1
U.S.	29.4	36.1	19.1	7.4	8.0

Note: Figures are percentages and include workers 16 years old and over; (1) Metropolitan Statistical Area - see Appendix A for areas included
Source: Census 2000, Summary File 3

Travel Time Index

Area	1982	1993	2002	2003
Urban Area[1]	1.10	1.24	1.40	1.40
Average[2]	1.12	1.28	1.37	1.37

Note: Travel Time Index - The ratio of travel time in the peak period to the travel time at free-flow conditions. A value of 1.35 indicates a 20-minute free-flow trip takes 27 minutes in the peak. Free-flow speeds (60 mph on freeways and 35 mph on principal arterials) are used as the comparison threshold; (1) Covers the Denver-Aurora, CO urban area; (2) average of 85 urban areas
Source: Texas Transportation Institute, The 2005 Urban Mobility Report, May 2005

Public Transportation

Agency name:	Denver Regional Transportation District (RTD)
Vehicle type:	Bus
Average fleet age in years:	6.7
No. operated in max. service:	928
Vehicle type:	Demand response
Average fleet age in years:	2.6
No. operated in max. service:	330
Vehicle type:	Light rail
Average fleet age in years:	5.7
No. operated in max. service:	46
Vehicle type:	Vanpool
Average fleet age in years:	0.0
No. operated in max. service:	126

Source: Federal Transit Administration, National Transit Database, 2005

Air Transportation

Airport name and code:	Denver International (DEN)
Domestic service (2006)	
Passenger airlines[1]:	45
Passenger enplanements:	21,864,651
Freight carriers[2]:	30
Freight (lbs.):	259,741,180
International service (2005)	
Passenger airlines[1]:	21
Passenger enplanements:	819,590
Freight carriers[2]:	10
Freight (lbs.):	11,520,105

Note: (1) Includes all major, minor and commuter airlines that carried at least one passenger during the year; (2) Includes all airlines and freight carriers that transported at least one pound of freight during the year
Source: Bureau of Transportation Statistics, The Intermodal Transportation Database, Air Carriers: T-100 International Market, 2004; Bureau of Transportation Statistics, The Intermodal Transportation Database, Air Carriers: T-100 Domestic Market, 2005

Other Transportation Statistics

Interstate highways:	I-25; I-70; I-76
Amtrak service:	Yes
Major waterways/ports:	None

Source: Editor & Publisher Market Guide, 2006; Amtrak.com; Rand McNally 2006 Road Atlas

BUSINESSES

Major Business Headquarters

Company Name	2006 Rankings	
	Fortune[1]	Forbes[2]
Leprino Foods	-	149
MDC Holdings	437	-
MediaNews Group	-	265
Newmont Mining	461	-
Qwest Communications	160	-
TransMontaigne	269	-
TransMontaigne	-	15

Note: (1) Fortune 500 - companies that produce a 10-K are ranked 1 to 500 based on 2005 revenue; (2) Forbes Largest Private Companies - all private companies with at least $1 billion in annual revenue are ranked 1 to 394; companies listed are located in the city; dashes indicate no ranking
Source: Fortune, April 17, 2006; Forbes, November 9, 2006

Best Companies to Work For

PCL Construction (HQ), headquartered in Denver, is among the "100 Best Companies to Work For." Criteria: More than 105,000 employees from 446 companies responded to a 57-question survey created by the Great Place to Work Institute. Two-thirds of a company's score is based on the survey, which covers topics such as attitudes towards management, job satisfaction, and camaraderie. The remaining third of the score comes from each company's responses to the Institute's Culture Audit, which includes detailed questions about demographic makeup, pay and benefits programs, and open-ended questions about the company's people-management philosophy, internal communications, opportunities, compensation practices, diversity programs, etc. Any company that is at least seven years old and has a minimum of 1,000 U.S. employees is eligible. The top three U.S. locations are shown for companies with more than one location. *Fortune, "100 Best Companies to Work for 2007," January 22, 2007*

Pinnacol Assurance; University of Colorado Hospital, headquartered in Denver, are among the "50 Best Employers for Workers Over 50." Criteria: recruiting practices; opportunities for training, education, and career development; workplace accommodations; alternative work options, such as flexible scheduling, job sharing, and phased retirement; employee health and pension benefits; and retiree benefits. Any employer with at least 50 employees based in the U.S. is eligible. This includes for-profit companies, not-for-profit organizations, and government employers. *AARP, "AARP Best Employers for Workers Over 50," 2006*

Fast-Growing Businesses

According to *Inc.*, Denver is home to three of America's 500 fastest-growing private companies: **C&A Holding Co; JCB Partners; Mont Blanc Gourmet**. Criteria: must be an independent, privately-held, U.S. corporation, proprietorship or partnership; net sales of at least $600,000 in FY2002; four-year operating/sales history; holding companies, regulated banks, and utilities were excluded. *Inc., "America's 500 Fastest-Growing Private Companies," September 2006*

Denver is home to two of *Business Week's* "Hot Growth Companies:" **Cimarex Energy; St. Mary Land & Exploration**. To qualify, a company must have annual sales of more than $50 million and less than $1.5 billion, a current market value greater than $25 million, a current stock price of at least $5, and be actively traded. Banks, insurers, real estate firms, and utilities are excluded. So are companies with declines in current financial results or in stock price, as well as companies where other developments raise questions about future performance. Companies were selected based on three-year results in sales growth, earnings growth, and return on invested capital. *Business Week, June 5, 2006*

According to *Fortune*, Denver is home to two of America's 100 fastest-growing companies: **Cimarex Energy; St. Mary Land & Exploration**. Companies were ranked based on earnings-per-share growth, revenue growth and total return over the previous three years. Criteria for inclusion: public companies with sales of at least $50 million. Companies that lost money in the most recent quarter, or ended in the red for the past four quarters as a whole, were not eligible. Limited partnerships and REITs were also not considered. *Fortune, "America's Fastest-Growing Companies," September 18, 2006*

According to Deloitte & Touche LLP, Denver is home to one of North America's 500 fastest-growing high-technology companies: **3t Systems**. Companies are ranked by percentage growth in revenue over a five-year period. Criteria for inclusion: company must be headquartered within North America; company must own proprietary intellectual property or proprietary technology that contributes to a significant portion of the company's operating revenue or devotes a significant proportion of revenues to research and development of technology; company must have been in business for a minumum of five years with 2001 operating revenues of at least $50,000 USD or $75,000 CD and 2005 operating revenues of at least $5 million USD/CD. *Deloitte & Touche LLP, 2006 Technology Fast 500*

Women-Owned Businesses: 1997 and 2002

Year	All Firms		Firms with Paid Employees			
	Firms	Sales ($000)	Firms	Sales ($000)	Employees	Payroll ($000)
1997	15,060	3,126,822	2,743	2,773,235	29,642	668,540
2002	16,015	3,045,879	3,132	2,672,671	27,081	714,333

Note: Figures cover firms located in the city; Women-owned business are defined as firms in which women own 51% or more of the stock or equity of the company; (a) Withheld to avoid disclosing data for individual companies; (b) Withheld because estimate did not meet publication standards; n/a not available
Source: 1997 Economic Census, Survey of Minority- and Women-Owned Business Enterprises; 2002 Economic Census, Survey of Business Owners (released February 9, 2006)

Minority Business Opportunity

Three of the 500 largest Hispanic-owned companies in the U.S. are located in Denver. *Hispanic Business, "Hispanic Business 500," June 2006*

Denver is home to one company which is on the Hispanic Business Fastest-Growing 100 list (greatest sales growth over the past five years): **A&N Quality Products**. *Hispanic Business, July/August 2006*

HOTELS

Hotels/Motels

Area	Hotels/Motels	Average Minimum Rates ($)		
		Tourist	First-Class	Deluxe
City	90	87	102	126

Source: OAG Travel Planner Online, Spring 2006

EVENT SITES

Stadiums, Arenas, and Auditoriums

Name	Capacity
Coors Field	50,247
Denver Coliseum	11,500
Denver Performing Arts Complex	2,000
McNichols Sports Arena	18,500
Mile High Stadium	76,123
University of Denver's Magness Arena	8,000

Source: www.officialtravelguide.com; www.eventective.com; original research

Hotels/Conference Centers

Name	Guest Rooms	Exhibit Space (sq. ft.)	Meeting Space (sq. ft.)
Adam's Mark Denver Hotel	1,225	43,000	133,000
Holiday Inn Denver International	256	50,000	70,000

Source: www.officialtravelguide.com; www.eventective.com; original research

Living Environment

COST OF LIVING

Cost of Living Index

Year	Composite Index	Groceries	Housing	Utilities	Trans-portation	Health Care	Misc. Goods/ Services
2004	105.2	107.1	111.3	90.9	103.5	117.1	101.9
2005	102.3	107.7	106.6	91.6	96.4	107.3	100.8
2006	101.9	104.7	107.1	99.7	96.5	104.8	98.6

Note: U.S. = 100; Figures are for the Metropolitan Statistical Area - see Appendix B for areas included
Source: The Council for Community and Economic Research (formerly ACCRA), Cost of Living Index, 2004, 2005 and 2006 4-Quarter Averages

HOUSING

House Price Index (HPI)

Area	National Ranking[2]	Quarterly Change (%)	One-Year Change (%)	Five-Year Change (%)
MSA[1]	231	0.30	1.32	16.75
U.S.[3]	-	1.12	5.87	55.21

Note: The HPI is a weighted repeat sales index. It measures average price changes in repeat sales or refinancings on the same properties. This information is obtained by reviewing repeat mortgage transactions on single-family properties whose mortgages have been purchased or securitized by Fannie Mae or Freddie Mac in January 1975; (1) Metropolitan Statistical Area - see Appendix B for areas included; (2) Rankings are based on annual percentage change for all metro areas containing at least 15,000 transactions over the last 10 years and ranges from 1 to 282; (3) figures based on a weighted division average; all figures are for the period ending December 31, 2006
Source: Office of Federal Housing Enterprise Oversight, House Price Index, March 1, 2007

House Price Valuations

Area	Q4 1999	Q4 2000	Q4 2001	Q4 2002	Q4 2003	Q4 2004	Q4 2005	Q4 2006
MSA[1]	-3.6	-1.3	2.6	7.8	10.6	8.6	10.9	9.1

Note: Figures show the percentage of over- or under-valuation of single family homes relative to statistically normal house values (e.g. a value of 23.6 indicates that house values are 23.6% overvalued). Statistically normal house values are based on house prices, interest rates, household incomes, population densities, and any historical premiums or discounts metropolitan areas have exhibited over time; (1) Figures cover the Metropolitan Statistical Area - see Appendix B for areas included
Source: Global Insight/National City Corporation, House Prices in America, March 2007

Median Home Prices

Area	2004	2005	2006p	Percent Change 2005 to 2006
Metro Area[1]	239.1	247.1	249.5	1.0
U.S. Average	195.2	219.0	222.0	1.4

Note: Figures are median sales prices of existing single-family homes in thousands of dollars; (p) preliminary; n/a not available; (1) Covers the Denver-Aurora, CO Metropolitan Statistical Area - see Appendix B for areas included
Source: National Association of Realtors, Metropolitan Area Prices, 4th Quarter 2006

Housing: Year Structure Built

Area	1990 -2000	1980 -1989	1970 -1979	1960 -1969	1950 -1959	1940 -1949	Before 1940	Median Year
City	7.5	8.9	16.3	14.3	18.6	9.9	24.5	1958
MSA[1]	19.4	18.0	23.7	13.2	12.4	4.4	9.0	1975
U.S.	17.0	15.8	18.5	13.7	12.7	7.3	15.0	1971

Note: Figures are percentages; (1) Metropolitan Statistical Area - see Appendix A for areas included
Source: Census 2000, Summary File 3

Average New Home Price

Area	2004	2005	2006
MSA[1]	293,715	303,831	331,381
U.S.	253,574	275,712	299,269

Note: Figures, in dollars, are based on a new home with 2,400 sq. ft. of living area on an 8,000 sq. ft. lot;
(1) Metropolitan Statistical Area - see Appendix B for areas included
Source: The Council for Community and Economic Research (formerly ACCRA), Cost of Living Index, 2004,
2005 and 2006 4-Quarter Averages

Average Apartment Rent

Area	2004	2005	2006
MSA[1]	745	720	742
U.S.	716	740	766

Note: Figures, in dollars per month, are based on an unfurnished two bedroom, 1-1/2 or 2 bath apartment,
approximately 950 sq. ft., excluding utilities except water; (1) Metropolitan Statistical Area - see Appendix B for
areas included
Source: The Council for Community and Economic Research (formerly ACCRA), Cost of Living Index, 2004,
2005 and 2006 4-Quarter Averages

RESIDENTIAL UTILITIES

Average Residential Utility Costs

Area	All Electric ($/mth)	Part Electric ($/mth)	Other Energy ($/mth)	Phone ($/mth)
MSA[1]	–	82.67	78.83	24.94
U.S.	136.00	76.53	90.52	25.87

Note: (1) Metropolitan Statistical Area - see Appendix B for areas included
Source: The Council for Community and Economic Research (formerly ACCRA), Cost of Living Index, 2006
4-Quarter Average

HEALTH

Average Health Care Costs

Area	Optometrist ($/visit)	Doctor ($/visit)	Dentist ($/visit)
MSA[1]	77.98	85.77	75.42
U.S.	76.38	76.10	68.72

Note: Optometrist—based on a full vision eye exam for an established adult patient;
Doctor—based on a general practitioner's routine exam of an established patient;
Dentist—based on adult teeth cleaning and periodic oral exam;
(1) Metropolitan Statistical Area - see Appendix B for areas included
Source: The Council for Community and Economic Research (formerly ACCRA), Cost of Living Index, 2006
4-Quarter Average

Mortality Rates

ICD-10 Sub-Chapter	ICD-10 Code	Age-Adjusted Death Rate per 100,000 population[1]	U.S. Age-Adjusted Death Rate per 100,000 population
Malignant neoplasms	C00-C97	180.4	185.8
Ischaemic heart diseases	I20-I25	120.0	150.2
Other forms of heart disease	I30-I51	31.8	50.8
Cerebrovascular diseases	I60-I69	42.0	50.0
Chronic lower respiratory diseases	J40-J47	48.7	41.1
Diabetes mellitus	E10-E14	21.2	24.5
Other degenerative diseases of the nervous system	G30-G31	23.7	22.3
Other external causes of accidental injury	W00-X59	37.9	21.2
Influenza and pneumonia	J10-J18	20.7	19.8
Hypertensive diseases	I10-I13	11.2	18.1

Note: ICD-10 = International Classification of Diseases 10th Revision; (1) Figures cover Denver County, CO
Source: Centers for Disease Control and Prevention, National Center for Health Statistics. Compressed
Mortality File 1999-2004. CDC WONDER On-line Database, compiled from Compressed Mortality File
1999-2004 Series 20 No. 2J, 2007.

Health Risk Data

Item	Area[1] (%)	U.S. (%)
Adults who have been told they have high blood pressure	19.5	25.5
Adults who have been told they have high blood cholesterol	32.0	35.6
Adults who have been told they have diabetes[2]	4.5	7.3
Adults who have been told they have arthritis	21.5	27.0
Adults who have been told they currently have asthma	8.5	8.0
Adults who are current smokers	19.8	20.6

Note: (1) Figures cover the Metropolitan Statistical Area - see Appendix B for areas included; (2) Figures do not include pregnancy-related diabetes, pre-diabetes or borderline diabetes
Source: Centers for Disease Control and Prevention, Behavioral Risk Factor Surveillance System, SMART: Selected Metropolitan/Micropolitan Area Trends, 2005

Distribution of Office-Based Physicians

Area	Total	Family/ General Practice	Specialties		
			Medical	Surgical	Other
CMSA[1] (number)	4,996	705	1,775	1,064	1,452
CMSA[1] (rate per 10,000 pop.)	18.7	2.6	6.7	4.0	5.4
Metro Average[2] (rate per 10,000 pop.)	19.4	2.1	7.5	4.5	5.3

Note: Data as of December 31, 2004; (1) Denver-Boulder-Greeley, CO Consolidated Metropolitan Statistical Area includes the following counties: Adams; Arapahoe; Boulder; Denver; Douglas; Jefferson; Weld; (2) Average of the 79 unique MSAs and CMSAs in this book
Source: American Medical Association, Physician Characteristics & Distribution in the U.S., 2006

Hospitals

Denver has the following hospitals: 8 general medical and surgical; 1 psychiatric; 1 long-term acute care; 1 other specialty; 1 children's general.
AHA Guide to the Healthcare Field 2007

According to *U.S. News*, the Denver metro area is home to five of the best hospitals in the U.S.: **Children's Hospital; Denver Health Medical Center; National Jewish Medical and Research Center; Rose Medical Center; University of Colorado Hospital**; *U.S. News Online, "America's Best Hospitals 2006"*

EDUCATION

Public School District Statistics

District Name	Schls	Pupils	Pupil/ Teacher Ratio	Minority Pupils[1] (%)	Free Lunch Eligible[2] (%)	IEP[3] (%)
Denver County 1	151	72,410	17.9	80.6	55.1	12.9
Mapleton 1	9	5,703	20.0	65.9	38.1	9.5

Note: Table includes regular local school districts with 2,000 or more students; (1) Percentage of students that are not white, non-Hispanic; (2) Percentage of students that are eligible for the free lunch program; (3) Percentage of students that have an Individualized Education Program.
Source: U.S. Department of Education, National Center for Education Statistics, Common Core of Data, Local Education Agency (School District) Universe Survey: School Year 2004-2005; U.S. Department of Education, National Center for Education Statistics, Common Core of Data, Public Elementary/Secondary School Universe Survey: School Year 2004-2005

Top Public High Schools

High School Name	Index[1]	Rank[1]	Subsidized Lunch (%)[2]	E&E (%)[3]
D'Evelyn	1.958	377	n/a	n/a
East	2.155	308	26.0	25.9
George Washington	2.955	125	n/a	n/a**

Note: (1) Public schools are ranked according to a ratio that is the number of Advanced Placement and/or International Baccalaureate tests taken by all students at a school in 2005 divided by the number of graduating seniors. All of the schools on the list have an index of at least 1.000; they are in the top five percent of public schools measured this way. The rankings range from 1 to 1,236; (2) Percentage of students receiving federally subsidized meals; (3) E & E stands for equity and excellence percentage: the portion of all graduating seniors at a school that had at least one passing grade on one AP or IB test; (*) Gave just IB tests; (**) Gave both IB and AP tests. AP and IB participation are indicators of a school's efforts to get students to excel and prepare for college; n/a not available
Source: Newsweek Online, May 23, 2006

Educational Quality

School District	Education Quotient[1]	Graduate Outcome[2]	Community Index[3]	Resource Index[4]	Rating[5]
Denver County 1	9	4	42	67	Red

Note: Scores are national percentile rankings and range from 1 (worst) to 99 (best); (1) Combination of the Graduate Outcome, Community and Resource Indexes weighted to reflect the greater importance of the Graduate Outcome and Resource Index; (2) Based on graduation rates and college board scores (SAT/ACT); (3) Based on the surrounding community's level of affluence and adult education; (4) Based on teacher salaries, per-pupil expenditures and student-teacher ratios; (5) School districts receive one of five rankings: Gold Medal (top 16 percent of districts evaluated); Blue Ribbon (top third); Green Light (average); Yellow Light (bottom 25 percent); Red Light (bottom 10 percent).
Source: Expansion Management, "2007 Education Quotient," January 2007

Highest Level of Education

Area	Less than H.S.	H.S. Diploma	Some College, No Deg.	Associate Degree	Bachelors Degree	Masters Degree	Profess. School Degree	Doctorate Degree
City	21.4	20.2	19.7	5.0	21.7	7.7	3.2	1.2
MSA[1]	13.2	21.8	23.8	6.8	23.2	7.8	2.3	1.0
U.S.	19.4	28.4	21.2	6.4	15.7	5.9	2.0	1.0

Note: Figures are 2006 estimated percentages and cover persons age 25 and over; (1) Metropolitan Statistical Area - see Appendix B for areas included
Source: Claritas, Inc.

Educational Attainment by Race

Area	High School Graduate (%)					Bachelor's Degree (%)				
	Total	White	Black	Asian	Hisp.[2]	Total	White	Black	Asian	Hisp.[2]
City	78.9	85.1	79.7	77.0	46.1	34.5	42.0	17.8	40.7	7.8
MSA[1]	86.4	89.6	83.6	79.8	55.9	34.2	37.3	21.0	40.6	10.6
U.S.	80.4	83.6	72.3	80.4	52.4	24.4	26.1	14.3	44.1	10.4

Note: Figures shown cover persons 25 years old and over; (1) Metropolitan Statistical Area - see Appendix A for areas included; (2) people of Hispanic origin can be of any race
Source: Census 2000, Summary File 3

School Enrollment by Type

Area	Grades KG to 8				Grades 9 to 12			
	Public		Private		Public		Private	
	Enrollment	%	Enrollment	%	Enrollment	%	Enrollment	%
City	53,202	87.7	7,484	12.3	20,810	89.6	2,412	10.4
MSA[1]	250,673	90.0	27,814	10.0	104,095	91.3	9,939	8.7
U.S.	33,526,011	88.7	4,285,121	11.3	14,848,628	90.6	1,532,323	9.4

Note: Figures shown cover persons 3 years old and over; (1) Metropolitan Statistical Area - see Appendix A for areas included
Source: Census 2000, Summary File 3

School Enrollment by Race

Area	Grades KG to 8 (%)				Grades 9 to 12 (%)			
	White	Black	Asian	Hisp.[1]	White	Black	Asian	Hisp.[1]
City	47.5	16.5	2.1	49.0	48.7	16.8	3.5	45.0
MSA[2]	73.1	6.9	2.7	24.9	74.5	6.6	3.4	21.9
U.S.	68.5	15.5	3.3	16.8	68.8	15.5	3.8	15.7

Note: Figures shown cover persons 3 years old and over; (1) people of Hispanic origin can be of any race; (2) Metropolitan Statistical Area - see Appendix A for areas included
Source: Census 2000, Summary File 3

Average Salaries of Public School Teachers

District	2004-05		2005-06		Percent Change 2004-05 to 2005-06
	Dollars	Rank[1]	Dollars	Rank[1]	
COLORADO	43,949	23	45,616	23	3.79
U.S. Average	47,674	-	49,109	-	3.01

Note: (1) State rank ranges from 1 to 51.
Source: National Education Association, Rankings & Estimates: Rankings of the States 2005 and Estimates of School Statistics 2006, November 2006

Higher Education

Four-Year Colleges			Two-Year Colleges			Medical Schools[1]	Law Schools[2]	Voc/ Tech[3]
Public	Private Non-profit	Private For-profit	Public	Private Non-profit	Private For-profit			
2	7	7	1	0	4	1	1	3

Note: Figures cover institutions located within the city limits; (1) includes schools accredited by the Liaison Committee on Medical Education and the American Osteopathic Association; (2) includes American Bar Association-accredited law schools; (3) includes all schools with programs that are less than 2 years
Source: National Center for Education Statistics, The Integrated Postsecondary Education System (IPEDS) Peer Analysis System, 2006; www.usnews.com, America's Best Graduate Schools 2008, Medical School Directory; www.usnews.com, America's Best Graduate Schools 2008, Law School Directory

PRESIDENTIAL ELECTION

2004 Presidential Election Results

Area	Bush	Kerry	Nader	Other
Denver County	29.3	69.6	0.6	0.6
U.S.	50.7	48.3	0.4	0.6

Note: Results are percentages and may not add to 100% due to rounding
Source: Dave Leip's Atlas of U.S. Presidential Elections, www.uselectionatlas.org

MAJOR EMPLOYERS

Major Employers

Company Name	Industry	Type of Site
Home Depot	Management services	Branch
Ball Metal Beverage Cont Corp	Metal cans	Headquarters
First Data	Data processing and preparation	Branch
IBM	Computers, peripherals, and software	Branch
IPS Financial Services	Functions related to depository banking	Headquarters
Conmed Electrosurgery	Electromedical equipment	Single
Echostar Communications Corp	Cable and other pay television services	Headquarters
Lockheed Martin	Search and navigation equipment	Branch
Lockheed Martin	Aircraft	Branch
Safety Dept	Public order and safety, nec	Branch
Eastern Colo Healthcare Sys	Administration of veterans' affairs	Branch
University Hospital	General medical and surgical hospitals	Headquarters
Colorado Dept of Transportation	Regulation, administration of transportation	Branch
Comcast Corporation	Cable and other pay television services	Branch
JD Edwards & Company	Prepackaged software	Headquarters
American Tourister	Luggage	Headquarters
United	Air transportation, scheduled	Branch
Denver Post Office	U.S. Postal Service	Branch
Alpine Access Inc	Business consulting, nec	Single

Note: Companies shown are located within the metropolitan area and have 2,500 or more employees; nec = not elsewhere classified.
Source: www.zapdata.com, January 2007

PUBLIC SAFETY

Crime Rate

Area	All Crimes	Violent Crimes				Property Crimes		
		Murder	Forcible Rape	Robbery	Aggrav. Assault	Burglary	Larceny -Theft	Motor Vehicle Theft
City	6,800.8	10.5	58.1	253.7	473.5	1,303.7	3,280.1	1,421.3
Suburbs[1]	4,305.8	3.2	41.8	81.9	207.1	653.8	2,688.7	629.4
Metro[2]	4,902.0	5.0	45.7	123.0	270.7	809.1	2,830.0	818.6
U.S.	3,899.0	5.6	31.7	140.7	291.1	726.7	2,286.3	416.7

Note: Figures are crimes per 100,000 population; (1) All areas within the metro area that are located outside the city limits; (2) Metropolitan Statistical Area - see Appendix B for areas included
Source: FBI Uniform Crime Reports, 2005

Hate Crimes

Area	Number of Quarters Reported	Bias Motivation				
		Race	Religion	Sexual Orientation	Ethnicity	Disability
City	4	4	2	4	2	0

Source: Federal Bureau of Investigation, Hate Crime Statistics 2005

RECREATION

Culture

Dance[1]	Theatre[1]	Instrumental Music[1]	Vocal Music[1]	Series/ Festivals	Museums	Zoos
7	13	3	3	2	17	1

Note: (1) number of professional perfoming groups
Source: The Grey House Performing Arts Directory, 2007; Official Museum Directory, 2007

Professional Sports Teams

Major League Baseball	National Basketball Association	National Football League	National Hockey League	Major League Soccer	Women's National Basketball Association
1	1	1	1	1	0

Note: Includes teams located in the Denver metro area.
Source: www.sportsvenues.com, Listing of Venues by State/Province and City, 2006

MEDIA

Newspapers

Name	Target Audience	Frequency	Circulation
Colorado Leader	General	Non-Daily	2,200
Colorado Statesman	General	Non-Daily	13,000
The Daily Journal	n/a	Daily	6,500
Denver Catholic Register	Catholic/Hispanic	Non-Daily	89,000
Denver Daily News	n/a	Daily	10,000
Denver Herald Dispatch	General	Non-Daily	8,500
The Denver Post	n/a	Daily	301,107
Denver Weekly News	Black/General	Non-Daily	10,000
Intermountain Jewish News	Jewish/Religious	Non-Daily	50,000
La Voz Hispana de Colorado	Hispanic	Non-Daily	18,250
Northglenn-Thornton Sentinel	General	Non-Daily	5,500
Rocky Mountain News	n/a	Daily	301,004
Washington Park Profile	General	Non-Daily	18,200
Westminster Window	General	Non-Daily	5,200
Westword	Alternative/General	Non-Daily	108,000

Note: Includes newspapers whose offices are located in the city and whose circulations are 1,000 or more; n/a not available
Source: BurrellesLuce, MediaContacts Online, January 2006

Television Stations

Name	Ch.	Network(s)	Type	Ownership
KWGN	2	WBN	Commercial	Tribune Broadcasting Company
KCNC	4	CBS	Commercial	CBS Broadcasting Company
KRMA	6	PBS	Public	Rocky Mountain Public Broadcasting Network
KMGH	7	ABC	Commercial	The McGraw-Hill Companies
KACT	8	n/a	Non-comm.	City of Aurora
KUSA	9	NBC	Commercial	Gannett Broadcasting
KBDI	12	PBS	Public	Front Range Educational Media Corp.
KTVJ	14	Univision	Commercial	Roberts Broadcasting Inc.
KTVD	20	UPN	Commercial	Channel 20 TV Company
KDEN	25	n/a	Commercial	Flinn Broadcasting Corporation
KDVR	31	Fox	Commercial	Fox Television Stations Inc.
KRMT	41	n/a	Non-comm.	Word of God Fellowship
KCEC	50	Univision	Commercial	Golden Hills Broadcasting
KWHD	53	n/a	Commercial	LeSea Inc.
KPXC	59	Pax	Commercial	Paxson Communications Corporation
KMAS	63	Telemundo	Commercial	n/a

Note: Stations included cover the Denver DMA (Designated Market Area); n/a not available
BurrellesLuce, MediaContacts Online, January 2006

Major AM Radio Stations

Call Letters	Freq. (kHz)	Station Type	Target Audience	Station Format	Music Format
KLZ	560	n/a	General/Religious	News/Talk	n/a
KIIX	600	Commercial	General	Sports/Talk	n/a
KHOW	630	n/a	General	Music/News/Talk	n/a
KLTT	670	n/a	General/Religious	Talk	n/a
KNUS	710	n/a	General	News/Sports/Talk	n/a
KKZN	760	n/a	General	Sports/Talk	n/a
KOA	850	n/a	General	Music/News/Sports/Talk	n/a
KPOF	910	Non-Comm	General/Religious	Educational/Music	Classical
KLMR	920	n/a	General	Music/News/Sports/Talk	n/a
KOGA	930	n/a	General	n/a	n/a
KKFN	950	n/a	General	Music/Sports/Talk	n/a
KRKS	990	Commercial	General/Religious	News/Talk	n/a
KSIR	1010	Commercial	General	News/Sports/Talk	n/a
KLMO	1060	Commercial	General	Talk	n/a
KMXA	1090	n/a	General/Hispanic	Music/Talk	n/a
KCUV	1150	n/a	General/Hispanic	Sports	n/a
KVCU	1190	College	General	Ed/Music/News/Sports	Urban Contemp.
KLVZ	1220	n/a	General/Religious	Music	n/a
KRAL	1240	Commercial	General	Music/News	Adult Contemp.
KIML	1270	Commercial	General	Music/News/Sports	n/a
KBNO	1280	n/a	Hispanic	Music/News/Talk	n/a
KOWB	1290	n/a	General	News/Talk	n/a
KFKA	1310	Commercial	General	Ed/News/Sports/Talk	n/a
KCOL	1410	Commercial	General	News/Talk	n/a
KRDZ	1440	Commercial	General	Music/News/Sports	Oldies
KADZ	1550	Commercial	Children/Religious	Music/Talk	Adult Contemp.
KCKK	1600	n/a	General	Music	n/a
KBJD	1650	Commercial	General	News/Talk	n/a

Note: Stations included cover the Denver DMA (Designated Market Area); n/a not available
Source: BurrellesLuce, MediaContacts Online, January 2006

Major FM Radio Stations

Call Letters	Freq. (mHz)	Station Type	Target Audience	Station Format	Music Format
KLDV	91.1	Non-Comm	Religious	Music	Christian
KUNC	91.5	n/a	General	Ed/Music/News/Talk	Jazz
KUWR	91.9	College	General	Music/News/Talk	Jazz
KLGT	92.9	n/a	General/Religious	n/a	n/a
KTCL	93.3	n/a	General	Music	n/a
KLMR	93.3	n/a	General	Music/News/Sports	A.O. Rock
KRAI	93.7	Commercial	General	Music/News	Adult Contemp.
KRKS	94.7	Commercial	General/Religious	Music/News/Talk	Christian
KCGY	95.1	n/a	General	Music/Sports	n/a
KFMD	95.7	n/a	General	Music	n/a
KGLL	96.1	Commercial	General	Music	Top 40
KAML	96.9	n/a	General	Music/News/Sports	Classic Rock
KBCO	97.3	Commercial	General	Music/News	Classic Rock
KQSK	97.5	Commercial	General	Music/News	Country
KYGO	98.5	n/a	General	Music	n/a
KSID	98.7	n/a	General	Music/News/Sports	n/a
KUAD	99.1	Commercial	General	Music	Country
KOGA	99.7	n/a	General	Music/News	n/a
KIMN	100.3	n/a	General	n/a	n/a
KGWY	100.7	Commercial	General	Music/News/Sports	Country
KOSI	101.1	n/a	General	Music	n/a
KPNY	102.1	Commercial	General	Music/News	Adult Contemp.
KRFX	103.5	n/a	General	Music/News/Sports	n/a
KJCD	104.3	n/a	General	Music/News/Talk	n/a
KNNG	104.7	Commercial	General	Music/News	Country
KXKL	105.1	n/a	General	Music/News	n/a
KIMX	105.5	n/a	General/Women	Music/News/Sports	n/a
KVAY	105.7	Commercial	General	Music	Oldies
KALC	105.9	Commercial	General	Music	Adult Contemp.
KAAQ	105.9	n/a	General	Music/News/Sports	n/a
KMCX	106.5	Commercial	General	Music/News	Country
KBPI	106.7	n/a	General	Music/News/Talk	n/a
KQKS	107.5	Commercial	General	Music	Urban Contemp.

Note: Stations included cover the Denver DMA (Designated Market Area); n/a not available
BurrellesLuce, MediaContacts Online, January 2006

CLIMATE

Average and Extreme Temperatures

Temperature	Jan	Feb	Mar	Apr	May	Jun	Jul	Aug	Sep	Oct	Nov	Dec	Yr.
Extreme High (°F)	73	76	84	90	93	102	103	100	97	89	79	75	103
Average High (°F)	43	47	52	62	71	81	88	86	77	67	52	45	64
Average Temp. (°F)	30	34	39	48	58	67	73	72	63	52	39	32	51
Average Low (°F)	16	20	25	34	44	53	59	57	48	37	25	18	37
Extreme Low (°F)	-25	-25	-10	-2	22	30	43	41	17	3	-8	-25	-25

Note: Figures cover the years 1948-1992
Source: National Climatic Data Center, International Station Meteorological Climate Summary, 9/96

Average Precipitation/Snowfall/Humidity

Precip./Humidity	Jan	Feb	Mar	Apr	May	Jun	Jul	Aug	Sep	Oct	Nov	Dec	Yr.
Avg. Precip. (in.)	0.6	0.6	1.3	1.7	2.5	1.7	1.9	1.5	1.1	1.0	0.9	0.6	15.5
Avg. Snowfall (in.)	9	7	14	9	2	Tr	0	0	2	4	9	8	63
Avg. Rel. Hum. 5am (%)	62	65	67	66	70	68	67	68	66	63	66	63	66
Avg. Rel. Hum. 5pm (%)	49	44	40	35	38	34	34	34	32	34	47	50	39

Note: Figures cover the years 1948-1992; Tr = Trace amounts (<0.05 in. of rain; <0.5 in. of snow)
Source: National Climatic Data Center, International Station Meteorological Climate Summary, 9/96

Weather Conditions

Temperature			Daytime Sky			Precipitation		
10°F & below	32°F & below	90°F & above	Clear	Partly cloudy	Cloudy	0.01 inch or more precip.	0.1 inch or more snow/ice	Thunder-storms
24	155	33	99	177	89	90	38	39

Note: Figures are average number of days per year and cover the years 1948-1992
Source: National Climatic Data Center, International Station Meteorological Climate Summary, 9/96

HAZARDOUS WASTE

Superfund Sites

Denver has four hazardous waste sites on the EPA's Superfund Final National Priorities List: **Broderick Wood Products; Chemical Sales Co.; Denver Radium Site; Vasquez Boulevard and I-70.** *U.S. Environmental Protection Agency, Final National Priorities List, March 20, 2007*

AIR & WATER QUALITY

Air Quality Index

Area	Percent of Days when Air Quality was...[2]				AQI Statistics	
	Good	Moderate	Unhealthy for Sensitive Groups	Unhealthy	Maximum	Median
MSA[1]	54.0	44.7	1.4	0.0	116	49

Note: The Air Quality Index (AQI) is an index for reporting daily air quality. EPA calculates the AQI for five major air pollutants regulated by the Clean Air Act: ground-level ozone, particle pollution (also known as particulate matter), carbon monoxide, sulfur dioxide, and nitrogen dioxide. The AQI runs from 0 to 500. The higher the AQI value, the greater the level of air pollution and the greater the health concern. There are six AQI categories: "Good" The AQI is between 0 and 50. Air quality is considered satisfactory; "Moderate" The AQI is between 51 and 100. Air quality is acceptable; "Unhealthy for Sensitive Groups" When AQI values are between 101 and 150, members of sensitive groups may experience health effects; "Unhealthy" When AQI values are between 151 and 200 everyone may begin to experience health effects; "Very Unhealthy" AQI values between 201 and 300 trigger a health alert; "Hazardous" AQI values over 300 trigger health warnings of emergency conditions; (1) Metropolitan Statistical Area - see Appendix A for areas included; (2) Based on 365 days with AQI data in 2005.
Source: U.S. Environmental Protection Agency, Air Quality Index Report, 2005

Air Quality Index Pollutants

Area	Percent of Days when AQI Pollutant was...[2]					
	Carbon Monoxide	Nitrogen Dioxide	Ozone	Sulfur Dioxide	Particulate Matter 2.5	Particulate Matter 10
MSA[1]	0.0	0.0	45.5	0.0	34.8	19.7

Note: The Air Quality Index (AQI) is an index for reporting daily air quality. EPA calculates the AQI for five major air pollutants regulated by the Clean Air Act: ground-level ozone, particle pollution (also known as particulate matter), carbon monoxide, sulfur dioxide, and nitrogen dioxide. The AQI runs from 0 to 500. The higher the AQI value, the greater the level of air pollution and the greater the health concern; (1) Metropolitan Statistical Area - see Appendix A for areas included; (2) Based on 365 days with AQI data in 2005.
Source: U.S. Environmental Protection Agency, Air Quality Index Report, 2005

Number of Days with Air Quality Index Values Greater than 100

Area	Trend Sites (23)								All Sites (82)
	1998	1999	2000	2001	2002	2003	2004	2005	2005
MSA[1]	7	3	2	8	7	16	0	1	2

Note: An AQI value greater than 100 indicates that air quality would have been in the unhealthful range on that day. Data from exceptional events are not included. These counts are presented in two ways. First, the counts are based on sites having an adequate record of monitoring data during the trend period (trend sites). These counts represent the relative change in the number of days with AQI values greater than 100. In the last column, the counts are based on all sites with data in the most recent year (because it is possible for a site to have data in the most recent year but not enough data to be a trend site); (1) Metropolitan Statistical Area - see Appendix A for areas included; n/a not available.
Source: U.S. Environmental Protection Agency, Air Trends Fact Book 2005

Maximum Pollutant Concentrations

	Particulate Matter 10 (ug/m^3)	Particulate Matter 2.5 (ug/m^3)	Ozone 1-hour (ppm)	Carbon Monoxide (ppm)	Sulfur Dioxide (ppm)	Nitrogen Dioxide (ppm)	Lead (ug/m^3)
MSA[1] Level	97	27	0.103	3	0.009	0.028	0.56
NAAQS[2]	150	65	0.125	9	0.140	0.053	1.50
Met NAAQS[2]	Yes	Yes	Yes	Yes	Yes	Yes	Yes

Note: Data from exceptional events are not included; (1) Metropolitan Statistical Area - see Appendix A for areas included; (2) National Ambient Air Quality Standards; n/a not available
Units: ppm = parts per million; ug/m^3 = micrograms per cubic meter
Source: U.S. Environmental Protection Agency, Air Trends Fact Book 2005

Watershed Health

The U.S. Environmental Protection Agency monitors the health of the aquatic resources for the nation's 2,000+ watersheds. **The Middle South Platte-Cherry Creek watershed serves the Denver area and received an overall Index of Watershed Indicators (IWI) score of 1 (better quality - low vulnerability).** The IWI score is based on seven condition and nine vulnerability indicators. The overall IWI score ranges from 1 (best health) to 6 (worst health). The Condition Indicators include: designated use attainment, fish and wildlife consumption advisories, source water condition, contaminated sediments, ambient water quality, and wetlands loss index. The Vulnerability Indicators include: aquatic species at risk, conventional and toxic loads over permitted limits, urban and agricultural runoff potential, population change, hydrologic modification, estuarine pollution susceptibility, and air deposition. *Note: The IWI is no longer being updated by the U.S. EPA. Source: U.S. Environmental Protection Agency, Index of Watershed Indicators, October 26, 2001*

Drinking Water

Water System Name	Pop. Served	Primary Water Source Type	Number of Violations in 2006[a]		
			Health Based	Significant Monitoring	Monitoring
Denver Water Board	1,000,000	Surface	None	None	None

Note: (a) Based on violation data from January 1, 2006 to December 31, 2006
Source: U.S. Environmental Protection Agency, Office of Ground Water and Drinking Water, Safe Drinking Water Information System (data extracted April 12, 2007)

Denver tap water is alkaline, 53% of supply hard, 47% of supply soft. The West Slope is fluoridated, the East Slope is not fluoridated.
Editor & Publisher Market Guide, 2005

Eugene, Oregon

Background

In 1846, Eugene F. Skinner, for whom the city is named, and his family settled in the lush Willamette Valley. In 1853, the town was named the seat of the newly created Lane County. The city was incorporated in 1862, and in 1876 the University of Oregon was established.

Eugene is now Oregon's second-largest city and was a major processing and shipping center for lumber until the decline of the timber industry in the 1980s. Eugene's economy struggled for a time, but by the latter 1990s, recovery was in full swing.

The city now enjoys a diverse economic base, with 10,000 businesses in and around Eugene. Government, education, and health care remain the largest providers of jobs. The city's major employers are the state's two major universities — University of Oregon in Eugene and Oregon State University in Corvallis, plus Hynix Semiconductor (formerly Hyundai Electronics), Bi-Mart Corp., Symantec, Monaco Coach Corp., Sacred Heart Medical Center, and Roseburg Forest Products. The local economy is also considerably bolstered by many small and medium-sized businesses employing 20 or fewer workers.

Eugene Airport, also known as Mahlon Sweet Field, is owned and operated by the City of Eugene, and is the fifth-largest airport in the Pacific Northwest. In addition to commercial flights, it also has an expanded air cargo facility to serve the growing demands of the region. Airport improvements are being implemented in line with a Master Plan drawn up in 1990 which features both short and long-term needs. Most recently, a new 6,000-foot runway was completed, and several taxiways have been rehabilitated, allowing two aircraft to land or take off at the same time.

The Eugene/Springfield area boasts nearly 100 organizations and facilities providing performing, literary, ethnic, and visual arts activities. The state-of-the-art Hult Center is home to resident ballet, symphony, opera, and musical theater companies and also attracts top performers from around the world. There are seven area museums and over a dozen galleries featuring local, national, and international artists' work. The Lane Education Service District (ESD) Planetarium is the second-largest facility of its kind in the Northwest, seating 125 under a 40-foot dome. The University of Oregon's natural history museum has been renovated and reopened.

Other fairs, festivals, and special events occur throughout the year, including the Lane County Fair, the Oregon Country Fair, Art in the Vineyard, the Asian Celebration, and the internationally acclaimed Oregon Bach Festival. The Lane County Ice Arena hosts world-class skaters, three Olympic Track and Field Trials, the Olympic Scientific Congress, the World Veterans' Championships, and the International Music Educator's Society.

Located in the famed South Willamette Valley wine country, Eugene is home to nine wineries and within easy reach of dozens more; there are more than 200 wineries in the entire Willamette Valley. The cool climate is particularly congenial to the early-ripening pinot noir grape, but chardonnay and pinot gris are also grown here.

In addition to the University of Oregon, several colleges are located in Eugene, such as Eugene Bible College, Northwest Christian College, and Lane Community College. The city offers a wide variety of restaurants such as Italian, German, and Thai, and plenty of shops, cinemas, and nightclubs.

In a recent community survey when residents were asked what they most liked about Eugene, respondents replied: Friendly people (13 percent), scenery/terrain (12 percent), followed by outdoor recreation (11 percent), central location (11 percent), climate/weather (10 percent), and size of the city (10 percent).

The Coast Range, west of the city, acts as a barrier to coastal fog, but active storms cross with little hindrance. To the east, the Cascade Range, which lures skiers to the area, blocks all but the strongest continental air masses. When eastern air does flow into the valley during dry, hot summer weather, an extreme fire hazard can develop. In the winter, however, clear, sunny days and cool, frosty nights result. Temperatures are largely controlled by maritime air from the Pacific Ocean, so that long periods of extremely hot or cold weather never occur.

Rankings

GeneralRankings

- Eugene was ranked #21 out of 331 metro areas in *Cities Ranked & Rated*. Criteria: cost of living; climate; crime; transportation; economy and jobs; education; arts and culture; health and healthcare; leisure. *Cities Ranked & Rated, 1st Edition, 2004*

- The Eugene area was selected as one of "60 Cheap Places to Live" in the U.S. The area appeared in the "IQ Campuses" (emerging centers of biotech and infotech) category. *Forbes.com, August 20, 2004*

Business/Finance Rankings

- Eugene was selected as one of the best places to start and grow a company by *Entrepreneur* and the National Policy Research Council. The Eugene metro area ranked #58 out of 63 mid-size metro areas. Criteria: business formation and growth (firms started four to 14 years ago that still employ at least 5 people and experienced rapid growth over the last four years). *Entrepreneur/National Policy Research Council, "Hot Cities for Entrepreneurs," September 2006*

- The Eugene metro area was selected as one of the "25 Hottest Housing Markets" in the U.S. The area ranked #58 out of 156 markets with a home price appreciation rate of 10.5%. Criteria: year-over-year change of median sales price of existing single-family homes between the 4th quarter of 2005 and the 4th quarter of 2006. *National Association of Realtors, Median Sales Price of Existing Single-Family Homes for Metropolitan Areas, 4th Quarter 2006*

- The Eugene metro area appeared on the Milken Institute "2005 Best Performing Cities" index. Rank: #96 out of 200 large metro areas. Criteria: job growth; wage and salary growth; high-tech output growth. *Milken Institute, "2005 Best Performing Cities," February 2006*

- *Forbes* ranked the 200 most populous metro areas in the U.S. in terms of the "Best Places for Business and Careers." The Eugene metro area was ranked #39. Criteria: business costs (labor, energy, tax and office space expenses); living costs (housing, transportation, food and other household expenditures); education levels of the work force; job growth; income growth; migration trends; crime rates; and culture/leisure. *Forbes, April 23, 2007*

Health/Environment Rankings

- The Eugene metro area appeared in *Country Home's* "2007 Best Green Places Report". The area ranked #18. Criteria included: air and watershed quality; miles of mass transit; green power; number of farmer's markets, organic producers and groceries. *Country Home, "2007 Best Green Places Report," April 2007*

- Sperling's BestPlaces ranked 331 metro areas and identified the most and least stressful U.S. cities. The Eugene metro area ranked #17 out of 114 mid-size metro areas (#1 = most stressful). Criteria: divorce rate; unemployment rate; violent and property crime; suicide rate; commute time; mental health; alcohol consumption; cloudy days. *www.BestPlaces.net, January 9, 2004*

- Eugene was highlighted as one of the top 25 cleanest metro areas for ozone air pollution in the U.S. The list represents cities with no monitored ozone air pollution in the unhealthful range. *American Lung Association, State of the Air 2006*

Women/Minorities Rankings

- *Ladies Home Journal* ranked America's 200 largest cities based on the qualities women surveyed care about most. Eugene ranked #38 out of 143 in the smaller city category (population under 300,000). Criteria: crime; lifestyle; education; jobs; health; child care; politics; and the economy. *Ladies Home Journal Online, "The Best Cities for Women 2002"*

■ Eugene was identified as one of the top 25 metropolitan statistical areas ranked by percentage of coupled households that are gay or lesbian." The area ranked #18. *Human Rights Campaign, "Gay and Lesbian Families in the United States: Same-Sex Unmarried Partner Households," August 1, 2001*

Seniors/Retirement Rankings

■ Eugene was profiled in the book *Where to Retire: America's Best and Most Affordable Places.* Cities were selected based on personal visits by the author and interviews with local residents coupled with statistics from various government agencies. *Where to Retire: America's Best and Most Affordable Places, 2006*

■ Eugene was identified as one of the "100 Most Popular Places to Retire" by *Where to Retire* magazine. The city ranked #85. Criteria: net retirees received from 1995-2000 (derived by subtracting all outbound retirees from inbound retirees for the county or county group - includes interstate moves only). *Where to Retire, "100 Most Popular Places to Retire," January/February 2007*

■ Eugene was profiled in the book *Retire in Style: 60 Outstanding Places Across the USA and Canada.* Criteria: landscape; climate; quality of life; cost of living; transportation; retail services; health care; community services; cultural and educational activities; recreational activities; work and volunteer activities; crime rates and public safety. *Retire in Style: 60 Outstanding Places Across the USA and Canada, 2005*

■ A.G. Edwards ranked America's 500 top-performing communities based on their residents' personal savings and investing behavior. The Eugene metro area ranked #467 with an index score of 95.34 (national average = 100.00). A dozen statistical factors were measured including: participation in retirement savings plans; personal debt levels; and home ownership. *A.G. Edwards, "2006 Nest Egg Index", September 6, 2006*

Children/Family Rankings

■ The Eugene metro area was selected as one of the "Best Cities for Relocating Families" by Worldwide ERC and Primacy Relocation. Criteria: tax rates; average home costs and home appreciation; ability to qualify for in-state tuition; service quality of local utilities; per-capita volunteerism; auto taxes; and quantity of fun, family-friendly events and venues. *Worldwide ERC and Primacy Relocation, "2006 Best Cities for Relocating Families"*

Safety Rankings

■ Allstate ranked the 200 largest cities in America in terms of driver safety. Eugene ranked #19. In addition, drivers were 13.6% less likely to have had an accident compared to the national average. Allstate researchers analyzed internal Property Damage reported claims over a two-year period (from January 2003 to December 2004) to ensure the findings would not be affected by external influences such as weather or road construction. A weighted average of the two-year numbers determined the annual percentages. The report defines an auto crash as any collision resulting in a property damage claim. *Allstate, "Allstate America's Best Drivers Report 2006," May 24, 2006*

■ *Ladies Home Journal* ranked America's 200 largest cities in terms of safety. Eugene ranked #66 out of 200. Criteria: violent crimes; crimes against property; and rape. *Ladies Home Journal Online, "The Best Cities for Women 2002"*

Sports/Recreation Rankings

■ The Eugene metro area appeared on *The Sporting News* list of the "Best Sports Cities 2006". The area ranked #69 out of 99 cities in North America. To be included in the rankings, a city must have at least one of the following: NCAA Division I basketball team; Class A minor league baseball team; training camp for a major league or NFL team; NASCAR Nextel Cup race; NCAA Division I-A bowl game; PGA Tour tournament; Triple Crown horse race. Once a city qualifies, a 12-month snapshot is taken of the sports atmosphere, putting a heavy premium on regular-season won-lost records; playoff berths, bowl appearances and tournament bids; championships; applicable power ratings; quality of competition; overall fan fervor; sports atmosphere and fan knowledge; abundance of teams (quality over quantity); stadium/arena quality; ticket availability and prices; franchise ownership; and the marquee appeal of athletes. *SportingNews.com, "Best Sports Cities 2006," August 1, 2006*

■ Eugene was chosen as one of "The 10 Best Cities for Mountain Bikers." The city was ranked #9. The criteria for making the list was two-fold: 1) great trails within or very close to the city; 2) the city had to be a place where people could actually live—with good jobs, decent schools, affordable housing, arts and sports, and a sense of community. *Mountain Bike, June 2001*

■ Eugene was chosen as one of America's best cities for bicycling. The city ranked #2 in the small city category (population 75,000 to 200,000). Criteria: cycling-friendly statistics (number of bike lanes and routes, number of bike racks, city bike projects completed and planned; bike culture (number of bike commuters, popular clubs, cool cycling events, renowned bike shops); climate/geography (the quality of roads and trails for riding, and how frequently mother nature lets riders enjoy them). *Bicycling, March 2006*

■ *Golf Digest* ranked 330 metro areas in the U.S. in terms of golf. The Eugene metro area was ranked #193. Criteria: access to golf; weather; value of golf; and quality of golf. *Golf Digest, "Metro Golf Rankings," August 2005*

Miscellaneous Rankings

■ Eugene was selected as one of "America's Best Vegetarian-Friendly Small Cities." The city was ranked #2. *www.peta.org, April 2006*

■ Sperling's BestPlaces in partnership with Pep Boys ranked 77 metro areas and identified "America's Most Drivable Cities." The Eugene metro area ranked #31. Criteria: climate; road roughness; urban mobility; gas prices. *Pep Boys, "America's Most Drivable Cities," April 9, 2003*

■ A study by Sperling's BestPlaces examined which U.S. metro areas were most affected by the fuel crunch in 2005. The Eugene metro area was selected as being one of the least impacted areas. The area ranked #3 out of 10. Criteria: average miles driven per day per peak traveler; average gallons of gas used per peak traveler; money spent on gas per driver. *Sperling's BestPlaces, www.bestplaces.net, September 29, 2005*

Business Environment

CITY FINANCES

City Government Finances

Component	2003-2004 ($000)	2003-2004 ($ per capita)
Total Revenues	480,350	3,421
Total Expenditures	440,686	3,139
Debt Outstanding	392,640	2,797
Cash and Securities	224,326	1,598

Source: U.S Census Bureau, Government Finances 2003-2004

City Government Revenue by Source

Source	2003-2004 ($000)	2003-2004 ($ per capita)
General Revenue		
From Federal Government	12,918	92
From State Government	9,243	66
From Local Governments	20,360	145
Taxes		
Property	80,078	570
Sales	20,963	149
Personal Income	0	0
License	0	0
Charges	64,539	460
Liquor Store	0	0
Utility	247,976	1,766
Employee Retirement	0	0
Other	24,273	173

Source: U.S Census Bureau, Government Finances 2003-2004

City Government Expenditures by Function

Function	2003-2004 ($000)	2003-2004 ($ per capita)	2003-2004 (%)
General Expenditures			
Airports	8,849	63	2.0
Corrections	0	0	0.0
Education	0	0	0.0
Fire Protection	20,562	146	4.7
Governmental Administration	48,980	349	11.1
Health	0	0	0.0
Highways	6,135	44	1.4
Hospitals	0	0	0.0
Housing and Community Development	10,554	75	2.4
Interest on General Debt	7,550	54	1.7
Libraries	8,090	58	1.8
Parking	2,074	15	0.5
Parks and Recreation	16,560	118	3.8
Police Protection	29,614	211	6.7
Public Welfare	0	0	0.0
Sewerage	20,250	144	4.6
Solid Waste Management	1,083	8	0.2
Liquor Store	0	0	0.0
Utility	222,738	1,587	50.5
Employee Retirement	0	0	0.0
Other	37,647	268	8.5

Source: U.S Census Bureau, Government Finances 2003-2004

Municipal Bond Ratings

Area	Moody's
City	Aaa

Source: Mergent Bond Record, January 2007 (unless noted otherwise)

DEMOGRAPHICS

Population Growth

Area	1990 Census	2000 Census	2006 Estimate	2011 Projection	Population Growth (%) 1990-2000	Population Growth (%) 2000-2011
City	118,073	137,893	144,090	149,543	16.8	8.4
MSA[1]	282,912	322,959	336,438	348,705	14.2	8.0
U.S.	248,709,873	281,421,906	298,021,266	312,383,955	13.2	11.0

Note: (1) Metropolitan Statistical Area - see Appendix B for areas included
Source: Claritas, Inc.

Number of Households and Average Household Size

Area	2006 Estimate	2006 Average Household Size
City	61,501	2.34
MSA[1]	137,577	2.45
U.S.	112,267,302	2.65

Note: (1) Metropolitan Statistical Area - see Appendix B for areas included
Source: Claritas, Inc.

Race and Ethnicity

Area	White Alone[2]	Black Alone[2]	Asian Alone[2]	Other Race Alone[2]	Hispanic[3]
City	86.2	1.4	4.5	8.0	6.0
MSA[1]	89.2	0.9	2.5	7.5	5.6
U.S.	73.3	12.4	4.2	10.1	14.5

Note: Figures are 2006 estimates; (1) Metropolitan Statistical Area - see Appendix B for areas included
(2) Alone is defined as not being in combination with one or more other races; (3) May be of any race.
Source: Claritas, Inc.

Segregation

City Index[2]	City Rank[3]	MSA[1] Index[2]	MSA[1] Rank[4]
25.5	100	37.9	308

Note: Figures are based on an analysis of Census 2000 data; (1) Metropolitan Statistical Area - see Appendix A for areas included; (2) White/Black Dissimilarity Index—the most commonly used measure of segregation between two groups, reflecting their relative distributions across neighborhoods within a city or metropolitan area. It can range in value from 0, indicating complete integration, to 100, indicating complete segregation; (3) Ranges from 1 (most segregated) to 100 (least segregated) and includes all the cities in this book; (4) Ranges from 1 (most segregated) to 318 (least segregated) and includes 318 metropolitan areas.
Source: www.CensusScope.org

Ancestry

Area	German	Irish[2]	English	American	Italian	Polish	French[3]	Scottish
City	20.3	13.1	14.8	4.8	3.7	2.0	4.1	3.8
MSA[1]	20.8	12.8	14.3	6.2	3.4	1.8	4.1	3.5
U.S.	15.2	10.9	8.7	7.3	5.6	3.2	3.0	1.7

Note: Figures include multiple ancestry (e.g. if a person reported being Irish and Italian, they were included in both columns); (1) Metropolitan Statistical Area - see Appendix A for areas included; (2) Includes Celtic; (3) Includes Alsatian but excludes Basque
Source: Census 2000, Summary File 3

Foreign-Born Population

Area	Percent of Population Born in — Any Foreign Country	Europe	Asia	Africa	Oceania[2]	Canada	Mexico	Latin America[3]
City	6.6	1.3	2.7	0.2	0.1	0.7	1.2	0.4
MSA[1]	4.9	1.1	1.6	0.1	0.1	0.5	1.3	0.3
U.S.	11.1	1.7	2.9	0.3	0.1	0.3	3.3	2.5

Note: (1) Metropolitan Statistical Area - see Appendix A for areas included; (2) Includes Australia, New Zealand subregion, Melanesia, Micronesia, Polynesia, and Oceania n.e.c; (3) Includes Central America (excluding Mexico), South America, and the Caribbean.
Source: Census 2000, Summary File 3

Marriage Status

Area	Never Married	Now Married (excluding Separated)	Separated	Widowed	Divorced
City	36.2	44.8	1.5	5.6	12.0
MSA[1]	28.1	52.2	1.6	5.9	12.1
U.S.	27.1	54.4	2.2	6.6	9.7

Note: Figures are percentages and cover the population 15 years of age and older;
(1) Metropolitan Statistical Area - see Appendix A for areas included
Source: Census 2000, Summary File 3

Age Distribution

Area	Percent of Population						
	Under Age 5	Age 5 to 17	Age 18 to 34	Age 35 to 49	Age 50 to 64	Age 65 to 79	80 Years and Over
City	5.3	15.3	31.9	21.6	13.8	8.2	3.9
MSA[1]	5.7	17.1	24.9	22.9	16.1	9.7	3.6
U.S.	6.8	18.9	23.7	23.5	14.8	9.2	3.2

Note: (1) Metropolitan Statistical Area - see Appendix A for areas included
Source: Census 2000, Summary File 3

Male/Female Ratio

Area	Males	Females	Males per 100 Females
City	70,589	73,501	96.0
MSA[1]	165,412	171,026	96.7
U.S.	146,712,712	151,308,554	97.0

Note: Figures are 2006 estimates; (1) Metropolitan Statistical Area -
see Appendix B for areas included
Source: Claritas, Inc.

Religion

Area	Catholic	Southern Baptist	United Methodist	ELCA[1]	LDS[2]	Presbyterian Church USA	Jewish Est.	Muslim Est.
County	4.8	1.3	1.0	1.3	2.6	0.5	1.0	0.2
U.S.	22.0	7.1	3.7	1.8	1.5	1.1	2.2	0.6

Note: Figures are the number of adherents as a percentage of the total population; Adherents are defined as all
members, including full members, their children and the estimated number of other participants who are not
considered members (e.g. the baptized, those not confirmed, those regularly attending services, etc.);
(1) Evangelical Lutheran Church in America; (2) The Church of Jesus Christ of Latter Day Saints
Source: Reprinted with permission from Religious Congregations and Membership in the United States 2000
(Nashville, Glenmary Research Center, 2002) Copyright Association of Statisticians of American Religious
Bodies. All rights reserved.

ECONOMY

Gross Metropolitan Product

Area	2002	2003	2004	2005	2005 Rank[2]
MSA[1]	10.3	10.6	11.9	12.8	148

Note: Figures are in billions of dollars; (1) Eugene-Springfield, OR Metropolitan Statistical Area - see
Appendix A for areas included; (2) Rank ranges from 1 to 361
Source: The U.S. Conference of Mayors, "U.S. Metro Economies: GMP - The Engines of America's Growth,"
January 2007

Economic Growth

Area	1995 GMP	2005 GMP	Average Annual Growth Rate	Growth Rate Rank[2]
MSA[1]	7.0	12.8	6.2	100

Note: Figures are in billions of dollars; GMP = Gross Metropolitan Product; (1) Eugene-Springfield, OR
Metropolitan Statistical Area - see Appendix A for areas included; (2) Rank ranges from 1 to 361
Source: The U.S. Conference of Mayors, "U.S. Metro Economies: GMP - The Engines of America's Growth,"
January 2007

INCOME

Per Capita/Median/Average Income

Area	Per Capita ($)	Median Household ($)	Average Household ($)
City	23,884	39,922	55,135
MSA[1]	22,815	42,403	55,209
U.S.	25,129	48,775	65,849

Note: Figures are 2006 estimates; (1) Metropolitan Statistical Area - see Appendix B for areas included
Source: Claritas, Inc.

Household Income Distribution

Area	\multicolumn{8}{c}{Percent of Households Earning}

Area	Under $15,000	$15,000 -24,999	$25,000 -34,999	$35,000 -49,999	$50,000 -74,999	$75,000 -99,000	$100,000 -149,999	$150,000 and up
City	18.9	13.1	12.6	16.6	17.5	8.9	7.8	4.7
MSA[1]	15.8	12.9	12.6	17.6	19.6	9.9	7.7	3.9
U.S.	13.3	11.0	11.3	15.7	19.5	11.8	11.0	6.4

Note: Figures are 2006 estimates; (1) Metropolitan Statistical Area - see Appendix B for areas included
Source: Claritas, Inc.

Poverty Rates by Age

Area	All Ages	Under 5 Years Old	5 to 17 Years Old	18 to 64 Years Old	65 Years and Over
City	17.1	1.1	2.1	13.0	0.9
MSA[1]	14.4	1.2	2.6	9.6	1.0
U.S.	12.4	1.2	3.0	6.9	1.2

Note: Figures are percent of population with income in 1999 below poverty level and only include population for whom poverty status is determined; (1) Metropolitan Statistical Area - see Appendix A for areas included
Source: Census 2000, Summary File 3

Personal Bankruptcy Filing Rate

Area	2003	2004	2005
Lane County	7.09	6.43	8.61
U.S.	5.57	5.31	6.88

Note: Numbers are per 1,000 population and include Chapter 7 and Chapter 13 filings
Source: Federal Deposit Insurance Corporation (FDIC), Regional Economic Conditions (RECON), 3/24/2006

EMPLOYMENT

Labor Force and Employment

Area	\multicolumn{3}{c}{Civilian Labor Force}			\multicolumn{3}{c}{Workers Employed}		

Area	Dec. 2005	Dec. 2006	% Chg.	Dec. 2005	Dec. 2006	% Chg.
City	77,688	79,681	2.6	74,134	76,252	2.9
MSA[1]	174,812	179,531	2.7	165,559	170,288	2.9
U.S.	149,874,000	152,571,000	1.8	142,918,000	146,081,000	2.2

Note: Data is not seasonally adjusted and covers workers 16 years of age and older;
(1) Metropolitan Statistical Area - see Appendix B for areas included
Source: Bureau of Labor Statistics, http://stats.bls.gov

Unemployment Rate

Area	\multicolumn{12}{c}{2006}

Area	Jan.	Feb.	Mar.	Apr.	May	Jun.	Jul.	Aug.	Sep.	Oct.	Nov.	Dec.
City	5.2	5.9	5.5	5.1	4.8	5.2	5.3	5.0	4.6	4.2	4.5	4.3
MSA[1]	6.0	6.6	6.2	5.7	5.4	5.6	5.8	5.5	5.1	4.7	5.1	5.1
U.S.	5.1	5.1	4.8	4.5	4.4	4.8	5.0	4.6	4.4	4.1	4.3	4.3

Note: Data is not seasonally adjusted and covers workers 16 years of age and older; All figures are percentages; (1) Metropolitan Statistical Area - see Appendix B for areas included
Source: Bureau of Labor Statistics, http://stats.bls.gov

Employment by Occupation

Occupation Classification	City (%)	MSA[1] (%)	U.S. (%)
Sales and Office	27.0	26.3	26.7
Professional and Related	26.4	20.4	20.2
Service	14.7	15.7	14.9
Production, Transportation, and Material Moving	11.9	15.5	14.6
Management, Business, and Financial	12.9	11.5	13.5
Construction, Extraction, and Maintenance	6.6	9.3	9.4
Farming, Forestry, and Fishing	0.5	1.3	0.7

Note: Figures cover employed civilians 16 years of age and older;
(1) Metropolitan Statistical Area - see Appendix A for areas included
Source: Census 2000, Summary File 3

Employment by Industry

Sector	MSA[1] Number of Employees	MSA[1] Percent of Total	U.S. Percent of Total
Government	29,200	18.7	16.3
Education and Health Services	19,800	12.7	13.2
Professional and Business Services	17,300	11.1	12.9
Retail Trade	20,300	13.0	11.5
Manufacturing	20,000	12.8	10.2
Leisure and Hospitality	14,100	9.0	9.5
Financial Activities	8,400	5.4	6.1
Construction	7,900	5.1	5.5
Wholesale Trade	5,900	3.8	4.3
Other Services	5,100	3.3	3.9
Transportation and Utilities	3,400	2.2	3.7
Information	3,800	2.4	2.2
Natural Resources and Mining	800	0.5	0.5

Note: Figures cover non-farm employment as of December 2006 and are not seasonally adjusted;
(1) Metropolitan Statistical Area - see Appendix B for areas included
Source: Bureau of Labor Statistics, http://stats.bls.gov

Occupations with Greatest Projected Employment Growth: 2002 - 2012

Occupation[1]	2002 Employment	2012 Projected Employment	Numeric Employment Change	Percent Employment Change
Retail Salespersons	50,120	57,600	7,480	14.9
Registered Nurses	26,980	34,030	7,050	26.1
Office Clerks, General	37,340	42,460	5,120	13.7
Cashiers	34,230	39,010	4,780	14.0
Janitors and Cleaners, Except Maids and Housekeeping Cleaners	22,840	26,570	3,730	16.3
Waiters and Waitresses	23,660	27,160	3,500	14.8
Combined Food Preparation and Serving Workers, Including Fast Food	23,280	26,560	3,280	14.1
Nursing Aides, Orderlies, and Attendants	12,180	15,210	3,030	24.9
Customer Service Representatives	18,180	21,200	3,020	16.6
General and Operations Managers	19,360	22,280	2,920	15.1

Note: Projections cover Oregon; (1) Sorted by numeric employment change
Source: www.projectionscentral.com, State Occupational Projections, 2002-2012 Long-Term Projections

Fastest Growing Occupations: 2002 - 2012

Occupation[1]	2002 Employment	2012 Projected Employment	Numeric Employment Change	Percent Employment Change
Pharmacy Technicians	3,560	4,650	1,090	30.6
Dental Laboratory Technicians	980	1,240	260	26.5
Pharmacists	3,080	3,890	810	26.3
Dental Hygienists	1,830	2,310	480	26.2
Dental Assistants	3,760	4,740	980	26.1
Registered Nurses	26,980	34,030	7,050	26.1
Medical Transcriptionists	1,750	2,190	440	25.1
Physical Therapists	1,640	2,050	410	25.0
Nursing Aides, Orderlies, and Attendants	12,180	15,210	3,030	24.9
Medical Records and Health Information Technicians	2,370	2,960	590	24.9

Note: Projections cover Oregon; (1) Sorted by percent employment change and excludes occupations with numeric employment change less than 200
Source: www.projectionscentral.com, State Occupational Projections, 2002-2012 Long-Term Projections

Average Wages

Occupation	$/Hr.	Occupation	$/Hr.
Accountants and Auditors	26.49	Maids and Housekeeping Cleaners	8.59
Automotive Mechanics	16.99	Maintenance and Repair Workers	15.82
Bookkeepers	14.02	Marketing Managers	35.48
Carpenters	18.34	Nuclear Medicine Technologists	n/a
Cashiers	9.54	Nurses, Licensed Practical	17.33
Clerks, General Office	12.04	Nurses, Registered	n/a
Clerks, Receptionists/Information	11.88	Nursing Aides/Orderlies/Attendants	11.14
Clerks, Shipping/Receiving	11.95	Packers and Packagers, Hand	9.32
Computer Programmers	27.30	Physical Therapists	31.49
Computer Support Specialists	17.61	Postal Service Mail Carriers	22.14
Computer Systems Analysts	28.49	Real Estate Brokers	n/a
Cooks, Restaurant	9.29	Retail Salespersons	12.12
Dentists	n/a	Sales Reps., Exc. Tech./Scientific	22.19
Electrical Engineers	36.13	Sales Reps., Tech./Scientific	30.49
Electricians	23.30	Secretaries, Exc. Legal/Med./Exec.	13.40
Financial Managers	42.52	Security Guards	10.24
First-Line Supervisors/Mgrs., Sales	17.40	Surgeons	n/a
Food Preparation Workers	9.07	Teacher Assistants	11.30
General and Operations Managers	42.73	Teachers, Elementary School	22.00
Hairdressers/Cosmetologists	n/a	Teachers, Secondary School	21.30
Internists	n/a	Telemarketers	9.25
Janitors and Cleaners	10.80	Truck Drivers, Heavy/Tractor-Trailer	14.63
Landscaping/Groundskeeping Workers	11.01	Truck Drivers, Light/Delivery Svcs.	12.98
Lawyers	51.19	Waiters and Waitresses	8.88

Note: Wage data is for May 2005 and covers the Eugene-Springfield, OR Metropolitan Statistics Area - see Appendix B for areas included. Hourly wages for elementary/secondary school teachers and teacher assistants were calculated by the editors from annual wage data assuming a 40 hour work week; n/a not available.
Source: Bureau of Labor Statistics, May 2005 Metro Area Occupational Employment and Wage Estimates

RESIDENTIAL REAL ESTATE

Building Permits

Area	Single-Family			Multi-Family			Total		
	2005	2006p	Pct. Chg.	2005	2006p	Pct. Chg.	2005	2006p	Pct. Chg.
City	756	528	-30.2	571	203	-64.4	1,327	731	-44.9
U.S.	1,682,000	1,380,000	-18.0	473,300	457,300	-3.4	2,155,300	1,837,300	-14.8

Note: (p) preliminary; figures represent new, privately-owned housing units authorized (unadjusted data); All permit data are based on estimates with imputation; U.S. figures are based on the new 20,000-place series.
Source: U.S. Census Bureau, Manufacturing, Mining, and Construction Statistics

Homeownership and Housing Vacancies

Area	Homeownership Rate[2] (%)			Rental Vacancy Rate[3] (%)			Homeowner Vacancy Rate[4] (%)		
	2004	2005	2006	2004	2005	2006	2004	2005	2006
MSA[1]	n/a	n/a	n/a	n/a	n/a	n/a	n/a	n/a	n/a
U.S.	69.0	68.9	68.8	10.2	9.8	9.7	1.7	1.9	2.4

Note: Comparable 2004 data was not available due to changes in metropolitan area definitions; (1) Metropolitan Statistical Area - see Appendix B for areas included; (2) The proportion of households that are owners; (3) The proportion of the rental inventory that is vacant for rent; (4) The proportion of the homeowner inventory that is vacant for sale; n/a not available
Source: U.S. Census Bureau, Housing Vacancies and Homeownership Annual Statistics: 2006

TAXES

State Corporate Income Tax Rates

State	Rate (%)	Number of Brackets	Low Bracket (Under $)	High Bracket (Over $)
Oregon	6.6	1	na	na

Note: Tax rates as of December 31, 2006; na not applicable
Source: Tax Foundation, www.taxfoundation.org

State Individual Income Tax Rates

State	Federal Deductibility	Marginal Rate (%)	Number of Brackets	Low Bracket (Under $)	High Bracket (Over $)
Oregon	Yes (z)	5.0-9.0 (r)	3	0	6,850

Note: Tax rates as of December 31, 2006; Brackets apply to single taxpayers and married people filing separately; na not applicable; (r) Indexed for Inflation; (z) Deduction limited to no more than $5,000.
Source: Tax Foundation, www.taxfoundation.org

Various State and Local Tax Rates

State and Local Sales and Use (%)	State Sales and Use (%)	Gasoline ($/gal.)	Cigarette ($/pack)	Spirits ($/gal.)	Table Wine ($/gal.)	Beer ($/gal.)
0	None	0.24	1.18	18.52 (b)	0.67	0.08

Note: Tax rates as of December 31, 2006; (b) States where the state government controls all sales. Excise tax rate is calculated using methodology designed by the Distilled Spirits Council of the United States (DISCUS).
Source: Tax Foundation, www.taxfoundation.org; The Sales Tax Clearinghouse, www.thestc.com

State Tax Burdens

Area	Combined State and Local Tax Burden		Combined Federal, State and Local Tax Burden	
	Percent	Rank	Percent	Rank
Oregon	9.9	35	30.2	28
U.S. Average	10.6	-	31.6	-

Note: Figures are for 2006 and measure taxes as a percentage of income
Source: Tax Foundation, www.taxfoundation.org

Internal Revenue Service Tax Audits

IRS District	Percent of Returns Audited				
	1996	1997	1998	1999	2000
Pacific Northwest	0.63	0.51	0.37	0.24	0.15
U.S.	0.66	0.61	0.46	0.31	0.20

Note: Figures cover IRS district audits of federal income tax returns filed by individuals. Geographic data on district audits after the year 2000 are being withheld by the IRS. TRAC is challenging this policy.
Source: Syracuse University, Transactional Records Access Clearinghouse (TRAC), "Odds of IRS District Tax Audit 2000"

**COMMERCIAL
UTILITIES**

Typical Monthly Electric Bills

Area	Commercial Service ($/month)		Industrial Service ($/month)	
	3 kW demand 1,000 kWh	40 kW demand 14,000 kWh	1,000 kW demand 200,000 kWh	50,000 kW demand 15,000,000 kWh
City	n/a	n/a	n/a	n/a
Average[1]	123	1,413	22,000	1,306,315

Note: Based on total rates in effect July 1, 2006; (1) average based on 196 utilities; n/a not available
Source: Edison Electric Institute, Typical Bills and Average Rates Report, Summer 2006

TRANSPORTATION

Means of Transportation to Work

Area	Car/Truck/Van		Public Transportation			Bicycle	Walked	Other Means	Worked at Home
	Drove Alone	Car-pooled	Bus	Subway	Railroad				
City	66.8	11.2	4.8	0.0	0.0	5.5	6.1	0.8	4.7
MSA[1]	71.6	12.2	3.2	0.0	0.0	3.0	4.2	0.6	5.1
U.S.	75.7	12.2	2.5	1.5	0.5	0.4	2.9	1.0	3.3

Note: Figures are percentages and cover workers 16 years of age and older;
(1) Metropolitan Statistical Area - see Appendix A for areas included
Source: Census 2000, Summary File 3

Travel Time to Work

Area	Less Than 15 Minutes	15 to 29 Minutes	30 to 44 Minutes	45 to 59 Minutes	60 Minutes or More
City	48.2	40.4	6.4	1.8	3.2
MSA[1]	39.8	41.1	11.6	3.0	4.5
U.S.	29.4	36.1	19.1	7.4	8.0

Note: Figures are percentages and include workers 16 years old and over; (1) Metropolitan Statistical Area -
see Appendix A for areas included
Source: Census 2000, Summary File 3

Travel Time Index

Area	1982	1993	2002	2003
Urban Area[1]	1.02	1.05	1.10	1.11
Average[2]	1.12	1.28	1.37	1.37

Note: Travel Time Index - The ratio of travel time in the peak period to the travel time at
free-flow conditions. A value of 1.35 indicates a 20-minute free-flow trip takes 27 minutes
in the peak. Free-flow speeds (60 mph on freeways and 35 mph on principal arterials)
are used as the comparison threshold; (1) Covers the Eugene, OR urban area;
(2) average of 85 urban areas
Source: Texas Transportation Institute, The 2005 Urban Mobility Report, May 2005

Public Transportation

Agency name:	Lane Transit District (LTD)
Vehicle type:	Bus
Average fleet age in years:	8.5
No. operated in max. service:	85
Vehicle type:	Demand response
Average fleet age in years:	4.5
No. operated in max. service:	23
Vehicle type:	Vanpool
Average fleet age in years:	4.0
No. operated in max. service:	3

Source: Federal Transit Administration, National Transit Database, 2005

Air Transportation

Airport name and code:	Mahlon Sweet Field (EUG)
Domestic service (2006)	
Passenger airlines[1]:	18
Passenger enplanements:	360,688
Freight carriers[2]:	6
Freight (lbs.):	1,343,573
International service (2005)	
Passenger airlines[1]:	1
Passenger enplanements:	10
Freight carriers[2]:	0
Freight (lbs.):	0

Note: (1) Includes all major, minor and commuter airlines that carried at least one passenger during the year; (2) Includes all airlines and freight carriers that transported at least one pound of freight during the year
Source: Bureau of Transportation Statistics, The Intermodal Transportation Database, Air Carriers: T-100 International Market, 2004; Bureau of Transportation Statistics, The Intermodal Transportation Database, Air Carriers: T-100 Domestic Market, 2005

Other Transportation Statistics

Interstate highways:	I-5
Amtrak service:	Yes
Major waterways/ports:	None

Source: Editor & Publisher Market Guide, 2006; Amtrak.com; Rand McNally 2006 Road Atlas

BUSINESSES

Major Business Headquarters

Company Name	2006 Rankings	
	Fortune[1]	Forbes[2]
No companies listed	-	-

Note: (1) Fortune 500 - companies that produce a 10-K are ranked 1 to 500 based on 2005 revenue; (2) Forbes Largest Private Companies - all private companies with at least $1 billion in annual revenue are ranked 1 to 394; companies listed are located in the city; dashes indicate no ranking
Source: Fortune, April 17, 2006; Forbes, November 9, 2006

Best Companies to Work For

Umpqua Bank, headquartered in Eugene, is among the "100 Best Companies to Work For." Criteria: More than 105,000 employees from 446 companies responded to a 57-question survey created by the Great Place to Work Institute. Two-thirds of a company's score is based on the survey, which covers topics such as attitudes towards management, job satisfaction, and camaraderie. The remaining third of the score comes from each company's responses to the Institute's Culture Audit, which includes detailed questions about demographic makeup, pay and benefits programs, and open-ended questions about the company's people-management philosophy, internal communications, opportunities, compensation practices, diversity programs, etc. Any company that is at least seven years old and has a minimum of 1,000 U.S. employees is eligible. The top three U.S. locations are shown for companies with more than one location. *Fortune, "100 Best Companies to Work for 2007," January 22, 2007*

Women-Owned Businesses: 1997 and 2002

Year	All Firms		Firms with Paid Employees			
	Firms	Sales ($000)	Firms	Sales ($000)	Employees	Payroll ($000)
1997	4,010	704,460	714	641,796	6,233	120,953
2002	4,188	526,077	796	465,374	4,623	96,663

Note: Figures cover firms located in the city; Women-owned business are defined as firms in which women own 51% or more of the stock or equity of the company; (a) Withheld to avoid disclosing data for individual companies; (b) Withheld because estimate did not meet publication standards; n/a not available
Source: 1997 Economic Census, Survey of Minority- and Women-Owned Business Enterprises; 2002 Economic Census, Survey of Business Owners (released February 9, 2006)

HOTELS

Hotels/Motels

Area	Hotels/Motels	Average Minimum Rates ($)		
		Tourist	First-Class	Deluxe
City	18	69	75	n/a

Note: n/a not available
Source: OAG Travel Planner Online, Spring 2006

EVENT SITES

Stadiums, Arenas, and Auditoriums

Name	Capacity
Hult Center for the Performing Arts	3,500

Source: www.officialtravelguide.com; www.eventective.com; original research

Hotels/Conference Centers

Name	Guest Rooms	Exhibit Space (sq. ft.)	Meeting Space (sq. ft.)
Eugene Hilton	272	30,000	30,000
Quinault Beach Resort	n/a	n/a	n/a

Note: n/a not available
Source: www.officialtravelguide.com; www.eventective.com; original research

Living Environment

COST OF LIVING

Cost of Living Index

Year	Composite Index	Groceries	Housing	Utilities	Trans-portation	Health Care	Misc. Goods/ Services
2004	n/a	n/a	n/a	n/a	n/a	n/a	n/a
2005	108.1	102.9	119.0	83.3	97.5	111.6	110.5
2006	109.1	95.2	127.8	83.6	108.1	114.5	106.4

Note: U.S. = 100
Source: The Council for Community and Economic Research (formerly ACCRA), Cost of Living Index, 2004, 2005 and 2006 4-Quarter Averages

HOUSING

House Price Index (HPI)

Area	National Ranking[2]	Quarterly Change (%)	One-Year Change (%)	Five-Year Change (%)
MSA[1]	37	0.31	11.38	65.51
U.S.[3]	-	1.12	5.87	55.21

Note: The HPI is a weighted repeat sales index. It measures average price changes in repeat sales or refinancings on the same properties. This information is obtained by reviewing repeat mortgage transactions on single-family properties whose mortgages have been purchased or securitized by Fannie Mae or Freddie Mac in January 1975; (1) Metropolitan Statistical Area - see Appendix B for areas included; (2) Rankings are based on annual percentage change for all metro areas containing at least 15,000 transactions over the last 10 years and ranges from 1 to 282; (3) figures based on a weighted division average; all figures are for the period ending December 31, 2006
Source: Office of Federal Housing Enterprise Oversight, House Price Index, March 1, 2007

House Price Valuations

Area	Q4 1999	Q4 2000	Q4 2001	Q4 2002	Q4 2003	Q4 2004	Q4 2005	Q4 2006
MSA[1]	5.9	5.6	6.9	7.0	11.7	17.3	31.7	37.8

Note: Figures show the percentage of over- or under-valuation of single family homes relative to statistically normal house values (e.g. a value of 23.6 indicates that house values are 23.6% overvalued). Statistically normal house values are based on house prices, interest rates, household incomes, population densities, and any historical premiums or discounts metropolitan areas have exhibited over time; (1) Figures cover the Metropolitan Statistical Area - see Appendix B for areas included
Source: Global Insight/National City Corporation, House Prices in America, March 2007

Median Home Prices

Area	2004	2005	2006p	Percent Change 2005 to 2006
Metro Area[1]	164.9	197.6	230.6	16.7
U.S. Average	195.2	219.0	222.0	1.4

Note: Figures are median sales prices of existing single-family homes in thousands of dollars; (p) preliminary; n/a not available; (1) Covers the Eugene-Springfield, OR Metropolitan Statistical Area - see Appendix B for areas included
Source: National Association of Realtors, Metropolitan Area Prices, 4th Quarter 2006

Housing: Year Structure Built

Area	1990 -2000	1980 -1989	1970 -1979	1960 -1969	1950 -1959	1940 -1949	Before 1940	Median Year
City	21.7	8.8	24.9	16.9	12.7	7.5	7.6	1972
MSA[1]	19.3	9.5	26.3	17.0	11.7	8.3	8.0	1972
U.S.	17.0	15.8	18.5	13.7	12.7	7.3	15.0	1971

Note: Figures are percentages; (1) Metropolitan Statistical Area - see Appendix A for areas included
Source: Census 2000, Summary File 3

Average New Home Price

Area	2004	2005	2006
City	n/a	344,564	396,167
U.S.	253,574	275,712	299,269

Note: Figures, in dollars, are based on a new home with 2,400 sq. ft. of living area on an 8,000 sq. ft. lot.
Source: The Council for Community and Economic Research (formerly ACCRA), Cost of Living Index, 2004, 2005 and 2006 4-Quarter Averages

Average Apartment Rent

Area	2004	2005	2006
City	n/a	754	768
U.S.	716	740	766

Note: Figures, in dollars per month, are based on an unfurnished two bedroom, 1-1/2 or 2 bath apartment, approximately 950 sq. ft. in size, excluding all utilities except water
Source: The Council for Community and Economic Research (formerly ACCRA), Cost of Living Index, 2004, 2005 and 2006 4-Quarter Averages

RESIDENTIAL UTILITIES

Average Residential Utility Costs

Area	All Electric ($/mth)	Part Electric ($/mth)	Other Energy ($/mth)	Phone ($/mth)
City	121.83	–	–	24.38
U.S.	136.00	76.53	90.52	25.87

Source: The Council for Community and Economic Research (formerly ACCRA), Cost of Living Index, 2006 4-Quarter Average

HEALTH

Average Health Care Costs

Area	Optometrist ($/visit)	Doctor ($/visit)	Dentist ($/visit)
City	107.71	105.56	77.61
U.S.	76.38	76.10	68.72

Note: Optometrist—based on a full vision eye exam for an established adult patient;
Doctor—based on a general practitioner's routine exam of an established patient;
Dentist—based on adult teeth cleaning and periodic oral exam.
Source: The Council for Community and Economic Research (formerly ACCRA), Cost of Living Index, 2006 4-Quarter Average

Mortality Rates

ICD-10 Sub-Chapter	ICD-10 Code	Age-Adjusted Death Rate per 100,000 population[1]	U.S. Age-Adjusted Death Rate per 100,000 population
Malignant neoplasms	C00-C97	193.2	185.8
Ischaemic heart diseases	I20-I25	94.5	150.2
Other forms of heart disease	I30-I51	47.5	50.8
Cerebrovascular diseases	I60-I69	54.0	50.0
Chronic lower respiratory diseases	J40-J47	49.5	41.1
Diabetes mellitus	E10-E14	26.1	24.5
Other degenerative diseases of the nervous system	G30-G31	32.2	22.3
Other external causes of accidental injury	W00-X59	21.9	21.2
Influenza and pneumonia	J10-J18	10.3	19.8
Hypertensive diseases	I10-I13	15.8	18.1

Note: ICD-10 = International Classification of Diseases 10th Revision; (1) Figures cover Lane County, OR
Source: Centers for Disease Control and Prevention, National Center for Health Statistics. Compressed Mortality File 1999-2004. CDC WONDER On-line Database, compiled from Compressed Mortality File 1999-2004 Series 20 No. 2J, 2007.

Health Risk Data

Item	Area[1] (%)	U.S. (%)
Adults who have been told they have high blood pressure	23.1	25.5
Adults who have been told they have high blood cholesterol	35.5	35.6
Adults who have been told they have diabetes[2]	7.5	7.3
Adults who have been told they have arthritis	29.1	27.0
Adults who have been told they currently have asthma	10.0	8.0
Adults who are current smokers	19.0	20.6

Note: (1) Figures cover the Metropolitan Statistical Area - see Appendix B for areas included; (2) Figures do not include pregnancy-related diabetes, pre-diabetes or borderline diabetes
Source: Centers for Disease Control and Prevention, Behaviorial Risk Factor Surveillance System, SMART: Selected Metropolitan/Micropolitan Area Trends, 2005

Distribution of Office-Based Physicians

Area	Total	Family/ General Practice	Specialties		
			Medical	Surgical	Other
MSA[1] (number)	688	137	211	151	189
MSA[1] (rate per 10,000 pop.)	20.9	4.2	6.4	4.6	5.7
Metro Average[2] (rate per 10,000 pop.)	19.4	2.1	7.5	4.5	5.3

Note: Data as of December 31, 2004; (1) Metropolitan Statistical Area - see Appendix A for areas included; (2) Average of the 79 unique MSAs and CMSAs in this book
Source: American Medical Association, Physician Characteristics & Distribution in the U.S., 2006

Hospitals

Eugene has the following hospitals: 1 general medical and surgical; 1 alcoholism and other chemical dependency.
AHA Guide to the Healthcare Field 2007

EDUCATION

Public School District Statistics

District Name	Schls	Pupils	Pupil/ Teacher Ratio	Minority Pupils[1] (%)	Free Lunch Eligible[2] (%)	IEP[3] (%)
Bethel Sd 52	11	5,748	22.0	21.0	28.3	17.4
Eugene Sd 4j	45	18,390	22.3	27.1	26.6	15.1

Note: Table includes regular local school districts with 2,000 or more students; (1) Percentage of students that are not white, non-Hispanic; (2) Percentage of students that are eligible for the free lunch program; (3) Percentage of students that have an Individualized Education Program.
Source: U.S. Department of Education, National Center for Education Statistics, Common Core of Data, Local Education Agency (School District) Universe Survey: School Year 2004-2005; U.S. Department of Education, National Center for Education Statistics, Common Core of Data, Public Elementary/Secondary School Universe Survey: School Year 2004-2005

Top Public High Schools

High School Name	Index[1]	Rank[1]	Subsidized Lunch (%)[2]	E&E (%)[3]
South Eugene	1.989	364	11.0	26.1**

Note: (1) Public schools are ranked according to a ratio that is the number of Advanced Placement and/or International Baccalaureate tests taken by all students at a school in 2005 divided by the number of graduating seniors. All of the schools on the list have an index of at least 1.000; they are in the top five percent of public schools measured this way. The rankings range from 1 to 1,236; (2) Percentage of students receiving federally subsidized meals; (3) E & E stands for equity and excellence percentage: the portion of all graduating seniors at a school that had at least one passing grade on one AP or IB test; (*) Gave just IB tests; (**) Gave both IB and AP tests. AP and IB participation are indicators of a school's efforts to get students to excel and prepare for college.
Source: Newsweek Online, May 23, 2006

Educational Quality

School District	Education Quotient[1]	Graduate Outcome[2]	Community Index[3]	Resource Index[4]	Rating[5]
Eugene 04J	87	94	59	25	Gold

Note: Scores are national percentile rankings and range from 1 (worst) to 99 (best); (1) Combination of the Graduate Outcome, Community and Resource Indexes weighted to reflect the greater importance of the Graduate Outcome and Resource Index; (2) Based on graduation rates and college board scores (SAT/ACT); (3) Based on the surrounding community's level of affluence and adult education; (4) Based on teacher salaries, per-pupil expenditures and student-teacher ratios; (5) School districts receive one of five rankings: Gold Medal (top 16 percent of districts evaluated); Blue Ribbon (top third); Green Light (average); Yellow Light (bottom 25 percent); Red Light (bottom 10 percent).
Source: Expansion Management, "2007 Education Quotient," January 2007

Highest Level of Education

Area	Less than H.S.	H.S. Diploma	Some College, No Deg.	Associate Degree	Bachelors Degree	Masters Degree	Profess. School Degree	Doctorate Degree
City	8.5	19.2	27.7	7.2	22.0	9.8	2.9	2.6
MSA[1]	12.4	25.7	28.9	7.3	15.7	6.6	1.9	1.5
U.S.	19.4	28.4	21.2	6.4	15.7	5.9	2.0	1.0

Note: Figures are 2006 estimated percentages and cover persons age 25 and over; (1) Metropolitan Statistical Area - see Appendix B for areas included
Source: Claritas, Inc.

Educational Attainment by Race

Area	High School Graduate (%)					Bachelor's Degree (%)				
	Total	White	Black	Asian	Hisp.[2]	Total	White	Black	Asian	Hisp.[2]
City	91.5	92.3	85.3	93.8	70.3	37.3	37.8	34.3	56.4	19.1
MSA[1]	87.5	88.2	84.5	88.0	64.8	25.5	25.6	29.2	49.4	15.8
U.S.	80.4	83.6	72.3	80.4	52.4	24.4	26.1	14.3	44.1	10.4

Note: Figures shown cover persons 25 years old and over; (1) Metropolitan Statistical Area - see Appendix A for areas included; (2) people of Hispanic origin can be of any race
Source: Census 2000, Summary File 3

School Enrollment by Type

Area	Grades KG to 8				Grades 9 to 12			
	Public		Private		Public		Private	
	Enrollment	%	Enrollment	%	Enrollment	%	Enrollment	%
City	13,156	90.3	1,418	9.7	5,815	90.0	645	10.0
MSA[1]	34,800	91.9	3,082	8.1	15,788	92.5	1,272	7.5
U.S.	33,526,011	88.7	4,285,121	11.3	14,848,628	90.6	1,532,323	9.4

Note: Figures shown cover persons 3 years old and over; (1) Metropolitan Statistical Area - see Appendix A for areas included
Source: Census 2000, Summary File 3

School Enrollment by Race

Area	Grades KG to 8 (%)				Grades 9 to 12 (%)			
	White	Black	Asian	Hisp.[1]	White	Black	Asian	Hisp.[1]
City	83.8	1.7	2.8	8.7	85.5	1.6	2.9	5.6
MSA[2]	87.2	1.1	1.6	7.4	89.2	0.8	1.7	5.1
U.S.	68.5	15.5	3.3	16.8	68.8	15.5	3.8	15.7

Note: Figures shown cover persons 3 years old and over; (1) people of Hispanic origin can be of any race; (2) Metropolitan Statistical Area - see Appendix A for areas included
Source: Census 2000, Summary File 3

Average Salaries of Public School Teachers

District	2004-05		2005-06		Percent Change 2004-05 to 2005-06
	Dollars	Rank[1]	Dollars	Rank[1]	
OREGON	48,330	15	48,981	16	1.35
U.S. Average	47,674	-	49,109	-	3.01

Note: (1) State rank ranges from 1 to 51.
Source: National Education Association, Rankings & Estimates: Rankings of the States 2005 and Estimates of School Statistics 2006, November 2006

Higher Education

Four-Year Colleges			Two-Year Colleges			Medical Schools[1]	Law Schools[2]	Voc/ Tech[3]
Public	Private Non-profit	Private For-profit	Public	Private Non-profit	Private For-profit			
1	3	0	1	0	0	0	1	0

Note: Figures cover institutions located within the city limits; (1) includes schools accredited by the Liaison Committee on Medical Education and the American Osteopathic Association; (2) includes American Bar Association-accredited law schools; (3) includes all schools with programs that are less than 2 years
Source: National Center for Education Statistics, The Integrated Postsecondary Education System (IPEDS) Peer Analysis System, 2006; www.usnews.com, America's Best Graduate Schools 2008, Medical School Directory; www.usnews.com, America's Best Graduate Schools 2008, Law School Directory

PRESIDENTIAL ELECTION

2004 Presidential Election Results

Area	Bush	Kerry	Nader	Other
Lane County	40.4	58.0	0.0	1.7
U.S.	50.7	48.3	0.4	0.6

Note: Results are percentages and may not add to 100% due to rounding
Source: Dave Leip's Atlas of U.S. Presidential Elections, www.uselectionatlas.org

MAJOR EMPLOYERS

Major Employers

Company Name	Industry	Type of Site
Accounting Department	General medical and surgical hospitals	Branch
County of Lane	Executive offices	Headquarters
DMV Field Office	Regulation, administration of transportation	Branch
Eugene Water & Electric Board	Electric and other services combined	Single
Georgia-Pacific	Hardwood veneer and plywood	Branch
H R Jones Veneer Inc	Softwood veneer and plywood	Headquarters
Hynix Semicdtr Mfg Amer Inc	Semiconductors and related devices	Single
KLCC-FM	Junior colleges	Headquarters
Lane County Finance	Finance, taxation, and monetary policy	Branch
McKenzie-Willamette Med Ctr	General medical and surgical hospitals	Headquarters
Monaco Coach Corporation	Motor homes	Headquarters
Oregon Timbrlnds Div/Containr	Hardwood dimension and flooring mills	Branch
Peace Health Medical Group	Offices and clinics of medical doctors	Single
Peacehealth	Offices and clinics of medical doctors	Branch
Peacehealth Oregen	General medical and surgical hospitals	Branch
Register Guard The	Newspapers	Headquarters
Rosboro Lumber Company	Softwood veneer and plywood	Single
Sacred Heart General Hospital	Offices of health practitioner	Branch
Symantec	Custom computer programming services	Branch
US Post Office	U.S. Postal Service	Branch
University of Oregon	Colleges and universities	Headquarters

Note: Companies shown are located within the metropolitan area and have 400 or more employees; nec = not elsewhere classified.
Source: www.zapdata.com, January 2007

PUBLIC SAFETY

Crime Rate

Area	All Crimes	Violent Crimes				Property Crimes		
		Murder	Forcible Rape	Robbery	Aggrav. Assault	Burglary	Larceny -Theft	Motor Vehicle Theft
City	7,078.3	3.5	37.4	82.3	103.8	1,109.1	4,593.6	1,148.6
Suburbs[1]	4,744.6	1.6	26.7	37.1	197.5	1,022.7	2,730.5	728.5
Metro[2]	5,748.8	2.4	31.3	56.6	157.2	1,059.9	3,532.2	909.3
U.S.	3,899.0	5.6	31.7	140.7	291.1	726.7	2,286.3	416.7

Note: Figures are crimes per 100,000 population; (1) All areas within the metro area that are located outside the city limits; (2) Metropolitan Statistical Area - see Appendix B for areas included
Source: FBI Uniform Crime Reports, 2005

Hate Crimes

Area	Number of Quarters Reported	Bias Motivation				
		Race	Religion	Sexual Orientation	Ethnicity	Disability
City	4	0	0	0	0	0

Source: Federal Bureau of Investigation, Hate Crime Statistics 2005

RECREATION

Culture

Dance[1]	Theatre[1]	Instrumental Music[1]	Vocal Music[1]	Series/ Festivals	Museums	Zoos
3	2	4	1	4	6	0

Note: (1) number of professional perfoming groups
Source: The Grey House Performing Arts Directory, 2007; Official Museum Directory, 2007

Professional Sports Teams

Major League Baseball	National Basketball Association	National Football League	National Hockey League	Major League Soccer	Women's National Basketball Association
0	0	0	0	0	0

Note: Includes teams located in the Eugene metro area.
Source: www.sportsvenues.com, Listing of Venues by State/Province and City, 2006

MEDIA

Newspapers

Name	Target Audience	Frequency	Circulation
Eugene Weekly	Alternative/General	Non-Daily	30,000
Oregon Commentator	General	Non-Daily	2,750
The Register-Guard	n/a	Daily	72,846

Note: Includes newspapers whose offices are located in the city and whose circulations are 500 or more; n/a not available
Source: BurrellesLuce, MediaContacts Online, January 2006

Television Stations

Name	Ch.	Network(s)	Type	Ownership
KPIC	4	CBS	Commercial	Fisher Broadcasting Inc.
KEZI	9	ABC	Commercial	KEZI Inc.
KCBY	11	CBS	Commercial	Fisher Broadcasting Inc.
KVAL	13	CBS	Commercial	Fisher Broadcasting Inc.
KMTR	16	NBC	Commercial	Clear Channel Communications Inc.
KMTZ	23	NBC	Commercial	Clear Channel Communications Inc.
KEVU	25	n/a	Commercial	California Oregon Broadcasting Inc.
KLSR	34	Fox	Commercial	California Oregon Broadcasting Inc.
KMTX	46	NBC	Commercial	Clear Channel Communications Inc.

Note: Stations included cover the Eugene DMA (Designated Market Area)
BurrellesLuce, MediaContacts Online, January 2006

Major AM Radio Stations

Call Letters	Freq. (kHz)	Station Type	Target Audience	Station Format	Music Format
KOAC	550	Non-Comm	General	News/Talk	World Music
KUGN	590	Commercial	General	Educational/Sports/Talk	n/a
KWRO	630	Commercial	General	News/Talk	n/a
KGRV	700	n/a	General/Religious	Music/Talk	n/a
KORE	1050	Commercial	Religious	Music/News/Talk	Christian
KPNW	1120	Commercial	General	News/Talk	n/a
KHSN	1230	Commercial	General	Music	Oldies
KQEN	1240	Commercial	General	Music/Talk	Adult Standards
KCST	1250	Commercial	General	Music/News/Sports	Adult Standards
KRVM	1280	Public	General	News/Talk	n/a
KSCR	1320	Commercial	General	News/Sports/Talk	n/a
KBBR	1340	Commercial	General	News/Talk	n/a
KNND	1400	Commercial	General	Educational/Music/Talk	Contemp. Country
KKXO	1450	Commercial	General	Music	Adult Standards
KRNR	1490	Commercial	General	Music/News/Sports	Country

Note: Stations included cover the Eugene DMA (Designated Market Area); n/a not available
Source: BurrellesLuce, MediaContacts Online, January 2006

Major FM Radio Stations

Call Letters	Freq. (mHz)	Station Type	Target Audience	Station Format	Music Format
KBVR	88.7	College	General/Hispanic	Music/News	Adult Contemp.
KLCC	89.7	College	General	Ed/Music/News/Talk	Urban Contemp.
KLCO	90.5	College	General	Music/News	World Music
KWAX	91.1	Public	General	Music	Classical
KKNU	93.1	n/a	General	Music	n/a
KMGE	94.5	n/a	General	Music	n/a
KOOS	94.9	Commercial	General	Music/News	Contemp. Country
KNRQ	95.3	Commercial	General	Music/News/Talk	Modern Rock
KZEL	96.1	Commercial	General	Music/News	Classic Rock
KSHR	97.3	Commercial	General	Music/News	Country
KKTT	97.9	Commercial	General	Music/News/Sports	Country
KYTT	98.7	Commercial	General/Religious	Music/News/Sports/Talk	Christian
KODZ	99.1	Commercial	General	Music	Oldies
KFLY	101.5	Commercial	General	Music	Classic Rock
KEHK	102.3	Commercial	General	Music/News	80's
KRSB	103.1	Commercial	General	Music/News	Country
KDUK	104.7	Commercial	General	Music/News/Talk	Top 40
KCST	106.9	Commercial	General	Music/News/Sports	Oldies
KACW	107.3	Commercial	General	Music	Top 40

Note: Stations included cover the Eugene DMA (Designated Market Area); n/a not available
BurrellesLuce, MediaContacts Online, January 2006

CLIMATE

Average and Extreme Temperatures

Temperature	Jan	Feb	Mar	Apr	May	Jun	Jul	Aug	Sep	Oct	Nov	Dec	Yr.
Extreme High (°F)	67	69	77	86	93	102	105	108	103	94	76	68	108
Average High (°F)	46	51	55	61	67	74	82	82	76	64	53	47	63
Average Temp. (°F)	40	44	46	50	55	61	67	67	62	53	46	41	53
Average Low (°F)	33	35	37	39	43	48	51	51	48	42	38	35	42
Extreme Low (°F)	-4	-3	20	27	28	32	39	38	32	19	12	-12	-12

Note: Figures cover the years 1948-1992
Source: National Climatic Data Center, International Station Meteorological Climate Summary, 9/96

Average Precipitation/Snowfall/Humidity

Precip./Humidity	Jan	Feb	Mar	Apr	May	Jun	Jul	Aug	Sep	Oct	Nov	Dec	Yr.
Avg. Precip. (in.)	7.8	5.6	5.3	3.0	2.2	1.4	0.4	0.8	1.4	3.6	7.6	8.2	47.3
Avg. Snowfall (in.)	4	1	1	Tr	Tr	0	0	0	0	Tr	Tr	1	7
Avg. Rel. Hum. 7am (%)	91	92	91	88	84	81	78	82	88	93	93	92	88
Avg. Rel. Hum. 4pm (%)	79	73	64	57	54	49	38	39	44	61	79	84	60

Note: Figures cover the years 1948-1992; Tr = Trace amounts (<0.05 in. of rain; <0.5 in. of snow)
Source: National Climatic Data Center, International Station Meteorological Climate Summary, 9/96

Weather Conditions

Temperature			Daytime Sky			Precipitation		
32°F & below	45°F & below	90°F & above	Clear	Partly cloudy	Cloudy	0.01 inch or more precip.	0.1 inch or more snow/ice	Thunder-storms
54	233	15	75	115	175	136	4	3

Note: Figures are average number of days per year and cover the years 1948-1992
Source: National Climatic Data Center, International Station Meteorological Climate Summary, 9/96

HAZARDOUS WASTE

Superfund Sites

Eugene has no sites on the EPA's Superfund Final National Priorities List.
U.S. Environmental Protection Agency, Final National Priorities List, March 20, 2007

AIR & WATER QUALITY

Air Quality Index

Area	Percent of Days when Air Quality was...[2]				AQI Statistics	
	Good	Moderate	Unhealthy for Sensitive Groups	Unhealthy	Maximum	Median
MSA[1]	69.9	23.6	6.3	0.3	155	36

Note: The Air Quality Index (AQI) is an index for reporting daily air quality. EPA calculates the AQI for five major air pollutants regulated by the Clean Air Act: ground-level ozone, particle pollution (also known as particulate matter), carbon monoxide, sulfur dioxide, and nitrogen dioxide. The AQI runs from 0 to 500. The higher the AQI value, the greater the level of air pollution and the greater the health concern. There are six AQI categories: "Good" The AQI is between 0 and 50. Air quality is considered satisfactory; "Moderate" The AQI is between 51 and 100. Air quality is acceptable; "Unhealthy for Sensitive Groups" When AQI values are between 101 and 150, members of sensitive groups may experience health effects; "Unhealthy" When AQI values are between 151 and 200 everyone may begin to experience health effects; "Very Unhealthy" AQI values between 201 and 300 trigger a health alert; "Hazardous" AQI values over 300 trigger health warnings of emergency conditions; (1) Metropolitan Statistical Area - see Appendix A for areas included; (2) Based on 365 days with AQI data in 2005.
Source: U.S. Environmental Protection Agency, Air Quality Index Report, 2005

Air Quality Index Pollutants

Area	Percent of Days when AQI Pollutant was...[2]					
	Carbon Monoxide	Nitrogen Dioxide	Ozone	Sulfur Dioxide	Particulate Matter 2.5	Particulate Matter 10
MSA[1]	0.3	0.0	36.2	0.0	63.0	0.5

Note: The Air Quality Index (AQI) is an index for reporting daily air quality. EPA calculates the AQI for five major air pollutants regulated by the Clean Air Act: ground-level ozone, particle pollution (also known as particulate matter), carbon monoxide, sulfur dioxide, and nitrogen dioxide. The AQI runs from 0 to 500. The higher the AQI value, the greater the level of air pollution and the greater the health concern; (1) Metropolitan Statistical Area - see Appendix A for areas included; (2) Based on 365 days with AQI data in 2005.
Source: U.S. Environmental Protection Agency, Air Quality Index Report, 2005

Number of Days with Air Quality Index Values Greater than 100

Area	Trend Sites								All Sites
	1998	1999	2000	2001	2002	2003	2004	2005	2005
MSA[1]	n/a	n/a	n/a	n/a	n/a	n/a	n/a	n/a	n/a

Note: An AQI value greater than 100 indicates that air quality would have been in the unhealthful range on that day. Data from exceptional events are not included. These counts are presented in two ways. First, the counts are based on sites having an adequate record of monitoring data during the trend period (trend sites). These counts represent the relative change in the number of days with AQI values greater than 100. In the last column, the counts are based on all sites with data in the most recent year (because it is possible for a site to have data in the most recent year but not enough data to be a trend site); (1) Metropolitan Statistical Area - see Appendix A for areas included; n/a not available.
Source: U.S. Environmental Protection Agency, Air Trends Fact Book 2005

Maximum Pollutant Concentrations

	Particulate Matter 10 (ug/m³)	Particulate Matter 2.5 (ug/m³)	Ozone 1-hour (ppm)	Carbon Monoxide (ppm)	Sulfur Dioxide (ppm)	Nitrogen Dioxide (ppm)	Lead (ug/m³)
MSA[1] Level	74	58	0.088	3	n/a	n/a	n/a
NAAQS[2]	150	65	0.125	9	0.140	0.053	1.50
Met NAAQS[2]	Yes	Yes	Yes	Yes	n/a	n/a	n/a

Note: Data from exceptional events are not included; (1) Metropolitan Statistical Area - see Appendix A for areas included; (2) National Ambient Air Quality Standards; n/a not available
Units: ppm = parts per million; ug/m³ = micrograms per cubic meter
Source: U.S. Environmental Protection Agency, Air Trends Fact Book 2005

Watershed Health

The U.S. Environmental Protection Agency monitors the health of the aquatic resources for the nation's 2,000+ watersheds. **The Upper Willamette watershed serves the Eugene area and received an overall Index of Watershed Indicators (IWI) score of 3 (less serious problems - low vulnerability).** The IWI score is based on seven condition and nine vulnerability indicators. The overall IWI score ranges from 1 (best health) to 6 (worst health). The Condition Indicators include: designated use attainment, fish and wildlife consumption advisories, source water condition, contaminated sediments, ambient water quality, and wetlands loss index. The Vulnerability Indicators include: aquatic species at risk, conventional and toxic loads over permitted limits, urban and agricultural runoff potential, population change, hydrologic modification, estuarine pollution susceptibility, and air deposition. *Note: The IWI is no longer being updated by the U.S. EPA. Source: U.S. Environmental Protection Agency, Index of Watershed Indicators, October 26, 2001*

Drinking Water

Water System Name	Pop. Served	Primary Water Source Type	Number of Violations in 2006[a]		
			Health Based	Significant Monitoring	Monitoring
Eugene Water & Electric Board	165,000	Surface	None	None	None

Note: (a) Based on violation data from January 1, 2006 to December 31, 2006
Source: U.S. Environmental Protection Agency, Office of Ground Water and Drinking Water, Safe Drinking Water Information System (data extracted April 12, 2007)

Eugene tap water is neutral, very soft.
Editor & Publisher Market Guide, 2005

Fort Collins, Colorado

Background

At 4,985 feet, Fort Collins lies high in the eastern base of the Rocky Mountains' front range along the Cache la Poudre River about one hour from Denver. Although not quite as large as Denver, Fort Collins, home to Colorado State University and its own symphony orchestra, offers virtually everything its citizens need, all within a spectacular landscape.

Fort Collins owes its name to Colonel William Collins of the Civil War era, who was sent with a regiment of Union soldiers to guard farmers and ranchers scattered throughout the valley, and to provide security for the Overland Stage trail. Originally called Camp Collins, the place remained a military reservation until 1866 and was incorporated in 1879.

The early economy of the town depended first on lumber, and then on the raising of livestock and produce, with alfalfa, grain, and sugar beets as the chief crops. Sugar refiners, dairies, and meat-packing plants bolstered the wealth of the town, as did the products of mining and quarrying. Fort Collins is still the commercial center for a rich agricultural region that produces hay, barley, and sugar beets.

Colorado State University, the land grant university of Colorado, was established in Fort Collins in 1879, and offers innumerable cultural, economic, and educational benefits to residents. More than 22,000 students are enrolled at CSU, which is the largest employer in the city. CSU offers a world-class range of undergraduate and graduate programs, and is an internationally recognized center for forestry, agricultural science, veterinary medicine, and civil engineering.

Fort Collins' businesses produce motion-picture film, combustion engines, prefabricated metal buildings, arc welders and rods, cement products, dental hygiene appliances, and miscellaneous plastics. Large employers in the area include Colorado State University, Hewlett-Packard, Eastman-Kodak, Intel, Agilent Technologies, Teledyne-Water Pik, LSI Logic, and Anheuser-Busch. With fabulous scenery, a symphony orchestra, and all the attractions of Denver an hour away, Fort Collins offers an attractive site for relocation. For outdoor sporting enthusiasts, the area is irresistible. The town is only a few hours from Colorado's world-famous ski areas, and cross-country skiing is nearby.

Gateway Park, 15 miles from Ft. Collins, offers several recreation opportunities, including a quarter-mile nature trail and a designated boat launching area. Lakes are easily accessible for all water sports, and the Cache la Poudre River itself offers some of the best trout fishing in Colorado. For hunters, the area is a paradise, with ample supplies of antelope, black bear, deer, elk, mountain lion, and small game.

Fort Collins also offers a great range of cultural amenities. The city's Lincoln Center presents year-round performances by a variety of artists. Old Town, a historic downtown shopping district, hosts a number of large festivals each year. Fort Collins Symphony, the Larimer Chorale, Open Stage Theatre, and the Canyon Concert Ballet call Fort Collins their home. The city also cultivates the visual arts, with "Arts in Public Places" sponsored by the city, and provides exhibits at the Lincoln Center, Fort Collins Museum, and private galleries.

Transportation in and around the city is convenient. The municipality operates its own bus service on 10 daily routes, and interstate bus service is available. Residents are served by three nearby airports, the Fort Collins Airpark, Fort Collins/Loveland Airport, and Denver International Airport, which is one of the nation's busiest airports.

Fort Collins features four distinct seasons and, though high in the foothills, is buffered from both summer and winter extremes of temperature. The most typical day in Fort Collins is warm and dry, and mild nights are the rule. The town enjoys 296 days per year of sun, and an annual snowfall of 51 inches. Rainfall is far less. Summers are comfortable, while winters are cold.

Rankings

GeneralRankings

- Fort Collins was ranked #128 out of 331 metro areas in *Cities Ranked & Rated*. Criteria: cost of living; climate; crime; transportation; economy and jobs; education; arts and culture; health and healthcare; leisure. *Cities Ranked & Rated, 1st Edition, 2004*

- Fort Collins was selected as one of the "Best Places to Live 2006" by *Money* magazine. The city ranked #1 out of 90 in the small city (under 300,000 population) category. Places were ranked using 38 quality-of-life indicators and six economic opportunity measures in the following categories: ease of living; health; education; crime; park space; arts and leisure. *Money, "Best Places to Live 2006"*

- The Fort Collins area was selected as one of "60 Cheap Places to Live" in the U.S. The area appeared in the "Steroid Cities" (fast-growing, business-friendly metro areas) category. *Forbes.com, August 20, 2004*

Business/Finance Rankings

- Fort Collins was selected as one of the best places to start and grow a company by *Entrepreneur* and the National Policy Research Council. The Fort Collins metro area ranked #23 out of 63 mid-size metro areas. Criteria: business formation and growth (firms started four to 14 years ago that still employ at least 5 people and experienced rapid growth over the last four years). *Entrepreneur/National Policy Research Council, "Hot Cities for Entrepreneurs," September 2006*

- Fort Collins was selected as one of 20 cities in North America that is doing its part to host green conventions by providing renewable energy, intelligent recycling programs, transportation that minimizes usage of fossil fuels, and plenty of parkland. The city was ranked #12. *Meetings and Conventions, "Natural Choices," August 2006*

- The Fort Collins metro area appeared on the Milken Institute "2005 Best Performing Cities" index. Rank: #46 out of 200 large metro areas. Criteria: job growth; wage and salary growth; high-tech output growth. *Milken Institute, "2005 Best Performing Cities," February 2006*

- The Fort Collins metro area was selected as one of "The Top 10 Boom Villages in America." *Business 2.0* magazine and econometric research firm Global Insight compared 319 metropolitan areas in the U.S. Criteria: a weighted formula that includes forecast growth rates in sectors that contain the economy's 10 most skilled occupational clusters; the prevalence of college degrees in the local workforce; median salary. The area ranked #2 among small metro areas. *Business 2.0 Magazine, March 2004*

- *Forbes* ranked the 200 most populous metro areas in the U.S. in terms of the "Best Places for Business and Careers." The Fort Collins metro area was ranked #28. Criteria: business costs (labor, energy, tax and office space expenses); living costs (housing, transportation, food and other household expenditures); education levels of the work force; job growth; income growth; migration trends; crime rates; and culture/leisure. *Forbes, April 23, 2007*

Health/Environment Rankings

- The Fort Collins metro area appeared in *Country Home's* "2007 Best Green Places Report". The area ranked #26. Criteria included: air and watershed quality; miles of mass transit; green power; number of farmer's markets, organic producers and groceries. *Country Home, "2007 Best Green Places Report," April 2007*

- Sperling's BestPlaces ranked 331 metro areas and identified the most and least stressful U.S. cities. The Fort Collins metro area ranked #88 out of 114 mid-size metro areas (#1 = most stressful). Criteria: divorce rate; unemployment rate; violent and property crime; suicide rate; commute time; mental health; alcohol consumption; cloudy days. *www.BestPlaces.net, January 9, 2004*

■ Fort Collins was highlighted as one of the top 25 cleanest metro areas for long-term particle pollution (PM 2.5) in the U.S. The area ranked #12. *American Lung Association, State of the Air 2006*

■ Fort Collins was given "Well City USA" project in process status by The Wellness Councils of America. The objective of the Well City USA initiative is to engage entire business communities in building healthy workforces. The primary requirement for achieving Well City USA designation is that 20% of a community's working population must be employed by either Bronze, Silver, Gold or Platinum designated Well Workplace Award winning companies. To date, nine communities have achieved Well City USA status and seven communities have Well City projects in progress. *The Wellness Councils of America, Well City USA, 2007*

Seniors/Retirement Rankings

■ Fort Collins was profiled in the book *Where to Retire: America's Best and Most Affordable Places.* Cities were selected based on personal visits by the author and interviews with local residents coupled with statistics from various government agencies. *Where to Retire: America's Best and Most Affordable Places, 2006*

■ Fort Collins was identified as one of the "100 Most Popular Places to Retire" by *Where to Retire* magazine. The city ranked #48. Criteria: net retirees received from 1995-2000 (derived by subtracting all outbound retirees from inbound retirees for the county or county group - includes interstate moves only). *Where to Retire, "100 Most Popular Places to Retire," January/February 2007*

■ Fort Collins was profiled in the book *Retire in Style: 60 Outstanding Places Across the USA and Canada.* Criteria: landscape; climate; quality of life; cost of living; transportation; retail services; health care; community services; cultural and educational activities; recreational activities; work and volunteer activities; crime rates and public safety. *Retire in Style: 60 Outstanding Places Across the USA and Canada, 2005*

■ Fort Collins was selected as one of the best places to retire by *Retirement Places Rated.* Criteria: cost of living; climate; personal safety; services; economy. The city was ranked #17 out of 200. *Retirement Places Rated, 6th Edition, 2004*

■ A.G. Edwards ranked America's 500 top-performing communities based on their residents' personal savings and investing behavior. The Fort Collins metro area ranked #75 with an index score of 108.03 (national average = 100.00). A dozen statistical factors were measured including: participation in retirement savings plans; personal debt levels; and home ownership. *A.G. Edwards, "2006 Nest Egg Index", September 6, 2006*

■ Fort Collins was selected as one of the "Best Places to Retire" by MSN House & Home. Criteria: affordability; climate; cultural amenities; medical care; easy access to outdoor recreation; and opportunities to keep learning. *Houseandhome.msn.com, "Best Places to Retire," September 2003*

Children/Family Rankings

■ The Fort Collins metro area was selected as one of the "Best Cities for Relocating Families" by Worldwide ERC and Primacy Relocation. Criteria: tax rates; average home costs and home appreciation; ability to qualify for in-state tuition; service quality of local utilities; per-capita volunteerism; auto taxes; and quantity of fun, family-friendly events and venues. *Worldwide ERC and Primacy Relocation, "2006 Best Cities for Relocating Families"*

■ Fort Collins was chosen as one of America's "100 Best Communities for Young People." The winners were selected based upon detailed information provided about each community's efforts to fulfill five essential promises critical to the well-being of young people: caring adults who are actively involved in their lives; safe places in which to learn and grow; a healthy start toward adulthood; an effective education that builds marketable skills; and opportunities to help others. *America's Promise, "100 Best Communities for Young People," September 26, 2005*

Safety Rankings

■ Allstate ranked the 200 largest cities in America in terms of driver safety. Fort Collins ranked #2. In addition, drivers were 24.0% less likely to have had an accident compared to the national average. Allstate researchers analyzed internal Property Damage reported claims over a two-year period (from January 2003 to December 2004) to ensure the findings would not be affected by external influences such as weather or road construction. A weighted average of the two-year numbers determined the annual percentages. The report defines an auto crash as any collision resulting in a property damage claim. *Allstate, "Allstate America's Best Drivers Report 2006," May 24, 2006*

Sports/Recreation Rankings

■ Fort Collins was chosen as one of America's 25 best cities for running. The city was ranked #25. Criteria: number of running clubs per city; amount of land set aside for park usage; air quality; weather; crime rates; and results from a *Runner's World* poll in which readers ranked their favorite running cities. *Runner's World, "The 25 Best Running Cities in America," July 2005*

■ *Golf Digest* ranked 330 metro areas in the U.S. in terms of golf. The Fort Collins metro area was ranked #305. Criteria: access to golf; weather; value of golf; and quality of golf. *Golf Digest, "Metro Golf Rankings," August 2005*

Miscellaneous Rankings

■ The Fort Collins metro area was identified one of "America's Smartest Cities" by *Forbes*. The area ranked #7. Criteria: 200 of the largest U.S. metro areas were ranked based on the percentage of the population age 25 and over with at least a bachelor's degree. *Forbes.com, "America's Smartest Cities," December 15, 2006*

■ Fort Collins was selected as a "Great College Town" by ePodunk. The city ranked #8 in the mid-sized city category. ePodunk.com looked at communities with four-year colleges and a total student enrollment of at least 1,500. Communities where the student ratio was too low or too high were ruled out, as were small cities with low rates of owner-occupied housing. Fifteen variables were then applied to assess arts and culture, recreation, intellectual activity, historic preservation, and cost of living. *www.ePodunk.com, April, 2002*

Business Environment

CITY FINANCES

City Government Finances

Component	2003-2004 ($000)	2003-2004 ($ per capita)
Total Revenues	303,486	2,434
Total Expenditures	295,979	2,374
Debt Outstanding	229,296	1,839
Cash and Securities	292,108	2,343

Source: U.S Census Bureau, Government Finances 2003-2004

City Government Revenue by Source

Source	2003-2004 ($000)	2003-2004 ($ per capita)
General Revenue		
From Federal Government	5,244	42
From State Government	12,325	99
From Local Governments	0	0
Taxes		
Property	17,024	137
Sales	74,873	601
Personal Income	0	0
License	91	1
Charges	53,940	433
Liquor Store	0	0
Utility	92,603	743
Employee Retirement	0	0
Other	47,386	380

Source: U.S Census Bureau, Government Finances 2003-2004

City Government Expenditures by Function

Function	2003-2004 ($000)	2003-2004 ($ per capita)	2003-2004 (%)
General Expenditures			
Airports	0	0	0.0
Corrections	0	0	0.0
Education	0	0	0.0
Fire Protection	12,683	102	4.3
Governmental Administration	16,535	133	5.6
Health	0	0	0.0
Highways	32,512	261	11.0
Hospitals	0	0	0.0
Housing and Community Development	2,882	23	1.0
Interest on General Debt	11,207	90	3.8
Libraries	6,060	49	2.0
Parking	1,378	11	0.5
Parks and Recreation	40,492	325	13.7
Police Protection	22,888	184	7.7
Public Welfare	0	0	0.0
Sewerage	11,290	91	3.8
Solid Waste Management	0	0	0.0
Liquor Store	0	0	0.0
Utility	113,287	909	38.3
Employee Retirement	0	0	0.0
Other	24,765	199	8.4

Source: U.S Census Bureau, Government Finances 2003-2004

Municipal Bond Ratings

Area	Moody's
City	A1 (1/2005)

Source: Mergent Bond Record, January 2007 (unless noted otherwise)

DEMOGRAPHICS

Population Growth

Area	1990 Census	2000 Census	2006 Estimate	2011 Projection	Population Growth (%) 1990-2000	Population Growth (%) 2000-2011
City	89,555	118,652	127,205	133,641	32.5	12.6
MSA[1]	186,136	251,494	272,172	288,180	35.1	14.6
U.S.	248,709,873	281,421,906	298,021,266	312,383,955	13.2	11.0

Note: (1) Metropolitan Statistical Area - see Appendix B for areas included
Source: Claritas, Inc.

Number of Households and Average Household Size

Area	2006 Estimate	2006 Average Household Size
City	49,388	2.58
MSA[1]	105,909	2.57
U.S.	112,267,302	2.65

Note: (1) Metropolitan Statistical Area - see Appendix B for areas included
Source: Claritas, Inc.

Race and Ethnicity

Area	White Alone[2]	Black Alone[2]	Asian Alone[2]	Other Race Alone[2]	Hispanic[3]
City	87.9	1.3	2.8	8.0	10.0
MSA[1]	90.1	0.8	1.8	7.3	9.5
U.S.	73.3	12.4	4.2	10.1	14.5

Note: Figures are 2006 estimates; (1) Metropolitan Statistical Area - see Appendix B for areas included
(2) Alone is defined as not being in combination with one or more other races; (3) May be of any race.
Source: Claritas, Inc.

Segregation

City Index[2]	City Rank[3]	MSA[1] Index[2]	MSA[1] Rank[4]
37.0	90	42.5	286

Note: Figures are based on an analysis of Census 2000 data; (1) Metropolitan Statistical Area - see Appendix A for areas included; (2) White/Black Dissimilarity Index—the most commonly used measure of segregation between two groups, reflecting their relative distributions across neighborhoods within a city or metropolitan area. It can range in value from 0, indicating complete integration, to 100, indicating complete segregation; (3) Ranges from 1 (most segregated) to 100 (least segregated) and includes all the cities in this book; (4) Ranges from 1 (most segregated) to 318 (least segregated) and includes 318 metropolitan areas.
Source: www.CensusScope.org

Ancestry

Area	German	Irish[2]	English	American	Italian	Polish	French[3]	Scottish
City	28.7	14.2	14.2	4.0	5.4	2.9	4.1	3.6
MSA[1]	29.7	14.0	14.4	4.9	4.5	2.6	3.9	3.2
U.S.	15.2	10.9	8.7	7.3	5.6	3.2	3.0	1.7

Note: Figures include multiple ancestry (e.g. if a person reported being Irish and Italian, they were included in both columns); (1) Metropolitan Statistical Area - see Appendix A for areas included; (2) Includes Celtic; (3) Includes Alsatian but excludes Basque
Source: Census 2000, Summary File 3

Foreign-Born Population

Area	Percent of Population Born in Any Foreign Country	Europe	Asia	Africa	Oceania[2]	Canada	Mexico	Latin America[3]
City	5.3	1.4	1.9	0.3	0.1	0.3	1.0	0.4
MSA[1]	4.3	1.0	1.2	0.1	0.0	0.3	1.3	0.3
U.S.	11.1	1.7	2.9	0.3	0.1	0.3	3.3	2.5

Note: (1) Metropolitan Statistical Area - see Appendix A for areas included; (2) Includes Australia, New Zealand subregion, Melanesia, Micronesia, Polynesia, and Oceania n.e.c; (3) Includes Central America (excluding Mexico), South America, and the Caribbean.
Source: Census 2000, Summary File 3

Marriage Status

Area	Never Married	Now Married (excluding Separated)	Separated	Widowed	Divorced
City	40.3	46.1	0.9	3.9	8.9
MSA[1]	30.3	55.0	1.0	4.2	9.6
U.S.	27.1	54.4	2.2	6.6	9.7

Note: Figures are percentages and cover the population 15 years of age and older;
(1) Metropolitan Statistical Area - see Appendix A for areas included
Source: Census 2000, Summary File 3

Age Distribution

Area	Percent of Population						
	Under Age 5	Age 5 to 17	Age 18 to 34	Age 35 to 49	Age 50 to 64	Age 65 to 79	80 Years and Over
City	6.0	15.3	39.0	21.6	10.2	5.5	2.3
MSA[1]	6.0	17.6	28.5	24.4	13.9	7.1	2.5
U.S.	6.8	18.9	23.7	23.5	14.8	9.2	3.2

Note: (1) Metropolitan Statistical Area - see Appendix A for areas included
Source: Census 2000, Summary File 3

Male/Female Ratio

Area	Males	Females	Males per 100 Females
City	63,877	63,328	100.9
MSA[1]	135,858	136,314	99.7
U.S.	146,712,712	151,308,554	97.0

Note: Figures are 2006 estimates; (1) Metropolitan Statistical Area -
see Appendix B for areas included
Source: Claritas, Inc.

Religion

Area	Catholic	Southern Baptist	United Methodist	ELCA[1]	LDS[2]	Presbyterian Church USA	Jewish Est.	Muslim Est.
County	12.8	0.9	2.1	2.1	2.5	1.8	0.4	0.5
U.S.	22.0	7.1	3.7	1.8	1.5	1.1	2.2	0.6

Note: Figures are the number of adherents as a percentage of the total population; Adherents are defined as all members, including full members, their children and the estimated number of other participants who are not considered members (e.g. the baptized, those not confirmed, those regularly attending services, etc.);
(1) Evangelical Lutheran Church in America; (2) The Church of Jesus Christ of Latter Day Saints
Source: Reprinted with permission from Religious Congregations and Membership in the United States 2000 (Nashville, Glenmary Research Center, 2002) Copyright Association of Statisticians of American Religious Bodies. All rights reserved.

ECONOMY

Gross Metropolitan Product

Area	2002	2003	2004	2005	2005 Rank[2]
MSA[1]	9.7	10.2	10.9	11.8	155

Note: Figures are in billions of dollars; (1) Fort Collins-Loveland, CO Metropolitan Statistical Area - see Appendix A for areas included; (2) Rank ranges from 1 to 361
Source: The U.S. Conference of Mayors, "U.S. Metro Economies: GMP - The Engines of America's Growth," January 2007

Economic Growth

Area	1995 GMP	2005 GMP	Average Annual Growth Rate	Growth Rate Rank[2]
MSA[1]	5.8	11.8	7.3	27

Note: Figures are in billions of dollars; GMP = Gross Metropolitan Product; (1) Fort Collins-Loveland, CO Metropolitan Statistical Area - see Appendix A for areas included; (2) Rank ranges from 1 to 361
Source: The U.S. Conference of Mayors, "U.S. Metro Economies: GMP - The Engines of America's Growth," January 2007

INCOME

Per Capita/Median/Average Income

Area	Per Capita ($)	Median Household ($)	Average Household ($)
City	27,199	54,018	69,027
MSA[1]	29,196	59,509	74,306
U.S.	25,129	48,775	65,849

Note: Figures are 2006 estimates; (1) Metropolitan Statistical Area - see Appendix B for areas included
Source: Claritas, Inc.

Household Income Distribution

Area	Percent of Households Earning							
	Under $15,000	$15,000 -24,999	$25,000 -34,999	$35,000 -49,999	$50,000 -74,999	$75,000 -99,000	$100,000 -149,999	$150,000 and up
City	11.6	10.5	10.1	14.7	19.5	13.2	13.9	6.6
MSA[1]	8.8	8.9	9.7	14.5	21.4	14.3	15.0	7.5
U.S.	13.3	11.0	11.3	15.7	19.5	11.8	11.0	6.4

Note: Figures are 2006 estimates; (1) Metropolitan Statistical Area - see Appendix B for areas included
Source: Claritas, Inc.

Poverty Rates by Age

Area	All Ages	Under 5 Years Old	5 to 17 Years Old	18 to 64 Years Old	65 Years and Over
City	14.0	0.7	1.2	11.6	0.5
MSA[1]	9.2	0.5	1.2	7.1	0.4
U.S.	12.4	1.2	3.0	6.9	1.2

Note: Figures are percent of population with income in 1999 below poverty level and only include population for whom poverty status is determined; (1) Metropolitan Statistical Area - see Appendix A for areas included
Source: Census 2000, Summary File 3

Personal Bankruptcy Filing Rate

Area	2003	2004	2005
Larimer County	5.12	5.80	8.13
U.S.	5.57	5.31	6.88

Note: Numbers are per 1,000 population and include Chapter 7 and Chapter 13 filings
Source: Federal Deposit Insurance Corporation (FDIC), Regional Economic Conditions (RECON), 3/24/2006

EMPLOYMENT

Labor Force and Employment

Area	Civilian Labor Force			Workers Employed		
	Dec. 2005	Dec. 2006	% Chg.	Dec. 2005	Dec. 2006	% Chg.
City	78,780	81,103	2.9	75,070	77,873	3.7
MSA[1]	165,256	170,299	3.1	158,492	164,409	3.7
U.S.	149,874,000	152,571,000	1.8	142,918,000	146,081,000	2.2

Note: Data is not seasonally adjusted and covers workers 16 years of age and older;
(1) Metropolitan Statistical Area - see Appendix B for areas included
Source: Bureau of Labor Statistics, http://stats.bls.gov

Unemployment Rate

Area	2006											
	Jan.	Feb.	Mar.	Apr.	May	Jun.	Jul.	Aug.	Sep.	Oct.	Nov.	Dec.
City	5.5	4.9	4.9	4.3	4.3	4.8	4.8	4.7	4.2	4.1	3.9	4.0
MSA[1]	4.8	4.3	4.3	3.8	3.8	4.1	4.2	4.1	3.6	3.6	3.4	3.5
U.S.	5.1	5.1	4.8	4.5	4.4	4.8	5.0	4.6	4.4	4.1	4.3	4.3

Note: Data is not seasonally adjusted and covers workers 16 years of age and older; All figures are percentages; (1) Metropolitan Statistical Area - see Appendix B for areas included
Source: Bureau of Labor Statistics, http://stats.bls.gov

Employment by Occupation

Occupation Classification	City (%)	MSA[1] (%)	U.S. (%)
Sales and Office	24.3	24.8	26.7
Professional and Related	28.7	25.3	20.2
Service	15.6	13.9	14.9
Production, Transportation, and Material Moving	9.7	11.5	14.6
Management, Business, and Financial	14.1	14.3	13.5
Construction, Extraction, and Maintenance	7.0	9.6	9.4
Farming, Forestry, and Fishing	0.5	0.5	0.7

Note: Figures cover employed civilians 16 years of age and older;
(1) Metropolitan Statistical Area - see Appendix A for areas included
Source: Census 2000, Summary File 3

Employment by Industry

Sector	MSA[1] Number of Employees	MSA[1] Percent of Total	U.S. Percent of Total
Government	28,100	20.8	16.3
Education and Health Services	14,400	10.7	13.2
Professional and Business Services	17,500	13.0	12.9
Retail Trade	17,800	13.2	11.5
Manufacturing	12,200	9.1	10.2
Leisure and Hospitality	15,200	11.3	9.5
Financial Activities	6,000	4.5	6.1
Construction	n/a	n/a	5.5
Wholesale Trade	3,100	2.3	4.3
Other Services	4,700	3.5	3.9
Transportation and Utilities	2,700	2.0	3.7
Information	2,500	1.9	2.2
Natural Resources and Mining	n/a	n/a	0.5

Note: Figures cover non-farm employment as of December 2006 and are not seasonally adjusted;
(1) Metropolitan Statistical Area - see Appendix B for areas included; n/a not available
Source: Bureau of Labor Statistics, http://stats.bls.gov

Occupations with Greatest Projected Employment Growth: 2002 - 2012

Occupation[1]	2002 Employment	2012 Projected Employment	Numeric Employment Change	Percent Employment Change
Retail Salespersons	84,250	100,890	16,640	19.8
Registered Nurses	30,350	43,380	13,030	42.9
Waiters and Waitresses	45,780	58,380	12,600	27.5
Customer Service Representatives	36,940	48,920	11,980	32.4
Combined Food Preparation and Serving Workers, Including Fast Food	38,320	50,090	11,770	30.7
Cashiers	53,660	64,910	11,250	21.0
Janitors and Cleaners, Except Maids and Housekeeping Cleaners	34,580	45,460	10,880	31.5
Postsecondary Teachers	19,560	29,660	10,100	51.6
Office Clerks, General	60,720	69,590	8,870	14.6
General and Operations Managers	32,920	40,890	7,970	24.2

Note: Projections cover Colorado; (1) Sorted by numeric employment change
Source: www.projectionscentral.com, State Occupational Projections, 2002-2012 Long-Term Projections

Fastest Growing Occupations: 2002 - 2012

Occupation[1]	2002 Employment	2012 Projected Employment	Numeric Employment Change	Percent Employment Change
Network Systems and Data Communications Analysts	4,980	8,280	3,300	66.3
Medical Assistants	5,780	9,440	3,660	63.3
Medical Records and Health Information Technicians	2,250	3,580	1,330	59.1
Pharmacists	3,020	4,780	1,760	58.3
Database Administrators	2,970	4,690	1,720	57.9
Cardiovascular Technologists and Technicians	530	830	300	56.6
Computer Software Engineers, Systems Software	9,470	14,600	5,130	54.2
Environmental Engineers	1,110	1,700	590	53.2
Computer Software Engineers, Applications	14,640	22,270	7,630	52.1
Physician Assistants	1,470	2,230	760	51.7

Note: Projections cover Colorado; (1) Sorted by percent employment change and excludes occupations with numeric employment change less than 250
Source: www.projectionscentral.com, State Occupational Projections, 2002-2012 Long-Term Projections

Average Wages

Occupation	$/Hr.	Occupation	$/Hr.
Accountants and Auditors	26.84	Maids and Housekeeping Cleaners	9.06
Automotive Mechanics	20.59	Maintenance and Repair Workers	15.26
Bookkeepers	15.45	Marketing Managers	33.58
Carpenters	15.95	Nuclear Medicine Technologists	n/a
Cashiers	8.85	Nurses, Licensed Practical	18.36
Clerks, General Office	11.98	Nurses, Registered	25.21
Clerks, Receptionists/Information	11.56	Nursing Aides/Orderlies/Attendants	11.08
Clerks, Shipping/Receiving	12.15	Packers and Packagers, Hand	8.54
Computer Programmers	30.27	Physical Therapists	25.37
Computer Support Specialists	20.61	Postal Service Mail Carriers	21.29
Computer Systems Analysts	36.15	Real Estate Brokers	30.71
Cooks, Restaurant	9.81	Retail Salespersons	10.72
Dentists	n/a	Sales Reps., Exc. Tech./Scientific	27.86
Electrical Engineers	29.31	Sales Reps., Tech./Scientific	31.20
Electricians	19.62	Secretaries, Exc. Legal/Med./Exec.	14.61
Financial Managers	44.65	Security Guards	10.33
First-Line Supervisors/Mgrs., Sales	18.50	Surgeons	n/a
Food Preparation Workers	8.87	Teacher Assistants	10.80
General and Operations Managers	39.10	Teachers, Elementary School	22.10
Hairdressers/Cosmetologists	11.69	Teachers, Secondary School	21.60
Internists	85.01	Telemarketers	10.57
Janitors and Cleaners	10.21	Truck Drivers, Heavy/Tractor-Trailer	20.05
Landscaping/Groundskeeping Workers	12.45	Truck Drivers, Light/Delivery Svcs.	12.09
Lawyers	37.33	Waiters and Waitresses	7.38

Note: Wage data is for May 2005 and covers the Fort Collins-Loveland, CO Metropolitan Statistics Area - see Appendix B for areas included. Hourly wages for elementary/secondary school teachers and teacher assistants were calculated by the editors from annual wage data assuming a 40 hour work week; n/a not available.
Source: Bureau of Labor Statistics, May 2005 Metro Area Occupational Employment and Wage Estimates

RESIDENTIAL REAL ESTATE

Building Permits

Area	Single-Family			Multi-Family			Total		
	2005	2006p	Pct. Chg.	2005	2006p	Pct. Chg.	2005	2006p	Pct. Chg.
City	732	466	-36.3	380	295	-22.4	1,112	761	-31.6
U.S.	1,682,000	1,380,000	-18.0	473,300	457,300	-3.4	2,155,300	1,837,300	-14.8

Note: (p) preliminary; figures represent new, privately-owned housing units authorized (unadjusted data); All permit data are based on estimates with imputation; U.S. figures are based on the new 20,000-place series.
Source: U.S. Census Bureau, Manufacturing, Mining, and Construction Statistics

Homeownership and Housing Vacancies

Area	Homeownership Rate[2] (%)			Rental Vacancy Rate[3] (%)			Homeowner Vacancy Rate[4] (%)		
	2004	2005	2006	2004	2005	2006	2004	2005	2006
MSA[1]	n/a	n/a	n/a	n/a	n/a	n/a	n/a	n/a	n/a
U.S.	69.0	68.9	68.8	10.2	9.8	9.7	1.7	1.9	2.4

Note: Comparable 2004 data was not available due to changes in metropolitan area definitions; (1) Metropolitan Statistical Area - see Appendix B for areas included; (2) The proportion of households that are owners; (3) The proportion of the rental inventory that is vacant for rent; (4) The proportion of the homeowner inventory that is vacant for sale; n/a not available
Source: U.S. Census Bureau, Housing Vacancies and Homeownership Annual Statistics: 2006

TAXES

State Corporate Income Tax Rates

State	Rate (%)	Number of Brackets	Low Bracket (Under $)	High Bracket (Over $)
Colorado	4.63	1	na	na

Note: Tax rates as of December 31, 2006; na not applicable
Source: Tax Foundation, www.taxfoundation.org

State Individual Income Tax Rates

State	Federal Deductibility	Marginal Rate (%)	Number of Brackets	Low Bracket (Under $)	High Bracket (Over $)
Colorado	No	4.63 (1)	1	na	na

Note: Tax rates as of December 31, 2006; Brackets apply to single taxpayers and married people filing separately; na not applicable; (1) 4.63% of federal taxable income.
Source: Tax Foundation, www.taxfoundation.org

Various State and Local Tax Rates

State and Local Sales and Use (%)	State Sales and Use (%)	Gasoline ($/gal.)	Cigarette ($/pack)	Spirits ($/gal.)	Table Wine ($/gal.)	Beer ($/gal.)
6.7	2.9	0.22	0.84	2.28	0.32	0.08

Note: Tax rates as of December 31, 2006
Source: Tax Foundation, www.taxfoundation.org; The Sales Tax Clearinghouse, www.thestc.com

State Tax Burdens

Area	Combined State and Local Tax Burden		Combined Federal, State and Local Tax Burden	
	Percent	Rank	Percent	Rank
Colorado	9.8	38	30.7	23
U.S. Average	10.6	-	31.6	-

Note: Figures are for 2006 and measure taxes as a percentage of income
Source: Tax Foundation, www.taxfoundation.org

Internal Revenue Service Tax Audits

IRS District	Percent of Returns Audited				
	1996	1997	1998	1999	2000
Rocky Mountain	0.73	0.67	0.49	0.28	0.20
U.S.	0.66	0.61	0.46	0.31	0.20

Note: Figures cover IRS district audits of federal income tax returns filed by individuals. Geographic data on district audits after the year 2000 are being withheld by the IRS. TRAC is challenging this policy.
Source: Syracuse University, Transactional Records Access Clearinghouse (TRAC), "Odds of IRS District Tax Audit 2000"

**COMMERCIAL
UTILITIES**

Typical Monthly Electric Bills

Area	Commercial Service ($/month)		Industrial Service ($/month)	
	3 kW demand 1,000 kWh	40 kW demand 14,000 kWh	1,000 kW demand 200,000 kWh	50,000 kW demand 15,000,000 kWh
City	n/a	n/a	n/a	n/a
Average[1]	123	1,413	22,000	1,306,315

Note: Based on total rates in effect July 1, 2006; (1) average based on 196 utilities; n/a not available
Source: Edison Electric Institute, Typical Bills and Average Rates Report, Summer 2006

TRANSPORTATION

Means of Transportation to Work

Area	Car/Truck/Van		Public Transportation			Bicycle	Walked	Other Means	Worked at Home
	Drove Alone	Car-pooled	Bus	Subway	Railroad				
City	75.3	10.2	1.4	0.0	0.0	4.4	3.6	0.6	4.3
MSA[1]	77.4	11.0	0.8	0.0	0.0	2.4	2.7	0.6	5.1
U.S.	75.7	12.2	2.5	1.5	0.5	0.4	2.9	1.0	3.3

Note: Figures are percentages and cover workers 16 years of age and older;
(1) Metropolitan Statistical Area - see Appendix A for areas included
Source: Census 2000, Summary File 3

Travel Time to Work

Area	Less Than 15 Minutes	15 to 29 Minutes	30 to 44 Minutes	45 to 59 Minutes	60 Minutes or More
City	45.6	38.9	7.8	2.8	4.9
MSA[1]	38.7	37.7	12.8	4.7	6.0
U.S.	29.4	36.1	19.1	7.4	8.0

Note: Figures are percentages and include workers 16 years old and over; (1) Metropolitan Statistical Area - see Appendix A for areas included
Source: Census 2000, Summary File 3

Public Transportation

Agency name:	Transfort
Vehicle type:	Bus
Average fleet age in years:	7.9
No. operated in max. service:	18
Vehicle type:	Demand response
Average fleet age in years:	4.8
No. operated in max. service:	19
Vehicle type:	Vanpool
Average fleet age in years:	0.6
No. operated in max. service:	13

Source: Federal Transit Administration, National Transit Database, 2005

Air Transportation

Airport name and code:	Denver International (60 miles south) (DEN)
Domestic service (2006)	
Passenger airlines[1]:	45
Passenger enplanements:	21,864,651
Freight carriers[2]:	30
Freight (lbs.):	259,741,180
International service (2005)	
Passenger airlines[1]:	21
Passenger enplanements:	819,590
Freight carriers[2]:	10
Freight (lbs.):	11,520,105

Note: (1) Includes all major, minor and commuter airlines that carried at least one passenger during the year;
(2) Includes all airlines and freight carriers that transported at least one pound of freight during the year
Source: Bureau of Transportation Statistics, The Intermodal Transportation Database, Air Carriers: T-100 International Market, 2004; Bureau of Transportation Statistics, The Intermodal Transportation Database, Air Carriers: T-100 Domestic Market, 2005

Other Transportation Statistics

Interstate highways:	I-25
Amtrak service:	Bus connection
Major waterways/ports:	None

Source: Editor & Publisher Market Guide, 2006; Amtrak.com; Rand McNally 2006 Road Atlas

BUSINESSES

Major Business Headquarters

Company Name	2006 Rankings	
	Fortune[1]	Forbes[2]
No companies listed	-	-

Note: (1) Fortune 500 - companies that produce a 10-K are ranked 1 to 500 based on 2005 revenue; (2) Forbes Largest Private Companies - all private companies with at least $1 billion in annual revenue are ranked 1 to 394; companies listed are located in the city; dashes indicate no ranking
Source: Fortune, April 17, 2006; Forbes, November 9, 2006

Women-Owned Businesses: 1997 and 2002

Year	All Firms		Firms with Paid Employees			
	Firms	Sales ($000)	Firms	Sales ($000)	Employees	Payroll ($000)
1997	3,237	166,493	319	115,056	1,775	31,199
2002	3,141	321,189	511	254,768	3,691	73,008

Note: Figures cover firms located in the city; Women-owned business are defined as firms in which women own 51% or more of the stock or equity of the company; (a) Withheld to avoid disclosing data for individual companies; (b) Withheld because estimate did not meet publication standards; n/a not available
Source: 1997 Economic Census, Survey of Minority- and Women-Owned Business Enterprises; 2002 Economic Census, Survey of Business Owners (released February 9, 2006)

Minority Business Opportunity

One of the 500 largest Hispanic-owned companies in the U.S. are located in Fort Collins.
Hispanic Business, "Hispanic Business 500," June 2006

HOTELS

Hotels/Motels

Area	Hotels/Motels	Average Minimum Rates ($)		
		Tourist	First-Class	Deluxe
City	20	49	79	n/a

Note: n/a not available
Source: OAG Travel Planner Online, Spring 2006

EVENT SITES

Stadiums, Arenas, and Auditoriums

Name	Capacity
Colorado State University	9,000

Source: www.officialtravelguide.com; www.eventective.com; original research

Hotels/Conference Centers

Name	Guest Rooms	Exhibit Space (sq. ft.)	Meeting Space (sq. ft.)
Fort Collins Marriott	230	7,260	16,154

Source: www.officialtravelguide.com; www.eventective.com; original research

Living Environment

COST OF LIVING

Cost of Living Index

Year	Composite Index	Groceries	Housing	Utilities	Trans-portation	Health Care	Misc. Goods/ Services
2004	102.3	107.4	104.8	90.0	108.0	104.0	99.9
2005	102.2	107.9	102.9	86.7	104.8	104.7	103.0
2006	103.4	111.1	105.5	81.4	99.3	105.4	106.0

Note: U.S. = 100
Source: The Council for Community and Economic Research (formerly ACCRA), Cost of Living Index, 2004, 2005 and 2006 4-Quarter Averages

HOUSING

House Price Index (HPI)

Area	National Ranking[2]	Quarterly Change (%)	One-Year Change (%)	Five-Year Change (%)
MSA[1]	240	-1.19	0.85	17.10
U.S.[3]	-	1.12	5.87	55.21

Note: The HPI is a weighted repeat sales index. It measures average price changes in repeat sales or refinancings on the same properties. This information is obtained by reviewing repeat mortgage transactions on single-family properties whose mortgages have been purchased or securitized by Fannie Mae or Freddie Mac in January 1975; (1) Metropolitan Statistical Area - see Appendix B for areas included; (2) Rankings are based on annual percentage change for all metro areas containing at least 15,000 transactions over the last 10 years and ranges from 1 to 282; (3) figures based on a weighted division average; all figures are for the period ending December 31, 2006
Source: Office of Federal Housing Enterprise Oversight, House Price Index, March 1, 2007

House Price Valuations

Area	Q4 1999	Q4 2000	Q4 2001	Q4 2002	Q4 2003	Q4 2004	Q4 2005	Q4 2006
MSA[1]	-0.4	0.7	5.5	11.3	15.6	11.5	12.1	9.9

Note: Figures show the percentage of over- or under-valuation of single family homes relative to statistically normal house values (e.g. a value of 23.6 indicates that house values are 23.6% overvalued). Statistically normal house values are based on house prices, interest rates, household incomes, population densities, and any historical premiums or discounts metropolitan areas have exhibited over time; (1) Figures cover the Metropolitan Statistical Area - see Appendix B for areas included
Source: Global Insight/National City Corporation, House Prices in America, March 2007

Median Home Prices

Area	2004	2005	2006p	Percent Change 2005 to 2006
Metro Area[1]	n/a	n/a	n/a	n/a
U.S. Average	195.2	219.0	222.0	1.4

Note: Figures are median sales prices of existing single-family homes in thousands of dollars; (p) preliminary; n/a not available; (1) Covers the Fort Collins-Loveland, CO Metropolitan Statistical Area - see Appendix B for areas included
Source: National Association of Realtors, Metropolitan Area Prices, 4th Quarter 2006

Housing: Year Structure Built

Area	1990 -2000	1980 -1989	1970 -1979	1960 -1969	1950 -1959	1940 -1949	Before 1940	Median Year
City	30.4	20.2	25.0	10.2	5.2	2.3	6.6	1980
MSA[1]	29.5	17.7	26.9	10.3	5.2	2.6	8.0	1979
U.S.	17.0	15.8	18.5	13.7	12.7	7.3	15.0	1971

Note: Figures are percentages; (1) Metropolitan Statistical Area - see Appendix A for areas included
Source: Census 2000, Summary File 3

Average New Home Price

Area	2004	2005	2006
City	263,818	285,303	318,828
U.S.	253,574	275,712	299,269

Note: Figures, in dollars, are based on a new home with 2,400 sq. ft. of living area on an 8,000 sq. ft. lot.
Source: The Council for Community and Economic Research (formerly ACCRA), Cost of Living Index, 2004, 2005 and 2006 4-Quarter Averages

Average Apartment Rent

Area	2004	2005	2006
City	812	806	756
U.S.	716	740	766

Note: Figures, in dollars per month, are based on an unfurnished two bedroom, 1-1/2 or 2 bath apartment, approximately 950 sq. ft. in size, excluding all utilities except water
Source: The Council for Community and Economic Research (formerly ACCRA), Cost of Living Index, 2004, 2005 and 2006 4-Quarter Averages

RESIDENTIAL UTILITIES

Average Residential Utility Costs

Area	All Electric ($/mth)	Part Electric ($/mth)	Other Energy ($/mth)	Phone ($/mth)
City	–	35.57	78.30	25.04
U.S.	136.00	76.53	90.52	25.87

Source: The Council for Community and Economic Research (formerly ACCRA), Cost of Living Index, 2006 4-Quarter Average

HEALTH

Average Health Care Costs

Area	Optometrist ($/visit)	Doctor ($/visit)	Dentist ($/visit)
City	86.45	78.44	72.95
U.S.	76.38	76.10	68.72

Note: Optometrist—based on a full vision eye exam for an established adult patient;
Doctor—based on a general practitioner's routine exam of an established patient;
Dentist—based on adult teeth cleaning and periodic oral exam.
Source: The Council for Community and Economic Research (formerly ACCRA), Cost of Living Index, 2006 4-Quarter Average

Mortality Rates

ICD-10 Sub-Chapter	ICD-10 Code	Age-Adjusted Death Rate per 100,000 population[1]	U.S. Age-Adjusted Death Rate per 100,000 population
Malignant neoplasms	C00-C97	145.2	185.8
Ischaemic heart diseases	I20-I25	102.8	150.2
Other forms of heart disease	I30-I51	44.2	50.8
Cerebrovascular diseases	I60-I69	46.1	50.0
Chronic lower respiratory diseases	J40-J47	36.1	41.1
Diabetes mellitus	E10-E14	20.4	24.5
Other degenerative diseases of the nervous system	G30-G31	20.3	22.3
Other external causes of accidental injury	W00-X59	23.5	21.2
Influenza and pneumonia	J10-J18	12.0	19.8
Hypertensive diseases	I10-I13	12.9	18.1

Note: ICD-10 = International Classification of Diseases 10th Revision; (1) Figures cover Larimer County, CO
Source: Centers for Disease Control and Prevention, National Center for Health Statistics. Compressed Mortality File 1999-2004. CDC WONDER On-line Database, compiled from Compressed Mortality File 1999-2004 Series 20 No. 2J, 2007.

Health Risk Data

Item	Area[1] (%)	U.S. (%)
Adults who have been told they have high blood pressure	n/a	25.5
Adults who have been told they have high blood cholesterol	n/a	35.6
Adults who have been told they have diabetes[2]	n/a	7.3
Adults who have been told they have arthritis	n/a	27.0
Adults who have been told they currently have asthma	n/a	8.0
Adults who are current smokers	n/a	20.6

Note: (1) Figures cover the Metropolitan Statistical Area - see Appendix B for areas included; n/a not available;
(2) Figures do not include pregnancy-related diabetes, pre-diabetes or borderline diabetes
Source: Centers for Disease Control and Prevention, Behaviorial Risk Factor Surveillance System, SMART:
Selected Metropolitan/Micropolitan Area Trends, 2005

Distribution of Office-Based Physicians

Area	Total	Family/ General Practice	Specialties		
			Medical	Surgical	Other
MSA[1] (number)	501	131	128	121	121
MSA[1] (rate per 10,000 pop.)	19.0	5.0	4.8	4.6	4.6
Metro Average[2] (rate per 10,000 pop.)	19.4	2.1	7.5	4.5	5.3

Note: Data as of December 31, 2004; (1) Metropolitan Statistical Area - see Appendix A for areas included;
(2) Average of the 79 unique MSAs and CMSAs in this book
Source: American Medical Association, Physician Characteristics & Distribution in the U.S., 2006

Hospitals

Fort Collins has the following hospitals: 1 general medical and surgical.
AHA Guide to the Healthcare Field 2007

EDUCATION

Public School District Statistics

District Name	Schls	Pupils	Pupil/ Teacher Ratio	Minority Pupils[1] (%)	Free Lunch Eligible[2] (%)	IEP[3] (%)
Poudre R-1	52	25,000	16.8	20.8	16.4	9.9

Note: Table includes regular local school districts with 2,000 or more students; (1) Percentage of students that
are not white, non-Hispanic; (2) Percentage of students that are eligible for the free lunch program;
(3) Percentage of students that have an Individualized Education Program.
Source: U.S. Department of Education, National Center for Education Statistics, Common Core of Data, Local
Education Agency (School District) Universe Survey: School Year 2004-2005; U.S. Department of Education,
National Center for Education Statistics, Common Core of Data, Public Elementary/Secondary School Universe
Survey: School Year 2004-2005

Top Public High Schools

High School Name	Index[1]	Rank[1]	Subsidized Lunch (%)[2]	E&E (%)[3]
Poudre	2.141	314	19.0	18.3**

Note: (1) Public schools are ranked according to a ratio that is the number of Advanced Placement and/or
International Baccalaureate tests taken by all students at a school in 2005 divided by the number of graduating
seniors. All of the schools on the list have an index of at least 1.000; they are in the top five percent of public
schools measured this way. The rankings range from 1 to 1,236; (2) Percentage of students receiving federally
subsidized meals; (3) E & E stands for equity and excellence percentage: the portion of all graduating seniors
at a school that had at least one passing grade on one AP or IB test; (*) Gave just IB tests; (**) Gave both IB
and AP tests. AP and IB participation are indicators of a school's efforts to get students to excel and prepare for
college.
Source: Newsweek Online, May 23, 2006

Educational Quality

School District	Education Quotient[1]	Graduate Outcome[2]	Community Index[3]	Resource Index[4]	Rating[5]
Poudre R-1	53	48	68	66	Green

Note: Scores are national percentile rankings and range from 1 (worst) to 99 (best); (1) Combination of the Graduate Outcome, Community and Resource Indexes weighted to reflect the greater importance of the Graduate Outcome and Resource Index; (2) Based on graduation rates and college board scores (SAT/ACT); (3) Based on the surrounding community's level of affluence and adult education; (4) Based on teacher salaries, per-pupil expenditures and student-teacher ratios; (5) School districts receive one of five rankings: Gold Medal (top 16 percent of districts evaluated); Blue Ribbon (top third); Green Light (average); Yellow Light (bottom 25 percent); Red Light (bottom 10 percent).
Source: Expansion Management, "2007 Education Quotient," January 2007

Highest Level of Education

Area	Less than H.S.	H.S. Diploma	Some College, No Deg.	Associate Degree	Bachelors Degree	Masters Degree	Profess. School Degree	Doctorate Degree
City	5.8	16.0	22.7	6.6	30.5	12.3	2.4	3.7
MSA[1]	7.5	20.9	24.3	7.2	25.6	10.0	2.0	2.6
U.S.	19.4	28.4	21.2	6.4	15.7	5.9	2.0	1.0

Note: Figures are 2006 estimated percentages and cover persons age 25 and over; (1) Metropolitan Statistical Area - see Appendix B for areas included
Source: Claritas, Inc.

Educational Attainment by Race

Area	High School Graduate (%)					Bachelor's Degree (%)				
	Total	White	Black	Asian	Hisp.[2]	Total	White	Black	Asian	Hisp.[2]
City	94.0	95.1	90.4	92.6	69.4	48.4	49.4	40.0	68.1	22.0
MSA[1]	92.3	93.3	91.7	89.9	66.2	39.5	40.2	39.4	62.0	17.4
U.S.	80.4	83.6	72.3	80.4	52.4	24.4	26.1	14.3	44.1	10.4

Note: Figures shown cover persons 25 years old and over; (1) Metropolitan Statistical Area - see Appendix A for areas included; (2) people of Hispanic origin can be of any race
Source: Census 2000, Summary File 3

School Enrollment by Type

Area	Grades KG to 8				Grades 9 to 12			
	Public		Private		Public		Private	
	Enrollment	%	Enrollment	%	Enrollment	%	Enrollment	%
City	11,716	91.9	1,037	8.1	5,017	94.6	286	5.4
MSA[1]	27,705	89.6	3,226	10.4	12,585	93.9	818	6.1
U.S.	33,526,011	88.7	4,285,121	11.3	14,848,628	90.6	1,532,323	9.4

Note: Figures shown cover persons 3 years old and over; (1) Metropolitan Statistical Area - see Appendix A for areas included
Source: Census 2000, Summary File 3

School Enrollment by Race

Area	Grades KG to 8 (%)				Grades 9 to 12 (%)			
	White	Black	Asian	Hisp.[1]	White	Black	Asian	Hisp.[1]
City	87.4	1.0	1.9	10.0	88.5	1.2	1.3	11.0
MSA[2]	89.5	0.7	1.3	10.4	90.4	0.6	1.5	10.5
U.S.	68.5	15.5	3.3	16.8	68.8	15.5	3.8	15.7

Note: Figures shown cover persons 3 years old and over; (1) people of Hispanic origin can be of any race; (2) Metropolitan Statistical Area - see Appendix A for areas included
Source: Census 2000, Summary File 3

Average Salaries of Public School Teachers

District	2004-05 Dollars	2004-05 Rank[1]	2005-06 Dollars	2005-06 Rank[1]	Percent Change 2004-05 to 2005-06
COLORADO	43,949	23	45,616	23	3.79
U.S. Average	47,674	-	49,109	-	3.01

Note: (1) State rank ranges from 1 to 51.
Source: National Education Association, Rankings & Estimates: Rankings of the States 2005 and Estimates of School Statistics 2006, November 2006

Higher Education

Four-Year Colleges Public	Four-Year Colleges Private Non-profit	Four-Year Colleges Private For-profit	Two-Year Colleges Public	Two-Year Colleges Private Non-profit	Two-Year Colleges Private For-profit	Medical Schools[1]	Law Schools[2]	Voc/ Tech[3]
1	0	1	0	0	2	0	0	1

Note: Figures cover institutions located within the city limits; (1) includes schools accredited by the Liaison Committee on Medical Education and the American Osteopathic Association; (2) includes American Bar Association-accredited law schools; (3) includes all schools with programs that are less than 2 years
Source: National Center for Education Statistics, The Integrated Postsecondary Education System (IPEDS) Peer Analysis System, 2006; www.usnews.com, America's Best Graduate Schools 2008, Medical School Directory; www.usnews.com, America's Best Graduate Schools 2008, Law School Directory

PRESIDENTIAL ELECTION

2004 Presidential Election Results

Area	Bush	Kerry	Nader	Other
Larimer County	51.8	46.6	0.7	0.9
U.S.	50.7	48.3	0.4	0.6

Note: Results are percentages and may not add to 100% due to rounding
Source: Dave Leip's Atlas of U.S. Presidential Elections, www.uselectionatlas.org

MAJOR EMPLOYERS

Major Employers

Company Name	Industry	Type of Site
Advanced Energy Industries	Electronic components, nec	Headquarters
Anheuser-Busch	Malt beverages	Branch
CSU Coop Extension	Regulation of agricultural marketing	Branch
Center Partners Inc	Computer related services, nec	Headquarters
Colorado State University	Colleges and universities	Headquarters
Fort Collins/Loveland Muni Airport	Executive offices	Headquarters
Fort Collins	Electric services	Branch
HP	Computer storage devices	Branch
LSI Logic Corporation	Semiconductors and related devices	Branch
Lachat Instruments	Analytical instruments	Headquarters
McKee Medical Center	General medical and surgical hospitals	Branch
Poudre School District	Elementary and secondary schools	Headquarters
Poudre Valley Hospital	General medical and surgical hospitals	Branch
Wal-Mart	Department stores	Branch
Woodward Governor Company	Aircraft parts and equipment, nec	Branch

Note: Companies shown are located within the metropolitan area and have 400 or more employees; nec = not elsewhere classified.
Source: www.zapdata.com, January 2007

PUBLIC SAFETY

Crime Rate

Area	All Crimes	Violent Crimes				Property Crimes		
		Murder	Forcible Rape	Robbery	Aggrav. Assault	Burglary	Larceny -Theft	Motor Vehicle Theft
City	3,787.9	1.6	91.7	44.3	205.9	593.5	2,516.2	334.8
Suburbs[1]	2,764.3	2.1	32.7	18.1	97.3	420.5	2,035.2	158.5
Metro[2]	3,247.6	1.8	60.5	30.4	148.6	502.2	2,262.3	241.7
U.S.	3,899.0	5.6	31.7	140.7	291.1	726.7	2,286.3	416.7

Note: Figures are crimes per 100,000 population; (1) All areas within the metro area that are located outside the city limits; (2) Metropolitan Statistical Area - see Appendix B for areas included
Source: FBI Uniform Crime Reports, 2005

Hate Crimes

Area	Number of Quarters Reported	Bias Motivation				
		Race	Religion	Sexual Orientation	Ethnicity	Disability
City	4	0	1	0	0	0

Source: Federal Bureau of Investigation, Hate Crime Statistics 2005

RECREATION

Culture

Dance[1]	Theatre[1]	Instrumental Music[1]	Vocal Music[1]	Series/ Festivals	Museums	Zoos
1	1	2	2	0	4	0

Note: (1) number of professional perfoming groups
Source: The Grey House Performing Arts Directory, 2007; Official Museum Directory, 2007

Professional Sports Teams

Major League Baseball	National Basketball Association	National Football League	National Hockey League	Major League Soccer	Women's National Basketball Association
0	0	0	0	0	0

Note: Includes teams located in the Fort Collins metro area.
Source: www.sportsvenues.com, Listing of Venues by State/Province and City, 2006

MEDIA

Newspapers

Name	Target Audience	Frequency	Circulation
The Coloradoan	n/a	Daily	29,055
Fort Collins Weekly	General	Non-Daily	20,000

Note: Includes newspapers whose offices are located in the city and whose circulations are 500 or more; n/a not available
Source: BurrellesLuce, MediaContacts Online, January 2006

Television Stations

Name	Ch.	Network(s)	Type	Ownership
KWGN	2	WBN	Commercial	Tribune Broadcasting Company
KCNC	4	CBS	Commercial	CBS Broadcasting Company
KRMA	6	PBS	Public	Rocky Mountain Public Broadcasting Network
KMGH	7	ABC	Commercial	The McGraw-Hill Companies
KACT	8	n/a	Non-comm.	City of Aurora
KUSA	9	NBC	Commercial	Gannett Broadcasting
KBDI	12	PBS	Public	Front Range Educational Media Corp.
KTVJ	14	Univision	Commercial	Roberts Broadcasting Inc.
KTVD	20	UPN	Commercial	Channel 20 TV Company
KDEN	25	n/a	Commercial	Flinn Broadcasting Corporation
KDVR	31	Fox	Commercial	Fox Television Stations Inc.
KRMT	41	n/a	Non-comm.	Word of God Fellowship
KCEC	50	Univision	Commercial	Golden Hills Broadcasting
KWHD	53	n/a	Commercial	LeSea Inc.
KPXC	59	Pax	Commercial	Paxson Communications Corporation
KMAS	63	Telemundo	Commercial	n/a

Note: Stations included cover the Denver DMA (Designated Market Area); n/a not available
BurrellesLuce, MediaContacts Online, January 2006

Major AM Radio Stations

Call Letters	Freq. (kHz)	Station Type	Target Audience	Station Format	Music Format
KLZ	560	n/a	General/Religious	News/Talk	n/a
KIIX	600	Commercial	General	Sports/Talk	n/a
KHOW	630	n/a	General	Music/News/Talk	n/a
KLTT	670	n/a	General/Religious	Talk	n/a
KNUS	710	n/a	General	News/Sports/Talk	n/a
KKZN	760	n/a	General	Sports/Talk	n/a
KOA	850	n/a	General	Music/News/Sports/Talk	n/a
KPOF	910	Non-Comm	General/Religious	Educational/Music	Classical
KLMR	920	n/a	General	Music/News/Sports/Talk	n/a
KOGA	930	n/a	General	n/a	n/a
KKFN	950	n/a	General	Music/Sports/Talk	n/a
KRKS	990	Commercial	General/Religious	News/Talk	n/a
KSIR	1010	Commercial	General	News/Sports/Talk	n/a
KLMO	1060	Commercial	General	Talk	n/a
KMXA	1090	n/a	General/Hispanic	Music/Talk	n/a
KCUV	1150	n/a	General/Hispanic	Sports	n/a
KVCU	1190	College	General	Ed/Music/News/Sports	Urban Contemp.
KLVZ	1220	n/a	General/Religious	Music	n/a
KRAL	1240	Commercial	General	Music/News	Adult Contemp.
KIML	1270	Commercial	General	Music/News/Sports	n/a
KBNO	1280	n/a	Hispanic	Music/News/Talk	n/a
KOWB	1290	n/a	General	News/Talk	n/a
KFKA	1310	Commercial	General	Ed/News/Sports/Talk	n/a
KCOL	1410	Commercial	General	News/Talk	n/a
KRDZ	1440	Commercial	General	Music/News/Sports	Oldies
KADZ	1550	Commercial	Children/Religious	Music/Talk	Adult Contemp.
KCKK	1600	n/a	General	Music	n/a
KBJD	1650	Commercial	General	News/Talk	n/a

Note: Stations included cover the Denver DMA (Designated Market Area); n/a not available
Source: BurrellesLuce, MediaContacts Online, January 2006

Major FM Radio Stations

Call Letters	Freq. (mHz)	Station Type	Target Audience	Station Format	Music Format
KLDV	91.1	Non-Comm	Religious	Music	Christian
KUNC	91.5	n/a	General	Ed/Music/News/Talk	Jazz
KUWR	91.9	College	General	Music/News/Talk	Jazz
KLGT	92.9	n/a	General/Religious	n/a	n/a
KTCL	93.3	n/a	General	Music	n/a
KLMR	93.3	n/a	General	Music/News/Sports	A.O. Rock
KRAI	93.7	Commercial	General	Music/News	Adult Contemp.
KRKS	94.7	Commercial	General/Religious	Music/News/Talk	Christian
KCGY	95.1	n/a	General	Music/Sports	n/a
KFMD	95.7	n/a	General	Music	n/a
KGLL	96.1	Commercial	General	Music	Top 40
KAML	96.9	n/a	General	Music/News/Sports	Classic Rock
KBCO	97.3	Commercial	General	Music/News	Classic Rock
KQSK	97.5	Commercial	General	Music/News	Country
KYGO	98.5	n/a	General	Music	n/a
KSID	98.7	n/a	General	Music/News/Sports	n/a
KUAD	99.1	Commercial	General	Music	Country
KOGA	99.7	n/a	General	Music/News	n/a
KIMN	100.3	n/a	General	n/a	n/a
KGWY	100.7	Commercial	General	Music/News/Sports	Country
KOSI	101.1	n/a	General	Music	n/a
KPNY	102.1	Commercial	General	Music/News	Adult Contemp.
KRFX	103.5	n/a	General	Music/News/Sports	n/a
KJCD	104.3	n/a	General	Music/News/Talk	n/a
KNNG	104.7	Commercial	General	Music/News	Country
KXKL	105.1	n/a	General	Music/News	n/a
KIMX	105.5	n/a	General/Women	Music/News/Sports	n/a
KVAY	105.7	Commercial	General	Music	Oldies
KALC	105.9	Commercial	General	Music	Adult Contemp.
KAAQ	105.9	n/a	General	Music/News/Sports	n/a
KMCX	106.5	Commercial	General	Music/News	Country
KBPI	106.7	n/a	General	Music/News/Talk	n/a
KQKS	107.5	Commercial	General	Music	Urban Contemp.

Note: Stations included cover the Denver DMA (Designated Market Area); n/a not available
BurrellesLuce, MediaContacts Online, January 2006

CLIMATE

Average and Extreme Temperatures

Temperature	Jan	Feb	Mar	Apr	May	Jun	Jul	Aug	Sep	Oct	Nov	Dec	Yr.
Extreme High (°F)	73	76	84	90	93	102	103	100	97	89	79	75	103
Average High (°F)	43	47	52	62	71	81	88	86	77	67	52	45	64
Average Temp. (°F)	30	34	39	48	58	67	73	72	63	52	39	32	51
Average Low (°F)	16	20	25	34	44	53	59	57	48	37	25	18	37
Extreme Low (°F)	-25	-25	-10	-2	22	30	43	41	17	3	-8	-25	-25

Note: Figures cover the years 1948-1992
Source: National Climatic Data Center, International Station Meteorological Climate Summary, 9/96

Average Precipitation/Snowfall/Humidity

Precip./Humidity	Jan	Feb	Mar	Apr	May	Jun	Jul	Aug	Sep	Oct	Nov	Dec	Yr.
Avg. Precip. (in.)	0.6	0.6	1.3	1.7	2.5	1.7	1.9	1.5	1.1	1.0	0.9	0.6	15.5
Avg. Snowfall (in.)	9	7	14	9	2	Tr	0	0	2	4	9	8	63
Avg. Rel. Hum. 5am (%)	62	65	67	66	70	68	67	68	66	63	66	63	66
Avg. Rel. Hum. 5pm (%)	49	44	40	35	38	34	34	34	32	34	47	50	39

Note: Figures cover the years 1948-1992; Tr = Trace amounts (<0.05 in. of rain; <0.5 in. of snow)
Source: National Climatic Data Center, International Station Meteorological Climate Summary, 9/96

Weather Conditions

Temperature			Daytime Sky			Precipitation		
10°F & below	32°F & below	90°F & above	Clear	Partly cloudy	Cloudy	0.01 inch or more precip.	0.1 inch or more snow/ice	Thunder-storms
24	155	33	99	177	89	90	38	39

Note: Figures are average number of days per year and cover the years 1948-1992
Source: National Climatic Data Center, International Station Meteorological Climate Summary, 9/96

HAZARDOUS WASTE

Superfund Sites

Fort Collins has no sites on the EPA's Superfund Final National Priorities List.
U.S. Environmental Protection Agency, Final National Priorities List, March 20, 2007

AIR & WATER QUALITY

Air Quality Index

Area	Percent of Days when Air Quality was...[2]				AQI Statistics	
	Good	Moderate	Unhealthy for Sensitive Groups	Unhealthy	Maximum	Median
MSA[1]	90.4	9.6	0.0	0.0	100	39

Note: The Air Quality Index (AQI) is an index for reporting daily air quality. EPA calculates the AQI for five major air pollutants regulated by the Clean Air Act: ground-level ozone, particle pollution (also known as particulate matter), carbon monoxide, sulfur dioxide, and nitrogen dioxide. The AQI runs from 0 to 500. The higher the AQI value, the greater the level of air pollution and the greater the health concern. There are six AQI categories: "Good" The AQI is between 0 and 50. Air quality is considered satisfactory; "Moderate" The AQI is between 51 and 100. Air quality is acceptable; "Unhealthy for Sensitive Groups" When AQI values are between 101 and 150, members of sensitive groups may experience health effects; "Unhealthy" When AQI values are between 151 and 200 everyone may begin to experience health effects; "Very Unhealthy" AQI values between 201 and 300 trigger a health alert; "Hazardous" AQI values over 300 trigger health warnings of emergency conditions; (1) Metropolitan Statistical Area - see Appendix A for areas included; (2) Based on 365 days with AQI data in 2005.
Source: U.S. Environmental Protection Agency, Air Quality Index Report, 2005

Air Quality Index Pollutants

Area	Percent of Days when AQI Pollutant was...[2]					
	Carbon Monoxide	Nitrogen Dioxide	Ozone	Sulfur Dioxide	Particulate Matter 2.5	Particulate Matter 10
MSA[1]	0.3	0.0	95.1	0.0	3.8	0.8

Note: The Air Quality Index (AQI) is an index for reporting daily air quality. EPA calculates the AQI for five major air pollutants regulated by the Clean Air Act: ground-level ozone, particle pollution (also known as particulate matter), carbon monoxide, sulfur dioxide, and nitrogen dioxide. The AQI runs from 0 to 500. The higher the AQI value, the greater the level of air pollution and the greater the health concern; (1) Metropolitan Statistical Area - see Appendix A for areas included; (2) Based on 365 days with AQI data in 2005.
Source: U.S. Environmental Protection Agency, Air Quality Index Report, 2005

Number of Days with Air Quality Index Values Greater than 100

Area	Trend Sites								All Sites
	1998	1999	2000	2001	2002	2003	2004	2005	2005
MSA[1]	n/a	n/a	n/a	n/a	n/a	n/a	n/a	n/a	n/a

Note: An AQI value greater than 100 indicates that air quality would have been in the unhealthful range on that day. Data from exceptional events are not included. These counts are presented in two ways. First, the counts are based on sites having an adequate record of monitoring data during the trend period (trend sites). These counts represent the relative change in the number of days with AQI values greater than 100. In the last column, the counts are based on all sites with data in the most recent year (because it is possible for a site to have data in the most recent year but not enough data to be a trend site); (1) Metropolitan Statistical Area - see Appendix A for areas included; n/a not available.
Source: U.S. Environmental Protection Agency, Air Trends Fact Book 2005

Maximum Pollutant Concentrations

	Particulate Matter 10 (ug/m^3)	Particulate Matter 2.5 (ug/m^3)	Ozone 1-hour (ppm)	Carbon Monoxide (ppm)	Sulfur Dioxide (ppm)	Nitrogen Dioxide (ppm)	Lead (ug/m^3)
MSA[1] Level	46	16	0.102	2	n/a	n/a	n/a
NAAQS[2]	150	65	0.125	9	0.140	0.053	1.50
Met NAAQS[2]	Yes	Yes	Yes	Yes	n/a	n/a	n/a

Note: Data from exceptional events are not included; (1) Metropolitan Statistical Area - see Appendix A for areas included; (2) National Ambient Air Quality Standards; n/a not available
Units: ppm = parts per million; ug/m^3 = micrograms per cubic meter
Source: U.S. Environmental Protection Agency, Air Trends Fact Book 2005

Watershed Health

The U.S. Environmental Protection Agency monitors the health of the aquatic resources for the nation's 2,000+ watersheds. **The Cache La Poudre watershed serves the Fort Collins area and received an overall Index of Watershed Indicators (IWI) score of 1 (better quality - low vulnerability).** The IWI score is based on seven condition and nine vulnerability indicators. The overall IWI score ranges from 1 (best health) to 6 (worst health). The Condition Indicators include: designated use attainment, fish and wildlife consumption advisories, source water condition, contaminated sediments, ambient water quality, and wetlands loss index. The Vulnerability Indicators include: aquatic species at risk, conventional and toxic loads over permitted limits, urban and agricultural runoff potential, population change, hydrologic modification, estuarine pollution susceptibility, and air deposition. *Note: The IWI is no longer being updated by the U.S. EPA. Source: U.S. Environmental Protection Agency, Index of Watershed Indicators, October 26, 2001*

Drinking Water

Water System Name	Pop. Served	Primary Water Source Type	Health Based	Significant Monitoring	Monitoring
			Number of Violations in 2006[a]		
City of Fort Collins	125,500	Surface	None	None	None

Note: (a) Based on violation data from January 1, 2006 to December 31, 2006
Source: U.S. Environmental Protection Agency, Office of Ground Water and Drinking Water, Safe Drinking Water Information System (data extracted April 12, 2007)

Fort Collins tap water is alkaline, very soft.
Editor & Publisher Market Guide, 2005

Honolulu, Hawaii

Background

Honolulu, whose name in Hawaiian means "sheltered harbor," is the capital of Hawaii and the seat of Honolulu County. The city sits in one of the most famously attractive areas of the world, on the island of Oahu, with the extinct volcano Diamond Head and Waikiki Beach to the east, and two mountain ranges, the Koolau and the Waianae, in the background. Honolulu is the economic hub of Hawaii, a major seaport and, most importantly, home to its $10 billion tourist industry.

Traditionally home to fishing and horticultural tribal groups, the Hawaiian islands were politically united under the reign of King Kamehameha I, who first moved his triumphant court to Waikiki and subsequently to a site in what is now downtown Honolulu (1804). It was during his time that the port became a center for the sandalwood trade, thus establishing the region as an international presence even before the political interventions of non-Hawaiians.

European activity dates from 1794, when the English sea captain William Brown entered Honolulu, dubbing it Fair Harbor, though many of the Europeans who followed called it Brown's Harbor. Two decades later, the first missionaries arrived. American Congregationalists were followed by French Catholics and, even later, Mormons and Anglicans. By the end of the nineteenth century, non-Hawaiians owned most of the land. This economic situation was soon echoed in the area's political developments, which culminated in the 1898 annexation of Hawaii by the United States.

As is true for many strategically located cities, the events of World War II had a profound effect on Honolulu. The Japanese attack on December 7, 1941, forever etched the name of Pearl Harbor into the national memory. During the war, existing military bases were expanded and new bases built, providing considerable economic stimuli. The Vietnam War also had a dramatic effect on Honolulu; by the end of the twentieth century, military families accounted for 10 percent of the population.

Today, the U.S. military is still a major employer in the city employing more than 45,000 personnel throughout the state. Nearby are the Nimitz-MacArthur Pacific Command Center, Hickam Air Force Base and the Tripler Army Medical Center. Fruit, primarily pineapple, processing and light manufacturing are also important to the economy. Aquaculture, which includes cultivated species of shellfish, finfish and algae, has grown in recent years. There is a small but fast-growing biotechnology sector.

Increasingly, however, tourism has been the private-sector mainstay of Honolulu's economy, with most of the millions of tourists who visit Hawaii annually coming through its port or airport. Honolulu is a required stop for any holiday ship cruising these waters, and it is also the center for the inter-island air services that ferry tourists to various resort locations.

The center of Honolulu's downtown district is dominated by the Iolani Palace, once home to Hawaii's original royal family. Nearby are the State Capitol Building and the State Supreme Court Building, known as Aliiolani Hall. The Aloha Tower Development Corporation, a state agency tasked with redeveloping underused state property, continues its work with plans to modernize the mixed-use space in and around the Aloha Tower Complex along the city's piers.

Honolulu, as it has grown along the southern coast of Oahu, has established a mix of residential zones, with single-family dwellings and relatively small multi-unit buildings. The result is that large parts of what is a major metropolitan area feel like cozy neighborhoods. In fact, Honolulu is governed in part through the device of a Neighborhood Board System, which insures maximal local input with regard to planning decisions and city services.

Cultural amenities include the Bishop Museum, the Honolulu Academy of Arts, and the Contemporary Museum, which together offer world-class collections in Polynesian art and artifacts, Japanese, Chinese, and Korean art, and modern art from the world over. Honolulu also hosts a symphony orchestra, he oldest US symphony orchestra west of the Rocky Mountains, which performs at the Neal S. Blaisdell Center.

Honolulu's weather is subtropical, with temperatures moderated by the surrounding ocean and the trade winds. There are only slight variations in temperature from summer to winter. Rain is moderate, though heavier in summer, when it sometimes comes in the form of quick showers while the sun is shining — an effect known locally as "liquid sunshine."

Rankings

General Rankings

- Honolulu was ranked #5 out of 331 metro areas in *Cities Ranked & Rated*. Criteria: cost of living; climate; crime; transportation; economy and jobs; education; arts and culture; health and healthcare; leisure. *Cities Ranked & Rated, 1st Edition, 2004*

- Honolulu was selected as one of the top places to live in the U.S. according to Harris Interactive. The city ranked #6 out of 10. Criteria: 3,685 U.S. adults were polled as to where they would choose to live if they could live anywhere in the country. *Harris Interactive, September 6, 2006*

- Mercer Human Resources Consulting ranked 215 cities worldwide in terms of overall quality of life. Honolulu ranked #27. Criteria: political, social, economic, and socio-cultural factors; medical and health considerations; schools and education; public services and transportation; recreation; consumer goods; housing; and natural environment. *Mercer Human Resources Consulting, April 3, 2006*

- *Condé Nast Traveler* polled nearly 28,000 readers for travel satisfaction. American cities were ranked based on the following criteria: friendliness; ambiance; culture/sites; restaurants; lodging; and shopping. Honolulu appeared in the top 10, ranking #7. *Condé Nast Traveler, Readers' Choice Awards 2006*

Business/Finance Rankings

- Honolulu was selected as one of the best places to start and grow a company by *Entrepreneur* and the National Policy Research Council. The Honolulu metro area ranked #19 out of 63 mid-size metro areas. Criteria: business formation and growth (firms started four to 14 years ago that still employ at least 5 people and experienced rapid growth over the last four years). *Entrepreneur/National Policy Research Council, "Hot Cities for Entrepreneurs," September 2006*

- Intel, in partnership with Sperling's BestPlaces, ranked the 80 "Best Cities for Teleworking" in America. The Honolulu metro area ranked #8 among mid-sized metro areas. The study identifies cities that hold the greatest potential for teleworking based on a host of factors including typical commuting times, fuel prices, availability of broadband Internet access and percentage of the population in telework friendly jobs. The study also factored in extreme climate and natural hazards. *Intel, "Best Cities for Teleworking," March 30, 2006*

- Honolulu was selected as one of 20 cities in North America that is doing its part to host green conventions by providing renewable energy, intelligent recycling programs, transportation that minimizes usage of fossil fuels, and plenty of parkland. The city was ranked #14. *Meetings and Conventions, "Natural Choices," August 2006*

- The Honolulu metro area appeared on the Milken Institute "2005 Best Performing Cities" index. Rank: #56 out of 200 large metro areas. Criteria: job growth; wage and salary growth; high-tech output growth. *Milken Institute, "2005 Best Performing Cities," February 2006*

- The Honolulu metro area was selected as one of "The Best Cities for Doing Business in America." *Inc.* magazine measured employment growth in 393 regions using the following criteria: recent growth trend; mid-term growth; long-term trend; and current year growth. The Honolulu metro area ranked #26 among mid-sized metro areas and #120 overall. *Inc., May 2006*

- Honolulu was identified as one of the 100 "Most Unwired Cities" in the U.S. The area ranked #73 out of the 100 largest metro areas in the U.S. Criteria: number of public and commercial wireless access points (hotspots); airports with wireless Internet access; broadband availability; local wireless networks; and wireless email devices. *Intel, "Most Unwired Cities Survey," June 7, 2005*

- *Forbes* ranked the 200 most populous metro areas in the U.S. in terms of the "Best Places for Business and Careers." The Honolulu metro area was ranked #138. Criteria: business costs (labor, energy, tax and office space expenses); living costs (housing, transportation, food and other household expenditures); education levels of the work force; job growth; income growth; migration trends; crime rates; and culture/leisure. *Forbes, April 23, 2007*

- *Kiplinger's Personal Finance* ranked 101 U.S. cities in terms of their total tax burdens. Honolulu ranked #70 (#1 had the lowest overall tax burden). Criteria: state income tax; property tax; sales tax; personal property tax; and gasoline tax. *Kiplinger's Personal Finance, July 2004*

- *Fortune* ranked the 100 largest metro areas in the U.S. in terms of projected median home price change in 2006. The Honolulu metro area ranked #54. *Fortune, "The Top 100: Is the Party Over?" December 26, 2005*

- Honolulu was identified as one of the top 10 richest major cities in the U.S. The city ranked #10. Criteria: 2004 median household income. *Forbes, "Richest Cities in the U.S.," October 27, 2005*

Health/Environment Rankings

- The Honolulu metro area appeared in *Country Home's* "2007 Best Green Places Report". The area ranked #95. Criteria included: air and watershed quality; miles of mass transit; green power; number of farmer's markets, organic producers and groceries. *Country Home, "2007 Best Green Places Report," April 2007*

- The American Podiatric Medical Association and *Prevention* magazine ranked America's 100 most populated cities based on fitness-walker friendliness. The best cities have safe streets, beautiful places to walk, mild weather and good air quality. Honolulu ranked #14. *Prevention, "The Best Walking Cities of 2007," April 2007; American Podiatric Medical Association, "2007 Best Fitness-Walking Cities"*

- Honolulu was selected as one of "greenest" cities in the U.S. Criteria: good water- and air-quality; efficient use of resources; renewable energy leadership; accessible and reliable public transportation; green building practices; number of parks and greenbelts; access to locally-grown fresh food through farmers' markets and community supported agriculture groups; and affordability. *The Green Guide Institute, "The Top 10 Green Cities in the U.S.: 2005," April 19, 2005*

- Honolulu was selected as one of the 25 fittest cities in America by *Men's Fitness Online*. It ranked #2 out of America's 50 largest cities. Criteria: gyms/sporting goods; nutrition; exercise/sports; overweight/sedentary; junk food; alcohol; smoking; television; air and water quality; climate; geography; commute time; parks/open space; recreation facilities; health care; motivation; civic legislation and leadership. *Men's Fitness Online, America's Fittest/Fattest Cities 2006*

- Honolulu was selected as one of "America's Healthiest Cities" by *Natural Health* magazine. The city was ranked #22 out of the 50 largest urban areas in the U.S. Twenty-six criteria in the following four categories were examined: whether the city boasts natural offerings; how well the city promotes its residents' physical health; whether the city offers a healthy environment; how well the city fosters a sense of community. *Natural Health, April 2003*

- *Men's Health* ranked the nation's largest 100 cities in terms of the *Best (and Worst) Cities for Men*. Honolulu was ranked #2. Criteria: 24 statistical parameters of long life in the categories of health, quality of life, and fitness. *Men's Health, January/February 2007*

- *Men's Health* ranked 100 U.S. cities in terms of the quality of their tap water. Honolulu was ranked #10 and received a grade of A. Criteria: levels of total coliform bacteria, arsenic, lead, total trihalomethanes (linked to cancer), and halo-acetic acids, plus the number of EPA water-system violations from 1995 to 2005. *Men's Health, March 2007*

- Ortho-McNeil Neurologics, in partnership with Sperling's BestPlaces, analyzed 110 metro areas and identified those U.S. cities with the highest prevalence of factors that are most commonly associated with migraine headaches. The Honolulu metro area ranked #103. Criteria: number of migraine-related drug prescriptions per capita; lifestyle factors that can contribute to migraines; environmental factors that can trigger migraines; and consumption of migraine-triggering foods. *Ortho-McNeil Neurologics, "America's Migraine Hot Spots," March 14, 2006*

- Sperling's BestPlaces ranked 331 metro areas and identified the most and least stressful U.S. cities. The Honolulu metro area ranked #92 out of the 100 largest metro areas (#1 = most stressful). Criteria: divorce rate; unemployment rate; violent and property crime; suicide rate; commute time; mental health; alcohol consumption; cloudy days. *www.BestPlaces.net, January 9, 2004*

- Sperling's BestPlaces in partnership with Vistakon ranked the 100 largest metro areas and identified "America's 10 Best Cities for Comfortable Eyes." The Honolulu metro area ranked #7. Criteria: altitude; sunny days; wind; extreme temperatures; humidity; pollution; commute time; computer use. *Vistakon, "America's Best and Worst Cities for Comfortable Eyes," June 15, 2004*

- Honolulu was highlighted as one of the top 25 cleanest metro areas for long-term particle pollution (PM 2.5) in the U.S. The area ranked #3. *American Lung Association, State of the Air 2006*

- Honolulu was highlighted as one of the top 25 cleanest metro areas for ozone air pollution in the U.S. The list represents cities with no monitored ozone air pollution in the unhealthful range. *American Lung Association, State of the Air 2006*

Women/Minorities Rankings

- Honolulu was ranked #1 out of 100 metro areas in *SELF Magazine's* ranking of "America's Best Places for Women." A panel of experts came up with nearly 40 criteria including: drinking and smoking rates; depression; unemployment; parks; crime; disease; healthcare insurance coverage; air quality; and commute times. *SELF Magazine, "America's Best Places for Women 2006," December 2006*

- *Ladies Home Journal* ranked America's 200 largest cities based on the qualities women surveyed care about most. Honolulu ranked #3 out of 57 in the big city category (population over 300,000). Criteria: crime; lifestyle; education; jobs; health; child care; politics; and the economy. *Ladies Home Journal Online, "The Best Cities for Women 2002"*

Seniors/Retirement Rankings

- A.G. Edwards ranked America's 500 top-performing communities based on their residents' personal savings and investing behavior. The Honolulu metro area ranked #93 with an index score of 107.14 (national average = 100.00). A dozen statistical factors were measured including: participation in retirement savings plans; personal debt levels; and home ownership. *A.G. Edwards, "2006 Nest Egg Index", September 6, 2006*

Children/Family Rankings

- *Zero Population Growth* ranked 100 cities in terms of children's health, safety, and economic well-being. Honolulu was ranked #26 out of 80 Large Cities (remainder of the 100 largest cities in the U.S.) and was given a grade of B+. Criteria: total population and population growth; percent of population under 18 years of age; percent of births to teens; infant mortality rate; percent of eligible women not receiving Title X services; contraceptive equity indicator; percent of children without health insurance; percent of city residents over age 25 with a high-school diploma; ration of PopEd (Population Connection's Education Program) teachers trained; sexuality education indicator; proficiency in reading and math; percent of kids living in poverty; percent growth in urbanized land; violent crime rate; recycling. *Population Connection, Kid Friendly Cities: Report Card 2004*

- *Fit Pregnancy* magazine ranked the 50 best U.S. cities in which to have a baby. Honolulu was ranked #23. Criteria: fertility services; maternal and infant health risk; access to hospitals and doctors; safety; affordability; stroller friendliness; and birthing options. *Fit Pregnancy, February/March, 2006*

- Honolulu was chosen as one of America's "100 Best Communities for Young People." The winners were selected based upon detailed information provided about each community's efforts to fulfill five essential promises critical to the well-being of young people: caring adults who are actively involved in their lives; safe places in which to learn and grow; a healthy start toward adulthood; an effective education that builds marketable skills; and opportunities to help others. *America's Promise, "100 Best Communities for Young People," September 26, 2005*

Safety Rankings

- Farmers Insurance Group of Companies, in partnership with Sperling's BestPlaces, ranked 331 metro areas and identified the "Most Secure U.S. Place to Live." The Honolulu metro area ranked #5 out of the top 20 in the large city category (500,000 or more residents). Criteria: crime rates; risk of natural disasters; and job loss numbers. *Farmers Insurance Group, "25 Most Secure U.S. Place to Live," June 6, 2005*

- Allstate ranked the 200 largest cities in America in terms of driver safety. Honolulu ranked #133. In addition, drivers were 16.7% more likely to have had an accident compared to the national average. Allstate researchers analyzed internal Property Damage reported claims over a two-year period (from January 2003 to December 2004) to ensure the findings would not be affected by external influences such as weather or road construction. A weighted average of the two-year numbers determined the annual percentages. The report defines an auto crash as any collision resulting in a property damage claim. *Allstate, "Allstate America's Best Drivers Report 2006," May 24, 2006*

- Honolulu was identified as one of the safest places in the U.S. in terms of its vulnerability to natural disasters and weather extremes. The city ranked #1 out of 10. Sperling's BestPlaces analyzed data to show a metro areas' relative tendency to experience natural disasters (hail, tornados, high winds, hurricanes, earthquakes, and brush fires) or extreme weather (abundant rain or snowfall or days that are below freezing or above 90 degrees Fahrenheit). *Forbes, "Safest and Least Safe Places in the U.S.," August 30, 2005*

- Honolulu was identified as one of the safest large cities in America by Morgan Quitno. All 32 cities with populations of 500,000 or more that reported crime rates in 2005 for murder, rape, robbery, aggravated assault, burglary, and motor vehicle thefts were ranked. The city ranked #2 out of the top 10. *www.morganquitno.com, 13th Annual America's Safest (and Most Dangerous) Cities Awards*

- *Ladies Home Journal* ranked America's 200 largest cities in terms of safety. Honolulu ranked #23 out of 200. Criteria: violent crimes; crimes against property; and rape. *Ladies Home Journal Online, "The Best Cities for Women 2002"*

Sports/Recreation Rankings

- Honolulu was chosen as one of America's 25 best cities for running. The city was ranked #19. Criteria: number of running clubs per city; amount of land set aside for park usage; air quality; weather; crime rates; and results from a *Runner's World* poll in which readers ranked their favorite running cities. *Runner's World, "The 25 Best Running Cities in America," July 2005*

- *Golf Digest* ranked 330 metro areas in the U.S. in terms of golf. The Honolulu metro area was ranked #222. Criteria: access to golf; weather; value of golf; and quality of golf. *Golf Digest, "Metro Golf Rankings," August 2005*

Dating/Romance Rankings

■ The Honolulu metro area was selected as one of the "Best Cities for Relocating Singles" by Worldwide ERC and Primacy Relocation. The area ranked #88 out of the 100 largest metro areas in the U.S. Areas were selected based on the following criteria: Population Criteria (local percentage and growth trends of unmarried residents aged 25-34; male-female ratios; the number of newcomers to the area; diversity and density); Economic Criteria (job growth vs. unemployment rates; apartment rental costs; fee and occupancy rates for temporary housing and mini-storage; higher education costs, including in-state and out-of-state tuition requirements; vehicle tax rates and quality of service from utility providers); Quality-of-Life Criteria (level of per capita volunteering; quality and quantity of collegiate and professional sports with fun, fan-friendly venues; number of Starbucks and other coffee shops; quality or popularity of restaurants, nightspots, health clubs, and online dating; moderate climates with sustainable water supplies). *Worldwide ERC and Primacy Relocation, "2006 Best Cities for Relocating Singles," October 11, 2006*

■ Honolulu was selected as one of "America's Favorite Cities" in the "top cities for honeymoons" category. The city was ranked #1 out of 25. Criteria: *Travel + Leisure* magazine and AOL's Travel Channel conducted an online survey of nearly half a million AOL members to find out what travelers think about twenty-five American cities. Results shown above are according to visitors to the city, not locals. *Travel + Leisure and AOL's Travel Channel, "America's Favorite Cities," March 22, 2004*

■ Sperling's BestPlaces in partnership with AXE Deodorant Bodyspray ranked 80 metro areas and identified "America's Best (and Worst) Cities for Dating." The Honolulu metro area ranked #10. Criteria: percentage of singles ages 18-24; population density; dating venues per capita. *AXE Deodorant Bodyspray, "America's Best (and Worst) Cities for Dating," May, 2004*

Miscellaneous Rankings

■ Honolulu was determined to be one of America's smartest cities. The city ranked #15 in the large city category (200,000+ adults 25 years and older). Criteria: the editors rated the collective brainpower of U.S communities based on the educational attainment of its residents. *American City Business Journals, www.bizjournals.com, June 12, 2006*

■ Honolulu was selected as one of the "Top 100 Sweatiest Summer Cities". The city was ranked #23. The ranking was based on the average male/female height/weight, average high temperature, and average relative humidity levels for 2002 in each of the cities during June, July and August. The sweat level was analyzed based on the assumption that the individual was walking for one hour. *Procter & Gamble, Old Spice, June 18, 2003*

■ Honolulu was selected as one of "America's Favorite Cities" in the "friendliest people" category. The city was ranked #2 out of 25. Criteria: *Travel + Leisure* magazine and AOL's Travel Channel conducted an online survey of nearly a million AOL members to find out what travelers think about twenty-five American cities. Results shown above are according to visitors to the city, not locals. *Travel + Leisure and AOL's Travel Channel, "America's Favorite Cities," March 22, 2004*

■ Honolulu was selected as one of "America's Favorite Cities" in the "cities with the most attractive people" category. The city was ranked #2 out of 25. Criteria: *Travel + Leisure* magazine and AOL's Travel Channel conducted an online survey of nearly a million AOL members to find out what travelers think about twenty-five American cities. Results shown above are according to visitors to the city, not locals. *Travel + Leisure and AOL's Travel Channel, "America's Favorite Cities," March 22, 2004*

■ Honolulu was selected as one of "America's Favorite Cities" in the "top cities for cleanliness" category. The city was ranked #2 out of 25. Criteria: *Travel + Leisure* magazine and AOL's Travel Channel conducted an online survey of nearly half a million AOL members to find out what travelers think about twenty-five American cities. Results shown above are according to visitors to the city, not locals. *Travel + Leisure and AOL's Travel Channel, "America's Favorite Cities," March 22, 2004*

- Sperling's BestPlaces in partnership with Pep Boys ranked 77 metro areas and identified "America's Most Drivable Cities." The Honolulu metro area ranked #57. Criteria: climate; road roughness; urban mobility; gas prices. *Pep Boys, "America's Most Drivable Cities," April 9, 2003*

- Honolulu was selected as one of "America's Most Literate Cities." The city ranked #22 out of the 70 largest U.S. cities. Criteria: number of booksellers; library resources; Internet resources; educational attainment; periodical publishing resources; newspaper circulation. *Central Connecticut State University, "America's Most Literate Cities 2006"*

- Scarborough Research, a leading market research firm, identified the top local markets for coffee bar patronage. The Honolulu DMA (Designated Market Area) ranked in the top 10 with 18% of adults reporting that they have used any coffee house/bar during the past 30 days. *Scarborough Research, Scarborough USA+ 2004 Release 1*

Business Environment

CITY FINANCES

City Government Finances

Component	2003-2004 ($000)	2003-2004 ($ per capita)
Total Revenues	1,237,146	1,381
Total Expenditures	1,477,156	1,649
Debt Outstanding	2,720,376	3,036
Cash and Securities	521,968	583

Source: U.S Census Bureau, Government Finances 2003-2004

City Government Revenue by Source

Source	2003-2004 ($000)	2003-2004 ($ per capita)
General Revenue		
From Federal Government	136,720	153
From State Government	63,437	71
From Local Governments	319	0
Taxes		
Property	434,029	484
Sales	97,507	109
Personal Income	0	0
License	54,364	61
Charges	237,386	265
Liquor Store	0	0
Utility	135,672	151
Employee Retirement	0	0
Other	77,712	87

Source: U.S Census Bureau, Government Finances 2003-2004

City Government Expenditures by Function

Function	2003-2004 ($000)	2003-2004 ($ per capita)	2003-2004 (%)
General Expenditures			
Airports	0	0	0.0
Corrections	0	0	0.0
Education	0	0	0.0
Fire Protection	65,049	73	4.4
Governmental Administration	91,124	102	6.2
Health	19,705	22	1.3
Highways	78,153	87	5.3
Hospitals	0	0	0.0
Housing and Community Development	46,057	51	3.1
Interest on General Debt	99,493	111	6.7
Libraries	0	0	0.0
Parking	4,341	5	0.3
Parks and Recreation	96,994	108	6.6
Police Protection	175,897	196	11.9
Public Welfare	0	0	0.0
Sewerage	146,085	163	9.9
Solid Waste Management	128,349	143	8.7
Liquor Store	0	0	0.0
Utility	345,431	386	23.4
Employee Retirement	0	0	0.0
Other	180,478	201	12.2

Source: U.S Census Bureau, Government Finances 2003-2004

Municipal Bond Ratings

Area	Moody's
City	Aaa

Source: Mergent Bond Record, January 2007 (unless noted otherwise)

DEMOGRAPHICS

Population Growth

Area	1990 Census	2000 Census	2006 Estimate	2011 Projection	Population Growth (%) 1990-2000	Population Growth (%) 2000-2011
City	376,465	371,657	379,336	387,662	-1.3	4.3
MSA[1]	836,231	876,156	909,408	940,689	4.8	7.4
U.S.	248,709,873	281,421,906	298,021,266	312,383,955	13.2	11.0

Note: (1) Metropolitan Statistical Area - see Appendix B for areas included
Source: Claritas, Inc.

Number of Households and Average Household Size

Area	2006 Estimate	2006 Average Household Size
City	145,319	2.61
MSA[1]	300,924	3.02
U.S.	112,267,302	2.65

Note: (1) Metropolitan Statistical Area - see Appendix B for areas included
Source: Claritas, Inc.

Race and Ethnicity

Area	White Alone[2]	Black Alone[2]	Asian Alone[2]	Other Race Alone[2]	Hispanic[3]
City	19.1	2.0	56.3	22.6	4.7
MSA[1]	20.5	2.9	46.5	30.1	7.2
U.S.	73.3	12.4	4.2	10.1	14.5

Note: Figures are 2006 estimates; (1) Metropolitan Statistical Area - see Appendix B for areas included
(2) Alone is defined as not being in combination with one or more other races; (3) May be of any race.
Source: Claritas, Inc.

Segregation

City		MSA[1]	
Index[2]	Rank[3]	Index[2]	Rank[4]
49.4	69	44.0	281

Note: Figures are based on an analysis of Census 2000 data; (1) Metropolitan Statistical Area - see Appendix A for areas included; (2) White/Black Dissimilarity Index—the most commonly used measure of segregation between two groups, reflecting their relative distributions across neighborhoods within a city or metropolitan area. It can range in value from 0, indicating complete integration, to 100, indicating complete segregation; (3) Ranges from 1 (most segregated) to 100 (least segregated) and includes all the cities in this book; (4) Ranges from 1 (most segregated) to 318 (least segregated) and includes 318 metropolitan areas.
Source: www.CensusScope.org

Ancestry

Area	German	Irish[2]	English	American	Italian	Polish	French[3]	Scottish
City	4.6	3.4	3.8	1.2	1.5	0.7	1.3	0.9
MSA[1]	5.3	4.0	3.8	1.4	1.7	0.8	1.3	0.9
U.S.	15.2	10.9	8.7	7.3	5.6	3.2	3.0	1.7

Note: Figures include multiple ancestry (e.g. if a person reported being Irish and Italian, they were included in both columns); (1) Metropolitan Statistical Area - see Appendix A for areas included; (2) Includes Celtic; (3) Includes Alsatian but excludes Basque
Source: Census 2000, Summary File 3

Foreign-Born Population

Area	Any Foreign Country	Percent of Population Born in Europe	Asia	Africa	Oceania[2]	Canada	Mexico	Latin America[3]
City	25.3	1.1	21.7	0.1	1.5	0.3	0.1	0.4
MSA[1]	19.2	0.8	16.4	0.1	1.2	0.3	0.2	0.4
U.S.	11.1	1.7	2.9	0.3	0.1	0.3	3.3	2.5

Note: (1) Metropolitan Statistical Area - see Appendix A for areas included; (2) Includes Australia, New Zealand subregion, Melanesia, Micronesia, Polynesia, and Oceania n.e.c; (3) Includes Central America (excluding Mexico), South America, and the Caribbean.
Source: Census 2000, Summary File 3

Marriage Status

Area	Never Married	Now Married (excluding Separated)	Separated	Widowed	Divorced
City	31.6	49.7	1.7	7.2	9.7
MSA[1]	30.7	53.4	1.6	5.9	8.4
U.S.	27.1	54.4	2.2	6.6	9.7

Note: Figures are percentages and cover the population 15 years of age and older;
(1) Metropolitan Statistical Area - see Appendix A for areas included
Source: Census 2000, Summary File 3

Age Distribution

Area	Percent of Population						
	Under Age 5	Age 5 to 17	Age 18 to 34	Age 35 to 49	Age 50 to 64	Age 65 to 79	80 Years and Over
City	5.0	14.1	23.3	23.1	16.5	13.0	5.0
MSA[1]	6.4	17.3	24.8	23.1	14.9	10.2	3.3
U.S.	6.8	18.9	23.7	23.5	14.8	9.2	3.2

Note: (1) Metropolitan Statistical Area - see Appendix A for areas included
Source: Census 2000, Summary File 3

Male/Female Ratio

Area	Males	Females	Males per 100 Females
City	184,264	195,072	94.5
MSA[1]	452,910	456,498	99.2
U.S.	146,712,712	151,308,554	97.0

Note: Figures are 2006 estimates; (1) Metropolitan Statistical Area -
see Appendix B for areas included
Source: Claritas, Inc.

Religion

Area	Catholic	Southern Baptist	United Methodist	ELCA[1]	LDS[2]	Presbyterian Church USA	Jewish Est.	Muslim Est.
County	17.6	1.9	0.8	0.3	3.3	0.0	0.7	0.1
U.S.	22.0	7.1	3.7	1.8	1.5	1.1	2.2	0.6

Note: Figures are the number of adherents as a percentage of the total population; Adherents are defined as all members, including full members, their children and the estimated number of other participants who are not considered members (e.g. the baptized, those not confirmed, those regularly attending services, etc.);
(1) Evangelical Lutheran Church in America; (2) The Church of Jesus Christ of Latter Day Saints
Source: Reprinted with permission from Religious Congregations and Membership in the United States 2000 (Nashville, Glenmary Research Center, 2002) Copyright Association of Statisticians of American Religious Bodies. All rights reserved.

ECONOMY

Gross Metropolitan Product

Area	2002	2003	2004	2005	2005 Rank[2]
MSA[1]	33.0	35.1	38.0	40.9	53

Note: Figures are in billions of dollars; (1) Honolulu, HI Metropolitan Statistical Area - see Appendix A for areas included; (2) Rank ranges from 1 to 361
Source: The U.S. Conference of Mayors, "U.S. Metro Economies: GMP - The Engines of America's Growth," January 2007

Economic Growth

Area	1995 GMP	2005 GMP	Average Annual Growth Rate	Growth Rate Rank[2]
MSA[1]	28.5	40.9	3.7	329

Note: Figures are in billions of dollars; GMP = Gross Metropolitan Product; (1) Honolulu, HI Metropolitan Statistical Area - see Appendix A for areas included; (2) Rank ranges from 1 to 361
Source: The U.S. Conference of Mayors, "U.S. Metro Economies: GMP - The Engines of America's Growth," January 2007

INCOME

Per Capita/Median/Average Income

Area	Per Capita ($)	Median Household ($)	Average Household ($)
City	27,514	49,419	70,534
MSA[1]	25,565	59,606	75,432
U.S.	25,129	48,775	65,849

Note: Figures are 2006 estimates; (1) Metropolitan Statistical Area - see Appendix B for areas included
Source: Claritas, Inc.

Household Income Distribution

Area	Percent of Households Earning							
	Under $15,000	$15,000 -24,999	$25,000 -34,999	$35,000 -49,999	$50,000 -74,999	$75,000 -99,000	$100,000 -149,999	$150,000 and up
City	13.7	10.0	11.2	15.8	17.6	11.1	12.0	8.7
MSA[1]	10.0	8.3	9.7	14.5	19.5	13.9	15.4	8.6
U.S.	13.3	11.0	11.3	15.7	19.5	11.8	11.0	6.4

Note: Figures are 2006 estimates; (1) Metropolitan Statistical Area - see Appendix B for areas included
Source: Claritas, Inc.

Poverty Rates by Age

Area	All Ages	Under 5 Years Old	5 to 17 Years Old	18 to 64 Years Old	65 Years and Over
City	11.8	0.8	2.1	7.3	1.5
MSA[1]	9.9	0.9	2.2	5.8	1.0
U.S.	12.4	1.2	3.0	6.9	1.2

Note: Figures are percent of population with income in 1999 below poverty level and only include population for whom poverty status is determined; (1) Metropolitan Statistical Area - see Appendix A for areas included
Source: Census 2000, Summary File 3

Personal Bankruptcy Filing Rate

Area	2003	2004	2005
Honolulu County	3.04	2.43	3.45
U.S.	5.57	5.31	6.88

Note: Numbers are per 1,000 population and include Chapter 7 and Chapter 13 filings
Source: Federal Deposit Insurance Corporation (FDIC), Regional Economic Conditions (RECON), 3/24/2006

EMPLOYMENT

Labor Force and Employment

Area	Civilian Labor Force			Workers Employed		
	Dec. 2005	Dec. 2006	% Chg.	Dec. 2005	Dec. 2006	% Chg.
City	453,851	464,522	2.4	443,437	457,288	3.1
MSA[1]	453,851	464,522	2.4	443,437	457,288	3.1
U.S.	149,874,000	152,571,000	1.8	142,918,000	146,081,000	2.2

Note: Data is not seasonally adjusted and covers workers 16 years of age and older;
(1) Metropolitan Statistical Area - see Appendix B for areas included
Source: Bureau of Labor Statistics, http://stats.bls.gov

Unemployment Rate

Area	2006											
	Jan.	Feb.	Mar.	Apr.	May	Jun.	Jul.	Aug.	Sep.	Oct.	Nov.	Dec.
City	2.2	2.2	2.4	2.7	2.7	3.6	3.2	2.7	2.6	1.9	2.2	1.6
MSA[1]	2.2	2.2	2.4	2.7	2.7	3.6	3.2	2.7	2.6	1.9	2.2	1.6
U.S.	5.1	5.1	4.8	4.5	4.4	4.8	5.0	4.6	4.4	4.1	4.3	4.3

Note: Data is not seasonally adjusted and covers workers 16 years of age and older; All figures are percentages; (1) Metropolitan Statistical Area - see Appendix B for areas included
Source: Bureau of Labor Statistics, http://stats.bls.gov

Employment by Occupation

Occupation Classification	City (%)	MSA[1] (%)	U.S. (%)
Sales and Office	29.8	29.1	26.7
Professional and Related	21.4	20.4	20.2
Service	20.2	19.6	14.9
Production, Transportation, and Material Moving	7.8	8.8	14.6
Management, Business, and Financial	14.3	13.4	13.5
Construction, Extraction, and Maintenance	6.1	8.1	9.4
Farming, Forestry, and Fishing	0.5	0.7	0.7

Note: Figures cover employed civilians 16 years of age and older;
(1) Metropolitan Statistical Area - see Appendix A for areas included
Source: Census 2000, Summary File 3

Employment by Industry

Sector	MSA[1] Number of Employees	MSA[1] Percent of Total	U.S. Percent of Total
Government	99,600	21.4	16.3
Education and Health Services	57,100	12.3	13.2
Professional and Business Services	65,300	14.0	12.9
Retail Trade	49,200	10.6	11.5
Manufacturing	11,600	2.5	10.2
Leisure and Hospitality	63,300	13.6	9.5
Financial Activities	23,100	5.0	6.1
Construction	n/a	n/a	5.5
Wholesale Trade	14,500	3.1	4.3
Other Services	21,100	4.5	3.9
Transportation and Utilities	25,600	5.5	3.7
Information	9,400	2.0	2.2
Natural Resources and Mining	n/a	n/a	0.5

Note: Figures cover non-farm employment as of December 2006 and are not seasonally adjusted;
(1) Metropolitan Statistical Area - see Appendix B for areas included; n/a not available
Source: Bureau of Labor Statistics, http://stats.bls.gov

Occupations with Greatest Projected Employment Growth: 2002 - 2012

Occupation[1]	2002 Employment	2012 Projected Employment	Numeric Employment Change	Percent Employment Change
Security Guards	9,370	12,090	2,720	29.0
Waiters and Waitresses	15,270	17,700	2,430	15.9
Postsecondary Teachers	5,850	7,930	2,080	35.6
Retail Salespersons	21,360	23,250	1,890	8.8
Maids and Housekeeping Cleaners	9,830	11,700	1,870	19.0
Registered Nurses	7,700	9,550	1,850	24.0
Janitors and Cleaners, Except Maids and Housekeeping Cleaners	12,270	14,030	1,760	14.3
Combined Food Preparation and Serving Workers, Including Fast Food	8,740	10,440	1,700	19.5
Medical Assistants	3,590	5,180	1,590	44.3
Construction Laborers	3,960	5,310	1,350	34.1

Note: Projections cover Hawaii; (1) Sorted by numeric employment change
Source: www.projectionscentral.com, State Occupational Projections, 2002-2012 Long-Term Projections

Fastest Growing Occupations: 2002 - 2012

Occupation[1]	2002 Employment	2012 Projected Employment	Numeric Employment Change	Percent Employment Change
Sailors and Marine Oilers	200	420	220	110.0
Network Systems and Data Communications Analysts	670	990	320	47.8
Self-Enrichment Education Teachers	1,630	2,370	740	45.4
Social and Human Service Assistants	1,780	2,580	800	44.9
Medical Assistants	3,590	5,180	1,590	44.3
Medical Records and Health Information Technicians	560	790	230	41.1
Network and Computer Systems Administrators	680	950	270	39.7
Transportation Attendants, Except Flight Attendants and Baggage Porters	780	1,070	290	37.2
Postsecondary Teachers	5,850	7,930	2,080	35.6
Nursing Aides, Orderlies, and Attendants	3,310	4,450	1,140	34.4

Note: Projections cover Hawaii; (1) Sorted by percent employment change and excludes occupations with numeric employment change less than 200
Source: www.projectionscentral.com, State Occupational Projections, 2002-2012 Long-Term Projections

Average Wages

Occupation	$/Hr.	Occupation	$/Hr.
Accountants and Auditors	23.89	Maids and Housekeeping Cleaners	11.95
Automotive Mechanics	17.90	Maintenance and Repair Workers	16.70
Bookkeepers	15.14	Marketing Managers	39.44
Carpenters	25.59	Nuclear Medicine Technologists	n/a
Cashiers	8.78	Nurses, Licensed Practical	18.60
Clerks, General Office	11.39	Nurses, Registered	31.84
Clerks, Receptionists/Information	11.26	Nursing Aides/Orderlies/Attendants	12.11
Clerks, Shipping/Receiving	13.28	Packers and Packagers, Hand	8.81
Computer Programmers	26.88	Physical Therapists	31.14
Computer Support Specialists	18.32	Postal Service Mail Carriers	23.16
Computer Systems Analysts	33.13	Real Estate Brokers	38.26
Cooks, Restaurant	10.96	Retail Salespersons	10.57
Dentists	n/a	Sales Reps., Exc. Tech./Scientific	20.29
Electrical Engineers	36.54	Sales Reps., Tech./Scientific	29.03
Electricians	28.49	Secretaries, Exc. Legal/Med./Exec.	15.28
Financial Managers	42.84	Security Guards	10.05
First-Line Supervisors/Mgrs., Sales	17.97	Surgeons	n/a
Food Preparation Workers	9.70	Teacher Assistants	9.60
General and Operations Managers	46.33	Teachers, Elementary School	20.40
Hairdressers/Cosmetologists	12.36	Teachers, Secondary School	22.50
Internists	87.82	Telemarketers	n/a
Janitors and Cleaners	9.98	Truck Drivers, Heavy/Tractor-Trailer	18.05
Landscaping/Groundskeeping Workers	11.76	Truck Drivers, Light/Delivery Svcs.	12.80
Lawyers	44.92	Waiters and Waitresses	10.25

Note: Wage data is for May 2005 and covers the Honolulu, HI Metropolitan Statistics Area - see Appendix B for areas included. Hourly wages for elementary/secondary school teachers and teacher assistants were calculated by the editors from annual wage data assuming a 40 hour work week; n/a not available.
Source: Bureau of Labor Statistics, May 2005 Metro Area Occupational Employment and Wage Estimates

RESIDENTIAL REAL ESTATE

Building Permits

Area	Single-Family			Multi-Family			Total		
	2005	2006p	Pct. Chg.	2005	2006p	Pct. Chg.	2005	2006p	Pct. Chg.
Co.	2,079	1,727	-16.9	1,909	879	-54.0	3,988	2,606	-34.7
U.S.	1,682,000	1,380,000	-18.0	473,300	457,300	-3.4	2,155,300	1,837,300	-14.8

Note: (p) preliminary; figures cover Honolulu County and represent new, privately-owned housing units authorized (unadjusted data); All permit data are based on estimates with imputation; U.S. figures are based on the new 20,000-place series.
Source: U.S. Census Bureau, Manufacturing, Mining, and Construction Statistics

Homeownership and Housing Vacancies

Area	Homeownership Rate[2] (%)			Rental Vacancy Rate[3] (%)			Homeowner Vacancy Rate[4] (%)		
	2004	2005	2006	2004	2005	2006	2004	2005	2006
MSA[1]	n/a	58.0	58.4	n/a	3.9	3.9	n/a	0.6	0.8
U.S.	69.0	68.9	68.8	10.2	9.8	9.7	1.7	1.9	2.4

Note: Comparable 2004 data was not available due to changes in metropolitan area definitions; (1) Metropolitan Statistical Area - see Appendix B for areas included; (2) The proportion of households that are owners; (3) The proportion of the rental inventory that is vacant for rent; (4) The proportion of the homeowner inventory that is vacant for sale; n/a not available
Source: U.S. Census Bureau, Housing Vacancies and Homeownership Annual Statistics: 2006

TAXES

State Corporate Income Tax Rates

State	Rate (%)	Number of Brackets	Low Bracket (Under $)	High Bracket (Over $)
Hawaii	4.4-6.4	3	0	100,000

Note: Tax rates as of December 31, 2006; na not applicable; 4% capital gains rate.
Source: Tax Foundation, www.taxfoundation.org

State Individual Income Tax Rates

State	Federal Deductibility	Marginal Rate (%)	Number of Brackets	Low Bracket (Under $)	High Bracket (Over $)
Hawaii	No	1.4-8.25	9	0	40,000

Note: Tax rates as of December 31, 2006; Brackets apply to single taxpayers and married people filing separately; na not applicable
Source: Tax Foundation, www.taxfoundation.org

Various State and Local Tax Rates

State and Local Sales and Use (%)	State Sales and Use (%)	Gasoline ($/gal.)	Cigarette ($/pack)	Spirits ($/gal.)	Table Wine ($/gal.)	Beer ($/gal.)
4.5	4.0	0.16	1.60 (n)	5.98	1.38	0.93

Note: Tax rates as of December 31, 2006; (n) Hawaii will continue to increase its tax $.20 each Sept. 30 until Sept. 30, 2011 when the tax will reach $2.60.
Source: Tax Foundation, www.taxfoundation.org; The Sales Tax Clearinghouse, www.thestc.com

State Tax Burdens

Area	Combined State and Local Tax Burden		Combined Federal, State and Local Tax Burden	
	Percent	Rank	Percent	Rank
Hawaii	11.7	5	31.2	17
U.S. Average	10.6	-	31.6	-

Note: Figures are for 2006 and measure taxes as a percentage of income
Source: Tax Foundation, www.taxfoundation.org

Internal Revenue Service Tax Audits

IRS District	Percent of Returns Audited				
	1996	1997	1998	1999	2000
Pacific Northwest	0.63	0.51	0.37	0.24	0.15
U.S.	0.66	0.61	0.46	0.31	0.20

Note: Figures cover IRS district audits of federal income tax returns filed by individuals. Geographic data on district audits after the year 2000 are being withheld by the IRS. TRAC is challenging this policy.
Source: Syracuse University, Transactional Records Access Clearinghouse (TRAC), "Odds of IRS District Tax Audit 2000"

COMMERCIAL UTILITIES

Typical Monthly Electric Bills

Area	Commercial Service ($/month)		Industrial Service ($/month)	
	3 kW demand 1,000 kWh	40 kW demand 14,000 kWh	1,000 kW demand 200,000 kWh	50,000 kW demand 15,000,000 kWh
City	244	2,619	41,906	2,748,101
Average[1]	123	1,413	22,000	1,306,315

Note: Based on total rates in effect July 1, 2006; (1) average based on 196 utilities
Source: Edison Electric Institute, Typical Bills and Average Rates Report, Summer 2006

TRANSPORTATION

Means of Transportation to Work

Area	Car/Truck/Van		Public Transportation			Bicycle	Walked	Other Means	Worked at Home
	Drove Alone	Car-pooled	Bus	Subway	Railroad				
City	57.7	18.1	11.3	0.0	0.0	1.2	6.6	2.0	3.1
MSA[1]	61.4	19.4	8.1	0.0	0.0	0.9	5.6	1.7	2.9
U.S.	75.7	12.2	2.5	1.5	0.5	0.4	2.9	1.0	3.3

Note: Figures are percentages and cover workers 16 years of age and older;
(1) Metropolitan Statistical Area - see Appendix A for areas included
Source: Census 2000, Summary File 3

Travel Time to Work

Area	Less Than 15 Minutes	15 to 29 Minutes	30 to 44 Minutes	45 to 59 Minutes	60 Minutes or More
City	26.2	42.2	21.6	5.4	4.6
MSA[1]	23.5	34.3	23.8	9.5	8.9
U.S.	29.4	36.1	19.1	7.4	8.0

Note: Figures are percentages and include workers 16 years old and over; (1) Metropolitan Statistical Area -
see Appendix A for areas included
Source: Census 2000, Summary File 3

Travel Time Index

Area	1982	1993	2002	2003
Urban Area[1]	1.10	1.21	1.18	1.19
Average[2]	1.12	1.28	1.37	1.37

Note: Travel Time Index - The ratio of travel time in the peak period to the travel time at
free-flow conditions. A value of 1.35 indicates a 20-minute free-flow trip takes 27 minutes
in the peak. Free-flow speeds (60 mph on freeways and 35 mph on principal arterials)
are used as the comparison threshold; (1) Covers the Honolulu, HI urban area;
(2) average of 85 urban areas
Source: Texas Transportation Institute, The 2005 Urban Mobility Report, May 2005

Public Transportation

Agency name:	City and County of Honolulu Dept. of Transportation Services (DTS)
Vehicle type:	Bus
Average fleet age in years:	7.3
No. operated in max. service:	416
Vehicle type:	Demand response
Average fleet age in years:	4.8
No. operated in max. service:	157

Source: Federal Transit Administration, National Transit Database, 2005

Air Transportation

Airport name and code:	Honolulu International (HNL)
Domestic service (2006)	
Passenger airlines[1]:	19
Passenger enplanements:	7,799,207
Freight carriers[2]:	19
Freight (lbs.):	338,153,318
International service (2005)	
Passenger airlines[1]:	24
Passenger enplanements:	2,027,966
Freight carriers[2]:	26
Freight (lbs.):	126,022,855

Note: (1) Includes all major, minor and commuter airlines that carried at least one passenger during the year; (2) Includes all airlines and freight carriers that transported at least one pound of freight during the year
Source: Bureau of Transportation Statistics, The Intermodal Transportation Database, Air Carriers: T-100 International Market, 2004; Bureau of Transportation Statistics, The Intermodal Transportation Database, Air Carriers: T-100 Domestic Market, 2005

Other Transportation Statistics

Interstate highways:	None
Amtrak service:	No
Major waterways/ports:	Port of Honolulu

Source: Editor & Publisher Market Guide, 2006; Amtrak.com; Rand McNally 2006 Road Atlas

BUSINESSES

Major Business Headquarters

Company Name	2006 Rankings	
	Fortune[1]	Forbes[2]
No companies listed	-	-

Note: (1) Fortune 500 - companies that produce a 10-K are ranked 1 to 500 based on 2005 revenue; (2) Forbes Largest Private Companies - all private companies with at least $1 billion in annual revenue are ranked 1 to 394; companies listed are located in the city; dashes indicate no ranking
Source: Fortune, April 17, 2006; Forbes, November 9, 2006

Women-Owned Businesses: 1997 and 2002

Year	All Firms		Firms with Paid Employees			
	Firms	Sales ($000)	Firms	Sales ($000)	Employees	Payroll ($000)
1997	9,967	1,733,983	2,025	1,510,138	15,589	319,683
2002	10,926	2,459,498	2,187	2,159,353	19,716	434,323

Note: Figures cover firms located in the city; Women-owned business are defined as firms in which women own 51% or more of the stock or equity of the company; (a) Withheld to avoid disclosing data for individual companies; (b) Withheld because estimate did not meet publication standards; n/a not available
Source: 1997 Economic Census, Survey of Minority- and Women-Owned Business Enterprises; 2002 Economic Census, Survey of Business Owners (released February 9, 2006)

HOTELS

Hotels/Motels

Area	Hotels/Motels	Average Minimum Rates ($)		
		Tourist	First-Class	Deluxe
City	100	131	183	268

Source: OAG Travel Planner Online, Spring 2006

EVENT SITES

Stadiums, Arenas, and Auditoriums

Name	Capacity
Aloha Stadium	50,000
Neal S. Blaisdell Center	8,805

Source: www.officialtravelguide.com; www.eventective.com; original research

Convention Centers

Name	Overall Space (sq. ft.)	Exhibit Space (sq. ft.)	Meeting Space (sq. ft.)	Meeting Rooms
Hawaii Convention Center	n/a	149,768	200,000	47

Note: n/a not available
Source: www.officialtravelguide.com; www.eventective.com; original research

Hotels/Conference Centers

Name	Guest Rooms	Exhibit Space (sq. ft.)	Meeting Space (sq. ft.)
Ala Moana Hotel	1,152	6,890	14,575
Hilton Hawaiian Village	3,386	100,000	100,000
Pacific Beach Hotel	830	12,702	21,784
Radisson Hotel Waikiki	620	12,104	12,104
Renaissance Ilikai Waikiki	783	15,340	25,000
Royal Hawaiian Hotel	528	n/a	12,250
Sheraton Waikiki Hotel	1,852	110,000	46,100

Note: n/a not available
Source: www.officialtravelguide.com; www.eventective.com; original research

Living Environment

COST OF LIVING

Cost of Living Index

Year	Composite Index	Groceries	Housing	Utilities	Trans-portation	Health Care	Misc. Goods/Services
2004	162.0	153.9	239.8	142.0	133.9	123.5	115.2
2005	159.8	152.8	233.4	140.3	118.9	111.8	123.0
2006	161.3	154.4	248.5	116.3	118.1	110.3	125.3

Note: U.S. = 100
Source: The Council for Community and Economic Research (formerly ACCRA), Cost of Living Index, 2004, 2005 and 2006 4-Quarter Averages

HOUSING

House Price Index (HPI)

Area	National Ranking[2]	Quarterly Change (%)	One-Year Change (%)	Five-Year Change (%)
MSA[1]	89	-2.04	7.49	101.08
U.S.[3]	-	1.12	5.87	55.21

Note: The HPI is a weighted repeat sales index. It measures average price changes in repeat sales or refinancings on the same properties. This information is obtained by reviewing repeat mortgage transactions on single-family properties whose mortgages have been purchased or securitized by Fannie Mae or Freddie Mac in January 1975; (1) Metropolitan Statistical Area - see Appendix B for areas included; (2) Rankings are based on annual percentage change for all metro areas containing at least 15,000 transactions over the last 10 years and ranges from 1 to 282; (3) figures based on a weighted division average; all figures are for the period ending December 31, 2006
Source: Office of Federal Housing Enterprise Oversight, House Price Index, March 1, 2007

House Price Valuations

Area	Q4 1999	Q4 2000	Q4 2001	Q4 2002	Q4 2003	Q4 2004	Q4 2005	Q4 2006
MSA[1]	-14.1	-13.4	-7.8	-3.3	5.4	17.1	34.2	35.4

Note: Figures show the percentage of over- or under-valuation of single family homes relative to statistically normal house values (e.g. a value of 23.6 indicates that house values are 23.6% overvalued). Statistically normal house values are based on house prices, interest rates, household incomes, population densities, and any historical premiums or discounts metropolitan areas have exhibited over time; (1) Figures cover the Metropolitan Statistical Area - see Appendix B for areas included
Source: Global Insight/National City Corporation, House Prices in America, March 2007

Median Home Prices

Area	2004	2005	2006p	Percent Change 2005 to 2006
Metro Area[1]	460.0	590.0	630.0	6.8
U.S. Average	195.2	219.0	222.0	1.4

Note: Figures are median sales prices of existing single-family homes in thousands of dollars; (p) preliminary; n/a not available; (1) Covers the Honolulu, HI Metropolitan Statistical Area - see Appendix B for areas included
Source: National Association of Realtors, Metropolitan Area Prices, 4th Quarter 2006

Housing: Year Structure Built

Area	1990-2000	1980-1989	1970-1979	1960-1969	1950-1959	1940-1949	Before 1940	Median Year
City	9.2	10.4	28.5	24.8	14.4	6.5	6.1	1969
MSA[1]	14.7	13.1	26.5	22.5	13.2	5.6	4.4	1972
U.S.	17.0	15.8	18.5	13.7	12.7	7.3	15.0	1971

Note: Figures are percentages; (1) Metropolitan Statistical Area - see Appendix A for areas included
Source: Census 2000, Summary File 3

Average New Home Price

Area	2004	2005	2006
City	616,368	637,967	747,077
U.S.	253,574	275,712	299,269

Note: Figures, in dollars, are based on a new home with 2,400 sq. ft. of living area on an 8,000 sq. ft. lot.
Source: The Council for Community and Economic Research (formerly ACCRA), Cost of Living Index, 2004, 2005 and 2006 4-Quarter Averages

Average Apartment Rent

Area	2004	2005	2006
City	1,693	1,853	1,933
U.S.	716	740	766

Note: Figures, in dollars per month, are based on an unfurnished two bedroom, 1-1/2 or 2 bath apartment, approximately 950 sq. ft. in size, excluding all utilities except water
Source: The Council for Community and Economic Research (formerly ACCRA), Cost of Living Index, 2004, 2005 and 2006 4-Quarter Averages

RESIDENTIAL UTILITIES

Average Residential Utility Costs

Area	All Electric ($/mth)	Part Electric ($/mth)	Other Energy ($/mth)	Phone ($/mth)
City	208.87	–	–	23.83
U.S.	136.00	76.53	90.52	25.87

Source: The Council for Community and Economic Research (formerly ACCRA), Cost of Living Index, 2006 4-Quarter Average

HEALTH

Average Health Care Costs

Area	Optometrist ($/visit)	Doctor ($/visit)	Dentist ($/visit)
City	84.22	83.93	71.06
U.S.	76.38	76.10	68.72

Note: Optometrist—based on a full vision eye exam for an established adult patient; Doctor—based on a general practitioner's routine exam of an established patient; Dentist—based on adult teeth cleaning and periodic oral exam.
Source: The Council for Community and Economic Research (formerly ACCRA), Cost of Living Index, 2006 4-Quarter Average

Mortality Rates

ICD-10 Sub-Chapter	ICD-10 Code	Age-Adjusted Death Rate per 100,000 population[1]	U.S. Age-Adjusted Death Rate per 100,000 population
Malignant neoplasms	C00-C97	142.8	185.8
Ischaemic heart diseases	I20-I25	85.4	150.2
Other forms of heart disease	I30-I51	69.5	50.8
Cerebrovascular diseases	I60-I69	47.9	50.0
Chronic lower respiratory diseases	J40-J47	17.6	41.1
Diabetes mellitus	E10-E14	12.3	24.5
Other degenerative diseases of the nervous system	G30-G31	9.8	22.3
Other external causes of accidental injury	W00-X59	18.3	21.2
Influenza and pneumonia	J10-J18	14.6	19.8
Hypertensive diseases	I10-I13	12.9	18.1

Note: ICD-10 = International Classification of Diseases 10th Revision; (1) Figures cover Honolulu County, HI
Source: Centers for Disease Control and Prevention, National Center for Health Statistics. Compressed Mortality File 1999-2004. CDC WONDER On-line Database, compiled from Compressed Mortality File 1999-2004 Series 20 No. 2J, 2007.

Health Risk Data

Item	Area[1] (%)	U.S. (%)
Adults who have been told they have high blood pressure	24.5	25.5
Adults who have been told they have high blood cholesterol	34.6	35.6
Adults who have been told they have diabetes[2]	7.1	7.3
Adults who have been told they have arthritis	21.0	27.0
Adults who have been told they currently have asthma	7.0	8.0
Adults who are current smokers	16.0	20.6

Note: (1) Figures cover the Metropolitan Statistical Area - see Appendix B for areas included; (2) Figures do not include pregnancy-related diabetes, pre-diabetes or borderline diabetes
Source: Centers for Disease Control and Prevention, Behaviorial Risk Factor Surveillance System, SMART: Selected Metropolitan/Micropolitan Area Trends, 2005

Distribution of Office-Based Physicians

Area	Total	Family/ General Practice	Specialties		
			Medical	Surgical	Other
MSA[1] (number)	2,163	203	875	494	591
MSA[1] (rate per 10,000 pop.)	24.5	2.3	9.9	5.6	6.7
Metro Average[2] (rate per 10,000 pop.)	19.4	2.1	7.5	4.5	5.3

Note: Data as of December 31, 2004; (1) Metropolitan Statistical Area - see Appendix A for areas included;
(2) Average of the 79 unique MSAs and CMSAs in this book
Source: American Medical Association, Physician Characteristics & Distribution in the U.S., 2006

Hospitals

Honolulu has the following hospitals: 6 general medical and surgical; 1 obstetrics and
gynecology; 1 rehabilitation; 1 other specialty; 1 children's other specialty.
AHA Guide to the Healthcare Field 2007

EDUCATION

Public School District Statistics

District Name	Schls	Pupils	Pupil/ Teacher Ratio	Minority Pupils[1] (%)	Free Lunch Eligible[2] (%)	IEP[3] (%)
Hawaii Department Of Education	285	183,185	16.4	79.9	30.7	12.4

Note: Table includes regular local school districts with 2,000 or more students; (1) Percentage of students that
are not white, non-Hispanic; (2) Percentage of students that are eligible for the free lunch program;
(3) Percentage of students that have an Individualized Education Program.
Source: U.S. Department of Education, National Center for Education Statistics, Common Core of Data, Local
Education Agency (School District) Universe Survey: School Year 2004-2005; U.S. Department of Education,
National Center for Education Statistics, Common Core of Data, Public Elementary/Secondary School Universe
Survey: School Year 2004-2005

Educational Quality

School District	Education Quotient[1]	Graduate Outcome[2]	Community Index[3]	Resource Index[4]	Rating[5]
Hawaii Dept. of Education	49	43	57	70	Green

Note: Scores are national percentile rankings and range from 1 (worst) to 99 (best); (1) Combination of the
Graduate Outcome, Community and Resource Indexes weighted to reflect the greater importance of the
Graduate Outcome and Resource Index; (2) Based on graduation rates and college board scores (SAT/ACT);
(3) Based on the surrounding community's level of affluence and adult education; (4) Based on teacher salaries,
per-pupil expenditures and student-teacher ratios; (5) School districts receive one of five rankings: Gold Medal
(top 16 percent of districts evaluated); Blue Ribbon (top third); Green Light (average); Yellow Light (bottom 25
percent); Red Light (bottom 10 percent).
Source: Expansion Management, "2007 Education Quotient," January 2007

Highest Level of Education

Area	Less than H.S.	H.S. Diploma	Some College, No Deg.	Associate Degree	Bachelors Degree	Masters Degree	Profess. School Degree	Doctorate Degree
City	16.8	25.9	19.5	6.8	20.4	6.4	2.7	1.4
MSA[1]	15.2	27.7	21.3	7.9	19.0	5.8	2.1	1.0
U.S.	19.4	28.4	21.2	6.4	15.7	5.9	2.0	1.0

Note: Figures are 2006 estimated percentages and cover persons age 25 and over; (1) Metropolitan Statistical
Area - see Appendix B for areas included
Source: Claritas, Inc.

Educational Attainment by Race

Area	High School Graduate (%)					Bachelor's Degree (%)				
	Total	White	Black	Asian	Hisp.[2]	Total	White	Black	Asian	Hisp.[2]
City	83.4	93.3	90.0	79.4	83.6	31.1	44.3	23.6	29.6	18.9
MSA[1]	84.8	93.5	93.0	80.8	84.3	27.9	39.6	20.9	28.2	15.1
U.S.	80.4	83.6	72.3	80.4	52.4	24.4	26.1	14.3	44.1	10.4

Note: Figures shown cover persons 25 years old and over; (1) Metropolitan Statistical Area - see Appendix A
for areas included; (2) people of Hispanic origin can be of any race
Source: Census 2000, Summary File 3

School Enrollment by Type

Area	Grades KG to 8				Grades 9 to 12			
	Public		Private		Public		Private	
	Enrollment	%	Enrollment	%	Enrollment	%	Enrollment	%
City	29,361	79.6	7,541	20.4	13,054	74.2	4,550	25.8
MSA[1]	89,045	82.9	18,407	17.1	38,196	79.4	9,908	20.6
U.S.	33,526,011	88.7	4,285,121	11.3	14,848,628	90.6	1,532,323	9.4

Note: Figures shown cover persons 3 years old and over; (1) Metropolitan Statistical Area - see Appendix A for areas included
Source: Census 2000, Summary File 3

School Enrollment by Race

Area	Grades KG to 8 (%)				Grades 9 to 12 (%)			
	White	Black	Asian	Hisp.[1]	White	Black	Asian	Hisp.[1]
City	12.2	1.7	46.0	7.2	10.7	1.8	54.7	5.4
MSA[2]	14.7	2.2	34.3	10.2	11.5	1.6	41.7	9.4
U.S.	68.5	15.5	3.3	16.8	68.8	15.5	3.8	15.7

Note: Figures shown cover persons 3 years old and over; (1) people of Hispanic origin can be of any race; (2) Metropolitan Statistical Area - see Appendix A for areas included
Source: Census 2000, Summary File 3

Average Salaries of Public School Teachers

District	2004-05		2005-06		Percent Change 2004-05 to 2005-06
	Dollars	Rank[1]	Dollars	Rank[1]	
HAWAII	46,149	19	51,599	14	11.81
U.S. Average	47,674	-	49,109	-	3.01

Note: (1) State rank ranges from 1 to 51.
Source: National Education Association, Rankings & Estimates: Rankings of the States 2005 and Estimates of School Statistics 2006, November 2006

Higher Education

Four-Year Colleges			Two-Year Colleges			Medical Schools[1]	Law Schools[2]	Voc/Tech[3]
Public	Private Non-profit	Private For-profit	Public	Private Non-profit	Private For-profit			
1	3	4	2	2	1	1	1	4

Note: Figures cover institutions located within the city limits; (1) includes schools accredited by the Liaison Committee on Medical Education and the American Osteopathic Association; (2) includes American Bar Association-accredited law schools; (3) includes all schools with programs that are less than 2 years
Source: National Center for Education Statistics, The Integrated Postsecondary Education System (IPEDS) Peer Analysis System, 2006; www.usnews.com, America's Best Graduate Schools 2008, Medical School Directory; www.usnews.com, America's Best Graduate Schools 2008, Law School Directory

PRESIDENTIAL ELECTION

2004 Presidential Election Results

Area	Bush	Kerry	Nader	Other
Honolulu County	48.3	51.1	0.0	0.6
U.S.	50.7	48.3	0.4	0.6

Note: Results are percentages and may not add to 100% due to rounding
Source: Dave Leip's Atlas of U.S. Presidential Elections, www.uselectionatlas.org

**MAJOR
EMPLOYERS**

Major Employers

Company Name	Industry	Type of Site
Amparo R Ringor	Offices and clinics of medical doctors	Branch
College of Engineering	Colleges and universities	Branch
Hawaiian Electric Company Inc	Electric services	Branch
Hmsa	Hospital and medical service plans	Headquarters
Kamehameha School	Elementary and secondary schools	Branch
Kuakini Health System	General medical and surgical hospitals	Headquarters
Naval Cmpt Tlcom Area Mstr Stn	National security	Branch
Polynesian Cultural Center	Amusement and recreation, nec	Headquarters
Sheraton	Hotels and motels	Headquarters
St Francis Medical Center	General medical and surgical hospitals	Headquarters
St Francis Medical Center West	General medical and surgical hospitals	Single
US Navy Pub Wrks Cntr-Parl Hbr	National security	Branch
University Press	Colleges and universities	Headquarters

Note: Companies shown are located within the metropolitan area and have 1,100 or more employees; nec = not elsewhere classified.
Source: www.zapdata.com, January 2007

PUBLIC SAFETY

Crime Rate

Area	All Crimes	Violent Crimes				Property Crimes		
		Murder	Forcible Rape	Robbery	Aggrav. Assault	Burglary	Larceny -Theft	Motor Vehicle Theft
County[3]	4,947.9	1.7	25.8	92.6	162.9	683.4	3,233.4	748.2
Suburbs[1]	n/a	n/a	n/a	n/a	n/a	n/a	n/a	n/a
Metro[2]	4,947.9	1.7	25.8	92.6	162.9	683.4	3,233.4	748.2
U.S.	3,899.0	5.6	31.7	140.7	291.1	726.7	2,286.3	416.7

Note: Figures are crimes per 100,000 population; (1) All areas within the metro area that are located outside the city limits; (2) Metropolitan Statistical Area - see Appendix B for areas included; (3) Figures are for Honolulu County; n/a not available
Source: FBI Uniform Crime Reports, 2005

Hate Crimes

Area	Number of Quarters Reported	Bias Motivation				
		Race	Religion	Sexual Orientation	Ethnicity	Disability
City	n/a	n/a	n/a	n/a	n/a	n/a

Note: n/a not available.
Source: Federal Bureau of Investigation, Hate Crime Statistics 2005

RECREATION

Culture

Dance[1]	Theatre[1]	Instrumental Music[1]	Vocal Music[1]	Series/ Festivals	Museums	Zoos
1	4	6	4	2	17	1

Note: (1) number of professional perfoming groups
Source: The Grey House Performing Arts Directory, 2007; Official Museum Directory, 2007

Professional Sports Teams

Major League Baseball	National Basketball Association	National Football League	National Hockey League	Major League Soccer	Women's National Basketball Association
0	0	0	0	0	0

Note: Includes teams located in the Honolulu metro area.
Source: www.sportsvenues.com, Listing of Venues by State/Province and City, 2006

MEDIA

Newspapers

Name	Target Audience	Frequency	Circulation
The Fil-Am Courier Online	Asian/Christian/Gen.	Non-Daily	22,000
Hawaii Hochi	n/a	Daily	5,500
The Honolulu Advertiser	n/a	Daily	143,983
Honolulu Star-Bulletin	n/a	Daily	64,000
Honolulu Weekly	Alternative	Non-Daily	45,000
Philippine Times	Asian	Non-Daily	10,000

Note: Includes newspapers whose offices are located in the city and whose circulations are 1,000 or more; n/a not available
Source: BurrellesLuce, MediaContacts Online, January 2006

Television Stations

Name	Ch.	Network(s)	Type	Ownership
KHON	2	Fox	Commercial	Emmis Communications Corporation
KGMV	3	CBS	Commercial	Emmis Communications Corporation
KITV	4	ABC	Commercial	Hearst-Argyle Broadcasting
KFVE	5	WBN	Commercial	Raycom Media Inc.
KHVO	6	ABC	Commercial	Hearst-Argyle Broadcasting
KAII	7	Fox	Commercial	Emmis Communications Corporation
KGMB	9	CBS	Commercial	Emmis Communications Corporation
KMEB	10	PBS	Public	Hawaii Public Broadcasting Authority
KHAW	11	Fox	Commercial	Emmis Communications Corporation
KHET	11	PBS	Public	Hawaii Public Broadcasting Authority
KMAU	12	ABC	Commercial	Hearst-Argyle Broadcasting
KHNL	13	NBC	Commercial	Raycom Media Inc.
KWHE	14	n/a	Commercial	Le Sea Broadcasting Corporation
KWHH	14	n/a	Commercial	Lesea Broadcasting Corporation
KOGG	15	NBC	Commercial	Raycom Media Inc.
KIKU	20	n/a	Commercial	International Media Group
KWHM	21	n/a	Commercial	Le Sea Broadcasting Corporation
KAAH	26	n/a	Non-comm.	Trinity Broadcasting Network
KBFD	32	n/a	Commercial	Allen Broadcasting Corporation
KPXO	66	Pax	Commercial	Paxson Communications Corporation

Note: Stations included cover the Honolulu DMA (Designated Market Area)
BurrellesLuce, MediaContacts Online, January 2006

Major AM Radio Stations

Call Letters	Freq. (kHz)	Station Type	Target Audience	Station Format	Music Format
KQNG	570	Commercial	General	News/Talk	n/a
KSSK	590	Commercial	General	Music/News/Sports	Adult Contemp.
KIPA	620	Commercial	General	Music/News/Sports	World Music
KHNR	650	n/a	General	News/Sports/Talk	n/a
KPUA	670	Commercial	General	News/Sports/Talk	n/a
KUMU	690	n/a	Children	Music	n/a
KUAI	720	Commercial	General	Music/News/Sports	Adult Contemp.
KKON	790	Commercial	General	Music/News/Sports	Oldies
KHVH	830	n/a	General	Ed/News/Sports/Talk	n/a
KGU	870	Commercial	General/Religious	Ed/Music/News/Sports/Talk	Gospel
KNUI	900	Commercial	General	Music/News	World Music
KHBZ	990	Commercial	General	Music/Talk	Oldies
KLHT	1040	Commercial	General/Religious	Educational/Music	Christian
KAHU	1060	Commercial	General	Educational/Music	Adult Contemp.
KWAI	1080	Commercial	General	News/Talk	n/a
KAOI	1110	Commercial	General	News/Sports/Talk	n/a
KZOO	1210	Commercial	General	Ed/Music/News/Talk	World Music
KNDI	1270	Commercial	Ethnic/General	Music/News	World Music
KCCN	1420	Commercial	General	News/Sports	n/a
KRTR	1460	Commercial	General	Music/News	Adult Contemp.
KUMU	1500	Commercial	General	Music/News	Oldies

Note: Stations included cover the Honolulu DMA (Designated Market Area); n/a not available
Source: BurrellesLuce, MediaContacts Online, January 2006

Major FM Radio Stations

Call Letters	Freq. (mHz)	Station Type	Target Audience	Station Format	Music Format
KHPR	88.1	Public	General	Music/News/Talk	Classical
KANO	91.1	n/a	General	Music/News/Talk	n/a
KSSK	92.3	Commercial	General	Music	Adult Contemp.
KQMQ	93.1	n/a	General	News/Talk	Rhythm & Blues
KQNG	93.5	n/a	General	Music/News/Sports	n/a
KPOA	93.5	Commercial	General	Music	World Music
KLUA	93.9	n/a	General	Music/News	n/a
KIKI	93.9	n/a	General	Music/News/Talk	Urban Contemp.
KWXX	94.7	n/a	General	Music	n/a
KUMU	94.7	Commercial	General	n/a	n/a
KAOI	95.1	Commercial	General	Music	Soft Rock
KAIM	95.5	Commercial	Christian/General	Ed/Music/News/Talk	Gospel
KRTR	96.3	Commercial	General	Music/News	Adult Contemp.
KFMN	96.9	Commercial	General	Music/News/Talk	Alternative
KNWB	97.1	n/a	General	Music/News	n/a
KPOI	97.5	n/a	General	Music	n/a
KKBG	97.9	Commercial	General	Music/News	Adult Contemp.
KMVI	98.3	Commercial	General	Music/News/Sports	Urban Contemp.
KDNN	98.5	n/a	General	Music/News	n/a
KNUI	99.9	Commercial	General	Music/News	Adult Contemp.
KAPA	100.3	Commercial	General	Music/News/Sports/Talk	World Music
KCCN	100.3	Commercial	General	Music/News	World Music
KLHI	101.1	Commercial	General	Music/News	Alternative
KAOY	101.5	n/a	General	News/Sports	n/a
KUCD	101.9	n/a	General	Music/News/Sports	n/a
KDDB	102.7	n/a	General	Music/News/Sports	n/a
KNUQ	103.7	Commercial	General	Music/News/Talk	World Music
KPHW	104.3	Commercial	General	Music/News/Talk	Urban Contemp.
KONI	104.7	Commercial	General	Music/News/Talk	Oldies
KINE	105.1	Commercial	General	Music/News/Sports	World Music
KAHA	105.9	Commercial	General	Music/News/Talk	Classic Rock
KLEO	106.1	Commercial	General	Music/News/Sports/Talk	Adult Contemp.

Note: Stations included cover the Honolulu DMA (Designated Market Area); n/a not available
BurrellesLuce, MediaContacts Online, January 2006

CLIMATE

Average and Extreme Temperatures

Temperature	Jan	Feb	Mar	Apr	May	Jun	Jul	Aug	Sep	Oct	Nov	Dec	Yr.
Extreme High (°F)	87	88	89	89	93	92	92	93	94	94	93	89	94
Average High (°F)	80	80	81	82	84	86	87	88	88	86	84	81	84
Average Temp. (°F)	73	73	74	76	77	79	80	81	81	79	77	74	77
Average Low (°F)	66	66	67	69	70	72	73	74	73	72	70	67	70
Extreme Low (°F)	52	53	55	56	60	65	66	67	66	64	57	54	52

Note: Figures cover the years 1949-1990
Source: National Climatic Data Center, International Station Meteorological Climate Summary, 9/96

Average Precipitation/Snowfall/Humidity

Precip./Humidity	Jan	Feb	Mar	Apr	May	Jun	Jul	Aug	Sep	Oct	Nov	Dec	Yr.
Avg. Precip. (in.)	3.7	2.5	2.8	1.4	1.0	0.4	0.5	0.6	0.7	2.0	2.8	3.7	22.4
Avg. Snowfall (in.)	0	0	0	0	0	0	0	0	0	0	0	0	0
Avg. Rel. Hum. 5am (%)	82	80	78	77	76	75	75	75	76	78	79	80	78
Avg. Rel. Hum. 5pm (%)	66	64	62	61	60	58	58	58	60	63	66	66	62

Note: Figures cover the years 1949-1990; Tr = Trace amounts (<0.05 in. of rain; <0.5 in. of snow)
Source: National Climatic Data Center, International Station Meteorological Climate Summary, 9/96

Weather Conditions

Temperature			Daytime Sky			Precipitation		
32°F & below	45°F & below	90°F & above	Clear	Partly cloudy	Cloudy	0.01 inch or more precip.	0.1 inch or more snow/ice	Thunder-storms
0	0	23	25	286	54	98	0	7

Note: Figures are average number of days per year and cover the years 1949-1990
Source: National Climatic Data Center, International Station Meteorological Climate Summary, 9/96

HAZARDOUS WASTE

Superfund Sites

Honolulu has no sites on the EPA's Superfund Final National Priorities List.
U.S. Environmental Protection Agency, Final National Priorities List, March 20, 2007

AIR & WATER QUALITY

Air Quality Index

Area	Percent of Days when Air Quality was...[2]				AQI Statistics	
	Good	Moderate	Unhealthy for Sensitive Groups	Unhealthy	Maximum	Median
MSA[1]	98.6	0.8	0.3	0.3	164	20

Note: The Air Quality Index (AQI) is an index for reporting daily air quality. EPA calculates the AQI for five major air pollutants regulated by the Clean Air Act: ground-level ozone, particle pollution (also known as particulate matter), carbon monoxide, sulfur dioxide, and nitrogen dioxide. The AQI runs from 0 to 500. The higher the AQI value, the greater the level of air pollution and the greater the health concern. There are six AQI categories: "Good" The AQI is between 0 and 50. Air quality is considered satisfactory; "Moderate" The AQI is between 51 and 100. Air quality is acceptable; "Unhealthy for Sensitive Groups" When AQI values are between 101 and 150, members of sensitive groups may experience health effects; "Unhealthy" When AQI values are between 151 and 200 everyone may begin to experience health effects; "Very Unhealthy" AQI values between 201 and 300 trigger a health alert; "Hazardous" AQI values over 300 trigger health warnings of emergency conditions; (1) Metropolitan Statistical Area - see Appendix A for areas included; (2) Based on 365 days with AQI data in 2005.
Source: U.S. Environmental Protection Agency, Air Quality Index Report, 2005

Air Quality Index Pollutants

Area	Percent of Days when AQI Pollutant was...[2]					
	Carbon Monoxide	Nitrogen Dioxide	Ozone	Sulfur Dioxide	Particulate Matter 2.5	Particulate Matter 10
MSA[1]	1.1	0.0	44.4	0.0	17.5	37.0

Note: The Air Quality Index (AQI) is an index for reporting daily air quality. EPA calculates the AQI for five major air pollutants regulated by the Clean Air Act: ground-level ozone, particle pollution (also known as particulate matter), carbon monoxide, sulfur dioxide, and nitrogen dioxide. The AQI runs from 0 to 500. The higher the AQI value, the greater the level of air pollution and the greater the health concern; (1) Metropolitan Statistical Area - see Appendix A for areas included; (2) Based on 365 days with AQI data in 2005.
Source: U.S. Environmental Protection Agency, Air Quality Index Report, 2005

Number of Days with Air Quality Index Values Greater than 100

Area	Trend Sites (11)								All Sites (30)
	1998	1999	2000	2001	2002	2003	2004	2005	2005
MSA[1]	0	2	2	2	2	2	2	3	3

Note: An AQI value greater than 100 indicates that air quality would have been in the unhealthful range on that day. Data from exceptional events are not included. These counts are presented in two ways. First, the counts are based on sites having an adequate record of monitoring data during the trend period (trend sites). These counts represent the relative change in the number of days with AQI values greater than 100. In the last column, the counts are based on all sites with data in the most recent year (because it is possible for a site to have data in the most recent year but not enough data to be a trend site); (1) Metropolitan Statistical Area - see Appendix A for areas included; n/a not available.
Source: U.S. Environmental Protection Agency, Air Trends Fact Book 2005

Maximum Pollutant Concentrations

	Particulate Matter 10 (ug/m^3)	Particulate Matter 2.5 (ug/m^3)	Ozone 1-hour (ppm)	Carbon Monoxide (ppm)	Sulfur Dioxide (ppm)	Nitrogen Dioxide (ppm)	Lead (ug/m^3)
MSA[1] Level	99	11	0.055	2	0.008	0.005	0.00
NAAQS[2]	150	65	0.125	9	0.140	0.053	1.50
Met NAAQS[2]	Yes	Yes	Yes	Yes	Yes	Yes	Yes

Note: Data from exceptional events are not included; (1) Metropolitan Statistical Area - see Appendix A for areas included; (2) National Ambient Air Quality Standards; n/a not available
Units: ppm = parts per million; ug/m^3 = micrograms per cubic meter
Source: U.S. Environmental Protection Agency, Air Trends Fact Book 2005

Watershed Health

The U.S. Environmental Protection Agency monitors the health of the aquatic resources for the nation's 2,000+ watersheds. **The Oahu watershed serves the Honolulu area and received an overall Index of Watershed Indicators (IWI) score of 3 (less serious problems - low vulnerability).** The IWI score is based on seven condition and nine vulnerability indicators. The overall IWI score ranges from 1 (best health) to 6 (worst health). The Condition Indicators include: designated use attainment, fish and wildlife consumption advisories, source water condition, contaminated sediments, ambient water quality, and wetlands loss index. The Vulnerability Indicators include: aquatic species at risk, conventional and toxic loads over permitted limits, urban and agricultural runoff potential, population change, hydrologic modification, estuarine pollution susceptibility, and air deposition. *Note: The IWI is no longer being updated by the U.S. EPA. Source: U.S. Environmental Protection Agency, Index of Watershed Indicators, October 26, 2001*

Drinking Water

Water System Name	Pop. Served	Primary Water Source Type	Number of Violations in 2006[a]		
			Health Based	Significant Monitoring	Monitoring
BWS Honolulu-Windward-Pearl Harbor	606,905	(b)	None	None	None

Note: (a) Based on violation data from January 1, 2006 to December 31, 2006; (b) Ground water under direct influence of surface water
Source: U.S. Environmental Protection Agency, Office of Ground Water and Drinking Water, Safe Drinking Water Information System (data extracted April 12, 2007)

Honolulu tap water is alkaline, soft and not fluoridated.
Editor & Publisher Market Guide, 2005

Irvine, California

Background

Irvine, in Orange County, California, is located on the southern portion of the vast Los Angeles-Riverside-Orange County metropolitan area. The city offers a mix of careful urban and residential planning coupled with a shrewd eye to the Pacific Rim's ever-expanding opportunities for improvements in the economic sphere and quality of life.

The area is rich in pre-colonial, Spanish, Mexican, and American history. Gabrielino Indians, a tribe of the Shoshonean language group, occupied the Irvine area for some 2,000 years before Europeans arrived, and subsisted well on a rich supply of shellfish, water fowl, and game animals. The Gabrielino were basket weavers, and also made fine jewelry from locally available seashells and stones.

Gaspar de Portola, leading a Spanish expedition into the area in 1769, ended the Gabrielino way of life, establishing forts, missions, and cattle-herding, and the king of Spain began to allocate land to missions and private individuals. Three large grants made up the land that later became the Irvine Ranch. In the years after California's acquisition by the United States, this vast plot was extensively litigated in a maze of conflicting land claims, but by 1878, James Irvine controlled the property, 110,000 acres stretching 23 miles from the Pacific Ocean to the Santa Ana River.

At the end of the nineteenth century, the ranch had shifted its focus from grazing to a mixed agricultural operation producing field crops and olive and citrus orchards, and by 1918 almost 60,000 acres were devoted exclusively to the cultivation of lima beans. From this time on, the pace of development quickened dramatically. Marine air facilities were built during World War II on land sold to the government by the Irvine Company, and by 1947 the company started to parcel out small sections of the ranch for residential and commercial use.

In 1959, the University of California received a large plot from the Irvine Company for the establishment of a new campus, and it can be said that Irvine is one of the few American communities to have been largely planned around the expansion of a university system. In 1970, the Irvine Business Complex was developed, along with the residential sites of Turtle Rock, University Park, Culverdale, The Ranch, and Walnut.

The University has further strengthened its ties to businesses in the community with the launch of a 180-acre University Research Park and the Irvine Biomedical Research Center.

In 1971, voting residents of these smaller communities elected to incorporate, forming a city considerably larger than had been envisioned by the original university planners. By 1980, the city hosted a population of 64,000, and took up a total area of 42 square miles. By 2004, it had reached a population of 178,317, reaching beyond the planned halfway point of its projected growth.

Irvine is now a self-sufficient, independent city whose economy depends on a mix of industries and services, including biotechnology products, electronics, and computer components. Major employers operating here include Allergan, Inc., Blizzard Entertainment, Toshiba, St. John Knits, Inc., and Parker Hannifin Corp. Irvine continues to carefully plan its efforts to preserve aspects of its natural environment, but nonetheless offers unique access to the great Los Angeles-Riverside-Orange County megalopolis. A major convenience for traveling Irvinites is that the fully modern John Wayne Airport is located just at the western edge of the city.

The city is home to the Ayn Rand Institute, the Verizon Wireless Amphitheater, and the Irvine Fine Arts Center devoted to visual arts programming.

Irvine specifically, and Orange County generally, feature southern California's famously salubrious climate. The sun shines almost all the time, temperatures are moderate, and rainfall is rare.

Rankings

General Rankings

- Santa Ana was ranked #65 out of 331 metro areas in *Cities Ranked & Rated*. Criteria: cost of living; climate; crime; transportation; economy and jobs; education; arts and culture; health and healthcare; leisure. *Cities Ranked & Rated, 1st Edition, 2004*

- The U.S. Conference of Mayors and Waste Management sponsors the City Livability Awards Program. The awards recognize and honor mayors for exemplary leadership in developing and implementing programs that improve the quality of life in America's cities. Irvine received an Honorable Mention Citation in the large cities category. *U.S Conference of Mayors, "2006 City Livability Awards"*

Business/Finance Rankings

- Los Angeles was selected as one of the best places to start and grow a company by *Entrepreneur* and the National Policy Research Council. The Los Angeles metro area ranked #27 out of 50 large metro areas. Criteria: business formation and growth (firms started four to 14 years ago that still employ at least 5 people and experienced rapid growth over the last four years). *Entrepreneur/National Policy Research Council, "Hot Cities for Entrepreneurs," September 2006*

- Intel, in partnership with Sperling's BestPlaces, ranked the 80 "Best Cities for Teleworking" in America. The Los Angeles metro area ranked #13 among extra large metro areas. The study identifies cities that hold the greatest potential for teleworking based on a host of factors including typical commuting times, fuel prices, availability of broadband Internet access and percentage of the population in telework friendly jobs. The study also factored in extreme climate and natural hazards. *Intel, "Best Cities for Teleworking," March 30, 2006*

- The Santa Ana metro area appeared on the Milken Institute "2005 Best Performing Cities" index. Rank: #17 out of 200 large metro areas. Criteria: job growth; wage and salary growth; high-tech output growth. *Milken Institute, "2005 Best Performing Cities," February 2006*

- The Santa Ana metro area was selected as one of "The Best Cities for Doing Business in America." *Inc.* magazine measured employment growth in 393 regions using the following criteria: recent growth trend; mid-term growth; long-term trend; and current year growth. The Santa Ana metro area ranked #17 among large metro areas and #124 overall. *Inc., May 2006*

- Santa Ana was identified as one of the 100 "Most Unwired Cities" in the U.S. The area ranked #10 out of the 100 largest metro areas in the U.S. Criteria: number of public and commercial wireless access points (hotspots); airports with wireless Internet access; broadband availability; local wireless networks; and wireless email devices. *Intel, "Most Unwired Cities Survey," June 7, 2005*

- Los Angeles was ranked #10 out of 125 regions worldwide in terms of its "Knowledge Competitiveness Index." The index attempts to measure the knowledge-based development taking place throughout the world and is based on 19 measures of economic performance that indicate a region's ability to translate its knowledge capacity into economic value. *Robert Huggins Associates, World Knowledge Competitiveness Index 2005*

- *Forbes* ranked the 200 most populous metro areas in the U.S. in terms of the "Best Places for Business and Careers." The Santa Ana metro area was ranked #70. Criteria: business costs (labor, energy, tax and office space expenses); living costs (housing, transportation, food and other household expenditures); education levels of the work force; job growth; income growth; migration trends; crime rates; and culture/leisure. *Forbes, April 23, 2007*

- *Fortune* ranked the 100 largest metro areas in the U.S. in terms of projected median home price change in 2006. The Santa Ana metro area ranked #98. *Fortune, "The Top 100: Is the Party Over?" December 26, 2005*

- Los Angeles was identified as one of the "Most Overpriced Places in the U.S." The area ranked #10 out of the nations 150 largest metro areas. Criteria: job growth; income growth; cost of living; and housing affordability. *Forbes.com, "Most Overpriced Places in the U.S. 2005"*

Health/EnvironmentRankings

■ Doctors at the Harvard School of Public Health ranked 40 metropolitan areas based on data from the government-sponsored Hospital Quality Alliance program. The program tracks the performance of individual hospitals in treating patients for three common health problems: heart attacks, congestive heart failure, and pneumonia. The Santa Ana metro area ranked #15 in quality of care for heart attacks, #13 for congestive heart failure, and #23 for pneumonia. *New England Journal of Medicine, July 21, 2005*

■ *Reader's Digest* ranked the 50 largest metro areas in the U.S. in terms of how "clean" they are. The Los Angeles metro area ranked #42. Criteria: air quality; water quality; toxic industrial pollution; Superfund sites; and sanitation. *Reader's Digest, "The 50 Cleanest (and Dirtiest) Cities in America," July 2005*

■ *Business Week* identified the 15 metro areas that saw the steepest declines in ground-level ozone pollution between 1990 and 2005. The Santa Ana metro area ranked #1. *Business Week, "America's Most Cleaned-Up Metro Areas," March 23, 2007*

■ The Santa Ana metro area appeared in *Country Home's* "2007 Best Green Places Report". The area ranked #83. Criteria included: air and watershed quality; miles of mass transit; green power; number of farmer's markets, organic producers and groceries. *Country Home, "2007 Best Green Places Report," April 2007*

■ Wyeth Consumer Healthcare, in partnership with Sperling's BestPlaces, ranked the nation's 50 most populous metro areas in terms of five key health factors. The Santa Ana metro area ranked #8. Criteria: physical activity, health status, nutrition, lifestyle pursuits; and mental wellness. *Wyeth Consumer Healthcare, "Centrum Healthiest Cities Study," April 19, 2005*

■ HealthGrades surveyed over 41,000 individuals on doctor satisfaction and ranked the 20 largest metro areas based on the highest "definitely yes" responses to the question "Do you trust the physician to make decisions/recommendations that are in your best interest?" The Los Angeles metro area ranked #17. *HealthGrades.com, "Top Cities in Doctor-Trust," September 7, 2006*

■ Irvine was named the winner of the 2002 Accessible America contest by the National Organization on Disability. The city was honored for its sucessful design of accessible programs, services and facilities for its citizens and visitors with disabilities.

■ Los Angeles was identified as a "2007 Asthma Capital." The area ranked #12 out of the nation's 100 largest metropolitan areas. Twelve factors were used to identify the most challenging places to live for people with asthma: estimated prevalence; self-reported prevalence; crude death rate for asthma; annual pollen score; annual air quality; public smoking laws; number of board-certified asthma specialists; school inhaler access laws; rescue medication use; controller medication use; uninsured rate; poverty rate. *Asthma and Allergy Foundation of America, "2007 Asthma Capitals"*

■ Los Angeles was identified as a "Spring Allergy Capital." The area ranked #20 out of 100. Three groups of factors were used to identify the most severe cities for people with allergies during the spring season: annual pollen levels; medicine utilization; access to board-certified allergists. *Asthma and Allergy Foundation of America, "2007 Spring Allergy Capital Rankings"*

■ Los Angeles was identified as a "Fall Allergy Capital." The area ranked #61 out of 100. Three groups of factors were used to identify the most severe cities for people with allergies during the fall season: annual pollen levels; medicine utilization; access to board-certified allergists. *Asthma and Allergy Foundation of America, "2006 Fall Allergy Capital Rankings"*

■ Ortho-McNeil Neurologics, in partnership with Sperling's BestPlaces, analyzed 110 metro areas and identified those U.S. cities with the highest prevalence of factors that are most commonly associated with migraine headaches. The Santa Ana metro area ranked #102. Criteria: number of migraine-related drug prescriptions per capita; lifestyle factors that can contribute to migraines; environmental factors that can trigger migraines; and consumption of migraine-triggering foods. *Ortho-McNeil Neurologics, "America's Migraine Hot Spots," March 14, 2006*

- Sperling's BestPlaces ranked 331 metro areas and identified the most and least stressful U.S. cities. The Santa Ana metro area ranked #98 out of the 100 largest metro areas (#1 = most stressful). Criteria: divorce rate; unemployment rate; violent and property crime; suicide rate; commute time; mental health; alcohol consumption; cloudy days. *www.BestPlaces.net, January 9, 2004*

- HealthGrades evaluated the performance of America's 25 most populous metropolitan areas by measuring the outcomes of five of the highest volume and most widely studied procedures and diagnoses: coronary artery bypass graft surgery; percutaneus coronary interventions; acute myocardial infarction/heart attack in angioplasty-capable hospitals; congestive heart failure; and community acquired pneumonia. The Los Angeles metro area ranked #10. *HealthGrades, "HealthGrades Hospital Quality in America Study," October 12, 2004*

- Los Angeles was highlighted as one of the 25 metro areas most polluted by year-round particle pollution (PM 2.5) in the U.S. The area ranked #1. *American Lung Association, State of the Air 2006*

- Los Angeles was highlighted as one of the 25 most ozone-polluted metro areas in the U.S. The area ranked #2. *American Lung Association, State of the Air 2006*

- Los Angeles was selected as one of "America's Top 10 Low-Carb Cities" by *LowCarbiz Magazine*. Criteria: abundance of low-carb products; restaurants with low-carb menu items; health practitioners supportive of carb-cutting regimens; local culture generally conducive to exercise and health. *LowCarbiz Magazine, April 2004*

- Santa Ana was selected as one of "America's Pet Healthiest Cities" by Purina. The city ranked #4 out of 50. Criteria: veterinary services; environment; legislation; preventative care; obesity/body condition. *Purina Pet Institute, "America's Pet Healthiest Cities," May 20, 2003*

Women/Minorities Rankings

- Santa Ana was ranked #4 out of 100 metro areas in *SELF Magazine's* ranking of "America's Best Places for Women." A panel of experts came up with nearly 40 criteria including: drinking and smoking rates; depression; unemployment; parks; crime; disease; healthcare insurance coverage; air quality; and commute times. *SELF Magazine, "America's Best Places for Women 2006," December 2006*

- *Ladies Home Journal* ranked America's 200 largest cities based on the qualities women surveyed care about most. Irvine ranked #5 out of 143 in the smaller city category (population under 300,000). Criteria: crime; lifestyle; education; jobs; health; child care; politics; and the economy. *Ladies Home Journal Online, "The Best Cities for Women 2002"*

- Los Angeles appeared on a list of the top 10 metro areas with the highest concentration of same-sex households. The area ranked #7. *Urban Institute Press, The Gay and Lesbian Atlas, May 2004*

- Los Angeles appeared on a list of the top 10 metro areas with the highest concentration of gay male couples. The area ranked #7. *Urban Institute Press, The Gay and Lesbian Atlas, May 2004*

- Los Angeles was identified as one of the top 25 metropolitan statistical areas ranked by percentage of coupled households that are gay or lesbian." The area ranked #19. *Human Rights Campaign, "Gay and Lesbian Families in the United States: Same-Sex Unmarried Partner Households," August 1, 2001*

Seniors/Retirement Rankings

- Sperling's BestPlaces in partnership with Bankers Life & Casualty Company designed a survey to identify the top 50 metro areas in the U.S. that offer the best overall qualities for senior living. The Santa Ana metro area ranked #47. The following criteria were statistically weighted to reflect the needs of the senior population: health; disease; economics; social; environment; spiritual; transportation; housing; and crime. *Bankers Life & Casualty Company, "Best Cities for Seniors 2005"*

■ A.G. Edwards ranked America's 500 top-performing communities based on their residents' personal savings and investing behavior. The Santa Ana metro area ranked #443 with an index score of 95.92 (national average = 100.00). A dozen statistical factors were measured including: participation in retirement savings plans; personal debt levels; and home ownership. *A.G. Edwards, "2006 Nest Egg Index", September 6, 2006*

Children/Family Rankings

■ The Santa Ana metro area was selected as one of the "Best Cities for Relocating Families" by Worldwide ERC and Primacy Relocation. Criteria: tax rates; average home costs and home appreciation; ability to qualify for in-state tuition; service quality of local utilities; per-capita volunteerism; auto taxes; and quantity of fun, family-friendly events and venues. *Worldwide ERC and Primacy Relocation, "2006 Best Cities for Relocating Families"*

■ Irvine was chosen as one of America's "100 Best Communities for Young People." The winners were selected based upon detailed information provided about each community's efforts to fulfill five essential promises critical to the well-being of young people: caring adults who are actively involved in their lives; safe places in which to learn and grow; a healthy start toward adulthood; an effective education that builds marketable skills; and opportunities to help others. *America's Promise, "100 Best Communities for Young People," September 26, 2005*

Safety Rankings

■ Allstate ranked the 200 largest cities in America in terms of driver safety. Irvine ranked #157. In addition, drivers were 23.7% more likely to have had an accident compared to the national average. Allstate researchers analyzed internal Property Damage reported claims over a two-year period (from January 2003 to December 2004) to ensure the findings would not be affected by external influences such as weather or road construction. A weighted average of the two-year numbers determined the annual percentages. The report defines an auto crash as any collision resulting in a property damage claim. *Allstate, "Allstate America's Best Drivers Report 2006," May 24, 2006*

■ Santa Ana was identified as one of the most dangerous large metro areas for pedestrians in the U.S. The area ranked #20 out of the nations 50 largest metro areas. Criteria: average yearly pedestrian fatalities per capita (for the years 2002 and 2003) adjusted for the number of walkers. *Surface Transportation Policy Project, "Mean Streets 2004"*

■ Irvine was identified as one of the safest cities in America by Morgan Quitno. All 371 cities with populations over 75,000 that reported crime rates in 2005 for murder, rape, robbery, aggravated assault, burglary, and motor vehicle thefts were ranked. The city ranked #7 out of the top 25. *www.morganquitno.com, 13th Annual America's Safest (and Most Dangerous) Cities Awards*

■ Irvine was identified as one of the safest mid-size cities in America by Morgan Quitno. All 213 cities with populations of 100,000 to 499,999 that reported crime rates in 2005 for murder, rape, robbery, aggravated assault, burglary, and motor vehicle thefts were ranked. The city ranked #2 out of the top 10. *www.morganquitno.com, 13th Annual America's Safest (and Most Dangerous) Cities Awards*

■ *Ladies Home Journal* ranked America's 200 largest cities in terms of safety. Irvine ranked #7 out of 200. Criteria: violent crimes; crimes against property; and rape. *Ladies Home Journal Online, "The Best Cities for Women 2002"*

Sports/Recreation Rankings

- The Los Angeles metro area appeared on *The Sporting News* list of the "Best Sports Cities 2006". The area ranked #8 out of 99 cities in North America. To be included in the rankings, a city must have at least one of the following: NCAA Division I basketball team; Class A minor league baseball team; training camp for a major league or NFL team; NASCAR Nextel Cup race; NCAA Division I-A bowl game; PGA Tour tournament; Triple Crown horse race. Once a city qualifies, a 12-month snapshot is taken of the sports atmosphere, putting a heavy premium on regular-season won-lost records; playoff berths, bowl appearances and tournament bids; championships; applicable power ratings; quality of competition; overall fan fervor; sports atmosphere and fan knowledge; abundance of teams (quality over quantity); stadium/arena quality; ticket availability and prices; franchise ownership; and the marquee appeal of athletes. *SportingNews.com, "Best Sports Cities 2006," August 1, 2006*

- Scarborough Research, a leading market research firm, identified the top local markets for avid NBA fans. The Los Angeles DMA (Designated Market Area) ranked in the top 10 with 15% of consumers 18 years and over reporting that they are "very interested in the NBA". *Scarborough Research, Scarborough USA+ 2005 Release 2*

- The Santa Ana metro area was selected by *Cranium* as one of the "Top 50 Fun Cities" in America. The area ranked #2. Criteria includes: number of sports teams, restaurants, and dance performances; number of toy stores; city budget spent on recreation. *Cranium, November 4, 2003*

- *Golf Digest* ranked 330 metro areas in the U.S. in terms of golf. The Santa Ana metro area was ranked #286. Criteria: access to golf; weather; value of golf; and quality of golf. *Golf Digest, "Metro Golf Rankings," August 2005*

Dating/Romance Rankings

- The Los Angeles metro area was selected as one of the "Best Cities for Relocating Singles" by Worldwide ERC and Primacy Relocation. The area ranked #28 out of the 100 largest metro areas in the U.S. Areas were selected based on the following criteria: Population Criteria (local percentage and growth trends of unmarried residents aged 25-34; male-female ratios; the number of newcomers to the area; diversity and density); Economic Criteria (job growth vs. unemployment rates; apartment rental costs; fee and occupancy rates for temporary housing and mini-storage; higher education costs, including in-state and out-of-state tuition requirements; vehicle tax rates and quality of service from utility providers); Quality-of-Life Criteria (level of per capita volunteering; quality and quantity of collegiate and professional sports with fun, fan-friendly venues; number of Starbucks and other coffee shops; quality or popularity of restaurants, nightspots, health clubs, and online dating; moderate climates with sustainable water supplies). *Worldwide ERC and Primacy Relocation, "2006 Best Cities for Relocating Singles," October 11, 2006*

- *Forbes* ranked the 40 most populous metro areas in the U.S. in terms of the "Best Cities for Singles." The Los Angeles metro area was ranked #19. Criteria: number of singles; cost of living alone; nightlife; culture; job growth; coolness; and online dating. *Forbes.com, July 25, 2006*

- Sperling's BestPlaces in partnership with AXE Deodorant Bodyspray ranked 80 metro areas and identified "America's Best (and Worst) Cities for Dating." The Santa Ana metro area ranked #59. Criteria: percentage of singles ages 18-24; population density; dating venues per capita. *AXE Deodorant Bodyspray, "America's Best (and Worst) Cities for Dating," May, 2004*

- The Santa Ana metro area was selected as one of the "10 Best Cities for Singles" by AOL CityGuide. The area ranked #3 out of 10.Criteria: over 300 cities were evaluated based on the quantity and quality of places for singles to meet other singles, such as bars and restaurants, cultural and sporting events, and online personals. *AOL CityGuide, "10 Best Cities for Singles," February 12, 2004*

Miscellaneous Rankings

- Irvine was determined to be one of America's smartest cities. The city ranked #10 in the small city category (50,000 to 100,000 adults 25 years and older). Criteria: the editors rated the collective brainpower of U.S communities based on the educational attainment of its residents. *American City Business Journals, www.bizjournals.com, June 12, 2006*

- Avis Rent-A-Car and Motorola, in partnership with Sperling's BestPlaces, ranked the nation's 75 most populous metro areas in terms of how difficult they are to navigate. The Los Angeles metro area ranked #7 with #1 being the most challenging. Criteria: street layouts; overall design and layout; travel time index; percent of congested freeway and street lane miles; bodies of water; complexity of directions needed to travel from major airports to city center; annual delay per person; days of snow exceeding 1.5 inches; and days of rain exceeding 0.5 inch. *Avis Rent-A-Car and Motorola, "America's Most Challenging Cities to Navigate," August 3, 2004*

- The Los Angeles metro area appeared on *Forbes* list of "America's Drunkest Cities". The area ranked #23. Criteria: 35 of the largest continental U.S. metro areas were chosen based on availability of data and geographic diversity. Each metro was ranked in five areas: state laws; drinkers; heavy drinkers; binge drinkers; and alcoholism. *Forbes.com, "America's Drunkest Cities," August 22, 2006*

- Sperling's BestPlaces in partnership with Pep Boys ranked 77 metro areas and identified "America's Most Drivable Cities." The Los Angeles metro area ranked #77. Criteria: climate; road roughness; urban mobility; gas prices. *Pep Boys, "America's Most Drivable Cities," April 9, 2003*

- Los Angeles was ranked #13 out of 268 metro areas in terms of its Creativity Index. The Creativity Index is a mix of four equally weighted factors: the Creative Class (scientists, engineers, architects, designers, writers, artists, musicians, or any profession where creativity is a key factor) share of the workforce; innovation, measured as patents per capita; high-tech industry, using the Milken Institute's Tech Pole Index; and diversity, measured by the Gay Index (a reasonable proxy for an areas' openness to different kinds of people and ideas). *The Rise of the Creative Class, 2002*

- State Farm Insurance, in partnership with Sperling's BestPlaces, analyzed several key factors that contribute to overall family preparedness. The Santa Ana metro area ranked #43 out of the nation's 50 most populous metro areas. Criteria: quality of life; life insurance coverage; and investments. *State Farm Life Insurance, "Fiscally Fit Cities Report," July 20, 2004*

- Scarborough Research, a leading market research firm, identified the top local markets for coffee bar patronage. The Los Angeles DMA (Designated Market Area) ranked in the top 10 with 19% of adults reporting that they have used any coffee house/bar during the past 30 days. *Scarborough Research, Scarborough USA+ 2004 Release 1*

Business Environment

City Government Finances

Component	2003-2004 ($000)	2003-2004 ($ per capita)
Total Revenues	161,840	998
Total Expenditures	201,732	1,244
Debt Outstanding	979,284	6,040
Cash and Securities	466,060	2,875

Source: U.S Census Bureau, Government Finances 2003-2004

City Government Revenue by Source

Source	2003-2004 ($000)	2003-2004 ($ per capita)
General Revenue		
From Federal Government	1,559	10
From State Government	17,534	108
From Local Governments	3,860	24
Taxes		
Property	17,245	106
Sales	63,964	395
Personal Income	0	0
License	0	0
Charges	32,549	201
Liquor Store	0	0
Utility	0	0
Employee Retirement	0	0
Other	25,129	155

Source: U.S Census Bureau, Government Finances 2003-2004

City Government Expenditures by Function

Function	2003-2004 ($000)	2003-2004 ($ per capita)	2003-2004 (%)
General Expenditures			
Airports	0	0	0.0
Corrections	0	0	0.0
Education	0	0	0.0
Fire Protection	0	0	0.0
Governmental Administration	11,161	69	5.5
Health	1,320	8	0.7
Highways	40,141	248	19.9
Hospitals	0	0	0.0
Housing and Community Development	1,479	9	0.7
Interest on General Debt	53,400	329	26.5
Libraries	0	0	0.0
Parking	0	0	0.0
Parks and Recreation	38,920	240	19.3
Police Protection	37,453	231	18.6
Public Welfare	0	0	0.0
Sewerage	0	0	0.0
Solid Waste Management	0	0	0.0
Liquor Store	0	0	0.0
Utility	0	0	0.0
Employee Retirement	0	0	0.0
Other	17,858	110	8.9

Source: U.S Census Bureau, Government Finances 2003-2004

Municipal Bond Ratings

Area	Moody's
City	n/a

Source: Mergent Bond Record, January 2007 (unless noted otherwise)

DEMOGRAPHICS

Population Growth

Area	1990 Census	2000 Census	2006 Estimate	2011 Projection	Population Growth (%) 1990-2000	Population Growth (%) 2000-2011
City	111,754	143,072	189,775	225,209	28.0	57.4
MSA[1]	11,273,720	12,365,627	13,155,105	13,873,953	9.7	12.2
U.S.	248,709,873	281,421,906	298,021,266	312,383,955	13.2	11.0

Note: (1) Metropolitan Statistical Area - see Appendix B for areas included
Source: Claritas, Inc.

Number of Households and Average Household Size

Area	2006 Estimate	2006 Average Household Size
City	66,776	2.84
MSA[1]	4,284,258	3.07
U.S.	112,267,302	2.65

Note: (1) Metropolitan Statistical Area - see Appendix B for areas included
Source: Claritas, Inc.

Race and Ethnicity

Area	White Alone[2]	Black Alone[2]	Asian Alone[2]	Other Race Alone[2]	Hispanic[3]
City	53.9	1.3	36.9	7.9	7.4
MSA[1]	50.5	7.4	13.4	28.6	43.8
U.S.	73.3	12.4	4.2	10.1	14.5

Note: Figures are 2006 estimates; (1) Metropolitan Statistical Area - see Appendix B for areas included
(2) Alone is defined as not being in combination with one or more other races; (3) May be of any race.
Source: Claritas, Inc.

Segregation

City Index[2]	City Rank[3]	MSA[1] Index[2]	MSA[1] Rank[4]
37.3	89	43.8	282

Note: Figures are based on an analysis of Census 2000 data; (1) Metropolitan Statistical Area - see Appendix A for areas included; (2) White/Black Dissimilarity Index—the most commonly used measure of segregation between two groups, reflecting their relative distributions across neighborhoods within a city or metropolitan area. It can range in value from 0, indicating complete integration, to 100, indicating complete segregation; (3) Ranges from 1 (most segregated) to 100 (least segregated) and includes all the cities in this book; (4) Ranges from 1 (most segregated) to 318 (least segregated) and includes 318 metropolitan areas.
Source: www.CensusScope.org

Ancestry

Area	German	Irish[2]	English	American	Italian	Polish	French[3]	Scottish
City	11.6	8.2	10.3	3.2	4.7	2.4	2.4	2.1
MSA[1]	11.7	8.7	8.9	3.5	4.7	1.9	2.6	1.9
U.S.	15.2	10.9	8.7	7.3	5.6	3.2	3.0	1.7

Note: Figures include multiple ancestry (e.g. if a person reported being Irish and Italian, they were included in both columns); (1) Metropolitan Statistical Area - see Appendix A for areas included; (2) Includes Celtic; (3) Includes Alsatian but excludes Basque
Source: Census 2000, Summary File 3

Foreign-Born Population

Area	Percent of Population Born in Any Foreign Country	Europe	Asia	Africa	Oceania[2]	Canada	Mexico	Latin America[3]
City	32.1	3.1	24.3	1.1	0.2	0.9	1.1	1.3
MSA[1]	29.9	2.0	10.9	0.4	0.2	0.6	13.7	2.1
U.S.	11.1	1.7	2.9	0.3	0.1	0.3	3.3	2.5

Note: (1) Metropolitan Statistical Area - see Appendix A for areas included; (2) Includes Australia, New Zealand subregion, Melanesia, Micronesia, Polynesia, and Oceania n.e.c; (3) Includes Central America (excluding Mexico), South America, and the Caribbean.
Source: Census 2000, Summary File 3

Marriage Status

Area	Never Married	Now Married (excluding Separated)	Separated	Widowed	Divorced
City	33.3	53.2	1.2	3.6	8.7
MSA[1]	28.4	55.4	2.1	5.1	9.1
U.S.	27.1	54.4	2.2	6.6	9.7

Note: Figures are percentages and cover the population 15 years of age and older;
(1) Metropolitan Statistical Area - see Appendix A for areas included
Source: Census 2000, Summary File 3

Age Distribution

Area	Percent of Population						
	Under Age 5	Age 5 to 17	Age 18 to 34	Age 35 to 49	Age 50 to 64	Age 65 to 79	80 Years and Over
City	5.6	17.8	29.2	25.7	14.5	5.4	1.8
MSA[1]	7.5	19.4	25.6	24.0	13.7	7.3	2.5
U.S.	6.8	18.9	23.7	23.5	14.8	9.2	3.2

Note: (1) Metropolitan Statistical Area - see Appendix A for areas included
Source: Census 2000, Summary File 3

Male/Female Ratio

Area	Males	Females	Males per 100 Females
City	92,347	97,428	94.8
MSA[1]	6,518,886	6,636,219	98.2
U.S.	146,712,712	151,308,554	97.0

Note: Figures are 2006 estimates; (1) Metropolitan Statistical Area -
see Appendix B for areas included
Source: Claritas, Inc.

Religion

Area	Catholic	Southern Baptist	United Methodist	ELCA[1]	LDS[2]	Presbyterian Church USA	Jewish Est.	Muslim Est.
County	27.4	1.2	0.6	0.8	1.7	0.9	2.1	1.4
U.S.	22.0	7.1	3.7	1.8	1.5	1.1	2.2	0.6

Note: Figures are the number of adherents as a percentage of the total population; Adherents are defined as all members, including full members, their children and the estimated number of other participants who are not considered members (e.g. the baptized, those not confirmed, those regularly attending services, etc.);
(1) Evangelical Lutheran Church in America; (2) The Church of Jesus Christ of Latter Day Saints
Source: Reprinted with permission from Religious Congregations and Membership in the United States 2000 (Nashville, Glenmary Research Center, 2002) Copyright Association of Statisticians of American Religious Bodies. All rights reserved.

ECONOMY

Gross Metropolitan Product

Area	2002	2003	2004	2005	2005 Rank[2]
MSA[1]	502.1	528.0	567.6	604.8	2

Note: Figures are in billions of dollars; (1) Los Angeles-Long Beach-Santa Ana, CA Metropolitan Statistical Area - see Appendix A for areas included; (2) Rank ranges from 1 to 361
Source: The U.S. Conference of Mayors, "U.S. Metro Economies: GMP - The Engines of America's Growth," January 2007

Economic Growth

Area	1995 GMP	2005 GMP	Average Annual Growth Rate	Growth Rate Rank[2]
MSA[1]	354.1	604.8	5.5	160

Note: Figures are in billions of dollars; GMP = Gross Metropolitan Product; (1) Los Angeles-Long Beach-Santa Ana, CA Metropolitan Statistical Area - see Appendix A for areas included; (2) Rank ranges from 1 to 361
Source: The U.S. Conference of Mayors, "U.S. Metro Economies: GMP - The Engines of America's Growth," January 2007

INCOME

Per Capita/Median/Average Income

Area	Per Capita ($)	Median Household ($)	Average Household ($)
City	38,301	85,125	107,885
MSA[1]	24,259	51,573	73,593
U.S.	25,129	48,775	65,849

Note: Figures are 2006 estimates; (1) Metropolitan Statistical Area - see Appendix B for areas included
Source: Claritas, Inc.

Household Income Distribution

Area	Under $15,000	$15,000 -24,999	$25,000 -34,999	$35,000 -49,999	$50,000 -74,999	$75,000 -99,000	$100,000 -149,999	$150,000 and up
City	7.8	4.9	5.2	9.3	16.8	14.9	21.0	20.2
MSA[1]	13.3	10.5	10.5	14.5	17.8	11.7	12.4	9.2
U.S.	13.3	11.0	11.3	15.7	19.5	11.8	11.0	6.4

Note: Figures are 2006 estimates; (1) Metropolitan Statistical Area - see Appendix B for areas included
Source: Claritas, Inc.

Poverty Rates by Age

Area	All Ages	Under 5 Years Old	5 to 17 Years Old	18 to 64 Years Old	65 Years and Over
City	9.1	0.4	1.2	7.1	0.4
MSA[1]	10.3	1.0	2.6	6.1	0.6
U.S.	12.4	1.2	3.0	6.9	1.2

Note: Figures are percent of population with income in 1999 below poverty level and only include population for whom poverty status is determined; (1) Metropolitan Statistical Area - see Appendix A for areas included
Source: Census 2000, Summary File 3

Personal Bankruptcy Filing Rate

Area	2003	2004	2005
Orange County	3.10	2.56	3.90
U.S.	5.57	5.31	6.88

Note: Numbers are per 1,000 population and include Chapter 7 and Chapter 13 filings
Source: Federal Deposit Insurance Corporation (FDIC), Regional Economic Conditions (RECON), 3/24/2006

EMPLOYMENT

Labor Force and Employment

Area	Civilian Labor Force			Workers Employed		
	Dec. 2005	Dec. 2006	% Chg.	Dec. 2005	Dec. 2006	% Chg.
City	84,898	85,560	0.8	82,908	83,559	0.8
MD[1]	1,610,610	1,623,137	0.8	1,559,722	1,571,968	0.8
U.S.	149,874,000	152,571,000	1.8	142,918,000	146,081,000	2.2

Note: Data is not seasonally adjusted and covers workers 16 years of age and older;
(1) Metropolitan Division - see Appendix B for areas included
Source: Bureau of Labor Statistics, http://stats.bls.gov

Unemployment Rate

Area	2006											
	Jan.	Feb.	Mar.	Apr.	May	Jun.	Jul.	Aug.	Sep.	Oct.	Nov.	Dec.
City	2.6	2.6	2.5	2.4	2.4	2.8	2.8	2.6	2.5	2.3	2.5	2.3
MD[1]	3.5	3.6	3.4	3.2	3.2	3.7	3.8	3.6	3.4	3.1	3.4	3.2
U.S.	5.1	5.1	4.8	4.5	4.4	4.8	5.0	4.6	4.4	4.1	4.3	4.3

Note: Data is not seasonally adjusted and covers workers 16 years of age and older; All figures are percentages; (1) Metropolitan Division - see Appendix B for areas included
Source: Bureau of Labor Statistics, http://stats.bls.gov

Employment by Occupation

Occupation Classification	City (%)	MSA[1] (%)	U.S. (%)
Sales and Office	28.1	28.7	26.7
Professional and Related	33.2	20.5	20.2
Service	7.6	13.2	14.9
Production, Transportation, and Material Moving	4.3	12.5	14.6
Management, Business, and Financial	24.5	17.6	13.5
Construction, Extraction, and Maintenance	2.4	7.3	9.4
Farming, Forestry, and Fishing	0.1	0.3	0.7

Note: Figures cover employed civilians 16 years of age and older;
(1) Metropolitan Statistical Area - see Appendix A for areas included
Source: Census 2000, Summary File 3

Employment by Industry

Sector	MSA[1]		U.S.
	Number of Employees	Percent of Total	Percent of Total
Government	159,700	10.4	16.3
Education and Health Services	143,600	9.3	13.2
Professional and Business Services	278,200	18.1	12.9
Retail Trade	167,300	10.9	11.5
Manufacturing	183,100	11.9	10.2
Leisure and Hospitality	169,800	11.0	9.5
Financial Activities	138,800	9.0	6.1
Construction	107,500	7.0	5.5
Wholesale Trade	83,000	5.4	4.3
Other Services	47,800	3.1	3.9
Transportation and Utilities	29,400	1.9	3.7
Information	31,300	2.0	2.2
Natural Resources and Mining	600	<0.1	0.5

Note: Figures cover non-farm employment as of December 2006 and are not seasonally adjusted;
(1) Metropolitan Statistical Area - see Appendix B for areas included
Source: Bureau of Labor Statistics, http://stats.bls.gov

Occupations with Greatest Projected Employment Growth: 2002 - 2012

Occupation[1]	2002 Employment	2012 Projected Employment	Numeric Employment Change	Percent Employment Change
Retail Salespersons	435,400	513,200	77,800	17.9
Postsecondary Teachers	154,500	217,700	63,200	40.9
Combined Food Preparation and Serving Workers, Including Fast Food	215,100	277,300	62,200	28.9
Cashiers	358,800	420,700	61,900	17.3
Registered Nurses	201,600	258,400	56,800	28.2
Waiters and Waitresses	214,000	264,900	50,900	23.8
Customer Service Representatives	197,500	244,900	47,400	24.0
Office Clerks, General	400,300	446,500	46,200	11.5
General and Operations Managers	224,000	267,000	43,000	19.2
Teacher Assistants	179,600	222,300	42,700	23.8

Note: Projections cover California; (1) Sorted by numeric employment change
Source: www.projectionscentral.com, State Occupational Projections, 2002-2012 Long-Term Projections

Fastest Growing Occupations: 2002 - 2012

Occupation[1]	2002 Employment	2012 Projected Employment	Numeric Employment Change	Percent Employment Change
Physical Therapist Aides	4,200	6,800	2,600	61.9
Dental Hygienists	16,600	26,200	9,600	57.8
Dental Assistants	42,700	67,100	24,400	57.1
Tapers	9,200	14,400	5,200	56.5
Drywall and Ceiling Tile Installers	26,800	41,800	15,000	56.0
Tile and Marble Setters	8,600	13,400	4,800	55.8
Network Systems and Data Communications Analysts	20,300	31,600	11,300	55.7
Physical Therapist Assistants	3,900	6,000	2,100	53.8
Fitness Trainers and Aerobics Instructors	24,000	35,700	11,700	48.8
Self-Enrichment Education Teachers	24,200	35,800	11,600	47.9

Note: Projections cover California; (1) Sorted by percent employment change and excludes occupations with numeric employment change less than 1500
Source: www.projectionscentral.com, State Occupational Projections, 2002-2012 Long-Term Projections

Average Wages

Occupation	$/Hr.	Occupation	$/Hr.
Accountants and Auditors	29.68	Maids and Housekeeping Cleaners	8.51
Automotive Mechanics	18.99	Maintenance and Repair Workers	15.90
Bookkeepers	17.10	Marketing Managers	54.37
Carpenters	22.19	Nuclear Medicine Technologists	33.79
Cashiers	9.67	Nurses, Licensed Practical	21.07
Clerks, General Office	13.14	Nurses, Registered	32.98
Clerks, Receptionists/Information	12.24	Nursing Aides/Orderlies/Attendants	10.77
Clerks, Shipping/Receiving	12.97	Packers and Packagers, Hand	8.89
Computer Programmers	34.87	Physical Therapists	33.40
Computer Support Specialists	22.63	Postal Service Mail Carriers	22.56
Computer Systems Analysts	36.36	Real Estate Brokers	n/a
Cooks, Restaurant	10.42	Retail Salespersons	12.12
Dentists	n/a	Sales Reps., Exc. Tech./Scientific	30.12
Electrical Engineers	37.65	Sales Reps., Tech./Scientific	35.34
Electricians	21.33	Secretaries, Exc. Legal/Med./Exec.	15.95
Financial Managers	52.95	Security Guards	10.50
First-Line Supervisors/Mgrs., Sales	18.67	Surgeons	78.92
Food Preparation Workers	8.80	Teacher Assistants	13.90
General and Operations Managers	54.14	Teachers, Elementary School	26.70
Hairdressers/Cosmetologists	9.83	Teachers, Secondary School	30.80
Internists	83.84	Telemarketers	13.36
Janitors and Cleaners	10.61	Truck Drivers, Heavy/Tractor-Trailer	18.16
Landscaping/Groundskeeping Workers	10.47	Truck Drivers, Light/Delivery Svcs.	12.31
Lawyers	64.36	Waiters and Waitresses	8.25

Note: Wage data is for May 2005 and covers the Santa Ana-Anaheim-Irvine, CA Metropolitan Division - see Appendix B for areas included. Hourly wages for elementary/secondary school teachers and teacher assistants were calculated by the editors from annual wage data assuming a 40 hour work week; n/a not available.
Source: Bureau of Labor Statistics, May 2005 Metro Area Occupational Employment and Wage Estimates

RESIDENTIAL REAL ESTATE

Building Permits

Area	Single-Family			Multi-Family			Total		
	2005	2006p	Pct. Chg.	2005	2006p	Pct. Chg.	2005	2006p	Pct. Chg.
City	1,164	593	-49.1	1,691	2,922	72.8	2,855	3,515	23.1
U.S.	1,682,000	1,380,000	-18.0	473,300	457,300	-3.4	2,155,300	1,837,300	-14.8

Note: (p) preliminary; figures represent new, privately-owned housing units authorized (unadjusted data); All permit data are based on estimates with imputation; U.S. figures are based on the new 20,000-place series.
Source: U.S. Census Bureau, Manufacturing, Mining, and Construction Statistics

Homeownership and Housing Vacancies

Area	Homeownership Rate[2] (%)			Rental Vacancy Rate[3] (%)			Homeowner Vacancy Rate[4] (%)		
	2004	2005	2006	2004	2005	2006	2004	2005	2006
MSA[1]	n/a	54.6	54.4	n/a	4.4	4.0	n/a	0.9	1.2
U.S.	69.0	68.9	68.8	10.2	9.8	9.7	1.7	1.9	2.4

Note: Comparable 2004 data was not available due to changes in metropolitan area definitions; (1) Metropolitan Statistical Area - see Appendix B for areas included; (2) The proportion of households that are owners; (3) The proportion of the rental inventory that is vacant for rent; (4) The proportion of the homeowner inventory that is vacant for sale; n/a not available
Source: U.S. Census Bureau, Housing Vacancies and Homeownership Annual Statistics: 2006

TAXES

State Corporate Income Tax Rates

State	Rate (%)	Number of Brackets	Low Bracket (Under $)	High Bracket (Over $)
California	8.84	1	na	na

Note: Tax rates as of December 31, 2006; na not applicable; 10.84% on financial institutions. Minimum tax is $800. The tax rate on S-Corporations is 1.5% (3.5% for financial S-Corporations).
Source: Tax Foundation, www.taxfoundation.org

State Individual Income Tax Rates

State	Federal Deductibility	Marginal Rate (%)	Number of Brackets	Low Bracket (Under $)	High Bracket (Over $)
California	No	1.0-10.3 (p)(r)	7	0	1,000,000

Note: Tax rates as of December 31, 2006; Brackets apply to single taxpayers and married people filing separately; na not applicable; (p) California's $1,000,000 bracket not doubled for married taxpayers; (r) Indexed for Inflation.
Source: Tax Foundation, www.taxfoundation.org

Various State and Local Tax Rates

State and Local Sales and Use (%)	State Sales and Use (%)	Gasoline ($/gal.)	Cigarette ($/pack)	Spirits ($/gal.)	Table Wine ($/gal.)	Beer ($/gal.)
7.75	6.25	0.192 (m)	0.87	3.3	0.20	0.20

Note: Tax rates as of December 31, 2006; (m) Additional cents per gallon taxes added this year that were not included in previous years' tables.
Source: Tax Foundation, www.taxfoundation.org; The Sales Tax Clearinghouse, www.thestc.com

State Tax Burdens

Area	Combined State and Local Tax Burden		Combined Federal, State and Local Tax Burden	
	Percent	Rank	Percent	Rank
California	10.9	15	32.7	9
U.S. Average	10.6	-	31.6	-

Note: Figures are for 2006 and measure taxes as a percentage of income
Source: Tax Foundation, www.taxfoundation.org

Internal Revenue Service Tax Audits

IRS District	Percent of Returns Audited				
	1996	1997	1998	1999	2000
Southern California	1.62	1.34	0.88	0.69	0.47
U.S.	0.66	0.61	0.46	0.31	0.20

Note: Figures cover IRS district audits of federal income tax returns filed by individuals. Geographic data on district audits after the year 2000 are being withheld by the IRS. TRAC is challenging this policy.
Source: Syracuse University, Transactional Records Access Clearinghouse (TRAC), "Odds of IRS District Tax Audit 2000"

**COMMERCIAL
REAL ESTATE**

Office Market

Market Area	Inventory (sq. ft.)	Vacant (sq. ft.)	Vac. Rate (%)	Under Constr. (sq. ft.)	Asking Rent ($/sf)	
					Class A	Class B
Orange County	69,431,428	5,051,303	7.3	3,677,726	35.28	25.92

Source: Grubb & Ellis, Office Markets Trends, 4th Quarter 2006

Industrial Market

Market Area	Inventory (sq. ft.)	Vacant (sq. ft.)	Vac. Rate (%)	Under Constr. (sq. ft.)	Asking Rent ($/sf)	
					WH/Dist	R&D/Flex
Orange County	269,303,801	9,458,963	3.5	998,530	8.28	14.52

Source: Grubb & Ellis, Industrial Markets Trends, 4th Quarter 2006

**COMMERCIAL
UTILITIES**

Typical Monthly Electric Bills

Area	Commercial Service ($/month)		Industrial Service ($/month)	
	3 kW demand 1,000 kWh	40 kW demand 14,000 kWh	1,000 kW demand 200,000 kWh	50,000 kW demand 15,000,000 kWh
City	215	2,636	60,545	2,448,677
Average[1]	123	1,413	22,000	1,306,315

Note: Based on total rates in effect July 1, 2006; (1) average based on 196 utilities
Source: Edison Electric Institute, Typical Bills and Average Rates Report, Summer 2006

TRANSPORTATION

Means of Transportation to Work

Area	Car/Truck/Van		Public Transportation			Bicycle	Walked	Other Means	Worked at Home
	Drove Alone	Car-pooled	Bus	Subway	Railroad				
City	79.2	8.2	0.5	0.0	0.1	1.1	4.8	0.7	5.4
MSA[1]	76.5	13.3	2.5	0.0	0.2	0.8	2.0	0.9	3.7
U.S.	75.7	12.2	2.5	1.5	0.5	0.4	2.9	1.0	3.3

Note: Figures are percentages and cover workers 16 years of age and older;
(1) Metropolitan Statistical Area - see Appendix A for areas included
Source: Census 2000, Summary File 3

Travel Time to Work

Area	Less Than 15 Minutes	15 to 29 Minutes	30 to 44 Minutes	45 to 59 Minutes	60 Minutes or More
City	29.9	44.5	14.1	5.0	6.5
MSA[1]	22.1	37.6	23.8	8.0	8.5
U.S.	29.4	36.1	19.1	7.4	8.0

Note: Figures are percentages and include workers 16 years old and over; (1) Metropolitan Statistical Area -
see Appendix A for areas included
Source: Census 2000, Summary File 3

Travel Time Index

Area	1982	1993	2002	2003
Urban Area[1]	1.30	1.73	1.77	1.75
Average[2]	1.12	1.28	1.37	1.37

Note: Travel Time Index - The ratio of travel time in the peak period to the travel time at
free-flow conditions. A value of 1.35 indicates a 20-minute free-flow trip takes 27 minutes
in the peak. Free-flow speeds (60 mph on freeways and 35 mph on principal arterials)
are used as the comparison threshold; (1) Covers the Los Angeles-Long Beach-Santa Ana, CA urban area;
(2) average of 85 urban areas
Source: Texas Transportation Institute, The 2005 Urban Mobility Report, May 2005

Public Transportation

Agency name:	Orange County Transportation Authority (OCTA)
Vehicle type:	Bus
Average fleet age in years:	7.6
No. operated in max. service:	553
Vehicle type:	Demand response
Average fleet age in years:	0.0
No. operated in max. service:	280

Source: Federal Transit Administration, National Transit Database, 2005

Air Transportation

Airport name and code:	John Wayne International (Santa Ana) (SNA)
Domestic service (2006)	
Passenger airlines[1]:	14
Passenger enplanements:	4,774,301
Freight carriers[2]:	14
Freight (lbs.):	29,128,721
International service (2005)	
Passenger airlines[1]:	5
Passenger enplanements:	1,195
Freight carriers[2]:	0
Freight (lbs.):	0

Note: (1) Includes all major, minor and commuter airlines that carried at least one passenger during the year; (2) Includes all airlines and freight carriers that transported at least one pound of freight during the year
Source: Bureau of Transportation Statistics, The Intermodal Transportation Database, Air Carriers: T-100 International Market, 2004; Bureau of Transportation Statistics, The Intermodal Transportation Database, Air Carriers: T-100 Domestic Market, 2005

Other Transportation Statistics

Interstate highways:	I-5
Amtrak service:	Yes
Major waterways/ports:	Near the Pacific Ocean (5 miles)

Source: Editor & Publisher Market Guide, 2006; Amtrak.com; Rand McNally 2006 Road Atlas

BUSINESSES

Major Business Headquarters

Company Name	2006 Rankings	
	Fortune[1]	Forbes[2]
Golden State Foods	-	137
Standard Pacific	493	-

Note: (1) Fortune 500 - companies that produce a 10-K are ranked 1 to 500 based on 2005 revenue; (2) Forbes Largest Private Companies - all private companies with at least $1 billion in annual revenue are ranked 1 to 394; companies listed are located in the city; dashes indicate no ranking
Source: Fortune, April 17, 2006; Forbes, November 9, 2006

Best Companies to Work For

Alcon Laboratories; Standard Pacific (HQ), headquartered in Irvine, are among the "100 Best Companies to Work For." Criteria: More than 105,000 employees from 446 companies responded to a 57-question survey created by the Great Place to Work Institute. Two-thirds of a company's score is based on the survey, which covers topics such as attitudes towards management, job satisfaction, and camaraderie. The remaining third of the score comes from each company's responses to the Institute's Culture Audit, which includes detailed questions about demographic makeup, pay and benefits programs, and open-ended questions about the company's people-management philosophy, internal communications, opportunities, compensation practices, diversity programs, etc. Any company that is at least seven years old and has a minimum of 1,000 U.S. employees is eligible. The top three U.S. locations are shown for companies with more than one location. *Fortune, "100 Best Companies to Work for 2007," January 22, 2007*

Standard Pacific Corp, headquartered in Irvine, is among the "100 Best Places to Work in IT." To qualify, companies, both public and private, had to have 2005 revenue of $250 million or greater and employ a minimum of 500 people in the U.S., with a minimum of 100 IT employees in the U.S. Companies were selected based on average salary and bonus increases, the percentage of IT employees receiving promotions, IT staff turnover rates, training and development, and the percentage of women and minorities in IT staff and management positions. In addition, information was collected on how the organizations reward outstanding performance, how their retention programs are structured and what benefits they offer. *Computerworld, "100 Best Places to Work in IT 2006," June 19, 2006*

Fast-Growing Businesses

According to *Inc.*, Irvine is home to three of America's 500 fastest-growing private companies: **Agile360; HireRight; RealtyTrac**. Criteria: must be an independent, privately-held, U.S. corporation, proprietorship or partnership; net sales of at least $600,000 in FY2002; four-year operating/sales history; holding companies, regulated banks, and utilities were excluded. *Inc., "America's 500 Fastest-Growing Private Companies," September 2006*

Irvine is home to one of *Business Week's* "Hot Growth Companies:" **Quality Systems**. To qualify, a company must have annual sales of more than $50 million and less than $1.5 billion, a current market value greater than $25 million, a current stock price of at least $5, and be actively traded. Banks, insurers, real estate firms, and utilities are excluded. So are companies with declines in current financial results or in stock price, as well as companies where other developments raise questions about future performance. Companies were selected based on three-year results in sales growth, earnings growth, and return on invested capital. *Business Week, June 5, 2006*

According to *Fortune*, Irvine is home to three of America's 100 fastest-growing companies: **Commercial Capital Bancorp; Epicor Software; Quality Systems**. Companies were ranked based on earnings-per-share growth, revenue growth and total return over the previous three years. Criteria for inclusion: public companies with sales of at least $50 million. Companies that lost money in the most recent quarter, or ended in the red for the past four quarters as a whole, were not eligible. Limited partnerships and REITs were also not considered. *Fortune, "America's Fastest-Growing Companies," September 18, 2006*

According to *Business 2.0*, Irvine is home to three of America's 100 fastest-growing technology companies: **Epicor Software; Microsemi; Quality Systems**. The 100 Fastest-Growing Technology Companies (B2 100) is a yearly ranking published by Business 2.0 magazine of businesses whose inventiveness and quick reflexes are helping them to set the pace for the economy. To find the B2 100, Zacks Investment Research of Chicago ranked 2,000 publicly traded companies using a rigorous combination of four financial criteria: growth in revenue, profit, and operating cash flow during the past three years; and the 12-month stock market return as of March 31, 2006. *Business 2.0, "100 Fastest-Growing Tech Companies 2006," June 2006*

According to Deloitte & Touche LLP, Irvine is home to five of North America's 500 fastest-growing high-technology companies: **BIOLASE Technology; HireRight; IntraLase Corp; Masimo Corporation; RealtyTrac**. Companies are ranked by percentage growth in revenue over a five-year period. Criteria for inclusion: company must be headquartered within North America; company must own proprietary intellectual property or proprietary technology that contributes to a significant portion of the company's operating revenue or devotes a significant proportion of revenues to research and development of technology; company must have been in business for a minumum of five years with 2001 operating revenues of at least $50,000 USD or $75,000 CD and 2005 operating revenues of at least $5 million USD/CD. *Deloitte & Touche LLP, 2006 Technology Fast 500*

Women-Owned Businesses: 1997 and 2002

Year	All Firms		Firms with Paid Employees			
	Firms	Sales ($000)	Firms	Sales ($000)	Employees	Payroll ($000)
1997	3,949	1,089,865	844	968,805	4,864	175,860
2002	4,663	1,985,466	(b)	(b)	(b)	(b)

Note: Figures cover firms located in the city; Women-owned business are defined as firms in which women own 51% or more of the stock or equity of the company; (a) Withheld to avoid disclosing data for individual companies; (b) Withheld because estimate did not meet publication standards; n/a not available
Source: 1997 Economic Census, Survey of Minority- and Women-Owned Business Enterprises; 2002 Economic Census, Survey of Business Owners (released February 9, 2006)

Minority Business Opportunity

Two of the 500 largest Hispanic-owned companies in the U.S. are located in Irvine. *Hispanic Business, "Hispanic Business 500," June 2006*

HOTELS

Hotels/Motels

Area	Hotels/Motels	Average Minimum Rates ($)		
		Tourist	First-Class	Deluxe
City	15	n/a	144	n/a

Note: n/a not available
Source: OAG Travel Planner Online, Spring 2006

EVENT SITES

Stadiums, Arenas, and Auditoriums

Name	Capacity
Bren Events Center	5,710

Source: www.officialtravelguide.com; www.eventective.com; original research

Hotels/Conference Centers

Name	Guest Rooms	Exhibit Space (sq. ft.)	Meeting Space (sq. ft.)
Hilton Irvine/Orange County Airport	289	26,000	26,000
Hyatt Regency Irvine	536	30,000	36,000
Irvine Marriott at John Wayne Airport	485	12,960	26,000
Orange County Airport Hilton	n/a	n/a	n/a

Note: n/a not available
Source: www.officialtravelguide.com; www.eventective.com; original research

Living Environment

COST OF LIVING

Cost of Living Index

Year	Composite Index	Groceries	Housing	Utilities	Trans- portation	Health Care	Misc. Goods/ Services
2004	146.0	114.8	229.7	110.7	118.6	110.2	106.0
2005	153.9	125.7	250.0	112.7	115.2	117.0	110.8
2006	155.3	130.9	258.5	106.7	113.3	115.7	112.2

Note: U.S. = 100; Figures are for Orange County
Source: The Council for Community and Economic Research (formerly ACCRA), Cost of Living Index, 2004, 2005 and 2006 4-Quarter Averages

HOUSING

House Price Index (HPI)

Area	National Ranking[2]	Quarterly Change (%)	One-Year Change (%)	Five-Year Change (%)
MD[1]	124	-0.28	5.53	115.47
U.S.[3]	-	1.12	5.87	55.21

Note: The HPI is a weighted repeat sales index. It measures average price changes in repeat sales or refinancings on the same properties. This information is obtained by reviewing repeat mortgage transactions on single-family properties whose mortgages have been purchased or securitized by Fannie Mae or Freddie Mac in January 1975; (1) Metropolitan Division - see Appendix B for areas included; (2) Rankings are based on annual percentage change for all metro areas containing at least 15,000 transactions over the last 10 years and ranges from 1 to 282; (3) figures based on a weighted division average; all figures are for the period ending December 31, 2006
Source: Office of Federal Housing Enterprise Oversight, House Price Index, March 1, 2007

House Price Valuations

Area	Q4 1999	Q4 2000	Q4 2001	Q4 2002	Q4 2003	Q4 2004	Q4 2005	Q4 2006
MSA[1]	-21.3	-19.2	-13.4	-3.6	7.2	22.2	34.3	33.5

Note: Figures show the percentage of over- or under-valuation of single family homes relative to statistically normal house values (e.g. a value of 23.6 indicates that house values are 23.6% overvalued). Statistically normal house values are based on house prices, interest rates, household incomes, population densities, and any historical premiums or discounts metropolitan areas have exhibited over time; (1) Figures cover the Metropolitan Statistical Area - see Appendix B for areas included
Source: Global Insight/National City Corporation, House Prices in America, March 2007

Median Home Prices

Area	2004	2005	2006p	Percent Change 2005 to 2006
Metro Area[1]	627.3	691.9	709.0	2.5
U.S. Average	195.2	219.0	222.0	1.4

Note: Figures are median sales prices of existing single-family homes in thousands of dollars; (p) preliminary; n/a not available; (1) Covers the Santa Ana-Anaheim-Irvine, CA Metropolitan Division - see Appendix B for areas included
Source: National Association of Realtors, Metropolitan Area Prices, 4th Quarter 2006

Housing: Year Structure Built

Area	1990 -2000	1980 -1989	1970 -1979	1960 -1969	1950 -1959	1940 -1949	Before 1940	Median Year
City	26.1	32.4	35.5	4.9	0.6	0.4	0.1	1983
MSA[1]	14.1	17.5	27.6	22.6	12.8	3.0	2.5	1973
U.S.	17.0	15.8	18.5	13.7	12.7	7.3	15.0	1971

Note: Figures are percentages; (1) Metropolitan Statistical Area - see Appendix A for areas included
Source: Census 2000, Summary File 3

Average New Home Price

Area	2004	2005	2006
City[1]	602,884	724,959	809,450
U.S.	253,574	275,712	299,269

Note: Figures, in dollars, are based on a new home with 2,400 sq. ft. of living area on an 8,000 sq. ft. lot;
(1) Orange County
Source: The Council for Community and Economic Research (formerly ACCRA), Cost of Living Index, 2004,
2005 and 2006 4-Quarter Averages

Average Apartment Rent

Area	2004	2005	2006
City[1]	1,353	1,403	1,508
U.S.	716	740	766

Note: Figures, in dollars per month, are based on an unfurnished two bedroom, 1-1/2 or 2 bath apartment,
approximately 950 sq. ft. in size, excluding all utilities except water; (1) Orange County
Source: The Council for Community and Economic Research (formerly ACCRA), Cost of Living Index, 2004,
2005 and 2006 4-Quarter Averages

RESIDENTIAL
UTILITIES

Average Residential Utility Costs

Area	All Electric ($/mth)	Part Electric ($/mth)	Other Energy ($/mth)	Phone ($/mth)
City[1]	–	102.95	65.09	28.11
U.S.	136.00	76.53	90.52	25.87

Note: (1) Orange County
Source: The Council for Community and Economic Research (formerly ACCRA), Cost of Living Index, 2006
4-Quarter Average

HEALTH

Average Health Care Costs

Area	Optometrist ($/visit)	Doctor ($/visit)	Dentist ($/visit)
City[1]	86.49	99.29	79.35
U.S.	76.38	76.10	68.72

Note: Optometrist—based on a full vision eye exam for an established adult patient;
Doctor—based on a general practitioner's routine exam of an established patient;
Dentist—based on adult teeth cleaning and periodic oral exam;
(1) Orange County
Source: The Council for Community and Economic Research (formerly ACCRA), Cost of Living Index, 2006
4-Quarter Average

Mortality Rates

ICD-10 Sub-Chapter	ICD-10 Code	Age-Adjusted Death Rate per 100,000 population[1]	U.S. Age-Adjusted Death Rate per 100,000 population
Malignant neoplasms	C00-C97	149.1	185.8
Ischaemic heart diseases	I20-I25	151.4	150.2
Other forms of heart disease	I30-I51	32.1	50.8
Cerebrovascular diseases	I60-I69	53.4	50.0
Chronic lower respiratory diseases	J40-J47	33.9	41.1
Diabetes mellitus	E10-E14	16.6	24.5
Other degenerative diseases of the nervous system	G30-G31	21.9	22.3
Other external causes of accidental injury	W00-X59	13.3	21.2
Influenza and pneumonia	J10-J18	25.1	19.8
Hypertensive diseases	I10-I13	17.3	18.1

Note: ICD-10 = International Classification of Diseases 10th Revision; (1) Figures cover Orange County, CA
Source: Centers for Disease Control and Prevention, National Center for Health Statistics. Compressed
Mortality File 1999-2004. CDC WONDER On-line Database, compiled from Compressed Mortality File
1999-2004 Series 20 No. 2J, 2007.

Health Risk Data

Item	Area[1] (%)	U.S. (%)
Adults who have been told they have high blood pressure	22.0	25.5
Adults who have been told they have high blood cholesterol	32.7	35.6
Adults who have been told they have diabetes[2]	3.5	7.3
Adults who have been told they have arthritis	21.0	27.0
Adults who have been told they currently have asthma	8.0	8.0
Adults who are current smokers	13.6	20.6

Note: (1) Figures cover the Metropolitan Division - see Appendix B for areas included; (2) Figures do not include pregnancy-related diabetes, pre-diabetes or borderline diabetes
Source: Centers for Disease Control and Prevention, Behaviorial Risk Factor Surveillance System, SMART: Selected Metropolitan/Micropolitan Area Trends, 2005

Distribution of Office-Based Physicians

Area	Total	Family/ General Practice	Specialties		
			Medical	Surgical	Other
CMSA[1] (number)	28,914	3,817	10,675	6,649	7,773
CMSA[1] (rate per 10,000 pop.)	17.1	2.3	6.3	3.9	4.6
Metro Average[2] (rate per 10,000 pop.)	19.4	2.1	7.5	4.5	5.3

Note: Data as of December 31, 2004; (1) Los Angeles-Riverside-Orange, CA Consolidated Metropolitan Statistical Area includes the following counties: Los Angeles; Orange; Riverside; San Bernardino; Ventura; (2) Average of the 79 unique MSAs and CMSAs in this book
Source: American Medical Association, Physician Characteristics & Distribution in the U.S., 2006

Hospitals

Irvine has the following hospitals: 1 general medical and surgical.
AHA Guide to the Healthcare Field 2007

According to *U.S. News*, the Santa Ana metro area is home to one of the best hospitals in the U.S.: **University of California - Irvine Medical Center (Orange)**; *U.S. News Online, "America's Best Hospitals 2006"*

EDUCATION

Public School District Statistics

District Name	Schls	Pupils	Pupil/ Teacher Ratio	Minority Pupils[1] (%)	Free Lunch Eligible[2] (%)	IEP[3] (%)
Irvine Unified	33	25,158	22.6	53.9	4.8	9.0

Note: Table includes regular local school districts with 2,000 or more students; (1) Percentage of students that are not white, non-Hispanic; (2) Percentage of students that are eligible for the free lunch program; (3) Percentage of students that have an Individualized Education Program.
Source: U.S. Department of Education, National Center for Education Statistics, Common Core of Data, Local Education Agency (School District) Universe Survey: School Year 2004-2005; U.S. Department of Education, National Center for Education Statistics, Common Core of Data, Public Elementary/Secondary School Universe Survey: School Year 2004-2005

Top Public High Schools

High School Name	Index[1]	Rank[1]	Subsidized Lunch (%)[2]	E&E (%)[3]
Irvine	1.180	1,044	n/a	n/a
Northwood	2.190	296	2.4	55.8
University	2.748	156	6.0	60.8
Woodbridge	1.066	1,156	5.3	28.0

Note: (1) Public schools are ranked according to a ratio that is the number of Advanced Placement and/or International Baccalaureate tests taken by all students at a school in 2005 divided by the number of graduating seniors. All of the schools on the list have an index of at least 1.000; they are in the top five percent of public schools measured this way. The rankings range from 1 to 1,236; (2) Percentage of students receiving federally subsidized meals; (3) E & E stands for equity and excellence percentage: the portion of all graduating seniors at a school that had at least one passing grade on one AP or IB test; (*) Gave just IB tests; (**) Gave both IB and AP tests. AP and IB participation are indicators of a school's efforts to get students to excel and prepare for college; n/a not available
Source: Newsweek Online, May 23, 2006

Educational Quality

School District	Education Quotient[1]	Graduate Outcome[2]	Community Index[3]	Resource Index[4]	Rating[5]
Irvine Unified	90	96	91	32	Gold

Note: Scores are national percentile rankings and range from 1 (worst) to 99 (best); (1) Combination of the Graduate Outcome, Community and Resource Indexes weighted to reflect the greater importance of the Graduate Outcome and Resource Index; (2) Based on graduation rates and college board scores (SAT/ACT); (3) Based on the surrounding community's level of affluence and adult education; (4) Based on teacher salaries, per-pupil expenditures and student-teacher ratios; (5) School districts receive one of five rankings: Gold Medal (top 16 percent of districts evaluated); Blue Ribbon (top third); Green Light (average); Yellow Light (bottom 25 percent); Red Light (bottom 10 percent).
Source: Expansion Management, "2007 Education Quotient," January 2007

Highest Level of Education

Area	Less than H.S.	H.S. Diploma	Some College, No Deg.	Associate Degree	Bachelors Degree	Masters Degree	Profess. School Degree	Doctorate Degree
City	4.6	10.2	18.1	8.2	34.4	15.7	4.8	4.1
MSA[1]	28.2	18.5	20.6	6.6	17.0	5.6	2.4	1.0
U.S.	19.4	28.4	21.2	6.4	15.7	5.9	2.0	1.0

Note: Figures are 2006 estimated percentages and cover persons age 25 and over; (1) Metropolitan Statistical Area - see Appendix B for areas included
Source: Claritas, Inc.

Educational Attainment by Race

Area	High School Graduate (%)					Bachelor's Degree (%)				
	Total	White	Black	Asian	Hisp.[2]	Total	White	Black	Asian	Hisp.[2]
City	95.3	96.3	96.3	94.5	86.6	58.4	57.0	35.7	67.2	38.6
MSA[1]	79.5	86.0	88.1	81.2	45.1	30.8	33.4	27.6	41.4	8.5
U.S.	80.4	83.6	72.3	80.4	52.4	24.4	26.1	14.3	44.1	10.4

Note: Figures shown cover persons 25 years old and over; (1) Metropolitan Statistical Area - see Appendix A for areas included; (2) people of Hispanic origin can be of any race
Source: Census 2000, Summary File 3

School Enrollment by Type

Area	Grades KG to 8				Grades 9 to 12			
	Public		Private		Public		Private	
	Enrollment	%	Enrollment	%	Enrollment	%	Enrollment	%
City	16,380	91.9	1,441	8.1	7,620	95.7	345	4.3
MSA[1]	358,527	88.6	45,927	11.4	154,346	93.5	10,681	6.5
U.S.	33,526,011	88.7	4,285,121	11.3	14,848,628	90.6	1,532,323	9.4

Note: Figures shown cover persons 3 years old and over; (1) Metropolitan Statistical Area - see Appendix A for areas included
Source: Census 2000, Summary File 3

School Enrollment by Race

Area	Grades KG to 8 (%)				Grades 9 to 12 (%)			
	White	Black	Asian	Hisp.[1]	White	Black	Asian	Hisp.[1]
City	60.3	1.4	27.3	8.6	60.0	1.3	27.9	9.1
MSA[2]	58.6	1.6	11.8	42.5	56.2	1.9	14.8	38.8
U.S.	68.5	15.5	3.3	16.8	68.8	15.5	3.8	15.7

Note: Figures shown cover persons 3 years old and over; (1) people of Hispanic origin can be of any race; (2) Metropolitan Statistical Area - see Appendix A for areas included
Source: Census 2000, Summary File 3

Average Salaries of Public School Teachers

District	2004-05		2005-06		Percent Change 2004-05 to 2005-06
	Dollars	Rank[1]	Dollars	Rank[1]	
CALIFORNIA	57,876	2	59,345	3	2.54
U.S. Average	47,674	-	49,109	-	3.01

Note: (1) State rank ranges from 1 to 51.
Source: National Education Association, Rankings & Estimates: Rankings of the States 2005 and Estimates of School Statistics 2006, November 2006

Higher Education

Four-Year Colleges			Two-Year Colleges			Medical Schools[1]	Law Schools[2]	Voc/Tech[3]
Public	Private Non-profit	Private For-profit	Public	Private Non-profit	Private For-profit			
1	1	0	1	0	1	1	0	1

Note: Figures cover institutions located within the city limits; (1) includes schools accredited by the Liaison Committee on Medical Education and the American Osteopathic Association; (2) includes American Bar Association-accredited law schools; (3) includes all schools with programs that are less than 2 years
Source: National Center for Education Statistics, The Integrated Postsecondary Education System (IPEDS) Peer Analysis System, 2006; www.usnews.com, America's Best Graduate Schools 2008, Medical School Directory; www.usnews.com, America's Best Graduate Schools 2008, Law School Directory

PRESIDENTIAL ELECTION

2004 Presidential Election Results

Area	Bush	Kerry	Nader	Other
Orange County	59.7	39.0	0.2	1.1
U.S.	50.7	48.3	0.4	0.6

Note: Results are percentages and may not add to 100% due to rounding
Source: Dave Leip's Atlas of U.S. Presidential Elections, www.uselectionatlas.org

MAJOR EMPLOYERS

Major Employers

Company Name	Industry	Type of Site
Disney	Motion picture and video production	Headquarters
Experian	Credit reporting services	Headquarters
Fluor Corp	Engineering services	Headquarters
HMF Corp	Fabricated structural metal	Single
Ingram Micro Inc	Computers, peripherals, and software	Headquarters
Irvine Medical Center	Telephone communication, except radio	Branch
Marine Corps Air Station El Toro	National security	Branch
Mercury Insurance	Fire, marine, and casualty insurance	Single
Saint Joseph Hospital	General medical and surgical hospitals	Headquarters
St John Boutiques	Women's, junior's, and misses' dresses	Branch
St Jude Medical Center	General medical and surgical hospitals	Headquarters
St Jude Medical Ctr Purch Dept	Medical and hospital equipment	Branch
UCI Medical Center	General medical and surgical hospitals	Branch

Note: Companies shown are located within the metropolitan area and have 2,500 or more employees; nec = not elsewhere classified.
Source: www.zapdata.com, January 2007

PUBLIC SAFETY

Crime Rate

Area	All Crimes	Violent Crimes				Property Crimes		
		Murder	Forcible Rape	Robbery	Aggrav. Assault	Burglary	Larceny -Theft	Motor Vehicle Theft
City	1,880.8	1.1	9.5	23.4	50.1	395.0	1,231.7	169.9
Suburbs[1]	2,728.5	2.6	14.9	95.8	183.0	448.8	1,531.7	451.6
Metro[2]	2,677.9	2.5	14.6	91.5	175.0	445.6	1,513.8	434.8
U.S.	3,899.0	5.6	31.7	140.7	291.1	726.7	2,286.3	416.7

Note: Figures are crimes per 100,000 population; (1) All areas within the metro area that are located outside the city limits; (2) Metropolitan Division - see Appendix B for areas included
Source: FBI Uniform Crime Reports, 2005

Hate Crimes

Area	Number of Quarters Reported	Bias Motivation				
		Race	Religion	Sexual Orientation	Ethnicity	Disability
City	4	2	0	0	0	0

Source: Federal Bureau of Investigation, Hate Crime Statistics 2005

RECREATION

Culture

Dance[1]	Theatre[1]	Instrumental Music[1]	Vocal Music[1]	Series/ Festivals	Museums	Zoos
1	1	1	0	2	3	0

Note: (1) number of professional perfoming groups
Source: The Grey House Performing Arts Directory, 2007; Official Museum Directory, 2007

Professional Sports Teams

Major League Baseball	National Basketball Association	National Football League	National Hockey League	Major League Soccer	Women's National Basketball Association
2	2	0	2	2	1

Note: Includes teams located in the Los Angeles-Anaheim metro area.
Source: www.sportsvenues.com, Listing of Venues by State/Province and City, 2006

MEDIA

Newspapers

Name	Target Audience	Frequency	Circulation
The Irvine World News	General	Non-Daily	49,700

Note: Includes newspapers whose offices are located in the city and whose circulations are 500 or more
Source: BurrellesLuce, MediaContacts Online, January 2006

Television Stations

Name	Ch.	Network(s)	Type	Ownership
KCBS	2	CBS	Commercial	CBS
KNBC	4	NBC	Commercial	General Electric Corporation
KTLA	5	WBN	Commercial	Tribune Broadcasting Company
KABC	7	ABC	Commercial	ABC Inc.
KCAL	9	CBS	Commercial	Viacom International Inc.
KTTV	11	Fox	Commercial	Fox Television Stations Inc.
KCOP	13	UPN	Commercial	Fox Television Stations Inc.
KSCI	18	n/a	Commercial	International Media Group
KWHY	22	Telemundo	Commercial	Telemundo Group Inc.
KVCR	24	PBS	Public	San Bernardino Community College District
KCET	28	PBS	Public	Community Television of Southern California
KPXN	30	Pax	Commercial	Paxson Communications Corporation
KVMD	31	APT	Commercial	n/a
KNET	38	n/a	Commercial	Venture Technology Group LLC.
KFTR	46	n/a	Commercial	Univision Communications Inc.
KOCE	50	PBS	Public	Coast Community College District
KVEA	52	Telemundo	Commercial	Telemundo Group Inc.
KDOC	56	n/a	Commercial	Golden Orange Broadcasting Company Inc.
KJLA	57	n/a	Commercial	Costa de Oro Television
KLCS	58	PBS	Public	Los Angeles Unified School District
KRCA	62	n/a	Commercial	Liberman Broadcasting
KADY	63	UPN	Commercial	Biltmore Broadcasting
KHIZ	64	n/a	Commercial	Sunbelt Broadcasting Company
KNLA	68	UPN	Non-comm.	Venture Technology Group LLC.

Note: Stations included cover the Los Angeles DMA (Designated Market Area)
BurrellesLuce, MediaContacts Online, January 2006

Major AM Radio Stations

Call Letters	Freq. (kHz)	Station Type	Target Audience	Station Format	Music Format
KLAC	570	Commercial	General	Sports/Talk	n/a
KAVL	610	Commercial	General	News/Sports/Talk	n/a
KFI	640	n/a	General	Music/News/Talk	n/a
KIRN	670	Commercial	Ethnic	Music/News/Talk	International
KDIS	710	Commercial	Children	Music/News	Top 40
KBRT	740	n/a	General/Religious	Talk	n/a
KABC	790	n/a	General	Music/News/Talk	n/a
KRLA	870	n/a	General	Talk	n/a
KOXR	910	n/a	Hispanic	News/Sports/Talk	n/a
KKHJ	930	Commercial	General/Hispanic	Music	Latin
KIXW	960	n/a	Hispanic	Talk	n/a
KFWB	980	Commercial	General	News/Sports	n/a
KTNQ	1020	n/a	Hispanic	News/Sports	n/a
KNX	1070	Commercial	General	News/Sports	n/a
KSPN	1110	Public	General	Music/Sports	Classical
KXTA	1150	Commercial	General	Sports/Talk	n/a
KXMX	1190	n/a	Hispanic	Music/Talk	n/a
KSUR	1260	n/a	General	Music	n/a
KKDD	1290	Commercial	Children	Educational/Music	Easy Listening
KAZN	1300	Commercial	Asian	Ed/Music/News/Sports/Talk	Easy Listening
KWKW	1330	n/a	Hispanic	Sports/Talk	n/a
KWRM	1370	Commercial	Hispanic	Ed/Music/News/Sports	Latin
KLTX	1390	Commercial	Christian/Gen/Hisp	Music/Talk	Latin
KCAL	1410	n/a	General/Hispanic	Music	n/a
KTYM	1460	Commercial	Black/General/Rel	Music/Talk	Gospel
KUTY	1470	Commercial	General/Hispanic	Music/News/Sports	Latin
KWIZ	1480	n/a	Asian	Music/News/Talk	n/a
KMZT	1510	n/a	General	Music	n/a
KVTA	1520	n/a	Hispanic	n/a	n/a
KHPY	1530	Commercial	General	Music	Oldies
KMPC	1540	Commercial	General/Men	Sports/Talk	n/a
KPRO	1570	Commercial	General/Religious	Music/Talk	Gospel
KMNY	1600	Commercial	Asian	Educational/News/Talk	n/a

Note: Stations included cover the Los Angeles DMA (Designated Market Area); n/a not available
Source: BurrellesLuce, MediaContacts Online, January 2006

Major FM Radio Stations

Call Letters	Freq. (mHz)	Station Type	Target Audience	Station Format	Music Format
KPFK	90.7	Non-Comm	General/Hispanic	Educational/Music	World Music
KCBS	93.1	Commercial	General	Music/News/Talk	Classic Rock
KFRG	95.1	n/a	General	Music/News/Talk	n/a
KLOS	95.5	n/a	General	Music/News/Talk	n/a
KXOL	96.3	n/a	General/Hispanic	n/a	n/a
KLSX	97.1	Commercial	General	Music/Sports/Talk	Classical
KSSE	97.5	Commercial	General/Hispanic	Music	Top 40
KLAX	97.9	n/a	General/Hispanic	Music/News/Talk	n/a
KYSR	98.7	n/a	General	Music/Talk	n/a
KKBT	100.3	Commercial	Black	Music/News/Talk	Urban Contemp.
KRTH	101.1	n/a	General	Music/News	n/a
KBIG	104.3	Commercial	General	Music	Adult Contemp.
KCAQ	104.7	n/a	General	Music	n/a
KPWR	105.9	n/a	General	Music/News/Talk	n/a

Note: Stations included cover the Los Angeles DMA (Designated Market Area); n/a not available
BurrellesLuce, MediaContacts Online, January 2006

CLIMATE

Average and Extreme Temperatures

Temperature	Jan	Feb	Mar	Apr	May	Jun	Jul	Aug	Sep	Oct	Nov	Dec	Yr.
Extreme High (°F)	89	91	97	108	102	107	112	104	112	105	95	93	112
Average High (°F)	68	69	69	72	73	77	82	83	83	79	73	68	75
Average Temp. (°F)	56	58	58	61	64	68	72	74	72	67	61	56	64
Average Low (°F)	44	46	48	50	55	59	62	64	61	56	48	43	53
Extreme Low (°F)	28	29	31	34	38	42	45	48	44	30	32	25	25

Note: Figures cover the years 1945-1995
Source: National Climatic Data Center, International Station Meteorological Climate Summary, 9/96

Average Precipitation/Snowfall/Humidity

Precip./Humidity	Jan	Feb	Mar	Apr	May	Jun	Jul	Aug	Sep	Oct	Nov	Dec	Yr.
Avg. Precip. (in.)	2.7	2.4	2.2	0.8	0.2	0.1	Tr	0.1	0.4	0.3	1.3	1.5	11.9
Avg. Snowfall (in.)	0	0	0	0	0	0	0	0	0	0	0	Tr	Tr
Avg. Rel. Hum. 7am (%)	78	81	82	79	77	79	80	81	81	80	79	79	80
Avg. Rel. Hum. 4pm (%)	56	57	57	55	58	59	57	57	56	57	56	57	57

Note: Figures cover the years 1945-1995; Tr = Trace amounts (<0.05 in. of rain; <0.5 in. of snow)
Source: National Climatic Data Center, International Station Meteorological Climate Summary, 9/96

Weather Conditions

Temperature			Daytime Sky			Precipitation		
10°F & below	32°F & below	90°F & above	Clear	Partly cloudy	Cloudy	0.01 inch or more precip.	0.1 inch or more snow/ice	Thunder-storms
0	2	18	95	192	78	41	0	4

Note: Figures are average number of days per year and cover the years 1945-1995
Source: National Climatic Data Center, International Station Meteorological Climate Summary, 9/96

HAZARDOUS WASTE

Superfund Sites

Irvine has no sites on the EPA's Superfund Final National Priorities List.
U.S. Environmental Protection Agency, Final National Priorities List, March 20, 2007

AIR & WATER QUALITY

Air Quality Index

Area	Percent of Days when Air Quality was...[2]				AQI Statistics	
	Good	Moderate	Unhealthy for Sensitive Groups	Unhealthy	Maximum	Median
MSA[1]	66.0	31.5	2.5	0.0	129	44

Note: The Air Quality Index (AQI) is an index for reporting daily air quality. EPA calculates the AQI for five major air pollutants regulated by the Clean Air Act: ground-level ozone, particle pollution (also known as particulate matter), carbon monoxide, sulfur dioxide, and nitrogen dioxide. The AQI runs from 0 to 500. The higher the AQI value, the greater the level of air pollution and the greater the health concern. There are six AQI categories: "Good" The AQI is between 0 and 50. Air quality is considered satisfactory; "Moderate" The AQI is between 51 and 100. Air quality is acceptable; "Unhealthy for Sensitive Groups" When AQI values are between 101 and 150, members of sensitive groups may experience health effects; "Unhealthy" When AQI values are between 151 and 200 everyone may begin to experience health effects; "Very Unhealthy" AQI values between 201 and 300 trigger a health alert; "Hazardous" AQI values over 300 trigger health warnings of emergency conditions; (1) Metropolitan Statistical Area - see Appendix A for areas included; (2) Based on 365 days with AQI data in 2005.
Source: U.S. Environmental Protection Agency, Air Quality Index Report, 2005

Air Quality Index Pollutants

Area	Percent of Days when AQI Pollutant was...[2]					
	Carbon Monoxide	Nitrogen Dioxide	Ozone	Sulfur Dioxide	Particulate Matter 2.5	Particulate Matter 10
MSA[1]	1.9	0.0	49.3	0.0	48.5	0.3

Note: The Air Quality Index (AQI) is an index for reporting daily air quality. EPA calculates the AQI for five major air pollutants regulated by the Clean Air Act: ground-level ozone, particle pollution (also known as particulate matter), carbon monoxide, sulfur dioxide, and nitrogen dioxide. The AQI runs from 0 to 500. The higher the AQI value, the greater the level of air pollution and the greater the health concern; (1) Metropolitan Statistical Area - see Appendix A for areas included; (2) Based on 365 days with AQI data in 2005.
Source: U.S. Environmental Protection Agency, Air Quality Index Report, 2005

Number of Days with Air Quality Index Values Greater than 100

Area	Trend Sites (8)								All Sites (30)
	1998	1999	2000	2001	2002	2003	2004	2005	2005
MSA[1]	5	4	5	6	4	5	3	0	9

Note: An AQI value greater than 100 indicates that air quality would have been in the unhealthful range on that day. Data from exceptional events are not included. These counts are presented in two ways. First, the counts are based on sites having an adequate record of monitoring data during the trend period (trend sites). These counts represent the relative change in the number of days with AQI values greater than 100. In the last column, the counts are based on all sites with data in the most recent year (because it is possible for a site to have data in the most recent year but not enough data to be a trend site); (1) Metropolitan Statistical Area - see Appendix A for areas included; n/a not available.
Source: U.S. Environmental Protection Agency, Air Trends Fact Book 2005

Maximum Pollutant Concentrations

	Particulate Matter 10 (ug/m^3)	Particulate Matter 2.5 (ug/m^3)	Ozone 1-hour (ppm)	Carbon Monoxide (ppm)	Sulfur Dioxide (ppm)	Nitrogen Dioxide (ppm)	Lead (ug/m^3)
MSA[1] Level	54	42	0.107	3	0.007	0.025	n/a
NAAQS[2]	150	65	0.125	9	0.140	0.053	1.50
Met NAAQS[2]	Yes	Yes	Yes	Yes	Yes	Yes	n/a

Note: Data from exceptional events are not included; (1) Metropolitan Statistical Area - see Appendix A for areas included; (2) National Ambient Air Quality Standards; n/a not available
Units: ppm = parts per million; ug/m^3 = micrograms per cubic meter
Source: U.S. Environmental Protection Agency, Air Trends Fact Book 2005

Watershed Health

The U.S. Environmental Protection Agency monitors the health of the aquatic resources for the nation's 2,000+ watersheds. **The Newport Bay watershed serves the Irvine area and received an overall Index of Watershed Indicators (IWI) score of 5 (more serious problems - low vulnerability)**. The IWI score is based on seven condition and nine vulnerability indicators. The overall IWI score ranges from 1 (best health) to 6 (worst health). The Condition Indicators include: designated use attainment, fish and wildlife consumption advisories, source water condition, contaminated sediments, ambient water quality, and wetlands loss index. The Vulnerability Indicators include: aquatic species at risk, conventional and toxic loads over permitted limits, urban and agricultural runoff potential, population change, hydrologic modification, estuarine pollution susceptibility, and air deposition. *Note: The IWI is no longer being updated by the U.S. EPA. Source: U.S. Environmental Protection Agency, Index of Watershed Indicators, October 26, 2001*

Drinking Water

Water System Name	Pop. Served	Primary Water Source Type	Number of Violations in 2006[a]		
			Health Based	Significant Monitoring	Monitoring
Irvine Ranch Water District	316,000	Purchased surface	None	None	None

Note: (a) Based on violation data from January 1, 2006 to December 31, 2006
Source: U.S. Environmental Protection Agency, Office of Ground Water and Drinking Water, Safe Drinking Water Information System (data extracted April 12, 2007)

Irvine tap water is not available.
Editor & Publisher Market Guide, 2005

Las Vegas, Nevada

Background

Upright citizens can accuse Las Vegas of many vices, but not of hypocrisy. Back in 1931, the city officials of this desert town, located 225 miles northeast of Los Angeles, saw gambling to be a growing popular pastime. To capitalize upon that trend, the city simply legalized it. Gambling, combined with spectacular, neon-lit entertainment, lures more than 28 million visitors a year to it's more than 1,700 casinos and 125,000 hotel rooms.

Before Wayne Newton ever saw his name in lights or Siegfried and Roy made white tigers disappear, Las Vegas was a temporary stopping place for a diverse group of people. In the early 1880s, Las Vegas was a watering hole for those on the trail to California. Areas of the Las Vegas Valley contained artesian wells that supported extensive green meadows, or vega in Spanish, hence the name Las Vegas. In 1855 the area was settled by Mormon missionaries, but they left two years later. Finally, in the late 1800s, the land was used for ranching.

In the beginning of the twentieth century, the seeds of the present Las Vegas began to sprout. In 1905 the arrival of the Union Pacific Railroad sprinkled businesses, saloons, and gambling houses along it tracks; the city was formally founded on May 15, 1905. Then, during the Great Depression, men working on the nearby Hoover Dam spent their extra money in the establishments. Finally, gambling was legalized, hydroelectric power from the Hoover Dam lit the city in neon, and hotels began to complete for the brightest stars and the plushest surroundings. Las Vegas was an overnight success, much like the dreams of many people who come to the city and hope to get rich quick. The dream has thus far endured, and in 2005 the city celebrated its centennial with a suitably festive media blitz, many special events, and the world's largest birthday cake-130,000 pounds.

Las Vegas is home to the World Series of Poker, which began in Texas in 1969. The most recent champion, Jamie Gold, pocketed $12 million.

For the past 25 years, senior citizens have constituted the fastest-growing segment of the Las Vegas population, as people over 60 years arrive to take advantage of the dry climate, reasonably priced housing, low property taxes, no sales tax, and plenty of entertainment. Today, the state leads the nation in growth of its senior citizen population, and this is expected to continue. Many programs exist to ensure their comfort and welfare, including quality economic, legal, and medical plans.

In 2005 the World Market Center opened. It is intended to be the nation's preeminent furniture wholesale showroom and marketplace, and is meant to compete with the current furniture market capital of High Point, North Carolina. In recent years, four megahotels and many smaller projects have been completed. At least $6 billion has been spent in hotel and casino construction. At the highest point of this activity, some 3,000 people moved to the city each month, most of them in construction and casino-related work. The recently completed $3.7 million Durango Drive Improvement project has helped to ease traffic congestion. The project included new ramps, a trails system underpass, new auxiliary lanes, and a new traffic signal system.

One of the more serious problems facing Las Vegas, because of its remarkable population growth, is the city's diminishing water supply. Las Vegas uses approximately 325 gallons daily per person, more than any city in the world. The city has raised water rates and encourages conservation by homeowners and businesses through desert landscaping, which can reduce water use by as much as 80 percent.

Las Vegas is located near the center of a broad desert valley, which is almost surrounded by mountains ranging from 2,000 to 10,000 feet. The four seasons are well defined. Summers display desert conditions with extreme high temperatures, but nights are relatively cool due to the closeness of the mountains. For about two weeks almost every summer, warm, moist air predominates, causing higher-than-average humidity and scattered, sever thunderstorms. Winters are generally mild and pleasant with clear skies prevailing. Strong winds, associated with major storms, usually reach the valley from the southwest or through the pass from the northwest. Winds over 50 miles per hour are infrequent but, when they do occur, are the most troublesome of the elements because of the dust and sand they stir up.

Rankings

General Rankings

■ Las Vegas was ranked #129 out of 331 metro areas in *Cities Ranked & Rated*. Criteria: cost of living; climate; crime; transportation; economy and jobs; education; arts and culture; health and healthcare; leisure. *Cities Ranked & Rated, 1st Edition, 2004*

■ Las Vegas was selected as one of the top places to live in the U.S. according to Harris Interactive. The city ranked #5 out of 10. Criteria: 3,685 U.S. adults were polled as to where they would choose to live if they could live anywhere in the country. *Harris Interactive, September 6, 2006*

■ Las Vegas was selected as one of the "50 Best Places to Live" by *Men's Journal*. The city ranked #1 in the "Sunniest Places" category. Criteria: number of mostly sunny days per year. *Men's Journal, April 2007*

■ The Las Vegas area was selected as one of "60 Cheap Places to Live" in the U.S. The area appeared in the "Steroid Cities" (fast-growing, business-friendly metro areas) category. *Forbes.com, August 20, 2004*

■ The U.S. Conference of Mayors and Waste Management sponsors the City Livability Awards Program. The awards recognize and honor mayors for exemplary leadership in developing and implementing programs that improve the quality of life in America's cities. Las Vegas received an Honorable Mention Citation in the large cities category. *U.S Conference of Mayors, "2006 City Livability Awards"*

Business/Finance Rankings

■ Las Vegas was selected as one of the best places to start and grow a company by *Entrepreneur* and the National Policy Research Council. The Las Vegas metro area ranked #4 out of 50 large metro areas. Criteria: business formation and growth (firms started four to 14 years ago that still employ at least 5 people and experienced rapid growth over the last four years). *Entrepreneur/National Policy Research Council, "Hot Cities for Entrepreneurs," September 2006*

■ Intel, in partnership with Sperling's BestPlaces, ranked the 80 "Best Cities for Teleworking" in America. The Las Vegas metro area ranked #20 among large metro areas. The study identifies cities that hold the greatest potential for teleworking based on a host of factors including typical commuting times, fuel prices, availability of broadband Internet access and percentage of the population in telework friendly jobs. The study also factored in extreme climate and natural hazards. *Intel, "Best Cities for Teleworking," March 30, 2006*

■ The Las Vegas metro area appeared on the Milken Institute "2005 Best Performing Cities" index. Rank: #11 out of 200 large metro areas. Criteria: job growth; wage and salary growth; high-tech output growth. *Milken Institute, "2005 Best Performing Cities," February 2006*

■ The Las Vegas metro area was selected as one of "The Best Cities for Doing Business in America." *Inc.* magazine measured employment growth in 393 regions using the following criteria: recent growth trend; mid-term growth; long-term trend; and current year growth. The Las Vegas metro area ranked #1 among large metro areas and #9 overall. *Inc., May 2006*

■ Las Vegas was identified as one of the 100 "Most Unwired Cities" in the U.S. The area ranked #42 out of the 100 largest metro areas in the U.S. Criteria: number of public and commercial wireless access points (hotspots); airports with wireless Internet access; broadband availability; local wireless networks; and wireless email devices. *Intel, "Most Unwired Cities Survey," June 7, 2005*

■ Las Vegas was ranked #68 out of 125 regions worldwide in terms of its "Knowledge Competitiveness Index." The index attempts to measure the knowledge-based development taking place throughout the world and is based on 19 measures of economic performance that indicate a region's ability to translate its knowledge capacity into economic value. *Robert Huggins Associates, World Knowledge Competitiveness Index 2005*

- *Forbes* ranked the 200 most populous metro areas in the U.S. in terms of the "Best Places for Business and Careers." The Las Vegas metro area was ranked #136. Criteria: business costs (labor, energy, tax and office space expenses); living costs (housing, transportation, food and other household expenditures); education levels of the work force; job growth; income growth; migration trends; crime rates; and culture/leisure. *Forbes, April 23, 2007*

- *Kiplinger's Personal Finance* ranked 101 U.S. cities in terms of their total tax burdens. Las Vegas ranked #10 (#1 had the lowest overall tax burden). Criteria: state income tax; property tax; sales tax; personal property tax; and gasoline tax. *Kiplinger's Personal Finance, July 2004*

- *Fortune* ranked the 100 largest metro areas in the U.S. in terms of projected median home price change in 2006. The Las Vegas metro area ranked #100. *Fortune, "The Top 100: Is the Party Over?" December 26, 2005*

Health/Environment Rankings

- *Reader's Digest* ranked the 50 largest metro areas in the U.S. in terms of how "clean" they are. The Las Vegas metro area ranked #13. Criteria: air quality; water quality; toxic industrial pollution; Superfund sites; and sanitation. *Reader's Digest, "The 50 Cleanest (and Dirtiest) Cities in America," July 2005*

- Sanofi-aventis, in partnership with Sperling's BestPlaces, ranked the 50 worst cities for respiratory infections in the U.S. Las Vegas ranked #23. Criteria: prevalence of sinusitis, pharyngitis (sore throat), bronchitis, acute upper respiratory infections, pneumonia, otitis media (middle ear infection), other respiratory tract infections and the common cold; total per capita prescriptions written for oral antibiotics for respiratory tract infections; and prevalence of state level antibiotic resistance. *Sanofi-aventis, "America's Worst Cities for Respiratory Infections," December 6, 2005*

- The Las Vegas metro area appeared in *Country Home's* "2007 Best Green Places Report". The area ranked #125. Criteria included: air and watershed quality; miles of mass transit; green power; number of farmer's markets, organic producers and groceries. *Country Home, "2007 Best Green Places Report," April 2007*

- Wyeth Consumer Healthcare, in partnership with Sperling's BestPlaces, ranked the nation's 50 most populous metro areas in terms of five key health factors. The Las Vegas metro area ranked #42. Criteria: physical activity, health status, nutrition, lifestyle pursuits; and mental wellness. *Wyeth Consumer Healthcare, "Centrum Healthiest Cities Study," April 19, 2005*

- The American Podiatric Medical Association and *Prevention* magazine ranked America's 100 most populated cities based on fitness-walker friendliness. The best cities have safe streets, beautiful places to walk, mild weather and good air quality. Las Vegas ranked #15. *Prevention, "The Best Walking Cities of 2007," April 2007; American Podiatric Medical Association, "2007 Best Fitness-Walking Cities"*

- Las Vegas was selected as one of the 25 fattest cities in America by *Men's Fitness Online*. It ranked #2 out of America's 50 largest cities. Criteria: gyms/sporting goods; nutrition; exercise/sports; overweight/sedentary; junk food; alcohol; smoking; television; air and water quality; climate; geography; commute time; parks/open space; recreation facilities; health care; motivation; civic legislation and leadership. *Men's Fitness Online, America's Fittest/Fattest Cities 2006*

- Las Vegas was identified as a "2007 Asthma Capital." The area ranked #49 out of the nation's 100 largest metropolitan areas. Twelve factors were used to identify the most challenging places to live for people with asthma: estimated prevalence; self-reported prevalence; crude death rate for asthma; annual pollen score; annual air quality; public smoking laws; number of board-certified asthma specialists; school inhaler access laws; rescue medication use; controller medication use; uninsured rate; poverty rate. *Asthma and Allergy Foundation of America, "2007 Asthma Capitals"*

- Las Vegas was identified as a "Spring Allergy Capital." The area ranked #19 out of 100. Three groups of factors were used to identify the most severe cities for people with allergies during the spring season: annual pollen levels; medicine utilization; access to board-certified allergists. *Asthma and Allergy Foundation of America, "2007 Spring Allergy Capital Rankings"*

- Las Vegas was identified as a "Fall Allergy Capital." The area ranked #25 out of 100. Three groups of factors were used to identify the most severe cities for people with allergies during the fall season: annual pollen levels; medicine utilization; access to board-certified allergists. *Asthma and Allergy Foundation of America, "2006 Fall Allergy Capital Rankings"*

- Las Vegas was selected as one of "America's Healthiest Cities" by *Natural Health* magazine. The city was ranked #20 out of the 50 largest urban areas in the U.S. Twenty-six criteria in the following four categories were examined: whether the city boasts natural offerings; how well the city promotes its residents' physical health; whether the city offers a healthy environment; how well the city fosters a sense of community. *Natural Health, April 2003*

- *Men's Health* ranked the nation's largest 100 cities in terms of the *Best (and Worst) Cities for Men*. Las Vegas was ranked #33. Criteria: 24 statistical parameters of long life in the categories of health, quality of life, and fitness. *Men's Health, January/February 2007*

- *Men's Health* ranked 100 U.S. cities in terms of the quality of their tap water. Las Vegas was ranked #77 and received a grade of C. Criteria: levels of total coliform bacteria, arsenic, lead, total trihalomethanes (linked to cancer), and halo-acetic acids, plus the number of EPA water-system violations from 1995 to 2005. *Men's Health, March 2007*

- Ortho-McNeil Neurologics, in partnership with Sperling's BestPlaces, analyzed 110 metro areas and identified those U.S. cities with the highest prevalence of factors that are most commonly associated with migraine headaches. The Las Vegas metro area ranked #77. Criteria: number of migraine-related drug prescriptions per capita; lifestyle factors that can contribute to migraines; environmental factors that can trigger migraines; and consumption of migraine-triggering foods. *Ortho-McNeil Neurologics, "America's Migraine Hot Spots," March 14, 2006*

- Sperling's BestPlaces ranked 331 metro areas and identified the most and least stressful U.S. cities. The Las Vegas metro area ranked #4 out of the 100 largest metro areas (#1 = most stressful). Criteria: divorce rate; unemployment rate; violent and property crime; suicide rate; commute time; mental health; alcohol consumption; cloudy days. *www.BestPlaces.net, January 9, 2004*

- Sperling's BestPlaces "Sleep in the City" study ranked America's 50 most populated metropolitan areas in getting a good night's sleep. The Las Vegas metro area ranked #7 in terms of the "Worst Cities for Sleep". Criteria: happiness index (derived from the responses to eight questions on the CDC BRFSS); number of days residents didn't get enough rest or sleep during the past month; average length of daily commute; divorce rates; unemployment rates. *www.BestPlaces.net, October 18, 2004*

- Sperling's BestPlaces in partnership with Vistakon ranked the 100 largest metro areas and identified "America's 10 Worst Cities for Comfortable Eyes." The Las Vegas metro area ranked #5. Criteria: altitude; sunny days; wind; extreme temperatures; humidity; pollution; commute time; computer use. *Vistakon, "America's Best and Worst Cities for Comfortable Eyes," June 15, 2004*

- Las Vegas was selected as one of "America's Top 10 Low-Carb Cities" by *LowCarbiz Magazine*. Criteria: abundance of low-carb products; restaurants with low-carb menu items; health practitioners supportive of carb-cutting regimens; local culture generally conducive to exercise and health. *LowCarbiz Magazine, April 2004*

- Las Vegas was selected as one of "America's Pet Healthiest Cities" by Purina. The city ranked #18 out of 50. Criteria: veterinary services; environment; legislation; preventative care; obesity/body condition. *Purina Pet Institute, "America's Pet Healthiest Cities," May 20, 2003*

■ According to research conducted by Malibu Wellness of 100 major U.S. cities' local water quality reports, Las Vegas was selected as one of 10 color-unfriendly cities in terms of hair color application and longevity. Criteria: quantity of minerals found in the water supply (lower ppm is better for hair color); type of oxidizers such as chlorine; and pH levels. *Malibu Wellness, Wellness e-Letter, "Best & Worst Cities for Hair Color," February 2005*

Women/Minorities Rankings

■ Las Vegas was ranked #74 out of 100 metro areas in *SELF Magazine's* ranking of "America's Best Places for Women." A panel of experts came up with nearly 40 criteria including: drinking and smoking rates; depression; unemployment; parks; crime; disease; healthcare insurance coverage; air quality; and commute times. *SELF Magazine, "America's Best Places for Women 2006," December 2006*

■ *Ladies Home Journal* ranked America's 200 largest cities based on the qualities women surveyed care about most. Las Vegas ranked #40 out of 57 in the big city category (population over 300,000). Criteria: crime; lifestyle; education; jobs; health; child care; politics; and the economy. *Ladies Home Journal Online, "The Best Cities for Women 2002"*

■ Las Vegas was profiled in the book *50 Fabulous Gay-Friendly Places to Live.* Criteria: an active gay community; positive gay health programs; youth outreach; gay-friendly politics; gay-owned and gay-friendly businesses; employment opportunities; fun nightlife; cultural opportunities; recreational opportunities; housing options. *50 Fabulous Gay-Friendly Places to Live, 2005*

■ Las Vegas was selected as one of the "Top 10 Cities for Hispanics to Live In." The city was ranked #10. The cities were selected based on data from the following sources: U.S. Census; *Forbes*; *Fortune*; *Money*; local newspapers; natives and residents; www.bestplaces.net; www.findyourspot.com. *Hispanic Magazine, July/August 2004*

Seniors/Retirement Rankings

■ Las Vegas was profiled in the book *Where to Retire: America's Best and Most Affordable Places.* Cities were selected based on personal visits by the author and interviews with local residents coupled with statistics from various government agencies. *Where to Retire: America's Best and Most Affordable Places, 2006*

■ Las Vegas was identified as one of the "100 Most Popular Places to Retire" by *Where to Retire* magazine. The city ranked #3. Criteria: net retirees received from 1995-2000 (derived by subtracting all outbound retirees from inbound retirees for the county or county group - includes interstate moves only). *Where to Retire, "100 Most Popular Places to Retire," January/February 2007*

■ Las Vegas was profiled in the book *Retire in Style: 60 Outstanding Places Across the USA and Canada.* Criteria: landscape; climate; quality of life; cost of living; transportation; retail services; health care; community services; cultural and educational activities; recreational activities; work and volunteer activities; crime rates and public safety. *Retire in Style: 60 Outstanding Places Across the USA and Canada, 2005*

■ Sperling's BestPlaces in partnership with Bankers Life & Casualty Company designed a survey to identify the top 50 metro areas in the U.S. that offer the best overall qualities for senior living. The Las Vegas metro area ranked #41. The following criteria were statistically weighted to reflect the needs of the senior population: health; disease; economics; social; environment; spiritual; transportation; housing; and crime. *Bankers Life & Casualty Company, "Best Cities for Seniors 2005"*

■ Las Vegas was selected as one of the best places to retire by *Retirement Places Rated.* Criteria: cost of living; climate; personal safety; services; economy. The city was ranked #145 out of 200. *Retirement Places Rated, 6th Edition, 2004*

■ A.G. Edwards ranked America's 500 top-performing communities based on their residents' personal savings and investing behavior. The Las Vegas metro area ranked #339 with an index score of 98.76 (national average = 100.00). A dozen statistical factors were measured including: participation in retirement savings plans; personal debt levels; and home ownership. *A.G. Edwards, "2006 Nest Egg Index", September 6, 2006*

Children/Family Rankings

■ The Las Vegas metro area was selected as one of the "Best Cities for Relocating Families" by Worldwide ERC and Primacy Relocation. Criteria: tax rates; average home costs and home appreciation; ability to qualify for in-state tuition; service quality of local utilities; per-capita volunteerism; auto taxes; and quantity of fun, family-friendly events and venues. *Worldwide ERC and Primacy Relocation, "2006 Best Cities for Relocating Families"*

■ *Zero Population Growth* ranked 100 cities in terms of children's health, safety, and economic well-being. Las Vegas was ranked #68 out of 80 Large Cities (remainder of the 100 largest cities in the U.S.) and was given a grade of C+. Criteria: total population and population growth; percent of population under 18 years of age; percent of births to teens; infant mortality rate; percent of eligible women not receiving Title X services; contraceptive equity indicator; percent of children without health insurance; percent of city residents over age 25 with a high-school diploma; ration of PopEd (Population Connection's Education Program) teachers trained; sexuality education indicator; proficiency in reading and math; percent of kids living in poverty; percent growth in urbanized land; violent crime rate; recycling. *Population Connection, Kid Friendly Cities: Report Card 2004*

■ *Fit Pregnancy* magazine ranked the 50 best U.S. cities in which to have a baby. Las Vegas was ranked #50. Criteria: fertility services; maternal and infant health risk; access to hospitals and doctors; safety; affordability; stroller friendliness; and birthing options. *Fit Pregnancy, February/March, 2006*

Safety Rankings

■ Allstate ranked the 200 largest cities in America in terms of driver safety. Las Vegas ranked #154. In addition, drivers were 22.6% more likely to have had an accident compared to the national average. Allstate researchers analyzed internal Property Damage reported claims over a two-year period (from January 2003 to December 2004) to ensure the findings would not be affected by external influences such as weather or road construction. A weighted average of the two-year numbers determined the annual percentages. The report defines an auto crash as any collision resulting in a property damage claim. *Allstate, "Allstate America's Best Drivers Report 2006," May 24, 2006*

■ Las Vegas was identified as one of the most dangerous large metro areas for pedestrians in the U.S. The area ranked #11 out of the nations 50 largest metro areas. Criteria: average yearly pedestrian fatalities per capita (for the years 2002 and 2003) adjusted for the number of walkers. *Surface Transportation Policy Project, "Mean Streets 2004"*

■ *Ladies Home Journal* ranked America's 200 largest cities in terms of safety. Las Vegas ranked #93 out of 200. Criteria: violent crimes; crimes against property; and rape. *Ladies Home Journal Online, "The Best Cities for Women 2002"*

Sports/Recreation Rankings

■ The Las Vegas metro area appeared on *The Sporting News* list of the "Best Sports Cities 2006". The area ranked #80 out of 99 cities in North America. To be included in the rankings, a city must have at least one of the following: NCAA Division I basketball team; Class A minor league baseball team; training camp for a major league or NFL team; NASCAR Nextel Cup race; NCAA Division I-A bowl game; PGA Tour tournament; Triple Crown horse race. Once a city qualifies, a 12-month snapshot is taken of the sports atmosphere, putting a heavy premium on regular-season won-lost records; playoff berths, bowl appearances and tournament bids; championships; applicable power ratings; quality of competition; overall fan fervor; sports atmosphere and fan knowledge; abundance of teams (quality over quantity); stadium/arena quality; ticket availability and prices; franchise ownership; and the marquee appeal of athletes. *SportingNews.com, "Best Sports Cities 2006," August 1, 2006*

■ The Las Vegas metro area was selected by *Cranium* as one of the "Top 50 Fun Cities" in America. The area ranked #25. Criteria includes: number of sports teams, restaurants, and dance performances; number of toy stores; city budget spent on recreation. *Cranium, November 4, 2003*

■ *Golf Digest* ranked 330 metro areas in the U.S. in terms of golf. The Las Vegas metro area was ranked #218. Criteria: access to golf; weather; value of golf; and quality of golf. *Golf Digest, "Metro Golf Rankings," August 2005*

Dating/Romance Rankings

■ The Las Vegas metro area was selected as one of the "Best Cities for Relocating Singles" by Worldwide ERC and Primacy Relocation. The area ranked #53 out of the 100 largest metro areas in the U.S. Areas were selected based on the following criteria: Population Criteria (local percentage and growth trends of unmarried residents aged 25-34; male-female ratios; the number of newcomers to the area; diversity and density); Economic Criteria (job growth vs. unemployment rates; apartment rental costs; fee and occupancy rates for temporary housing and mini-storage; higher education costs, including in-state and out-of-state tuition requirements; vehicle tax rates and quality of service from utility providers); Quality-of-Life Criteria (level of per capita volunteering; quality and quantity of collegiate and professional sports with fun, fan-friendly venues; number of Starbucks and other coffee shops; quality or popularity of restaurants, nightspots, health clubs, and online dating; moderate climates with sustainable water supplies). *Worldwide ERC and Primacy Relocation, "2006 Best Cities for Relocating Singles," October 11, 2006*

■ *Forbes* ranked the 40 most populous metro areas in the U.S. in terms of the "Best Cities for Singles." The Las Vegas metro area was ranked #21. Criteria: number of singles; cost of living alone; nightlife; culture; job growth; coolness; and online dating. *Forbes.com, July 25, 2006*

■ Sperling's BestPlaces in partnership with AXE Deodorant Bodyspray ranked 80 metro areas and identified "America's Best (and Worst) Cities for Dating." The Las Vegas metro area ranked #52. Criteria: percentage of singles ages 18-24; population density; dating venues per capita. *AXE Deodorant Bodyspray, "America's Best (and Worst) Cities for Dating," May, 2004*

Culture/Performing Arts Rankings

■ Las Vegas was selected as one of "America's Top 25 Arts Destinations." The city ranked #18 in the mid-sized city (population 100,000 to 499,999) category. Criteria: readers' top choices for arts travel destinations based on the richness and variety of visual arts sites, activities and events. *American Style, June 2006*

■ Scarborough Research, a leading market research firm, identified the top local markets for rock concert attendance. The Las Vegas DMA (Designated Market Area) ranked in the top 25 with 14% of consumers, 18 years old and over, reporting that they have attended a rock concert during the past year. *Scarborough Research, Scarborough USA+ 2003 Release 2*

Miscellaneous Rankings

■ Las Vegas was determined to be one of America's smartest cities. The city ranked #44 in the large city category (200,000+ adults 25 years and older). Criteria: the editors rated the collective brainpower of U.S communities based on the educational attainment of its residents. *American City Business Journals, www.bizjournals.com, June 12, 2006*

■ Las Vegas was selected as one of the "Top 100 Sweatiest Summer Cities". The city was ranked #12. The ranking was based on the average male/female height/weight, average high temperature, and average relative humidity levels for 2002 in each of the cities during June, July and August. The sweat level was analyzed based on the assumption that the individual was walking for one hour. *Procter & Gamble, Old Spice, June 18, 2003*

- Las Vegas was selected as one of America's "20 Meanest Cities" by the National Coalition for the Homeless and The National Law Center on Homelessness & Poverty. The city was ranked #5. Criteria: the number of anti-homeless laws; the enforcement of those laws and severities of penalties; the general political climate towards homeless people; local advocate support for the meanest designation; the city's history of criminalization measures; and the existence of pending or recently enacted criminalization legislation. *National Coalition for the Homeless and The National Law Center on Homelessness & Poverty, "A Dream Denied: The Criminalization of Homelessness in U.S. Cities," January 2006*

- The Las Vegas metro area appeared on *Forbes* list of "America's Drunkest Cities". The area ranked #14. Criteria: 35 of the largest continental U.S. metro areas were chosen based on availability of data and geographic diversity. Each metro was ranked in five areas: state laws; drinkers; heavy drinkers; binge drinkers; and alcoholism. *Forbes.com, "America's Drunkest Cities," August 22, 2006*

- Las Vegas appeared on ApartmentRatings.com "Top Cities for Renters List 2006". The area ranked #129 out of 138. Criteria: renter satisfaction; affordability; and vacancy. *ApartmentRatings.com, "Top Cities for Renters List 2006"*

- Sperling's BestPlaces in partnership with Pep Boys ranked 77 metro areas and identified "America's Most Drivable Cities." The Las Vegas metro area ranked #42. Criteria: climate; road roughness; urban mobility; gas prices. *Pep Boys, "America's Most Drivable Cities," April 9, 2003*

- Las Vegas was ranked #117 out of 268 metro areas in terms of its Creativity Index. The Creativity Index is a mix of four equally weighted factors: the Creative Class (scientists, engineers, architects, designers, writers, artists, musicians, or any profession where creativity is a key factor) share of the workforce; innovation, measured as patents per capita; high-tech industry, using the Milken Institute's Tech Pole Index; and diversity, measured by the Gay Index (a reasonable proxy for an areas' openness to different kinds of people and ideas). *The Rise of the Creative Class, 2002*

- Las Vegas was selected as one of "America's Most Literate Cities." The city ranked #40 out of the 70 largest U.S. cities. Criteria: number of booksellers; library resources; Internet resources; educational attainment; periodical publishing resources; newspaper circulation. *Central Connecticut State University, "America's Most Literate Cities 2006"*

- State Farm Insurance, in partnership with Sperling's BestPlaces, analyzed several key factors that contribute to overall family preparedness. The Las Vegas metro area ranked #27 out of the nation's 50 most populous metro areas. Criteria: quality of life; life insurance coverage; and investments. *State Farm Life Insurance, "Fiscally Fit Cities Report," July 20, 2004*

- Las Vegas was selected as having one of the highest number of Starbucks stores per capita in the U.S. The city appeared in the large city category. Criteria: U.S. cities with populations of 10,000 or more were analyzed with regards to the number of Starbucks stores per capita. Supermarkets and other stores selling coffee beans were not included. *ePodunk.com, "Coffee Quotients," March 2005*

- A study by Sperling's BestPlaces examined which U.S. metro areas were most affected by the fuel crunch in 2005. The Las Vegas metro area was selected as being one of the least impacted areas. The area ranked #7 out of 10. Criteria: average miles driven per day per peak traveler; average gallons of gas used per peak traveler; money spent on gas per driver. *Sperling's BestPlaces, www.bestplaces.net, September 29, 2005*

Business Environment

CITY FINANCES

City Government Finances

Component	2003-2004 ($000)	2003-2004 ($ per capita)
Total Revenues	757,224	1,489
Total Expenditures	663,547	1,305
Debt Outstanding	346,786	682
Cash and Securities	456,632	898

Source: U.S Census Bureau, Government Finances 2003-2004

City Government Revenue by Source

Source	2003-2004 ($000)	2003-2004 ($ per capita)
General Revenue		
From Federal Government	10,885	21
From State Government	217,949	429
From Local Governments	68,140	134
Taxes		
Property	100,007	197
Sales	49,102	97
Personal Income	0	0
License	0	0
Charges	173,284	341
Liquor Store	0	0
Utility	651	1
Employee Retirement	0	0
Other	137,206	270

Source: U.S Census Bureau, Government Finances 2003-2004

City Government Expenditures by Function

Function	2003-2004 ($000)	2003-2004 ($ per capita)	2003-2004 (%)
General Expenditures			
Airports	0	0	0.0
Corrections	29,532	58	4.5
Education	0	0	0.0
Fire Protection	92,978	183	14.0
Governmental Administration	132,015	260	19.9
Health	2,422	5	0.4
Highways	75,422	148	11.4
Hospitals	819	2	0.1
Housing and Community Development	25,000	49	3.8
Interest on General Debt	24,070	47	3.6
Libraries	0	0	0.0
Parking	4,243	8	0.6
Parks and Recreation	64,462	127	9.7
Police Protection	112,724	222	17.0
Public Welfare	906	2	0.1
Sewerage	33,721	66	5.1
Solid Waste Management	4,664	9	0.7
Liquor Store	0	0	0.0
Utility	1,233	2	0.2
Employee Retirement	0	0	0.0
Other	59,336	117	8.9

Source: U.S Census Bureau, Government Finances 2003-2004

Municipal Bond Ratings

Area	Moody's
City	Aaa

Source: Mergent Bond Record, January 2007 (unless noted otherwise)

DEMOGRAPHICS

Population Growth

Area	1990 Census	2000 Census	2006 Estimate	2011 Projection	Population Growth (%) 1990-2000	Population Growth (%) 2000-2011
City	261,374	478,434	557,484	636,036	83.0	32.9
MSA[1]	741,459	1,375,765	1,752,385	2,083,252	85.5	51.4
U.S.	248,709,873	281,421,906	298,021,266	312,383,955	13.2	11.0

Note: (1) Metropolitan Statistical Area - see Appendix B for areas included
Source: Claritas, Inc.

Number of Households and Average Household Size

Area	2006 Estimate	2006 Average Household Size
City	202,372	2.75
MSA[1]	643,950	2.72
U.S.	112,267,302	2.65

Note: (1) Metropolitan Statistical Area - see Appendix B for areas included
Source: Claritas, Inc.

Race and Ethnicity

Area	White Alone[2]	Black Alone[2]	Asian Alone[2]	Other Race Alone[2]	Hispanic[3]
City	65.5	10.9	5.6	18.0	29.0
MSA[1]	67.6	9.5	6.5	16.5	26.1
U.S.	73.3	12.4	4.2	10.1	14.5

Note: Figures are 2006 estimates; (1) Metropolitan Statistical Area - see Appendix B for areas included
(2) Alone is defined as not being in combination with one or more other races; (3) May be of any race.
Source: Claritas, Inc.

Segregation

City Index[2]	City Rank[3]	MSA[1] Index[2]	MSA[1] Rank[4]
42.4	78	47.4	254

Note: Figures are based on an analysis of Census 2000 data; (1) Metropolitan Statistical Area - see Appendix A for areas included; (2) White/Black Dissimilarity Index—the most commonly used measure of segregation between two groups, reflecting their relative distributions across neighborhoods within a city or metropolitan area. It can range in value from 0, indicating complete integration, to 100, indicating complete segregation; (3) Ranges from 1 (most segregated) to 100 (least segregated) and includes all the cities in this book; (4) Ranges from 1 (most segregated) to 318 (least segregated) and includes 318 metropolitan areas.
Source: www.CensusScope.org

Ancestry

Area	German	Irish[2]	English	American	Italian	Polish	French[3]	Scottish
City	12.2	9.8	8.4	4.5	6.7	2.5	2.8	1.7
MSA[1]	13.4	10.5	9.3	5.0	6.6	2.6	3.0	1.7
U.S.	15.2	10.9	8.7	7.3	5.6	3.2	3.0	1.7

Note: Figures include multiple ancestry (e.g. if a person reported being Irish and Italian, they were included in both columns); (1) Metropolitan Statistical Area - see Appendix A for areas included; (2) Includes Celtic; (3) Includes Alsatian but excludes Basque
Source: Census 2000, Summary File 3

Foreign-Born Population

Area	Any Foreign Country	Percent of Population Born in Europe	Asia	Africa	Oceania[2]	Canada	Mexico	Latin America[3]
City	18.9	1.9	3.6	0.2	0.1	0.6	10.0	2.6
MSA[1]	16.5	1.7	3.8	0.3	0.1	0.6	7.9	2.2
U.S.	11.1	1.7	2.9	0.3	0.1	0.3	3.3	2.5

Note: (1) Metropolitan Statistical Area - see Appendix A for areas included; (2) Includes Australia, New Zealand subregion, Melanesia, Micronesia, Polynesia, and Oceania n.e.c; (3) Includes Central America (excluding Mexico), South America, and the Caribbean.
Source: Census 2000, Summary File 3

Marriage Status

Area	Never Married	Now Married (excluding Separated)	Separated	Widowed	Divorced
City	25.7	52.1	2.7	5.6	13.9
MSA[1]	24.7	53.3	2.5	5.8	13.7
U.S.	27.1	54.4	2.2	6.6	9.7

Note: Figures are percentages and cover the population 15 years of age and older;
(1) Metropolitan Statistical Area - see Appendix A for areas included
Source: Census 2000, Summary File 3

Age Distribution

Area	Percent of Population						
	Under Age 5	Age 5 to 17	Age 18 to 34	Age 35 to 49	Age 50 to 64	Age 65 to 79	80 Years and Over
City	7.6	18.1	25.1	22.7	15.0	9.5	2.0
MSA[1]	7.3	17.9	24.2	22.7	16.1	9.7	2.1
U.S.	6.8	18.9	23.7	23.5	14.8	9.2	3.2

Note: (1) Metropolitan Statistical Area - see Appendix A for areas included
Source: Census 2000, Summary File 3

Male/Female Ratio

Area	Males	Females	Males per 100 Females
City	283,237	274,247	103.3
MSA[1]	889,679	862,706	103.1
U.S.	146,712,712	151,308,554	97.0

Note: Figures are 2006 estimates; (1) Metropolitan Statistical Area -
see Appendix B for areas included
Source: Claritas, Inc.

Religion

Area	Catholic	Southern Baptist	United Methodist	ELCA[1]	LDS[2]	Presbyterian Church USA	Jewish Est.	Muslim Est.
County	17.2	1.9	0.4	0.6	6.0	0.3	5.5	0.1
U.S.	22.0	7.1	3.7	1.8	1.5	1.1	2.2	0.6

Note: Figures are the number of adherents as a percentage of the total population; Adherents are defined as all members, including full members, their children and the estimated number of other participants who are not considered members (e.g. the baptized, those not confirmed, those regularly attending services, etc.);
(1) Evangelical Lutheran Church in America; (2) The Church of Jesus Christ of Latter Day Saints
Source: Reprinted with permission from Religious Congregations and Membership in the United States 2000 (Nashville, Glenmary Research Center, 2002) Copyright Association of Statisticians of American Religious Bodies. All rights reserved.

ECONOMY

Gross Metropolitan Product

Area	2002	2003	2004	2005	2005 Rank[2]
MSA[1]	56.1	61.8	69.5	78.8	29

Note: Figures are in billions of dollars; (1) Las Vegas-Paradise, NV Metropolitan Statistical Area - see Appendix A for areas included; (2) Rank ranges from 1 to 361
Source: The U.S. Conference of Mayors, "U.S. Metro Economies: GMP - The Engines of America's Growth," January 2007

Economic Growth

Area	1995 GMP	2005 GMP	Average Annual Growth Rate	Growth Rate Rank[2]
MSA[1]	31.7	78.8	9.5	3

Note: Figures are in billions of dollars; GMP = Gross Metropolitan Product; (1) Las Vegas-Paradise, NV Metropolitan Statistical Area - see Appendix A for areas included; (2) Rank ranges from 1 to 361
Source: The U.S. Conference of Mayors, "U.S. Metro Economies: GMP - The Engines of America's Growth," January 2007

INCOME

Per Capita/Median/Average Income

Area	Per Capita ($)	Median Household ($)	Average Household ($)
City	23,819	48,879	64,687
MSA[1]	24,531	51,001	66,118
U.S.	25,129	48,775	65,849

Note: Figures are 2006 estimates; (1) Metropolitan Statistical Area - see Appendix B for areas included
Source: Claritas, Inc.

Household Income Distribution

Area								
	Under $15,000	$15,000 -24,999	$25,000 -34,999	$35,000 -49,999	$50,000 -74,999	$75,000 -99,000	$100,000 -149,999	$150,000 and up
City	11.7	11.0	12.0	16.6	20.2	12.1	11.0	5.5
MSA[1]	10.3	10.2	11.5	17.1	21.3	12.7	11.2	5.6
U.S.	13.3	11.0	11.3	15.7	19.5	11.8	11.0	6.4

Note: Figures are 2006 estimates; (1) Metropolitan Statistical Area - see Appendix B for areas included
Source: Claritas, Inc.

Poverty Rates by Age

Area	All Ages	Under 5 Years Old	5 to 17 Years Old	18 to 64 Years Old	65 Years and Over
City	11.9	1.3	2.8	6.9	0.9
MSA[1]	11.1	1.2	2.6	6.4	0.9
U.S.	12.4	1.2	3.0	6.9	1.2

Note: Figures are percent of population with income in 1999 below poverty level and only include population for whom poverty status is determined; (1) Metropolitan Statistical Area - see Appendix A for areas included
Source: Census 2000, Summary File 3

Personal Bankruptcy Filing Rate

Area	2003	2004	2005
Clark County	9.97	7.71	10.70
U.S.	5.57	5.31	6.88

Note: Numbers are per 1,000 population and include Chapter 7 and Chapter 13 filings
Source: Federal Deposit Insurance Corporation (FDIC), Regional Economic Conditions (RECON), 3/24/2006

EMPLOYMENT

Labor Force and Employment

Area	Civilian Labor Force			Workers Employed		
	Dec. 2005	Dec. 2006	% Chg.	Dec. 2005	Dec. 2006	% Chg.
City	274,701	296,422	7.9	264,892	283,721	7.1
MSA[1]	875,790	945,220	7.9	845,466	905,562	7.1
U.S.	149,874,000	152,571,000	1.8	142,918,000	146,081,000	2.2

Note: Data is not seasonally adjusted and covers workers 16 years of age and older;
(1) Metropolitan Statistical Area - see Appendix B for areas included
Source: Bureau of Labor Statistics, http://stats.bls.gov

Unemployment Rate

Area	2006											
	Jan.	Feb.	Mar.	Apr.	May	Jun.	Jul.	Aug.	Sep.	Oct.	Nov.	Dec.
City	4.1	4.0	3.8	4.1	3.7	4.5	4.7	4.2	4.2	4.1	4.2	4.3
MSA[1]	3.9	3.8	3.7	4.0	3.6	4.3	4.6	4.1	4.0	4.0	4.0	4.2
U.S.	5.1	5.1	4.8	4.5	4.4	4.8	5.0	4.6	4.4	4.1	4.3	4.3

Note: Data is not seasonally adjusted and covers workers 16 years of age and older; All figures are percentages; (1) Metropolitan Statistical Area - see Appendix B for areas included
Source: Bureau of Labor Statistics, http://stats.bls.gov

Employment by Occupation

Occupation Classification	City (%)	MSA[1] (%)	U.S. (%)
Sales and Office	27.5	27.8	26.7
Professional and Related	14.4	13.2	20.2
Service	26.3	26.7	14.9
Production, Transportation, and Material Moving	9.0	9.8	14.6
Management, Business, and Financial	11.1	10.8	13.5
Construction, Extraction, and Maintenance	11.5	11.5	9.4
Farming, Forestry, and Fishing	0.1	0.1	0.7

Note: Figures cover employed civilians 16 years of age and older;
(1) Metropolitan Statistical Area - see Appendix A for areas included
Source: Census 2000, Summary File 3

Employment by Industry

Sector	MSA[1] Number of Employees	MSA[1] Percent of Total	U.S. Percent of Total
Government	97,300	10.4	16.3
Education and Health Services	61,700	6.6	13.2
Professional and Business Services	116,900	12.5	12.9
Retail Trade	103,500	11.0	11.5
Manufacturing	27,700	3.0	10.2
Leisure and Hospitality	272,500	29.1	9.5
Financial Activities	52,000	5.5	6.1
Construction	107,900	11.5	5.5
Wholesale Trade	24,100	2.6	4.3
Other Services	26,100	2.8	3.9
Transportation and Utilities	35,600	3.8	3.7
Information	11,400	1.2	2.2
Natural Resources and Mining	400	<0.1	0.5

Note: Figures cover non-farm employment as of December 2006 and are not seasonally adjusted;
(1) Metropolitan Statistical Area - see Appendix B for areas included
Source: Bureau of Labor Statistics, http://stats.bls.gov

Occupations with Greatest Projected Employment Growth: 2002 - 2012

Occupation[1]	2002 Employment	2012 Projected Employment	Numeric Employment Change	Percent Employment Change
Retail Salespersons	34,060	49,430	15,370	45.1
Cashiers	35,760	50,760	15,000	41.9
Waiters and Waitresses	33,510	47,570	14,060	42.0
Gaming Dealers	22,650	35,170	12,520	55.3
Janitors and Cleaners, Except Maids and Housekeeping Cleaners	26,650	37,430	10,780	40.5
Maids and Housekeeping Cleaners	23,100	32,830	9,730	42.1
Carpenters	18,320	26,310	7,990	43.6
Registered Nurses	15,360	23,220	7,860	51.2
Combined Food Preparation and Serving Workers, Including Fast Food	13,330	20,970	7,640	57.3
Laborers and Freight, Stock, and Material Movers, Hand	26,520	33,270	6,750	25.5

Note: Projections cover Nevada; (1) Sorted by numeric employment change
Source: www.projectionscentral.com, State Occupational Projections, 2002-2012 Long-Term Projections

Fastest Growing Occupations: 2002 - 2012

Occupation[1]	2002 Employment	2012 Projected Employment	Numeric Employment Change	Percent Employment Change
Personal Financial Advisors	940	1,640	700	74.5
Network Systems and Data Communications Analysts	970	1,690	720	74.2
Pharmacists	1,900	3,280	1,380	72.6
Social and Human Service Assistants	720	1,230	510	70.8
Loan Officers	2,540	4,310	1,770	69.7
Fitness Trainers and Aerobics Instructors	990	1,670	680	68.7
Respiratory Therapists	680	1,140	460	67.6
Medical Records and Health Information Technicians	1,090	1,820	730	67.0
Private Detectives and Investigators	610	1,010	400	65.6
Bill and Account Collectors	4,900	8,050	3,150	64.3

Note: Projections cover Nevada; (1) Sorted by percent employment change and excludes occupations with numeric employment change less than 200
Source: www.projectionscentral.com, State Occupational Projections, 2002-2012 Long-Term Projections

Average Wages

Occupation	$/Hr.	Occupation	$/Hr.
Accountants and Auditors	25.42	Maids and Housekeeping Cleaners	11.02
Automotive Mechanics	18.43	Maintenance and Repair Workers	17.73
Bookkeepers	14.40	Marketing Managers	43.15
Carpenters	19.87	Nuclear Medicine Technologists	28.89
Cashiers	9.19	Nurses, Licensed Practical	18.49
Clerks, General Office	11.68	Nurses, Registered	28.59
Clerks, Receptionists/Information	11.45	Nursing Aides/Orderlies/Attendants	11.96
Clerks, Shipping/Receiving	13.91	Packers and Packagers, Hand	8.54
Computer Programmers	30.23	Physical Therapists	34.38
Computer Support Specialists	16.64	Postal Service Mail Carriers	21.74
Computer Systems Analysts	34.63	Real Estate Brokers	n/a
Cooks, Restaurant	12.60	Retail Salespersons	11.82
Dentists	n/a	Sales Reps., Exc. Tech./Scientific	26.49
Electrical Engineers	37.71	Sales Reps., Tech./Scientific	37.54
Electricians	23.57	Secretaries, Exc. Legal/Med./Exec.	14.63
Financial Managers	42.23	Security Guards	11.09
First-Line Supervisors/Mgrs., Sales	17.72	Surgeons	92.53
Food Preparation Workers	10.70	Teacher Assistants	11.40
General and Operations Managers	52.77	Teachers, Elementary School	16.90
Hairdressers/Cosmetologists	11.55	Teachers, Secondary School	19.40
Internists	86.54	Telemarketers	10.29
Janitors and Cleaners	10.82	Truck Drivers, Heavy/Tractor-Trailer	18.22
Landscaping/Groundskeeping Workers	11.47	Truck Drivers, Light/Delivery Svcs.	13.49
Lawyers	52.69	Waiters and Waitresses	8.48

Note: Wage data is for May 2005 and covers the Las Vegas-Paradise, NV Metropolitan Statistics Area - see Appendix B for areas included. Hourly wages for elementary/secondary school teachers and teacher assistants were calculated by the editors from annual wage data assuming a 40 hour work week; n/a not available.
Source: Bureau of Labor Statistics, May 2005 Metro Area Occupational Employment and Wage Estimates

RESIDENTIAL REAL ESTATE

Building Permits

Area	Single-Family			Multi-Family			Total		
	2005	2006ᴾ	Pct. Chg.	2005	2006ᴾ	Pct. Chg.	2005	2006ᴾ	Pct. Chg.
City	4,271	2,998	-29.8	2,287	2,204	-3.6	6,558	5,202	-20.7
U.S.	1,682,000	1,380,000	-18.0	473,300	457,300	-3.4	2,155,300	1,837,300	-14.8

Note: (p) preliminary; figures represent new, privately-owned housing units authorized (unadjusted data); All permit data are based on estimates with imputation; U.S. figures are based on the new 20,000-place series.
Source: U.S. Census Bureau, Manufacturing, Mining, and Construction Statistics

Homeownership and Housing Vacancies

Area	Homeownership Rate[2] (%)			Rental Vacancy Rate[3] (%)			Homeowner Vacancy Rate[4] (%)		
	2004	2005	2006	2004	2005	2006	2004	2005	2006
MSA[1]	n/a	61.4	63.3	n/a	9.0	9.6	n/a	3.8	2.8
U.S.	69.0	68.9	68.8	10.2	9.8	9.7	1.7	1.9	2.4

Note: Comparable 2004 data was not available due to changes in metropolitan area definitions; (1) Metropolitan Statistical Area - see Appendix B for areas included; (2) The proportion of households that are owners; (3) The proportion of the rental inventory that is vacant for rent; (4) The proportion of the homeowner inventory that is vacant for sale; n/a not available
Source: U.S. Census Bureau, Housing Vacancies and Homeownership Annual Statistics: 2006

TAXES

State Corporate Income Tax Rates

State	Rate (%)	Number of Brackets	Low Bracket (Under $)	High Bracket (Over $)
Nevada	None	na	na	na

Note: Tax rates as of December 31, 2006; na not applicable
Source: Tax Foundation, www.taxfoundation.org

State Individual Income Tax Rates

State	Federal Deductibility	Marginal Rate (%)	Number of Brackets	Low Bracket (Under $)	High Bracket (Over $)
Nevada	No	None	na	na	na

Note: Tax rates as of December 31, 2006; Brackets apply to single taxpayers and married people filing separately; na not applicable
Source: Tax Foundation, www.taxfoundation.org

Various State and Local Tax Rates

State and Local Sales and Use (%)	State Sales and Use (%)	Gasoline ($/gal.)	Cigarette ($/pack)	Spirits ($/gal.)	Table Wine ($/gal.)	Beer ($/gal.)
7.75	6.5	0.238 (m)	0.8	3.6	0.70	0.16

Note: Tax rates as of December 31, 2006; (m) Additional cents per gallon taxes added this year that were not included in previous years' tables.
Source: Tax Foundation, www.taxfoundation.org; The Sales Tax Clearinghouse, www.thestc.com

State Tax Burdens

Area	Combined State and Local Tax Burden		Combined Federal, State and Local Tax Burden	
	Percent	Rank	Percent	Rank
Nevada	9.5	43	31.6	14
U.S. Average	10.6	-	31.6	-

Note: Figures are for 2006 and measure taxes as a percentage of income
Source: Tax Foundation, www.taxfoundation.org

Internal Revenue Service Tax Audits

IRS District	Percent of Returns Audited				
	1996	1997	1998	1999	2000
Southwest	0.80	0.81	0.61	0.36	0.29
U.S.	0.66	0.61	0.46	0.31	0.20

Note: Figures cover IRS district audits of federal income tax returns filed by individuals. Geographic data on district audits after the year 2000 are being withheld by the IRS. TRAC is challenging this policy.
Source: Syracuse University, Transactional Records Access Clearinghouse (TRAC), "Odds of IRS District Tax Audit 2000"

**COMMERCIAL
UTILITIES**

Typical Monthly Electric Bills

Area	Commercial Service ($/month)		Industrial Service ($/month)	
	3 kW demand 1,000 kWh	40 kW demand 14,000 kWh	1,000 kW demand 200,000 kWh	50,000 kW demand 15,000,000 kWh
City	109	1,238	17,378	1,203,734
Average[1]	123	1,413	22,000	1,306,315

Note: Based on total rates in effect July 1, 2006; (1) average based on 196 utilities
Source: Edison Electric Institute, Typical Bills and Average Rates Report, Summer 2006

TRANSPORTATION

Means of Transportation to Work

Area	Car/Truck/Van		Public Transportation			Bicycle	Walked	Other Means	Worked at Home
	Drove Alone	Car-pooled	Bus	Subway	Railroad				
City	73.8	15.1	4.7	0.0	0.0	0.4	2.2	1.5	2.4
MSA[1]	74.5	15.0	3.9	0.0	0.0	0.5	2.4	1.3	2.3
U.S.	75.7	12.2	2.5	1.5	0.5	0.4	2.9	1.0	3.3

Note: Figures are percentages and cover workers 16 years of age and older;
(1) Metropolitan Statistical Area - see Appendix A for areas included
Source: Census 2000, Summary File 3

Travel Time to Work

Area	Less Than 15 Minutes	15 to 29 Minutes	30 to 44 Minutes	45 to 59 Minutes	60 Minutes or More
City	19.7	45.9	24.5	4.6	5.3
MSA[1]	24.4	45.2	20.9	4.2	5.2
U.S.	29.4	36.1	19.1	7.4	8.0

Note: Figures are percentages and include workers 16 years old and over; (1) Metropolitan Statistical Area -
see Appendix A for areas included
Source: Census 2000, Summary File 3

Travel Time Index

Area	1982	1993	2002	2003
Urban Area[1]	1.07	1.24	1.36	1.39
Average[2]	1.12	1.28	1.37	1.37

Note: Travel Time Index - The ratio of travel time in the peak period to the travel time at
free-flow conditions. A value of 1.35 indicates a 20-minute free-flow trip takes 27 minutes
in the peak. Free-flow speeds (60 mph on freeways and 35 mph on principal arterials)
are used as the comparison threshold; (1) Covers the Las Vegas, NV urban area;
(2) average of 85 urban areas
Source: Texas Transportation Institute, The 2005 Urban Mobility Report, May 2005

Public Transportation

Agency name:	Regional Transportation Commission of Southern Nevada (RTC)
Vehicle type:	Bus
Average fleet age in years:	8.6
No. operated in max. service:	270
Vehicle type:	Demand response
Average fleet age in years:	2.9
No. operated in max. service:	172

Source: Federal Transit Administration, National Transit Database, 2005

Air Transportation

Airport name and code:	McCarran International (LAS)
Domestic service (2006)	
Passenger airlines[1]:	39
Passenger enplanements:	20,972,537
Freight carriers[2]:	27
Freight (lbs.):	101,349,654
International service (2005)	
Passenger airlines[1]:	35
Passenger enplanements:	837,093
Freight carriers[2]:	14
Freight (lbs.):	3,951,806

Note: (1) Includes all major, minor and commuter airlines that carried at least one passenger during the year; (2) Includes all airlines and freight carriers that transported at least one pound of freight during the year
Source: Bureau of Transportation Statistics, The Intermodal Transportation Database, Air Carriers: T-100 International Market, 2004; Bureau of Transportation Statistics, The Intermodal Transportation Database, Air Carriers: T-100 Domestic Market, 2005

Other Transportation Statistics

Interstate highways:	I-15
Amtrak service:	Bus connection
Major waterways/ports:	None

Source: Editor & Publisher Market Guide, 2006; Amtrak.com; Rand McNally 2006 Road Atlas

BUSINESSES

Major Business Headquarters

Company Name	2006 Rankings	
	Fortune[1]	Forbes[2]
Harrah's Entertainment	309	-
MGM Mirage	334	-
Tang Industries	-	252

Note: (1) Fortune 500 - companies that produce a 10-K are ranked 1 to 500 based on 2005 revenue; (2) Forbes Largest Private Companies - all private companies with at least $1 billion in annual revenue are ranked 1 to 394; companies listed are located in the city; dashes indicate no ranking
Source: Fortune, April 17, 2006; Forbes, November 9, 2006

Best Companies to Work For

Station Casinos (HQ), headquartered in Las Vegas, is among the "100 Best Companies to Work For." Criteria: More than 105,000 employees from 446 companies responded to a 57-question survey created by the Great Place to Work Institute. Two-thirds of a company's score is based on the survey, which covers topics such as attitudes towards management, job satisfaction, and camaraderie. The remaining third of the score comes from each company's responses to the Institute's Culture Audit, which includes detailed questions about demographic makeup, pay and benefits programs, and open-ended questions about the company's people-management philosophy, internal communications, opportunities, compensation practices, diversity programs, etc. Any company that is at least seven years old and has a minimum of 1,000 U.S. employees is eligible. The top three U.S. locations are shown for companies with more than one location. *Fortune, "100 Best Companies to Work for 2007," January 22, 2007*

MGM Mirage, headquartered in Las Vegas, is among the "50 Best Companies for Minorities." Criteria: 1,200 of the largest U.S employers were surveyed. Those companies were analyzed on information such as the number of minorities in the workforce and on the board, and the rate at which minority employees are hired (and fired). *Fortune, "50 Best Companies for Minorities," June 28, 2004*

Harrah's Entertainment Inc, headquartered in Las Vegas, is among the "100 Best Places to Work in IT." To qualify, companies, both public and private, had to have 2005 revenue of $250 million or greater and employ a minimum of 500 people in the U.S., with a minimum of 100 IT employees in the U.S. Companies were selected based on average salary and bonus increases, the percentage of IT employees receiving promotions, IT staff turnover rates, training and development, and the percentage of women and minorities in IT staff and management positions. In addition, information was collected on how the organizations reward outstanding performance, how their retention programs are structured and what benefits they offer. *Computerworld, "100 Best Places to Work in IT 2006," June 19, 2006*

Fast-Growing Businesses

According to *Inc.*, Las Vegas is home to three of America's 500 fastest-growing private companies: **Allegiant Air; Silver State Mortgage; Zappos.com**. Criteria: must be an independent, privately-held, U.S. corporation, proprietorship or partnership; net sales of at least $600,000 in FY2002; four-year operating/sales history; holding companies, regulated banks, and utilities were excluded. *Inc., "America's 500 Fastest-Growing Private Companies," September 2006*

Women-Owned Businesses: 1997 and 2002

Year	All Firms		Firms with Paid Employees			
	Firms	Sales ($000)	Firms	Sales ($000)	Employees	Payroll ($000)
1997	8,008	1,470,420	1,179	1,265,005	12,914	241,532
2002	10,869	1,786,147	1,495	1,378,102	12,579	309,974

Note: Figures cover firms located in the city; Women-owned business are defined as firms in which women own 51% or more of the stock or equity of the company; (a) Withheld to avoid disclosing data for individual companies; (b) Withheld because estimate did not meet publication standards; n/a not available
Source: 1997 Economic Census, Survey of Minority- and Women-Owned Business Enterprises; 2002 Economic Census, Survey of Business Owners (released February 9, 2006)

Minority Business Opportunity

One of the 500 largest Hispanic-owned companies in the U.S. are located in Las Vegas. *Hispanic Business, "Hispanic Business 500," June 2006*

HOTELS

Hotels/Motels

Area	Hotels/Motels	Average Minimum Rates ($)		
		Tourist	First-Class	Deluxe
City	187	38	67	100

Source: OAG Travel Planner Online, Spring 2006

The Las Vegas metro area is home to four of the top 187 hotels in the U.S. according to *Travel & Leisure*: **Bellagio** (#46); **Four Seasons, Las Vegas** (#56); **Wynn Las Vegas** (#104); **The Venetian** (#142). Criteria: service; location; rooms; food; and value. *Travel & Leisure, "The T+L 500, 2007"*

EVENT SITES

Stadiums, Arenas, and Auditoriums

Name	Capacity
Cashman Field Center	9,000
Las Vegas Motor Speedway	8,000
Star of the Desert Arena	6,500
Thomas & Mack Center and Sam Boyd Stadium	42,500

Source: www.officialtravelguide.com; www.eventective.com; original research

Hotels/Conference Centers

Name	Guest Rooms	Exhibit Space (sq. ft.)	Meeting Space (sq. ft.)
Aladdin Resort and Casino	2,567	n/a	75,000
Bally's Las Vegas	2,814	110,503	175,000
Bellagio	3,933	114,632	200,000
Caesars Palace	2,571	54,000	170,000
Las Vegas Hilton	2,956	150,000	220,000
Mandalay Bay Resort and Casino	1,117	n/a	20,000
Paris Las Vegas Casino Resort	2,916	n/a	85,000
Rio All-Suite Casino Resort	2,582	100,000	100,000
Riviera Hotel & Casino	2,100	90,000	160,000
The Venetian Resort Hotel Casino	4,027	n/a	1,800,000
Tropicana Resort and Casino	1,878	100,000	100,000

Note: n/a not available
Source: www.officialtravelguide.com; www.eventective.com; original research

Living Environment

COST OF LIVING

Cost of Living Index

Year	Composite Index	Groceries	Housing	Utilities	Trans-portation	Health Care	Misc. Goods/ Services
2004	108.8	110.9	116.3	88.5	110.5	125.4	104.5
2005	113.1	104.2	134.3	105.1	107.9	110.2	102.8
2006	109.2	99.4	130.0	112.1	105.1	105.7	96.9

Note: U.S. = 100
Source: The Council for Community and Economic Research (formerly ACCRA), Cost of Living Index, 2004, 2005 and 2006 4-Quarter Averages

HOUSING

House Price Index (HPI)

Area	National Ranking[2]	Quarterly Change (%)	One-Year Change (%)	Five-Year Change (%)
MSA[1]	133	0.06	5.36	102.61
U.S.[3]	-	1.12	5.87	55.21

Note: The HPI is a weighted repeat sales index. It measures average price changes in repeat sales or refinancings on the same properties. This information is obtained by reviewing repeat mortgage transactions on single-family properties whose mortgages have been purchased or securitized by Fannie Mae or Freddie Mac in January 1975; (1) Metropolitan Statistical Area - see Appendix B for areas included; (2) Rankings are based on annual percentage change for all metro areas containing at least 15,000 transactions over the last 10 years and ranges from 1 to 282; (3) figures based on a weighted division average; all figures are for the period ending December 31, 2006
Source: Office of Federal Housing Enterprise Oversight, House Price Index, March 1, 2007

House Price Valuations

Area	Q4 1999	Q4 2000	Q4 2001	Q4 2002	Q4 2003	Q4 2004	Q4 2005	Q4 2006
MSA[1]	-18.2	-15.4	-10.6	-8.1	-1.4	19.5	31.4	31.1

Note: Figures show the percentage of over- or under-valuation of single family homes relative to statistically normal house values (e.g. a value of 23.6 indicates that house values are 23.6% overvalued). Statistically normal house values are based on house prices, interest rates, household incomes, population densities, and any historical premiums or discounts metropolitan areas have exhibited over time; (1) Figures cover the Metropolitan Statistical Area - see Appendix B for areas included
Source: Global Insight/National City Corporation, House Prices in America, March 2007

Median Home Prices

Area	2004	2005	2006p	Percent Change 2005 to 2006
Metro Area[1]	266.4	304.7	317.4	4.2
U.S. Average	195.2	219.0	222.0	1.4

Note: Figures are median sales prices of existing single-family homes in thousands of dollars; (p) preliminary; n/a not available; (1) Covers the Las Vegas-Paradise, NV Metropolitan Statistical Area - see Appendix B for areas included
Source: National Association of Realtors, Metropolitan Area Prices, 4th Quarter 2006

Housing: Year Structure Built

Area	1990 -2000	1980 -1989	1970 -1979	1960 -1969	1950 -1959	1940 -1949	Before 1940	Median Year
City	48.9	19.0	13.2	10.9	5.9	1.6	0.6	1989
MSA[1]	47.0	21.7	17.9	8.4	3.5	1.0	0.6	1989
U.S.	17.0	15.8	18.5	13.7	12.7	7.3	15.0	1971

Note: Figures are percentages; (1) Metropolitan Statistical Area - see Appendix A for areas included
Source: Census 2000, Summary File 3

Average New Home Price

Area	2004	2005	2006
City	301,867	383,147	400,837
U.S.	253,574	275,712	299,269

Note: Figures, in dollars, are based on a new home with 2,400 sq. ft. of living area on an 8,000 sq. ft. lot.
Source: The Council for Community and Economic Research (formerly ACCRA), Cost of Living Index, 2004, 2005 and 2006 4-Quarter Averages

Average Apartment Rent

Area	2004	2005	2006
City	783	823	867
U.S.	716	740	766

Note: Figures, in dollars per month, are based on an unfurnished two bedroom, 1-1/2 or 2 bath apartment, approximately 950 sq. ft. in size, excluding all utilities except water
Source: The Council for Community and Economic Research (formerly ACCRA), Cost of Living Index, 2004, 2005 and 2006 4-Quarter Averages

RESIDENTIAL UTILITIES

Average Residential Utility Costs

Area	All Electric ($/mth)	Part Electric ($/mth)	Other Energy ($/mth)	Phone ($/mth)
City	–	112.35	58.02	30.84
U.S.	136.00	76.53	90.52	25.87

Source: The Council for Community and Economic Research (formerly ACCRA), Cost of Living Index, 2006 4-Quarter Average

HEALTH

Average Health Care Costs

Area	Optometrist ($/visit)	Doctor ($/visit)	Dentist ($/visit)
City	85.93	88.83	73.50
U.S.	76.38	76.10	68.72

Note: Optometrist—based on a full vision eye exam for an established adult patient;
Doctor—based on a general practitioner's routine exam of an established patient;
Dentist—based on adult teeth cleaning and periodic oral exam.
Source: The Council for Community and Economic Research (formerly ACCRA), Cost of Living Index, 2006 4-Quarter Average

Mortality Rates

ICD-10 Sub-Chapter	ICD-10 Code	Age-Adjusted Death Rate per 100,000 population[1]	U.S. Age-Adjusted Death Rate per 100,000 population
Malignant neoplasms	C00-C97	194.9	185.8
Ischaemic heart diseases	I20-I25	127.6	150.2
Other forms of heart disease	I30-I51	97.7	50.8
Cerebrovascular diseases	I60-I69	54.2	50.0
Chronic lower respiratory diseases	J40-J47	52.1	41.1
Diabetes mellitus	E10-E14	11.7	24.5
Other degenerative diseases of the nervous system	G30-G31	18.5	22.3
Other external causes of accidental injury	W00-X59	26.6	21.2
Influenza and pneumonia	J10-J18	22.0	19.8
Hypertensive diseases	I10-I13	17.4	18.1

Note: ICD-10 = International Classification of Diseases 10th Revision; (1) Figures cover Clark County, NV
Source: Centers for Disease Control and Prevention, National Center for Health Statistics. Compressed Mortality File 1999-2004. CDC WONDER On-line Database, compiled from Compressed Mortality File 1999-2004 Series 20 No. 2J, 2007.

Health Risk Data

Item	Area[1] (%)	U.S. (%)
Adults who have been told they have high blood pressure	23.7	25.5
Adults who have been told they have high blood cholesterol	40.0	35.6
Adults who have been told they have diabetes[2]	7.2	7.3
Adults who have been told they have arthritis	24.6	27.0
Adults who have been told they currently have asthma	6.8	8.0
Adults who are current smokers	23.5	20.6

Note: (1) Figures cover the Metropolitan Statistical Area - see Appendix B for areas included; (2) Figures do not include pregnancy-related diabetes, pre-diabetes or borderline diabetes
Source: Centers for Disease Control and Prevention, Behaviorial Risk Factor Surveillance System, SMART: Selected Metropolitan/Micropolitan Area Trends, 2005

Distribution of Office-Based Physicians

Area	Total	Family/ General Practice	Specialties		
			Medical	Surgical	Other
MSA[1] (number)	2,535	308	978	558	691
MSA[1] (rate per 10,000 pop.)	14.8	1.8	5.7	3.3	4.0
Metro Average[2] (rate per 10,000 pop.)	19.4	2.1	7.5	4.5	5.3

Note: Data as of December 31, 2004; (1) Metropolitan Statistical Area - see Appendix A for areas included; (2) Average of the 79 unique MSAs and CMSAs in this book
Source: American Medical Association, Physician Characteristics & Distribution in the U.S., 2006

Hospitals

Las Vegas has the following hospitals: 7 general medical and surgical; 2 psychiatric; 2 rehabilitation; 3 long-term acute care; 1 other specialty.
AHA Guide to the Healthcare Field 2007

EDUCATION

Public School District Statistics

District Name	Schls	Pupils	Pupil/ Teacher Ratio	Minority Pupils[1] (%)	Free Lunch Eligible[2] (%)	IEP[3] (%)
Clark County School District	308	283,221	19.9	n/a	n/a	10.7

Note: Table includes regular local school districts with 2,000 or more students; (1) Percentage of students that are not white, non-Hispanic; (2) Percentage of students that are eligible for the free lunch program; (3) Percentage of students that have an Individualized Education Program.
Source: U.S. Department of Education, National Center for Education Statistics, Common Core of Data, Local Education Agency (School District) Universe Survey: School Year 2004-2005; U.S. Department of Education, National Center for Education Statistics, Common Core of Data, Public Elementary/Secondary School Universe Survey: School Year 2004-2005

Educational Quality

School District	Education Quotient[1]	Graduate Outcome[2]	Community Index[3]	Resource Index[4]	Rating[5]
Clark County	24	31	35	2	Yellow

Note: Scores are national percentile rankings and range from 1 (worst) to 99 (best); (1) Combination of the Graduate Outcome, Community and Resource Indexes weighted to reflect the greater importance of the Graduate Outcome and Resource Index; (2) Based on graduation rates and college board scores (SAT/ACT); (3) Based on the surrounding community's level of affluence and adult education; (4) Based on teacher salaries, per-pupil expenditures and student-teacher ratios; (5) School districts receive one of five rankings: Gold Medal (top 16 percent of districts evaluated); Blue Ribbon (top third); Green Light (average); Yellow Light (bottom 25 percent); Red Light (bottom 10 percent).
Source: Expansion Management, "2007 Education Quotient," January 2007

Highest Level of Education

Area	Less than H.S.	H.S. Diploma	Some College, No Deg.	Associate Degree	Bachelors Degree	Masters Degree	Profess. School Degree	Doctorate Degree
City	20.4	28.7	25.8	5.8	12.6	4.1	2.1	0.6
MSA[1]	18.9	29.3	27.2	5.9	12.4	4.0	1.7	0.6
U.S.	19.4	28.4	21.2	6.4	15.7	5.9	2.0	1.0

Note: Figures are 2006 estimated percentages and cover persons age 25 and over; (1) Metropolitan Statistical Area - see Appendix B for areas included
Source: Claritas, Inc.

Educational Attainment by Race

Area	High School Graduate (%)					Bachelor's Degree (%)				
	Total	White	Black	Asian	Hisp.[2]	Total	White	Black	Asian	Hisp.[2]
City	78.5	82.7	76.1	83.2	44.6	18.2	19.8	12.5	30.2	6.1
MSA[1]	79.2	82.2	78.5	81.5	47.9	16.4	17.2	11.9	27.2	6.4
U.S.	80.4	83.6	72.3	80.4	52.4	24.4	26.1	14.3	44.1	10.4

Note: Figures shown cover persons 25 years old and over; (1) Metropolitan Statistical Area - see Appendix A for areas included; (2) people of Hispanic origin can be of any race
Source: Census 2000, Summary File 3

School Enrollment by Type

Area	Grades KG to 8				Grades 9 to 12			
	Public		Private		Public		Private	
	Enrollment	%	Enrollment	%	Enrollment	%	Enrollment	%
City	58,821	93.1	4,349	6.9	22,255	93.9	1,435	6.1
MSA[1]	190,592	94.6	10,904	5.4	72,968	94.8	3,972	5.2
U.S.	33,526,011	88.7	4,285,121	11.3	14,848,628	90.6	1,532,323	9.4

Note: Figures shown cover persons 3 years old and over; (1) Metropolitan Statistical Area - see Appendix A for areas included
Source: Census 2000, Summary File 3

School Enrollment by Race

Area	Grades KG to 8 (%)				Grades 9 to 12 (%)			
	White	Black	Asian	Hisp.[1]	White	Black	Asian	Hisp.[1]
City	62.3	13.1	3.4	32.3	63.0	13.3	4.5	29.8
MSA[2]	66.2	10.5	3.6	29.2	67.1	10.0	4.8	25.8
U.S.	68.5	15.5	3.3	16.8	68.8	15.5	3.8	15.7

Note: Figures shown cover persons 3 years old and over; (1) people of Hispanic origin can be of any race; (2) Metropolitan Statistical Area - see Appendix A for areas included
Source: Census 2000, Summary File 3

Average Salaries of Public School Teachers

District	2004-05		2005-06		Percent Change 2004-05 to 2005-06
	Dollars	Rank[1]	Dollars	Rank[1]	
NEVADA	43,394	25	44,426	26	2.38
U.S. Average	47,674	-	49,109	-	3.01

Note: (1) State rank ranges from 1 to 51.
Source: National Education Association, Rankings & Estimates: Rankings of the States 2005 and Estimates of School Statistics 2006, November 2006

Higher Education

Four-Year Colleges			Two-Year Colleges			Medical Schools[1]	Law Schools[2]	Voc/Tech[3]
Public	Private Non-profit	Private For-profit	Public	Private Non-profit	Private For-profit			
2	0	1	0	1	6	0	1	6

Note: Figures cover institutions located within the city limits; (1) includes schools accredited by the Liaison Committee on Medical Education and the American Osteopathic Association; (2) includes American Bar Association-accredited law schools; (3) includes all schools with programs that are less than 2 years
Source: National Center for Education Statistics, The Integrated Postsecondary Education System (IPEDS) Peer Analysis System, 2006; www.usnews.com, America's Best Graduate Schools 2008, Medical School Directory; www.usnews.com, America's Best Graduate Schools 2008, Law School Directory

PRESIDENTIAL ELECTION

2004 Presidential Election Results

Area	Bush	Kerry	Nader	Other
Clark County	46.8	51.7	0.6	1.0
U.S.	50.7	48.3	0.4	0.6

Note: Results are percentages and may not add to 100% due to rounding
Source: Dave Leip's Atlas of U.S. Presidential Elections, www.uselectionatlas.org

MAJOR EMPLOYERS

Major Employers

Company Name	Industry	Type of Site
Aladdin Resort & Casino	Hotels and motels	Single
Barrick Gaming Operations LLC	Hotels and motels	Single
Caesars Palace Hotel & Casino	Hotels and motels	Headquarters
Circus Circus Hotel & Casino	Hotels and motels	Headquarters
Coast Hotels and Casinos Inc	Hotels and motels	Headquarters
Columbia Sunrise Chld Hosp	General medical and surgical hospitals	Headquarters
Excalibur Hotel & Casino	Hotels and motels	Single
Fremont Hotel and Casino	Hotels and motels	Single
Harrahs Las Vegas Inc	Hotels and motels	Single
Hilton	Hotels and motels	Headquarters
Imperial Palace Hotel & Casino	Hotels and motels	Single
Ivantage Network Solutions	Business consulting, nec	Headquarters
Las Vegas City of	Executive offices	Headquarters
MGM Grand Hotel Inc	Hotels and motels	Headquarters
Mandalay Bay Resort & Casino	Hotels and motels	Single
Mirage Resorts Incorporated	Hotels and motels	Headquarters
Monte Carlo Resort & Casino	Hotels and motels	Headquarters
New York New York	Hotels and motels	Single
Parball Corporation	Hotels and motels	Headquarters
Paris Project Office	Hotels and motels	Single
Primadonna Corp	Hotels and motels	Single
Ramada Inn	Hotels and motels	Single
Rio Suite Hotel & Casino	Hotels and motels	Single
Riverside Resort and Casino	Coin-operated amusement devices	Single
Sams Town Ht & Gambling Hall	Hotels and motels	Branch
Stardust Resort & Casino	Hotels and motels	Headquarters
Station Casinos Inc	Hotels and motels	Headquarters
Sun Coast Hotel & Casino	Hotels and motels	Branch
Sunset Station	Hotels and motels	Branch
The Bellagio Resort	Hotels and motels	Headquarters
The Venetian Resort Ht Casino	Hotels and motels	Single
Tower Shops at Stratosphere	Hotels and motels	Headquarters
US Dept of the Air Force	National security	Branch
University Medical Center	General medical and surgical hospitals	Headquarters

Note: Companies shown are located within the metropolitan area and have 2,000 or more employees; nec = not elsewhere classified.
Source: www.zapdata.com, January 2007

PUBLIC SAFETY

Crime Rate

Area	All Crimes	Violent Crimes				Property Crimes		
		Murder	Forcible Rape	Robbery	Aggrav. Assault	Burglary	Larceny -Theft	Motor Vehicle Theft
City	5,581.9	11.3	48.1	272.6	411.6	1,121.0	2,160.8	1,556.5
Suburbs[1]	4,402.9	7.0	25.4	136.1	299.8	924.9	2,043.7	966.0
Metro[2]	5,288.0	10.3	42.4	238.6	383.7	1,072.1	2,131.6	1,409.3
U.S.	3,899.0	5.6	31.7	140.7	291.1	726.7	2,286.3	416.7

Note: Figures are crimes per 100,000 population; (1) All areas within the metro area that are located outside the city limits; (2) Metropolitan Statistical Area - see Appendix B for areas included
Source: FBI Uniform Crime Reports, 2005

Hate Crimes

Area	Number of Quarters Reported	Bias Motivation				
		Race	Religion	Sexual Orientation	Ethnicity	Disability
Area[2]	4	31	12	5	16	1

Note: (2) Figures cover Las Vegas Metropolitan Police Department.
Source: Federal Bureau of Investigation, Hate Crime Statistics 2005

RECREATION

Culture

Dance[1]	Theatre[1]	Instrumental Music[1]	Vocal Music[1]	Series/ Festivals	Museums	Zoos
1	2	4	1	2	14	0

Note: (1) number of professional performing groups
Source: The Grey House Performing Arts Directory, 2007; Official Museum Directory, 2007

Professional Sports Teams

Major League Baseball	National Basketball Association	National Football League	National Hockey League	Major League Soccer	Women's National Basketball Association
0	0	0	0	0	0

Note: Includes teams located in the Las Vegas metro area.
Source: www.sportsvenues.com, Listing of Venues by State/Province and City, 2006

MEDIA

Newspapers

Name	Target Audience	Frequency	Circulation
El Mundo	General/Hispanic	Non-Daily	25,000
Las Vegas Review-Journal	n/a	Daily	207,178
Nevada Daily Legal News	n/a	Daily	2,500

Note: Includes newspapers whose offices are located in the city and whose circulations are 1,000 or more; n/a not available
Source: BurrellesLuce, MediaContacts Online, January 2006

Television Stations

Name	Ch.	Network(s)	Type	Ownership
KLBC	2	UPN	Commercial	n/a
KVBC	3	NBC	Commercial	Sunbelt Broadcasting Company
KVVU	5	Fox	Commercial	Meredith Communications LLC
KLAS	8	CBS	Commercial	Landmark Communications
KLVX	10	PBS	Public	Clark County School District
KTNV	13	ABC	Commercial	Journal Broadcast Group
KINC	15	n/a	Commercial	Entravision Communications
KVWB	21	WBN	Commercial	Sinclair Broadcast Group
KTUD	25	UPN	Commercial	n/a
KFBT	33	WBN	Commercial	Sinclair Broadcast Group
KBLR	39	Telemundo	Commercial	Summit Media Broadcasting LLC

Note: Stations included cover the Las Vegas DMA (Designated Market Area)
BurrellesLuce, MediaContacts Online, January 2006

Major AM Radio Stations

Call Letters	Freq. (kHz)	Station Type	Target Audience	Station Format	Music Format
KNMX	540	Commercial	General/Hisp/Rel	Music/Talk	Latin
KDWN	720	Commercial	General	News/Talk	n/a
KXNT	840	Commercial	General	Talk	n/a
KLSQ	870	Commercial	General/Hispanic	Music/News	Oldies
KBAD	920	Commercial	General	Talk	n/a
KNUU	970	n/a	General	News/Talk	n/a
KKVV	1060	Commercial	General/Religious	News/Talk	n/a
KSFN	1140	Commercial	General	Sports/Talk	n/a
KLAV	1230	Commercial	General	Talk	n/a
KDOX	1280	Commercial	General/Hispanic	Music/News	Latin
KRLV	1340	Commercial	General/Hispanic	News/Sports/Talk	n/a
KSHP	1400	Commercial	General	Sports/Talk	n/a
KENO	1460	n/a	General	News/Sports/Talk	n/a

Note: Stations included cover the Las Vegas DMA (Designated Market Area); n/a not available
Source: BurrellesLuce, MediaContacts Online, January 2006

Major FM Radio Stations

Call Letters	Freq. (mHz)	Station Type	Target Audience	Station Format	Music Format
KCEP	88.1	Non-Comm	Black/General	Ed/Music/News/Talk	Urban Contemp.
KILA	90.5	Non-Comm	General/Religious	Music/Talk	Christian
KUNV	91.5	Commercial	General	Educational/Music	Jazz
KOMP	92.3	Commercial	General	Music	Modern Rock
KRCY	92.7	Commercial	General	Music/News	Oldies
KQOL	93.1	n/a	General	Music/News/Talk	n/a
KMXB	94.1	Commercial	General	Music/News/Talk	Adult Contemp.
KWNR	95.5	Commercial	General	Music	Country
KKLZ	96.3	n/a	General	Music/News/Sports	n/a
KXPT	97.1	Commercial	General	Music	Classic Rock
KVEG	97.5	Commercial	General/Women	Music/News	Urban Contemp.
KLUC	98.5	Commercial	General	Music/News/Talk	Rhythm & Blues
KMZQ	100.5	Commercial	General	Music/News	Adult Contemp.
KISF	103.5	n/a	General	Music	n/a
KJUL	104.3	n/a	General	Music/News/Sports	n/a
KRRN	105.1	Commercial	General/Hispanic	Music	Latin
KSNE	106.5	Commercial	General	Music	Adult Contemp.
KXTE	107.5	Commercial	General/Young Adult	Music/News/Talk	Modern Rock

Note: Stations included cover the Las Vegas DMA (Designated Market Area); n/a not available
BurrellesLuce, MediaContacts Online, January 2006

CLIMATE

Average and Extreme Temperatures

Temperature	Jan	Feb	Mar	Apr	May	Jun	Jul	Aug	Sep	Oct	Nov	Dec	Yr.
Extreme High (°F)	77	87	91	99	109	115	116	116	113	103	87	77	116
Average High (°F)	56	62	69	78	88	99	104	102	94	81	66	57	80
Average Temp. (°F)	45	50	56	65	74	84	90	88	80	68	54	46	67
Average Low (°F)	33	38	43	51	60	69	76	74	66	54	41	34	53
Extreme Low (°F)	8	16	23	31	40	49	60	56	43	26	21	11	8

Note: Figures cover the years 1948-1990
Source: National Climatic Data Center, International Station Meteorological Climate Summary, 9/96

Average Precipitation/Snowfall/Humidity

Precip./Humidity	Jan	Feb	Mar	Apr	May	Jun	Jul	Aug	Sep	Oct	Nov	Dec	Yr.
Avg. Precip. (in.)	0.5	0.4	0.4	0.2	0.2	0.1	0.4	0.5	0.3	0.2	0.4	0.3	4.0
Avg. Snowfall (in.)	1	Tr	Tr	Tr	0	0	0	0	0	0	Tr	Tr	1
Avg. Rel. Hum. 7am (%)	59	52	41	31	26	20	26	31	30	36	47	56	38
Avg. Rel. Hum. 4pm (%)	32	25	20	15	13	10	14	16	16	18	26	31	20

Note: Figures cover the years 1948-1990; Tr = Trace amounts (<0.05 in. of rain; <0.5 in. of snow)
Source: National Climatic Data Center, International Station Meteorological Climate Summary, 9/96

Weather Conditions

Temperature			Daytime Sky			Precipitation		
10°F & below	32°F & below	90°F & above	Clear	Partly cloudy	Cloudy	0.01 inch or more precip.	0.1 inch or more snow/ice	Thunder-storms
< 1	37	134	185	132	48	27	2	13

Note: Figures are average number of days per year and cover the years 1948-1990
Source: National Climatic Data Center, International Station Meteorological Climate Summary, 9/96

HAZARDOUS WASTE

Superfund Sites

Las Vegas has no sites on the EPA's Superfund Final National Priorities List.
U.S. Environmental Protection Agency, Final National Priorities List, March 20, 2007

AIR & WATER QUALITY

Air Quality Index

Area	Percent of Days when Air Quality was...[2]				AQI Statistics	
	Good	Moderate	Unhealthy for Sensitive Groups	Unhealthy	Maximum	Median
MSA[1]	46.8	49.9	2.7	0.5	181	52

Note: The Air Quality Index (AQI) is an index for reporting daily air quality. EPA calculates the AQI for five major air pollutants regulated by the Clean Air Act: ground-level ozone, particle pollution (also known as particulate matter), carbon monoxide, sulfur dioxide, and nitrogen dioxide. The AQI runs from 0 to 500. The higher the AQI value, the greater the level of air pollution and the greater the health concern. There are six AQI categories: "Good" The AQI is between 0 and 50. Air quality is considered satisfactory; "Moderate" The AQI is between 51 and 100. Air quality is acceptable; "Unhealthy for Sensitive Groups" When AQI values are between 101 and 150, members of sensitive groups may experience health effects; "Unhealthy" When AQI values are between 151 and 200 everyone may begin to experience health effects; "Very Unhealthy" AQI values between 201 and 300 trigger a health alert; "Hazardous" AQI values over 300 trigger health warnings of emergency conditions; (1) Metropolitan Statistical Area - see Appendix A for areas included; (2) Based on 365 days with AQI data in 2005.
Source: U.S. Environmental Protection Agency, Air Quality Index Report, 2005

Air Quality Index Pollutants

Area	Percent of Days when AQI Pollutant was...[2]					
	Carbon Monoxide	Nitrogen Dioxide	Ozone	Sulfur Dioxide	Particulate Matter 2.5	Particulate Matter 10
MSA[1]	0.3	0.0	54.8	0.0	20.8	24.1

Note: The Air Quality Index (AQI) is an index for reporting daily air quality. EPA calculates the AQI for five major air pollutants regulated by the Clean Air Act: ground-level ozone, particle pollution (also known as particulate matter), carbon monoxide, sulfur dioxide, and nitrogen dioxide. The AQI runs from 0 to 500. The higher the AQI value, the greater the level of air pollution and the greater the health concern; (1) Metropolitan Statistical Area - see Appendix A for areas included; (2) Based on 365 days with AQI data in 2005.
Source: U.S. Environmental Protection Agency, Air Quality Index Report, 2005

Number of Days with Air Quality Index Values Greater than 100

Area	Trend Sites (9)								All Sites (86)
	1998	1999	2000	2001	2002	2003	2004	2005	2005
MSA[1]	0	0	0	1	2	3	1	2	10

Note: An AQI value greater than 100 indicates that air quality would have been in the unhealthful range on that day. Data from exceptional events are not included. These counts are presented in two ways. First, the counts are based on sites having an adequate record of monitoring data during the trend period (trend sites). These counts represent the relative change in the number of days with AQI values greater than 100. In the last column, the counts are based on all sites with data in the most recent year (because it is possible for a site to have data in the most recent year but not enough data to be a trend site); (1) Metropolitan Statistical Area - see Appendix A for areas included; n/a not available.
Source: U.S. Environmental Protection Agency, Air Trends Fact Book 2005

Maximum Pollutant Concentrations

	Particulate Matter 10 (ug/m³)	Particulate Matter 2.5 (ug/m³)	Ozone 1-hour (ppm)	Carbon Monoxide (ppm)	Sulfur Dioxide (ppm)	Nitrogen Dioxide (ppm)	Lead (ug/m³)
MSA[1] Level	142	29	0.116	5	0.008	0.020	n/a
NAAQS[2]	150	65	0.125	9	0.140	0.053	1.50
Met NAAQS[2]	Yes	Yes	Yes	Yes	Yes	Yes	n/a

Note: Data from exceptional events are not included; (1) Metropolitan Statistical Area - see Appendix A for areas included; (2) National Ambient Air Quality Standards; n/a not available
Units: ppm = parts per million; ug/m³ = micrograms per cubic meter
Source: U.S. Environmental Protection Agency, Air Trends Fact Book 2005

Watershed Health

The U.S. Environmental Protection Agency monitors the health of the aquatic resources for the nation's 2,000+ watersheds. **The Las Vegas Wash watershed serves the Las Vegas area and received an overall Index of Watershed Indicators (IWI) score of 3 (less serious problems - low vulnerability).** The IWI score is based on seven condition and nine vulnerability indicators. The overall IWI score ranges from 1 (best health) to 6 (worst health). The Condition Indicators include: designated use attainment, fish and wildlife consumption advisories, source water condition, contaminated sediments, ambient water quality, and wetlands loss index. The Vulnerability Indicators include: aquatic species at risk, conventional and toxic loads over permitted limits, urban and agricultural runoff potential, population change, hydrologic modification, estuarine pollution susceptibility, and air deposition. *Note: The IWI is no longer being updated by the U.S. EPA. Source: U.S. Environmental Protection Agency, Index of Watershed Indicators, October 26, 2001*

Drinking Water

Water System Name	Pop. Served	Primary Water Source Type	Number of Violations in 2006[a]		
			Health Based	Significant Monitoring	Monitoring
Las Vegas Valley Water District	1,181,263	Purchased surface	None	None	None

Note: (a) Based on violation data from January 1, 2006 to December 31, 2006
Source: U.S. Environmental Protection Agency, Office of Ground Water and Drinking Water, Safe Drinking Water Information System (data extracted April 12, 2007)

Las Vegas tap water is alkaline, hard.
Editor & Publisher Market Guide, 2005

Los Angeles, California

Background

There is as much to say about Los Angeles as there are unincorporated and incorporated municipalities under its jurisdiction. The city is immense, and in the words of one of its residents, "If you want a life in LA, you need a car."

Los Angeles acquired its many neighborhoods and communities such as Hollywood, Glendale, Burbank, and Alhambra when those cities wanted to share in the water piped into Los Angeles from the Owens River. To obtain it, the cities were required to join the Los Angeles municipal system. Due to those annexations, Los Angeles is now one of the largest U.S. cities in both acreage and population. It is also one of the most racially diverse.

The city tries to connect the communities in its far-flung empire through a rather Byzantine system of freeways which gives Los Angeles its reputation as a congested, car-oriented culture, where people have to schedule their days around the three-hour rush hour.

Despite these nightmares, Los Angeles is a city with a diversified economy and 325 days of sunshine a year. What was founded in 1781 as a sleepy pueblo of 44 people, with chickens roaming the footpaths, is now a city leading the nation in commerce, transportation, finance, and, especially, entertainment — with three-quarters of all motion pictures made in the United States still produced in the Los Angeles area, and headquarters of such major studios as MGM and Universal located in "municipalities" unto themselves.

Playa Vista, the first new community to be established on the Westside of Los Angeles in more than 50 years, is home to Electronic Arts, the world's leading video game publisher. Lincoln Properties is planning to build office buildings totaling more than 820,000 square feet in the eastern portion of Playa Vista community known as "The Campus at Playa Vista." The National Basketball Association Clippers will have its training facility at the Campus, which will also be home to a basketball-themed public park. The residential portion of Playa Vista is nearly complete.

The arts are center-stage in Los Angeles. The new home of the Getty Center and Museum, an architectural masterpiece designed by Richard Meier and built on a commanding hill, is a dramatic venue for visual arts and other events. The Los Angeles Opera, under the direction of Placido Domingo, offers a lively season of operas as well as recitals by such luminaries as Cecilia Bartoli and Renee Fleming. The Los Angeles Philharmonic now performs in the Walt Disney Concert Hall, dedicated in October 2003. This hall was designed by Frank Gehry, famous as the architect of the Guggenheim Museum at Bilbao.

The downtown's first modern industrial park, The Los Angeles World Trade Center, is a 20-acre project that is downtown's only foreign trade zone.

Inland and up foothill slopes, both high and low temperatures become more extreme and the average relative humidity drops. Relative humidity is frequently high near the coast, but may be quite low along the foothills. Most rain falls November through March, while the summers are very dry. Destructive flash floods occasionally develop in and below some mountain canyons. Snow is often visible on the nearby mountains in the winter, but is extremely rare in the coastal basin. Thunderstorms are infrequent.

The climate of Los Angeles is normally pleasant and mild throughout the year, with unusual differences in temperature, humidity, cloudiness, fog, rain, and sunshine over fairly short distances in the metro area. Low clouds are common at night and in the morning along the coast during spring and summer. Near the foothills, clouds form later in the day and clear earlier. Annual percentages of fog and cloudiness are greatest near the ocean. Sunshine totals are highest on the inland side of the city.

At times, high concentrations of air pollution affect the Los Angeles coastal basin and adjacent areas, when lack of air movement combines with an atmospheric inversion. In the fall and winter, the Santa Ana winds pick up considerable amounts of dust and can blow strongly in the northern and eastern sections of the city and in outlying areas in the north and east; these rarely reach coastal sections of the city.

Rankings

General Rankings

■ Los Angeles was ranked #54 out of 331 metro areas in *Cities Ranked & Rated*. Criteria: cost of living; climate; crime; transportation; economy and jobs; education; arts and culture; health and healthcare; leisure. *Cities Ranked & Rated, 1st Edition, 2004*

■ Los Angeles was selected as one of the top places to live in the U.S. according to Harris Interactive. The city ranked #11 out of 10. Criteria: 3,685 U.S. adults were polled as to where they would choose to live if they could live anywhere in the country. *Harris Interactive, September 6, 2006*

■ Los Angeles was selected as one of the "50 Best Places to Live" by *Men's Journal*. The city ranked #1 in the "Best Adventure Cities" category. Criteria: proximity to national parks, rock climbing, surfing, biking, skiing, and other active-pursuit options. *Men's Journal, April 2007*

Business/Finance Rankings

■ Los Angeles was selected as one of the best places to start and grow a company by *Entrepreneur* and the National Policy Research Council. The Los Angeles metro area ranked #27 out of 50 large metro areas. Criteria: business formation and growth (firms started four to 14 years ago that still employ at least 5 people and experienced rapid growth over the last four years). *Entrepreneur/National Policy Research Council, "Hot Cities for Entrepreneurs," September 2006*

■ Intel, in partnership with Sperling's BestPlaces, ranked the 80 "Best Cities for Teleworking" in America. The Los Angeles metro area ranked #13 among extra large metro areas. The study identifies cities that hold the greatest potential for teleworking based on a host of factors including typical commuting times, fuel prices, availability of broadband Internet access and percentage of the population in telework friendly jobs. The study also factored in extreme climate and natural hazards. *Intel, "Best Cities for Teleworking," March 30, 2006*

■ Los Angeles was selected as one of the four best U.S. cities for real estate investment. The city ranked #3. *Association of Foreign Investors in Real Estate, AFIRE Foreign Investment Survey 2006*

■ The Los Angeles metro area appeared on the Milken Institute "2005 Best Performing Cities" index. Rank: #124 out of 200 large metro areas. Criteria: job growth; wage and salary growth; high-tech output growth. *Milken Institute, "2005 Best Performing Cities," February 2006*

■ The Los Angeles metro area was selected as one of "The Best Cities for Doing Business in America." *Inc.* magazine measured employment growth in 393 regions using the following criteria: recent growth trend; mid-term growth; long-term trend; and current year growth. The Los Angeles metro area ranked #46 among large metro areas and #279 overall. *Inc., May 2006*

■ Los Angeles was identified as one of the 100 "Most Unwired Cities" in the U.S. The area ranked #24 out of the 100 largest metro areas in the U.S. Criteria: number of public and commercial wireless access points (hotspots); airports with wireless Internet access; broadband availability; local wireless networks; and wireless email devices. *Intel, "Most Unwired Cities Survey," June 7, 2005*

■ Los Angeles was ranked #10 out of 125 regions worldwide in terms of its "Knowledge Competitiveness Index." The index attempts to measure the knowledge-based development taking place throughout the world and is based on 19 measures of economic performance that indicate a region's ability to translate its knowledge capacity into economic value. *Robert Huggins Associates, World Knowledge Competitiveness Index 2005*

■ *Forbes* ranked the 200 most populous metro areas in the U.S. in terms of the "Best Places for Business and Careers." The Los Angeles metro area was ranked #159. Criteria: business costs (labor, energy, tax and office space expenses); living costs (housing, transportation, food and other household expenditures); education levels of the work force; job growth; income growth; migration trends; crime rates; and culture/leisure. *Forbes, April 23, 2007*

- Mercer Human Resources Consulting ranked 50 urban areas worldwide in terms of cost-of-living. Los Angeles ranked #44 (the lower the ranking, the higher the cost-of-living). The survey measured the comparative cost of over 200 items (i.e. housing, food, clothing, household goods, transportation, and entertainment) in each location. *Mercer Human Resources Consulting, "Cost of Living Survey 2005"*

- *Kiplinger's Personal Finance* ranked 101 U.S. cities in terms of their total tax burdens. Los Angeles ranked #86 (#1 had the lowest overall tax burden). Criteria: state income tax; property tax; sales tax; personal property tax; and gasoline tax. *Kiplinger's Personal Finance, July 2004*

- *Fortune* ranked the 100 largest metro areas in the U.S. in terms of projected median home price change in 2006. The Los Angeles metro area ranked #95. *Fortune, "The Top 100: Is the Party Over?" December 26, 2005*

- Los Angeles was identified as one of the "Most Overpriced Places in the U.S." The area ranked #10 out of the nations 150 largest metro areas. Criteria: job growth; income growth; cost of living; and housing affordability. *Forbes.com, "Most Overpriced Places in the U.S. 2005"*

Health/Environment Rankings

- Doctors at the Harvard School of Public Health ranked 40 metropolitan areas based on data from the government-sponsored Hospital Quality Alliance program. The program tracks the performance of individual hospitals in treating patients for three common health problems: heart attacks, congestive heart failure, and pneumonia. The Los Angeles metro area ranked #19 in quality of care for heart attacks, #30 for congestive heart failure, and #39 for pneumonia. *New England Journal of Medicine, July 21, 2005*

- *Reader's Digest* ranked the 50 largest metro areas in the U.S. in terms of how "clean" they are. The Los Angeles metro area ranked #42. Criteria: air quality; water quality; toxic industrial pollution; Superfund sites; and sanitation. *Reader's Digest, "The 50 Cleanest (and Dirtiest) Cities in America," July 2005*

- *Business Week* identified the 15 metro areas that saw the steepest declines in ground-level ozone pollution between 1990 and 2005. The Los Angeles metro area ranked #7. *Business Week, "America's Most Cleaned-Up Metro Areas," March 23, 2007*

- Sanofi-aventis, in partnership with Sperling's BestPlaces, ranked the 50 worst cities for respiratory infections in the U.S. Los Angeles ranked #48. Criteria: prevalence of sinusitis, pharyngitis (sore throat), bronchitis, acute upper respiratory infections, pneumonia, otitis media (middle ear infection), other respiratory tract infections and the common cold; total per capita prescriptions written for oral antibiotics for respiratory tract infections; and prevalence of state level antibiotic resistance. *Sanofi-aventis, "America's Worst Cities for Respiratory Infections," December 6, 2005*

- The Los Angeles metro area appeared in *Country Home's* "2007 Best Green Places Report". The area ranked #66. Criteria included: air and watershed quality; miles of mass transit; green power; number of farmer's markets, organic producers and groceries. *Country Home, "2007 Best Green Places Report," April 2007*

- Wyeth Consumer Healthcare, in partnership with Sperling's BestPlaces, ranked the nation's 50 most populous metro areas in terms of five key health factors. The Los Angeles metro area ranked #23. Criteria: physical activity, health status, nutrition, lifestyle pursuits; and mental wellness. *Wyeth Consumer Healthcare, "Centrum Healthiest Cities Study," April 19, 2005*

- HealthGrades identified the 10 best cities for nursing home care in the U.S. Los Angeles ranked #1. Criteria: proportion of facilities that had four or more actual harm violations from health or complaint surveys in the last four years. *www.HealthGrades.com, "Best and Worst Cities for Nursing Home Care," March 16, 2004*

- HealthGrades surveyed over 41,000 individuals on doctor satisfaction and ranked the 20 largest metro areas based on the highest "definitely yes" responses to the question "Do you trust the physician to make decisions/recommendations that are in your best interest?" The Los Angeles metro area ranked #17. *HealthGrades.com, "Top Cities in Doctor-Trust," September 7, 2006*

- The American Podiatric Medical Association and *Prevention* magazine ranked America's 100 most populated cities based on fitness-walker friendliness. The best cities have safe streets, beautiful places to walk, mild weather and good air quality. Los Angeles ranked #61. *Prevention, "The Best Walking Cities of 2007," April 2007; American Podiatric Medical Association, "2007 Best Fitness-Walking Cities"*

- Los Angeles was selected as one of the 25 fattest cities in America by *Men's Fitness Online*. It ranked #3 out of America's 50 largest cities. Criteria: gyms/sporting goods; nutrition; exercise/sports; overweight/sedentary; junk food; alcohol; smoking; television; air and water quality; climate; geography; commute time; parks/open space; recreation facilities; health care; motivation; civic legislation and leadership. *Men's Fitness Online, America's Fittest/Fattest Cities 2006*

- Los Angeles was identified as a "2007 Asthma Capital." The area ranked #12 out of the nation's 100 largest metropolitan areas. Twelve factors were used to identify the most challenging places to live for people with asthma: estimated prevalence; self-reported prevalence; crude death rate for asthma; annual pollen score; annual air quality; public smoking laws; number of board-certified asthma specialists; school inhaler access laws; rescue medication use; controller medication use; uninsured rate; poverty rate. *Asthma and Allergy Foundation of America, "2007 Asthma Capitals"*

- Los Angeles was identified as a "Spring Allergy Capital." The area ranked #20 out of 100. Three groups of factors were used to identify the most severe cities for people with allergies during the spring season: annual pollen levels; medicine utilization; access to board-certified allergists. *Asthma and Allergy Foundation of America, "2007 Spring Allergy Capital Rankings"*

- Los Angeles was identified as a "Fall Allergy Capital." The area ranked #61 out of 100. Three groups of factors were used to identify the most severe cities for people with allergies during the fall season: annual pollen levels; medicine utilization; access to board-certified allergists. *Asthma and Allergy Foundation of America, "2006 Fall Allergy Capital Rankings"*

- Los Angeles was selected as one of "America's Healthiest Cities" by *Natural Health* magazine. The city was ranked #47 out of the 50 largest urban areas in the U.S. Twenty-six criteria in the following four categories were examined: whether the city boasts natural offerings; how well the city promotes its residents' physical health; whether the city offers a healthy environment; how well the city fosters a sense of community. *Natural Health, April 2003*

- *Men's Health* ranked the nation's largest 100 cities in terms of the *Best (and Worst) Cities for Men*. Los Angeles was ranked #26. Criteria: 24 statistical parameters of long life in the categories of health, quality of life, and fitness. *Men's Health, January/February 2007*

- *Men's Health* ranked 100 U.S. cities in terms of the quality of their tap water. Los Angeles was ranked #97 and received a grade of F. Criteria: levels of total coliform bacteria, arsenic, lead, total trihalomethanes (linked to cancer), and halo-acetic acids, plus the number of EPA water-system violations from 1995 to 2005. *Men's Health, March 2007*

- Ortho-McNeil Neurologics, in partnership with Sperling's BestPlaces, analyzed 110 metro areas and identified those U.S. cities with the highest prevalence of factors that are most commonly associated with migraine headaches. The Los Angeles metro area ranked #102. Criteria: number of migraine-related drug prescriptions per capita; lifestyle factors that can contribute to migraines; environmental factors that can trigger migraines; and consumption of migraine-triggering foods. *Ortho-McNeil Neurologics, "America's Migraine Hot Spots," March 14, 2006*

- Sperling's BestPlaces ranked 331 metro areas and identified the most and least stressful U.S. cities. The Los Angeles metro area ranked #32 out of the 100 largest metro areas (#1 = most stressful). Criteria: divorce rate; unemployment rate; violent and property crime; suicide rate; commute time; mental health; alcohol consumption; cloudy days. *www.BestPlaces.net, January 9, 2004*

- HealthGrades evaluated the performance of America's 25 most populous metropolitan areas by measuring the outcomes of five of the highest volume and most widely studied procedures and diagnoses: coronary artery bypass graft surgery; percutaneus coronary interventions; acute myocardial infarction/heart attack in angioplasty-capable hospitals; congestive heart failure; and community acquired pneumonia. The Los Angeles metro area ranked #10. *HealthGrades, "HealthGrades Hospital Quality in America Study," October 12, 2004*

- Los Angeles was highlighted as one of the 25 metro areas most polluted by year-round particle pollution (PM 2.5) in the U.S. The area ranked #1. *American Lung Association, State of the Air 2006*

- Los Angeles was highlighted as one of the 25 most ozone-polluted metro areas in the U.S. The area ranked #2. *American Lung Association, State of the Air 2006*

- Los Angeles was selected as one of "America's Top 10 Low-Carb Cities" by *LowCarbiz Magazine*. Criteria: abundance of low-carb products; restaurants with low-carb menu items; health practitioners supportive of carb-cutting regimens; local culture generally conducive to exercise and health. *LowCarbiz Magazine, April 2004*

- Los Angeles was selected as one of "America's Pet Healthiest Cities" by Purina. The city ranked #17 out of 50. Criteria: veterinary services; environment; legislation; preventative care; obesity/body condition. *Purina Pet Institute, "America's Pet Healthiest Cities," May 20, 2003*

Women/Minorities Rankings

- Los Angeles was ranked #28 out of 100 metro areas in *SELF Magazine's* ranking of "America's Best Places for Women." A panel of experts came up with nearly 40 criteria including: drinking and smoking rates; depression; unemployment; parks; crime; disease; healthcare insurance coverage; air quality; and commute times. *SELF Magazine, "America's Best Places for Women 2006," December 2006*

- *Ladies Home Journal* ranked America's 200 largest cities based on the qualities women surveyed care about most. Los Angeles ranked #27 out of 57 in the big city category (population over 300,000). Criteria: crime; lifestyle; education; jobs; health; child care; politics; and the economy. *Ladies Home Journal Online, "The Best Cities for Women 2002"*

- Los Angeles appeared on a list of the top 10 metro areas with the highest concentration of same-sex households. The area ranked #7. *Urban Institute Press, The Gay and Lesbian Atlas, May 2004*

- Los Angeles was profiled in the book *50 Fabulous Gay-Friendly Places to Live*. Criteria: an active gay community; positive gay health programs; youth outreach; gay-friendly politics; gay-owned and gay-friendly businesses; employment opportunities; fun nightlife; cultural opportunities; recreational opportunities; housing options. *50 Fabulous Gay-Friendly Places to Live, 2005*

- Los Angeles was selected as one of "America's Top Lesbian Cities" by Gay.com. The city ranked #2 out of 5. *Gay.com*

- Los Angeles appeared on a list of the top 10 metro areas with the highest concentration of gay male couples. The area ranked #7. *Urban Institute Press, The Gay and Lesbian Atlas, May 2004*

- Los Angeles was identified as one of the top 25 metropolitan statistical areas ranked by percentage of coupled households that are gay or lesbian." The area ranked #19. *Human Rights Campaign, "Gay and Lesbian Families in the United States: Same-Sex Unmarried Partner Households," August 1, 2001*

- Los Angeles was selected as one of the "Best Cities for Black Families." The city ranked #6 out of 20. For six months, bet.com compiled data on African Americans in those U.S. cities with the largest Black populations. The data involved the following: infant mortality; high school graduation; median income; homeownership; unemployment; business ownership; poverty rates; AIDS infection rates; percentage of children in single parent, typically fatherless, households; teen pregnancy; economic segregation index; violent and property crime. *www.bet.com, October 1, 2002*

- Los Angeles was selected as one of the "Top 10 Cities for Hispanics to Live In." The city was ranked #8. The cities were selected based on data from the following sources: U.S. Census; *Forbes*; *Fortune*; *Money*; local newspapers; natives and residents; www.bestplaces.net; www.findyourspot.com. *Hispanic Magazine, July/August 2004*

Seniors/Retirement Rankings

- Los Angeles was profiled in the book *Where to Retire: America's Best and Most Affordable Places*. Cities were selected based on personal visits by the author and interviews with local residents coupled with statistics from various government agencies. *Where to Retire: America's Best and Most Affordable Places, 2006*

- Sperling's BestPlaces in partnership with Bankers Life & Casualty Company designed a survey to identify the top 50 metro areas in the U.S. that offer the best overall qualities for senior living. The Los Angeles metro area ranked #17. The following criteria were statistically weighted to reflect the needs of the senior population: health; disease; economics; social; environment; spiritual; transportation; housing; and crime. *Bankers Life & Casualty Company, "Best Cities for Seniors 2005"*

- A.G. Edwards ranked America's 500 top-performing communities based on their residents' personal savings and investing behavior. The Los Angeles metro area ranked #443 with an index score of 95.92 (national average = 100.00). A dozen statistical factors were measured including: participation in retirement savings plans; personal debt levels; and home ownership. *A.G. Edwards, "2006 Nest Egg Index", September 6, 2006*

Children/Family Rankings

- *Zero Population Growth* ranked 100 cities in terms of children's health, safety, and economic well-being. Los Angeles was ranked #10 out of 20 Major Cities (main city in a metro area with population of greater than 2.5 million) and was given a grade of B. Criteria: total population and population growth; percent of population under 18 years of age; percent of births to teens; infant mortality rate; percent of eligible women not receiving Title X services; contraceptive equity indicator; percent of children without health insurance; percent of city residents over age 25 with a high-school diploma; ration of PopEd (Population Connection's Education Program) teachers trained; sexuality education indicator; proficiency in reading and math; percent of kids living in poverty; percent growth in urbanized land; violent crime rate; recycling. *Population Connection, Kid Friendly Cities: Report Card 2004*

- *Fit Pregnancy* magazine ranked the 50 best U.S. cities in which to have a baby. Los Angeles was ranked #34. Criteria: fertility services; maternal and infant health risk; access to hospitals and doctors; safety; affordability; stroller friendliness; and birthing options. *Fit Pregnancy, February/March, 2006*

Safety Rankings

- Allstate ranked the 200 largest cities in America in terms of driver safety. Los Angeles ranked #184. In addition, drivers were 42.9% more likely to have had an accident compared to the national average. Allstate researchers analyzed internal Property Damage reported claims over a two-year period (from January 2003 to December 2004) to ensure the findings would not be affected by external influences such as weather or road construction. A weighted average of the two-year numbers determined the annual percentages. The report defines an auto crash as any collision resulting in a property damage claim. *Allstate, "Allstate America's Best Drivers Report 2006," May 24, 2006*

- Los Angeles was identified as one of the most dangerous large metro areas for pedestrians in the U.S. The area ranked #20 out of the nations 50 largest metro areas. Criteria: average yearly pedestrian fatalities per capita (for the years 2002 and 2003) adjusted for the number of walkers. *Surface Transportation Policy Project, "Mean Streets 2004"*

- *Ladies Home Journal* ranked America's 200 largest cities in terms of safety. Los Angeles ranked #126 out of 200. Criteria: violent crimes; crimes against property; and rape. *Ladies Home Journal Online, "The Best Cities for Women 2002"*

Sports/Recreation Rankings

- The Los Angeles metro area appeared on *The Sporting News* list of the "Best Sports Cities 2006". The area ranked #8 out of 99 cities in North America. To be included in the rankings, a city must have at least one of the following: NCAA Division I basketball team; Class A minor league baseball team; training camp for a major league or NFL team; NASCAR Nextel Cup race; NCAA Division I-A bowl game; PGA Tour tournament; Triple Crown horse race. Once a city qualifies, a 12-month snapshot is taken of the sports atmosphere, putting a heavy premium on regular-season won-lost records; playoff berths, bowl appearances and tournament bids; championships; applicable power ratings; quality of competition; overall fan fervor; sports atmosphere and fan knowledge; abundance of teams (quality over quantity); stadium/arena quality; ticket availability and prices; franchise ownership; and the marquee appeal of athletes. *SportingNews.com, "Best Sports Cities 2006," August 1, 2006*

- Scarborough Research, a leading market research firm, identified the top local markets for avid NBA fans. The Los Angeles DMA (Designated Market Area) ranked in the top 10 with 15% of consumers 18 years and over reporting that they are "very interested in the NBA". *Scarborough Research, Scarborough USA+ 2005 Release 2*

- The Los Angeles metro area was selected by *Cranium* as one of the "Top 50 Fun Cities" in America. The area ranked #26. Criteria includes: number of sports teams, restaurants, and dance performances; number of toy stores; city budget spent on recreation. *Cranium, November 4, 2003*

- *Golf Digest* ranked 330 metro areas in the U.S. in terms of golf. The Los Angeles metro area was ranked #246. Criteria: access to golf; weather; value of golf; and quality of golf. *Golf Digest, "Metro Golf Rankings," August 2005*

Dating/Romance Rankings

- Los Angeles was selected as one of the "Best Cities for Dating" by Love@AOL. The area ranked #2 out of 10. Criteria: Love@AOL surveyed singles and looked at a wide range of dating characteristics such as: are there lots of places to take a date; how easy is it to find a date; and when you're dating, do you acknowledge Valentine's Day? *Love@AOL, "2006 Dating Trends Survey: Best Cities for Dating"*

- The Los Angeles metro area was selected as one of the "Best Cities for Relocating Singles" by Worldwide ERC and Primacy Relocation. The area ranked #28 out of the 100 largest metro areas in the U.S. Areas were selected based on the following criteria: Population Criteria (local percentage and growth trends of unmarried residents aged 25-34; male-female ratios; the number of newcomers to the area; diversity and density); Economic Criteria (job growth vs. unemployment rates; apartment rental costs; fee and occupancy rates for temporary housing and mini-storage; higher education costs, including in-state and out-of-state tuition requirements; vehicle tax rates and quality of service from utility providers); Quality-of-Life Criteria (level of per capita volunteering; quality and quantity of collegiate and professional sports with fun, fan-friendly venues; number of Starbucks and other coffee shops; quality or popularity of restaurants, nightspots, health clubs, and online dating; moderate climates with sustainable water supplies). *Worldwide ERC and Primacy Relocation, "2006 Best Cities for Relocating Singles," October 11, 2006*

- *Forbes* ranked the 40 most populous metro areas in the U.S. in terms of the "Best Cities for Singles." The Los Angeles metro area was ranked #19. Criteria: number of singles; cost of living alone; nightlife; culture; job growth; coolness; and online dating. *Forbes.com, July 25, 2006*

- Sperling's BestPlaces in partnership with AXE Deodorant Bodyspray ranked 80 metro areas and identified "America's Best (and Worst) Cities for Dating." The Los Angeles metro area ranked #32. Criteria: percentage of singles ages 18-24; population density; dating venues per capita. *AXE Deodorant Bodyspray, "America's Best (and Worst) Cities for Dating," May, 2004*

- The Los Angeles metro area was selected as one of the "10 Best Cities for Singles" by AOL CityGuide. The area ranked #2 out of 10.Criteria: over 300 cities were evaluated based on the quantity and quality of places for singles to meet other singles, such as bars and restaurants, cultural and sporting events, and online personals. *AOL CityGuide, "10 Best Cities for Singles," February 12, 2004*

Culture/Performing Arts Rankings

- Los Angeles was selected as one of "The Top 10 American Cities to be a Moviemaker.". The city was ranked #6. *MovieMaker Magazine, Winter 2006, Issue No. 61*

- Los Angeles was selected as one of "America's Top 25 Arts Destinations." The city ranked #12 in the big city (population 500,000 and over) category. Criteria: readers' top choices for arts travel destinations based on the richness and variety of visual arts sites, activities and events. *American Style, June 2006*

Miscellaneous Rankings

- Los Angeles was selected as one of the "Least Courteous Cities (Worst Road Rage)" in the U.S. by AutoVantage. The city ranked #4. Criteria: 2,040 consumers were interviewed in 20 major metropolitan areas about their views on road rage. *AutoVantage, "In The Driver's Seat Road Rage Survey," May 16, 2006*

- Los Angeles was determined to be one of America's smartest cities. The city ranked #41 in the large city category (200,000+ adults 25 years and older). Criteria: the editors rated the collective brainpower of U.S communities based on the educational attainment of its residents. *American City Business Journals, www.bizjournals.com, June 12, 2006*

- Los Angeles was selected as one of the "Top 100 Sweatiest Summer Cities". The city was ranked #94. The ranking was based on the average male/female height/weight, average high temperature, and average relative humidity levels for 2002 in each of the cities during June, July and August. The sweat level was analyzed based on the assumption that the individual was walking for one hour. *Procter & Gamble, Old Spice, June 18, 2003*

- Avis Rent-A-Car and Motorola, in partnership with Sperling's BestPlaces, ranked the nation's 75 most populous metro areas in terms of how difficult they are to navigate. The Los Angeles metro area ranked #7 with #1 being the most challenging. Criteria: street layouts; overall design and layout; travel time index; percent of congested freeway and street lane miles; bodies of water; complexity of directions needed to travel from major airports to city center; annual delay per person; days of snow exceeding 1.5 inches; and days of rain exceeding 0.5 inch. *Avis Rent-A-Car and Motorola, "America's Most Challenging Cities to Navigate," August 3, 2004*

- Los Angeles was selected as one of America's "20 Meanest Cities" by the National Coalition for the Homeless and The National Law Center on Homelessness & Poverty. The city was ranked #18. Criteria: the number of anti-homeless laws; the enforcement of those laws and severities of penalties; the general political climate towards homeless people; local advocate support for the meanest designation; the city's history of criminalization measures; and the existence of pending or recently enacted criminalization legislation. *National Coalition for the Homeless and The National Law Center on Homelessness & Poverty, "A Dream Denied: The Criminalization of Homelessness in U.S. Cities," January 2006*

- The Los Angeles metro area appeared on *Forbes* list of "America's Drunkest Cities". The area ranked #23. Criteria: 35 of the largest continental U.S. metro areas were chosen based on availability of data and geographic diversity. Each metro was ranked in five areas: state laws; drinkers; heavy drinkers; binge drinkers; and alcoholism. *Forbes.com, "America's Drunkest Cities," August 22, 2006*

- Los Angeles appeared on ApartmentRatings.com "Top Cities for Renters List 2006". The area ranked #132 out of 138. Criteria: renter satisfaction; affordability; and vacancy. *ApartmentRatings.com, "Top Cities for Renters List 2006"*

■ Sperling's BestPlaces in partnership with Pep Boys ranked 77 metro areas and identified "America's Most Drivable Cities." The Los Angeles metro area ranked #77. Criteria: climate; road roughness; urban mobility; gas prices. *Pep Boys, "America's Most Drivable Cities," April 9, 2003*

■ Los Angeles was ranked #13 out of 268 metro areas in terms of its Creativity Index. The Creativity Index is a mix of four equally weighted factors: the Creative Class (scientists, engineers, architects, designers, writers, artists, musicians, or any profession where creativity is a key factor) share of the workforce; innovation, measured as patents per capita; high-tech industry, using the Milken Institute's Tech Pole Index; and diversity, measured by the Gay Index (a reasonable proxy for an areas' openness to different kinds of people and ideas). *The Rise of the Creative Class, 2002*

■ Los Angeles was selected as one of "America's Most Literate Cities." The city ranked #57 out of the 70 largest U.S. cities. Criteria: number of booksellers; library resources; Internet resources; educational attainment; periodical publishing resources; newspaper circulation. *Central Connecticut State University, "America's Most Literate Cities 2006"*

■ State Farm Insurance, in partnership with Sperling's BestPlaces, analyzed several key factors that contribute to overall family preparedness. The Los Angeles metro area ranked #48 out of the nation's 50 most populous metro areas. Criteria: quality of life; life insurance coverage; and investments. *State Farm Life Insurance, "Fiscally Fit Cities Report," July 20, 2004*

■ Scarborough Research, a leading market research firm, identified the top local markets for coffee bar patronage. The Los Angeles DMA (Designated Market Area) ranked in the top 10 with 19% of adults reporting that they have used any coffee house/bar during the past 30 days. *Scarborough Research, Scarborough USA+ 2004 Release 1*

Business Environment

CITY FINANCES

City Government Finances

Component	2003-2004 ($000)	2003-2004 ($ per capita)
Total Revenues	13,471,129	3,546
Total Expenditures	10,895,644	2,868
Debt Outstanding	14,633,205	3,852
Cash and Securities	17,370,041	4,572

Source: U.S Census Bureau, Government Finances 2003-2004

City Government Revenue by Source

Source	2003-2004 ($000)	2003-2004 ($ per capita)
General Revenue		
From Federal Government	300,006	79
From State Government	539,651	142
From Local Governments	138,270	36
Taxes		
Property	991,214	261
Sales	1,061,088	279
Personal Income	0	0
License	0	0
Charges	2,299,553	605
Liquor Store	0	0
Utility	2,918,015	768
Employee Retirement	3,812,418	1,004
Other	1,410,914	371

Source: U.S Census Bureau, Government Finances 2003-2004

City Government Expenditures by Function

Function	2003-2004 ($000)	2003-2004 ($ per capita)	2003-2004 (%)
General Expenditures			
Airports	719,881	189	6.6
Corrections	0	0	0.0
Education	0	0	0.0
Fire Protection	432,992	114	4.0
Governmental Administration	408,530	108	3.7
Health	50,008	13	0.5
Highways	341,414	90	3.1
Hospitals	0	0	0.0
Housing and Community Development	207,002	54	1.9
Interest on General Debt	395,951	104	3.6
Libraries	74,114	20	0.7
Parking	25,667	7	0.2
Parks and Recreation	326,300	86	3.0
Police Protection	1,208,608	318	11.1
Public Welfare	0	0	0.0
Sewerage	564,861	149	5.2
Solid Waste Management	226,913	60	2.1
Liquor Store	0	0	0.0
Utility	3,154,488	830	29.0
Employee Retirement	1,339,969	353	12.3
Other	1,418,946	374	13.0

Source: U.S Census Bureau, Government Finances 2003-2004

Municipal Bond Ratings

Area	Moody's
City	Aaa

Source: Mergent Bond Record, January 2007 (unless noted otherwise)

DEMOGRAPHICS

Population Growth

Area	1990 Census	2000 Census	2006 Estimate	2011 Projection	Population Growth (%)	
					1990-2000	2000-2011
City	3,487,671	3,694,820	3,910,145	4,110,733	5.9	11.3
MSA[1]	11,273,720	12,365,627	13,155,105	13,873,953	9.7	12.2
U.S.	248,709,873	281,421,906	298,021,266	312,383,955	13.2	11.0

Note: (1) Metropolitan Statistical Area - see Appendix B for areas included
Source: Claritas, Inc.

Number of Households and Average Household Size

Area	2006 Estimate	2006 Average Household Size
City	1,342,430	2.91
MSA[1]	4,284,258	3.07
U.S.	112,267,302	2.65

Note: (1) Metropolitan Statistical Area - see Appendix B for areas included
Source: Claritas, Inc.

Race and Ethnicity

Area	White Alone[2]	Black Alone[2]	Asian Alone[2]	Other Race Alone[2]	Hispanic[3]
City	46.1	10.1	10.4	33.4	49.5
MSA[1]	50.5	7.4	13.4	28.6	43.8
U.S.	73.3	12.4	4.2	10.1	14.5

Note: Figures are 2006 estimates; (1) Metropolitan Statistical Area - see Appendix B for areas included
(2) Alone is defined as not being in combination with one or more other races; (3) May be of any race.
Source: Claritas, Inc.

Segregation

City		MSA[1]	
Index[2]	Rank[3]	Index[2]	Rank[4]
74.0	14	70.5	53

Note: Figures are based on an analysis of Census 2000 data; (1) Metropolitan Statistical Area - see Appendix A for areas included; (2) White/Black Dissimilarity Index—the most commonly used measure of segregation between two groups, reflecting their relative distributions across neighborhoods within a city or metropolitan area. It can range in value from 0, indicating complete integration, to 100, indicating complete segregation; (3) Ranges from 1 (most segregated) to 100 (least segregated) and includes all the cities in this book; (4) Ranges from 1 (most segregated) to 318 (least segregated) and includes 318 metropolitan areas.
Source: www.CensusScope.org

Ancestry

Area	German	Irish[2]	English	American	Italian	Polish	French[3]	Scottish
City	4.5	3.8	3.5	2.6	2.6	1.5	1.3	0.8
MSA[1]	5.8	4.6	4.4	2.5	2.8	1.3	1.5	1.0
U.S.	15.2	10.9	8.7	7.3	5.6	3.2	3.0	1.7

Note: Figures include multiple ancestry (e.g. if a person reported being Irish and Italian, they were included in both columns); (1) Metropolitan Statistical Area - see Appendix A for areas included; (2) Includes Celtic; (3) Includes Alsatian but excludes Basque
Source: Census 2000, Summary File 3

Foreign-Born Population

Area	Percent of Population Born in							
	Any Foreign Country	Europe	Asia	Africa	Oceania[2]	Canada	Mexico	Latin America[3]
City	40.9	2.7	10.2	0.6	0.1	0.4	16.9	10.1
MSA[1]	36.2	2.0	10.7	0.5	0.1	0.4	16.0	6.5
U.S.	11.1	1.7	2.9	0.3	0.1	0.3	3.3	2.5

Note: (1) Metropolitan Statistical Area - see Appendix A for areas included; (2) Includes Australia, New Zealand subregion, Melanesia, Micronesia, Polynesia, and Oceania n.e.c; (3) Includes Central America (excluding Mexico), South America, and the Caribbean.
Source: Census 2000, Summary File 3

Marriage Status

Area	Never Married	Now Married (excluding Separated)	Separated	Widowed	Divorced
City	37.1	45.5	3.5	5.4	8.4
MSA[1]	34.1	48.8	3.1	5.5	8.5
U.S.	27.1	54.4	2.2	6.6	9.7

Note: Figures are percentages and cover the population 15 years of age and older;
(1) Metropolitan Statistical Area - see Appendix A for areas included
Source: Census 2000, Summary File 3

Age Distribution

Area	Percent of Population						
	Under Age 5	Age 5 to 17	Age 18 to 34	Age 35 to 49	Age 50 to 64	Age 65 to 79	80 Years and Over
City	7.6	18.9	29.1	22.7	12.1	7.2	2.5
MSA[1]	7.7	20.3	26.7	23.0	12.6	7.3	2.4
U.S.	6.8	18.9	23.7	23.5	14.8	9.2	3.2

Note: (1) Metropolitan Statistical Area - see Appendix A for areas included
Source: Census 2000, Summary File 3

Male/Female Ratio

Area	Males	Females	Males per 100 Females
City	1,950,821	1,959,324	99.6
MSA[1]	6,518,886	6,636,219	98.2
U.S.	146,712,712	151,308,554	97.0

Note: Figures are 2006 estimates; (1) Metropolitan Statistical Area -
see Appendix B for areas included
Source: Claritas, Inc.

Religion

Area	Catholic	Southern Baptist	United Methodist	ELCA[1]	LDS[2]	Presbyterian Church USA	Jewish Est.	Muslim Est.
County	40.0	1.2	0.6	0.3	1.0	0.6	5.9	1.0
U.S.	22.0	7.1	3.7	1.8	1.5	1.1	2.2	0.6

Note: Figures are the number of adherents as a percentage of the total population; Adherents are defined as all
members, including full members, their children and the estimated number of other participants who are not
considered members (e.g. the baptized, those not confirmed, those regularly attending services, etc.);
(1) Evangelical Lutheran Church in America; (2) The Church of Jesus Christ of Latter Day Saints
Source: Reprinted with permission from Religious Congregations and Membership in the United States 2000
(Nashville, Glenmary Research Center, 2002) Copyright Association of Statisticians of American Religious
Bodies. All rights reserved.

ECONOMY

Gross Metropolitan Product

Area	2002	2003	2004	2005	2005 Rank[2]
MSA[1]	502.1	528.0	567.6	604.8	2

Note: Figures are in billions of dollars; (1) Los Angeles-Long Beach-Santa Ana, CA Metropolitan Statistical
Area - see Appendix A for areas included; (2) Rank ranges from 1 to 361
Source: The U.S. Conference of Mayors, "U.S. Metro Economies: GMP - The Engines of America's Growth,"
January 2007

Economic Growth

Area	1995 GMP	2005 GMP	Average Annual Growth Rate	Growth Rate Rank[2]
MSA[1]	354.1	604.8	5.5	160

Note: Figures are in billions of dollars; GMP = Gross Metropolitan Product; (1) Los Angeles-Long Beach-Santa Ana, CA Metropolitan Statistical Area - see Appendix A for areas included; (2) Rank ranges from 1 to 361
Source: The U.S. Conference of Mayors, "U.S. Metro Economies: GMP - The Engines of America's Growth," January 2007

INCOME

Per Capita/Median/Average Income

Area	Per Capita ($)	Median Household ($)	Average Household ($)
City	22,274	41,076	63,909
MSA[1]	24,259	51,573	73,593
U.S.	25,129	48,775	65,849

Note: Figures are 2006 estimates; (1) Metropolitan Statistical Area - see Appendix B for areas included
Source: Claritas, Inc.

Household Income Distribution

Area	Percent of Households Earning							
	Under $15,000	$15,000 -24,999	$25,000 -34,999	$35,000 -49,999	$50,000 -74,999	$75,000 -99,000	$100,000 -149,999	$150,000 and up
City	18.9	13.1	12.1	14.7	15.6	9.1	9.0	7.5
MSA[1]	13.3	10.5	10.5	14.5	17.8	11.7	12.4	9.2
U.S.	13.3	11.0	11.3	15.7	19.5	11.8	11.0	6.4

Note: Figures are 2006 estimates; (1) Metropolitan Statistical Area - see Appendix B for areas included
Source: Claritas, Inc.

Poverty Rates by Age

Area	All Ages	Under 5 Years Old	5 to 17 Years Old	18 to 64 Years Old	65 Years and Over
City	22.1	2.4	5.7	12.8	1.2
MSA[1]	17.9	1.9	4.9	10.1	1.0
U.S.	12.4	1.2	3.0	6.9	1.2

Note: Figures are percent of population with income in 1999 below poverty level and only include population for whom poverty status is determined; (1) Metropolitan Statistical Area - see Appendix A for areas included
Source: Census 2000, Summary File 3

Personal Bankruptcy Filing Rate

Area	2003	2004	2005
Los Angeles County	4.26	3.41	4.90
U.S.	5.57	5.31	6.88

Note: Numbers are per 1,000 population and include Chapter 7 and Chapter 13 filings
Source: Federal Deposit Insurance Corporation (FDIC), Regional Economic Conditions (RECON), 3/24/2006

EMPLOYMENT

Labor Force and Employment

Area	Civilian Labor Force			Workers Employed		
	Dec. 2005	Dec. 2006	% Chg.	Dec. 2005	Dec. 2006	% Chg.
City	1,900,522	1,886,424	-0.7	1,794,288	1,798,788	0.3
MD[1]	4,895,787	4,873,751	-0.5	4,652,703	4,670,475	0.4
U.S.	149,874,000	152,571,000	1.8	142,918,000	146,081,000	2.2

Note: Data is not seasonally adjusted and covers workers 16 years of age and older; (1) Metropolitan Division - see Appendix B for areas included
Source: Bureau of Labor Statistics, http://stats.bls.gov

Unemployment Rate

Area	2006											
	Jan.	Feb.	Mar.	Apr.	May	Jun.	Jul.	Aug.	Sep.	Oct.	Nov.	Dec.
City	6.0	6.1	5.3	5.0	5.4	5.2	5.6	5.6	5.3	4.7	4.5	4.6
MD[1]	5.2	5.2	4.7	4.5	4.6	4.7	5.3	5.1	4.7	4.2	4.2	4.2
U.S.	5.1	5.1	4.8	4.5	4.4	4.8	5.0	4.6	4.4	4.1	4.3	4.3

Note: Data is not seasonally adjusted and covers workers 16 years of age and older; All figures are percentages; (1) Metropolitan Division - see Appendix B for areas included
Source: Bureau of Labor Statistics, http://stats.bls.gov

Employment by Occupation

Occupation Classification	City (%)	MSA[1] (%)	U.S. (%)
Sales and Office	26.7	27.6	26.7
Professional and Related	21.6	20.9	20.2
Service	16.0	14.7	14.9
Production, Transportation, and Material Moving	15.2	15.5	14.6
Management, Business, and Financial	12.6	13.4	13.5
Construction, Extraction, and Maintenance	7.7	7.8	9.4
Farming, Forestry, and Fishing	0.2	0.2	0.7

Note: Figures cover employed civilians 16 years of age and older;
(1) Metropolitan Statistical Area - see Appendix A for areas included
Source: Census 2000, Summary File 3

Employment by Industry

Sector	MSA[1] Number of Employees	MSA[1] Percent of Total	U.S. Percent of Total
Government	597,100	14.4	16.3
Education and Health Services	495,000	11.9	13.2
Professional and Business Services	604,600	14.6	12.9
Retail Trade	446,700	10.8	11.5
Manufacturing	458,100	11.0	10.2
Leisure and Hospitality	389,700	9.4	9.5
Financial Activities	249,200	6.0	6.1
Construction	155,500	3.7	5.5
Wholesale Trade	226,800	5.5	4.3
Other Services	147,000	3.5	3.9
Transportation and Utilities	169,800	4.1	3.7
Information	211,700	5.1	2.2
Natural Resources and Mining	4,000	0.1	0.5

Note: Figures cover non-farm employment as of December 2006 and are not seasonally adjusted;
(1) Metropolitan Statistical Area - see Appendix B for areas included
Source: Bureau of Labor Statistics, http://stats.bls.gov

Occupations with Greatest Projected Employment Growth: 2002 - 2012

Occupation[1]	2002 Employment	2012 Projected Employment	Numeric Employment Change	Percent Employment Change
Retail Salespersons	435,400	513,200	77,800	17.9
Postsecondary Teachers	154,500	217,700	63,200	40.9
Combined Food Preparation and Serving Workers, Including Fast Food	215,100	277,300	62,200	28.9
Cashiers	358,800	420,700	61,900	17.3
Registered Nurses	201,600	258,400	56,800	28.2
Waiters and Waitresses	214,000	264,900	50,900	23.8
Customer Service Representatives	197,500	244,900	47,400	24.0
Office Clerks, General	400,300	446,500	46,200	11.5
General and Operations Managers	224,000	267,000	43,000	19.2
Teacher Assistants	179,600	222,300	42,700	23.8

Note: Projections cover California; (1) Sorted by numeric employment change
Source: www.projectionscentral.com, State Occupational Projections, 2002-2012 Long-Term Projections

Fastest Growing Occupations: 2002 - 2012

Occupation[1]	2002 Employment	2012 Projected Employment	Numeric Employment Change	Percent Employment Change
Physical Therapist Aides	4,200	6,800	2,600	61.9
Dental Hygienists	16,600	26,200	9,600	57.8
Dental Assistants	42,700	67,100	24,400	57.1
Tapers	9,200	14,400	5,200	56.5
Drywall and Ceiling Tile Installers	26,800	41,800	15,000	56.0
Tile and Marble Setters	8,600	13,400	4,800	55.8
Network Systems and Data Communications Analysts	20,300	31,600	11,300	55.7
Physical Therapist Assistants	3,900	6,000	2,100	53.8
Fitness Trainers and Aerobics Instructors	24,000	35,700	11,700	48.8
Self-Enrichment Education Teachers	24,200	35,800	11,600	47.9

Note: Projections cover California; (1) Sorted by percent employment change and excludes occupations with numeric employment change less than 1500
Source: www.projectionscentral.com, State Occupational Projections, 2002-2012 Long-Term Projections

Average Wages

Occupation	$/Hr.	Occupation	$/Hr.
Accountants and Auditors	29.07	Maids and Housekeeping Cleaners	9.26
Automotive Mechanics	18.97	Maintenance and Repair Workers	16.91
Bookkeepers	16.17	Marketing Managers	52.80
Carpenters	21.85	Nuclear Medicine Technologists	32.04
Cashiers	9.61	Nurses, Licensed Practical	20.09
Clerks, General Office	12.32	Nurses, Registered	32.53
Clerks, Receptionists/Information	11.69	Nursing Aides/Orderlies/Attendants	10.47
Clerks, Shipping/Receiving	12.37	Packers and Packagers, Hand	8.61
Computer Programmers	34.18	Physical Therapists	32.19
Computer Support Specialists	20.95	Postal Service Mail Carriers	22.72
Computer Systems Analysts	33.42	Real Estate Brokers	44.55
Cooks, Restaurant	10.33	Retail Salespersons	11.91
Dentists	n/a	Sales Reps., Exc. Tech./Scientific	25.59
Electrical Engineers	39.22	Sales Reps., Tech./Scientific	32.45
Electricians	23.80	Secretaries, Exc. Legal/Med./Exec.	15.49
Financial Managers	50.04	Security Guards	10.74
First-Line Supervisors/Mgrs., Sales	18.64	Surgeons	80.56
Food Preparation Workers	8.72	Teacher Assistants	12.80
General and Operations Managers	52.97	Teachers, Elementary School	24.70
Hairdressers/Cosmetologists	12.76	Teachers, Secondary School	27.40
Internists	77.11	Telemarketers	12.12
Janitors and Cleaners	10.53	Truck Drivers, Heavy/Tractor-Trailer	17.08
Landscaping/Groundskeeping Workers	12.23	Truck Drivers, Light/Delivery Svcs.	12.62
Lawyers	64.38	Waiters and Waitresses	8.34

Note: Wage data is for May 2005 and covers the Los Angeles-Long Beach-Glendale, CA Metropolitan Division - see Appendix B for areas included. Hourly wages for elementary/secondary school teachers and teacher assistants were calculated by the editors from annual wage data assuming a 40 hour work week; n/a not available.
Source: Bureau of Labor Statistics, May 2005 Metro Area Occupational Employment and Wage Estimates

RESIDENTIAL REAL ESTATE

Building Permits

Area	Single-Family			Multi-Family			Total		
	2005	2006p	Pct. Chg.	2005	2006p	Pct. Chg.	2005	2006p	Pct. Chg.
City	2,482	2,421	-2.5	6,723	12,027	78.9	9,205	14,448	57.0
U.S.	1,682,000	1,380,000	-18.0	473,300	457,300	-3.4	2,155,300	1,837,300	-14.8

Note: (p) preliminary; figures represent new, privately-owned housing units authorized (unadjusted data); All permit data are based on estimates with imputation; U.S. figures are based on the new 20,000-place series.
Source: U.S. Census Bureau, Manufacturing, Mining, and Construction Statistics

Homeownership and Housing Vacancies

Area	Homeownership Rate[2] (%)			Rental Vacancy Rate[3] (%)			Homeowner Vacancy Rate[4] (%)		
	2004	2005	2006	2004	2005	2006	2004	2005	2006
MSA[1]	n/a	54.6	54.4	n/a	4.4	4.0	n/a	0.9	1.2
U.S.	69.0	68.9	68.8	10.2	9.8	9.7	1.7	1.9	2.4

Note: Comparable 2004 data was not available due to changes in metropolitan area definitions; (1) Metropolitan Statistical Area - see Appendix B for areas included; (2) The proportion of households that are owners; (3) The proportion of the rental inventory that is vacant for rent; (4) The proportion of the homeowner inventory that is vacant for sale; n/a not available
Source: U.S. Census Bureau, Housing Vacancies and Homeownership Annual Statistics: 2006

TAXES

State Corporate Income Tax Rates

State	Rate (%)	Number of Brackets	Low Bracket (Under $)	High Bracket (Over $)
California	8.84	1	na	na

Note: Tax rates as of December 31, 2006; na not applicable; 10.84% on financial institutions. Minimum tax is $800. The tax rate on S-Corporations is 1.5% (3.5% for financial S-Corporations).
Source: Tax Foundation, www.taxfoundation.org

State Individual Income Tax Rates

State	Federal Deductibility	Marginal Rate (%)	Number of Brackets	Low Bracket (Under $)	High Bracket (Over $)
California	No	1.0-10.3 (p)(r)	7	0	1,000,000

Note: Tax rates as of December 31, 2006; Brackets apply to single taxpayers and married people filing separately; na not applicable; (p) California's $1,000,000 bracket not doubled for married taxpayers; (r) Indexed for Inflation.
Source: Tax Foundation, www.taxfoundation.org

Various State and Local Tax Rates

State and Local Sales and Use (%)	State Sales and Use (%)	Gasoline ($/gal.)	Cigarette ($/pack)	Spirits ($/gal.)	Table Wine ($/gal.)	Beer ($/gal.)
8.25	6.25	0.192 (m)	0.87	3.3	0.20	0.20

Note: Tax rates as of December 31, 2006; (m) Additional cents per gallon taxes added this year that were not included in previous years' tables.
Source: Tax Foundation, www.taxfoundation.org; The Sales Tax Clearinghouse, www.thestc.com

State Tax Burdens

Area	Combined State and Local Tax Burden		Combined Federal, State and Local Tax Burden	
	Percent	Rank	Percent	Rank
California	10.9	15	32.7	9
U.S. Average	10.6	-	31.6	-

Note: Figures are for 2006 and measure taxes as a percentage of income
Source: Tax Foundation, www.taxfoundation.org

Internal Revenue Service Tax Audits

IRS District	Percent of Returns Audited				
	1996	1997	1998	1999	2000
Los Angeles	1.59	1.54	0.98	0.67	0.48
U.S.	0.66	0.61	0.46	0.31	0.20

Note: Figures cover IRS district audits of federal income tax returns filed by individuals. Geographic data on district audits after the year 2000 are being withheld by the IRS. TRAC is challenging this policy.
Source: Syracuse University, Transactional Records Access Clearinghouse (TRAC), "Odds of IRS District Tax Audit 2000"

**COMMERCIAL
REAL ESTATE**

Office Market

Market Area	Inventory (sq. ft.)	Vacant (sq. ft.)	Vac. Rate (%)	Under Constr. (sq. ft.)	Asking Rent ($/sf) Class A	Asking Rent ($/sf) Class B
Los Angeles	182,865,799	17,209,996	9.4	1,549,591	34.32	26.88

Source: Grubb & Ellis, Office Markets Trends, 4th Quarter 2006

Industrial Market

Market Area	Inventory (sq. ft.)	Vacant (sq. ft.)	Vac. Rate (%)	Under Constr. (sq. ft.)	Asking Rent ($/sf) WH/Dist	Asking Rent ($/sf) R&D/Flex
Los Angeles	983,352,491	14,782,403	1.5	5,468,450	7.20	10.44

Source: Grubb & Ellis, Industrial Markets Trends, 4th Quarter 2006

**COMMERCIAL
UTILITIES**

Typical Monthly Electric Bills

Area	Commercial Service ($/month) 3 kW demand 1,000 kWh	Commercial Service ($/month) 40 kW demand 14,000 kWh	Industrial Service ($/month) 1,000 kW demand 200,000 kWh	Industrial Service ($/month) 50,000 kW demand 15,000,000 kWh
City	n/a	n/a	n/a	n/a
Average[1]	123	1,413	22,000	1,306,315

Note: Based on total rates in effect July 1, 2006; (1) average based on 196 utilities; n/a not available
Source: Edison Electric Institute, Typical Bills and Average Rates Report, Summer 2006

TRANSPORTATION

Means of Transportation to Work

Area	Car/Truck/Van Drove Alone	Car/Truck/Van Car-pooled	Public Transportation Bus	Public Transportation Subway	Public Transportation Railroad	Bicycle	Walked	Other Means	Worked at Home
City	65.7	14.7	9.7	0.2	0.1	0.6	3.6	1.2	4.1
MSA[1]	70.4	15.1	6.1	0.2	0.2	0.6	2.9	1.1	3.5
U.S.	75.7	12.2	2.5	1.5	0.5	0.4	2.9	1.0	3.3

Note: Figures are percentages and cover workers 16 years of age and older;
(1) Metropolitan Statistical Area - see Appendix A for areas included
Source: Census 2000, Summary File 3

Travel Time to Work

Area	Less Than 15 Minutes	15 to 29 Minutes	30 to 44 Minutes	45 to 59 Minutes	60 Minutes or More
City	18.9	35.6	25.7	9.3	10.6
MSA[1]	20.7	34.6	24.1	9.7	10.9
U.S.	29.4	36.1	19.1	7.4	8.0

Note: Figures are percentages and include workers 16 years old and over; (1) Metropolitan Statistical Area -
see Appendix A for areas included
Source: Census 2000, Summary File 3

Travel Time Index

Area	1982	1993	2002	2003
Urban Area[1]	1.30	1.73	1.77	1.75
Average[2]	1.12	1.28	1.37	1.37

Note: Travel Time Index - The ratio of travel time in the peak period to the travel time at
free-flow conditions. A value of 1.35 indicates a 20-minute free-flow trip takes 27 minutes
in the peak. Free-flow speeds (60 mph on freeways and 35 mph on principal arterials)
are used as the comparison threshold; (1) Covers the Los Angeles-Long Beach-Santa Ana, CA urban area;
(2) average of 85 urban areas
Source: Texas Transportation Institute, The 2005 Urban Mobility Report, May 2005

Public Transportation

Agency name:	Los Angeles Co. Metro Transportation Authority (LACMTA)
Vehicle type:	Bus
Average fleet age in years:	7.2
No. operated in max. service:	2,256
Vehicle type:	Heavy rail
Average fleet age in years:	9.0
No. operated in max. service:	70
Vehicle type:	Light rail
Average fleet age in years:	12.1
No. operated in max. service:	96
Agency name:	City of Los Angeles Department of Transportation (LADOT)
Vehicle type:	Bus
Average fleet age in years:	8.4
No. operated in max. service:	224
Vehicle type:	Demand response
Average fleet age in years:	3.5
No. operated in max. service:	164
Agency name:	LACMTA - Small Operators
Vehicle type:	Bus
Average fleet age in years:	5.4
No. operated in max. service:	171
Vehicle type:	Demand Response
Average fleet age in years:	5.0
No. operated in max. service:	211

Source: Federal Transit Administration, National Transit Database, 2005

Air Transportation

Airport name and code:	Los Angeles International (LAX)
Domestic service (2006)	
Passenger airlines[1]:	34
Passenger enplanements:	21,339,036
Freight carriers[2]:	43
Freight (lbs.):	941,663,753
International service (2005)	
Passenger airlines[1]:	63
Passenger enplanements:	8,133,442
Freight carriers[2]:	74
Freight (lbs.):	807,999,284

*Note: (1) Includes all major, minor and commuter airlines that carried at least one passenger during the year;
(2) Includes all airlines and freight carriers that transported at least one pound of freight during the year
Source: Bureau of Transportation Statistics, The Intermodal Transportation Database, Air Carriers: T-100
International Market, 2004; Bureau of Transportation Statistics, The Intermodal Transportation Database, Air
Carriers: T-100 Domestic Market, 2005*

Other Transportation Statistics

Interstate highways:	I-10; I-5
Amtrak service:	Yes
Major waterways/ports:	Port of Los Angeles

Source: Editor & Publisher Market Guide, 2006; Amtrak.com; Rand McNally 2006 Road Atlas

BUSINESSES

Major Business Headquarters

Company Name	2006 Rankings	
	Fortune[1]	Forbes[2]
Aecom Technology	-	82
Capital Group Cos	-	20
KB Home	254	-
Latham & Watkins	-	270
Metro-Goldwyn-Mayer	-	242
Murdock Holding Company	-	30
Northrop Grumman	67	-
Occidental Petroleum	133	-
Roll International	-	258
Topa Equities	-	314

Note: (1) Fortune 500 - companies that produce a 10-K are ranked 1 to 500 based on 2005 revenue; (2) Forbes Largest Private Companies - all private companies with at least $1 billion in annual revenue are ranked 1 to 394; companies listed are located in the city; dashes indicate no ranking
Source: Fortune, April 17, 2006; Forbes, November 9, 2006

Best Companies to Work For

Arnold & Porter; Four Seasons Hotels; IKEA North America, headquartered in Los Angeles, are among the "100 Best Companies to Work For." Criteria: More than 105,000 employees from 446 companies responded to a 57-question survey created by the Great Place to Work Institute. Two-thirds of a company's score is based on the survey, which covers topics such as attitudes towards management, job satisfaction, and camaraderie. The remaining third of the score comes from each company's responses to the Institute's Culture Audit, which includes detailed questions about demographic makeup, pay and benefits programs, and open-ended questions about the company's people-management philosophy, internal communications, opportunities, compensation practices, diversity programs, etc. Any company that is at least seven years old and has a minimum of 1,000 U.S. employees is eligible. The top three U.S. locations are shown for companies with more than one location. *Fortune, "100 Best Companies to Work for 2007," January 22, 2007*

The Capital Group Cos, headquartered in Los Angeles, is among the "100 Best Places to Work in IT." To qualify, companies, both public and private, had to have 2005 revenue of $250 million or greater and employ a minimum of 500 people in the U.S., with a minimum of 100 IT employees in the U.S. Companies were selected based on average salary and bonus increases, the percentage of IT employees receiving promotions, IT staff turnover rates, training and development, and the percentage of women and minorities in IT staff and management positions. In addition, information was collected on how the organizations reward outstanding performance, how their retention programs are structured and what benefits they offer. *Computerworld, "100 Best Places to Work in IT 2006," June 19, 2006*

Fast-Growing Businesses

According to *Inc.*, Los Angeles is home to seven of America's 500 fastest-growing private companies: **American Apparel; Ancillary Care Management; Kurtzman Carson Consultants; Odesus; Outsource Partners International; SCI Real Estate Investments; Segue Electronics**. Criteria: must be an independent, privately-held, U.S. corporation, proprietorship or partnership; net sales of at least $600,000 in FY2002; four-year operating/sales history; holding companies, regulated banks, and utilities were excluded. *Inc., "America's 500 Fastest-Growing Private Companies," September 2006*

Los Angeles is home to three of *Business Week's* "Hot Growth Companies:" **Guess?; Korn/Ferry International; PeopleSupport**. To qualify, a company must have annual sales of more than $50 million and less than $1.5 billion, a current market value greater than $25 million, a current stock price of at least $5, and be actively traded. Banks, insurers, real estate firms, and utilities are excluded. So are companies with declines in current financial results or in stock price, as well as companies where other developments raise questions about future performance. Companies were selected based on three-year results in sales growth, earnings growth, and return on invested capital. *Business Week, June 5, 2006*

According to *Fortune*, Los Angeles is home to two of America's 100 fastest-growing companies: **Reliance Steel & Aluminum; Wilshire Bancorp**. Companies were ranked based on earnings-per-share growth, revenue growth and total return over the previous three years. Criteria for inclusion: public companies with sales of at least $50 million. Companies that lost money in the most recent quarter, or ended in the red for the past four quarters as a whole, were not eligible. Limited partnerships and REITs were also not considered. *Fortune, "America's Fastest-Growing Companies," September 18, 2006*

According to *Business 2.0*, Los Angeles is home to one of America's 100 fastest-growing technology companies: **J2 Global Communications**. The 100 Fastest-Growing Technology Companies (B2 100) is a yearly ranking published by Business 2.0 magazine of businesses whose inventiveness and quick reflexes are helping them to set the pace for the economy. To find the B2 100, Zacks Investment Research of Chicago ranked 2,000 publicly traded companies using a rigorous combination of four financial criteria: growth in revenue, profit, and operating cash flow during the past three years; and the 12-month stock market return as of March 31, 2006. *Business 2.0, "100 Fastest-Growing Tech Companies 2006," June 2006*

According to Deloitte & Touche LLP, Los Angeles is home to three of North America's 500 fastest-growing high-technology companies: **PeopleSupport; PriceGrabber.com; SOA Software**. Companies are ranked by percentage growth in revenue over a five-year period. Criteria for inclusion: company must be headquartered within North America; company must own proprietary intellectual property or proprietary technology that contributes to a significant portion of the company's operating revenue or devotes a significant proportion of revenues to research and development of technology; company must have been in business for a minumum of five years with 2001 operating revenues of at least $50,000 USD or $75,000 CD and 2005 operating revenues of at least $5 million USD/CD. *Deloitte & Touche LLP, 2006 Technology Fast 500*

Women-Owned Businesses: 1997 and 2002

Year	All Firms		Firms with Paid Employees			
	Firms	Sales ($000)	Firms	Sales ($000)	Employees	Payroll ($000)
1997	89,619	10,908,035	12,502	8,801,155	92,217	2,801,479
2002	117,713	15,705,184	15,634	12,676,899	105,192	3,115,879

Note: Figures cover firms located in the city; Women-owned business are defined as firms in which women own 51% or more of the stock or equity of the company; (a) Withheld to avoid disclosing data for individual companies; (b) Withheld because estimate did not meet publication standards; n/a not available
Source: 1997 Economic Census, Survey of Minority- and Women-Owned Business Enterprises; 2002 Economic Census, Survey of Business Owners (released February 9, 2006)

Minority Business Opportunity

Los Angeles is home to two companies which are on the Black Enterprise Industrial/Service 100 list (100 largest companies based on gross sales): **Americus Credit Group**; **Marc Wear**. Criteria: operational in previous calendar year; at least 51% black-owned and manufactures/owns the product it sells or provides industrial or consumer services. Brokerages, real estate firms and firms that provide professional services are not eligible. *Black Enterprise, www.blackenterprise.com, B.E. 100s, 2006*

Los Angeles is home to one company which is on the Black Enterprise Bank 25 list (25 largest banks based on total assets, capital, deposits and loans, including mortgage-backed securities for the calendar year): **Broadway Federal Bank**. Criteria: commercial banks or savings and loans that are classified by the Federal Reserve as black institutions and have been fully operational for the previous calendar year. *Black Enterprise, www.blackenterprise.com, B.E. 100s, 2006*

Nine of the 500 largest Hispanic-owned companies in the U.S. are located in Los Angeles. *Hispanic Business, "Hispanic Business 500," June 2006*

Los Angeles is home to two companies which are on the Hispanic Business Fastest-Growing 100 list (greatest sales growth over the past five years): **TELACU Industries**; **E.J. De La Rosa & Co.**. *Hispanic Business, July/August 2006*

HOTELS

Hotels/Motels

Area	Hotels/Motels	Average Minimum Rates ($)		
		Tourist	First-Class	Deluxe
City	111	78	124	266

Source: OAG Travel Planner Online, Spring 2006

The Los Angeles metro area is home to seven of the top 187 hotels in the U.S. according to *Travel & Leisure*: **Hotel Bel-Air** (#11); **Peninsula Beverly Hills** (#12); **Beverly Wilshire** (#45); **Raffles L'Ermitage, Beverly Hills** (#84); **Beverly Hills Hotel & Bungalows** (#93); **Shutters on the Beach** (#157); **Four Seasons Hotel Los Angeles at Beverly Hills** (#168). Criteria: service; location; rooms; food; and value. *Travel & Leisure, "The T+L 500, 2007"*

EVENT SITES

Stadiums, Arenas, and Auditoriums

Name	Capacity
Dodger Stadium	56,000
Los Angeles Sports Arena	92,516
Music Center of L.A. County	6,015
Shrine Auditorium	6,300
The Grand Olympic Auditorium	7,500
The Greek Theatre	5,700

Source: www.officialtravelguide.com; www.eventective.com; original research

Convention Centers

Name	Overall Space (sq. ft.)	Exhibit Space (sq. ft.)	Meeting Space (sq. ft.)	Meeting Rooms
Los Angeles Convention & Exhibition Center	n/a	147,000	770,000	54

Note: n/a not available
Source: www.officialtravelguide.com; www.eventective.com; original research

Hotels/Conference Centers

Name	Guest Rooms	Exhibit Space (sq. ft.)	Meeting Space (sq. ft.)
Burbank Airport Hilton and Convention Center	1,234	n/a	55,000
Regal Biltmore Hotel	n/a	n/a	n/a
The Westin Bonaventure Hotel and Suites	1,354	25,116	100,000
The Westin Century Plaza Hotel and Tower	727	23,000	100,000

Note: n/a not available
Source: www.officialtravelguide.com; www.eventective.com; original research

Living Environment

COST OF LIVING

Cost of Living Index

Year	Composite Index	Groceries	Housing	Utilities	Trans-portation	Health Care	Misc. Goods/ Services
2004	152.2	118.7	239.3	125.5	115.9	102.7	111.8
2005	156.1	126.5	257.6	113.5	113.2	116.1	110.8
2006	155.6	131.3	265.8	102.6	111.8	114.7	108.6

Note: U.S. = 100; Figures are for the Metropolitan Statistical Area - see Appendix B for areas included
Source: The Council for Community and Economic Research (formerly ACCRA), Cost of Living Index, 2004, 2005 and 2006 4-Quarter Averages

HOUSING

House Price Index (HPI)

Area	National Ranking[2]	Quarterly Change (%)	One-Year Change (%)	Five-Year Change (%)
MD[1]	53	0.13	9.20	131.90
U.S.[3]	-	1.12	5.87	55.21

Note: The HPI is a weighted repeat sales index. It measures average price changes in repeat sales or refinancings on the same properties. This information is obtained by reviewing repeat mortgage transactions on single-family properties whose mortgages have been purchased or securitized by Fannie Mae or Freddie Mac in January 1975; (1) Metropolitan Division - see Appendix B for areas included; (2) Rankings are based on annual percentage change for all metro areas containing at least 15,000 transactions over the last 10 years and ranges from 1 to 282; (3) figures based on a weighted division average; all figures are for the period ending December 31, 2006
Source: Office of Federal Housing Enterprise Oversight, House Price Index, March 1, 2007

House Price Valuations

Area	Q4 1999	Q4 2000	Q4 2001	Q4 2002	Q4 2003	Q4 2004	Q4 2005	Q4 2006
MSA[1]	-17.7	-16.1	-11.9	-0.7	13.0	29.8	48.9	51.5

Note: Figures show the percentage of over- or under-valuation of single family homes relative to statistically normal house values (e.g. a value of 23.6 indicates that house values are 23.6% overvalued). Statistically normal house values are based on house prices, interest rates, household incomes, population densities, and any historical premiums or discounts metropolitan areas have exhibited over time; (1) Figures cover the Metropolitan Statistical Area - see Appendix B for areas included
Source: Global Insight/National City Corporation, House Prices in America, March 2007

Median Home Prices

Area	2004	2005	2006p	Percent Change 2005 to 2006
Metro Area[1]	446.4	529.0	584.8	10.5
U.S. Average	195.2	219.0	222.0	1.4

Note: Figures are median sales prices of existing single-family homes in thousands of dollars; (p) preliminary; n/a not available; (1) Covers the Los Angeles-Long Beach-Santa Ana, CA Metropolitan Statistical Area - see Appendix B for areas included
Source: National Association of Realtors, Metropolitan Area Prices, 4th Quarter 2006

Housing: Year Structure Built

Area	1990 -2000	1980 -1989	1970 -1979	1960 -1969	1950 -1959	1940 -1949	Before 1940	Median Year
City	6.2	11.1	15.0	17.5	20.5	13.0	16.7	1960
MSA[1]	6.9	12.3	15.6	17.8	22.3	12.2	12.9	1961
U.S.	17.0	15.8	18.5	13.7	12.7	7.3	15.0	1971

Note: Figures are percentages; (1) Metropolitan Statistical Area - see Appendix A for areas included
Source: Census 2000, Summary File 3

Average New Home Price

Area	2004	2005	2006
MSA[1]	632,766	744,157	833,405
U.S.	253,574	275,712	299,269

Note: Figures, in dollars, are based on a new home with 2,400 sq. ft. of living area on an 8,000 sq. ft. lot; (1) Metropolitan Statistical Area - see Appendix B for areas included
Source: The Council for Community and Economic Research (formerly ACCRA), Cost of Living Index, 2004, 2005 and 2006 4-Quarter Averages

Average Apartment Rent

Area	2004	2005	2006
MSA[1]	1,441	1,513	1,619
U.S.	716	740	766

Note: Figures, in dollars per month, are based on an unfurnished two bedroom, 1-1/2 or 2 bath apartment, approximately 950 sq. ft., excluding utilities except water; (1) Metropolitan Statistical Area - see Appendix B for areas included
Source: The Council for Community and Economic Research (formerly ACCRA), Cost of Living Index, 2004, 2005 and 2006 4-Quarter Averages

RESIDENTIAL UTILITIES

Average Residential Utility Costs

Area	All Electric ($/mth)	Part Electric ($/mth)	Other Energy ($/mth)	Phone ($/mth)
MSA[1]	–	101.56	60.89	26.41
U.S.	136.00	76.53	90.52	25.87

Note: (1) Metropolitan Statistical Area - see Appendix B for areas included
Source: The Council for Community and Economic Research (formerly ACCRA), Cost of Living Index, 2006 4-Quarter Average

HEALTH

Average Health Care Costs

Area	Optometrist ($/visit)	Doctor ($/visit)	Dentist ($/visit)
MSA[1]	82.74	97.67	80.22
U.S.	76.38	76.10	68.72

Note: Optometrist—based on a full vision eye exam for an established adult patient;
Doctor—based on a general practitioner's routine exam of an established patient;
Dentist—based on adult teeth cleaning and periodic oral exam;
(1) Metropolitan Statistical Area - see Appendix B for areas included
Source: The Council for Community and Economic Research (formerly ACCRA), Cost of Living Index, 2006 4-Quarter Average

Mortality Rates

ICD-10 Sub-Chapter	ICD-10 Code	Age-Adjusted Death Rate per 100,000 population[1]	U.S. Age-Adjusted Death Rate per 100,000 population
Malignant neoplasms	C00-C97	159.6	185.8
Ischaemic heart diseases	I20-I25	175.8	150.2
Other forms of heart disease	I30-I51	29.2	50.8
Cerebrovascular diseases	I60-I69	50.1	50.0
Chronic lower respiratory diseases	J40-J47	34.3	41.1
Diabetes mellitus	E10-E14	26.5	24.5
Other degenerative diseases of the nervous system	G30-G31	16.7	22.3
Other external causes of accidental injury	W00-X59	13.2	21.2
Influenza and pneumonia	J10-J18	27.8	19.8
Hypertensive diseases	I10-I13	21.0	18.1

Note: ICD-10 = International Classification of Diseases 10th Revision; (1) Figures cover Los Angeles County, CA
Source: Centers for Disease Control and Prevention, National Center for Health Statistics. Compressed Mortality File 1999-2004. CDC WONDER On-line Database, compiled from Compressed Mortality File 1999-2004 Series 20 No. 2J, 2007.

Health Risk Data

Item	Area[1] (%)	U.S. (%)
Adults who have been told they have high blood pressure	26.3	25.5
Adults who have been told they have high blood cholesterol	39.3	35.6
Adults who have been told they have diabetes[2]	6.7	7.3
Adults who have been told they have arthritis	19.5	27.0
Adults who have been told they currently have asthma	6.0	8.0
Adults who are current smokers	15.6	20.6

Note: (1) Figures cover the Metropolitan Division - see Appendix B for areas included; (2) Figures do not include pregnancy-related diabetes, pre-diabetes or borderline diabetes
Source: Centers for Disease Control and Prevention, Behaviorial Risk Factor Surveillance System, SMART: Selected Metropolitan/Micropolitan Area Trends, 2005

Distribution of Office-Based Physicians

Area	Total	Family/ General Practice	Specialties Medical	Specialties Surgical	Specialties Other
CMSA[1] (number)	28,914	3,817	10,675	6,649	7,773
CMSA[1] (rate per 10,000 pop.)	17.1	2.3	6.3	3.9	4.6
Metro Average[2] (rate per 10,000 pop.)	19.4	2.1	7.5	4.5	5.3

Note: Data as of December 31, 2004; (1) Los Angeles-Riverside-Orange, CA Consolidated Metropolitan Statistical Area includes the following counties: Los Angeles; Orange; Riverside; San Bernardino; Ventura; (2) Average of the 79 unique MSAs and CMSAs in this book
Source: American Medical Association, Physician Characteristics & Distribution in the U.S., 2006

Hospitals

Los Angeles has the following hospitals: 36 general medical and surgical; 2 psychiatric; 1 tuberculosis and other respiratory disease; 1 prison; 1 cancer; 2 long-term acute care; 1 children's general; 1 children's orthopedic.
AHA Guide to the Healthcare Field 2007

According to *U.S. News,* the Los Angeles metro area is home to eight of the best hospitals in the U.S.: **Cedars-Sinai Medical Center; Childrens Hospital Los Angeles; Doheny Eye Institute - USC University Hospital; Jules Stein Eye Institute - UCLA Medical Center; Mattel Children's Hospital at UCLA; UCLA Medical Center; UCLA's Neuropsychiatric Hospital; USC University Hospital;** *U.S. News Online, "America's Best Hospitals 2006"*

EDUCATION

Public School District Statistics

District Name	Schls	Pupils	Pupil/ Teacher Ratio	Minority Pupils[1] (%)	Free Lunch Eligible[2] (%)	IEP[3] (%)
Los Angeles Unified	760	741,367	21.1	91.0	66.9	11.2

Note: Table includes regular local school districts with 2,000 or more students; (1) Percentage of students that are not white, non-Hispanic; (2) Percentage of students that are eligible for the free lunch program; (3) Percentage of students that have an Individualized Education Program.
Source: U.S. Department of Education, National Center for Education Statistics, Common Core of Data, Local Education Agency (School District) Universe Survey: School Year 2004-2005; U.S. Department of Education, National Center for Education Statistics, Common Core of Data, Public Elementary/Secondary School Universe Survey: School Year 2004-2005

Top Public High Schools

High School Name	Index[1]	Rank[1]	Subsidized Lunch (%)[2]	E&E (%)[3]
Downtown Business Magnet	1.709	528	81.5	n/a
Eagle Rock	1.898	416	63.8	30.5
Foshay Learning Center	1.888	421	85.3	5.6
Francisco Bravo Medical Magnet	2.028	351	85.5	n/a
Franklin	1.220	999	79.7	n/a
Fremont	1.552	665	70.8	n/a
Garfield	1.046	1,173	77.5	n/a
Granada Hills	1.691	545	26.0	n/a
Hamilton	1.444	753	49.2	n/a
Lincoln	1.392	811	83.8	n/a
Locke	1.048	1,172	71.4	n/a
Los Angeles Center for Enriched Studies	3.964	45	34.0	69.0
Manual Arts	1.352	845	86.2	n/a
Marshall	1.910	404	72.5	n/a
North Hollywood	2.435	213	74.0	42.6
Thomas Jefferson	1.119	1,104	91.2	n/a
University	1.225	996	56.8	n/a
Woodrow Wilson	1.137	1,083	77.9	n/a

Note: (1) Public schools are ranked according to a ratio that is the number of Advanced Placement and/or International Baccalaureate tests taken by all students at a school in 2005 divided by the number of graduating seniors. All of the schools on the list have an index of at least 1.000; they are in the top five percent of public schools measured this way. The rankings range from 1 to 1,236; (2) Percentage of students receiving federally subsidized meals; (3) E & E stands for equity and excellence percentage: the portion of all graduating seniors at a school that had at least one passing grade on one AP or IB test; (*) Gave just IB tests; (**) Gave both IB and AP tests. AP and IB participation are indicators of a school's efforts to get students to excel and prepare for college; n/a not available
Source: Newsweek Online, May 23, 2006

Educational Quality

School District	Education Quotient[1]	Graduate Outcome[2]	Community Index[3]	Resource Index[4]	Rating[5]
Los Angeles Unified	7	6	14	58	Red

Note: Scores are national percentile rankings and range from 1 (worst) to 99 (best); (1) Combination of the Graduate Outcome, Community and Resource Indexes weighted to reflect the greater importance of the Graduate Outcome and Resource Index; (2) Based on graduation rates and college board scores (SAT/ACT); (3) Based on the surrounding community's level of affluence and adult education; (4) Based on teacher salaries, per-pupil expenditures and student-teacher ratios; (5) School districts receive one of five rankings: Gold Medal (top 16 percent of districts evaluated); Blue Ribbon (top third); Green Light (average); Yellow Light (bottom 25 percent); Red Light (bottom 10 percent).
Source: Expansion Management, "2007 Education Quotient," January 2007

Highest Level of Education

Area	Less than H.S.	H.S. Diploma	Some College, No Deg.	Associate Degree	Bachelors Degree	Masters Degree	Profess. School Degree	Doctorate Degree
City	33.8	17.4	18.3	5.3	16.3	5.2	2.7	1.0
MSA[1]	28.2	18.5	20.6	6.6	17.0	5.6	2.4	1.0
U.S.	19.4	28.4	21.2	6.4	15.7	5.9	2.0	1.0

Note: Figures are 2006 estimated percentages and cover persons age 25 and over; (1) Metropolitan Statistical Area - see Appendix B for areas included
Source: Claritas, Inc.

Educational Attainment by Race

Area	High School Graduate (%)					Bachelor's Degree (%)				
	Total	White	Black	Asian	Hisp.[2]	Total	White	Black	Asian	Hisp.[2]
City	66.6	75.6	76.0	82.1	35.5	25.5	32.7	17.1	42.4	6.1
MSA[1]	69.9	77.0	79.3	82.4	42.1	24.9	29.3	17.8	42.9	6.8
U.S.	80.4	83.6	72.3	80.4	52.4	24.4	26.1	14.3	44.1	10.4

Note: Figures shown cover persons 25 years old and over; (1) Metropolitan Statistical Area - see Appendix A for areas included; (2) people of Hispanic origin can be of any race
Source: Census 2000, Summary File 3

School Enrollment by Type

| Area | Grades KG to 8 | | | | Grades 9 to 12 | | | |
| | Public | | Private | | Public | | Private | |
	Enrollment	%	Enrollment	%	Enrollment	%	Enrollment	%
City	454,318	86.5	70,607	13.5	201,618	89.3	24,200	10.7
MSA[1]	1,261,035	88.4	164,761	11.6	560,595	91.0	55,347	9.0
U.S.	33,526,011	88.7	4,285,121	11.3	14,848,628	90.6	1,532,323	9.4

Note: Figures shown cover persons 3 years old and over; (1) Metropolitan Statistical Area - see Appendix A for areas included
Source: Census 2000, Summary File 3

School Enrollment by Race

| Area | Grades KG to 8 (%) | | | | Grades 9 to 12 (%) | | | |
	White	Black	Asian	Hisp.[1]	White	Black	Asian	Hisp.[1]
City	39.1	11.7	6.5	62.8	36.8	11.9	8.0	61.5
MSA[2]	41.8	10.5	9.1	57.7	39.8	10.3	11.2	55.9
U.S.	68.5	15.5	3.3	16.8	68.8	15.5	3.8	15.7

Note: Figures shown cover persons 3 years old and over; (1) people of Hispanic origin can be of any race; (2) Metropolitan Statistical Area - see Appendix A for areas included
Source: Census 2000, Summary File 3

Average Salaries of Public School Teachers

| District | 2004-05 | | 2005-06 | | Percent Change 2004-05 to 2005-06 |
	Dollars	Rank[1]	Dollars	Rank[1]	
CALIFORNIA	57,876	2	59,345	3	2.54
U.S. Average	47,674	-	49,109	-	3.01

Note: (1) State rank ranges from 1 to 51.
Source: National Education Association, Rankings & Estimates: Rankings of the States 2005 and Estimates of School Statistics 2006, November 2006

Higher Education

| Four-Year Colleges | | | Two-Year Colleges | | | Medical Schools[1] | Law Schools[2] | Voc/ Tech[3] |
Public	Private Non-profit	Private For-profit	Public	Private Non-profit	Private For-profit			
2	18	6	4	1	2	2	4	26

Note: Figures cover institutions located within the city limits; (1) includes schools accredited by the Liaison Committee on Medical Education and the American Osteopathic Association; (2) includes American Bar Association-accredited law schools; (3) includes all schools with programs that are less than 2 years
Source: National Center for Education Statistics, The Integrated Postsecondary Education System (IPEDS) Peer Analysis System, 2006; www.usnews.com, America's Best Graduate Schools 2008, Medical School Directory; www.usnews.com, America's Best Graduate Schools 2008, Law School Directory

PRESIDENTIAL ELECTION

2004 Presidential Election Results

Area	Bush	Kerry	Nader	Other
Los Angeles County	35.6	63.1	0.1	1.2
U.S.	50.7	48.3	0.4	0.6

Note: Results are percentages and may not add to 100% due to rounding
Source: Dave Leip's Atlas of U.S. Presidential Elections, www.uselectionatlas.org

MAJOR EMPLOYERS

Major Employers

Company Name	Industry	Type of Site
Boeing	Airports, flying fields, and services	Branch
Caltech	Colleges and universities	Headquarters
Cedars-Sinai Home Care	General medical and surgical hospitals	Branch
Cedars-Sinai Medical Center	General medical and surgical hospitals	Branch
City of Los Angeles	Executive offices	Headquarters
County of Los Angeles	Executive offices	Headquarters
Fox Entertainment Group Inc	Motion picture and video production	Single
General Motors	New and used car dealers	Branch
Information Systems Tech Bur	Courts	Single
LAC USC County Medical Center	Colleges and universities	Branch
MCA Music	Motion picture and video production	Headquarters
Memorial Health Services	General medical and surgical hospitals	Headquarters
Prolease Pacific Inc	Accounting, auditing, and bookkeeping	Single
Raytheon	Search and navigation equipment	Branch
Team One	Employment agencies	Single
Toyota Motor Sales USA Inc	Automobiles and other motor vehicles	Headquarters
US Post Office	U.S. Postal Service	Branch
USC	Colleges and universities	Headquarters
Walt Disney Company	Television broadcasting stations	Branch
Warner Bros Entertainment	Motion picture and video production	Headquarters

Note: Companies shown are located within the metropolitan area and have 5,000 or more employees; nec = not elsewhere classified.
Source: www.zapdata.com, January 2007

PUBLIC SAFETY

Crime Rate

Area	All Crimes	Violent Crimes				Property Crimes		
		Murder	Forcible Rape	Robbery	Aggrav. Assault	Burglary	Larceny -Theft	Motor Vehicle Theft
City	3,850.4	12.6	28.5	356.4	423.0	583.6	1,704.2	741.9
Suburbs[1]	3,317.7	9.5	20.9	210.3	323.3	591.4	1,479.1	683.2
Metro[2]	3,523.8	10.7	23.8	266.8	361.9	588.4	1,566.2	705.9
U.S.	3,899.0	5.6	31.7	140.7	291.1	726.7	2,286.3	416.7

Note: Figures are crimes per 100,000 population; (1) All areas within the metro area that are located outside the city limits; (2) Metropolitan Division - see Appendix B for areas included
Source: FBI Uniform Crime Reports, 2005

Hate Crimes

Area	Number of Quarters Reported	Bias Motivation				
		Race	Religion	Sexual Orientation	Ethnicity	Disability
City	4	104	34	42	39	0

Source: Federal Bureau of Investigation, Hate Crime Statistics 2005

RECREATION

Culture

Dance[1]	Theatre[1]	Instrumental Music[1]	Vocal Music[1]	Series/ Festivals	Museums	Zoos
19	32	7	5	13	40	1

Note: (1) number of professional perfoming groups
Source: The Grey House Performing Arts Directory, 2007; Official Museum Directory, 2007

Professional Sports Teams

Major League Baseball	National Basketball Association	National Football League	National Hockey League	Major League Soccer	Women's National Basketball Association
2	2	0	2	2	1

Note: Includes teams located in the Los Angeles-Anaheim metro area.
Source: www.sportsvenues.com, Listing of Venues by State/Province and City, 2006

MEDIA

Newspapers

Name	Target Audience	Frequency	Circulation
The African Times	Black	Non-Daily	85,000
The Argonaut	General	Non-Daily	40,000
Belvedere Citizen	General/Hispanic	Non-Daily	95,994
California Examiner	General	Non-Daily	95,000
Carson Wave	Black/General	Non-Daily	40,000
Central News/Journal/Star Wave	General	Non-Daily	230,000
Hollywood Reporter	n/a	Daily	40,366
Inglewood Hawthorne Wave	Black/General	Non-Daily	42,400
Investor's Business Daily	n/a	Daily	233,645
The Jewish Journal	General/Jewish	Non-Daily	55,000
Korean Central Daily	n/a	Daily	70,000
LA Weekly	Alternative/General	Non-Daily	225,000
La Ola	Hispanic	Non-Daily	415,000
La Opinion	n/a	Daily	126,628
La Voz Libre	General/Hispanic	Non-Daily	44,500
Los Angeles Downtown News	General	Non-Daily	47,000
Los Angeles Times	n/a	Daily	983,727
Lynwood Press	Black/General/Hisp.	Non-Daily	42,400
The Nikkei Weekly	Asian/Ethnic	Non-Daily	40,000
The Tidings	General/Religious	Non-Daily	40,000
Vida Nueva	General/Hispanic	Non-Daily	100,000
World Reporter	Asian/General	Non-Daily	50,000

Note: Includes newspapers whose offices are located in the city and whose circulations are 40,000 or more; n/a not available
Source: BurrellesLuce, MediaContacts Online, January 2006

Television Stations

Name	Ch.	Network(s)	Type	Ownership
KCBS	2	CBS	Commercial	CBS
KNBC	4	NBC	Commercial	General Electric Corporation
KTLA	5	WBN	Commercial	Tribune Broadcasting Company
KABC	7	ABC	Commercial	ABC Inc.
KCAL	9	CBS	Commercial	Viacom International Inc.
KTTV	11	Fox	Commercial	Fox Television Stations Inc.
KCOP	13	UPN	Commercial	Fox Television Stations Inc.
KSCI	18	n/a	Commercial	International Media Group
KWHY	22	Telemundo	Commercial	Telemundo Group Inc.
KVCR	24	PBS	Public	San Bernardino Community College District
KCET	28	PBS	Public	Community Television of Southern California
KPXN	30	Pax	Commercial	Paxson Communications Corporation
KVMD	31	APT	Commercial	n/a
KNET	38	n/a	Commercial	Venture Technology Group LLC.
KFTR	46	n/a	Commercial	Univision Communications Inc.
KOCE	50	PBS	Public	Coast Community College District
KVEA	52	Telemundo	Commercial	Telemundo Group Inc.
KDOC	56	n/a	Commercial	Golden Orange Broadcasting Company Inc.
KJLA	57	n/a	Commercial	Costa de Oro Television
KLCS	58	PBS	Public	Los Angeles Unified School District
KRCA	62	n/a	Commercial	Liberman Broadcasting
KADY	63	UPN	Commercial	Biltmore Broadcasting
KHIZ	64	n/a	Commercial	Sunbelt Broadcasting Company
KNLA	68	UPN	Non-comm.	Venture Technology Group LLC.

Note: Stations included cover the Los Angeles DMA (Designated Market Area)
BurrellesLuce, MediaContacts Online, January 2006

Major AM Radio Stations

Call Letters	Freq. (kHz)	Station Type	Target Audience	Station Format	Music Format
KLAC	570	Commercial	General	Sports/Talk	n/a
KAVL	610	Commercial	General	News/Sports/Talk	n/a
KFI	640	n/a	General	Music/News/Talk	n/a
KIRN	670	Commercial	Ethnic	Music/News/Talk	International
KDIS	710	Commercial	Children	Music/News	Top 40
KBRT	740	n/a	General/Religious	Talk	n/a
KABC	790	n/a	General	Music/News/Talk	n/a
KRLA	870	n/a	General	Talk	n/a
KOXR	910	n/a	Hispanic	News/Sports/Talk	n/a
KKHJ	930	Commercial	General/Hispanic	Music	Latin
KIXW	960	n/a	Hispanic	Talk	n/a
KFWB	980	Commercial	General	News/Sports	n/a
KTNQ	1020	n/a	Hispanic	News/Sports	n/a
KNX	1070	Commercial	General	News/Sports	n/a
KSPN	1110	Public	General	Music/Sports	Classical
KXTA	1150	Commercial	General	Sports/Talk	n/a
KXMX	1190	n/a	Hispanic	Music/Talk	n/a
KSUR	1260	n/a	General	Music	n/a
KKDD	1290	Commercial	Children	Educational/Music	Easy Listening
KAZN	1300	Commercial	Asian	Ed/Music/News/Sports/Talk	Easy Listening
KWKW	1330	n/a	Hispanic	Sports/Talk	n/a
KWRM	1370	Commercial	Hispanic	Ed/Music/News/Sports	Latin
KLTX	1390	Commercial	Christian/Gen/Hisp	Music/Talk	Latin
KCAL	1410	n/a	General/Hispanic	Music	n/a
KTYM	1460	Commercial	Black/General/Rel	Music/Talk	Gospel
KUTY	1470	Commercial	General/Hispanic	Music/News/Sports	Latin
KWIZ	1480	n/a	Asian	Music/News/Talk	n/a
KMZT	1510	n/a	General	Music	n/a
KVTA	1520	n/a	Hispanic	n/a	n/a
KHPY	1530	Commercial	General	Music	Oldies
KMPC	1540	Commercial	General/Men	Sports/Talk	n/a
KPRO	1570	Commercial	General/Religious	Music/Talk	Gospel
KMNY	1600	Commercial	Asian	Educational/News/Talk	n/a

Note: Stations included cover the Los Angeles DMA (Designated Market Area); n/a not available
Source: BurrellesLuce, MediaContacts Online, January 2006

Major FM Radio Stations

Call Letters	Freq. (mHz)	Station Type	Target Audience	Station Format	Music Format
KPFK	90.7	Non-Comm	General/Hispanic	Educational/Music	World Music
KCBS	93.1	Commercial	General	Music/News/Talk	Classic Rock
KFRG	95.1	n/a	General	Music/News/Talk	n/a
KLOS	95.5	n/a	General	Music/News/Talk	n/a
KXOL	96.3	n/a	General/Hispanic	n/a	n/a
KLSX	97.1	Commercial	General	Music/Sports/Talk	Classical
KSSE	97.5	Commercial	General/Hispanic	Music	Top 40
KLAX	97.9	n/a	General/Hispanic	Music/News/Talk	n/a
KYSR	98.7	n/a	General	Music/Talk	n/a
KKBT	100.3	Commercial	Black	Music/News/Talk	Urban Contemp.
KRTH	101.1	n/a	General	Music/News	n/a
KBIG	104.3	Commercial	General	Music	Adult Contemp.
KCAQ	104.7	n/a	General	Music	n/a
KPWR	105.9	n/a	General	Music/News/Talk	n/a

Note: Stations included cover the Los Angeles DMA (Designated Market Area); n/a not available
BurrellesLuce, MediaContacts Online, January 2006

CLIMATE

Average and Extreme Temperatures

Temperature	Jan	Feb	Mar	Apr	May	Jun	Jul	Aug	Sep	Oct	Nov	Dec	Yr.
Extreme High (°F)	88	92	95	102	97	104	97	98	110	106	101	94	110
Average High (°F)	65	66	65	67	69	72	75	76	76	74	71	66	70
Average Temp. (°F)	56	57	58	60	63	66	69	70	70	67	62	57	63
Average Low (°F)	47	49	50	53	56	59	63	64	63	59	52	48	55
Extreme Low (°F)	27	34	37	43	45	48	52	51	47	43	38	32	27

Note: Figures cover the years 1947-1990
Source: National Climatic Data Center, International Station Meteorological Climate Summary, 9/96

Average Precipitation/Snowfall/Humidity

Precip./Humidity	Jan	Feb	Mar	Apr	May	Jun	Jul	Aug	Sep	Oct	Nov	Dec	Yr.
Avg. Precip. (in.)	2.6	2.3	1.8	0.8	0.1	Tr	Tr	0.1	0.2	0.3	1.5	1.5	11.3
Avg. Snowfall (in.)	Tr	0	0	0	0	0	0	0	0	0	0	0	Tr
Avg. Rel. Hum. 7am (%)	69	72	76	76	77	80	80	81	80	76	69	67	75
Avg. Rel. Hum. 4pm (%)	60	62	64	64	66	67	67	68	67	66	61	60	64

Note: Figures cover the years 1947-1990; Tr = Trace amounts (<0.05 in. of rain; <0.5 in. of snow)
Source: National Climatic Data Center, International Station Meteorological Climate Summary, 9/96

Weather Conditions

Temperature			Daytime Sky			Precipitation		
10°F & below	32°F & below	90°F & above	Clear	Partly cloudy	Cloudy	0.01 inch or more precip.	0.1 inch or more snow/ice	Thunder-storms
0	< 1	5	131	125	109	34	0	1

Note: Figures are average number of days per year and cover the years 1947-1990
Source: National Climatic Data Center, International Station Meteorological Climate Summary, 9/96

HAZARDOUS WASTE

Superfund Sites

Los Angeles has two hazardous waste sites on the EPA's Superfund Final National Priorities List: **Del Amo**; **San Fernando Valley (Area 4)**. *U.S. Environmental Protection Agency, Final National Priorities List, March 20, 2007*

AIR & WATER QUALITY

Air Quality Index

Area	Percent of Days when Air Quality was...[2]				AQI Statistics	
	Good	Moderate	Unhealthy for Sensitive Groups	Unhealthy	Maximum	Median
MSA[1]	32.9	45.8	17.0	4.4	207	62

Note: The Air Quality Index (AQI) is an index for reporting daily air quality. EPA calculates the AQI for five major air pollutants regulated by the Clean Air Act: ground-level ozone, particle pollution (also known as particulate matter), carbon monoxide, sulfur dioxide, and nitrogen dioxide. The AQI runs from 0 to 500. The higher the AQI value, the greater the level of air pollution and the greater the health concern. There are six AQI categories: "Good" The AQI is between 0 and 50. Air quality is considered satisfactory; "Moderate" The AQI is between 51 and 100. Air quality is acceptable; "Unhealthy for Sensitive Groups" When AQI values are between 101 and 150, members of sensitive groups may experience health effects; "Unhealthy" When AQI values are between 151 and 200 everyone may begin to experience health effects; "Very Unhealthy" AQI values between 201 and 300 trigger a health alert; "Hazardous" AQI values over 300 trigger health warnings of emergency conditions; (1) Metropolitan Statistical Area - see Appendix A for areas included; (2) Based on 365 days with AQI data in 2005.
Source: U.S. Environmental Protection Agency, Air Quality Index Report, 2005

Air Quality Index Pollutants

Area	Percent of Days when AQI Pollutant was...[2]					
	Carbon Monoxide	Nitrogen Dioxide	Ozone	Sulfur Dioxide	Particulate Matter 2.5	Particulate Matter 10
MSA[1]	1.6	0.0	51.5	0.0	45.2	1.6

Note: The Air Quality Index (AQI) is an index for reporting daily air quality. EPA calculates the AQI for five major air pollutants regulated by the Clean Air Act: ground-level ozone, particle pollution (also known as particulate matter), carbon monoxide, sulfur dioxide, and nitrogen dioxide. The AQI runs from 0 to 500. The higher the AQI value, the greater the level of air pollution and the greater the health concern; (1) Metropolitan Statistical Area - see Appendix A for areas included; (2) Based on 365 days with AQI data in 2005.
Source: U.S. Environmental Protection Agency, Air Quality Index Report, 2005

Number of Days with Air Quality Index Values Greater than 100

Area	Trend Sites (52)								All Sites (120)
	1998	1999	2000	2001	2002	2003	2004	2005	2005
MSA[1]	49	54	63	81	81	88	65	45	80

Note: An AQI value greater than 100 indicates that air quality would have been in the unhealthful range on that day. Data from exceptional events are not included. These counts are presented in two ways. First, the counts are based on sites having an adequate record of monitoring data during the trend period (trend sites). These counts represent the relative change in the number of days with AQI values greater than 100. In the last column, the counts are based on all sites with data in the most recent year (because it is possible for a site to have data in the most recent year but not enough data to be a trend site); (1) Metropolitan Statistical Area - see Appendix A for areas included; n/a not available.
Source: U.S. Environmental Protection Agency, Air Trends Fact Book 2005

Maximum Pollutant Concentrations

	Particulate Matter 10 (ug/m^3)	Particulate Matter 2.5 (ug/m^3)	Ozone 1-hour (ppm)	Carbon Monoxide (ppm)	Sulfur Dioxide (ppm)	Nitrogen Dioxide (ppm)	Lead (ug/m^3)
MSA[1] Level	79	53	0.171	6	0.010	0.031	0.02
NAAQS[2]	150	65	0.125	9	0.140	0.053	1.50
Met NAAQS[2]	Yes	Yes	No	Yes	Yes	Yes	Yes

Note: Data from exceptional events are not included; (1) Metropolitan Statistical Area - see Appendix A for areas included; (2) National Ambient Air Quality Standards; n/a not available
Units: ppm = parts per million; ug/m^3 = micrograms per cubic meter
Source: U.S. Environmental Protection Agency, Air Trends Fact Book 2005

Watershed Health

The U.S. Environmental Protection Agency monitors the health of the aquatic resources for the nation's 2,000+ watersheds. **The Los Angeles watershed serves the Los Angeles area and received an overall Index of Watershed Indicators (IWI) score of 3 (less serious problems - low vulnerability).** The IWI score is based on seven condition and nine vulnerability indicators. The overall IWI score ranges from 1 (best health) to 6 (worst health). The Condition Indicators include: designated use attainment, fish and wildlife consumption advisories, source water condition, contaminated sediments, ambient water quality, and wetlands loss index. The Vulnerability Indicators include: aquatic species at risk, conventional and toxic loads over permitted limits, urban and agricultural runoff potential, population change, hydrologic modification, estuarine pollution susceptibility, and air deposition. *Note: The IWI is no longer being updated by the U.S. EPA. Source: U.S. Environmental Protection Agency, Index of Watershed Indicators, October 26, 2001*

Drinking Water

Water System Name	Pop. Served	Primary Water Source Type	Number of Violations in 2006[a]		
			Health Based	Significant Monitoring	Monitoring
LA Dept of Water & Power	4,000,000	Surface	None	None	None

Note: (a) Based on violation data from January 1, 2006 to December 31, 2006
Source: U.S. Environmental Protection Agency, Office of Ground Water and Drinking Water, Safe Drinking Water Information System (data extracted April 12, 2007)

Los Angeles tap water hardness ranges from 4.2-15.1 gpg. The alkalinity also varies, ranging from 5.4-8.6 gpg. The Owens River Aqueduct accounts for approximately 70% of the water supply and is slightly alkaline and moderately soft with 4.2 gpg total hardness.
Editor & Publisher Market Guide, 2005

Phoenix, Arizona

Background

Phoenix, the arid "Valley of the Sun," and the capital of Arizona, was named by the English soldier and prospector, "Lord Darell" Duppa for the mythical bird of ancient Greek/Phoenician lore. According to the legend, the Phoenix was a beautiful bird that destroyed itself with its own flames. When nothing remained but embers, it would rise again from the ashes, more awesome and beautiful than before. Like the romantic tale, Duppa hoped that his city of Phoenix would rise again from the mysteriously abandoned Hohokam village.

Many might agree that Phoenix fulfilled Duppa's wish. Within 15 years after its second founding in 1867, Phoenix had grown to be an important supply point for the mining districts of north-central Arizona, as well as an important trading site for farmers, cattlemen, and prospectors.

Around this time, Phoenix entered its Wild West phase, complete with stagecoaches, saloons, gambling houses, soldiers, cowboys, miners, and the pungent air of outlawry. Two public hangings near the end of the 1800s set a dramatic example, and helped turn the tide.

Today, Phoenix is just as exciting as ever, but more law-abiding, and many continue to be attracted to Phoenix's natural beauty. Despite occasional sprawling suburbs and shopping malls, the sophisticated blend of Spanish, Native American, and cowboy culture is obvious in the city's architecture, arts, and crafts.

Downtown Phoenix underwent a major renaissance in the 1990s with the completion of a history museum, an expanded art museum, a new central library, and a renovated concert hall. The $48 million Arizona Science Center opened in 1998, as did Chase Field, where, in 2001, the Arizona Diamondbacks won their first World Series.

Phoenix is the country's sixth-largest city, with more than one million people, while the Phoenix metro area population has grown to nearly four million. This increase in population continues to make Phoenix an attractive location for companies that are expanding into the fields of electronics and communications. Indeed, Intel and Motorola have major facilities right outside the city.

The city is currently building Valley Metro Rail, a light rail project, which is scheduled for completion in 2008. Interest has also been expressed in Phoenix and several neighboring cities for the creation of a commuter rail system operating on existing railroad lines.

Contrary to some thinking, the Phoenix Chamber of Commerce reports that ample water sources are available to support the growth of Greater Phoenix well into the twenty-second century. Sources include seven reservoirs, local groundwater aquifers, and Colorado River water supplied through the Central Arizona Project Canal.

Temperatures in Phoenix are mild in winter and very hot in summer. However, with the low humidity, the summer heat is somewhat more bearable than one might expect. Rainfall is slight and comes in two seasons. In winter rain comes on winds from the Pacific, ending by April. In summer, especially during July and August, there are severe thunderstorms from the southeast.

Rankings

GeneralRankings

- Phoenix was ranked #273 out of 331 metro areas in *Cities Ranked & Rated*. Criteria: cost of living; climate; crime; transportation; economy and jobs; education; arts and culture; health and healthcare; leisure. *Cities Ranked & Rated, 1st Edition, 2004*

- The Phoenix metro area was selected one of America's "Top 10 Metros Overall" by *Expansion Management* in their 4th annual Mayor's Challenge ranking of metro areas that have achieved solid ratings across the board in numerous *EM* studies during the past 12 months. The area ranked #10. Criteria: education (with emphasis on college board test results and high school graduation rates); availability of quality healthcare services and the cost to employers; quality of life; logistics workforce and companies; transportation infrastructure; quality and quantity of highly educated technical workers; and business climate. *Expansion Management, August 2006*

- Phoenix was selected as one of the top places to live in the U.S. according to Harris Interactive. The city ranked #12 out of 10. Criteria: 3,685 U.S. adults were polled as to where they would choose to live if they could live anywhere in the country. *Harris Interactive, September 6, 2006*

- Phoenix was selected as one of "America's Best Places to Live" by monstermoving.com. The top 10 cities were selected based on the fact that they appear repeatedly on other publications' "Top Cities" lists. *www.monstermoving.com, February 26, 2004*

- Phoenix was selected as one of the "50 Best Places to Live" by *Men's Journal*. The city ranked #2 in the "Sunniest Places" category. Criteria: number of mostly sunny days per year. *Men's Journal, April 2007*

- The Phoenix area was selected as one of "60 Cheap Places to Live" in the U.S. The area appeared in the "Steroid Cities" (fast-growing, business-friendly metro areas) category. *Forbes.com, August 20, 2004*

Business/Finance Rankings

- Phoenix was selected as one of the best places to start and grow a company by *Entrepreneur* and the National Policy Research Council. The Phoenix metro area ranked #1 out of 50 large metro areas. Criteria: business formation and growth (firms started four to 14 years ago that still employ at least 5 people and experienced rapid growth over the last four years). *Entrepreneur/National Policy Research Council, "Hot Cities for Entrepreneurs," September 2006*

- The Phoenix metro area was selected as one of "America's 50 Hottest Cities" for business relocations and expansions. Criteria: industry's most prominent site selection consultants were asked to list their top city choices for relocating and expanding manufacturing companies, taking into consideration such factors as the business climate, work force quality, operating costs, incentive programs, and the ease of working with local political and economic development officials. *Expansion Management, January-February 2007*

- The Phoenix metro area was cited as one of America's "Most Picture Perfect Metros" by *Plant Sites and Parks* magazine. Each year *PSP* readers rank the metro areas they consider best bets for their companies to relocate or expand to in the coming year. The area ranked #4 out of 10. *Plant Sites and Parks, March 2004*

- Intel, in partnership with Sperling's BestPlaces, ranked the 80 "Best Cities for Teleworking" in America. The Phoenix metro area ranked #15 among extra large metro areas. The study identifies cities that hold the greatest potential for teleworking based on a host of factors including typical commuting times, fuel prices, availability of broadband Internet access and percentage of the population in telework friendly jobs. The study also factored in extreme climate and natural hazards. *Intel, "Best Cities for Teleworking," March 30, 2006*

- The Phoenix metro area appeared on the Milken Institute "2005 Best Performing Cities" index. Rank: #15 out of 200 large metro areas. Criteria: job growth; wage and salary growth; high-tech output growth. *Milken Institute, "2005 Best Performing Cities," February 2006*

- The Phoenix metro area was selected as one of "The Best Cities for Doing Business in America." *Inc.* magazine measured employment growth in 393 regions using the following criteria: recent growth trend; mid-term growth; long-term trend; and current year growth. The Phoenix metro area ranked #6 among large metro areas and #36 overall. *Inc., May 2006*

- The Phoenix metro area was selected as one of "The Top 20 Boom Towns in America." *Business 2.0* magazine and econometric research firm Global Insight compared 319 metropolitan areas in the U.S. and ranked the 61 with populations over 1 million. Criteria: a weighted formula that includes forecast growth rates in sectors that contain the economy's 10 most skilled occupational clusters; the prevalence of college degrees in the local workforce; median salary. The area ranked #12 among large metro areas. *Business 2.0 Magazine, March 2004*

- Phoenix was identified as one of the 100 "Most Unwired Cities" in the U.S. The area ranked #55 out of the 100 largest metro areas in the U.S. Criteria: number of public and commercial wireless access points (hotspots); airports with wireless Internet access; broadband availability; local wireless networks; and wireless email devices. *Intel, "Most Unwired Cities Survey," June 7, 2005*

- Phoenix was ranked #38 out of 125 regions worldwide in terms of its "Knowledge Competitiveness Index." The index attempts to measure the knowledge-based development taking place throughout the world and is based on 19 measures of economic performance that indicate a region's ability to translate its knowledge capacity into economic value. *Robert Huggins Associates, World Knowledge Competitiveness Index 2005*

- *Forbes* ranked the 200 most populous metro areas in the U.S. in terms of the "Best Places for Business and Careers." The Phoenix metro area was ranked #55. Criteria: business costs (labor, energy, tax and office space expenses); living costs (housing, transportation, food and other household expenditures); education levels of the work force; job growth; income growth; migration trends; crime rates; and culture/leisure. *Forbes, April 23, 2007*

- Phoenix was selected as a 2006 Digital Cities Survey winner. The city ranked #10 in the large city (250,000 or more population) category. The survey examined and assessed how city governments are utilizing information technology to operate and deliver quality service to their customers and citizens. Survey questions focused on implementation and adoption of online service delivery; planning and governance; and the infrastructure and architecture that make the transformation to digital government possible. *Center for Digital Government, "2006 Digital Cities Survey"*

- *Kiplinger's Personal Finance* ranked 101 U.S. cities in terms of their total tax burdens. Phoenix ranked #18 (#1 had the lowest overall tax burden). Criteria: state income tax; property tax; sales tax; personal property tax; and gasoline tax. *Kiplinger's Personal Finance, July 2004*

- *Fortune* ranked the 100 largest metro areas in the U.S. in terms of projected median home price change in 2006. The Phoenix metro area ranked #68. *Fortune, "The Top 100: Is the Party Over?" December 26, 2005*

Health/Environment Rankings

- Doctors at the Harvard School of Public Health ranked 40 metropolitan areas based on data from the government-sponsored Hospital Quality Alliance program. The program tracks the performance of individual hospitals in treating patients for three common health problems: heart attacks, congestive heart failure, and pneumonia. The Phoenix metro area ranked #24 in quality of care for heart attacks, #15 for congestive heart failure, and #8 for pneumonia. *New England Journal of Medicine, July 21, 2005*

- *Reader's Digest* ranked the 50 largest metro areas in the U.S. in terms of how "clean" they are. The Phoenix metro area ranked #36. Criteria: air quality; water quality; toxic industrial pollution; Superfund sites; and sanitation. *Reader's Digest, "The 50 Cleanest (and Dirtiest) Cities in America," July 2005*

- Sanofi-aventis, in partnership with Sperling's BestPlaces, ranked the 50 worst cities for respiratory infections in the U.S. Phoenix ranked #45. Criteria: prevalence of sinusitis, pharyngitis (sore throat), bronchitis, acute upper respiratory infections, pneumonia, otitis media (middle ear infection), other respiratory tract infections and the common cold; total per capita prescriptions written for oral antibiotics for respiratory tract infections; and prevalence of state level antibiotic resistance. *Sanofi-aventis, "America's Worst Cities for Respiratory Infections," December 6, 2005*

- The Phoenix metro area appeared in *Country Home's* "2007 Best Green Places Report". The area ranked #115. Criteria included: air and watershed quality; miles of mass transit; green power; number of farmer's markets, organic producers and groceries. *Country Home, "2007 Best Green Places Report," April 2007*

- Wyeth Consumer Healthcare, in partnership with Sperling's BestPlaces, ranked the nation's 50 most populous metro areas in terms of five key health factors. The Phoenix metro area ranked #21. Criteria: physical activity, health status, nutrition, lifestyle pursuits; and mental wellness. *Wyeth Consumer Healthcare, "Centrum Healthiest Cities Study," April 19, 2005*

- HealthGrades surveyed over 41,000 individuals on doctor satisfaction and ranked the 20 largest metro areas based on the highest "definitely yes" responses to the question "Do you trust the physician to make decisions/recommendations that are in your best interest?" The Phoenix metro area ranked #13. *HealthGrades.com, "Top Cities in Doctor-Trust," September 7, 2006*

- The American Podiatric Medical Association and *Prevention* magazine ranked America's 100 most populated cities based on fitness-walker friendliness. The best cities have safe streets, beautiful places to walk, mild weather and good air quality. Phoenix ranked #36. *Prevention, "The Best Walking Cities of 2007," April 2007; American Podiatric Medical Association, "2007 Best Fitness-Walking Cities"*

- Phoenix was named the winner of the 2003 Accessible America contest by the National Organization on Disability. The city was honored for its sucessful design of accessible programs, services and facilities for its citizens and visitors with disabilities.

- Phoenix was selected as one of the 25 fittest cities in America by *Men's Fitness Online*. It ranked #15 out of America's 50 largest cities. Criteria: gyms/sporting goods; nutrition; exercise/sports; overweight/sedentary; junk food; alcohol; smoking; television; air and water quality; climate; geography; commute time; parks/open space; recreation facilities; health care; motivation; civic legislation and leadership. *Men's Fitness Online, America's Fittest/Fattest Cities 2006*

- Phoenix was identified as a "2007 Asthma Capital." The area ranked #44 out of the nation's 100 largest metropolitan areas. Twelve factors were used to identify the most challenging places to live for people with asthma: estimated prevalence; self-reported prevalence; crude death rate for asthma; annual pollen score; annual air quality; public smoking laws; number of board-certified asthma specialists; school inhaler access laws; rescue medication use; controller medication use; uninsured rate; poverty rate. *Asthma and Allergy Foundation of America, "2007 Asthma Capitals"*

- Phoenix was identified as a "Spring Allergy Capital." The area ranked #21 out of 100. Three groups of factors were used to identify the most severe cities for people with allergies during the spring season: annual pollen levels; medicine utilization; access to board-certified allergists. *Asthma and Allergy Foundation of America, "2007 Spring Allergy Capital Rankings"*

- Phoenix was identified as a "Fall Allergy Capital." The area ranked #63 out of 100. Three groups of factors were used to identify the most severe cities for people with allergies during the fall season: annual pollen levels; medicine utilization; access to board-certified allergists. *Asthma and Allergy Foundation of America, "2006 Fall Allergy Capital Rankings"*

- Phoenix was selected as one of "America's Healthiest Cities" by *Natural Health* magazine. The city was ranked #45 out of the 50 largest urban areas in the U.S. Twenty-six criteria in the following four categories were examined: whether the city boasts natural offerings; how well the city promotes its residents' physical health; whether the city offers a healthy environment; how well the city fosters a sense of community. *Natural Health, April 2003*

■ *Men's Health* ranked the nation's largest 100 cities in terms of the *Best (and Worst) Cities for Men.* Phoenix was ranked #31. Criteria: 24 statistical parameters of long life in the categories of health, quality of life, and fitness. *Men's Health, January/February 2007*

■ *Men's Health* ranked 100 U.S. cities in terms of the quality of their tap water. Phoenix was ranked #100 and received a grade of F. Criteria: levels of total coliform bacteria, arsenic, lead, total trihalomethanes (linked to cancer), and halo-acetic acids, plus the number of EPA water-system violations from 1995 to 2005. *Men's Health, March 2007*

■ GlaxoSmithKline, in partnership with Sperling's BestPlaces, analyzed the nation's 100 largest metro areas and identified 25 asthma "hot spots" where high prevalence makes the condition a key issue and environmental triggers and other factors can make living with asthma a particular challenge. The Phoenix metro area ranked #3 with #1 being the most challenging place to live. Criteria: asthma prevalence; asthma mortality; pollen scores; number of asthma specialists per capita; ratio of prescriptions for rescue medications to prescriptions for controller medications (an indicator of proper asthma treatment); air pollution; smoking laws; climate; and prevalence of tobacco use. *GlaxoSmithKline, "Asthma Hot Spots," October 29, 2002*

■ Ortho-McNeil Neurologics, in partnership with Sperling's BestPlaces, analyzed 110 metro areas and identified those U.S. cities with the highest prevalence of factors that are most commonly associated with migraine headaches. The Phoenix metro area ranked #54. Criteria: number of migraine-related drug prescriptions per capita; lifestyle factors that can contribute to migraines; environmental factors that can trigger migraines; and consumption of migraine-triggering foods. *Ortho-McNeil Neurologics, "America's Migraine Hot Spots," March 14, 2006*

■ Sperling's BestPlaces ranked 331 metro areas and identified the most and least stressful U.S. cities. The Phoenix metro area ranked #20 out of the 100 largest metro areas (#1 = most stressful). Criteria: divorce rate; unemployment rate; violent and property crime; suicide rate; commute time; mental health; alcohol consumption; cloudy days. *www.BestPlaces.net, January 9, 2004*

■ Sperling's BestPlaces in partnership with Vistakon ranked the 100 largest metro areas and identified "America's 10 Worst Cities for Comfortable Eyes." The Phoenix metro area ranked #9. Criteria: altitude; sunny days; wind; extreme temperatures; humidity; pollution; commute time; computer use. *Vistakon, "America's Best and Worst Cities for Comfortable Eyes," June 15, 2004*

■ HealthGrades evaluated the performance of America's 25 most populous metropolitan areas by measuring the outcomes of five of the highest volume and most widely studied procedures and diagnoses: coronary artery bypass graft surgery; percutaneus coronary interventions; acute myocardial infarction/heart attack in angioplasty-capable hospitals; congestive heart failure; and community acquired pneumonia. The Phoenix metro area ranked #4. *HealthGrades, "HealthGrades Hospital Quality in America Study," October 12, 2004*

■ Phoenix was selected as one of "America's Top 10 Low-Carb Cities" by *LowCarbiz Magazine.* Criteria: abundance of low-carb products; restaurants with low-carb menu items; health practitioners supportive of carb-cutting regimens; local culture generally conducive to exercise and health. *LowCarbiz Magazine, April 2004*

■ Phoenix was selected as one of "America's Pet Healthiest Cities" by Purina. The city ranked #23 out of 50. Criteria: veterinary services; environment; legislation; preventative care; obesity/body condition. *Purina Pet Institute, "America's Pet Healthiest Cities," May 20, 2003*

■ According to research conducted by Malibu Wellness of 100 major U.S. cities' local water quality reports, Phoenix was selected as one of 10 color-unfriendly cities in terms of hair color application and longevity. Criteria: quantity of minerals found in the water supply (lower ppm is better for hair color); type of oxidizers such as chlorine; and pH levels. *Malibu Wellness, Wellness e-Letter, "Best & Worst Cities for Hair Color," February 2005*

Women/Minorities Rankings

■ Phoenix was ranked #64 out of 100 metro areas in *SELF Magazine's* ranking of "America's Best Places for Women." A panel of experts came up with nearly 40 criteria including: drinking and smoking rates; depression; unemployment; parks; crime; disease; healthcare insurance coverage; air quality; and commute times. *SELF Magazine, "America's Best Places for Women 2006," December 2006*

■ *Ladies Home Journal* ranked America's 200 largest cities based on the qualities women surveyed care about most. Phoenix ranked #41 out of 57 in the big city category (population over 300,000). Criteria: crime; lifestyle; education; jobs; health; child care; politics; and the economy. *Ladies Home Journal Online, "The Best Cities for Women 2002"*

■ Phoenix was profiled in the book *50 Fabulous Gay-Friendly Places to Live.* Criteria: an active gay community; positive gay health programs; youth outreach; gay-friendly politics; gay-owned and gay-friendly businesses; employment opportunities; fun nightlife; cultural opportunities; recreational opportunities; housing options. *50 Fabulous Gay-Friendly Places to Live, 2005*

■ Phoenix was selected as one of "America's Top Lesbian Cities" by Gay.com. The city ranked #5 out of 5. *Gay.com*

Seniors/Retirement Rankings

■ Phoenix was identified as one of the "100 Most Popular Places to Retire" by *Where to Retire* magazine. The city ranked #1. Criteria: net retirees received from 1995-2000 (derived by subtracting all outbound retirees from inbound retirees for the county or county group - includes interstate moves only). *Where to Retire, "100 Most Popular Places to Retire," January/February 2007*

■ Sperling's BestPlaces in partnership with Bankers Life & Casualty Company designed a survey to identify the top 50 metro areas in the U.S. that offer the best overall qualities for senior living. The Phoenix metro area ranked #35. The following criteria were statistically weighted to reflect the needs of the senior population: health; disease; economics; social; environment; spiritual; transportation; housing; and crime. *Bankers Life & Casualty Company, "Best Cities for Seniors 2005"*

■ A.G. Edwards ranked America's 500 top-performing communities based on their residents' personal savings and investing behavior. The Phoenix metro area ranked #248 with an index score of 101.82 (national average = 100.00). A dozen statistical factors were measured including: participation in retirement savings plans; personal debt levels; and home ownership. *A.G. Edwards, "2006 Nest Egg Index", September 6, 2006*

Children/Family Rankings

■ The Phoenix metro area was selected as one of the "Best Cities for Relocating Families" by Worldwide ERC and Primacy Relocation. Criteria: tax rates; average home costs and home appreciation; ability to qualify for in-state tuition; service quality of local utilities; per-capita volunteerism; auto taxes; and quantity of fun, family-friendly events and venues. *Worldwide ERC and Primacy Relocation, "2006 Best Cities for Relocating Families"*

■ *Zero Population Growth* ranked 100 cities in terms of children's health, safety, and economic well-being. Phoenix was ranked #18 out of 20 Major Cities (main city in a metro area with population of greater than 2.5 million) and was given a grade of C. Criteria: total population and population growth; percent of population under 18 years of age; percent of births to teens; infant mortality rate; percent of eligible women not receiving Title X services; contraceptive equity indicator; percent of children without health insurance; percent of city residents over age 25 with a high-school diploma; ration of PopEd (Population Connection's Education Program) teachers trained; sexuality education indicator; proficiency in reading and math; percent of kids living in poverty; percent growth in urbanized land; violent crime rate; recycling. *Population Connection, Kid Friendly Cities: Report Card 2004*

■ *Fit Pregnancy* magazine ranked the 50 best U.S. cities in which to have a baby. Phoenix was ranked #38. Criteria: fertility services; maternal and infant health risk; access to hospitals and doctors; safety; affordability; stroller friendliness; and birthing options. *Fit Pregnancy, February/March, 2006*

Safety Rankings

■ Allstate ranked the 200 largest cities in America in terms of driver safety. Phoenix ranked #75. In addition, drivers were 3.6% more likely to have had an accident compared to the national average. Allstate researchers analyzed internal Property Damage reported claims over a two-year period (from January 2003 to December 2004) to ensure the findings would not be affected by external influences such as weather or road construction. A weighted average of the two-year numbers determined the annual percentages. The report defines an auto crash as any collision resulting in a property damage claim. *Allstate, "Allstate America's Best Drivers Report 2006," May 24, 2006*

■ Phoenix was identified as one of the most dangerous large metro areas for pedestrians in the U.S. The area ranked #10 out of the nations 50 largest metro areas. Criteria: average yearly pedestrian fatalities per capita (for the years 2002 and 2003) adjusted for the number of walkers. *Surface Transportation Policy Project, "Mean Streets 2004"*

■ *Ladies Home Journal* ranked America's 200 largest cities in terms of safety. Phoenix ranked #95 out of 200. Criteria: violent crimes; crimes against property; and rape. *Ladies Home Journal Online, "The Best Cities for Women 2002"*

Sports/Recreation Rankings

■ The Phoenix metro area appeared on *The Sporting News* list of the "Best Sports Cities 2006". The area ranked #10 out of 99 cities in North America. To be included in the rankings, a city must have at least one of the following: NCAA Division I basketball team; Class A minor league baseball team; training camp for a major league or NFL team; NASCAR Nextel Cup race; NCAA Division I-A bowl game; PGA Tour tournament; Triple Crown horse race. Once a city qualifies, a 12-month snapshot is taken of the sports atmosphere, putting a heavy premium on regular-season won-lost records; playoff berths, bowl appearances and tournament bids; championships; applicable power ratings; quality of competition; overall fan fervor; sports atmosphere and fan knowledge; abundance of teams (quality over quantity); stadium/arena quality; ticket availability and prices; franchise ownership; and the marquee appeal of athletes. *SportingNews.com, "Best Sports Cities 2006," August 1, 2006*

■ Phoenix was chosen as one of America's 25 best cities for running. The city was ranked #22. Criteria: number of running clubs per city; amount of land set aside for park usage; air quality; weather; crime rates; and results from a *Runner's World* poll in which readers ranked their favorite running cities. *Runner's World, "The 25 Best Running Cities in America," July 2005*

■ Phoenix was chosen as one of America's best cities for bicycling. The city ranked #0 in the very large city category (population 1 million or more). Criteria: cycling-friendly statistics (number of bike lanes and routes, number of bike racks, city bike projects completed and planned; bike culture (number of bike commuters, popular clubs, cool cycling events, renowned bike shops); climate/geography (the quality of roads and trails for riding, and how frequently mother nature lets riders enjoy them). *Bicycling, March 2006*

■ Scarborough Research, a leading market research firm, identified the top local markets for avid NBA fans. The Phoenix DMA (Designated Market Area) ranked in the top 10 with 14% of consumers 18 years and over reporting that they are "very interested in the NBA". *Scarborough Research, Scarborough USA+ 2005 Release 2*

■ The Phoenix metro area was selected by *Cranium* as one of the "Top 50 Fun Cities" in America. The area ranked #49. Criteria includes: number of sports teams, restaurants, and dance performances; number of toy stores; city budget spent on recreation. *Cranium, November 4, 2003*

■ *Golf Digest* ranked 330 metro areas in the U.S. in terms of golf. The Phoenix metro area was ranked #153. Criteria: access to golf; weather; value of golf; and quality of golf. *Golf Digest, "Metro Golf Rankings," August 2005*

Dating/Romance Rankings

■ The Phoenix metro area was selected as one of the "Best Cities for Relocating Singles" by Worldwide ERC and Primacy Relocation. The area ranked #17 out of the 100 largest metro areas in the U.S. Areas were selected based on the following criteria: Population Criteria (local percentage and growth trends of unmarried residents aged 25-34; male-female ratios; the number of newcomers to the area; diversity and density); Economic Criteria (job growth vs. unemployment rates; apartment rental costs; fee and occupancy rates for temporary housing and mini-storage; higher education costs, including in-state and out-of-state tuition requirements; vehicle tax rates and quality of service from utility providers); Quality-of-Life Criteria (level of per capita volunteering; quality and quantity of collegiate and professional sports with fun, fan-friendly venues; number of Starbucks and other coffee shops; quality or popularity of restaurants, nightspots, health clubs, and online dating; moderate climates with sustainable water supplies). *Worldwide ERC and Primacy Relocation, "2006 Best Cities for Relocating Singles," October 11, 2006*

■ *Forbes* ranked the 40 most populous metro areas in the U.S. in terms of the "Best Cities for Singles." The Phoenix metro area was ranked #3. Criteria: number of singles; cost of living alone; nightlife; culture; job growth; coolness; and online dating. *Forbes.com, July 25, 2006*

■ Sperling's BestPlaces in partnership with AXE Deodorant Bodyspray ranked 80 metro areas and identified "America's Best (and Worst) Cities for Dating." The Phoenix metro area ranked #21. Criteria: percentage of singles ages 18-24; population density; dating venues per capita. *AXE Deodorant Bodyspray, "America's Best (and Worst) Cities for Dating," May, 2004*

Culture/Performing Arts Rankings

■ Phoenix was selected as one of "The Top Ten Cities that Rock." The city was ranked #9. Criteria: overall music scene; retail music stores; live music venues. *Esquire, March 2004*

■ Phoenix was selected as one of "America's Top 25 Arts Destinations." The city ranked #15 in the big city (population 500,000 and over) category. Criteria: readers' top choices for arts travel destinations based on the richness and variety of visual arts sites, activities and events. *American Style, June 2006*

■ Scarborough Research, a leading market research firm, identified the top local markets for rock concert attendance. The Phoenix DMA (Designated Market Area) ranked in the top 25 with 15% of consumers, 18 years old and over, reporting that they have attended a rock concert during the past year. *Scarborough Research, Scarborough USA+ 2003 Release 2*

Miscellaneous Rankings

■ Phoenix was selected as one of the "Least Courteous Cities (Worst Road Rage)" in the U.S. by AutoVantage. The city ranked #2. Criteria: 2,040 consumers were interviewed in 20 major metropolitan areas about their views on road rage. *AutoVantage, "In The Driver's Seat Road Rage Survey," May 16, 2006*

■ Phoenix was determined to be one of America's smartest cities. The city ranked #36 in the large city category (200,000+ adults 25 years and older). Criteria: the editors rated the collective brainpower of U.S communities based on the educational attainment of its residents. *American City Business Journals, www.bizjournals.com, June 12, 2006*

■ Phoenix was identified as one of North America's most accommodating cities for travelers with pets. The city was ranked #5. Criteria: number of AAA Approved and Diamond rated pet-friendly hotels. *AAA, Traveling with your Pet: The AAA PetBook, 2006*

■ Phoenix was selected as one of the "Top 100 Sweatiest Summer Cities". The city was ranked #1. The ranking was based on the average male/female height/weight, average high temperature, and average relative humidity levels for 2002 in each of the cities during June, July and August. The sweat level was analyzed based on the assumption that the individual was walking for one hour. *Procter & Gamble, Old Spice, June 18, 2003*

■ Phoenix was selected as one of America's "20 Meanest Cities" by the National Coalition for the Homeless and The National Law Center on Homelessness & Poverty. The city was ranked #17. Criteria: the number of anti-homeless laws; the enforcement of those laws and severities of penalties; the general political climate towards homeless people; local advocate support for the meanest designation; the city's history of criminalization measures; and the existence of pending or recently enacted criminalization legislation. *National Coalition for the Homeless and The National Law Center on Homelessness & Poverty, "A Dream Denied: The Criminalization of Homelessness in U.S. Cities," January 2006*

■ The Phoenix metro area appeared on *Forbes* list of "America's Drunkest Cities". The area ranked #22. Criteria: 35 of the largest continental U.S. metro areas were chosen based on availability of data and geographic diversity. Each metro was ranked in five areas: state laws; drinkers; heavy drinkers; binge drinkers; and alcoholism. *Forbes.com, "America's Drunkest Cities," August 22, 2006*

■ Phoenix appeared on ApartmentRatings.com "Top Cities for Renters List 2006". The area ranked #109 out of 138. Criteria: renter satisfaction; affordability; and vacancy. *ApartmentRatings.com, "Top Cities for Renters List 2006"*

■ Sperling's BestPlaces in partnership with Pep Boys ranked 77 metro areas and identified "America's Most Drivable Cities." The Phoenix metro area ranked #37. Criteria: climate; road roughness; urban mobility; gas prices. *Pep Boys, "America's Most Drivable Cities," April 9, 2003*

■ Phoenix was ranked #22 out of 268 metro areas in terms of its Creativity Index. The Creativity Index is a mix of four equally weighted factors: the Creative Class (scientists, engineers, architects, designers, writers, artists, musicians, or any profession where creativity is a key factor) share of the workforce; innovation, measured as patents per capita; high-tech industry, using the Milken Institute's Tech Pole Index; and diversity, measured by the Gay Index (a reasonable proxy for an areas' openness to different kinds of people and ideas). *The Rise of the Creative Class, 2002*

■ Phoenix was selected as one of "America's Most Literate Cities." The city ranked #59 out of the 70 largest U.S. cities. Criteria: number of booksellers; library resources; Internet resources; educational attainment; periodical publishing resources; newspaper circulation. *Central Connecticut State University, "America's Most Literate Cities 2006"*

■ State Farm Insurance, in partnership with Sperling's BestPlaces, analyzed several key factors that contribute to overall family preparedness. The Phoenix metro area ranked #10 out of the nation's 50 most populous metro areas. Criteria: quality of life; life insurance coverage; and investments. *State Farm Life Insurance, "Fiscally Fit Cities Report," July 20, 2004*

Business Environment

CITY FINANCES

City Government Finances

Component	2003-2004 ($000)	2003-2004 ($ per capita)
Total Revenues	2,861,824	2,086
Total Expenditures	2,874,330	2,095
Debt Outstanding	4,791,916	3,493
Cash and Securities	4,250,560	3,098

Source: U.S Census Bureau, Government Finances 2003-2004

City Government Revenue by Source

Source	2003-2004 ($000)	2003-2004 ($ per capita)
General Revenue		
From Federal Government	416,141	303
From State Government	405,241	295
From Local Governments	46,519	34
Taxes		
Property	224,177	163
Sales	539,758	393
Personal Income	0	0
License	0	0
Charges	539,699	393
Liquor Store	0	0
Utility	246,806	180
Employee Retirement	226,930	165
Other	216,553	158

Source: U.S Census Bureau, Government Finances 2003-2004

City Government Expenditures by Function

Function	2003-2004 ($000)	2003-2004 ($ per capita)	2003-2004 (%)
General Expenditures			
Airports	520,614	379	18.1
Corrections	11,006	8	0.4
Education	20,326	15	0.7
Fire Protection	178,015	130	6.2
Governmental Administration	127,597	93	4.4
Health	0	0	0.0
Highways	67,423	49	2.3
Hospitals	0	0	0.0
Housing and Community Development	111,964	82	3.9
Interest on General Debt	187,998	137	6.5
Libraries	34,084	25	1.2
Parking	2,171	2	0.1
Parks and Recreation	291,940	213	10.2
Police Protection	343,443	250	11.9
Public Welfare	0	0	0.0
Sewerage	128,769	94	4.5
Solid Waste Management	86,519	63	3.0
Liquor Store	0	0	0.0
Utility	487,779	356	17.0
Employee Retirement	79,221	58	2.8
Other	195,461	142	6.8

Source: U.S Census Bureau, Government Finances 2003-2004

Municipal Bond Ratings

Area	Moody's
City	Aa1 (1/2006)

Source: Mergent Bond Record, January 2007 (unless noted otherwise)

DEMOGRAPHICS

Population Growth

Area	1990 Census	2000 Census	2006 Estimate	2011 Projection	Population Growth (%) 1990-2000	Population Growth (%) 2000-2011
City	989,873	1,321,045	1,425,284	1,537,377	33.5	16.4
MSA[1]	2,238,480	3,251,876	3,865,907	4,394,608	45.3	35.1
U.S.	248,709,873	281,421,906	298,021,266	312,383,955	13.2	11.0

Note: (1) Metropolitan Statistical Area - see Appendix B for areas included
Source: Claritas, Inc.

Number of Households and Average Household Size

Area	2006 Estimate	2006 Average Household Size
City	500,680	2.85
MSA[1]	1,408,131	2.75
U.S.	112,267,302	2.65

Note: (1) Metropolitan Statistical Area - see Appendix B for areas included
Source: Claritas, Inc.

Race and Ethnicity

Area	White Alone[2]	Black Alone[2]	Asian Alone[2]	Other Race Alone[2]	Hispanic[3]
City	66.4	5.2	2.2	26.2	40.8
MSA[1]	73.8	3.9	2.4	19.9	29.3
U.S.	73.3	12.4	4.2	10.1	14.5

Note: Figures are 2006 estimates; (1) Metropolitan Statistical Area - see Appendix B for areas included
(2) Alone is defined as not being in combination with one or more other races; (3) May be of any race.
Source: Claritas, Inc.

Segregation

City Index[2]	City Rank[3]	MSA[1] Index[2]	MSA[1] Rank[4]
54.4	63	49.1	244

Note: Figures are based on an analysis of Census 2000 data; (1) Metropolitan Statistical Area - see Appendix A
for areas included; (2) White/Black Dissimilarity Index—the most commonly used measure of segregation
between two groups, reflecting their relative distributions across neighborhoods within a city or metropolitan
area. It can range in value from 0, indicating complete integration, to 100, indicating complete segregation; (3)
Ranges from 1 (most segregated) to 100 (least segregated) and includes all the cities in this book; (4) Ranges
from 1 (most segregated) to 318 (least segregated) and includes 318 metropolitan areas.
Source: www.CensusScope.org

Ancestry

Area	German	Irish[2]	English	American	Italian	Polish	French[3]	Scottish
City	13.7	9.4	8.0	4.0	4.4	2.4	2.4	1.6
MSA[1]	16.2	10.5	10.3	4.6	4.9	2.7	2.9	1.9
U.S.	15.2	10.9	8.7	7.3	5.6	3.2	3.0	1.7

Note: Figures include multiple ancestry (e.g. if a person reported being Irish and Italian, they were included in
both columns); (1) Metropolitan Statistical Area - see Appendix A for areas included; (2) Includes Celtic; (3)
Includes Alsatian but excludes Basque
Source: Census 2000, Summary File 3

Foreign-Born Population

Area	Percent of Population Born in Any Foreign Country	Europe	Asia	Africa	Oceania[2]	Canada	Mexico	Latin America[3]
City	19.5	1.6	1.7	0.2	0.1	0.4	14.4	1.1
MSA[1]	14.1	1.5	1.8	0.2	0.1	0.6	9.2	0.8
U.S.	11.1	1.7	2.9	0.3	0.1	0.3	3.3	2.5

Note: (1) Metropolitan Statistical Area - see Appendix A for areas included; (2) Includes Australia, New
Zealand subregion, Melanesia, Micronesia, Polynesia, and Oceania n.e.c; (3) Includes Central America
(excluding Mexico), South America, and the Caribbean.
Source: Census 2000, Summary File 3

Marriage Status

Area	Never Married	Now Married (excluding Separated)	Separated	Widowed	Divorced
City	29.9	51.0	2.4	4.8	11.9
MSA[1]	26.5	55.0	1.9	5.6	11.0
U.S.	27.1	54.4	2.2	6.6	9.7

Note: Figures are percentages and cover the population 15 years of age and older;
(1) Metropolitan Statistical Area - see Appendix A for areas included
Source: Census 2000, Summary File 3

Age Distribution

Area	Percent of Population						
	Under Age 5	Age 5 to 17	Age 18 to 34	Age 35 to 49	Age 50 to 64	Age 65 to 79	80 Years and Over
City	8.6	20.3	28.0	22.9	12.2	6.1	1.9
MSA[1]	7.7	19.0	25.8	22.0	13.5	9.0	3.0
U.S.	6.8	18.9	23.7	23.5	14.8	9.2	3.2

Note: (1) Metropolitan Statistical Area - see Appendix A for areas included
Source: Census 2000, Summary File 3

Male/Female Ratio

Area	Males	Females	Males per 100 Females
City	727,168	698,116	104.2
MSA[1]	1,946,170	1,919,737	101.4
U.S.	146,712,712	151,308,554	97.0

Note: Figures are 2006 estimates; (1) Metropolitan Statistical Area -
see Appendix B for areas included
Source: Claritas, Inc.

Religion

Area	Catholic	Southern Baptist	United Meth-odist	ELCA[1]	LDS[2]	Presby-terian Church USA	Jewish Est.	Muslim Est.
County	17.3	2.5	1.1	1.7	5.0	0.6	2.0	0.3
U.S.	22.0	7.1	3.7	1.8	1.5	1.1	2.2	0.6

Note: Figures are the number of adherents as a percentage of the total population; Adherents are defined as all members, including full members, their children and the estimated number of other participants who are not considered members (e.g. the baptized, those not confirmed, those regularly attending services, etc.); (1) Evangelical Lutheran Church in America; (2) The Church of Jesus Christ of Latter Day Saints Source: Reprinted with permission from Religious Congregations and Membership in the United States 2000 (Nashville, Glenmary Research Center, 2002) Copyright Association of Statisticians of American Religious Bodies. All rights reserved.

ECONOMY

Gross Metropolitan Product

Area	2002	2003	2004	2005	2005 Rank[2]
MSA[1]	120.3	128.0	136.2	153.2	14

Note: Figures are in billions of dollars; (1) Phoenix-Mesa-Scottsdale, AZ Metropolitan Statistical Area - see Appendix A for areas included; (2) Rank ranges from 1 to 361
Source: The U.S. Conference of Mayors, "U.S. Metro Economies: GMP - The Engines of America's Growth," January 2007

Economic Growth

Area	1995 GMP	2005 GMP	Average Annual Growth Rate	Growth Rate Rank[2]
MSA[1]	73.6	153.2	7.6	19

Note: Figures are in billions of dollars; GMP = Gross Metropolitan Product; (1) Phoenix-Mesa-Scottsdale, AZ Metropolitan Statistical Area - see Appendix A for areas included; (2) Rank ranges from 1 to 361
Source: The U.S. Conference of Mayors, "U.S. Metro Economies: GMP - The Engines of America's Growth," January 2007

INCOME

Per Capita/Median/Average Income

Area	Per Capita ($)	Median Household ($)	Average Household ($)
City	22,355	45,862	62,924
MSA[1]	25,352	52,008	68,998
U.S.	25,129	48,775	65,849

Note: Figures are 2006 estimates; (1) Metropolitan Statistical Area - see Appendix B for areas included
Source: Claritas, Inc.

Household Income Distribution

Area	Under $15,000	$15,000 -24,999	$25,000 -34,999	$35,000 -49,999	$50,000 -74,999	$75,000 -99,000	$100,000 -149,999	$150,000 and up
				Percent of Households Earning				
City	12.5	12.0	12.9	17.5	19.1	10.6	9.6	5.9
MSA[1]	10.2	10.2	11.4	16.5	20.6	12.5	11.9	6.8
U.S.	13.3	11.0	11.3	15.7	19.5	11.8	11.0	6.4

Note: Figures are 2006 estimates; (1) Metropolitan Statistical Area - see Appendix B for areas included
Source: Claritas, Inc.

Poverty Rates by Age

Area	All Ages	Under 5 Years Old	5 to 17 Years Old	18 to 64 Years Old	65 Years and Over
City	15.8	2.1	4.1	8.8	0.8
MSA[1]	12.0	1.4	3.0	6.7	0.9
U.S.	12.4	1.2	3.0	6.9	1.2

Note: Figures are percent of population with income in 1999 below poverty level and only include population for whom poverty status is determined; (1) Metropolitan Statistical Area - see Appendix A for areas included
Source: Census 2000, Summary File 3

Personal Bankruptcy Filing Rate

Area	2003	2004	2005
Maricopa County	6.18	6.03	7.24
U.S.	5.57	5.31	6.88

Note: Numbers are per 1,000 population and include Chapter 7 and Chapter 13 filings
Source: Federal Deposit Insurance Corporation (FDIC), Regional Economic Conditions (RECON), 3/24/2006

EMPLOYMENT

Labor Force and Employment

Area	Civilian Labor Force			Workers Employed		
	Dec. 2005	Dec. 2006	% Chg.	Dec. 2005	Dec. 2006	% Chg.
City	805,650	837,762	4.0	770,833	805,427	4.5
MSA[1]	1,952,929	2,032,289	4.1	1,880,490	1,964,883	4.5
U.S.	149,874,000	152,571,000	1.8	142,918,000	146,081,000	2.2

Note: Data is not seasonally adjusted and covers workers 16 years of age and older;
(1) Metropolitan Statistical Area - see Appendix B for areas included
Source: Bureau of Labor Statistics, http://stats.bls.gov

Unemployment Rate

Area	2006											
	Jan.	Feb.	Mar.	Apr.	May	Jun.	Jul.	Aug.	Sep.	Oct.	Nov.	Dec.
City	5.2	4.6	4.1	4.2	3.8	4.6	4.8	3.6	3.9	3.9	3.9	3.9
MSA[1]	4.5	3.9	3.5	3.6	3.3	3.9	4.1	3.1	3.3	3.4	3.3	3.3
U.S.	5.1	5.1	4.8	4.5	4.4	4.8	5.0	4.6	4.4	4.1	4.3	4.3

Note: Data is not seasonally adjusted and covers workers 16 years of age and older; All figures are percentages; (1) Metropolitan Statistical Area - see Appendix B for areas included
Source: Bureau of Labor Statistics, http://stats.bls.gov

Employment by Occupation

Occupation Classification	City (%)	MSA[1] (%)	U.S. (%)
Sales and Office	29.1	29.5	26.7
Professional and Related	17.6	19.0	20.2
Service	15.9	14.9	14.9
Production, Transportation, and Material Moving	12.0	11.1	14.6
Management, Business, and Financial	13.2	14.4	13.5
Construction, Extraction, and Maintenance	12.0	10.6	9.4
Farming, Forestry, and Fishing	0.3	0.5	0.7

Note: Figures cover employed civilians 16 years of age and older;
(1) Metropolitan Statistical Area - see Appendix A for areas included
Source: Census 2000, Summary File 3

Employment by Industry

Sector	MSA[1] Number of Employees	MSA[1] Percent of Total	U.S. Percent of Total
Government	242,100	12.4	16.3
Education and Health Services	199,400	10.2	13.2
Professional and Business Services	335,400	17.1	12.9
Retail Trade	242,900	12.4	11.5
Manufacturing	139,800	7.1	10.2
Leisure and Hospitality	186,400	9.5	9.5
Financial Activities	158,400	8.1	6.1
Construction	190,800	9.7	5.5
Wholesale Trade	89,200	4.6	4.3
Other Services	74,800	3.8	3.9
Transportation and Utilities	65,200	3.3	3.7
Information	31,900	1.6	2.2
Natural Resources and Mining	2,800	0.1	0.5

Note: Figures cover non-farm employment as of December 2006 and are not seasonally adjusted;
(1) Metropolitan Statistical Area - see Appendix B for areas included
Source: Bureau of Labor Statistics, http://stats.bls.gov

Occupations with Greatest Projected Employment Growth: 2002 - 2012

Occupation[1]	2002 Employment	2012 Projected Employment	Numeric Employment Change	Percent Employment Change
Cashiers	63,550	85,240	21,690	34.1
Registered Nurses	34,190	54,330	20,140	58.9
Combined Food Preparation and Serving Workers, Including Fast Food	48,950	63,360	14,410	29.4
Retail Salespersons	67,560	81,370	13,810	20.4
Customer Service Representatives	45,870	59,210	13,340	29.1
Carpenters	33,870	44,580	10,710	31.6
Landscaping and Groundskeeping Workers	30,700	39,990	9,290	30.3
Nursing Aides, Orderlies, and Attendants	18,390	27,620	9,230	50.2
Postsecondary Teachers	29,790	38,960	9,170	30.8
Medical Assistants	10,950	19,540	8,590	78.4

Note: Projections cover Arizona; (1) Sorted by numeric employment change
Source: www.projectionscentral.com, State Occupational Projections, 2002-2012 Long-Term Projections

Fastest Growing Occupations: 2002 - 2012

Occupation[1]	2002 Employment	2012 Projected Employment	Numeric Employment Change	Percent Employment Change
Emergency Medical Technicians and Paramedics	1,540	3,220	1,680	109.1
Medical Assistants	10,950	19,540	8,590	78.4
Physician Assistants	2,110	3,740	1,630	77.3
Medical Records and Health Information Technicians	3,000	5,190	2,190	73.0
Respiratory Therapy Technicians	680	1,170	490	72.1
Dental Hygienists	1,680	2,880	1,200	71.4
Respiratory Therapists	1,380	2,350	970	70.3
Dental Assistants	5,280	8,980	3,700	70.1
Home Health Aides	10,390	17,560	7,170	69.0
Physical Therapist Aides	1,490	2,450	960	64.4

Note: Projections cover Arizona; (1) Sorted by percent employment change and excludes occupations with numeric employment change less than 300
Source: www.projectionscentral.com, State Occupational Projections, 2002-2012 Long-Term Projections

Average Wages

Occupation	$/Hr.	Occupation	$/Hr.
Accountants and Auditors	24.71	Maids and Housekeeping Cleaners	8.07
Automotive Mechanics	18.71	Maintenance and Repair Workers	14.95
Bookkeepers	14.70	Marketing Managers	39.27
Carpenters	16.41	Nuclear Medicine Technologists	27.21
Cashiers	9.12	Nurses, Licensed Practical	18.89
Clerks, General Office	12.50	Nurses, Registered	27.38
Clerks, Receptionists/Information	11.15	Nursing Aides/Orderlies/Attendants	10.73
Clerks, Shipping/Receiving	10.44	Packers and Packagers, Hand	7.90
Computer Programmers	29.39	Physical Therapists	30.04
Computer Support Specialists	21.41	Postal Service Mail Carriers	21.55
Computer Systems Analysts	31.83	Real Estate Brokers	43.89
Cooks, Restaurant	9.95	Retail Salespersons	11.77
Dentists	n/a	Sales Reps., Exc. Tech./Scientific	22.88
Electrical Engineers	36.74	Sales Reps., Tech./Scientific	25.55
Electricians	17.32	Secretaries, Exc. Legal/Med./Exec.	12.69
Financial Managers	41.31	Security Guards	10.33
First-Line Supervisors/Mgrs., Sales	18.04	Surgeons	78.30
Food Preparation Workers	9.61	Teacher Assistants	9.60
General and Operations Managers	42.41	Teachers, Elementary School	16.00
Hairdressers/Cosmetologists	11.75	Teachers, Secondary School	18.80
Internists	84.23	Telemarketers	10.14
Janitors and Cleaners	8.71	Truck Drivers, Heavy/Tractor-Trailer	18.29
Landscaping/Groundskeeping Workers	9.52	Truck Drivers, Light/Delivery Svcs.	13.12
Lawyers	47.56	Waiters and Waitresses	7.79

Note: Wage data is for May 2005 and covers the Phoenix-Mesa-Scottsdale, AZ Metropolitan Statistics Area - see Appendix B for areas included. Hourly wages for elementary/secondary school teachers and teacher assistants were calculated by the editors from annual wage data assuming a 40 hour work week; n/a not available.
Source: Bureau of Labor Statistics, May 2005 Metro Area Occupational Employment and Wage Estimates

RESIDENTIAL REAL ESTATE

Building Permits

Area	Single-Family			Multi-Family			Total		
	2005	2006p	Pct. Chg.	2005	2006p	Pct. Chg.	2005	2006p	Pct. Chg.
City	12,391	9,025	-27.2	2,752	2,244	-18.5	15,143	11,269	-25.6
U.S.	1,682,000	1,380,000	-18.0	473,300	457,300	-3.4	2,155,300	1,837,300	-14.8

Note: (p) preliminary; figures represent new, privately-owned housing units authorized (unadjusted data); All permit data are based on estimates with imputation; U.S. figures are based on the new 20,000-place series.
Source: U.S. Census Bureau, Manufacturing, Mining, and Construction Statistics

Homeownership and Housing Vacancies

Area	Homeownership Rate[2] (%)			Rental Vacancy Rate[3] (%)			Homeowner Vacancy Rate[4] (%)		
	2004	2005	2006	2004	2005	2006	2004	2005	2006
MSA[1]	n/a	71.2	72.5	n/a	11.2	9.1	n/a	1.0	3.1
U.S.	69.0	68.9	68.8	10.2	9.8	9.7	1.7	1.9	2.4

Note: Comparable 2004 data was not available due to changes in metropolitan area definitions; (1) Metropolitan Statistical Area - see Appendix B for areas included; (2) The proportion of households that are owners; (3) The proportion of the rental inventory that is vacant for rent; (4) The proportion of the homeowner inventory that is vacant for sale; n/a not available
Source: U.S. Census Bureau, Housing Vacancies and Homeownership Annual Statistics: 2006

TAXES

State Corporate Income Tax Rates

State	Rate (%)	Number of Brackets	Low Bracket (Under $)	High Bracket (Over $)
Arizona	6.968	1	na	na

Note: Tax rates as of December 31, 2006; na not applicable; Minimum tax is $50.
Source: Tax Foundation, www.taxfoundation.org

State Individual Income Tax Rates

State	Federal Deductibility	Marginal Rate (%)	Number of Brackets	Low Bracket (Under $)	High Bracket (Over $)
Arizona	No	2.87-5.04	5	0	150,000

Note: Tax rates as of December 31, 2006; Brackets apply to single taxpayers and married people filing separately; na not applicable
Source: Tax Foundation, www.taxfoundation.org

Various State and Local Tax Rates

State and Local Sales and Use (%)	State Sales and Use (%)	Gasoline ($/gal.)	Cigarette ($/pack)	Spirits ($/gal.)	Table Wine ($/gal.)	Beer ($/gal.)
8.1	5.6	0.19 (m)	2	3	0.84	0.16

Note: Tax rates as of December 31, 2006; (m) Additional cents per gallon taxes added this year that were not included in previous years' tables.
Source: Tax Foundation, www.taxfoundation.org; The Sales Tax Clearinghouse, www.thestc.com

State Tax Burdens

Area	Combined State and Local Tax Burden		Combined Federal, State and Local Tax Burden	
	Percent	Rank	Percent	Rank
Arizona	10.1	32	29.9	29
U.S. Average	10.6	-	31.6	-

Note: Figures are for 2006 and measure taxes as a percentage of income
Source: Tax Foundation, www.taxfoundation.org

Internal Revenue Service Tax Audits

IRS District	Percent of Returns Audited				
	1996	1997	1998	1999	2000
Southwest	0.80	0.81	0.61	0.36	0.29
U.S.	0.66	0.61	0.46	0.31	0.20

Note: Figures cover IRS district audits of federal income tax returns filed by individuals. Geographic data on district audits after the year 2000 are being withheld by the IRS. TRAC is challenging this policy.
Source: Syracuse University, Transactional Records Access Clearinghouse (TRAC), "Odds of IRS District Tax Audit 2000"

**COMMERCIAL
REAL ESTATE**

Office Market

Market Area	Inventory (sq. ft.)	Vacant (sq. ft.)	Vac. Rate (%)	Under Constr. (sq. ft.)	Asking Rent ($/sf)	
					Class A	Class B
Phoenix	57,524,717	7,316,897	12.7	4,089,448	27.69	21.84

Source: Grubb & Ellis, Office Markets Trends, 4th Quarter 2006

Industrial Market

Market Area	Inventory (sq. ft.)	Vacant (sq. ft.)	Vac. Rate (%)	Under Constr. (sq. ft.)	Asking Rent ($/sf)	
					WH/Dist	R&D/Flex
Phoenix	248,538,713	16,241,395	6.5	4,971,854	6.00	12.24

Source: Grubb & Ellis, Industrial Markets Trends, 4th Quarter 2006

**COMMERCIAL
UTILITIES**

Typical Monthly Electric Bills

Area	Commercial Service ($/month)		Industrial Service ($/month)	
	3 kW demand 1,000 kWh	40 kW demand 14,000 kWh	1,000 kW demand 200,000 kWh	50,000 kW demand 15,000,000 kWh
City	146	1,407	22,221	1,273,053
Average[1]	123	1,413	22,000	1,306,315

Note: Based on total rates in effect July 1, 2006; (1) average based on 196 utilities
Source: Edison Electric Institute, Typical Bills and Average Rates Report, Summer 2006

TRANSPORTATION

Means of Transportation to Work

Area	Car/Truck/Van		Public Transportation			Bicycle	Walked	Other Means	Worked at Home
	Drove Alone	Car-pooled	Bus	Subway	Railroad				
City	71.7	17.4	3.0	0.0	0.0	0.9	2.2	1.5	3.3
MSA[1]	74.6	15.3	1.8	0.0	0.0	0.9	2.1	1.4	3.7
U.S.	75.7	12.2	2.5	1.5	0.5	0.4	2.9	1.0	3.3

Note: Figures are percentages and cover workers 16 years of age and older;
(1) Metropolitan Statistical Area - see Appendix A for areas included
Source: Census 2000, Summary File 3

Travel Time to Work

Area	Less Than 15 Minutes	15 to 29 Minutes	30 to 44 Minutes	45 to 59 Minutes	60 Minutes or More
City	22.5	38.4	25.1	7.9	6.1
MSA[1]	23.8	37.0	24.1	8.8	6.3
U.S.	29.4	36.1	19.1	7.4	8.0

Note: Figures are percentages and include workers 16 years old and over; (1) Metropolitan Statistical Area -
see Appendix A for areas included
Source: Census 2000, Summary File 3

Travel Time Index

Area	1982	1993	2002	2003
Urban Area[1]	1.13	1.27	1.35	1.35
Average[2]	1.12	1.28	1.37	1.37

Note: Travel Time Index - The ratio of travel time in the peak period to the travel time at
free-flow conditions. A value of 1.35 indicates a 20-minute free-flow trip takes 27 minutes
in the peak. Free-flow speeds (60 mph on freeways and 35 mph on principal arterials)
are used as the comparison threshold; (1) Covers the Phoenix, AZ urban area;
(2) average of 85 urban areas
Source: Texas Transportation Institute, The 2005 Urban Mobility Report, May 2005

Public Transportation

Agency name:	City of Phoenix Public Transit Dept. (Valley Metro)
Vehicle type:	Bus
Average fleet age in years:	6.9
No. operated in max. service:	411
Vehicle type:	Demand response
Average fleet age in years:	3.2
No. operated in max. service:	130
Agency name:	Phoenix - VPSI Inc.
Vehicle type:	Vanpool
Average fleet age in years:	2.1
No. operated in max. service:	3

Source: Federal Transit Administration, National Transit Database, 2005

Air Transportation

Airport name and code:	Phoenix Sky Harbor International (PHX)
Domestic service (2006)	
Passenger airlines[1]:	33
Passenger enplanements:	19,715,316
Freight carriers[2]:	32
Freight (lbs.):	261,231,406
International service (2005)	
Passenger airlines[1]:	14
Passenger enplanements:	871,348
Freight carriers[2]:	10
Freight (lbs.):	5,993,068

*Note: (1) Includes all major, minor and commuter airlines that carried at least one passenger during the year;
(2) Includes all airlines and freight carriers that transported at least one pound of freight during the year
Source: Bureau of Transportation Statistics, The Intermodal Transportation Database, Air Carriers: T-100
International Market, 2004; Bureau of Transportation Statistics, The Intermodal Transportation Database, Air
Carriers: T-100 Domestic Market, 2005*

Other Transportation Statistics

Interstate highways:	I-10; I-17
Amtrak service:	Bus connection
Major waterways/ports:	None

Source: Editor & Publisher Market Guide, 2006; Amtrak.com; Rand McNally 2006 Road Atlas

BUSINESSES

Major Business Headquarters

Company Name	2006 Rankings	
	Fortune[1]	Forbes[2]
Phelps Dodge	260	-
Shamrock Foods	-	240

*Note: (1) Fortune 500 - companies that produce a 10-K are ranked 1 to 500 based on 2005 revenue; (2) Forbes
Largest Private Companies - all private companies with at least $1 billion in annual revenue are ranked 1 to
394; companies listed are located in the city; dashes indicate no ranking
Source: Fortune, April 17, 2006; Forbes, November 9, 2006*

Best Companies to Work For

**American Express; Kimley-Horn & Assoc; Mayo Clinic; PCL Construction; Perkins
Coie; Standard Pacific**, headquartered in Phoenix, are among the "100 Best Companies to
Work For." Criteria: More than 105,000 employees from 446 companies responded to a
57-question survey created by the Great Place to Work Institute. Two-thirds of a company's
score is based on the survey, which covers topics such as attitudes towards management, job
satisfaction, and camaraderie. The remaining third of the score comes from each company's
responses to the Institute's Culture Audit, which includes detailed questions about
demographic makeup, pay and benefits programs, and open-ended questions about the
company's people-management philosophy, internal communications, opportunities,
compensation practices, diversity programs, etc. Any company that is at least seven years old
and has a minimum of 1,000 U.S. employees is eligible. The top three U.S. locations are
shown for companies with more than one location. *Fortune, "100 Best Companies to Work
for 2007," January 22, 2007*

Fast-Growing Businesses

According to *Inc.*, Phoenix is home to six of America's 500 fastest-growing private companies: **Abacus 247; Ambient Weather; IPower; Jobing.com; PremierGarage; Schaller Anderson**. Criteria: must be an independent, privately-held, U.S. corporation, proprietorship or partnership; net sales of at least $600,000 in FY2002; four-year operating/sales history; holding companies, regulated banks, and utilities were excluded. *Inc., "America's 500 Fastest-Growing Private Companies," September 2006*

Phoenix is home to one of *Business Week's* "Hot Growth Companies:" **Radyne**. To qualify, a company must have annual sales of more than $50 million and less than $1.5 billion, a current market value greater than $25 million, a current stock price of at least $5, and be actively traded. Banks, insurers, real estate firms, and utilities are excluded. So are companies with declines in current financial results or in stock price, as well as companies where other developments raise questions about future performance. Companies were selected based on three-year results in sales growth, earnings growth, and return on invested capital. *Business Week, June 5, 2006*

According to *Fortune*, Phoenix is home to two of America's 100 fastest-growing companies: **Phelps Dodge; Southern Copper**. Companies were ranked based on earnings-per-share growth, revenue growth and total return over the previous three years. Criteria for inclusion: public companies with sales of at least $50 million. Companies that lost money in the most recent quarter, or ended in the red for the past four quarters as a whole, were not eligible. Limited partnerships and REITs were also not considered. *Fortune, "America's Fastest-Growing Companies," September 18, 2006*

Women-Owned Businesses: 1997 and 2002

Year	All Firms		Firms with Paid Employees			
	Firms	Sales ($000)	Firms	Sales ($000)	Employees	Payroll ($000)
1997	22,535	3,862,069	3,401	3,442,585	32,044	633,523
2002	25,212	4,865,840	4,042	4,268,508	38,338	991,667

Note: Figures cover firms located in the city; Women-owned business are defined as firms in which women own 51% or more of the stock or equity of the company; (a) Withheld to avoid disclosing data for individual companies; (b) Withheld because estimate did not meet publication standards; n/a not available
Source: 1997 Economic Census, Survey of Minority- and Women-Owned Business Enterprises; 2002 Economic Census, Survey of Business Owners (released February 9, 2006)

HOTELS

Hotels/Motels

Area	Hotels/Motels	Average Minimum Rates ($)		
		Tourist	First-Class	Deluxe
City	132	57	102	190

Source: OAG Travel Planner Online, Spring 2006

The Phoenix metro area is home to five of the top 187 hotels in the U.S. according to *Travel & Leisure*: **The Phoenician** (#55); **Boulders Resort & Golden Door Spa** (#59); **Four Seasons Resort at Troon North** (#115); **Sanctuary on Camelback Mountain Resort & Spa** (#123); **Royal Palms Resort & Spa** (#136). Criteria: service; location; rooms; food; and value. *Travel & Leisure, "The T+L 500, 2007"*

EVENT SITES

Stadiums, Arenas, and Auditoriums

Name	Capacity
Fountain Hills Community Center	1,100
Phoenix Civic Plaza	36,320

Source: www.officialtravelguide.com; www.eventective.com; original research

Hotels/Conference Centers

Name	Guest Rooms	Exhibit Space (sq. ft.)	Meeting Space (sq. ft.)
Black Canyon Conference Center by Sodexho	n/a	n/a	n/a
Crowne Plaza North Phoenix	250	10,000	10,000
Days Inn Phoenix Airport	220	12,000	10,000
Wells Fargo Conference Center	n/a	n/a	n/a

Note: n/a not available

Source: www.officialtravelguide.com; www.eventective.com; original research

Living Environment

COST OF LIVING

Cost of Living Index

Year	Composite Index	Groceries	Housing	Utilities	Trans-portation	Health Care	Misc. Goods/ Services
2004	98.5	100.2	91.1	92.0	108.9	108.3	102.0
2005	98.0	98.0	93.2	92.0	104.1	100.8	101.7
2006	101.4	98.9	104.8	91.6	103.2	101.3	101.9

Note: U.S. = 100
Source: The Council for Community and Economic Research (formerly ACCRA), Cost of Living Index, 2004, 2005 and 2006 4-Quarter Averages

HOUSING

House Price Index (HPI)

Area	National Ranking[2]	Quarterly Change (%)	One-Year Change (%)	Five-Year Change (%)
MSA[1]	60	0.78	9.04	99.79
U.S.[3]	-	1.12	5.87	55.21

Note: The HPI is a weighted repeat sales index. It measures average price changes in repeat sales or refinancings on the same properties. This information is obtained by reviewing repeat mortgage transactions on single-family properties whose mortgages have been purchased or securitized by Fannie Mae or Freddie Mac in January 1975; (1) Metropolitan Statistical Area - see Appendix B for areas included; (2) Rankings are based on annual percentage change for all metro areas containing at least 15,000 transactions over the last 10 years and ranges from 1 to 282; (3) figures based on a weighted division average; all figures are for the period ending December 31, 2006
Source: Office of Federal Housing Enterprise Oversight, House Price Index, March 1, 2007

House Price Valuations

Area	Q4 1999	Q4 2000	Q4 2001	Q4 2002	Q4 2003	Q4 2004	Q4 2005	Q4 2006
MSA[1]	-10.1	-9.1	-5.8	-2.9	0.4	7.7	37.3	40.6

Note: Figures show the percentage of over- or under-valuation of single family homes relative to statistically normal house values (e.g. a value of 23.6 indicates that house values are 23.6% overvalued). Statistically normal house values are based on house prices, interest rates, household incomes, population densities, and any historical premiums or discounts metropolitan areas have exhibited over time; (1) Figures cover the Metropolitan Statistical Area - see Appendix B for areas included
Source: Global Insight/National City Corporation, House Prices in America, March 2007

Median Home Prices

Area	2004	2005	2006p	Percent Change 2005 to 2006
Metro Area[1]	169.4	247.4	268.2	8.4
U.S. Average	195.2	219.0	222.0	1.4

Note: Figures are median sales prices of existing single-family homes in thousands of dollars; (p) preliminary; n/a not available; (1) Covers the Phoenix-Mesa-Scottsdale, AZ Metropolitan Statistical Area - see Appendix B for areas included
Source: National Association of Realtors, Metropolitan Area Prices, 4th Quarter 2006

Housing: Year Structure Built

Area	1990 -2000	1980 -1989	1970 -1979	1960 -1969	1950 -1959	1940 -1949	Before 1940	Median Year
City	20.0	22.9	25.1	13.4	12.5	3.6	2.5	1977
MSA[1]	30.4	25.5	23.2	10.4	7.1	2.0	1.4	1982
U.S.	17.0	15.8	18.5	13.7	12.7	7.3	15.0	1971

Note: Figures are percentages; (1) Metropolitan Statistical Area - see Appendix A for areas included
Source: Census 2000, Summary File 3

Average New Home Price

Area	2004	2005	2006
City	228,919	256,927	318,810
U.S.	253,574	275,712	299,269

Note: Figures, in dollars, are based on a new home with 2,400 sq. ft. of living area on an 8,000 sq. ft. lot.
Source: The Council for Community and Economic Research (formerly ACCRA), Cost of Living Index, 2004, 2005 and 2006 4-Quarter Averages

Average Apartment Rent

Area	2004	2005	2006
City	682	697	751
U.S.	716	740	766

Note: Figures, in dollars per month, are based on an unfurnished two bedroom, 1-1/2 or 2 bath apartment, approximately 950 sq. ft. in size, excluding all utilities except water
Source: The Council for Community and Economic Research (formerly ACCRA), Cost of Living Index, 2004, 2005 and 2006 4-Quarter Averages

RESIDENTIAL UTILITIES

Average Residential Utility Costs

Area	All Electric ($/mth)	Part Electric ($/mth)	Other Energy ($/mth)	Phone ($/mth)
City	149.46	–	–	22.62
U.S.	136.00	76.53	90.52	25.87

Source: The Council for Community and Economic Research (formerly ACCRA), Cost of Living Index, 2006 4-Quarter Average

HEALTH

Average Health Care Costs

Area	Optometrist ($/visit)	Doctor ($/visit)	Dentist ($/visit)
City	94.16	72.47	71.68
U.S.	76.38	76.10	68.72

Note: Optometrist—based on a full vision eye exam for an established adult patient;
Doctor—based on a general practitioner's routine exam of an established patient;
Dentist—based on adult teeth cleaning and periodic oral exam.
Source: The Council for Community and Economic Research (formerly ACCRA), Cost of Living Index, 2006 4-Quarter Average

Mortality Rates

ICD-10 Sub-Chapter	ICD-10 Code	Age-Adjusted Death Rate per 100,000 population[1]	U.S. Age-Adjusted Death Rate per 100,000 population
Malignant neoplasms	C00-C97	164.2	185.8
Ischaemic heart diseases	I20-I25	150.1	150.2
Other forms of heart disease	I30-I51	22.4	50.8
Cerebrovascular diseases	I60-I69	43.5	50.0
Chronic lower respiratory diseases	J40-J47	42.4	41.1
Diabetes mellitus	E10-E14	19.2	24.5
Other degenerative diseases of the nervous system	G30-G31	36.3	22.3
Other external causes of accidental injury	W00-X59	26.7	21.2
Influenza and pneumonia	J10-J18	18.5	19.8
Hypertensive diseases	I10-I13	18.6	18.1

Note: ICD-10 = International Classification of Diseases 10th Revision; (1) Figures cover Maricopa County, AZ
Source: Centers for Disease Control and Prevention, National Center for Health Statistics. Compressed Mortality File 1999-2004. CDC WONDER On-line Database, compiled from Compressed Mortality File 1999-2004 Series 20 No. 2J, 2007.

Health Risk Data

Item	Area[1] (%)	U.S. (%)
Adults who have been told they have high blood pressure	20.5	25.5
Adults who have been told they have high blood cholesterol	32.1	35.6
Adults who have been told they have diabetes[2]	7.0	7.3
Adults who have been told they have arthritis	25.3	27.0
Adults who have been told they currently have asthma	6.8	8.0
Adults who are current smokers	20.3	20.6

Note: (1) Figures cover the Metropolitan Statistical Area - see Appendix B for areas included; (2) Figures do not include pregnancy-related diabetes, pre-diabetes or borderline diabetes
Source: Centers for Disease Control and Prevention, Behaviorial Risk Factor Surveillance System, SMART: Selected Metropolitan/Micropolitan Area Trends, 2005

Distribution of Office-Based Physicians

Area	Total	Family/ General Practice	Specialties		
			Medical	Surgical	Other
MSA[1] (number)	5,759	737	2,017	1,369	1,636
MSA[1] (rate per 10,000 pop.)	16.7	2.1	5.8	4.0	4.7
Metro Average[2] (rate per 10,000 pop.)	19.4	2.1	7.5	4.5	5.3

Note: Data as of December 31, 2004; (1) Metropolitan Statistical Area - see Appendix A for areas included; (2) Average of the 79 unique MSAs and CMSAs in this book
Source: American Medical Association, Physician Characteristics & Distribution in the U.S., 2006

Hospitals

Phoenix has the following hospitals: 14 general medical and surgical; 2 psychiatric; 1 heart; 1 surgical; 3 long-term acute care; 1 other specialty; 1 children's general.
AHA Guide to the Healthcare Field 2007

According to *U.S. News,* the Phoenix metro area is home to three of the best hospitals in the U.S.: **Banner Good Samaritan Medical Center**; **Mayo Clinic Arizona**; **Saint Joseph's Hospital and Medical Center**; *U.S. News Online, "America's Best Hospitals 2006"*

EDUCATION

Public School District Statistics

District Name	Schls	Pupils	Pupil/ Teacher Ratio	Minority Pupils[1] (%)	Free Lunch Eligible[2] (%)	IEP[3] (%)
Alhambra Elementary District	15	14,928	19.7	86.9	84.9	18.7
Balsz Elementary District	5	3,436	16.9	91.1	71.8	17.5
Cartwright Elementary District	25	20,009	19.8	91.8	81.3	21.0
Creighton Elementary District	10	8,248	16.6	91.7	88.8	17.8
Deer Valley Unified District	36	33,318	20.1	20.2	6.2	21.2
Fowler Elementary District	6	3,779	18.7	88.3	80.3	19.0
Isaac Elementary District	14	8,805	19.2	97.6	n/a	17.5
Madison Elementary District	9	5,272	16.9	45.1	39.5	19.5
Murphy Elementary District	4	2,566	17.5	97.1	92.8	22.4
Osborn Elementary District	6	3,755	17.3	85.8	88.6	24.8
Paradise Valley Unified District	48	35,202	19.0	26.3	22.4	19.1
Pendergast Elementary District	13	10,457	19.4	70.9	47.3	14.6
Phoenix Elementary District	18	8,212	18.8	94.6	77.2	22.7
Phoenix Union High School District	14	24,776	19.7	89.4	61.6	17.0
Roosevelt Elementary District	22	12,461	19.0	96.4	81.4	21.5
Scottsdale Unified District	33	26,356	18.6	20.8	15.6	16.1
Washington Elementary School District	32	24,280	19.0	54.7	61.2	19.3

Note: Table includes regular local school districts with 2,000 or more students; (1) Percentage of students that are not white, non-Hispanic; (2) Percentage of students that are eligible for the free lunch program; (3) Percentage of students that have an Individualized Education Program.
Source: U.S. Department of Education, National Center for Education Statistics, Common Core of Data, Local Education Agency (School District) Universe Survey: School Year 2004-2005; U.S. Department of Education, National Center for Education Statistics, Common Core of Data, Public Elementary/Secondary School Universe Survey: School Year 2004-2005

Top Public High Schools

High School Name	Index[1]	Rank[1]	Subsidized Lunch (%)[2]	E&E (%)[3]
North Canyon	1.052	1,169	34.0	43.5**

Note: (1) Public schools are ranked according to a ratio that is the number of Advanced Placement and/or International Baccalaureate tests taken by all students at a school in 2005 divided by the number of graduating seniors. All of the schools on the list have an index of at least 1.000; they are in the top five percent of public schools measured this way. The rankings range from 1 to 1,236; (2) Percentage of students receiving federally subsidized meals; (3) E & E stands for equity and excellence percentage: the portion of all graduating seniors at a school that had at least one passing grade on one AP or IB test; (*) Gave just IB tests; (**) Gave both IB and AP tests. AP and IB participation are indicators of a school's efforts to get students to excel and prepare for college.
Source: Newsweek Online, May 23, 2006

Educational Quality

School District	Education Quotient[1]	Graduate Outcome[2]	Community Index[3]	Resource Index[4]	Rating[5]
Deer Valley Unified	68	77	61	3	Blue

Note: Scores are national percentile rankings and range from 1 (worst) to 99 (best); (1) Combination of the Graduate Outcome, Community and Resource Indexes weighted to reflect the greater importance of the Graduate Outcome and Resource Index; (2) Based on graduation rates and college board scores (SAT/ACT); (3) Based on the surrounding community's level of affluence and adult education; (4) Based on teacher salaries, per-pupil expenditures and student-teacher ratios; (5) School districts receive one of five rankings: Gold Medal (top 16 percent of districts evaluated); Blue Ribbon (top third); Green Light (average); Yellow Light (bottom 25 percent); Red Light (bottom 10 percent).
Source: Expansion Management, "2007 Education Quotient," January 2007

Highest Level of Education

Area	Less than H.S.	H.S. Diploma	Some College, No Deg.	Associate Degree	Bachelors Degree	Masters Degree	Profess. School Degree	Doctorate Degree
City	23.6	22.8	24.4	6.6	15.1	4.9	1.9	0.6
MSA[1]	17.9	23.4	26.6	7.1	16.7	5.8	1.8	0.8
U.S.	19.4	28.4	21.2	6.4	15.7	5.9	2.0	1.0

Note: Figures are 2006 estimated percentages and cover persons age 25 and over; (1) Metropolitan Statistical Area - see Appendix B for areas included
Source: Claritas, Inc.

Educational Attainment by Race

Area	High School Graduate (%)					Bachelor's Degree (%)				
	Total	White	Black	Asian	Hisp.[2]	Total	White	Black	Asian	Hisp.[2]
City	76.6	82.5	77.5	80.1	43.1	22.7	26.1	15.2	42.1	6.1
MSA[1]	81.9	86.3	81.6	84.9	49.3	25.1	27.3	19.4	46.6	7.8
U.S.	80.4	83.6	72.3	80.4	52.4	24.4	26.1	14.3	44.1	10.4

Note: Figures shown cover persons 25 years old and over; (1) Metropolitan Statistical Area - see Appendix A for areas included; (2) people of Hispanic origin can be of any race
Source: Census 2000, Summary File 3

School Enrollment by Type

Area	Grades KG to 8				Grades 9 to 12			
	Public		Private		Public		Private	
	Enrollment	%	Enrollment	%	Enrollment	%	Enrollment	%
City	180,398	93.3	12,894	6.7	68,750	92.8	5,365	7.2
MSA[1]	414,735	93.4	29,200	6.6	163,065	93.8	10,740	6.2
U.S.	33,526,011	88.7	4,285,121	11.3	14,848,628	90.6	1,532,323	9.4

Note: Figures shown cover persons 3 years old and over; (1) Metropolitan Statistical Area - see Appendix A for areas included
Source: Census 2000, Summary File 3

School Enrollment by Race

Area	Grades KG to 8 (%)				Grades 9 to 12 (%)			
	White	Black	Asian	Hisp.[1]	White	Black	Asian	Hisp.[1]
City	62.9	5.8	1.6	45.6	64.9	6.2	2.1	40.5
MSA[2]	68.7	4.4	1.7	35.6	70.9	4.6	2.0	31.5
U.S.	68.5	15.5	3.3	16.8	68.8	15.5	3.8	15.7

Note: Figures shown cover persons 3 years old and over; (1) people of Hispanic origin can be of any race; (2) Metropolitan Statistical Area - see Appendix A for areas included
Source: Census 2000, Summary File 3

Average Salaries of Public School Teachers

District	2004-05		2005-06		Percent Change 2004-05 to 2005-06
	Dollars	Rank[1]	Dollars	Rank[1]	
ARIZONA	42,905	27	44,672	25	4.12
U.S. Average	47,674	-	49,109	-	3.01

Note: (1) State rank ranges from 1 to 51.
Source: National Education Association, Rankings & Estimates: Rankings of the States 2005 and Estimates of School Statistics 2006, November 2006

Higher Education

Four-Year Colleges			Two-Year Colleges			Medical Schools[1]	Law Schools[2]	Voc/ Tech[3]
Public	Private Non-profit	Private For-profit	Public	Private Non-profit	Private For-profit			
1	6	10	5	0	6	0	0	5

Note: Figures cover institutions located within the city limits; (1) includes schools accredited by the Liaison Committee on Medical Education and the American Osteopathic Association; (2) includes American Bar Association-accredited law schools; (3) includes all schools with programs that are less than 2 years
Source: National Center for Education Statistics, The Integrated Postsecondary Education System (IPEDS) Peer Analysis System, 2006; www.usnews.com, America's Best Graduate Schools 2008, Medical School Directory; www.usnews.com, America's Best Graduate Schools 2008, Law School Directory

PRESIDENTIAL ELECTION

2004 Presidential Election Results

Area	Bush	Kerry	Nader	Other
Maricopa County	57.0	42.3	0.1	0.6
U.S.	50.7	48.3	0.4	0.6

Note: Results are percentages and may not add to 100% due to rounding
Source: Dave Leip's Atlas of U.S. Presidential Elections, www.uselectionatlas.org

MAJOR EMPLOYERS

Major Employers

Company Name	Industry	Type of Site
American Express	Business services, nec	Branch
American Express	Foreign trade and international banks	Branch
Bashas Distribution Center	General warehousing and storage	Branch
Board of Regents Arizona	Colleges and universities	Headquarters
Chase Bankcard Services Inc	State commercial banks	Single
Chase Manhattan	National commercial banks	Branch
Checkmate	Help supply services	Headquarters
City of Phoenix	Executive offices	Headquarters
General Dynmics C4 Systems Inc	Engineering services	Headquarters
Hamilton Hallmark	Electronic parts and equipment, nec	Headquarters
Intel	Semiconductors and related devices	Branch
MDHC	Aircraft	Single
Maricopa Integrated Health Sys	General medical and surgical hospitals	Branch
Motorola	Radio and t.v. communications equipment	Branch
Motorola Semiconductor Disc	Semiconductors and related devices	Branch
Motorola Semiconductor Logic	Semiconductors and related devices	Branch
Police Dept-Chiefs Office	Police protection	Branch
Scottsdale Healthcare Corp	Specialty outpatient clinics, nec	Branch
Sheriffs Office	Police protection	Branch
St Josephs Hospital & Med Ctr	General medical and surgical hospitals	Branch
Swift Transportation Co Inc	Trucking, except local	Headquarters

Note: Companies shown are located within the metropolitan area and have 2,300 or more employees; nec = not elsewhere classified.
Source: www.zapdata.com, January 2007

PUBLIC SAFETY

Crime Rate

Area	All Crimes	Violent Crimes				Property Crimes		
		Murder	Forcible Rape	Robbery	Aggrav. Assault	Burglary	Larceny -Theft	Motor Vehicle Theft
City	7,094.0	15.0	36.4	289.0	388.8	1,108.6	3,583.0	1,673.3
Suburbs[1]	4,918.9	4.4	31.6	84.9	258.7	967.0	2,809.4	762.9
Metro[2]	5,749.1	8.4	33.4	162.8	308.4	1,021.0	3,104.6	1,110.4
U.S.	3,899.0	5.6	31.7	140.7	291.1	726.7	2,286.3	416.7

Note: Figures are crimes per 100,000 population; (1) All areas within the metro area that are located outside the city limits; (2) Metropolitan Statistical Area - see Appendix B for areas included
Source: FBI Uniform Crime Reports, 2005

Hate Crimes

Area	Number of Quarters Reported	Bias Motivation				
		Race	Religion	Sexual Orientation	Ethnicity	Disability
City	n/a	n/a	n/a	n/a	n/a	n/a

Note: n/a not available.
Source: Federal Bureau of Investigation, Hate Crime Statistics 2005

RECREATION

Culture

Dance[1]	Theatre[1]	Instrumental Music[1]	Vocal Music[1]	Series/ Festivals	Museums	Zoos
1	1	2	4	3	15	1

Note: (1) number of professional perfoming groups
Source: The Grey House Performing Arts Directory, 2007; Official Museum Directory, 2007

Professional Sports Teams

Major League Baseball	National Basketball Association	National Football League	National Hockey League	Major League Soccer	Women's National Basketball Association
1	1	1	1	0	1

Note: Includes teams located in the Phoenix-Scottsdale metro area.
Source: www.sportsvenues.com, Listing of Venues by State/Province and City, 2006

MEDIA

Newspapers

Name	Target Audience	Frequency	Circulation
Ahwatukee Foothills News	General	Non-Daily	27,500
Arizona Informant	Black/General	Non-Daily	15,000
The Arizona Republic	n/a	Daily	496,373
The Catholic Sun	Catholic/Religious	Non-Daily	109,000
Jewish News of Greater Phoenix	General/Jewish	Non-Daily	20,000
La Voz	Hispanic	Non-Daily	40,625
New Times	General	Non-Daily	140,000

Note: Includes newspapers whose offices are located in the city and whose circulations are 10,000 or more; n/a not available
Source: BurrellesLuce, MediaContacts Online, January 2006

Television Stations

Name	Ch.	Network(s)	Type	Ownership
KNAZ	2	NBC	Commercial	Gannett Broadcasting
KTVK	3	n/a	Commercial	Belo Corporation
KMOH	6	NBC	Commercial	Gannett Broadcasting
KAZ	7	n/a	Commercial	n/a
KAET	8	PBS	Public	Arizona Board of Regents
KSAZ	10	Fox	Commercial	Fox Television Stations Inc.
KPNX	12	NBC	Commercial	Gannett Broadcasting
KNXV	15	ABC	Commercial	Scripps Howard Inc.
KPAZ	21	n/a	Non-comm.	Paul F. Crouch
KCVA	30	n/a	Commercial	Kenneth Casey
KTVW	33	Univision	Commercial	Univision Television Group
KPHO	41	CBS	Commercial	Meredith Communications LLC
KUTP	45	UPN	Commercial	United Television Inc.
KPPX	51	n/a	Commercial	Paxson Communications Corporation
KASW	61	WBN	Commercial	Brooks Broadcasting
KDRX	64	Telemundo	Commercial	Hispanic Broadcasters of Arizona Inc.

Note: Stations included cover the Phoenix DMA (Designated Market Area)
BurrellesLuce, MediaContacts Online, January 2006

Major AM Radio Stations

Call Letters	Freq. (kHz)	Station Type	Target Audience	Station Format	Music Format
KFYI	550	Commercial	General	Talk	n/a
KTAR	620	Commercial	General	News/Talk	n/a
KAZM	780	Commercial	General	Music/News	Adult Contemp.
KGME	910	Commercial	General	Sports	n/a
KAFF	930	Commercial	General	Music/News/Talk	Country
KKNT	960	Commercial	General	News/Talk	n/a
KVWM	970	n/a	General	Music	n/a
KFLG	1000	Commercial	General	Music	Country
KDUS	1060	n/a	General	Sports/Talk	n/a
KFNX	1100	Commercial	General	Talk	n/a
KMYL	1190	Commercial	General	News/Talk	n/a
KASC	1260	College	General	Music/News/Sports	Alternative
KDJI	1270	Commercial	General	Music/News/Sports	Oldies
KXEG	1280	Commercial	General/Religious	Educational/Music	Christian
KXAM	1310	Commercial	General	Talk	n/a
KAZG	1440	Commercial	General	Music	Oldies
KPHX	1480	n/a	General/Hispanic	Music/News/Sports	n/a
KZZZ	1490	Commercial	General	News/Talk	n/a
KFNN	1510	n/a	General	Music/News/Talk	n/a
KASA	1540	Commercial	Hispanic/Religious	Music/Talk	Latin
KMIK	1580	Commercial	Children	Ed/Music/News/Sports	Top 40

Note: Stations included cover the Phoenix DMA (Designated Market Area); n/a not available
Source: BurrellesLuce, MediaContacts Online, January 2006

Major FM Radio Stations

Call Letters	Freq. (mHz)	Station Type	Target Audience	Station Format	Music Format
KUYI	88.1	n/a	General/Native Amer	Music/News/Talk	Top 40
KNAU	88.7	College	General	Music/News	n/a
KFLR	90.3	n/a	General/Religious	Music/News/Sports	n/a
KGCB	90.9	n/a	General/Religious	Music/News/Sports/Talk	n/a
KJZZ	91.5	College	General	Music/Talk	Jazz
KZUA	92.1	Commercial	General	Music/News/Sports	Country
KKFR	92.3	n/a	General	Music	n/a
KJJJ	92.7	n/a	General	Music/News/Sports	n/a
KAFF	92.9	n/a	General	Music/News	n/a
KDKB	93.3	Commercial	General	Music/News/Sports/Talk	A.O. Rock
KMGN	93.9	n/a	General	Music/News	n/a
KXKQ	94.1	n/a	General	Music/News	n/a
KOOL	94.5	n/a	General/Women	Music/News/Sports	n/a
KZZZ	94.7	Commercial	General	News/Sports/Talk	n/a
KYOT	95.5	n/a	General	Music/News/Talk	n/a
KRFM	96.5	n/a	General	Music	n/a
KWMX	96.7	n/a	General	n/a	n/a
KMXP	96.9	Commercial	General	Music/News/Talk	Adult Top 40
KRXS	97.3	n/a	General	Music/News	n/a
KVNA	97.5	n/a	General	Music	n/a
KLUK	97.9	Commercial	General	Music	Classic Rock
KUPD	97.9	Commercial	General	Music	A.O. Rock
KKLD	98.3	n/a	General	Music/News/Sports	n/a
KKLT	98.7	Commercial	General	Music	Adult Contemp.
KFMM	99.1	Commercial	General	Educational/Music/News	Country
KAJM	99.3	Commercial	General	Music/News/Talk	Rhythm & Blues
KESZ	99.9	Commercial	General	Music/News/Talk	Adult Contemp.
KSLX	100.7	Commercial	General	Music	Classic Rock
KNRJ	101.1	Commercial	General	Music	Top 40
KRRK	101.1	n/a	General	Music/News/Talk	n/a
KZON	101.5	n/a	General	Music/News/Talk	n/a
KAHM	102.1	Commercial	General	Music	Easy Listening
KNIX	102.5	Commercial	General	Music/News	Country
KQST	102.9	Commercial	General	Music/News/Talk	Top 40
KLNZ	103.5	n/a	General/Hispanic	Music	n/a
KEDJ	103.9	Commercial	Hispanic	Music	Alternative
KZZP	104.7	Commercial	General	Music/Talk	Top 40
KFLX	105.1	n/a	General/Men	News/Sports	A.O. Rock
KHOT	105.9	Commercial	General/Hispanic	Music	Latin
KPPV	106.7	n/a	General	Music/News	n/a
KNKK	107.1	Commercial	General	Music	Adult Contemp.
KSED	107.5	n/a	General	n/a	n/a
KMLE	107.9	Commercial	General	Music	Country

Note: Stations included cover the Phoenix DMA (Designated Market Area); n/a not available
BurrellesLuce, MediaContacts Online, January 2006

CLIMATE

Average and Extreme Temperatures

Temperature	Jan	Feb	Mar	Apr	May	Jun	Jul	Aug	Sep	Oct	Nov	Dec	Yr.
Extreme High (°F)	88	92	100	105	113	122	118	116	118	107	93	88	122
Average High (°F)	66	70	75	84	93	103	105	103	99	88	75	67	86
Average Temp. (°F)	53	57	62	70	78	88	93	91	85	74	62	54	72
Average Low (°F)	40	44	48	55	63	72	80	78	72	60	48	41	59
Extreme Low (°F)	17	22	25	37	40	51	66	61	47	34	27	22	17

Note: Figures cover the years 1948-1990
Source: National Climatic Data Center, International Station Meteorological Climate Summary, 9/96

Average Precipitation/Snowfall/Humidity

Precip./Humidity	Jan	Feb	Mar	Apr	May	Jun	Jul	Aug	Sep	Oct	Nov	Dec	Yr.
Avg. Precip. (in.)	0.7	0.6	0.8	0.3	0.1	0.1	0.8	1.0	0.7	0.6	0.6	0.9	7.3
Avg. Snowfall (in.)	Tr	Tr	0	0	0	0	0	0	0	0	0	Tr	Tr
Avg. Rel. Hum. 5am (%)	68	63	56	45	37	33	47	53	50	53	59	66	53
Avg. Rel. Hum. 5pm (%)	34	28	24	17	14	12	21	24	23	24	28	34	24

Note: Figures cover the years 1948-1990; Tr = Trace amounts (<0.05 in. of rain; <0.5 in. of snow)
Source: National Climatic Data Center, International Station Meteorological Climate Summary, 9/96

Weather Conditions

Temperature			Daytime Sky			Precipitation		
10°F & below	32°F & below	90°F & above	Clear	Partly cloudy	Cloudy	0.01 inch or more precip.	0.1 inch or more snow/ice	Thunder-storms
0	10	167	186	125	54	37	< 1	23

Note: Figures are average number of days per year and cover the years 1948-1990
Source: National Climatic Data Center, International Station Meteorological Climate Summary, 9/96

HAZARDOUS WASTE

Superfund Sites

Phoenix has one hazardous waste site on the EPA's Superfund Final National Priorities List: **Motorola, Inc. (52nd Street Plant)**. *U.S. Environmental Protection Agency, Final National Priorities List, March 20, 2007*

AIR & WATER QUALITY

Air Quality Index

Area	Percent of Days when Air Quality was...[2]				AQI Statistics	
	Good	Moderate	Unhealthy for Sensitive Groups	Unhealthy	Maximum	Median
MSA[1]	21.6	68.5	9.9	0.0	140	67

Note: The Air Quality Index (AQI) is an index for reporting daily air quality. EPA calculates the AQI for five major air pollutants regulated by the Clean Air Act: ground-level ozone, particle pollution (also known as particulate matter), carbon monoxide, sulfur dioxide, and nitrogen dioxide. The AQI runs from 0 to 500. The higher the AQI value, the greater the level of air pollution and the greater the health concern. There are six AQI categories: "Good" The AQI is between 0 and 50. Air quality is considered satisfactory; "Moderate" The AQI is between 51 and 100. Air quality is acceptable; "Unhealthy for Sensitive Groups" When AQI values are between 101 and 150, members of sensitive groups may experience health effects; "Unhealthy" When AQI values are between 151 and 200 everyone may begin to experience health effects; "Very Unhealthy" AQI values between 201 and 300 trigger a health alert; "Hazardous" AQI values over 300 trigger health warnings of emergency conditions; (1) Metropolitan Statistical Area - see Appendix A for areas included; (2) Based on 365 days with AQI data in 2005.
Source: U.S. Environmental Protection Agency, Air Quality Index Report, 2005

Air Quality Index Pollutants

Area	Percent of Days when AQI Pollutant was...[2]					
	Carbon Monoxide	Nitrogen Dioxide	Ozone	Sulfur Dioxide	Particulate Matter 2.5	Particulate Matter 10
MSA[1]	0.8	0.0	36.7	0.0	2.2	60.3

Note: The Air Quality Index (AQI) is an index for reporting daily air quality. EPA calculates the AQI for five major air pollutants regulated by the Clean Air Act: ground-level ozone, particle pollution (also known as particulate matter), carbon monoxide, sulfur dioxide, and nitrogen dioxide. The AQI runs from 0 to 500. The higher the AQI value, the greater the level of air pollution and the greater the health concern; (1) Metropolitan Statistical Area - see Appendix A for areas included; (2) Based on 365 days with AQI data in 2005.
Source: U.S. Environmental Protection Agency, Air Quality Index Report, 2005

Number of Days with Air Quality Index Values Greater than 100

Area	Trend Sites (25)								All Sites (145)
	1998	1999	2000	2001	2002	2003	2004	2005	2005
MSA[1]	14	9	11	7	8	8	1	4	19

Note: An AQI value greater than 100 indicates that air quality would have been in the unhealthful range on that day. Data from exceptional events are not included. These counts are presented in two ways. First, the counts are based on sites having an adequate record of monitoring data during the trend period (trend sites). These counts represent the relative change in the number of days with AQI values greater than 100. In the last column, the counts are based on all sites with data in the most recent year (because it is possible for a site to have data in the most recent year but not enough data to be a trend site); (1) Metropolitan Statistical Area - see Appendix A for areas included; n/a not available.
Source: U.S. Environmental Protection Agency, Air Trends Fact Book 2005

Maximum Pollutant Concentrations

	Particulate Matter 10 (ug/m³)	Particulate Matter 2.5 (ug/m³)	Ozone 1-hour (ppm)	Carbon Monoxide (ppm)	Sulfur Dioxide (ppm)	Nitrogen Dioxide (ppm)	Lead (ug/m³)
MSA[1] Level	200	41	0.115	5	0.007	0.032	n/a
NAAQS[2]	150	65	0.125	9	0.140	0.053	1.50
Met NAAQS[2]	No	Yes	Yes	Yes	Yes	Yes	n/a

Note: Data from exceptional events are not included; (1) Metropolitan Statistical Area - see Appendix A for areas included; (2) National Ambient Air Quality Standards; n/a not available
Units: ppm = parts per million; ug/m³ = micrograms per cubic meter
Source: U.S. Environmental Protection Agency, Air Trends Fact Book 2005

Watershed Health

The U.S. Environmental Protection Agency monitors the health of the aquatic resources for the nation's 2,000+ watersheds. **The Lower Salt watershed serves the Phoenix area and received an overall Index of Watershed Indicators (IWI) score of 2 (better quality - high vulnerability).** The IWI score is based on seven condition and nine vulnerability indicators. The overall IWI score ranges from 1 (best health) to 6 (worst health). The Condition Indicators include: designated use attainment, fish and wildlife consumption advisories, source water condition, contaminated sediments, ambient water quality, and wetlands loss index. The Vulnerability Indicators include: aquatic species at risk, conventional and toxic loads over permitted limits, urban and agricultural runoff potential, population change, hydrologic modification, estuarine pollution susceptibility, and air deposition. *Note: The IWI is no longer being updated by the U.S. EPA. Source: U.S. Environmental Protection Agency, Index of Watershed Indicators, October 26, 2001*

Drinking Water

Water System Name	Pop. Served	Primary Water Source Type	Number of Violations in 2006[a]		
			Health Based	Significant Monitoring	Monitoring
City of Phoenix	1,200,000	Surface	None	None	None

Note: (a) Based on violation data from January 1, 2006 to December 31, 2006
Source: U.S. Environmental Protection Agency, Office of Ground Water and Drinking Water, Safe Drinking Water Information System (data extracted April 12, 2007)

Phoenix tap water is alkaline, approximately 11 grains of hardness per gallon and fluoridated.
Editor & Publisher Market Guide, 2005

Portland, Oregon

Background

Portland is the kind of city that inspires civic pride and the desire to preserve. For who among us could be indifferent to the magnificent views of the Cascade Mountains, the mild climate, and the historical brick structures that blend so well with its more contemporary structures?

Nature is undisputedly "Queen" in Portland. The symbol of the city, she is embodied in Portlandia, a statue of an earth-mother kneeling among her sculpture animal children. The number of activities, such as fishing, skiing, and hunting, as well as the number of outdoor zoological gardens, attest to the mindset of the typical Portlander. And to think that in 1845 Portland held the unromantic name of "Stumptown!"

For the concerned citizen looking for a place that espouses the ideals of the early 1990s television series *Northern Exposure,* Portland may be its real-world, big city counterpart. Portland is a major industrial and commercial center that can still boast clean air and water within its city limits as many of the factories use the electricity generated by mountain rivers; thus, little soot or smoke is belched out. The largest employers in the city are in the health services and Oregon State University.

Portland is a major cultural center, with art museums such as the Portland Art Museum and the Oregon Museum of Science and Industry, and fine educational institutions such as Reed College and the University of Portland. The site where Portland's PGE Park sports stadium now stands was first used for athletic competition in 1893, when the Multnomah Amateur Athletic Club rented a piece of Tanner Creek Gulch pasture there. More recently, in 2001, the PGE was given a $38.5 facelift, and now meets more contemporary tastes and standards, with accommodations that include a field level bar and grill and pavilion suites, all state-of-the-art and seismic code compliant.

The Portland area's regional government is referred to as Metro and includes 24 cities and parts of three counties. Established in the late 1970s, it is the nation's first and only elected regional government. It attempts to control growth by using its authority over land use, transportation, and the environment. This experiment in urban planning is designed to protect farms, forests, and open space. Portland today has a downtown area that caters to pedestrians and includes a heavily used city park where once there was a freeway. Visible from the air is a clear line against sprawl — with cities on one side and open spaces on the other.

Portland is Oregon's biggest city, and has long been considered a shining example of effective sprawl control. Urban planners and visiting city officials see Portland as a "role model for twenty-first century urban development." The city, with its seven-member Metro Council, faces the question of whether further growth will be more sprawling or more dense for Portland and other communities inside the UGB (urban growth boundary), with homebuilders and other advocates on one side of the debate and local officials on the other side.

Finally, Portland's well-organized mass-transit system makes living there all the more enjoyable; this is a city that takes history, progress, and environmental protection seriously.

In 2000, the Portland Art Museum completed its "Program for the Millennium," a multi-stage expansion program that brought total exhibition space to 240,000 square feet. In 2004 work was begun to restore the North Building, a former Masonic Temple acquired in 1991. Completed in 2005, the restoration both preserves the original structure and provides space for the Portland Art Museum's Center for Modern and Contemporary Art.

Portland has a very definite winter rainfall climate, with the most rain falling October through May. The winter season is marked by relatively mild temperatures, cloudy skies, and rain with southeasterly surface winds predominating. Summer produces pleasant, mild temperatures with very little precipitation. Fall and spring are transitional. Fall and early winter bring the most frequent fog. Destructive storms are infrequent, with thunderstorms occurring once a month through the spring and summer.

Rankings

GeneralRankings

■ Portland was ranked #12 out of 331 metro areas in *Cities Ranked & Rated*. Criteria: cost of living; climate; crime; transportation; economy and jobs; education; arts and culture; health and healthcare; leisure. *Cities Ranked & Rated, 1st Edition, 2004*

■ Portland was selected as one of the "Top Cities for Recent Grads" by eGrad.com. The city ranked #1. Criteria: eGrad.com conducted a nationwide survey in which a representative sample of recent graduates commented on the pros and cons of their new towns. Topics ranged from affordability, to housing, to employment, to general satisfaction. *eGrad.com, "Top Cities for Recent Grads 2004"*

■ Portland was selected as one of the top places to live in the U.S. according to Harris Interactive. The city ranked #12 out of 10. Criteria: 3,685 U.S. adults were polled as to where they would choose to live if they could live anywhere in the country. *Harris Interactive, September 6, 2006*

■ Portland was selected as one of the "50 Best Places to Live" by *Men's Journal*. The city ranked #5 in the "Best Downtowns" category. These city centers were selected based on the fact that you can enjoy all the amenities of urban living, find a range of great housing options, and still get your fix of active puruits. *Men's Journal, April 2007*

■ Mercer Human Resources Consulting ranked 215 cities worldwide in terms of overall quality of life. Portland ranked #43. Criteria: political, social, economic, and socio-cultural factors; medical and health considerations; schools and education; public services and transportation; recreation; consumer goods; housing; and natural environment. *Mercer Human Resources Consulting, April 3, 2006*

■ Portland was selected as one of "60 Cheap Places to Live" in the U.S. The city appeared in the "Bohemian Bargains" (lively inner cities) category. *Forbes.com, August 20, 2004*

Business/Finance Rankings

■ Portland was selected as one of the best places to start and grow a company by *Entrepreneur* and the National Policy Research Council. The Portland metro area ranked #36 out of 50 large metro areas. Criteria: business formation and growth (firms started four to 14 years ago that still employ at least 5 people and experienced rapid growth over the last four years). *Entrepreneur/National Policy Research Council, "Hot Cities for Entrepreneurs," September 2006*

■ The Portland metro area was selected as one of "America's 50 Hottest Cities" for business relocations and expansions. Criteria: industry's most prominent site selection consultants were asked to list their top city choices for relocating and expanding manufacturing companies, taking into consideration such factors as the business climate, work force quality, operating costs, incentive programs, and the ease of working with local political and economic development officials. *Expansion Management, January-February 2007*

■ The Portland metro area was selected as one of the "Top 40 Real Estate Markets" for expanding or relocating businesses. The area ranked #40 out of 40. Criteria: rental costs; purchase prices; and vacancy rates of office and warehouse space. *Expansion Management, October 2006*

■ Intel, in partnership with Sperling's BestPlaces, ranked the 80 "Best Cities for Teleworking" in America. The Portland metro area ranked #16 among large metro areas. The study identifies cities that hold the greatest potential for teleworking based on a host of factors including typical commuting times, fuel prices, availability of broadband Internet access and percentage of the population in telework friendly jobs. The study also factored in extreme climate and natural hazards. *Intel, "Best Cities for Teleworking," March 30, 2006*

■ Portland was identified as one of "The Most Inventive Towns in America". The city ranked #13. Criteria: places with the most patents overall, combining those of large companies and individual inventors. *The Wall Street Journal, July 22-23, 2006*

- Portland was selected as one of 20 cities in North America that is doing its part to host green conventions by providing renewable energy, intelligent recycling programs, transportation that minimizes usage of fossil fuels, and plenty of parkland. The city was ranked #1. *Meetings and Conventions, "Natural Choices," August 2006*

- The Portland metro area was selected as one of the "25 Hottest Housing Markets" in the U.S. The area ranked #1 out of 156 markets with a home price appreciation rate of 11.2%. Criteria: year-over-year change of median sales price of existing single-family homes between the 4th quarter of 2005 and the 4th quarter of 2006. *National Association of Realtors, Median Sales Price of Existing Single-Family Homes for Metropolitan Areas, 4th Quarter 2006*

- The Portland metro area appeared on the Milken Institute "2005 Best Performing Cities" index. Rank: #95 out of 200 large metro areas. Criteria: job growth; wage and salary growth; high-tech output growth. *Milken Institute, "2005 Best Performing Cities," February 2006*

- The Portland metro area was selected as one of "The Best Cities for Doing Business in America." *Inc.* magazine measured employment growth in 393 regions using the following criteria: recent growth trend; mid-term growth; long-term trend; and current year growth. The Portland metro area ranked #24 among large metro areas and #169 overall. *Inc., May 2006*

- Portland was identified as one of the top 10 metro areas with the greatest number of *Inc. 500* companies per million residents. The area ranked #4. *Inc., September 2006*

- Portland was identified as one of the 100 "Most Unwired Cities" in the U.S. The area ranked #4 out of the 100 largest metro areas in the U.S. Criteria: number of public and commercial wireless access points (hotspots); airports with wireless Internet access; broadband availability; local wireless networks; and wireless email devices. *Intel, "Most Unwired Cities Survey," June 7, 2005*

- Portland was ranked #18 out of 125 regions worldwide in terms of its "Knowledge Competitiveness Index." The index attempts to measure the knowledge-based development taking place throughout the world and is based on 19 measures of economic performance that indicate a region's ability to translate its knowledge capacity into economic value. *Robert Huggins Associates, World Knowledge Competitiveness Index 2005*

- *Forbes* ranked the 200 most populous metro areas in the U.S. in terms of the "Best Places for Business and Careers." The Portland metro area was ranked #45. Criteria: business costs (labor, energy, tax and office space expenses); living costs (housing, transportation, food and other household expenditures); education levels of the work force; job growth; income growth; migration trends; crime rates; and culture/leisure. *Forbes, April 23, 2007*

- *Kiplinger's Personal Finance* ranked 101 U.S. cities in terms of their total tax burdens. Portland ranked #87 (#1 had the lowest overall tax burden). Criteria: state income tax; property tax; sales tax; personal property tax; and gasoline tax. *Kiplinger's Personal Finance, July 2004*

- *Fortune* ranked the 100 largest metro areas in the U.S. in terms of projected median home price change in 2006. The Portland metro area ranked #59. *Fortune, "The Top 100: Is the Party Over?" December 26, 2005*

- Portland was identified as one of the "Most Overpriced Places in the U.S." The area ranked #3 out of the nations 150 largest metro areas. Criteria: job growth; income growth; cost of living; and housing affordability. *Forbes.com, "Most Overpriced Places in the U.S. 2005"*

Health/Environment Rankings

- *Reader's Digest* ranked the 50 largest metro areas in the U.S. in terms of how "clean" they are. The Portland metro area ranked #1. Criteria: air quality; water quality; toxic industrial pollution; Superfund sites; and sanitation. *Reader's Digest, "The 50 Cleanest (and Dirtiest) Cities in America," July 2005*

- *Business Week* identified the 15 metro areas that saw the steepest declines in ground-level ozone pollution between 1990 and 2005. The Portland metro area ranked #10. *Business Week, "America's Most Cleaned-Up Metro Areas," March 23, 2007*

- Sanofi-aventis, in partnership with Sperling's BestPlaces, ranked the 50 worst cities for respiratory infections in the U.S. Portland ranked #47. Criteria: prevalence of sinusitis, pharyngitis (sore throat), bronchitis, acute upper respiratory infections, pneumonia, otitis media (middle ear infection), other respiratory tract infections and the common cold; total per capita prescriptions written for oral antibiotics for respiratory tract infections; and prevalence of state level antibiotic resistance. *Sanofi-aventis, "America's Worst Cities for Respiratory Infections," December 6, 2005*

- The Portland metro area appeared in *Country Home's* "2007 Best Green Places Report". The area ranked #40. Criteria included: air and watershed quality; miles of mass transit; green power; number of farmer's markets, organic producers and groceries. *Country Home, "2007 Best Green Places Report," April 2007*

- Wyeth Consumer Healthcare, in partnership with Sperling's BestPlaces, ranked the nation's 50 most populous metro areas in terms of five key health factors. The Portland metro area ranked #16. Criteria: physical activity, health status, nutrition, lifestyle pursuits; and mental wellness. *Wyeth Consumer Healthcare, "Centrum Healthiest Cities Study," April 19, 2005*

- The American Podiatric Medical Association and *Prevention* magazine ranked America's 100 most populated cities based on fitness-walker friendliness. The best cities have safe streets, beautiful places to walk, mild weather and good air quality. Portland ranked #19. *Prevention, "The Best Walking Cities of 2007," April 2007; American Podiatric Medical Association, "2007 Best Fitness-Walking Cities"*

- Portland was selected as one of "The Top 10 Greenest Cities" in the U.S." Criteria: cities that are obsessed with clean air and clean water, renewable energy, reliable city buses, trams, streetcars and subways, a growing number of parks, greenbelts, farmer's markets, and opportunities for community involvement. *Homestore.com, "The Top 10 Greenest Cities," April 2006*

- Portland was selected as one of "greenest" cities in the U.S. Criteria: good water- and air-quality; efficient use of resources; renewable energy leadership; accessible and reliable public transportation; green building practices; number of parks and greenbelts; access to locally-grown fresh food through farmers' markets and community supported agriculture groups; and affordability. *The Green Guide Institute, "The Top 10 Green Cities in the U.S.: 2005," April 19, 2005*

- Portland was selected as one of the 25 fittest cities in America by *Men's Fitness Online*. It ranked #17 out of America's 50 largest cities. Criteria: gyms/sporting goods; nutrition; exercise/sports; overweight/sedentary; junk food; alcohol; smoking; television; air and water quality; climate; geography; commute time; parks/open space; recreation facilities; health care; motivation; civic legislation and leadership. *Men's Fitness Online, America's Fittest/Fattest Cities 2006*

- Portland was identified as a "2007 Asthma Capital." The area ranked #75 out of the nation's 100 largest metropolitan areas. Twelve factors were used to identify the most challenging places to live for people with asthma: estimated prevalence; self-reported prevalence; crude death rate for asthma; annual pollen score; annual air quality; public smoking laws; number of board-certified asthma specialists; school inhaler access laws; rescue medication use; controller medication use; uninsured rate; poverty rate. *Asthma and Allergy Foundation of America, "2007 Asthma Capitals"*

- Portland was identified as a "Spring Allergy Capital." The area ranked #84 out of 100. Three groups of factors were used to identify the most severe cities for people with allergies during the spring season: annual pollen levels; medicine utilization; access to board-certified allergists. *Asthma and Allergy Foundation of America, "2007 Spring Allergy Capital Rankings"*

- Portland was identified as a "Fall Allergy Capital." The area ranked #98 out of 100. Three groups of factors were used to identify the most severe cities for people with allergies during the fall season: annual pollen levels; medicine utilization; access to board-certified allergists. *Asthma and Allergy Foundation of America, "2006 Fall Allergy Capital Rankings"*

- Portland was selected as one of "America's Healthiest Cities" by *Natural Health* magazine. The city was ranked #6 out of the 50 largest urban areas in the U.S. Twenty-six criteria in the following four categories were examined: whether the city boasts natural offerings; how well the city promotes its residents' physical health; whether the city offers a healthy environment; how well the city fosters a sense of community. *Natural Health, April 2003*

- *Men's Health* ranked the nation's largest 100 cities in terms of the *Best (and Worst) Cities for Men*. Portland was ranked #35. Criteria: 24 statistical parameters of long life in the categories of health, quality of life, and fitness. *Men's Health, January/February 2007*

- *Men's Health* ranked 100 U.S. cities in terms of the quality of their tap water. Portland was ranked #72 and received a grade of C. Criteria: levels of total coliform bacteria, arsenic, lead, total trihalomethanes (linked to cancer), and halo-acetic acids, plus the number of EPA water-system violations from 1995 to 2005. *Men's Health, March 2007*

- GlaxoSmithKline, in partnership with Sperling's BestPlaces, analyzed the nation's 100 largest metro areas and identified 25 asthma "hot spots" where high prevalence makes the condition a key issue and environmental triggers and other factors can make living with asthma a particular challenge. The Portland metro area ranked #19 with #1 being the most challenging place to live. Criteria: asthma prevalence; asthma mortality; pollen scores; number of asthma specialists per capita; ratio of prescriptions for rescue medications to prescriptions for controller medications (an indicator of proper asthma treatment); air pollution; smoking laws; climate; and prevalence of tobacco use. *GlaxoSmithKline, "Asthma Hot Spots," October 29, 2002*

- Ortho-McNeil Neurologics, in partnership with Sperling's BestPlaces, analyzed 110 metro areas and identified those U.S. cities with the highest prevalence of factors that are most commonly associated with migraine headaches. The Portland metro area ranked #70. Criteria: number of migraine-related drug prescriptions per capita; lifestyle factors that can contribute to migraines; environmental factors that can trigger migraines; and consumption of migraine-triggering foods. *Ortho-McNeil Neurologics, "America's Migraine Hot Spots," March 14, 2006*

- Sperling's BestPlaces ranked 331 metro areas and identified the most and least stressful U.S. cities. The Portland metro area ranked #6 out of the 100 largest metro areas (#1 = most stressful). Criteria: divorce rate; unemployment rate; violent and property crime; suicide rate; commute time; mental health; alcohol consumption; cloudy days. *www.BestPlaces.net, January 9, 2004*

- Sperling's BestPlaces in partnership with Vistakon ranked the 100 largest metro areas and identified "America's 10 Best Cities for Comfortable Eyes." The Portland metro area ranked #5. Criteria: altitude; sunny days; wind; extreme temperatures; humidity; pollution; commute time; computer use. *Vistakon, "America's Best and Worst Cities for Comfortable Eyes," June 15, 2004*

- HealthGrades evaluated the performance of America's 25 most populous metropolitan areas by measuring the outcomes of five of the highest volume and most widely studied procedures and diagnoses: coronary artery bypass graft surgery; percutaneus coronary interventions; acute myocardial infarction/heart attack in angioplasty-capable hospitals; congestive heart failure; and community acquired pneumonia. The Portland metro area ranked #25. *HealthGrades, "HealthGrades Hospital Quality in America Study," October 12, 2004*

- Portland was selected as one of "America's Top 10 Low-Carb Cities" by *LowCarbiz Magazine*. Criteria: abundance of low-carb products; restaurants with low-carb menu items; health practitioners supportive of carb-cutting regimens; local culture generally conducive to exercise and health. *LowCarbiz Magazine, April 2004*

- Portland was selected as one of "America's Pet Healthiest Cities" by Purina. The city ranked #3 out of 50. Criteria: veterinary services; environment; legislation; preventative care; obesity/body condition. *Purina Pet Institute, "America's Pet Healthiest Cities," May 20, 2003*

- According to research conducted by Malibu Wellness of 100 major U.S. cities' local water quality reports, Portland is one of the two "Best Cities for Hair Color" in terms of hair color application and longevity. Criteria: quantity of minerals found in the water supply (lower ppm is better for hair color); type of oxidizers such as chlorine; and pH levels. *Malibu Wellness, Wellness e-Letter, "Best & Worst Cities for Hair Color," February 2005*

Women/Minorities Rankings

- Portland was ranked #32 out of 100 metro areas in *SELF Magazine's* ranking of "America's Best Places for Women." A panel of experts came up with nearly 40 criteria including: drinking and smoking rates; depression; unemployment; parks; crime; disease; healthcare insurance coverage; air quality; and commute times. *SELF Magazine, "America's Best Places for Women 2006," December 2006*

- *Ladies Home Journal* ranked America's 200 largest cities based on the qualities women surveyed care about most. Portland ranked #21 out of 57 in the big city category (population over 300,000). Criteria: crime; lifestyle; education; jobs; health; child care; politics; and the economy. *Ladies Home Journal Online, "The Best Cities for Women 2002"*

- Portland was profiled in the book *50 Fabulous Gay-Friendly Places to Live*. Criteria: an active gay community; positive gay health programs; youth outreach; gay-friendly politics; gay-owned and gay-friendly businesses; employment opportunities; fun nightlife; cultural opportunities; recreational opportunities; housing options. *50 Fabulous Gay-Friendly Places to Live, 2005*

- Portland was selected as one of "America's Top Lesbian Cities" by Gay.com. The city ranked #4 out of 5. *Gay.com*

- Portland was identified as one of the top 25 metropolitan statistical areas ranked by percentage of coupled households that are gay or lesbian." The area ranked #20. *Human Rights Campaign, "Gay and Lesbian Families in the United States: Same-Sex Unmarried Partner Households," August 1, 2001*

Seniors/Retirement Rankings

- Portland was profiled in the book *Where to Retire: America's Best and Most Affordable Places*. Cities were selected based on personal visits by the author and interviews with local residents coupled with statistics from various government agencies. *Where to Retire: America's Best and Most Affordable Places, 2006*

- Portland was profiled in the book *Retire in Style: 60 Outstanding Places Across the USA and Canada*. Criteria: landscape; climate; quality of life; cost of living; transportation; retail services; health care; community services; cultural and educational activities; recreational activities; work and volunteer activities; crime rates and public safety. *Retire in Style: 60 Outstanding Places Across the USA and Canada, 2005*

- Sperling's BestPlaces in partnership with Bankers Life & Casualty Company designed a survey to identify the top 50 metro areas in the U.S. that offer the best overall qualities for senior living. The Portland metro area ranked #1. The following criteria were statistically weighted to reflect the needs of the senior population: health; disease; economics; social; environment; spiritual; transportation; housing; and crime. *Bankers Life & Casualty Company, "Best Cities for Seniors 2005"*

- A.G. Edwards ranked America's 500 top-performing communities based on their residents' personal savings and investing behavior. The Portland metro area ranked #153 with an index score of 104.86 (national average = 100.00). A dozen statistical factors were measured including: participation in retirement savings plans; personal debt levels; and home ownership. *A.G. Edwards, "2006 Nest Egg Index", September 6, 2006*

Children/FamilyRankings

■ *Zero Population Growth* ranked 100 cities in terms of children's health, safety, and economic well-being. Portland was ranked #16 out of 80 Large Cities (remainder of the 100 largest cities in the U.S.) and was given a grade of A-. Criteria: total population and population growth; percent of population under 18 years of age; percent of births to teens; infant mortality rate; percent of eligible women not receiving Title X services; contraceptive equity indicator; percent of children without health insurance; percent of city residents over age 25 with a high-school diploma; ration of PopEd (Population Connection's Education Program) teachers trained; sexuality education indicator; proficiency in reading and math; percent of kids living in poverty; percent growth in urbanized land; violent crime rate; recycling. *Population Connection, Kid Friendly Cities: Report Card 2004*

■ *Fit Pregnancy* magazine ranked the 50 best U.S. cities in which to have a baby. Portland was ranked #1. Criteria: fertility services; maternal and infant health risk; access to hospitals and doctors; safety; affordability; stroller friendliness; and birthing options. *Fit Pregnancy, February/March, 2006*

Safety Rankings

■ Allstate ranked the 200 largest cities in America in terms of driver safety. Portland ranked #89. In addition, drivers were 6.6% more likely to have had an accident compared to the national average. Allstate researchers analyzed internal Property Damage reported claims over a two-year period (from January 2003 to December 2004) to ensure the findings would not be affected by external influences such as weather or road construction. A weighted average of the two-year numbers determined the annual percentages. The report defines an auto crash as any collision resulting in a property damage claim. *Allstate, "Allstate America's Best Drivers Report 2006," May 24, 2006*

■ Portland was identified as one of the most dangerous large metro areas for pedestrians in the U.S. The area ranked #39 out of the nations 50 largest metro areas. Criteria: average yearly pedestrian fatalities per capita (for the years 2002 and 2003) adjusted for the number of walkers. *Surface Transportation Policy Project, "Mean Streets 2004"*

■ *Ladies Home Journal* ranked America's 200 largest cities in terms of safety. Portland ranked #161 out of 200. Criteria: violent crimes; crimes against property; and rape. *Ladies Home Journal Online, "The Best Cities for Women 2002"*

Sports/Recreation Rankings

■ The Portland metro area appeared on *The Sporting News* list of the "Best Sports Cities 2006". The area ranked #58 out of 99 cities in North America. To be included in the rankings, a city must have at least one of the following: NCAA Division I basketball team; Class A minor league baseball team; training camp for a major league or NFL team; NASCAR Nextel Cup race; NCAA Division I-A bowl game; PGA Tour tournament; Triple Crown horse race. Once a city qualifies, a 12-month snapshot is taken of the sports atmosphere, putting a heavy premium on regular-season won-lost records; playoff berths, bowl appearances and tournament bids; championships; applicable power ratings; quality of competition; overall fan fervor; sports atmosphere and fan knowledge; abundance of teams (quality over quantity); stadium/arena quality; ticket availability and prices; franchise ownership; and the marquee appeal of athletes. *SportingNews.com, "Best Sports Cities 2006," August 1, 2006*

■ Portland was selected as a "dream city" runner-up by readers of *Backpacker* magazine. *Backpacker, "2nd Annual Readers' Choice Awards," February 2006*

■ Portland was chosen as one of America's 25 best cities for running. The city was ranked #10. Criteria: number of running clubs per city; amount of land set aside for park usage; air quality; weather; crime rates; and results from a *Runner's World* poll in which readers ranked their favorite running cities. *Runner's World, "The 25 Best Running Cities in America," July 2005*

■ Portland was chosen as one of "The 10 Best Cities for Mountain Bikers." The city was ranked #6. The criteria for making the list was two-fold: 1) great trails within or very close to the city; 2) the city had to be a place where people could actually live—with good jobs, decent schools, affordable housing, arts and sports, and a sense of community. *Mountain Bike, June 2001*

- Portland was selected as one of "10 Great Biking Cities." Editors at the Washington Post asked Adventure Cycling Association, a non-profit bike organization in Montana, and *Bicycling* magazine for their suggestions on the most bike-friendly cities in the country. *Washington Post, October 1, 2006*

- Portland was chosen as one of America's best cities for bicycling. The city ranked #0 in the large city category (population 500,000 to 1 million) and was selected as the best U.S. cycling city overall. Criteria: cycling-friendly statistics (number of bike lanes and routes, number of bike racks, city bike projects completed and planned; bike culture (number of bike commuters, popular clubs, cool cycling events, renowned bike shops); climate/geography (the quality of roads and trails for riding, and how frequently mother nature lets riders enjoy them). *Bicycling, March 2006*

- The Portland metro area was selected by *Cranium* as one of the "Top 50 Fun Cities" in America. The area ranked #11. Criteria includes: number of sports teams, restaurants, and dance performances; number of toy stores; city budget spent on recreation. *Cranium, November 4, 2003*

- *Golf Digest* ranked 330 metro areas in the U.S. in terms of golf. The Portland metro area was ranked #302. Criteria: access to golf; weather; value of golf; and quality of golf. *Golf Digest, "Metro Golf Rankings," August 2005*

Dating/Romance Rankings

- The Portland metro area was selected as one of the "Best Cities for Relocating Singles" by Worldwide ERC and Primacy Relocation. The area ranked #8 out of the 100 largest metro areas in the U.S. Areas were selected based on the following criteria: Population Criteria (local percentage and growth trends of unmarried residents aged 25-34; male-female ratios; the number of newcomers to the area; diversity and density); Economic Criteria (job growth vs. unemployment rates; apartment rental costs; fee and occupancy rates for temporary housing and mini-storage; higher education costs, including in-state and out-of-state tuition requirements; vehicle tax rates and quality of service from utility providers); Quality-of-Life Criteria (level of per capita volunteering; quality and quantity of collegiate and professional sports with fun, fan-friendly venues; number of Starbucks and other coffee shops; quality or popularity of restaurants, nightspots, health clubs, and online dating; moderate climates with sustainable water supplies). *Worldwide ERC and Primacy Relocation, "2006 Best Cities for Relocating Singles," October 11, 2006*

- *Forbes* ranked the 40 most populous metro areas in the U.S. in terms of the "Best Cities for Singles." The Portland metro area was ranked #27. Criteria: number of singles; cost of living alone; nightlife; culture; job growth; coolness; and online dating. *Forbes.com, July 25, 2006*

- Sperling's BestPlaces in partnership with AXE Deodorant Bodyspray ranked 80 metro areas and identified "America's Best (and Worst) Cities for Dating." The Portland metro area ranked #15. Criteria: percentage of singles ages 18-24; population density; dating venues per capita. *AXE Deodorant Bodyspray, "America's Best (and Worst) Cities for Dating," May, 2004*

Culture/Performing Arts Rankings

- Portland was selected as one of "The Top 10 American Cities to be a Moviemaker.". The city was ranked #3. *MovieMaker Magazine, Winter 2006, Issue No. 61*

- Portland was selected as one of "America's Top 25 Arts Destinations." The city ranked #10 in the big city (population 500,000 and over) category. Criteria: readers' top choices for arts travel destinations based on the richness and variety of visual arts sites, activities and events. *American Style, June 2006*

- Scarborough Research, a leading market research firm, identified the top local markets for rock concert attendance. The Portland DMA (Designated Market Area) ranked in the top 25 with 16% of consumers, 18 years old and over, reporting that they have attended a rock concert during the past year. *Scarborough Research, Scarborough USA+ 2003 Release 2*

Miscellaneous Rankings

■ Portland was selected as the best all-around city for dogs in *Dog Fancy's* DogTown USA contest. Criteria: access to top veterinary professionals, dog parks, and canine-friendly businesses; shelter-euthanasia rates; and owner responsibility. *Dog Fancy, "DogTown USA," 2006*

■ Portland was determined to be one of America's smartest cities. The city ranked #9 in the large city category (200,000+ adults 25 years and older). Criteria: the editors rated the collective brainpower of U.S communities based on the educational attainment of its residents. *American City Business Journals, www.bizjournals.com, June 12, 2006*

■ Portland was selected as one of the "Top 100 Sweatiest Summer Cities". The city was ranked #95. The ranking was based on the average male/female height/weight, average high temperature, and average relative humidity levels for 2002 in each of the cities during June, July and August. The sweat level was analyzed based on the assumption that the individual was walking for one hour. *Procter & Gamble, Old Spice, June 18, 2003*

■ Portland was selected as one of the "Top 10 Most Independent Cities for Homesellers" in 2005. The city was ranked #8. The cities listed had more consumers choosing to sell their homes free of interference from a real-estate broker than anywhere else. Data was based on geographical information for listings posted on ForSaleByOwner.com from July 2004 - July 2005. *ForSaleByOwner.com, August 3, 2005*

■ The Portland metro area appeared on *Forbes* list of "America's Drunkest Cities". The area ranked #19. Criteria: 35 of the largest continental U.S. metro areas were chosen based on availability of data and geographic diversity. Each metro was ranked in five areas: state laws; drinkers; heavy drinkers; binge drinkers; and alcoholism. *Forbes.com, "America's Drunkest Cities," August 22, 2006*

■ Portland appeared on ApartmentRatings.com "Top Cities for Renters List 2006". The area ranked #70 out of 138. Criteria: renter satisfaction; affordability; and vacancy. *ApartmentRatings.com, "Top Cities for Renters List 2006"*

■ Portland was selected as one of "America's Best Vegetarian-Friendly Large Cities." The city was ranked #1. *www.peta.org, April 2006*

■ Portland was selected as one of "America's Favorite Cities" in the "top cities for cleanliness" category. The city was ranked #3 out of 25. Criteria: *Travel + Leisure* magazine and AOL's Travel Channel conducted an online survey of nearly half a million AOL members to find out what travelers think about twenty-five American cities. Results shown above are according to visitors to the city, not locals. *Travel + Leisure and AOL's Travel Channel, "America's Favorite Cities," March 22, 2004*

■ Sperling's BestPlaces in partnership with Pep Boys ranked 77 metro areas and identified "America's Most Drivable Cities." The Portland metro area ranked #58. Criteria: climate; road roughness; urban mobility; gas prices. *Pep Boys, "America's Most Drivable Cities," April 9, 2003*

■ Portland was ranked #18 out of 268 metro areas in terms of its Creativity Index. The Creativity Index is a mix of four equally weighted factors: the Creative Class (scientists, engineers, architects, designers, writers, artists, musicians, or any profession where creativity is a key factor) share of the workforce; innovation, measured as patents per capita; high-tech industry, using the Milken Institute's Tech Pole Index; and diversity, measured by the Gay Index (a reasonable proxy for an areas' openness to different kinds of people and ideas). *The Rise of the Creative Class, 2002*

■ Portland was selected as one of "America's Most Literate Cities." The city ranked #10 out of the 70 largest U.S. cities. Criteria: number of booksellers; library resources; Internet resources; educational attainment; periodical publishing resources; newspaper circulation. *Central Connecticut State University, "America's Most Literate Cities 2006"*

- State Farm Insurance, in partnership with Sperling's BestPlaces, analyzed several key factors that contribute to overall family preparedness. The Portland metro area ranked #2 out of the nation's 50 most populous metro areas. Criteria: quality of life; life insurance coverage; and investments. *State Farm Life Insurance, "Fiscally Fit Cities Report," July 20, 2004*

- Scarborough Research, a leading market research firm, identified the top local markets for coffee bar patronage. The Portland DMA (Designated Market Area) ranked in the top 10 with 21% of adults reporting that they have used any coffee house/bar during the past 30 days. *Scarborough Research, Scarborough USA+ 2004 Release 1*

- Portland was selected as having one of the highest number of Starbucks stores per capita in the U.S. The city appeared in the large city category. Criteria: U.S. cities with populations of 10,000 or more were analyzed with regards to the number of Starbucks stores per capita. Supermarkets and other stores selling coffee beans were not included. *ePodunk.com, "Coffee Quotients," March 2005*

- A study by Sperling's BestPlaces examined which U.S. metro areas were most affected by the fuel crunch in 2005. The Portland metro area was selected as being one of the least impacted areas. The area ranked #9 out of 10. Criteria: average miles driven per day per peak traveler; average gallons of gas used per peak traveler; money spent on gas per driver. *Sperling's BestPlaces, www.bestplaces.net, September 29, 2005*

Business Environment

CITY FINANCES

City Government Finances

Component	2003-2004 ($000)	2003-2004 ($ per capita)
Total Revenues	881,299	1,634
Total Expenditures	1,058,637	1,962
Debt Outstanding	2,249,611	4,170
Cash and Securities	574,994	1,066

Source: U.S Census Bureau, Government Finances 2003-2004

City Government Revenue by Source

Source	2003-2004 ($000)	2003-2004 ($ per capita)
General Revenue		
From Federal Government	43,164	80
From State Government	42,607	79
From Local Governments	56,011	104
Taxes		
Property	228,524	424
Sales	54,807	102
Personal Income	0	0
License	0	0
Charges	236,768	439
Liquor Store	0	0
Utility	80,478	149
Employee Retirement	726	1
Other	138,214	256

Source: U.S Census Bureau, Government Finances 2003-2004

City Government Expenditures by Function

Function	2003-2004 ($000)	2003-2004 ($ per capita)	2003-2004 (%)
General Expenditures			
Airports	0	0	0.0
Corrections	0	0	0.0
Education	0	0	0.0
Fire Protection	73,143	136	6.9
Governmental Administration	64,783	120	6.1
Health	0	0	0.0
Highways	109,126	202	10.3
Hospitals	0	0	0.0
Housing and Community Development	46,590	86	4.4
Interest on General Debt	84,083	156	7.9
Libraries	0	0	0.0
Parking	5,020	9	0.5
Parks and Recreation	76,200	141	7.2
Police Protection	126,522	235	12.0
Public Welfare	0	0	0.0
Sewerage	245,268	455	23.2
Solid Waste Management	2,528	5	0.2
Liquor Store	0	0	0.0
Utility	93,683	174	8.8
Employee Retirement	75,384	140	7.1
Other	56,307	104	5.3

Source: U.S Census Bureau, Government Finances 2003-2004

Municipal Bond Ratings

Area	Moody's
City	Aaa (1/2006)

Source: Mergent Bond Record, January 2007 (unless noted otherwise)

DEMOGRAPHICS

Population Growth

Area	1990 Census	2000 Census	2006 Estimate	2011 Projection	Population Growth (%)	
					1990-2000	2000-2011
City	485,833	529,121	541,219	557,910	8.9	5.4
MSA[1]	1,523,741	1,927,881	2,104,306	2,251,340	26.5	16.8
U.S.	248,709,873	281,421,906	298,021,266	312,383,955	13.2	11.0

Note: (1) Metropolitan Statistical Area - see Appendix B for areas included
Source: Claritas, Inc.

Number of Households and Average Household Size

Area	2006 Estimate	2006 Average Household Size
City	228,778	2.37
MSA[1]	812,600	2.59
U.S.	112,267,302	2.65

Note: (1) Metropolitan Statistical Area - see Appendix B for areas included
Source: Claritas, Inc.

Race and Ethnicity

Area	White Alone[2]	Black Alone[2]	Asian Alone[2]	Other Race Alone[2]	Hispanic[3]
City	76.1	6.4	6.8	10.6	8.8
MSA[1]	82.4	2.7	5.2	9.7	9.4
U.S.	73.3	12.4	4.2	10.1	14.5

Note: Figures are 2006 estimates; (1) Metropolitan Statistical Area - see Appendix B for areas included
(2) Alone is defined as not being in combination with one or more other races; (3) May be of any race.
Source: Claritas, Inc.

Segregation

City		MSA[1]	
Index[2]	Rank[3]	Index[2]	Rank[4]
57.0	59	55.8	189

Note: Figures are based on an analysis of Census 2000 data; (1) Metropolitan Statistical Area - see Appendix A for areas included; (2) White/Black Dissimilarity Index—the most commonly used measure of segregation between two groups, reflecting their relative distributions across neighborhoods within a city or metropolitan area. It can range in value from 0, indicating complete integration, to 100, indicating complete segregation; (3) Ranges from 1 (most segregated) to 100 (least segregated) and includes all the cities in this book; (4) Ranges from 1 (most segregated) to 318 (least segregated) and includes 318 metropolitan areas.
Source: www.CensusScope.org

Ancestry

Area	German	Irish[2]	English	American	Italian	Polish	French[3]	Scottish
City	18.8	12.2	11.7	3.8	3.7	1.9	3.5	3.2
MSA[1]	20.8	11.8	12.7	5.5	3.5	1.8	3.7	3.1
U.S.	15.2	10.9	8.7	7.3	5.6	3.2	3.0	1.7

Note: Figures include multiple ancestry (e.g. if a person reported being Irish and Italian, they were included in both columns); (1) Metropolitan Statistical Area - see Appendix A for areas included; (2) Includes Celtic; (3) Includes Alsatian but excludes Basque
Source: Census 2000, Summary File 3

Foreign-Born Population

Area	Percent of Population Born in							
	Any Foreign Country	Europe	Asia	Africa	Oceania[2]	Canada	Mexico	Latin America[3]
City	13.0	3.3	5.0	0.5	0.3	0.6	2.5	0.9
MSA[1]	10.9	2.5	3.6	0.2	0.2	0.6	3.1	0.6
U.S.	11.1	1.7	2.9	0.3	0.1	0.3	3.3	2.5

Note: (1) Metropolitan Statistical Area - see Appendix A for areas included; (2) Includes Australia, New Zealand subregion, Melanesia, Micronesia, Polynesia, and Oceania n.e.c; (3) Includes Central America (excluding Mexico), South America, and the Caribbean.
Source: Census 2000, Summary File 3

Marriage Status

Area	Never Married	Now Married (excluding Separated)	Separated	Widowed	Divorced
City	34.6	44.1	2.0	5.9	13.3
MSA[1]	26.8	54.6	1.7	5.3	11.6
U.S.	27.1	54.4	2.2	6.6	9.7

Note: Figures are percentages and cover the population 15 years of age and older;
(1) Metropolitan Statistical Area - see Appendix A for areas included
Source: Census 2000, Summary File 3

Age Distribution

Area	Percent of Population						
	Under Age 5	Age 5 to 17	Age 18 to 34	Age 35 to 49	Age 50 to 64	Age 65 to 79	80 Years and Over
City	6.0	15.0	28.5	24.9	14.0	8.0	3.6
MSA[1]	7.0	18.4	24.8	24.7	14.7	7.4	3.0
U.S.	6.8	18.9	23.7	23.5	14.8	9.2	3.2

Note: (1) Metropolitan Statistical Area - see Appendix A for areas included
Source: Census 2000, Summary File 3

Male/Female Ratio

Area	Males	Females	Males per 100 Females
City	268,271	272,948	98.3
MSA[1]	1,047,771	1,056,535	99.2
U.S.	146,712,712	151,308,554	97.0

Note: Figures are 2006 estimates; (1) Metropolitan Statistical Area -
see Appendix B for areas included
Source: Claritas, Inc.

Religion

Area	Catholic	Southern Baptist	United Methodist	ELCA[1]	LDS[2]	Presbyterian Church USA	Jewish Est.	Muslim Est.
County	22.7	0.7	0.9	1.2	1.6	1.6	2.9	0.6
U.S.	22.0	7.1	3.7	1.8	1.5	1.1	2.2	0.6

Note: Figures are the number of adherents as a percentage of the total population; Adherents are defined as all members, including full members, their children and the estimated number of other participants who are not considered members (e.g. the baptized, those not confirmed, those regularly attending services, etc.);
(1) Evangelical Lutheran Church in America; (2) The Church of Jesus Christ of Latter Day Saints
Source: Reprinted with permission from Religious Congregations and Membership in the United States 2000 (Nashville, Glenmary Research Center, 2002) Copyright Association of Statisticians of American Religious Bodies. All rights reserved.

ECONOMY

Gross Metropolitan Product

Area	2002	2003	2004	2005	2005 Rank[2]
MSA[1]	70.3	72.1	80.0	85.7	26

Note: Figures are in billions of dollars; (1) Portland-Vancouver-Beaverton, OR-WA Metropolitan Statistical Area - see Appendix A for areas included; (2) Rank ranges from 1 to 361
Source: The U.S. Conference of Mayors, "U.S. Metro Economies: GMP - The Engines of America's Growth," January 2007

Economic Growth

Area	1995 GMP	2005 GMP	Average Annual Growth Rate	Growth Rate Rank[2]
MSA[1]	47.4	85.7	6.1	112

Note: Figures are in billions of dollars; GMP = Gross Metropolitan Product; (1)
Portland-Vancouver-Beaverton, OR-WA Metropolitan Statistical Area - see Appendix A for areas included; (2)
Rank ranges from 1 to 361
Source: The U.S. Conference of Mayors, "U.S. Metro Economies: GMP - The Engines of America's Growth,"
January 2007

INCOME

Per Capita/Median/Average Income

Area	Per Capita ($)	Median Household ($)	Average Household ($)
City	26,832	47,046	62,627
MSA[1]	26,897	54,266	69,014
U.S.	25,129	48,775	65,849

Note: Figures are 2006 estimates; (1) Metropolitan Statistical Area - see Appendix B for areas included
Source: Claritas, Inc.

Household Income Distribution

Area				Percent of Households Earning			
	Under $15,000	$15,000 -24,999	$25,000 -34,999	$35,000 -49,999	$50,000 -74,999	$75,000 -99,000	$100,000 -149,999	$150,000 and up
City	13.6	11.1	11.8	16.8	19.9	11.3	10.0	5.5
MSA[1]	9.8	9.4	10.7	16.4	21.6	13.4	12.3	6.4
U.S.	13.3	11.0	11.3	15.7	19.5	11.8	11.0	6.4

Note: Figures are 2006 estimates; (1) Metropolitan Statistical Area - see Appendix B for areas included
Source: Claritas, Inc.

Poverty Rates by Age

Area	All Ages	Under 5 Years Old	5 to 17 Years Old	18 to 64 Years Old	65 Years and Over
City	13.1	1.0	2.4	8.4	1.2
MSA[1]	9.5	0.9	2.0	5.7	0.7
U.S.	12.4	1.2	3.0	6.9	1.2

Note: Figures are percent of population with income in 1999 below poverty level and only include population
for whom poverty status is determined; (1) Metropolitan Statistical Area - see Appendix A for areas included
Source: Census 2000, Summary File 3

Personal Bankruptcy Filing Rate

Area	2003	2004	2005
Multnomah County	6.85	6.80	9.36
U.S.	5.57	5.31	6.88

Note: Numbers are per 1,000 population and include Chapter 7 and Chapter 13 filings
Source: Federal Deposit Insurance Corporation (FDIC), Regional Economic Conditions (RECON), 3/24/2006

EMPLOYMENT

Labor Force and Employment

Area	Civilian Labor Force			Workers Employed		
	Dec. 2005	Dec. 2006	% Chg.	Dec. 2005	Dec. 2006	% Chg.
City	295,816	302,337	2.2	280,606	287,513	2.5
MSA[1]	1,109,417	1,130,606	1.9	1,055,669	1,077,585	2.1
U.S.	149,874,000	152,571,000	1.8	142,918,000	146,081,000	2.2

Note: Data is not seasonally adjusted and covers workers 16 years of age and older;
(1) Metropolitan Statistical Area - see Appendix B for areas included
Source: Bureau of Labor Statistics, http://stats.bls.gov

Unemployment Rate

Area	2006											
	Jan.	Feb.	Mar.	Apr.	May	Jun.	Jul.	Aug.	Sep.	Oct.	Nov.	Dec.
City	5.6	6.1	5.9	5.6	5.5	5.6	5.4	5.2	5.0	4.6	5.0	4.9
MSA[1]	5.3	6.0	5.6	5.2	5.0	5.3	5.3	5.2	4.8	4.4	4.7	4.7
U.S.	5.1	5.1	4.8	4.5	4.4	4.8	5.0	4.6	4.4	4.1	4.3	4.3

Note: Data is not seasonally adjusted and covers workers 16 years of age and older; All figures are percentages; (1) Metropolitan Statistical Area - see Appendix B for areas included
Source: Bureau of Labor Statistics, http://stats.bls.gov

Employment by Occupation

Occupation Classification	City (%)	MSA[1] (%)	U.S. (%)
Sales and Office	26.5	27.3	26.7
Professional and Related	23.6	20.7	20.2
Service	15.0	13.6	14.9
Production, Transportation, and Material Moving	14.0	14.3	14.6
Management, Business, and Financial	13.6	14.6	13.5
Construction, Extraction, and Maintenance	7.0	8.8	9.4
Farming, Forestry, and Fishing	0.2	0.7	0.7

Note: Figures cover employed civilians 16 years of age and older;
(1) Metropolitan Statistical Area - see Appendix A for areas included
Source: Census 2000, Summary File 3

Employment by Industry

Sector	MSA[1]		U.S.
	Number of Employees	Percent of Total	Percent of Total
Government	142,300	13.7	16.3
Education and Health Services	127,000	12.3	13.2
Professional and Business Services	135,700	13.1	12.9
Retail Trade	114,700	11.1	11.5
Manufacturing	127,700	12.3	10.2
Leisure and Hospitality	94,500	9.1	9.5
Financial Activities	70,700	6.8	6.1
Construction	64,400	6.2	5.5
Wholesale Trade	58,400	5.6	4.3
Other Services	35,800	3.5	3.9
Transportation and Utilities	38,500	3.7	3.7
Information	24,200	2.3	2.2
Natural Resources and Mining	1,700	0.2	0.5

Note: Figures cover non-farm employment as of December 2006 and are not seasonally adjusted;
(1) Metropolitan Statistical Area - see Appendix B for areas included
Source: Bureau of Labor Statistics, http://stats.bls.gov

Occupations with Greatest Projected Employment Growth: 2002 - 2012

Occupation[1]	2002 Employment	2012 Projected Employment	Numeric Employment Change	Percent Employment Change
Retail Salespersons	50,120	57,600	7,480	14.9
Registered Nurses	26,980	34,030	7,050	26.1
Office Clerks, General	37,340	42,460	5,120	13.7
Cashiers	34,230	39,010	4,780	14.0
Janitors and Cleaners, Except Maids and Housekeeping Cleaners	22,840	26,570	3,730	16.3
Waiters and Waitresses	23,660	27,160	3,500	14.8
Combined Food Preparation and Serving Workers, Including Fast Food	23,280	26,560	3,280	14.1
Nursing Aides, Orderlies, and Attendants	12,180	15,210	3,030	24.9
Customer Service Representatives	18,180	21,200	3,020	16.6
General and Operations Managers	19,360	22,280	2,920	15.1

Note: Projections cover Oregon; (1) Sorted by numeric employment change
Source: www.projectionscentral.com, State Occupational Projections, 2002-2012 Long-Term Projections

Fastest Growing Occupations: 2002 - 2012

Occupation[1]	2002 Employment	2012 Projected Employment	Numeric Employment Change	Percent Employment Change
Pharmacy Technicians	3,560	4,650	1,090	30.6
Dental Laboratory Technicians	980	1,240	260	26.5
Pharmacists	3,080	3,890	810	26.3
Dental Hygienists	1,830	2,310	480	26.2
Dental Assistants	3,760	4,740	980	26.1
Registered Nurses	26,980	34,030	7,050	26.1
Medical Transcriptionists	1,750	2,190	440	25.1
Physical Therapists	1,640	2,050	410	25.0
Nursing Aides, Orderlies, and Attendants	12,180	15,210	3,030	24.9
Medical Records and Health Information Technicians	2,370	2,960	590	24.9

Note: Projections cover Oregon; (1) Sorted by percent employment change and excludes occupations with numeric employment change less than 200
Source: www.projectionscentral.com, State Occupational Projections, 2002-2012 Long-Term Projections

Average Wages

Occupation	$/Hr.	Occupation	$/Hr.
Accountants and Auditors	27.34	Maids and Housekeeping Cleaners	8.99
Automotive Mechanics	16.46	Maintenance and Repair Workers	17.04
Bookkeepers	15.79	Marketing Managers	43.80
Carpenters	19.86	Nuclear Medicine Technologists	31.99
Cashiers	10.07	Nurses, Licensed Practical	20.12
Clerks, General Office	13.04	Nurses, Registered	30.09
Clerks, Receptionists/Information	12.14	Nursing Aides/Orderlies/Attendants	11.59
Clerks, Shipping/Receiving	13.89	Packers and Packagers, Hand	9.56
Computer Programmers	30.37	Physical Therapists	31.51
Computer Support Specialists	21.40	Postal Service Mail Carriers	21.77
Computer Systems Analysts	33.41	Real Estate Brokers	n/a
Cooks, Restaurant	10.51	Retail Salespersons	12.39
Dentists	n/a	Sales Reps., Exc. Tech./Scientific	26.87
Electrical Engineers	40.71	Sales Reps., Tech./Scientific	34.11
Electricians	27.95	Secretaries, Exc. Legal/Med./Exec.	14.41
Financial Managers	47.39	Security Guards	11.09
First-Line Supervisors/Mgrs., Sales	19.54	Surgeons	63.57
Food Preparation Workers	9.89	Teacher Assistants	12.10
General and Operations Managers	47.48	Teachers, Elementary School	22.30
Hairdressers/Cosmetologists	11.98	Teachers, Secondary School	22.90
Internists	79.19	Telemarketers	10.88
Janitors and Cleaners	10.72	Truck Drivers, Heavy/Tractor-Trailer	17.39
Landscaping/Groundskeeping Workers	11.39	Truck Drivers, Light/Delivery Svcs.	13.66
Lawyers	44.80	Waiters and Waitresses	9.90

Note: Wage data is for May 2005 and covers the Portland-Vancouver-Beaverton, OR-WA Metropolitan Statistics Area - see Appendix B for areas included. Hourly wages for elementary/secondary school teachers and teacher assistants were calculated by the editors from annual wage data assuming a 40 hour work week; n/a not available.
Source: Bureau of Labor Statistics, May 2005 Metro Area Occupational Employment and Wage Estimates

RESIDENTIAL REAL ESTATE

Building Permits

Area	Single-Family			Multi-Family			Total		
	2005	2006p	Pct. Chg.	2005	2006p	Pct. Chg.	2005	2006p	Pct. Chg.
City	981	1,256	28.0	2,755	2,295	-16.7	3,736	3,551	-5.0
U.S.	1,682,000	1,380,000	-18.0	473,300	457,300	-3.4	2,155,300	1,837,300	-14.8

Note: (p) preliminary; figures represent new, privately-owned housing units authorized (unadjusted data); All permit data are based on estimates with imputation; U.S. figures are based on the new 20,000-place series.
Source: U.S. Census Bureau, Manufacturing, Mining, and Construction Statistics

Homeownership and Housing Vacancies

Area	Homeownership Rate[2] (%)			Rental Vacancy Rate[3] (%)			Homeowner Vacancy Rate[4] (%)		
	2004	2005	2006	2004	2005	2006	2004	2005	2006
MSA[1]	n/a	68.3	66.0	n/a	9.7	7.1	n/a	1.6	1.7
U.S.	69.0	68.9	68.8	10.2	9.8	9.7	1.7	1.9	2.4

Note: Comparable 2004 data was not available due to changes in metropolitan area definitions; (1) Metropolitan Statistical Area - see Appendix B for areas included; (2) The proportion of households that are owners; (3) The proportion of the rental inventory that is vacant for rent; (4) The proportion of the homeowner inventory that is vacant for sale; n/a not available
Source: U.S. Census Bureau, Housing Vacancies and Homeownership Annual Statistics: 2006

TAXES

State Corporate Income Tax Rates

State	Rate (%)	Number of Brackets	Low Bracket (Under $)	High Bracket (Over $)
Oregon	6.6	1	na	na

Note: Tax rates as of December 31, 2006; na not applicable
Source: Tax Foundation, www.taxfoundation.org

State Individual Income Tax Rates

State	Federal Deductibility	Marginal Rate (%)	Number of Brackets	Low Bracket (Under $)	High Bracket (Over $)
Oregon	Yes (z)	5.0-9.0 (r)	3	0	6,850

Note: Tax rates as of December 31, 2006; Brackets apply to single taxpayers and married people filing separately; na not applicable; (r) Indexed for Inflation; (z) Deduction limited to no more than $5,000.
Source: Tax Foundation, www.taxfoundation.org

Various State and Local Tax Rates

State and Local Sales and Use (%)	State Sales and Use (%)	Gasoline ($/gal.)	Cigarette ($/pack)	Spirits ($/gal.)	Table Wine ($/gal.)	Beer ($/gal.)
0	None	0.24	1.18	18.52 (b)	0.67	0.08

Note: Tax rates as of December 31, 2006; (b) States where the state government controls all sales. Excise tax rate is calculated using methodology designed by the Distilled Spirits Council of the United States (DISCUS).
Source: Tax Foundation, www.taxfoundation.org; The Sales Tax Clearinghouse, www.thestc.com

State Tax Burdens

Area	Combined State and Local Tax Burden		Combined Federal, State and Local Tax Burden	
	Percent	Rank	Percent	Rank
Oregon	9.9	35	30.2	28
U.S. Average	10.6	-	31.6	-

Note: Figures are for 2006 and measure taxes as a percentage of income
Source: Tax Foundation, www.taxfoundation.org

Internal Revenue Service Tax Audits

IRS District	Percent of Returns Audited				
	1996	1997	1998	1999	2000
Pacific Northwest	0.63	0.51	0.37	0.24	0.15
U.S.	0.66	0.61	0.46	0.31	0.20

Note: Figures cover IRS district audits of federal income tax returns filed by individuals. Geographic data on district audits after the year 2000 are being withheld by the IRS. TRAC is challenging this policy.
Source: Syracuse University, Transactional Records Access Clearinghouse (TRAC), "Odds of IRS District Tax Audit 2000"

**COMMERCIAL
REAL ESTATE**

Office Market

Market Area	Inventory (sq. ft.)	Vacant (sq. ft.)	Vac. Rate (%)	Under Constr. (sq. ft.)	Asking Rent ($/sf) Class A	Class B
Portland	42,466,578	4,977,352	11.7	820,370	23.60	18.43

Source: Grubb & Ellis, Office Markets Trends, 4th Quarter 2006

Industrial Market

Market Area	Inventory (sq. ft.)	Vacant (sq. ft.)	Vac. Rate (%)	Under Constr. (sq. ft.)	Asking Rent ($/sf) WH/Dist	R&D/Flex
Portland	133,802,776	8,364,335	6.3	1,299,787	4.44	8.88

Source: Grubb & Ellis, Industrial Markets Trends, 4th Quarter 2006

**COMMERCIAL
UTILITIES**

Typical Monthly Electric Bills

Area	Commercial Service ($/month) 3 kW demand 1,000 kWh	40 kW demand 14,000 kWh	Industrial Service ($/month) 1,000 kW demand 200,000 kWh	50,000 kW demand 15,000,000 kWh
City	96	1,006	15,384	870,428
Average[1]	123	1,413	22,000	1,306,315

Note: Based on total rates in effect July 1, 2006; (1) average based on 196 utilities
Source: Edison Electric Institute, Typical Bills and Average Rates Report, Summer 2006

TRANSPORTATION

Means of Transportation to Work

Area	Car/Truck/Van Drove Alone	Car-pooled	Public Transportation Bus	Subway	Railroad	Bicycle	Walked	Other Means	Worked at Home
City	63.7	11.9	11.3	0.4	0.2	1.8	5.2	1.3	4.3
MSA[1]	73.1	11.5	5.3	0.4	0.2	0.8	3.0	1.1	4.6
U.S.	75.7	12.2	2.5	1.5	0.5	0.4	2.9	1.0	3.3

Note: Figures are percentages and cover workers 16 years of age and older;
(1) Metropolitan Statistical Area - see Appendix A for areas included
Source: Census 2000, Summary File 3

Travel Time to Work

Area	Less Than 15 Minutes	15 to 29 Minutes	30 to 44 Minutes	45 to 59 Minutes	60 Minutes or More
City	25.5	45.6	19.2	4.9	4.8
MSA[1]	26.3	40.0	21.1	7.0	5.5
U.S.	29.4	36.1	19.1	7.4	8.0

Note: Figures are percentages and include workers 16 years old and over; (1) Metropolitan Statistical Area - see Appendix A for areas included
Source: Census 2000, Summary File 3

Travel Time Index

Area	1982	1993	2002	2003
Urban Area[1]	1.05	1.24	1.38	1.37
Average[2]	1.12	1.28	1.37	1.37

Note: Travel Time Index - The ratio of travel time in the peak period to the travel time at free-flow conditions. A value of 1.35 indicates a 20-minute free-flow trip takes 27 minutes in the peak. Free-flow speeds (60 mph on freeways and 35 mph on principal arterials) are used as the comparison threshold; (1) Covers the Portland, OR-WA urban area; (2) average of 85 urban areas
Source: Texas Transportation Institute, The 2005 Urban Mobility Report, May 2005

Public Transportation

Agency name:	Tri-County Metropolitan Transportation District of Oregon (Tri-Met)
Vehicle type:	Bus
Average fleet age in years:	9.0
No. operated in max. service:	536
Vehicle type:	Light rail
Average fleet age in years:	10.5
No. operated in max. service:	87
Vehicle type:	Demand response
Average fleet age in years:	5.6
No. operated in max. service:	233

Source: Federal Transit Administration, National Transit Database, 2005

Air Transportation

Airport name and code:	Portland International (PDX)
Domestic service (2006)	
Passenger airlines[1]:	28
Passenger enplanements:	6,677,006
Freight carriers[2]:	28
Freight (lbs.):	231,611,095
International service (2005)	
Passenger airlines[1]:	13
Passenger enplanements:	259,879
Freight carriers[2]:	13
Freight (lbs.):	30,296,081

Note: (1) Includes all major, minor and commuter airlines that carried at least one passenger during the year; (2) Includes all airlines and freight carriers that transported at least one pound of freight during the year
Source: Bureau of Transportation Statistics, The Intermodal Transportation Database, Air Carriers: T-100 International Market, 2004; Bureau of Transportation Statistics, The Intermodal Transportation Database, Air Carriers: T-100 Domestic Market, 2005

Other Transportation Statistics

Interstate highways:	I-5; I-80
Amtrak service:	Yes
Major waterways/ports:	Port of Portland

Source: Editor & Publisher Market Guide, 2006; Amtrak.com; Rand McNally 2006 Road Atlas

BUSINESSES

Major Business Headquarters

Company Name	2006 Rankings	
	Fortune[1]	Forbes[2]
Columbia Forest Prods	-	373
Hampton Affiliates	-	286
Knowledge Learning	-	219
North Pacific Group	-	308

Note: (1) Fortune 500 - companies that produce a 10-K are ranked 1 to 500 based on 2005 revenue; (2) Forbes Largest Private Companies - all private companies with at least $1 billion in annual revenue are ranked 1 to 394; companies listed are located in the city; dashes indicate no ranking
Source: Fortune, April 17, 2006; Forbes, November 9, 2006

Best Companies to Work For

Perkins Coie; Umpqua Bank (HQ), headquartered in Portland, are among the "100 Best Companies to Work For." Criteria: More than 105,000 employees from 446 companies responded to a 57-question survey created by the Great Place to Work Institute. Two-thirds of a company's score is based on the survey, which covers topics such as attitudes towards management, job satisfaction, and camaraderie. The remaining third of the score comes from each company's responses to the Institute's Culture Audit, which includes detailed questions about demographic makeup, pay and benefits programs, and open-ended questions about the company's people-management philosophy, internal communications, opportunities, compensation practices, diversity programs, etc. Any company that is at least seven years old and has a minimum of 1,000 U.S. employees is eligible. The top three U.S. locations are shown for companies with more than one location. *Fortune, "100 Best Companies to Work for 2007," January 22, 2007*

Fast-Growing Businesses

According to *Inc.*, Portland is home to two of America's 500 fastest-growing private companies: **Jive Software; Wellpartner**. Criteria: must be an independent, privately-held, U.S. corporation, proprietorship or partnership; net sales of at least $600,000 in FY2002; four-year operating/sales history; holding companies, regulated banks, and utilities were excluded. *Inc., "America's 500 Fastest-Growing Private Companies," September 2006*

According to *Fortune*, Portland is home to one of America's 100 fastest-growing companies: **Schnitzer Steel**. Companies were ranked based on earnings-per-share growth, revenue growth and total return over the previous three years. Criteria for inclusion: public companies with sales of at least $50 million. Companies that lost money in the most recent quarter, or ended in the red for the past four quarters as a whole, were not eligible. Limited partnerships and REITs were also not considered. *Fortune, "America's Fastest-Growing Companies," September 18, 2006*

Women-Owned Businesses: 1997 and 2002

Year	All Firms		Firms with Paid Employees			
	Firms	Sales ($000)	Firms	Sales ($000)	Employees	Payroll ($000)
1997	16,477	2,442,464	2,722	2,120,149	21,072	432,706
2002	17,900	3,207,362	3,155	2,797,873	22,098	540,495

Note: Figures cover firms located in the city; Women-owned business are defined as firms in which women own 51% or more of the stock or equity of the company; (a) Withheld to avoid disclosing data for individual companies; (b) Withheld because estimate did not meet publication standards; n/a not available
Source: 1997 Economic Census, Survey of Minority- and Women-Owned Business Enterprises; 2002 Economic Census, Survey of Business Owners (released February 9, 2006)

Minority Business Opportunity

One of the 500 largest Hispanic-owned companies in the U.S. are located in Portland. *Hispanic Business, "Hispanic Business 500," June 2006*

Portland is home to one company which is on the Hispanic Business Fastest-Growing 100 list (greatest sales growth over the past five years): **Fulfillment Corporation of America**. *Hispanic Business, July/August 2006*

HOTELS

Hotels/Motels

Area	Hotels/Motels	Average Minimum Rates ($)		
		Tourist	First-Class	Deluxe
City	90	70	96	194

Source: OAG Travel Planner Online, Spring 2006

The Portland metro area is home to two of the top 187 hotels in the U.S. according to *Travel & Leisure*: **Heathman Hotel** (#160); **5th Avenue Suites Hotel** (#175). Criteria: service; location; rooms; food; and value. *Travel & Leisure, "The T+L 500, 2007"*

EVENT SITES

Stadiums, Arenas, and Auditoriums

Name	Capacity
Civic Stadium/Portland Center for the Performing Arts	30,000
Portland Center for the Performing Arts	3,300
Portland Civic Stadium	25,000
Portland Memorial Coliseum	12,000
Rose Garden	21,700

Source: www.officialtravelguide.com; www.eventective.com; original research

Convention Centers

Name	Overall Space (sq. ft.)	Exhibit Space (sq. ft.)	Meeting Space (sq. ft.)	Meeting Rooms
Oregon Convention Center	n/a	22,800	255,000	50

Note: n/a not available
Source: www.officialtravelguide.com; www.eventective.com; original research

Living Environment

COST OF LIVING

Cost of Living Index

Year	Composite Index	Groceries	Housing	Utilities	Trans-portation	Health Care	Misc. Goods/ Services
2004	112.4	116.5	110.8	114.3	110.1	132.7	110.0
2005	113.5	120.8	112.1	118.0	108.2	112.0	112.2
2006	116.8	116.6	125.4	114.3	106.0	112.8	114.2

Note: U.S. = 100; Figures are for the Metropolitan Statistical Area - see Appendix B for areas included
Source: The Council for Community and Economic Research (formerly ACCRA), Cost of Living Index, 2004, 2005 and 2006 4-Quarter Averages

HOUSING

House Price Index (HPI)

Area	National Ranking[2]	Quarterly Change (%)	One-Year Change (%)	Five-Year Change (%)
MSA[1]	22	1.51	13.45	66.86
U.S.[3]	-	1.12	5.87	55.21

Note: The HPI is a weighted repeat sales index. It measures average price changes in repeat sales or refinancings on the same properties. This information is obtained by reviewing repeat mortgage transactions on single-family properties whose mortgages have been purchased or securitized by Fannie Mae or Freddie Mac in January 1975; (1) Metropolitan Statistical Area - see Appendix B for areas included; (2) Rankings are based on annual percentage change for all metro areas containing at least 15,000 transactions over the last 10 years and ranges from 1 to 282; (3) figures based on a weighted division average; all figures are for the period ending December 31, 2006
Source: Office of Federal Housing Enterprise Oversight, House Price Index, March 1, 2007

House Price Valuations

Area	Q4 1999	Q4 2000	Q4 2001	Q4 2002	Q4 2003	Q4 2004	Q4 2005	Q4 2006
MSA[1]	1.2	0.3	4.2	8.4	12.8	18.1	33.7	42.8

Note: Figures show the percentage of over- or under-valuation of single family homes relative to statistically normal house values (e.g. a value of 23.6 indicates that house values are 23.6% overvalued). Statistically normal house values are based on house prices, interest rates, household incomes, population densities, and any historical premiums or discounts metropolitan areas have exhibited over time; (1) Figures cover the Metropolitan Statistical Area - see Appendix B for areas included
Source: Global Insight/National City Corporation, House Prices in America, March 2007

Median Home Prices

Area	2004	2005	2006p	Percent Change 2005 to 2006
Metro Area[1]	206.5	244.9	280.8	14.7
U.S. Average	195.2	219.0	222.0	1.4

Note: Figures are median sales prices of existing single-family homes in thousands of dollars; (p) preliminary; n/a not available; (1) Covers the Portland-Vancouver-Beaverton, OR-WA Metropolitan Statistical Area - see Appendix B for areas included
Source: National Association of Realtors, Metropolitan Area Prices, 4th Quarter 2006

Housing: Year Structure Built

Area	1990 -2000	1980 -1989	1970 -1979	1960 -1969	1950 -1959	1940 -1949	Before 1940	Median Year
City	10.1	5.7	12.1	11.5	14.9	11.5	34.0	1953
MSA[1]	24.6	13.0	20.9	11.3	9.1	6.5	14.7	1974
U.S.	17.0	15.8	18.5	13.7	12.7	7.3	15.0	1971

Note: Figures are percentages; (1) Metropolitan Statistical Area - see Appendix A for areas included
Source: Census 2000, Summary File 3

Average New Home Price

Area	2004	2005	2006
MSA[1]	284,436	318,686	389,049
U.S.	253,574	275,712	299,269

Note: Figures, in dollars, are based on a new home with 2,400 sq. ft. of living area on an 8,000 sq. ft. lot;
(1) Metropolitan Statistical Area - see Appendix B for areas included
Source: The Council for Community and Economic Research (formerly ACCRA), Cost of Living Index, 2004,
2005 and 2006 4-Quarter Averages

Average Apartment Rent

Area	2004	2005	2006
MSA[1]	777	781	862
U.S.	716	740	766

Note: Figures, in dollars per month, are based on an unfurnished two bedroom, 1-1/2 or 2 bath apartment,
approximately 950 sq. ft., excluding utilities except water; (1) Metropolitan Statistical Area - see Appendix B for
areas included
Source: The Council for Community and Economic Research (formerly ACCRA), Cost of Living Index, 2004,
2005 and 2006 4-Quarter Averages

RESIDENTIAL
UTILITIES

Average Residential Utility Costs

Area	All Electric ($/mth)	Part Electric ($/mth)	Other Energy ($/mth)	Phone ($/mth)
MSA[1]	–	90.15	89.10	30.08
U.S.	136.00	76.53	90.52	25.87

Note: (1) Metropolitan Statistical Area - see Appendix B for areas included
Source: The Council for Community and Economic Research (formerly ACCRA), Cost of Living Index, 2006
4-Quarter Average

HEALTH

Average Health Care Costs

Area	Optometrist ($/visit)	Doctor ($/visit)	Dentist ($/visit)
MSA[1]	84.34	88.30	81.12
U.S.	76.38	76.10	68.72

Note: Optometrist—based on a full vision eye exam for an established adult patient;
Doctor—based on a general practitioner's routine exam of an established patient;
Dentist—based on adult teeth cleaning and periodic oral exam;
(1) Metropolitan Statistical Area - see Appendix B for areas included
Source: The Council for Community and Economic Research (formerly ACCRA), Cost of Living Index, 2006
4-Quarter Average

Mortality Rates

ICD-10 Sub-Chapter	ICD-10 Code	Age-Adjusted Death Rate per 100,000 population[1]	U.S. Age-Adjusted Death Rate per 100,000 population
Malignant neoplasms	C00-C97	194.1	185.8
Ischaemic heart diseases	I20-I25	119.5	150.2
Other forms of heart disease	I30-I51	51.8	50.8
Cerebrovascular diseases	I60-I69	64.6	50.0
Chronic lower respiratory diseases	J40-J47	41.4	41.1
Diabetes mellitus	E10-E14	32.2	24.5
Other degenerative diseases of the nervous system	G30-G31	30.3	22.3
Other external causes of accidental injury	W00-X59	26.8	21.2
Influenza and pneumonia	J10-J18	12.1	19.8
Hypertensive diseases	I10-I13	16.1	18.1

Note: ICD-10 = International Classification of Diseases 10th Revision; (1) Figures cover Multnomah County,
OR
Source: Centers for Disease Control and Prevention, National Center for Health Statistics. Compressed
Mortality File 1999-2004. CDC WONDER On-line Database, compiled from Compressed Mortality File
1999-2004 Series 20 No. 2J, 2007.

Health Risk Data

Item	Area[1] (%)	U.S. (%)
Adults who have been told they have high blood pressure	21.5	25.5
Adults who have been told they have high blood cholesterol	34.2	35.6
Adults who have been told they have diabetes[2]	6.0	7.3
Adults who have been told they have arthritis	24.0	27.0
Adults who have been told they currently have asthma	10.0	8.0
Adults who are current smokers	17.5	20.6

Note: (1) Figures cover the Metropolitan Statistical Area - see Appendix B for areas included; (2) Figures do not include pregnancy-related diabetes, pre-diabetes or borderline diabetes
Source: Centers for Disease Control and Prevention, Behaviorial Risk Factor Surveillance System, SMART: Selected Metropolitan/Micropolitan Area Trends, 2005

Distribution of Office-Based Physicians

Area	Total	Family/ General Practice	Specialties		
			Medical	Surgical	Other
CMSA[1] (number)	4,451	598	1,587	1,026	1,240
CMSA[1] (rate per 10,000 pop.)	18.6	2.5	6.6	4.3	5.2
Metro Average[2] (rate per 10,000 pop.)	19.4	2.1	7.5	4.5	5.3

Note: Data as of December 31, 2004; (1) Portland-Salem, OR-WA Consolidated Metropolitan Statistical Area includes the following counties: Oregon (Clackamas, Columbia, Marion, Multnomah, Polk, Washington, Yamhill); Washington (Clark);
(2) Average of the 79 unique MSAs and CMSAs in this book
Source: American Medical Association, Physician Characteristics & Distribution in the U.S., 2006

Hospitals

Portland has the following hospitals: 8 general medical and surgical; 1 surgical.
AHA Guide to the Healthcare Field 2007

According to *U.S. News,* the Portland metro area is home to one of the best hospitals in the U.S.: **Oregon Health and Science University Hospital**; *U.S. News Online, "America's Best Hospitals 2006"*

EDUCATION

Public School District Statistics

District Name	Schls	Pupils	Pupil/ Teacher Ratio	Minority Pupils[1] (%)	Free Lunch Eligible[2] (%)	IEP[3] (%)
Centennial Sd 28j	10	6,409	19.4	28.6	52.2	13.9
David Douglas Sd 40	14	9,572	20.7	35.9	58.6	12.7
Parkrose Sd 3	6	3,473	20.2	44.7	49.1	13.4
Portland Sd 1j	105	47,649	17.9	40.3	36.6	14.3

Note: Table includes regular local school districts with 2,000 or more students; (1) Percentage of students that are not white, non-Hispanic; (2) Percentage of students that are eligible for the free lunch program; (3) Percentage of students that have an Individualized Education Program.
Source: U.S. Department of Education, National Center for Education Statistics, Common Core of Data, Local Education Agency (School District) Universe Survey: School Year 2004-2005; U.S. Department of Education, National Center for Education Statistics, Common Core of Data, Public Elementary/Secondary School Universe Survey: School Year 2004-2005

Top Public High Schools

High School Name	Index[1]	Rank[1]	Subsidized Lunch (%)[2]	E&E (%)[3]
Lincoln	1.131	1,091	9.1	n/a**
Woodrow Wilson	1.319	890	14.8	20.5

Note: (1) Public schools are ranked according to a ratio that is the number of Advanced Placement and/or International Baccalaureate tests taken by all students at a school in 2005 divided by the number of graduating seniors. All of the schools on the list have an index of at least 1.000; they are in the top five percent of public schools measured this way. The rankings range from 1 to 1,236; (2) Percentage of students receiving federally subsidized meals; (3) E & E stands for equity and excellence percentage: the portion of all graduating seniors at a school that had at least one passing grade on one AP or IB test; (*) Gave just IB tests; (**) Gave both IB and AP tests. AP and IB participation are indicators of a school's efforts to get students to excel and prepare for college; n/a not available
Source: Newsweek Online, May 23, 2006

Educational Quality

School District	Education Quotient[1]	Graduate Outcome[2]	Community Index[3]	Resource Index[4]	Rating[5]
Portland 1J	72	72	70	48	Blue

Note: Scores are national percentile rankings and range from 1 (worst) to 99 (best); (1) Combination of the Graduate Outcome, Community and Resource Indexes weighted to reflect the greater importance of the Graduate Outcome and Resource Index; (2) Based on graduation rates and college board scores (SAT/ACT); (3) Based on the surrounding community's level of affluence and adult education; (4) Based on teacher salaries, per-pupil expenditures and student-teacher ratios; (5) School districts receive one of five rankings: Gold Medal (top 16 percent of districts evaluated); Blue Ribbon (top third); Green Light (average); Yellow Light (bottom 25 percent); Red Light (bottom 10 percent).
Source: Expansion Management, "2007 Education Quotient," January 2007

Highest Level of Education

Area	Less than H.S.	H.S. Diploma	Some College, No Deg.	Associate Degree	Bachelors Degree	Masters Degree	Profess. School Degree	Doctorate Degree
City	14.5	22.5	25.0	5.8	21.1	7.2	2.8	1.2
MSA[1]	12.7	23.9	27.7	7.0	19.2	6.5	2.1	0.9
U.S.	19.4	28.4	21.2	6.4	15.7	5.9	2.0	1.0

Note: Figures are 2006 estimated percentages and cover persons age 25 and over; (1) Metropolitan Statistical Area - see Appendix B for areas included
Source: Claritas, Inc.

Educational Attainment by Race

Area	High School Graduate (%)					Bachelor's Degree (%)				
	Total	White	Black	Asian	Hisp.[2]	Total	White	Black	Asian	Hisp.[2]
City	85.7	88.8	78.4	68.5	59.5	32.6	35.5	15.3	26.7	14.5
MSA[1]	87.2	89.4	80.4	79.1	53.7	28.8	29.6	18.0	38.3	11.8
U.S.	80.4	83.6	72.3	80.4	52.4	24.4	26.1	14.3	44.1	10.4

Note: Figures shown cover persons 25 years old and over; (1) Metropolitan Statistical Area - see Appendix A for areas included; (2) people of Hispanic origin can be of any race
Source: Census 2000, Summary File 3

School Enrollment by Type

Area	Grades KG to 8				Grades 9 to 12			
	Public		Private		Public		Private	
	Enrollment	%	Enrollment	%	Enrollment	%	Enrollment	%
City	48,210	87.7	6,772	12.3	21,811	89.2	2,630	10.8
MSA[1]	219,761	88.8	27,653	11.2	95,236	91.4	8,906	8.6
U.S.	33,526,011	88.7	4,285,121	11.3	14,848,628	90.6	1,532,323	9.4

Note: Figures shown cover persons 3 years old and over; (1) Metropolitan Statistical Area - see Appendix A for areas included
Source: Census 2000, Summary File 3

School Enrollment by Race

Area	Grades KG to 8 (%)				Grades 9 to 12 (%)			
	White	Black	Asian	Hisp.[1]	White	Black	Asian	Hisp.[1]
City	68.0	9.7	7.1	9.9	68.3	11.0	8.0	8.0
MSA[2]	80.1	3.1	4.4	9.9	81.9	3.4	4.8	7.7
U.S.	68.5	15.5	3.3	16.8	68.8	15.5	3.8	15.7

Note: Figures shown cover persons 3 years old and over; (1) people of Hispanic origin can be of any race; (2) Metropolitan Statistical Area - see Appendix A for areas included
Source: Census 2000, Summary File 3

Average Salaries of Public School Teachers

District	2004-05 Dollars	2004-05 Rank[1]	2005-06 Dollars	2005-06 Rank[1]	Percent Change 2004-05 to 2005-06
OREGON	48,330	15	48,981	16	1.35
U.S. Average	47,674	-	49,109	-	3.01

Note: (1) State rank ranges from 1 to 51.
Source: National Education Association, Rankings & Estimates: Rankings of the States 2005 and Estimates of School Statistics 2006, November 2006

Higher Education

Four-Year Colleges Public	Four-Year Colleges Private Non-profit	Four-Year Colleges Private For-profit	Two-Year Colleges Public	Two-Year Colleges Private Non-profit	Two-Year Colleges Private For-profit	Medical Schools[1]	Law Schools[2]	Voc/ Tech[3]
2	15	3	1	1	6	1	1	2

Note: Figures cover institutions located within the city limits; (1) includes schools accredited by the Liaison Committee on Medical Education and the American Osteopathic Association; (2) includes American Bar Association-accredited law schools; (3) includes all schools with programs that are less than 2 years
Source: National Center for Education Statistics, The Integrated Postsecondary Education System (IPEDS) Peer Analysis System, 2006; www.usnews.com, America's Best Graduate Schools 2008, Medical School Directory; www.usnews.com, America's Best Graduate Schools 2008, Law School Directory

PRESIDENTIAL ELECTION

2004 Presidential Election Results

Area	Bush	Kerry	Nader	Other
Multnomah County	27.1	71.6	0.0	1.3
U.S.	50.7	48.3	0.4	0.6

Note: Results are percentages and may not add to 100% due to rounding
Source: Dave Leip's Atlas of U.S. Presidential Elections, www.uselectionatlas.org

MAJOR EMPLOYERS

Major Employers

Company Name	Industry	Type of Site
Adventist Medical Center	General medical and surgical hospitals	Headquarters
Alaska Pipe and Supply	Plumbing and hydronic heating supplies	Branch
Ameriquest Mortgage	Mortgage bankers and correspondents	Branch
Archdiocese of Portland	Religious organizations	Headquarters
Croet	Colleges and universities	Headquarters
Denton Plastics Inc	Refuse systems	Single
Emanual Hospital	General medical and surgical hospitals	Headquarters
Intel	Miscellaneous fabricated wire products	Branch
Intel	Process control instruments	Branch
Intel	Semiconductors and related devices	Branch
Mentor Graphics Corporation	Computer integrated systems design	Branch
Nike	Rubber and plastics footwear	Headquarters
PCC Structurals Inc	Copper foundries	Branch
Portland Community College	Junior colleges	Headquarters
Portland State University	Colleges and universities	Headquarters
Portland VAMC	Administration of veterans' affairs	Branch
Precision Cast Products	Aircraft parts and equipment, nec	Headquarters
Regence Blcross Blueshield Ore	Accident and health insurance	Headquarters
Shaw Environmental & Infrastructure	Single-family housing construction	Branch
Southwest Washington Med Ctr	General medical and surgical hospitals	Headquarters
St Vincents Hosp & Med Cntr	General medical and surgical hospitals	Branch
Stancorp Mrtg Investors LLC	Life insurance	Single
US Post Office	U.S. Postal Service	Branch

Note: Companies shown are located within the metropolitan area and have 1,700 or more employees; nec = not elsewhere classified.
Source: www.zapdata.com, January 2007

PUBLIC SAFETY

Crime Rate

Area	All Crimes	Violent Crimes				Property Crimes		
		Murder	Forcible Rape	Robbery	Aggrav. Assault	Burglary	Larceny -Theft	Motor Vehicle Theft
City	7,680.2	3.7	60.1	210.4	439.7	1,132.7	4,773.2	1,060.3
Suburbs[1]	3,708.7	2.3	37.3	50.6	102.5	569.1	2,516.1	430.9
Metro[2]	4,734.9	2.6	43.2	91.9	189.6	714.7	3,099.4	593.5
U.S.	3,899.0	5.6	31.7	140.7	291.1	726.7	2,286.3	416.7

Note: Figures are crimes per 100,000 population; (1) All areas within the metro area that are located outside the city limits; (2) Metropolitan Statistical Area - see Appendix B for areas included
Source: FBI Uniform Crime Reports, 2005

Hate Crimes

Area	Number of Quarters Reported	Bias Motivation				
		Race	Religion	Sexual Orientation	Ethnicity	Disability
City	4	35	6	20	11	0

Source: Federal Bureau of Investigation, Hate Crime Statistics 2005

RECREATION

Culture

Dance[1]	Theatre[1]	Instrumental Music[1]	Vocal Music[1]	Series/ Festivals	Museums	Zoos
3	7	12	1	7	8	1

Note: (1) number of professional performing groups
Source: The Grey House Performing Arts Directory, 2007; Official Museum Directory, 2007

Professional Sports Teams

Major League Baseball	National Basketball Association	National Football League	National Hockey League	Major League Soccer	Women's National Basketball Association
0	1	0	0	0	0

Note: Includes teams located in the Portland metro area.
Source: www.sportsvenues.com, Listing of Venues by State/Province and City, 2006

MEDIA

Newspapers

Name	Target Audience	Frequency	Circulation
Beaverton Valley Times	General	Non-Daily	7,036
The Bee	General	Non-Daily	16,000
Catholic Sentinel	Catholic	Non-Daily	14,702
The Clackamas Review/The Oregon City News	General	Non-Daily	44,900
Daily Journal of Commerce	n/a	Daily	4,786
El Centinela	Catholic/Hispanic	Non-Daily	8,200
El Hispanic News	Hispanic	Non-Daily	12,000
The Jewish Review	Jewish	Non-Daily	10,000
The Oregonian	n/a	Daily	335,562
Portland Mercury	General	Non-Daily	30,000
Portland Observer Weekly	General	Non-Daily	30,000
Portland Tribune	General	Non-Daily	200,000
Sherwood Gazette	General	Non-Daily	10,000
The Skanner	Black/General	Non-Daily	40,000
St. Johns Review	General	Non-Daily	3,700
Tigard Times	General	Non-Daily	8,500
Tualatin Times	General	Non-Daily	3,300
Willamette Week	Alternative/General	Non-Daily	85,000

Note: Includes newspapers whose offices are located in the city and whose circulations are 1,000 or more; n/a not available
Source: BurrellesLuce, MediaContacts Online, January 2006

Television Stations

Name	Ch.	Network(s)	Type	Ownership
KATU	2	ABC	Commercial	Fisher Broadcasting Inc.
KOAB	3	PBS	Public	Oregon Public Broadcasting Inc.
KOIN	6	CBS	Commercial	Emmis Communications Corporation
KOAC	7	PBS	Public	Oregon Public Broadcasting Inc.
KGW	8	NBC	Commercial	Belo Corporation
KOPB	10	PBS	Public	Oregon Public Broadcasting Inc.
KPTV	12	Fox/UPN	Commercial	Meredith Communications LLC
KTVR	13	PBS	Public	Oregon Public Broadcasting Inc.
KPXG	22	Pax	Commercial	Paxson Communications Corporation
KNMT	24	n/a	Non-comm.	National Minority Television Inc.
KEPB	28	PBS	Public	Oregon Public Broadcasting Inc.
KWBP	32	WBN	Commercial	Acme Television Holdings
KPDX	49	Fox	Commercial	Meredith Communications LLC

Note: Stations included cover the Portland DMA (Designated Market Area)
BurrellesLuce, MediaContacts Online, January 2006

Major AM Radio Stations

Call Letters	Freq. (kHz)	Station Type	Target Audience	Station Format	Music Format
KTLK	620	Commercial	General	Music/News/Talk	Adult Contemp.
KXL	750	n/a	General	News/Talk	n/a
KPAM	860	n/a	General/Men	News/Talk	n/a
KOTK	910	n/a	General	Talk	n/a
KFXX	910	n/a	General	Sports/Talk	n/a
KWBY	940	Commercial	General/Hispanic	Educational/Music	Latin
KCMD	970	Commercial	General	Comedy	n/a
KEX	1190	Commercial	General/Men/Women	News	n/a
KBAM	1270	n/a	General	Music/News	n/a
KKSL	1290	Commercial	General/Religious	Educational/Music	Gospel
KNPT	1310	n/a	General	News/Sports/Talk	n/a
KKPZ	1330	Commercial	General/Religious	Educational	n/a
KUIK	1360	Commercial	Hispanic	News/Sports/Talk	n/a
KBNP	1410	Commercial	General	n/a	n/a
KYKN	1430	Commercial	General	News/Talk	n/a
KODL	1440	Commercial	General	Music/News	Adult Standards
KKSN	1520	Commercial	General	Music/News/Sports	Adult Standards
KKAD	1550	Commercial	General	News/Talk	n/a
KMBD	1590	Commercial	General	News/Sports/Talk	n/a

Note: Stations included cover the Portland DMA (Designated Market Area); n/a not available
Source: BurrellesLuce, MediaContacts Online, January 2006

Major FM Radio Stations

Call Letters	Freq. (mHz)	Station Type	Target Audience	Station Format	Music Format
KMHD	89.1	College	General	Music	n/a
KBPS	89.9	n/a	General	Music/News	n/a
KBOO	90.7	Non-Comm	Ethnic/General	Music/Sports/Talk	World Music
KOPB	91.5	Public	General	Educational/News	n/a
KGON	92.3	n/a	General/Men	Music/News	n/a
KAST	92.9	Commercial	General	Music	Adult Contemp.
KPDQ	93.7	Commercial	General/Religious	Music/Talk	Gospel
KTIL	94.1	Commercial	General	Music/News	Easy Listening
KUKN	94.5	Commercial	General	Music	Country
KKBC	95.3	Commercial	General	Music	Oldies
KXJM	95.5	n/a	General	Music/News/Talk	n/a
KKSN	97.1	Commercial	General	Music	Oldies
KUPL	98.7	n/a	General	Music/Talk	n/a
KUBQ	98.7	Commercial	General	Music	Top 40
KWJJ	99.5	Commercial	General	Music	Country
KRKT	99.9	Commercial	General	Music/News	Country
KKRZ	100.3	Commercial	General	Music	Top 40
KPPT	100.7	Commercial	General	Music	Classic Rock
KUFO	101.1	n/a	General	Music	n/a
KINK	101.9	Commercial	General	Music/Talk	Alternative
KCRX	102.3	Commercial	General	Music/News/Sports	Classic Rock
KYTE	102.7	n/a	General	Music	n/a
KKCW	103.3	Commercial	General	Music	Adult Contemp.
KXPC	103.7	n/a	General	Music/News	n/a
KVAS	103.9	Commercial	General	Music/News	Country
KMCQ	104.5	Commercial	General	Music/News	Adult Contemp.
KCMB	104.7	Commercial	General	Music/News	Country
KRSK	105.1	Commercial	General	Music	Adult Contemp.
KLOO	106.1	n/a	General	Music/News	n/a
KVMX	107.5	n/a	General	Music	n/a
KHPE	107.9	n/a	General/Religious	Educational/Music/Talk	n/a

Note: Stations included cover the Portland DMA (Designated Market Area); n/a not available
BurrellesLuce, MediaContacts Online, January 2006

CLIMATE

Average and Extreme Temperatures

Temperature	Jan	Feb	Mar	Apr	May	Jun	Jul	Aug	Sep	Oct	Nov	Dec	Yr.
Extreme High (°F)	65	71	83	93	100	102	107	107	105	92	73	64	107
Average High (°F)	45	50	56	61	68	73	80	79	74	64	53	46	62
Average Temp. (°F)	39	43	48	52	58	63	68	68	63	55	46	41	54
Average Low (°F)	34	36	39	42	48	53	57	57	52	46	40	36	45
Extreme Low (°F)	-2	-3	19	29	29	39	43	44	34	26	13	6	-3

Note: Figures cover the years 1926-1992
Source: National Climatic Data Center, International Station Meteorological Climate Summary, 9/96

Average Precipitation/Snowfall/Humidity

Precip./Humidity	Jan	Feb	Mar	Apr	May	Jun	Jul	Aug	Sep	Oct	Nov	Dec	Yr.
Avg. Precip. (in.)	5.5	4.2	3.8	2.4	2.0	1.5	0.5	0.9	1.7	3.0	5.5	6.6	37.5
Avg. Snowfall (in.)	3	1	1	Tr	Tr	0	0	0	0	0	1	2	7
Avg. Rel. Hum. 7am (%)	85	86	86	84	80	78	77	81	87	90	88	87	84
Avg. Rel. Hum. 4pm (%)	75	67	60	55	53	50	45	45	49	61	74	79	59

Note: Figures cover the years 1926-1992; Tr = Trace amounts (<0.05 in. of rain; <0.5 in. of snow)
Source: National Climatic Data Center, International Station Meteorological Climate Summary, 9/96

Weather Conditions

Temperature			Daytime Sky			Precipitation		
5°F & below	32°F & below	90°F & above	Clear	Partly cloudy	Cloudy	0.01 inch or more precip.	0.1 inch or more snow/ice	Thunder-storms
<1	37	11	67	116	182	152	4	7

Note: Figures are average number of days per year and cover the years 1926-1992
Source: National Climatic Data Center, International Station Meteorological Climate Summary, 9/96

HAZARDOUS WASTE

Superfund Sites

Portland has three hazardous waste sites on the EPA's Superfund Final National Priorities List: **Harbor Oil Inc.**; **Mccormick & Baxter Creosoting Co. (Portland Plant)**; **Portland Harbor**. *U.S. Environmental Protection Agency, Final National Priorities List, March 20, 2007*

AIR & WATER QUALITY

Air Quality Index

Area	Percent of Days when Air Quality was...[2]				AQI Statistics	
	Good	Moderate	Unhealthy for Sensitive Groups	Unhealthy	Maximum	Median
MSA[1]	75.1	23.0	1.9	0.0	150	34

Note: The Air Quality Index (AQI) is an index for reporting daily air quality. EPA calculates the AQI for five major air pollutants regulated by the Clean Air Act: ground-level ozone, particle pollution (also known as particulate matter), carbon monoxide, sulfur dioxide, and nitrogen dioxide. The AQI runs from 0 to 500. The higher the AQI value, the greater the level of air pollution and the greater health concern. There are six AQI categories: "Good" The AQI is between 0 and 50. Air quality is considered satisfactory; "Moderate" The AQI is between 51 and 100. Air quality is acceptable; "Unhealthy for Sensitive Groups" When AQI values are between 101 and 150, members of sensitive groups may experience health effects; "Unhealthy" When AQI values are between 151 and 200 everyone may begin to experience health effects; "Very Unhealthy" AQI values between 201 and 300 trigger a health alert; "Hazardous" AQI values over 300 trigger health warnings of emergency conditions; (1) Metropolitan Statistical Area - see Appendix A for areas included; (2) Based on 365 days with AQI data in 2005.
Source: U.S. Environmental Protection Agency, Air Quality Index Report, 2005

Air Quality Index Pollutants

Area	Percent of Days when AQI Pollutant was...[2]					
	Carbon Monoxide	Nitrogen Dioxide	Ozone	Sulfur Dioxide	Particulate Matter 2.5	Particulate Matter 10
MSA[1]	1.4	0.0	32.1	0.0	65.8	0.8

Note: The Air Quality Index (AQI) is an index for reporting daily air quality. EPA calculates the AQI for five major air pollutants regulated by the Clean Air Act: ground-level ozone, particle pollution (also known as particulate matter), carbon monoxide, sulfur dioxide, and nitrogen dioxide. The AQI runs from 0 to 500. The higher the AQI value, the greater the level of air pollution and the greater the health concern; (1) Metropolitan Statistical Area - see Appendix A for areas included; (2) Based on 365 days with AQI data in 2005.
Source: U.S. Environmental Protection Agency, Air Quality Index Report, 2005

Number of Days with Air Quality Index Values Greater than 100

Area	Trend Sites (14)								All Sites (49)
	1998	1999	2000	2001	2002	2003	2004	2005	2005
MSA[1]	3	5	7	3	6	0	3	4	4

Note: An AQI value greater than 100 indicates that air quality would have been in the unhealthful range on that day. Data from exceptional events are not included. These counts are presented in two ways. First, the counts are based on sites having an adequate record of monitoring data during the trend period (trend sites). These counts represent the relative change in the number of days with AQI values greater than 100. In the last column, the counts are based on all sites with data in the most recent year (because it is possible for a site to have data in the most recent year but not enough data to be a trend site); (1) Metropolitan Statistical Area - see Appendix A for areas included; n/a not available.
Source: U.S. Environmental Protection Agency, Air Trends Fact Book 2005

Maximum Pollutant Concentrations

	Particulate Matter 10 (ug/m³)	Particulate Matter 2.5 (ug/m³)	Ozone 1-hour (ppm)	Carbon Monoxide (ppm)	Sulfur Dioxide (ppm)	Nitrogen Dioxide (ppm)	Lead (ug/m³)
MSA[1] Level	54	26	0.091	5	0.006	n/a	n/a
NAAQS[2]	150	65	0.125	9	0.140	0.053	1.50
Met NAAQS[2]	Yes	Yes	Yes	Yes	Yes	n/a	n/a

Note: Data from exceptional events are not included; (1) Metropolitan Statistical Area - see Appendix A for areas included; (2) National Ambient Air Quality Standards; n/a not available
Units: ppm = parts per million; ug/m³ = micrograms per cubic meter
Source: U.S. Environmental Protection Agency, Air Trends Fact Book 2005

Watershed Health

The U.S. Environmental Protection Agency monitors the health of the aquatic resources for the nation's 2,000+ watersheds. **The Lower Willamette watershed serves the Portland area and received an overall Index of Watershed Indicators (IWI) score of 5 (more serious problems - low vulnerability)**. The IWI score is based on seven condition and nine vulnerability indicators. The overall IWI score ranges from 1 (best health) to 6 (worst health). The Condition Indicators include: designated use attainment, fish and wildlife consumption advisories, source water condition, contaminated sediments, ambient water quality, and wetlands loss index. The Vulnerability Indicators include: aquatic species at risk, conventional and toxic loads over permitted limits, urban and agricultural runoff potential, population change, hydrologic modification, estuarine pollution susceptibility, and air deposition. *Note: The IWI is no longer being updated by the U.S. EPA. Source: U.S. Environmental Protection Agency, Index of Watershed Indicators, October 26, 2001*

Drinking Water

Water System Name	Pop. Served	Primary Water Source Type	Number of Violations in 2006[a]		
			Health Based	Significant Monitoring	Monitoring
Portland Bureau of Water Works	539,200	Surface	None	None	None

Note: (a) Based on violation data from January 1, 2006 to December 31, 2006
Source: U.S. Environmental Protection Agency, Office of Ground Water and Drinking Water, Safe Drinking Water Information System (data extracted April 12, 2007)

Portland tap water is neutral, very soft and not fluoridated.
Editor & Publisher Market Guide, 2005

Provo, Utah

Background

Provo is situated on the Provo River at a site that was once under the waters of Lake Bonneville in a prehistoric period. Year after year, Provo enjoys one of the country's highest employment rates, a growing high-tech economy, a minuscule crime rate, and a magnificent natural environment. The seat of Utah County, it lies at the base of the steep Wasatch Mountains, with Provo Peak rising to a height of 11,054 feet just east of the city, making Provo convenient to many of Utah's famed ski areas and to the Uinta National Forest.

The Spanish missionaries Francisco Silvestre Velez de Escalante and Francisco Atanasio Dominguez, exploring for a more direct route from present-day New Mexico to California, were probably the first Europeans to view the area, but they did not stay long or establish a permanent mission. They did, however, note that the area could easily be irrigated and developed into an important agricultural settlement. Etienne Prevot, a Canadian trapper and explorer, likewise visited but did not settle, though he too remarked on the beauty and potential of the site. They also noted the presence of the site's original inhabitants, the Ute Indians, who held an important fish festival on the river every spring.

Permanent European settlement of Provo is strongly linked to Mormon history. In 1849, John S. Higbee, with 30 families in a wagon train, left the larger Salt Lake City community to move north. As they arrived at the site, they confronted a group of Ute, with whom white settlers had already been in some conflict. A short-lived peace agreement gave way to further conflict and a series of battles, after which the Indians agreed to resettlement. Peace ensued, and Provo was not subject to long periods of Indian hostilities as were many other young Western towns.

Irrigation has been central to Provo's success, and in the very year of Higbee's arrival, two large canals were dug, taking water from the Provo River. Thereafter, grain mills were constructed to serve the needs of nearby farmers. Important rail links were completed in the 1870s connecting Provo to Salt Lake City and to the Union Pacific System, and giving impetus to the region's agricultural and mining industries.

Provo's growth then took off, with an electric generating plant built in 1890, and in 1914, an interurban commuter rail service established between Provo and Salt Lake City. The town had become a major regional industrial center, with ironworks, flour mills, and brickyards. Today, industries include computer hardware and software (Novell, Inc.), food processing, clothing, and electronic equipment.

Provo's industrial dynamism and creativity is reflected in the careers of two of its favorite sons. Dr. Harvey Fletcher, who was associated with Bell Laboratories, was the inventor of many aids to the deaf and hearing-impaired, and was an important early leader of the National Acoustic Association. Philo T. Farnsworth, born in Beaver, Utah, but raised in Provo, was a college student in 1924 when he developed the fundamental concepts of television at the age of 18.

Provo is home to Farnsworth's alma mater, Brigham Young University, a private university operated by The Church of Jesus Christ of Latter-day Saints. The school was founded in 1875 and has earned national respect for everything from its football team and undergraduate liberal arts program to its graduate programs in business and law.

In 2001, Provo resident Larry H. Miller donated the Larry H. Miller Field to Brigham Young University. Initially, the stadium hosted the Provo Angels minor league professional baseball team, but the stadium in recent years has been used as a training and competitive facility by other teams, including the Brigham Young Cougars.

The climate of Provo is semi-arid continental. Summers are generally hot and dry. Winters are cold but not severe. Precipitation is generally light, with most of the rain falling in the spring.

Rankings

General Rankings

- Provo was ranked #146 out of 331 metro areas in *Cities Ranked & Rated*. Criteria: cost of living; climate; crime; transportation; economy and jobs; education; arts and culture; health and healthcare; leisure. *Cities Ranked & Rated, 1st Edition, 2004*

- The Provo area was selected as one of "60 Cheap Places to Live" in the U.S. The area appeared in the "Steroid Cities" (fast-growing, business-friendly metro areas) category. *Forbes.com, August 20, 2004*

Business/Finance Rankings

- Provo was selected as one of the best places to start and grow a company by *Entrepreneur* and the National Policy Research Council. The Provo metro area ranked #32 out of 63 mid-size metro areas. Criteria: business formation and growth (firms started four to 14 years ago that still employ at least 5 people and experienced rapid growth over the last four years). *Entrepreneur/National Policy Research Council, "Hot Cities for Entrepreneurs," September 2006*

- The Provo metro area appeared on the Milken Institute "2005 Best Performing Cities" index. Rank: #23 out of 200 large metro areas. Criteria: job growth; wage and salary growth; high-tech output growth. *Milken Institute, "2005 Best Performing Cities," February 2006*

- The Provo metro area was selected as one of "The Best Cities for Doing Business in America." *Inc.* magazine measured employment growth in 393 regions using the following criteria: recent growth trend; mid-term growth; long-term trend; and current year growth. The Provo metro area ranked #9 among mid-sized metro areas and #40 overall. *Inc., May 2006*

- Provo was identified as one of the top 10 metro areas with the greatest number of *Inc. 500* companies per million residents. The area ranked #1. *Inc., September 2006*

- *Forbes* ranked the 200 most populous metro areas in the U.S. in terms of the "Best Places for Business and Careers." The Provo metro area was ranked #2. Criteria: business costs (labor, energy, tax and office space expenses); living costs (housing, transportation, food and other household expenditures); education levels of the work force; job growth; income growth; migration trends; crime rates; and culture/leisure. *Forbes, April 23, 2007*

- Provo was identified as one of the top 20 metro areas with the highest rate of home price appreciation in 2006. The area ranked #3 with a one-year price appreciation of 19.9% through the 4th quarter 2006. *Office of Federal Housing Enterprise Oversight, House Price Index, 4th Quarter 2006*

Health/Environment Rankings

- The Provo metro area appeared in *Country Home's* "2007 Best Green Places Report". The area ranked #62. Criteria included: air and watershed quality; miles of mass transit; green power; number of farmer's markets, organic producers and groceries. *Country Home, "2007 Best Green Places Report," April 2007*

- Ortho-McNeil Neurologics, in partnership with Sperling's BestPlaces, analyzed 110 metro areas and identified those U.S. cities with the highest prevalence of factors that are most commonly associated with migraine headaches. The Provo metro area ranked #85. Criteria: number of migraine-related drug prescriptions per capita; lifestyle factors that can contribute to migraines; environmental factors that can trigger migraines; and consumption of migraine-triggering foods. *Ortho-McNeil Neurologics, "America's Migraine Hot Spots," March 14, 2006*

- Sperling's BestPlaces ranked 331 metro areas and identified the most and least stressful U.S. cities. The Provo metro area ranked #114 out of 114 mid-size metro areas (#1 = most stressful). Criteria: divorce rate; unemployment rate; violent and property crime; suicide rate; commute time; mental health; alcohol consumption; cloudy days. *www.BestPlaces.net, January 9, 2004*

Seniors/Retirement Rankings

■ A.G. Edwards ranked America's 500 top-performing communities based on their residents' personal savings and investing behavior. The Provo metro area ranked #224 with an index score of 102.67 (national average = 100.00). A dozen statistical factors were measured including: participation in retirement savings plans; personal debt levels; and home ownership. *A.G. Edwards, "2006 Nest Egg Index", September 6, 2006*

Children/Family Rankings

■ The Provo metro area was selected as one of the "Best Cities for Relocating Families" by Worldwide ERC and Primacy Relocation. Criteria: tax rates; average home costs and home appreciation; ability to qualify for in-state tuition; service quality of local utilities; per-capita volunteerism; auto taxes; and quantity of fun, family-friendly events and venues. *Worldwide ERC and Primacy Relocation, "2006 Best Cities for Relocating Families"*

Safety Rankings

■ Farmers Insurance Group of Companies, in partnership with Sperling's BestPlaces, ranked 331 metro areas and identified the "Most Secure U.S. Place to Live." The Provo metro area ranked #8 out of the top 20 in the mid-size city category (150,000 to 500,000 residents). Criteria: crime rates; risk of natural disasters; and job loss numbers. *Farmers Insurance Group, "25 Most Secure U.S. Place to Live," June 6, 2005*

Sports/Recreation Rankings

■ *Golf Digest* ranked 330 metro areas in the U.S. in terms of golf. The Provo metro area was ranked #232. Criteria: access to golf; weather; value of golf; and quality of golf. *Golf Digest, "Metro Golf Rankings," August 2005*

Miscellaneous Rankings

■ Provo was selected as a "Great College Town" by ePodunk. The city ranked #10 in the mid-sized city category. ePodunk.com looked at communities with four-year colleges and a total student enrollment of at least 1,500. Communities where the student ratio was too low or too high were ruled out, as were small cities with low rates of owner-occupied housing. Fifteen variables were then applied to assess arts and culture, recreation, intellectual activity, historic preservation, and cost of living. *www.ePodunk.com, April, 2002*

Business Environment

CITY FINANCES

City Government Finances

Component	2003-2004 ($000)	2003-2004 ($ per capita)
Total Revenues	121,738	1,158
Total Expenditures	126,812	1,206
Debt Outstanding	122,265	1,163
Cash and Securities	107,844	1,025

Source: U.S Census Bureau, Government Finances 2003-2004

City Government Revenue by Source

Source	2003-2004 ($000)	2003-2004 ($ per capita)
General Revenue		
From Federal Government	10,970	104
From State Government	3,522	33
From Local Governments	193	2
Taxes		
Property	12,020	114
Sales	19,307	184
Personal Income	0	0
License	0	0
Charges	18,364	175
Liquor Store	0	0
Utility	49,723	473
Employee Retirement	0	0
Other	7,639	73

Source: U.S Census Bureau, Government Finances 2003-2004

City Government Expenditures by Function

Function	2003-2004 ($000)	2003-2004 ($ per capita)	2003-2004 (%)
General Expenditures			
Airports	2,370	23	1.9
Corrections	0	0	0.0
Education	0	0	0.0
Fire Protection	7,052	67	5.6
Governmental Administration	8,371	80	6.6
Health	0	0	0.0
Highways	6,373	61	5.0
Hospitals	0	0	0.0
Housing and Community Development	10,035	95	7.9
Interest on General Debt	2,738	26	2.2
Libraries	3,336	32	2.6
Parking	0	0	0.0
Parks and Recreation	5,505	52	4.3
Police Protection	11,760	112	9.3
Public Welfare	0	0	0.0
Sewerage	7,192	68	5.7
Solid Waste Management	2,532	24	2.0
Liquor Store	0	0	0.0
Utility	51,882	493	40.9
Employee Retirement	0	0	0.0
Other	7,666	73	6.0

Source: U.S Census Bureau, Government Finances 2003-2004

Municipal Bond Ratings

Area	Moody's
City	Aaa

Source: Mergent Bond Record, January 2007 (unless noted otherwise)

DEMOGRAPHICS

Population Growth

Area	1990 Census	2000 Census	2006 Estimate	2011 Projection	Population Growth (%)	
					1990-2000	2000-2011
City	87,148	105,166	109,959	114,999	20.7	9.3
MSA[1]	269,407	376,774	454,396	515,085	39.9	36.7
U.S.	248,709,873	281,421,906	298,021,266	312,383,955	13.2	11.0

Note: (1) Metropolitan Statistical Area - see Appendix B for areas included
Source: Claritas, Inc.

Number of Households and Average Household Size

Area	2006 Estimate	2006 Average Household Size
City	31,498	3.49
MSA[1]	124,826	3.64
U.S.	112,267,302	2.65

Note: (1) Metropolitan Statistical Area - see Appendix B for areas included
Source: Claritas, Inc.

Race and Ethnicity

Area	White Alone[2]	Black Alone[2]	Asian Alone[2]	Other Race Alone[2]	Hispanic[3]
City	86.2	0.4	2.0	11.3	14.0
MSA[1]	91.3	0.3	1.2	7.3	8.5
U.S.	73.3	12.4	4.2	10.1	14.5

Note: Figures are 2006 estimates; (1) Metropolitan Statistical Area - see Appendix B for areas included
(2) Alone is defined as not being in combination with one or more other races; (3) May be of any race.
Source: Claritas, Inc.

Segregation

City		MSA[1]	
Index[2]	Rank[3]	Index[2]	Rank[4]
36.9	91	46.0	263

Note: Figures are based on an analysis of Census 2000 data; (1) Metropolitan Statistical Area - see Appendix A
for areas included; (2) White/Black Dissimilarity Index—the most commonly used measure of segregation
between two groups, reflecting their relative distributions across neighborhoods within a city or metropolitan
area. It can range in value from 0, indicating complete integration, to 100, indicating complete segregation; (3)
Ranges from 1 (most segregated) to 100 (least segregated) and includes all the cities in this book; (4) Ranges
from 1 (most segregated) to 318 (least segregated) and includes 318 metropolitan areas.
Source: www.CensusScope.org

Ancestry

Area	German	Irish[2]	English	American	Italian	Polish	French[3]	Scottish
City	11.5	4.7	30.4	4.6	2.4	0.6	2.3	4.9
MSA[1]	10.8	4.7	33.5	6.9	2.1	0.5	2.2	4.8
U.S.	15.2	10.9	8.7	7.3	5.6	3.2	3.0	1.7

Note: Figures include multiple ancestry (e.g. if a person reported being Irish and Italian, they were included in
both columns); (1) Metropolitan Statistical Area - see Appendix A for areas included; (2) Includes Celtic; (3)
Includes Alsatian but excludes Basque
Source: Census 2000, Summary File 3

Foreign-Born Population

Area	Percent of Population Born in							
	Any Foreign Country	Europe	Asia	Africa	Oceania[2]	Canada	Mexico	Latin America[3]
City	9.6	0.9	1.5	0.2	0.3	0.7	3.8	2.2
MSA[1]	6.3	0.7	0.9	0.1	0.2	0.6	2.5	1.4
U.S.	11.1	1.7	2.9	0.3	0.1	0.3	3.3	2.5

Note: (1) Metropolitan Statistical Area - see Appendix A for areas included; (2) Includes Australia, New
Zealand subregion, Melanesia, Micronesia, Polynesia, and Oceania n.e.c; (3) Includes Central America
(excluding Mexico), South America, and the Caribbean.
Source: Census 2000, Summary File 3

Marriage Status

Area	Never Married	Now Married (excluding Separated)	Separated	Widowed	Divorced
City	47.2	45.9	0.6	2.4	3.9
MSA[1]	32.6	58.6	0.8	3.0	4.9
U.S.	27.1	54.4	2.2	6.6	9.7

Note: Figures are percentages and cover the population 15 years of age and older;
(1) Metropolitan Statistical Area - see Appendix A for areas included
Source: Census 2000, Summary File 3

Age Distribution

Area	Percent of Population						
	Under Age 5	Age 5 to 17	Age 18 to 34	Age 35 to 49	Age 50 to 64	Age 65 to 79	80 Years and Over
City	8.6	13.5	56.5	10.0	5.7	4.0	1.7
MSA[1]	10.9	23.0	36.0	15.4	8.2	4.8	1.7
U.S.	6.8	18.9	23.7	23.5	14.8	9.2	3.2

Note: (1) Metropolitan Statistical Area - see Appendix A for areas included
Source: Census 2000, Summary File 3

Male/Female Ratio

Area	Males	Females	Males per 100 Females
City	52,988	56,971	93.0
MSA[1]	225,398	228,998	98.4
U.S.	146,712,712	151,308,554	97.0

Note: Figures are 2006 estimates; (1) Metropolitan Statistical Area -
see Appendix B for areas included
Source: Claritas, Inc.

Religion

Area	Catholic	Southern Baptist	United Methodist	ELCA[1]	LDS[2]	Presbyterian Church USA	Jewish Est.	Muslim Est.
County	1.0	0.1	0.0	0.0	88.1	0.1	0.0	0.0
U.S.	22.0	7.1	3.7	1.8	1.5	1.1	2.2	0.6

Note: Figures are the number of adherents as a percentage of the total population; Adherents are defined as all
members, including full members, their children and the estimated number of other participants who are not
considered members (e.g. the baptized, those not confirmed, those regularly attending services, etc.);
(1) Evangelical Lutheran Church in America; (2) The Church of Jesus Christ of Latter Day Saints
Source: Reprinted with permission from Religious Congregations and Membership in the United States 2000
(Nashville, Glenmary Research Center, 2002) Copyright Association of Statisticians of American Religious
Bodies. All rights reserved.

ECONOMY

Gross Metropolitan Product

Area	2002	2003	2004	2005	2005 Rank[2]
MSA[1]	9.9	10.5	11.6	12.9	146

Note: Figures are in billions of dollars; (1) Provo-Orem, UT Metropolitan Statistical Area - see Appendix A for
areas included; (2) Rank ranges from 1 to 361
Source: The U.S. Conference of Mayors, "U.S. Metro Economies: GMP - The Engines of America's Growth,"
January 2007

Economic Growth

Area	1995 GMP	2005 GMP	Average Annual Growth Rate	Growth Rate Rank[2]
MSA[1]	6.5	12.9	7.0	41

Note: Figures are in billions of dollars; GMP = Gross Metropolitan Product; (1) Provo-Orem, UT Metropolitan
Statistical Area - see Appendix A for areas included; (2) Rank ranges from 1 to 361
Source: The U.S. Conference of Mayors, "U.S. Metro Economies: GMP - The Engines of America's Growth,"
January 2007

INCOME

Per Capita/Median/Average Income

Area	Per Capita ($)	Median Household ($)	Average Household ($)
City	15,179	38,674	51,756
MSA[1]	18,489	53,785	66,823
U.S.	25,129	48,775	65,849

Note: Figures are 2006 estimates; (1) Metropolitan Statistical Area - see Appendix B for areas included
Source: Claritas, Inc.

Household Income Distribution

Area	Under $15,000	$15,000 -24,999	$25,000 -34,999	$35,000 -49,999	$50,000 -74,999	$75,000 -99,000	$100,000 -149,999	$150,000 and up
				Percent of Households Earning				
City	14.1	16.0	15.1	19.5	16.7	8.2	7.1	3.3
MSA[1]	8.0	9.7	11.1	17.7	23.0	13.2	12.0	5.3
U.S.	13.3	11.0	11.3	15.7	19.5	11.8	11.0	6.4

Note: Figures are 2006 estimates; (1) Metropolitan Statistical Area - see Appendix B for areas included
Source: Claritas, Inc.

Poverty Rates by Age

Area	All Ages	Under 5 Years Old	5 to 17 Years Old	18 to 64 Years Old	65 Years and Over
City	26.8	1.5	2.0	23.0	0.3
MSA[1]	12.0	1.1	1.9	8.6	0.3
U.S.	12.4	1.2	3.0	6.9	1.2

Note: Figures are percent of population with income in 1999 below poverty level and only include population for whom poverty status is determined; (1) Metropolitan Statistical Area - see Appendix A for areas included
Source: Census 2000, Summary File 3

Personal Bankruptcy Filing Rate

Area	2003	2004	2005
Utah County	6.64	5.98	6.35
U.S.	5.57	5.31	6.88

Note: Numbers are per 1,000 population and include Chapter 7 and Chapter 13 filings
Source: Federal Deposit Insurance Corporation (FDIC), Regional Economic Conditions (RECON), 3/24/2006

EMPLOYMENT

Labor Force and Employment

Area	Civilian Labor Force			Workers Employed		
	Dec. 2005	Dec. 2006	% Chg.	Dec. 2005	Dec. 2006	% Chg.
City	63,382	65,520	3.4	61,165	64,038	4.7
MSA[1]	209,912	217,254	3.5	203,273	212,819	4.7
U.S.	149,874,000	152,571,000	1.8	142,918,000	146,081,000	2.2

Note: Data is not seasonally adjusted and covers workers 16 years of age and older;
(1) Metropolitan Statistical Area - see Appendix B for areas included
Source: Bureau of Labor Statistics, http://stats.bls.gov

Unemployment Rate

Area	2006											
	Jan.	Feb.	Mar.	Apr.	May	Jun.	Jul.	Aug.	Sep.	Oct.	Nov.	Dec.
City	4.3	4.3	3.7	3.5	3.5	3.5	3.7	3.6	2.7	2.4	2.5	2.3
MSA[1]	3.9	3.9	3.3	3.2	3.1	3.1	3.3	3.3	2.4	2.1	2.2	2.0
U.S.	5.1	5.1	4.8	4.5	4.4	4.8	5.0	4.6	4.4	4.1	4.3	4.3

Note: Data is not seasonally adjusted and covers workers 16 years of age and older; All figures are percentages; (1) Metropolitan Statistical Area - see Appendix B for areas included
Source: Bureau of Labor Statistics, http://stats.bls.gov

Employment by Occupation

Occupation Classification	City (%)	MSA[1] (%)	U.S. (%)
Sales and Office	28.8	27.7	26.7
Professional and Related	28.6	24.3	20.2
Service	16.1	14.0	14.9
Production, Transportation, and Material Moving	9.4	11.4	14.6
Management, Business, and Financial	9.7	12.2	13.5
Construction, Extraction, and Maintenance	7.1	10.1	9.4
Farming, Forestry, and Fishing	0.2	0.3	0.7

Note: Figures cover employed civilians 16 years of age and older;
(1) Metropolitan Statistical Area - see Appendix A for areas included
Source: Census 2000, Summary File 3

Employment by Industry

Sector	MSA[1]		U.S.
	Number of Employees	Percent of Total	Percent of Total
Government	25,300	13.5	16.3
Education and Health Services	40,000	21.4	13.2
Professional and Business Services	22,800	12.2	12.9
Retail Trade	24,000	12.8	11.5
Manufacturing	19,200	10.3	10.2
Leisure and Hospitality	13,400	7.2	9.5
Financial Activities	6,600	3.5	6.1
Construction	n/a	n/a	5.5
Wholesale Trade	4,700	2.5	4.3
Other Services	4,100	2.2	3.9
Transportation and Utilities	2,200	1.2	3.7
Information	8,000	4.3	2.2
Natural Resources and Mining	n/a	n/a	0.5

Note: Figures cover non-farm employment as of December 2006 and are not seasonally adjusted;
(1) Metropolitan Statistical Area - see Appendix B for areas included; n/a not available
Source: Bureau of Labor Statistics, http://stats.bls.gov

Occupations with Greatest Projected Employment Growth: 2002 - 2012

Occupation[1]	2002 Employment	2012 Projected Employment	Numeric Employment Change	Percent Employment Change
Retail Salespersons	38,530	48,730	10,200	26.5
Customer Service Representatives	23,440	33,210	9,770	41.7
Cashiers	29,130	38,670	9,540	32.7
Combined Food Preparation and Serving Workers, Including Fast Food	15,360	23,580	8,220	53.5
Waiters and Waitresses	16,730	24,740	8,010	47.9
Registered Nurses	15,180	22,000	6,820	44.9
Janitors and Cleaners, Except Maids and Housekeeping Cleaners	18,530	24,650	6,120	33.0
Truck Drivers, Heavy and Tractor-Trailer	18,170	24,150	5,980	32.9
Carpenters	15,180	20,710	5,530	36.4
Teacher Assistants	14,480	19,970	5,490	37.9

Note: Projections cover Utah; (1) Sorted by numeric employment change
Source: www.projectionscentral.com, State Occupational Projections, 2002-2012 Long-Term Projections

Fastest Growing Occupations: 2002 - 2012

Occupation[1]	2002 Employment	2012 Projected Employment	Numeric Employment Change	Percent Employment Change
Network Systems and Data Communications Analysts	1,300	2,270	970	74.6
Medical Assistants	3,300	5,590	2,290	69.4
Home Health Aides	2,080	3,510	1,430	68.8
Pharmacists	1,870	3,120	1,250	66.8
Physical Therapist Aides	670	1,110	440	65.7
Personal and Home Care Aides	2,150	3,520	1,370	63.7
Social and Human Service Assistants	4,200	6,870	2,670	63.6
Computer Software Engineers, Systems Software	1,920	3,140	1,220	63.5
Physician Assistants	410	660	250	61.0
Architects, Except Landscape and Naval	730	1,170	440	60.3

Note: Projections cover Utah; (1) Sorted by percent employment change and excludes occupations with numeric employment change less than 200
Source: www.projectionscentral.com, State Occupational Projections, 2002-2012 Long-Term Projections

Average Wages

Occupation	$/Hr.	Occupation	$/Hr.
Accountants and Auditors	24.01	Maids and Housekeeping Cleaners	7.69
Automotive Mechanics	17.77	Maintenance and Repair Workers	15.02
Bookkeepers	13.31	Marketing Managers	42.12
Carpenters	14.81	Nuclear Medicine Technologists	n/a
Cashiers	7.74	Nurses, Licensed Practical	15.16
Clerks, General Office	9.99	Nurses, Registered	25.43
Clerks, Receptionists/Information	9.68	Nursing Aides/Orderlies/Attendants	8.64
Clerks, Shipping/Receiving	10.69	Packers and Packagers, Hand	7.85
Computer Programmers	27.33	Physical Therapists	28.87
Computer Support Specialists	17.91	Postal Service Mail Carriers	21.15
Computer Systems Analysts	26.55	Real Estate Brokers	55.71
Cooks, Restaurant	9.15	Retail Salespersons	10.21
Dentists	n/a	Sales Reps., Exc. Tech./Scientific	22.27
Electrical Engineers	26.96	Sales Reps., Tech./Scientific	27.46
Electricians	14.95	Secretaries, Exc. Legal/Med./Exec.	11.31
Financial Managers	36.20	Security Guards	11.81
First-Line Supervisors/Mgrs., Sales	16.73	Surgeons	n/a
Food Preparation Workers	7.53	Teacher Assistants	9.80
General and Operations Managers	37.95	Teachers, Elementary School	17.30
Hairdressers/Cosmetologists	10.89	Teachers, Secondary School	19.20
Internists	91.57	Telemarketers	11.86
Janitors and Cleaners	10.51	Truck Drivers, Heavy/Tractor-Trailer	17.28
Landscaping/Groundskeeping Workers	9.32	Truck Drivers, Light/Delivery Svcs.	11.15
Lawyers	50.69	Waiters and Waitresses	7.55

Note: Wage data is for May 2005 and covers the Provo-Orem, UT Metropolitan Statistics Area - see Appendix B for areas included. Hourly wages for elementary/secondary school teachers and teacher assistants were calculated by the editors from annual wage data assuming a 40 hour work week; n/a not available.
Source: Bureau of Labor Statistics, May 2005 Metro Area Occupational Employment and Wage Estimates

RESIDENTIAL REAL ESTATE

Building Permits

Area	Single-Family			Multi-Family			Total		
	2005	2006p	Pct. Chg.	2005	2006p	Pct. Chg.	2005	2006p	Pct. Chg.
City	260	286	10.0	104	275	164.4	364	561	54.1
U.S.	1,682,000	1,380,000	-18.0	473,300	457,300	-3.4	2,155,300	1,837,300	-14.8

Note: (p) preliminary; figures represent new, privately-owned housing units authorized (unadjusted data); All permit data are based on estimates with imputation; U.S. figures are based on the new 20,000-place series.
Source: U.S. Census Bureau, Manufacturing, Mining, and Construction Statistics

Homeownership and Housing Vacancies

Area	Homeownership Rate[2] (%)			Rental Vacancy Rate[3] (%)			Homeowner Vacancy Rate[4] (%)		
	2004	2005	2006	2004	2005	2006	2004	2005	2006
MSA[1]	n/a	n/a	n/a	n/a	n/a	n/a	n/a	n/a	n/a
U.S.	69.0	68.9	68.8	10.2	9.8	9.7	1.7	1.9	2.4

Note: Comparable 2004 data was not available due to changes in metropolitan area definitions; (1) Metropolitan Statistical Area - see Appendix B for areas included; (2) The proportion of households that are owners; (3) The proportion of the rental inventory that is vacant for rent; (4) The proportion of the homeowner inventory that is vacant for sale; n/a not available
Source: U.S. Census Bureau, Housing Vacancies and Homeownership Annual Statistics: 2006

TAXES

State Corporate Income Tax Rates

State	Rate (%)	Number of Brackets	Low Bracket (Under $)	High Bracket (Over $)
Utah	5.0	1	na	na

Note: Tax rates as of December 31, 2006; na not applicable; Minimum tax is $100.
Source: Tax Foundation, www.taxfoundation.org

State Individual Income Tax Rates

State	Federal Deductibility	Marginal Rate (%)	Number of Brackets	Low Bracket (Under $)	High Bracket (Over $)
Utah	Yes	2.3-6.98 (cc)	6	0	5,000

Note: Tax rates as of December 31, 2006; Brackets apply to single taxpayers and married people filing separately; na not applicable; (cc) In 2007 an optional 5.35% flat tax will be available.
Source: Tax Foundation, www.taxfoundation.org

Various State and Local Tax Rates

State and Local Sales and Use (%)	State Sales and Use (%)	Gasoline ($/gal.)	Cigarette ($/pack)	Spirits ($/gal.)	Table Wine ($/gal.)	Beer ($/gal.)
6.5	4.75	0.25	0.70	9.66 (b)	(i)	0.41

Note: Tax rates as of December 31, 2006; (b) States where the state government controls all sales. Excise tax rate is calculated using methodology designed by the Distilled Spirits Council of the United States (DISCUS); (i) Products are subject to ad valorem mark-up and excise taxes. Only license state volume-based tax rates are shown. Some control states also levy volume-based taxes in addition to their percentage ad valorem taxes.
Source: Tax Foundation, www.taxfoundation.org; The Sales Tax Clearinghouse, www.thestc.com

State Tax Burdens

Area	Combined State and Local Tax Burden		Combined Federal, State and Local Tax Burden	
	Percent	Rank	Percent	Rank
Utah	10.5	22	29.5	34
U.S. Average	10.6	-	31.6	-

Note: Figures are for 2006 and measure taxes as a percentage of income
Source: Tax Foundation, www.taxfoundation.org

Internal Revenue Service Tax Audits

IRS District	Percent of Returns Audited				
	1996	1997	1998	1999	2000
Rocky Mountain	0.73	0.67	0.49	0.28	0.20
U.S.	0.66	0.61	0.46	0.31	0.20

Note: Figures cover IRS district audits of federal income tax returns filed by individuals. Geographic data on district audits after the year 2000 are being withheld by the IRS. TRAC is challenging this policy.
Source: Syracuse University, Transactional Records Access Clearinghouse (TRAC), "Odds of IRS District Tax Audit 2000"

COMMERCIAL
UTILITIES

Typical Monthly Electric Bills

Area	Commercial Service ($/month)		Industrial Service ($/month)	
	3 kW demand 1,000 kWh	40 kW demand 14,000 kWh	1,000 kW demand 200,000 kWh	50,000 kW demand 15,000,000 kWh
City	n/a	n/a	n/a	n/a
Average[1]	123	1,413	22,000	1,306,315

Note: Based on total rates in effect July 1, 2006; (1) average based on 196 utilities; n/a not available
Source: Edison Electric Institute, Typical Bills and Average Rates Report, Summer 2006

TRANSPORTATION

Means of Transportation to Work

Area	Car/Truck/Van		Public Transportation			Bicycle	Walked	Other Means	Worked at Home
	Drove Alone	Car-pooled	Bus	Subway	Railroad				
City	63.2	15.5	1.7	0.0	0.0	1.9	12.8	0.6	4.1
MSA[1]	72.5	14.9	1.3	0.0	0.0	0.8	4.9	0.5	5.0
U.S.	75.7	12.2	2.5	1.5	0.5	0.4	2.9	1.0	3.3

Note: Figures are percentages and cover workers 16 years of age and older;
(1) Metropolitan Statistical Area - see Appendix A for areas included
Source: Census 2000, Summary File 3

Travel Time to Work

Area	Less Than 15 Minutes	15 to 29 Minutes	30 to 44 Minutes	45 to 59 Minutes	60 Minutes or More
City	55.7	32.3	5.6	3.1	3.3
MSA[1]	45.0	35.9	10.7	4.2	4.2
U.S.	29.4	36.1	19.1	7.4	8.0

Note: Figures are percentages and include workers 16 years old and over; (1) Metropolitan Statistical Area -
see Appendix A for areas included
Source: Census 2000, Summary File 3

Public Transportation

Agency name:	None

Source: Federal Transit Administration, National Transit Database, 2005

Air Transportation

Airport name and code:	Salt Lake City International (50 miles north) (SLC)
Domestic service (2006)	
Passenger airlines[1]:	31
Passenger enplanements:	10,041,732
Freight carriers[2]:	23
Freight (lbs.):	170,594,605
International service (2005)	
Passenger airlines[1]:	19
Passenger enplanements:	193,314
Freight carriers[2]:	6
Freight (lbs.):	505,225

Note: (1) Includes all major, minor and commuter airlines that carried at least one passenger during the year;
(2) Includes all airlines and freight carriers that transported at least one pound of freight during the year
Source: Bureau of Transportation Statistics, The Intermodal Transportation Database, Air Carriers: T-100
International Market, 2004; Bureau of Transportation Statistics, The Intermodal Transportation Database, Air
Carriers: T-100 Domestic Market, 2005

Other Transportation Statistics

Interstate highways:	I-15
Amtrak service:	Yes
Major waterways/ports:	None

Source: Editor & Publisher Market Guide, 2006; Amtrak.com; Rand McNally 2006 Road Atlas

BUSINESSES

Major Business Headquarters

Company Name	2006 Rankings	
	Fortune[1]	Forbes[2]
No companies listed	-	-

Note: (1) Fortune 500 - companies that produce a 10-K are ranked 1 to 500 based on 2005 revenue; (2) Forbes Largest Private Companies - all private companies with at least $1 billion in annual revenue are ranked 1 to 394; companies listed are located in the city; dashes indicate no ranking
Source: Fortune, April 17, 2006; Forbes, November 9, 2006

Fast-Growing Businesses

According to *Inc.*, Provo is home to two of America's 500 fastest-growing private companies: **Atlas Marketing Group; VitalSmarts**. Criteria: must be an independent, privately-held, U.S. corporation, proprietorship or partnership; net sales of at least $600,000 in FY2002; four-year operating/sales history; holding companies, regulated banks, and utilities were excluded. *Inc., "America's 500 Fastest-Growing Private Companies,"September 2006*

Women-Owned Businesses: 1997 and 2002

Year	All Firms		Firms with Paid Employees			
	Firms	Sales ($000)	Firms	Sales ($000)	Employees	Payroll ($000)
1997	1,296	96,158	189	79,596	1,552	23,983
2002	1,602	148,200	191	108,453	1,241	23,443

Note: Figures cover firms located in the city; Women-owned business are defined as firms in which women own 51% or more of the stock or equity of the company; (a) Withheld to avoid disclosing data for individual companies; (b) Withheld because estimate did not meet publication standards; n/a not available
Source: 1997 Economic Census, Survey of Minority- and Women-Owned Business Enterprises; 2002 Economic Census, Survey of Business Owners (released February 9, 2006)

HOTELS

Hotels/Motels

Area	Hotels/Motels	Average Minimum Rates ($)		
		Tourist	First-Class	Deluxe
City	19	63	81	n/a

Note: n/a not available
Source: OAG Travel Planner Online, Spring 2006

EVENT SITES

Stadiums, Arenas, and Auditoriums

Name	Capacity
Marriott Center/Cougar Stadium	65,000

Source: www.officialtravelguide.com; www.eventective.com; original research

Hotels/Conference Centers

Name	Guest Rooms	Exhibit Space (sq. ft.)	Meeting Space (sq. ft.)
Provo Marriott	330	8,000	28,000

Source: www.officialtravelguide.com; www.eventective.com; original research

Living Environment

COST OF LIVING

Cost of Living Index

Year	Composite Index	Groceries	Housing	Utilities	Trans-portation	Health Care	Misc. Goods/ Services
2004	n/a	n/a	n/a	n/a	n/a	n/a	n/a
2005	n/a	n/a	n/a	n/a	n/a	n/a	n/a
2006	n/a	n/a	n/a	n/a	n/a	n/a	n/a

Note: U.S. = 100; n/a not available
Source: The Council for Community and Economic Research (formerly ACCRA), Cost of Living Index, 2004, 2005 and 2006 4-Quarter Averages

HOUSING

House Price Index (HPI)

Area	National Ranking[2]	Quarterly Change (%)	One-Year Change (%)	Five-Year Change (%)
MSA[1]	3	4.18	19.92	38.59
U.S.[3]	-	1.12	5.87	55.21

Note: The HPI is a weighted repeat sales index. It measures average price changes in repeat sales or refinancings on the same properties. This information is obtained by reviewing repeat mortgage transactions on single-family properties whose mortgages have been purchased or securitized by Fannie Mae or Freddie Mac in January 1975; (1) Metropolitan Statistical Area - see Appendix B for areas included; (2) Rankings are based on annual percentage change for all metro areas containing at least 15,000 transactions over the last 10 years and ranges from 1 to 282; (3) figures based on a weighted division average; all figures are for the period ending December 31, 2006
Source: Office of Federal Housing Enterprise Oversight, House Price Index, March 1, 2007

House Price Valuations

Area	Q4 1999	Q4 2000	Q4 2001	Q4 2002	Q4 2003	Q4 2004	Q4 2005	Q4 2006
MSA[1]	4.1	4.5	6.8	9.0	9.3	8.4	10.7	18.8

Note: Figures show the percentage of over- or under-valuation of single family homes relative to statistically normal house values (e.g. a value of 23.6 indicates that house values are 23.6% overvalued). Statistically normal house values are based on house prices, interest rates, household incomes, population densities, and any historical premiums or discounts metropolitan areas have exhibited over time; (1) Figures cover the Metropolitan Statistical Area - see Appendix B for areas included
Source: Global Insight/National City Corporation, House Prices in America, March 2007

Median Home Prices

Area	2004	2005	2006p	Percent Change 2005 to 2006
Metro Area[1]	n/a	n/a	n/a	n/a
U.S. Average	195.2	219.0	222.0	1.4

Note: Figures are median sales prices of existing single-family homes in thousands of dollars; (p) preliminary; n/a not available; (1) Covers the Provo-Orem, UT Metropolitan Statistical Area - see Appendix B for areas included
Source: National Association of Realtors, Metropolitan Area Prices, 4th Quarter 2006

Housing: Year Structure Built

Area	1990 -2000	1980 -1989	1970 -1979	1960 -1969	1950 -1959	1940 -1949	Before 1940	Median Year
City	24.0	12.7	24.1	13.9	10.5	6.7	8.2	1974
MSA[1]	33.9	12.7	22.8	9.1	8.4	5.4	7.8	1978
U.S.	17.0	15.8	18.5	13.7	12.7	7.3	15.0	1971

Note: Figures are percentages; (1) Metropolitan Statistical Area - see Appendix A for areas included
Source: Census 2000, Summary File 3

Average New Home Price

Area	2004	2005	2006
City[1]	n/a	n/a	n/a
U.S.	253,574	275,712	299,269

Note: n/a not available
Source: The Council for Community and Economic Research (formerly ACCRA), Cost of Living Index, 2004, 2005 and 2006 4-Quarter Averages

Average Apartment Rent

Area	2004	2005	2006
City[1]	n/a	n/a	n/a
U.S.	716	740	766

Note: n/a not available
Source: The Council for Community and Economic Research (formerly ACCRA), Cost of Living Index, 2004, 2005 and 2006 4-Quarter Averages

RESIDENTIAL UTILITIES

Average Residential Utility Costs

Area	All Electric ($/mth)	Part Electric ($/mth)	Other Energy ($/mth)	Phone ($/mth)
City	n/a	n/a	n/a	n/a
U.S.	136.00	76.53	90.52	25.87

Note: n/a not available
Source: The Council for Community and Economic Research (formerly ACCRA), Cost of Living Index, 2006 4-Quarter Average

HEALTH

Average Health Care Costs

Area	Optometrist ($/visit)	Doctor ($/visit)	Dentist ($/visit)
City	n/a	n/a	n/a
U.S.	76.38	76.10	68.72

Note: n/a not available
Source: The Council for Community and Economic Research (formerly ACCRA), Cost of Living Index, 2006 4-Quarter Average

Mortality Rates

ICD-10 Sub-Chapter	ICD-10 Code	Age-Adjusted Death Rate per 100,000 population[1]	U.S. Age-Adjusted Death Rate per 100,000 population
Malignant neoplasms	C00-C97	120.9	185.8
Ischaemic heart diseases	I20-I25	86.2	150.2
Other forms of heart disease	I30-I51	68.5	50.8
Cerebrovascular diseases	I60-I69	50.2	50.0
Chronic lower respiratory diseases	J40-J47	22.9	41.1
Diabetes mellitus	E10-E14	25.7	24.5
Other degenerative diseases of the nervous system	G30-G31	33.3	22.3
Other external causes of accidental injury	W00-X59	15.5	21.2
Influenza and pneumonia	J10-J18	20.2	19.8
Hypertensive diseases	I10-I13	10.8	18.1

Note: ICD-10 = International Classification of Diseases 10th Revision; (1) Figures cover Utah County, UT
Source: Centers for Disease Control and Prevention, National Center for Health Statistics. Compressed Mortality File 1999-2004. CDC WONDER On-line Database, compiled from Compressed Mortality File 1999-2004 Series 20 No. 2J, 2007.

Health Risk Data

Item	Area[1] (%)	U.S. (%)
Adults who have been told they have high blood pressure	13.1	25.5
Adults who have been told they have high blood cholesterol	29.2	35.6
Adults who have been told they have diabetes[2]	6.3	7.3
Adults who have been told they have arthritis	17.5	27.0
Adults who have been told they currently have asthma	6.1	8.0
Adults who are current smokers	6.7	20.6

Note: (1) Figures cover the Metropolitan Statistical Area - see Appendix B for areas included; (2) Figures do not include pregnancy-related diabetes, pre-diabetes or borderline diabetes
Source: Centers for Disease Control and Prevention, Behaviorial Risk Factor Surveillance System, SMART: Selected Metropolitan/Micropolitan Area Trends, 2005

Distribution of Office-Based Physicians

Area	Total	Family/ General Practice	Specialties		
			Medical	Surgical	Other
MSA[1] (number)	448	88	126	118	116
MSA[1] (rate per 10,000 pop.)	11.6	2.3	3.3	3.0	3.0
Metro Average[2] (rate per 10,000 pop.)	19.4	2.1	7.5	4.5	5.3

Note: Data as of December 31, 2004; (1) Metropolitan Statistical Area - see Appendix A for areas included; (2) Average of the 79 unique MSAs and CMSAs in this book
Source: American Medical Association, Physician Characteristics & Distribution in the U.S., 2006

Hospitals

Provo has the following hospitals: 1 general medical and surgical; 1 psychiatric.
AHA Guide to the Healthcare Field 2007

EDUCATION

Public School District Statistics

District Name	Schls	Pupils	Pupil/ Teacher Ratio	Minority Pupils[1] (%)	Free Lunch Eligible[2] (%)	IEP[3] (%)
Provo District	26	13,380	21.2	28.1	34.1	12.9

Note: Table includes regular local school districts with 2,000 or more students; (1) Percentage of students that are not white, non-Hispanic; (2) Percentage of students that are eligible for the free lunch program; (3) Percentage of students that have an Individualized Education Program.
Source: U.S. Department of Education, National Center for Education Statistics, Common Core of Data, Local Education Agency (School District) Universe Survey: School Year 2004-2005; U.S. Department of Education, National Center for Education Statistics, Common Core of Data, Public Elementary/Secondary School Universe Survey: School Year 2004-2005

Educational Quality

School District	Education Quotient[1]	Graduate Outcome[2]	Community Index[3]	Resource Index[4]	Rating[5]
Provo	n/a	n/a	n/a	n/a	n/a

Note: Scores are national percentile rankings and range from 1 (worst) to 99 (best); (1) Combination of the Graduate Outcome, Community and Resource Indexes weighted to reflect the greater importance of the Graduate Outcome and Resource Index; (2) Based on graduation rates and college board scores (SAT/ACT); (3) Based on the surrounding community's level of affluence and adult education; (4) Based on teacher salaries, per-pupil expenditures and student-teacher ratios; (5) School districts receive one of five rankings: Gold Medal (top 16 percent of districts evaluated); Blue Ribbon (top third); Green Light (average); Yellow Light (bottom 25 percent); Red Light (bottom 10 percent).
Source: Expansion Management, "2007 Education Quotient," January 2007

Highest Level of Education

Area	Less than H.S.	H.S. Diploma	Some College, No Deg.	Associate Degree	Bachelors Degree	Masters Degree	Profess. School Degree	Doctorate Degree
City	10.1	14.2	30.4	9.1	25.1	6.3	1.6	3.1
MSA[1]	8.8	19.5	30.7	9.8	21.6	6.3	1.6	1.8
U.S.	19.4	28.4	21.2	6.4	15.7	5.9	2.0	1.0

Note: Figures are 2006 estimated percentages and cover persons age 25 and over; (1) Metropolitan Statistical Area - see Appendix B for areas included
Source: Claritas, Inc.

Educational Attainment by Race

Area	High School Graduate (%)					Bachelor's Degree (%)				
	Total	White	Black	Asian	Hisp.[2]	Total	White	Black	Asian	Hisp.[2]
City	89.4	92.1	75.4	88.5	62.4	35.7	37.3	25.4	51.7	15.5
MSA[1]	90.9	92.2	78.7	91.5	62.8	31.5	32.1	25.7	48.7	16.2
U.S.	80.4	83.6	72.3	80.4	52.4	24.4	26.1	14.3	44.1	10.4

Note: Figures shown cover persons 25 years old and over; (1) Metropolitan Statistical Area - see Appendix A for areas included; (2) people of Hispanic origin can be of any race
Source: Census 2000, Summary File 3

School Enrollment by Type

Area	Grades KG to 8				Grades 9 to 12			
	Public		Private		Public		Private	
	Enrollment	%	Enrollment	%	Enrollment	%	Enrollment	%
City	9,048	96.1	366	3.9	4,330	93.4	304	6.6
MSA[1]	56,391	96.9	1,786	3.1	24,610	96.2	976	3.8
U.S.	33,526,011	88.7	4,285,121	11.3	14,848,628	90.6	1,532,323	9.4

Note: Figures shown cover persons 3 years old and over; (1) Metropolitan Statistical Area - see Appendix A for areas included
Source: Census 2000, Summary File 3

School Enrollment by Race

Area	Grades KG to 8 (%)				Grades 9 to 12 (%)			
	White	Black	Asian	Hisp.[1]	White	Black	Asian	Hisp.[1]
City	83.7	0.7	0.8	18.1	90.3	0.2	1.1	11.9
MSA[2]	91.8	0.5	0.6	7.5	93.6	0.2	0.6	6.1
U.S.	68.5	15.5	3.3	16.8	68.8	15.5	3.8	15.7

Note: Figures shown cover persons 3 years old and over; (1) people of Hispanic origin can be of any race; (2) Metropolitan Statistical Area - see Appendix A for areas included
Source: Census 2000, Summary File 3

Average Salaries of Public School Teachers

District	2004-05		2005-06		Percent Change 2004-05 to 2005-06
	Dollars	Rank[1]	Dollars	Rank[1]	
UTAH	39,456	39	40,316	43	2.18
U.S. Average	47,674	-	49,109	-	3.01

Note: (1) State rank ranges from 1 to 51.
Source: National Education Association, Rankings & Estimates: Rankings of the States 2005 and Estimates of School Statistics 2006, November 2006

Higher Education

Four-Year Colleges			Two-Year Colleges			Medical Schools[1]	Law Schools[2]	Voc/ Tech[3]
Public	Private Non-profit	Private For-profit	Public	Private Non-profit	Private For-profit			
0	1	0	0	0	4	0	1	0

Note: Figures cover institutions located within the city limits; (1) includes schools accredited by the Liaison Committee on Medical Education and the American Osteopathic Association; (2) includes American Bar Association-accredited law schools; (3) includes all schools with programs that are less than 2 years
Source: National Center for Education Statistics, The Integrated Postsecondary Education System (IPEDS) Peer Analysis System, 2006; www.usnews.com, America's Best Graduate Schools 2008, Medical School Directory; www.usnews.com, America's Best Graduate Schools 2008, Law School Directory

PRESIDENTIAL ELECTION

2004 Presidential Election Results

Area	Bush	Kerry	Nader	Other
Utah County	86.0	11.6	0.9	1.5
U.S.	50.7	48.3	0.4	0.6

Note: Results are percentages and may not add to 100% due to rounding
Source: Dave Leip's Atlas of U.S. Presidential Elections, www.uselectionatlas.org

MAJOR EMPLOYERS

Major Employers

Company Name	Industry	Type of Site
Brigham Young University	Colleges and universities	Headquarters
City of Provo	Executive offices	Headquarters
Geneva Steel	Blast furnaces and steel mills	Headquarters
Micron Technology	Semiconductors and related devices	Branch
Morinda Holdings Inc	Groceries and related products, nec	Single
Natures Sunshine	Pharmaceutical preparations	Headquarters
Nestle USA-Prepared Foods Div	Frozen specialties, nec	Branch
Neways International	Medicinals and botanicals	Headquarters
Novell Inc	Prepackaged software	Headquarters
Nu Skin Enterprises Inc	Drugs, proprietaries, and sundries	Headquarters
Nu Skin International Inc	Management services	Headquarters
Nu Skin United States Inc	Drugs, proprietaries, and sundries	Headquarters
Phone Directories Company	Miscellaneous publishing	Headquarters
Tahitian Noni International	Groceries and related products, nec	Headquarters
Thanksgiving Point	Eating places	Single
Utah State Development Center	Elementary and secondary schools	Branch
Utah State Hospital	Psychiatric hospitals	Branch
Utah Valley State College	Colleges and universities	Headquarters
Western Wats	Business services, nec	Single

Note: Companies shown are located within the metropolitan area and have 500 or more employees; nec = not elsewhere classified.
Source: www.zapdata.com, January 2007

PUBLIC SAFETY

Crime Rate

Area	All Crimes	Violent Crimes				Property Crimes		
		Murder	Forcible Rape	Robbery	Aggrav. Assault	Burglary	Larceny -Theft	Motor Vehicle Theft
City	3,379.2	2.9	53.4	16.5	103.9	653.5	2,347.0	202.0
Suburbs[1]	3,128.2	0.6	25.4	10.8	52.9	513.2	2,363.0	162.4
Metro[2]	3,188.9	1.2	32.1	12.2	65.2	547.1	2,359.1	172.0
U.S.	3,899.0	5.6	31.7	140.7	291.1	726.7	2,286.3	416.7

Note: Figures are crimes per 100,000 population; (1) All areas within the metro area that are located outside the city limits; (2) Metropolitan Statistical Area - see Appendix B for areas included
Source: FBI Uniform Crime Reports, 2005

Hate Crimes

Area	Number of Quarters Reported	Bias Motivation				
		Race	Religion	Sexual Orientation	Ethnicity	Disability
City	4	0	0	1	0	0

Source: Federal Bureau of Investigation, Hate Crime Statistics 2005

RECREATION

Culture

Dance[1]	Theatre[1]	Instrumental Music[1]	Vocal Music[1]	Series/ Festivals	Museums	Zoos
0	0	1	0	1	5	0

Note: (1) number of professional perfoming groups
Source: The Grey House Performing Arts Directory, 2007; Official Museum Directory, 2007

Professional Sports Teams

Major League Baseball	National Basketball Association	National Football League	National Hockey League	Major League Soccer	Women's National Basketball Association
0	0	0	0	0	0

Note: Includes teams located in the Provo metro area.
Source: www.sportsvenues.com, Listing of Venues by State/Province and City, 2006

MEDIA

Newspapers

Name	Target Audience	Frequency	Circulation
The Daily Herald	n/a	Daily	42,467

Note: Includes newspapers whose offices are located in the city and whose circulations are 500 or more; n/a not available
Source: BurrellesLuce, MediaContacts Online, January 2006

Television Stations

Name	Ch.	Network(s)	Type	Ownership
KUTV	2	CBS	Commercial	CBS
KCSG	4	Pax	Commercial	n/a
KTVX	4	ABC	Commercial	n/a
KSL	5	NBC	Commercial	Bonneville International Corporation
KUED	7	PBS	Public	University of Utah
KUEN	9	n/a	Public	Utah State Board of Regents
KENV	10	NBC	Commercial	Sunbelt Broadcasting Company
KBYU	11	PBS	Public	Brigham Young University
KDLQ	13	Fox/ABC	Commercial	n/a
KSTU	13	Fox	Commercial	Fox Television Stations Inc.
KJZZ	14	n/a	Commercial	Larry H. Miller Communications
KUPX	16	Pax	Commercial	Paxson Communications Corporation
KUEW	18	PBS	n/a	University of Utah
KUWB	30	WBN	Commercial	Acme Television Holdings

Note: Stations included cover the Salt Lake City DMA (Designated Market Area)
BurrellesLuce, MediaContacts Online, January 2006

Major AM Radio Stations

Call Letters	Freq. (kHz)	Station Type	Target Audience	Station Format	Music Format
KNRS	570	Commercial	General	News/Talk	n/a
KSUB	590	n/a	General	News/Sports/Talk	n/a
KVNU	610	Commercial	General	News/Talk	n/a
KMTI	650	Commercial	General	Music/News/Sports/Talk	Country
KOAL	750	n/a	General	News/Sports/Talk	n/a
KBEE	860	Commercial	General	Music/Talk	Country
KDXU	890	Commercial	General	News/Talk	n/a
KALL	910	Commercial	General	News	n/a
KMER	950	Commercial	General	News	n/a
KOVO	960	Commercial	General	Sports/Talk	n/a
KSVC	980	Commercial	General	News/Sports/Talk	n/a
KKDS	1060	Commercial	General	Music/News	Adult Contemp.
KAFL	1080	Commercial	General	Music	Country
KANN	1120	Non-Comm	Religious	Educational/Music/News	Christian
KSL	1160	Commercial	General	News/Talk	n/a
KUNF	1210	Commercial	General	Music/News	Easy Listening
KRSV	1210	Commercial	General	Music/News/Sports	Country
KEVA	1240	Commercial	General	News	n/a
KNEU	1250	Commercial	General	Music/News	Country
KZNS	1280	Commercial	General	News/Sports/Talk	n/a
KFNZ	1320	n/a	General/Men	Music/Sports	n/a
KRKK	1360	n/a	General	Music/News	n/a
KSOP	1370	Commercial	General	Music/News	Country
KLGN	1390	Commercial	General	Music/News/Sports/Talk	Adult Standards
KLO	1430	Commercial	General	Music/News/Sports/Talk	n/a
KXOL	1660	n/a	General	Music	n/a

Note: Stations included cover the Salt Lake City DMA (Designated Market Area); n/a not available
Source: BurrellesLuce, MediaContacts Online, January 2006

Major FM Radio Stations

Call Letters	Freq. (mHz)	Station Type	Target Audience	Station Format	Music Format
KBYU	89.1	College	General	Music/News	Classical
KUER	90.1	College	General	Music/News	Jazz
KUSU	91.5	College	General	Educational/Music/News	Classic Rock
KBLQ	92.9	Commercial	General	Music/News/Sports	Soft Rock
KCYQ	93.7	Commercial	General	Music	Country
KODJ	94.1	Commercial	General	Music	Oldies
KVFX	94.5	Commercial	General	Music	Adult Contemp.
KZHT	94.9	Commercial	General/Women	Music	Top 40
KXBN	94.9	Commercial	General	Music	Top 40
KYCS	95.1	Commercial	General	Music/News	Adult Contemp.
KYFO	95.5	Non-Comm	General	Music/Talk	Christian
KFNN	95.7	Commercial	General	Music/News	Adult Contemp.
KXRK	96.3	n/a	Gay/Lesbian	Music	n/a
KQSW	96.5	Commercial	General	Music/News	Country
KISN	97.1	Commercial	General	Music	Adult Contemp.
KREC	98.1	Commercial	General	Educational/Music/News	Adult Contemp.
KBEE	98.7	n/a	General	Music/News/Sports	n/a
KURR	99.5	Commercial	General/Native Amer	Music/Talk	Classic Rock
KONY	101.1	Commercial	General	Music	Contemp. Country
KXFF	102.9	n/a	n/a	n/a	n/a
KUDD	103.9	Commercial	General/Women	Music	Top 40
KSIT	104.5	Commercial	General	Music/News	Classic Rock
KNFL	104.9	n/a	General	Music	Oldies
KENZ	107.5	n/a	General	Music	n/a

Note: Stations included cover the Salt Lake City DMA (Designated Market Area); n/a not available
BurrellesLuce, MediaContacts Online, January 2006

CLIMATE

Average and Extreme Temperatures

Temperature	Jan	Feb	Mar	Apr	May	Jun	Jul	Aug	Sep	Oct	Nov	Dec	Yr.
Extreme High (°F)	62	69	78	85	93	104	107	104	100	89	75	67	107
Average High (°F)	37	43	52	62	72	83	93	90	80	66	50	38	64
Average Temp. (°F)	28	34	41	50	59	69	78	76	65	53	40	30	52
Average Low (°F)	19	24	31	38	46	54	62	61	51	40	30	22	40
Extreme Low (°F)	-22	-14	2	15	25	35	40	37	27	16	-14	-15	-22

Note: Figures cover the years 1948-1990
Source: National Climatic Data Center, International Station Meteorological Climate Summary, 9/96

Average Precipitation/Snowfall/Humidity

Precip./Humidity	Jan	Feb	Mar	Apr	May	Jun	Jul	Aug	Sep	Oct	Nov	Dec	Yr.
Avg. Precip. (in.)	1.3	1.2	1.8	2.0	1.7	0.9	0.8	0.9	1.1	1.3	1.3	1.4	15.6
Avg. Snowfall (in.)	13	10	11	6	1	Tr	0	0	Tr	2	6	13	63
Avg. Rel. Hum. 5am (%)	79	77	71	67	66	60	53	54	60	68	75	79	67
Avg. Rel. Hum. 5pm (%)	69	59	47	38	33	26	22	23	28	40	59	71	43

Note: Figures cover the years 1948-1990; Tr = Trace amounts (<0.05 in. of rain; <0.5 in. of snow)
Source: National Climatic Data Center, International Station Meteorological Climate Summary, 9/96

Weather Conditions

Temperature			Daytime Sky			Precipitation		
5°F & below	32°F & below	90°F & above	Clear	Partly cloudy	Cloudy	0.01 inch or more precip.	0.1 inch or more snow/ice	Thunder-storms
7	128	56	94	152	119	92	38	38

Note: Figures are average number of days per year and cover the years 1948-1990
Source: National Climatic Data Center, International Station Meteorological Climate Summary, 9/96

HAZARDOUS WASTE

Superfund Sites

Provo has no sites on the EPA's Superfund Final National Priorities List.
U.S. Environmental Protection Agency, Final National Priorities List, March 20, 2007

AIR & WATER QUALITY

Air Quality Index

Area	Percent of Days when Air Quality was...[2]				AQI Statistics	
	Good	Moderate	Unhealthy for Sensitive Groups	Unhealthy	Maximum	Median
MSA[1]	77.8	20.5	1.4	0.3	169	38

Note: The Air Quality Index (AQI) is an index for reporting daily air quality. EPA calculates the AQI for five major air pollutants regulated by the Clean Air Act: ground-level ozone, particle pollution (also known as particulate matter), carbon monoxide, sulfur dioxide, and nitrogen dioxide. The AQI runs from 0 to 500. The higher the AQI value, the greater the level of air pollution and the greater the health concern. There are six AQI categories: "Good" The AQI is between 0 and 50. Air quality is considered satisfactory; "Moderate" The AQI is between 51 and 100. Air quality is acceptable; "Unhealthy for Sensitive Groups" When AQI values are between 101 and 150, members of sensitive groups may experience health effects; "Unhealthy" When AQI values are between 151 and 200 everyone may begin to experience health effects; "Very Unhealthy" AQI values between 201 and 300 trigger a health alert; "Hazardous" AQI values over 300 trigger health warnings of emergency conditions; (1) Metropolitan Statistical Area - see Appendix A for areas included; (2) Based on 365 days with AQI data in 2005.
Source: U.S. Environmental Protection Agency, Air Quality Index Report, 2005

Air Quality Index Pollutants

Area	Percent of Days when AQI Pollutant was...[2]					
	Carbon Monoxide	Nitrogen Dioxide	Ozone	Sulfur Dioxide	Particulate Matter 2.5	Particulate Matter 10
MSA[1]	6.8	0.0	36.2	0.0	43.6	13.4

Note: The Air Quality Index (AQI) is an index for reporting daily air quality. EPA calculates the AQI for five major air pollutants regulated by the Clean Air Act: ground-level ozone, particle pollution (also known as particulate matter), carbon monoxide, sulfur dioxide, and nitrogen dioxide. The AQI runs from 0 to 500. The higher the AQI value, the greater the level of air pollution and the greater the health concern; (1) Metropolitan Statistical Area - see Appendix A for areas included; (2) Based on 365 days with AQI data in 2005.
Source: U.S. Environmental Protection Agency, Air Quality Index Report, 2005

Number of Days with Air Quality Index Values Greater than 100

Area	Trend Sites								All Sites
	1998	1999	2000	2001	2002	2003	2004	2005	2005
MSA[1]	n/a	n/a	n/a	n/a	n/a	n/a	n/a	n/a	n/a

Note: An AQI value greater than 100 indicates that air quality would have been in the unhealthful range on that day. Data from exceptional events are not included. These counts are presented in two ways. First, the counts are based on sites having an adequate record of monitoring data during the trend period (trend sites). These counts represent the relative change in the number of days with AQI values greater than 100. In the last column, the counts are based on all sites with data in the most recent year (because it is possible for a site to have data in the most recent year but not enough data to be a trend site); (1) Metropolitan Statistical Area - see Appendix A for areas included; n/a not available.
Source: U.S. Environmental Protection Agency, Air Trends Fact Book 2005

Maximum Pollutant Concentrations

	Particulate Matter 10 (ug/m^3)	Particulate Matter 2.5 (ug/m^3)	Ozone 1-hour (ppm)	Carbon Monoxide (ppm)	Sulfur Dioxide (ppm)	Nitrogen Dioxide (ppm)	Lead (ug/m^3)
MSA[1] Level	77	37	0.114	3	n/a	0.021	n/a
NAAQS[2]	150	65	0.125	9	0.140	0.053	1.50
Met NAAQS[2]	Yes	Yes	Yes	Yes	n/a	Yes	n/a

Note: Data from exceptional events are not included; (1) Metropolitan Statistical Area - see Appendix A for areas included; (2) National Ambient Air Quality Standards; n/a not available
Units: ppm = parts per million; ug/m^3 = micrograms per cubic meter
Source: U.S. Environmental Protection Agency, Air Trends Fact Book 2005

Watershed Health

The U.S. Environmental Protection Agency monitors the health of the aquatic resources for the nation's 2,000+ watersheds. **The Provo watershed serves the Provo area and received an overall Index of Watershed Indicators (IWI) score of 3 (less serious problems - low vulnerability)**. The IWI score is based on seven condition and nine vulnerability indicators. The overall IWI score ranges from 1 (best health) to 6 (worst health). The Condition Indicators include: designated use attainment, fish and wildlife consumption advisories, source water condition, contaminated sediments, ambient water quality, and wetlands loss index. The Vulnerability Indicators include: aquatic species at risk, conventional and toxic loads over permitted limits, urban and agricultural runoff potential, population change, hydrologic modification, estuarine pollution susceptibility, and air deposition. *Note: The IWI is no longer being updated by the U.S. EPA. Source: U.S. Environmental Protection Agency, Index of Watershed Indicators, October 26, 2001*

Drinking Water

Water System Name	Pop. Served	Primary Water Source Type	Number of Violations in 2006[a]		
			Health Based	Significant Monitoring	Monitoring
Provo City	110,000	Ground	None	None	None

Note: (a) Based on violation data from January 1, 2006 to December 31, 2006
Source: U.S. Environmental Protection Agency, Office of Ground Water and Drinking Water, Safe Drinking Water Information System (data extracted April 12, 2007)

Provo tap water is alkaline and hard.
Editor & Publisher Market Guide, 2005

Reno, Nevada

Background

Dubbed the "Biggest Little City in the World," Reno is known as a mecca for tourists wanting to gamble, but it is so much more. Washoes and Paiutes roamed the area before white explorers led by the famed John C. Fremont arrived in the nineteenth century. Due to the Truckee River running through it, the area became a stopping point for people hurrying to California to take advantage of the 1849 gold rush. In 1859, prospectors discovered the Comstock Lode — a massive vein of gold and silver forty miles to the south of the Truckee.

A shrewd entrepreneur by the name of Charles Fuller built a toll bridge across the river for prospectors desperate to reach the lode. He also built a hotel. Floods kept destroying Fuller's bridge, and he sold the land to Myron Lake in 1861, who constructed another bridge around which a settlement grew. Lake turned over to the Central Pacific Railroad several dozen acres of his land, on the condition that half of the transcontinental railroad would run through the area. Here the town of Reno was founded in 1868 and named after Jesse Lee Reno, a valiant Union officer killed during the Civil War. Reno became an important shipping point for the mines of the Comstock Lode.

By 1900, the lode was in decline and Reno had to look to other commercial ventures. One was the quick divorce — a six weeks' residency requirement was approved by the state legislature in 1931. In a continuing effort to jumpstart the state's economy during the Great Depression, Nevada legalized gambling in 1931. As the number of gambling houses increased in Reno, so did its population.

The Reno Arch (on which is emblazoned the city's nickname) welcomes tourists to an array of glittering casinos and hotels. The tourist and gambling industry are still quite important to the area's commerce, but many downtown casinos have closed, sparking a movement to turn the empty buildings into residential space. Out-of-state developers have purchased the Comstock and the Sundowner, amongst others, in hopes of turning them into upscale condos.

Other commercial ventures have been attracted to Reno's business-friendly environment, which includes no corporate or personal income taxes, nor unitary, inventory, or franchise taxes. Companies such as Microsoft Licensing, and John Deere have either expanded in or relocated to the Reno metropolitan area. Ralston Foods, International Game Technology, and R.R. Donnelly & Sons have been located in the area for some time. Reno is also an important distribution center, and there are many light-manufacturing industries in the area.

The city also hosts ArtTown, in which music, visual arts, film, dance, theater and historical tours are the featured highlights of the month of July. This is among the country's largest visual and performing arts festivals.

The $105 million expansion of the Reno-Sparks Convention Center was completed in 2002. This expanded the facility from 320,000 square feet to one-half million square feet.

Located on a semi-arid plateau to the east of the Sierra Nevada mountains, Reno offers a generally health climate with short, albeit hot, summers and relatively mild winters. Temperatures can vary widely from day to night. More than half of the city's precipitation falls as a rain-snow mixture during winter. Located at the edge of the Sierra Nevada, snows can pile up but tends to melt within a few days. Reno sees relatively little rain.

Rankings

General Rankings

■ Reno was ranked #9 out of 331 metro areas in *Cities Ranked & Rated*. Criteria: cost of living; climate; crime; transportation; economy and jobs; education; arts and culture; health and healthcare; leisure. *Cities Ranked & Rated, 1st Edition, 2004*

■ The Reno area was selected as one of "60 Cheap Places to Live" in the U.S. The area appeared in the "Steroid Cities" (fast-growing, business-friendly metro areas) category. *Forbes.com, August 20, 2004*

Business/Finance Rankings

■ Reno was selected as one of the best places to start and grow a company by *Entrepreneur* and the National Policy Research Council. The Reno metro area ranked #36 out of 63 mid-size metro areas. Criteria: business formation and growth (firms started four to 14 years ago that still employ at least 5 people and experienced rapid growth over the last four years). *Entrepreneur/National Policy Research Council, "Hot Cities for Entrepreneurs," September 2006*

■ The Reno metro area was selected as one of "America's 50 Hottest Cities" for business relocations and expansions. Criteria: industry's most prominent site selection consultants were asked to list their top city choices for relocating and expanding manufacturing companies, taking into consideration such factors as the business climate, work force quality, operating costs, incentive programs, and the ease of working with local political and economic development officials. *Expansion Management, January-February 2007*

■ The Reno metro area appeared on the Milken Institute "2005 Best Performing Cities" index. Rank: #21 out of 200 large metro areas. Criteria: job growth; wage and salary growth; high-tech output growth. *Milken Institute, "2005 Best Performing Cities," February 2006*

■ The Reno metro area was selected as one of "The Best Cities for Doing Business in America." *Inc.* magazine measured employment growth in 393 regions using the following criteria: recent growth trend; mid-term growth; long-term trend; and current year growth. The Reno metro area ranked #5 among mid-sized metro areas and #25 overall. *Inc., May 2006*

■ *Forbes* ranked the 200 most populous metro areas in the U.S. in terms of the "Best Places for Business and Careers." The Reno metro area was ranked #118. Criteria: business costs (labor, energy, tax and office space expenses); living costs (housing, transportation, food and other household expenditures); education levels of the work force; job growth; income growth; migration trends; crime rates; and culture/leisure. *Forbes, April 23, 2007*

Health/Environment Rankings

■ The Reno metro area appeared in *Country Home's* "2007 Best Green Places Report". The area ranked #131. Criteria included: air and watershed quality; miles of mass transit; green power; number of farmer's markets, organic producers and groceries. *Country Home, "2007 Best Green Places Report," April 2007*

■ The American Podiatric Medical Association and *Prevention* magazine ranked America's 100 most populated cities based on fitness-walker friendliness. The best cities have safe streets, beautiful places to walk, mild weather and good air quality. Reno ranked #28. *Prevention, "The Best Walking Cities of 2007," April 2007; American Podiatric Medical Association, "2007 Best Fitness-Walking Cities"*

■ Sperling's BestPlaces ranked 331 metro areas and identified the most and least stressful U.S. cities. The Reno metro area ranked #64 out of 114 mid-size metro areas (#1 = most stressful). Criteria: divorce rate; unemployment rate; violent and property crime; suicide rate; commute time; mental health; alcohol consumption; cloudy days. *www.BestPlaces.net, January 9, 2004*

■ Reno was highlighted as one of the top 25 cleanest metro areas for long-term particle pollution (PM 2.5) in the U.S. The area ranked #21. *American Lung Association, State of the Air 2006*

Women/MinoritiesRankings

■ *Ladies Home Journal* ranked America's 200 largest cities based on the qualities women surveyed care about most. Reno ranked #63 out of 143 in the smaller city category (population under 300,000). Criteria: crime; lifestyle; education; jobs; health; child care; politics; and the economy. *Ladies Home Journal Online, "The Best Cities for Women 2002"*

Seniors/Retirement Rankings

■ Reno was profiled in the book *Where to Retire: America's Best and Most Affordable Places.* Cities were selected based on personal visits by the author and interviews with local residents coupled with statistics from various government agencies. *Where to Retire: America's Best and Most Affordable Places, 2006*

■ Reno was identified as one of the "100 Most Popular Places to Retire" by *Where to Retire* magazine. The city ranked #55. Criteria: net retirees received from 1995-2000 (derived by subtracting all outbound retirees from inbound retirees for the county or county group - includes interstate moves only). *Where to Retire, "100 Most Popular Places to Retire," January/February 2007*

■ Reno was profiled in the book *Retire in Style: 60 Outstanding Places Across the USA and Canada.* Criteria: landscape; climate; quality of life; cost of living; transportation; retail services; health care; community services; cultural and educational activities; recreational activities; work and volunteer activities; crime rates and public safety. *Retire in Style: 60 Outstanding Places Across the USA and Canada, 2005*

■ Reno was selected as one of the best places to retire by *Retirement Places Rated.* Criteria: cost of living; climate; personal safety; services; economy. The city was ranked #51 out of 200. *Retirement Places Rated, 6th Edition, 2004*

■ A.G. Edwards ranked America's 500 top-performing communities based on their residents' personal savings and investing behavior. The Reno metro area ranked #226 with an index score of 102.59 (national average = 100.00). A dozen statistical factors were measured including: participation in retirement savings plans; personal debt levels; and home ownership. *A.G. Edwards, "2006 Nest Egg Index", September 6, 2006*

Safety Rankings

■ Allstate ranked the 200 largest cities in America in terms of driver safety. Reno ranked #36. In addition, drivers were 6.9% less likely to have had an accident compared to the national average. Allstate researchers analyzed internal Property Damage reported claims over a two-year period (from January 2003 to December 2004) to ensure the findings would not be affected by external influences such as weather or road construction. A weighted average of the two-year numbers determined the annual percentages. The report defines an auto crash as any collision resulting in a property damage claim. *Allstate, "Allstate America's Best Drivers Report 2006," May 24, 2006*

■ *Ladies Home Journal* ranked America's 200 largest cities in terms of safety. Reno ranked #84 out of 200. Criteria: violent crimes; crimes against property; and rape. *Ladies Home Journal Online, "The Best Cities for Women 2002"*

Sports/Recreation Rankings

■ The Reno metro area appeared on *The Sporting News* list of the "Best Sports Cities 2006". The area ranked #82 out of 99 cities in North America. To be included in the rankings, a city must have at least one of the following: NCAA Division I basketball team; Class A minor league baseball team; training camp for a major league or NFL team; NASCAR Nextel Cup race; NCAA Division I-A bowl game; PGA Tour tournament; Triple Crown horse race. Once a city qualifies, a 12-month snapshot is taken of the sports atmosphere, putting a heavy premium on regular-season won-lost records; playoff berths, bowl appearances and tournament bids; championships; applicable power ratings; quality of competition; overall fan fervor; sports atmosphere and fan knowledge; abundance of teams (quality over quantity); stadium/arena quality; ticket availability and prices; franchise ownership; and the marquee appeal of athletes. *SportingNews.com, "Best Sports Cities 2006," August 1, 2006*

- *Golf Digest* ranked 330 metro areas in the U.S. in terms of golf. The Reno metro area was ranked #141. Criteria: access to golf; weather; value of golf; and quality of golf. *Golf Digest, "Metro Golf Rankings," August 2005*

Miscellaneous Rankings

- Reno appeared on ApartmentRatings.com "Top Cities for Renters List 2006". The area ranked #101 out of 138. Criteria: renter satisfaction; affordability; and vacancy. *ApartmentRatings.com, "Top Cities for Renters List 2006"*

Business Environment

CITY FINANCES

City Government Finances

Component	2003-2004 ($000)	2003-2004 ($ per capita)
Total Revenues	260,459	1,369
Total Expenditures	325,108	1,709
Debt Outstanding	618,406	3,251
Cash and Securities	484,874	2,549

Source: U.S Census Bureau, Government Finances 2003-2004

City Government Revenue by Source

Source	2003-2004 ($000)	2003-2004 ($ per capita)
General Revenue		
From Federal Government	4,280	22
From State Government	69,235	364
From Local Governments	17,122	90
Taxes		
Property	52,257	275
Sales	21,972	115
Personal Income	0	0
License	0	0
Charges	53,330	280
Liquor Store	0	0
Utility	0	0
Employee Retirement	0	0
Other	42,263	222

Source: U.S Census Bureau, Government Finances 2003-2004

City Government Expenditures by Function

Function	2003-2004 ($000)	2003-2004 ($ per capita)	2003-2004 (%)
General Expenditures			
Airports	0	0	0.0
Corrections	0	0	0.0
Education	0	0	0.0
Fire Protection	42,803	225	13.2
Governmental Administration	16,964	89	5.2
Health	2,027	11	0.6
Highways	34,265	180	10.5
Hospitals	0	0	0.0
Housing and Community Development	8,237	43	2.5
Interest on General Debt	20,975	110	6.5
Libraries	0	0	0.0
Parking	0	0	0.0
Parks and Recreation	37,480	197	11.5
Police Protection	47,406	249	14.6
Public Welfare	0	0	0.0
Sewerage	48,995	258	15.1
Solid Waste Management	0	0	0.0
Liquor Store	0	0	0.0
Utility	0	0	0.0
Employee Retirement	0	0	0.0
Other	65,956	347	20.3

Source: U.S Census Bureau, Government Finances 2003-2004

Municipal Bond Ratings

Area	Moody's
City	Aaa (1/2006)

Source: Mergent Bond Record, January 2007 (unless noted otherwise)

DEMOGRAPHICS

Population Growth

Area	1990 Census	2000 Census	2006 Estimate	2011 Projection	Population Growth (%) 1990-2000	Population Growth (%) 2000-2011
City	139,950	180,480	204,313	226,382	29.0	25.4
MSA[1]	257,193	342,885	399,472	449,914	33.3	31.2
U.S.	248,709,873	281,421,906	298,021,266	312,383,955	13.2	11.0

Note: (1) Metropolitan Statistical Area - see Appendix B for areas included
Source: Claritas, Inc.

Number of Households and Average Household Size

Area	2006 Estimate	2006 Average Household Size
City	83,036	2.46
MSA[1]	153,697	2.60
U.S.	112,267,302	2.65

Note: (1) Metropolitan Statistical Area - see Appendix B for areas included
Source: Claritas, Inc.

Race and Ethnicity

Area	White Alone[2]	Black Alone[2]	Asian Alone[2]	Other Race Alone[2]	Hispanic[3]
City	74.3	2.6	5.9	17.2	23.2
MSA[1]	77.6	2.2	4.8	15.4	20.0
U.S.	73.3	12.4	4.2	10.1	14.5

Note: Figures are 2006 estimates; (1) Metropolitan Statistical Area - see Appendix B for areas included
(2) Alone is defined as not being in combination with one or more other races; (3) May be of any race.
Source: Claritas, Inc.

Segregation

City Index[2]	City Rank[3]	MSA[1] Index[2]	MSA[1] Rank[4]
41.6	79	44.1	279

Note: Figures are based on an analysis of Census 2000 data; (1) Metropolitan Statistical Area - see Appendix A for areas included; (2) White/Black Dissimilarity Index—the most commonly used measure of segregation between two groups, reflecting their relative distributions across neighborhoods within a city or metropolitan area. It can range in value from 0, indicating complete integration, to 100, indicating complete segregation; (3) Ranges from 1 (most segregated) to 100 (least segregated) and includes all the cities in this book; (4) Ranges from 1 (most segregated) to 318 (least segregated) and includes 318 metropolitan areas.
Source: www.CensusScope.org

Ancestry

Area	German	Irish[2]	English	American	Italian	Polish	French[3]	Scottish
City	15.9	12.7	11.4	4.5	6.6	1.7	3.5	2.6
MSA[1]	17.1	13.8	12.6	4.6	6.8	1.9	3.9	2.6
U.S.	15.2	10.9	8.7	7.3	5.6	3.2	3.0	1.7

Note: Figures include multiple ancestry (e.g. if a person reported being Irish and Italian, they were included in both columns); (1) Metropolitan Statistical Area - see Appendix A for areas included; (2) Includes Celtic; (3) Includes Alsatian but excludes Basque
Source: Census 2000, Summary File 3

Foreign-Born Population

Area	Any Foreign Country	Percent of Population Born in Europe	Asia	Africa	Oceania[2]	Canada	Mexico	Latin America[3]
City	17.3	1.6	4.2	0.2	0.3	0.5	8.3	2.2
MSA[1]	14.1	1.4	3.4	0.1	0.3	0.5	6.7	1.7
U.S.	11.1	1.7	2.9	0.3	0.1	0.3	3.3	2.5

Note: (1) Metropolitan Statistical Area - see Appendix A for areas included; (2) Includes Australia, New Zealand subregion, Melanesia, Micronesia, Polynesia, and Oceania n.e.c; (3) Includes Central America (excluding Mexico), South America, and the Caribbean.
Source: Census 2000, Summary File 3

Marriage Status

Area	Never Married	Now Married (excluding Separated)	Separated	Widowed	Divorced
City	29.1	46.6	2.5	5.9	15.9
MSA[1]	25.7	52.1	1.9	5.4	14.9
U.S.	27.1	54.4	2.2	6.6	9.7

Note: Figures are percentages and cover the population 15 years of age and older;
(1) Metropolitan Statistical Area - see Appendix A for areas included
Source: Census 2000, Summary File 3

Age Distribution

Area	Percent of Population						
	Under Age 5	Age 5 to 17	Age 18 to 34	Age 35 to 49	Age 50 to 64	Age 65 to 79	80 Years and Over
City	6.7	16.5	27.3	23.3	14.9	8.6	2.7
MSA[1]	6.8	18.0	24.1	24.8	15.9	8.3	2.3
U.S.	6.8	18.9	23.7	23.5	14.8	9.2	3.2

Note: (1) Metropolitan Statistical Area - see Appendix A for areas included
Source: Census 2000, Summary File 3

Male/Female Ratio

Area	Males	Females	Males per 100 Females
City	104,406	99,907	104.5
MSA[1]	202,304	197,168	102.6
U.S.	146,712,712	151,308,554	97.0

Note: Figures are 2006 estimates; (1) Metropolitan Statistical Area -
see Appendix B for areas included
Source: Claritas, Inc.

Religion

Area	Catholic	Southern Baptist	United Methodist	ELCA[1]	LDS[2]	Presbyterian Church USA	Jewish Est.	Muslim Est.
County	16.2	1.1	0.8	0.6	3.5	0.5	0.6	0.2
U.S.	22.0	7.1	3.7	1.8	1.5	1.1	2.2	0.6

Note: Figures are the number of adherents as a percentage of the total population; Adherents are defined as all members, including full members, their children and the estimated number of other participants who are not considered members (e.g. the baptized, those not confirmed, those regularly attending services, etc.);
(1) Evangelical Lutheran Church in America; (2) The Church of Jesus Christ of Latter Day Saints
Source: Reprinted with permission from Religious Congregations and Membership in the United States 2000 (Nashville, Glenmary Research Center, 2002) Copyright Association of Statisticians of American Religious Bodies. All rights reserved.

ECONOMY

Gross Metropolitan Product

Area	2002	2003	2004	2005	2005 Rank[2]
MSA[1]	15.4	16.6	18.2	19.9	94

Note: Figures are in billions of dollars; (1) Reno-Sparks, NV Metropolitan Statistical Area - see Appendix A for areas included; (2) Rank ranges from 1 to 361
Source: The U.S. Conference of Mayors, "U.S. Metro Economies: GMP - The Engines of America's Growth," January 2007

Economic Growth

Area	1995 GMP	2005 GMP	Average Annual Growth Rate	Growth Rate Rank[2]
MSA[1]	10.7	19.9	6.5	78

Note: Figures are in billions of dollars; GMP = Gross Metropolitan Product; (1) Reno-Sparks, NV Metropolitan Statistical Area - see Appendix A for areas included; (2) Rank ranges from 1 to 361
Source: The U.S. Conference of Mayors, "U.S. Metro Economies: GMP - The Engines of America's Growth," January 2007

INCOME

Per Capita/Median/Average Income

Area	Per Capita ($)	Median Household ($)	Average Household ($)
City	25,135	46,125	61,031
MSA[1]	27,321	53,466	70,291
U.S.	25,129	48,775	65,849

Note: Figures are 2006 estimates; (1) Metropolitan Statistical Area - see Appendix B for areas included
Source: Claritas, Inc.

Household Income Distribution

Area	Percent of Households Earning							
	Under $15,000	$15,000 -24,999	$25,000 -34,999	$35,000 -49,999	$50,000 -74,999	$75,000 -99,000	$100,000 -149,999	$150,000 and up
City	12.7	11.9	12.8	17.0	20.2	11.2	9.3	4.9
MSA[1]	9.9	9.7	11.4	16.0	21.1	13.0	12.1	6.7
U.S.	13.3	11.0	11.3	15.7	19.5	11.8	11.0	6.4

Note: Figures are 2006 estimates; (1) Metropolitan Statistical Area - see Appendix B for areas included
Source: Claritas, Inc.

Poverty Rates by Age

Area	All Ages	Under 5 Years Old	5 to 17 Years Old	18 to 64 Years Old	65 Years and Over
City	12.6	1.5	2.4	7.8	0.8
MSA[1]	10.0	1.1	2.1	6.1	0.6
U.S.	12.4	1.2	3.0	6.9	1.2

Note: Figures are percent of population with income in 1999 below poverty level and only include population for whom poverty status is determined; (1) Metropolitan Statistical Area - see Appendix A for areas included
Source: Census 2000, Summary File 3

Personal Bankruptcy Filing Rate

Area	2003	2004	2005
Washoe County	6.96	6.08	7.62
U.S.	5.57	5.31	6.88

Note: Numbers are per 1,000 population and include Chapter 7 and Chapter 13 filings
Source: Federal Deposit Insurance Corporation (FDIC), Regional Economic Conditions (RECON), 3/24/2006

EMPLOYMENT

Labor Force and Employment

Area	Civilian Labor Force			Workers Employed		
	Dec. 2005	Dec. 2006	% Chg.	Dec. 2005	Dec. 2006	% Chg.
City	108,392	115,919	6.9	104,634	111,352	6.4
MSA[1]	212,680	227,537	7.0	205,431	218,620	6.4
U.S.	149,874,000	152,571,000	1.8	142,918,000	146,081,000	2.2

Note: Data is not seasonally adjusted and covers workers 16 years of age and older;
(1) Metropolitan Statistical Area - see Appendix B for areas included
Source: Bureau of Labor Statistics, http://stats.bls.gov

Unemployment Rate

Area	2006											
	Jan.	Feb.	Mar.	Apr.	May	Jun.	Jul.	Aug.	Sep.	Oct.	Nov.	Dec.
City	4.5	4.2	4.2	4.2	3.7	4.1	4.4	3.8	3.8	3.7	3.8	3.9
MSA[1]	4.5	4.1	4.1	4.1	3.6	4.0	4.2	3.7	3.7	3.6	3.7	3.9
U.S.	5.1	5.1	4.8	4.5	4.4	4.8	5.0	4.6	4.4	4.1	4.3	4.3

Note: Data is not seasonally adjusted and covers workers 16 years of age and older; All figures are percentages; (1) Metropolitan Statistical Area - see Appendix B for areas included
Source: Bureau of Labor Statistics, http://stats.bls.gov

Employment by Occupation

Occupation Classification	City (%)	MSA[1] (%)	U.S. (%)
Sales and Office	29.1	28.9	26.7
Professional and Related	17.3	16.6	20.2
Service	22.0	19.9	14.9
Production, Transportation, and Material Moving	11.0	12.1	14.6
Management, Business, and Financial	11.9	12.9	13.5
Construction, Extraction, and Maintenance	8.5	9.5	9.4
Farming, Forestry, and Fishing	0.2	0.2	0.7

Note: Figures cover employed civilians 16 years of age and older;
(1) Metropolitan Statistical Area - see Appendix A for areas included
Source: Census 2000, Summary File 3

Employment by Industry

Sector	MSA[1] Number of Employees	MSA[1] Percent of Total	U.S. Percent of Total
Government	29,800	13.0	16.3
Education and Health Services	20,300	8.9	13.2
Professional and Business Services	31,200	13.6	12.9
Retail Trade	25,400	11.1	11.5
Manufacturing	14,700	6.4	10.2
Leisure and Hospitality	39,900	17.4	9.5
Financial Activities	10,700	4.7	6.1
Construction	22,900	10.0	5.5
Wholesale Trade	11,000	4.8	4.3
Other Services	7,300	3.2	3.9
Transportation and Utilities	12,500	5.5	3.7
Information	2,700	1.2	2.2
Natural Resources and Mining	400	0.2	0.5

Note: Figures cover non-farm employment as of December 2006 and are not seasonally adjusted;
(1) Metropolitan Statistical Area - see Appendix B for areas included
Source: Bureau of Labor Statistics, http://stats.bls.gov

Occupations with Greatest Projected Employment Growth: 2002 - 2012

Occupation[1]	2002 Employment	2012 Projected Employment	Numeric Employment Change	Percent Employment Change
Retail Salespersons	34,060	49,430	15,370	45.1
Cashiers	35,760	50,760	15,000	41.9
Waiters and Waitresses	33,510	47,570	14,060	42.0
Gaming Dealers	22,650	35,170	12,520	55.3
Janitors and Cleaners, Except Maids and Housekeeping Cleaners	26,650	37,430	10,780	40.5
Maids and Housekeeping Cleaners	23,100	32,830	9,730	42.1
Carpenters	18,320	26,310	7,990	43.6
Registered Nurses	15,360	23,220	7,860	51.2
Combined Food Preparation and Serving Workers, Including Fast Food	13,330	20,970	7,640	57.3
Laborers and Freight, Stock, and Material Movers, Hand	26,520	33,270	6,750	25.5

Note: Projections cover Nevada; (1) Sorted by numeric employment change
Source: www.projectionscentral.com, State Occupational Projections, 2002-2012 Long-Term Projections

Fastest Growing Occupations: 2002 - 2012

Occupation[1]	2002 Employment	2012 Projected Employment	Numeric Employment Change	Percent Employment Change
Personal Financial Advisors	940	1,640	700	74.5
Network Systems and Data Communications Analysts	970	1,690	720	74.2
Pharmacists	1,900	3,280	1,380	72.6
Social and Human Service Assistants	720	1,230	510	70.8
Loan Officers	2,540	4,310	1,770	69.7
Fitness Trainers and Aerobics Instructors	990	1,670	680	68.7
Respiratory Therapists	680	1,140	460	67.6
Medical Records and Health Information Technicians	1,090	1,820	730	67.0
Private Detectives and Investigators	610	1,010	400	65.6
Bill and Account Collectors	4,900	8,050	3,150	64.3

Note: Projections cover Nevada; (1) Sorted by percent employment change and excludes occupations with numeric employment change less than 200
Source: www.projectionscentral.com, State Occupational Projections, 2002-2012 Long-Term Projections

Average Wages

Occupation	$/Hr.	Occupation	$/Hr.
Accountants and Auditors	24.29	Maids and Housekeeping Cleaners	8.45
Automotive Mechanics	18.67	Maintenance and Repair Workers	15.96
Bookkeepers	14.27	Marketing Managers	42.37
Carpenters	20.62	Nuclear Medicine Technologists	n/a
Cashiers	8.85	Nurses, Licensed Practical	20.36
Clerks, General Office	11.67	Nurses, Registered	29.46
Clerks, Receptionists/Information	11.71	Nursing Aides/Orderlies/Attendants	12.06
Clerks, Shipping/Receiving	12.88	Packers and Packagers, Hand	10.28
Computer Programmers	29.62	Physical Therapists	31.92
Computer Support Specialists	16.84	Postal Service Mail Carriers	21.90
Computer Systems Analysts	29.24	Real Estate Brokers	n/a
Cooks, Restaurant	10.45	Retail Salespersons	11.84
Dentists	n/a	Sales Reps., Exc. Tech./Scientific	24.26
Electrical Engineers	33.16	Sales Reps., Tech./Scientific	35.56
Electricians	21.08	Secretaries, Exc. Legal/Med./Exec.	14.54
Financial Managers	41.40	Security Guards	10.56
First-Line Supervisors/Mgrs., Sales	19.32	Surgeons	n/a
Food Preparation Workers	9.51	Teacher Assistants	n/a
General and Operations Managers	48.75	Teachers, Elementary School	n/a
Hairdressers/Cosmetologists	10.52	Teachers, Secondary School	n/a
Internists	89.86	Telemarketers	11.09
Janitors and Cleaners	9.59	Truck Drivers, Heavy/Tractor-Trailer	19.19
Landscaping/Groundskeeping Workers	11.30	Truck Drivers, Light/Delivery Svcs.	15.07
Lawyers	56.08	Waiters and Waitresses	6.93

Note: Wage data is for May 2005 and covers the Reno-Sparks, NV Metropolitan Statistics Area - see Appendix B for areas included. Hourly wages for elementary/secondary school teachers and teacher assistants were calculated by the editors from annual wage data assuming a 40 hour work week; n/a not available.
Source: Bureau of Labor Statistics, May 2005 Metro Area Occupational Employment and Wage Estimates

RESIDENTIAL REAL ESTATE

Building Permits

Area	Single-Family			Multi-Family			Total		
	2005	2006ᵖ	Pct. Chg.	2005	2006ᵖ	Pct. Chg.	2005	2006ᵖ	Pct. Chg.
City	2,885	1,497	-48.1	1,025	273	-73.4	3,910	1,770	-54.7
U.S.	1,682,000	1,380,000	-18.0	473,300	457,300	-3.4	2,155,300	1,837,300	-14.8

Note: (p) preliminary; figures represent new, privately-owned housing units authorized (unadjusted data); All permit data are based on estimates with imputation; U.S. figures are based on the new 20,000-place series.
Source: U.S. Census Bureau, Manufacturing, Mining, and Construction Statistics

Homeownership and Housing Vacancies

Area	Homeownership Rate[2] (%)			Rental Vacancy Rate[3] (%)			Homeowner Vacancy Rate[4] (%)		
	2004	2005	2006	2004	2005	2006	2004	2005	2006
MSA[1]	n/a	n/a	n/a	n/a	n/a	n/a	n/a	n/a	n/a
U.S.	69.0	68.9	68.8	10.2	9.8	9.7	1.7	1.9	2.4

Note: Comparable 2004 data was not available due to changes in metropolitan area definitions; (1) Metropolitan Statistical Area - see Appendix B for areas included; (2) The proportion of households that are owners; (3) The proportion of the rental inventory that is vacant for rent; (4) The proportion of the homeowner inventory that is vacant for sale; n/a not available
Source: U.S. Census Bureau, Housing Vacancies and Homeownership Annual Statistics: 2006

TAXES

State Corporate Income Tax Rates

State	Rate (%)	Number of Brackets	Low Bracket (Under $)	High Bracket (Over $)
Nevada	None	na	na	na

Note: Tax rates as of December 31, 2006; na not applicable
Source: Tax Foundation, www.taxfoundation.org

State Individual Income Tax Rates

State	Federal Deductibility	Marginal Rate (%)	Number of Brackets	Low Bracket (Under $)	High Bracket (Over $)
Nevada	No	None	na	na	na

Note: Tax rates as of December 31, 2006; Brackets apply to single taxpayers and married people filing separately; na not applicable
Source: Tax Foundation, www.taxfoundation.org

Various State and Local Tax Rates

State and Local Sales and Use (%)	State Sales and Use (%)	Gasoline ($/gal.)	Cigarette ($/pack)	Spirits ($/gal.)	Table Wine ($/gal.)	Beer ($/gal.)
7.375	6.5	0.238 (m)	0.8	3.6	0.70	0.16

Note: Tax rates as of December 31, 2006; (m) Additional cents per gallon taxes added this year that were not included in previous years' tables.
Source: Tax Foundation, www.taxfoundation.org; The Sales Tax Clearinghouse, www.thestc.com

State Tax Burdens

Area	Combined State and Local Tax Burden		Combined Federal, State and Local Tax Burden	
	Percent	Rank	Percent	Rank
Nevada	9.5	43	31.6	14
U.S. Average	10.6	-	31.6	-

Note: Figures are for 2006 and measure taxes as a percentage of income
Source: Tax Foundation, www.taxfoundation.org

Internal Revenue Service Tax Audits

IRS District	Percent of Returns Audited				
	1996	1997	1998	1999	2000
Southwest	0.80	0.81	0.61	0.36	0.29
U.S.	0.66	0.61	0.46	0.31	0.20

Note: Figures cover IRS district audits of federal income tax returns filed by individuals. Geographic data on district audits after the year 2000 are being withheld by the IRS. TRAC is challenging this policy.
Source: Syracuse University, Transactional Records Access Clearinghouse (TRAC), "Odds of IRS District Tax Audit 2000"

**COMMERCIAL
UTILITIES**

Typical Monthly Electric Bills

Area	Commercial Service ($/month)		Industrial Service ($/month)	
	3 kW demand 1,000 kWh	40 kW demand 14,000 kWh	1,000 kW demand 200,000 kWh	50,000 kW demand 15,000,000 kWh
City	140	1,665	28,916	1,838,767
Average[1]	123	1,413	22,000	1,306,315

Note: Based on total rates in effect July 1, 2006; (1) average based on 196 utilities
Source: Edison Electric Institute, Typical Bills and Average Rates Report, Summer 2006

TRANSPORTATION

Means of Transportation to Work

Area	Car/Truck/Van		Public Transportation			Bicycle	Walked	Other Means	Worked at Home
	Drove Alone	Car-pooled	Bus	Subway	Railroad				
City	72.6	14.3	4.1	0.0	0.0	0.9	4.4	1.2	2.4
MSA[1]	75.3	13.8	3.0	0.0	0.0	0.7	3.2	1.2	2.9
U.S.	75.7	12.2	2.5	1.5	0.5	0.4	2.9	1.0	3.3

Note: Figures are percentages and cover workers 16 years of age and older;
(1) Metropolitan Statistical Area - see Appendix A for areas included
Source: Census 2000, Summary File 3

Travel Time to Work

Area	Less Than 15 Minutes	15 to 29 Minutes	30 to 44 Minutes	45 to 59 Minutes	60 Minutes or More
City	41.4	45.8	7.0	2.4	3.4
MSA[1]	35.2	49.2	9.5	2.7	3.3
U.S.	29.4	36.1	19.1	7.4	8.0

Note: Figures are percentages and include workers 16 years old and over; (1) Metropolitan Statistical Area -
see Appendix A for areas included
Source: Census 2000, Summary File 3

Public Transportation

Agency name:	Regional Transportation Commission of Washoe County (RTC)
Vehicle type:	Bus
Average fleet age in years:	6.4
No. operated in max. service:	60
Vehicle type:	Demand response
Average fleet age in years:	4.1
No. operated in max. service:	36

Source: Federal Transit Administration, National Transit Database, 2005

Air Transportation

Airport name and code:	Reno-Tahoe International (RNO)
Domestic service (2006)	
Passenger airlines[1]:	24
Passenger enplanements:	2,439,170
Freight carriers[2]:	18
Freight (lbs.):	62,142,903
International service (2005)	
Passenger airlines[1]:	5
Passenger enplanements:	987
Freight carriers[2]:	0
Freight (lbs.):	0

Note: (1) Includes all major, minor and commuter airlines that carried at least one passenger during the year;
(2) Includes all airlines and freight carriers that transported at least one pound of freight during the year
Source: Bureau of Transportation Statistics, The Intermodal Transportation Database, Air Carriers: T-100
International Market, 2004; Bureau of Transportation Statistics, The Intermodal Transportation Database, Air
Carriers: T-100 Domestic Market, 2005

Other Transportation Statistics

Interstate highways:	I-80
Amtrak service:	Yes
Major waterways/ports:	None

Source: Editor & Publisher Market Guide, 2006; Amtrak.com; Rand McNally 2006 Road Atlas

BUSINESSES

Major Business Headquarters

Company Name	2006 Rankings	
	Fortune[1]	Forbes[2]
No companies listed	-	-

Note: (1) Fortune 500 - companies that produce a 10-K are ranked 1 to 500 based on 2005 revenue; (2) Forbes Largest Private Companies - all private companies with at least $1 billion in annual revenue are ranked 1 to 394; companies listed are located in the city; dashes indicate no ranking
Source: Fortune, April 17, 2006; Forbes, November 9, 2006

Best Companies to Work For

Granite Construction, headquartered in Reno, is among the "100 Best Companies to Work For." Criteria: More than 105,000 employees from 446 companies responded to a 57-question survey created by the Great Place to Work Institute. Two-thirds of a company's score is based on the survey, which covers topics such as attitudes towards management, job satisfaction, and camaraderie. The remaining third of the score comes from each company's responses to the Institute's Culture Audit, which includes detailed questions about demographic makeup, pay and benefits programs, and open-ended questions about the company's people-management philosophy, internal communications, opportunities, compensation practices, diversity programs, etc. Any company that is at least seven years old and has a minimum of 1,000 U.S. employees is eligible. The top three U.S. locations are shown for companies with more than one location. *Fortune, "100 Best Companies to Work for 2007," January 22, 2007*

Fast-Growing Businesses

According to *Inc.*, Reno is home to one of America's 500 fastest-growing private companies: **Alere Medical**. Criteria: must be an independent, privately-held, U.S. corporation, proprietorship or partnership; net sales of at least $600,000 in FY2002; four-year operating/sales history; holding companies, regulated banks, and utilities were excluded. *Inc., "America's 500 Fastest-Growing Private Companies," September 2006*

Women-Owned Businesses: 1997 and 2002

Year	All Firms		Firms with Paid Employees			
	Firms	Sales ($000)	Firms	Sales ($000)	Employees	Payroll ($000)
1997	4,012	779,110	940	693,353	7,200	196,484
2002	4,862	877,757	833	761,990	7,409	214,765

Note: Figures cover firms located in the city; Women-owned business are defined as firms in which women own 51% or more of the stock or equity of the company; (a) Withheld to avoid disclosing data for individual companies; (b) Withheld because estimate did not meet publication standards; n/a not available
Source: 1997 Economic Census, Survey of Minority- and Women-Owned Business Enterprises; 2002 Economic Census, Survey of Business Owners (released February 9, 2006)

HOTELS

Hotels/Motels

Area	Hotels/Motels	Average Minimum Rates ($)		
		Tourist	First-Class	Deluxe
City	51	37	48	n/a

Note: n/a not available
Source: OAG Travel Planner Online, Spring 2006

EVENT SITES

Stadiums, Arenas, and Auditoriums

Name	Capacity
Lawlor Events Center	11,600
Pioneer Center for Performing Arts	1,434

Source: www.officialtravelguide.com; www.eventective.com; original research

Convention Centers

Name	Overall Space (sq. ft.)	Exhibit Space (sq. ft.)	Meeting Space (sq. ft.)	Meeting Rooms
Reno-Sparks Convention Center	500,000	110,000	381,000	53

Source: www.officialtravelguide.com; www.eventective.com; original research

Hotels/Conference Centers

Name	Guest Rooms	Exhibit Space (sq. ft.)	Meeting Space (sq. ft.)
Reno Hilton	1,995	200,000	200,000
Silver Legacy Resort Casino	1,712	70,000	90,000

Source: www.officialtravelguide.com; www.eventective.com; original research

Living Environment

COST OF LIVING

Cost of Living Index

Year	Composite Index	Groceries	Housing	Utilities	Trans-portation	Health Care	Misc. Goods/ Services
2004	103.9	102.3	101.4	102.9	119.1	101.2	103.4
2005	110.8	106.4	117.1	108.8	111.1	111.9	107.5
2006	109.7	110.8	119.2	95.3	102.8	114.8	107.1

Note: U.S. = 100; Figures are for Reno-Sparks
Source: The Council for Community and Economic Research (formerly ACCRA), Cost of Living Index, 2004, 2005 and 2006 4-Quarter Averages

HOUSING

House Price Index (HPI)

Area	National Ranking[2]	Quarterly Change (%)	One-Year Change (%)	Five-Year Change (%)
MSA[1]	265	-0.33	-0.84	96.03
U.S.[3]	-	1.12	5.87	55.21

Note: The HPI is a weighted repeat sales index. It measures average price changes in repeat sales or refinancings on the same properties. This information is obtained by reviewing repeat mortgage transactions on single-family properties whose mortgages have been purchased or securitized by Fannie Mae or Freddie Mac in January 1975; (1) Metropolitan Statistical Area - see Appendix B for areas included; (2) Rankings are based on annual percentage change for all metro areas containing at least 15,000 transactions over the last 10 years and ranges from 1 to 282; (3) figures based on a weighted division average; all figures are for the period ending December 31, 2006
Source: Office of Federal Housing Enterprise Oversight, House Price Index, March 1, 2007

House Price Valuations

Area	Q4 1999	Q4 2000	Q4 2001	Q4 2002	Q4 2003	Q4 2004	Q4 2005	Q4 2006
MSA[1]	-16.8	-17.7	-14.1	-6.8	2.3	20.4	42.5	34.7

Note: Figures show the percentage of over- or under-valuation of single family homes relative to statistically normal house values (e.g. a value of 23.6 indicates that house values are 23.6% overvalued). Statistically normal house values are based on house prices, interest rates, household incomes, population densities, and any historical premiums or discounts metropolitan areas have exhibited over time; (1) Figures cover the Metropolitan Statistical Area - see Appendix B for areas included
Source: Global Insight/National City Corporation, House Prices in America, March 2007

Median Home Prices

Area	2004	2005	2006p	Percent Change 2005 to 2006
Metro Area[1]	284.3	349.9	347.2	-0.8
U.S. Average	195.2	219.0	222.0	1.4

Note: Figures are median sales prices of existing single-family homes in thousands of dollars; (p) preliminary; n/a not available; (1) Covers the Reno-Sparks, NV Metropolitan Statistical Area - see Appendix B for areas included
Source: National Association of Realtors, Metropolitan Area Prices, 4th Quarter 2006

Housing: Year Structure Built

Area	1990 -2000	1980 -1989	1970 -1979	1960 -1969	1950 -1959	1940 -1949	Before 1940	Median Year
City	25.0	18.4	22.8	14.8	9.3	5.0	4.6	1977
MSA[1]	27.3	20.6	25.0	13.0	7.3	3.5	3.3	1979
U.S.	17.0	15.8	18.5	13.7	12.7	7.3	15.0	1971

Note: Figures are percentages; (1) Metropolitan Statistical Area - see Appendix A for areas included
Source: Census 2000, Summary File 3

Average New Home Price

Area	2004	2005	2006
City[1]	251,332	329,739	369,178
U.S.	253,574	275,712	299,269

Note: Figures, in dollars, are based on a new home with 2,400 sq. ft. of living area on an 8,000 sq. ft. lot;
(1) Reno-Sparks
Source: The Council for Community and Economic Research (formerly ACCRA), Cost of Living Index, 2004,
2005 and 2006 4-Quarter Averages

Average Apartment Rent

Area	2004	2005	2006
City[1]	825	838	749
U.S.	716	740	766

Note: Figures, in dollars per month, are based on an unfurnished two bedroom, 1-1/2 or 2 bath apartment,
approximately 950 sq. ft. in size, excluding all utilities except water; (1) Reno-Sparks
Source: The Council for Community and Economic Research (formerly ACCRA), Cost of Living Index, 2004,
2005 and 2006 4-Quarter Averages

RESIDENTIAL UTILITIES

Average Residential Utility Costs

Area	All Electric ($/mth)	Part Electric ($/mth)	Other Energy ($/mth)	Phone ($/mth)
City[1]	–	77.85	91.10	20.06
U.S.	136.00	76.53	90.52	25.87

Note: (1) Reno-Sparks
Source: The Council for Community and Economic Research (formerly ACCRA), Cost of Living Index, 2006
4-Quarter Average

HEALTH

Average Health Care Costs

Area	Optometrist ($/visit)	Doctor ($/visit)	Dentist ($/visit)
City[1]	87.50	82.06	93.88
U.S.	76.38	76.10	68.72

Note: Optometrist—based on a full vision eye exam for an established adult patient;
Doctor—based on a general practitioner's routine exam of an established patient;
Dentist—based on adult teeth cleaning and periodic oral exam;
(1) Reno-Sparks
Source: The Council for Community and Economic Research (formerly ACCRA), Cost of Living Index, 2006
4-Quarter Average

Mortality Rates

ICD-10 Sub-Chapter	ICD-10 Code	Age-Adjusted Death Rate per 100,000 population[1]	U.S. Age-Adjusted Death Rate per 100,000 population
Malignant neoplasms	C00-C97	178.1	185.8
Ischaemic heart diseases	I20-I25	127.5	150.2
Other forms of heart disease	I30-I51	51.8	50.8
Cerebrovascular diseases	I60-I69	54.1	50.0
Chronic lower respiratory diseases	J40-J47	70.0	41.1
Diabetes mellitus	E10-E14	14.5	24.5
Other degenerative diseases of the nervous system	G30-G31	13.2	22.3
Other external causes of accidental injury	W00-X59	18.3	21.2
Influenza and pneumonia	J10-J18	16.3	19.8
Hypertensive diseases	I10-I13	50.6	18.1

Note: ICD-10 = International Classification of Diseases 10th Revision; (1) Figures cover Washoe County, NV
Source: Centers for Disease Control and Prevention, National Center for Health Statistics. Compressed
Mortality File 1999-2004. CDC WONDER On-line Database, compiled from Compressed Mortality File
1999-2004 Series 20 No. 2J, 2007.

Health Risk Data

Item	Area[1] (%)	U.S. (%)
Adults who have been told they have high blood pressure	22.1	25.5
Adults who have been told they have high blood cholesterol	35.3	35.6
Adults who have been told they have diabetes[2]	5.6	7.3
Adults who have been told they have arthritis	23.5	27.0
Adults who have been told they currently have asthma	8.0	8.0
Adults who are current smokers	20.1	20.6

Note: (1) Figures cover the Metropolitan Statistical Area - see Appendix B for areas included; (2) Figures do not include pregnancy-related diabetes, pre-diabetes or borderline diabetes
Source: Centers for Disease Control and Prevention, Behaviorial Risk Factor Surveillance System, SMART: Selected Metropolitan/Micropolitan Area Trends, 2005

Distribution of Office-Based Physicians

Area	Total	Family/ General Practice	Specialties		
			Medical	Surgical	Other
MSA[1] (number)	772	102	215	209	246
MSA[1] (rate per 10,000 pop.)	21.7	2.9	6.0	5.9	6.9
Metro Average[2] (rate per 10,000 pop.)	19.4	2.1	7.5	4.5	5.3

Note: Data as of December 31, 2004; (1) Metropolitan Statistical Area - see Appendix A for areas included; (2) Average of the 79 unique MSAs and CMSAs in this book
Source: American Medical Association, Physician Characteristics & Distribution in the U.S., 2006

Hospitals

Reno has the following hospitals: 4 general medical and surgical; 1 psychiatric; 1 rehabilitation; 1 long-term acute care; 1 children's psychiatric.
AHA Guide to the Healthcare Field 2007

EDUCATION

Public School District Statistics

District Name	Schls	Pupils	Pupil/ Teacher Ratio	Minority Pupils[1] (%)	Free Lunch Eligible[2] (%)	IEP[3] (%)
Washoe County School District	100	63,322	18.1	n/a	n/a	12.6

Note: Table includes regular local school districts with 2,000 or more students; (1) Percentage of students that are not white, non-Hispanic; (2) Percentage of students that are eligible for the free lunch program; (3) Percentage of students that have an Individualized Education Program.
Source: U.S. Department of Education, National Center for Education Statistics, Common Core of Data, Local Education Agency (School District) Universe Survey: School Year 2004-2005; U.S. Department of Education, National Center for Education Statistics, Common Core of Data, Public Elementary/Secondary School Universe Survey: School Year 2004-2005

Top Public High Schools

High School Name	Index[1]	Rank[1]	Subsidized Lunch (%)[2]	E&E (%)[3]
Galena	1.708	531	14.0	n/a
McQueen	1.772	488	9.8	26.1
North Valleys	1.179	1,045	26.8	11.6
Reno	1.568	650	11.9	30.5
Wooster	1.760	495	39.0	n/a**

Note: (1) Public schools are ranked according to a ratio that is the number of Advanced Placement and/or International Baccalaureate tests taken by all students at a school in 2005 divided by the number of graduating seniors. All of the schools on the list have an index of at least 1.000; they are in the top five percent of public schools measured this way. The rankings range from 1 to 1,236; (2) Percentage of students receiving federally subsidized meals; (3) E & E stands for equity and excellence percentage: the portion of all graduating seniors at a school that had at least one passing grade on one AP or IB test; (*) Gave just IB tests; (**) Gave both IB and AP tests. AP and IB participation are indicators of a school's efforts to get students to excel and prepare for college; n/a not available
Source: Newsweek Online, May 23, 2006

Educational Quality

School District	Education Quotient[1]	Graduate Outcome[2]	Community Index[3]	Resource Index[4]	Rating[5]
Washoe County	47	54	47	4	Green

Note: Scores are national percentile rankings and range from 1 (worst) to 99 (best); (1) Combination of the Graduate Outcome, Community and Resource Indexes weighted to reflect the greater importance of the Graduate Outcome and Resource Index; (2) Based on graduation rates and college board scores (SAT/ACT); (3) Based on the surrounding community's level of affluence and adult education; (4) Based on teacher salaries, per-pupil expenditures and student-teacher ratios; (5) School districts receive one of five rankings: Gold Medal (top 16 percent of districts evaluated); Blue Ribbon (top third); Green Light (average); Yellow Light (bottom 25 percent); Red Light (bottom 10 percent).
Source: Expansion Management, "2007 Education Quotient," January 2007

Highest Level of Education

Area	Less than H.S.	H.S. Diploma	Some College, No Deg.	Associate Degree	Bachelors Degree	Masters Degree	Profess. School Degree	Doctorate Degree
City	17.3	23.7	27.3	6.8	16.6	5.3	2.0	1.0
MSA[1]	15.6	25.2	28.2	7.2	15.9	5.0	1.9	0.9
U.S.	19.4	28.4	21.2	6.4	15.7	5.9	2.0	1.0

Note: Figures are 2006 estimated percentages and cover persons age 25 and over; (1) Metropolitan Statistical Area - see Appendix B for areas included
Source: Claritas, Inc.

Educational Attainment by Race

Area	High School Graduate (%)					Bachelor's Degree (%)				
	Total	White	Black	Asian	Hisp.[2]	Total	White	Black	Asian	Hisp.[2]
City	82.4	86.4	82.6	83.7	42.6	25.0	26.9	15.2	34.6	6.6
MSA[1]	83.9	87.3	84.2	83.2	45.9	23.7	25.2	16.7	34.2	6.9
U.S.	80.4	83.6	72.3	80.4	52.4	24.4	26.1	14.3	44.1	10.4

Note: Figures shown cover persons 25 years old and over; (1) Metropolitan Statistical Area - see Appendix A for areas included; (2) people of Hispanic origin can be of any race
Source: Census 2000, Summary File 3

School Enrollment by Type

Area	Grades KG to 8				Grades 9 to 12			
	Public		Private		Public		Private	
	Enrollment	%	Enrollment	%	Enrollment	%	Enrollment	%
City	20,254	94.4	1,201	5.6	8,597	92.7	679	7.3
MSA[1]	41,138	94.0	2,646	6.0	17,229	93.4	1,216	6.6
U.S.	33,526,011	88.7	4,285,121	11.3	14,848,628	90.6	1,532,323	9.4

Note: Figures shown cover persons 3 years old and over; (1) Metropolitan Statistical Area - see Appendix A for areas included
Source: Census 2000, Summary File 3

School Enrollment by Race

Area	Grades KG to 8 (%)				Grades 9 to 12 (%)			
	White	Black	Asian	Hisp.[1]	White	Black	Asian	Hisp.[1]
City	69.5	2.4	4.7	29.5	68.0	3.3	6.0	28.9
MSA[2]	74.2	2.0	3.8	25.1	74.0	3.0	4.4	22.4
U.S.	68.5	15.5	3.3	16.8	68.8	15.5	3.8	15.7

Note: Figures shown cover persons 3 years old and over; (1) people of Hispanic origin can be of any race; (2) Metropolitan Statistical Area - see Appendix A for areas included
Source: Census 2000, Summary File 3

Average Salaries of Public School Teachers

District	2004-05 Dollars	2004-05 Rank[1]	2005-06 Dollars	2005-06 Rank[1]	Percent Change 2004-05 to 2005-06
NEVADA	43,394	25	44,426	26	2.38
U.S. Average	47,674	-	49,109	-	3.01

Note: (1) State rank ranges from 1 to 51.
Source: National Education Association, Rankings & Estimates: Rankings of the States 2005 and Estimates of School Statistics 2006, November 2006

Higher Education

Four-Year Colleges Public	Four-Year Colleges Private Non-profit	Four-Year Colleges Private For-profit	Two-Year Colleges Public	Two-Year Colleges Private Non-profit	Two-Year Colleges Private For-profit	Medical Schools[1]	Law Schools[2]	Voc/ Tech[3]
1	0	2	1	0	1	1	0	1

Note: Figures cover institutions located within the city limits; (1) includes schools accredited by the Liaison Committee on Medical Education and the American Osteopathic Association; (2) includes American Bar Association-accredited law schools; (3) includes all schools with programs that are less than 2 years
Source: National Center for Education Statistics, The Integrated Postsecondary Education System (IPEDS) Peer Analysis System, 2006; www.usnews.com, America's Best Graduate Schools 2008, Medical School Directory; www.usnews.com, America's Best Graduate Schools 2008, Law School Directory

PRESIDENTIAL ELECTION

2004 Presidential Election Results

Area	Bush	Kerry	Nader	Other
Washoe County	51.3	47.0	0.6	1.1
U.S.	50.7	48.3	0.4	0.6

Note: Results are percentages and may not add to 100% due to rounding
Source: Dave Leip's Atlas of U.S. Presidential Elections, www.uselectionatlas.org

MAJOR EMPLOYERS

Major Employers

Company Name	Industry	Type of Site
152nd Tactical Reconnaissance Group	National security	Branch
Boomtown Casino-Family Fun Ctr	Amusement and recreation, nec	Single
Carson City Sports Book	Hotels and motels	Single
Circus Circus	Eating places	Branch
City of Reno	Executive offices	Headquarters
County of Washoe	Executive offices	Headquarters
El Dorado Hotel & Casino	Hotels and motels	Single
Fitzgeralds Gaming Corporation	Hotels and motels	Branch
Harrahs	Hotels and motels	Branch
Hilton	Hotels and motels	Single
Hyatt Hotel	Hotels and motels	Branch
IGT	Manufacturing industries, nec	Headquarters
Nevada Power Company	Electric services	Headquarters
Saint Marys Eye Institute	General medical and surgical hospitals	Headquarters
Sierra Nevada Healthcare Sys	Administration of veterans' affairs	Branch
Sierra Pacific Power Company	Electric services	Headquarters
Silver Legacy Resort & Casino	Hotels and motels	Single
University of Nevada Reno	Administration of social & manpower programs	Single
Washoe County Sheriffs Office	Police protection	Branch

Note: Companies shown are located within the metropolitan area and have 700 or more employees; nec = not elsewhere classified.
Source: www.zapdata.com, January 2007

PUBLIC SAFETY

Crime Rate

Area	All Crimes	Violent Crimes				Property Crimes		
		Murder	Forcible Rape	Robbery	Aggrav. Assault	Burglary	Larceny -Theft	Motor Vehicle Theft
City	6,108.5	3.9	53.7	205.6	478.1	935.8	3,686.0	745.3
Suburbs[1]	3,068.1	3.1	34.2	61.2	212.0	688.9	1,697.1	371.7
Metro[2]	4,633.5	3.5	44.3	135.5	349.0	816.0	2,721.1	564.0
U.S.	3,899.0	5.6	31.7	140.7	291.1	726.7	2,286.3	416.7

Note: Figures are crimes per 100,000 population; (1) All areas within the metro area that are located outside the city limits; (2) Metropolitan Statistical Area - see Appendix B for areas included
Source: FBI Uniform Crime Reports, 2005

Hate Crimes

Area	Number of Quarters Reported	Bias Motivation				
		Race	Religion	Sexual Orientation	Ethnicity	Disability
City	4	1	2	1	3	0

Source: Federal Bureau of Investigation, Hate Crime Statistics 2005

RECREATION

Culture

Dance[1]	Theatre[1]	Instrumental Music[1]	Vocal Music[1]	Series/ Festivals	Museums	Zoos
0	1	2	1	2	5	1

Note: (1) number of professional perfoming groups
Source: The Grey House Performing Arts Directory, 2007; Official Museum Directory, 2007

Professional Sports Teams

Major League Baseball	National Basketball Association	National Football League	National Hockey League	Major League Soccer	Women's National Basketball Association
0	0	0	0	0	0

Note: Includes teams located in the Reno metro area.
Source: www.sportsvenues.com, Listing of Venues by State/Province and City, 2006

MEDIA

Newspapers

Name	Target Audience	Frequency	Circulation
Ahora	Hispanic	Non-Daily	10,000
Reno Gazette-Journal	n/a	Daily	66,269
Reno News & Review	Alternative/General	Non-Daily	27,000

Note: Includes newspapers whose offices are located in the city and whose circulations are 500 or more; n/a not available
Source: BurrellesLuce, MediaContacts Online, January 2006

Television Stations

Name	Ch.	Network(s)	Type	Ownership
KTVN	2	CBS	Commercial	Sarkes Tarzian Inc.
KRNV	4	NBC	Commercial	Sierra Broadcasting Company
KNPB	5	PBS	Public	Channel 5 Public Broadcasting Inc.
KOLO	8	ABC	Commercial	Stephens Group Inc.
KRXI	11	Fox	Commercial	Cox Enterprises Inc.
KAME	21	Fox/UPN	Commercial	Broadcast Development L.L.C.
KREN	27	WBN	Commercial	Pappas Telecasting Companies

Note: Stations included cover the Reno DMA (Designated Market Area)
BurrellesLuce, MediaContacts Online, January 2006

Major AM Radio Stations

Call Letters	Freq. (kHz)	Station Type	Target Audience	Station Format	Music Format
KHIT	630	Commercial	General	Music	Country
KKOH	780	Commercial	General	Talk	n/a
KVLV	980	Commercial	General	Music/News	Country
KPLY	1230	Commercial	General	News	n/a
KSUE	1240	Commercial	General	News/Sports/Talk	n/a
KPTL	1300	Commercial	General	Music/News	Oldies
KWNA	1400	Commercial	General	Music/News	Oldies
KOZZ	1450	n/a	General	Sports	n/a
KOWL	1490	Commercial	General	News/Talk	n/a
KIHM	1590	Non-Comm	General/Religious	Educational/Music	Christian
KQLO	1590	Commercial	General/Hispanic	Educational/Music	Top 40

Note: Stations included cover the Reno DMA (Designated Market Area); n/a not available
Source: BurrellesLuce, MediaContacts Online, January 2006

Major FM Radio Stations

Call Letters	Freq. (mHz)	Station Type	Target Audience	Station Format	Music Format
KUNR	88.7	College	General	Music/News	Jazz
KNIS	91.3	Non-Comm	General/Religious	Educational/Music	Christian
KJZS	92.1	Commercial	General	Music	Jazz
KNHK	92.9	Commercial	General	Music/News/Talk	Classic Rock
KJDX	93.3	Commercial	General	Music/News	Country
KWYL	93.7	Commercial	General	Music	Urban Contemp.
KRLT	93.9	Commercial	General	Music	Adult Contemp.
KNEV	95.5	Commercial	General	Music	Alternative
KLCA	96.5	Commercial	General	Music	Adult Contemp.
KWNZ	97.3	Commercial	General	Music	Urban Contemp.
KVLV	99.3	Commercial	General	Music/News	Adult Contemp.
KGVM	99.3	Commercial	General	Music/News	Adult Contemp.
KRZQ	100.9	Commercial	General	Music/Talk	Alternative
KRNV	101.7	Commercial	General/Hispanic	Music/News	Latin
KHJQ	102.1	Commercial	General	Music	Top 40
KODS	103.7	Commercial	General	Music	Oldies
KDOT	104.5	Commercial	General	Music	Modern Rock
KOZZ	105.7	n/a	General	Music	n/a
KMMT	106.5	Commercial	General	Music/News	Adult Contemp.
KRNO	106.9	Commercial	General	Music	Soft Rock

Note: Stations included cover the Reno DMA (Designated Market Area); n/a not available
BurrellesLuce, MediaContacts Online, January 2006

CLIMATE

Average and Extreme Temperatures

Temperature	Jan	Feb	Mar	Apr	May	Jun	Jul	Aug	Sep	Oct	Nov	Dec	Yr.
Extreme High (°F)	70	75	83	89	96	103	104	105	101	91	77	70	105
Average High (°F)	45	51	56	64	73	82	91	89	81	70	55	46	67
Average Temp. (°F)	32	38	41	48	56	63	70	68	61	51	40	33	50
Average Low (°F)	19	23	26	31	38	44	49	47	40	32	25	20	33
Extreme Low (°F)	-16	-16	0	13	18	25	33	24	20	8	1	-16	-16

Note: Figures cover the years 1949-1992
Source: National Climatic Data Center, International Station Meteorological Climate Summary, 9/96

Average Precipitation/Snowfall/Humidity

Precip./Humidity	Jan	Feb	Mar	Apr	May	Jun	Jul	Aug	Sep	Oct	Nov	Dec	Yr.
Avg. Precip. (in.)	1.0	0.9	0.7	0.4	0.7	0.4	0.3	0.2	0.3	0.4	0.8	1.0	7.2
Avg. Snowfall (in.)	6	5	4	1	1	Tr	0	0	Tr	Tr	2	4	24
Avg. Rel. Hum. 7am (%)	79	77	71	61	55	51	49	55	64	72	78	80	66
Avg. Rel. Hum. 4pm (%)	51	41	34	27	26	22	19	19	22	27	41	51	32

Note: Figures cover the years 1949-1992; Tr = Trace amounts (<0.05 in. of rain; <0.5 in. of snow)
Source: National Climatic Data Center, International Station Meteorological Climate Summary, 9/96

Weather Conditions

Temperature			Daytime Sky			Precipitation		
10°F & below	32°F & below	90°F & above	Clear	Partly cloudy	Cloudy	0.01 inch or more precip.	0.1 inch or more snow/ice	Thunder-storms
14	178	50	143	139	83	50	17	14

Note: Figures are average number of days per year and cover the years 1949-1992
Source: National Climatic Data Center, International Station Meteorological Climate Summary, 9/96

HAZARDOUS WASTE

Superfund Sites

Reno has no sites on the EPA's Superfund Final National Priorities List.
U.S. Environmental Protection Agency, Final National Priorities List, March 20, 2007

AIR & WATER QUALITY

Air Quality Index

Area	Percent of Days when Air Quality was...[2]				AQI Statistics	
	Good	Moderate	Unhealthy for Sensitive Groups	Unhealthy	Maximum	Median
MSA[1]	63.3	35.6	1.1	0.0	146	46

Note: The Air Quality Index (AQI) is an index for reporting daily air quality. EPA calculates the AQI for five major air pollutants regulated by the Clean Air Act: ground-level ozone, particle pollution (also known as particulate matter), carbon monoxide, sulfur dioxide, and nitrogen dioxide. The AQI runs from 0 to 500. The higher the AQI value, the greater the level of air pollution and the greater the health concern. There are six AQI categories: "Good" The AQI is between 0 and 50. Air quality is considered satisfactory; "Moderate" The AQI is between 51 and 100. Air quality is acceptable; "Unhealthy for Sensitive Groups" When AQI values are between 101 and 150, members of sensitive groups may experience health effects; "Unhealthy" When AQI values are between 151 and 200 everyone may begin to experience health effects; "Very Unhealthy" AQI values between 201 and 300 trigger a health alert; "Hazardous" AQI values over 300 trigger health warnings of emergency conditions; (1) Metropolitan Statistical Area - see Appendix A for areas included; (2) Based on 365 days with AQI data in 2005.
Source: U.S. Environmental Protection Agency, Air Quality Index Report, 2005

Air Quality Index Pollutants

Area	Percent of Days when AQI Pollutant was...[2]					
	Carbon Monoxide	Nitrogen Dioxide	Ozone	Sulfur Dioxide	Particulate Matter 2.5	Particulate Matter 10
MSA[1]	0.3	0.0	48.2	0.0	5.5	46.0

Note: The Air Quality Index (AQI) is an index for reporting daily air quality. EPA calculates the AQI for five major air pollutants regulated by the Clean Air Act: ground-level ozone, particle pollution (also known as particulate matter), carbon monoxide, sulfur dioxide, and nitrogen dioxide. The AQI runs from 0 to 500. The higher the AQI value, the greater the level of air pollution and the greater the health concern; (1) Metropolitan Statistical Area - see Appendix A for areas included; (2) Based on 365 days with AQI data in 2005.
Source: U.S. Environmental Protection Agency, Air Quality Index Report, 2005

Number of Days with Air Quality Index Values Greater than 100

Area	Trend Sites								All Sites
	1998	1999	2000	2001	2002	2003	2004	2005	2005
MSA[1]	n/a	n/a	n/a	n/a	n/a	n/a	n/a	n/a	n/a

Note: An AQI value greater than 100 indicates that air quality would have been in the unhealthful range on that day. Data from exceptional events are not included. These counts are presented in two ways. First, the counts are based on sites having an adequate record of monitoring data during the trend period (trend sites). These counts represent the relative change in the number of days with AQI values greater than 100. In the last column, the counts are based on all sites with data in the most recent year (because it is possible for a site to have data in the most recent year but not enough data to be a trend site); (1) Metropolitan Statistical Area - see Appendix A for areas included; n/a not available.
Source: U.S. Environmental Protection Agency, Air Trends Fact Book 2005

Maximum Pollutant Concentrations

	Particulate Matter 10 (ug/m³)	Particulate Matter 2.5 (ug/m³)	Ozone 1-hour (ppm)	Carbon Monoxide (ppm)	Sulfur Dioxide (ppm)	Nitrogen Dioxide (ppm)	Lead (ug/m³)
MSA[1] Level	142	41	0.081	3	n/a	n/a	n/a
NAAQS[2]	150	65	0.125	9	0.140	0.053	1.50
Met NAAQS[2]	Yes	Yes	Yes	Yes	n/a	n/a	n/a

Note: Data from exceptional events are not included; (1) Metropolitan Statistical Area - see Appendix A for areas included; (2) National Ambient Air Quality Standards; n/a not available
Units: ppm = parts per million; ug/m³ = micrograms per cubic meter
Source: U.S. Environmental Protection Agency, Air Trends Fact Book 2005

Watershed Health

The U.S. Environmental Protection Agency monitors the health of the aquatic resources for the nation's 2,000+ watersheds. **The Truckee watershed serves the Reno area and received an overall Index of Watershed Indicators (IWI) score of 3 (less serious problems - low vulnerability).** The IWI score is based on seven condition and nine vulnerability indicators. The overall IWI score ranges from 1 (best health) to 6 (worst health). The Condition Indicators include: designated use attainment, fish and wildlife consumption advisories, source water condition, contaminated sediments, ambient water quality, and wetlands loss index. The Vulnerability Indicators include: aquatic species at risk, conventional and toxic loads over permitted limits, urban and agricultural runoff potential, population change, hydrologic modification, estuarine pollution susceptibility, and air deposition. *Note: The IWI is no longer being updated by the U.S. EPA. Source: U.S. Environmental Protection Agency, Index of Watershed Indicators, October 26, 2001*

Drinking Water

Water System Name	Pop. Served	Primary Water Source Type	Number of Violations in 2006[a]		
			Health Based	Significant Monitoring	Monitoring
Truckee Meadows Water Authority	315,000	Surface	None	None	None

Note: (a) Based on violation data from January 1, 2006 to December 31, 2006
Source: U.S. Environmental Protection Agency, Office of Ground Water and Drinking Water, Safe Drinking Water Information System (data extracted April 12, 2007)

Reno tap water is alkaline, very soft and not fluoridated.
Editor & Publisher Market Guide, 2005

Sacramento, California

Background

Sacramento is the capital of California and the seat of Sacramento County. It lies at the juncture of the Sacramento and American rivers, an international attraction for rafters and kayakers, and is bracketed by two mountain ranges, with the Coastal Range rising on the west and the Sierra Nevada range on the east. As the seat of state government and a hub of traditional and new economic activity, the city offers great opportunities to its current residents and to newcomers.

Sacramento was settled by a Swiss soldier, Captain John Augustus Sutter, in 1839, when he received permission of the then-Mexican government to establish a new colony. The beautiful 50,000-acre land grant included a wide swath of the rich and fertile valley between the two rivers, and Sutter's ranch, trading post, and agricultural projects were soon productive and profitable. When, in 1846, American troops occupied the area, Sutter was well-positioned to take advantage, and his trade soon extended well up the northern coast.

One of Sutter's employees, a carpenter named James W. Marshall, discovered gold at the mill at Columa, and "Sutter's Mill" subsequently came to symbolize everything associated with America's first gold rush. Sutter first tried to expand into mining supplies, but was only meagerly rewarded. He then ceded land along the Sacramento River to his son, who drew up plans for the establishment of the town that became the city we know today.

Sacramento was a natural center for the supply of miners, but it did not become a thriving town easily. It was plagued by floods, as well as fire and a cholera epidemic. The flooding has since been well controlled by dam projects, which also now supply electricity to a wide area, but the town's early and dismal record did little to recommend it as the young state's new capital. However, Sutter managed to fight off a daunting list of candidates for that designation, and in 1854, Sacramento became California's capital.

The state Renaissance Revival capitol building is breathtaking. The domed granite structure is built on a sloping terrace, with a park full of trees and flowers surrounding the building. The tree-lined streets laid out in front are broad and straight, and eye-pleasing camellias decorate the scenery in random patterns.

Sutter's Fort State Historical Monument features a restoration of Sutter's original ranch and trading post, and a designated Old Sacramento Historical Area preserves many buildings from the gold rush period and thereafter. At the city's Crocker Art Museum, currently undergoing a huge expansion tripling the existing space, visitors can view an extensive collection of works by, among others, Durer, Michelangelo, Rembrandt, and Leonardo da Vinci. Sacramento's symphony and the Sacramento Ballet are active, professional, and well-attended. The space and aviation industries contribute as well to the area's economy, and components for America's first satellite were built there

Raley Field, a baseball stadium completed in 2000, is home to the Sacramento River Rats. In addition, the town hosts two basketball teams that play at the ARCO arena, Sacramento is also home to the California State University at Sacramento, McGeorge School of Law, and three colleges, Cosumnes River, Sacramento City, and Sierra College. In addition, the University of California at Davis is within comfortable commuting distance.

The Sacramento Intermodal Transportation Facility Project (SITF), an integrated transportation plan, saw its first phase completed in late 2004. By late 2006, a link on the Amtrak/Folsom reached the downtown Sacramento Valley Station, connecting light rail with inter-city services and local and commuter buses. Further links, south to Cosumnes River College and north to Sacramento International Airport, are planned and should be completed by 2014. The city is currently revitalizing the riverfront for mixed-use projects.

Sacramento has a mild climate with abundant sunshine. A nearly cloud-free sky prevails throughout the summer months, which are usually dry, with warm to hot afternoons and mostly mild nights. Thunderstorms, which are few in number, occur mainly in the spring. Heavy fog develops mostly in midwinter, never in summer, and seldom in spring or fall.

Rankings

GeneralRankings

- Sacramento was ranked #85 out of 331 metro areas in *Cities Ranked & Rated*. Criteria: cost of living; climate; crime; transportation; economy and jobs; education; arts and culture; health and healthcare; leisure. *Cities Ranked & Rated, 1st Edition, 2004*

- Sacramento was selected as one of the "50 Best Places to Live" by *Men's Journal*. The city ranked #5 in the "Best Adventure Cities" category. Criteria: proximity to national parks, rock climbing, surfing, biking, skiing, and other active-pursuit options. *Men's Journal, April 2007*

- Sacramento was selected as one of "60 Cheap Places to Live" in the U.S. The city appeared in the "Bohemian Bargains" (lively inner cities) category. *Forbes.com, August 20, 2004*

Business/Finance Rankings

- Sacramento was selected as one of the best places to start and grow a company by *Entrepreneur* and the National Policy Research Council. The Sacramento metro area ranked #34 out of 50 large metro areas. Criteria: business formation and growth (firms started four to 14 years ago that still employ at least 5 people and experienced rapid growth over the last four years). *Entrepreneur/National Policy Research Council, "Hot Cities for Entrepreneurs," September 2006*

- Intel, in partnership with Sperling's BestPlaces, ranked the 80 "Best Cities for Teleworking" in America. The Sacramento metro area ranked #6 among large metro areas. The study identifies cities that hold the greatest potential for teleworking based on a host of factors including typical commuting times, fuel prices, availability of broadband Internet access and percentage of the population in telework friendly jobs. The study also factored in extreme climate and natural hazards. *Intel, "Best Cities for Teleworking," March 30, 2006*

- Sacramento was selected as one of 20 cities in North America that is doing its part to host green conventions by providing renewable energy, intelligent recycling programs, transportation that minimizes usage of fossil fuels, and plenty of parkland. The city was ranked #19. *Meetings and Conventions, "Natural Choices," August 2006*

- The Sacramento metro area appeared on the Milken Institute "2005 Best Performing Cities" index. Rank: #34 out of 200 large metro areas. Criteria: job growth; wage and salary growth; high-tech output growth. *Milken Institute, "2005 Best Performing Cities," February 2006*

- The Sacramento metro area was selected as one of "The Best Cities for Doing Business in America." *Inc.* magazine measured employment growth in 393 regions using the following criteria: recent growth trend; mid-term growth; long-term trend; and current year growth. The Sacramento metro area ranked #19 among large metro areas and #132 overall. *Inc., May 2006*

- The Sacramento metro area was selected as one of "The Top 20 Boom Towns in America." *Business 2.0* magazine and econometric research firm Global Insight compared 319 metropolitan areas in the U.S. and ranked the 61 with populations over 1 million. Criteria: a weighted formula that includes forecast growth rates in sectors that contain the economy's 10 most skilled occupational clusters; the prevalence of college degrees in the local workforce; median salary. The area ranked #11 among large metro areas. *Business 2.0 Magazine, March 2004*

- Sacramento was identified as one of the 100 "Most Unwired Cities" in the U.S. The area ranked #18 out of the 100 largest metro areas in the U.S. Criteria: number of public and commercial wireless access points (hotspots); airports with wireless Internet access; broadband availability; local wireless networks; and wireless email devices. *Intel, "Most Unwired Cities Survey," June 7, 2005*

- Sacramento was ranked #11 out of 125 regions worldwide in terms of its "Knowledge Competitiveness Index." The index attempts to measure the knowledge-based development taking place throughout the world and is based on 19 measures of economic performance that indicate a region's ability to translate its knowledge capacity into economic value. *Robert Huggins Associates, World Knowledge Competitiveness Index 2005*

- *Forbes* ranked the 200 most populous metro areas in the U.S. in terms of the "Best Places for Business and Careers." The Sacramento metro area was ranked #89. Criteria: business costs (labor, energy, tax and office space expenses); living costs (housing, transportation, food and other household expenditures); education levels of the work force; job growth; income growth; migration trends; crime rates; and culture/leisure. *Forbes, April 23, 2007*

- *Fortune* ranked the 100 largest metro areas in the U.S. in terms of projected median home price change in 2006. The Sacramento metro area ranked #94. *Fortune, "The Top 100: Is the Party Over?" December 26, 2005*

Health/Environment Rankings

- *Reader's Digest* ranked the 50 largest metro areas in the U.S. in terms of how "clean" they are. The Sacramento metro area ranked #12. Criteria: air quality; water quality; toxic industrial pollution; Superfund sites; and sanitation. *Reader's Digest, "The 50 Cleanest (and Dirtiest) Cities in America," July 2005*

- Sanofi-aventis, in partnership with Sperling's BestPlaces, ranked the 50 worst cities for respiratory infections in the U.S. Sacramento ranked #50. Criteria: prevalence of sinusitis, pharyngitis (sore throat), bronchitis, acute upper respiratory infections, pneumonia, otitis media (middle ear infection), other respiratory tract infections and the common cold; total per capita prescriptions written for oral antibiotics for respiratory tract infections; and prevalence of state level antibiotic resistance. *Sanofi-aventis, "America's Worst Cities for Respiratory Infections," December 6, 2005*

- The Sacramento metro area appeared in *Country Home's* "2007 Best Green Places Report". The area ranked #103. Criteria included: air and watershed quality; miles of mass transit; green power; number of farmer's markets, organic producers and groceries. *Country Home, "2007 Best Green Places Report," April 2007*

- Wyeth Consumer Healthcare, in partnership with Sperling's BestPlaces, ranked the nation's 50 most populous metro areas in terms of five key health factors. The Sacramento metro area ranked #7. Criteria: physical activity, health status, nutrition, lifestyle pursuits; and mental wellness. *Wyeth Consumer Healthcare, "Centrum Healthiest Cities Study," April 19, 2005*

- The American Podiatric Medical Association and *Prevention* magazine ranked America's 100 most populated cities based on fitness-walker friendliness. The best cities have safe streets, beautiful places to walk, mild weather and good air quality. Sacramento ranked #52. *Prevention, "The Best Walking Cities of 2007," April 2007; American Podiatric Medical Association, "2007 Best Fitness-Walking Cities"*

- Sacramento was selected as one of the 25 fittest cities in America by *Men's Fitness Online*. It ranked #11 out of America's 50 largest cities. Criteria: gyms/sporting goods; nutrition; exercise/sports; overweight/sedentary; junk food; alcohol; smoking; television; air and water quality; climate; geography; commute time; parks/open space; recreation facilities; health care; motivation; civic legislation and leadership. *Men's Fitness Online, America's Fittest/Fattest Cities 2006*

- Sacramento was identified as a "2007 Asthma Capital." The area ranked #64 out of the nation's 100 largest metropolitan areas. Twelve factors were used to identify the most challenging places to live for people with asthma: estimated prevalence; self-reported prevalence; crude death rate for asthma; annual pollen score; annual air quality; public smoking laws; number of board-certified asthma specialists; school inhaler access laws; rescue medication use; controller medication use; uninsured rate; poverty rate. *Asthma and Allergy Foundation of America, "2007 Asthma Capitals"*

- Sacramento was identified as a "Spring Allergy Capital." The area ranked #50 out of 100. Three groups of factors were used to identify the most severe cities for people with allergies during the spring season: annual pollen levels; medicine utilization; access to board-certified allergists. *Asthma and Allergy Foundation of America, "2007 Spring Allergy Capital Rankings"*

- Sacramento was identified as a "Fall Allergy Capital." The area ranked #64 out of 100. Three groups of factors were used to identify the most severe cities for people with allergies during the fall season: annual pollen levels; medicine utilization; access to board-certified allergists. *Asthma and Allergy Foundation of America, "2006 Fall Allergy Capital Rankings"*

- Sacramento was selected as one of "America's Healthiest Cities" by *Natural Health* magazine. The city was ranked #15 out of the 50 largest urban areas in the U.S. Twenty-six criteria in the following four categories were examined: whether the city boasts natural offerings; how well the city promotes its residents' physical health; whether the city offers a healthy environment; how well the city fosters a sense of community. *Natural Health, April 2003*

- *Men's Health* ranked the nation's largest 100 cities in terms of the *Best (and Worst) Cities for Men*. Sacramento was ranked #25. Criteria: 24 statistical parameters of long life in the categories of health, quality of life, and fitness. *Men's Health, January/February 2007*

- *Men's Health* ranked 100 U.S. cities in terms of the quality of their tap water. Sacramento was ranked #53 and received a grade of C. Criteria: levels of total coliform bacteria, arsenic, lead, total trihalomethanes (linked to cancer), and halo-acetic acids, plus the number of EPA water-system violations from 1995 to 2005. *Men's Health, March 2007*

- GlaxoSmithKline, in partnership with Sperling's BestPlaces, analyzed the nation's 100 largest metro areas and identified 25 asthma "hot spots" where high prevalence makes the condition a key issue and environmental triggers and other factors can make living with asthma a particular challenge. The Sacramento metro area ranked #25 with #1 being the most challenging place to live. Criteria: asthma prevalence; asthma mortality; pollen scores; number of asthma specialists per capita; ratio of prescriptions for rescue medications to prescriptions for controller medications (an indicator of proper asthma treatment); air pollution; smoking laws; climate; and prevalence of tobacco use. *GlaxoSmithKline, "Asthma Hot Spots," October 29, 2002*

- Ortho-McNeil Neurologics, in partnership with Sperling's BestPlaces, analyzed 110 metro areas and identified those U.S. cities with the highest prevalence of factors that are most commonly associated with migraine headaches. The Sacramento metro area ranked #57. Criteria: number of migraine-related drug prescriptions per capita; lifestyle factors that can contribute to migraines; environmental factors that can trigger migraines; and consumption of migraine-triggering foods. *Ortho-McNeil Neurologics, "America's Migraine Hot Spots," March 14, 2006*

- Sperling's BestPlaces ranked 331 metro areas and identified the most and least stressful U.S. cities. The Sacramento metro area ranked #36 out of the 100 largest metro areas (#1 = most stressful). Criteria: divorce rate; unemployment rate; violent and property crime; suicide rate; commute time; mental health; alcohol consumption; cloudy days. *www.BestPlaces.net, January 9, 2004*

- HealthGrades evaluated the performance of America's 25 most populous metropolitan areas by measuring the outcomes of five of the highest volume and most widely studied procedures and diagnoses: coronary artery bypass graft surgery; percutaneus coronary interventions; acute myocardial infarction/heart attack in angioplasty-capable hospitals; congestive heart failure; and community acquired pneumonia. The Sacramento metro area ranked #20. *HealthGrades, "HealthGrades Hospital Quality in America Study," October 12, 2004*

- Sacramento was highlighted as one of the 25 most ozone-polluted metro areas in the U.S. The area ranked #7. *American Lung Association, State of the Air 2006*

- Sacramento was selected as one of "America's Pet Healthiest Cities" by Purina. The city ranked #27 out of 50. Criteria: veterinary services; environment; legislation; preventative care; obesity/body condition. *Purina Pet Institute, "America's Pet Healthiest Cities," May 20, 2003*

- According to research conducted by Malibu Wellness of 100 major U.S. cities' local water quality reports, Sacramento was selected as a top-ranked color-friendly city in terms of hair color application and longevity. Criteria: quantity of minerals found in the water supply (lower ppm is better for hair color); type of oxidizers such as chlorine; and pH levels. *Malibu Wellness, Wellness e-Letter, "Best & Worst Cities for Hair Color," February 2005*

Women/MinoritiesRankings

■ Sacramento was ranked #31 out of 100 metro areas in *SELF Magazine's* ranking of "America's Best Places for Women." A panel of experts came up with nearly 40 criteria including: drinking and smoking rates; depression; unemployment; parks; crime; disease; healthcare insurance coverage; air quality; and commute times. *SELF Magazine, "America's Best Places for Women 2006," December 2006*

■ *Ladies Home Journal* ranked America's 200 largest cities based on the qualities women surveyed care about most. Sacramento ranked #26 out of 57 in the big city category (population over 300,000). Criteria: crime; lifestyle; education; jobs; health; child care; politics; and the economy. *Ladies Home Journal Online, "The Best Cities for Women 2002"*

■ Sacramento was profiled in the book *50 Fabulous Gay-Friendly Places to Live.* Criteria: an active gay community; positive gay health programs; youth outreach; gay-friendly politics; gay-owned and gay-friendly businesses; employment opportunities; fun nightlife; cultural opportunities; recreational opportunities; housing options. *50 Fabulous Gay-Friendly Places to Live, 2005*

■ Sacramento was identified as one of the top 25 metropolitan statistical areas ranked by percentage of coupled households that are gay or lesbian." The area ranked #22. *Human Rights Campaign, "Gay and Lesbian Families in the United States: Same-Sex Unmarried Partner Households," August 1, 2001*

Seniors/Retirement Rankings

■ Sperling's Best Places in partnership with Bankers Life & Casualty Company designed a survey to identify the top 50 metro areas in the U.S. that offer the best overall qualities for senior living. The Sacramento metro area ranked #45. The following criteria were statistically weighted to reflect the needs of the senior population: health; disease; economics; social; environment; spiritual; transportation; housing; and crime. *Bankers Life & Casualty Company, "Best Cities for Seniors 2005"*

■ A.G. Edwards ranked America's 500 top-performing communities based on their residents' personal savings and investing behavior. The Sacramento metro area ranked #374 with an index score of 97.65 (national average = 100.00). A dozen statistical factors were measured including: participation in retirement savings plans; personal debt levels; and home ownership. *A.G. Edwards, "2006 Nest Egg Index", September 6, 2006*

Children/Family Rankings

■ *Zero Population Growth* ranked 100 cities in terms of children's health, safety, and economic well-being. Sacramento was ranked #37 out of 80 Large Cities (remainder of the 100 largest cities in the U.S.) and was given a grade of B. Criteria: total population and population growth; percent of population under 18 years of age; percent of births to teens; infant mortality rate; percent of eligible women not receiving Title X services; contraceptive equity indicator; percent of children without health insurance; percent of city residents over age 25 with a high-school diploma; ration of PopEd (Population Connection's Education Program) teachers trained; sexuality education indicator; proficiency in reading and math; percent of kids living in poverty; percent growth in urbanized land; violent crime rate; recycling. *Population Connection, Kid Friendly Cities: Report Card 2004*

■ *Fit Pregnancy* magazine ranked the 50 best U.S. cities in which to have a baby. Sacramento was ranked #10. Criteria: fertility services; maternal and infant health risk; access to hospitals and doctors; safety; affordability; stroller friendliness; and birthing options. *Fit Pregnancy, February/March, 2006*

Safety Rankings

■ Farmers Insurance Group of Companies, in partnership with Sperling's BestPlaces, ranked 331 metro areas and identified the "Most Secure U.S. Place to Live." The Sacramento metro area ranked #7 out of the top 20 in the large city category (500,000 or more residents). Criteria: crime rates; risk of natural disasters; and job loss numbers. *Farmers Insurance Group, "25 Most Secure U.S. Place to Live," June 6, 2005*

- Allstate ranked the 200 largest cities in America in terms of driver safety. Sacramento ranked #172. In addition, drivers were 28.2% more likely to have had an accident compared to the national average. Allstate researchers analyzed internal Property Damage reported claims over a two-year period (from January 2003 to December 2004) to ensure the findings would not be affected by external influences such as weather or road construction. A weighted average of the two-year numbers determined the annual percentages. The report defines an auto crash as any collision resulting in a property damage claim. *Allstate, "Allstate America's Best Drivers Report 2006," May 24, 2006*

- Sacramento was identified as one of the most dangerous large metro areas for pedestrians in the U.S. The area ranked #16 out of the nations 50 largest metro areas. Criteria: average yearly pedestrian fatalities per capita (for the years 2002 and 2003) adjusted for the number of walkers. *Surface Transportation Policy Project, "Mean Streets 2004"*

- *Ladies Home Journal* ranked America's 200 largest cities in terms of safety. Sacramento ranked #100 out of 200. Criteria: violent crimes; crimes against property; and rape. *Ladies Home Journal Online, "The Best Cities for Women 2002"*

Sports/Recreation Rankings

- The Sacramento metro area appeared on *The Sporting News* list of the "Best Sports Cities 2006". The area ranked #47 out of 99 cities in North America. To be included in the rankings, a city must have at least one of the following: NCAA Division I basketball team; Class A minor league baseball team; training camp for a major league or NFL team; NASCAR Nextel Cup race; NCAA Division I-A bowl game; PGA Tour tournament; Triple Crown horse race. Once a city qualifies, a 12-month snapshot is taken of the sports atmosphere, putting a heavy premium on regular-season won-lost records; playoff berths, bowl appearances and tournament bids; championships; applicable power ratings; quality of competition; overall fan fervor; sports atmosphere and fan knowledge; abundance of teams (quality over quantity); stadium/arena quality; ticket availability and prices; franchise ownership; and the marquee appeal of athletes. *SportingNews.com, "Best Sports Cities 2006," August 1, 2006*

- Scarborough Research, a leading market research firm, identified the top local markets for avid NBA fans. The Sacramento DMA (Designated Market Area) ranked in the top 10 with 19% of consumers 18 years and over reporting that they are "very interested in the NBA". *Scarborough Research, Scarborough USA+ 2005 Release 2*

- The Sacramento metro area was selected by *Cranium* as one of the "Top 50 Fun Cities" in America. The area ranked #23. Criteria includes: number of sports teams, restaurants, and dance performances; number of toy stores; city budget spent on recreation. *Cranium, November 4, 2003*

- *Golf Digest* ranked 330 metro areas in the U.S. in terms of golf. The Sacramento metro area was ranked #257. Criteria: access to golf; weather; value of golf; and quality of golf. *Golf Digest, "Metro Golf Rankings," August 2005*

Dating/Romance Rankings

- The Sacramento metro area was selected as one of the "Best Cities for Relocating Singles" by Worldwide ERC and Primacy Relocation. The area ranked #66 out of the 100 largest metro areas in the U.S. Areas were selected based on the following criteria: Population Criteria (local percentage and growth trends of unmarried residents aged 25-34; male-female ratios; the number of newcomers to the area; diversity and density); Economic Criteria (job growth vs. unemployment rates; apartment rental costs; fee and occupancy rates for temporary housing and mini-storage; higher education costs, including in-state and out-of-state tuition requirements; vehicle tax rates and quality of service from utility providers); Quality-of-Life Criteria (level of per capita volunteering; quality and quantity of collegiate and professional sports with fun, fan-friendly venues; number of Starbucks and other coffee shops; quality or popularity of restaurants, nightspots, health clubs, and online dating; moderate climates with sustainable water supplies). *Worldwide ERC and Primacy Relocation, "2006 Best Cities for Relocating Singles," October 11, 2006*

- *Forbes* ranked the 40 most populous metro areas in the U.S. in terms of the "Best Cities for Singles." The Sacramento metro area was ranked #13. Criteria: number of singles; cost of living alone; nightlife; culture; job growth; coolness; and online dating. *Forbes.com, July 25, 2006*

- Sperling's BestPlaces in partnership with AXE Deodorant Bodyspray ranked 80 metro areas and identified "America's Best (and Worst) Cities for Dating." The Sacramento metro area ranked #40. Criteria: percentage of singles ages 18-24; population density; dating venues per capita. *AXE Deodorant Bodyspray, "America's Best (and Worst) Cities for Dating," May, 2004*

Miscellaneous Rankings

- Sacramento was determined to be one of America's smartest cities. The city ranked #30 in the large city category (200,000+ adults 25 years and older). Criteria: the editors rated the collective brainpower of U.S communities based on the educational attainment of its residents. *American City Business Journals, www.bizjournals.com, June 12, 2006*

- Sacramento was selected as one of the "Top 100 Sweatiest Summer Cities". The city was ranked #72. The ranking was based on the average male/female height/weight, average high temperature, and average relative humidity levels for 2002 in each of the cities during June, July and August. The sweat level was analyzed based on the assumption that the individual was walking for one hour. *Procter & Gamble, Old Spice, June 18, 2003*

- Sacramento appeared on ApartmentRatings.com "Top Cities for Renters List 2006". The area ranked #115 out of 138. Criteria: renter satisfaction; affordability; and vacancy. *ApartmentRatings.com, "Top Cities for Renters List 2006"*

- Sperling's BestPlaces in partnership with Pep Boys ranked 77 metro areas and identified "America's Most Drivable Cities." The Sacramento metro area ranked #59. Criteria: climate; road roughness; urban mobility; gas prices. *Pep Boys, "America's Most Drivable Cities," April 9, 2003*

- Sacramento was ranked #26 out of 268 metro areas in terms of its Creativity Index. The Creativity Index is a mix of four equally weighted factors: the Creative Class (scientists, engineers, architects, designers, writers, artists, musicians, or any profession where creativity is a key factor) share of the workforce; innovation, measured as patents per capita; high-tech industry, using the Milken Institute's Tech Pole Index; and diversity, measured by the Gay Index (a reasonable proxy for an areas' openness to different kinds of people and ideas). *The Rise of the Creative Class, 2002*

- Sacramento was selected as one of "America's Most Literate Cities." The city ranked #28 out of the 70 largest U.S. cities. Criteria: number of booksellers; library resources; Internet resources; educational attainment; periodical publishing resources; newspaper circulation. *Central Connecticut State University, "America's Most Literate Cities 2006"*

- State Farm Insurance, in partnership with Sperling's BestPlaces, analyzed several key factors that contribute to overall family preparedness. The Sacramento metro area ranked #19 out of the nation's 50 most populous metro areas. Criteria: quality of life; life insurance coverage; and investments. *State Farm Life Insurance, "Fiscally Fit Cities Report," July 20, 2004*

- Scarborough Research, a leading market research firm, identified the top local markets for reality television. The Sacramento DMA (Designated Market Area) ranked in the top 10 with 26% of consumers reporting that they "typically watch" reality-dating, reality-talent, or reality-adventure television shows. *Scarborough Research, Scarborough USA+ 2004 Release 1*

- Scarborough Research, a leading market research firm, identified the top local markets for coffee bar patronage. The Sacramento DMA (Designated Market Area) ranked in the top 10 with 20% of adults reporting that they have used any coffee house/bar during the past 30 days. *Scarborough Research, Scarborough USA+ 2004 Release 1*

Business Environment

CITY FINANCES

City Government Finances

Component	2003-2004 ($000)	2003-2004 ($ per capita)
Total Revenues	824,332	1,894
Total Expenditures	853,717	1,961
Debt Outstanding	1,356,601	3,117
Cash and Securities	1,283,794	2,950

Source: U.S Census Bureau, Government Finances 2003-2004

City Government Revenue by Source

Source	2003-2004 ($000)	2003-2004 ($ per capita)
General Revenue		
From Federal Government	53,705	123
From State Government	60,622	139
From Local Governments	0	0
Taxes		
Property	99,171	228
Sales	156,737	360
Personal Income	0	0
License	0	0
Charges	219,159	504
Liquor Store	0	0
Utility	45,969	106
Employee Retirement	14,799	34
Other	174,170	400

Source: U.S Census Bureau, Government Finances 2003-2004

City Government Expenditures by Function

Function	2003-2004 ($000)	2003-2004 ($ per capita)	2003-2004 (%)
General Expenditures			
Airports	0	0	0.0
Corrections	4,499	10	0.5
Education	0	0	0.0
Fire Protection	62,668	144	7.3
Governmental Administration	100,800	232	11.8
Health	13,175	30	1.5
Highways	109,179	251	12.8
Hospitals	0	0	0.0
Housing and Community Development	66,370	152	7.8
Interest on General Debt	59,892	138	7.0
Libraries	7,759	18	0.9
Parking	11,284	26	1.3
Parks and Recreation	80,256	184	9.4
Police Protection	111,189	255	13.0
Public Welfare	0	0	0.0
Sewerage	29,765	68	3.5
Solid Waste Management	43,961	101	5.1
Liquor Store	0	0	0.0
Utility	87,580	201	10.3
Employee Retirement	26,772	62	3.1
Other	38,568	89	4.5

Source: U.S Census Bureau, Government Finances 2003-2004

Municipal Bond Ratings

Area	Moody's
City	Aaa

Source: Mergent Bond Record, January 2007 (unless noted otherwise)

DEMOGRAPHICS

Population Growth

Area	1990 Census	2000 Census	2006 Estimate	2011 Projection	Population Growth (%) 1990-2000	Population Growth (%) 2000-2011
City	368,923	407,018	468,468	515,264	10.3	26.6
MSA[1]	1,481,126	1,796,857	2,068,151	2,280,011	21.3	26.9
U.S.	248,709,873	281,421,906	298,021,266	312,383,955	13.2	11.0

Note: (1) Metropolitan Statistical Area - see Appendix B for areas included
Source: Claritas, Inc.

Number of Households and Average Household Size

Area	2006 Estimate	2006 Average Household Size
City	176,122	2.66
MSA[1]	763,086	2.71
U.S.	112,267,302	2.65

Note: (1) Metropolitan Statistical Area - see Appendix B for areas included
Source: Claritas, Inc.

Race and Ethnicity

Area	White Alone[2]	Black Alone[2]	Asian Alone[2]	Other Race Alone[2]	Hispanic[3]
City	45.2	14.5	18.2	22.0	24.5
MSA[1]	66.5	7.2	10.5	15.9	17.5
U.S.	73.3	12.4	4.2	10.1	14.5

Note: Figures are 2006 estimates; (1) Metropolitan Statistical Area - see Appendix B for areas included
(2) Alone is defined as not being in combination with one or more other races; (3) May be of any race.
Source: Claritas, Inc.

Segregation

City Index[2]	City Rank[3]	MSA[1] Index[2]	MSA[1] Rank[4]
49.1	70	59.6	150

Note: Figures are based on an analysis of Census 2000 data; (1) Metropolitan Statistical Area - see Appendix A for areas included; (2) White/Black Dissimilarity Index—the most commonly used measure of segregation between two groups, reflecting their relative distributions across neighborhoods within a city or metropolitan area. It can range in value from 0, indicating complete integration, to 100, indicating complete segregation; (3) Ranges from 1 (most segregated) to 100 (least segregated) and includes all the cities in this book; (4) Ranges from 1 (most segregated) to 318 (least segregated) and includes 318 metropolitan areas.
Source: www.CensusScope.org

Ancestry

Area	German	Irish[2]	English	American	Italian	Polish	French[3]	Scottish
City	8.4	6.8	6.3	3.1	3.8	0.8	2.1	1.3
MSA[1]	14.4	10.7	10.7	4.6	5.4	1.4	3.3	2.2
U.S.	15.2	10.9	8.7	7.3	5.6	3.2	3.0	1.7

Note: Figures include multiple ancestry (e.g. if a person reported being Irish and Italian, they were included in both columns); (1) Metropolitan Statistical Area - see Appendix A for areas included; (2) Includes Celtic; (3) Includes Alsatian but excludes Basque
Source: Census 2000, Summary File 3

Foreign-Born Population

Area	Any Foreign Country	Europe	Asia	Africa	Oceania[2]	Canada	Mexico	Latin America[3]
City	20.3	2.0	9.9	0.3	1.0	0.2	6.0	0.9
MSA[1]	13.9	2.7	5.9	0.2	0.4	0.4	3.6	0.7
U.S.	11.1	1.7	2.9	0.3	0.1	0.3	3.3	2.5

Note: (1) Metropolitan Statistical Area - see Appendix A for areas included; (2) Includes Australia, New Zealand subregion, Melanesia, Micronesia, Polynesia, and Oceania n.e.c; (3) Includes Central America (excluding Mexico), South America, and the Caribbean.
Source: Census 2000, Summary File 3

Marriage Status

Area	Never Married	Now Married (excluding Separated)	Separated	Widowed	Divorced
City	33.4	44.5	3.1	6.8	12.2
MSA[1]	26.8	53.1	2.4	5.9	11.8
U.S.	27.1	54.4	2.2	6.6	9.7

Note: Figures are percentages and cover the population 15 years of age and older;
(1) Metropolitan Statistical Area - see Appendix A for areas included
Source: Census 2000, Summary File 3

Age Distribution

Area	Percent of Population						
	Under Age 5	Age 5 to 17	Age 18 to 34	Age 35 to 49	Age 50 to 64	Age 65 to 79	80 Years and Over
City	7.0	20.2	25.6	22.8	13.0	8.2	3.2
MSA[1]	6.9	20.3	22.4	24.4	14.4	8.7	2.9
U.S.	6.8	18.9	23.7	23.5	14.8	9.2	3.2

Note: (1) Metropolitan Statistical Area - see Appendix A for areas included
Source: Census 2000, Summary File 3

Male/Female Ratio

Area	Males	Females	Males per 100 Females
City	228,538	239,930	95.3
MSA[1]	1,016,122	1,052,029	96.6
U.S.	146,712,712	151,308,554	97.0

Note: Figures are 2006 estimates; (1) Metropolitan Statistical Area - see Appendix B for areas included
Source: Claritas, Inc.

Religion

Area	Catholic	Southern Baptist	United Methodist	ELCA[1]	LDS[2]	Presbyterian Church USA	Jewish Est.	Muslim Est.
County	18.3	1.7	0.6	0.7	2.5	0.9	1.4	0.5
U.S.	22.0	7.1	3.7	1.8	1.5	1.1	2.2	0.6

Note: Figures are the number of adherents as a percentage of the total population; Adherents are defined as all members, including full members, their children and the estimated number of other participants who are not considered members (e.g. the baptized, those not confirmed, those regularly attending services, etc.); (1) Evangelical Lutheran Church in America; (2) The Church of Jesus Christ of Latter Day Saints Source: Reprinted with permission from Religious Congregations and Membership in the United States 2000 (Nashville, Glenmary Research Center, 2002) Copyright Association of Statisticians of American Religious Bodies. All rights reserved.

ECONOMY

Gross Metropolitan Product

Area	2002	2003	2004	2005	2005 Rank[2]
MSA[1]	73.5	78.8	85.3	91.6	24

Note: Figures are in billions of dollars; (1) Sacramento—Arden-Arcade—Roseville, CA Metropolitan Statistical Area - see Appendix A for areas included; (2) Rank ranges from 1 to 361 Source: The U.S. Conference of Mayors, "U.S. Metro Economies: GMP - The Engines of America's Growth," January 2007

Economic Growth

Area	1995 GMP	2005 GMP	Average Annual Growth Rate	Growth Rate Rank[2]
MSA[1]	45.8	91.6	7.2	33

Note: Figures are in billions of dollars; GMP = Gross Metropolitan Product; (1)
Sacramento—Arden-Arcade—Roseville, CA Metropolitan Statistical Area - see Appendix A for areas included;
(2) Rank ranges from 1 to 361
Source: The U.S. Conference of Mayors, "U.S. Metro Economies: GMP - The Engines of America's Growth,"
January 2007

INCOME

Per Capita/Median/Average Income

Area	Per Capita ($)	Median Household ($)	Average Household ($)
City	21,721	43,480	57,010
MSA[1]	26,098	54,161	69,937
U.S.	25,129	48,775	65,849

Note: Figures are 2006 estimates; (1) Metropolitan Statistical Area - see Appendix B for areas included
Source: Claritas, Inc.

Household Income Distribution

Area	Under $15,000	$15,000 -24,999	$25,000 -34,999	$35,000 -49,999	$50,000 -74,999	$75,000 -99,000	$100,000 -149,999	$150,000 and up
City	16.4	12.2	11.9	16.7	18.8	10.3	9.2	4.5
MSA[1]	11.1	9.7	10.3	15.5	20.0	13.0	13.3	7.0
U.S.	13.3	11.0	11.3	15.7	19.5	11.8	11.0	6.4

Note: Figures are 2006 estimates; (1) Metropolitan Statistical Area - see Appendix B for areas included
Source: Claritas, Inc.

Poverty Rates by Age

Area	All Ages	Under 5 Years Old	5 to 17 Years Old	18 to 64 Years Old	65 Years and Over
City	20.0	2.1	6.0	10.9	1.0
MSA[1]	12.2	1.2	3.5	6.8	0.7
U.S.	12.4	1.2	3.0	6.9	1.2

Note: Figures are percent of population with income in 1999 below poverty level and only include population
for whom poverty status is determined; (1) Metropolitan Statistical Area - see Appendix A for areas included
Source: Census 2000, Summary File 3

Personal Bankruptcy Filing Rate

Area	2003	2004	2005
Sacramento County	4.54	4.12	5.99
U.S.	5.57	5.31	6.88

Note: Numbers are per 1,000 population and include Chapter 7 and Chapter 13 filings
Source: Federal Deposit Insurance Corporation (FDIC), Regional Economic Conditions (RECON), 3/24/2006

EMPLOYMENT

Labor Force and Employment

Area	Civilian Labor Force			Workers Employed		
	Dec. 2005	Dec. 2006	% Chg.	Dec. 2005	Dec. 2006	% Chg.
City	213,136	216,594	1.6	202,773	205,391	1.3
MSA[1]	1,032,494	1,048,457	1.5	990,211	1,002,996	1.3
U.S.	149,874,000	152,571,000	1.8	142,918,000	146,081,000	2.2

Note: Data is not seasonally adjusted and covers workers 16 years of age and older;
(1) Metropolitan Statistical Area - see Appendix B for areas included
Source: Bureau of Labor Statistics, http://stats.bls.gov

Unemployment Rate

Area	2006											
	Jan.	Feb.	Mar.	Apr.	May	Jun.	Jul.	Aug.	Sep.	Oct.	Nov.	Dec.
City	5.6	5.7	5.5	5.4	5.1	5.7	5.8	5.4	5.2	4.9	5.2	5.2
MSA[1]	4.7	4.8	4.7	4.6	4.2	4.7	4.7	4.4	4.2	3.9	4.3	4.3
U.S.	5.1	5.1	4.8	4.5	4.4	4.8	5.0	4.6	4.4	4.1	4.3	4.3

Note: Data is not seasonally adjusted and covers workers 16 years of age and older; All figures are percentages; (1) Metropolitan Statistical Area - see Appendix B for areas included
Source: Bureau of Labor Statistics, http://stats.bls.gov

Employment by Occupation

Occupation Classification	City (%)	MSA[1] (%)	U.S. (%)
Sales and Office	28.6	29.1	26.7
Professional and Related	22.5	21.6	20.2
Service	16.2	14.8	14.9
Production, Transportation, and Material Moving	11.0	9.7	14.6
Management, Business, and Financial	13.7	15.3	13.5
Construction, Extraction, and Maintenance	7.6	9.1	9.4
Farming, Forestry, and Fishing	0.4	0.4	0.7

Note: Figures cover employed civilians 16 years of age and older;
(1) Metropolitan Statistical Area - see Appendix A for areas included
Source: Census 2000, Summary File 3

Employment by Industry

Sector	MSA[1]		U.S.
	Number of Employees	Percent of Total	Percent of Total
Government	232,700	25.5	16.3
Education and Health Services	93,500	10.2	13.2
Professional and Business Services	107,400	11.8	12.9
Retail Trade	105,000	11.5	11.5
Manufacturing	49,100	5.4	10.2
Leisure and Hospitality	87,200	9.5	9.5
Financial Activities	65,400	7.2	6.1
Construction	69,800	7.6	5.5
Wholesale Trade	29,000	3.2	4.3
Other Services	28,900	3.2	3.9
Transportation and Utilities	24,600	2.7	3.7
Information	20,200	2.2	2.2
Natural Resources and Mining	800	0.1	0.5

Note: Figures cover non-farm employment as of December 2006 and are not seasonally adjusted;
(1) Metropolitan Statistical Area - see Appendix B for areas included
Source: Bureau of Labor Statistics, http://stats.bls.gov

Occupations with Greatest Projected Employment Growth: 2002 - 2012

Occupation[1]	2002 Employment	2012 Projected Employment	Numeric Employment Change	Percent Employment Change
Retail Salespersons	435,400	513,200	77,800	17.9
Postsecondary Teachers	154,500	217,700	63,200	40.9
Combined Food Preparation and Serving Workers, Including Fast Food	215,100	277,300	62,200	28.9
Cashiers	358,800	420,700	61,900	17.3
Registered Nurses	201,600	258,400	56,800	28.2
Waiters and Waitresses	214,000	264,900	50,900	23.8
Customer Service Representatives	197,500	244,900	47,400	24.0
Office Clerks, General	400,300	446,500	46,200	11.5
General and Operations Managers	224,000	267,000	43,000	19.2
Teacher Assistants	179,600	222,300	42,700	23.8

Note: Projections cover California; (1) Sorted by numeric employment change
Source: www.projectionscentral.com, State Occupational Projections, 2002-2012 Long-Term Projections

Fastest Growing Occupations: 2002 - 2012

Occupation[1]	2002 Employment	2012 Projected Employment	Numeric Employment Change	Percent Employment Change
Physical Therapist Aides	4,200	6,800	2,600	61.9
Dental Hygienists	16,600	26,200	9,600	57.8
Dental Assistants	42,700	67,100	24,400	57.1
Tapers	9,200	14,400	5,200	56.5
Drywall and Ceiling Tile Installers	26,800	41,800	15,000	56.0
Tile and Marble Setters	8,600	13,400	4,800	55.8
Network Systems and Data Communications Analysts	20,300	31,600	11,300	55.7
Physical Therapist Assistants	3,900	6,000	2,100	53.8
Fitness Trainers and Aerobics Instructors	24,000	35,700	11,700	48.8
Self-Enrichment Education Teachers	24,200	35,800	11,600	47.9

Note: Projections cover California; (1) Sorted by percent employment change and excludes occupations with numeric employment change less than 1500
Source: www.projectionscentral.com, State Occupational Projections, 2002-2012 Long-Term Projections

Average Wages

Occupation	$/Hr.	Occupation	$/Hr.
Accountants and Auditors	27.79	Maids and Housekeeping Cleaners	9.34
Automotive Mechanics	18.02	Maintenance and Repair Workers	17.14
Bookkeepers	16.56	Marketing Managers	46.33
Carpenters	22.56	Nuclear Medicine Technologists	38.25
Cashiers	10.09	Nurses, Licensed Practical	21.17
Clerks, General Office	13.59	Nurses, Registered	33.16
Clerks, Receptionists/Information	11.87	Nursing Aides/Orderlies/Attendants	12.64
Clerks, Shipping/Receiving	12.91	Packers and Packagers, Hand	9.88
Computer Programmers	30.79	Physical Therapists	37.87
Computer Support Specialists	24.59	Postal Service Mail Carriers	20.97
Computer Systems Analysts	31.88	Real Estate Brokers	33.02
Cooks, Restaurant	10.78	Retail Salespersons	11.67
Dentists	n/a	Sales Reps., Exc. Tech./Scientific	26.58
Electrical Engineers	36.11	Sales Reps., Tech./Scientific	30.99
Electricians	21.80	Secretaries, Exc. Legal/Med./Exec.	14.79
Financial Managers	42.58	Security Guards	10.17
First-Line Supervisors/Mgrs., Sales	18.64	Surgeons	72.51
Food Preparation Workers	9.29	Teacher Assistants	11.10
General and Operations Managers	48.36	Teachers, Elementary School	24.90
Hairdressers/Cosmetologists	10.37	Teachers, Secondary School	25.70
Internists	64.31	Telemarketers	13.12
Janitors and Cleaners	11.12	Truck Drivers, Heavy/Tractor-Trailer	18.09
Landscaping/Groundskeeping Workers	10.67	Truck Drivers, Light/Delivery Svcs.	13.19
Lawyers	48.15	Waiters and Waitresses	7.99

Note: Wage data is for May 2005 and covers the Sacramento—Arden-Arcade—Roseville, CA Metropolitan Statistics Area - see Appendix B for areas included. Hourly wages for elementary/secondary school teachers and teacher assistants were calculated by the editors from annual wage data assuming a 40 hour work week; n/a not available.
Source: Bureau of Labor Statistics, May 2005 Metro Area Occupational Employment and Wage Estimates

RESIDENTIAL REAL ESTATE

Building Permits

Area	Single-Family			Multi-Family			Total		
	2005	2006p	Pct. Chg.	2005	2006p	Pct. Chg.	2005	2006p	Pct. Chg.
City	1,856	1,785	-3.8	1,236	1,749	41.5	3,092	3,534	14.3
U.S.	1,682,000	1,380,000	-18.0	473,300	457,300	-3.4	2,155,300	1,837,300	-14.8

Note: (p) preliminary; figures represent new, privately-owned housing units authorized (unadjusted data); All permit data are based on estimates with imputation; U.S. figures are based on the new 20,000-place series.
Source: U.S. Census Bureau, Manufacturing, Mining, and Construction Statistics

Homeownership and Housing Vacancies

Area	Homeownership Rate[2] (%)			Rental Vacancy Rate[3] (%)			Homeowner Vacancy Rate[4] (%)		
	2004	2005	2006	2004	2005	2006	2004	2005	2006
MSA[1]	n/a	64.1	64.2	n/a	8.5	12.7	n/a	1.2	3.3
U.S.	69.0	68.9	68.8	10.2	9.8	9.7	1.7	1.9	2.4

Note: Comparable 2004 data was not available due to changes in metropolitan area definitions; (1) Metropolitan Statistical Area - see Appendix B for areas included; (2) The proportion of households that are owners; (3) The proportion of the rental inventory that is vacant for rent; (4) The proportion of the homeowner inventory that is vacant for sale; n/a not available
Source: U.S. Census Bureau, Housing Vacancies and Homeownership Annual Statistics: 2006

TAXES

State Corporate Income Tax Rates

State	Rate (%)	Number of Brackets	Low Bracket (Under $)	High Bracket (Over $)
California	8.84	1	na	na

Note: Tax rates as of December 31, 2006; na not applicable; 10.84% on financial institutions. Minimum tax is $800. The tax rate on S-Corporations is 1.5% (3.5% for financial S-Corporations).
Source: Tax Foundation, www.taxfoundation.org

State Individual Income Tax Rates

State	Federal Deductibility	Marginal Rate (%)	Number of Brackets	Low Bracket (Under $)	High Bracket (Over $)
California	No	1.0-10.3 (p)(r)	7	0	1,000,000

Note: Tax rates as of December 31, 2006; Brackets apply to single taxpayers and married people filing separately; na not applicable; (p) California's $1,000,000 bracket not doubled for married taxpayers; (r) Indexed for Inflation.
Source: Tax Foundation, www.taxfoundation.org

Various State and Local Tax Rates

State and Local Sales and Use (%)	State Sales and Use (%)	Gasoline ($/gal.)	Cigarette ($/pack)	Spirits ($/gal.)	Table Wine ($/gal.)	Beer ($/gal.)
7.75	6.25	0.192 (m)	0.87	3.3	0.20	0.20

Note: Tax rates as of December 31, 2006; (m) Additional cents per gallon taxes added this year that were not included in previous years' tables.
Source: Tax Foundation, www.taxfoundation.org; The Sales Tax Clearinghouse, www.thestc.com

State Tax Burdens

Area	Combined State and Local Tax Burden		Combined Federal, State and Local Tax Burden	
	Percent	Rank	Percent	Rank
California	10.9	15	32.7	9
U.S. Average	10.6	-	31.6	-

Note: Figures are for 2006 and measure taxes as a percentage of income
Source: Tax Foundation, www.taxfoundation.org

Internal Revenue Service Tax Audits

IRS District	Percent of Returns Audited				
	1996	1997	1998	1999	2000
Northern California	1.24	1.34	1.08	0.60	0.41
U.S.	0.66	0.61	0.46	0.31	0.20

Note: Figures cover IRS district audits of federal income tax returns filed by individuals. Geographic data on district audits after the year 2000 are being withheld by the IRS. TRAC is challenging this policy.
Source: Syracuse University, Transactional Records Access Clearinghouse (TRAC), "Odds of IRS District Tax Audit 2000"

**COMMERCIAL
REAL ESTATE**

Office Market

| Market Area | Inventory (sq. ft.) | Vacant (sq. ft.) | Vac. Rate (%) | Under Constr. (sq. ft.) | Asking Rent ($/sf) | |
					Class A	Class B
Sacramento	50,328,201	7,533,291	15.0	1,332,922	25.56	21.12

Source: Grubb & Ellis, Office Markets Trends, 4th Quarter 2006

Industrial Market

| Market Area | Inventory (sq. ft.) | Vacant (sq. ft.) | Vac. Rate (%) | Under Constr. (sq. ft.) | Asking Rent ($/sf) | |
					WH/Dist	R&D/Flex
Sacramento	125,043,341	15,460,248	12.4	869,962	4.92	9.12

Source: Grubb & Ellis, Industrial Markets Trends, 4th Quarter 2006

**COMMERCIAL
UTILITIES**

Typical Monthly Electric Bills

| Area | Commercial Service ($/month) | | Industrial Service ($/month) | |
	3 kW demand 1,000 kWh	40 kW demand 14,000 kWh	1,000 kW demand 200,000 kWh	50,000 kW demand 15,000,000 kWh
City	n/a	n/a	n/a	n/a
Average[1]	123	1,413	22,000	1,306,315

Note: Based on total rates in effect July 1, 2006; (1) average based on 196 utilities; n/a not available
Source: Edison Electric Institute, Typical Bills and Average Rates Report, Summer 2006

TRANSPORTATION

Means of Transportation to Work

| Area | Car/Truck/Van | | Public Transportation | | | Bicycle | Walked | Other Means | Worked at Home |
	Drove Alone	Car-pooled	Bus	Subway	Railroad				
City	71.0	16.3	3.8	0.1	0.1	1.4	2.8	1.5	2.9
MSA[1]	76.2	13.6	2.0	0.1	0.2	0.7	2.0	1.2	4.1
U.S.	75.7	12.2	2.5	1.5	0.5	0.4	2.9	1.0	3.3

Note: Figures are percentages and cover workers 16 years of age and older;
(1) Metropolitan Statistical Area - see Appendix A for areas included
Source: Census 2000, Summary File 3

Travel Time to Work

Area	Less Than 15 Minutes	15 to 29 Minutes	30 to 44 Minutes	45 to 59 Minutes	60 Minutes or More
City	27.5	45.6	17.3	4.4	5.3
MSA[1]	25.2	39.3	21.7	6.9	6.8
U.S.	29.4	36.1	19.1	7.4	8.0

Note: Figures are percentages and include workers 16 years old and over; (1) Metropolitan Statistical Area -
see Appendix A for areas included
Source: Census 2000, Summary File 3

Travel Time Index

Area	1982	1993	2002	2003
Urban Area[1]	1.07	1.19	1.34	1.37
Average[2]	1.12	1.28	1.37	1.37

Note: Travel Time Index - The ratio of travel time in the peak period to the travel time at
free-flow conditions. A value of 1.35 indicates a 20-minute free-flow trip takes 27 minutes
in the peak. Free-flow speeds (60 mph on freeways and 35 mph on principal arterials)
are used as the comparison threshold; (1) Covers the Sacramento, CA urban area;
(2) average of 85 urban areas
Source: Texas Transportation Institute, The 2005 Urban Mobility Report, May 2005

Public Transportation

Agency name:	Sacramento Regional Transit District (Sacramento RT)
Vehicle type:	Bus
Average fleet age in years:	7.0
No. operated in max. service:	226
Vehicle type:	Light rail
Average fleet age in years:	9.1
No. operated in max. service:	56
Vehicle type:	Demand response
Average fleet age in years:	3.7
No. operated in max. service:	98

Source: Federal Transit Administration, National Transit Database, 2005

Air Transportation

Airport name and code:	Sacramento International (SMF)
Domestic service (2006)	
Passenger airlines[1]:	25
Passenger enplanements:	5,124,307
Freight carriers[2]:	18
Freight (lbs.):	64,462,043
International service (2005)	
Passenger airlines[1]:	5
Passenger enplanements:	59,887
Freight carriers[2]:	1
Freight (lbs.):	7,720

Note: (1) Includes all major, minor and commuter airlines that carried at least one passenger during the year; (2) Includes all airlines and freight carriers that transported at least one pound of freight during the year Source: Bureau of Transportation Statistics, The Intermodal Transportation Database, Air Carriers: T-100 International Market, 2004; Bureau of Transportation Statistics, The Intermodal Transportation Database, Air Carriers: T-100 Domestic Market, 2005

Other Transportation Statistics

Interstate highways:	I-5; I-80
Amtrak service:	Yes
Major waterways/ports:	None

Source: Editor & Publisher Market Guide, 2006; Amtrak.com; Rand McNally 2006 Road Atlas

BUSINESSES

Major Business Headquarters

Company Name	2006 Rankings	
	Fortune[1]	Forbes[2]
No companies listed	-	-

Note: (1) Fortune 500 - companies that produce a 10-K are ranked 1 to 500 based on 2005 revenue; (2) Forbes Largest Private Companies - all private companies with at least $1 billion in annual revenue are ranked 1 to 394; companies listed are located in the city; dashes indicate no ranking Source: Fortune, April 17, 2006; Forbes, November 9, 2006

Best Companies to Work For

Granite Construction, headquartered in Sacramento, is among the "100 Best Companies to Work For." Criteria: More than 105,000 employees from 446 companies responded to a 57-question survey created by the Great Place to Work Institute. Two-thirds of a company's score is based on the survey, which covers topics such as attitudes towards management, job satisfaction, and camaraderie. The remaining third of the score comes from each company's responses to the Institute's Culture Audit, which includes detailed questions about demographic makeup, pay and benefits programs, and open-ended questions about the company's people-management philosophy, internal communications, opportunities, compensation practices, diversity programs, etc. Any company that is at least seven years old and has a minimum of 1,000 U.S. employees is eligible. The top three U.S. locations are shown for companies with more than one location. *Fortune, "100 Best Companies to Work for 2007," January 22, 2007*

Sutter Health, headquartered in Sacramento, is among the "100 Best Places to Work in IT." To qualify, companies, both public and private, had to have 2005 revenue of $250 million or greater and employ a minimum of 500 people in the U.S., with a minimum of 100 IT employees in the U.S. Companies were selected based on average salary and bonus increases, the percentage of IT employees receiving promotions, IT staff turnover rates, training and development, and the percentage of women and minorities in IT staff and management positions. In addition, information was collected on how the organizations reward outstanding performance, how their retention programs are structured and what benefits they offer. *Computerworld, "100 Best Places to Work in IT 2006," June 19, 2006*

Fast-Growing Businesses

According to *Inc.*, Sacramento is home to one of America's 500 fastest-growing private companies: **CoreLogic Systems**. Criteria: must be an independent, privately-held, U.S. corporation, proprietorship or partnership; net sales of at least $600,000 in FY2002; four-year operating/sales history; holding companies, regulated banks, and utilities were excluded. *Inc., "America's 500 Fastest-Growing Private Companies,"September 2006*

According to Deloitte & Touche LLP, Sacramento is home to one of North America's 500 fastest-growing high-technology companies: **CoreLogic**. Companies are ranked by percentage growth in revenue over a five-year period. Criteria for inclusion: company must be headquartered within North America; company must own proprietary intellectual property or proprietary technology that contributes to a significant portion of the company's operating revenue or devotes a significant proportion of revenues to research and development of technology; company must have been in business for a minumum of five years with 2001 operating revenues of at least $50,000 USD or $75,000 CD and 2005 operating revenues of at least $5 million USD/CD. *Deloitte & Touche LLP, 2006 Technology Fast 500*

Women-Owned Businesses: 1997 and 2002

Year	All Firms		Firms with Paid Employees			
	Firms	Sales ($000)	Firms	Sales ($000)	Employees	Payroll ($000)
1997	8,287	1,656,984	1,574	1,475,946	11,286	267,713
2002	9,421	1,069,147	1,308	850,242	8,780	238,649

Note: *Figures cover firms located in the city; Women-owned business are defined as firms in which women own 51% or more of the stock or equity of the company; (a) Withheld to avoid disclosing data for individual companies; (b) Withheld because estimate did not meet publication standards; n/a not available*
Source: *1997 Economic Census, Survey of Minority- and Women-Owned Business Enterprises; 2002 Economic Census, Survey of Business Owners (released February 9, 2006)*

Minority Business Opportunity

Two of the 500 largest Hispanic-owned companies in the U.S. are located in Sacramento. *Hispanic Business, "Hispanic Business 500," June 2006*

HOTELS

Hotels/Motels

Area	Hotels/Motels	Average Minimum Rates ($)		
		Tourist	First-Class	Deluxe
City	64	64	102	130

Source: *OAG Travel Planner Online, Spring 2006*

EVENT SITES

Convention Centers

Name	Overall Space (sq. ft.)	Exhibit Space (sq. ft.)	Meeting Space (sq. ft.)	Meeting Rooms
Sacramento Convention Center	460,000	24,000	134,000	31

Source: *www.officialtravelguide.com; www.eventective.com; original research*

Hotels/Conference Centers

Name	Guest Rooms	Exhibit Space (sq. ft.)	Meeting Space (sq. ft.)
Hilton Sacramento Arden West	331	5,700	18,850
Holiday Inn Sacramento Northeast	230	15,000	15,000
Hyatt Regency Sacramento	503	n/a	41,037

Note: n/a not available
Source: www.officialtravelguide.com; www.eventective.com; original research

Living Environment

COST OF LIVING

Cost of Living Index

Year	Composite Index	Groceries	Housing	Utilities	Trans-portation	Health Care	Misc. Goods/ Services
2004	n/a	n/a	n/a	n/a	n/a	n/a	n/a
2005	n/a	n/a	n/a	n/a	n/a	n/a	n/a
2006	122.8	121.9	163.7	94.8	105.5	113.6	104.4

Note: U.S. = 100
Source: The Council for Community and Economic Research (formerly ACCRA), Cost of Living Index, 2004, 2005 and 2006 4-Quarter Averages

HOUSING

House Price Index (HPI)

Area	National Ranking[2]	Quarterly Change (%)	One-Year Change (%)	Five-Year Change (%)
MSA[1]	274	-1.20	-2.41	88.66
U.S.[3]	-	1.12	5.87	55.21

Note: The HPI is a weighted repeat sales index. It measures average price changes in repeat sales or refinancings on the same properties. This information is obtained by reviewing repeat mortgage transactions on single-family properties whose mortgages have been purchased or securitized by Fannie Mae or Freddie Mac in January 1975; (1) Metropolitan Statistical Area - see Appendix B for areas included; (2) Rankings are based on annual percentage change for all metro areas containing at least 15,000 transactions over the last 10 years and ranges from 1 to 282; (3) figures based on a weighted division average; all figures are for the period ending December 31, 2006
Source: Office of Federal Housing Enterprise Oversight, House Price Index, March 1, 2007

House Price Valuations

Area	Q4 1999	Q4 2000	Q4 2001	Q4 2002	Q4 2003	Q4 2004	Q4 2005	Q4 2006
MSA[1]	-19.9	-14.9	-5.2	6.0	17.2	33.7	49.1	41.2

Note: Figures show the percentage of over- or under-valuation of single family homes relative to statistically normal house values (e.g. a value of 23.6 indicates that house values are 23.6% overvalued). Statistically normal house values are based on house prices, interest rates, household incomes, population densities, and any historical premiums or discounts metropolitan areas have exhibited over time; (1) Figures cover the Metropolitan Statistical Area - see Appendix B for areas included
Source: Global Insight/National City Corporation, House Prices in America, March 2007

Median Home Prices

Area	2004	2005	2006[p]	Percent Change 2005 to 2006
Metro Area[1]	317.0	375.9	374.8	-0.3
U.S. Average	195.2	219.0	222.0	1.4

Note: Figures are median sales prices of existing single-family homes in thousands of dollars; (p) preliminary; n/a not available; (1) Covers the Sacramento—Arden-Arcade—Roseville, CA Metropolitan Statistical Area - see Appendix B for areas included
Source: National Association of Realtors, Metropolitan Area Prices, 4th Quarter 2006

Housing: Year Structure Built

Area	1990 -2000	1980 -1989	1970 -1979	1960 -1969	1950 -1959	1940 -1949	Before 1940	Median Year
City	9.0	18.4	18.4	15.2	15.5	10.6	13.0	1967
MSA[1]	19.4	20.5	22.9	14.5	12.3	5.1	5.3	1976
U.S.	17.0	15.8	18.5	13.7	12.7	7.3	15.0	1971

Note: Figures are percentages; (1) Metropolitan Statistical Area - see Appendix A for areas included
Source: Census 2000, Summary File 3

Average New Home Price

Area	2004	2005	2006
City	n/a	n/a	508,892
U.S.	253,574	275,712	299,269

Note: Figures, in dollars, are based on a new home with 2,400 sq. ft. of living area on an 8,000 sq. ft. lot.
Source: The Council for Community and Economic Research (formerly ACCRA), Cost of Living Index, 2004, 2005 and 2006 4-Quarter Averages

Average Apartment Rent

Area	2004	2005	2006
City	n/a	n/a	934
U.S.	716	740	766

Note: Figures, in dollars per month, are based on an unfurnished two bedroom, 1-1/2 or 2 bath apartment, approximately 950 sq. ft. in size, excluding all utilities except water
Source: The Council for Community and Economic Research (formerly ACCRA), Cost of Living Index, 2004, 2005 and 2006 4-Quarter Averages

RESIDENTIAL UTILITIES

Average Residential Utility Costs

Area	All Electric ($/mth)	Part Electric ($/mth)	Other Energy ($/mth)	Phone ($/mth)
City	–	147.59	29.75	17.91
U.S.	136.00	76.53	90.52	25.87

Source: The Council for Community and Economic Research (formerly ACCRA), Cost of Living Index, 2006 4-Quarter Average

HEALTH

Average Health Care Costs

Area	Optometrist ($/visit)	Doctor ($/visit)	Dentist ($/visit)
City	108.09	85.51	79.87
U.S.	76.38	76.10	68.72

Note: Optometrist—based on a full vision eye exam for an established adult patient;
Doctor—based on a general practitioner's routine exam of an established patient;
Dentist—based on adult teeth cleaning and periodic oral exam.
Source: The Council for Community and Economic Research (formerly ACCRA), Cost of Living Index, 2006 4-Quarter Average

Mortality Rates

ICD-10 Sub-Chapter	ICD-10 Code	Age-Adjusted Death Rate per 100,000 population[1]	U.S. Age-Adjusted Death Rate per 100,000 population
Malignant neoplasms	C00-C97	181.5	185.8
Ischaemic heart diseases	I20-I25	155.3	150.2
Other forms of heart disease	I30-I51	31.8	50.8
Cerebrovascular diseases	I60-I69	63.4	50.0
Chronic lower respiratory diseases	J40-J47	47.3	41.1
Diabetes mellitus	E10-E14	20.5	24.5
Other degenerative diseases of the nervous system	G30-G31	24.7	22.3
Other external causes of accidental injury	W00-X59	21.4	21.2
Influenza and pneumonia	J10-J18	24.7	19.8
Hypertensive diseases	I10-I13	25.5	18.1

Note: ICD-10 = International Classification of Diseases 10th Revision; (1) Figures cover Sacramento County, CA
Source: Centers for Disease Control and Prevention, National Center for Health Statistics. Compressed Mortality File 1999-2004. CDC WONDER On-line Database, compiled from Compressed Mortality File 1999-2004 Series 20 No. 2J, 2007.

Health Risk Data

Item	Area[1] (%)	U.S. (%)
Adults who have been told they have high blood pressure	n/a	25.5
Adults who have been told they have high blood cholesterol	n/a	35.6
Adults who have been told they have diabetes[2]	n/a	7.3
Adults who have been told they have arthritis	n/a	27.0
Adults who have been told they currently have asthma	n/a	8.0
Adults who are current smokers	n/a	20.6

Note: (1) Figures cover the Metropolitan Statistical Area - see Appendix B for areas included; n/a not available;
(2) Figures do not include pregnancy-related diabetes, pre-diabetes or borderline diabetes
Source: Centers for Disease Control and Prevention, Behaviorial Risk Factor Surveillance System, SMART:
Selected Metropolitan/Micropolitan Area Trends, 2005

Distribution of Office-Based Physicians

Area	Total	Family/ General Practice	Specialties Medical	Specialties Surgical	Specialties Other
CMSA[1] (number)	3,783	563	1,317	847	1,056
CMSA[1] (rate per 10,000 pop.)	19.5	2.9	6.8	4.4	5.4
Metro Average[2] (rate per 10,000 pop.)	19.4	2.1	7.5	4.5	5.3

Note: Data as of December 31, 2004; (1) Sacramento-Yolo, CA Consolidated Metropolitan Statistical Area
includes the following counties: El Dorado; Placer; Sacramento; Yolo;
(2) Average of the 79 unique MSAs and CMSAs in this book
Source: American Medical Association, Physician Characteristics & Distribution in the U.S., 2006

Hospitals

Sacramento has the following hospitals: 6 general medical and surgical; 3 psychiatric; 1
children's general.
AHA Guide to the Healthcare Field 2007

According to *U.S. News,* the Sacramento metro area is home to one of the best hospitals in the
U.S.: **University of California - Davis Medical Center**; *U.S. News Online, "America's Best
Hospitals 2006"*

EDUCATION

Public School District Statistics

District Name	Schls	Pupils	Pupil/ Teacher Ratio	Minority Pupils[1] (%)	Free Lunch Eligible[2] (%)	IEP[3] (%)
Grant Joint Union High	18	13,558	21.8	63.3	47.8	11.4
Natomas Unified	14	9,743	21.3	73.4	28.3	9.3
North Sacramento Elementary	11	5,108	17.7	81.4	72.8	11.5
Robla Elementary	5	2,173	18.2	74.0	60.5	15.3
Sacramento City Unified	91	51,420	19.5	78.0	54.0	12.2

Note: Table includes regular local school districts with 2,000 or more students; (1) Percentage of students that
are not white, non-Hispanic; (2) Percentage of students that are eligible for the free lunch program;
(3) Percentage of students that have an Individualized Education Program.
Source: U.S. Department of Education, National Center for Education Statistics, Common Core of Data, Local
Education Agency (School District) Universe Survey: School Year 2004-2005; U.S. Department of Education,
National Center for Education Statistics, Common Core of Data, Public Elementary/Secondary School Universe
Survey: School Year 2004-2005

Top Public High Schools

High School Name	Index[1]	Rank[1]	Subsidized Lunch (%)[2]	E&E (%)[3]
Kennedy	1.413	786	33.4	13.6
Mira Loma	2.336	249	35.0	12.5**
Rio Americano	1.439	758	7.2	28.8

Note: (1) Public schools are ranked according to a ratio that is the number of Advanced Placement and/or International Baccalaureate tests taken by all students at a school in 2005 divided by the number of graduating seniors. All of the schools on the list have an index of at least 1.000; they are in the top five percent of public schools measured this way. The rankings range from 1 to 1,236; (2) Percentage of students receiving federally subsidized meals; (3) E & E stands for equity and excellence percentage: the portion of all graduating seniors at a school that had at least one passing grade on one AP or IB test; (*) Gave just IB tests; (**) Gave both IB and AP tests. AP and IB participation are indicators of a school's efforts to get students to excel and prepare for college.
Source: Newsweek Online, May 23, 2006

Educational Quality

School District	Education Quotient[1]	Graduate Outcome[2]	Community Index[3]	Resource Index[4]	Rating[5]
Sacramento City Unified	11	11	23	49	Yellow

Note: Scores are national percentile rankings and range from 1 (worst) to 99 (best); (1) Combination of the Graduate Outcome, Community and Resource Indexes weighted to reflect the greater importance of the Graduate Outcome and Resource Index; (2) Based on graduation rates and college board scores (SAT/ACT); (3) Based on the surrounding community's level of affluence and adult education; (4) Based on teacher salaries, per-pupil expenditures and student-teacher ratios; (5) School districts receive one of five rankings: Gold Medal (top 16 percent of districts evaluated); Blue Ribbon (top third); Green Light (average); Yellow Light (bottom 25 percent); Red Light (bottom 10 percent).
Source: Expansion Management, "2007 Education Quotient," January 2007

Highest Level of Education

Area	Less than H.S.	H.S. Diploma	Some College, No Deg.	Associate Degree	Bachelors Degree	Masters Degree	Profess. School Degree	Doctorate Degree
City	22.6	21.5	24.0	8.0	15.4	5.1	2.6	0.8
MSA[1]	15.2	22.1	27.0	8.8	17.8	5.7	2.3	1.0
U.S.	19.4	28.4	21.2	6.4	15.7	5.9	2.0	1.0

Note: Figures are 2006 estimated percentages and cover persons age 25 and over; (1) Metropolitan Statistical Area - see Appendix B for areas included
Source: Claritas, Inc.

Educational Attainment by Race

Area	High School Graduate (%)					Bachelor's Degree (%)				
	Total	White	Black	Asian	Hisp.[2]	Total	White	Black	Asian	Hisp.[2]
City	77.3	84.1	80.6	65.6	57.2	23.9	29.6	13.6	25.6	10.3
MSA[1]	85.0	88.7	83.1	73.8	63.6	25.9	27.8	16.2	31.6	12.3
U.S.	80.4	83.6	72.3	80.4	52.4	24.4	26.1	14.3	44.1	10.4

Note: Figures shown cover persons 25 years old and over; (1) Metropolitan Statistical Area - see Appendix A for areas included; (2) people of Hispanic origin can be of any race
Source: Census 2000, Summary File 3

School Enrollment by Type

Area	Grades KG to 8				Grades 9 to 12			
	Public		Private		Public		Private	
	Enrollment	%	Enrollment	%	Enrollment	%	Enrollment	%
City	54,640	92.1	4,702	7.9	23,025	91.2	2,210	8.8
MSA[1]	213,241	90.3	22,784	9.7	93,412	92.7	7,388	7.3
U.S.	33,526,011	88.7	4,285,121	11.3	14,848,628	90.6	1,532,323	9.4

Note: Figures shown cover persons 3 years old and over; (1) Metropolitan Statistical Area - see Appendix A for areas included
Source: Census 2000, Summary File 3

School Enrollment by Race

Area	Grades KG to 8 (%)				Grades 9 to 12 (%)			
	White	Black	Asian	Hisp.[1]	White	Black	Asian	Hisp.[1]
City	32.7	21.1	19.3	28.5	34.1	18.5	23.4	24.6
MSA[2]	61.7	9.9	9.5	19.4	63.2	9.0	11.1	17.1
U.S.	68.5	15.5	3.3	16.8	68.8	15.5	3.8	15.7

Note: Figures shown cover persons 3 years old and over; (1) people of Hispanic origin can be of any race; (2) Metropolitan Statistical Area - see Appendix A for areas included
Source: Census 2000, Summary File 3

Average Salaries of Public School Teachers

District	2004-05		2005-06		Percent Change 2004-05 to 2005-06
	Dollars	Rank[1]	Dollars	Rank[1]	
CALIFORNIA	57,876	2	59,345	3	2.54
U.S. Average	47,674	-	49,109	-	3.01

Note: (1) State rank ranges from 1 to 51.
Source: National Education Association, Rankings & Estimates: Rankings of the States 2005 and Estimates of School Statistics 2006, November 2006

Higher Education

Four-Year Colleges			Two-Year Colleges			Medical Schools[1]	Law Schools[2]	Voc/Tech[3]
Public	Private Non-profit	Private For-profit	Public	Private Non-profit	Private For-profit			
1	1	1	4	0	4	0	1	6

Note: Figures cover institutions located within the city limits; (1) includes schools accredited by the Liaison Committee on Medical Education and the American Osteopathic Association; (2) includes American Bar Association-accredited law schools; (3) includes all schools with programs that are less than 2 years
Source: National Center for Education Statistics, The Integrated Postsecondary Education System (IPEDS) Peer Analysis System, 2006; www.usnews.com, America's Best Graduate Schools 2008, Medical School Directory; www.usnews.com, America's Best Graduate Schools 2008, Law School Directory

PRESIDENTIAL ELECTION

2004 Presidential Election Results

Area	Bush	Kerry	Nader	Other
Sacramento County	49.3	49.5	0.2	1.0
U.S.	50.7	48.3	0.4	0.6

Note: Results are percentages and may not add to 100% due to rounding
Source: Dave Leip's Atlas of U.S. Presidential Elections, www.uselectionatlas.org

MAJOR EMPLOYERS

Major Employers

Company Name	Industry	Type of Site
California Dept of Justice	Legal counsel and prosecution	Branch
California State Prison at Folsom	Correctional institutions	Branch
Caltrans	Regulation, administration of transportation	Headquarters
DMV Budget and Analysis	Regulation, administration of transportation	Headquarters
Employment Development CA Dept	Administration of social & manpower programs	Headquarters
Food & Agriculture Cal Dept	Regulation of agricultural marketing	Branch
Information Sources Inc	Custom computer programming services	Headquarters
Intel	Semiconductors and related devices	Branch
Office of Water Programs	Social services, nec	Single
Sacramento Bee	Newspapers	Headquarters
Sutter Medical Center	Building maintenance services, nec	Branch
UCD Medical Center	Medical laboratories	Branch

Note: Companies shown are located within the metropolitan area and have 2,000 or more employees; nec = not elsewhere classified.
Source: www.zapdata.com, January 2007

PUBLIC SAFETY

Crime Rate

Area	All Crimes	Violent Crimes				Property Crimes		
		Murder	Forcible Rape	Robbery	Aggrav. Assault	Burglary	Larceny -Theft	Motor Vehicle Theft
City	6,854.3	11.4	37.2	441.2	661.4	1,277.1	2,912.4	1,513.5
Suburbs[1]	3,988.7	4.6	24.4	103.3	269.3	807.4	2,024.4	755.3
Metro[2]	4,634.3	6.1	27.2	179.4	357.6	913.3	2,224.5	926.1
U.S.	3,899.0	5.6	31.7	140.7	291.1	726.7	2,286.3	416.7

Note: Figures are crimes per 100,000 population; (1) All areas within the metro area that are located outside the city limits; (2) Metropolitan Statistical Area - see Appendix B for areas included
Source: FBI Uniform Crime Reports, 2005

Hate Crimes

Area	Number of Quarters Reported	Bias Motivation				
		Race	Religion	Sexual Orientation	Ethnicity	Disability
City	4	28	3	11	7	1

Source: Federal Bureau of Investigation, Hate Crime Statistics 2005

RECREATION

Culture

Dance[1]	Theatre[1]	Instrumental Music[1]	Vocal Music[1]	Series/ Festivals	Museums	Zoos
1	8	3	4	5	16	1

Note: (1) number of professional performing groups
Source: The Grey House Performing Arts Directory, 2007; Official Museum Directory, 2007

Professional Sports Teams

Major League Baseball	National Basketball Association	National Football League	National Hockey League	Major League Soccer	Women's National Basketball Association
0	1	0	0	0	1

Note: Includes teams located in the Sacramento metro area.
Source: www.sportsvenues.com, Listing of Venues by State/Province and City, 2006

MEDIA

Newspapers

Name	Target Audience	Frequency	Circulation
Catholic Herald	Catholic/Religious	Non-Daily	49,000
The Daily Recorder	n/a	Daily	1,100
El Heraldo Catolico	Hispanic/Religious	Non-Daily	34,000
El Hispano	General/Hispanic	Non-Daily	20,150
The Sacramento Bee	n/a	Daily	293,705
Sacramento/The Happening	General	Non-Daily	63,000
Sacramento News & Review	Alternative/General	Non-Daily	90,000
Sacramento Observer	Black	Non-Daily	50,000

Note: Includes newspapers whose offices are located in the city and whose circulations are 1,000 or more; n/a not available
Source: BurrellesLuce, MediaContacts Online, January 2006

Television Stations

Name	Ch.	Network(s)	Type	Ownership
KCRA	3	NBC	Commercial	Hearst-Argyle Broadcasting
KVIE	6	PBS	Public	KVIE
KXTV	10	ABC	Commercial	Gannett Broadcasting
KOVR	13	CBS	Commercial	Sinclair Broadcast Group
KUVS	19	Univision	Commercial	Univision Communications Inc.
KSPX	29	n/a	Commercial	Paxson Communications Corporation
KMAX	31	UPN	Commercial	Paramount Communications Inc.
KTXL	40	Fox	Commercial	Tribune Broadcasting Company
KNSO	51	Telemundo	Commercial	Sainte Partners II LP
KQCA	58	WBN	Commercial	Hearst-Argyle Broadcasting

Note: Stations included cover the Sacramento-Stockton-Modesto DMA (Designated Market Area)
BurrellesLuce, MediaContacts Online, January 2006

Major AM Radio Stations

Call Letters	Freq. (kHz)	Station Type	Target Audience	Station Format	Music Format
KSTE	650	n/a	General	Music/News/Talk	n/a
KFIA	710	n/a	General	Talk	n/a
KCBC	770	n/a	General	Educational	n/a
KNCO	830	Commercial	General	News/Talk	n/a
KVIN	920	n/a	General	Music	n/a
KAHI	950	n/a	General	Music/News/Talk	n/a
KESP	970	n/a	General	News/Sports	n/a
KLVP	1040	Commercial	Religious	Music	Christian
KLIB	1110	n/a	Ethnic/Hispanic	News/Sports/Talk	n/a
KHTK	1140	n/a	General/Men	Music/Sports/Talk	n/a
KWG	1230	n/a	General/Hispanic	n/a	n/a
KJAX	1280	n/a	General	News/Sports	n/a
KCTC	1320	Commercial	General	Music	Adult Standards
KFIV	1360	n/a	General	n/a	n/a
KPCO	1370	Commercial	General	Music	Adult Standards
KTKZ	1380	Commercial	General	News/Sports/Talk	n/a
KMYC	1410	Commercial	General	Talk	n/a
KSTN	1420	n/a	General	Music/News/Sports	n/a
KVML	1450	n/a	General	News/Talk	n/a
KFBK	1530	Commercial	General	News/Talk	n/a
KCVR	1570	Commercial	General/Hispanic	Music/News	Latin
KSSU	1580	College	General	Music/Sports/Talk	Adult Contemp.
KUBA	1600	n/a	General	Music/News	n/a

Note: Stations included cover the Sacramento-Stockton-Modesto DMA (Designated Market Area); n/a not available
Source: BurrellesLuce, MediaContacts Online, January 2006

Major FM Radio Stations

Call Letters	Freq. (mHz)	Station Type	Target Audience	Station Format	Music Format
KXJZ	88.9	College	General	Music/Talk	Jazz
KKTO	90.5	College	General	Music/News	Jazz
KXPR	90.9	College	General	Music/News	Classical
KGBY	92.5	n/a	General	Music	n/a
KSSJ	94.7	n/a	General	Music	n/a
KHOP	95.1	n/a	General	Sports	n/a
KYMX	96.1	n/a	General	Music	n/a
KSEG	96.9	n/a	General	Music/News/Sports	n/a
KRCX	99.9	n/a	Hispanic	Ed/Music/News/Sports/Talk	n/a
KCIV	99.9	n/a	General/Religious	Educational/News/Talk	n/a
KZZO	100.5	n/a	General	Music	n/a
KHYL	101.1	n/a	General	Music/News/Sports	n/a
KSFM	102.5	Commercial	General/Young Adult	Music/News/Talk	Rhythm & Blues
KATM	103.3	n/a	General	Music	n/a
KHKK	104.1	n/a	General	Music/News/Talk	n/a
KRRE	104.3	n/a	Hispanic	Music/News	n/a
KNCI	105.1	n/a	General	Music/News/Talk	n/a
KWOD	106.5	Commercial	General	Music/News/Talk	Alternative
KDND	107.9	Commercial	General	Music	Top 40

Note: Stations included cover the Sacramento-Stockton-Modesto DMA (Designated Market Area); n/a not available
BurrellesLuce, MediaContacts Online, January 2006

CLIMATE

Average and Extreme Temperatures

Temperature	Jan	Feb	Mar	Apr	May	Jun	Jul	Aug	Sep	Oct	Nov	Dec	Yr.
Extreme High (°F)	70	76	88	93	105	115	114	109	108	101	87	72	115
Average High (°F)	53	60	64	71	80	87	93	91	87	78	63	53	73
Average Temp. (°F)	45	51	54	59	65	72	76	75	72	64	53	46	61
Average Low (°F)	38	41	43	46	50	55	58	58	56	50	43	38	48
Extreme Low (°F)	20	23	26	32	34	41	48	48	43	35	26	18	18

Note: Figures cover the years 1947-1990
Source: National Climatic Data Center, International Station Meteorological Climate Summary, 9/96

Average Precipitation/Snowfall/Humidity

Precip./Humidity	Jan	Feb	Mar	Apr	May	Jun	Jul	Aug	Sep	Oct	Nov	Dec	Yr.
Avg. Precip. (in.)	3.6	2.8	2.4	1.3	0.4	0.1	Tr	0.1	0.3	1.0	2.4	2.8	17.3
Avg. Snowfall (in.)	Tr	Tr	Tr	Tr	0	0	0	0	0	0	0	Tr	Tr
Avg. Rel. Hum. 7am (%)	90	88	84	78	71	67	68	73	75	80	87	90	79
Avg. Rel. Hum. 4pm (%)	70	59	51	43	36	31	28	29	31	39	57	70	45

Note: Figures cover the years 1947-1990; Tr = Trace amounts (<0.05 in. of rain; <0.5 in. of snow)
Source: National Climatic Data Center, International Station Meteorological Climate Summary, 9/96

Weather Conditions

Temperature			Daytime Sky			Precipitation		
10°F & below	32°F & below	90°F & above	Clear	Partly cloudy	Cloudy	0.01 inch or more precip.	0.1 inch or more snow/ice	Thunder-storms
0	21	73	175	111	79	58	< 1	2

Note: Figures are average number of days per year and cover the years 1947-1990
Source: National Climatic Data Center, International Station Meteorological Climate Summary, 9/96

HAZARDOUS WASTE

Superfund Sites

Sacramento has one hazardous waste site on the EPA's Superfund Final National Priorities List: **Sacramento Army Depot**. *U.S. Environmental Protection Agency, Final National Priorities List, March 20, 2007*

AIR & WATER
QUALITY

Air Quality Index

Area	Percent of Days when Air Quality was...[2]				AQI Statistics	
	Good	Moderate	Unhealthy for Sensitive Groups	Unhealthy	Maximum	Median
MSA[1]	22.2	62.7	12.1	3.0	182	61

Note: The Air Quality Index (AQI) is an index for reporting daily air quality. EPA calculates the AQI for five major air pollutants regulated by the Clean Air Act: ground-level ozone, particle pollution (also known as particulate matter), carbon monoxide, sulfur dioxide, and nitrogen dioxide. The AQI runs from 0 to 500. The higher the AQI value, the greater the level of air pollution and the greater the health concern. There are six AQI categories: "Good" The AQI is between 0 and 50. Air quality is considered satisfactory; "Moderate" The AQI is between 51 and 100. Air quality is acceptable; "Unhealthy for Sensitive Groups" When AQI values are between 101 and 150, members of sensitive groups may experience health effects; "Unhealthy" When AQI values are between 151 and 200 everyone may begin to experience health effects; "Very Unhealthy" AQI values between 201 and 300 trigger a health alert; "Hazardous" AQI values over 300 trigger health warnings of emergency conditions; (1) Metropolitan Statistical Area - see Appendix A for areas included; (2) Based on 365 days with AQI data in 2005.
Source: U.S. Environmental Protection Agency, Air Quality Index Report, 2005

Air Quality Index Pollutants

Area	Percent of Days when AQI Pollutant was...[2]					
	Carbon Monoxide	Nitrogen Dioxide	Ozone	Sulfur Dioxide	Particulate Matter 2.5	Particulate Matter 10
MSA[1]	0.0	0.0	33.7	0.0	65.8	0.5

Note: The Air Quality Index (AQI) is an index for reporting daily air quality. EPA calculates the AQI for five major air pollutants regulated by the Clean Air Act: ground-level ozone, particle pollution (also known as particulate matter), carbon monoxide, sulfur dioxide, and nitrogen dioxide. The AQI runs from 0 to 500. The higher the AQI value, the greater the level of air pollution and the greater the health concern; (1) Metropolitan Statistical Area - see Appendix A for areas included; (2) Based on 365 days with AQI data in 2005.
Source: U.S. Environmental Protection Agency, Air Quality Index Report, 2005

Number of Days with Air Quality Index Values Greater than 100

Area	Trend Sites (21)								All Sites (91)
	1998	1999	2000	2001	2002	2003	2004	2005	2005
MSA[1]	27	56	41	46	57	35	26	39	53

Note: An AQI value greater than 100 indicates that air quality would have been in the unhealthful range on that day. Data from exceptional events are not included. These counts are presented in two ways. First, the counts are based on sites having an adequate record of monitoring data during the trend period (trend sites). These counts represent the relative change in the number of days with AQI values greater than 100. In the last column, the counts are based on all sites with data in the most recent year (because it is possible for a site to have data in the most recent year but not enough data to be a trend site); (1) Metropolitan Statistical Area - see Appendix A for areas included; n/a not available.
Source: U.S. Environmental Protection Agency, Air Trends Fact Book 2005

Maximum Pollutant Concentrations

	Particulate Matter 10 (ug/m³)	Particulate Matter 2.5 (ug/m³)	Ozone 1-hour (ppm)	Carbon Monoxide (ppm)	Sulfur Dioxide (ppm)	Nitrogen Dioxide (ppm)	Lead (ug/m³)
MSA[1] Level	67	49	0.129	4	0.002	0.016	n/a
NAAQS[2]	150	65	0.125	9	0.140	0.053	1.50
Met NAAQS[2]	Yes	Yes	No	Yes	Yes	Yes	n/a

Note: Data from exceptional events are not included; (1) Metropolitan Statistical Area - see Appendix A for areas included; (2) National Ambient Air Quality Standards; n/a not available
Units: ppm = parts per million; ug/m³ = micrograms per cubic meter
Source: U.S. Environmental Protection Agency, Air Trends Fact Book 2005

Watershed Health

The U.S. Environmental Protection Agency monitors the health of the aquatic resources for the nation's 2,000+ watersheds. **The Lower Sacramento watershed serves the Sacramento area and received an overall Index of Watershed Indicators (IWI) score of 3 (less serious problems - low vulnerability).** The IWI score is based on seven condition and nine vulnerability indicators. The overall IWI score ranges from 1 (best health) to 6 (worst health). The Condition Indicators include: designated use attainment, fish and wildlife consumption advisories, source water condition, contaminated sediments, ambient water quality, and wetlands loss index. The Vulnerability Indicators include: aquatic species at risk, conventional and toxic loads over permitted limits, urban and agricultural runoff potential, population change, hydrologic modification, estuarine pollution susceptibility, and air deposition. *Note: The IWI is no longer being updated by the U.S. EPA. Source: U.S. Environmental Protection Agency, Index of Watershed Indicators, October 26, 2001*

Drinking Water

Water System Name	Pop. Served	Primary Water Source Type	Number of Violations in 2006[a]		
			Health Based	Significant Monitoring	Monitoring
City of Sacramento	454,330	Surface	None	None	None

Note: (a) Based on violation data from January 1, 2006 to December 31, 2006
Source: U.S. Environmental Protection Agency, Office of Ground Water and Drinking Water, Safe Drinking Water Information System (data extracted April 12, 2007)

Sacramento tap water is varies, soft to hard and not fluoridated.
Editor & Publisher Market Guide, 2005

Salt Lake City, Utah

Background

One cannot disassociate Salt Lake City, Utah's largest city and state capital, from its Mormon, or Church of Jesus Christ of Latter Day Saints, origins. The city was founded by Brigham Young on July 24, 1847, as a place of refuge from mainstream ostracism for the Morman's polygamous lifestyle.

Brigham Young decided to lead his people to a "land that nobody wanted," so they could exercise their form of worship in peace. Two scouts, Orson Pratt and Erastus Snow, located the site for Brigham Young, who declared: "This is the place." The site that was to be called Salt Lake City was breathtaking. The area was bordered on the east and southwest by the dramatic peaks of the Wasatch Range, and on the northwest by the Great Salt Lake.

The land was too dry and hard for farming, but Mormon industry diverted the flow of mountain streams to irrigate the land, and the valley turned into a prosperous agricultural region. A little more than 10 years after its incorporation as a city, the U.S. government was still suspicious of its Mormon residents. Fort Douglas was erected in 1862, manned by federal troops to keep an eye on the Mormons and their polygamous practices. In 1869, the completion of the Transcontinental Railroad brought mining, industry, and other non-Mormon interests to Salt Lake City. As for polygamy, the Mormon Church made it illegal in 1890.

While mining played a major role in the early development of Salt Lake City, major industry sectors now include construction, trade, transportation, communications, finance, insurance, and real estate. The University of Utah Research Park located here finds tenants occupying 35 new buildings and employing 6,300.

In 2006, the LDS Church, which owns the ZCMI Center Mall and Crossroads Mall, announced plans to demolish the malls, a skyscraper, and several other buildings to make way for the $1 billion City Creek Center redevelopment. It will combine several new office and residential buildings, one of which will be the third-tallest building in the city, around an outdoor shopping center and is expected to be completed in 2011.

Salt Lake City hosted the 2002 Winter Olympics, which proved economically successful. In preparation for the Olympics, the city underwent a major highway expansion that included the widening of Interstate 15 to accommodate more lanes and more interchanges. The city also has a new $350 million light rail system that operates for 20 miles and runs through the downtown with the addition of commuter rail in 2008. The Gateway is a new mixed-use development that includes shops, restaurants, and the Clark Planetarium with its 3-D IMAX(r) theater, "star theater," and exhibits.

The NBA's Utah Jazz plays at the EnergySolutions Arena and Real Salt Lake of Major League Soccer that began play in 2005 and currently plays at Rice-Eccles Stadium at the University of Utah.

The nearby mountain ranges and the Great Salt Lake greatly influence climatic conditions. Temperatures are moderated by the lake in winter, and storm activity is enhanced by both the lake and the mountains. Salt Lake City normally has a semi-arid continental climate with four well-defined seasons. Summers are hot and dry, while winters are cold, but generally not severe. Mountains to the north and east act as a barrier to frequent invasions of cold air. Heavy fog can develop when there is a temperature inversion in winter and may persist for several days at a time.

Rankings

General Rankings

- Salt Lake City was ranked #84 out of 331 metro areas in *Cities Ranked & Rated*. Criteria: cost of living; climate; crime; transportation; economy and jobs; education; arts and culture; health and healthcare; leisure. *Cities Ranked & Rated, 1st Edition, 2004*

- Salt Lake City was selected as one of the "Top Cities for Recent Grads" by eGrad.com. The city ranked #4. Criteria: eGrad.com conducted a nationwide survey in which a representative sample of recent graduates commented on the pros and cons of their new towns. Topics ranged from affordability, to housing, to employment, to general satisfaction. *eGrad.com, "Top Cities for Recent Grads 2004"*

- The Salt Lake City metro area was selected as one of "America's Best Places to Live and Work" by *Employment Review*. The area ranked #10 out of 20. Criteria: unemployment rate; projected job growth; cost of living; and industry specific data. *Employment Review, www.bestjobsusa.com, 2003*

Business/Finance Rankings

- Salt Lake City was selected as one of the best places to start and grow a company by *Entrepreneur* and the National Policy Research Council. The Salt Lake City metro area ranked #42 out of 50 large metro areas. Criteria: business formation and growth (firms started four to 14 years ago that still employ at least 5 people and experienced rapid growth over the last four years). *Entrepreneur/National Policy Research Council, "Hot Cities for Entrepreneurs," September 2006*

- The Salt Lake City metro area was selected as one of the "Top 40 Real Estate Markets" for expanding or relocating businesses. The area ranked #23 out of 40. Criteria: rental costs; purchase prices; and vacancy rates of office and warehouse space. *Expansion Management, October 2006*

- Intel, in partnership with Sperling's BestPlaces, ranked the 80 "Best Cities for Teleworking" in America. The Salt Lake City metro area ranked #16 among mid-sized metro areas. The study identifies cities that hold the greatest potential for teleworking based on a host of factors including typical commuting times, fuel prices, availability of broadband Internet access and percentage of the population in telework friendly jobs. The study also factored in extreme climate and natural hazards. *Intel, "Best Cities for Teleworking," March 30, 2006*

- Salt Lake City was selected as one of 20 cities in North America that is doing its part to host green conventions by providing renewable energy, intelligent recycling programs, transportation that minimizes usage of fossil fuels, and plenty of parkland. The city was ranked #8. *Meetings and Conventions, "Natural Choices," August 2006*

- The Salt Lake City metro area was selected as one of the "25 Hottest Housing Markets" in the U.S. The area ranked #8 out of 156 markets with a home price appreciation rate of 22.7%. Criteria: year-over-year change of median sales price of existing single-family homes between the 4th quarter of 2005 and the 4th quarter of 2006. *National Association of Realtors, Median Sales Price of Existing Single-Family Homes for Metropolitan Areas, 4th Quarter 2006*

- The Salt Lake City metro area appeared on the Milken Institute "2005 Best Performing Cities" index. Rank: #87 out of 200 large metro areas. Criteria: job growth; wage and salary growth; high-tech output growth. *Milken Institute, "2005 Best Performing Cities," February 2006*

- The Salt Lake City metro area was selected as one of "The Best Cities for Doing Business in America." *Inc.* magazine measured employment growth in 393 regions using the following criteria: recent growth trend; mid-term growth; long-term trend; and current year growth. The Salt Lake City metro area ranked #15 among large metro areas and #98 overall. *Inc., May 2006*

- Salt Lake City was identified as one of the top 10 metro areas with the greatest number of *Inc. 500* companies per million residents. The area ranked #10. *Inc., September 2006*

■ Salt Lake City was identified as one of the 100 "Most Unwired Cities" in the U.S. The area ranked #33 out of the 100 largest metro areas in the U.S. Criteria: number of public and commercial wireless access points (hotspots); airports with wireless Internet access; broadband availability; local wireless networks; and wireless email devices. *Intel, "Most Unwired Cities Survey," June 7, 2005*

■ Salt Lake City was ranked #34 out of 125 regions worldwide in terms of its "Knowledge Competitiveness Index." The index attempts to measure the knowledge-based development taking place throughout the world and is based on 19 measures of economic performance that indicate a region's ability to translate its knowledge capacity into economic value. *Robert Huggins Associates, World Knowledge Competitiveness Index 2005*

■ *Forbes* ranked the 200 most populous metro areas in the U.S. in terms of the "Best Places for Business and Careers." The Salt Lake City metro area was ranked #77. Criteria: business costs (labor, energy, tax and office space expenses); living costs (housing, transportation, food and other household expenditures); education levels of the work force; job growth; income growth; migration trends; crime rates; and culture/leisure. *Forbes, April 23, 2007*

■ Salt Lake City was selected as a 2006 Digital Cities Survey winner. The city ranked #4 in the mid-sized city (125,000 to 249,999 population) category. The survey examined and assessed how city governments are utilizing information technology to operate and deliver quality service to their customers and citizens. Survey questions focused on implementation and adoption of online service delivery; planning and governance; and the infrastructure and architecture that make the transformation to digital government possible. *Center for Digital Government, "2006 Digital Cities Survey"*

■ Salt Lake City was identified as one of the top 20 metro areas with the highest rate of home price appreciation in 2006. The area ranked #4 with a one-year price appreciation of 19.8% through the 4th quarter 2006. *Office of Federal Housing Enterprise Oversight, House Price Index, 4th Quarter 2006*

■ *Kiplinger's Personal Finance* ranked 101 U.S. cities in terms of their total tax burdens. Salt Lake City ranked #59 (#1 had the lowest overall tax burden). Criteria: state income tax; property tax; sales tax; personal property tax; and gasoline tax. *Kiplinger's Personal Finance, July 2004*

■ *Fortune* ranked the 100 largest metro areas in the U.S. in terms of projected median home price change in 2006. The Salt Lake City metro area ranked #20. *Fortune, "The Top 100: Is the Party Over?" December 26, 2005*

Health/Environment Rankings

■ *Reader's Digest* ranked the 50 largest metro areas in the U.S. in terms of how "clean" they are. The Salt Lake City metro area ranked #18. Criteria: air quality; water quality; toxic industrial pollution; Superfund sites; and sanitation. *Reader's Digest, "The 50 Cleanest (and Dirtiest) Cities in America," July 2005*

■ Sanofi-aventis, in partnership with Sperling's BestPlaces, ranked the 50 worst cities for respiratory infections in the U.S. Salt Lake City ranked #24. Criteria: prevalence of sinusitis, pharyngitis (sore throat), bronchitis, acute upper respiratory infections, pneumonia, otitis media (middle ear infection), other respiratory tract infections and the common cold; total per capita prescriptions written for oral antibiotics for respiratory tract infections; and prevalence of state level antibiotic resistance. *Sanofi-aventis, "America's Worst Cities for Respiratory Infections," December 6, 2005*

■ The Salt Lake City metro area appeared in *Country Home's* "2007 Best Green Places Report". The area ranked #174. Criteria included: air and watershed quality; miles of mass transit; green power; number of farmer's markets, organic producers and groceries. *Country Home, "2007 Best Green Places Report," April 2007*

■ Wyeth Consumer Healthcare, in partnership with Sperling's BestPlaces, ranked the nation's 50 most populous metro areas in terms of five key health factors. The Salt Lake City metro area ranked #5. Criteria: physical activity, health status, nutrition, lifestyle pursuits; and mental wellness. *Wyeth Consumer Healthcare, "Centrum Healthiest Cities Study," April 19, 2005*

- Salt Lake City was identified as one of "America's Heart-Healthiest Cities" by *Men's Journal*. The city ranked #3 out of 8. Criteria: easy access to the outdoors; strong park and trail system; clear culture of activity (i.e. outdoor festivals, street fairs, bike racks and local distance races); city should be dense (good walkability), but not big (too stressful). *Men's Journal, "Where You Live is Key," August 2006*

- Salt Lake City was identified as a "2007 Asthma Capital." The area ranked #33 out of the nation's 100 largest metropolitan areas. Twelve factors were used to identify the most challenging places to live for people with asthma: estimated prevalence; self-reported prevalence; crude death rate for asthma; annual pollen score; annual air quality; public smoking laws; number of board-certified asthma specialists; school inhaler access laws; rescue medication use; controller medication use; uninsured rate; poverty rate. *Asthma and Allergy Foundation of America, "2007 Asthma Capitals"*

- Salt Lake City was identified as a "Spring Allergy Capital." The area ranked #60 out of 100. Three groups of factors were used to identify the most severe cities for people with allergies during the spring season: annual pollen levels; medicine utilization; access to board-certified allergists. *Asthma and Allergy Foundation of America, "2007 Spring Allergy Capital Rankings"*

- Salt Lake City was identified as a "Fall Allergy Capital." The area ranked #72 out of 100. Three groups of factors were used to identify the most severe cities for people with allergies during the fall season: annual pollen levels; medicine utilization; access to board-certified allergists. *Asthma and Allergy Foundation of America, "2006 Fall Allergy Capital Rankings"*

- *Men's Health* ranked the nation's largest 100 cities in terms of the *Best (and Worst) Cities for Men.* Salt Lake City was ranked #14. Criteria: 24 statistical parameters of long life in the categories of health, quality of life, and fitness. *Men's Health, January/February 2007*

- *Men's Health* ranked 100 U.S. cities in terms of the quality of their tap water. Salt Lake City was ranked #82 and received a grade of D. Criteria: levels of total coliform bacteria, arsenic, lead, total trihalomethanes (linked to cancer), and halo-acetic acids, plus the number of EPA water-system violations from 1995 to 2005. *Men's Health, March 2007*

- Ortho-McNeil Neurologics, in partnership with Sperling's BestPlaces, analyzed 110 metro areas and identified those U.S. cities with the highest prevalence of factors that are most commonly associated with migraine headaches. The Salt Lake City metro area ranked #21. Criteria: number of migraine-related drug prescriptions per capita; lifestyle factors that can contribute to migraines; environmental factors that can trigger migraines; and consumption of migraine-triggering foods. *Ortho-McNeil Neurologics, "America's Migraine Hot Spots," March 14, 2006*

- Sperling's BestPlaces ranked 331 metro areas and identified the most and least stressful U.S. cities. The Salt Lake City metro area ranked #64 out of the 100 largest metro areas (#1 = most stressful). Criteria: divorce rate; unemployment rate; violent and property crime; suicide rate; commute time; mental health; alcohol consumption; cloudy days. *www.BestPlaces.net, January 9, 2004*

- Sperling's BestPlaces in partnership with Vistakon ranked the 100 largest metro areas and identified "America's 10 Worst Cities for Comfortable Eyes." The Salt Lake City metro area ranked #3. Criteria: altitude; sunny days; wind; extreme temperatures; humidity; pollution; commute time; computer use. *Vistakon, "America's Best and Worst Cities for Comfortable Eyes," June 15, 2004*

- Salt Lake City was selected as one of "America's Pet Healthiest Cities" by Purina. The city ranked #10 out of 50. Criteria: veterinary services; environment; legislation; preventative care; obesity/body condition. *Purina Pet Institute, "America's Pet Healthiest Cities," May 20, 2003*

- According to research conducted by Malibu Wellness of 100 major U.S. cities' local water quality reports, Salt Lake City was selected as one of 10 color-unfriendly cities in terms of hair color application and longevity. Criteria: quantity of minerals found in the water supply (lower ppm is better for hair color); type of oxidizers such as chlorine; and pH levels. *Malibu Wellness, Wellness e-Letter, "Best & Worst Cities for Hair Color," February 2005*

Women/Minorities Rankings

■ Salt Lake City was ranked #37 out of 100 metro areas in *SELF Magazine's* ranking of "America's Best Places for Women." A panel of experts came up with nearly 40 criteria including: drinking and smoking rates; depression; unemployment; parks; crime; disease; healthcare insurance coverage; air quality; and commute times. *SELF Magazine, "America's Best Places for Women 2006," December 2006*

■ *Ladies Home Journal* ranked America's 200 largest cities based on the qualities women surveyed care about most. Salt Lake City ranked #119 out of 143 in the smaller city category (population under 300,000). Criteria: crime; lifestyle; education; jobs; health; child care; politics; and the economy. *Ladies Home Journal Online, "The Best Cities for Women 2002"*

■ Salt Lake City was profiled in the book *50 Fabulous Gay-Friendly Places to Live.* Criteria: an active gay community; positive gay health programs; youth outreach; gay-friendly politics; gay-owned and gay-friendly businesses; employment opportunities; fun nightlife; cultural opportunities; recreational opportunities; housing options. *50 Fabulous Gay-Friendly Places to Live, 2005*

Seniors/Retirement Rankings

■ Salt Lake City was profiled in the book *Where to Retire: America's Best and Most Affordable Places.* Cities were selected based on personal visits by the author and interviews with local residents coupled with statistics from various government agencies. *Where to Retire: America's Best and Most Affordable Places, 2006*

■ Sperling's BestPlaces in partnership with Bankers Life & Casualty Company designed a survey to identify the top 50 metro areas in the U.S. that offer the best overall qualities for senior living. The Salt Lake City metro area ranked #12. The following criteria were statistically weighted to reflect the needs of the senior population: health; disease; economics; social; environment; spiritual; transportation; housing; and crime. *Bankers Life & Casualty Company, "Best Cities for Seniors 2005"*

■ A.G. Edwards ranked America's 500 top-performing communities based on their residents' personal savings and investing behavior. The Salt Lake City metro area ranked #116 with an index score of 106.43 (national average = 100.00). A dozen statistical factors were measured including: participation in retirement savings plans; personal debt levels; and home ownership. *A.G. Edwards, "2006 Nest Egg Index", September 6, 2006*

Children/Family Rankings

■ The Salt Lake City metro area was selected as one of the "Best Cities for Relocating Families" by Worldwide ERC and Primacy Relocation. Criteria: tax rates; average home costs and home appreciation; ability to qualify for in-state tuition; service quality of local utilities; per-capita volunteerism; auto taxes; and quantity of fun, family-friendly events and venues. *Worldwide ERC and Primacy Relocation, "2006 Best Cities for Relocating Families"*

■ Salt Lake City was highlighted in the Forbes.com article "The Best Education in the Biggest Cities." The city ranked #2 out of 8. Criteria: the 100 largest school districts in the most populous cities in the U.S. were evaluated in three categories: high school graduation rate; affordability of housing; best access to educational resources. *Forbes.com, February 13, 2004*

Safety Rankings

■ Allstate ranked the 200 largest cities in America in terms of driver safety. Salt Lake City ranked #77. In addition, drivers were 4.4% more likely to have had an accident compared to the national average. Allstate researchers analyzed internal Property Damage reported claims over a two-year period (from January 2003 to December 2004) to ensure the findings would not be affected by external influences such as weather or road construction. A weighted average of the two-year numbers determined the annual percentages. The report defines an auto crash as any collision resulting in a property damage claim. *Allstate, "Allstate America's Best Drivers Report 2006," May 24, 2006*

■ Salt Lake City was identified as one of the most dangerous large metro areas for pedestrians in the U.S. The area ranked #31 out of the nations 50 largest metro areas. Criteria: average yearly pedestrian fatalities per capita (for the years 2002 and 2003) adjusted for the number of walkers. *Surface Transportation Policy Project, "Mean Streets 2004"*

■ *Ladies Home Journal* ranked America's 200 largest cities in terms of safety. Salt Lake City ranked #131 out of 200. Criteria: violent crimes; crimes against property; and rape. *Ladies Home Journal Online, "The Best Cities for Women 2002"*

Sports/Recreation Rankings

■ The Salt Lake City metro area appeared on *The Sporting News* list of the "Best Sports Cities 2006". The area ranked #30 out of 99 cities in North America. To be included in the rankings, a city must have at least one of the following: NCAA Division I basketball team; Class A minor league baseball team; training camp for a major league or NFL team; NASCAR Nextel Cup race; NCAA Division I-A bowl game; PGA Tour tournament; Triple Crown horse race. Once a city qualifies, a 12-month snapshot is taken of the sports atmosphere, putting a heavy premium on regular-season won-lost records; playoff berths, bowl appearances and tournament bids; championships; applicable power ratings; quality of competition; overall fan fervor; sports atmosphere and fan knowledge; abundance of teams (quality over quantity); stadium/arena quality; ticket availability and prices; franchise ownership; and the marquee appeal of athletes. *SportingNews.com, "Best Sports Cities 2006," August 1, 2006*

■ Salt Lake City was chosen as one of America's 25 best cities for running. The city was ranked #18. Criteria: number of running clubs per city; amount of land set aside for park usage; air quality; weather; crime rates; and results from a *Runner's World* poll in which readers ranked their favorite running cities. *Runner's World, "The 25 Best Running Cities in America," July 2005*

■ Scarborough Research, a leading market research firm, identified the top local markets for avid NBA fans. The Salt Lake City DMA (Designated Market Area) ranked in the top 10 with 13% of consumers 18 years and over reporting that they are "very interested in the NBA". *Scarborough Research, Scarborough USA+ 2005 Release 2*

■ The Salt Lake City metro area was selected by *Cranium* as one of the "Top 50 Fun Cities" in America. The area ranked #9. Criteria includes: number of sports teams, restaurants, and dance performances; number of toy stores; city budget spent on recreation. *Cranium, November 4, 2003*

■ *Golf Digest* ranked 330 metro areas in the U.S. in terms of golf. The Salt Lake City metro area was ranked #210. Criteria: access to golf; weather; value of golf; and quality of golf. *Golf Digest, "Metro Golf Rankings," August 2005*

Dating/Romance Rankings

■ The Salt Lake City metro area was selected as one of the "Best Cities for Relocating Singles" by Worldwide ERC and Primacy Relocation. The area ranked #37 out of the 100 largest metro areas in the U.S. Areas were selected based on the following criteria: Population Criteria (local percentage and growth trends of unmarried residents aged 25-34; male-female ratios; the number of newcomers to the area; diversity and density); Economic Criteria (job growth vs. unemployment rates; apartment rental costs; fee and occupancy rates for temporary housing and mini-storage; higher education costs, including in-state and out-of-state tuition requirements; vehicle tax rates and quality of service from utility providers); Quality-of-Life Criteria (level of per capita volunteering; quality and quantity of collegiate and professional sports with fun, fan-friendly venues; number of Starbucks and other coffee shops; quality or popularity of restaurants, nightspots, health clubs, and online dating; moderate climates with sustainable water supplies). *Worldwide ERC and Primacy Relocation, "2006 Best Cities for Relocating Singles," October 11, 2006*

■ *Forbes* ranked the 40 most populous metro areas in the U.S. in terms of the "Best Cities for Singles." The Salt Lake City metro area was ranked #36. Criteria: number of singles; cost of living alone; nightlife; culture; job growth; coolness; and online dating. *Forbes.com, July 25, 2006*

■ Sperling's BestPlaces in partnership with AXE Deodorant Bodyspray ranked 80 metro areas and identified "America's Best (and Worst) Cities for Dating." The Salt Lake City metro area ranked #41. Criteria: percentage of singles ages 18-24; population density; dating venues per capita. *AXE Deodorant Bodyspray, "America's Best (and Worst) Cities for Dating," May, 2004*

Culture/Performing Arts Rankings

■ Salt Lake City was selected as one of "America's Top 25 Arts Destinations." The city ranked #14 in the mid-sized city (population 100,000 to 499,999) category. Criteria: readers' top choices for arts travel destinations based on the richness and variety of visual arts sites, activities and events. *American Style, June 2006*

■ Scarborough Research, a leading market research firm, identified the top local markets for rock concert attendance. The Salt Lake City DMA (Designated Market Area) ranked in the top 25 with 14% of consumers, 18 years old and over, reporting that they have attended a rock concert during the past year. *Scarborough Research, Scarborough USA+ 2003 Release 2*

Miscellaneous Rankings

■ Salt Lake City was selected as one of the "Top 100 Sweatiest Summer Cities". The city was ranked #58. The ranking was based on the average male/female height/weight, average high temperature, and average relative humidity levels for 2002 in each of the cities during June, July and August. The sweat level was analyzed based on the assumption that the individual was walking for one hour. *Procter & Gamble, Old Spice, June 18, 2003*

■ Salt Lake City was selected as one of "America's Best Vegetarian-Friendly Small Cities." The city was ranked #3. *www.peta.org, April 2006*

■ Sperling's BestPlaces in partnership with Pep Boys ranked 77 metro areas and identified "America's Most Drivable Cities." The Salt Lake City metro area ranked #51. Criteria: climate; road roughness; urban mobility; gas prices. *Pep Boys, "America's Most Drivable Cities," April 9, 2003*

■ Salt Lake City was ranked #41 out of 268 metro areas in terms of its Creativity Index. The Creativity Index is a mix of four equally weighted factors: the Creative Class (scientists, engineers, architects, designers, writers, artists, musicians, or any profession where creativity is a key factor) share of the workforce; innovation, measured as patents per capita; high-tech industry, using the Milken Institute's Tech Pole Index; and diversity, measured by the Gay Index (a reasonable proxy for an areas' openness to different kinds of people and ideas). *The Rise of the Creative Class, 2002*

■ Salt Lake City was selected as one of America's best-mannered cities. The area ranked in the top 10 at #10. The list is based on thousands of letters and faxes received by etiquette expert Marjabelle Young Stewart. *The Associated Press, January 15, 2005*

■ State Farm Insurance, in partnership with Sperling's BestPlaces, analyzed several key factors that contribute to overall family preparedness. The Salt Lake City metro area ranked #1 out of the nation's 50 most populous metro areas. Criteria: quality of life; life insurance coverage; and investments. *State Farm Life Insurance, "Fiscally Fit Cities Report," July 20, 2004*

Business Environment

CITY FINANCES

City Government Finances

Component	2003-2004 ($000)	2003-2004 ($ per capita)
Total Revenues	449,157	2,478
Total Expenditures	431,341	2,380
Debt Outstanding	366,333	2,021
Cash and Securities	411,111	2,268

Source: U.S Census Bureau, Government Finances 2003-2004

City Government Revenue by Source

Source	2003-2004 ($000)	2003-2004 ($ per capita)
General Revenue		
From Federal Government	12,048	66
From State Government	9,435	52
From Local Governments	3,709	20
Taxes		
Property	96,603	533
Sales	64,665	357
Personal Income	0	0
License	0	0
Charges	158,099	872
Liquor Store	0	0
Utility	44,881	248
Employee Retirement	0	0
Other	59,717	329

Source: U.S Census Bureau, Government Finances 2003-2004

City Government Expenditures by Function

Function	2003-2004 ($000)	2003-2004 ($ per capita)	2003-2004 (%)
General Expenditures			
Airports	111,667	616	25.9
Corrections	0	0	0.0
Education	0	0	0.0
Fire Protection	27,527	152	6.4
Governmental Administration	24,959	138	5.8
Health	0	0	0.0
Highways	40,195	222	9.3
Hospitals	0	0	0.0
Housing and Community Development	33,616	185	7.8
Interest on General Debt	20,688	114	4.8
Libraries	11,582	64	2.7
Parking	0	0	0.0
Parks and Recreation	11,864	65	2.8
Police Protection	43,321	239	10.0
Public Welfare	0	0	0.0
Sewerage	24,659	136	5.7
Solid Waste Management	15,116	83	3.5
Liquor Store	0	0	0.0
Utility	45,742	252	10.6
Employee Retirement	0	0	0.0
Other	20,405	113	4.7

Source: U.S Census Bureau, Government Finances 2003-2004

Municipal Bond Ratings

Area	Moody's
City	Aaa

Source: Mergent Bond Record, January 2007 (unless noted otherwise)

DEMOGRAPHICS

Population Growth

Area	1990 Census	2000 Census	2006 Estimate	2011 Projection	Population Growth (%)	
					1990-2000	2000-2011
City	159,796	181,743	177,325	175,202	13.7	-3.6
MSA[1]	768,075	968,858	1,033,776	1,086,733	26.1	12.2
U.S.	248,709,873	281,421,906	298,021,266	312,383,955	13.2	11.0

Note: (1) Metropolitan Statistical Area - see Appendix B for areas included
Source: Claritas, Inc.

Number of Households and Average Household Size

Area	2006 Estimate	2006 Average Household Size
City	69,884	2.54
MSA[1]	338,691	3.05
U.S.	112,267,302	2.65

Note: (1) Metropolitan Statistical Area - see Appendix B for areas included
Source: Claritas, Inc.

Race and Ethnicity

Area	White Alone[2]	Black Alone[2]	Asian Alone[2]	Other Race Alone[2]	Hispanic[3]
City	76.9	2.0	3.8	17.4	23.8
MSA[1]	84.6	1.2	2.7	11.5	14.5
U.S.	73.3	12.4	4.2	10.1	14.5

Note: Figures are 2006 estimates; (1) Metropolitan Statistical Area - see Appendix B for areas included
(2) Alone is defined as not being in combination with one or more other races; (3) May be of any race.
Source: Claritas, Inc.

Segregation

City		MSA[1]	
Index[2]	Rank[3]	Index[2]	Rank[4]
44.7	74	47.8	252

Note: Figures are based on an analysis of Census 2000 data; (1) Metropolitan Statistical Area - see Appendix A
for areas included; (2) White/Black Dissimilarity Index—the most commonly used measure of segregation
between two groups, reflecting their relative distributions across neighborhoods within a city or metropolitan
area. It can range in value from 0, indicating complete integration, to 100, indicating complete segregation; (3)
Ranges from 1 (most segregated) to 100 (least segregated) and includes all the cities in this book; (4) Ranges
from 1 (most segregated) to 318 (least segregated) and includes 318 metropolitan areas.
Source: www.CensusScope.org

Ancestry

Area	German	Irish[2]	English	American	Italian	Polish	French[3]	Scottish
City	10.8	6.7	20.9	4.3	2.8	1.0	2.4	4.3
MSA[1]	12.0	6.2	27.4	6.4	2.8	0.8	2.3	4.3
U.S.	15.2	10.9	8.7	7.3	5.6	3.2	3.0	1.7

Note: Figures include multiple ancestry (e.g. if a person reported being Irish and Italian, they were included in
both columns); (1) Metropolitan Statistical Area - see Appendix A for areas included; (2) Includes Celtic; (3)
Includes Alsatian but excludes Basque
Source: Census 2000, Summary File 3

Foreign-Born Population

Area	Percent of Population Born in							
	Any Foreign Country	Europe	Asia	Africa	Oceania[2]	Canada	Mexico	Latin America[3]
City	18.3	3.1	3.0	0.7	1.0	0.4	8.5	1.7
MSA[1]	8.6	1.5	1.7	0.2	0.4	0.3	3.5	1.1
U.S.	11.1	1.7	2.9	0.3	0.1	0.3	3.3	2.5

Note: (1) Metropolitan Statistical Area - see Appendix A for areas included; (2) Includes Australia, New
Zealand subregion, Melanesia, Micronesia, Polynesia, and Oceania n.e.c; (3) Includes Central America
(excluding Mexico), South America, and the Caribbean.
Source: Census 2000, Summary File 3

Marriage Status

Area	Never Married	Now Married (excluding Separated)	Separated	Widowed	Divorced
City	34.7	46.9	1.9	5.7	10.8
MSA[1]	27.6	57.6	1.4	4.1	9.3
U.S.	27.1	54.4	2.2	6.6	9.7

Note: Figures are percentages and cover the population 15 years of age and older;
(1) Metropolitan Statistical Area - see Appendix A for areas included
Source: Census 2000, Summary File 3

Age Distribution

Area	Percent of Population						
	Under Age 5	Age 5 to 17	Age 18 to 34	Age 35 to 49	Age 50 to 64	Age 65 to 79	80 Years and Over
City	7.8	15.6	35.0	20.4	10.1	7.4	3.7
MSA[1]	9.1	22.2	28.1	20.9	11.4	6.2	2.1
U.S.	6.8	18.9	23.7	23.5	14.8	9.2	3.2

Note: (1) Metropolitan Statistical Area - see Appendix A for areas included
Source: Census 2000, Summary File 3

Male/Female Ratio

Area	Males	Females	Males per 100 Females
City	90,322	87,003	103.8
MSA[1]	522,851	510,925	102.3
U.S.	146,712,712	151,308,554	97.0

Note: Figures are 2006 estimates; (1) Metropolitan Statistical Area -
see Appendix B for areas included
Source: Claritas, Inc.

Religion

Area	Catholic	Southern Baptist	United Methodist	ELCA[1]	LDS[2]	Presbyterian Church USA	Jewish Est.	Muslim Est.
County	6.0	0.6	0.5	0.4	56.0	0.4	0.5	0.4
U.S.	22.0	7.1	3.7	1.8	1.5	1.1	2.2	0.6

Note: Figures are the number of adherents as a percentage of the total population; Adherents are defined as all
members, including full members, their children and the estimated number of other participants who are not
considered members (e.g. the baptized, those not confirmed, those regularly attending services, etc.);
(1) Evangelical Lutheran Church in America; (2) The Church of Jesus Christ of Latter Day Saints
Source: Reprinted with permission from Religious Congregations and Membership in the United States 2000
(Nashville, Glenmary Research Center, 2002) Copyright Association of Statisticians of American Religious
Bodies. All rights reserved.

ECONOMY

Gross Metropolitan Product

Area	2002	2003	2004	2005	2005 Rank[2]
MSA[1]	38.2	39.5	42.2	46.4	48

Note: Figures are in billions of dollars; (1) Salt Lake City, UT Metropolitan Statistical Area - see Appendix A
for areas included; (2) Rank ranges from 1 to 361
Source: The U.S. Conference of Mayors, "U.S. Metro Economies: GMP - The Engines of America's Growth,"
January 2007

Economic Growth

Area	1995 GMP	2005 GMP	Average Annual Growth Rate	Growth Rate Rank[2]
MSA[1]	25.1	46.4	6.4	88

Note: Figures are in billions of dollars; GMP = Gross Metropolitan Product; (1) Salt Lake City, UT
Metropolitan Statistical Area - see Appendix A for areas included; (2) Rank ranges from 1 to 361
Source: The U.S. Conference of Mayors, "U.S. Metro Economies: GMP - The Engines of America's Growth,"
January 2007

INCOME

Per Capita/Median/Average Income

Area	Per Capita ($)	Median Household ($)	Average Household ($)
City	24,535	43,564	61,491
MSA[1]	24,295	58,289	73,468
U.S.	25,129	48,775	65,849

Note: Figures are 2006 estimates; (1) Metropolitan Statistical Area - see Appendix B for areas included
Source: Claritas, Inc.

Household Income Distribution

Area	Under $15,000	$15,000 -24,999	$25,000 -34,999	$35,000 -49,999	$50,000 -74,999	$75,000 -99,000	$100,000 -149,999	$150,000 and up
City	15.2	12.9	12.7	16.0	18.5	9.9	8.8	5.9
MSA[1]	7.9	8.4	10.0	16.2	22.8	14.2	13.6	7.0
U.S.	13.3	11.0	11.3	15.7	19.5	11.8	11.0	6.4

Note: Figures are 2006 estimates; (1) Metropolitan Statistical Area - see Appendix B for areas included
Source: Claritas, Inc.

Poverty Rates by Age

Area	All Ages	Under 5 Years Old	5 to 17 Years Old	18 to 64 Years Old	65 Years and Over
City	15.3	1.5	3.0	9.9	0.9
MSA[1]	7.7	1.0	1.9	4.4	0.4
U.S.	12.4	1.2	3.0	6.9	1.2

Note: Figures are percent of population with income in 1999 below poverty level and only include population for whom poverty status is determined; (1) Metropolitan Statistical Area - see Appendix A for areas included
Source: Census 2000, Summary File 3

Personal Bankruptcy Filing Rate

Area	2003	2004	2005
Salt Lake County	11.25	10.60	10.89
U.S.	5.57	5.31	6.88

Note: Numbers are per 1,000 population and include Chapter 7 and Chapter 13 filings
Source: Federal Deposit Insurance Corporation (FDIC), Regional Economic Conditions (RECON), 3/24/2006

EMPLOYMENT

Labor Force and Employment

Area	Civilian Labor Force			Workers Employed		
	Dec. 2005	Dec. 2006	% Chg.	Dec. 2005	Dec. 2006	% Chg.
City	107,103	109,813	2.5	102,630	106,870	4.1
MSA[1]	566,884	582,605	2.8	546,818	569,410	4.1
U.S.	149,874,000	152,571,000	1.8	142,918,000	146,081,000	2.2

Note: Data is not seasonally adjusted and covers workers 16 years of age and older;
(1) Metropolitan Statistical Area - see Appendix B for areas included
Source: Bureau of Labor Statistics, http://stats.bls.gov

Unemployment Rate

Area	2006											
	Jan.	Feb.	Mar.	Apr.	May	Jun.	Jul.	Aug.	Sep.	Oct.	Nov.	Dec.
City	4.8	5.0	4.3	4.1	4.0	4.0	4.1	4.1	3.2	2.8	2.9	2.7
MSA[1]	4.1	4.2	3.6	3.5	3.4	3.4	3.4	3.5	2.7	2.4	2.5	2.3
U.S.	5.1	5.1	4.8	4.5	4.4	4.8	5.0	4.6	4.4	4.1	4.3	4.3

Note: Data is not seasonally adjusted and covers workers 16 years of age and older; All figures are percentages; (1) Metropolitan Statistical Area - see Appendix B for areas included
Source: Bureau of Labor Statistics, http://stats.bls.gov

Employment by Occupation

Occupation Classification	City (%)	MSA[1] (%)	U.S. (%)
Sales and Office	26.4	30.8	26.7
Professional and Related	25.7	19.1	20.2
Service	15.4	13.0	14.9
Production, Transportation, and Material Moving	12.0	13.3	14.6
Management, Business, and Financial	12.7	13.6	13.5
Construction, Extraction, and Maintenance	7.6	10.0	9.4
Farming, Forestry, and Fishing	0.1	0.2	0.7

Note: Figures cover employed civilians 16 years of age and older;
(1) Metropolitan Statistical Area - see Appendix A for areas included
Source: Census 2000, Summary File 3

Employment by Industry

| Sector | MSA[1] | | U.S. |
	Number of Employees	Percent of Total	Percent of Total
Government	93,200	14.7	16.3
Education and Health Services	58,100	9.1	13.2
Professional and Business Services	102,400	16.1	12.9
Retail Trade	72,000	11.3	11.5
Manufacturing	56,000	8.8	10.2
Leisure and Hospitality	57,900	9.1	9.5
Financial Activities	50,600	8.0	6.1
Construction	n/a	n/a	5.5
Wholesale Trade	30,100	4.7	4.3
Other Services	19,100	3.0	3.9
Transportation and Utilities	30,300	4.8	3.7
Information	18,900	3.0	2.2
Natural Resources and Mining	n/a	n/a	0.5

Note: Figures cover non-farm employment as of December 2006 and are not seasonally adjusted;
(1) Metropolitan Statistical Area - see Appendix B for areas included; n/a not available
Source: Bureau of Labor Statistics, http://stats.bls.gov

Occupations with Greatest Projected Employment Growth: 2002 - 2012

Occupation[1]	2002 Employment	2012 Projected Employment	Numeric Employment Change	Percent Employment Change
Retail Salespersons	38,530	48,730	10,200	26.5
Customer Service Representatives	23,440	33,210	9,770	41.7
Cashiers	29,130	38,670	9,540	32.7
Combined Food Preparation and Serving Workers, Including Fast Food	15,360	23,580	8,220	53.5
Waiters and Waitresses	16,730	24,740	8,010	47.9
Registered Nurses	15,180	22,000	6,820	44.9
Janitors and Cleaners, Except Maids and Housekeeping Cleaners	18,530	24,650	6,120	33.0
Truck Drivers, Heavy and Tractor-Trailer	18,170	24,150	5,980	32.9
Carpenters	15,180	20,710	5,530	36.4
Teacher Assistants	14,480	19,970	5,490	37.9

Note: Projections cover Utah; (1) Sorted by numeric employment change
Source: www.projectionscentral.com, State Occupational Projections, 2002-2012 Long-Term Projections

Fastest Growing Occupations: 2002 - 2012

Occupation[1]	2002 Employment	2012 Projected Employment	Numeric Employment Change	Percent Employment Change
Network Systems and Data Communications Analysts	1,300	2,270	970	74.6
Medical Assistants	3,300	5,590	2,290	69.4
Home Health Aides	2,080	3,510	1,430	68.8
Pharmacists	1,870	3,120	1,250	66.8
Physical Therapist Aides	670	1,110	440	65.7
Personal and Home Care Aides	2,150	3,520	1,370	63.7
Social and Human Service Assistants	4,200	6,870	2,670	63.6
Computer Software Engineers, Systems Software	1,920	3,140	1,220	63.5
Physician Assistants	410	660	250	61.0
Architects, Except Landscape and Naval	730	1,170	440	60.3

Note: Projections cover Utah; (1) Sorted by percent employment change and excludes occupations with numeric employment change less than 200
Source: www.projectionscentral.com, State Occupational Projections, 2002-2012 Long-Term Projections

Average Wages

Occupation	$/Hr.	Occupation	$/Hr.
Accountants and Auditors	24.19	Maids and Housekeeping Cleaners	8.69
Automotive Mechanics	17.09	Maintenance and Repair Workers	15.79
Bookkeepers	14.01	Marketing Managers	40.30
Carpenters	15.06	Nuclear Medicine Technologists	24.29
Cashiers	8.65	Nurses, Licensed Practical	16.88
Clerks, General Office	11.25	Nurses, Registered	26.06
Clerks, Receptionists/Information	10.90	Nursing Aides/Orderlies/Attendants	10.05
Clerks, Shipping/Receiving	12.34	Packers and Packagers, Hand	7.78
Computer Programmers	32.86	Physical Therapists	29.10
Computer Support Specialists	18.29	Postal Service Mail Carriers	21.64
Computer Systems Analysts	31.26	Real Estate Brokers	29.53
Cooks, Restaurant	10.24	Retail Salespersons	11.44
Dentists	n/a	Sales Reps., Exc. Tech./Scientific	25.12
Electrical Engineers	37.56	Sales Reps., Tech./Scientific	32.91
Electricians	18.57	Secretaries, Exc. Legal/Med./Exec.	12.93
Financial Managers	39.35	Security Guards	11.53
First-Line Supervisors/Mgrs., Sales	17.50	Surgeons	n/a
Food Preparation Workers	7.83	Teacher Assistants	8.90
General and Operations Managers	42.78	Teachers, Elementary School	20.20
Hairdressers/Cosmetologists	10.39	Teachers, Secondary School	20.30
Internists	n/a	Telemarketers	8.28
Janitors and Cleaners	9.27	Truck Drivers, Heavy/Tractor-Trailer	18.74
Landscaping/Groundskeeping Workers	10.35	Truck Drivers, Light/Delivery Svcs.	12.51
Lawyers	53.41	Waiters and Waitresses	8.53

Note: Wage data is for May 2005 and covers the Salt Lake City, UT Metropolitan Statistics Area - see Appendix B for areas included. Hourly wages for elementary/secondary school teachers and teacher assistants were calculated by the editors from annual wage data assuming a 40 hour work week; n/a not available.
Source: Bureau of Labor Statistics, May 2005 Metro Area Occupational Employment and Wage Estimates

RESIDENTIAL REAL ESTATE

Building Permits

Area	Single-Family			Multi-Family			Total		
	2005	2006p	Pct. Chg.	2005	2006p	Pct. Chg.	2005	2006p	Pct. Chg.
City	96	117	21.9	830	191	-77.0	926	308	-66.7
U.S.	1,682,000	1,380,000	-18.0	473,300	457,300	-3.4	2,155,300	1,837,300	-14.8

Note: (p) preliminary; figures represent new, privately-owned housing units authorized (unadjusted data); All permit data are based on estimates with imputation; U.S. figures are based on the new 20,000-place series.
Source: U.S. Census Bureau, Manufacturing, Mining, and Construction Statistics

Homeownership and Housing Vacancies

Area	Homeownership Rate[2] (%)			Rental Vacancy Rate[3] (%)			Homeowner Vacancy Rate[4] (%)		
	2004	2005	2006	2004	2005	2006	2004	2005	2006
MSA[1]	n/a	68.8	69.6	n/a	7.0	4.7	n/a	1.5	2.7
U.S.	69.0	68.9	68.8	10.2	9.8	9.7	1.7	1.9	2.4

Note: Comparable 2004 data was not available due to changes in metropolitan area definitions; (1) Metropolitan Statistical Area - see Appendix B for areas included; (2) The proportion of households that are owners; (3) The proportion of the rental inventory that is vacant for rent; (4) The proportion of the homeowner inventory that is vacant for sale; n/a not available
Source: U.S. Census Bureau, Housing Vacancies and Homeownership Annual Statistics: 2006

TAXES

State Corporate Income Tax Rates

State	Rate (%)	Number of Brackets	Low Bracket (Under $)	High Bracket (Over $)
Utah	5.0	1	na	na

Note: Tax rates as of December 31, 2006; na not applicable; Minimum tax is $100.
Source: Tax Foundation, www.taxfoundation.org

State Individual Income Tax Rates

State	Federal Deductibility	Marginal Rate (%)	Number of Brackets	Low Bracket (Under $)	High Bracket (Over $)
Utah	Yes	2.3-6.98 (cc)	6	0	5,000

Note: Tax rates as of December 31, 2006; Brackets apply to single taxpayers and married people filing separately; na not applicable; (cc) In 2007 an optional 5.35% flat tax will be available.
Source: Tax Foundation, www.taxfoundation.org

Various State and Local Tax Rates

State and Local Sales and Use (%)	State Sales and Use (%)	Gasoline ($/gal.)	Cigarette ($/pack)	Spirits ($/gal.)	Table Wine ($/gal.)	Beer ($/gal.)
6.85	4.75	0.25	0.70	9.66 (b)	(i)	0.41

Note: Tax rates as of December 31, 2006; (b) States where the state government controls all sales. Excise tax rate is calculated using methodology designed by the Distilled Spirits Council of the United States (DISCUS); (i) Products are subject to ad valorem mark-up and excise taxes. Only license state volume-based tax rates are shown. Some control states also levy volume-based taxes in addition to their percentage ad valorem taxes.
Source: Tax Foundation, www.taxfoundation.org; The Sales Tax Clearinghouse, www.thestc.com

State Tax Burdens

Area	Combined State and Local Tax Burden		Combined Federal, State and Local Tax Burden	
	Percent	Rank	Percent	Rank
Utah	10.5	22	29.5	34
U.S. Average	10.6	-	31.6	-

Note: Figures are for 2006 and measure taxes as a percentage of income
Source: Tax Foundation, www.taxfoundation.org

Internal Revenue Service Tax Audits

IRS District	Percent of Returns Audited				
	1996	1997	1998	1999	2000
Rocky Mountain	0.73	0.67	0.49	0.28	0.20
U.S.	0.66	0.61	0.46	0.31	0.20

Note: Figures cover IRS district audits of federal income tax returns filed by individuals. Geographic data on district audits after the year 2000 are being withheld by the IRS. TRAC is challenging this policy.
Source: Syracuse University, Transactional Records Access Clearinghouse (TRAC), "Odds of IRS District Tax Audit 2000"

COMMERCIAL
UTILITIES

Typical Monthly Electric Bills

Area	Commercial Service ($/month)		Industrial Service ($/month)	
	3 kW demand 1,000 kWh	40 kW demand 14,000 kWh	1,000 kW demand 200,000 kWh	50,000 kW demand 15,000,000 kWh
City	92	917	18,586	872,187
Average[1]	123	1,413	22,000	1,306,315

Note: Based on total rates in effect July 1, 2006; (1) average based on 196 utilities
Source: Edison Electric Institute, Typical Bills and Average Rates Report, Summer 2006

TRANSPORTATION

Means of Transportation to Work

Area	Car/Truck/Van		Public Transportation			Bicycle	Walked	Other Means	Worked at Home
	Drove Alone	Car-pooled	Bus	Subway	Railroad				
City	69.3	13.9	5.9	0.0	0.1	1.5	4.9	1.1	3.2
MSA[1]	77.2	13.1	2.5	0.1	0.2	0.4	1.8	0.9	3.8
U.S.	75.7	12.2	2.5	1.5	0.5	0.4	2.9	1.0	3.3

Note: Figures are percentages and cover workers 16 years of age and older;
(1) Metropolitan Statistical Area - see Appendix A for areas included
Source: Census 2000, Summary File 3

Travel Time to Work

Area	Less Than 15 Minutes	15 to 29 Minutes	30 to 44 Minutes	45 to 59 Minutes	60 Minutes or More
City	38.1	43.7	12.2	2.8	3.2
MSA[1]	29.2	43.6	18.0	4.8	4.4
U.S.	29.4	36.1	19.1	7.4	8.0

Note: Figures are percentages and include workers 16 years old and over; (1) Metropolitan Statistical Area -
see Appendix A for areas included
Source: Census 2000, Summary File 3

Travel Time Index

Area	1982	1993	2002	2003
Urban Area[1]	1.03	1.13	1.26	1.28
Average[2]	1.12	1.28	1.37	1.37

Note: Travel Time Index - The ratio of travel time in the peak period to the travel time at
free-flow conditions. A value of 1.35 indicates a 20-minute free-flow trip takes 27 minutes
in the peak. Free-flow speeds (60 mph on freeways and 35 mph on principal arterials)
are used as the comparison threshold; (1) Covers the Salt Lake City, UT urban area;
(2) average of 85 urban areas
Source: Texas Transportation Institute, The 2005 Urban Mobility Report, May 2005

Public Transportation

Agency name:	Utah Transit Authority (UTA)
Vehicle type:	Bus
Average fleet age in years:	7.4
No. operated in max. service:	384
Vehicle type:	Light rail
Average fleet age in years:	7.9
No. operated in max. service:	42
Vehicle type:	Demand response
Average fleet age in years:	3.6
No. operated in max. service:	146
Vehicle type:	Vanpool
Average fleet age in years:	3.2
No. operated in max. service:	288

Source: Federal Transit Administration, National Transit Database, 2005

Air Transportation

Airport name and code:	Salt Lake City International (SLC)
Domestic service (2006)	
Passenger airlines[1]:	31
Passenger enplanements:	10,041,732
Freight carriers[2]:	23
Freight (lbs.):	170,594,605
International service (2005)	
Passenger airlines[1]:	19
Passenger enplanements:	193,314
Freight carriers[2]:	6
Freight (lbs.):	505,225

*Note: (1) Includes all major, minor and commuter airlines that carried at least one passenger during the year;
(2) Includes all airlines and freight carriers that transported at least one pound of freight during the year
Source: Bureau of Transportation Statistics, The Intermodal Transportation Database, Air Carriers: T-100
International Market, 2004; Bureau of Transportation Statistics, The Intermodal Transportation Database, Air
Carriers: T-100 Domestic Market, 2005*

Other Transportation Statistics

Interstate highways:	I-15; I-80; I-84
Amtrak service:	Yes
Major waterways/ports:	None

Source: Editor & Publisher Market Guide, 2006; Amtrak.com; Rand McNally 2006 Road Atlas

BUSINESSES

Major Business Headquarters

Company Name	2006 Rankings	
	Fortune[1]	Forbes[2]
Alsco	-	333
Huntsman	172	-
Sinclair Oil	-	38

*Note: (1) Fortune 500 - companies that produce a 10-K are ranked 1 to 500 based on 2005 revenue; (2) Forbes
Largest Private Companies - all private companies with at least $1 billion in annual revenue are ranked 1 to
394; companies listed are located in the city; dashes indicate no ranking
Source: Fortune, April 17, 2006; Forbes, November 9, 2006*

Fast-Growing Businesses

According to *Inc.*, Salt Lake City is home to three of America's 500 fastest-growing private
companies: **Diamond Wireless; Spring Communications; Universal Accounting Center**.
Criteria: must be an independent, privately-held, U.S. corporation, proprietorship or
partnership; net sales of at least $600,000 in FY2002; four-year operating/sales history;
holding companies, regulated banks, and utilities were excluded. *Inc., "America's 500
Fastest-Growing Private Companies," September 2006*

According to Deloitte & Touche LLP, Salt Lake City is home to one of North America's 500
fastest-growing high-technology companies: **FatPipe Networks**. Companies are ranked by
percentage growth in revenue over a five-year period. Criteria for inclusion: company must be
headquartered within North America; company must own proprietary intellectual property or
proprietary technology that contributes to a significant portion of the company's operating
revenue or devotes a significant proportion of revenues to research and development of
technology; company must have been in business for a minumum of five years with 2001
operating revenues of at least $50,000 USD or $75,000 CD and 2005 operating revenues of at
least $5 million USD/CD. *Deloitte & Touche LLP, 2006 Technology Fast 500*

Women-Owned Businesses: 1997 and 2002

Year	All Firms		Firms with Paid Employees			
	Firms	Sales ($000)	Firms	Sales ($000)	Employees	Payroll ($000)
1997	4,092	1,317,798	779	1,236,223	11,473	261,256
2002	4,402	1,348,201	888	1,238,626	8,633	261,892

*Note: Figures cover firms located in the city; Women-owned business are defined as firms in which women own
51% or more of the stock or equity of the company; (a) Withheld to avoid disclosing data for individual
companies; (b) Withheld because estimate did not meet publication standards; n/a not available
Source: 1997 Economic Census, Survey of Minority- and Women-Owned Business Enterprises; 2002 Economic
Census, Survey of Business Owners (released February 9, 2006)*

HOTELS

Hotels/Motels

Area	Hotels/Motels	Average Minimum Rates ($)		
		Tourist	First-Class	Deluxe
City	77	61	93	168

Source: OAG Travel Planner Online, Spring 2006

EVENT SITES

Stadiums, Arenas, and Auditoriums

Name	Capacity
Capitol Theatre	1,987
Delta Center	20,400
Jon M. Huntsman Center	15,000

Source: www.officialtravelguide.com; www.eventective.com; original research

Convention Centers

Name	Overall Space (sq. ft.)	Exhibit Space (sq. ft.)	Meeting Space (sq. ft.)	Meeting Rooms
Salt Palace Convention Center	679,000	164,000	515,000	53

Source: www.officialtravelguide.com; www.eventective.com; original research

Hotels/Conference Centers

Name	Guest Rooms	Exhibit Space (sq. ft.)	Meeting Space (sq. ft.)
Hilton City Center	499	n/a	24,000
Little America Hotel & Towers Downtown	850	12,000	22,000
Salt Lake City Marriott Downtown	359	8,355	15,309
The Grand America	775	48,000	75,000

Note: n/a not available
Source: www.officialtravelguide.com; www.eventective.com; original research

Living Environment

COST OF LIVING

Cost of Living Index

Year	Composite Index	Groceries	Housing	Utilities	Trans-portation	Health Care	Misc. Goods/ Services
2004	99.1	102.9	94.9	91.1	101.3	103.0	102.2
2005	96.0	105.7	90.6	89.2	98.4	99.1	97.9
2006	99.2	104.1	95.5	91.4	97.8	94.2	103.5

Note: U.S. = 100
Source: The Council for Community and Economic Research (formerly ACCRA), Cost of Living Index, 2004, 2005 and 2006 4-Quarter Averages

HOUSING

House Price Index (HPI)

Area	National Ranking[2]	Quarterly Change (%)	One-Year Change (%)	Five-Year Change (%)
MSA[1]	4	3.34	19.76	48.98
U.S.[3]	-	1.12	5.87	55.21

Note: The HPI is a weighted repeat sales index. It measures average price changes in repeat sales or refinancings on the same properties. This information is obtained by reviewing repeat mortgage transactions on single-family properties whose mortgages have been purchased or securitized by Fannie Mae or Freddie Mac in January 1975; (1) Metropolitan Statistical Area - see Appendix B for areas included; (2) Rankings are based on annual percentage change for all metro areas containing at least 15,000 transactions over the last 10 years and ranges from 1 to 282; (3) figures based on a weighted division average; all figures are for the period ending December 31, 2006
Source: Office of Federal Housing Enterprise Oversight, House Price Index, March 1, 2007

House Price Valuations

Area	Q4 1999	Q4 2000	Q4 2001	Q4 2002	Q4 2003	Q4 2004	Q4 2005	Q4 2006
MSA[1]	5.5	2.0	-0.3	0.6	0.9	0.6	5.6	12.3

Note: Figures show the percentage of over- or under-valuation of single family homes relative to statistically normal house values (e.g. a value of 23.6 indicates that house values are 23.6% overvalued). Statistically normal house values are based on house prices, interest rates, household incomes, population densities, and any historical premiums or discounts metropolitan areas have exhibited over time; (1) Figures cover the Metropolitan Statistical Area - see Appendix B for areas included
Source: Global Insight/National City Corporation, House Prices in America, March 2007

Median Home Prices

Area	2004	2005	2006p	Percent Change 2005 to 2006
Metro Area[1]	158.0	173.9	203.0	16.7
U.S. Average	195.2	219.0	222.0	1.4

Note: Figures are median sales prices of existing single-family homes in thousands of dollars; (p) preliminary; n/a not available; (1) Covers the Salt Lake City, UT Metropolitan Statistical Area - see Appendix B for areas included
Source: National Association of Realtors, Metropolitan Area Prices, 4th Quarter 2006

Housing: Year Structure Built

Area	1990 -2000	1980 -1989	1970 -1979	1960 -1969	1950 -1959	1940 -1949	Before 1940	Median Year
City	7.3	7.6	13.6	11.1	15.2	13.4	31.7	1953
MSA[1]	22.0	16.4	22.5	11.9	11.7	6.0	9.4	1975
U.S.	17.0	15.8	18.5	13.7	12.7	7.3	15.0	1971

Note: Figures are percentages; (1) Metropolitan Statistical Area - see Appendix A for areas included
Source: Census 2000, Summary File 3

Average New Home Price

Area	2004	2005	2006
City	231,740	246,254	287,756
U.S.	253,574	275,712	299,269

Note: Figures, in dollars, are based on a new home with 2,400 sq. ft. of living area on an 8,000 sq. ft. lot.
Source: The Council for Community and Economic Research (formerly ACCRA), Cost of Living Index, 2004, 2005 and 2006 4-Quarter Averages

Average Apartment Rent

Area	2004	2005	2006
City	784	736	723
U.S.	716	740	766

Note: Figures, in dollars per month, are based on an unfurnished two bedroom, 1-1/2 or 2 bath apartment, approximately 950 sq. ft. in size, excluding all utilities except water
Source: The Council for Community and Economic Research (formerly ACCRA), Cost of Living Index, 2004, 2005 and 2006 4-Quarter Averages

RESIDENTIAL
UTILITIES

Average Residential Utility Costs

Area	All Electric ($/mth)	Part Electric ($/mth)	Other Energy ($/mth)	Phone ($/mth)
City	–	50.02	76.47	28.35
U.S.	136.00	76.53	90.52	25.87

Source: The Council for Community and Economic Research (formerly ACCRA), Cost of Living Index, 2006 4-Quarter Average

HEALTH

Average Health Care Costs

Area	Optometrist ($/visit)	Doctor ($/visit)	Dentist ($/visit)
City	73.29	78.79	58.52
U.S.	76.38	76.10	68.72

Note: Optometrist—based on a full vision eye exam for an established adult patient;
Doctor—based on a general practitioner's routine exam of an established patient;
Dentist—based on adult teeth cleaning and periodic oral exam.
Source: The Council for Community and Economic Research (formerly ACCRA), Cost of Living Index, 2006 4-Quarter Average

Mortality Rates

ICD-10 Sub-Chapter	ICD-10 Code	Age-Adjusted Death Rate per 100,000 population[1]	U.S. Age-Adjusted Death Rate per 100,000 population
Malignant neoplasms	C00-C97	147.1	185.8
Ischaemic heart diseases	I20-I25	86.3	150.2
Other forms of heart disease	I30-I51	66.8	50.8
Cerebrovascular diseases	I60-I69	46.5	50.0
Chronic lower respiratory diseases	J40-J47	36.9	41.1
Diabetes mellitus	E10-E14	26.7	24.5
Other degenerative diseases of the nervous system	G30-G31	15.5	22.3
Other external causes of accidental injury	W00-X59	17.3	21.2
Influenza and pneumonia	J10-J18	22.0	19.8
Hypertensive diseases	I10-I13	10.1	18.1

Note: ICD-10 = International Classification of Diseases 10th Revision; (1) Figures cover Salt Lake County, UT
Source: Centers for Disease Control and Prevention, National Center for Health Statistics. Compressed Mortality File 1999-2004. CDC WONDER On-line Database, compiled from Compressed Mortality File 1999-2004 Series 20 No. 2J, 2007.

Health Risk Data

Item	Area[1] (%)	U.S. (%)
Adults who have been told they have high blood pressure	19.2	25.5
Adults who have been told they have high blood cholesterol	33.0	35.6
Adults who have been told they have diabetes[2]	5.3	7.3
Adults who have been told they have arthritis	21.8	27.0
Adults who have been told they currently have asthma	8.6	8.0
Adults who are current smokers	13.6	20.6

Note: (1) Figures cover the Metropolitan Statistical Area - see Appendix B for areas included; (2) Figures do not include pregnancy-related diabetes, pre-diabetes or borderline diabetes
Source: Centers for Disease Control and Prevention, Behaviorial Risk Factor Surveillance System, SMART: Selected Metropolitan/Micropolitan Area Trends, 2005

Distribution of Office-Based Physicians

Area	Total	Family/ General Practice	Specialties		
			Medical	Surgical	Other
MSA[1] (number)	2,021	262	667	490	602
MSA[1] (rate per 10,000 pop.)	14.8	1.9	4.9	3.6	4.4
Metro Average[2] (rate per 10,000 pop.)	19.4	2.1	7.5	4.5	5.3

Note: Data as of December 31, 2004; (1) Metropolitan Statistical Area - see Appendix A for areas included; (2) Average of the 79 unique MSAs and CMSAs in this book
Source: American Medical Association, Physician Characteristics & Distribution in the U.S., 2006

Hospitals

Salt Lake City has the following hospitals: 5 general medical and surgical; 1 psychiatric; 1 children's general; 1 children's orthopedic.
AHA Guide to the Healthcare Field 2007

According to *U.S. News*, the Salt Lake City metro area is home to two of the best hospitals in the U.S.: **LDS Hospital; University of Utah Hospitals and Clinics**; *U.S. News Online, "America's Best Hospitals 2006"*

EDUCATION

Public School District Statistics

District Name	Schls	Pupils	Pupil/ Teacher Ratio	Minority Pupils[1] (%)	Free Lunch Eligible[2] (%)	IEP[3] (%)
Granite District	115	68,783	22.0	30.4	31.6	12.9
Salt Lake District	45	23,600	19.9	50.7	45.9	14.0

Note: Table includes regular local school districts with 2,000 or more students; (1) Percentage of students that are not white, non-Hispanic; (2) Percentage of students that are eligible for the free lunch program; (3) Percentage of students that have an Individualized Education Program.
Source: U.S. Department of Education, National Center for Education Statistics, Common Core of Data, Local Education Agency (School District) Universe Survey: School Year 2004-2005; U.S. Department of Education, National Center for Education Statistics, Common Core of Data, Public Elementary/Secondary School Universe Survey: School Year 2004-2005

Top Public High Schools

High School Name	Index[1]	Rank[1]	Subsidized Lunch (%)[2]	E&E (%)[3]
Brighton	1.137	1,082	8.0	n/a
Highland	1.829	450	47.0	23.7
Olympus	1.214	1,006	9.0	35.1
Skyline	1.783	477	5.0	45.5**
West	2.639	169	58.0	n/a**

Note: (1) Public schools are ranked according to a ratio that is the number of Advanced Placement and/or International Baccalaureate tests taken by all students at a school in 2005 divided by the number of graduating seniors. All of the schools on the list have an index of at least 1.000; they are in the top five percent of public schools measured this way. The rankings range from 1 to 1,236; (2) Percentage of students receiving federally subsidized meals; (3) E & E stands for equity and excellence percentage: the portion of all graduating seniors at a school that had at least one passing grade on one AP or IB test; (*) Gave just IB tests; (**) Gave both IB and AP tests. AP and IB participation are indicators of a school's efforts to get students to excel and prepare for college; n/a not available
Source: Newsweek Online, May 23, 2006

Educational Quality

School District	Education Quotient[1]	Graduate Outcome[2]	Community Index[3]	Resource Index[4]	Rating[5]
Granite	29	37	39	1	Green

Note: Scores are national percentile rankings and range from 1 (worst) to 99 (best); (1) Combination of the Graduate Outcome, Community and Resource Indexes weighted to reflect the greater importance of the Graduate Outcome and Resource Index; (2) Based on graduation rates and college board scores (SAT/ACT); (3) Based on the surrounding community's level of affluence and adult education; (4) Based on teacher salaries, per-pupil expenditures and student-teacher ratios; (5) School districts receive one of five rankings: Gold Medal (top 16 percent of districts evaluated); Blue Ribbon (top third); Green Light (average); Yellow Light (bottom 25 percent); Red Light (bottom 10 percent).
Source: Expansion Management, "2007 Education Quotient," January 2007

Highest Level of Education

Area	Less than H.S.	H.S. Diploma	Some College, No Deg.	Associate Degree	Bachelors Degree	Masters Degree	Profess. School Degree	Doctorate Degree
City	16.6	19.6	22.7	6.1	20.8	8.0	3.7	2.6
MSA[1]	12.7	24.2	28.1	7.6	18.5	5.7	2.1	1.1
U.S.	19.4	28.4	21.2	6.4	15.7	5.9	2.0	1.0

Note: Figures are 2006 estimated percentages and cover persons age 25 and over; (1) Metropolitan Statistical Area - see Appendix B for areas included
Source: Claritas, Inc.

Educational Attainment by Race

Area	High School Graduate (%)					Bachelor's Degree (%)				
	Total	White	Black	Asian	Hisp.[2]	Total	White	Black	Asian	Hisp.[2]
City	83.4	87.7	76.5	77.2	47.5	34.9	38.0	16.2	45.5	9.4
MSA[1]	87.5	89.9	83.0	78.2	56.5	26.5	27.6	19.5	34.8	9.4
U.S.	80.4	83.6	72.3	80.4	52.4	24.4	26.1	14.3	44.1	10.4

Note: Figures shown cover persons 25 years old and over; (1) Metropolitan Statistical Area - see Appendix A for areas included; (2) people of Hispanic origin can be of any race
Source: Census 2000, Summary File 3

School Enrollment by Type

Area	Grades KG to 8				Grades 9 to 12			
	Public		Private		Public		Private	
	Enrollment	%	Enrollment	%	Enrollment	%	Enrollment	%
City	18,258	90.9	1,820	9.1	7,946	91.4	743	8.6
MSA[1]	189,691	94.4	11,196	5.6	93,135	95.6	4,302	4.4
U.S.	33,526,011	88.7	4,285,121	11.3	14,848,628	90.6	1,532,323	9.4

Note: Figures shown cover persons 3 years old and over; (1) Metropolitan Statistical Area - see Appendix A for areas included
Source: Census 2000, Summary File 3

School Enrollment by Race

Area	Grades KG to 8 (%)				Grades 9 to 12 (%)			
	White	Black	Asian	Hisp.[1]	White	Black	Asian	Hisp.[1]
City	68.8	3.2	3.0	29.5	72.1	3.9	3.2	22.0
MSA[2]	85.4	1.1	1.7	12.7	87.1	1.0	2.1	10.6
U.S.	68.5	15.5	3.3	16.8	68.8	15.5	3.8	15.7

Note: Figures shown cover persons 3 years old and over; (1) people of Hispanic origin can be of any race; (2) Metropolitan Statistical Area - see Appendix A for areas included
Source: Census 2000, Summary File 3

Average Salaries of Public School Teachers

District	2004-05		2005-06		Percent Change 2004-05 to 2005-06
	Dollars	Rank[1]	Dollars	Rank[1]	
UTAH	39,456	39	40,316	43	2.18
U.S. Average	47,674	-	49,109	-	3.01

Note: (1) State rank ranges from 1 to 51.
Source: National Education Association, Rankings & Estimates: Rankings of the States 2005 and Estimates of School Statistics 2006, November 2006

Higher Education

Four-Year Colleges			Two-Year Colleges			Medical Schools[1]	Law Schools[2]	Voc/ Tech[3]
Public	Private Non-profit	Private For-profit	Public	Private Non-profit	Private For-profit			
1	2	1	1	1	2	1	1	6

Note: Figures cover institutions located within the city limits; (1) includes schools accredited by the Liaison Committee on Medical Education and the American Osteopathic Association; (2) includes American Bar Association-accredited law schools; (3) includes all schools with programs that are less than 2 years
Source: National Center for Education Statistics, The Integrated Postsecondary Education System (IPEDS) Peer Analysis System, 2006; www.usnews.com, America's Best Graduate Schools 2008, Medical School Directory; www.usnews.com, America's Best Graduate Schools 2008, Law School Directory

PRESIDENTIAL ELECTION

2004 Presidential Election Results

Area	Bush	Kerry	Nader	Other
Salt Lake County	59.6	37.5	1.7	1.2
U.S.	50.7	48.3	0.4	0.6

Note: Results are percentages and may not add to 100% due to rounding
Source: Dave Leip's Atlas of U.S. Presidential Elections, www.uselectionatlas.org

MAJOR EMPLOYERS

Major Employers

Company Name	Industry	Type of Site
Convergys	Business services, nec	Branch
Discover Financial Svcs Del	Short-term business credit	Branch
Edo Electro Ceramic Products	Search and navigation equipment	Single
Kennecott Holding Corporation	Copper ores	Headquarters
Marketstar Corporation	Management consulting services	Single
Mormon Church	Religious organizations	Headquarters
National Guard Utah	National security	Headquarters
Primary Childrens Medical Ctr	Specialty hospitals, except psychiatric	Branch
Salt Lake City School District	Management consulting services	Branch
Service Center	Finance, taxation, and monetary policy	Branch
US Post Office	U.S. Postal Service	Branch
University Utah Hsptals Clnics	General medical and surgical hospitals	Headquarters
Weber State University	Colleges and universities	Headquarters

Note: Companies shown are located within the metropolitan area and have 1,750 or more employees; nec = not elsewhere classified.
Source: www.zapdata.com, January 2007

PUBLIC SAFETY

Crime Rate

Area	All Crimes	Violent Crimes				Property Crimes		
		Murder	Forcible Rape	Robbery	Aggrav. Assault	Burglary	Larceny -Theft	Motor Vehicle Theft
City	9,284.7	5.4	39.0	225.9	424.6	1,176.4	6,287.3	1,126.1
Suburbs[1]	4,840.4	2.8	46.9	43.5	162.1	671.0	3,465.6	448.6
Metro[2]	5,619.5	3.2	45.5	75.5	208.1	759.6	3,960.2	567.3
U.S.	3,899.0	5.6	31.7	140.7	291.1	726.7	2,286.3	416.7

Note: Figures are crimes per 100,000 population; (1) All areas within the metro area that are located outside the city limits; (2) Metropolitan Statistical Area - see Appendix B for areas included
Source: FBI Uniform Crime Reports, 2005

Hate Crimes

Area	Number of Quarters Reported	Bias Motivation				
		Race	Religion	Sexual Orientation	Ethnicity	Disability
City	4	7	1	5	5	0

Source: Federal Bureau of Investigation, Hate Crime Statistics 2005

RECREATION

Culture

Dance[1]	Theatre[1]	Instrumental Music[1]	Vocal Music[1]	Series/ Festivals	Museums	Zoos
5	5	8	5	6	10	1

Note: (1) number of professional perfoming groups
Source: The Grey House Performing Arts Directory, 2007; Official Museum Directory, 2007

Professional Sports Teams

Major League Baseball	National Basketball Association	National Football League	National Hockey League	Major League Soccer	Women's National Basketball Association
0	1	0	0	1	0

Note: Includes teams located in the Salt Lake City metro area.
Source: www.sportsvenues.com, Listing of Venues by State/Province and City, 2006

MEDIA

Newspapers

Name	Target Audience	Frequency	Circulation
The Deseret Morning News	n/a	Daily	73,954
The Event Newsweekly	Alternative	Non-Daily	36,000
Intermountain Catholic	Catholic/Religious	Non-Daily	13,667
Intermountain Commercial Record/Salt Lake Times	General	Non-Daily	3,000
Salt Lake City Weekly	Alternative	Non-Daily	60,000
The Salt Lake Tribune	n/a	Daily	136,317

Note: Includes newspapers whose offices are located in the city and whose circulations are 1,000 or more; n/a not available
Source: BurrellesLuce, MediaContacts Online, January 2006

Television Stations

Name	Ch.	Network(s)	Type	Ownership
KUTV	2	CBS	Commercial	CBS
KCSG	4	Pax	Commercial	n/a
KTVX	4	ABC	Commercial	n/a
KSL	5	NBC	Commercial	Bonneville International Corporation
KUED	7	PBS	Public	University of Utah
KUEN	9	n/a	Public	Utah State Board of Regents
KENV	10	NBC	Commercial	Sunbelt Broadcasting Company
KBYU	11	PBS	Public	Brigham Young University
KDLQ	13	Fox/ABC	Commercial	n/a
KSTU	13	Fox	Commercial	Fox Television Stations Inc.
KJZZ	14	n/a	Commercial	Larry H. Miller Communications
KUPX	16	Pax	Commercial	Paxson Communications Corporation
KUEW	18	PBS	n/a	University of Utah
KUWB	30	WBN	Commercial	Acme Television Holdings

Note: Stations included cover the Salt Lake City DMA (Designated Market Area)
BurrellesLuce, MediaContacts Online, January 2006

Major AM Radio Stations

Call Letters	Freq. (kHz)	Station Type	Target Audience	Station Format	Music Format
KNRS	570	Commercial	General	News/Talk	n/a
KSUB	590	n/a	General	News/Sports/Talk	n/a
KVNU	610	Commercial	General	News/Talk	n/a
KMTI	650	Commercial	General	Music/News/Sports/Talk	Country
KOAL	750	n/a	General	News/Sports/Talk	n/a
KBEE	860	Commercial	General	Music/Talk	Country
KDXU	890	Commercial	General	News/Talk	n/a
KALL	910	Commercial	General	News	n/a
KMER	950	Commercial	General	News	n/a
KOVO	960	Commercial	General	Sports/Talk	n/a
KSVC	980	Commercial	General	News/Sports/Talk	n/a
KKDS	1060	Commercial	General	Music/News	Adult Contemp.
KAFL	1080	Commercial	General	Music	Country
KANN	1120	Non-Comm	Religious	Educational/Music/News	Christian
KSL	1160	Commercial	General	News/Talk	n/a
KUNF	1210	Commercial	General	Music/News	Easy Listening
KRSV	1210	Commercial	General	Music/News/Sports	Country
KEVA	1240	Commercial	General	News	n/a
KNEU	1250	Commercial	General	Music/News	Country
KZNS	1280	Commercial	General	News/Sports/Talk	n/a
KFNZ	1320	n/a	General/Men	Music/Sports	n/a
KRKK	1360	n/a	General	Music/News	n/a
KSOP	1370	Commercial	General	Music/News	Country
KLGN	1390	Commercial	General	Music/News/Sports/Talk	Adult Standards
KLO	1430	Commercial	General	Music/News/Sports/Talk	n/a
KXOL	1660	n/a	General	Music	n/a

Note: Stations included cover the Salt Lake City DMA (Designated Market Area); n/a not available
Source: BurrellesLuce, MediaContacts Online, January 2006

Major FM Radio Stations

Call Letters	Freq. (mHz)	Station Type	Target Audience	Station Format	Music Format
KBYU	89.1	College	General	Music/News	Classical
KUER	90.1	College	General	Music/News	Jazz
KUSU	91.5	College	General	Educational/Music/News	Classic Rock
KBLQ	92.9	Commercial	General	Music/News/Sports	Soft Rock
KCYQ	93.7	Commercial	General	Music	Country
KODJ	94.1	Commercial	General	Music	Oldies
KVFX	94.5	Commercial	General	Music	Adult Contemp.
KZHT	94.9	Commercial	General/Women	Music	Top 40
KXBN	94.9	Commercial	General	Music	Top 40
KYCS	95.1	Commercial	General	Music/News	Adult Contemp.
KYFO	95.5	Non-Comm	General	Music/Talk	Christian
KFNN	95.7	Commercial	General	Music/News	Adult Contemp.
KXRK	96.3	n/a	Gay/Lesbian	Music	n/a
KQSW	96.5	Commercial	General	Music/News	Country
KISN	97.1	Commercial	General	Music	Adult Contemp.
KREC	98.1	Commercial	General	Educational/Music/News	Adult Contemp.
KBEE	98.7	n/a	General	Music/News/Sports	n/a
KURR	99.5	Commercial	General/Native Amer	Music/Talk	Classic Rock
KONY	101.1	Commercial	General	Music	Contemp. Country
KXFF	102.9	n/a	n/a	n/a	n/a
KUDD	103.9	Commercial	General/Women	Music	Top 40
KSIT	104.5	Commercial	General	Music/News	Classic Rock
KNFL	104.9	n/a	General	Music	Oldies
KENZ	107.5	n/a	General	Music	n/a

Note: Stations included cover the Salt Lake City DMA (Designated Market Area); n/a not available
BurrellesLuce, MediaContacts Online, January 2006

CLIMATE

Average and Extreme Temperatures

Temperature	Jan	Feb	Mar	Apr	May	Jun	Jul	Aug	Sep	Oct	Nov	Dec	Yr.
Extreme High (°F)	62	69	78	85	93	104	107	104	100	89	75	67	107
Average High (°F)	37	43	52	62	72	83	93	90	80	66	50	38	64
Average Temp. (°F)	28	34	41	50	59	69	78	76	65	53	40	30	52
Average Low (°F)	19	24	31	38	46	54	62	61	51	40	30	22	40
Extreme Low (°F)	-22	-14	2	15	25	35	40	37	27	16	-14	-15	-22

Note: Figures cover the years 1948-1990
Source: National Climatic Data Center, International Station Meteorological Climate Summary, 9/96

Average Precipitation/Snowfall/Humidity

Precip./Humidity	Jan	Feb	Mar	Apr	May	Jun	Jul	Aug	Sep	Oct	Nov	Dec	Yr.
Avg. Precip. (in.)	1.3	1.2	1.8	2.0	1.7	0.9	0.8	0.9	1.1	1.3	1.3	1.4	15.6
Avg. Snowfall (in.)	13	10	11	6	1	Tr	0	0	Tr	2	6	13	63
Avg. Rel. Hum. 5am (%)	79	77	71	67	66	60	53	54	60	68	75	79	67
Avg. Rel. Hum. 5pm (%)	69	59	47	38	33	26	22	23	28	40	59	71	43

Note: Figures cover the years 1948-1990; Tr = Trace amounts (<0.05 in. of rain; <0.5 in. of snow)
Source: National Climatic Data Center, International Station Meteorological Climate Summary, 9/96

Weather Conditions

Temperature			Daytime Sky			Precipitation		
5°F & below	32°F & below	90°F & above	Clear	Partly cloudy	Cloudy	0.01 inch or more precip.	0.1 inch or more snow/ice	Thunder-storms
7	128	56	94	152	119	92	38	38

Note: Figures are average number of days per year and cover the years 1948-1990
Source: National Climatic Data Center, International Station Meteorological Climate Summary, 9/96

HAZARDOUS WASTE

Superfund Sites

Salt Lake City has three hazardous waste sites on the EPA's Superfund Final National Priorities List: **Portland Cement (Kiln Dust 2 & 3)**; **Utah Power & Light/American Barrel Co.**; **Wasatch Chemical Co. (Lot 6)**. *U.S. Environmental Protection Agency, Final National Priorities List, March 20, 2007*

AIR & WATER QUALITY

Air Quality Index

Area	Percent of Days when Air Quality was...[2]				AQI Statistics	
	Good	Moderate	Unhealthy for Sensitive Groups	Unhealthy	Maximum	Median
MSA[1]	58.4	32.9	8.5	0.3	159	46

Note: The Air Quality Index (AQI) is an index for reporting daily air quality. EPA calculates the AQI for five major air pollutants regulated by the Clean Air Act: ground-level ozone, particle pollution (also known as particulate matter), carbon monoxide, sulfur dioxide, and nitrogen dioxide. The AQI runs from 0 to 500. The higher the AQI value, the greater the level of air pollution and the greater the health concern. There are six AQI categories: "Good" The AQI is between 0 and 50. Air quality is considered satisfactory; "Moderate" The AQI is between 51 and 100. Air quality is acceptable; "Unhealthy for Sensitive Groups" When AQI values are between 101 and 150, members of sensitive groups may experience health effects; "Unhealthy" When AQI values are between 151 and 200 everyone may begin to experience health effects; "Very Unhealthy" AQI values between 201 and 300 trigger a health alert; "Hazardous" AQI values over 300 trigger health warnings of emergency conditions; (1) Metropolitan Statistical Area - see Appendix A for areas included; (2) Based on 365 days with AQI data in 2005.
Source: U.S. Environmental Protection Agency, Air Quality Index Report, 2005

Air Quality Index Pollutants

| Area | Percent of Days when AQI Pollutant was...[2] | | | | | |
	Carbon Monoxide	Nitrogen Dioxide	Ozone	Sulfur Dioxide	Particulate Matter 2.5	Particulate Matter 10
MSA[1]	5.2	0.0	33.2	0.0	46.3	15.3

Note: The Air Quality Index (AQI) is an index for reporting daily air quality. EPA calculates the AQI for five major air pollutants regulated by the Clean Air Act: ground-level ozone, particle pollution (also known as particulate matter), carbon monoxide, sulfur dioxide, and nitrogen dioxide. The AQI runs from 0 to 500. The higher the AQI value, the greater the level of air pollution and the greater the health concern; (1) Metropolitan Statistical Area - see Appendix A for areas included; (2) Based on 365 days with AQI data in 2005.
Source: U.S. Environmental Protection Agency, Air Quality Index Report, 2005

Number of Days with Air Quality Index Values Greater than 100

| Area | Trend Sites (13) | | | | | | | | All Sites (70) |
	1998	1999	2000	2001	2002	2003	2004	2005	2005
MSA[1]	12	13	20	27	33	10	37	26	34

Note: An AQI value greater than 100 indicates that air quality would have been in the unhealthful range on that day. Data from exceptional events are not included. These counts are presented in two ways. First, the counts are based on sites having an adequate record of monitoring data during the trend period (trend sites). These counts represent the relative change in the number of days with AQI values greater than 100. In the last column, the counts are based on all sites with data in the most recent year (because it is possible for a site to have data in the most recent year but not enough data to be a trend site); (1) Metropolitan Statistical Area - see Appendix A for areas included; n/a not available.
Source: U.S. Environmental Protection Agency, Air Trends Fact Book 2005

Maximum Pollutant Concentrations

	Particulate Matter 10 (ug/m^3)	Particulate Matter 2.5 (ug/m^3)	Ozone 1-hour (ppm)	Carbon Monoxide (ppm)	Sulfur Dioxide (ppm)	Nitrogen Dioxide (ppm)	Lead (ug/m^3)
MSA[1] Level	123	44	0.121	5	0.012	0.024	0.08
NAAQS[2]	150	65	0.125	9	0.140	0.053	1.50
Met NAAQS[2]	Yes	Yes	Yes	Yes	Yes	Yes	Yes

Note: Data from exceptional events are not included; (1) Metropolitan Statistical Area - see Appendix A for areas included; (2) National Ambient Air Quality Standards; n/a not available
Units: ppm = parts per million; ug/m^3 = micrograms per cubic meter
Source: U.S. Environmental Protection Agency, Air Trends Fact Book 2005

Watershed Health

The U.S. Environmental Protection Agency monitors the health of the aquatic resources for the nation's 2,000+ watersheds. **The Jordan watershed serves the Salt Lake City area and received an overall Index of Watershed Indicators (IWI) score of 3 (less serious problems - low vulnerability).** The IWI score is based on seven condition and nine vulnerability indicators. The overall IWI score ranges from 1 (best health) to 6 (worst health). The Condition Indicators include: designated use attainment, fish and wildlife consumption advisories, source water condition, contaminated sediments, ambient water quality, and wetlands loss index. The Vulnerability Indicators include: aquatic species at risk, conventional and toxic loads over permitted limits, urban and agricultural runoff potential, population change, hydrologic modification, estuarine pollution susceptibility, and air deposition. *Note: The IWI is no longer being updated by the U.S. EPA. Source: U.S. Environmental Protection Agency, Index of Watershed Indicators, October 26, 2001*

Drinking Water

| Water System Name | Pop. Served | Primary Water Source Type | Number of Violations in 2006[a] | | |
			Health Based	Significant Monitoring	Monitoring
Salt Lake City Water System	312,000	Surface	None	None	None

Note: (a) Based on violation data from January 1, 2006 to December 31, 2006
Source: U.S. Environmental Protection Agency, Office of Ground Water and Drinking Water, Safe Drinking Water Information System (data extracted April 12, 2007)

Salt Lake City tap water is alkaline, hard and not fluoridated.
Editor & Publisher Market Guide, 2005

San Diego, California

Background

San Diego is the archetypal southern California city. Located 100 miles south of Los Angeles, near the Mexican border, San Diego is characterized by sunny days, an excellent harbor, a populous citizenry that alludes to its Spanish heritage, and recreational activities based on ideal weather conditions.

San Diego was first claimed in 1542 for Spain by Juan Rodriquez Cabrillo, a Portuguese navigator in the service of the Spanish crown. The site remained uneventful until 1769, when Spanish colonizer, Gaspar de Portola, established the first European settlement in California. Accompanying de Portola was a Franciscan monk named Junipero Serra, who established the Mission Basilica San Diega de Alcala, the first of a chain of missions along the California Coast.

After San Diego fell under the U.S. flag during the Mexican War of 1846, the city existed in relative isolation, deferring status and importance to its sister cities in the north, Los Angeles and San Francisco. Even when San Francisco businessman Alonzo Horton bought 1,000 acres of land near the harbor to establish a logical and practical downtown there, San Diego remained secondary to both these cities, and saw a decrease in population from 40,000 in 1880 to 17,000 at the turn of the century.

World War II repopulated the city, when the Navy moved one of its bases from Pearl Harbor to San Diego. The naval base brought personnel and a number of related industries, such as nuclear and oceanographic research, and aviation development. In celebration of this past, the famed IMidway, a 1,000-foot World War II aircraft carrier, has undergone a $6.5 million reconstruction and has been moved to Navy Pier, where it opened in 2004 as a floating museum.

Today, San Diego is the second most populous city in California, with plenty of outdoor activities, jobs, fine educational institutions, theaters, and museums with which to attract new residents, young and old alike. San Diego's downtown redevelopment agency has transformed what was largely an abandoned downtown into a glittering showcase of waterfront skyscrapers, live-work loft developments, five-star hotels, and many cafes, restaurants, and shops. The once-industrial East Village adjacent to PETCO ballpark is now the new frontier in San Diego's downtown urban renewal.

According to recent studies, the western part of the U.S., from Seattle to the Silicon Valley, and from San Diego to Denver, is becoming the center for all the hot growth industries, namely telecommunications, biomedical products, software, and financial services. San Diego leads the country in biotechnology companies that are attracting venture capital.

The San Diego Convention Center underwent expansion in 2001 that increased exhibit space from 250,000 to 615,000 square feet. The water supply system, always a significant issue in this part of California, has been upgraded and improved in recent years. The San Diego International Airport, at present trends, will shift from serving 16 million passengers in 2004 to serving more than 27 million by 2030, and appropriate airport renovations are being discussed.

San Diego summers are cool and winters are warm in comparison with other locations along the same general latitude, due to the Pacific Ocean. A marked feature of the climate is the wide variation in temperature. In nearby valleys, for example, daytime temperatures are much warmer in summer and noticeably cooler on winter nights than in the city proper. As is usual on the Pacific Coast, nighttime and early morning cloudiness is the norm. Considerable fog occurs along the coast, especially during the winter months.

Rankings

General Rankings

- San Diego was ranked #74 out of 331 metro areas in *Cities Ranked & Rated*. Criteria: cost of living; climate; crime; transportation; economy and jobs; education; arts and culture; health and healthcare; leisure. *Cities Ranked & Rated, 1st Edition, 2004*

- San Diego was selected as one of the "Top Cities for Recent Grads" by eGrad.com. The city ranked #5. Criteria: eGrad.com conducted a nationwide survey in which a representative sample of recent graduates commented on the pros and cons of their new towns. Topics ranged from affordability, to housing, to employment, to general satisfaction. *eGrad.com, "Top Cities for Recent Grads 2004"*

- San Diego was selected as one of the top places to live in the U.S. according to Harris Interactive. The city ranked #3 out of 10. Criteria: 3,685 U.S. adults were polled as to where they would choose to live if they could live anywhere in the country. *Harris Interactive, September 6, 2006*

- The San Diego metro area was selected as one of "America's Best Places to Live and Work" by *Employment Review*. The area ranked #9 out of 20. Criteria: unemployment rate; projected job growth; cost of living; and industry specific data. *Employment Review, www.bestjobsusa.com, 2003*

- San Diego was selected as one of the "Best Places to Live 2006" by *Money* magazine. The city ranked #5 out of 10 in the big city (300,000+ population) category. Places were ranked using 38 quality-of-life indicators and six economic opportunity measures in the following categories: ease of living; health; education; crime; park space; arts and leisure. *Money, "Best Places to Live 2006"*

- San Diego was selected as one of the "50 Best Places to Live" by *Men's Journal*. The city ranked #2 in the "Best Downtowns" category. These city centers were selected based on the fact that you can enjoy all the amenities of urban living, find a range of great housing options, and still get your fix of active puruits. *Men's Journal, April 2007*

- San Diego was selected as one of "America's 30 Most Livable Communities" by the non-profit group, Partners for Livable Communities. Criteria: environmental quality; parkland; ability to train new workers; job market; education; and use of the arts for economic development. *Partners for Livable Communities, www.mostlivable.org, April 20, 2004*

Business/Finance Rankings

- San Diego was selected as one of the best places to start and grow a company by *Entrepreneur* and the National Policy Research Council. The San Diego metro area ranked #20 out of 50 large metro areas. Criteria: business formation and growth (firms started four to 14 years ago that still employ at least 5 people and experienced rapid growth over the last four years). *Entrepreneur/National Policy Research Council, "Hot Cities for Entrepreneurs," September 2006*

- The San Diego metro area was selected as one of "America's 50 Hottest Cities" for business relocations and expansions. Criteria: industry's most prominent site selection consultants were asked to list their top city choices for relocating and expanding manufacturing companies, taking into consideration such factors as the business climate, work force quality, operating costs, incentive programs, and the ease of working with local political and economic development officials. *Expansion Management, January-February 2007*

- The San Diego metro area was cited as one of America's "Most Picture Perfect Metros" by *Plant Sites and Parks* magazine. Each year *PSP* readers rank the metro areas they consider best bets for their companies to relocate or expand to in the coming year. The area ranked #7 out of 10. *Plant Sites and Parks, March 2004*

- Intel, in partnership with Sperling's BestPlaces, ranked the 80 "Best Cities for Teleworking" in America. The San Diego metro area ranked #4 among large metro areas. The study identifies cities that hold the greatest potential for teleworking based on a host of factors including typical commuting times, fuel prices, availability of broadband Internet access and percentage of the population in telework friendly jobs. The study also factored in extreme climate and natural hazards. *Intel, "Best Cities for Teleworking," March 30, 2006*

- San Diego was identified as one of "The Most Inventive Towns in America". The city ranked #6. Criteria: places with the most patents overall, combining those of large companies and individual inventors. *The Wall Street Journal, July 22-23, 2006*

- The San Diego metro area appeared on the Milken Institute "2005 Best Performing Cities" index. Rank: #29 out of 200 large metro areas. Criteria: job growth; wage and salary growth; high-tech output growth. *Milken Institute, "2005 Best Performing Cities," February 2006*

- The San Diego metro area was selected as one of "The Best Cities for Doing Business in America." *Inc.* magazine measured employment growth in 393 regions using the following criteria: recent growth trend; mid-term growth; long-term trend; and current year growth. The San Diego metro area ranked #20 among large metro areas and #133 overall. *Inc., May 2006*

- The San Diego metro area was selected as one of "The Top 20 Boom Towns in America." *Business 2.0* magazine and econometric research firm Global Insight compared 319 metropolitan areas in the U.S. and ranked the 61 with populations over 1 million. Criteria: a weighted formula that includes forecast growth rates in sectors that contain the economy's 10 most skilled occupational clusters; the prevalence of college degrees in the local workforce; median salary. The area ranked #17 among large metro areas. *Business 2.0 Magazine, March 2004*

- San Diego was identified as one of the 100 "Most Unwired Cities" in the U.S. The area ranked #11 out of the 100 largest metro areas in the U.S. Criteria: number of public and commercial wireless access points (hotspots); airports with wireless Internet access; broadband availability; local wireless networks; and wireless email devices. *Intel, "Most Unwired Cities Survey," June 7, 2005*

- San Diego was ranked #7 out of 125 regions worldwide in terms of its "Knowledge Competitiveness Index." The index attempts to measure the knowledge-based development taking place throughout the world and is based on 19 measures of economic performance that indicate a region's ability to translate its knowledge capacity into economic value. *Robert Huggins Associates, World Knowledge Competitiveness Index 2005*

- *Forbes* ranked the 200 most populous metro areas in the U.S. in terms of the "Best Places for Business and Careers." The San Diego metro area was ranked #92. Criteria: business costs (labor, energy, tax and office space expenses); living costs (housing, transportation, food and other household expenditures); education levels of the work force; job growth; income growth; migration trends; crime rates; and culture/leisure. *Forbes, April 23, 2007*

- San Diego was selected as a 2006 Digital Cities Survey winner. The city ranked #7 in the large city (250,000 or more population) category. The survey examined and assessed how city governments are utilizing information technology to operate and deliver quality service to their customers and citizens. Survey questions focused on implementation and adoption of online service delivery; planning and governance; and the infrastructure and architecture that make the transformation to digital government possible. *Center for Digital Government, "2006 Digital Cities Survey"*

- *Fortune* ranked the 100 largest metro areas in the U.S. in terms of projected median home price change in 2006. The San Diego metro area ranked #99. *Fortune, "The Top 100: Is the Party Over?" December 26, 2005*

- San Diego was identified as one of the top 10 richest major cities in the U.S. The city ranked #5. Criteria: 2004 median household income. *Forbes, "Richest Cities in the U.S.," October 27, 2005*

Health/EnvironmentRankings

■ Doctors at the Harvard School of Public Health ranked 40 metropolitan areas based on data from the government-sponsored Hospital Quality Alliance program. The program tracks the performance of individual hospitals in treating patients for three common health problems: heart attacks, congestive heart failure, and pneumonia. The San Diego metro area ranked #31 in quality of care for heart attacks, #36 for congestive heart failure, and #38 for pneumonia. *New England Journal of Medicine, July 21, 2005*

■ *Reader's Digest* ranked the 50 largest metro areas in the U.S. in terms of how "clean" they are. The San Diego metro area ranked #10. Criteria: air quality; water quality; toxic industrial pollution; Superfund sites; and sanitation. *Reader's Digest, "The 50 Cleanest (and Dirtiest) Cities in America," July 2005*

■ *Business Week* identified the 15 metro areas that saw the steepest declines in ground-level ozone pollution between 1990 and 2005. The San Diego metro area ranked #3. *Business Week, "America's Most Cleaned-Up Metro Areas," March 23, 2007*

■ The San Diego metro area appeared in *Country Home's* "2007 Best Green Places Report". The area ranked #12. Criteria included: air and watershed quality; miles of mass transit; green power; number of farmer's markets, organic producers and groceries. *Country Home, "2007 Best Green Places Report," April 2007*

■ Wyeth Consumer Healthcare, in partnership with Sperling's BestPlaces, ranked the nation's 50 most populous metro areas in terms of five key health factors. The San Diego metro area ranked #12. Criteria: physical activity, health status, nutrition, lifestyle pursuits; and mental wellness. *Wyeth Consumer Healthcare, "Centrum Healthiest Cities Study," April 19, 2005*

■ HealthGrades identified the 10 best cities for nursing home care in the U.S. San Diego ranked #5. Criteria: proportion of facilities that had four or more actual harm violations from health or complaint surveys in the last four years. *www.HealthGrades.com, "Best and Worst Cities for Nursing Home Care," March 16, 2004*

■ HealthGrades surveyed over 41,000 individuals on doctor satisfaction and ranked the 20 largest metro areas based on the highest "definitely yes" responses to the question "Do you trust the physician to make decisions/recommendations that are in your best interest?" The San Diego metro area ranked #16. *HealthGrades.com, "Top Cities in Doctor-Trust," September 7, 2006*

■ The American Podiatric Medical Association and *Prevention* magazine ranked America's 100 most populated cities based on fitness-walker friendliness. The best cities have safe streets, beautiful places to walk, mild weather and good air quality. San Diego ranked #7. *Prevention, "The Best Walking Cities of 2007," April 2007; American Podiatric Medical Association, "2007 Best Fitness-Walking Cities"*

■ San Diego was selected as one of the 25 fattest cities in America by *Men's Fitness Online*. It ranked #21 out of America's 50 largest cities. Criteria: gyms/sporting goods; nutrition; exercise/sports; overweight/sedentary; junk food; alcohol; smoking; television; air and water quality; climate; geography; commute time; parks/open space; recreation facilities; health care; motivation; civic legislation and leadership. *Men's Fitness Online, America's Fittest/Fattest Cities 2006*

■ San Diego was identified as a "2007 Asthma Capital." The area ranked #63 out of the nation's 100 largest metropolitan areas. Twelve factors were used to identify the most challenging places to live for people with asthma: estimated prevalence; self-reported prevalence; crude death rate for asthma; annual pollen score; annual air quality; public smoking laws; number of board-certified asthma specialists; school inhaler access laws; rescue medication use; controller medication use; uninsured rate; poverty rate. *Asthma and Allergy Foundation of America, "2007 Asthma Capitals"*

■ San Diego was identified as a "Spring Allergy Capital." The area ranked #54 out of 100. Three groups of factors were used to identify the most severe cities for people with allergies during the spring season: annual pollen levels; medicine utilization; access to board-certified allergists. *Asthma and Allergy Foundation of America, "2007 Spring Allergy Capital Rankings"*

- San Diego was identified as a "Fall Allergy Capital." The area ranked #69 out of 100. Three groups of factors were used to identify the most severe cities for people with allergies during the fall season: annual pollen levels; medicine utilization; access to board-certified allergists. *Asthma and Allergy Foundation of America, "2006 Fall Allergy Capital Rankings"*

- San Diego was selected as one of "America's Healthiest Cities" by *Natural Health* magazine. The city was ranked #27 out of the 50 largest urban areas in the U.S. Twenty-six criteria in the following four categories were examined: whether the city boasts natural offerings; how well the city promotes its residents' physical health; whether the city offers a healthy environment; how well the city fosters a sense of community. *Natural Health, April 2003*

- *Men's Health* ranked the nation's largest 100 cities in terms of the *Best (and Worst) Cities for Men*. San Diego was ranked #4. Criteria: 24 statistical parameters of long life in the categories of health, quality of life, and fitness. *Men's Health, January/February 2007*

- *Men's Health* ranked 100 U.S. cities in terms of the quality of their tap water. San Diego was ranked #68 and received a grade of C. Criteria: levels of total coliform bacteria, arsenic, lead, total trihalomethanes (linked to cancer), and halo-acetic acids, plus the number of EPA water-system violations from 1995 to 2005. *Men's Health, March 2007*

- Ortho-McNeil Neurologics, in partnership with Sperling's BestPlaces, analyzed 110 metro areas and identified those U.S. cities with the highest prevalence of factors that are most commonly associated with migraine headaches. The San Diego metro area ranked #99. Criteria: number of migraine-related drug prescriptions per capita; lifestyle factors that can contribute to migraines; environmental factors that can trigger migraines; and consumption of migraine-triggering foods. *Ortho-McNeil Neurologics, "America's Migraine Hot Spots," March 14, 2006*

- Sperling's BestPlaces ranked 331 metro areas and identified the most and least stressful U.S. cities. The San Diego metro area ranked #75 out of the 100 largest metro areas (#1 = most stressful). Criteria: divorce rate; unemployment rate; violent and property crime; suicide rate; commute time; mental health; alcohol consumption; cloudy days. *www.BestPlaces.net, January 9, 2004*

- Sperling's BestPlaces "Sleep in the City" study ranked America's 50 most populated metropolitan areas in getting a good night's sleep. The San Diego metro area ranked #3 in terms of the "Best Cities for Sleep". Criteria: happiness index (derived from the responses to eight questions on the CDC BRFSS); number of days residents didn't get enough rest or sleep during the past month; average length of daily commute; divorce rates; unemployment rates. *www.BestPlaces.net, October 18, 2004*

- HealthGrades evaluated the performance of America's 25 most populous metropolitan areas by measuring the outcomes of five of the highest volume and most widely studied procedures and diagnoses: coronary artery bypass graft surgery; percutaneus coronary interventions; acute myocardial infarction/heart attack in angioplasty-capable hospitals; congestive heart failure; and community acquired pneumonia. The San Diego metro area ranked #11. *HealthGrades, "HealthGrades Hospital Quality in America Study," October 12, 2004*

- San Diego was selected as one of "America's Pet Healthiest Cities" by Purina. The city ranked #34 out of 50. Criteria: veterinary services; environment; legislation; preventative care; obesity/body condition. *Purina Pet Institute, "America's Pet Healthiest Cities," May 20, 2003*

Women/Minorities Rankings

- San Diego was ranked #17 out of 100 metro areas in *SELF Magazine's* ranking of "America's Best Places for Women." A panel of experts came up with nearly 40 criteria including: drinking and smoking rates; depression; unemployment; parks; crime; disease; healthcare insurance coverage; air quality; and commute times. *SELF Magazine, "America's Best Places for Women 2006," December 2006*

- *Ladies Home Journal* ranked America's 200 largest cities based on the qualities women surveyed care about most. San Diego ranked #9 out of 57 in the big city category (population over 300,000). Criteria: crime; lifestyle; education; jobs; health; child care; politics; and the economy. *Ladies Home Journal Online, "The Best Cities for Women 2002"*

- San Diego was identified as one of the top 25 metropolitan statistical areas ranked by percentage of coupled households that are gay or lesbian." The area ranked #17. *Human Rights Campaign, "Gay and Lesbian Families in the United States: Same-Sex Unmarried Partner Households," August 1, 2001*

- San Diego was selected as one of the "Top 10 Cities for Hispanics to Live In." The city was ranked #3. The cities were selected based on data from the following sources: U.S. Census; *Forbes*; *Fortune*; *Money*; local newspapers; natives and residents; www.bestplaces.net; www.findyourspot.com. *Hispanic Magazine, July/August 2004*

Seniors/Retirement Rankings

- San Diego was profiled in the book *Where to Retire: America's Best and Most Affordable Places*. Cities were selected based on personal visits by the author and interviews with local residents coupled with statistics from various government agencies. *Where to Retire: America's Best and Most Affordable Places, 2006*

- Sperling's BestPlaces in partnership with Bankers Life & Casualty Company designed a survey to identify the top 50 metro areas in the U.S. that offer the best overall qualities for senior living. The San Diego metro area ranked #34. The following criteria were statistically weighted to reflect the needs of the senior population: health; disease; economics; social; environment; spiritual; transportation; housing; and crime. *Bankers Life & Casualty Company, "Best Cities for Seniors 2005"*

- The San Diego metro area was selected as one of "The 15 Best Places to Live the Good Life." Criteria: availability of jobs; affordable housing; culture and entertainment; access to outdoor recreation; safety; colleges and universities; sense of community; proximity to comprehensive, well-regarded health care facilities; good public high schools; ease of getting around. *AARP The Magazine, May/June 2003*

- A.G. Edwards ranked America's 500 top-performing communities based on their residents' personal savings and investing behavior. The San Diego metro area ranked #282 with an index score of 100.50 (national average = 100.00). A dozen statistical factors were measured including: participation in retirement savings plans; personal debt levels; and home ownership. *A.G. Edwards, "2006 Nest Egg Index", September 6, 2006*

Children/Family Rankings

- *Zero Population Growth* ranked 100 cities in terms of children's health, safety, and economic well-being. San Diego was ranked #3 out of 20 Major Cities (main city in a metro area with population of greater than 2.5 million) and was given a grade of A-. Criteria: total population and population growth; percent of population under 18 years of age; percent of births to teens; infant mortality rate; percent of eligible women not receiving Title X services; contraceptive equity indicator; percent of children without health insurance; percent of city residents over age 25 with a high-school diploma; ration of PopEd (Population Connection's Education Program) teachers trained; sexuality education indicator; proficiency in reading and math; percent of kids living in poverty; percent growth in urbanized land; violent crime rate; recycling. *Population Connection, Kid Friendly Cities: Report Card 2004*

- San Diego was highlighted in the Forbes.com article "The Best Education in the Biggest Cities." The city ranked #8 out of 8. Criteria: the 100 largest school districts in the most populous cities in the U.S. were evaluated in three categories: high school graduation rate; affordability of housing; best access to educational resources. *Forbes.com, February 13, 2004*

- *Fit Pregnancy* magazine ranked the 50 best U.S. cities in which to have a baby. San Diego was ranked #12. Criteria: fertility services; maternal and infant health risk; access to hospitals and doctors; safety; affordability; stroller friendliness; and birthing options. *Fit Pregnancy, February/March, 2006*

Safety Rankings

■ Allstate ranked the 200 largest cities in America in terms of driver safety. San Diego ranked #113. In addition, drivers were 11.9% more likely to have had an accident compared to the national average. Allstate researchers analyzed internal Property Damage reported claims over a two-year period (from January 2003 to December 2004) to ensure the findings would not be affected by external influences such as weather or road construction. A weighted average of the two-year numbers determined the annual percentages. The report defines an auto crash as any collision resulting in a property damage claim. *Allstate, "Allstate America's Best Drivers Report 2006," May 24, 2006*

■ San Diego was identified as one of the most dangerous large metro areas for pedestrians in the U.S. The area ranked #28 out of the nations 50 largest metro areas. Criteria: average yearly pedestrian fatalities per capita (for the years 2002 and 2003) adjusted for the number of walkers. *Surface Transportation Policy Project, "Mean Streets 2004"*

■ San Diego was identified as one of the safest large cities in America by Morgan Quitno. All 32 cities with populations of 500,000 or more that reported crime rates in 2005 for murder, rape, robbery, aggravated assault, burglary, and motor vehicle thefts were ranked. The city ranked #6 out of the top 10. *www.morganquitno.com, 13th Annual America's Safest (and Most Dangerous) Cities Awards*

■ *Ladies Home Journal* ranked America's 200 largest cities in terms of safety. San Diego ranked #51 out of 200. Criteria: violent crimes; crimes against property; and rape. *Ladies Home Journal Online, "The Best Cities for Women 2002"*

Sports/Recreation Rankings

■ The San Diego metro area appeared on *The Sporting News* list of the "Best Sports Cities 2006". The area ranked #22 out of 99 cities in North America. To be included in the rankings, a city must have at least one of the following: NCAA Division I basketball team; Class A minor league baseball team; training camp for a major league or NFL team; NASCAR Nextel Cup race; NCAA Division I-A bowl game; PGA Tour tournament; Triple Crown horse race. Once a city qualifies, a 12-month snapshot is taken of the sports atmosphere, putting a heavy premium on regular-season won-lost records; playoff berths, bowl appearances and tournament bids; championships; applicable power ratings; quality of competition; overall fan fervor; sports atmosphere and fan knowledge; abundance of teams (quality over quantity); stadium/arena quality; ticket availability and prices; franchise ownership; and the marquee appeal of athletes. *SportingNews.com, "Best Sports Cities 2006," August 1, 2006*

■ San Diego was chosen as one of America's 25 best cities for running. The city was ranked #2. Criteria: number of running clubs per city; amount of land set aside for park usage; air quality; weather; crime rates; and results from a *Runner's World* poll in which readers ranked their favorite running cities. *Runner's World, "The 25 Best Running Cities in America," July 2005*

■ San Diego was chosen as one of America's best cities for bicycling. The city ranked #1 in the very large city category (population 1 million or more). Criteria: cycling-friendly statistics (number of bike lanes and routes, number of bike racks, city bike projects completed and planned; bike culture (number of bike commuters, popular clubs, cool cycling events, renowned bike shops); climate/geography (the quality of roads and trails for riding, and how frequently mother nature lets riders enjoy them). *Bicycling, March 2006*

■ The San Diego metro area was selected by *Cranium* as one of the "Top 50 Fun Cities" in America. The area ranked #18. Criteria includes: number of sports teams, restaurants, and dance performances; number of toy stores; city budget spent on recreation. *Cranium, November 4, 2003*

■ *Golf Digest* ranked 330 metro areas in the U.S. in terms of golf. The San Diego metro area was ranked #285. Criteria: access to golf; weather; value of golf; and quality of golf. *Golf Digest, "Metro Golf Rankings," August 2005*

Dating/Romance Rankings

- The San Diego metro area was selected as one of the "Best Cities for Relocating Singles" by Worldwide ERC and Primacy Relocation. The area ranked #14 out of the 100 largest metro areas in the U.S. Areas were selected based on the following criteria: Population Criteria (local percentage and growth trends of unmarried residents aged 25-34; male-female ratios; the number of newcomers to the area; diversity and density); Economic Criteria (job growth vs. unemployment rates; apartment rental costs; fee and occupancy rates for temporary housing and mini-storage; higher education costs, including in-state and out-of-state tuition requirements; vehicle tax rates and quality of service from utility providers); Quality-of-Life Criteria (level of per capita volunteering; quality and quantity of collegiate and professional sports with fun, fan-friendly venues; number of Starbucks and other coffee shops; quality or popularity of restaurants, nightspots, health clubs, and online dating; moderate climates with sustainable water supplies). *Worldwide ERC and Primacy Relocation, "2006 Best Cities for Relocating Singles," October 11, 2006*

- *Forbes* ranked the 40 most populous metro areas in the U.S. in terms of the "Best Cities for Singles." The San Diego metro area was ranked #18. Criteria: number of singles; cost of living alone; nightlife; culture; job growth; coolness; and online dating. *Forbes.com, July 25, 2006*

- Sperling's BestPlaces in partnership with AXE Deodorant Bodyspray ranked 80 metro areas and identified "America's Best (and Worst) Cities for Dating." The San Diego metro area ranked #3. Criteria: percentage of singles ages 18-24; population density; dating venues per capita. *AXE Deodorant Bodyspray, "America's Best (and Worst) Cities for Dating," May, 2004*

Culture/Performing Arts Rankings

- San Diego was selected as one of "America's Top 25 Arts Destinations." The city ranked #16 in the big city (population 500,000 and over) category. Criteria: readers' top choices for arts travel destinations based on the richness and variety of visual arts sites, activities and events. *American Style, June 2006*

- Scarborough Research, a leading market research firm, identified the top local markets for rock concert attendance. The San Diego DMA (Designated Market Area) ranked in the top 25 with 16% of consumers, 18 years old and over, reporting that they have attended a rock concert during the past year. *Scarborough Research, Scarborough USA+ 2003 Release 2*

Miscellaneous Rankings

- San Diego was selected as a runner-up in *Dog Fancy's* DogTown USA contest. Criteria: access to top veterinary professionals, dog parks, and canine-friendly businesses; shelter-euthanasia rates; and owner responsibility. *Dog Fancy, "DogTown USA," 2006*

- San Diego was determined to be one of America's smartest cities. The city ranked #7 in the large city category (200,000+ adults 25 years and older). Criteria: the editors rated the collective brainpower of U.S communities based on the educational attainment of its residents. *American City Business Journals, www.bizjournals.com, June 12, 2006*

- San Diego was selected as one of the "Top 100 Sweatiest Summer Cities". The city was ranked #96. The ranking was based on the average male/female height/weight, average high temperature, and average relative humidity levels for 2002 in each of the cities during June, July and August. The sweat level was analyzed based on the assumption that the individual was walking for one hour. *Procter & Gamble, Old Spice, June 18, 2003*

- San Diego appeared on ApartmentRatings.com "Top Cities for Renters List 2006". The area ranked #131 out of 138. Criteria: renter satisfaction; affordability; and vacancy. *ApartmentRatings.com, "Top Cities for Renters List 2006"*

- San Diego was selected as one of "America's Favorite Cities" in the "cities with the most attractive people" category. The city was ranked #1 out of 25. Criteria: *Travel + Leisure* magazine and AOL's Travel Channel conducted an online survey of nearly half a million AOL members to find out what travelers think about twenty-five American cities. Results shown above are according to visitors to the city, not locals. *Travel + Leisure and AOL's Travel Channel, "America's Favorite Cities," March 22, 2004*

- Sperling's BestPlaces in partnership with Pep Boys ranked 77 metro areas and identified "America's Most Drivable Cities." The San Diego metro area ranked #64. Criteria: climate; road roughness; urban mobility; gas prices. *Pep Boys, "America's Most Drivable Cities," April 9, 2003*

- San Diego was ranked #3 out of 268 metro areas in terms of its Creativity Index. The Creativity Index is a mix of four equally weighted factors: the Creative Class (scientists, engineers, architects, designers, writers, artists, musicians, or any profession where creativity is a key factor) share of the workforce; innovation, measured as patents per capita; high-tech industry, using the Milken Institute's Tech Pole Index; and diversity, measured by the Gay Index (a reasonable proxy for an areas' openness to different kinds of people and ideas). *The Rise of the Creative Class, 2002*

- San Diego was selected as one of "America's Most Literate Cities." The city ranked #26 out of the 70 largest U.S. cities. Criteria: number of booksellers; library resources; Internet resources; educational attainment; periodical publishing resources; newspaper circulation. *Central Connecticut State University, "America's Most Literate Cities 2006"*

- San Diego was selected as one of America's best-mannered cities. The area ranked in the top 10 at #2. The list is based on thousands of letters and faxes received by etiquette expert Marjabelle Young Stewart. *The Associated Press, January 15, 2005*

- State Farm Insurance, in partnership with Sperling's BestPlaces, analyzed several key factors that contribute to overall family preparedness. The San Diego metro area ranked #37 out of the nation's 50 most populous metro areas. Criteria: quality of life; life insurance coverage; and investments. *State Farm Life Insurance, "Fiscally Fit Cities Report," July 20, 2004*

- Scarborough Research, a leading market research firm, identified the top local markets for coffee bar patronage. The San Diego DMA (Designated Market Area) ranked in the top 10 with 20% of adults reporting that they have used any coffee house/bar during the past 30 days. *Scarborough Research, Scarborough USA+ 2004 Release 1*

Business Environment

CITY FINANCES

City Government Finances

Component	2003-2004 ($000)	2003-2004 ($ per capita)
Total Revenues	3,036,138	2,411
Total Expenditures	2,522,806	2,003
Debt Outstanding	2,770,970	2,200
Cash and Securities	3,923,463	3,115

Source: U.S Census Bureau, Government Finances 2003-2004

City Government Revenue by Source

Source	2003-2004 ($000)	2003-2004 ($ per capita)
General Revenue		
From Federal Government	221,309	176
From State Government	180,474	143
From Local Governments	90,792	72
Taxes		
Property	267,996	213
Sales	388,650	309
Personal Income	0	0
License	0	0
Charges	425,746	338
Liquor Store	0	0
Utility	252,502	200
Employee Retirement	687,296	546
Other	521,373	414

Source: U.S Census Bureau, Government Finances 2003-2004

City Government Expenditures by Function

Function	2003-2004 ($000)	2003-2004 ($ per capita)	2003-2004 (%)
General Expenditures			
Airports	4,599	4	0.2
Corrections	8,283	7	0.3
Education	0	0	0.0
Fire Protection	142,940	113	5.7
Governmental Administration	100,291	80	4.0
Health	13,936	11	0.6
Highways	141,959	113	5.6
Hospitals	0	0	0.0
Housing and Community Development	313,665	249	12.4
Interest on General Debt	100,798	80	4.0
Libraries	50,819	40	2.0
Parking	4,950	4	0.2
Parks and Recreation	190,484	151	7.6
Police Protection	272,289	216	10.8
Public Welfare	0	0	0.0
Sewerage	408,951	325	16.2
Solid Waste Management	57,613	46	2.3
Liquor Store	0	0	0.0
Utility	443,651	352	17.6
Employee Retirement	184,891	147	7.3
Other	82,687	66	3.3

Source: U.S Census Bureau, Government Finances 2003-2004

Municipal Bond Ratings

Area	Moody's
City	Aaa

Source: Mergent Bond Record, January 2007 (unless noted otherwise)

DEMOGRAPHICS

Population Growth

Area	1990 Census	2000 Census	2006 Estimate	2011 Projection	Population Growth (%)	
					1990-2000	2000-2011
City	1,111,048	1,223,400	1,294,273	1,369,292	10.1	11.9
MSA[1]	2,498,016	2,813,833	2,996,862	3,182,742	12.6	13.1
U.S.	248,709,873	281,421,906	298,021,266	312,383,955	13.2	11.0

Note: (1) Metropolitan Statistical Area - see Appendix B for areas included
Source: Claritas, Inc.

Number of Households and Average Household Size

Area	2006 Estimate	2006 Average Household Size
City	477,188	2.71
MSA[1]	1,055,563	2.84
U.S.	112,267,302	2.65

Note: (1) Metropolitan Statistical Area - see Appendix B for areas included
Source: Claritas, Inc.

Race and Ethnicity

Area	White Alone[2]	Black Alone[2]	Asian Alone[2]	Other Race Alone[2]	Hispanic[3]
City	58.9	6.7	14.7	19.6	27.8
MSA[1]	64.2	5.1	9.9	20.8	29.6
U.S.	73.3	12.4	4.2	10.1	14.5

Note: Figures are 2006 estimates; (1) Metropolitan Statistical Area - see Appendix B for areas included
(2) Alone is defined as not being in combination with one or more other races; (3) May be of any race.
Source: Claritas, Inc.

Segregation

City		MSA[1]	
Index[2]	Rank[3]	Index[2]	Rank[4]
63.6	36	58.2	171

Note: Figures are based on an analysis of Census 2000 data; (1) Metropolitan Statistical Area - see Appendix A for areas included; (2) White/Black Dissimilarity Index—the most commonly used measure of segregation between two groups, reflecting their relative distributions across neighborhoods within a city or metropolitan area. It can range in value from 0, indicating complete integration, to 100, indicating complete segregation; (3) Ranges from 1 (most segregated) to 100 (least segregated) and includes all the cities in this book; (4) Ranges from 1 (most segregated) to 318 (least segregated) and includes 318 metropolitan areas.
Source: www.CensusScope.org

Ancestry

Area	German	Irish[2]	English	American	Italian	Polish	French[3]	Scottish
City	10.8	8.7	8.0	3.2	4.6	2.1	2.4	1.8
MSA[1]	12.6	9.6	9.0	3.8	4.7	2.0	2.8	2.0
U.S.	15.2	10.9	8.7	7.3	5.6	3.2	3.0	1.7

Note: Figures include multiple ancestry (e.g. if a person reported being Irish and Italian, they were included in both columns); (1) Metropolitan Statistical Area - see Appendix A for areas included; (2) Includes Celtic; (3) Includes Alsatian but excludes Basque
Source: Census 2000, Summary File 3

Foreign-Born Population

Area	Percent of Population Born in							
	Any Foreign Country	Europe	Asia	Africa	Oceania[2]	Canada	Mexico	Latin America[3]
City	25.7	2.4	10.5	0.8	0.2	0.5	10.1	1.2
MSA[1]	21.6	2.0	7.0	0.4	0.1	0.5	10.4	1.0
U.S.	11.1	1.7	2.9	0.3	0.1	0.3	3.3	2.5

Note: (1) Metropolitan Statistical Area - see Appendix A for areas included; (2) Includes Australia, New Zealand subregion, Melanesia, Micronesia, Polynesia, and Oceania n.e.c; (3) Includes Central America (excluding Mexico), South America, and the Caribbean.
Source: Census 2000, Summary File 3

Marriage Status

Area	Never Married	Now Married (excluding Separated)	Separated	Widowed	Divorced
City	35.0	47.5	2.4	4.9	10.2
MSA[1]	30.2	52.0	2.3	5.3	10.2
U.S.	27.1	54.4	2.2	6.6	9.7

Note: Figures are percentages and cover the population 15 years of age and older;
(1) Metropolitan Statistical Area - see Appendix A for areas included
Source: Census 2000, Summary File 3

Age Distribution

Area	Percent of Population						
	Under Age 5	Age 5 to 17	Age 18 to 34	Age 35 to 49	Age 50 to 64	Age 65 to 79	80 Years and Over
City	6.7	17.2	30.0	23.3	12.4	7.8	2.6
MSA[1]	7.0	18.6	26.9	23.5	12.8	8.3	2.9
U.S.	6.8	18.9	23.7	23.5	14.8	9.2	3.2

Note: (1) Metropolitan Statistical Area - see Appendix A for areas included
Source: Census 2000, Summary File 3

Male/Female Ratio

Area	Males	Females	Males per 100 Females
City	652,780	641,493	101.8
MSA[1]	1,506,333	1,490,529	101.1
U.S.	146,712,712	151,308,554	97.0

Note: Figures are 2006 estimates; (1) Metropolitan Statistical Area -
see Appendix B for areas included
Source: Claritas, Inc.

Religion

Area	Catholic	Southern Baptist	United Methodist	ELCA[1]	LDS[2]	Presbyterian Church USA	Jewish Est.	Muslim Est.
County	29.5	1.0	0.7	0.6	1.6	0.9	2.5	0.3
U.S.	22.0	7.1	3.7	1.8	1.5	1.1	2.2	0.6

Note: Figures are the number of adherents as a percentage of the total population; Adherents are defined as all
members, including full members, their children and the estimated number of other participants who are not
considered members (e.g. the baptized, those not confirmed, those regularly attending services, etc.);
(1) Evangelical Lutheran Church in America; (2) The Church of Jesus Christ of Latter Day Saints
Source: Reprinted with permission from Religious Congregations and Membership in the United States 2000
(Nashville, Glenmary Research Center, 2002) Copyright Association of Statisticians of American Religious
Bodies. All rights reserved.

ECONOMY

Gross Metropolitan Product

Area	2002	2003	2004	2005	2005 Rank[2]
MSA[1]	117.0	124.4	134.5	143.4	16

Note: Figures are in billions of dollars; (1) San Diego-Carlsbad-San Marcos, CA Metropolitan Statistical Area -
see Appendix A for areas included; (2) Rank ranges from 1 to 361
Source: The U.S. Conference of Mayors, "U.S. Metro Economies: GMP - The Engines of America's Growth,"
January 2007

Economic Growth

Area	1995 GMP	2005 GMP	Average Annual Growth Rate	Growth Rate Rank[2]
MSA[1]	73.8	143.4	6.9	49

Note: Figures are in billions of dollars; GMP = Gross Metropolitan Product; (1) San Diego-Carlsbad-San
Marcos, CA Metropolitan Statistical Area - see Appendix A for areas included; (2) Rank ranges from 1 to 361
Source: The U.S. Conference of Mayors, "U.S. Metro Economies: GMP - The Engines of America's Growth,"
January 2007

INCOME

Per Capita/Median/Average Income

Area	Per Capita ($)	Median Household ($)	Average Household ($)
City	27,624	53,762	73,544
MSA[1]	26,918	55,945	74,929
U.S.	25,129	48,775	65,849

Note: Figures are 2006 estimates; (1) Metropolitan Statistical Area - see Appendix B for areas included
Source: Claritas, Inc.

Household Income Distribution

Area	Percent of Households Earning							
	Under $15,000	$15,000 -24,999	$25,000 -34,999	$35,000 -49,999	$50,000 -74,999	$75,000 -99,000	$100,000 -149,999	$150,000 and up
City	11.8	10.2	10.6	14.7	18.5	12.4	13.2	8.7
MSA[1]	10.2	9.7	10.5	15.0	19.4	12.9	13.7	8.7
U.S.	13.3	11.0	11.3	15.7	19.5	11.8	11.0	6.4

Note: Figures are 2006 estimates; (1) Metropolitan Statistical Area - see Appendix B for areas included
Source: Claritas, Inc.

Poverty Rates by Age

Area	All Ages	Under 5 Years Old	5 to 17 Years Old	18 to 64 Years Old	65 Years and Over
City	14.6	1.4	3.5	8.9	0.8
MSA[1]	12.4	1.2	3.2	7.3	0.8
U.S.	12.4	1.2	3.0	6.9	1.2

Note: Figures are percent of population with income in 1999 below poverty level and only include population for whom poverty status is determined; (1) Metropolitan Statistical Area - see Appendix A for areas included
Source: Census 2000, Summary File 3

Personal Bankruptcy Filing Rate

Area	2003	2004	2005
San Diego County	3.79	3.55	4.98
U.S.	5.57	5.31	6.88

Note: Numbers are per 1,000 population and include Chapter 7 and Chapter 13 filings
Source: Federal Deposit Insurance Corporation (FDIC), Regional Economic Conditions (RECON), 3/24/2006

EMPLOYMENT

Labor Force and Employment

Area	Civilian Labor Force			Workers Employed		
	Dec. 2005	Dec. 2006	% Chg.	Dec. 2005	Dec. 2006	% Chg.
City	677,288	681,145	0.6	652,670	655,815	0.5
MSA[1]	1,517,188	1,525,826	0.6	1,462,017	1,469,060	0.5
U.S.	149,874,000	152,571,000	1.8	142,918,000	146,081,000	2.2

Note: Data is not seasonally adjusted and covers workers 16 years of age and older;
(1) Metropolitan Statistical Area - see Appendix B for areas included
Source: Bureau of Labor Statistics, http://stats.bls.gov

Unemployment Rate

Area	2006											
	Jan.	Feb.	Mar.	Apr.	May	Jun.	Jul.	Aug.	Sep.	Oct.	Nov.	Dec.
City	4.0	4.1	3.8	3.7	3.6	4.2	4.3	4.1	3.9	3.6	3.9	3.7
MSA[1]	4.0	4.1	3.9	3.7	3.7	4.2	4.3	4.1	3.9	3.6	3.9	3.7
U.S.	5.1	5.1	4.8	4.5	4.4	4.8	5.0	4.6	4.4	4.1	4.3	4.3

Note: Data is not seasonally adjusted and covers workers 16 years of age and older; All figures are percentages; (1) Metropolitan Statistical Area - see Appendix B for areas included
Source: Bureau of Labor Statistics, http://stats.bls.gov

Employment by Occupation

Occupation Classification	City (%)	MSA[1] (%)	U.S. (%)
Sales and Office	26.4	27.2	26.7
Professional and Related	26.8	22.8	20.2
Service	15.9	16.1	14.9
Production, Transportation, and Material Moving	9.0	9.9	14.6
Management, Business, and Financial	15.0	14.9	13.5
Construction, Extraction, and Maintenance	6.7	8.7	9.4
Farming, Forestry, and Fishing	0.2	0.5	0.7

Note: Figures cover employed civilians 16 years of age and older;
(1) Metropolitan Statistical Area - see Appendix A for areas included
Source: Census 2000, Summary File 3

Employment by Industry

Sector	MSA[1] Number of Employees	MSA[1] Percent of Total	U.S. Percent of Total
Government	222,500	16.9	16.3
Education and Health Services	126,500	9.6	13.2
Professional and Business Services	217,300	16.5	12.9
Retail Trade	153,800	11.7	11.5
Manufacturing	102,900	7.8	10.2
Leisure and Hospitality	157,900	12.0	9.5
Financial Activities	82,000	6.2	6.1
Construction	89,200	6.8	5.5
Wholesale Trade	45,200	3.4	4.3
Other Services	49,700	3.8	3.9
Transportation and Utilities	28,800	2.2	3.7
Information	37,400	2.8	2.2
Natural Resources and Mining	500	<0.1	0.5

Note: Figures cover non-farm employment as of December 2006 and are not seasonally adjusted;
(1) Metropolitan Statistical Area - see Appendix B for areas included
Source: Bureau of Labor Statistics, http://stats.bls.gov

Occupations with Greatest Projected Employment Growth: 2002 - 2012

Occupation[1]	2002 Employment	2012 Projected Employment	Numeric Employment Change	Percent Employment Change
Retail Salespersons	435,400	513,200	77,800	17.9
Postsecondary Teachers	154,500	217,700	63,200	40.9
Combined Food Preparation and Serving Workers, Including Fast Food	215,100	277,300	62,200	28.9
Cashiers	358,800	420,700	61,900	17.3
Registered Nurses	201,600	258,400	56,800	28.2
Waiters and Waitresses	214,000	264,900	50,900	23.8
Customer Service Representatives	197,500	244,900	47,400	24.0
Office Clerks, General	400,300	446,500	46,200	11.5
General and Operations Managers	224,000	267,000	43,000	19.2
Teacher Assistants	179,600	222,300	42,700	23.8

Note: Projections cover California; (1) Sorted by numeric employment change
Source: www.projectionscentral.com, State Occupational Projections, 2002-2012 Long-Term Projections

Fastest Growing Occupations: 2002 - 2012

Occupation[1]	2002 Employment	2012 Projected Employment	Numeric Employment Change	Percent Employment Change
Physical Therapist Aides	4,200	6,800	2,600	61.9
Dental Hygienists	16,600	26,200	9,600	57.8
Dental Assistants	42,700	67,100	24,400	57.1
Tapers	9,200	14,400	5,200	56.5
Drywall and Ceiling Tile Installers	26,800	41,800	15,000	56.0
Tile and Marble Setters	8,600	13,400	4,800	55.8
Network Systems and Data Communications Analysts	20,300	31,600	11,300	55.7
Physical Therapist Assistants	3,900	6,000	2,100	53.8
Fitness Trainers and Aerobics Instructors	24,000	35,700	11,700	48.8
Self-Enrichment Education Teachers	24,200	35,800	11,600	47.9

Note: Projections cover California; (1) Sorted by percent employment change and excludes occupations with numeric employment change less than 1500
Source: www.projectionscentral.com, State Occupational Projections, 2002-2012 Long-Term Projections

Average Wages

Occupation	$/Hr.	Occupation	$/Hr.
Accountants and Auditors	27.79	Maids and Housekeeping Cleaners	8.76
Automotive Mechanics	20.53	Maintenance and Repair Workers	16.67
Bookkeepers	16.39	Marketing Managers	53.93
Carpenters	20.90	Nuclear Medicine Technologists	35.36
Cashiers	9.69	Nurses, Licensed Practical	19.26
Clerks, General Office	12.14	Nurses, Registered	31.92
Clerks, Receptionists/Information	11.49	Nursing Aides/Orderlies/Attendants	11.37
Clerks, Shipping/Receiving	12.80	Packers and Packagers, Hand	8.69
Computer Programmers	36.67	Physical Therapists	32.95
Computer Support Specialists	21.53	Postal Service Mail Carriers	22.27
Computer Systems Analysts	34.88	Real Estate Brokers	n/a
Cooks, Restaurant	10.24	Retail Salespersons	11.93
Dentists	n/a	Sales Reps., Exc. Tech./Scientific	28.88
Electrical Engineers	41.15	Sales Reps., Tech./Scientific	36.22
Electricians	22.92	Secretaries, Exc. Legal/Med./Exec.	15.37
Financial Managers	45.29	Security Guards	10.57
First-Line Supervisors/Mgrs., Sales	18.48	Surgeons	83.08
Food Preparation Workers	8.27	Teacher Assistants	12.20
General and Operations Managers	52.85	Teachers, Elementary School	28.80
Hairdressers/Cosmetologists	11.99	Teachers, Secondary School	27.90
Internists	59.63	Telemarketers	12.92
Janitors and Cleaners	10.25	Truck Drivers, Heavy/Tractor-Trailer	18.31
Landscaping/Groundskeeping Workers	10.99	Truck Drivers, Light/Delivery Svcs.	12.66
Lawyers	53.55	Waiters and Waitresses	8.40

Note: Wage data is for May 2005 and covers the San Diego-Carlsbad-San Marcos, CA Metropolitan Statistics Area - see Appendix B for areas included. Hourly wages for elementary/secondary school teachers and teacher assistants were calculated by the editors from annual wage data assuming a 40 hour work week; n/a not available.
Source: Bureau of Labor Statistics, May 2005 Metro Area Occupational Employment and Wage Estimates

RESIDENTIAL REAL ESTATE

Building Permits

Area	Single-Family			Multi-Family			Total		
	2005	2006p	Pct. Chg.	2005	2006p	Pct. Chg.	2005	2006p	Pct. Chg.
City	1,059	815	-23.0	3,880	1,693	-56.4	4,939	2,508	-49.2
U.S.	1,682,000	1,380,000	-18.0	473,300	457,300	-3.4	2,155,300	1,837,300	-14.8

Note: (p) preliminary; figures represent new, privately-owned housing units authorized (unadjusted data); All permit data are based on estimates with imputation; U.S. figures are based on the new 20,000-place series.
Source: U.S. Census Bureau, Manufacturing, Mining, and Construction Statistics

Homeownership and Housing Vacancies

Area	Homeownership Rate[2] (%)			Rental Vacancy Rate[3] (%)			Homeowner Vacancy Rate[4] (%)		
	2004	2005	2006	2004	2005	2006	2004	2005	2006
MSA[1]	n/a	60.5	61.2	n/a	6.3	7.3	n/a	2.1	2.8
U.S.	69.0	68.9	68.8	10.2	9.8	9.7	1.7	1.9	2.4

Note: Comparable 2004 data was not available due to changes in metropolitan area definitions; (1) Metropolitan Statistical Area - see Appendix B for areas included; (2) The proportion of households that are owners; (3) The proportion of the rental inventory that is vacant for rent; (4) The proportion of the homeowner inventory that is vacant for sale; n/a not available
Source: U.S. Census Bureau, Housing Vacancies and Homeownership Annual Statistics: 2006

TAXES

State Corporate Income Tax Rates

State	Rate (%)	Number of Brackets	Low Bracket (Under $)	High Bracket (Over $)
California	8.84	1	na	na

Note: Tax rates as of December 31, 2006; na not applicable; 10.84% on financial institutions. Minimum tax is $800. The tax rate on S-Corporations is 1.5% (3.5% for financial S-Corporations).
Source: Tax Foundation, www.taxfoundation.org

State Individual Income Tax Rates

State	Federal Deductibility	Marginal Rate (%)	Number of Brackets	Low Bracket (Under $)	High Bracket (Over $)
California	No	1.0-10.3 (p)(r)	7	0	1,000,000

Note: Tax rates as of December 31, 2006; Brackets apply to single taxpayers and married people filing separately; na not applicable; (p) California's $1,000,000 bracket not doubled for married taxpayers; (r) Indexed for Inflation.
Source: Tax Foundation, www.taxfoundation.org

Various State and Local Tax Rates

State and Local Sales and Use (%)	State Sales and Use (%)	Gasoline ($/gal.)	Cigarette ($/pack)	Spirits ($/gal.)	Table Wine ($/gal.)	Beer ($/gal.)
7.75	6.25	0.192 (m)	0.87	3.3	0.20	0.20

Note: Tax rates as of December 31, 2006; (m) Additional cents per gallon taxes added this year that were not included in previous years' tables.
Source: Tax Foundation, www.taxfoundation.org; The Sales Tax Clearinghouse, www.thestc.com

State Tax Burdens

Area	Combined State and Local Tax Burden		Combined Federal, State and Local Tax Burden	
	Percent	Rank	Percent	Rank
California	10.9	15	32.7	9
U.S. Average	10.6	-	31.6	-

Note: Figures are for 2006 and measure taxes as a percentage of income
Source: Tax Foundation, www.taxfoundation.org

Internal Revenue Service Tax Audits

IRS District	Percent of Returns Audited				
	1996	1997	1998	1999	2000
Southern California	1.62	1.34	0.88	0.69	0.47
U.S.	0.66	0.61	0.46	0.31	0.20

Note: Figures cover IRS district audits of federal income tax returns filed by individuals. Geographic data on district audits after the year 2000 are being withheld by the IRS. TRAC is challenging this policy.
Source: Syracuse University, Transactional Records Access Clearinghouse (TRAC), "Odds of IRS District Tax Audit 2000"

COMMERCIAL REAL ESTATE

Office Market

Market Area	Inventory (sq. ft.)	Vacant (sq. ft.)	Vac. Rate (%)	Under Constr. (sq. ft.)	Asking Rent ($/sf)	
					Class A	Class B
San Diego	65,570,681	6,639,781	10.1	3,415,630	36.60	28.08

Source: Grubb & Ellis, Office Markets Trends, 4th Quarter 2006

Industrial Market

Market Area	Inventory (sq. ft.)	Vacant (sq. ft.)	Vac. Rate (%)	Under Constr. (sq. ft.)	Asking Rent ($/sf)	
					WH/Dist	R&D/Flex
San Diego	57,675,042	4,521,299	7.8	1,288,494	8.16	13.32

Source: Grubb & Ellis, Industrial Markets Trends, 4th Quarter 2006

COMMERCIAL UTILITIES

Typical Monthly Electric Bills

Area	Commercial Service ($/month)		Industrial Service ($/month)	
	3 kW demand 1,000 kWh	40 kW demand 14,000 kWh	1,000 kW demand 200,000 kWh	50,000 kW demand 15,000,000 kWh
City	n/a	n/a	n/a	n/a
Average[1]	123	1,413	22,000	1,306,315

Note: Based on total rates in effect July 1, 2006; (1) average based on 196 utilities; n/a not available
Source: Edison Electric Institute, Typical Bills and Average Rates Report, Summer 2006

TRANSPORTATION

Means of Transportation to Work

Area	Car/Truck/Van		Public Transportation			Bicycle	Walked	Other Means	Worked at Home
	Drove Alone	Car-pooled	Bus	Subway	Railroad				
City	74.0	12.2	3.8	0.0	0.0	0.7	3.6	1.5	4.0
MSA[1]	73.9	13.0	2.9	0.0	0.2	0.6	3.4	1.6	4.4
U.S.	75.7	12.2	2.5	1.5	0.5	0.4	2.9	1.0	3.3

Note: Figures are percentages and cover workers 16 years of age and older;
(1) Metropolitan Statistical Area - see Appendix A for areas included
Source: Census 2000, Summary File 3

Travel Time to Work

Area	Less Than 15 Minutes	15 to 29 Minutes	30 to 44 Minutes	45 to 59 Minutes	60 Minutes or More
City	25.1	46.2	19.8	4.4	4.6
MSA[1]	24.7	40.7	21.6	6.7	6.4
U.S.	29.4	36.1	19.1	7.4	8.0

Note: Figures are percentages and include workers 16 years old and over; (1) Metropolitan Statistical Area - see Appendix A for areas included
Source: Census 2000, Summary File 3

Travel Time Index

Area	1982	1993	2002	2003
Urban Area[1]	1.06	1.22	1.40	1.41
Average[2]	1.12	1.28	1.37	1.37

Note: Travel Time Index - The ratio of travel time in the peak period to the travel time at free-flow conditions. A value of 1.35 indicates a 20-minute free-flow trip takes 27 minutes in the peak. Free-flow speeds (60 mph on freeways and 35 mph on principal arterials) are used as the comparison threshold; (1) Covers the San Diego, CA urban area; (2) average of 85 urban areas
Source: Texas Transportation Institute, The 2005 Urban Mobility Report, May 2005

Public Transportation

Agency name:	San Diego Metropolitan Transit System (MTS)
Vehicle type:	Bus
Average fleet age in years:	7.6
No. operated in max. service:	211
Agency name:	North San Diego County Transit District (NCTD)
Vehicle type:	Bus
Average fleet age in years:	6.8
No. operated in max. service:	149
Vehicle type:	Commuter rail
Average fleet age in years:	8.4
No. operated in max. service:	28
Vehicle type:	Demand response
Average fleet age in years:	2.1
No. operated in max. service:	30
Agency name:	MTS Contract Services (MCS)
Vehicle type:	Bus
Average fleet age in years:	6.8
No. operated in max. service:	207
Vehicle type:	Demand response
Average fleet age in years:	5.0
No. operated in max. service:	107
Agency name:	San Diego Association of Governments (SANDAG)
Vehicle type:	Vanpool
Average fleet age in years:	1.5
No. operated in max. service:	423
Agency name:	San Diego Trolley Inc.
Vehicle type:	Light rail
Average fleet age in years:	15.2
No. operated in max. service:	83

Source: Federal Transit Administration, National Transit Database, 2005

Air Transportation

Airport name and code:	San Diego International-Lindbergh Field (SAN)
Domestic service (2006)	
Passenger airlines[1]:	30
Passenger enplanements:	8,541,050
Freight carriers[2]:	27
Freight (lbs.):	146,454,356
International service (2005)	
Passenger airlines[1]:	11
Passenger enplanements:	162,929
Freight carriers[2]:	2
Freight (lbs.):	55,048

Note: (1) Includes all major, minor and commuter airlines that carried at least one passenger during the year; (2) Includes all airlines and freight carriers that transported at least one pound of freight during the year
Source: Bureau of Transportation Statistics, The Intermodal Transportation Database, Air Carriers: T-100 International Market, 2004; Bureau of Transportation Statistics, The Intermodal Transportation Database, Air Carriers: T-100 Domestic Market, 2005

Other Transportation Statistics

Interstate highways:	I-5; I-8; I-15
Amtrak service:	Yes
Major waterways/ports:	San Diego Harbor

Source: Editor & Publisher Market Guide, 2006; Amtrak.com; Rand McNally 2006 Road Atlas

BUSINESSES

Major Business Headquarters

Company Name	2006 Rankings	
	Fortune[1]	Forbes[2]
LPL Financial Services	-	287
Petco Animal Supplies	-	176
Qualcomm	381	-
Science Applications Int'l	285	-
Sempra Energy	197	-

Note: (1) Fortune 500 - companies that produce a 10-K are ranked 1 to 500 based on 2005 revenue; (2) Forbes Largest Private Companies - all private companies with at least $1 billion in annual revenue are ranked 1 to 394; companies listed are located in the city; dashes indicate no ranking
Source: Fortune, April 17, 2006; Forbes, November 9, 2006

Best Companies to Work For

Booz Allen Hamilton; Intuit; Nordstrom; Qualcomm (HQ), headquartered in San Diego, are among the "100 Best Companies to Work For." Criteria: More than 105,000 employees from 446 companies responded to a 57-question survey created by the Great Place to Work Institute. Two-thirds of a company's score is based on the survey, which covers topics such as attitudes towards management, job satisfaction, and camaraderie. The remaining third of the score comes from each company's responses to the Institute's Culture Audit, which includes detailed questions about demographic makeup, pay and benefits programs, and open-ended questions about the company's people-management philosophy, internal communications, opportunities, compensation practices, diversity programs, etc. Any company that is at least seven years old and has a minimum of 1,000 U.S. employees is eligible. The top three U.S. locations are shown for companies with more than one location. *Fortune, "100 Best Companies to Work for 2007," January 22, 2007*

Scripps Health, headquartered in San Diego, is among the "100 Best Companies for Working Mothers." Criteria: workforce profile; compensation; child care; flexibility; time off and leaves; family-friendly programs; and company culture. This year *Working Mother* gave particular weight to flex and time off. *Working Mother, "100 Best Companies," October 2006*

Scripps Health, headquartered in San Diego, is among the "50 Best Employers for Workers Over 50." Criteria: recruiting practices; opportunities for training, education, and career development; workplace accommodations; alternative work options, such as flexible scheduling, job sharing, and phased retirement; employee health and pension benefits; and retiree benefits. Any employer with at least 50 employees based in the U.S. is eligible. This includes for-profit companies, not-for-profit organizations, and government employers. *AARP, "AARP Best Employers for Workers Over 50," 2006*

Sempra Energy, headquartered in San Diego, is among the "50 Best Companies for Minorities." Criteria: 1,200 of the largest U.S employers were surveyed. Those companies were analyzed on information such as the number of minorities in the workforce and on the board, and the rate at which minority employees are hired (and fired). *Fortune, "50 Best Companies for Minorities," June 28, 2004*

Qualcomm Inc; Sharp HealthCare<D, headquartered in San Diego, are among the "100 Best Places to Work in IT." To qualify, companies, both public and private, had to have 2005 revenue of $250 million or greater and employ a minimum of 500 people in the U.S., with a minimum of 100 IT employees in the U.S. Companies were selected based on average salary and bonus increases, the percentage of IT employees receiving promotions, IT staff turnover rates, training and development, and the percentage of women and minorities in IT staff and management positions. In addition, information was collected on how the organizations reward outstanding performance, how their retention programs are structured and what benefits they offer. *Computerworld, "100 Best Places to Work in IT 2006," June 19, 2006*

Fast-Growing Businesses

According to *Inc.*, San Diego is home to six of America's 500 fastest-growing private companies: **Advanced Planning Services; Blue Tech; Chassis Plans; DriveCam; Five Point Capital; The Active Network**. Criteria: must be an independent, privately-held, U.S. corporation, proprietorship or partnership; net sales of at least $600,000 in FY2002; four-year operating/sales history; holding companies, regulated banks, and utilities were excluded. *Inc., "America's 500 Fastest-Growing Private Companies," September 2006*

San Diego is home to two of *Business Week's* "Hot Growth Companies:" **Gen-Probe; InfoSonics**. To qualify, a company must have annual sales of more than $50 million and less than $1.5 billion, a current market value greater than $25 million, a current stock price of at least $5, and be actively traded. Banks, insurers, real estate firms, and utilities are excluded. So are companies with declines in current financial results or in stock price, as well as companies where other developments raise questions about future performance. Companies were selected based on three-year results in sales growth, earnings growth, and return on invested capital. *Business Week, June 5, 2006*

According to *Business 2.0*, San Diego is home to three of America's 100 fastest-growing technology companies: **Biosite; Qualcomm; Websense**. The 100 Fastest-Growing Technology Companies (B2 100) is a yearly ranking published by Business 2.0 magazine of businesses whose inventiveness and quick reflexes are helping them to set the pace for the economy. To find the B2 100, Zacks Investment Research of Chicago ranked 2,000 publicly traded companies using a rigorous combination of four financial criteria: growth in revenue, profit, and operating cash flow during the past three years; and the 12-month stock market return as of March 31, 2006. *Business 2.0, "100 Fastest-Growing Tech Companies 2006," June 2006*

According to Deloitte & Touche LLP, San Diego is home to 18 of North America's 500 fastest-growing high-technology companies: **Althea Technologies; American Technology Corporation; Biosite Incorporated; Continuous Computing Corporation; Cypress Bioscience; Dalrada Financial Corporation; Illumina; Information Systems Laboratories; Inovio Biomedical Corporation; KES; Kintera; Leap Wireless International; Ligand Pharmaceuticals; Novatel Wireless; NuVasive; SGX Pharmaceuticals; The Active Network; Websense**. Companies are ranked by percentage growth in revenue over a five-year period. Criteria for inclusion: company must be headquartered within North America; company must own proprietary intellectual property or proprietary technology that contributes to a significant portion of the company's operating revenue or devotes a significant proportion of revenues to research and development of technology; company must have been in business for a minumum of five years with 2001 operating revenues of at least $50,000 USD or $75,000 CD and 2005 operating revenues of at least $5 million USD/CD. *Deloitte & Touche LLP, 2006 Technology Fast 500*

Women-Owned Businesses: 1997 and 2002

Year	All Firms		Firms with Paid Employees			
	Firms	Sales ($000)	Firms	Sales ($000)	Employees	Payroll ($000)
1997	26,895	3,644,814	3,583	2,873,723	38,673	775,990
2002	32,513	5,056,910	4,753	4,292,952	51,252	1,311,990

Note: Figures cover firms located in the city; Women-owned business are defined as firms in which women own 51% or more of the stock or equity of the company; (a) Withheld to avoid disclosing data for individual companies; (b) Withheld because estimate did not meet publication standards; n/a not available
Source: 1997 Economic Census, Survey of Minority- and Women-Owned Business Enterprises; 2002 Economic Census, Survey of Business Owners (released February 9, 2006)

Minority Business Opportunity

One of the 500 largest Hispanic-owned companies in the U.S. are located in San Diego. *Hispanic Business, "Hispanic Business 500," June 2006*

San Diego is home to one company which is on the Hispanic Business Fastest-Growing 100 list (greatest sales growth over the past five years): **WSA Distributors**. *Hispanic Business, July/August 2006*

HOTELS

Hotels/Motels

Area	Hotels/Motels	Average Minimum Rates ($)		
		Tourist	First-Class	Deluxe
City	190	86	120	248

Source: OAG Travel Planner Online, Spring 2006

The San Diego metro area is home to four of the top 187 hotels in the U.S. according to *Travel & Leisure*: **Rancho Valencia Resort & Spa** (#53); **Four Seasons Resort Aviara** (#146); **The Lodge at Torrey Pines** (#178); **Hotel Solamar** (#186). Criteria: service; location; rooms; food; and value. *Travel & Leisure, "The T+L 500, 2007"*

EVENT SITES

Stadiums, Arenas, and Auditoriums

Name	Capacity
Open Air Theatre/Student Activity Center	12,000
San Diego Jack Murphy Stadium/Qualcomm Stadium	71,294
San Diego Sports Arena	14,000
Starlight Musical Theatre	43,000

Source: www.officialtravelguide.com; www.eventective.com; original research

Convention Centers

Name	Overall Space (sq. ft.)	Exhibit Space (sq. ft.)	Meeting Space (sq. ft.)	Meeting Rooms
San Diego Convention Center	1,104,309	204,114	615,701	72

Source: www.officialtravelguide.com; www.eventective.com; original research

Hotels/Conference Centers

Name	Guest Rooms	Exhibit Space (sq. ft.)	Meeting Space (sq. ft.)
Hotel Del Coronado	n/a	n/a	n/a
San Diego Marriott Hotel & Marina	1,358	25,254	110,000
Sheraton San Diego Hotel & Marina	1,045	18,700	73,000

Note: n/a not available
Source: www.officialtravelguide.com; www.eventective.com; original research

Living Environment

COST OF LIVING

Cost of Living Index

Year	Composite Index	Groceries	Housing	Utilities	Trans-portation	Health Care	Misc. Goods/ Services
2004	140.9	118.0	207.6	92.5	125.0	116.1	111.5
2005	149.4	116.2	236.6	97.1	116.6	121.5	116.0
2006	147.1	116.7	230.4	98.2	113.3	119.4	118.5

Note: U.S. = 100
Source: The Council for Community and Economic Research (formerly ACCRA), Cost of Living Index, 2004, 2005 and 2006 4-Quarter Averages

HOUSING

House Price Index (HPI)

Area	National Ranking[2]	Quarterly Change (%)	One-Year Change (%)	Five-Year Change (%)
MSA[1]	260	-0.90	-0.18	92.27
U.S.[3]	-	1.12	5.87	55.21

Note: The HPI is a weighted repeat sales index. It measures average price changes in repeat sales or refinancings on the same properties. This information is obtained by reviewing repeat mortgage transactions on single-family properties whose mortgages have been purchased or securitized by Fannie Mae or Freddie Mac in January 1975; (1) Metropolitan Statistical Area - see Appendix B for areas included; (2) Rankings are based on annual percentage change for all metro areas containing at least 15,000 transactions over the last 10 years and ranges from 1 to 282; (3) figures based on a weighted division average; all figures are for the period ending December 31, 2006
Source: Office of Federal Housing Enterprise Oversight, House Price Index, March 1, 2007

House Price Valuations

Area	Q4 1999	Q4 2000	Q4 2001	Q4 2002	Q4 2003	Q4 2004	Q4 2005	Q4 2006
MSA[1]	-19.4	-14.9	-9.3	2.8	15.0	30.6	37.0	29.6

Note: Figures show the percentage of over- or under-valuation of single family homes relative to statistically normal house values (e.g. a value of 23.6 indicates that house values are 23.6% overvalued). Statistically normal house values are based on house prices, interest rates, household incomes, population densities, and any historical premiums or discounts metropolitan areas have exhibited over time; (1) Figures cover the Metropolitan Statistical Area - see Appendix B for areas included
Source: Global Insight/National City Corporation, House Prices in America, March 2007

Median Home Prices

Area	2004	2005	2006p	Percent Change 2005 to 2006
Metro Area[1]	551.6	604.3	601.8	-0.4
U.S. Average	195.2	219.0	222.0	1.4

Note: Figures are median sales prices of existing single-family homes in thousands of dollars; (p) preliminary; n/a not available; (1) Covers the San Diego-Carlsbad-San Marcos, CA Metropolitan Statistical Area - see Appendix B for areas included
Source: National Association of Realtors, Metropolitan Area Prices, 4th Quarter 2006

Housing: Year Structure Built

Area	1990 -2000	1980 -1989	1970 -1979	1960 -1969	1950 -1959	1940 -1949	Before 1940	Median Year
City	12.3	19.6	24.0	15.4	14.8	6.2	7.7	1972
MSA[1]	13.9	21.9	26.3	15.0	12.9	4.9	5.1	1975
U.S.	17.0	15.8	18.5	13.7	12.7	7.3	15.0	1971

Note: Figures are percentages; (1) Metropolitan Statistical Area - see Appendix A for areas included
Source: Census 2000, Summary File 3

Average New Home Price

Area	2004	2005	2006
City	544,750	673,257	712,092
U.S.	253,574	275,712	299,269

Note: Figures, in dollars, are based on a new home with 2,400 sq. ft. of living area on an 8,000 sq. ft. lot.
Source: The Council for Community and Economic Research (formerly ACCRA), Cost of Living Index, 2004, 2005 and 2006 4-Quarter Averages

Average Apartment Rent

Area	2004	2005	2006
City	1,330	1,515	1,595
U.S.	716	740	766

Note: Figures, in dollars per month, are based on an unfurnished two bedroom, 1-1/2 or 2 bath apartment, approximately 950 sq. ft. in size, excluding all utilities except water
Source: The Council for Community and Economic Research (formerly ACCRA), Cost of Living Index, 2004, 2005 and 2006 4-Quarter Averages

RESIDENTIAL UTILITIES

Average Residential Utility Costs

Area	All Electric ($/mth)	Part Electric ($/mth)	Other Energy ($/mth)	Phone ($/mth)
City	–	83.75	73.45	25.22
U.S.	136.00	76.53	90.52	25.87

Source: The Council for Community and Economic Research (formerly ACCRA), Cost of Living Index, 2006 4-Quarter Average

HEALTH

Average Health Care Costs

Area	Optometrist ($/visit)	Doctor ($/visit)	Dentist ($/visit)
City	103.80	85.43	92.87
U.S.	76.38	76.10	68.72

Note: Optometrist—based on a full vision eye exam for an established adult patient;
Doctor—based on a general practitioner's routine exam of an established patient;
Dentist—based on adult teeth cleaning and periodic oral exam.
Source: The Council for Community and Economic Research (formerly ACCRA), Cost of Living Index, 2006 4-Quarter Average

Mortality Rates

ICD-10 Sub-Chapter	ICD-10 Code	Age-Adjusted Death Rate per 100,000 population[1]	U.S. Age-Adjusted Death Rate per 100,000 population
Malignant neoplasms	C00-C97	172.1	185.8
Ischaemic heart diseases	I20-I25	135.5	150.2
Other forms of heart disease	I30-I51	39.0	50.8
Cerebrovascular diseases	I60-I69	51.5	50.0
Chronic lower respiratory diseases	J40-J47	39.6	41.1
Diabetes mellitus	E10-E14	19.8	24.5
Other degenerative diseases of the nervous system	G30-G31	40.1	22.3
Other external causes of accidental injury	W00-X59	16.6	21.2
Influenza and pneumonia	J10-J18	17.1	19.8
Hypertensive diseases	I10-I13	21.3	18.1

Note: ICD-10 = International Classification of Diseases 10th Revision; (1) Figures cover San Diego County, CA
Source: Centers for Disease Control and Prevention, National Center for Health Statistics. Compressed Mortality File 1999-2004. CDC WONDER On-line Database, compiled from Compressed Mortality File 1999-2004 Series 20 No. 2J, 2007.

Health Risk Data

Item	Area[1] (%)	U.S. (%)
Adults who have been told they have high blood pressure	23.1	25.5
Adults who have been told they have high blood cholesterol	34.7	35.6
Adults who have been told they have diabetes[2]	7.1	7.3
Adults who have been told they have arthritis	21.0	27.0
Adults who have been told they currently have asthma	5.5	8.0
Adults who are current smokers	17.0	20.6

Note: (1) Figures cover the Metropolitan Statistical Area - see Appendix B for areas included; (2) Figures do not include pregnancy-related diabetes, pre-diabetes or borderline diabetes
Source: Centers for Disease Control and Prevention, Behaviorial Risk Factor Surveillance System, SMART: Selected Metropolitan/Micropolitan Area Trends, 2005

Distribution of Office-Based Physicians

Area	Total	Family/ General Practice	Specialties		
			Medical	Surgical	Other
MSA[1] (number)	6,085	809	2,072	1,414	1,790
MSA[1] (rate per 10,000 pop.)	21.0	2.8	7.2	4.9	6.2
Metro Average[2] (rate per 10,000 pop.)	19.4	2.1	7.5	4.5	5.3

Note: Data as of December 31, 2004; (1) Metropolitan Statistical Area - see Appendix A for areas included; (2) Average of the 79 unique MSAs and CMSAs in this book
Source: American Medical Association, Physician Characteristics & Distribution in the U.S., 2006

Hospitals

San Diego has the following hospitals: 7 general medical and surgical; 3 psychiatric; 1 obstetrics and gynecology; 1 rehabilitation; 2 long-term acute care; 1 other specialty; 1 children's general.
AHA Guide to the Healthcare Field 2007

According to *U.S. News,* the San Diego metro area is home to one of the best hospitals in the U.S.: **University of California - San Diego Medical Center**; *U.S. News Online, "America's Best Hospitals 2006"*

EDUCATION

Public School District Statistics

District Name	Schls	Pupils	Pupil/ Teacher Ratio	Minority Pupils[1] (%)	Free Lunch Eligible[2] (%)	IEP[3] (%)
San Diego Unified	221	134,709	18.7	74.2	42.6	12.1

Note: Table includes regular local school districts with 2,000 or more students; (1) Percentage of students that are not white, non-Hispanic; (2) Percentage of students that are eligible for the free lunch program; (3) Percentage of students that have an Individualized Education Program.
Source: U.S. Department of Education, National Center for Education Statistics, Common Core of Data, Local Education Agency (School District) Universe Survey: School Year 2004-2005; U.S. Department of Education, National Center for Education Statistics, Common Core of Data, Public Elementary/Secondary School Universe Survey: School Year 2004-2005

Top Public High Schools

High School Name	Index[1]	Rank[1]	Subsidized Lunch (%)[2]	E&E (%)[3]
Clairemont	1.465	731	35.6	n/a
Gompers	1.086	1,137	64.3	n/a
Madison	1.490	716	55.9	n/a
Mira Mesa	1.887	422	26.2	n/a
Mission Bay	1.747	502	55.8	n/a
Mount Carmel	1.424	769	11.6	n/a
Muir	1.368	831	65.0	n/a
Patrick Henry	2.308	257	24.9	n/a
Point Loma	1.806	464	32.1	n/a
Rancho Bernardo	1.897	417	4.0	n/a
San Diego High School of International Studies	4.576	22	47.0	n/a*
School of Creative and Performing Arts	3.049	111	40.6	n/a
Scripps Ranch	2.319	251	18.0	n/a
Serra	2.976	119	n/a	n/a
Torrey Pines	3.056	110	4.0	48.8
University City	2.616	173	25.0	23.9

Note: (1) Public schools are ranked according to a ratio that is the number of Advanced Placement and/or International Baccalaureate tests taken by all students at a school in 2005 divided by the number of graduating seniors. All of the schools on the list have an index of at least 1.000; they are in the top five percent of public schools measured this way. The rankings range from 1 to 1,236; (2) Percentage of students receiving federally subsidized meals; (3) E & E stands for equity and excellence percentage: the portion of all graduating seniors at a school that had at least one passing grade on one AP or IB test; (*) Gave just IB tests; (**) Gave both IB and AP tests. AP and IB participation are indicators of a school's efforts to get students to excel and prepare for college; n/a not available
Source: Newsweek Online, May 23, 2006

Educational Quality

School District	Education Quotient[1]	Graduate Outcome[2]	Community Index[3]	Resource Index[4]	Rating[5]
San Diego Unified	26	22	55	61	Green

Note: Scores are national percentile rankings and range from 1 (worst) to 99 (best); (1) Combination of the Graduate Outcome, Community and Resource Indexes weighted to reflect the greater importance of the Graduate Outcome and Resource Index; (2) Based on graduation rates and college board scores (SAT/ACT); (3) Based on the surrounding community's level of affluence and adult education; (4) Based on teacher salaries, per-pupil expenditures and student-teacher ratios; (5) School districts receive one of five rankings: Gold Medal (top 16 percent of districts evaluated); Blue Ribbon (top third); Green Light (average); Yellow Light (bottom 25 percent); Red Light (bottom 10 percent).
Source: Expansion Management, "2007 Education Quotient," January 2007

Highest Level of Education

Area	Less than H.S.	H.S. Diploma	Some College, No Deg.	Associate Degree	Bachelors Degree	Masters Degree	Profess. School Degree	Doctorate Degree
City	17.1	16.8	23.2	7.5	22.0	8.0	3.2	2.2
MSA[1]	17.3	19.6	25.5	7.6	19.0	6.8	2.6	1.5
U.S.	19.4	28.4	21.2	6.4	15.7	5.9	2.0	1.0

Note: Figures are 2006 estimated percentages and cover persons age 25 and over; (1) Metropolitan Statistical Area - see Appendix B for areas included
Source: Claritas, Inc.

Educational Attainment by Race

Area	High School Graduate (%)					Bachelor's Degree (%)				
	Total	White	Black	Asian	Hisp.[2]	Total	White	Black	Asian	Hisp.[2]
City	82.8	88.8	83.4	80.0	52.4	35.0	40.9	15.7	38.4	11.9
MSA[1]	82.6	87.7	86.1	81.3	53.5	29.5	33.1	16.3	37.2	10.7
U.S.	80.4	83.6	72.3	80.4	52.4	24.4	26.1	14.3	44.1	10.4

Note: Figures shown cover persons 25 years old and over; (1) Metropolitan Statistical Area - see Appendix A for areas included; (2) people of Hispanic origin can be of any race
Source: Census 2000, Summary File 3

School Enrollment by Type

Area	Grades KG to 8				Grades 9 to 12			
	Public		Private		Public		Private	
	Enrollment	%	Enrollment	%	Enrollment	%	Enrollment	%
City	139,884	91.0	13,786	9.0	59,532	93.0	4,489	7.0
MSA[1]	345,699	90.9	34,480	9.1	149,710	93.8	9,945	6.2
U.S.	33,526,011	88.7	4,285,121	11.3	14,848,628	90.6	1,532,323	9.4

Note: Figures shown cover persons 3 years old and over; (1) Metropolitan Statistical Area - see Appendix A for areas included
Source: Census 2000, Summary File 3

School Enrollment by Race

Area	Grades KG to 8 (%)				Grades 9 to 12 (%)			
	White	Black	Asian	Hisp.[1]	White	Black	Asian	Hisp.[1]
City	47.8	10.3	13.2	38.5	45.8	9.9	15.9	36.8
MSA[2]	57.2	7.0	7.8	38.2	56.6	6.7	9.5	35.9
U.S.	68.5	15.5	3.3	16.8	68.8	15.5	3.8	15.7

Note: Figures shown cover persons 3 years old and over; (1) people of Hispanic origin can be of any race; (2) Metropolitan Statistical Area - see Appendix A for areas included
Source: Census 2000, Summary File 3

Average Salaries of Public School Teachers

District	2004-05		2005-06		Percent Change 2004-05 to 2005-06
	Dollars	Rank[1]	Dollars	Rank[1]	
CALIFORNIA	57,876	2	59,345	3	2.54
U.S. Average	47,674	-	49,109	-	3.01

Note: (1) State rank ranges from 1 to 51.
Source: National Education Association, Rankings & Estimates: Rankings of the States 2005 and Estimates of School Statistics 2006, November 2006

Higher Education

Four-Year Colleges			Two-Year Colleges			Medical Schools[1]	Law Schools[2]	Voc/ Tech[3]
Public	Private Non-profit	Private For-profit	Public	Private Non-profit	Private For-profit			
1	8	9	3	0	5	1	3	9

Note: Figures cover institutions located within the city limits; (1) includes schools accredited by the Liaison Committee on Medical Education and the American Osteopathic Association; (2) includes American Bar Association-accredited law schools; (3) includes all schools with programs that are less than 2 years
Source: National Center for Education Statistics, The Integrated Postsecondary Education System (IPEDS) Peer Analysis System, 2006; www.usnews.com, America's Best Graduate Schools 2008, Medical School Directory; www.usnews.com, America's Best Graduate Schools 2008, Law School Directory

PRESIDENTIAL ELECTION

2004 Presidential Election Results

Area	Bush	Kerry	Nader	Other
San Diego County	52.5	46.4	0.1	1.0
U.S.	50.7	48.3	0.4	0.6

Note: Results are percentages and may not add to 100% due to rounding
Source: Dave Leip's Atlas of U.S. Presidential Elections, www.uselectionatlas.org

**MAJOR
EMPLOYERS**

Major Employers

Company Name	Industry	Type of Site
Health & Human Services	Administration of social & manpower programs	Branch
Nassco	Shipbuilding and repairing	Single
Naval Air Systems Command Ctr	National security	Branch
Naval Amphibious Base	National security	Branch
Naval Medical Center	Offices and clinics of medical doctors	Branch
Palomar Community COllege	Junior colleges	Headquarters
Police Dept-Headquarters	Police protection	Branch
SAIC	Commercial physical research	Headquarters
Safeskin Surgical Glove	Fabricated rubber products, nec	Headquarters
San Diego Healthcare Sys 664	Administration of veterans' affairs	Branch
Scripps Clinic - Torrey Pines	Skilled nursing care facilities	Branch
Sharp Memorial Hospital	General medical and surgical hospitals	Headquarters
Sheriffs Dept	Police protection	Branch
Solar Turbines Incorporated	Turbines and turbine generator sets	Headquarters
UCSD Medical Center	Medical laboratories	Branch
UCSD Medical Center	Offices and clinics of medical doctors	Branch
UCSD Medical Center University	Offices and clinics of medical doctors	Single

Note: Companies shown are located within the metropolitan area and have 2,500 or more employees; nec = not elsewhere classified.
Source: www.zapdata.com, January 2007

PUBLIC SAFETY

Crime Rate

Area	All Crimes	Violent Crimes				Property Crimes		
		Murder	Forcible Rape	Robbery	Aggrav. Assault	Burglary	Larceny -Theft	Motor Vehicle Theft
City	4,151.7	4.0	29.6	146.4	339.1	586.6	1,934.8	1,111.3
Suburbs[1]	3,493.4	2.8	26.1	123.8	278.9	607.7	1,762.6	691.6
Metro[2]	3,777.2	3.3	27.6	133.5	304.8	598.6	1,836.8	872.5
U.S.	3,899.0	5.6	31.7	140.7	291.1	726.7	2,286.3	416.7

Note: Figures are crimes per 100,000 population; (1) All areas within the metro area that are located outside the city limits; (2) Metropolitan Statistical Area - see Appendix B for areas included
Source: FBI Uniform Crime Reports, 2005

Hate Crimes

Area	Number of Quarters Reported	Bias Motivation				
		Race	Religion	Sexual Orientation	Ethnicity	Disability
City	4	18	5	10	8	0

Source: Federal Bureau of Investigation, Hate Crime Statistics 2005

RECREATION

Culture

Dance[1]	Theatre[1]	Instrumental Music[1]	Vocal Music[1]	Series/ Festivals	Museums	Zoos
6	9	6	5	6	27	1

Note: (1) number of professional perfoming groups
Source: The Grey House Performing Arts Directory, 2007; Official Museum Directory, 2007

Professional Sports Teams

Major League Baseball	National Basketball Association	National Football League	National Hockey League	Major League Soccer	Women's National Basketball Association
1	0	1	0	0	0

Note: Includes teams located in the San Diego metro area.
Source: www.sportsvenues.com, Listing of Venues by State/Province and City, 2006

MEDIA

Newspapers

Name	Target Audience	Frequency	Circulation
Old California Gazette	General	Non-Daily	75,000
San Diego Navy Dispatch	General	Non-Daily	25,000
San Diego Reader	Alternative/General	Non-Daily	158,000
The San Diego Union-Tribune	n/a	Daily	339,032
San Diego Voice & Viewpoint	Black/General	Non-Daily	25,000
Southern Cross	Catholic/Gen./Relig.	Non-Daily	32,000

Note: Includes newspapers whose offices are located in the city and whose circulations are 25,000 or more; n/a not available
Source: BurrellesLuce, MediaContacts Online, January 2006

Television Stations

Name	Ch.	Network(s)	Type	Ownership
XETV	6	Fox	Commercial	Grupo Televisa
KFMB	8	CBS	Commercial	Midwest TV Ltd.
KGTV	10	ABC	Commercial	The McGraw-Hill Companies
KPBS	15	PBS	Public	San Diego State University
KNSD	39	NBC	Commercial	General Electric Corporation
KUSI	51	n/a	Commercial	McKinnon Broadcasting Company
KSWB	69	WBN	Commercial	Tribune Broadcasting Company

Note: Stations included cover the San Diego DMA (Designated Market Area)
BurrellesLuce, MediaContacts Online, January 2006

Major AM Radio Stations

Call Letters	Freq. (kHz)	Station Type	Target Audience	Station Format	Music Format
KOGO	600	Commercial	General	News/Sports/Talk	n/a
XTRA	690	n/a	Men	Sports/Talk	Adult Standards
KFMB	760	n/a	General	News/Sports/Talk	n/a
KECR	910	Non-Comm	General/Religious	Music	Christian
KCEO	1000	Commercial	General	Educational/Talk	n/a
KURS	1040	n/a	Hispanic	Ed/Music/News/Sports/Talk	n/a
KSDO	1130	n/a	General	Music/Talk	n/a
KCBQ	1170	Commercial	General	Talk	n/a
KPRZ	1210	Commercial	General/Rel/Women	Talk	n/a
KSON	1240	n/a	Children/General	Music/News	n/a
KKSM	1320	College	General	Music	Alternative
KPOP	1360	Commercial	General	Music	Adult Standards
KFSD	1450	n/a	General	Music	n/a

Note: Stations included cover the San Diego DMA (Designated Market Area); n/a not available
Source: BurrellesLuce, MediaContacts Online, January 2006

Major FM Radio Stations

Call Letters	Freq. (mHz)	Station Type	Target Audience	Station Format	Music Format
XHTZ	90.3	Commercial	General/Young Adult	Music	Urban Contemp.
XTRA	91.1	n/a	Young Adult	Music/News/Talk	n/a
XHRM	92.5	Commercial	General	Music	Oldies
KMYI	94.1	Commercial	General	n/a	n/a
KBZT	94.9	n/a	General	Music/News	n/a
KOCO	95.7	n/a	General	Music	n/a
KYXY	96.5	Commercial	General	Music/News	Soft Rock
KSON	97.3	n/a	General	Music/News/Talk	n/a
KIFM	98.1	n/a	General	Music/News	n/a
KFMB	100.7	Commercial	General	n/a	n/a
KGB	101.5	Commercial	General	Music	Classic Rock
KPRI	102.1	Commercial	General	Music	Alternative
KLQV	102.9	Commercial	General/Hispanic	Music/News	Adult Contemp.
KPLN	103.7	Commercial	General/Men	Music/News/Sports	Classic Rock
XLTN	104.5	n/a	General/Hispanic	Music	n/a
KIOZ	105.3	Commercial	General	Music	Middle of the Rd.
KLNV	106.5	n/a	Hispanic	Music	n/a

Note: Stations included cover the San Diego DMA (Designated Market Area); n/a not available
BurrellesLuce, MediaContacts Online, January 2006

CLIMATE

Average and Extreme Temperatures

Temperature	Jan	Feb	Mar	Apr	May	Jun	Jul	Aug	Sep	Oct	Nov	Dec	Yr.
Extreme High (°F)	88	88	93	98	96	101	95	98	111	107	97	88	111
Average High (°F)	65	66	66	68	69	72	76	77	77	74	71	66	71
Average Temp. (°F)	57	58	59	62	64	67	71	72	71	67	62	58	64
Average Low (°F)	48	50	52	55	58	61	65	66	65	60	53	49	57
Extreme Low (°F)	29	36	39	44	48	51	55	58	51	43	38	34	29

Note: Figures cover the years 1948-1990
Source: National Climatic Data Center, International Station Meteorological Climate Summary, 9/96

Average Precipitation/Snowfall/Humidity

Precip./Humidity	Jan	Feb	Mar	Apr	May	Jun	Jul	Aug	Sep	Oct	Nov	Dec	Yr.
Avg. Precip. (in.)	1.9	1.4	1.7	0.8	0.2	0.1	Tr	0.1	0.2	0.4	1.2	1.4	9.5
Avg. Snowfall (in.)	Tr	0	0	0	0	0	0	0	0	0	0	Tr	Tr
Avg. Rel. Hum. 7am (%)	70	72	73	72	73	77	79	79	78	74	69	68	74
Avg. Rel. Hum. 4pm (%)	57	58	59	59	63	66	65	66	65	63	60	58	62

Note: Figures cover the years 1948-1990; Tr = Trace amounts (<0.05 in. of rain; <0.5 in. of snow)
Source: National Climatic Data Center, International Station Meteorological Climate Summary, 9/96

Weather Conditions

Temperature			Daytime Sky			Precipitation		
10°F & below	32°F & below	90°F & above	Clear	Partly cloudy	Cloudy	0.01 inch or more precip.	0.1 inch or more snow/ice	Thunder-storms
0	< 1	4	115	126	124	40	0	5

Note: Figures are average number of days per year and cover the years 1948-1990
Source: National Climatic Data Center, International Station Meteorological Climate Summary, 9/96

HAZARDOUS WASTE

Superfund Sites

San Diego has no sites on the EPA's Superfund Final National Priorities List.
U.S. Environmental Protection Agency, Final National Priorities List, March 20, 2007

AIR & WATER QUALITY

Air Quality Index

Area	Percent of Days when Air Quality was...[2]				AQI Statistics	
	Good	Moderate	Unhealthy for Sensitive Groups	Unhealthy	Maximum	Median
MSA[1]	53.4	44.1	2.5	0.0	111	49

Note: The Air Quality Index (AQI) is an index for reporting daily air quality. EPA calculates the AQI for five major air pollutants regulated by the Clean Air Act: ground-level ozone, particle pollution (also known as particulate matter), carbon monoxide, sulfur dioxide, and nitrogen dioxide. The AQI runs from 0 to 500. The higher the AQI value, the greater the level of air pollution and the greater the health concern. There are six AQI categories: "Good" The AQI is between 0 and 50. Air quality is considered satisfactory; "Moderate" The AQI is between 51 and 100. Air quality is acceptable; "Unhealthy for Sensitive Groups" When AQI values are between 101 and 150, members of sensitive groups may experience health effects; "Unhealthy" When AQI values are between 151 and 200 everyone may begin to experience health effects; "Very Unhealthy" AQI values between 201 and 300 trigger a health alert; "Hazardous" AQI values over 300 trigger health warnings of emergency conditions; (1) Metropolitan Statistical Area - see Appendix A for areas included; (2) Based on 365 days with AQI data in 2005.
Source: U.S. Environmental Protection Agency, Air Quality Index Report, 2005

Air Quality Index Pollutants

Area	Percent of Days when AQI Pollutant was...[2]					
	Carbon Monoxide	Nitrogen Dioxide	Ozone	Sulfur Dioxide	Particulate Matter 2.5	Particulate Matter 10
MSA[1]	1.1	0.0	59.5	0.0	34.2	5.2

Note: The Air Quality Index (AQI) is an index for reporting daily air quality. EPA calculates the AQI for five major air pollutants regulated by the Clean Air Act: ground-level ozone, particle pollution (also known as particulate matter), carbon monoxide, sulfur dioxide, and nitrogen dioxide. The AQI runs from 0 to 500. The higher the AQI value, the greater the level of air pollution and the greater the health concern; (1) Metropolitan Statistical Area - see Appendix A for areas included; (2) Based on 365 days with AQI data in 2005.
Source: U.S. Environmental Protection Agency, Air Quality Index Report, 2005

Number of Days with Air Quality Index Values Greater than 100

Area	Trend Sites (29)								All Sites (57)
	1998	1999	2000	2001	2002	2003	2004	2005	2005
MSA[1]	32	33	31	30	20	20	16	7	9

Note: An AQI value greater than 100 indicates that air quality would have been in the unhealthful range on that day. Data from exceptional events are not included. These counts are presented in two ways. First, the counts are based on sites having an adequate record of monitoring data during the trend period (trend sites). These counts represent the relative change in the number of days with AQI values greater than 100. In the last column, the counts are based on all sites with data in the most recent year (because it is possible for a site to have data in the most recent year but not enough data to be a trend site); (1) Metropolitan Statistical Area - see Appendix A for areas included; n/a not available.
Source: U.S. Environmental Protection Agency, Air Trends Fact Book 2005

Maximum Pollutant Concentrations

	Particulate Matter 10 (ug/m³)	Particulate Matter 2.5 (ug/m³)	Ozone 1-hour (ppm)	Carbon Monoxide (ppm)	Sulfur Dioxide (ppm)	Nitrogen Dioxide (ppm)	Lead (ug/m³)
MSA[1] Level	154	30	0.106	4	0.013	0.024	n/a
NAAQS[2]	150	65	0.125	9	0.140	0.053	1.50
Met NAAQS[2]	No	Yes	Yes	Yes	Yes	Yes	n/a

Note: Data from exceptional events are not included; (1) Metropolitan Statistical Area - see Appendix A for areas included; (2) National Ambient Air Quality Standards; n/a not available
Units: ppm = parts per million; ug/m³ = micrograms per cubic meter
Source: U.S. Environmental Protection Agency, Air Trends Fact Book 2005

Watershed Health

The U.S. Environmental Protection Agency monitors the health of the aquatic resources for the nation's 2,000+ watersheds. **The San Diego watershed serves the San Diego area and received an overall Index of Watershed Indicators (IWI) score of 2 (better quality - high vulnerability).** The IWI score is based on seven condition and nine vulnerability indicators. The overall IWI score ranges from 1 (best health) to 6 (worst health). The Condition Indicators include: designated use attainment, fish and wildlife consumption advisories, source water condition, contaminated sediments, ambient water quality, and wetlands loss index. The

Vulnerability Indicators include: aquatic species at risk, conventional and toxic loads over permitted limits, urban and agricultural runoff potential, population change, hydrologic modification, estuarine pollution susceptibility, and air deposition. *Note: The IWI is no longer being updated by the U.S. EPA. Source: U.S. Environmental Protection Agency, Index of Watershed Indicators, October 26, 2001*

Drinking Water

Water System Name	Pop. Served	Primary Water Source Type	Number of Violations in 2006[a]		
			Health Based	Significant Monitoring	Monitoring
City of San Diego	1,305,736	Surface	None	None	None

Note: (a) Based on violation data from January 1, 2006 to December 31, 2006
Source: U.S. Environmental Protection Agency, Office of Ground Water and Drinking Water, Safe Drinking Water Information System (data extracted April 12, 2007)

San Diego tap water is hard and not fluoridated.
Editor & Publisher Market Guide, 2005

San Francisco, California

Background

San Francisco is one of the most beautiful cities in the world. It is blessed with a mild climate, one of the best landlocked harbors in the world, and a strong sense of civic pride shaped by its unique history. It has been said that San Francisco is "Paris, but populated with Americans, most of them smiling."

The hilly peninsula known today as San Francisco and its bay was largely ignored by explorers during the sixteenth and seventeenth centuries. Until the 1760s, no European had seen the "Golden Gate," or the narrow strip of water leading into what was to become one of the greatest harbors in the world. However, even with the eventual discovery of that prime piece of real estate, San Francisco remained a quiet and pastoral settlement for nearly 90 years.

The discovery of gold in the Sierra Nevada foothills in 1848 changed San Francisco forever. Every hopeful adventurer from around the world docked in San Francisco, aspiring to make his fortune. San Francisco had entered its phase as a rowdy, frontier, gold-prospecting town, with plenty of bachelors, amusing themselves at the gambling houses and saloons.

When the supply of gold dwindled, many of the men went back to their native countries, but some stayed and continued to live in the ethnic neighborhoods they had created — neighborhoods that still exist today, such as Chinatown, the Italian District, and the Japan Center.

The charm of San Francisco lies in its cosmopolitan, yet cohesive, flavor. Ever mindful of its citizenry, newspapers in San Francisco range from English, Irish, Spanish, and Swiss to Chinese, Japanese, and Korean, with many community newspapers in between. In addition, the city has long been home to a significant gay community.

The San Francisco Bay Area is one of the major economic regions of the United States, with one of the highest percentages of college-educated adults in the nation, which translates into a high per-capita real income. The Bay Area is also home to 20 percent of California's environmental companies, and leads the state with the largest concentration of biotech companies. A former warehouse district in San Francisco has become the center for nearly 400 multimedia and Internet-related companies. Before the Internet crash in 2000, this industry cluster, combined with the concentration of multimedia activity in the Bay Area, had produced jobs for nearly 60,000 people. In terms of world trade, high-tech exports from the Silicon Valley area accounted for almost one-third of the nation's high-technology exports.

AT&T Park, home of the San Francisco Giants major league baseball team, was completed in 2000. The 42,000-seat stadium cost $306 million. The city offers excellent convention facilities with its Moscone Center, where a third building, Moscone West, was completed in 2003, bringing exhibit space to 770,000 square feet. The center was named for Mayor George Moscone, who championed controversial causes and who was murdered in office in 1978, along with gay activist Harvey Milk.

The Fine Arts Museums of San Francisco include the de Young, which is the city's oldest museum, and the Legion of Honor, a beautiful Beaux-arts museum which is home to Rodin's *Thinker*. In 2005, the de Young Museum reopened in a new building in Golden Gate Park, replacing an earlier structure damaged by the 1989 earthquake.

Also damaged in that quake was the main facility of the California Academy of Sciences, which oversees the Steinhart Aquarium, the Morrison Planetarium and the Natural History Museum. And a new facility by architect Renzo Piano, designed to be seismically safe and environmentally friendly, will open in 2008.

San Francisco is known as the "Air-Conditioned City" with cool pleasant summers and mild winters. It has greater climatic variability than any other urban area of the same size in the country. Sea fogs and associated low stratus clouds are most common in the summertime, when it is not unusual to see perched on the Golden Gate Bridge a low cloud illuminated by the sun.

Rankings

General Rankings

- San Francisco was ranked #107 out of 331 metro areas in *Cities Ranked & Rated*. Criteria: cost of living; climate; crime; transportation; economy and jobs; education; arts and culture; health and healthcare; leisure. *Cities Ranked & Rated, 1st Edition, 2004*

- San Francisco was selected as one of "America's Top 100 Places to Live" by Relocate-America.com. Nominations were accepted throughout the year for cities and towns considered to be "great places to live." The nominations, along with key data regarding education, employment, economy, crime, parks, recreation and housing were reviewed, rated and judged by the Relocate-America.com editorial staff. *Relocate-America.com, "Relocate America's Top 100 Places to Live in 2006"*

- San Francisco was selected as one of the "Top Cities for Recent Grads" by eGrad.com. The city ranked #3. Criteria: eGrad.com conducted a nationwide survey in which a representative sample of recent graduates commented on the pros and cons of their new towns. Topics ranged from affordability, to housing, to employment, to general satisfaction. *eGrad.com, "Top Cities for Recent Grads 2004"*

- San Francisco was selected as one of the top places to live in the U.S. according to Harris Interactive. The city ranked #2 out of 10. Criteria: 3,685 U.S. adults were polled as to where they would choose to live if they could live anywhere in the country. *Harris Interactive, September 6, 2006*

- San Francisco was selected as one of "America's Best Places to Live" by monstermoving.com. The top 10 cities were selected based on the fact that they appear repeatedly on other publications' "Top Cities" lists. *www.monstermoving.com, February 26, 2004*

- San Francisco was selected as one of the "50 Best Places to Live" by *Men's Journal*. The city ranked #3 in the "Best Adventure Cities" category. Criteria: proximity to national parks, rock climbing, surfing, biking, skiing, and other active-pursuit options. *Men's Journal, April 2007*

- Mercer Human Resources Consulting ranked 215 cities worldwide in terms of overall quality of life. San Francisco ranked #28. Criteria: political, social, economic, and socio-cultural factors; medical and health considerations; schools and education; public services and transportation; recreation; consumer goods; housing; and natural environment. *Mercer Human Resources Consulting, April 3, 2006*

- San Francisco appeared on *Travel & Leisure's* list of the ten best cities in the continental U.S. and Canada. The city was ranked #2. Criteria: activities/attractions; culture/arts; restaurants/food; people; and value. *Travel & Leisure, "The World's Best Awards 2006"*

- *Condé Nast Traveler* polled nearly 28,000 readers for travel satisfaction. American cities were ranked based on the following criteria: friendliness; ambiance; culture/sites; restaurants; lodging; and shopping. San Francisco appeared in the top 10, ranking #1. *Condé Nast Traveler, Readers' Choice Awards 2006*

- San Francisco was selected as one of the "Best Places to Live" by MSN House & Home. The city appeared in the best big city category. Criteria: lively economy; diverse cultural amenities; and abundant recreational activities. *Houseandhome.msn.com, "Best Places to Live," September 2003*

Business/Finance Rankings

- San Francisco was selected as one of the best places to start and grow a company by *Entrepreneur* and the National Policy Research Council. The San Francisco metro area ranked #28 out of 50 large metro areas. Criteria: business formation and growth (firms started four to 14 years ago that still employ at least 5 people and experienced rapid growth over the last four years). *Entrepreneur/National Policy Research Council, "Hot Cities for Entrepreneurs," September 2006*

■ The San Francisco metro area was selected one of America's "Top 10 Knowledge Worker Metros." The area ranked #8. Criteria: degree holders (bachelors, masters, professional, and Ph.D.) as a percent of the workforce; science and engineering workers as a percent of the workforce; number of patents issued; number and type of colleges in each metro area. *Expansion Management, April 2006*

■ Intel, in partnership with Sperling's BestPlaces, ranked the 80 "Best Cities for Teleworking" in America. The San Francisco metro area ranked #5 among extra large metro areas. The study identifies cities that hold the greatest potential for teleworking based on a host of factors including typical commuting times, fuel prices, availability of broadband Internet access and percentage of the population in telework friendly jobs. The study also factored in extreme climate and natural hazards. *Intel, "Best Cities for Teleworking," March 30, 2006*

■ San Francisco was identified as one of "The Most Inventive Towns in America". The city ranked #12. Criteria: places with the most patents overall, combining those of large companies and individual inventors. *The Wall Street Journal, July 22-23, 2006*

■ San Francisco was selected as one of 20 cities in North America that is doing its part to host green conventions by providing renewable energy, intelligent recycling programs, transportation that minimizes usage of fossil fuels, and plenty of parkland. The city was ranked #2. *Meetings and Conventions, "Natural Choices," August 2006*

■ San Francisco was selected as one of the four best U.S. cities for real estate investment. The city ranked #4. *Association of Foreign Investors in Real Estate, AFIRE Foreign Investment Survey 2006*

■ The San Francisco metro area appeared on the Milken Institute "2005 Best Performing Cities" index. Rank: #173 out of 200 large metro areas. Criteria: job growth; wage and salary growth; high-tech output growth. *Milken Institute, "2005 Best Performing Cities," February 2006*

■ The San Francisco metro area was selected as one of "The Best Cities for Doing Business in America." *Inc.* magazine measured employment growth in 393 regions using the following criteria: recent growth trend; mid-term growth; long-term trend; and current year growth. The San Francisco metro area ranked #60 among large metro areas and #358 overall. *Inc., May 2006*

■ The San Francisco metro area was selected as one of "The Top 20 Boom Towns in America." *Business 2.0* magazine and econometric research firm Global Insight compared 319 metropolitan areas in the U.S. and ranked the 61 with populations over 1 million. Criteria: a weighted formula that includes forecast growth rates in sectors that contain the economy's 10 most skilled occupational clusters; the prevalence of college degrees in the local workforce; median salary. The area ranked #7 among large metro areas. *Business 2.0 Magazine, March 2004*

■ San Francisco was identified as one of the 100 "Most Unwired Cities" in the U.S. The area ranked #2 out of the 100 largest metro areas in the U.S. Criteria: number of public and commercial wireless access points (hotspots); airports with wireless Internet access; broadband availability; local wireless networks; and wireless email devices. *Intel, "Most Unwired Cities Survey," June 7, 2005*

■ San Francisco was ranked #3 out of 125 regions worldwide in terms of its "Knowledge Competitiveness Index." The index attempts to measure the knowledge-based development taking place throughout the world and is based on 19 measures of economic performance that indicate a region's ability to translate its knowledge capacity into economic value. *Robert Huggins Associates, World Knowledge Competitiveness Index 2005*

■ *Forbes* ranked the 200 most populous metro areas in the U.S. in terms of the "Best Places for Business and Careers." The San Francisco metro area was ranked #175. Criteria: business costs (labor, energy, tax and office space expenses); living costs (housing, transportation, food and other household expenditures); education levels of the work force; job growth; income growth; migration trends; crime rates; and culture/leisure. *Forbes, April 23, 2007*

- Mercer Human Resources Consulting ranked 50 urban areas worldwide in terms of cost-of-living. San Francisco ranked #50 (the lower the ranking, the higher the cost-of-living). The survey measured the comparative cost of over 200 items (i.e. housing, food, clothing, household goods, transportation, and entertainment) in each location. *Mercer Human Resources Consulting, "Cost of Living Survey 2005"*

- *Fortune* ranked the 100 largest metro areas in the U.S. in terms of projected median home price change in 2006. The San Francisco metro area ranked #83. *Fortune, "The Top 100: Is the Party Over?" December 26, 2005*

- San Francisco was identified as one of the "Most Overpriced Places in the U.S." The area ranked #7 out of the nations 150 largest metro areas. Criteria: job growth; income growth; cost of living; and housing affordability. *Forbes.com, "Most Overpriced Places in the U.S. 2005"*

- San Francisco was identified as one of the top 10 richest major cities in the U.S. The city ranked #3. Criteria: 2004 median household income. *Forbes, "Richest Cities in the U.S.," October 27, 2005*

Health/Environment Rankings

- *Reader's Digest* ranked the 50 largest metro areas in the U.S. in terms of how "clean" they are. The San Francisco metro area ranked #5. Criteria: air quality; water quality; toxic industrial pollution; Superfund sites; and sanitation. *Reader's Digest, "The 50 Cleanest (and Dirtiest) Cities in America," July 2005*

- The San Francisco metro area appeared in *Country Home's* "2007 Best Green Places Report". The area ranked #19. Criteria included: air and watershed quality; miles of mass transit; green power; number of farmer's markets, organic producers and groceries. *Country Home, "2007 Best Green Places Report," April 2007*

- Wyeth Consumer Healthcare, in partnership with Sperling's BestPlaces, ranked the nation's 50 most populous metro areas in terms of five key health factors. The San Francisco metro area ranked #3. Criteria: physical activity, health status, nutrition, lifestyle pursuits; and mental wellness. *Wyeth Consumer Healthcare, "Centrum Healthiest Cities Study," April 19, 2005*

- HealthGrades identified the 10 best cities for nursing home care in the U.S. San Francisco ranked #6. Criteria: proportion of facilities that had four or more actual harm violations from health or complaint surveys in the last four years. *www.HealthGrades.com, "Best and Worst Cities for Nursing Home Care," March 16, 2004*

- HealthGrades surveyed over 41,000 individuals on doctor satisfaction and ranked the 20 largest metro areas based on the highest "definitely yes" responses to the question "Do you trust the physician to make decisions/recommendations that are in your best interest?" The San Francisco metro area ranked #20. *HealthGrades.com, "Top Cities in Doctor-Trust," September 7, 2006*

- The American Podiatric Medical Association and *Prevention* magazine ranked America's 100 most populated cities based on fitness-walker friendliness. The best cities have safe streets, beautiful places to walk, mild weather and good air quality. San Francisco ranked #3. *Prevention, "The Best Walking Cities of 2007," April 2007; American Podiatric Medical Association, "2007 Best Fitness-Walking Cities"*

- San Francisco was selected as one of "The Top 10 Greenest Cities" in the U.S." Criteria: cities that are obsessed with clean air and clean water, renewable energy, reliable city buses, trams, streetcars and subways, a growing number of parks, greenbelts, farmer's markets, and opportunities for community involvement. *Homestore.com, "The Top 10 Greenest Cities," April 2006*

- San Francisco was selected as one of "greenest" cities in the U.S. Criteria: good water- and air-quality; efficient use of resources; renewable energy leadership; accessible and reliable public transportation; green building practices; number of parks and greenbelts; access to locally-grown fresh food through farmers' markets and community supported agriculture groups; and affordability. *The Green Guide Institute, "The Top 10 Green Cities in the U.S.: 2005," April 19, 2005*

- San Francisco was selected as one of the 25 fittest cities in America by *Men's Fitness Online.* It ranked #7 out of America's 50 largest cities. Criteria: gyms/sporting goods; nutrition; exercise/sports; overweight/sedentary; junk food; alcohol; smoking; television; air and water quality; climate; geography; commute time; parks/open space; recreation facilities; health care; motivation; civic legislation and leadership. *Men's Fitness Online, America's Fittest/Fattest Cities 2006*

- San Francisco was identified as a "2007 Asthma Capital." The area ranked #91 out of the nation's 100 largest metropolitan areas. Twelve factors were used to identify the most challenging places to live for people with asthma: estimated prevalence; self-reported prevalence; crude death rate for asthma; annual pollen score; annual air quality; public smoking laws; number of board-certified asthma specialists; school inhaler access laws; rescue medication use; controller medication use; uninsured rate; poverty rate. *Asthma and Allergy Foundation of America, "2007 Asthma Capitals"*

- San Francisco was identified as a "Spring Allergy Capital." The area ranked #27 out of 100. Three groups of factors were used to identify the most severe cities for people with allergies during the spring season: annual pollen levels; medicine utilization; access to board-certified allergists. *Asthma and Allergy Foundation of America, "2007 Spring Allergy Capital Rankings"*

- San Francisco was identified as a "Fall Allergy Capital." The area ranked #74 out of 100. Three groups of factors were used to identify the most severe cities for people with allergies during the fall season: annual pollen levels; medicine utilization; access to board-certified allergists. *Asthma and Allergy Foundation of America, "2006 Fall Allergy Capital Rankings"*

- San Francisco was selected as one of "America's Healthiest Cities" by *Natural Health* magazine. The city was ranked #1 out of the 50 largest urban areas in the U.S. Twenty-six criteria in the following four categories were examined: whether the city boasts natural offerings; how well the city promotes its residents' physical health; whether the city offers a healthy environment; how well the city fosters a sense of community. *Natural Health, April 2003*

- *Men's Health* ranked the nation's largest 100 cities in terms of the *Best (and Worst) Cities for Men.* San Francisco was ranked #6. Criteria: 24 statistical parameters of long life in the categories of health, quality of life, and fitness. *Men's Health, January/February 2007*

- *Men's Health* ranked 100 U.S. cities in terms of the quality of their tap water. San Francisco was ranked #21 and received a grade of B. Criteria: levels of total coliform bacteria, arsenic, lead, total trihalomethanes (linked to cancer), and halo-acetic acids, plus the number of EPA water-system violations from 1995 to 2005. *Men's Health, March 2007*

- Ortho-McNeil Neurologics, in partnership with Sperling's BestPlaces, analyzed 110 metro areas and identified those U.S. cities with the highest prevalence of factors that are most commonly associated with migraine headaches. The San Francisco metro area ranked #96. Criteria: number of migraine-related drug prescriptions per capita; lifestyle factors that can contribute to migraines; environmental factors that can trigger migraines; and consumption of migraine-triggering foods. *Ortho-McNeil Neurologics, "America's Migraine Hot Spots," March 14, 2006*

- Sperling's BestPlaces ranked 331 metro areas and identified the most and least stressful U.S. cities. The San Francisco metro area ranked #42 out of the 100 largest metro areas (#1 = most stressful). Criteria: divorce rate; unemployment rate; violent and property crime; suicide rate; commute time; mental health; alcohol consumption; cloudy days. *www.BestPlaces.net, January 9, 2004*

- Sperling's BestPlaces "Sleep in the City" study ranked America's 50 most populated metropolitan areas in getting a good night's sleep. The San Francisco metro area ranked #9 in terms of the "Worst Cities for Sleep". Criteria: happiness index (derived from the responses to eight questions on the CDC BRFSS); number of days residents didn't get enough rest or sleep during the past month; average length of daily commute; divorce rates; unemployment rates. *www.BestPlaces.net, October 18, 2004*

■ Sperling's BestPlaces in partnership with Vistakon ranked the 100 largest metro areas and identified "America's 10 Best Cities for Comfortable Eyes." The San Francisco metro area ranked #6. Criteria: altitude; sunny days; wind; extreme temperatures; humidity; pollution; commute time; computer use. *Vistakon, "America's Best and Worst Cities for Comfortable Eyes," June 15, 2004*

■ HealthGrades evaluated the performance of America's 25 most populous metropolitan areas by measuring the outcomes of five of the highest volume and most widely studied procedures and diagnoses: coronary artery bypass graft surgery; percutaneus coronary interventions; acute myocardial infarction/heart attack in angioplasty-capable hospitals; congestive heart failure; and community acquired pneumonia. The San Francisco metro area ranked #22. *HealthGrades, "HealthGrades Hospital Quality in America Study," October 12, 2004*

■ San Francisco was selected as one of "America's Top 10 Low-Carb Cities" by *LowCarbiz Magazine*. Criteria: abundance of low-carb products; restaurants with low-carb menu items; health practitioners supportive of carb-cutting regimens; local culture generally conducive to exercise and health. *LowCarbiz Magazine, April 2004*

■ San Francisco was selected as one of "America's Pet Healthiest Cities" by Purina. The city ranked #5 out of 50. Criteria: veterinary services; environment; legislation; preventative care; obesity/body condition. *Purina Pet Institute, "America's Pet Healthiest Cities," May 20, 2003*

■ According to research conducted by Malibu Wellness of 100 major U.S. cities' local water quality reports, San Francisco was selected as a top-ranked color-friendly city in terms of hair color application and longevity. However, because high pH levels in the water do not allow hair cuticles to close down tightly, color does not last as long as in other top-ranked cities. Criteria: quantity of minerals found in the water supply (lower ppm is better for hair color); type of oxidizers such as chlorine; and pH levels. *Malibu Wellness, Wellness e-Letter, "Best & Worst Cities for Hair Color," February 2005*

Women/Minorities Rankings

■ San Francisco was ranked #7 out of 100 metro areas in *SELF Magazine's* ranking of "America's Best Places for Women." A panel of experts came up with nearly 40 criteria including: drinking and smoking rates; depression; unemployment; parks; crime; disease; healthcare insurance coverage; air quality; and commute times. *SELF Magazine, "America's Best Places for Women 2006," December 2006*

■ *Ladies Home Journal* ranked America's 200 largest cities based on the qualities women surveyed care about most. San Francisco ranked #24 out of 57 in the big city category (population over 300,000). Criteria: crime; lifestyle; education; jobs; health; child care; politics; and the economy. *Ladies Home Journal Online, "The Best Cities for Women 2002"*

■ San Francisco appeared on a list of the top 10 metro areas with the highest concentration of same-sex households. The area ranked #1. *Urban Institute Press, The Gay and Lesbian Atlas, May 2004*

■ San Francisco was profiled in the book *50 Fabulous Gay-Friendly Places to Live*. Criteria: an active gay community; positive gay health programs; youth outreach; gay-friendly politics; gay-owned and gay-friendly businesses; employment opportunities; fun nightlife; cultural opportunities; recreational opportunities; housing options. *50 Fabulous Gay-Friendly Places to Live, 2005*

■ San Francisco was selected as one of "America's Top Lesbian Cities" by Gay.com. The city ranked #3 out of 5. *Gay.com*

■ San Francisco appeared on a list of the top 10 metro areas with the highest concentration of gay male couples. The area ranked #1. *Urban Institute Press, The Gay and Lesbian Atlas, May 2004*

■ San Francisco appeared on a list of the top 10 metro areas with the highest concentration of lesbian couples. The area ranked #4. *Urban Institute Press, The Gay and Lesbian Atlas, May 2004*

- San Francisco appeared on a list of the top 10 metro areas with the highest concentration of African-American same-sex couples among all African-American households. The area ranked #1. *Urban Institute Press, The Gay and Lesbian Atlas, May 2004*

- San Francisco appeared on a list of the top 10 metro areas with the highest concentration of Hispanic same-sex couples among all Hispanic households. The area ranked #1. *Urban Institute Press, The Gay and Lesbian Atlas, May 2004*

- San Francisco was identified as one of the top 25 metropolitan statistical areas ranked by percentage of coupled households that are gay or lesbian." The area ranked #1. *Human Rights Campaign, "Gay and Lesbian Families in the United States: Same-Sex Unmarried Partner Households," August 1, 2001*

Seniors/Retirement Rankings

- Sperling'sBestPlacesinpartnershipwithBankersLife&CasualtyCompanydesigneda surveytoidentifythetop50metroareasintheU.S.thatofferthebestoverallqualitiesfor seniorliving.TheSanFranciscometroarearanked#3.Thefollowingcriteriawerestatistically weightedtoreflecttheneedsofthesenior population: health; disease; economics; social; environment;spiritual;transportation;housing;andcrime*Bankers Life & Casualty Company, "Best Cities for Seniors 2005"*

- A.G. Edwards ranked America's 500 top-performing communities based on their residents' personal savings and investing behavior. The San Francisco metro area ranked #9 with an index score of 116.42 (national average = 100.00). A dozen statistical factors were measured including: participation in retirement savings plans; personal debt levels; and home ownership. *A.G. Edwards, "2006 Nest Egg Index", September 6, 2006*

Children/Family Rankings

- The San Francisco metro area was selected as one of the "Best Cities for Relocating Families" by Worldwide ERC and Primacy Relocation. Criteria: tax rates; average home costs and home appreciation; ability to qualify for in-state tuition; service quality of local utilities; per-capita volunteerism; auto taxes; and quantity of fun, family-friendly events and venues. *Worldwide ERC and Primacy Relocation, "2006 Best Cities for Relocating Families"*

- *Zero Population Growth* ranked 100 cities in terms of children's health, safety, and economic well-being. San Francisco was ranked #4 out of 20 Major Cities (main city in a metro area with population of greater than 2.5 million) and was given a grade of A-. Criteria: total population and population growth; percent of population under 18 years of age; percent of births to teens; infant mortality rate; percent of eligible women not receiving Title X services; contraceptive equity indicator; percent of children without health insurance; percent of city residents over age 25 with a high-school diploma; ration of PopEd (Population Connection's Education Program) teachers trained; sexuality education indicator; proficiency in reading and math; percent of kids living in poverty; percent growth in urbanized land; violent crime rate; recycling. *Population Connection, Kid Friendly Cities: Report Card 2004*

- *Fit Pregnancy* magazine ranked the 50 best U.S. cities in which to have a baby. San Francisco was ranked #4. Criteria: fertility services; maternal and infant health risk; access to hospitals and doctors; safety; affordability; stroller friendliness; and birthing options. *Fit Pregnancy, February/March, 2006*

Safety Rankings

- Allstate ranked the 200 largest cities in America in terms of driver safety. San Francisco ranked #189. In addition, drivers were 53.8% more likely to have had an accident compared to the national average. Allstate researchers analyzed internal Property Damage reported claims over a two-year period (from January 2003 to December 2004) to ensure the findings would not be affected by external influences such as weather or road construction. A weighted average of the two-year numbers determined the annual percentages. The report defines an auto crash as any collision resulting in a property damage claim. *Allstate, "Allstate America's Best Drivers Report 2006," May 24, 2006*

- San Francisco was identified as one of the most dangerous large metro areas for pedestrians in the U.S. The area ranked #37 out of the nations 50 largest metro areas. Criteria: average yearly pedestrian fatalities per capita (for the years 2002 and 2003) adjusted for the number of walkers. *Surface Transportation Policy Project, "Mean Streets 2004"*

- *Ladies Home Journal* ranked America's 200 largest cities in terms of safety. San Francisco ranked #86 out of 200. Criteria: violent crimes; crimes against property; and rape. *Ladies Home Journal Online, "The Best Cities for Women 2002"*

Sports/Recreation Rankings

- The San Francisco metro area appeared on *The Sporting News* list of the "Best Sports Cities 2006". The area ranked #43 out of 99 cities in North America. To be included in the rankings, a city must have at least one of the following: NCAA Division I basketball team; Class A minor league baseball team; training camp for a major league or NFL team; NASCAR Nextel Cup race; NCAA Division I-A bowl game; PGA Tour tournament; Triple Crown horse race. Once a city qualifies, a 12-month snapshot is taken of the sports atmosphere, putting a heavy premium on regular-season won-lost records; playoff berths, bowl appearances and tournament bids; championships; applicable power ratings; quality of competition; overall fan fervor; sports atmosphere and fan knowledge; abundance of teams (quality over quantity); stadium/arena quality; ticket availability and prices; franchise ownership; and the marquee appeal of athletes. *SportingNews.com, "Best Sports Cities 2006," August 1, 2006*

- San Francisco was chosen as one of America's 25 best cities for running. The city was ranked #1. Criteria: number of running clubs per city; amount of land set aside for park usage; air quality; weather; crime rates; and results from a *Runner's World* poll in which readers ranked their favorite running cities. *Runner's World, "The 25 Best Running Cities in America," July 2005*

- San Francisco was selected as one of "10 Great Biking Cities." Editors at the Washington Post asked Adventure Cycling Association, a non-profit bike organization in Montana, and *Bicycling* magazine for their suggestions on the most bike-friendly cities in the country. *Washington Post, October 1, 2006*

- San Francisco was chosen as one of America's best cities for bicycling. The city ranked #0 in the large city category (population 500,000 to 1 million). Criteria: cycling-friendly statistics (number of bike lanes and routes, number of bike racks, city bike projects completed and planned; bike culture (number of bike commuters, popular clubs, cool cycling events, renowned bike shops); climate/geography (the quality of roads and trails for riding, and how frequently mother nature lets riders enjoy them). *Bicycling, March 2006*

- The San Francisco metro area was selected by *Cranium* as one of the "Top 50 Fun Cities" in America. The area ranked #12. Criteria includes: number of sports teams, restaurants, and dance performances; number of toy stores; city budget spent on recreation. *Cranium, November 4, 2003*

- *Golf Digest* ranked 330 metro areas in the U.S. in terms of golf. The San Francisco metro area was ranked #311. Criteria: access to golf; weather; value of golf; and quality of golf. *Golf Digest, "Metro Golf Rankings," August 2005*

Dating/Romance Rankings

- San Francisco was selected as one of the "Best Cities for Dating" by Love@AOL. The area ranked #8 out of 10. Criteria: Love@AOL surveyed singles and looked at a wide range of dating characteristics such as: are there lots of places to take a date; how easy is it to find a date; and when you're dating, do you acknowledge Valentine's Day? *Love@AOL, "2006 Dating Trends Survey: Best Cities for Dating"*

- The San Francisco metro area was selected as one of the "Top Ten U.S. Cities for Finding a Rich, Single Man" by Teasley, a Manhattan-based marketing consulting firm. The area ranked #1. Criteria: high single-male to single-female ratios and higher income to cost-of-living ratios. *Teasley, February 10, 2004*

■ The San Francisco metro area was selected as one of the "Best Cities for Relocating Singles" by Worldwide ERC and Primacy Relocation. The area ranked #16 out of the 100 largest metro areas in the U.S. Areas were selected based on the following criteria: Population Criteria (local percentage and growth trends of unmarried residents aged 25-34; male-female ratios; the number of newcomers to the area; diversity and density); Economic Criteria (job growth vs. unemployment rates; apartment rental costs; fee and occupancy rates for temporary housing and mini-storage; higher education costs, including in-state and out-of-state tuition requirements; vehicle tax rates and quality of service from utility providers); Quality-of-Life Criteria (level of per capita volunteering; quality and quantity of collegiate and professional sports with fun, fan-friendly venues; number of Starbucks and other coffee shops; quality or popularity of restaurants, nightspots, health clubs, and online dating; moderate climates with sustainable water supplies). *Worldwide ERC and Primacy Relocation, "2006 Best Cities for Relocating Singles," October 11, 2006*

■ San Francisco was selected as one of "America's Favorite Cities" in the "top cities for honeymoons" category. The city was ranked #3 out of 25. Criteria: *Travel + Leisure* magazine and AOL's Travel Channel conducted an online survey of nearly half a million AOL members to find out what travelers think about twenty-five American cities. Results shown above are according to visitors to the city, not locals. *Travel + Leisure and AOL's Travel Channel, "America's Favorite Cities," March 22, 2004*

■ *Forbes* ranked the 40 most populous metro areas in the U.S. in terms of the "Best Cities for Singles." The San Francisco metro area was ranked #4. Criteria: number of singles; cost of living alone; nightlife; culture; job growth; coolness; and online dating. *Forbes.com, July 25, 2006*

■ Sperling's BestPlaces in partnership with AXE Deodorant Bodyspray ranked 80 metro areas and identified "America's Best (and Worst) Cities for Dating." The San Francisco metro area ranked #38. Criteria: percentage of singles ages 18-24; population density; dating venues per capita. *AXE Deodorant Bodyspray, "America's Best (and Worst) Cities for Dating," May, 2004*

■ The San Francisco metro area was selected as one of the "10 Best Cities for Singles" by AOL CityGuide. The area ranked #6 out of 10.Criteria: over 300 cities were evaluated based on the quantity and quality of places for singles to meet other singles, such as bars and restaurants, cultural and sporting events, and online personals. *AOL CityGuide, "10 Best Cities for Singles," February 12, 2004*

Culture/Performing Arts Rankings

■ San Francisco was selected as one of "The Top Ten Cities that Rock." The city was ranked #10. Criteria: overall music scene; retail music stores; live music venues. *Esquire, March 2004*

■ San Francisco was selected as one of "America's Top 25 Arts Destinations." The city ranked #4 in the big city (population 500,000 and over) category. Criteria: readers' top choices for arts travel destinations based on the richness and variety of visual arts sites, activities and events. *American Style, June 2006*

■ Scarborough Research, a leading market research firm, identified the top local markets for rock concert attendance. The San Francisco DMA (Designated Market Area) ranked in the top 25 with 19% of consumers, 18 years old and over, reporting that they have attended a rock concert during the past year. *Scarborough Research, Scarborough USA+ 2003 Release 2*

Miscellaneous Rankings

■ San Francisco was determined to be one of America's smartest cities. The city ranked #2 in the large city category (200,000+ adults 25 years and older). Criteria: the editors rated the collective brainpower of U.S communities based on the educational attainment of its residents. *American City Business Journals, www.bizjournals.com, June 12, 2006*

- San Francisco was selected as one of the "Top 100 Sweatiest Summer Cities". The city was ranked #100. The ranking was based on the average male/female height/weight, average high temperature, and average relative humidity levels for 2002 in each of the cities during June, July and August. The sweat level was analyzed based on the assumption that the individual was walking for one hour. *Procter & Gamble, Old Spice, June 18, 2003*

- Avis Rent-A-Car and Motorola, in partnership with Sperling's BestPlaces, ranked the nation's 75 most populous metro areas in terms of how difficult they are to navigate. The San Francisco metro area ranked #3 with #1 being the most challenging. Criteria: street layouts; overall design and layout; travel time index; percent of congested freeway and street lane miles; bodies of water; complexity of directions needed to travel from major airports to city center; annual delay per person; days of snow exceeding 1.5 inches; and days of rain exceeding 0.5 inch. *Avis Rent-A-Car and Motorola, "America's Most Challenging Cities to Navigate," August 3, 2004*

- San Francisco was selected as one of America's "20 Meanest Cities" by the National Coalition for the Homeless and The National Law Center on Homelessness & Poverty. The city was ranked #11. Criteria: the number of anti-homeless laws; the enforcement of those laws and severities of penalties; the general political climate towards homeless people; local advocate support for the meanest designation; the city's history of criminalization measures; and the existence of pending or recently enacted criminalization legislation. *National Coalition for the Homeless and The National Law Center on Homelessness & Poverty, "A Dream Denied: The Criminalization of Homelessness in U.S. Cities," January 2006*

- The San Francisco metro area appeared on *Forbes* list of "America's Drunkest Cities". The area ranked #20. Criteria: 35 of the largest continental U.S. metro areas were chosen based on availability of data and geographic diversity. Each metro was ranked in five areas: state laws; drinkers; heavy drinkers; binge drinkers; and alcoholism. *Forbes.com, "America's Drunkest Cities," August 22, 2006*

- The San Francisco metro area was identified one of "America's Smartest Cities" by *Forbes*. The area ranked #5. Criteria: 200 of the largest U.S. metro areas were ranked based on the percentage of the population age 25 and over with at least a bachelor's degree. *Forbes.com, "America's Smartest Cities," December 15, 2006*

- San Francisco appeared on ApartmentRatings.com "Top Cities for Renters List 2006". The area ranked #134 out of 138. Criteria: renter satisfaction; affordability; and vacancy. *ApartmentRatings.com, "Top Cities for Renters List 2006"*

- San Francisco was selected as one of "America's Best Vegetarian-Friendly Large Cities." The city was ranked #3. *www.peta.org, April 2006*

- San Francisco was selected as one of "America's Favorite Cities" in the "cities with the most attractive people" category. The city was ranked #3 out of 25. Criteria: *Travel + Leisure* magazine and AOL's Travel Channel conducted an online survey of nearly half a million AOL members to find out what travelers think about twenty-five American cities. Results shown above are according to visitors to the city, not locals. *Travel + Leisure and AOL's Travel Channel, "America's Favorite Cities," March 22, 2004*

- San Francisco was selected as one of "America's Favorite Cities" in the "top cities for shopping" category. The city was ranked #3 out of 25. Criteria: *Travel + Leisure* magazine and AOL's Travel Channel conducted an online survey of nearly half a million AOL members to find out what travelers think about twenty-five American cities. Results shown above are according to visitors to the city, not locals. *Travel + Leisure and AOL's Travel Channel, "America's Favorite Cities," March 22, 2004*

- San Francisco was selected as one of "America's Favorite Cities" in the "top cities for dining out" category. The city was ranked #2 out of 25. Criteria: *Travel + Leisure* magazine and AOL's Travel Channel conducted an online survey of nearly half a million AOL members to find out what travelers think about twenty-five American cities. Results shown above are according to visitors to the city, not locals. *Travel + Leisure and AOL's Travel Channel, "America's Favorite Cities," March 22, 2004*

- Sperling's BestPlaces in partnership with Pep Boys ranked 77 metro areas and identified "America's Most Drivable Cities." The San Francisco metro area ranked #76. Criteria: climate; road roughness; urban mobility; gas prices. *Pep Boys, "America's Most Drivable Cities," April 9, 2003*

- San Francisco was ranked #1 out of 268 metro areas in terms of its Creativity Index. The Creativity Index is a mix of four equally weighted factors: the Creative Class (scientists, engineers, architects, designers, writers, artists, musicians, or any profession where creativity is a key factor) share of the workforce; innovation, measured as patents per capita; high-tech industry, using the Milken Institute's Tech Pole Index; and diversity, measured by the Gay Index (a reasonable proxy for an areas' openness to different kinds of people and ideas). *The Rise of the Creative Class, 2002*

- San Francisco was selected as one of "America's Most Literate Cities." The city ranked #9 out of the 70 largest U.S. cities. Criteria: number of booksellers; library resources; Internet resources; educational attainment; periodical publishing resources; newspaper circulation. *Central Connecticut State University, "America's Most Literate Cities 2006"*

- San Francisco was identified as one of the "Most Liberal Places in America" by ePodunk. Criteria: individual contributions to PACs; election returns; gay households; local government resolutions opposing combat in Iraq; local officials performing gay marriages; Congressional District voting history *www.ePodunk.com, January 3, 2005*

- State Farm Insurance, in partnership with Sperling's BestPlaces, analyzed several key factors that contribute to overall family preparedness. The San Francisco metro area ranked #29 out of the nation's 50 most populous metro areas. Criteria: quality of life; life insurance coverage; and investments. *State Farm Life Insurance, "Fiscally Fit Cities Report," July 20, 2004*

- Scarborough Research, a leading market research firm, identified the top local markets for reality television. The San Francisco DMA (Designated Market Area) ranked in the top 10 with 26% of consumers reporting that they "typically watch" reality-dating, reality-talent, or reality- adventure television shows. *Scarborough Research, Scarborough USA+ 2004 Release 1*

- Scarborough Research, a leading market research firm, identified the top local markets for coffee bar patronage. The San Francisco DMA (Designated Market Area) ranked in the top 10 with 26% of adults reporting that they have used any coffee house/bar during the past 30 days. *Scarborough Research, Scarborough USA+ 2004 Release 1*

Business Environment

CITY FINANCES

City Government Finances

Component	2003-2004 ($000)	2003-2004 ($ per capita)
Total Revenues	8,595,792	11,250
Total Expenditures	7,222,105	9,452
Debt Outstanding	8,153,482	10,671
Cash and Securities	8,382,004	10,971

Source: U.S Census Bureau, Government Finances 2003-2004

City Government Revenue by Source

Source	2003-2004 ($000)	2003-2004 ($ per capita)
General Revenue		
From Federal Government	381,450	499
From State Government	1,368,062	1,791
From Local Governments	651,795	853
Taxes		
Property	761,594	997
Sales	526,710	689
Personal Income	0	0
License	0	0
Charges	1,348,961	1,766
Liquor Store	0	0
Utility	477,216	625
Employee Retirement	1,916,854	2,509
Other	1,163,150	1,522

Source: U.S Census Bureau, Government Finances 2003-2004

City Government Expenditures by Function

Function	2003-2004 ($000)	2003-2004 ($ per capita)	2003-2004 (%)
General Expenditures			
Airports	589,800	772	8.2
Corrections	138,136	181	1.9
Education	104,183	136	1.4
Fire Protection	201,072	263	2.8
Governmental Administration	294,537	385	4.1
Health	687,650	900	9.5
Highways	146,964	192	2.0
Hospitals	623,284	816	8.6
Housing and Community Development	183,918	241	2.5
Interest on General Debt	610,010	798	8.4
Libraries	52,786	69	0.7
Parking	78,707	103	1.1
Parks and Recreation	114,833	150	1.6
Police Protection	351,466	460	4.9
Public Welfare	415,375	544	5.8
Sewerage	208,644	273	2.9
Solid Waste Management	87,419	114	1.2
Liquor Store	0	0	0.0
Utility	1,129,499	1,478	15.6
Employee Retirement	496,383	650	6.9
Other	707,439	926	9.8

Source: U.S Census Bureau, Government Finances 2003-2004

Municipal Bond Ratings

Area	Moody's
City	Aaa

Source: Mergent Bond Record, January 2007 (unless noted otherwise)

DEMOGRAPHICS

Population Growth

Area	1990 Census	2000 Census	2006 Estimate	2011 Projection	Population Growth (%)	
					1990-2000	2000-2011
City	723,959	776,733	750,596	746,548	7.3	-3.9
MSA[1]	3,686,592	4,123,740	4,184,673	4,270,050	11.9	3.5
U.S.	248,709,873	281,421,906	298,021,266	312,383,955	13.2	11.0

Note: (1) Metropolitan Statistical Area - see Appendix B for areas included
Source: Claritas, Inc.

Number of Households and Average Household Size

Area	2006 Estimate	2006 Average Household Size
City	318,072	2.36
MSA[1]	1,555,486	2.69
U.S.	112,267,302	2.65

Note: (1) Metropolitan Statistical Area - see Appendix B for areas included
Source: Claritas, Inc.

Race and Ethnicity

Area	White Alone[2]	Black Alone[2]	Asian Alone[2]	Other Race Alone[2]	Hispanic[3]
City	48.4	7.1	33.1	11.4	14.0
MSA[1]	53.9	8.8	21.6	15.7	19.5
U.S.	73.3	12.4	4.2	10.1	14.5

Note: Figures are 2006 estimates; (1) Metropolitan Statistical Area - see Appendix B for areas included
(2) Alone is defined as not being in combination with one or more other races; (3) May be of any race.
Source: Claritas, Inc.

Segregation

City		MSA[1]	
Index[2]	Rank[3]	Index[2]	Rank[4]
62.2	42	65.6	94

Note: Figures are based on an analysis of Census 2000 data; (1) Metropolitan Statistical Area - see Appendix A for areas included; (2) White/Black Dissimilarity Index—the most commonly used measure of segregation between two groups, reflecting their relative distributions across neighborhoods within a city or metropolitan area. It can range in value from 0, indicating complete integration, to 100, indicating complete segregation; (3) Ranges from 1 (most segregated) to 100 (least segregated) and includes all the cities in this book; (4) Ranges from 1 (most segregated) to 318 (least segregated) and includes 318 metropolitan areas.
Source: www.CensusScope.org

Ancestry

Area	German	Irish[2]	English	American	Italian	Polish	French[3]	Scottish
City	7.7	8.9	6.1	1.6	5.0	1.8	2.3	1.8
MSA[1]	9.7	10.1	7.8	2.1	6.8	1.9	2.7	2.1
U.S.	15.2	10.9	8.7	7.3	5.6	3.2	3.0	1.7

Note: Figures include multiple ancestry (e.g. if a person reported being Irish and Italian, they were included in both columns); (1) Metropolitan Statistical Area - see Appendix A for areas included; (2) Includes Celtic; (3) Includes Alsatian but excludes Basque
Source: Census 2000, Summary File 3

Foreign-Born Population

Area	Percent of Population Born in							
	Any Foreign Country	Europe	Asia	Africa	Oceania[2]	Canada	Mexico	Latin America[3]
City	36.8	5.1	22.6	0.4	0.4	0.5	3.0	4.9
MSA[1]	32.1	4.6	16.6	0.4	0.7	0.6	4.7	4.6
U.S.	11.1	1.7	2.9	0.3	0.1	0.3	3.3	2.5

Note: (1) Metropolitan Statistical Area - see Appendix A for areas included; (2) Includes Australia, New Zealand subregion, Melanesia, Micronesia, Polynesia, and Oceania n.e.c; (3) Includes Central America (excluding Mexico), South America, and the Caribbean.
Source: Census 2000, Summary File 3

Marriage Status

Area	Never Married	Now Married (excluding Separated)	Separated	Widowed	Divorced
City	44.8	38.6	1.9	6.1	8.6
MSA[1]	35.8	47.1	1.8	6.1	9.3
U.S.	27.1	54.4	2.2	6.6	9.7

Note: Figures are percentages and cover the population 15 years of age and older;
(1) Metropolitan Statistical Area - see Appendix A for areas included
Source: Census 2000, Summary File 3

Age Distribution

Area	Percent of Population						
	Under Age 5	Age 5 to 17	Age 18 to 34	Age 35 to 49	Age 50 to 64	Age 65 to 79	80 Years and Over
City	4.0	10.4	32.1	25.0	14.6	10.0	3.8
MSA[1]	5.1	13.5	26.7	25.6	15.8	9.6	3.6
U.S.	6.8	18.9	23.7	23.5	14.8	9.2	3.2

Note: (1) Metropolitan Statistical Area - see Appendix A for areas included
Source: Census 2000, Summary File 3

Male/Female Ratio

Area	Males	Females	Males per 100 Females
City	381,372	369,224	103.3
MSA[1]	2,072,695	2,111,978	98.1
U.S.	146,712,712	151,308,554	97.0

Note: Figures are 2006 estimates; (1) Metropolitan Statistical Area -
see Appendix B for areas included
Source: Claritas, Inc.

Religion

Area	Catholic	Southern Baptist	United Methodist	ELCA[1]	LDS[2]	Presbyterian Church USA	Jewish Est.	Muslim Est.
County	23.3	0.4	1.7	0.2	0.2	0.5	6.4	2.9
U.S.	22.0	7.1	3.7	1.8	1.5	1.1	2.2	0.6

Note: Figures are the number of adherents as a percentage of the total population; Adherents are defined as all members, including full members, their children and the estimated number of other participants who are not considered members (e.g. the baptized, those not confirmed, those regularly attending services, etc.);
(1) Evangelical Lutheran Church in America; (2) The Church of Jesus Christ of Latter Day Saints
Source: Reprinted with permission from Religious Congregations and Membership in the United States 2000 (Nashville, Glenmary Research Center, 2002) Copyright Association of Statisticians of American Religious Bodies. All rights reserved.

ECONOMY

Gross Metropolitan Product

Area	2002	2003	2004	2005	2005 Rank[2]
MSA[1]	186.1	190.8	201.5	213.5	9

Note: Figures are in billions of dollars; (1) San Francisco-Oakland-Fremont, CA Metropolitan Statistical Area - see Appendix A for areas included; (2) Rank ranges from 1 to 361
Source: The U.S. Conference of Mayors, "U.S. Metro Economies: GMP - The Engines of America's Growth," January 2007

Economic Growth

Area	1995 GMP	2005 GMP	Average Annual Growth Rate	Growth Rate Rank[2]
MSA[1]	129.6	213.5	5.1	209

Note: Figures are in billions of dollars; GMP = Gross Metropolitan Product; (1) San Francisco-Oakland-Fremont, CA Metropolitan Statistical Area - see Appendix A for areas included; (2) Rank ranges from 1 to 361
Source: The U.S. Conference of Mayors, "U.S. Metro Economies: GMP - The Engines of America's Growth," January 2007

INCOME

Per Capita/Median/Average Income

Area	Per Capita ($)	Median Household ($)	Average Household ($)
City	40,769	67,024	94,966
MSA[1]	36,175	70,806	96,333
U.S.	25,129	48,775	65,849

Note: Figures are 2006 estimates; (1) Metropolitan Statistical Area - see Appendix B for areas included
Source: Claritas, Inc.

Household Income Distribution

Area	Percent of Households Earning							
	Under $15,000	$15,000 -24,999	$25,000 -34,999	$35,000 -49,999	$50,000 -74,999	$75,000 -99,000	$100,000 -149,999	$150,000 and up
City	12.4	7.5	7.3	11.6	16.5	12.4	16.2	16.1
MSA[1]	9.2	6.9	7.3	11.9	17.6	13.9	17.5	15.7
U.S.	13.3	11.0	11.3	15.7	19.5	11.8	11.0	6.4

Note: Figures are 2006 estimates; (1) Metropolitan Statistical Area - see Appendix B for areas included
Source: Claritas, Inc.

Poverty Rates by Age

Area	All Ages	Under 5 Years Old	5 to 17 Years Old	18 to 64 Years Old	65 Years and Over
City	11.3	0.5	1.5	7.9	1.4
MSA[1]	8.4	0.5	1.3	5.7	1.0
U.S.	12.4	1.2	3.0	6.9	1.2

Note: Figures are percent of population with income in 1999 below poverty level and only include population for whom poverty status is determined; (1) Metropolitan Statistical Area - see Appendix A for areas included
Source: Census 2000, Summary File 3

Personal Bankruptcy Filing Rate

Area	2003	2004	2005
San Francisco County	2.73	2.55	4.05
U.S.	5.57	5.31	6.88

Note: Numbers are per 1,000 population and include Chapter 7 and Chapter 13 filings
Source: Federal Deposit Insurance Corporation (FDIC), Regional Economic Conditions (RECON), 3/24/2006

EMPLOYMENT

Labor Force and Employment

Area	Civilian Labor Force			Workers Employed		
	Dec. 2005	Dec. 2006	% Chg.	Dec. 2005	Dec. 2006	% Chg.
City	422,324	427,973	1.3	404,691	411,536	1.7
MD[1]	919,312	932,195	1.4	884,278	899,235	1.7
U.S.	149,874,000	152,571,000	1.8	142,918,000	146,081,000	2.2

Note: Data is not seasonally adjusted and covers workers 16 years of age and older;
(1) Metropolitan Division - see Appendix B for areas included
Source: Bureau of Labor Statistics, http://stats.bls.gov

Unemployment Rate

Area	2006											
	Jan.	Feb.	Mar.	Apr.	May	Jun.	Jul.	Aug.	Sep.	Oct.	Nov.	Dec.
City	4.7	4.7	4.4	4.2	4.1	4.6	4.7	4.5	4.1	3.8	4.0	3.8
MD[1]	4.3	4.3	4.1	3.9	3.8	4.3	4.3	4.1	3.8	3.5	3.7	3.5
U.S.	5.1	5.1	4.8	4.5	4.4	4.8	5.0	4.6	4.4	4.1	4.3	4.3

Note: Data is not seasonally adjusted and covers workers 16 years of age and older; All figures are
percentages; (1) Metropolitan Division - see Appendix B for areas included
Source: Bureau of Labor Statistics, http://stats.bls.gov

Employment by Occupation

Occupation Classification	City (%)	MSA[1] (%)	U.S. (%)
Sales and Office	25.6	26.1	26.7
Professional and Related	28.4	26.5	20.2
Service	14.3	13.7	14.9
Production, Transportation, and Material Moving	7.5	7.5	14.6
Management, Business, and Financial	20.0	20.2	13.5
Construction, Extraction, and Maintenance	4.2	5.8	9.4
Farming, Forestry, and Fishing	0.1	0.2	0.7

Note: Figures cover employed civilians 16 years of age and older;
(1) Metropolitan Statistical Area - see Appendix A for areas included
Source: Census 2000, Summary File 3

Employment by Industry

Sector	MSA[1] Number of Employees	MSA[1] Percent of Total	U.S. Percent of Total
Government	132,900	13.5	16.3
Education and Health Services	106,200	10.8	13.2
Professional and Business Services	195,600	19.9	12.9
Retail Trade	100,900	10.3	11.5
Manufacturing	44,300	4.5	10.2
Leisure and Hospitality	121,700	12.4	9.5
Financial Activities	90,400	9.2	6.1
Construction	43,500	4.4	5.5
Wholesale Trade	26,800	2.7	4.3
Other Services	38,200	3.9	3.9
Transportation and Utilities	43,100	4.4	3.7
Information	39,000	4.0	2.2
Natural Resources and Mining	300	<0.1	0.5

Note: Figures cover non-farm employment as of December 2006 and are not seasonally adjusted;
(1) Metropolitan Statistical Area - see Appendix B for areas included
Source: Bureau of Labor Statistics, http://stats.bls.gov

Occupations with Greatest Projected Employment Growth: 2002 - 2012

Occupation[1]	2002 Employment	2012 Projected Employment	Numeric Employment Change	Percent Employment Change
Retail Salespersons	435,400	513,200	77,800	17.9
Postsecondary Teachers	154,500	217,700	63,200	40.9
Combined Food Preparation and Serving Workers, Including Fast Food	215,100	277,300	62,200	28.9
Cashiers	358,800	420,700	61,900	17.3
Registered Nurses	201,600	258,400	56,800	28.2
Waiters and Waitresses	214,000	264,900	50,900	23.8
Customer Service Representatives	197,500	244,900	47,400	24.0
Office Clerks, General	400,300	446,500	46,200	11.5
General and Operations Managers	224,000	267,000	43,000	19.2
Teacher Assistants	179,600	222,300	42,700	23.8

Note: Projections cover California; (1) Sorted by numeric employment change
Source: www.projectionscentral.com, State Occupational Projections, 2002-2012 Long-Term Projections

Fastest Growing Occupations: 2002 - 2012

Occupation[1]	2002 Employment	2012 Projected Employment	Numeric Employment Change	Percent Employment Change
Physical Therapist Aides	4,200	6,800	2,600	61.9
Dental Hygienists	16,600	26,200	9,600	57.8
Dental Assistants	42,700	67,100	24,400	57.1
Tapers	9,200	14,400	5,200	56.5
Drywall and Ceiling Tile Installers	26,800	41,800	15,000	56.0
Tile and Marble Setters	8,600	13,400	4,800	55.8
Network Systems and Data Communications Analysts	20,300	31,600	11,300	55.7
Physical Therapist Assistants	3,900	6,000	2,100	53.8
Fitness Trainers and Aerobics Instructors	24,000	35,700	11,700	48.8
Self-Enrichment Education Teachers	24,200	35,800	11,600	47.9

Note: Projections cover California; (1) Sorted by percent employment change and excludes occupations with numeric employment change less than 1500
Source: www.projectionscentral.com, State Occupational Projections, 2002-2012 Long-Term Projections

Average Wages

Occupation	$/Hr.	Occupation	$/Hr.
Accountants and Auditors	32.01	Maids and Housekeeping Cleaners	12.53
Automotive Mechanics	24.36	Maintenance and Repair Workers	20.97
Bookkeepers	18.99	Marketing Managers	61.07
Carpenters	24.70	Nuclear Medicine Technologists	39.17
Cashiers	10.98	Nurses, Licensed Practical	25.05
Clerks, General Office	14.08	Nurses, Registered	38.64
Clerks, Receptionists/Information	14.25	Nursing Aides/Orderlies/Attendants	15.48
Clerks, Shipping/Receiving	14.79	Packers and Packagers, Hand	8.98
Computer Programmers	41.65	Physical Therapists	35.03
Computer Support Specialists	28.99	Postal Service Mail Carriers	22.65
Computer Systems Analysts	39.38	Real Estate Brokers	72.33
Cooks, Restaurant	12.10	Retail Salespersons	12.71
Dentists	n/a	Sales Reps., Exc. Tech./Scientific	32.32
Electrical Engineers	43.32	Sales Reps., Tech./Scientific	36.86
Electricians	32.98	Secretaries, Exc. Legal/Med./Exec.	18.45
Financial Managers	57.88	Security Guards	12.49
First-Line Supervisors/Mgrs., Sales	19.64	Surgeons	70.48
Food Preparation Workers	10.16	Teacher Assistants	15.00
General and Operations Managers	56.87	Teachers, Elementary School	26.30
Hairdressers/Cosmetologists	16.07	Teachers, Secondary School	29.00
Internists	76.80	Telemarketers	14.63
Janitors and Cleaners	11.98	Truck Drivers, Heavy/Tractor-Trailer	19.82
Landscaping/Groundskeeping Workers	15.47	Truck Drivers, Light/Delivery Svcs.	15.06
Lawyers	64.24	Waiters and Waitresses	9.04

Note: Wage data is for May 2005 and covers the San Francisco-San Mateo-Redwood City, CA Metropolitan Division - see Appendix B for areas included. Hourly wages for elementary/secondary school teachers and teacher assistants were calculated by the editors from annual wage data assuming a 40 hour work week; n/a not available.
Source: Bureau of Labor Statistics, May 2005 Metro Area Occupational Employment and Wage Estimates

RESIDENTIAL REAL ESTATE

Building Permits

Area	Single-Family			Multi-Family			Total		
	2005	2006p	Pct. Chg.	2005	2006p	Pct. Chg.	2005	2006p	Pct. Chg.
City	51	95	86.3	2,487	2,303	-7.4	2,538	2,398	-5.5
U.S.	1,682,000	1,380,000	-18.0	473,300	457,300	-3.4	2,155,300	1,837,300	-14.8

Note: (p) preliminary; figures represent new, privately-owned housing units authorized (unadjusted data); All permit data are based on estimates with imputation; U.S. figures are based on the new 20,000-place series.
Source: U.S. Census Bureau, Manufacturing, Mining, and Construction Statistics

Homeownership and Housing Vacancies

Area	Homeownership Rate[2] (%)			Rental Vacancy Rate[3] (%)			Homeowner Vacancy Rate[4] (%)		
	2004	2005	2006	2004	2005	2006	2004	2005	2006
MSA[1]	n/a	57.8	59.4	n/a	8.0	6.9	n/a	1.6	2.4
U.S.	69.0	68.9	68.8	10.2	9.8	9.7	1.7	1.9	2.4

Note: Comparable 2004 data was not available due to changes in metropolitan area definitions; (1) Metropolitan Statistical Area - see Appendix B for areas included; (2) The proportion of households that are owners; (3) The proportion of the rental inventory that is vacant for rent; (4) The proportion of the homeowner inventory that is vacant for sale; n/a not available
Source: U.S. Census Bureau, Housing Vacancies and Homeownership Annual Statistics: 2006

TAXES

State Corporate Income Tax Rates

State	Rate (%)	Number of Brackets	Low Bracket (Under $)	High Bracket (Over $)
California	8.84	1	na	na

Note: Tax rates as of December 31, 2006; na not applicable; 10.84% on financial institutions. Minimum tax is $800. The tax rate on S-Corporations is 1.5% (3.5% for financial S-Corporations).
Source: Tax Foundation, www.taxfoundation.org

State Individual Income Tax Rates

State	Federal Deductibility	Marginal Rate (%)	Number of Brackets	Low Bracket (Under $)	High Bracket (Over $)
California	No	1.0-10.3 (p)(r)	7	0	1,000,000

Note: Tax rates as of December 31, 2006; Brackets apply to single taxpayers and married people filing separately; na not applicable; (p) California's $1,000,000 bracket not doubled for married taxpayers; (r) Indexed for Inflation.
Source: Tax Foundation, www.taxfoundation.org

Various State and Local Tax Rates

State and Local Sales and Use (%)	State Sales and Use (%)	Gasoline ($/gal.)	Cigarette ($/pack)	Spirits ($/gal.)	Table Wine ($/gal.)	Beer ($/gal.)
8.5	6.25	0.192 (m)	0.87	3.3	0.20	0.20

Note: Tax rates as of December 31, 2006; (m) Additional cents per gallon taxes added this year that were not included in previous years' tables.
Source: Tax Foundation, www.taxfoundation.org; The Sales Tax Clearinghouse, www.thestc.com

State Tax Burdens

Area	Combined State and Local Tax Burden		Combined Federal, State and Local Tax Burden	
	Percent	Rank	Percent	Rank
California	10.9	15	32.7	9
U.S. Average	10.6	-	31.6	-

Note: Figures are for 2006 and measure taxes as a percentage of income
Source: Tax Foundation, www.taxfoundation.org

Internal Revenue Service Tax Audits

IRS District	Percent of Returns Audited				
	1996	1997	1998	1999	2000
Northern California	1.24	1.34	1.08	0.60	0.41
U.S.	0.66	0.61	0.46	0.31	0.20

Note: Figures cover IRS district audits of federal income tax returns filed by individuals. Geographic data on district audits after the year 2000 are being withheld by the IRS. TRAC is challenging this policy.
Source: Syracuse University, Transactional Records Access Clearinghouse (TRAC), "Odds of IRS District Tax Audit 2000"

COMMERCIAL REAL ESTATE

Office Market

Market Area	Inventory (sq. ft.)	Vacant (sq. ft.)	Vac. Rate (%)	Under Constr. (sq. ft.)	Asking Rent ($/sf)	
					Class A	Class B
San Francisco	62,596,121	8,078,487	12.9	1,354,476	39.48	29.18

Source: Grubb & Ellis, Office Markets Trends, 4th Quarter 2006

COMMERCIAL UTILITIES

Typical Monthly Electric Bills

Area	Commercial Service ($/month)		Industrial Service ($/month)	
	3 kW demand 1,000 kWh	40 kW demand 14,000 kWh	1,000 kW demand 200,000 kWh	50,000 kW demand 15,000,000 kWh
City	187	2,316	28,589	1,738,772
Average[1]	123	1,413	22,000	1,306,315

Note: Based on total rates in effect July 1, 2006; (1) average based on 196 utilities
Source: Edison Electric Institute, Typical Bills and Average Rates Report, Summer 2006

TRANSPORTATION

Means of Transportation to Work

Area	Car/Truck/Van		Public Transportation			Bicycle	Walked	Other Means	Worked at Home
	Drove Alone	Car-pooled	Bus	Subway	Railroad				
City	40.5	10.8	21.4	6.0	0.6	2.0	9.4	4.8	4.6
MSA[1]	56.5	11.6	12.3	3.7	0.9	1.4	5.6	3.1	4.8
U.S.	75.7	12.2	2.5	1.5	0.5	0.4	2.9	1.0	3.3

Note: Figures are percentages and cover workers 16 years of age and older;
(1) Metropolitan Statistical Area - see Appendix A for areas included
Source: Census 2000, Summary File 3

Travel Time to Work

Area	Less Than 15 Minutes	15 to 29 Minutes	30 to 44 Minutes	45 to 59 Minutes	60 Minutes or More
City	14.9	35.0	27.4	11.3	11.4
MSA[1]	19.1	34.5	25.0	10.8	10.6
U.S.	29.4	36.1	19.1	7.4	8.0

Note: Figures are percentages and include workers 16 years old and over; (1) Metropolitan Statistical Area - see Appendix A for areas included
Source: Census 2000, Summary File 3

Travel Time Index

Area	1982	1993	2002	2003
Urban Area[1]	1.21	1.44	1.55	1.54
Average[2]	1.12	1.28	1.37	1.37

Note: Travel Time Index - The ratio of travel time in the peak period to the travel time at free-flow conditions. A value of 1.35 indicates a 20-minute free-flow trip takes 27 minutes in the peak. Free-flow speeds (60 mph on freeways and 35 mph on principal arterials) are used as the comparison threshold; (1) Covers the San Francisco-Oakland, CA urban area; (2) average of 85 urban areas
Source: Texas Transportation Institute, The 2005 Urban Mobility Report, May 2005

Public Transportation

Agency name:	San Francisco Municipal Railway (MUNI)
Vehicle type:	Bus
Average fleet age in years:	7.6
No. operated in max. service:	396
Vehicle type:	Trolleybus
Average fleet age in years:	8.1
No. operated in max. service:	259
Vehicle type:	Light rail
Average fleet age in years:	19.5
No. operated in max. service:	127
Vehicle type:	Cable car
Average fleet age in years:	95.8
No. operated in max. service:	26
Agency name:	San Francisco Bay Area Rapid Transit District (BART)
Vehicle type:	Heavy rail
Average fleet age in years:	7.7
No. operated in max. service:	522
Agency name:	San Francisco Paratransit (ATC)
Vehicle type:	Demand response
Average fleet age in years:	5.2
No. operated in max. service:	1,514

Source: Federal Transit Administration, National Transit Database, 2005

Air Transportation

Airport name and code:	San Francisco International (SFO)
Domestic service (2006)	
Passenger airlines[1]:	28
Passenger enplanements:	12,184,603
Freight carriers[2]:	32
Freight (lbs.):	246,064,596
International service (2005)	
Passenger airlines[1]:	37
Passenger enplanements:	3,893,481
Freight carriers[2]:	32
Freight (lbs.):	284,577,207

Note: (1) Includes all major, minor and commuter airlines that carried at least one passenger during the year; (2) Includes all airlines and freight carriers that transported at least one pound of freight during the year
Source: Bureau of Transportation Statistics, The Intermodal Transportation Database, Air Carriers: T-100 International Market, 2004; Bureau of Transportation Statistics, The Intermodal Transportation Database, Air Carriers: T-100 Domestic Market, 2005

Other Transportation Statistics

Interstate highways:	I-80
Amtrak service:	Bus connection
Major waterways/ports:	Port of San Francisco

Source: Editor & Publisher Market Guide, 2006; Amtrak.com; Rand McNally 2006 Road Atlas

BUSINESSES

Major Business Headquarters

Company Name	2006 Rankings	
	Fortune[1]	Forbes[2]
Bechtel	-	9
Charles Schwab	418	-
Gap	139	-
Levi Strauss	484	53
Lucasfilm	-	257
McKesson	16	-
PG&E Corp.	200	-
Swinerton	-	193
Wells Fargo	46	-
Wilbur-Ellis	-	224

Note: (1) Fortune 500 - companies that produce a 10-K are ranked 1 to 500 based on 2005 revenue; (2) Forbes Largest Private Companies - all private companies with at least $1 billion in annual revenue are ranked 1 to 394; companies listed are located in the city; dashes indicate no ranking
Source: Fortune, April 17, 2006; Forbes, November 9, 2006

Best Companies to Work For

Adobe Systems; Bain & Co; Bingham McCutchen; Bright Horizons; Marriott International; Nordstrom; Russell Investment Group, headquartered in San Francisco, are among the "100 Best Companies to Work For." Criteria: More than 105,000 employees from 446 companies responded to a 57-question survey created by the Great Place to Work Institute. Two-thirds of a company's score is based on the survey, which covers topics such as attitudes towards management, job satisfaction, and camaraderie. The remaining third of the score comes from each company's responses to the Institute's Culture Audit, which includes detailed questions about demographic makeup, pay and benefits programs, and open-ended questions about the company's people-management philosophy, internal communications, opportunities, compensation practices, diversity programs, etc. Any company that is at least seven years old and has a minimum of 1,000 U.S. employees is eligible. The top three U.S. locations are shown for companies with more than one location. *Fortune, "100 Best Companies to Work for 2007," January 22, 2007*

Wells Fargo & Co, headquartered in San Francisco, is among the "100 Best Companies for Working Mothers." Criteria: workforce profile; compensation; child care; flexibility; time off and leaves; family-friendly programs; and company culture. This year *Working Mother* gave particular weight to flex and time off. *Working Mother, "100 Best Companies," October 2006*

Levi Strauss; PG&E Corporation; Union Bank of California, headquartered in San Francisco, are among the "50 Best Companies for Minorities." Criteria: 1,200 of the largest U.S employers were surveyed. Those companies were analyzed on information such as the number of minorities in the workforce and on the board, and the rate at which minority employees are hired (and fired). *Fortune, "50 Best Companies for Minorities," June 28, 2004*

Charles Schwab & Co, headquartered in San Francisco, is among the "100 Best Places to Work in IT." To qualify, companies, both public and private, had to have 2005 revenue of $250 million or greater and employ a minimum of 500 people in the U.S., with a minimum of 100 IT employees in the U.S. Companies were selected based on average salary and bonus increases, the percentage of IT employees receiving promotions, IT staff turnover rates, training and development, and the percentage of women and minorities in IT staff and management positions. In addition, information was collected on how the organizations reward outstanding performance, how their retention programs are structured and what benefits they offer. *Computerworld, "100 Best Places to Work in IT 2006," June 19, 2006*

Gap Inc, headquartered in San Francisco, is among the "Top 35 Companies for Executive Women." To be named to the NAFE Top 35, companies with a minimum of two women on the board complete a comprehensive application that focuses on the number of women in senior ranks (compared to men and to the company population), including questions about the programs and policies which support women's advancement. *National Association for Female Executives, "Top 35 Companies for Executive Women in 2007," March 7, 2006*

Fast-Growing Businesses

According to *Inc.*, San Francisco is home to seven of America's 500 fastest-growing private companies: **Calypso Technology; Headsets.com; LoopNet; Method Products; StarMine; StubHub; VerticalResponse**. Criteria: must be an independent, privately-held, U.S.

corporation, proprietorship or partnership; net sales of at least $600,000 in FY2002; four-year operating/sales history; holding companies, regulated banks, and utilities were excluded. *Inc., "America's 500 Fastest-Growing Private Companies," September 2006*

According to *Fortune*, San Francisco is home to one of America's 100 fastest-growing companies: **Building Materials Holding**. Companies were ranked based on earnings-per-share growth, revenue growth and total return over the previous three years. Criteria for inclusion: public companies with sales of at least $50 million. Companies that lost money in the most recent quarter, or ended in the red for the past four quarters as a whole, were not eligible. Limited partnerships and REITs were also not considered. *Fortune, "America's Fastest-Growing Companies," September 18, 2006*

According to Deloitte & Touche LLP, San Francisco is home to seven of North America's 500 fastest-growing high-technology companies: **Aptimus; LoopNet; MarketTools; Ninth House; ON24; StubHub; nCircle Network Security**. Companies are ranked by percentage growth in revenue over a five-year period. Criteria for inclusion: company must be headquartered within North America; company must own proprietary intellectual property or proprietary technology that contributes to a significant portion of the company's operating revenue or devotes a significant proportion of revenues to research and development of technology; company must have been in business for a minumum of five years with 2001 operating revenues of at least $50,000 USD or $75,000 CD and 2005 operating revenues of at least $5 million USD/CD. *Deloitte & Touche LLP, 2006 Technology Fast 500*

Women-Owned Businesses: 1997 and 2002

Year	All Firms		Firms with Paid Employees			
	Firms	Sales ($000)	Firms	Sales ($000)	Employees	Payroll ($000)
1997	25,426	4,055,266	4,965	3,418,020	28,083	791,324
2002	28,459	4,686,117	4,690	3,854,337	38,993	994,394

Note: Figures cover firms located in the city; Women-owned business are defined as firms in which women own 51% or more of the stock or equity of the company; (a) Withheld to avoid disclosing data for individual companies; (b) Withheld because estimate did not meet publication standards; n/a not available
Source: 1997 Economic Census, Survey of Minority- and Women-Owned Business Enterprises; 2002 Economic Census, Survey of Business Owners (released February 9, 2006)

Minority Business Opportunity

Four of the 500 largest Hispanic-owned companies in the U.S. are located in San Francisco. *Hispanic Business, "Hispanic Business 500," June 2006*

HOTELS

Hotels/Motels

Area	Hotels/Motels	Average Minimum Rates ($)		
		Tourist	First-Class	Deluxe
City	213	83	137	306

Source: OAG Travel Planner Online, Spring 2006

The San Francisco metro area is home to five of the top 187 hotels in the U.S. according to *Travel & Leisure*: **Campton Place** (#38); **Ritz-Carlton, San Francisco** (#48); **Four Seasons, San Francisco** (#58); **Mandarin Oriental, San Francisco** (#97); **Hotel Vitale** (#145). Criteria: service; location; rooms; food; and value. *Travel & Leisure, "The T+L 500, 2007"*

EVENT SITES

Stadiums, Arenas, and Auditoriums

Name	Capacity
3Com Park	63,000
Bill Graham Civic Auditorium	7,000
Fort Mason Center	4,500

Source: www.officialtravelguide.com; www.eventective.com; original research

Convention Centers

Name	Overall Space (sq. ft.)	Exhibit Space (sq. ft.)	Meeting Space (sq. ft.)	Meeting Rooms
Concourse Exhibition Center at Showplace Square	125,000	n/a	125,000	n/a
Moscone Convention Center	1,346,000	159,980	441,960	69

Note: n/a not available
Source: www.officialtravelguide.com; www.eventective.com; original research

Hotels/Conference Centers

Name	Guest Rooms	Exhibit Space (sq. ft.)	Meeting Space (sq. ft.)
Hilton San Francisco and Towers	2,046	110,000	110,000
Hyatt Regency San Francisco	805	17,064	67,000
San Francisco Conference Center	n/a	n/a	n/a
San Francisco Marriott	1,500	23,165	100,000
The Fairmont Hotel San Francisco	591	30,000	47,000

Note: n/a not available
Source: www.officialtravelguide.com; www.eventective.com; original research

Living Environment

COST OF LIVING

Cost of Living Index

Year	Composite Index	Groceries	Housing	Utilities	Trans-portation	Health Care	Misc. Goods/ Services
2004	178.2	134.6	308.7	109.1	127.3	120.2	120.0
2005	179.0	147.9	306.7	99.7	118.5	124.6	129.3
2006	171.2	143.6	284.5	90.9	114.5	124.4	135.4

Note: U.S. = 100
Source: The Council for Community and Economic Research (formerly ACCRA), Cost of Living Index, 2004, 2005 and 2006 4-Quarter Averages

HOUSING

House Price Index (HPI)

Area	National Ranking[2]	Quarterly Change (%)	One-Year Change (%)	Five-Year Change (%)
MD[1]	213	-1.19	2.06	58.13
U.S.[3]	-	1.12	5.87	55.21

Note: The HPI is a weighted repeat sales index. It measures average price changes in repeat sales or refinancings on the same properties. This information is obtained by reviewing repeat mortgage transactions on single-family properties whose mortgages have been purchased or securitized by Fannie Mae or Freddie Mac in January 1975; (1) Metropolitan Division - see Appendix B for areas included; (2) Rankings are based on annual percentage change for all metro areas containing at least 15,000 transactions over the last 10 years and ranges from 1 to 282; (3) figures based on a weighted division average; all figures are for the period ending December 31, 2006
Source: Office of Federal Housing Enterprise Oversight, House Price Index, March 1, 2007

House Price Valuations

Area	Q4 1999	Q4 2000	Q4 2001	Q4 2002	Q4 2003	Q4 2004	Q4 2005	Q4 2006
MSA[1]	-17.0	-9.0	-1.1	10.7	15.9	23.5	35.3	29.7

Note: Figures show the percentage of over- or under-valuation of single family homes relative to statistically normal house values (e.g. a value of 23.6 indicates that house values are 23.6% overvalued). Statistically normal house values are based on house prices, interest rates, household incomes, population densities, and any historical premiums or discounts metropolitan areas have exhibited over time; (1) Figures cover the Metropolitan Statistical Area - see Appendix B for areas included
Source: Global Insight/National City Corporation, House Prices in America, March 2007

Median Home Prices

Area	2004	2005	2006p	Percent Change 2005 to 2006
Metro Area[1]	641.7	715.7	736.8	2.9
U.S. Average	195.2	219.0	222.0	1.4

Note: Figures are median sales prices of existing single-family homes in thousands of dollars; (p) preliminary; n/a not available; (1) Covers the San Francisco-Oakland-Fremont, CA Metropolitan Statistical Area - see Appendix B for areas included
Source: National Association of Realtors, Metropolitan Area Prices, 4th Quarter 2006

Housing: Year Structure Built

Area	1990 -2000	1980 -1989	1970 -1979	1960 -1969	1950 -1959	1940 -1949	Before 1940	Median Year
City	4.1	4.9	7.0	9.4	11.4	13.2	49.9	1940
MSA[1]	5.5	7.3	12.8	15.2	17.5	12.1	29.6	1955
U.S.	17.0	15.8	18.5	13.7	12.7	7.3	15.0	1971

Note: Figures are percentages; (1) Metropolitan Statistical Area - see Appendix A for areas included
Source: Census 2000, Summary File 3

Average New Home Price

Area	2004	2005	2006
City	799,158	868,419	871,443
U.S.	253,574	275,712	299,269

Note: Figures, in dollars, are based on a new home with 2,400 sq. ft. of living area on an 8,000 sq. ft. lot.
Source: The Council for Community and Economic Research (formerly ACCRA), Cost of Living Index, 2004, 2005 and 2006 4-Quarter Averages

Average Apartment Rent

Area	2004	2005	2006
City	2,020	2,040	1,995
U.S.	716	740	766

Note: Figures, in dollars per month, are based on an unfurnished two bedroom, 1-1/2 or 2 bath apartment, approximately 950 sq. ft. in size, excluding all utilities except water
Source: The Council for Community and Economic Research (formerly ACCRA), Cost of Living Index, 2004, 2005 and 2006 4-Quarter Averages

RESIDENTIAL UTILITIES

Average Residential Utility Costs

Area	All Electric ($/mth)	Part Electric ($/mth)	Other Energy ($/mth)	Phone ($/mth)
City	–	72.80	63.66	25.44
U.S.	136.00	76.53	90.52	25.87

Source: The Council for Community and Economic Research (formerly ACCRA), Cost of Living Index, 2006 4-Quarter Average

HEALTH

Average Health Care Costs

Area	Optometrist ($/visit)	Doctor ($/visit)	Dentist ($/visit)
City	105.09	103.96	86.58
U.S.	76.38	76.10	68.72

Note: Optometrist—based on a full vision eye exam for an established adult patient;
Doctor—based on a general practitioner's routine exam of an established patient;
Dentist—based on adult teeth cleaning and periodic oral exam.
Source: The Council for Community and Economic Research (formerly ACCRA), Cost of Living Index, 2006 4-Quarter Average

Mortality Rates

ICD-10 Sub-Chapter	ICD-10 Code	Age-Adjusted Death Rate per 100,000 population[1]	U.S. Age-Adjusted Death Rate per 100,000 population
Malignant neoplasms	C00-C97	165.9	185.8
Ischaemic heart diseases	I20-I25	113.4	150.2
Other forms of heart disease	I30-I51	25.5	50.8
Cerebrovascular diseases	I60-I69	53.7	50.0
Chronic lower respiratory diseases	J40-J47	26.1	41.1
Diabetes mellitus	E10-E14	16.0	24.5
Other degenerative diseases of the nervous system	G30-G31	13.5	22.3
Other external causes of accidental injury	W00-X59	18.6	21.2
Influenza and pneumonia	J10-J18	25.8	19.8
Hypertensive diseases	I10-I13	26.1	18.1

Note: ICD-10 = International Classification of Diseases 10th Revision; (1) Figures cover San Francisco County, CA
Source: Centers for Disease Control and Prevention, National Center for Health Statistics. Compressed Mortality File 1999-2004. CDC WONDER On-line Database, compiled from Compressed Mortality File 1999-2004 Series 20 No. 2J, 2007.

Health Risk Data

Item	Area[1] (%)	U.S. (%)
Adults who have been told they have high blood pressure	26.5	25.5
Adults who have been told they have high blood cholesterol	36.2	35.6
Adults who have been told they have diabetes[2]	7.0	7.3
Adults who have been told they have arthritis	22.1	27.0
Adults who have been told they currently have asthma	9.5	8.0
Adults who are current smokers	15.8	20.6

Note: (1) Figures cover the Metropolitan Statistical Area - see Appendix B for areas included; (2) Figures do not include pregnancy-related diabetes, pre-diabetes or borderline diabetes
Source: Centers for Disease Control and Prevention, Behaviorial Risk Factor Surveillance System, SMART: Selected Metropolitan/Micropolitan Area Trends, 2005

Distribution of Office-Based Physicians

Area	Total	Family/ General Practice	Specialties Medical	Specialties Surgical	Specialties Other
CMSA[1] (number)	17,058	1,764	6,722	3,668	4,904
CMSA[1] (rate per 10,000 pop.)	24.5	2.5	9.7	5.3	7.1
Metro Average[2] (rate per 10,000 pop.)	19.4	2.1	7.5	4.5	5.3

Note: Data as of December 31, 2004; (1) San Francisco-Oakland-San Jose, CA Consolidated Metropolitan Statistical Area includes the following counties: Alameda; Contra Costa; Marin; Napa; San Francisco; San Mateo; Santa Clara; Santa Cruz; Solano; Sonoma;
(2) Average of the 79 unique MSAs and CMSAs in this book
Source: American Medical Association, Physician Characteristics & Distribution in the U.S., 2006

Hospitals

San Francisco has the following hospitals: 9 general medical and surgical; 1 other specialty.
AHA Guide to the Healthcare Field 2007

According to *U.S. News*, the San Francisco metro area is home to one of the best hospitals in the U.S.: **University of California - San Francisco Medical Center**; *U.S. News Online, "America's Best Hospitals 2006"*

EDUCATION

Public School District Statistics

District Name	Schls	Pupils	Pupil/ Teacher Ratio	Minority Pupils[1] (%)	Free Lunch Eligible[2] (%)	IEP[3] (%)
San Francisco Unified	120	57,144	18.0	90.7	40.2	12.3

Note: Table includes regular local school districts with 2,000 or more students; (1) Percentage of students that are not white, non-Hispanic; (2) Percentage of students that are eligible for the free lunch program; (3) Percentage of students that have an Individualized Education Program.
Source: U.S. Department of Education, National Center for Education Statistics, Common Core of Data, Local Education Agency (School District) Universe Survey: School Year 2004-2005; U.S. Department of Education, National Center for Education Statistics, Common Core of Data, Public Elementary/Secondary School Universe Survey: School Year 2004-2005

Top Public High Schools

High School Name	Index[1]	Rank[1]	Subsidized Lunch (%)[2]	E&E (%)[3]
Gateway	1.210	1,011	22.0	21.0
George Washington	2.127	316	42.0	27.0
Lowell	4.462	26	31.0	90.8
Mission	1.283	930	55.3	n/a

Note: (1) Public schools are ranked according to a ratio that is the number of Advanced Placement and/or International Baccalaureate tests taken by all students at a school in 2005 divided by the number of graduating seniors. All of the schools on the list have an index of at least 1.000; they are in the top five percent of public schools measured this way. The rankings range from 1 to 1,236; (2) Percentage of students receiving federally subsidized meals; (3) E & E stands for equity and excellence percentage: the portion of all graduating seniors at a school that had at least one passing grade on one AP or IB test; (*) Gave just IB tests; (**) Gave both IB and AP tests. AP and IB participation are indicators of a school's efforts to get students to excel and prepare for college; n/a not available
Source: Newsweek Online, May 23, 2006

Educational Quality

School District	Education Quotient[1]	Graduate Outcome[2]	Community Index[3]	Resource Index[4]	Rating[5]
San Francisco Unified	36	34	60	49	Green

Note: Scores are national percentile rankings and range from 1 (worst) to 99 (best); (1) Combination of the Graduate Outcome, Community and Resource Indexes weighted to reflect the greater importance of the Graduate Outcome and Resource Index; (2) Based on graduation rates and college board scores (SAT/ACT); (3) Based on the surrounding community's level of affluence and adult education; (4) Based on teacher salaries, per-pupil expenditures and student-teacher ratios; (5) School districts receive one of five rankings: Gold Medal (top 16 percent of districts evaluated); Blue Ribbon (top third); Green Light (average); Yellow Light (bottom 25 percent); Red Light (bottom 10 percent).
Source: Expansion Management, "2007 Education Quotient," January 2007

Highest Level of Education

Area	Less than H.S.	H.S. Diploma	Some College, No Deg.	Associate Degree	Bachelors Degree	Masters Degree	Profess. School Degree	Doctorate Degree
City	19.0	14.0	16.9	5.6	28.4	10.1	4.5	1.7
MSA[1]	16.1	17.6	21.3	6.8	24.0	9.1	3.3	1.9
U.S.	19.4	28.4	21.2	6.4	15.7	5.9	2.0	1.0

Note: Figures are 2006 estimated percentages and cover persons age 25 and over; (1) Metropolitan Statistical Area - see Appendix B for areas included
Source: Claritas, Inc.

Educational Attainment by Race

Area	High School Graduate (%)					Bachelor's Degree (%)				
	Total	White	Black	Asian	Hisp.[2]	Total	White	Black	Asian	Hisp.[2]
City	81.2	91.7	76.1	67.3	62.5	45.0	59.3	18.1	31.8	20.3
MSA[1]	84.2	91.3	75.9	75.6	59.2	43.6	51.3	18.5	38.9	16.2
U.S.	80.4	83.6	72.3	80.4	52.4	24.4	26.1	14.3	44.1	10.4

Note: Figures shown cover persons 25 years old and over; (1) Metropolitan Statistical Area - see Appendix A for areas included; (2) people of Hispanic origin can be of any race
Source: Census 2000, Summary File 3

School Enrollment by Type

Area	Grades KG to 8				Grades 9 to 12			
	Public		Private		Public		Private	
	Enrollment	%	Enrollment	%	Enrollment	%	Enrollment	%
City	42,881	72.8	16,049	27.2	24,540	83.1	4,991	16.9
MSA[1]	132,872	78.0	37,427	22.0	64,080	83.2	12,973	16.8
U.S.	33,526,011	88.7	4,285,121	11.3	14,848,628	90.6	1,532,323	9.4

Note: Figures shown cover persons 3 years old and over; (1) Metropolitan Statistical Area - see Appendix A for areas included
Source: Census 2000, Summary File 3

School Enrollment by Race

Area	Grades KG to 8 (%)				Grades 9 to 12 (%)			
	White	Black	Asian	Hisp.[1]	White	Black	Asian	Hisp.[1]
City	28.6	12.6	38.9	21.5	26.9	11.3	40.8	23.6
MSA[2]	48.4	6.7	23.4	25.0	44.9	6.9	26.0	25.5
U.S.	68.5	15.5	3.3	16.8	68.8	15.5	3.8	15.7

Note: Figures shown cover persons 3 years old and over; (1) people of Hispanic origin can be of any race; (2) Metropolitan Statistical Area - see Appendix A for areas included
Source: Census 2000, Summary File 3

Average Salaries of Public School Teachers

District	2004-05		2005-06		Percent Change 2004-05 to 2005-06
	Dollars	Rank[1]	Dollars	Rank[1]	
CALIFORNIA	57,876	2	59,345	3	2.54
U.S. Average	47,674	-	49,109	-	3.01

Note: (1) State rank ranges from 1 to 51.
Source: National Education Association, Rankings & Estimates: Rankings of the States 2005 and Estimates of School Statistics 2006, November 2006

Higher Education

Four-Year Colleges			Two-Year Colleges			Medical Schools[1]	Law Schools[2]	Voc/ Tech[3]
Public	Private Non-profit	Private For-profit	Public	Private Non-profit	Private For-profit			
3	10	2	1	1	3	1	3	3

Note: Figures cover institutions located within the city limits; (1) includes schools accredited by the Liaison Committee on Medical Education and the American Osteopathic Association; (2) includes American Bar Association-accredited law schools; (3) includes all schools with programs that are less than 2 years
Source: National Center for Education Statistics, The Integrated Postsecondary Education System (IPEDS) Peer Analysis System, 2006; www.usnews.com, America's Best Graduate Schools 2008, Medical School Directory; www.usnews.com, America's Best Graduate Schools 2008, Law School Directory

PRESIDENTIAL ELECTION

2004 Presidential Election Results

Area	Bush	Kerry	Nader	Other
San Francisco County	15.2	83.0	0.4	1.3
U.S.	50.7	48.3	0.4	0.6

Note: Results are percentages and may not add to 100% due to rounding
Source: Dave Leip's Atlas of U.S. Presidential Elections, www.uselectionatlas.org

MAJOR EMPLOYERS

Major Employers

Company Name	Industry	Type of Site
California Pacific Medical Ctr	General medical and surgical hospitals	Headquarters
City College of San Francisco	Junior colleges	Headquarters
Dept of Public Health City An	Administration of public health programs	Single
Firemans Fund Insurance Co	Fire, marine, and casualty insurance	Headquarters
Franklin Templeton Services	Investment advice	Single
GapKids	Family clothing stores	Headquarters
Macys	Department stores	Headquarters
Municipal Railway	Local and suburban transit	Branch
Municipal Railway Dept	Transportation services, nec	Branch
Oracle	Prepackaged software	Headquarters
PG&E	Electric services	Headquarters
Police Dept	Police protection	Branch
Public Health Dept	General medical and surgical hospitals	Branch
Thermal Controls	Electronic connectors	Headquarters
UCSF Medical Center	General medical and surgical hospitals	Branch
US Post Office	U.S. Postal Service	Branch
Union Pacific Railroad Company	Railroads, line-haul operating	Branch

Note: Companies shown are located within the metropolitan area and have 2,200 or more employees; nec = not elsewhere classified.
Source: www.zapdata.com, January 2007

PUBLIC SAFETY

Crime Rate

Area	All Crimes	Violent Crimes				Property Crimes		
		Murder	Forcible Rape	Robbery	Aggrav. Assault	Burglary	Larceny -Theft	Motor Vehicle Theft
City	5,373.1	12.8	23.0	410.9	352.3	828.6	2,654.5	1,091.1
Suburbs[1]	3,009.8	3.5	22.3	93.1	195.1	516.2	1,799.5	380.1
Metro[2]	4,050.8	7.6	22.6	233.1	264.3	653.8	2,176.1	693.3
U.S.	3,899.0	5.6	31.7	140.7	291.1	726.7	2,286.3	416.7

Note: Figures are crimes per 100,000 population; (1) All areas within the metro area that are located outside the city limits; (2) Metropolitan Division - see Appendix B for areas included
Source: FBI Uniform Crime Reports, 2005

Hate Crimes

Area	Number of Quarters Reported	Bias Motivation				
		Race	Religion	Sexual Orientation	Ethnicity	Disability
City	4	34	10	47	12	1

Source: Federal Bureau of Investigation, Hate Crime Statistics 2005

RECREATION

Culture

Dance[1]	Theatre[1]	Instrumental Music[1]	Vocal Music[1]	Series/ Festivals	Museums	Zoos
23	25	12	12	31	30	1

Note: (1) number of professional perfoming groups
Source: The Grey House Performing Arts Directory, 2007; Official Museum Directory, 2007

Professional Sports Teams

Major League Baseball	National Basketball Association	National Football League	National Hockey League	Major League Soccer	Women's National Basketball Association
2	1	2	0	0	0

Note: Includes teams located in the San Francisco-Oakland metro area.
Source: www.sportsvenues.com, Listing of Venues by State/Province and City, 2006

MEDIA

Newspapers

Name	Target Audience	Frequency	Circulation
AsianWeek	Asian/General	Non-Daily	50,000
California Voice	General	Non-Daily	37,325
El Bohemio News	Hispanic/Religious	Non-Daily	60,000
El Latino	Hispanic	Non-Daily	40,000
El Mensajero	General/Hispanic	Non-Daily	60,000
El Tecolote	General/Hispanic	Non-Daily	10,000
Hokubei Mainichi	n/a	Daily	10,000
J. (The Jewish News Weekly of Northern California)	Jewish/Religious	Non-Daily	25,000
Korea Times - San Francisco Edition	n/a	Daily	25,000
The New Fillmore	General	Non-Daily	20,000
New Mission News	General	Non-Daily	18,000
Oakland Metro Reporter	Black	Non-Daily	32,645
Russian Life	Ethnic/General	Non-Daily	15,000
SF Weekly	Alternative/General	Non-Daily	125,000
The San Francisco Bay Guardian	Alternative/General	Non-Daily	153,000
San Francisco Chronicle	n/a	Daily	480,587
San Francisco Examiner	n/a	Daily	50,634
San Francisco Independent	General	Non-Daily	379,000
San Francisco Metro Reporter	Black	Non-Daily	22,325
San Jose/Peninsula Reporter	Black	Non-Daily	19,575
The Sun Reporter	Black	Non-Daily	16,000
Sunset Beacon	General	Non-Daily	25,000

Note: Includes newspapers whose offices are located in the city and whose circulations are 10,000 or more; n/a not available
Source: BurrellesLuce, MediaContacts Online, January 2006

Television Stations

Name	Ch.	Network(s)	Type	Ownership
KTVU	2	Fox	Commercial	Cox Enterprises Inc.
KRON	4	n/a	Commercial	Young Broadcasting Inc.
KPIX	5	CBS	Commercial	CBS
KGO	7	ABC	Commercial	n/a
KFWU	8	n/a	Commercial	Pappas Telecasting Companies
KTSF	8	n/a	Commercial	Lincoln Broadcasting Company
KQED	9	PBS	Public	KQED Inc.
KNTV	11	NBC	Commercial	NBC TV Stations Division
KDTV	14	Univision	Commercial	Univision Television Group
KCU	15	NBC/Telem.	Commercial	Telemundo Group Inc.
KBWB	20	WBN	Commercial	Granite Broadcasting Corporation
KRCB	22	PBS	Public	Rural California Broadcasting Corp.
KMTP	32	n/a	Public	Minority Television Project
KICU	36	n/a	Commercial	Cox Enterprises Inc.
KCNS	38	n/a	Commercial	Shop at Home Inc.
KTNC	42	n/a	Commercial	Pappas Telecasting Companies
KBHK	44	UPN	Commercial	United Television Inc.
KSTS	48	Telemundo	Commercial	Telemundo Group Inc.
KFTY	50	n/a	Commercial	Clear Channel Communications Inc.
KTEH	54	PBS	Public	KTEH Foundation
KCSM	60	PBS	Public	San Mateo County Community College District
KKPX	65	Pax	Commercial	Paxson Communications Corporation
KTLN	68	n/a	Non-comm.	North Bay Television Inc.

Note: Stations included cover the San Francisco-Oakland-San Jose DMA (Designated Market Area); n/a not available
BurrellesLuce, MediaContacts Online, January 2006

Major AM Radio Stations

Call Letters	Freq. (kHz)	Station Type	Target Audience	Station Format	Music Format
KSFO	560	n/a	General	News/Talk	n/a
KNBR	680	n/a	General	Music/Sports/Talk	n/a
KLVB	730	Non-Comm	Religious	Educational/Music	Christian
KCBS	740	n/a	General	Music/News/Sports/Talk	n/a
KGO	810	n/a	General	News/Talk	n/a
KNEW	910	Commercial	General	Music/News/Talk	80's
KABL	960	Commercial	General	Music	Easy Listening
KNBR	1050	n/a	General/Men	Music/News/Sports/Talk	n/a
KFAX	1100	n/a	General/Religious	Music/Talk	n/a
KZSJ	1120	Commercial	Asian	Ed/Music/News/Sports/Talk	Latin
KLOK	1170	Commercial	General/Hispanic	Music	Latin
KDYA	1190	Commercial	Black/General/Rel	Music/News/Talk	Gospel
KEBR	1210	Non-Comm	Religious	Educational/Music/News	Christian
KDAC	1230	n/a	General/Hispanic	Music	n/a
KLLK	1250	n/a	General/Hispanic	Music/News	n/a
KOIT	1260	Commercial	General	Music	Adult Contemp.
KAZA	1290	n/a	General/Hispanic	Music/Sports	n/a
KSRO	1350	n/a	General	News/Talk	n/a
KZSF	1370	Commercial	General/Hispanic	Music/Sports	Latin
KVTO	1400	Commercial	General	Music/News/Sports/Talk	International
KUKI	1400	n/a	General/Hispanic	Music	n/a
KVVN	1430	Commercial	General	Music/News/Sports	International
KVON	1440	n/a	General	News/Sports/Talk	n/a
KEST	1450	Commercial	General	Music/News	International
KRRS	1460	n/a	Hispanic	Music/News/Talk	n/a
KSJX	1500	Commercial	Asian	Music/News/Sports	Classical
KYCY	1550	n/a	General	Music/News/Sports/Talk	n/a
KLIV	1590	Commercial	General	News/Sports	n/a
KDIA	1640	Commercial	General	Talk	n/a

Note: Stations included cover the San Francisco-Oakland-San Jose DMA (Designated Market Area); n/a not available
Source: BurrellesLuce, MediaContacts Online, January 2006

Major FM Radio Stations

Call Letters	Freq. (mHz)	Station Type	Target Audience	Station Format	Music Format
KECG	88.1	Commercial	Hispanic	Ed/Music/News/Sports	Rhythm & Blues
KQED	88.5	n/a	General	Music/News/Talk	World Music
KLVR	91.9	n/a	Religious	Educational/Music	n/a
KSJO	92.3	n/a	General	Music/News/Talk	n/a
KFGY	92.9	n/a	General	Music	n/a
KPFA	94.1	Non-Comm	General	Educational/Music/News	Middle of the Rd.
KRZZ	96.3	Commercial	General	News	n/a
KLLC	97.3	n/a	General	Music/News/Sports	n/a
KISQ	98.1	Commercial	General	Music	Rhythm & Blues
KLVS	99.3	Non-Comm	Religious	Educational/Music	Christian
KNTI	99.5	n/a	General	Music/News	n/a
KIOI	101.3	Commercial	General	Music	80's
KMEL	106.1	n/a	General/Young Adult	Music	n/a
KEZR	106.5	Commercial	General	Music/Talk	Adult Contemp.
KEAR	106.9	Non-Comm	Christian/General	Music/Talk	Gospel

Note: Stations included cover the San Francisco-Oakland-San Jose DMA (Designated Market Area); n/a not available
BurrellesLuce, MediaContacts Online, January 2006

CLIMATE

Average and Extreme Temperatures

Temperature	Jan	Feb	Mar	Apr	May	Jun	Jul	Aug	Sep	Oct	Nov	Dec	Yr.
Extreme High (°F)	72	77	85	92	97	106	105	98	103	99	85	75	106
Average High (°F)	56	59	61	64	66	70	71	72	73	70	63	56	65
Average Temp. (°F)	49	52	53	56	58	61	63	63	64	61	55	50	57
Average Low (°F)	42	44	45	47	49	52	53	54	54	51	47	42	49
Extreme Low (°F)	26	30	31	36	39	43	44	45	41	37	31	24	24

Note: Figures cover the years 1948-1990
Source: National Climatic Data Center, International Station Meteorological Climate Summary, 9/96

Average Precipitation/Snowfall/Humidity

Precip./Humidity	Jan	Feb	Mar	Apr	May	Jun	Jul	Aug	Sep	Oct	Nov	Dec	Yr.
Avg. Precip. (in.)	4.3	3.1	2.9	1.4	0.3	0.1	Tr	Tr	0.2	1.0	2.5	3.4	19.3
Avg. Snowfall (in.)	Tr	Tr	Tr	0	0	0	0	0	0	0	0	Tr	Tr
Avg. Rel. Hum. 7am (%)	86	85	82	79	78	77	81	83	83	83	85	86	82
Avg. Rel. Hum. 4pm (%)	67	65	63	61	61	60	60	62	60	60	64	68	63

Note: Figures cover the years 1948-1990; Tr = Trace amounts (<0.05 in. of rain; <0.5 in. of snow)
Source: National Climatic Data Center, International Station Meteorological Climate Summary, 9/96

Weather Conditions

Temperature			Daytime Sky			Precipitation		
10°F & below	32°F & below	90°F & above	Clear	Partly cloudy	Cloudy	0.01 inch or more precip.	0.1 inch or more snow/ice	Thunder-storms
0	6	4	136	130	99	63	< 1	5

Note: Figures are average number of days per year and cover the years 1948-1990
Source: National Climatic Data Center, International Station Meteorological Climate Summary, 9/96

HAZARDOUS WASTE

Superfund Sites

San Francisco has one hazardous waste site on the EPA's Superfund Final National Priorities List: **Treasure Island Naval Station-Hunters Point Annex**. *U.S. Environmental Protection Agency, Final National Priorities List, March 20, 2007*

AIR & WATER QUALITY

Air Quality Index

Area	Percent of Days when Air Quality was...[2]				AQI Statistics	
	Good	Moderate	Unhealthy for Sensitive Groups	Unhealthy	Maximum	Median
MSA[1]	85.8	13.4	0.8	0.0	107	30

Note: The Air Quality Index (AQI) is an index for reporting daily air quality. EPA calculates the AQI for five major air pollutants regulated by the Clean Air Act: ground-level ozone, particle pollution (also known as particulate matter), carbon monoxide, sulfur dioxide, and nitrogen dioxide. The AQI runs from 0 to 500. The higher the AQI value, the greater the level of air pollution and the greater the health concern. There are six AQI categories: "Good" The AQI is between 0 and 50. Air quality is considered satisfactory; "Moderate" The AQI is between 51 and 100. Air quality is acceptable; "Unhealthy for Sensitive Groups" When AQI values are between 101 and 150, members of sensitive groups may experience health effects; "Unhealthy" When AQI values are between 151 and 200 everyone may begin to experience health effects; "Very Unhealthy" AQI values between 201 and 300 trigger a health alert; "Hazardous" AQI values over 300 trigger health warnings of emergency conditions; (1) Metropolitan Statistical Area - see Appendix A for areas included; (2) Based on 365 days with AQI data in 2005.
Source: U.S. Environmental Protection Agency, Air Quality Index Report, 2005

Air Quality Index Pollutants

Area	Percent of Days when AQI Pollutant was...[2]					
	Carbon Monoxide	Nitrogen Dioxide	Ozone	Sulfur Dioxide	Particulate Matter 2.5	Particulate Matter 10
MSA[1]	0.3	0.0	54.0	0.0	45.8	0.0

Note: The Air Quality Index (AQI) is an index for reporting daily air quality. EPA calculates the AQI for five major air pollutants regulated by the Clean Air Act: ground-level ozone, particle pollution (also known as particulate matter), carbon monoxide, sulfur dioxide, and nitrogen dioxide. The AQI runs from 0 to 500. The higher the AQI value, the greater the level of air pollution and the greater the health concern; (1) Metropolitan Statistical Area - see Appendix A for areas included; (2) Based on 365 days with AQI data in 2005.
Source: U.S. Environmental Protection Agency, Air Quality Index Report, 2005

Number of Days with Air Quality Index Values Greater than 100

Area	Trend Sites (11)								All Sites (26)
	1998	1999	2000	2001	2002	2003	2004	2005	2005
MSA[1]	0	2	3	5	1	0	0	0	2

Note: An AQI value greater than 100 indicates that air quality would have been in the unhealthful range on that day. Data from exceptional events are not included. These counts are presented in two ways. First, the counts are based on sites having an adequate record of monitoring data during the trend period (trend sites). These counts represent the relative change in the number of days with AQI values greater than 100. In the last column, the counts are based on all sites with data in the most recent year (because it is possible for a site to have data in the most recent year but not enough data to be a trend site); (1) Metropolitan Statistical Area - see Appendix A for areas included; n/a not available.
Source: U.S. Environmental Protection Agency, Air Trends Fact Book 2005

Maximum Pollutant Concentrations

	Particulate Matter 10 (ug/m^3)	Particulate Matter 2.5 (ug/m^3)	Ozone 1-hour (ppm)	Carbon Monoxide (ppm)	Sulfur Dioxide (ppm)	Nitrogen Dioxide (ppm)	Lead (ug/m^3)
MSA[1] Level	70	33	0.075	3	0.006	0.016	n/a
NAAQS[2]	150	65	0.125	9	0.140	0.053	1.50
Met NAAQS[2]	Yes	Yes	Yes	Yes	Yes	Yes	n/a

Note: Data from exceptional events are not included; (1) Metropolitan Statistical Area - see Appendix A for areas included; (2) National Ambient Air Quality Standards; n/a not available
Units: ppm = parts per million; ug/m^3 = micrograms per cubic meter
Source: U.S. Environmental Protection Agency, Air Trends Fact Book 2005

Watershed Health

The U.S. Environmental Protection Agency monitors the health of the aquatic resources for the nation's 2,000+ watersheds. **The San Francisco Bay watershed serves the San Francisco area and received an overall Index of Watershed Indicators (IWI) score of 2 (better quality - high vulnerability).** The IWI score is based on seven condition and nine vulnerability indicators. The overall IWI score ranges from 1 (best health) to 6 (worst health). The Condition Indicators include: designated use attainment, fish and wildlife consumption advisories, source water condition, contaminated sediments, ambient water quality, and wetlands loss index. The Vulnerability Indicators include: aquatic species at risk, conventional and toxic loads over permitted limits, urban and agricultural runoff potential, population change, hydrologic modification, estuarine pollution susceptibility, and air deposition. *Note: The IWI is no longer being updated by the U.S. EPA. Source: U.S. Environmental Protection Agency, Index of Watershed Indicators, October 26, 2001*

Drinking Water

Water System Name	Pop. Served	Primary Water Source Type	Number of Violations in 2006[a]		
			Health Based	Significant Monitoring	Monitoring
San Francisco Public Utilities	2,400,000	Purchased surface	None	None	None

Note: (a) Based on violation data from January 1, 2006 to December 31, 2006
Source: U.S. Environmental Protection Agency, Office of Ground Water and Drinking Water, Safe Drinking Water Information System (data extracted April 12, 2007)

San Francisco tap water is alkaline, very soft and fluoridated.
Editor & Publisher Market Guide, 2005

San Jose, California

Background

Like many cities in the valleys of northern California, San Jose is an abundant cornucopia of wine grapes and produce. Situated only seven miles from the southernmost tip of San Francisco Bay, San Jose is flanked by the Santa Cruz Mountains to the west, and the Mount Hamilton arm of the Diablo Range to the east. The Coyote and Guadalupe rivers gently cut through this landscape, carrying water only in the spring.

San Jose was founded on November 29, 1777, by Spanish colonizers, and can rightfully claim to be the oldest civic settlement in California. Like its present-day role, San Jose was established by the Spanish to be a produce and cattle supplier to the nearby communities and presidios of San Francisco and Monterey.

After U.S. troops wrested the territory of California from Mexican rule, San Jose became its state capital. At the same time, the city served as a supply base to gold prospectors.

Today, San Jose retains much of its history. As in the past, it is still a major shipping and processing center for agricultural produce. Also, San Jose produces some of the best table wines in the country. To remind its citizens of its Spanish heritage, a replica of the Mission of Santa Clara stands on the grounds of the University of Santa Clara.

Due to annexation of surrounding communities after World War II, the population of San Jose has increased more than tenfold. With the additional industries of NASA research, and electronic components and motors production to attract people to the area, San Jose is rapidly becoming a family-oriented community of housing developments and shopping malls.

During the 1990s, San Jose was home to more than half of Silicon Valley's leading semiconductor, networking, and telecommunications companies, giving it the nickname "Capital of Silicon Valley." The newly renovated downtown became headquarters for Adobe Systems, a major developer of computer software, Cisco Systems, e-Bay and BEA Systems.

In the new century, San Jose suffered from the downturn in electronics and computer industries, but the city has developed numerous strategies, including economic incentives and redevelopment programs to solve unemployment and ensure that the city remains economically healthy and grows into the future.

The HP Pavilion, home of the San Jose Sharks hockey team, is one of the most active venues for events in the world, selling the most tickets to non-sporting events of any venue in the United States.

San Jose enjoys a Mediterranean, or dry summer subtropical, climate. The rain that does fall comes mostly during the months of November through March. Severe winter storms with gale winds and heavy rain occur occasionally. The summer weather is dominated by night and morning stratus clouds along with sea breezes blowing from the cold waters of the bay. During the winter months fog is common, causing difficult flying conditions. Inversions causing pollution are not common during the summer months, but become more frequent during the fall and winter.

Rankings

General Rankings

■ San Jose was ranked #168 out of 331 metro areas in *Cities Ranked & Rated*. Criteria: cost of living; climate; crime; transportation; economy and jobs; education; arts and culture; health and healthcare; leisure. *Cities Ranked & Rated, 1st Edition, 2004*

■ San Jose was selected as one of the "50 Best Places to Live" by *Men's Journal*. The city ranked #2 in the "Healthiest Places" category. Criteria: illness rates; eating habits; medical resources available. *Men's Journal, April 2007*

■ San Jose was selected as one of "America's 30 Most Livable Communities" by the non-profit group, Partners for Livable Communities. Criteria: environmental quality; parkland; ability to train new workers; job market; education; and use of the arts for economic development. *Partners for Livable Communities, www.mostlivable.org, April 20, 2004*

Business/Finance Rankings

■ San Jose was selected as one of the best places to start and grow a company by *Entrepreneur* and the National Policy Research Council. The San Jose metro area ranked #28 out of 50 large metro areas. Criteria: business formation and growth (firms started four to 14 years ago that still employ at least 5 people and experienced rapid growth over the last four years). *Entrepreneur/National Policy Research Council, "Hot Cities for Entrepreneurs," September 2006*

■ The San Jose metro area was selected as one of "America's 50 Hottest Cities" for business relocations and expansions. Criteria: industry's most prominent site selection consultants were asked to list their top city choices for relocating and expanding manufacturing companies, taking into consideration such factors as the business climate, work force quality, operating costs, incentive programs, and the ease of working with local political and economic development officials. *Expansion Management, January-February 2007*

■ The San Jose metro area was selected one of America's "Top 10 Knowledge Worker Metros." The area ranked #7. Criteria: degree holders (bachelors, masters, professional, and Ph.D.) as a percent of the workforce; science and engineering workers as a percent of the workforce; number of patents issued; number and type of colleges in each metro area. *Expansion Management, April 2006*

■ Intel, in partnership with Sperling's BestPlaces, ranked the 80 "Best Cities for Teleworking" in America. The San Jose metro area ranked #1 among large metro areas. The study identifies cities that hold the greatest potential for teleworking based on a host of factors including typical commuting times, fuel prices, availability of broadband Internet access and percentage of the population in telework friendly jobs. The study also factored in extreme climate and natural hazards. *Intel, "Best Cities for Teleworking," March 30, 2006*

■ San Jose was identified as one of "The Most Inventive Towns in America". The city ranked #1. Criteria: places with the most patents overall, combining those of large companies and individual inventors. *The Wall Street Journal, July 22-23, 2006*

■ The San Jose metro area appeared on the Milken Institute "2005 Best Performing Cities" index. Rank: #185 out of 200 large metro areas. Criteria: job growth; wage and salary growth; high-tech output growth. *Milken Institute, "2005 Best Performing Cities," February 2006*

■ The San Jose metro area was selected as one of "The Top 20 Boom Towns in America." *Business 2.0* magazine and econometric research firm Global Insight compared 319 metropolitan areas in the U.S. and ranked the 61 with populations over 1 million. Criteria: a weighted formula that includes forecast growth rates in sectors that contain the economy's 10 most skilled occupational clusters; the prevalence of college degrees in the local workforce; median salary. The area ranked #2 among large metro areas. *Business 2.0 Magazine, March 2004*

■ San Jose was identified as one of the 100 "Most Unwired Cities" in the U.S. The area ranked #2 out of the 100 largest metro areas in the U.S. Criteria: number of public and commercial wireless access points (hotspots); airports with wireless Internet access; broadband availability; local wireless networks; and wireless email devices. *Intel, "Most Unwired Cities Survey," June 7, 2005*

■ San Jose was ranked #1 out of 125 regions worldwide in terms of its "Knowledge Competitiveness Index." The index attempts to measure the knowledge-based development taking place throughout the world and is based on 19 measures of economic performance that indicate a region's ability to translate its knowledge capacity into economic value. *Robert Huggins Associates, World Knowledge Competitiveness Index 2005*

■ *Forbes* ranked the 200 most populous metro areas in the U.S. in terms of the "Best Places for Business and Careers." The San Jose metro area was ranked #183. Criteria: business costs (labor, energy, tax and office space expenses); living costs (housing, transportation, food and other household expenditures); education levels of the work force; job growth; income growth; migration trends; crime rates; and culture/leisure. *Forbes, April 23, 2007*

■ *Fortune* ranked the 100 largest metro areas in the U.S. in terms of projected median home price change in 2006. The San Jose metro area ranked #88. *Fortune, "The Top 100: Is the Party Over?" December 26, 2005*

■ San Jose was identified as one of the "Most Overpriced Places in the U.S." The area ranked #5 out of the nations 150 largest metro areas. Criteria: job growth; income growth; cost of living; and housing affordability. *Forbes.com, "Most Overpriced Places in the U.S. 2005"*

■ San Jose was identified as one of the top 10 richest major cities in the U.S. The city ranked #1. Criteria: 2004 median household income. *Forbes, "Richest Cities in the U.S.," October 27, 2005*

Health/Environment Rankings

■ *Reader's Digest* ranked the 50 largest metro areas in the U.S. in terms of how "clean" they are. The San Jose metro area ranked #2. Criteria: air quality; water quality; toxic industrial pollution; Superfund sites; and sanitation. *Reader's Digest, "The 50 Cleanest (and Dirtiest) Cities in America," July 2005*

■ The San Jose metro area appeared in *Country Home's* "2007 Best Green Places Report". The area ranked #178. Criteria included: air and watershed quality; miles of mass transit; green power; number of farmer's markets, organic producers and groceries. *Country Home, "2007 Best Green Places Report," April 2007*

■ Wyeth Consumer Healthcare, in partnership with Sperling's BestPlaces, ranked the nation's 50 most populous metro areas in terms of five key health factors. The San Jose metro area ranked #1. Criteria: physical activity, health status, nutrition, lifestyle pursuits; and mental wellness. *Wyeth Consumer Healthcare, "Centrum Healthiest Cities Study," April 19, 2005*

■ HealthGrades identified the 10 best cities for nursing home care in the U.S. San Jose ranked #10. Criteria: proportion of facilities that had four or more actual harm violations from health or complaint surveys in the last four years. *www.HealthGrades.com, "Best and Worst Cities for Nursing Home Care," March 16, 2004*

■ The American Podiatric Medical Association and *Prevention* magazine ranked America's 100 most populated cities based on fitness-walker friendliness. The best cities have safe streets, beautiful places to walk, mild weather and good air quality. San Jose ranked #8. *Prevention, "The Best Walking Cities of 2007," April 2007; American Podiatric Medical Association, "2007 Best Fitness-Walking Cities"*

■ San Jose was selected as one of the 25 fattest cities in America by *Men's Fitness Online*. It ranked #24 out of America's 50 largest cities. Criteria: gyms/sporting goods; nutrition; exercise/sports; overweight/sedentary; junk food; alcohol; smoking; television; air and water quality; climate; geography; commute time; parks/open space; recreation facilities; health care; motivation; civic legislation and leadership. *Men's Fitness Online, America's Fittest/Fattest Cities 2006*

- San Jose was selected as one of "America's Healthiest Cities" by *Natural Health* magazine. The city was ranked #43 out of the 50 largest urban areas in the U.S. Twenty-six criteria in the following four categories were examined: whether the city boasts natural offerings; how well the city promotes its residents' physical health; whether the city offers a healthy environment; how well the city fosters a sense of community. *Natural Health, April 2003*

- *Men's Health* ranked the nation's largest 100 cities in terms of the *Best (and Worst) Cities for Men*. San Jose was ranked #1. Criteria: 24 statistical parameters of long life in the categories of health, quality of life, and fitness. *Men's Health, January/February 2007*

- *Men's Health* ranked 100 U.S. cities in terms of the quality of their tap water. San Jose was ranked #65 and received a grade of C. Criteria: levels of total coliform bacteria, arsenic, lead, total trihalomethanes (linked to cancer), and halo-acetic acids, plus the number of EPA water-system violations from 1995 to 2005. *Men's Health, March 2007*

- Ortho-McNeil Neurologics, in partnership with Sperling's BestPlaces, analyzed 110 metro areas and identified those U.S. cities with the highest prevalence of factors that are most commonly associated with migraine headaches. The San Jose metro area ranked #96. Criteria: number of migraine-related drug prescriptions per capita; lifestyle factors that can contribute to migraines; environmental factors that can trigger migraines; and consumption of migraine-triggering foods. *Ortho-McNeil Neurologics, "America's Migraine Hot Spots," March 14, 2006*

- Sperling's BestPlaces ranked 331 metro areas and identified the most and least stressful U.S. cities. The San Jose metro area ranked #56 out of the 100 largest metro areas (#1 = most stressful). Criteria: divorce rate; unemployment rate; violent and property crime; suicide rate; commute time; mental health; alcohol consumption; cloudy days. *www.BestPlaces.net, January 9, 2004*

- San Jose was selected as one of "America's Pet Healthiest Cities" by Purina. The city ranked #38 out of 50. Criteria: veterinary services; environment; legislation; preventative care; obesity/body condition. *Purina Pet Institute, "America's Pet Healthiest Cities," May 20, 2003*

Women/Minorities Rankings

- San Jose was ranked #9 out of 100 metro areas in *SELF Magazine's* ranking of "America's Best Places for Women." A panel of experts came up with nearly 40 criteria including: drinking and smoking rates; depression; unemployment; parks; crime; disease; healthcare insurance coverage; air quality; and commute times. *SELF Magazine, "America's Best Places for Women 2006," December 2006*

- *Ladies Home Journal* ranked America's 200 largest cities based on the qualities women surveyed care about most. San Jose ranked #19 out of 57 in the big city category (population over 300,000). Criteria: crime; lifestyle; education; jobs; health; child care; politics; and the economy. *Ladies Home Journal Online, "The Best Cities for Women 2002"*

- San Jose was identified as one of the top 25 metropolitan statistical areas ranked by percentage of coupled households that are gay or lesbian." The area ranked #1. *Human Rights Campaign, "Gay and Lesbian Families in the United States: Same-Sex Unmarried Partner Households," August 1, 2001*

Seniors/Retirement Rankings

- Sperling's BestPlaces in partnership with Bankers Life & Casualty Company designed a survey to identify the top 50 metro areas in the U.S. that offer the best overall qualities for senior living. The San Jose metro area ranked #37. The following criteria were statistically weighted to reflect the needs of the senior population: health; disease; economics; social; environment; spiritual; transportation; housing; and crime. *Bankers Life & Casualty Company, "Best Cities for Seniors 2005"*

- A.G. Edwards ranked America's 500 top-performing communities based on their residents' personal savings and investing behavior. The San Jose metro area ranked #3 with an index score of 125.93 (national average = 100.00). A dozen statistical factors were measured including: participation in retirement savings plans; personal debt levels; and home ownership. *A.G. Edwards, "2006 Nest Egg Index", September 6, 2006*

Children/Family Rankings

- The San Jose metro area was selected as one of the "Best Cities for Relocating Families" by Worldwide ERC and Primacy Relocation. Criteria: tax rates; average home costs and home appreciation; ability to qualify for in-state tuition; service quality of local utilities; per-capita volunteerism; auto taxes; and quantity of fun, family-friendly events and venues. *Worldwide ERC and Primacy Relocation, "2006 Best Cities for Relocating Families"*

- *Zero Population Growth* ranked 100 cities in terms of children's health, safety, and economic well-being. San Jose was ranked #14 out of 80 Large Cities (remainder of the 100 largest cities in the U.S.) and was given a grade of A-. Criteria: total population and population growth; percent of population under 18 years of age; percent of births to teens; infant mortality rate; percent of eligible women not receiving Title X services; contraceptive equity indicator; percent of children without health insurance; percent of city residents over age 25 with a high-school diploma; ration of PopEd (Population Connection's Education Program) teachers trained; sexuality education indicator; proficiency in reading and math; percent of kids living in poverty; percent growth in urbanized land; violent crime rate; recycling. *Population Connection, Kid Friendly Cities: Report Card 2004*

- *Fit Pregnancy* magazine ranked the 50 best U.S. cities in which to have a baby. San Jose was ranked #15. Criteria: fertility services; maternal and infant health risk; access to hospitals and doctors; safety; affordability; stroller friendliness; and birthing options. *Fit Pregnancy, February/March, 2006*

- San Jose was chosen as one of America's "100 Best Communities for Young People." The winners were selected based upon detailed information provided about each community's efforts to fulfill five essential promises critical to the well-being of young people: caring adults who are actively involved in their lives; safe places in which to learn and grow; a healthy start toward adulthood; an effective education that builds marketable skills; and opportunities to help others. *America's Promise, "100 Best Communities for Young People," September 26, 2005*

Safety Rankings

- Allstate ranked the 200 largest cities in America in terms of driver safety. San Jose ranked #114. In addition, drivers were 12.0% more likely to have had an accident compared to the national average. Allstate researchers analyzed internal Property Damage reported claims over a two-year period (from January 2003 to December 2004) to ensure the findings would not be affected by external influences such as weather or road construction. A weighted average of the two-year numbers determined the annual percentages. The report defines an auto crash as any collision resulting in a property damage claim. *Allstate, "Allstate America's Best Drivers Report 2006," May 24, 2006*

- San Jose was identified as one of the most dangerous large metro areas for pedestrians in the U.S. The area ranked #37 out of the nations 50 largest metro areas. Criteria: average yearly pedestrian fatalities per capita (for the years 2002 and 2003) adjusted for the number of walkers. *Surface Transportation Policy Project, "Mean Streets 2004"*

- San Jose was identified as one of the safest large cities in America by Morgan Quitno. All 32 cities with populations of 500,000 or more that reported crime rates in 2005 for murder, rape, robbery, aggravated assault, burglary, and motor vehicle thefts were ranked. The city ranked #1 out of the top 10. *www.morganquitno.com, 13th Annual America's Safest (and Most Dangerous) Cities Awards*

- *Ladies Home Journal* ranked America's 200 largest cities in terms of safety. San Jose ranked #49 out of 200. Criteria: violent crimes; crimes against property; and rape. *Ladies Home Journal Online, "The Best Cities for Women 2002"*

Sports/Recreation Rankings

- The San Jose metro area appeared on *The Sporting News* list of the "Best Sports Cities 2006". The area ranked #24 out of 99 cities in North America. To be included in the rankings, a city must have at least one of the following: NCAA Division I basketball team; Class A minor league baseball team; training camp for a major league or NFL team; NASCAR Nextel Cup race; NCAA Division I-A bowl game; PGA Tour tournament; Triple Crown horse race. Once a city qualifies, a 12-month snapshot is taken of the sports atmosphere, putting a heavy premium on regular-season won-lost records; playoff berths, bowl appearances and tournament bids; championships; applicable power ratings; quality of competition; overall fan fervor; sports atmosphere and fan knowledge; abundance of teams (quality over quantity); stadium/arena quality; ticket availability and prices; franchise ownership; and the marquee appeal of athletes. *SportingNews.com, "Best Sports Cities 2006," August 1, 2006*

- The San Jose metro area was selected by *Cranium* as one of the "Top 50 Fun Cities" in America. The area ranked #3. Criteria includes: number of sports teams, restaurants, and dance performances; number of toy stores; city budget spent on recreation. *Cranium, November 4, 2003*

- *Golf Digest* ranked 330 metro areas in the U.S. in terms of golf. The San Jose metro area was ranked #309. Criteria: access to golf; weather; value of golf; and quality of golf. *Golf Digest, "Metro Golf Rankings," August 2005*

Dating/Romance Rankings

- The San Jose metro area was selected as one of the "Top Ten U.S. Cities for Finding a Rich, Single Man" by Teasley, a Manhattan-based marketing consulting firm. The area ranked #1. Criteria: high single-male to single-female ratios and higher income to cost-of-living ratios. *Teasley, February 10, 2004*

- The San Jose metro area was selected as one of the "Best Cities for Relocating Singles" by Worldwide ERC and Primacy Relocation. The area ranked #42 out of the 100 largest metro areas in the U.S. Areas were selected based on the following criteria: Population Criteria (local percentage and growth trends of unmarried residents aged 25-34; male-female ratios; the number of newcomers to the area; diversity and density); Economic Criteria (job growth vs. unemployment rates; apartment rental costs; fee and occupancy rates for temporary housing and mini-storage; higher education costs, including in-state and out-of-state tuition requirements; vehicle tax rates and quality of service from utility providers); Quality-of-Life Criteria (level of per capita volunteering; quality and quantity of collegiate and professional sports with fun, fan-friendly venues; number of Starbucks and other coffee shops; quality or popularity of restaurants, nightspots, health clubs, and online dating; moderate climates with sustainable water supplies). *Worldwide ERC and Primacy Relocation, "2006 Best Cities for Relocating Singles," October 11, 2006*

- Sperling's BestPlaces in partnership with AXE Deodorant Bodyspray ranked 80 metro areas and identified "America's Best (and Worst) Cities for Dating." The San Jose metro area ranked #39. Criteria: percentage of singles ages 18-24; population density; dating venues per capita. *AXE Deodorant Bodyspray, "America's Best (and Worst) Cities for Dating," May, 2004*

Culture/Performing Arts Rankings

- San Jose was selected as one of "America's Top 25 Arts Destinations." The city ranked #25 in the big city (population 500,000 and over) category. Criteria: readers' top choices for arts travel destinations based on the richness and variety of visual arts sites, activities and events. *American Style, June 2006*

Miscellaneous Rankings

- San Jose was determined to be one of America's smartest cities. The city ranked #16 in the large city category (200,000+ adults 25 years and older). Criteria: the editors rated the collective brainpower of U.S communities based on the educational attainment of its residents. *American City Business Journals, www.bizjournals.com, June 12, 2006*

- The San Jose metro area was identified one of "America's Smartest Cities" by *Forbes*. The area ranked #10. Criteria: 200 of the largest U.S. metro areas were ranked based on the percentage of the population age 25 and over with at least a bachelor's degree. *Forbes.com, "America's Smartest Cities," December 15, 2006*

- San Jose appeared on ApartmentRatings.com "Top Cities for Renters List 2006". The area ranked #118 out of 138. Criteria: renter satisfaction; affordability; and vacancy. *ApartmentRatings.com, "Top Cities for Renters List 2006"*

- Sperling's BestPlaces in partnership with Pep Boys ranked 77 metro areas and identified "America's Most Drivable Cities." The San Jose metro area ranked #67. Criteria: climate; road roughness; urban mobility; gas prices. *Pep Boys, "America's Most Drivable Cities," April 9, 2003*

- San Jose was selected as one of "America's Most Literate Cities." The city ranked #50 out of the 70 largest U.S. cities. Criteria: number of booksellers; library resources; Internet resources; educational attainment; periodical publishing resources; newspaper circulation. *Central Connecticut State University, "America's Most Literate Cities 2006"*

- State Farm Insurance, in partnership with Sperling's BestPlaces, analyzed several key factors that contribute to overall family preparedness. The San Jose metro area ranked #38 out of the nation's 50 most populous metro areas. Criteria: quality of life; life insurance coverage; and investments. *State Farm Life Insurance, "Fiscally Fit Cities Report," July 20, 2004*

- Scarborough Research, a leading market research firm, identified the top local markets for reality television. The San Jose DMA (Designated Market Area) ranked in the top 10 with 26% of consumers reporting that they "typically watch" reality-dating, reality-talent, or reality-adventure television shows. *Scarborough Research, Scarborough USA+ 2004 Release 1*

- Scarborough Research, a leading market research firm, identified the top local markets for coffee bar patronage. The San Jose DMA (Designated Market Area) ranked in the top 10 with 26% of adults reporting that they have used any coffee house/bar during the past 30 days. *Scarborough Research, Scarborough USA+ 2004 Release 1*

Business Environment

CITY FINANCES

City Government Finances

Component	2003-2004 ($000)	2003-2004 ($ per capita)
Total Revenues	1,955,012	2,171
Total Expenditures	1,888,466	2,097
Debt Outstanding	3,970,669	4,410
Cash and Securities	4,364,529	4,847

Source: U.S Census Bureau, Government Finances 2003-2004

City Government Revenue by Source

Source	2003-2004 ($000)	2003-2004 ($ per capita)
General Revenue		
From Federal Government	35,598	40
From State Government	93,541	104
From Local Governments	7,646	8
Taxes		
Property	278,552	309
Sales	240,776	267
Personal Income	0	0
License	0	0
Charges	387,978	431
Liquor Store	0	0
Utility	19,880	22
Employee Retirement	509,443	566
Other	381,598	424

Source: U.S Census Bureau, Government Finances 2003-2004

City Government Expenditures by Function

Function	2003-2004 ($000)	2003-2004 ($ per capita)	2003-2004 (%)
General Expenditures			
Airports	150,694	167	8.0
Corrections	0	0	0.0
Education	0	0	0.0
Fire Protection	109,059	121	5.8
Governmental Administration	291,186	323	15.4
Health	17,846	20	0.9
Highways	104,468	116	5.5
Hospitals	0	0	0.0
Housing and Community Development	267,110	297	14.1
Interest on General Debt	163,095	181	8.6
Libraries	51,010	57	2.7
Parking	9,338	10	0.5
Parks and Recreation	94,684	105	5.0
Police Protection	211,733	235	11.2
Public Welfare	0	0	0.0
Sewerage	111,527	124	5.9
Solid Waste Management	64,131	71	3.4
Liquor Store	0	0	0.0
Utility	39,431	44	2.1
Employee Retirement	135,302	150	7.2
Other	67,852	75	3.6

Source: U.S Census Bureau, Government Finances 2003-2004

Municipal Bond Ratings

Area	Moody's
City	Aaa

Source: Mergent Bond Record, January 2007 (unless noted otherwise)

DEMOGRAPHICS

Population Growth

Area	1990 Census	2000 Census	2006 Estimate	2011 Projection	Population Growth (%) 1990-2000	Population Growth (%) 2000-2011
City	784,324	894,943	915,192	938,342	14.1	4.8
MSA[1]	1,534,280	1,735,819	1,759,428	1,792,371	13.1	3.3
U.S.	248,709,873	281,421,906	298,021,266	312,383,955	13.2	11.0

Note: (1) Metropolitan Statistical Area - see Appendix B for areas included
Source: Claritas, Inc.

Number of Households and Average Household Size

Area	2006 Estimate	2006 Average Household Size
City	280,122	3.27
MSA[1]	581,696	3.02
U.S.	112,267,302	2.65

Note: (1) Metropolitan Statistical Area - see Appendix B for areas included
Source: Claritas, Inc.

Race and Ethnicity

Area	White Alone[2]	Black Alone[2]	Asian Alone[2]	Other Race Alone[2]	Hispanic[3]
City	43.0	3.2	30.9	22.9	31.1
MSA[1]	49.5	2.5	29.0	19.0	25.7
U.S.	73.3	12.4	4.2	10.1	14.5

Note: Figures are 2006 estimates; (1) Metropolitan Statistical Area - see Appendix B for areas included
(2) Alone is defined as not being in combination with one or more other races; (3) May be of any race.
Source: Claritas, Inc.

Segregation

City Index[2]	City Rank[3]	MSA[1] Index[2]	MSA[1] Rank[4]
44.0	76	45.9	264

Note: Figures are based on an analysis of Census 2000 data; (1) Metropolitan Statistical Area - see Appendix A
for areas included; (2) White/Black Dissimilarity Index—the most commonly used measure of segregation
between two groups, reflecting their relative distributions across neighborhoods within a city or metropolitan
area. It can range in value from 0, indicating complete integration, to 100, indicating complete segregation; (3)
Ranges from 1 (most segregated) to 100 (least segregated) and includes all the cities in this book; (4) Ranges
from 1 (most segregated) to 318 (least segregated) and includes 318 metropolitan areas.
Source: www.CensusScope.org

Ancestry

Area	German	Irish[2]	English	American	Italian	Polish	French[3]	Scottish
City	7.6	6.1	5.6	1.9	4.8	1.2	1.8	1.2
MSA[1]	9.2	7.1	7.2	2.3	5.2	1.5	2.2	1.6
U.S.	15.2	10.9	8.7	7.3	5.6	3.2	3.0	1.7

Note: Figures include multiple ancestry (e.g. if a person reported being Irish and Italian, they were included in
both columns); (1) Metropolitan Statistical Area - see Appendix A for areas included; (2) Includes Celtic; (3)
Includes Alsatian but excludes Basque
Source: Census 2000, Summary File 3

Foreign-Born Population

Area	Percent of Population Born in: Any Foreign Country	Europe	Asia	Africa	Oceania[2]	Canada	Mexico	Latin America[3]
City	36.9	2.5	20.4	0.6	0.2	0.4	11.1	1.7
MSA[1]	34.1	3.4	19.5	0.5	0.2	0.6	8.3	1.5
U.S.	11.1	1.7	2.9	0.3	0.1	0.3	3.3	2.5

Note: (1) Metropolitan Statistical Area - see Appendix A for areas included; (2) Includes Australia, New
Zealand subregion, Melanesia, Micronesia, Polynesia, and Oceania n.e.c; (3) Includes Central America
(excluding Mexico), South America, and the Caribbean.
Source: Census 2000, Summary File 3

Marriage Status

Area	Never Married	Now Married (excluding Separated)	Separated	Widowed	Divorced
City	31.2	54.0	2.0	4.4	8.4
MSA[1]	30.2	54.8	1.8	4.7	8.5
U.S.	27.1	54.4	2.2	6.6	9.7

Note: Figures are percentages and cover the population 15 years of age and older;
(1) Metropolitan Statistical Area - see Appendix A for areas included
Source: Census 2000, Summary File 3

Age Distribution

Area	Percent of Population						
	Under Age 5	Age 5 to 17	Age 18 to 34	Age 35 to 49	Age 50 to 64	Age 65 to 79	80 Years and Over
City	7.6	18.8	27.8	24.5	13.3	6.3	1.8
MSA[1]	7.0	17.7	26.9	25.0	13.9	7.2	2.3
U.S.	6.8	18.9	23.7	23.5	14.8	9.2	3.2

Note: (1) Metropolitan Statistical Area - see Appendix A for areas included
Source: Census 2000, Summary File 3

Male/Female Ratio

Area	Males	Females	Males per 100 Females
City	466,156	449,036	103.8
MSA[1]	894,153	865,275	103.3
U.S.	146,712,712	151,308,554	97.0

Note: Figures are 2006 estimates; (1) Metropolitan Statistical Area -
see Appendix B for areas included
Source: Claritas, Inc.

Religion

Area	Catholic	Southern Baptist	United Methodist	ELCA[1]	LDS[2]	Presbyterian Church USA	Jewish Est.	Muslim Est.
County	28.7	1.0	0.9	0.6	1.2	0.6	3.2	1.1
U.S.	22.0	7.1	3.7	1.8	1.5	1.1	2.2	0.6

Note: Figures are the number of adherents as a percentage of the total population; Adherents are defined as all members, including full members, their children and the estimated number of other participants who are not considered members (e.g. the baptized, those not confirmed, those regularly attending services, etc.);
(1) Evangelical Lutheran Church in America; (2) The Church of Jesus Christ of Latter Day Saints
Source: Reprinted with permission from Religious Congregations and Membership in the United States 2000 (Nashville, Glenmary Research Center, 2002) Copyright Association of Statisticians of American Religious Bodies. All rights reserved.

ECONOMY

Gross Metropolitan Product

Area	2002	2003	2004	2005	2005 Rank[2]
MSA[1]	82.6	82.8	87.6	93.6	23

Note: Figures are in billions of dollars; (1) San Jose-Sunnyvale-Santa Clara, CA Metropolitan Statistical Area - see Appendix A for areas included; (2) Rank ranges from 1 to 361
Source: The U.S. Conference of Mayors, "U.S. Metro Economies: GMP - The Engines of America's Growth," January 2007

Economic Growth

Area	1995 GMP	2005 GMP	Average Annual Growth Rate	Growth Rate Rank[2]
MSA[1]	59.4	93.6	4.7	256

Note: Figures are in billions of dollars; GMP = Gross Metropolitan Product; (1) San Jose-Sunnyvale-Santa Clara, CA Metropolitan Statistical Area - see Appendix A for areas included; (2) Rank ranges from 1 to 361
Source: The U.S. Conference of Mayors, "U.S. Metro Economies: GMP - The Engines of America's Growth," January 2007

INCOME

Per Capita/Median/Average Income

Area	Per Capita ($)	Median Household ($)	Average Household ($)
City	30,046	78,207	97,407
MSA[1]	35,989	83,053	107,853
U.S.	25,129	48,775	65,849

Note: Figures are 2006 estimates; (1) Metropolitan Statistical Area - see Appendix B for areas included
Source: Claritas, Inc.

Household Income Distribution

Area				Percent of Households Earning				
	Under $15,000	$15,000 -24,999	$25,000 -34,999	$35,000 -49,999	$50,000 -74,999	$75,000 -99,000	$100,000 -149,999	$150,000 and up
City	7.0	5.8	6.4	10.8	18.1	15.3	20.3	16.3
MSA[1]	6.6	5.4	6.1	10.2	17.1	14.7	20.2	19.8
U.S.	13.3	11.0	11.3	15.7	19.5	11.8	11.0	6.4

Note: Figures are 2006 estimates; (1) Metropolitan Statistical Area - see Appendix B for areas included
Source: Claritas, Inc.

Poverty Rates by Age

Area	All Ages	Under 5 Years Old	5 to 17 Years Old	18 to 64 Years Old	65 Years and Over
City	8.8	0.8	2.1	5.4	0.6
MSA[1]	7.5	0.6	1.6	4.7	0.6
U.S.	12.4	1.2	3.0	6.9	1.2

Note: Figures are percent of population with income in 1999 below poverty level and only include population for whom poverty status is determined; (1) Metropolitan Statistical Area - see Appendix A for areas included
Source: Census 2000, Summary File 3

Personal Bankruptcy Filing Rate

Area	2003	2004	2005
Santa Clara County	2.99	2.92	3.57
U.S.	5.57	5.31	6.88

Note: Numbers are per 1,000 population and include Chapter 7 and Chapter 13 filings
Source: Federal Deposit Insurance Corporation (FDIC), Regional Economic Conditions (RECON), 3/24/2006

EMPLOYMENT

Labor Force and Employment

Area	Civilian Labor Force			Workers Employed		
	Dec. 2005	Dec. 2006	% Chg.	Dec. 2005	Dec. 2006	% Chg.
City	429,206	434,007	1.1	407,861	413,837	1.5
MSA[1]	847,575	857,267	1.1	809,031	820,886	1.5
U.S.	149,874,000	152,571,000	1.8	142,918,000	146,081,000	2.2

Note: Data is not seasonally adjusted and covers workers 16 years of age and older;
(1) Metropolitan Statistical Area - see Appendix B for areas included
Source: Bureau of Labor Statistics, http://stats.bls.gov

Unemployment Rate

Area	2006											
	Jan.	Feb.	Mar.	Apr.	May	Jun.	Jul.	Aug.	Sep.	Oct.	Nov.	Dec.
City	5.5	5.6	5.3	5.0	4.9	5.5	5.6	5.3	5.0	4.6	5.0	4.6
MSA[1]	5.1	5.1	4.8	4.6	4.4	5.0	5.0	4.7	4.5	4.2	4.5	4.2
U.S.	5.1	5.1	4.8	4.5	4.4	4.8	5.0	4.6	4.4	4.1	4.3	4.3

Note: Data is not seasonally adjusted and covers workers 16 years of age and older; All figures are percentages; (1) Metropolitan Statistical Area - see Appendix B for areas included
Source: Bureau of Labor Statistics, http://stats.bls.gov

Employment by Occupation

Occupation Classification	City (%)	MSA[1] (%)	U.S. (%)
Sales and Office	24.4	22.7	26.7
Professional and Related	24.8	29.9	20.2
Service	12.3	10.5	14.9
Production, Transportation, and Material Moving	14.3	11.2	14.6
Management, Business, and Financial	16.1	18.6	13.5
Construction, Extraction, and Maintenance	7.9	6.6	9.4
Farming, Forestry, and Fishing	0.3	0.4	0.7

Note: Figures cover employed civilians 16 years of age and older;
(1) Metropolitan Statistical Area - see Appendix A for areas included
Source: Census 2000, Summary File 3

Employment by Industry

Sector	MSA[1] Number of Employees	Percent of Total	U.S. Percent of Total
Government	97,500	10.7	16.3
Education and Health Services	103,900	11.4	13.2
Professional and Business Services	169,000	18.6	12.9
Retail Trade	89,200	9.8	11.5
Manufacturing	170,900	18.8	10.2
Leisure and Hospitality	75,900	8.4	9.5
Financial Activities	37,300	4.1	6.1
Construction	48,000	5.3	5.5
Wholesale Trade	38,900	4.3	4.3
Other Services	25,200	2.8	3.9
Transportation and Utilities	13,200	1.5	3.7
Information	39,700	4.4	2.2
Natural Resources and Mining	200	<0.1	0.5

Note: Figures cover non-farm employment as of December 2006 and are not seasonally adjusted;
(1) Metropolitan Statistical Area - see Appendix B for areas included
Source: Bureau of Labor Statistics, http://stats.bls.gov

Occupations with Greatest Projected Employment Growth: 2002 - 2012

Occupation[1]	2002 Employment	2012 Projected Employment	Numeric Employment Change	Percent Employment Change
Retail Salespersons	435,400	513,200	77,800	17.9
Postsecondary Teachers	154,500	217,700	63,200	40.9
Combined Food Preparation and Serving Workers, Including Fast Food	215,100	277,300	62,200	28.9
Cashiers	358,800	420,700	61,900	17.3
Registered Nurses	201,600	258,400	56,800	28.2
Waiters and Waitresses	214,000	264,900	50,900	23.8
Customer Service Representatives	197,500	244,900	47,400	24.0
Office Clerks, General	400,300	446,500	46,200	11.5
General and Operations Managers	224,000	267,000	43,000	19.2
Teacher Assistants	179,600	222,300	42,700	23.8

Note: Projections cover California; (1) Sorted by numeric employment change
Source: www.projectionscentral.com, State Occupational Projections, 2002-2012 Long-Term Projections

Fastest Growing Occupations: 2002 - 2012

Occupation[1]	2002 Employment	2012 Projected Employment	Numeric Employment Change	Percent Employment Change
Physical Therapist Aides	4,200	6,800	2,600	61.9
Dental Hygienists	16,600	26,200	9,600	57.8
Dental Assistants	42,700	67,100	24,400	57.1
Tapers	9,200	14,400	5,200	56.5
Drywall and Ceiling Tile Installers	26,800	41,800	15,000	56.0
Tile and Marble Setters	8,600	13,400	4,800	55.8
Network Systems and Data Communications Analysts	20,300	31,600	11,300	55.7
Physical Therapist Assistants	3,900	6,000	2,100	53.8
Fitness Trainers and Aerobics Instructors	24,000	35,700	11,700	48.8
Self-Enrichment Education Teachers	24,200	35,800	11,600	47.9

Note: Projections cover California; (1) Sorted by percent employment change and excludes occupations with numeric employment change less than 1500
Source: www.projectionscentral.com, State Occupational Projections, 2002-2012 Long-Term Projections

Average Wages

Occupation	$/Hr.	Occupation	$/Hr.
Accountants and Auditors	33.71	Maids and Housekeeping Cleaners	11.05
Automotive Mechanics	22.52	Maintenance and Repair Workers	20.45
Bookkeepers	18.76	Marketing Managers	66.92
Carpenters	26.73	Nuclear Medicine Technologists	38.80
Cashiers	10.70	Nurses, Licensed Practical	24.84
Clerks, General Office	15.59	Nurses, Registered	42.28
Clerks, Receptionists/Information	14.82	Nursing Aides/Orderlies/Attendants	15.55
Clerks, Shipping/Receiving	14.87	Packers and Packagers, Hand	9.93
Computer Programmers	43.69	Physical Therapists	36.78
Computer Support Specialists	29.72	Postal Service Mail Carriers	22.07
Computer Systems Analysts	41.11	Real Estate Brokers	n/a
Cooks, Restaurant	10.55	Retail Salespersons	13.34
Dentists	n/a	Sales Reps., Exc. Tech./Scientific	34.28
Electrical Engineers	45.35	Sales Reps., Tech./Scientific	42.51
Electricians	30.70	Secretaries, Exc. Legal/Med./Exec.	17.73
Financial Managers	60.64	Security Guards	13.33
First-Line Supervisors/Mgrs., Sales	20.75	Surgeons	69.44
Food Preparation Workers	9.67	Teacher Assistants	13.80
General and Operations Managers	60.83	Teachers, Elementary School	25.70
Hairdressers/Cosmetologists	11.21	Teachers, Secondary School	29.30
Internists	58.26	Telemarketers	13.63
Janitors and Cleaners	11.59	Truck Drivers, Heavy/Tractor-Trailer	20.21
Landscaping/Groundskeeping Workers	13.86	Truck Drivers, Light/Delivery Svcs.	14.52
Lawyers	73.85	Waiters and Waitresses	8.18

Note: Wage data is for May 2005 and covers the San Jose-Sunnyvale-Santa Clara, CA Metropolitan Statistics Area - see Appendix B for areas included. Hourly wages for elementary/secondary school teachers and teacher assistants were calculated by the editors from annual wage data assuming a 40 hour work week; n/a not available.
Source: Bureau of Labor Statistics, May 2005 Metro Area Occupational Employment and Wage Estimates

RESIDENTIAL REAL ESTATE

Building Permits

Area	Single-Family			Multi-Family			Total		
	2005	2006p	Pct. Chg.	2005	2006p	Pct. Chg.	2005	2006p	Pct. Chg.
City	805	602	-25.2	1,970	2,373	20.5	2,775	2,975	7.2
U.S.	1,682,000	1,380,000	-18.0	473,300	457,300	-3.4	2,155,300	1,837,300	-14.8

Note: (p) preliminary; figures represent new, privately-owned housing units authorized (unadjusted data); All permit data are based on estimates with imputation; U.S. figures are based on the new 20,000-place series.
Source: U.S. Census Bureau, Manufacturing, Mining, and Construction Statistics

Homeownership and Housing Vacancies

Area	Homeownership Rate[2] (%)			Rental Vacancy Rate[3] (%)			Homeowner Vacancy Rate[4] (%)		
	2004	2005	2006	2004	2005	2006	2004	2005	2006
MSA[1]	n/a	59.2	59.4	n/a	6.7	6.0	n/a	1.5	1.6
U.S.	69.0	68.9	68.8	10.2	9.8	9.7	1.7	1.9	2.4

Note: Comparable 2004 data was not available due to changes in metropolitan area definitions; (1) Metropolitan Statistical Area - see Appendix B for areas included; (2) The proportion of households that are owners; (3) The proportion of the rental inventory that is vacant for rent; (4) The proportion of the homeowner inventory that is vacant for sale; n/a not available
Source: U.S. Census Bureau, Housing Vacancies and Homeownership Annual Statistics: 2006

TAXES

State Corporate Income Tax Rates

State	Rate (%)	Number of Brackets	Low Bracket (Under $)	High Bracket (Over $)
California	8.84	1	na	na

Note: Tax rates as of December 31, 2006; na not applicable; 10.84% on financial institutions. Minimum tax is $800. The tax rate on S-Corporations is 1.5% (3.5% for financial S-Corporations).
Source: Tax Foundation, www.taxfoundation.org

State Individual Income Tax Rates

State	Federal Deductibility	Marginal Rate (%)	Number of Brackets	Low Bracket (Under $)	High Bracket (Over $)
California	No	1.0-10.3 (p)(r)	7	0	1,000,000

Note: Tax rates as of December 31, 2006; Brackets apply to single taxpayers and married people filing separately; na not applicable; (p) California's $1,000,000 bracket not doubled for married taxpayers; (r) Indexed for Inflation.
Source: Tax Foundation, www.taxfoundation.org

Various State and Local Tax Rates

State and Local Sales and Use (%)	State Sales and Use (%)	Gasoline ($/gal.)	Cigarette ($/pack)	Spirits ($/gal.)	Table Wine ($/gal.)	Beer ($/gal.)
8.25	6.25	0.192 (m)	0.87	3.3	0.20	0.20

Note: Tax rates as of December 31, 2006; (m) Additional cents per gallon taxes added this year that were not included in previous years' tables.
Source: Tax Foundation, www.taxfoundation.org; The Sales Tax Clearinghouse, www.thestc.com

State Tax Burdens

Area	Combined State and Local Tax Burden		Combined Federal, State and Local Tax Burden	
	Percent	Rank	Percent	Rank
California	10.9	15	32.7	9
U.S. Average	10.6	-	31.6	-

Note: Figures are for 2006 and measure taxes as a percentage of income
Source: Tax Foundation, www.taxfoundation.org

Internal Revenue Service Tax Audits

IRS District	Percent of Returns Audited				
	1996	1997	1998	1999	2000
Central California	1.17	0.91	0.71	0.56	0.29
U.S.	0.66	0.61	0.46	0.31	0.20

Note: Figures cover IRS district audits of federal income tax returns filed by individuals. Geographic data on district audits after the year 2000 are being withheld by the IRS. TRAC is challenging this policy.
Source: Syracuse University, Transactional Records Access Clearinghouse (TRAC), "Odds of IRS District Tax Audit 2000"

COMMERCIAL REAL ESTATE

Office Market

Market Area	Inventory (sq. ft.)	Vacant (sq. ft.)	Vac. Rate (%)	Under Constr. (sq. ft.)	Asking Rent ($/sf)	
					Class A	Class B
San Jose	60,244,453	6,180,596	10.3	928,430	33.96	25.68

Source: Grubb & Ellis, Office Markets Trends, 4th Quarter 2006

Industrial Market

Market Area	Inventory (sq. ft.)	Vacant (sq. ft.)	Vac. Rate (%)	Under Constr. (sq. ft.)	Asking Rent ($/sf)	
					WH/Dist	R&D/Flex
San Jose	274,276,954	31,263,244	11.4	558,000	5.64	12.60

Source: Grubb & Ellis, Industrial Markets Trends, 4th Quarter 2006

COMMERCIAL UTILITIES

Typical Monthly Electric Bills

Area	Commercial Service ($/month)		Industrial Service ($/month)	
	3 kW demand 1,000 kWh	40 kW demand 14,000 kWh	1,000 kW demand 200,000 kWh	50,000 kW demand 15,000,000 kWh
City	187	2,316	28,589	1,738,772
Average[1]	123	1,413	22,000	1,306,315

Note: Based on total rates in effect July 1, 2006; (1) average based on 196 utilities
Source: Edison Electric Institute, Typical Bills and Average Rates Report, Summer 2006

TRANSPORTATION

Means of Transportation to Work

Area	Car/Truck/Van		Public Transportation			Bicycle	Walked	Other Means	Worked at Home
	Drove Alone	Car-pooled	Bus	Subway	Railroad				
City	76.4	14.1	3.3	0.1	0.4	0.6	1.4	1.3	2.5
MSA[1]	77.3	12.2	2.6	0.1	0.6	1.2	1.8	1.0	3.1
U.S.	75.7	12.2	2.5	1.5	0.5	0.4	2.9	1.0	3.3

Note: Figures are percentages and cover workers 16 years of age and older;
(1) Metropolitan Statistical Area - see Appendix A for areas included
Source: Census 2000, Summary File 3

Travel Time to Work

Area	Less Than 15 Minutes	15 to 29 Minutes	30 to 44 Minutes	45 to 59 Minutes	60 Minutes or More
City	16.8	39.9	26.4	9.3	7.5
MSA[1]	21.1	40.8	23.4	7.9	6.8
U.S.	29.4	36.1	19.1	7.4	8.0

Note: Figures are percentages and include workers 16 years old and over; (1) Metropolitan Statistical Area -
see Appendix A for areas included
Source: Census 2000, Summary File 3

Travel Time Index

Area	1982	1993	2002	2003
Urban Area[1]	1.18	1.34	1.39	1.37
Average[2]	1.12	1.28	1.37	1.37

Note: Travel Time Index - The ratio of travel time in the peak period to the travel time at
free-flow conditions. A value of 1.35 indicates a 20-minute free-flow trip takes 27 minutes
in the peak. Free-flow speeds (60 mph on freeways and 35 mph on principal arterials)
are used as the comparison threshold; (1) Covers the San Jose, CA urban area;
(2) average of 85 urban areas
Source: Texas Transportation Institute, The 2005 Urban Mobility Report, May 2005

Public Transportation

Agency name:	Santa Clara Valley Transportation Authority (VTA)
Vehicle type:	Bus
Average fleet age in years:	6.8
No. operated in max. service:	366
Vehicle type:	Light rail
Average fleet age in years:	4.7
No. operated in max. service:	34
Vehicle type:	Demand response
Average fleet age in years:	4.8
No. operated in max. service:	192

Source: Federal Transit Administration, National Transit Database, 2005

Air Transportation

Airport name and code:	San Jose International (SJC)
Domestic service (2006)	
Passenger airlines[1]:	28
Passenger enplanements:	5,145,446
Freight carriers[2]:	20
Freight (lbs.):	95,708,691
International service (2005)	
Passenger airlines[1]:	10
Passenger enplanements:	140,529
Freight carriers[2]:	3
Freight (lbs.):	6,114,869

Note: (1) Includes all major, minor and commuter airlines that carried at least one passenger during the year; (2) Includes all airlines and freight carriers that transported at least one pound of freight during the year
Source: Bureau of Transportation Statistics, The Intermodal Transportation Database, Air Carriers: T-100 International Market, 2004; Bureau of Transportation Statistics, The Intermodal Transportation Database, Air Carriers: T-100 Domestic Market, 2005

Other Transportation Statistics

Interstate highways:	I-80
Amtrak service:	Yes
Major waterways/ports:	None

Source: Editor & Publisher Market Guide, 2006; Amtrak.com; Rand McNally 2006 Road Atlas

BUSINESSES

Major Business Headquarters

Company Name	2006 Rankings	
	Fortune[1]	Forbes[2]
Calpine	275	-
Cisco Systems	83	-
Fry's Electronics	-	142
Ma Laboratories	-	317
Sanmina-SCI	198	-
eBay	458	-

Note: (1) Fortune 500 - companies that produce a 10-K are ranked 1 to 500 based on 2005 revenue; (2) Forbes Largest Private Companies - all private companies with at least $1 billion in annual revenue are ranked 1 to 394; companies listed are located in the city; dashes indicate no ranking
Source: Fortune, April 17, 2006; Forbes, November 9, 2006

Best Companies to Work For

Adobe Systems (HQ); Cisco Systems (HQ), headquartered in San Jose, are among the "100 Best Companies to Work For." Criteria: More than 105,000 employees from 446 companies responded to a 57-question survey created by the Great Place to Work Institute. Two-thirds of a company's score is based on the survey, which covers topics such as attitudes towards management, job satisfaction, and camaraderie. The remaining third of the score comes from each company's responses to the Institute's Culture Audit, which includes detailed questions about demographic makeup, pay and benefits programs, and open-ended questions about the company's people-management philosophy, internal communications, opportunities, compensation practices, diversity programs, etc. Any company that is at least seven years old and has a minimum of 1,000 U.S. employees is eligible. The top three U.S. locations are shown for companies with more than one location. *Fortune, "100 Best Companies to Work for 2007," January 22, 2007*

Knight-Ridder, headquartered in San Jose, is among the "50 Best Companies for Minorities." Criteria: 1,200 of the largest U.S employers were surveyed. Those companies were analyzed on information such as the number of minorities in the workforce and on the board, and the rate at which minority employees are hired (and fired). *Fortune, "50 Best Companies for Minorities," June 28, 2004*

Fast-Growing Businesses

According to *Inc.*, San Jose is home to one of America's 500 fastest-growing private companies: **2Wire**. Criteria: must be an independent, privately-held, U.S. corporation, proprietorship or partnership; net sales of at least $600,000 in FY2002; four-year operating/sales history; holding companies, regulated banks, and utilities were excluded. *Inc., "America's 500 Fastest-Growing Private Companies,"September 2006*

San Jose is home to one of *Business Week's* "Hot Growth Companies:" **Altera**. To qualify, a company must have annual sales of more than $50 million and less than $1.5 billion, a current market value greater than $25 million, a current stock price of at least $5, and be actively traded. Banks, insurers, real estate firms, and utilities are excluded. So are companies with declines in current financial results or in stock price, as well as companies where other developments raise questions about future performance. Companies were selected based on three-year results in sales growth, earnings growth, and return on invested capital. *Business Week, June 5, 2006*

According to *Business 2.0*, San Jose is home to five of America's 100 fastest-growing technology companies: **Adobe Systems; Business Objects; Laserscope; Secure Computing; eBay**. The 100 Fastest-Growing Technology Companies (B2 100) is a yearly ranking published by Business 2.0 magazine of businesses whose inventiveness and quick reflexes are helping them to set the pace for the economy. To find the B2 100, Zacks Investment Research of Chicago ranked 2,000 publicly traded companies using a rigorous combination of four financial criteria: growth in revenue, profit, and operating cash flow during the past three years; and the 12-month stock market return as of March 31, 2006. *Business 2.0, "100 Fastest-Growing Tech Companies 2006," June 2006*

According to Deloitte & Touche LLP, San Jose is home to 12 of North America's 500 fastest-growing high-technology companies: **Bookham; Laserscope; Notify Technology Corporation; Photon Dynamics; PortalPlayer; RAE Systems; Roamware; SiRF Technology Holdings; Silicon Optix; Terabeam; Tessera Technologies; VNUS Medical Technologies**. Companies are ranked by percentage growth in revenue over a five-year period. Criteria for inclusion: company must be headquartered within North America; company must own proprietary intellectual property or proprietary technology that contributes to a significant portion of the company's operating revenue or devotes a significant proportion of revenues to research and development of technology; company must have been in business for a minumum of five years with 2001 operating revenues of at least $50,000 USD or $75,000 CD and 2005 operating revenues of at least $5 million USD/CD. *Deloitte & Touche LLP, 2006 Technology Fast 500*

Women-Owned Businesses: 1997 and 2002

Year	All Firms		Firms with Paid Employees			
	Firms	Sales ($000)	Firms	Sales ($000)	Employees	Payroll ($000)
1997	14,818	3,235,544	2,158	2,919,703	17,093	560,493
2002	16,853	2,960,220	2,816	2,533,801	22,108	781,710

Note: Figures cover firms located in the city; Women-owned business are defined as firms in which women own 51% or more of the stock or equity of the company; (a) Withheld to avoid disclosing data for individual companies; (b) Withheld because estimate did not meet publication standards; n/a not available
Source: 1997 Economic Census, Survey of Minority- and Women-Owned Business Enterprises; 2002 Economic Census, Survey of Business Owners (released February 9, 2006)

Minority Business Opportunity

Two of the 500 largest Hispanic-owned companies in the U.S. are located in San Jose. *Hispanic Business, "Hispanic Business 500," June 2006*

San Jose is home to one company which is on the Hispanic Business Fastest-Growing 100 list (greatest sales growth over the past five years): **R.W. Garcia Co..** *Hispanic Business, July/August 2006*

HOTELS

Hotels/Motels

Area	Hotels/Motels	Average Minimum Rates ($)		
		Tourist	First-Class	Deluxe
City	59	85	115	n/a

Note: n/a not available
Source: OAG Travel Planner Online, Spring 2006

EVENT SITES

Stadiums, Arenas, and Auditoriums

Name	Capacity
Civic Auditorium San Jose Convention & Cultural Facilities	3,260
HP Pavilion at San Jose	20,000
Parkside Hall San Jose Convention & Cultural Facilities	1,800

Source: www.officialtravelguide.com; www.eventective.com; original research

Convention Centers

Name	Overall Space (sq. ft.)	Exhibit Space (sq. ft.)	Meeting Space (sq. ft.)	Meeting Rooms
Event Center of San Jose State	144,000	n/a	25,000	n/a
San Jose Convention Center - Parkside Hall	n/a	n/a	30,000	n/a
San Jose McEnery Convention Center	425,000	22,000	143,000	30

Note: n/a not available
Source: www.officialtravelguide.com; www.eventective.com; original research

Hotels/Conference Centers

Name	Guest Rooms	Exhibit Space (sq. ft.)	Meeting Space (sq. ft.)
Doubletree Hotel San Jose	505	30,000	30,000
Silicon Valley Conference Center	n/a	n/a	n/a
The Fairmont Hotel San Jose/Silicon Valley	805	21,800	45,000

Note: n/a not available
Source: www.officialtravelguide.com; www.eventective.com; original research

Living Environment

COST OF LIVING

Cost of Living Index

Year	Composite Index	Groceries	Housing	Utilities	Trans- portation	Health Care	Misc. Goods/ Services
2004	172.1	143.1	281.5	115.4	130.2	140.3	118.1
2005	167.8	143.8	270.5	110.8	122.8	120.1	125.0
2006	156.8	144.6	253.5	101.9	111.4	118.9	117.0

Note: U.S. = 100
Source: The Council for Community and Economic Research (formerly ACCRA), Cost of Living Index, 2004, 2005 and 2006 4-Quarter Averages

HOUSING

House Price Index (HPI)

Area	National Ranking[2]	Quarterly Change (%)	One-Year Change (%)	Five-Year Change (%)
MSA[1]	164	0.14	4.19	56.73
U.S.[3]	-	1.12	5.87	55.21

Note: The HPI is a weighted repeat sales index. It measures average price changes in repeat sales or refinancings on the same properties. This information is obtained by reviewing repeat mortgage transactions on single-family properties whose mortgages have been purchased or securitized by Fannie Mae or Freddie Mac in January 1975; (1) Metropolitan Statistical Area - see Appendix B for areas included; (2) Rankings are based on annual percentage change for all metro areas containing at least 15,000 transactions over the last 10 years and ranges from 1 to 282; (3) figures based on a weighted division average; all figures are for the period ending December 31, 2006
Source: Office of Federal Housing Enterprise Oversight, House Price Index, March 1, 2007

House Price Valuations

Area	Q4 1999	Q4 2000	Q4 2001	Q4 2002	Q4 2003	Q4 2004	Q4 2005	Q4 2006
MSA[1]	-18.6	-8.2	2.3	14.2	14.5	21.3	38.9	37.1

Note: Figures show the percentage of over- or under-valuation of single family homes relative to statistically normal house values (e.g. a value of 23.6 indicates that house values are 23.6% overvalued). Statistically normal house values are based on house prices, interest rates, household incomes, population densities, and any historical premiums or discounts metropolitan areas have exhibited over time; (1) Figures cover the Metropolitan Statistical Area - see Appendix B for areas included
Source: Global Insight/National City Corporation, House Prices in America, March 2007

Median Home Prices

Area	2004	2005	2006p	Percent Change 2005 to 2006
Metro Area[1]	698.5	744.5	775.0	4.1
U.S. Average	195.2	219.0	222.0	1.4

Note: Figures are median sales prices of existing single-family homes in thousands of dollars; (p) preliminary; n/a not available; (1) Covers the San Jose-Sunnyvale-Santa Clara, CA Metropolitan Statistical Area - see Appendix B for areas included
Source: National Association of Realtors, Metropolitan Area Prices, 4th Quarter 2006

Housing: Year Structure Built

Area	1990 -2000	1980 -1989	1970 -1979	1960 -1969	1950 -1959	1940 -1949	Before 1940	Median Year
City	12.3	14.8	28.5	23.6	11.9	3.8	5.2	1972
MSA[1]	11.5	13.4	25.2	22.8	16.6	5.2	5.3	1970
U.S.	17.0	15.8	18.5	13.7	12.7	7.3	15.0	1971

Note: Figures are percentages; (1) Metropolitan Statistical Area - see Appendix A for areas included
Source: Census 2000, Summary File 3

Average New Home Price

Area	2004	2005	2006
City	743,026	800,379	817,688
U.S.	253,574	275,712	299,269

Note: Figures, in dollars, are based on a new home with 2,400 sq. ft. of living area on an 8,000 sq. ft. lot.
Source: The Council for Community and Economic Research (formerly ACCRA), Cost of Living Index, 2004, 2005 and 2006 4-Quarter Averages

Average Apartment Rent

Area	2004	2005	2006
City	1,548	1,358	1,216
U.S.	716	740	766

Note: Figures, in dollars per month, are based on an unfurnished two bedroom, 1-1/2 or 2 bath apartment, approximately 950 sq. ft. in size, excluding all utilities except water
Source: The Council for Community and Economic Research (formerly ACCRA), Cost of Living Index, 2004, 2005 and 2006 4-Quarter Averages

RESIDENTIAL UTILITIES

Average Residential Utility Costs

Area	All Electric ($/mth)	Part Electric ($/mth)	Other Energy ($/mth)	Phone ($/mth)
City	–	108.52	62.30	23.96
U.S.	136.00	76.53	90.52	25.87

Source: The Council for Community and Economic Research (formerly ACCRA), Cost of Living Index, 2006 4-Quarter Average

HEALTH

Average Health Care Costs

Area	Optometrist ($/visit)	Doctor ($/visit)	Dentist ($/visit)
City	102.58	108.66	81.01
U.S.	76.38	76.10	68.72

Note: Optometrist—based on a full vision eye exam for an established adult patient;
Doctor—based on a general practitioner's routine exam of an established patient;
Dentist—based on adult teeth cleaning and periodic oral exam.
Source: The Council for Community and Economic Research (formerly ACCRA), Cost of Living Index, 2006 4-Quarter Average

Mortality Rates

ICD-10 Sub-Chapter	ICD-10 Code	Age-Adjusted Death Rate per 100,000 population[1]	U.S. Age-Adjusted Death Rate per 100,000 population
Malignant neoplasms	C00-C97	148.2	185.8
Ischaemic heart diseases	I20-I25	106.6	150.2
Other forms of heart disease	I30-I51	27.4	50.8
Cerebrovascular diseases	I60-I69	44.4	50.0
Chronic lower respiratory diseases	J40-J47	29.7	41.1
Diabetes mellitus	E10-E14	19.8	24.5
Other degenerative diseases of the nervous system	G30-G31	21.2	22.3
Other external causes of accidental injury	W00-X59	14.7	21.2
Influenza and pneumonia	J10-J18	20.2	19.8
Hypertensive diseases	I10-I13	23.9	18.1

Note: ICD-10 = International Classification of Diseases 10th Revision; (1) Figures cover Santa Clara County, CA
Source: Centers for Disease Control and Prevention, National Center for Health Statistics. Compressed Mortality File 1999-2004. CDC WONDER On-line Database, compiled from Compressed Mortality File 1999-2004 Series 20 No. 2J, 2007.

Health Risk Data

Item	Area[1] (%)	U.S. (%)
Adults who have been told they have high blood pressure	n/a	25.5
Adults who have been told they have high blood cholesterol	n/a	35.6
Adults who have been told they have diabetes[2]	n/a	7.3
Adults who have been told they have arthritis	n/a	27.0
Adults who have been told they currently have asthma	n/a	8.0
Adults who are current smokers	n/a	20.6

Note: (1) Figures cover the Metropolitan Statistical Area - see Appendix B for areas included; n/a not available;
(2) Figures do not include pregnancy-related diabetes, pre-diabetes or borderline diabetes
Source: Centers for Disease Control and Prevention, Behaviorial Risk Factor Surveillance System, SMART:
Selected Metropolitan/Micropolitan Area Trends, 2005

Distribution of Office-Based Physicians

Area	Total	Family/ General Practice	Specialties		
			Medical	Surgical	Other
CMSA[1] (number)	17,058	1,764	6,722	3,668	4,904
CMSA[1] (rate per 10,000 pop.)	24.5	2.5	9.7	5.3	7.1
Metro Average[2] (rate per 10,000 pop.)	19.4	2.1	7.5	4.5	5.3

Note: Data as of December 31, 2004; (1) San Francisco-Oakland-San Jose, CA Consolidated Metropolitan
Statistical Area includes the following counties: Alameda; Contra Costa; Marin; Napa; San Francisco; San
Mateo; Santa Clara; Santa Cruz; Solano; Sonoma;
(2) Average of the 79 unique MSAs and CMSAs in this book
Source: American Medical Association, Physician Characteristics & Distribution in the U.S., 2006

Hospitals

San Jose has the following hospitals: 5 general medical and surgical.
AHA Guide to the Healthcare Field 2007

EDUCATION

Public School District Statistics

District Name	Schls	Pupils	Pupil/ Teacher Ratio	Minority Pupils[1] (%)	Free Lunch Eligible[2] (%)	IEP[3] (%)
Alum Rock Union Elementary	26	13,604	19.2	96.5	64.3	11.5
Berryessa Union Elementary	14	8,419	21.3	90.1	18.6	8.4
Cambrian Elementary	6	2,897	20.5	42.5	17.1	8.2
Campbell Union High	7	7,803	25.8	46.0	10.4	10.6
East Side Union High	23	25,496	22.2	86.7	25.0	10.8
Evergreen Elementary	18	13,354	21.5	89.3	24.4	7.9
Franklin-Mckinley Elementary	15	9,837	19.9	97.0	60.3	8.1
Moreland Elementary	8	4,274	20.1	57.6	23.3	10.1
Mt. Pleasant Elementary	5	2,892	19.8	93.2	45.4	11.0
Oak Grove Elementary	20	11,714	21.0	73.5	31.1	10.1
San Jose Unified	55	31,874	19.2	71.4	33.9	11.8
Union Elementary	8	4,446	21.1	31.8	9.1	11.6

Note: Table includes regular local school districts with 2,000 or more students; (1) Percentage of students that
are not white, non-Hispanic; (2) Percentage of students that are eligible for the free lunch program;
(3) Percentage of students that have an Individualized Education Program.
Source: U.S. Department of Education, National Center for Education Statistics, Common Core of Data, Local
Education Agency (School District) Universe Survey: School Year 2004-2005; U.S. Department of Education,
National Center for Education Statistics, Common Core of Data, Public Elementary/Secondary School Universe
Survey: School Year 2004-2005

Top Public High Schools

High School Name	Index[1]	Rank[1]	Subsidized Lunch (%)[2]	E&E (%)[3]
Hill	1.458	740	69.0	28.0**
Leland	2.258	273	7.0	47.0
Lincoln	1.340	859	35.0	n/a
Lynbrook	1.747	501	16.0	58.0
Pioneer	1.351	847	17.2	n/a
San Jose High Academy	2.409	224	58.8	n/a*
Silver Creek	1.835	445	25.0	n/a
Willow Glen	1.147	1,070	37.0	23.5

Note: (1) Public schools are ranked according to a ratio that is the number of Advanced Placement and/or International Baccalaureate tests taken by all students at a school in 2005 divided by the number of graduating seniors. All of the schools on the list have an index of at least 1.000; they are in the top five percent of public schools measured this way. The rankings range from 1 to 1,236; (2) Percentage of students receiving federally subsidized meals; (3) E & E stands for equity and excellence percentage: the portion of all graduating seniors at a school that had at least one passing grade on one AP or IB test; (*) Gave just IB tests; (**) Gave both IB and AP tests. AP and IB participation are indicators of a school's efforts to get students to excel and prepare for college; n/a not available
Source: Newsweek Online, May 23, 2006

Educational Quality

School District	Education Quotient[1]	Graduate Outcome[2]	Community Index[3]	Resource Index[4]	Rating[5]
San Jose Unified	57	53	67	57	Green

Note: Scores are national percentile rankings and range from 1 (worst) to 99 (best); (1) Combination of the Graduate Outcome, Community and Resource Indexes weighted to reflect the greater importance of the Graduate Outcome and Resource Index; (2) Based on graduation rates and college board scores (SAT/ACT); (3) Based on the surrounding community's level of affluence and adult education; (4) Based on teacher salaries, per-pupil expenditures and student-teacher ratios; (5) School districts receive one of five rankings: Gold Medal (top 16 percent of districts evaluated); Blue Ribbon (top third); Green Light (average); Yellow Light (bottom 25 percent); Red Light (bottom 10 percent).
Source: Expansion Management, "2007 Education Quotient," January 2007

Highest Level of Education

Area	Less than H.S.	H.S. Diploma	Some College, No Deg.	Associate Degree	Bachelors Degree	Masters Degree	Profess. School Degree	Doctorate Degree
City	22.3	18.2	20.8	7.7	20.6	7.7	1.5	1.3
MSA[1]	17.4	16.2	19.9	7.4	23.4	11.2	2.2	2.4
U.S.	19.4	28.4	21.2	6.4	15.7	5.9	2.0	1.0

Note: Figures are 2006 estimated percentages and cover persons age 25 and over; (1) Metropolitan Statistical Area - see Appendix B for areas included
Source: Claritas, Inc.

Educational Attainment by Race

Area	High School Graduate (%)					Bachelor's Degree (%)				
	Total	White	Black	Asian	Hisp.[2]	Total	White	Black	Asian	Hisp.[2]
City	78.3	84.8	88.0	79.7	52.1	31.6	33.9	28.0	40.7	8.9
MSA[1]	83.4	88.4	88.6	84.8	55.1	40.5	42.5	29.7	51.3	11.0
U.S.	80.4	83.6	72.3	80.4	52.4	24.4	26.1	14.3	44.1	10.4

Note: Figures shown cover persons 25 years old and over; (1) Metropolitan Statistical Area - see Appendix A for areas included; (2) people of Hispanic origin can be of any race
Source: Census 2000, Summary File 3

School Enrollment by Type

Area	Grades KG to 8				Grades 9 to 12			
	Public		Private		Public		Private	
	Enrollment	%	Enrollment	%	Enrollment	%	Enrollment	%
City	106,741	88.9	13,294	11.1	49,044	91.1	4,769	8.9
MSA[1]	184,435	86.6	28,642	13.4	83,075	89.8	9,411	10.2
U.S.	33,526,011	88.7	4,285,121	11.3	14,848,628	90.6	1,532,323	9.4

Note: Figures shown cover persons 3 years old and over; (1) Metropolitan Statistical Area - see Appendix A for areas included
Source: Census 2000, Summary File 3

School Enrollment by Race

Area	Grades KG to 8 (%)				Grades 9 to 12 (%)			
	White	Black	Asian	Hisp.[1]	White	Black	Asian	Hisp.[1]
City	41.2	3.4	25.1	39.9	39.4	3.4	27.0	39.0
MSA[2]	47.3	2.6	24.3	32.8	45.3	3.1	25.2	33.5
U.S.	68.5	15.5	3.3	16.8	68.8	15.5	3.8	15.7

Note: Figures shown cover persons 3 years old and over; (1) people of Hispanic origin can be of any race; (2) Metropolitan Statistical Area - see Appendix A for areas included
Source: Census 2000, Summary File 3

Average Salaries of Public School Teachers

District	2004-05		2005-06		Percent Change 2004-05 to 2005-06
	Dollars	Rank[1]	Dollars	Rank[1]	
CALIFORNIA	57,876	2	59,345	3	2.54
U.S. Average	47,674	-	49,109	-	3.01

Note: (1) State rank ranges from 1 to 51.
Source: National Education Association, Rankings & Estimates: Rankings of the States 2005 and Estimates of School Statistics 2006, November 2006

Higher Education

Four-Year Colleges			Two-Year Colleges			Medical Schools[1]	Law Schools[2]	Voc/ Tech[3]
Public	Private Non-profit	Private For-profit	Public	Private Non-profit	Private For-profit			
1	3	2	2	0	0	0	0	2

Note: Figures cover institutions located within the city limits; (1) includes schools accredited by the Liaison Committee on Medical Education and the American Osteopathic Association; (2) includes American Bar Association-accredited law schools; (3) includes all schools with programs that are less than 2 years
Source: National Center for Education Statistics, The Integrated Postsecondary Education System (IPEDS) Peer Analysis System, 2006; www.usnews.com, America's Best Graduate Schools 2008, Medical School Directory; www.usnews.com, America's Best Graduate Schools 2008, Law School Directory

PRESIDENTIAL ELECTION

2004 Presidential Election Results

Area	Bush	Kerry	Nader	Other
Santa Clara County	34.6	63.9	0.2	1.2
U.S.	50.7	48.3	0.4	0.6

Note: Results are percentages and may not add to 100% due to rounding
Source: Dave Leip's Atlas of U.S. Presidential Elections, www.uselectionatlas.org

Major Employers

Company Name	Industry	Type of Site
AOL	Telephone communication, except radio	Branch
Advanced Crdiovascular Systems	Surgical and medical instruments	Single
Advanced Micro Devices Inc	Semiconductors and related devices	Headquarters
Asifco	Management services	Single
City of San Jose	Executive offices	Headquarters
HP	Commercial physical research	Branch
HP	Electronic computers	Headquarters
Hitachi Global Storage Tech	Computer storage devices	Headquarters
Intel	Semiconductors and related devices	Headquarters
LSI Logic	Semiconductors and related devices	Headquarters
National Semiconductor Corp	Semiconductors and related devices	Headquarters
Palo Alto Healthcare System	Administration of veterans' affairs	Branch
Space Systems/Loral Inc	Radio and t.v. communications equipment	Headquarters
Stanford Linear Accelrtr Ctr	Libraries	Branch
Stanford University Medical	General medical and surgical hospitals	Branch
Sun Microsystems	Custom computer programming services	Branch
Sun Microsystems	Electronic computers	Headquarters

Note: Companies shown are located within the metropolitan area and have 2,200 or more employees; nec = not elsewhere classified.
Source: www.zapdata.com, January 2007

Crime Rate

Area	All Crimes	Violent Crimes				Property Crimes		
		Murder	Forcible Rape	Robbery	Aggrav. Assault	Burglary	Larceny -Theft	Motor Vehicle Theft
City	2,901.8	2.9	28.9	97.1	254.7	444.7	1,468.8	604.8
Suburbs[1]	3,031.3	2.1	18.0	54.2	169.0	512.9	1,963.9	311.1
Metro[2]	2,964.1	2.5	23.7	76.5	213.5	477.5	1,706.7	463.7
U.S.	3,899.0	5.6	31.7	140.7	291.1	726.7	2,286.3	416.7

Note: Figures are crimes per 100,000 population; (1) All areas within the metro area that are located outside the city limits; (2) Metropolitan Statistical Area - see Appendix B for areas included
Source: FBI Uniform Crime Reports, 2005

Hate Crimes

Area	Number of Quarters Reported	Bias Motivation				
		Race	Religion	Sexual Orientation	Ethnicity	Disability
City	4	14	4	3	1	0

Source: Federal Bureau of Investigation, Hate Crime Statistics 2005

Culture

Dance[1]	Theatre[1]	Instrumental Music[1]	Vocal Music[1]	Series/ Festivals	Museums	Zoos
2	8	4	2	0	10	1

Note: (1) number of professional perfoming groups
Source: The Grey House Performing Arts Directory, 2007; Official Museum Directory, 2007

Professional Sports Teams

Major League Baseball	National Basketball Association	National Football League	National Hockey League	Major League Soccer	Women's National Basketball Association
0	0	0	1	1	0

Note: Includes teams located in the San Jose metro area.
Source: www.sportsvenues.com, Listing of Venues by State/Province and City, 2006

MEDIA

Newspapers

Name	Target Audience	Frequency	Circulation
Campbell Reporter	General	Non-Daily	18,000
Cupertino Courier	General	Non-Daily	18,600
El Observador	General/Hispanic	Non-Daily	36,240
El Vistazo	Hispanic	Non-Daily	35,000
La Oferta Review	Hispanic	Non-Daily	53,920
Metro	General	Non-Daily	105,000
Nuevo Mundo	General/Hispanic	Non-Daily	53,000
San Jose Mercury News	n/a	Daily	277,100
The Sunnyvale Sun	General	Non-Daily	18,000
Vietnam - The Daily News	n/a	Daily	13,000

Note: Includes newspapers whose offices are located in the city and whose circulations are 10,000 or more; n/a not available
Source: BurrellesLuce, MediaContacts Online, January 2006

Television Stations

Name	Ch.	Network(s)	Type	Ownership
KTVU	2	Fox	Commercial	Cox Enterprises Inc.
KRON	4	n/a	Commercial	Young Broadcasting Inc.
KPIX	5	CBS	Commercial	CBS
KGO	7	ABC	Commercial	n/a
KFWU	8	n/a	Commercial	Pappas Telecasting Companies
KTSF	8	n/a	Commercial	Lincoln Broadcasting Company
KQED	9	PBS	Public	KQED Inc.
KNTV	11	NBC	Commercial	NBC TV Stations Division
KDTV	14	Univision	Commercial	Univision Television Group
KCU	15	NBC/Telem.	Commercial	Telemundo Group Inc.
KBWB	20	WBN	Commercial	Granite Broadcasting Corporation
KRCB	22	PBS	Public	Rural California Broadcasting Corp.
KMTP	32	n/a	Public	Minority Television Project
KICU	36	n/a	Commercial	Cox Enterprises Inc.
KCNS	38	n/a	Commercial	Shop at Home Inc.
KTNC	42	n/a	Commercial	Pappas Telecasting Companies
KBHK	44	UPN	Commercial	United Television Inc.
KSTS	48	Telemundo	Commercial	Telemundo Group Inc.
KFTY	50	n/a	Commercial	Clear Channel Communications Inc.
KTEH	54	PBS	Public	KTEH Foundation
KCSM	60	PBS	Public	San Mateo County Community College District
KKPX	65	Pax	Commercial	Paxson Communications Corporation
KTLN	68	n/a	Non-comm.	North Bay Television Inc.

Note: Stations included cover the San Francisco-Oakland-San Jose DMA (Designated Market Area); n/a not available
BurrellesLuce, MediaContacts Online, January 2006

Major AM Radio Stations

Call Letters	Freq. (kHz)	Station Type	Target Audience	Station Format	Music Format
KSFO	560	n/a	General	News/Talk	n/a
KNBR	680	n/a	General	Music/Sports/Talk	n/a
KLVB	730	Non-Comm	Religious	Educational/Music	Christian
KCBS	740	n/a	General	Music/News/Sports/Talk	n/a
KGO	810	n/a	General	News/Talk	n/a
KNEW	910	Commercial	General	Music/News/Talk	80's
KABL	960	Commercial	General	Music	Easy Listening
KNBR	1050	n/a	General/Men	Music/News/Sports/Talk	n/a
KFAX	1100	n/a	General/Religious	Music/Talk	n/a
KZSJ	1120	Commercial	Asian	Ed/Music/News/Sports/Talk	Latin
KLOK	1170	Commercial	General/Hispanic	Music	Latin
KDYA	1190	Commercial	Black/General/Rel	Music/News/Talk	Gospel
KEBR	1210	Non-Comm	Religious	Educational/Music/News	Christian
KDAC	1230	n/a	General/Hispanic	Music	n/a
KLLK	1250	n/a	General/Hispanic	Music/News	n/a
KOIT	1260	Commercial	General	Music	Adult Contemp.
KAZA	1290	n/a	General/Hispanic	Music/Sports	n/a
KSRO	1350	n/a	General	News/Talk	n/a
KZSF	1370	Commercial	General/Hispanic	Music/Sports	Latin
KVTO	1400	Commercial	General	Music/News/Sports/Talk	International
KUKI	1400	n/a	General/Hispanic	Music	n/a
KVVN	1430	Commercial	General	Music/News/Sports	International
KVON	1440	n/a	General	News/Sports/Talk	n/a
KEST	1450	Commercial	General	Music/News	International
KRRS	1460	n/a	Hispanic	Music/News/Talk	n/a
KSJX	1500	Commercial	Asian	Music/News/Sports	Classical
KYCY	1550	n/a	General	Music/News/Sports/Talk	n/a
KLIV	1590	Commercial	General	News/Sports	n/a
KDIA	1640	Commercial	General	Talk	n/a

Note: Stations included cover the San Francisco-Oakland-San Jose DMA (Designated Market Area); n/a not available
Source: BurrellesLuce, MediaContacts Online, January 2006

Major FM Radio Stations

Call Letters	Freq. (mHz)	Station Type	Target Audience	Station Format	Music Format
KECG	88.1	Commercial	Hispanic	Ed/Music/News/Sports	Rhythm & Blues
KQED	88.5	n/a	General	Music/News/Talk	World Music
KLVR	91.9	n/a	Religious	Educational/Music	n/a
KSJO	92.3	n/a	General	Music/News/Talk	n/a
KFGY	92.9	n/a	General	Music	n/a
KPFA	94.1	Non-Comm	General	Educational/Music/News	Middle of the Rd.
KRZZ	96.3	Commercial	General	News	n/a
KLLC	97.3	n/a	General	Music/News/Sports	n/a
KISQ	98.1	Commercial	General	Music	Rhythm & Blues
KLVS	99.3	Non-Comm	Religious	Educational/Music	Christian
KNTI	99.5	n/a	General	Music/News	n/a
KIOI	101.3	Commercial	General	Music	80's
KMEL	106.1	n/a	General/Young Adult	Music	n/a
KEZR	106.5	Commercial	General	Music/Talk	Adult Contemp.
KEAR	106.9	Non-Comm	Christian/General	Music/Talk	Gospel

Note: Stations included cover the San Francisco-Oakland-San Jose DMA (Designated Market Area); n/a not available
BurrellesLuce, MediaContacts Online, January 2006

CLIMATE

Average and Extreme Temperatures

Temperature	Jan	Feb	Mar	Apr	May	Jun	Jul	Aug	Sep	Oct	Nov	Dec	Yr.
Extreme High (°F)	76	82	83	95	103	104	105	101	105	100	87	76	105
Average High (°F)	57	61	63	67	70	74	75	75	76	72	65	58	68
Average Temp. (°F)	50	53	55	58	61	65	66	67	66	63	56	50	59
Average Low (°F)	42	45	46	48	51	55	57	58	57	53	47	42	50
Extreme Low (°F)	21	26	30	32	38	43	45	47	41	33	29	23	21

Note: Figures cover the years 1945-1993
Source: National Climatic Data Center, International Station Meteorological Climate Summary, 9/96

Average Precipitation/Snowfall/Humidity

Precip./Humidity	Jan	Feb	Mar	Apr	May	Jun	Jul	Aug	Sep	Oct	Nov	Dec	Yr.
Avg. Precip. (in.)	2.7	2.3	2.2	0.9	0.3	0.1	Tr	Tr	0.2	0.7	1.7	2.3	13.5
Avg. Snowfall (in.)	Tr	Tr	Tr	0	0	0	0	0	0	0	0	Tr	Tr
Avg. Rel. Hum. 7am (%)	82	82	80	76	74	73	77	79	79	79	81	82	79
Avg. Rel. Hum. 4pm (%)	62	59	56	52	53	54	58	58	55	54	59	63	57

Note: Figures cover the years 1945-1993; Tr = Trace amounts (<0.05 in. of rain; <0.5 in. of snow)
Source: National Climatic Data Center, International Station Meteorological Climate Summary, 9/96

Weather Conditions

Temperature			Daytime Sky			Precipitation		
10°F & below	32°F & below	90°F & above	Clear	Partly cloudy	Cloudy	0.01 inch or more precip.	0.1 inch or more snow/ice	Thunder-storms
0	5	5	106	180	79	57	< 1	6

Note: Figures are average number of days per year and cover the years 1945-1993
Source: National Climatic Data Center, International Station Meteorological Climate Summary, 9/96

HAZARDOUS WASTE

Superfund Sites

San Jose has two hazardous waste sites on the EPA's Superfund Final National Priorities List: **Fairchild Semiconductor Corp. (South San Jose Plant); Lorentz Barrel & Drum Co..**
U.S. Environmental Protection Agency, Final National Priorities List, March 20, 2007

AIR & WATER QUALITY

Air Quality Index

Area	Percent of Days when Air Quality was...[2]				AQI Statistics	
	Good	Moderate	Unhealthy for Sensitive Groups	Unhealthy	Maximum	Median
MSA[1]	81.9	15.9	2.2	0.0	129	36

Note: The Air Quality Index (AQI) is an index for reporting daily air quality. EPA calculates the AQI for five major air pollutants regulated by the Clean Air Act: ground-level ozone, particle pollution (also known as particulate matter), carbon monoxide, sulfur dioxide, and nitrogen dioxide. The AQI runs from 0 to 500. The higher the AQI value, the greater the level of air pollution and the greater the health concern. There are six AQI categories: "Good" The AQI is between 0 and 50. Air quality is considered satisfactory; "Moderate" The AQI is between 51 and 100. Air quality is acceptable; "Unhealthy for Sensitive Groups" When AQI values are between 101 and 150, members of sensitive groups may experience health effects; "Unhealthy" When AQI values are between 151 and 200 everyone may begin to experience health effects; "Very Unhealthy" AQI values between 201 and 300 trigger a health alert; "Hazardous" AQI values over 300 trigger health warnings of emergency conditions; (1) Metropolitan Statistical Area - see Appendix A for areas included; (2) Based on 365 days with AQI data in 2005.
Source: U.S. Environmental Protection Agency, Air Quality Index Report, 2005

Air Quality Index Pollutants

Area	Percent of Days when AQI Pollutant was...[2]					
	Carbon Monoxide	Nitrogen Dioxide	Ozone	Sulfur Dioxide	Particulate Matter 2.5	Particulate Matter 10
MSA[1]	0.0	0.0	65.8	0.0	33.2	1.1

Note: The Air Quality Index (AQI) is an index for reporting daily air quality. EPA calculates the AQI for five major air pollutants regulated by the Clean Air Act: ground-level ozone, particle pollution (also known as particulate matter), carbon monoxide, sulfur dioxide, and nitrogen dioxide. The AQI runs from 0 to 500. The higher the AQI value, the greater the level of air pollution and the greater the health concern; (1) Metropolitan Statistical Area - see Appendix A for areas included; (2) Based on 365 days with AQI data in 2005.
Source: U.S. Environmental Protection Agency, Air Quality Index Report, 2005

Number of Days with Air Quality Index Values Greater than 100

Area	Trend Sites (5)								All Sites (31)
	1998	1999	2000	2001	2002	2003	2004	2005	2005
MSA[1]	5	17	20	12	9	6	2	6	10

Note: An AQI value greater than 100 indicates that air quality would have been in the unhealthful range on that day. Data from exceptional events are not included. These counts are presented in two ways. First, the counts are based on sites having an adequate record of monitoring data during the trend period (trend sites). These counts represent the relative change in the number of days with AQI values greater than 100. In the last column, the counts are based on all sites with data in the most recent year (because it is possible for a site to have data in the most recent year but not enough data to be a trend site); (1) Metropolitan Statistical Area - see Appendix A for areas included; n/a not available.
Source: U.S. Environmental Protection Agency, Air Trends Fact Book 2005

Maximum Pollutant Concentrations

	Particulate Matter 10 (ug/m³)	Particulate Matter 2.5 (ug/m³)	Ozone 1-hour (ppm)	Carbon Monoxide (ppm)	Sulfur Dioxide (ppm)	Nitrogen Dioxide (ppm)	Lead (ug/m³)
MSA[1] Level	67	40	0.104	3	n/a	0.019	n/a
NAAQS[2]	150	65	0.125	9	0.140	0.053	1.50
Met NAAQS[2]	Yes	Yes	Yes	Yes	n/a	Yes	n/a

Note: Data from exceptional events are not included; (1) Metropolitan Statistical Area - see Appendix A for areas included; (2) National Ambient Air Quality Standards; n/a not available
Units: ppm = parts per million; ug/m³ = micrograms per cubic meter
Source: U.S. Environmental Protection Agency, Air Trends Fact Book 2005

Watershed Health

The U.S. Environmental Protection Agency monitors the health of the aquatic resources for the nation's 2,000+ watersheds. **The Coyote watershed serves the San Jose area and received an overall Index of Watershed Indicators (IWI) score of 5 (more serious problems - low vulnerability).** The IWI score is based on seven condition and nine vulnerability indicators. The overall IWI score ranges from 1 (best health) to 6 (worst health). The Condition Indicators include: designated use attainment, fish and wildlife consumption advisories, source water condition, contaminated sediments, ambient water quality, and wetlands loss index. The Vulnerability Indicators include: aquatic species at risk, conventional and toxic loads over permitted limits, urban and agricultural runoff potential, population change, hydrologic modification, estuarine pollution susceptibility, and air deposition. *Note: The IWI is no longer being updated by the U.S. EPA. Source: U.S. Environmental Protection Agency, Index of Watershed Indicators, October 26, 2001*

Drinking Water

Water System Name	Pop. Served	Primary Water Source Type	Number of Violations in 2006[a]		
			Health Based	Significant Monitoring	Monitoring
San Jose Water Company	990,000	Surface	None	None	None

Note: (a) Based on violation data from January 1, 2006 to December 31, 2006
Source: U.S. Environmental Protection Agency, Office of Ground Water and Drinking Water, Safe Drinking Water Information System (data extracted April 12, 2007)

San Jose tap water is alkaline, very hard and not fluoridated.
Editor & Publisher Market Guide, 2005

Scottsdale, Arizona

Background

Scottsdale is located in Maricopa County in central Arizona, 10 miles east of Phoenix. The city is known as a center for electronics equipment, the aerial mapping industry, and fine clothing. Most notably, the town is also a major tourism destination and retirement center, with warm winters and strong sunshine most of the year.

From 800 to 1400 AD, the area's residents were the Hohokam Indians, who farmed using a sophisticated irrigation system involving more than 200 miles of canals. After the Hohokam culture declined, Pima and Maricopa Indians were the only inhabitants until the late 1880s, when white settlers established a permanent presence in what is now the town of Scottsdale. Army chaplain Winfield Scott and his wife were the first non-Indian farmers in the region, planting oranges, sweet potatoes, and peanuts.

In 1896, the population had reached a level that justified the establishment of the first school; a year later, J. L. Davis opened a general store, which also served as a post office. Year-round good weather made Scottsdale a natural resort location, and in 1909, the Ingleside Inn was built, the first of many such establishments to follow. Population growth, however, was slow — by 1951, the year of Scottsdale's incorporation as a city, the town had only 2,000 residents. The newly elected mayor, Malcolm White, was a great promoter of his new city, publicizing its old-fashioned virtues and magnificent scenery by dubbing it "The West's Most Western Town."

Scottsdale has distinguished itself in its efforts to preserve the beauty of the desert environment; there are more than 40 miles of walking and biking trails, and many golf courses connect to the Indian Bend Wash Greenbelt, an integrated flood-control and preservation project that avoids as much as possible the use of concrete.

The city is a golfer's paradise, with more than 125 courses in the area open almost year-round. Skiing is available to the north, and the spectacular Sonoran desert is just to the south. Tonto National Forest adjoins Scottsdale, which is also within easy driving distance of some of the nation's most revered natural treasures — Carefree/Cave Creek, McDowell Mountain Regional Park, Camel Back Mountain Park, Montezuma's Castle National Monument, Fort Verde State Historic Park, Casa Grande National Monument, and Picacho Peak State Park.

Taliesin West, the architectural school founded by Frank Lloyd Wright, is in Scottsdale, as is the Cosanti Foundation, which pursues the projects of the visionary architect Paolo Soleri.

The city continues to grow and improve. In 2003, development of the McDowell Mountain Ranch site as a major residential community was completed and the site is now fully occupied. In 2007, construction was completed on the Canal Bank improvement project, to bring pedestrian paths, landscaping, public art, and park-like areas to downtown.

The city is well known for its support of the arts, with more than 100 art galleries and craft shops. The Scottsdale Historical Museum documents the area's rich local history, and the Fleischer Museum exhibits Impressionist painting and sculpture. The city is home to its own symphony orchestra, and hosts a Dixieland Jazz Festival each November. The Scottsdale Museum of Contemporary Art opened in 1999. The town is also host to the world's largest golf tournament, the FBR Open, known as the "Greatest Show on Grass." WestWord, Scottsdales premier event facility, is undergoing improvement and adding new facilities.

The area features two important sites of interest to horticulturists — the Arboretum at Arizona State University and the Boyce Thompson Southwest Arboretum. Scottsdale is also convenient to Arizona State University and other major educational institutions.

Sunshine in Scottsdale is abundant. The climate is dry, with very hot summers and mild winters. What rainfall occurs generally comes during two seasons, from Thanksgiving to early April, when Pacific storms bring periodic rains, and during July and August, the thunderstorm season.

Rankings

General Rankings

■ Phoenix was ranked #273 out of 331 metro areas in *Cities Ranked & Rated*. Criteria: cost of living; climate; crime; transportation; economy and jobs; education; arts and culture; health and healthcare; leisure. *Cities Ranked & Rated, 1st Edition, 2004*

■ The Phoenix metro area was selected one of America's "Top 10 Metros Overall" by *Expansion Management* in their 4th annual Mayor's Challenge ranking of metro areas that have achieved solid ratings across the board in numerous *EM* studies during the past 12 months. The area ranked #10. Criteria: education (with emphasis on college board test results and high school graduation rates); availability of quality healthcare services and the cost to employers; quality of life; logistics workforce and companies; transportation infrastructure; quality and quantity of highly educated technical workers; and business climate. *Expansion Management, August 2006*

■ Scottsdale was selected as one of "America's Top 100 Places to Live" by Relocate-America.com. Nominations were accepted throughout the year for cities and towns considered to be "great places to live." The nominations, along with key data regarding education, employment, economy, crime, parks, recreation and housing were reviewed, rated and judged by the Relocate-America.com editorial staff. *Relocate-America.com, "Relocate America's Top 100 Places to Live in 2006"*

■ Scottsdale was selected as one of the "Best Places to Live 2006" by *Money* magazine. The city ranked #7 out of 90 in the small city (under 300,000 population) category. Places were ranked using 38 quality-of-life indicators and six economic opportunity measures in the following categories: ease of living; health; education; crime; park space; arts and leisure. *Money, "Best Places to Live 2006"*

Business/Finance Rankings

■ Phoenix was selected as one of the best places to start and grow a company by *Entrepreneur* and the National Policy Research Council. The Phoenix metro area ranked #1 out of 50 large metro areas. Criteria: business formation and growth (firms started four to 14 years ago that still employ at least 5 people and experienced rapid growth over the last four years). *Entrepreneur/National Policy Research Council, "Hot Cities for Entrepreneurs," September 2006*

■ The Phoenix metro area was selected as one of "America's 50 Hottest Cities" for business relocations and expansions. Criteria: industry's most prominent site selection consultants were asked to list their top city choices for relocating and expanding manufacturing companies, taking into consideration such factors as the business climate, work force quality, operating costs, incentive programs, and the ease of working with local political and economic development officials. *Expansion Management, January-February 2007*

■ The Phoenix metro area was cited as one of America's "Most Picture Perfect Metros" by *Plant Sites and Parks* magazine. Each year *PSP* readers rank the metro areas they consider best bets for their companies to relocate or expand to in the coming year. The area ranked #4 out of 10. *Plant Sites and Parks, March 2004*

■ Intel, in partnership with Sperling's BestPlaces, ranked the 80 "Best Cities for Teleworking" in America. The Phoenix metro area ranked #15 among extra large metro areas. The study identifies cities that hold the greatest potential for teleworking based on a host of factors including typical commuting times, fuel prices, availability of broadband Internet access and percentage of the population in telework friendly jobs. The study also factored in extreme climate and natural hazards. *Intel, "Best Cities for Teleworking," March 30, 2006*

■ The Phoenix metro area appeared on the Milken Institute "2005 Best Performing Cities" index. Rank: #15 out of 200 large metro areas. Criteria: job growth; wage and salary growth; high-tech output growth. *Milken Institute, "2005 Best Performing Cities," February 2006*

■ The Phoenix metro area was selected as one of "The Best Cities for Doing Business in America." *Inc.* magazine measured employment growth in 393 regions using the following criteria: recent growth trend; mid-term growth; long-term trend; and current year growth. The Phoenix metro area ranked #6 among large metro areas and #36 overall. *Inc., May 2006*

■ The Phoenix metro area was selected as one of "The Top 20 Boom Towns in America." *Business 2.0* magazine and econometric research firm Global Insight compared 319 metropolitan areas in the U.S. and ranked the 61 with populations over 1 million. Criteria: a weighted formula that includes forecast growth rates in sectors that contain the economy's 10 most skilled occupational clusters; the prevalence of college degrees in the local workforce; median salary. The area ranked #12 among large metro areas. *Business 2.0 Magazine, March 2004*

■ Phoenix was identified as one of the 100 "Most Unwired Cities" in the U.S. The area ranked #55 out of the 100 largest metro areas in the U.S. Criteria: number of public and commercial wireless access points (hotspots); airports with wireless Internet access; broadband availability; local wireless networks; and wireless email devices. *Intel, "Most Unwired Cities Survey," June 7, 2005*

■ Phoenix was ranked #38 out of 125 regions worldwide in terms of its "Knowledge Competitiveness Index." The index attempts to measure the knowledge-based development taking place throughout the world and is based on 19 measures of economic performance that indicate a region's ability to translate its knowledge capacity into economic value. *Robert Huggins Associates, World Knowledge Competitiveness Index 2005*

■ *Forbes* ranked the 200 most populous metro areas in the U.S. in terms of the "Best Places for Business and Careers." The Phoenix metro area was ranked #55. Criteria: business costs (labor, energy, tax and office space expenses); living costs (housing, transportation, food and other household expenditures); education levels of the work force; job growth; income growth; migration trends; crime rates; and culture/leisure. *Forbes, April 23, 2007*

■ *Fortune* ranked the 100 largest metro areas in the U.S. in terms of projected median home price change in 2006. The Phoenix metro area ranked #68. *Fortune, "The Top 100: Is the Party Over?" December 26, 2005*

Health/Environment Rankings

■ Doctors at the Harvard School of Public Health ranked 40 metropolitan areas based on data from the government-sponsored Hospital Quality Alliance program. The program tracks the performance of individual hospitals in treating patients for three common health problems: heart attacks, congestive heart failure, and pneumonia. The Phoenix metro area ranked #24 in quality of care for heart attacks, #15 for congestive heart failure, and #8 for pneumonia. *New England Journal of Medicine, July 21, 2005*

■ *Reader's Digest* ranked the 50 largest metro areas in the U.S. in terms of how "clean" they are. The Phoenix metro area ranked #36. Criteria: air quality; water quality; toxic industrial pollution; Superfund sites; and sanitation. *Reader's Digest, "The 50 Cleanest (and Dirtiest) Cities in America," July 2005*

■ The Phoenix metro area appeared in *Country Home's* "2007 Best Green Places Report". The area ranked #115. Criteria included: air and watershed quality; miles of mass transit; green power; number of farmer's markets, organic producers and groceries. *Country Home, "2007 Best Green Places Report," April 2007*

■ Wyeth Consumer Healthcare, in partnership with Sperling's BestPlaces, ranked the nation's 50 most populous metro areas in terms of five key health factors. The Phoenix metro area ranked #21. Criteria: physical activity, health status, nutrition, lifestyle pursuits; and mental wellness. *Wyeth Consumer Healthcare, "Centrum Healthiest Cities Study," April 19, 2005*

■ HealthGrades surveyed over 41,000 individuals on doctor satisfaction and ranked the 20 largest metro areas based on the highest "definitely yes" responses to the question "Do you trust the physician to make decisions/recommendations that are in your best interest?" The Phoenix metro area ranked #13. *HealthGrades.com, "Top Cities in Doctor-Trust," September 7, 2006*

- The American Podiatric Medical Association and *Prevention* magazine ranked America's 100 most populated cities based on fitness-walker friendliness. The best cities have safe streets, beautiful places to walk, mild weather and good air quality. Scottsdale ranked #16. *Prevention, "The Best Walking Cities of 2007," April 2007; American Podiatric Medical Association, "2007 Best Fitness-Walking Cities"*

- Phoenix was identified as a "2007 Asthma Capital." The area ranked #44 out of the nation's 100 largest metropolitan areas. Twelve factors were used to identify the most challenging places to live for people with asthma: estimated prevalence; self-reported prevalence; crude death rate for asthma; annual pollen score; annual air quality; public smoking laws; number of board-certified asthma specialists; school inhaler access laws; rescue medication use; controller medication use; uninsured rate; poverty rate. *Asthma and Allergy Foundation of America, "2007 Asthma Capitals"*

- Phoenix was identified as a "Spring Allergy Capital." The area ranked #21 out of 100. Three groups of factors were used to identify the most severe cities for people with allergies during the spring season: annual pollen levels; medicine utilization; access to board-certified allergists. *Asthma and Allergy Foundation of America, "2007 Spring Allergy Capital Rankings"*

- Phoenix was identified as a "Fall Allergy Capital." The area ranked #63 out of 100. Three groups of factors were used to identify the most severe cities for people with allergies during the fall season: annual pollen levels; medicine utilization; access to board-certified allergists. *Asthma and Allergy Foundation of America, "2006 Fall Allergy Capital Rankings"*

- GlaxoSmithKline, in partnership with Sperling's BestPlaces, analyzed the nation's 100 largest metro areas and identified 25 asthma "hot spots" where high prevalence makes the condition a key issue and environmental triggers and other factors can make living with asthma a particular challenge. The Phoenix metro area ranked #3 with #1 being the most challenging place to live. Criteria: asthma prevalence; asthma mortality; pollen scores; number of asthma specialists per capita; ratio of prescriptions for rescue medications to prescriptions for controller medications (an indicator of proper asthma treatment); air pollution; smoking laws; climate; and prevalence of tobacco use. *GlaxoSmithKline, "Asthma Hot Spots," October 29, 2002*

- Ortho-McNeil Neurologics, in partnership with Sperling's BestPlaces, analyzed 110 metro areas and identified those U.S. cities with the highest prevalence of factors that are most commonly associated with migraine headaches. The Phoenix metro area ranked #54. Criteria: number of migraine-related drug prescriptions per capita; lifestyle factors that can contribute to migraines; environmental factors that can trigger migraines; and consumption of migraine-triggering foods. *Ortho-McNeil Neurologics, "America's Migraine Hot Spots," March 14, 2006*

- Sperling's BestPlaces ranked 331 metro areas and identified the most and least stressful U.S. cities. The Phoenix metro area ranked #20 out of the 100 largest metro areas (#1 = most stressful). Criteria: divorce rate; unemployment rate; violent and property crime; suicide rate; commute time; mental health; alcohol consumption; cloudy days. *www.BestPlaces.net, January 9, 2004*

- Sperling's BestPlaces in partnership with Vistakon ranked the 100 largest metro areas and identified "America's 10 Worst Cities for Comfortable Eyes." The Phoenix metro area ranked #9. Criteria: altitude; sunny days; wind; extreme temperatures; humidity; pollution; commute time; computer use. *Vistakon, "America's Best and Worst Cities for Comfortable Eyes," June 15, 2004*

- HealthGrades evaluated the performance of America's 25 most populous metropolitan areas by measuring the outcomes of five of the highest volume and most widely studied procedures and diagnoses: coronary artery bypass graft surgery; percutaneus coronary interventions; acute myocardial infarction/heart attack in angioplasty-capable hospitals; congestive heart failure; and community acquired pneumonia. The Phoenix metro area ranked #4. *HealthGrades, "HealthGrades Hospital Quality in America Study," October 12, 2004*

■ Phoenix was selected as one of "America's Top 10 Low-Carb Cities" by *LowCarbiz Magazine*. Criteria: abundance of low-carb products; restaurants with low-carb menu items; health practitioners supportive of carb-cutting regimens; local culture generally conducive to exercise and health. *LowCarbiz Magazine, April 2004*

■ Phoenix was selected as one of "America's Pet Healthiest Cities" by Purina. The city ranked #23 out of 50. Criteria: veterinary services; environment; legislation; preventative care; obesity/body condition. *Purina Pet Institute, "America's Pet Healthiest Cities," May 20, 2003*

■ According to research conducted by Malibu Wellness of 100 major U.S. cities' local water quality reports, Scottsdale was selected as a color-unfriendly city. However, due to the fact that one side of the city receives much softer water, hair color application and longevity can be great in one area of the city, but suffers in another area. Criteria: quantity of minerals found in the water supply (lower ppm is better for hair color); type of oxidizers such as chlorine; and pH levels. *Malibu Wellness, Wellness e-Letter, "Best & Worst Cities for Hair Color," February 2005*

Women/Minorities Rankings

■ Phoenix was ranked #64 out of 100 metro areas in *SELF Magazine's* ranking of "America's Best Places for Women." A panel of experts came up with nearly 40 criteria including: drinking and smoking rates; depression; unemployment; parks; crime; disease; healthcare insurance coverage; air quality; and commute times. *SELF Magazine, "America's Best Places for Women 2006," December 2006*

■ *Ladies Home Journal* ranked America's 200 largest cities based on the qualities women surveyed care about most. Scottsdale ranked #45 out of 143 in the smaller city category (population under 300,000). Criteria: crime; lifestyle; education; jobs; health; child care; politics; and the economy. *Ladies Home Journal Online, "The Best Cities for Women 2002"*

Seniors/Retirement Rankings

■ Scottsdale was profiled in the book *Where to Retire: America's Best and Most Affordable Places*. Cities were selected based on personal visits by the author and interviews with local residents coupled with statistics from various government agencies. *Where to Retire: America's Best and Most Affordable Places, 2006*

■ Scottsdale was identified as one of the "100 Most Popular Places to Retire" by *Where to Retire* magazine. The city ranked #1. Criteria: net retirees received from 1995-2000 (derived by subtracting all outbound retirees from inbound retirees for the county or county group - includes interstate moves only). *Where to Retire, "100 Most Popular Places to Retire," January/February 2007*

■ Sperling's BestPlaces in partnership with Bankers Life & Casualty Company designed a survey to identify the top 50 metro areas in the U.S. that offer the best overall qualities for senior living. The Phoenix metro area ranked #35. The following criteria were statistically weighted to reflect the needs of the senior population: health; disease; economics; social; environment; spiritual; transportation; housing; and crime. *Bankers Life & Casualty Company, "Best Cities for Seniors 2005"*

■ Scottsdale was selected as one of the best places to retire by *Retirement Places Rated*. Criteria: cost of living; climate; personal safety; services; economy. The city was ranked #2 out of 200. *Retirement Places Rated, 6th Edition, 2004*

■ A.G. Edwards ranked America's 500 top-performing communities based on their residents' personal savings and investing behavior. The Phoenix metro area ranked #248 with an index score of 101.82 (national average = 100.00). A dozen statistical factors were measured including: participation in retirement savings plans; personal debt levels; and home ownership. *A.G. Edwards, "2006 Nest Egg Index", September 6, 2006*

Children/Family Rankings

■ The Phoenix metro area was selected as one of the "Best Cities for Relocating Families" by Worldwide ERC and Primacy Relocation. Criteria: tax rates; average home costs and home appreciation; ability to qualify for in-state tuition; service quality of local utilities; per-capita volunteerism; auto taxes; and quantity of fun, family-friendly events and venues. *Worldwide ERC and Primacy Relocation, "2006 Best Cities for Relocating Families"*

■ *Zero Population Growth* ranked 100 cities in terms of children's health, safety, and economic well-being. Scottsdale was ranked #34 out of 80 Large Cities (remainder of the 100 largest cities in the U.S.) and was given a grade of B+. Criteria: total population and population growth; percent of population under 18 years of age; percent of births to teens; infant mortality rate; percent of eligible women not receiving Title X services; contraceptive equity indicator; percent of children without health insurance; percent of city residents over age 25 with a high-school diploma; ration of PopEd (Population Connection's Education Program) teachers trained; sexuality education indicator; proficiency in reading and math; percent of kids living in poverty; percent growth in urbanized land; violent crime rate; recycling. *Population Connection, Kid Friendly Cities: Report Card 2004*

■ Scottsdale was chosen as one of America's "100 Best Communities for Young People." The winners were selected based upon detailed information provided about each community's efforts to fulfill five essential promises critical to the well-being of young people: caring adults who are actively involved in their lives; safe places in which to learn and grow; a healthy start toward adulthood; an effective education that builds marketable skills; and opportunities to help others. *America's Promise, "100 Best Communities for Young People," September 26, 2005*

Safety Rankings

■ Allstate ranked the 200 largest cities in America in terms of driver safety. Scottsdale ranked #51. In addition, drivers were 3.0% less likely to have had an accident compared to the national average. Allstate researchers analyzed internal Property Damage reported claims over a two-year period (from January 2003 to December 2004) to ensure the findings would not be affected by external influences such as weather or road construction. A weighted average of the two-year numbers determined the annual percentages. The report defines an auto crash as any collision resulting in a property damage claim. *Allstate, "Allstate America's Best Drivers Report 2006," May 24, 2006*

■ Phoenix was identified as one of the most dangerous large metro areas for pedestrians in the U.S. The area ranked #10 out of the nations 50 largest metro areas. Criteria: average yearly pedestrian fatalities per capita (for the years 2002 and 2003) adjusted for the number of walkers. *Surface Transportation Policy Project, "Mean Streets 2004"*

■ *Ladies Home Journal* ranked America's 200 largest cities in terms of safety. Scottsdale ranked #24 out of 200. Criteria: violent crimes; crimes against property; and rape. *Ladies Home Journal Online, "The Best Cities for Women 2002"*

Sports/Recreation Rankings

■ The Phoenix metro area appeared on *The Sporting News* list of the "Best Sports Cities 2006". The area ranked #10 out of 99 cities in North America. To be included in the rankings, a city must have at least one of the following: NCAA Division I basketball team; Class A minor league baseball team; training camp for a major league or NFL team; NASCAR Nextel Cup race; NCAA Division I-A bowl game; PGA Tour tournament; Triple Crown horse race. Once a city qualifies, a 12-month snapshot is taken of the sports atmosphere, putting a heavy premium on regular-season won-lost records; playoff berths, bowl appearances and tournament bids; championships; applicable power ratings; quality of competition; overall fan fervor; sports atmosphere and fan knowledge; abundance of teams (quality over quantity); stadium/arena quality; ticket availability and prices; franchise ownership; and the marquee appeal of athletes. *SportingNews.com, "Best Sports Cities 2006," August 1, 2006*

- Scarborough Research, a leading market research firm, identified the top local markets for avid NBA fans. The Phoenix DMA (Designated Market Area) ranked in the top 10 with 14% of consumers 18 years and over reporting that they are "very interested in the NBA". *Scarborough Research, Scarborough USA+ 2005 Release 2*

- The Phoenix metro area was selected by *Cranium* as one of the "Top 50 Fun Cities" in America. The area ranked #49. Criteria includes: number of sports teams, restaurants, and dance performances; number of toy stores; city budget spent on recreation. *Cranium, November 4, 2003*

- *Golf Digest* ranked 330 metro areas in the U.S. in terms of golf. The Phoenix metro area was ranked #153. Criteria: access to golf; weather; value of golf; and quality of golf. *Golf Digest, "Metro Golf Rankings," August 2005*

Dating/Romance Rankings

- The Phoenix metro area was selected as one of the "Best Cities for Relocating Singles" by Worldwide ERC and Primacy Relocation. The area ranked #17 out of the 100 largest metro areas in the U.S. Areas were selected based on the following criteria: Population Criteria (local percentage and growth trends of unmarried residents aged 25-34; male-female ratios; the number of newcomers to the area; diversity and density); Economic Criteria (job growth vs. unemployment rates; apartment rental costs; fee and occupancy rates for temporary housing and mini-storage; higher education costs, including in-state and out-of-state tuition requirements; vehicle tax rates and quality of service from utility providers); Quality-of-Life Criteria (level of per capita volunteering; quality and quantity of collegiate and professional sports with fun, fan-friendly venues; number of Starbucks and other coffee shops; quality or popularity of restaurants, nightspots, health clubs, and online dating; moderate climates with sustainable water supplies). *Worldwide ERC and Primacy Relocation, "2006 Best Cities for Relocating Singles," October 11, 2006*

- *Forbes* ranked the 40 most populous metro areas in the U.S. in terms of the "Best Cities for Singles." The Phoenix metro area was ranked #3. Criteria: number of singles; cost of living alone; nightlife; culture; job growth; coolness; and online dating. *Forbes.com, July 25, 2006*

- Sperling's BestPlaces in partnership with AXE Deodorant Bodyspray ranked 80 metro areas and identified "America's Best (and Worst) Cities for Dating." The Phoenix metro area ranked #21. Criteria: percentage of singles ages 18-24; population density; dating venues per capita. *AXE Deodorant Bodyspray, "America's Best (and Worst) Cities for Dating," May, 2004*

Culture/Performing Arts Rankings

- Scottsdale was selected as one of "America's Top 25 Arts Destinations." The city ranked #4 in the mid-sized city (population 100,000 to 499,999) category. Criteria: readers' top choices for arts travel destinations based on the richness and variety of visual arts sites, activities and events. *American Style, June 2006*

- Scarborough Research, a leading market research firm, identified the top local markets for rock concert attendance. The Phoenix DMA (Designated Market Area) ranked in the top 25 with 15% of consumers, 18 years old and over, reporting that they have attended a rock concert during the past year. *Scarborough Research, Scarborough USA+ 2003 Release 2*

Miscellaneous Rankings

- Scottsdale was determined to be one of America's smartest cities. The city ranked #5 in the mid-sized city category (100,000 to 200,000 adults 25 years and older). Criteria: the editors rated the collective brainpower of U.S communities based on the educational attainment of its residents. *American City Business Journals, www.bizjournals.com, June 12, 2006*

- The Phoenix metro area appeared on *Forbes* list of "America's Drunkest Cities". The area ranked #22. Criteria: 35 of the largest continental U.S. metro areas were chosen based on availability of data and geographic diversity. Each metro was ranked in five areas: state laws; drinkers; heavy drinkers; binge drinkers; and alcoholism. *Forbes.com, "America's Drunkest Cities," August 22, 2006*

- Scottsdale appeared on ApartmentRatings.com "Top Cities for Renters List 2006". The area ranked #119 out of 138. Criteria: renter satisfaction; affordability; and vacancy. *ApartmentRatings.com, "Top Cities for Renters List 2006"*

- Sperling's BestPlaces in partnership with Pep Boys ranked 77 metro areas and identified "America's Most Drivable Cities." The Phoenix metro area ranked #37. Criteria: climate; road roughness; urban mobility; gas prices. *Pep Boys, "America's Most Drivable Cities," April 9, 2003*

- Phoenix was ranked #22 out of 268 metro areas in terms of its Creativity Index. The Creativity Index is a mix of four equally weighted factors: the Creative Class (scientists, engineers, architects, designers, writers, artists, musicians, or any profession where creativity is a key factor) share of the workforce; innovation, measured as patents per capita; high-tech industry, using the Milken Institute's Tech Pole Index; and diversity, measured by the Gay Index (a reasonable proxy for an areas' openness to different kinds of people and ideas). *The Rise of the Creative Class, 2002*

- State Farm Insurance, in partnership with Sperling's BestPlaces, analyzed several key factors that contribute to overall family preparedness. The Phoenix metro area ranked #10 out of the nation's 50 most populous metro areas. Criteria: quality of life; life insurance coverage; and investments. *State Farm Life Insurance, "Fiscally Fit Cities Report," July 20, 2004*

- Scottsdale was selected as having one of the highest number of Starbucks stores per capita in the U.S. The city appeared in the large city category. Criteria: U.S. cities with populations of 10,000 or more were analyzed with regards to the number of Starbucks stores per capita. Supermarkets and other stores selling coffee beans were not included. *ePodunk.com, "Coffee Quotients," March 2005*

Business Environment

CITY FINANCES

City Government Finances

Component	2003-2004 ($000)	2003-2004 ($ per capita)
Total Revenues	479,834	2,224
Total Expenditures	442,333	2,050
Debt Outstanding	711,947	3,299
Cash and Securities	629,708	2,918

Source: U.S Census Bureau, Government Finances 2003-2004

City Government Revenue by Source

Source	2003-2004 ($000)	2003-2004 ($ per capita)
General Revenue		
From Federal Government	7,712	36
From State Government	55,082	255
From Local Governments	0	0
Taxes		
Property	54,978	255
Sales	135,793	629
Personal Income	0	0
License	0	0
Charges	53,371	247
Liquor Store	0	0
Utility	68,039	315
Employee Retirement	0	0
Other	104,859	486

Source: U.S Census Bureau, Government Finances 2003-2004

City Government Expenditures by Function

Function	2003-2004 ($000)	2003-2004 ($ per capita)	2003-2004 (%)
General Expenditures			
Airports	2,843	13	0.6
Corrections	0	0	0.0
Education	0	0	0.0
Fire Protection	19,234	89	4.3
Governmental Administration	34,544	160	7.8
Health	0	0	0.0
Highways	44,637	207	10.1
Hospitals	0	0	0.0
Housing and Community Development	7,249	34	1.6
Interest on General Debt	25,452	118	5.8
Libraries	7,839	36	1.8
Parking	0	0	0.0
Parks and Recreation	29,323	136	6.6
Police Protection	55,416	257	12.5
Public Welfare	0	0	0.0
Sewerage	25,638	119	5.8
Solid Waste Management	13,095	61	3.0
Liquor Store	0	0	0.0
Utility	91,078	422	20.6
Employee Retirement	0	0	0.0
Other	85,985	398	19.4

Source: U.S Census Bureau, Government Finances 2003-2004

Municipal Bond Ratings

Area	Moody's
City	Aaa (1/2006)

Source: Mergent Bond Record, January 2007 (unless noted otherwise)

DEMOGRAPHICS

Population Growth

Area	1990 Census	2000 Census	2006 Estimate	2011 Projection	Population Growth (%) 1990-2000	Population Growth (%) 2000-2011
City	130,300	202,705	223,930	245,298	55.6	21.0
MSA[1]	2,238,480	3,251,876	3,865,907	4,394,608	45.3	35.1
U.S.	248,709,873	281,421,906	298,021,266	312,383,955	13.2	11.0

Note: (1) Metropolitan Statistical Area - see Appendix B for areas included
Source: Claritas, Inc.

Number of Households and Average Household Size

Area	2006 Estimate	2006 Average Household Size
City	100,800	2.22
MSA[1]	1,408,131	2.75
U.S.	112,267,302	2.65

Note: (1) Metropolitan Statistical Area - see Appendix B for areas included
Source: Claritas, Inc.

Race and Ethnicity

Area	White Alone[2]	Black Alone[2]	Asian Alone[2]	Other Race Alone[2]	Hispanic[3]
City	90.2	1.6	2.5	5.8	8.5
MSA[1]	73.8	3.9	2.4	19.9	29.3
U.S.	73.3	12.4	4.2	10.1	14.5

Note: Figures are 2006 estimates; (1) Metropolitan Statistical Area - see Appendix B for areas included
(2) Alone is defined as not being in combination with one or more other races; (3) May be of any race.
Source: Claritas, Inc.

Segregation

City Index[2]	City Rank[3]	MSA[1] Index[2]	MSA[1] Rank[4]
28.8	98	49.1	244

Note: Figures are based on an analysis of Census 2000 data; (1) Metropolitan Statistical Area - see Appendix A for areas included; (2) White/Black Dissimilarity Index—the most commonly used measure of segregation between two groups, reflecting their relative distributions across neighborhoods within a city or metropolitan area. It can range in value from 0, indicating complete integration, to 100, indicating complete segregation; (3) Ranges from 1 (most segregated) to 100 (least segregated) and includes all the cities in this book; (4) Ranges from 1 (most segregated) to 318 (least segregated) and includes 318 metropolitan areas.
Source: www.CensusScope.org

Ancestry

Area	German	Irish[2]	English	American	Italian	Polish	French[3]	Scottish
City	20.6	14.1	13.4	4.5	8.5	4.4	3.7	2.9
MSA[1]	16.2	10.5	10.3	4.6	4.9	2.7	2.9	1.9
U.S.	15.2	10.9	8.7	7.3	5.6	3.2	3.0	1.7

Note: Figures include multiple ancestry (e.g. if a person reported being Irish and Italian, they were included in both columns); (1) Metropolitan Statistical Area - see Appendix A for areas included; (2) Includes Celtic; (3) Includes Alsatian but excludes Basque
Source: Census 2000, Summary File 3

Foreign-Born Population

Area	Percent of Population Born in Any Foreign Country	Europe	Asia	Africa	Oceania[2]	Canada	Mexico	Latin America[3]
City	9.5	2.9	2.1	0.3	0.1	1.4	2.2	0.6
MSA[1]	14.1	1.5	1.8	0.2	0.1	0.6	9.2	0.8
U.S.	11.1	1.7	2.9	0.3	0.1	0.3	3.3	2.5

Note: (1) Metropolitan Statistical Area - see Appendix A for areas included; (2) Includes Australia, New Zealand subregion, Melanesia, Micronesia, Polynesia, and Oceania n.e.c.; (3) Includes Central America (excluding Mexico), South America, and the Caribbean.
Source: Census 2000, Summary File 3

Marriage Status

Area	Never Married	Now Married (excluding Separated)	Separated	Widowed	Divorced
City	23.7	56.0	1.3	6.6	12.5
MSA[1]	26.5	55.0	1.9	5.6	11.0
U.S.	27.1	54.4	2.2	6.6	9.7

Note: Figures are percentages and cover the population 15 years of age and older;
(1) Metropolitan Statistical Area - see Appendix A for areas included
Source: Census 2000, Summary File 3

Age Distribution

Area	Percent of Population						
	Under Age 5	Age 5 to 17	Age 18 to 34	Age 35 to 49	Age 50 to 64	Age 65 to 79	80 Years and Over
City	5.0	14.2	20.9	23.6	19.4	13.0	3.9
MSA[1]	7.7	19.0	25.8	22.0	13.5	9.0	3.0
U.S.	6.8	18.9	23.7	23.5	14.8	9.2	3.2

Note: (1) Metropolitan Statistical Area - see Appendix A for areas included
Source: Census 2000, Summary File 3

Male/Female Ratio

Area	Males	Females	Males per 100 Females
City	108,626	115,304	94.2
MSA[1]	1,946,170	1,919,737	101.4
U.S.	146,712,712	151,308,554	97.0

Note: Figures are 2006 estimates; (1) Metropolitan Statistical Area -
see Appendix B for areas included
Source: Claritas, Inc.

Religion

Area	Catholic	Southern Baptist	United Methodist	ELCA[1]	LDS[2]	Presbyterian Church USA	Jewish Est.	Muslim Est.
County	17.3	2.5	1.1	1.7	5.0	0.6	2.0	0.3
U.S.	22.0	7.1	3.7	1.8	1.5	1.1	2.2	0.6

Note: Figures are the number of adherents as a percentage of the total population; Adherents are defined as all
members, including full members, their children and the estimated number of other participants who are not
considered members (e.g. the baptized, those not confirmed, those regularly attending services, etc.);
(1) Evangelical Lutheran Church in America; (2) The Church of Jesus Christ of Latter Day Saints
Source: Reprinted with permission from Religious Congregations and Membership in the United States 2000
(Nashville, Glenmary Research Center, 2002) Copyright Association of Statisticians of American Religious
Bodies. All rights reserved.

ECONOMY

Gross Metropolitan Product

Area	2002	2003	2004	2005	2005 Rank[2]
MSA[1]	120.3	128.0	136.2	153.2	14

Note: Figures are in billions of dollars; (1) Phoenix-Mesa-Scottsdale, AZ Metropolitan Statistical Area - see
Appendix A for areas included; (2) Rank ranges from 1 to 361
Source: The U.S. Conference of Mayors, "U.S. Metro Economies: GMP - The Engines of America's Growth,"
January 2007

Economic Growth

Area	1995 GMP	2005 GMP	Average Annual Growth Rate	Growth Rate Rank[2]
MSA[1]	73.6	153.2	7.6	19

Note: Figures are in billions of dollars; GMP = Gross Metropolitan Product; (1) Phoenix-Mesa-Scottsdale, AZ
Metropolitan Statistical Area - see Appendix A for areas included; (2) Rank ranges from 1 to 361
Source: The U.S. Conference of Mayors, "U.S. Metro Economies: GMP - The Engines of America's Growth,"
January 2007

INCOME

Per Capita/Median/Average Income

Area	Per Capita ($)	Median Household ($)	Average Household ($)
City	44,519	65,783	98,337
MSA[1]	25,352	52,008	68,998
U.S.	25,129	48,775	65,849

Note: Figures are 2006 estimates; (1) Metropolitan Statistical Area - see Appendix B for areas included
Source: Claritas, Inc.

Household Income Distribution

Area	Percent of Households Earning							
	Under $15,000	$15,000 -24,999	$25,000 -34,999	$35,000 -49,999	$50,000 -74,999	$75,000 -99,000	$100,000 -149,999	$150,000 and up
City	7.8	7.9	8.9	13.5	18.6	11.9	14.8	16.4
MSA[1]	10.2	10.2	11.4	16.5	20.6	12.5	11.9	6.8
U.S.	13.3	11.0	11.3	15.7	19.5	11.8	11.0	6.4

Note: Figures are 2006 estimates; (1) Metropolitan Statistical Area - see Appendix B for areas included
Source: Claritas, Inc.

Poverty Rates by Age

Area	All Ages	Under 5 Years Old	5 to 17 Years Old	18 to 64 Years Old	65 Years and Over
City	5.8	0.3	0.8	3.7	1.0
MSA[1]	12.0	1.4	3.0	6.7	0.9
U.S.	12.4	1.2	3.0	6.9	1.2

Note: Figures are percent of population with income in 1999 below poverty level and only include population for whom poverty status is determined; (1) Metropolitan Statistical Area - see Appendix A for areas included
Source: Census 2000, Summary File 3

Personal Bankruptcy Filing Rate

Area	2003	2004	2005
Maricopa County	6.18	6.03	7.24
U.S.	5.57	5.31	6.88

Note: Numbers are per 1,000 population and include Chapter 7 and Chapter 13 filings
Source: Federal Deposit Insurance Corporation (FDIC), Regional Economic Conditions (RECON), 3/24/2006

EMPLOYMENT

Labor Force and Employment

Area	Civilian Labor Force			Workers Employed		
	Dec. 2005	Dec. 2006	% Chg.	Dec. 2005	Dec. 2006	% Chg.
City	135,767	141,434	4.2	132,104	138,032	4.5
MSA[1]	1,952,929	2,032,289	4.1	1,880,490	1,964,883	4.5
U.S.	149,874,000	152,571,000	1.8	142,918,000	146,081,000	2.2

Note: Data is not seasonally adjusted and covers workers 16 years of age and older;
(1) Metropolitan Statistical Area - see Appendix B for areas included
Source: Bureau of Labor Statistics, http://stats.bls.gov

Unemployment Rate

Area	2006											
	Jan.	Feb.	Mar.	Apr.	May	Jun.	Jul.	Aug.	Sep.	Oct.	Nov.	Dec.
City	3.3	2.9	2.6	2.6	2.4	2.9	3.0	2.2	2.4	2.5	2.4	2.4
MSA[1]	4.5	3.9	3.5	3.6	3.3	3.9	4.1	3.1	3.3	3.4	3.3	3.3
U.S.	5.1	5.1	4.8	4.5	4.4	4.8	5.0	4.6	4.4	4.1	4.3	4.3

Note: Data is not seasonally adjusted and covers workers 16 years of age and older; All figures are percentages; (1) Metropolitan Statistical Area - see Appendix B for areas included
Source: Bureau of Labor Statistics, http://stats.bls.gov

Employment by Occupation

Occupation Classification	City (%)	MSA[1] (%)	U.S. (%)
Sales and Office	33.1	29.5	26.7
Professional and Related	22.9	19.0	20.2
Service	11.6	14.9	14.9
Production, Transportation, and Material Moving	4.5	11.1	14.6
Management, Business, and Financial	24.0	14.4	13.5
Construction, Extraction, and Maintenance	3.8	10.6	9.4
Farming, Forestry, and Fishing	0.0	0.5	0.7

Note: Figures cover employed civilians 16 years of age and older;
(1) Metropolitan Statistical Area - see Appendix A for areas included
Source: Census 2000, Summary File 3

Employment by Industry

Sector	MSA[1] Number of Employees	MSA[1] Percent of Total	U.S. Percent of Total
Government	242,100	12.4	16.3
Education and Health Services	199,400	10.2	13.2
Professional and Business Services	335,400	17.1	12.9
Retail Trade	242,900	12.4	11.5
Manufacturing	139,800	7.1	10.2
Leisure and Hospitality	186,400	9.5	9.5
Financial Activities	158,400	8.1	6.1
Construction	190,800	9.7	5.5
Wholesale Trade	89,200	4.6	4.3
Other Services	74,800	3.8	3.9
Transportation and Utilities	65,200	3.3	3.7
Information	31,900	1.6	2.2
Natural Resources and Mining	2,800	0.1	0.5

Note: Figures cover non-farm employment as of December 2006 and are not seasonally adjusted;
(1) Metropolitan Statistical Area - see Appendix B for areas included
Source: Bureau of Labor Statistics, http://stats.bls.gov

Occupations with Greatest Projected Employment Growth: 2002 - 2012

Occupation[1]	2002 Employment	2012 Projected Employment	Numeric Employment Change	Percent Employment Change
Cashiers	63,550	85,240	21,690	34.1
Registered Nurses	34,190	54,330	20,140	58.9
Combined Food Preparation and Serving Workers, Including Fast Food	48,950	63,360	14,410	29.4
Retail Salespersons	67,560	81,370	13,810	20.4
Customer Service Representatives	45,870	59,210	13,340	29.1
Carpenters	33,870	44,580	10,710	31.6
Landscaping and Groundskeeping Workers	30,700	39,990	9,290	30.3
Nursing Aides, Orderlies, and Attendants	18,390	27,620	9,230	50.2
Postsecondary Teachers	29,790	38,960	9,170	30.8
Medical Assistants	10,950	19,540	8,590	78.4

Note: Projections cover Arizona; (1) Sorted by numeric employment change
Source: www.projectionscentral.com, State Occupational Projections, 2002-2012 Long-Term Projections

Fastest Growing Occupations: 2002 - 2012

Occupation[1]	2002 Employment	2012 Projected Employment	Numeric Employment Change	Percent Employment Change
Emergency Medical Technicians and Paramedics	1,540	3,220	1,680	109.1
Medical Assistants	10,950	19,540	8,590	78.4
Physician Assistants	2,110	3,740	1,630	77.3
Medical Records and Health Information Technicians	3,000	5,190	2,190	73.0
Respiratory Therapy Technicians	680	1,170	490	72.1
Dental Hygienists	1,680	2,880	1,200	71.4
Respiratory Therapists	1,380	2,350	970	70.3
Dental Assistants	5,280	8,980	3,700	70.1
Home Health Aides	10,390	17,560	7,170	69.0
Physical Therapist Aides	1,490	2,450	960	64.4

Note: Projections cover Arizona; (1) Sorted by percent employment change and excludes occupations with numeric employment change less than 300
Source: www.projectionscentral.com, State Occupational Projections, 2002-2012 Long-Term Projections

Average Wages

Occupation	$/Hr.	Occupation	$/Hr.
Accountants and Auditors	24.71	Maids and Housekeeping Cleaners	8.07
Automotive Mechanics	18.71	Maintenance and Repair Workers	14.95
Bookkeepers	14.70	Marketing Managers	39.27
Carpenters	16.41	Nuclear Medicine Technologists	27.21
Cashiers	9.12	Nurses, Licensed Practical	18.89
Clerks, General Office	12.50	Nurses, Registered	27.38
Clerks, Receptionists/Information	11.15	Nursing Aides/Orderlies/Attendants	10.73
Clerks, Shipping/Receiving	10.44	Packers and Packagers, Hand	7.90
Computer Programmers	29.39	Physical Therapists	30.04
Computer Support Specialists	21.41	Postal Service Mail Carriers	21.55
Computer Systems Analysts	31.83	Real Estate Brokers	43.89
Cooks, Restaurant	9.95	Retail Salespersons	11.77
Dentists	n/a	Sales Reps., Exc. Tech./Scientific	22.88
Electrical Engineers	36.74	Sales Reps., Tech./Scientific	25.55
Electricians	17.32	Secretaries, Exc. Legal/Med./Exec.	12.69
Financial Managers	41.31	Security Guards	10.33
First-Line Supervisors/Mgrs., Sales	18.04	Surgeons	78.30
Food Preparation Workers	9.61	Teacher Assistants	9.60
General and Operations Managers	42.41	Teachers, Elementary School	16.00
Hairdressers/Cosmetologists	11.75	Teachers, Secondary School	18.80
Internists	84.23	Telemarketers	10.14
Janitors and Cleaners	8.71	Truck Drivers, Heavy/Tractor-Trailer	18.29
Landscaping/Groundskeeping Workers	9.52	Truck Drivers, Light/Delivery Svcs.	13.12
Lawyers	47.56	Waiters and Waitresses	7.79

Note: Wage data is for May 2005 and covers the Phoenix-Mesa-Scottsdale, AZ Metropolitan Statistics Area - see Appendix B for areas included. Hourly wages for elementary/secondary school teachers and teacher assistants were calculated by the editors from annual wage data assuming a 40 hour work week; n/a not available.
Source: Bureau of Labor Statistics, May 2005 Metro Area Occupational Employment and Wage Estimates

RESIDENTIAL REAL ESTATE

Building Permits

Area	Single-Family			Multi-Family			Total		
	2005	2006p	Pct. Chg.	2005	2006p	Pct. Chg.	2005	2006p	Pct. Chg.
City	1,282	909	-29.1	226	559	147.3	1,508	1,468	-2.7
U.S.	1,682,000	1,380,000	-18.0	473,300	457,300	-3.4	2,155,300	1,837,300	-14.8

Note: (p) preliminary; figures represent new, privately-owned housing units authorized (unadjusted data); All permit data are based on estimates with imputation; U.S. figures are based on the new 20,000-place series.
Source: U.S. Census Bureau, Manufacturing, Mining, and Construction Statistics

Homeownership and Housing Vacancies

Area	Homeownership Rate[2] (%)			Rental Vacancy Rate[3] (%)			Homeowner Vacancy Rate[4] (%)		
	2004	2005	2006	2004	2005	2006	2004	2005	2006
MSA[1]	n/a	71.2	72.5	n/a	11.2	9.1	n/a	1.0	3.1
U.S.	69.0	68.9	68.8	10.2	9.8	9.7	1.7	1.9	2.4

Note: Comparable 2004 data was not available due to changes in metropolitan area definitions; (1) Metropolitan Statistical Area - see Appendix B for areas included; (2) The proportion of households that are owners; (3) The proportion of the rental inventory that is vacant for rent; (4) The proportion of the homeowner inventory that is vacant for sale; n/a not available
Source: U.S. Census Bureau, Housing Vacancies and Homeownership Annual Statistics: 2006

TAXES

State Corporate Income Tax Rates

State	Rate (%)	Number of Brackets	Low Bracket (Under $)	High Bracket (Over $)
Arizona	6.968	1	na	na

Note: Tax rates as of December 31, 2006; na not applicable; Minimum tax is $50.
Source: Tax Foundation, www.taxfoundation.org

State Individual Income Tax Rates

State	Federal Deductibility	Marginal Rate (%)	Number of Brackets	Low Bracket (Under $)	High Bracket (Over $)
Arizona	No	2.87-5.04	5	0	150,000

Note: Tax rates as of December 31, 2006; Brackets apply to single taxpayers and married people filing separately; na not applicable
Source: Tax Foundation, www.taxfoundation.org

Various State and Local Tax Rates

State and Local Sales and Use (%)	State Sales and Use (%)	Gasoline ($/gal.)	Cigarette ($/pack)	Spirits ($/gal.)	Table Wine ($/gal.)	Beer ($/gal.)
7.95	5.6	0.19 (m)	2	3	0.84	0.16

Note: Tax rates as of December 31, 2006; (m) Additional cents per gallon taxes added this year that were not included in previous years' tables.
Source: Tax Foundation, www.taxfoundation.org; The Sales Tax Clearinghouse, www.thestc.com

State Tax Burdens

Area	Combined State and Local Tax Burden		Combined Federal, State and Local Tax Burden	
	Percent	Rank	Percent	Rank
Arizona	10.1	32	29.9	29
U.S. Average	10.6	-	31.6	-

Note: Figures are for 2006 and measure taxes as a percentage of income
Source: Tax Foundation, www.taxfoundation.org

Internal Revenue Service Tax Audits

IRS District	Percent of Returns Audited				
	1996	1997	1998	1999	2000
Southwest	0.80	0.81	0.61	0.36	0.29
U.S.	0.66	0.61	0.46	0.31	0.20

Note: Figures cover IRS district audits of federal income tax returns filed by individuals. Geographic data on district audits after the year 2000 are being withheld by the IRS. TRAC is challenging this policy.
Source: Syracuse University, Transactional Records Access Clearinghouse (TRAC), "Odds of IRS District Tax Audit 2000"

**COMMERCIAL
REAL ESTATE**

Office Market

Market Area	Inventory (sq. ft.)	Vacant (sq. ft.)	Vac. Rate (%)	Under Constr. (sq. ft.)	Asking Rent ($/sf)	
					Class A	Class B
Phoenix	57,524,717	7,316,897	12.7	4,089,448	27.69	21.84

Source: Grubb & Ellis, Office Markets Trends, 4th Quarter 2006

Industrial Market

Market Area	Inventory (sq. ft.)	Vacant (sq. ft.)	Vac. Rate (%)	Under Constr. (sq. ft.)	Asking Rent ($/sf)	
					WH/Dist	R&D/Flex
Phoenix	248,538,713	16,241,395	6.5	4,971,854	6.00	12.24

Source: Grubb & Ellis, Industrial Markets Trends, 4th Quarter 2006

**COMMERCIAL
UTILITIES**

Typical Monthly Electric Bills

Area	Commercial Service ($/month)		Industrial Service ($/month)	
	3 kW demand 1,000 kWh	40 kW demand 14,000 kWh	1,000 kW demand 200,000 kWh	50,000 kW demand 15,000,000 kWh
City	146	1,407	22,221	1,273,053
Average[1]	123	1,413	22,000	1,306,315

Note: Based on total rates in effect July 1, 2006; (1) average based on 196 utilities
Source: Edison Electric Institute, Typical Bills and Average Rates Report, Summer 2006

TRANSPORTATION

Means of Transportation to Work

Area	Car/Truck/Van		Public Transportation			Bicycle	Walked	Other Means	Worked at Home
	Drove Alone	Car-pooled	Bus	Subway	Railroad				
City	80.3	7.6	0.9	0.0	0.0	0.8	1.7	1.5	7.1
MSA[1]	74.6	15.3	1.8	0.0	0.0	0.9	2.1	1.4	3.7
U.S.	75.7	12.2	2.5	1.5	0.5	0.4	2.9	1.0	3.3

Note: Figures are percentages and cover workers 16 years of age and older;
(1) Metropolitan Statistical Area - see Appendix A for areas included
Source: Census 2000, Summary File 3

Travel Time to Work

Area	Less Than 15 Minutes	15 to 29 Minutes	30 to 44 Minutes	45 to 59 Minutes	60 Minutes or More
City	26.9	39.4	22.6	7.1	4.1
MSA[1]	23.8	37.0	24.1	8.8	6.3
U.S.	29.4	36.1	19.1	7.4	8.0

Note: Figures are percentages and include workers 16 years old and over; (1) Metropolitan Statistical Area -
see Appendix A for areas included
Source: Census 2000, Summary File 3

Travel Time Index

Area	1982	1993	2002	2003
Urban Area[1]	1.13	1.27	1.35	1.35
Average[2]	1.12	1.28	1.37	1.37

Note: Travel Time Index - The ratio of travel time in the peak period to the travel time at
free-flow conditions. A value of 1.35 indicates a 20-minute free-flow trip takes 27 minutes
in the peak. Free-flow speeds (60 mph on freeways and 35 mph on principal arterials)
are used as the comparison threshold; (1) Covers the Phoenix, AZ urban area;
(2) average of 85 urban areas
Source: Texas Transportation Institute, The 2005 Urban Mobility Report, May 2005

Public Transportation

Agency name:	City of Phoenix Public Transit Dept. (Valley Metro)
Vehicle type:	Bus
Average fleet age in years:	6.9
No. operated in max. service:	411
Vehicle type:	Demand response
Average fleet age in years:	3.2
No. operated in max. service:	130
Agency name:	Phoenix - VPSI Inc.
Vehicle type:	Vanpool
Average fleet age in years:	2.1
No. operated in max. service:	276

Source: Federal Transit Administration, National Transit Database, 2005

Air Transportation

Airport name and code:	Phoenix Sky Harbor International (PHX)
Domestic service (2006)	
Passenger airlines[1]:	33
Passenger enplanements:	19,715,316
Freight carriers[2]:	32
Freight (lbs.):	261,231,406
International service (2005)	
Passenger airlines[1]:	14
Passenger enplanements:	871,348
Freight carriers[2]:	10
Freight (lbs.):	5,993,068

Note: (1) Includes all major, minor and commuter airlines that carried at least one passenger during the year; (2) Includes all airlines and freight carriers that transported at least one pound of freight during the year
Source: Bureau of Transportation Statistics, The Intermodal Transportation Database, Air Carriers: T-100 International Market, 2004; Bureau of Transportation Statistics, The Intermodal Transportation Database, Air Carriers: T-100 Domestic Market, 2005

Other Transportation Statistics

Interstate highways:	I-10; I-17
Amtrak service:	No
Major waterways/ports:	None

Source: Editor & Publisher Market Guide, 2006; Amtrak.com; Rand McNally 2006 Road Atlas

BUSINESSES

Major Business Headquarters

Company Name	2006 Rankings	
	Fortune[1]	Forbes[2]
Allied Waste Industries	376	-
Discount Tire	-	190
Forever Living Products Intl	-	340
Hunt Construction Group	-	213
Services Group of America	-	127

Note: (1) Fortune 500 - companies that produce a 10-K are ranked 1 to 500 based on 2005 revenue; (2) Forbes Largest Private Companies - all private companies with at least $1 billion in annual revenue are ranked 1 to 394; companies listed are located in the city; dashes indicate no ranking
Source: Fortune, April 17, 2006; Forbes, November 9, 2006

Best Companies to Work For

Vanguard, headquartered in Scottsdale, is among the "100 Best Companies to Work For." Criteria: More than 105,000 employees from 446 companies responded to a 57-question survey created by the Great Place to Work Institute. Two-thirds of a company's score is based on the survey, which covers topics such as attitudes towards management, job satisfaction, and camaraderie. The remaining third of the score comes from each company's responses to the Institute's Culture Audit, which includes detailed questions about demographic makeup, pay and benefits programs, and open-ended questions about the company's people-management philosophy, internal communications, opportunities, compensation practices, diversity programs, etc. Any company that is at least seven years old and has a minimum of 1,000 U.S.

employees is eligible. The top three U.S. locations are shown for companies with more than one location. *Fortune, "100 Best Companies to Work for 2007," January 22, 2007*

Scottsdale Healthcare, headquartered in Scottsdale, is among the "50 Best Employers for Workers Over 50." Criteria: recruiting practices; opportunities for training, education, and career development; workplace accommodations; alternative work options, such as flexible scheduling, job sharing, and phased retirement; employee health and pension benefits; and retiree benefits. Any employer with at least 50 employees based in the U.S. is eligible. This includes for-profit companies, not-for-profit organizations, and government employers. *AARP, "AARP Best Employers for Workers Over 50," 2006*

Fast-Growing Businesses

According to *Inc.*, Scottsdale is home to five of America's 500 fastest-growing private companies: **DollarDays International; PatchLink; The Go Daddy Group; eTelecare Global Solutions; iCrossing**. Criteria: must be an independent, privately-held, U.S. corporation, proprietorship or partnership; net sales of at least $600,000 in FY2002; four-year operating/sales history; holding companies, regulated banks, and utilities were excluded. *Inc., "America's 500 Fastest-Growing Private Companies," September 2006*

According to *Fortune*, Scottsdale is home to one of America's 100 fastest-growing companies: **Meritage Homes**. Companies were ranked based on earnings-per-share growth, revenue growth and total return over the previous three years. Criteria for inclusion: public companies with sales of at least $50 million. Companies that lost money in the most recent quarter, or ended in the red for the past four quarters as a whole, were not eligible. Limited partnerships and REITs were also not considered. *Fortune, "America's Fastest-Growing Companies," September 18, 2006*

Women-Owned Businesses: 1997 and 2002

Year	All Firms		Firms with Paid Employees			
	Firms	Sales ($000)	Firms	Sales ($000)	Employees	Payroll ($000)
1997	6,643	822,517	1,166	649,529	6,394	145,071
2002	8,039	1,342,901	1,466	1,006,379	10,011	251,195

Note: Figures cover firms located in the city; Women-owned business are defined as firms in which women own 51% or more of the stock or equity of the company; (a) Withheld to avoid disclosing data for individual companies; (b) Withheld because estimate did not meet publication standards; n/a not available
Source: 1997 Economic Census, Survey of Minority- and Women-Owned Business Enterprises; 2002 Economic Census, Survey of Business Owners (released February 9, 2006)

HOTELS

Hotels/Motels

Area	Hotels/Motels	Average Minimum Rates ($)		
		Tourist	First-Class	Deluxe
City	67	69	110	180

Source: OAG Travel Planner Online, Spring 2006

The Phoenix metro area is home to five of the top 187 hotels in the U.S. according to *Travel & Leisure*: **The Phoenician** (#55); **Boulders Resort & Golden Door Spa** (#59); **Four Seasons Resort at Troon North** (#115); **Sanctuary on Camelback Mountain Resort & Spa** (#123); **Royal Palms Resort & Spa** (#136). Criteria: service; location; rooms; food; and value. *Travel & Leisure, "The T+L 500, 2007"*

EVENT SITES

Hotels/Conference Centers

Name	Guest Rooms	Exhibit Space (sq. ft.)	Meeting Space (sq. ft.)
Fairmont Scottsdale Princess	651	18,000	71,800
Hyatt Regency Scottsdale	493	70,000	70,000
Marriott's Camelback Inn Resort	n/a	n/a	n/a
Scottsdale Conference Resort	326	80,000	50,000
The Phoenician	654	27,000	64,000

Note: n/a not available
Source: www.officialtravelguide.com; www.eventective.com; original research

Living Environment

COST OF LIVING

Cost of Living Index

Year	Composite Index	Groceries	Housing	Utilities	Trans-portation	Health Care	Misc. Goods/Services
2004	98.5	100.2	91.1	92.0	108.9	108.3	102.0
2005	98.0	98.0	93.2	92.0	104.1	100.8	101.7
2006	101.4	98.9	104.8	91.6	103.2	101.3	101.9

Note: U.S. = 100; Figures are for Phoenix (data for Scottsdale was not available)
Source: The Council for Community and Economic Research (formerly ACCRA), Cost of Living Index, 2004, 2005 and 2006 4-Quarter Averages

HOUSING

House Price Index (HPI)

Area	National Ranking[2]	Quarterly Change (%)	One-Year Change (%)	Five-Year Change (%)
MSA[1]	60	0.78	9.04	99.79
U.S.[3]	-	1.12	5.87	55.21

Note: The HPI is a weighted repeat sales index. It measures average price changes in repeat sales or refinancings on the same properties. This information is obtained by reviewing repeat mortgage transactions on single-family properties whose mortgages have been purchased or securitized by Fannie Mae or Freddie Mac in January 1975; (1) Metropolitan Statistical Area - see Appendix B for areas included; (2) Rankings are based on annual percentage change for all metro areas containing at least 15,000 transactions over the last 10 years and ranges from 1 to 282; (3) figures based on a weighted division average; all figures are for the period ending December 31, 2006
Source: Office of Federal Housing Enterprise Oversight, House Price Index, March 1, 2007

House Price Valuations

Area	Q4 1999	Q4 2000	Q4 2001	Q4 2002	Q4 2003	Q4 2004	Q4 2005	Q4 2006
MSA[1]	-10.1	-9.1	-5.8	-2.9	0.4	7.7	37.3	40.6

Note: Figures show the percentage of over- or under-valuation of single family homes relative to statistically normal house values (e.g. a value of 23.6 indicates that house values are 23.6% overvalued). Statistically normal house values are based on house prices, interest rates, household incomes, population densities, and any historical premiums or discounts metropolitan areas have exhibited over time; (1) Figures cover the Metropolitan Statistical Area - see Appendix B for areas included
Source: Global Insight/National City Corporation, House Prices in America, March 2007

Median Home Prices

Area	2004	2005	2006p	Percent Change 2005 to 2006
Metro Area[1]	169.4	247.4	268.2	8.4
U.S. Average	195.2	219.0	222.0	1.4

Note: Figures are median sales prices of existing single-family homes in thousands of dollars; (p) preliminary; n/a not available; (1) Covers the Phoenix-Mesa-Scottsdale, AZ Metropolitan Statistical Area - see Appendix B for areas included
Source: National Association of Realtors, Metropolitan Area Prices, 4th Quarter 2006

Housing: Year Structure Built

Area	1990 -2000	1980 -1989	1970 -1979	1960 -1969	1950 -1959	1940 -1949	Before 1940	Median Year
City	37.7	23.8	19.1	12.4	6.1	0.4	0.3	1985
MSA[1]	30.4	25.5	23.2	10.4	7.1	2.0	1.4	1982
U.S.	17.0	15.8	18.5	13.7	12.7	7.3	15.0	1971

Note: Figures are percentages; (1) Metropolitan Statistical Area - see Appendix A for areas included
Source: Census 2000, Summary File 3

Average New Home Price

Area	2004	2005	2006
City[1]	228,919	256,927	318,810
U.S.	253,574	275,712	299,269

Note: Figures, in dollars, are based on a new home with 2,400 sq. ft. of living area on an 8,000 sq. ft. lot;
(1) Phoenix (data for Scottsdale was not available)
Source: The Council for Community and Economic Research (formerly ACCRA), Cost of Living Index, 2004,
2005 and 2006 4-Quarter Averages

Average Apartment Rent

Area	2004	2005	2006
City[1]	682	697	751
U.S.	716	740	766

Note: Figures, in dollars per month, are based on an unfurnished two bedroom, 1-1/2 or 2 bath apartment,
approximately 950 sq. ft. in size, excluding all utilities except water; (1) Phoenix (data for Scottsdale was not
available)
Source: The Council for Community and Economic Research (formerly ACCRA), Cost of Living Index, 2004,
2005 and 2006 4-Quarter Averages

RESIDENTIAL
UTILITIES

Average Residential Utility Costs

Area	All Electric ($/mth)	Part Electric ($/mth)	Other Energy ($/mth)	Phone ($/mth)
City[1]	149.46	–	–	22.62
U.S.	136.00	76.53	90.52	25.87

Note: (1) Phoenix (data for Scottsdale was not available)
Source: The Council for Community and Economic Research (formerly ACCRA), Cost of Living Index, 2006
4-Quarter Average

HEALTH

Average Health Care Costs

Area	Optometrist ($/visit)	Doctor ($/visit)	Dentist ($/visit)
City[1]	94.16	72.47	71.68
U.S.	76.38	76.10	68.72

Note: Optometrist—based on a full vision eye exam for an established adult patient;
Doctor—based on a general practitioner's routine exam of an established patient;
Dentist—based on adult teeth cleaning and periodic oral exam;
(1) Phoenix (data for Scottsdale was not available)
Source: The Council for Community and Economic Research (formerly ACCRA), Cost of Living Index, 2006
4-Quarter Average

Mortality Rates

ICD-10 Sub-Chapter	ICD-10 Code	Age-Adjusted Death Rate per 100,000 population[1]	U.S. Age-Adjusted Death Rate per 100,000 population
Malignant neoplasms	C00-C97	164.2	185.8
Ischaemic heart diseases	I20-I25	150.1	150.2
Other forms of heart disease	I30-I51	22.4	50.8
Cerebrovascular diseases	I60-I69	43.5	50.0
Chronic lower respiratory diseases	J40-J47	42.4	41.1
Diabetes mellitus	E10-E14	19.2	24.5
Other degenerative diseases of the nervous system	G30-G31	36.3	22.3
Other external causes of accidental injury	W00-X59	26.7	21.2
Influenza and pneumonia	J10-J18	18.5	19.8
Hypertensive diseases	I10-I13	18.6	18.1

Note: ICD-10 = International Classification of Diseases 10th Revision; (1) Figures cover Maricopa County, AZ
Source: Centers for Disease Control and Prevention, National Center for Health Statistics. Compressed
Mortality File 1999-2004. CDC WONDER On-line Database, compiled from Compressed Mortality File
1999-2004 Series 20 No. 2J, 2007.

Health Risk Data

Item	Area[1] (%)	U.S. (%)
Adults who have been told they have high blood pressure	20.5	25.5
Adults who have been told they have high blood cholesterol	32.1	35.6
Adults who have been told they have diabetes[2]	7.0	7.3
Adults who have been told they have arthritis	25.3	27.0
Adults who have been told they currently have asthma	6.8	8.0
Adults who are current smokers	20.3	20.6

Note: (1) Figures cover the Metropolitan Statistical Area - see Appendix B for areas included; (2) Figures do not include pregnancy-related diabetes, pre-diabetes or borderline diabetes
Source: Centers for Disease Control and Prevention, Behaviorial Risk Factor Surveillance System, SMART: Selected Metropolitan/Micropolitan Area Trends, 2005

Distribution of Office-Based Physicians

Area	Total	Family/ General Practice	Specialties		
			Medical	Surgical	Other
MSA[1] (number)	5,759	737	2,017	1,369	1,636
MSA[1] (rate per 10,000 pop.)	16.7	2.1	5.8	4.0	4.7
Metro Average[2] (rate per 10,000 pop.)	19.4	2.1	7.5	4.5	5.3

Note: Data as of December 31, 2004; (1) Metropolitan Statistical Area - see Appendix A for areas included; (2) Average of the 79 unique MSAs and CMSAs in this book
Source: American Medical Association, Physician Characteristics & Distribution in the U.S., 2006

Hospitals

Scottsdale has the following hospitals: 2 general medical and surgical; 1 psychiatric; 1 rehabilitation.
AHA Guide to the Healthcare Field 2007

According to *U.S. News,* the Phoenix metro area is home to three of the best hospitals in the U.S.: **Banner Good Samaritan Medical Center**; **Mayo Clinic Arizona**; **Saint Joseph's Hospital and Medical Center**; *U.S. News Online, "America's Best Hospitals 2006"*

EDUCATION

Public School District Statistics

District Name	Schls	Pupils	Pupil/ Teacher Ratio	Minority Pupils[1] (%)	Free Lunch Eligible[2] (%)	IEP[3] (%)
Cave Creek Unified District	7	5,518	19.9	9.7	4.8	13.1

Note: Table includes regular local school districts with 2,000 or more students; (1) Percentage of students that are not white, non-Hispanic; (2) Percentage of students that are eligible for the free lunch program; (3) Percentage of students that have an Individualized Education Program.
Source: U.S. Department of Education, National Center for Education Statistics, Common Core of Data, Local Education Agency (School District) Universe Survey: School Year 2004-2005; U.S. Department of Education, National Center for Education Statistics, Common Core of Data, Public Elementary/Secondary School Universe Survey: School Year 2004-2005

Top Public High Schools

High School Name	Index[1]	Rank[1]	Subsidized Lunch (%)[2]	E&E (%)[3]
Chaparral	1.118	1,106	<1.0	28.8

Note: (1) Public schools are ranked according to a ratio that is the number of Advanced Placement and/or International Baccalaureate tests taken by all students at a school in 2005 divided by the number of graduating seniors. All of the schools on the list have an index of at least 1.000; they are in the top five percent of public schools measured this way. The rankings range from 1 to 1,236; (2) Percentage of students receiving federally subsidized meals; (3) E & E stands for equity and excellence percentage: the portion of all graduating seniors at a school that had at least one passing grade on one AP or IB test; (*) Gave just IB tests; (**) Gave both IB and AP tests. AP and IB participation are indicators of a school's efforts to get students to excel and prepare for college.
Source: Newsweek Online, May 23, 2006

Educational Quality

School District	Education Quotient[1]	Graduate Outcome[2]	Community Index[3]	Resource Index[4]	Rating[5]
Scottsdale Unified	85	94	86	7	Gold

Note: Scores are national percentile rankings and range from 1 (worst) to 99 (best); (1) Combination of the Graduate Outcome, Community and Resource Indexes weighted to reflect the greater importance of the Graduate Outcome and Resource Index; (2) Based on graduation rates and college board scores (SAT/ACT); (3) Based on the surrounding community's level of affluence and adult education; (4) Based on teacher salaries, per-pupil expenditures and student-teacher ratios; (5) School districts receive one of five rankings: Gold Medal (top 16 percent of districts evaluated); Blue Ribbon (top third); Green Light (average); Yellow Light (bottom 25 percent); Red Light (bottom 10 percent).
Source: Expansion Management, "2007 Education Quotient," January 2007

Highest Level of Education

Area	Less than H.S.	H.S. Diploma	Some College, No Deg.	Associate Degree	Bachelors Degree	Masters Degree	Profess. School Degree	Doctorate Degree
City	6.2	16.1	26.2	6.6	29.8	9.7	3.9	1.5
MSA[1]	17.9	23.4	26.6	7.1	16.7	5.8	1.8	0.8
U.S.	19.4	28.4	21.2	6.4	15.7	5.9	2.0	1.0

Note: Figures are 2006 estimated percentages and cover persons age 25 and over; (1) Metropolitan Statistical Area - see Appendix B for areas included
Source: Claritas, Inc.

Educational Attainment by Race

Area	High School Graduate (%)					Bachelor's Degree (%)				
	Total	White	Black	Asian	Hisp.[2]	Total	White	Black	Asian	Hisp.[2]
City	93.5	94.3	92.6	92.6	69.8	44.1	44.6	41.6	58.1	21.3
MSA[1]	81.9	86.3	81.6	84.9	49.3	25.1	27.3	19.4	46.6	7.8
U.S.	80.4	83.6	72.3	80.4	52.4	24.4	26.1	14.3	44.1	10.4

Note: Figures shown cover persons 25 years old and over; (1) Metropolitan Statistical Area - see Appendix A for areas included; (2) people of Hispanic origin can be of any race
Source: Census 2000, Summary File 3

School Enrollment by Type

Area	Grades KG to 8				Grades 9 to 12			
	Public		Private		Public		Private	
	Enrollment	%	Enrollment	%	Enrollment	%	Enrollment	%
City	17,720	87.3	2,589	12.7	7,609	92.4	629	7.6
MSA[1]	414,735	93.4	29,200	6.6	163,065	93.8	10,740	6.2
U.S.	33,526,011	88.7	4,285,121	11.3	14,848,628	90.6	1,532,323	9.4

Note: Figures shown cover persons 3 years old and over; (1) Metropolitan Statistical Area - see Appendix A for areas included
Source: Census 2000, Summary File 3

School Enrollment by Race

Area	Grades KG to 8 (%)				Grades 9 to 12 (%)			
	White	Black	Asian	Hisp.[1]	White	Black	Asian	Hisp.[1]
City	89.0	1.2	1.9	10.3	89.1	1.6	2.7	9.3
MSA[2]	68.7	4.4	1.7	35.6	70.9	4.6	2.0	31.5
U.S.	68.5	15.5	3.3	16.8	68.8	15.5	3.8	15.7

Note: Figures shown cover persons 3 years old and over; (1) people of Hispanic origin can be of any race; (2) Metropolitan Statistical Area - see Appendix A for areas included
Source: Census 2000, Summary File 3

Average Salaries of Public School Teachers

District	2004-05 Dollars	2004-05 Rank[1]	2005-06 Dollars	2005-06 Rank[1]	Percent Change 2004-05 to 2005-06
ARIZONA	42,905	27	44,672	25	4.12
U.S. Average	47,674	-	49,109	-	3.01

Note: (1) State rank ranges from 1 to 51.
Source: National Education Association, Rankings & Estimates: Rankings of the States 2005 and Estimates of School Statistics 2006, November 2006

Higher Education

Four-Year Colleges Public	Private Non-profit	Private For-profit	Two-Year Colleges Public	Private Non-profit	Private For-profit	Medical Schools[1]	Law Schools[2]	Voc/ Tech[3]
0	0	1	1	0	0	0	0	3

Note: Figures cover institutions located within the city limits; (1) includes schools accredited by the Liaison Committee on Medical Education and the American Osteopathic Association; (2) includes American Bar Association-accredited law schools; (3) includes all schools with programs that are less than 2 years
Source: National Center for Education Statistics, The Integrated Postsecondary Education System (IPEDS) Peer Analysis System, 2006; www.usnews.com, America's Best Graduate Schools 2008, Medical School Directory; www.usnews.com, America's Best Graduate Schools 2008, Law School Directory

PRESIDENTIAL ELECTION

2004 Presidential Election Results

Area	Bush	Kerry	Nader	Other
Maricopa County	57.0	42.3	0.1	0.6
U.S.	50.7	48.3	0.4	0.6

Note: Results are percentages and may not add to 100% due to rounding
Source: Dave Leip's Atlas of U.S. Presidential Elections, www.uselectionatlas.org

MAJOR EMPLOYERS

Major Employers

Company Name	Industry	Type of Site
American Express	Business services, nec	Branch
American Express	Foreign trade and international banks	Branch
Bashas Distribution Center	General warehousing and storage	Branch
Board of Regents Arizona	Colleges and universities	Headquarters
Chase Bankcard Services Inc	State commercial banks	Single
Chase Manhattan	National commercial banks	Branch
Checkmate	Help supply services	Headquarters
City of Phoenix	Executive offices	Headquarters
General Dynmics C4 Systems Inc	Engineering services	Headquarters
Hamilton Hallmark	Electronic parts and equipment, nec	Headquarters
Intel	Semiconductors and related devices	Branch
MDHC	Aircraft	Single
Maricopa Integrated Health Sys	General medical and surgical hospitals	Branch
Motorola	Radio and t.v. communications equipment	Branch
Motorola Semiconductor Disc	Semiconductors and related devices	Branch
Motorola Semiconductor Logic	Semiconductors and related devices	Branch
Police Dept-Chiefs Office	Police protection	Branch
Scottsdale Healthcare Corp	Specialty outpatient clinics, nec	Branch
Sheriffs Office	Police protection	Branch
St Josephs Hospital & Med Ctr	General medical and surgical hospitals	Branch
Swift Transportation Co Inc	Trucking, except local	Headquarters

Note: Companies shown are located within the metropolitan area and have 2,300 or more employees; nec = not elsewhere classified.
Source: www.zapdata.com, January 2007

PUBLIC SAFETY

Crime Rate

Area	All Crimes	Violent Crimes				Property Crimes		
		Murder	Forcible Rape	Robbery	Aggrav. Assault	Burglary	Larceny -Theft	Motor Vehicle Theft
City	3,574.6	1.7	22.2	54.5	124.3	815.0	2,050.7	506.2
Suburbs[1]	5,887.1	8.9	34.1	169.7	320.1	1,034.1	3,171.6	1,148.7
Metro[2]	5,749.1	8.4	33.4	162.8	308.4	1,021.0	3,104.6	1,110.4
U.S.	3,899.0	5.6	31.7	140.7	291.1	726.7	2,286.3	416.7

Note: Figures are crimes per 100,000 population; (1) All areas within the metro area that are located outside the city limits; (2) Metropolitan Statistical Area - see Appendix B for areas included
Source: FBI Uniform Crime Reports, 2005

Hate Crimes

Area	Number of Quarters Reported	Bias Motivation				
		Race	Religion	Sexual Orientation	Ethnicity	Disability
City	4	0	2	0	0	0

Source: Federal Bureau of Investigation, Hate Crime Statistics 2005

RECREATION

Culture

Dance[1]	Theatre[1]	Instrumental Music[1]	Vocal Music[1]	Series/ Festivals	Museums	Zoos
0	0	1	0	2	4	0

Note: (1) number of professional perfoming groups
Source: The Grey House Performing Arts Directory, 2007; Official Museum Directory, 2007

Professional Sports Teams

Major League Baseball	National Basketball Association	National Football League	National Hockey League	Major League Soccer	Women's National Basketball Association
1	1	1	1	0	1

Note: Includes teams located in the Phoenix-Scottsdale metro area.
Source: www.sportsvenues.com, Listing of Venues by State/Province and City, 2006

MEDIA

Newspapers

Name	Target Audience	Frequency	Circulation
North Scottsdale Independent	General	Non-Daily	13,000
Northeast Phoenix Independent	General	Non-Daily	20,000
Paradise Valley Independent	General	Non-Daily	23,000
Scottsdale Tribune	n/a	Daily	18,387

Note: Includes newspapers whose offices are located in the city and whose circulations are 500 or more; n/a not available
Source: BurrellesLuce, MediaContacts Online, January 2006

Television Stations

Name	Ch.	Network(s)	Type	Ownership
KNAZ	2	NBC	Commercial	Gannett Broadcasting
KTVK	3	n/a	Commercial	Belo Corporation
KMOH	6	NBC	Commercial	Gannett Broadcasting
KAZ	7	n/a	Commercial	n/a
KAET	8	PBS	Public	Arizona Board of Regents
KSAZ	10	Fox	Commercial	Fox Television Stations Inc.
KPNX	12	NBC	Commercial	Gannett Broadcasting
KNXV	15	ABC	Commercial	Scripps Howard Inc.
KPAZ	21	n/a	Non-comm.	Paul F. Crouch
KCVA	30	n/a	Commercial	Kenneth Casey
KTVW	33	Univision	Commercial	Univision Television Group
KPHO	41	CBS	Commercial	Meredith Communications LLC
KUTP	45	UPN	Commercial	United Television Inc.
KPPX	51	n/a	Commercial	Paxson Communications Corporation
KASW	61	WBN	Commercial	Brooks Broadcasting
KDRX	64	Telemundo	Commercial	Hispanic Broadcasters of Arizona Inc.

Note: Stations included cover the Phoenix DMA (Designated Market Area)
BurrellesLuce, MediaContacts Online, January 2006

Major AM Radio Stations

Call Letters	Freq. (kHz)	Station Type	Target Audience	Station Format	Music Format
KFYI	550	Commercial	General	Talk	n/a
KTAR	620	Commercial	General	News/Talk	n/a
KAZM	780	Commercial	General	Music/News	Adult Contemp.
KGME	910	Commercial	General	Sports	n/a
KAFF	930	Commercial	General	Music/News/Talk	Country
KKNT	960	Commercial	General	News/Talk	n/a
KVWM	970	n/a	General	Music	n/a
KFLG	1000	Commercial	General	Music	Country
KDUS	1060	n/a	General	Sports/Talk	n/a
KFNX	1100	Commercial	General	Talk	n/a
KMYL	1190	Commercial	General	News/Talk	n/a
KASC	1260	College	General	Music/News/Sports	Alternative
KDJI	1270	Commercial	General	Music/News/Sports	Oldies
KXEG	1280	Commercial	General/Religious	Educational/Music	Christian
KXAM	1310	Commercial	General	Talk	n/a
KAZG	1440	Commercial	General	Music	Oldies
KPHX	1480	n/a	General/Hispanic	Music/News/Sports	n/a
KZZZ	1490	Commercial	General	News/Talk	n/a
KFNN	1510	n/a	General	Music/News/Talk	n/a
KASA	1540	Commercial	Hispanic/Religious	Music/Talk	Latin
KMIK	1580	Commercial	Children	Ed/Music/News/Sports	Top 40

Note: Stations included cover the Phoenix DMA (Designated Market Area); n/a not available
Source: BurrellesLuce, MediaContacts Online, January 2006

Major FM Radio Stations

Call Letters	Freq. (mHz)	Station Type	Target Audience	Station Format	Music Format
KUYI	88.1	n/a	General/Native Amer	Music/News/Talk	Top 40
KNAU	88.7	College	General	Music/News	n/a
KFLR	90.3	n/a	General/Religious	Music/News/Sports	n/a
KGCB	90.9	n/a	General/Religious	Music/News/Sports/Talk	n/a
KJZZ	91.5	College	General	Music/Talk	Jazz
KZUA	92.1	Commercial	General	Music/News/Sports	Country
KKFR	92.3	n/a	General	Music	n/a
KJJJ	92.7	n/a	General	Music/News/Sports	n/a
KAFF	92.9	n/a	General	Music/News	n/a
KDKB	93.3	Commercial	General	Music/News/Sports/Talk	A.O. Rock
KMGN	93.9	n/a	General	Music/News	n/a
KXKQ	94.1	n/a	General	Music/News	n/a
KOOL	94.5	n/a	General/Women	Music/News/Sports	n/a
KZZZ	94.7	Commercial	General	News/Sports/Talk	n/a
KYOT	95.5	n/a	General	Music/News/Talk	n/a
KRFM	96.5	n/a	General	Music	n/a
KWMX	96.7	n/a	General	n/a	n/a
KMXP	96.9	Commercial	General	Music/News/Talk	Adult Top 40
KRXS	97.3	n/a	General	Music/News	n/a
KVNA	97.5	n/a	General	Music	n/a
KLUK	97.9	Commercial	General	Music	Classic Rock
KUPD	97.9	Commercial	General	Music	A.O. Rock
KKLD	98.3	n/a	General	Music/News/Sports	n/a
KKLT	98.7	Commercial	General	Music	Adult Contemp.
KFMM	99.1	Commercial	General	Educational/Music/News	Country
KAJM	99.3	Commercial	General	Music/News/Talk	Rhythm & Blues
KESZ	99.9	Commercial	General	Music/News/Talk	Adult Contemp.
KSLX	100.7	Commercial	General	Music	Classic Rock
KNRJ	101.1	Commercial	General	Music	Top 40
KRRK	101.1	n/a	General	Music/News/Talk	n/a
KZON	101.5	n/a	General	Music/News/Talk	n/a
KAHM	102.1	Commercial	General	Music	Easy Listening
KNIX	102.5	Commercial	General	Music/News	Country
KQST	102.9	Commercial	General	Music/News/Talk	Top 40
KLNZ	103.5	n/a	General/Hispanic	Music	n/a
KEDJ	103.9	Commercial	Hispanic	Music	Alternative
KZZP	104.7	Commercial	General	Music/Talk	Top 40
KFLX	105.1	n/a	General/Men	News/Sports	A.O. Rock
KHOT	105.9	Commercial	General/Hispanic	Music	Latin
KPPV	106.7	n/a	General	Music/News	n/a
KNKK	107.1	Commercial	General	Music	Adult Contemp.
KSED	107.5	n/a	General	n/a	n/a
KMLE	107.9	Commercial	General	Music	Country

Note: Stations included cover the Phoenix DMA (Designated Market Area); n/a not available
BurrellesLuce, MediaContacts Online, January 2006

CLIMATE

Average and Extreme Temperatures

Temperature	Jan	Feb	Mar	Apr	May	Jun	Jul	Aug	Sep	Oct	Nov	Dec	Yr.
Extreme High (°F)	88	92	100	105	113	122	118	116	118	107	93	88	122
Average High (°F)	66	70	75	84	93	103	105	103	99	88	75	67	86
Average Temp. (°F)	53	57	62	70	78	88	93	91	85	74	62	54	72
Average Low (°F)	40	44	48	55	63	72	80	78	72	60	48	41	59
Extreme Low (°F)	17	22	25	37	40	51	66	61	47	34	27	22	17

Note: Figures cover the years 1948-1990
Source: National Climatic Data Center, International Station Meteorological Climate Summary, 9/96

Average Precipitation/Snowfall/Humidity

Precip./Humidity	Jan	Feb	Mar	Apr	May	Jun	Jul	Aug	Sep	Oct	Nov	Dec	Yr.
Avg. Precip. (in.)	0.7	0.6	0.8	0.3	0.1	0.1	0.8	1.0	0.7	0.6	0.6	0.9	7.3
Avg. Snowfall (in.)	Tr	Tr	0	0	0	0	0	0	0	0	0	Tr	Tr
Avg. Rel. Hum. 5am (%)	68	63	56	45	37	33	47	53	50	53	59	66	53
Avg. Rel. Hum. 5pm (%)	34	28	24	17	14	12	21	24	23	24	28	34	24

Note: Figures cover the years 1948-1990; Tr = Trace amounts (<0.05 in. of rain; <0.5 in. of snow)
Source: National Climatic Data Center, International Station Meteorological Climate Summary, 9/96

Weather Conditions

Temperature			Daytime Sky			Precipitation		
10°F & below	32°F & below	90°F & above	Clear	Partly cloudy	Cloudy	0.01 inch or more precip.	0.1 inch or more snow/ice	Thunder-storms
0	10	167	186	125	54	37	< 1	23

Note: Figures are average number of days per year and cover the years 1948-1990
Source: National Climatic Data Center, International Station Meteorological Climate Summary, 9/96

HAZARDOUS WASTE

Superfund Sites

Scottsdale has one hazardous waste site on the EPA's Superfund Final National Priorities List: **Indian Bend Wash Area**. *U.S. Environmental Protection Agency, Final National Priorities List, March 20, 2007*

AIR & WATER QUALITY

Air Quality Index

Area	Percent of Days when Air Quality was...[2]				AQI Statistics	
	Good	Moderate	Unhealthy for Sensitive Groups	Unhealthy	Maximum	Median
MSA[1]	21.6	68.5	9.9	0.0	140	67

Note: The Air Quality Index (AQI) is an index for reporting daily air quality. EPA calculates the AQI for five major air pollutants regulated by the Clean Air Act: ground-level ozone, particle pollution (also known as particulate matter), carbon monoxide, sulfur dioxide, and nitrogen dioxide. The AQI runs from 0 to 500. The higher the AQI value, the greater the level of air pollution and the greater the health concern. There are six AQI categories: "Good" The AQI is between 0 and 50. Air quality is considered satisfactory; "Moderate" The AQI is between 51 and 100. Air quality is acceptable; "Unhealthy for Sensitive Groups" When AQI values are between 101 and 150, members of sensitive groups may experience health effects; "Unhealthy" When AQI values are between 151 and 200 everyone may begin to experience health effects; "Very Unhealthy" AQI values between 201 and 300 trigger a health alert; "Hazardous" AQI values over 300 trigger health warnings of emergency conditions; (1) Metropolitan Statistical Area - see Appendix A for areas included; (2) Based on 365 days with AQI data in 2005.
Source: U.S. Environmental Protection Agency, Air Quality Index Report, 2005

Air Quality Index Pollutants

Area	Percent of Days when AQI Pollutant was...[2]					
	Carbon Monoxide	Nitrogen Dioxide	Ozone	Sulfur Dioxide	Particulate Matter 2.5	Particulate Matter 10
MSA[1]	0.8	0.0	36.7	0.0	2.2	60.3

Note: The Air Quality Index (AQI) is an index for reporting daily air quality. EPA calculates the AQI for five major air pollutants regulated by the Clean Air Act: ground-level ozone, particle pollution (also known as particulate matter), carbon monoxide, sulfur dioxide, and nitrogen dioxide. The AQI runs from 0 to 500. The higher the AQI value, the greater the level of air pollution and the greater the health concern; (1) Metropolitan Statistical Area - see Appendix A for areas included; (2) Based on 365 days with AQI data in 2005.
Source: U.S. Environmental Protection Agency, Air Quality Index Report, 2005

Number of Days with Air Quality Index Values Greater than 100

Area	Trend Sites (25)								All Sites (145)
	1998	1999	2000	2001	2002	2003	2004	2005	2005
MSA[1]	14	9	11	7	8	8	1	4	19

Note: An AQI value greater than 100 indicates that air quality would have been in the unhealthful range on that day. Data from exceptional events are not included. These counts are presented in two ways. First, the counts are based on sites having an adequate record of monitoring data during the trend period (trend sites). These counts represent the relative change in the number of days with AQI values greater than 100. In the last column, the counts are based on all sites with data in the most recent year (because it is possible for a site to have data in the most recent year but not enough data to be a trend site); (1) Metropolitan Statistical Area - see Appendix A for areas included; n/a not available.
Source: U.S. Environmental Protection Agency, Air Trends Fact Book 2005

Maximum Pollutant Concentrations

	Particulate Matter 10 (ug/m^3)	Particulate Matter 2.5 (ug/m^3)	Ozone 1-hour (ppm)	Carbon Monoxide (ppm)	Sulfur Dioxide (ppm)	Nitrogen Dioxide (ppm)	Lead (ug/m^3)
MSA[1] Level	200	41	0.115	5	0.007	0.032	n/a
NAAQS[2]	150	65	0.125	9	0.140	0.053	1.50
Met NAAQS[2]	No	Yes	Yes	Yes	Yes	Yes	n/a

Note: Data from exceptional events are not included; (1) Metropolitan Statistical Area - see Appendix A for areas included; (2) National Ambient Air Quality Standards; n/a not available
Units: ppm = parts per million; ug/m^3 = micrograms per cubic meter
Source: U.S. Environmental Protection Agency, Air Trends Fact Book 2005

Watershed Health

The U.S. Environmental Protection Agency monitors the health of the aquatic resources for the nation's 2,000+ watersheds. **The Lower Salt watershed serves the Scottsdale area and received an overall Index of Watershed Indicators (IWI) score of 2 (better quality - high vulnerability).** The IWI score is based on seven condition and nine vulnerability indicators. The overall IWI score ranges from 1 (best health) to 6 (worst health). The Condition Indicators include: designated use attainment, fish and wildlife consumption advisories, source water condition, contaminated sediments, ambient water quality, and wetlands loss index. The Vulnerability Indicators include: aquatic species at risk, conventional and toxic loads over permitted limits, urban and agricultural runoff potential, population change, hydrologic modification, estuarine pollution susceptibility, and air deposition. *Note: The IWI is no longer being updated by the U.S. EPA. Source: U.S. Environmental Protection Agency, Index of Watershed Indicators, October 26, 2001*

Drinking Water

Water System Name	Pop. Served	Primary Water Source Type	Number of Violations in 2006[a]		
			Health Based	Significant Monitoring	Monitoring
City of Scottsdale	180,000	Surface	None	None	1

Note: (a) Based on violation data from January 1, 2006 to December 31, 2006
Source: U.S. Environmental Protection Agency, Office of Ground Water and Drinking Water, Safe Drinking Water Information System (data extracted April 12, 2007)

Scottsdale tap water is alkaline and hard.
Editor & Publisher Market Guide, 2005

Seattle, Washington

Background

Perhaps it's hard to imagine, but the virgin hinterlands and wide curving arch of Elliot Bay of present-day Seattle were once named New York. The city was renamed Seattle in 1853, for the Native American Indian Chief Seattle, two years after its first five families from Illinois had settled into the narrow strip of land between Puget Sound and Lake Washington.

The lush, green forests of the "Emerald City," created by the infamously frequent rains and its many natural waterways, gave birth to Seattle's first major industry — lumber. However, this industry also bred a society of bearded, rabble-rousing bachelors. To alleviate that problem, Asa Mercer, president of the Territorial University, which later became the University of Washington, trekked back East and recruited marriageable women. Among those "Mercer girls" was Ms. Mercer herself. Seattle was settling down.

Today, the city does not rely on lumber as its major industry, but now boasts commercial aircraft production and missile research, due to the presence of Boeing on the outskirts of the city.

In addition, importing and exporting is a major revenue source. As the closest U.S. mainland port to Asia, Seattle has become a key trade center for goods such as cars, forest products, electronic equipment, bananas, and petroleum products. It is also home to the headquarters of Amazon.com, Nordstrom, Starbucks, and Safeco Corp.

On the technology front, Seattle seems to be moving in the direction of becoming the next Silicon Valley. It is predominantly a software town dominated by Microsoft in nearby Redmond, with its more than 30,000 employees. Early in 2003 Corbis, the online photo-archive company, moved its headquarters to the city's historic Pioneer Square. And an increase in the rise of young firms brings the feeling that the city is ready for more expansion and innovation.

The Seattle Seaport Terminal Project is actually comprised of a number of small-and-large-scale projects designed to improve the port's facilities for businesses, passengers, residents, and tourists. One phase of the project, a major renovation of Terminal 5, cost some $265 million and was completed by 1998. Other construction has included a Cruise Ship Terminal improvement, completed in 2000. The port authority is now in discussions to expand its container facilities. To date, more than $2 billion has been invested in port facilities improvements over the past fifteen years, and approximately that much again is expected to be invested in coming years.

Seattle has undergone a cultural and commercial reemergence of its downtown. Tourists and locals are drawn by luxury hotels, restaurants, a 16-screen movie theater, and other entertainment-oriented businesses, and the first in a nationwide chain of Game Works, computerized playgrounds for adults. In Center City Seattle, an estimated $761.6 million in development projects were completed in 2006, $2.3 billion are currently under construction, and another $281.2 million have been permitted.

The arts are a vital part of Seattle life. The world-famous Seattle Opera, now performing in a state-of-the-art hall dedicated in 2003, is perhaps best-known for its summer presentations of Wagner's *Ring* cycle. The Seattle Philharmonic Orchestra celebrated its 50th anniversary in 2004; its annual Bushnell Concerto Competition features promising new area musicians. The Seattle Museum recently constructed Olympic Sculpture Park, which turned disused waterfront property into a permanent green space with plantings native to Puget Sound. The Seattle Museum of Flight's remarkable collection - the largest on the West Coast — includes a Concorde, donated by British Airways, and the Boeing 707 used as Air Force One by presidents from Eisenhower to Nixon.

Seattle has a distinctly marine climate. The city's location on Puget Sound and between two mountain ranges ensures a mild climate year 'round, with only moderate variations in temperature. Summers are generally sunny and, while winters are rainy, most of the rain falls between October and March.

Rankings

General Rankings

■ Seattle was ranked #88 out of 331 metro areas in *Cities Ranked & Rated*. Criteria: cost of living; climate; crime; transportation; economy and jobs; education; arts and culture; health and healthcare; leisure. *Cities Ranked & Rated, 1st Edition, 2004*

■ The Seattle metro area was selected one of America's "Top 10 Metros Overall" by *Expansion Management* in their 4th annual Mayor's Challenge ranking of metro areas that have achieved solid ratings across the board in numerous *EM* studies during the past 12 months. The area ranked #8. Criteria: education (with emphasis on college board test results and high school graduation rates); availability of quality healthcare services and the cost to employers; quality of life; logistics workforce and companies; transportation infrastructure; quality and quantity of highly educated technical workers; and business climate. *Expansion Management, August 2006*

■ Seattle was selected as one of the top places to live in the U.S. according to Harris Interactive. The city ranked #4 out of 10. Criteria: 3,685 U.S. adults were polled as to where they would choose to live if they could live anywhere in the country. *Harris Interactive, September 6, 2006*

■ The Seattle metro area was selected as one of "America's Best Places to Live and Work" by *Employment Review*. The area ranked #17 out of 20. Criteria: unemployment rate; projected job growth; cost of living; and industry specific data. *Employment Review, www.bestjobsusa.com, 2003*

■ Seattle appeared on *Travel & Leisure's* list of the ten best cities in the continental U.S. and Canada. The city was ranked #10. Criteria: activities/attractions; culture/arts; restaurants/food; people; and value. *Travel & Leisure, "The World's Best Awards 2006"*

■ *Condé Nast Traveler* polled nearly 28,000 readers for travel satisfaction. American cities were ranked based on the following criteria: friendliness; ambiance; culture/sites; restaurants; lodging; and shopping. Seattle appeared in the top 10, ranking #9. *Condé Nast Traveler, Readers' Choice Awards 2006*

Business/Finance Rankings

■ Seattle was selected as one of the best places to start and grow a company by *Entrepreneur* and the National Policy Research Council. The Seattle metro area ranked #31 out of 50 large metro areas. Criteria: business formation and growth (firms started four to 14 years ago that still employ at least 5 people and experienced rapid growth over the last four years). *Entrepreneur/National Policy Research Council, "Hot Cities for Entrepreneurs," September 2006*

■ The Seattle metro area was selected as one of "America's 50 Hottest Cities" for business relocations and expansions. Criteria: industry's most prominent site selection consultants were asked to list their top city choices for relocating and expanding manufacturing companies, taking into consideration such factors as the business climate, work force quality, operating costs, incentive programs, and the ease of working with local political and economic development officials. *Expansion Management, January-February 2007*

■ Intel, in partnership with Sperling's BestPlaces, ranked the 80 "Best Cities for Teleworking" in America. The Seattle metro area ranked #10 among extra large metro areas. The study identifies cities that hold the greatest potential for teleworking based on a host of factors including typical commuting times, fuel prices, availability of broadband Internet access and percentage of the population in telework friendly jobs. The study also factored in extreme climate and natural hazards. *Intel, "Best Cities for Teleworking," March 30, 2006*

■ Seattle was identified as one of "The Most Inventive Towns in America". The city ranked #14. Criteria: places with the most patents overall, combining those of large companies and individual inventors. *The Wall Street Journal, July 22-23, 2006*

- Seattle was selected as one of 20 cities in North America that is doing its part to host green conventions by providing renewable energy, intelligent recycling programs, transportation that minimizes usage of fossil fuels, and plenty of parkland. The city was ranked #16. *Meetings and Conventions, "Natural Choices," August 2006*

- The Seattle metro area was selected as one of the "25 Hottest Housing Markets" in the U.S. The area ranked #16 out of 156 markets with a home price appreciation rate of 11.3%. Criteria: year-over-year change of median sales price of existing single-family homes between the 4th quarter of 2005 and the 4th quarter of 2006. *National Association of Realtors, Median Sales Price of Existing Single-Family Homes for Metropolitan Areas, 4th Quarter 2006*

- The Seattle metro area appeared on the Milken Institute "2005 Best Performing Cities" index. Rank: #127 out of 200 large metro areas. Criteria: job growth; wage and salary growth; high-tech output growth. *Milken Institute, "2005 Best Performing Cities," February 2006*

- The Seattle metro area was selected as one of "The Best Cities for Doing Business in America." *Inc.* magazine measured employment growth in 393 regions using the following criteria: recent growth trend; mid-term growth; long-term trend; and current year growth. The Seattle metro area ranked #28 among large metro areas and #179 overall. *Inc., May 2006*

- The Seattle metro area was selected as one of "The Top 20 Boom Towns in America." *Business 2.0* magazine and econometric research firm Global Insight compared 319 metropolitan areas in the U.S. and ranked the 61 with populations over 1 million. Criteria: a weighted formula that includes forecast growth rates in sectors that contain the economy's 10 most skilled occupational clusters; the prevalence of college degrees in the local workforce; median salary. The area ranked #9 among large metro areas. *Business 2.0 Magazine, March 2004*

- Seattle was identified as one of the 100 "Most Unwired Cities" in the U.S. The area ranked #1 out of the 100 largest metro areas in the U.S. Criteria: number of public and commercial wireless access points (hotspots); airports with wireless Internet access; broadband availability; local wireless networks; and wireless email devices. *Intel, "Most Unwired Cities Survey," June 7, 2005*

- Seattle was ranked #5 out of 125 regions worldwide in terms of its "Knowledge Competitiveness Index." The index attempts to measure the knowledge-based development taking place throughout the world and is based on 19 measures of economic performance that indicate a region's ability to translate its knowledge capacity into economic value. *Robert Huggins Associates, World Knowledge Competitiveness Index 2005*

- *Forbes* ranked the 200 most populous metro areas in the U.S. in terms of the "Best Places for Business and Careers." The Seattle metro area was ranked #62. Criteria: business costs (labor, energy, tax and office space expenses); living costs (housing, transportation, food and other household expenditures); education levels of the work force; job growth; income growth; migration trends; crime rates; and culture/leisure. *Forbes, April 23, 2007*

- Seattle was identified as one of the top 20 metro areas with the highest rate of home price appreciation in 2006. The area ranked #18 with a one-year price appreciation of 14.5% through the 4th quarter 2006. *Office of Federal Housing Enterprise Oversight, House Price Index, 4th Quarter 2006*

- *Kiplinger's Personal Finance* ranked 101 U.S. cities in terms of their total tax burdens. Seattle ranked #22 (#1 had the lowest overall tax burden). Criteria: state income tax; property tax; sales tax; personal property tax; and gasoline tax. *Kiplinger's Personal Finance, July 2004*

- *Fortune* ranked the 100 largest metro areas in the U.S. in terms of projected median home price change in 2006. The Seattle metro area ranked #65. *Fortune, "The Top 100: Is the Party Over?" December 26, 2005*

- Seattle was identified as one of the "Most Overpriced Places in the U.S." The area ranked #1 out of the nations 150 largest metro areas. Criteria: job growth; income growth; cost of living; and housing affordability. *Forbes.com, "Most Overpriced Places in the U.S. 2005"*

■ Seattle was identified as one of the top 10 richest major cities in the U.S. The city ranked #8. Criteria: 2004 median household income. *Forbes, "Richest Cities in the U.S.," October 27, 2005*

Health/Environment Rankings

■ *Reader's Digest* ranked the 50 largest metro areas in the U.S. in terms of how "clean" they are. The Seattle metro area ranked #27. Criteria: air quality; water quality; toxic industrial pollution; Superfund sites; and sanitation. *Reader's Digest, "The 50 Cleanest (and Dirtiest) Cities in America," July 2005*

■ *Business Week* identified the 15 metro areas that saw the steepest declines in ground-level ozone pollution between 1990 and 2005. The Seattle metro area ranked #2. *Business Week, "America's Most Cleaned-Up Metro Areas," March 23, 2007*

■ Sanofi-aventis, in partnership with Sperling's BestPlaces, ranked the 50 worst cities for respiratory infections in the U.S. Seattle ranked #44. Criteria: prevalence of sinusitis, pharyngitis (sore throat), bronchitis, acute upper respiratory infections, pneumonia, otitis media (middle ear infection), other respiratory tract infections and the common cold; total per capita prescriptions written for oral antibiotics for respiratory tract infections; and prevalence of state level antibiotic resistance. *Sanofi-aventis, "America's Worst Cities for Respiratory Infections," December 6, 2005*

■ The Seattle metro area appeared in *Country Home's* "2007 Best Green Places Report". The area ranked #32. Criteria included: air and watershed quality; miles of mass transit; green power; number of farmer's markets, organic producers and groceries. *Country Home, "2007 Best Green Places Report," April 2007*

■ Wyeth Consumer Healthcare, in partnership with Sperling's BestPlaces, ranked the nation's 50 most populous metro areas in terms of five key health factors. The Seattle metro area ranked #4. Criteria: physical activity, health status, nutrition, lifestyle pursuits; and mental wellness. *Wyeth Consumer Healthcare, "Centrum Healthiest Cities Study," April 19, 2005*

■ HealthGrades identified the 10 worst cities for nursing home care in the U.S. Seattle ranked #5. Criteria: proportion of facilities that had four or more actual harm violations from health or complaint surveys in the last four years. *www.HealthGrades.com, "Best and Worst Cities for Nursing Home Care," March 16, 2004*

■ HealthGrades surveyed over 41,000 individuals on doctor satisfaction and ranked the 20 largest metro areas based on the highest "definitely yes" responses to the question "Do you trust the physician to make decisions/recommendations that are in your best interest?" The Seattle metro area ranked #9. *HealthGrades.com, "Top Cities in Doctor-Trust," September 7, 2006*

■ The American Podiatric Medical Association and *Prevention* magazine ranked America's 100 most populated cities based on fitness-walker friendliness. The best cities have safe streets, beautiful places to walk, mild weather and good air quality. Seattle ranked #5. *Prevention, "The Best Walking Cities of 2007," April 2007; American Podiatric Medical Association, "2007 Best Fitness-Walking Cities"*

■ Seattle was selected as one of "greenest" cities in the U.S. Criteria: good water- and air-quality; efficient use of resources; renewable energy leadership; accessible and reliable public transportation; green building practices; number of parks and greenbelts; access to locally-grown fresh food through farmers' markets and community supported agriculture groups; and affordability. *The Green Guide Institute, "The Top 10 Green Cities in the U.S.: 2005," April 19, 2005*

■ Seattle was selected as one of the 25 fittest cities in America by *Men's Fitness Online*. It ranked #8 out of America's 50 largest cities. Criteria: gyms/sporting goods; nutrition; exercise/sports; overweight/sedentary; junk food; alcohol; smoking; television; air and water quality; climate; geography; commute time; parks/open space; recreation facilities; health care; motivation; civic legislation and leadership. *Men's Fitness Online, America's Fittest/Fattest Cities 2006*

- Seattle was identified as a "2007 Asthma Capital." The area ranked #100 out of the nation's 100 largest metropolitan areas. Twelve factors were used to identify the most challenging places to live for people with asthma: estimated prevalence; self-reported prevalence; crude death rate for asthma; annual pollen score; annual air quality; public smoking laws; number of board-certified asthma specialists; school inhaler access laws; rescue medication use; controller medication use; uninsured rate; poverty rate. *Asthma and Allergy Foundation of America, "2007 Asthma Capitals"*

- Seattle was identified as a "Spring Allergy Capital." The area ranked #96 out of 100. Three groups of factors were used to identify the most severe cities for people with allergies during the spring season: annual pollen levels; medicine utilization; access to board-certified allergists. *Asthma and Allergy Foundation of America, "2007 Spring Allergy Capital Rankings"*

- Seattle was identified as a "Fall Allergy Capital." The area ranked #94 out of 100. Three groups of factors were used to identify the most severe cities for people with allergies during the fall season: annual pollen levels; medicine utilization; access to board-certified allergists. *Asthma and Allergy Foundation of America, "2006 Fall Allergy Capital Rankings"*

- Seattle was selected as one of "America's Healthiest Cities" by *Natural Health* magazine. The city was ranked #3 out of the 50 largest urban areas in the U.S. Twenty-six criteria in the following four categories were examined: whether the city boasts natural offerings; how well the city promotes its residents' physical health; whether the city offers a healthy environment; how well the city fosters a sense of community. *Natural Health, April 2003*

- *Men's Health* ranked the nation's largest 100 cities in terms of the *Best (and Worst) Cities for Men.* Seattle was ranked #16. Criteria: 24 statistical parameters of long life in the categories of health, quality of life, and fitness. *Men's Health, January/February 2007*

- *Men's Health* ranked 100 U.S. cities in terms of the quality of their tap water. Seattle was ranked #86 and received a grade of D. Criteria: levels of total coliform bacteria, arsenic, lead, total trihalomethanes (linked to cancer), and halo-acetic acids, plus the number of EPA water-system violations from 1995 to 2005. *Men's Health, March 2007*

- Ortho-McNeil Neurologics, in partnership with Sperling's BestPlaces, analyzed 110 metro areas and identified those U.S. cities with the highest prevalence of factors that are most commonly associated with migraine headaches. The Seattle metro area ranked #59. Criteria: number of migraine-related drug prescriptions per capita; lifestyle factors that can contribute to migraines; environmental factors that can trigger migraines; and consumption of migraine-triggering foods. *Ortho-McNeil Neurologics, "America's Migraine Hot Spots," March 14, 2006*

- Sperling's BestPlaces ranked 331 metro areas and identified the most and least stressful U.S. cities. The Seattle metro area ranked #11 out of the 100 largest metro areas (#1 = most stressful). Criteria: divorce rate; unemployment rate; violent and property crime; suicide rate; commute time; mental health; alcohol consumption; cloudy days. *www.BestPlaces.net, January 9, 2004*

- Sperling's BestPlaces in partnership with Vistakon ranked the 100 largest metro areas and identified "America's 10 Best Cities for Comfortable Eyes." The Seattle metro area ranked #10. Criteria: altitude; sunny days; wind; extreme temperatures; humidity; pollution; commute time; computer use. *Vistakon, "America's Best and Worst Cities for Comfortable Eyes," June 15, 2004*

- HealthGrades evaluated the performance of America's 25 most populous metropolitan areas by measuring the outcomes of five of the highest volume and most widely studied procedures and diagnoses: coronary artery bypass graft surgery; percutaneus coronary interventions; acute myocardial infarction/heart attack in angioplasty-capable hospitals; congestive heart failure; and community acquired pneumonia. The Seattle metro area ranked #24. *HealthGrades, "HealthGrades Hospital Quality in America Study," October 12, 2004*

- Seattle was selected as one of "America's Top 10 Low-Carb Cities" by *LowCarbiz Magazine.* Criteria: abundance of low-carb products; restaurants with low-carb menu items; health practitioners supportive of carb-cutting regimens; local culture generally conducive to exercise and health. *LowCarbiz Magazine, April 2004*

- Seattle was selected as one of "America's Pet Healthiest Cities" by Purina. The city ranked #11 out of 50. Criteria: veterinary services; environment; legislation; preventative care; obesity/body condition. *Purina Pet Institute, "America's Pet Healthiest Cities," May 20, 2003*

- According to research conducted by Malibu Wellness of 100 major U.S. cities' local water quality reports, Seattle was selected as a top-ranked color-friendly city in terms of hair color application and longevity. Criteria: quantity of minerals found in the water supply (lower ppm is better for hair color); type of oxidizers such as chlorine; and pH levels. *Malibu Wellness, Wellness e-Letter, "Best & Worst Cities for Hair Color," February 2005*

Women/Minorities Rankings

- Seattle was ranked #18 out of 100 metro areas in *SELF Magazine's* ranking of "America's Best Places for Women." A panel of experts came up with nearly 40 criteria including: drinking and smoking rates; depression; unemployment; parks; crime; disease; healthcare insurance coverage; air quality; and commute times. *SELF Magazine, "America's Best Places for Women 2006," December 2006*

- *Ladies Home Journal* ranked America's 200 largest cities based on the qualities women surveyed care about most. Seattle ranked #25 out of 57 in the big city category (population over 300,000). Criteria: crime; lifestyle; education; jobs; health; child care; politics; and the economy. *Ladies Home Journal Online, "The Best Cities for Women 2002"*

- Seattle appeared on a list of the top 10 metro areas with the highest concentration of same-sex households. The area ranked #3. *Urban Institute Press, The Gay and Lesbian Atlas, May 2004*

- Seattle was profiled in the book *50 Fabulous Gay-Friendly Places to Live.* Criteria: an active gay community; positive gay health programs; youth outreach; gay-friendly politics; gay-owned and gay-friendly businesses; employment opportunities; fun nightlife; cultural opportunities; recreational opportunities; housing options. *50 Fabulous Gay-Friendly Places to Live, 2005*

- Seattle appeared on a list of the top 10 metro areas with the highest concentration of gay male couples. The area ranked #4. *Urban Institute Press, The Gay and Lesbian Atlas, May 2004*

- Seattle appeared on a list of the top 10 metro areas with the highest concentration of African-American same-sex couples among all African-American households. The area ranked #6. *Urban Institute Press, The Gay and Lesbian Atlas, May 2004*

- Seattle appeared on a list of the top 10 metro areas with the highest concentration of Hispanic same-sex couples among all Hispanic households. The area ranked #5. *Urban Institute Press, The Gay and Lesbian Atlas, May 2004*

- Seattle was identified as one of the top 25 metropolitan statistical areas ranked by percentage of coupled households that are gay or lesbian." The area ranked #10. *Human Rights Campaign, "Gay and Lesbian Families in the United States: Same-Sex Unmarried Partner Households," August 1, 2001*

Seniors/Retirement Rankings

- Seattle was profiled in the book *Where to Retire: America's Best and Most Affordable Places.* Cities were selected based on personal visits by the author and interviews with local residents coupled with statistics from various government agencies. *Where to Retire: America's Best and Most Affordable Places, 2006*

- Sperling's BestPlaces in partnership with Bankers Life & Casualty Company designed a survey to identify the top 50 metro areas in the U.S. that offer the best overall qualities for senior living. The Seattle metro area ranked #2. The following criteria were statistically weighted to reflect the needs of the senior population: health; disease; economics; social; environment; spiritual; transportation; housing; and crime. *Bankers Life & Casualty Company, "Best Cities for Seniors 2005"*

■ A.G. Edwards ranked America's 500 top-performing communities based on their residents' personal savings and investing behavior. The Seattle metro area ranked #73 with an index score of 108.06 (national average = 100.00). A dozen statistical factors were measured including: participation in retirement savings plans; personal debt levels; and home ownership. *A.G. Edwards, "2006 Nest Egg Index", September 6, 2006*

Children/Family Rankings

■ The Seattle metro area was selected as one of the "Best Cities for Relocating Families" by Worldwide ERC and Primacy Relocation. Criteria: tax rates; average home costs and home appreciation; ability to qualify for in-state tuition; service quality of local utilities; per-capita volunteerism; auto taxes; and quantity of fun, family-friendly events and venues. *Worldwide ERC and Primacy Relocation, "2006 Best Cities for Relocating Families"*

■ *Zero Population Growth* ranked 100 cities in terms of children's health, safety, and economic well-being. Seattle was ranked #1 out of 20 Major Cities (main city in a metro area with population of greater than 2.5 million) and was given a grade of A. Criteria: total population and population growth; percent of population under 18 years of age; percent of births to teens; infant mortality rate; percent of eligible women not receiving Title X services; contraceptive equity indicator; percent of children without health insurance; percent of city residents over age 25 with a high-school diploma; ration of PopEd (Population Connection's Education Program) teachers trained; sexuality education indicator; proficiency in reading and math; percent of kids living in poverty; percent growth in urbanized land; violent crime rate; recycling. *Population Connection, Kid Friendly Cities: Report Card 2004*

■ *Fit Pregnancy* magazine ranked the 50 best U.S. cities in which to have a baby. Seattle was ranked #6. Criteria: fertility services; maternal and infant health risk; access to hospitals and doctors; safety; affordability; stroller friendliness; and birthing options. *Fit Pregnancy, February/March, 2006*

Safety Rankings

■ Allstate ranked the 200 largest cities in America in terms of driver safety. Seattle ranked #165. In addition, drivers were 26.6% more likely to have had an accident compared to the national average. Allstate researchers analyzed internal Property Damage reported claims over a two-year period (from January 2003 to December 2004) to ensure the findings would not be affected by external influences such as weather or road construction. A weighted average of the two-year numbers determined the annual percentages. The report defines an auto crash as any collision resulting in a property damage claim. *Allstate, "Allstate America's Best Drivers Report 2006," May 24, 2006*

■ Seattle was identified as one of the most dangerous large metro areas for pedestrians in the U.S. The area ranked #40 out of the nations 50 largest metro areas. Criteria: average yearly pedestrian fatalities per capita (for the years 2002 and 2003) adjusted for the number of walkers. *Surface Transportation Policy Project, "Mean Streets 2004"*

■ *Ladies Home Journal* ranked America's 200 largest cities in terms of safety. Seattle ranked #96 out of 200. Criteria: violent crimes; crimes against property; and rape. *Ladies Home Journal Online, "The Best Cities for Women 2002"*

Sports/Recreation Rankings

■ The Seattle metro area appeared on *The Sporting News* list of the "Best Sports Cities 2006". The area ranked #15 out of 99 cities in North America. To be included in the rankings, a city must have at least one of the following: NCAA Division I basketball team; Class A minor league baseball team; training camp for a major league or NFL team; NASCAR Nextel Cup race; NCAA Division I-A bowl game; PGA Tour tournament; Triple Crown horse race. Once a city qualifies, a 12-month snapshot is taken of the sports atmosphere, putting a heavy premium on regular-season won-lost records; playoff berths, bowl appearances and tournament bids; championships; applicable power ratings; quality of competition; overall fan fervor; sports atmosphere and fan knowledge; abundance of teams (quality over quantity); stadium/arena quality; ticket availability and prices; franchise ownership; and the marquee appeal of athletes. *SportingNews.com, "Best Sports Cities 2006," August 1, 2006*

- Seattle was selected as a "dream city" runner-up by readers of *Backpacker* magazine. *Backpacker, "2nd Annual Readers' Choice Awards," February 2006*

- Seattle was chosen as one of America's 25 best cities for running. The city was ranked #12. Criteria: number of running clubs per city; amount of land set aside for park usage; air quality; weather; crime rates; and results from a *Runner's World* poll in which readers ranked their favorite running cities. *Runner's World, "The 25 Best Running Cities in America," July 2005*

- Seattle was selected as one of "10 Great Biking Cities." Editors at the Washington Post asked Adventure Cycling Association, a non-profit bike organization in Montana, and *Bicycling* magazine for their suggestions on the most bike-friendly cities in the country. *Washington Post, October 1, 2006*

- Seattle was chosen as one of America's best cities for bicycling. The city ranked #3 in the large city category (population 500,000 to 1 million). Criteria: cycling-friendly statistics (number of bike lanes and routes, number of bike racks, city bike projects completed and planned; bike culture (number of bike commuters, popular clubs, cool cycling events, renowned bike shops); climate/geography (the quality of roads and trails for riding, and how frequently mother nature lets riders enjoy them). *Bicycling, March 2006*

- The Seattle metro area was selected by *Cranium* as one of the "Top 50 Fun Cities" in America. The area ranked #10. Criteria includes: number of sports teams, restaurants, and dance performances; number of toy stores; city budget spent on recreation. *Cranium, November 4, 2003*

- *Golf Digest* ranked 330 metro areas in the U.S. in terms of golf. The Seattle metro area was ranked #315. Criteria: access to golf; weather; value of golf; and quality of golf. *Golf Digest, "Metro Golf Rankings," August 2005*

Dating/Romance Rankings

- The Seattle metro area was selected as one of the "Best Cities for Relocating Singles" by Worldwide ERC and Primacy Relocation. The area ranked #10 out of the 100 largest metro areas in the U.S. Areas were selected based on the following criteria: Population Criteria (local percentage and growth trends of unmarried residents aged 25-34; male-female ratios; the number of newcomers to the area; diversity and density); Economic Criteria (job growth vs. unemployment rates; apartment rental costs; fee and occupancy rates for temporary housing and mini-storage; higher education costs, including in-state and out-of-state tuition requirements; vehicle tax rates and quality of service from utility providers); Quality-of-Life Criteria (level of per capita volunteering; quality and quantity of collegiate and professional sports with fun, fan-friendly venues; number of Starbucks and other coffee shops; quality or popularity of restaurants, nightspots, health clubs, and online dating; moderate climates with sustainable water supplies). *Worldwide ERC and Primacy Relocation, "2006 Best Cities for Relocating Singles," October 11, 2006*

- *Forbes* ranked the 40 most populous metro areas in the U.S. in terms of the "Best Cities for Singles." The Seattle metro area was ranked #7. Criteria: number of singles; cost of living alone; nightlife; culture; job growth; coolness; and online dating. *Forbes.com, July 25, 2006*

- Sperling's BestPlaces in partnership with AXE Deodorant Bodyspray ranked 80 metro areas and identified "America's Best (and Worst) Cities for Dating." The Seattle metro area ranked #5. Criteria: percentage of singles ages 18-24; population density; dating venues per capita. *AXE Deodorant Bodyspray, "America's Best (and Worst) Cities for Dating," May, 2004*

Culture/Performing Arts Rankings

- Seattle was selected as one of "America's Top 25 Arts Destinations." The city ranked #6 in the big city (population 500,000 and over) category. Criteria: readers' top choices for arts travel destinations based on the richness and variety of visual arts sites, activities and events. *American Style, June 2006*

■ Scarborough Research, a leading market research firm, identified the top local markets for rock concert attendance. The Seattle DMA (Designated Market Area) ranked in the top 25 with 14% of consumers, 18 years old and over, reporting that they have attended a rock concert during the past year. *Scarborough Research, Scarborough USA+ 2003 Release 2*

Miscellaneous Rankings

■ Seattle was selected as one of the "Most Courteous Cities (Least Road Rage)" in the U.S. by AutoVantage. The city ranked #4. Criteria: 2,040 consumers were interviewed in 20 major metropolitan areas about their views on road rage. *AutoVantage, "In The Driver's Seat Road Rage Survey," May 16, 2006*

■ Seattle was determined to be one of America's smartest cities. The city ranked #1 in the large city category (200,000+ adults 25 years and older). Criteria: the editors rated the collective brainpower of U.S communities based on the educational attainment of its residents. *American City Business Journals, www.bizjournals.com, June 12, 2006*

■ Seattle was selected as one of the "Top 100 Sweatiest Summer Cities". The city was ranked #99. The ranking was based on the average male/female height/weight, average high temperature, and average relative humidity levels for 2002 in each of the cities during June, July and August. The sweat level was analyzed based on the assumption that the individual was walking for one hour. *Procter & Gamble, Old Spice, June 18, 2003*

■ Seattle was selected as one of the "Top 10 Most Independent Cities for Homesellers" in 2005. The city was ranked #10. The cities listed had more consumers choosing to sell their homes free of interference from a real-estate broker than anywhere else. Data was based on geographical information for listings posted on ForSaleByOwner.com from July 2004 - July 2005. *ForSaleByOwner.com, August 3, 2005*

■ Avis Rent-A-Car and Motorola, in partnership with Sperling's BestPlaces, ranked the nation's 75 most populous metro areas in terms of how difficult they are to navigate. The Seattle metro area ranked #8 with #1 being the most challenging. Criteria: street layouts; overall design and layout; travel time index; percent of congested freeway and street lane miles; bodies of water; complexity of directions needed to travel from major airports to city center; annual delay per person; days of snow exceeding 1.5 inches; and days of rain exceeding 0.5 inch. *Avis Rent-A-Car and Motorola, "America's Most Challenging Cities to Navigate," August 3, 2004*

■ The Seattle metro area appeared on *Forbes* list of "America's Drunkest Cities". The area ranked #12. Criteria: 35 of the largest continental U.S. metro areas were chosen based on availability of data and geographic diversity. Each metro was ranked in five areas: state laws; drinkers; heavy drinkers; binge drinkers; and alcoholism. *Forbes.com, "America's Drunkest Cities," August 22, 2006*

■ Seattle appeared on ApartmentRatings.com "Top Cities for Renters List 2006". The area ranked #89 out of 138. Criteria: renter satisfaction; affordability; and vacancy. *ApartmentRatings.com, "Top Cities for Renters List 2006"*

■ Seattle was selected as one of "America's Best Vegetarian-Friendly Large Cities." The city was ranked #2. *www.peta.org, April 2006*

■ Sperling's BestPlaces in partnership with Pep Boys ranked 77 metro areas and identified "America's Most Drivable Cities." The Seattle metro area ranked #69. Criteria: climate; road roughness; urban mobility; gas prices. *Pep Boys, "America's Most Drivable Cities," April 9, 2003*

■ Seattle was selected as a "Great College Town" by ePodunk. The city ranked #5 in the big city category. ePodunk.com looked at communities with four-year colleges and a total student enrollment of at least 1,500. Communities where the student ratio was too low or too high were ruled out, as were small cities with low rates of owner-occupied housing. Fifteen variables were then applied to assess arts and culture, recreation, intellectual activity, historic preservation, and cost of living. *www.ePodunk.com, April, 2002*

- Seattle was ranked #5 out of 268 metro areas in terms of its Creativity Index. The Creativity Index is a mix of four equally weighted factors: the Creative Class (scientists, engineers, architects, designers, writers, artists, musicians, or any profession where creativity is a key factor) share of the workforce; innovation, measured as patents per capita; high-tech industry, using the Milken Institute's Tech Pole Index; and diversity, measured by the Gay Index (a reasonable proxy for an areas' openness to different kinds of people and ideas). *The Rise of the Creative Class, 2002*

- Seattle was selected as one of "America's Most Literate Cities." The city ranked #1 out of the 70 largest U.S. cities. Criteria: number of booksellers; library resources; Internet resources; educational attainment; periodical publishing resources; newspaper circulation. *Central Connecticut State University, "America's Most Literate Cities 2006"*

- Seattle was selected as one of America's best-mannered cities. The area ranked in the top 10 at #3. The list is based on thousands of letters and faxes received by etiquette expert Marjabelle Young Stewart. *The Associated Press, January 15, 2005*

- Seattle was identified as one of the "Most Liberal Places in America" by ePodunk. Criteria: individual contributions to PACs; election returns; gay households; local government resolutions opposing combat in Iraq; local officials performing gay marriages; Congressional District voting history *www.ePodunk.com, January 3, 2005*

- State Farm Insurance, in partnership with Sperling's BestPlaces, analyzed several key factors that contribute to overall family preparedness. The Seattle metro area ranked #8 out of the nation's 50 most populous metro areas. Criteria: quality of life; life insurance coverage; and investments. *State Farm Life Insurance, "Fiscally Fit Cities Report," July 20, 2004*

- Scarborough Research, a leading market research firm, identified the top local markets for coffee bar patronage. The Seattle DMA (Designated Market Area) ranked in the top 10 with 23% of adults reporting that they have used any coffee house/bar during the past 30 days. *Scarborough Research, Scarborough USA+ 2004 Release 1*

- Seattle was selected as having one of the highest number of Starbucks stores per capita in the U.S. The city appeared in the large city category. Criteria: U.S. cities with populations of 10,000 or more were analyzed with regards to the number of Starbucks stores per capita. Supermarkets and other stores selling coffee beans were not included. *ePodunk.com, "Coffee Quotients," March 2005*

Business Environment

CITY FINANCES

City Government Finances

Component	2003-2004 ($000)	2003-2004 ($ per capita)
Total Revenues	2,512,388	4,404
Total Expenditures	2,478,034	4,344
Debt Outstanding	3,508,381	6,150
Cash and Securities	1,268,761	2,224

Source: U.S Census Bureau, Government Finances 2003-2004

City Government Revenue by Source

Source	2003-2004 ($000)	2003-2004 ($ per capita)
General Revenue		
From Federal Government	37,717	66
From State Government	92,336	162
From Local Governments	4,469	8
Taxes		
Property	268,301	470
Sales	278,282	488
Personal Income	0	0
License	0	0
Charges	345,721	606
Liquor Store	0	0
Utility	860,279	1,508
Employee Retirement	332,482	583
Other	292,801	513

Source: U.S Census Bureau, Government Finances 2003-2004

City Government Expenditures by Function

Function	2003-2004 ($000)	2003-2004 ($ per capita)	2003-2004 (%)
General Expenditures			
Airports	0	0	0.0
Corrections	12,810	22	0.5
Education	0	0	0.0
Fire Protection	105,396	185	4.3
Governmental Administration	105,080	184	4.2
Health	14,730	26	0.6
Highways	100,580	176	4.1
Hospitals	0	0	0.0
Housing and Community Development	35,656	63	1.4
Interest on General Debt	53,319	93	2.2
Libraries	137,160	240	5.5
Parking	2,612	5	0.1
Parks and Recreation	216,647	380	8.7
Police Protection	164,153	288	6.6
Public Welfare	35,609	62	1.4
Sewerage	144,477	253	5.8
Solid Waste Management	108,456	190	4.4
Liquor Store	0	0	0.0
Utility	971,758	1,704	39.2
Employee Retirement	86,778	152	3.5
Other	182,813	320	7.4

Source: U.S Census Bureau, Government Finances 2003-2004

Municipal Bond Ratings

Area	Moody's
City	n/a

Source: Mergent Bond Record, January 2007 (unless noted otherwise)

DEMOGRAPHICS

Population Growth

Area	1990 Census	2000 Census	2006 Estimate	2011 Projection	Population Growth (%)	
					1990-2000	2000-2011
City	516,262	563,374	578,033	594,270	9.1	5.5
MSA[1]	2,559,164	3,043,878	3,226,674	3,397,122	18.9	11.6
U.S.	248,709,873	281,421,906	298,021,266	312,383,955	13.2	11.0

Note: (1) Metropolitan Statistical Area - see Appendix B for areas included
Source: Claritas, Inc.

Number of Households and Average Household Size

Area	2006 Estimate	2006 Average Household Size
City	265,973	2.17
MSA[1]	1,270,402	2.54
U.S.	112,267,302	2.65

Note: (1) Metropolitan Statistical Area - see Appendix B for areas included
Source: Claritas, Inc.

Race and Ethnicity

Area	White Alone[2]	Black Alone[2]	Asian Alone[2]	Other Race Alone[2]	Hispanic[3]
City	68.6	7.9	14.5	9.1	6.3
MSA[1]	75.5	5.2	10.0	9.3	6.6
U.S.	73.3	12.4	4.2	10.1	14.5

Note: Figures are 2006 estimates; (1) Metropolitan Statistical Area - see Appendix B for areas included
(2) Alone is defined as not being in combination with one or more other races; (3) May be of any race.
Source: Claritas, Inc.

Segregation

City		MSA[1]	
Index[2]	Rank[3]	Index[2]	Rank[4]
64.2	33	57.9	172

Note: Figures are based on an analysis of Census 2000 data; (1) Metropolitan Statistical Area - see Appendix A for areas included; (2) White/Black Dissimilarity Index—the most commonly used measure of segregation between two groups, reflecting their relative distributions across neighborhoods within a city or metropolitan area. It can range in value from 0, indicating complete integration, to 100, indicating complete segregation; (3) Ranges from 1 (most segregated) to 100 (least segregated) and includes all the cities in this book; (4) Ranges from 1 (most segregated) to 318 (least segregated) and includes 318 metropolitan areas.
Source: www.CensusScope.org

Ancestry

Area	German	Irish[2]	English	American	Italian	Polish	French[3]	Scottish
City	15.2	11.9	11.3	2.5	3.9	2.2	3.3	3.5
MSA[1]	17.6	11.5	12.3	4.3	3.6	2.0	3.6	3.3
U.S.	15.2	10.9	8.7	7.3	5.6	3.2	3.0	1.7

Note: Figures include multiple ancestry (e.g. if a person reported being Irish and Italian, they were included in both columns); (1) Metropolitan Statistical Area - see Appendix A for areas included; (2) Includes Celtic; (3) Includes Alsatian but excludes Basque
Source: Census 2000, Summary File 3

Foreign-Born Population

Area	Percent of Population Born in							
	Any Foreign Country	Europe	Asia	Africa	Oceania[2]	Canada	Mexico	Latin America[3]
City	16.9	2.7	9.4	1.3	0.3	0.9	1.4	0.8
MSA[1]	13.8	2.8	6.9	0.7	0.2	1.0	1.5	0.6
U.S.	11.1	1.7	2.9	0.3	0.1	0.3	3.3	2.5

Note: (1) Metropolitan Statistical Area - see Appendix A for areas included; (2) Includes Australia, New Zealand subregion, Melanesia, Micronesia, Polynesia, and Oceania n.e.c.; (3) Includes Central America (excluding Mexico), South America, and the Caribbean.
Source: Census 2000, Summary File 3

Marriage Status

Area	Never Married	Now Married (excluding Separated)	Separated	Widowed	Divorced
City	41.8	39.9	1.6	5.4	11.4
MSA[1]	29.2	53.2	1.5	4.8	11.3
U.S.	27.1	54.4	2.2	6.6	9.7

Note: Figures are percentages and cover the population 15 years of age and older;
(1) Metropolitan Statistical Area - see Appendix A for areas included
Source: Census 2000, Summary File 3

Age Distribution

Area	Percent of Population						
	Under Age 5	Age 5 to 17	Age 18 to 34	Age 35 to 49	Age 50 to 64	Age 65 to 79	80 Years and Over
City	4.6	10.9	33.5	25.1	13.8	8.1	4.0
MSA[1]	6.3	17.4	25.2	26.1	14.7	7.4	2.9
U.S.	6.8	18.9	23.7	23.5	14.8	9.2	3.2

Note: (1) Metropolitan Statistical Area - see Appendix A for areas included
Source: Census 2000, Summary File 3

Male/Female Ratio

Area	Males	Females	Males per 100 Females
City	289,945	288,088	100.6
MSA[1]	1,609,994	1,616,680	99.6
U.S.	146,712,712	151,308,554	97.0

Note: Figures are 2006 estimates; (1) Metropolitan Statistical Area -
see Appendix B for areas included
Source: Claritas, Inc.

Religion

Area	Catholic	Southern Baptist	United Methodist	ELCA[1]	LDS[2]	Presbyterian Church USA	Jewish Est.	Muslim Est.
County	16.2	0.7	1.1	2.0	2.3	1.6	1.9	0.5
U.S.	22.0	7.1	3.7	1.8	1.5	1.1	2.2	0.6

Note: Figures are the number of adherents as a percentage of the total population; Adherents are defined as all
members, including full members, their children and the estimated number of other participants who are not
considered members (e.g. the baptized, those not confirmed, those regularly attending services, etc.);
(1) Evangelical Lutheran Church in America; (2) The Church of Jesus Christ of Latter Day Saints
Source: Reprinted with permission from Religious Congregations and Membership in the United States 2000
(Nashville, Glenmary Research Center, 2002) Copyright Association of Statisticians of American Religious
Bodies. All rights reserved.

ECONOMY

Gross Metropolitan Product

Area	2002	2003	2004	2005	2005 Rank[2]
MSA[1]	138.9	142.3	149.0	158.0	13

Note: Figures are in billions of dollars; (1) Seattle-Tacoma-Bellevue, WA Metropolitan Statistical Area - see
Appendix A for areas included; (2) Rank ranges from 1 to 361
Source: The U.S. Conference of Mayors, "U.S. Metro Economies: GMP - The Engines of America's Growth,"
January 2007

Economic Growth

Area	1995 GMP	2005 GMP	Average Annual Growth Rate	Growth Rate Rank[2]
MSA[1]	90.9	158.0	5.7	144

Note: Figures are in billions of dollars; GMP = Gross Metropolitan Product; (1) Seattle-Tacoma-Bellevue, WA
Metropolitan Statistical Area - see Appendix A for areas included; (2) Rank ranges from 1 to 361
Source: The U.S. Conference of Mayors, "U.S. Metro Economies: GMP - The Engines of America's Growth,"
January 2007

INCOME

Per Capita/Median/Average Income

Area	Per Capita ($)	Median Household ($)	Average Household ($)
City	33,136	50,252	70,554
MSA[1]	29,569	58,417	74,194
U.S.	25,129	48,775	65,849

Note: Figures are 2006 estimates; (1) Metropolitan Statistical Area - see Appendix B for areas included
Source: Claritas, Inc.

Household Income Distribution

Area	Percent of Households Earning							
	Under $15,000	$15,000 -24,999	$25,000 -34,999	$35,000 -49,999	$50,000 -74,999	$75,000 -99,000	$100,000 -149,999	$150,000 and up
City	13.1	10.0	11.0	15.7	18.6	11.9	11.7	8.0
MSA[1]	9.3	8.4	9.9	15.2	21.1	14.4	14.0	7.6
U.S.	13.3	11.0	11.3	15.7	19.5	11.8	11.0	6.4

Note: Figures are 2006 estimates; (1) Metropolitan Statistical Area - see Appendix B for areas included
Source: Claritas, Inc.

Poverty Rates by Age

Area	All Ages	Under 5 Years Old	5 to 17 Years Old	18 to 64 Years Old	65 Years and Over
City	11.8	0.6	1.7	8.3	1.2
MSA[1]	7.9	0.6	1.6	5.0	0.7
U.S.	12.4	1.2	3.0	6.9	1.2

Note: Figures are percent of population with income in 1999 below poverty level and only include population for whom poverty status is determined; (1) Metropolitan Statistical Area - see Appendix A for areas included
Source: Census 2000, Summary File 3

Personal Bankruptcy Filing Rate

Area	2003	2004	2005
King County	4.88	4.69	6.13
U.S.	5.57	5.31	6.88

Note: Numbers are per 1,000 population and include Chapter 7 and Chapter 13 filings
Source: Federal Deposit Insurance Corporation (FDIC), Regional Economic Conditions (RECON), 3/24/2006

EMPLOYMENT

Labor Force and Employment

Area	Civilian Labor Force			Workers Employed		
	Dec. 2005	Dec. 2006	% Chg.	Dec. 2005	Dec. 2006	% Chg.
City	353,519	360,482	2.0	338,552	346,799	2.4
MD[1]	1,384,455	1,408,918	1.8	1,323,572	1,350,252	2.0
U.S.	149,874,000	152,571,000	1.8	142,918,000	146,081,000	2.2

Note: Data is not seasonally adjusted and covers workers 16 years of age and older;
(1) Metropolitan Division - see Appendix B for areas included
Source: Bureau of Labor Statistics, http://stats.bls.gov

Unemployment Rate

Area	2006											
	Jan.	Feb.	Mar.	Apr.	May	Jun.	Jul.	Aug.	Sep.	Oct.	Nov.	Dec.
City	4.0	4.3	3.9	3.6	4.2	4.1	3.9	3.8	4.2	3.8	4.2	3.8
MD[1]	4.3	4.7	4.5	4.0	4.4	4.4	4.1	4.0	4.4	4.1	4.5	4.2
U.S.	5.1	5.1	4.8	4.5	4.4	4.8	5.0	4.6	4.4	4.1	4.3	4.3

Note: Data is not seasonally adjusted and covers workers 16 years of age and older; All figures are percentages; (1) Metropolitan Division - see Appendix B for areas included
Source: Bureau of Labor Statistics, http://stats.bls.gov

Employment by Occupation

Occupation Classification	City (%)	MSA[1] (%)	U.S. (%)
Sales and Office	24.4	26.4	26.7
Professional and Related	31.2	24.3	20.2
Service	13.9	13.1	14.9
Production, Transportation, and Material Moving	8.2	10.9	14.6
Management, Business, and Financial	17.2	16.6	13.5
Construction, Extraction, and Maintenance	4.9	8.3	9.4
Farming, Forestry, and Fishing	0.3	0.3	0.7

Note: Figures cover employed civilians 16 years of age and older;
(1) Metropolitan Statistical Area - see Appendix A for areas included
Source: Census 2000, Summary File 3

Employment by Industry

Sector	MSA[1] Number of Employees	MSA[1] Percent of Total	U.S. Percent of Total
Government	200,700	13.9	16.3
Education and Health Services	149,900	10.4	13.2
Professional and Business Services	208,500	14.4	12.9
Retail Trade	152,900	10.6	11.5
Manufacturing	163,800	11.3	10.2
Leisure and Hospitality	131,200	9.1	9.5
Financial Activities	90,000	6.2	6.1
Construction	93,000	6.4	5.5
Wholesale Trade	71,900	5.0	4.3
Other Services	50,300	3.5	3.9
Transportation and Utilities	51,600	3.6	3.7
Information	81,100	5.6	2.2
Natural Resources and Mining	1,100	0.1	0.5

Note: Figures cover non-farm employment as of December 2006 and are not seasonally adjusted;
(1) Metropolitan Statistical Area - see Appendix B for areas included
Source: Bureau of Labor Statistics, http://stats.bls.gov

Occupations with Greatest Projected Employment Growth: 2002 - 2012

Occupation[1]	2002 Employment	2012 Projected Employment	Numeric Employment Change	Percent Employment Change
Maids and Housekeeping Cleaners	42,770	57,330	14,560	34.0
Child Care Workers	42,180	56,290	14,110	33.5
Retail Salespersons	78,000	89,630	11,630	14.9
Cashiers	63,700	73,900	10,200	16.0
Janitors and Cleaners, Except Maids and Housekeeping Cleaners	44,260	54,430	10,170	23.0
Office Clerks, General	53,850	63,570	9,720	18.1
Registered Nurses	45,930	55,260	9,330	20.3
Combined Food Preparation and Serving Workers, Including Fast Food	48,250	56,000	7,750	16.1
Teacher Assistants	33,570	40,890	7,320	21.8
Waiters and Waitresses	42,670	49,900	7,230	16.9

Note: Projections cover Washington; (1) Sorted by numeric employment change
Source: www.projectionscentral.com, State Occupational Projections, 2002-2012 Long-Term Projections

Fastest Growing Occupations: 2002 - 2012

Occupation[1]	2002 Employment	2012 Projected Employment	Numeric Employment Change	Percent Employment Change
Veterinary Assistants and Laboratory Animal Caretakers	1,140	1,570	430	37.7
Medical Scientists, Except Epidemiologists	930	1,270	340	36.6
Veterinary Technologists and Technicians	930	1,270	340	36.6
Dental Laboratory Technicians	870	1,180	310	35.6
Veterinarians	1,210	1,640	430	35.5
Maids and Housekeeping Cleaners	42,770	57,330	14,560	34.0
Computer Software Engineers, Applications	15,890	21,220	5,330	33.5
Child Care Workers	42,180	56,290	14,110	33.5
Technical Writers	3,030	3,990	960	31.7
Computer Software Engineers, Systems Software	12,970	16,900	3,930	30.3

Note: Projections cover Washington; (1) Sorted by percent employment change and excludes occupations with numeric employment change less than 300
Source: www.projectionscentral.com, State Occupational Projections, 2002-2012 Long-Term Projections

Average Wages

Occupation	$/Hr.	Occupation	$/Hr.
Accountants and Auditors	29.34	Maids and Housekeeping Cleaners	9.81
Automotive Mechanics	21.00	Maintenance and Repair Workers	18.74
Bookkeepers	16.35	Marketing Managers	60.40
Carpenters	23.96	Nuclear Medicine Technologists	33.41
Cashiers	11.43	Nurses, Licensed Practical	20.88
Clerks, General Office	13.73	Nurses, Registered	32.89
Clerks, Receptionists/Information	12.41	Nursing Aides/Orderlies/Attendants	12.72
Clerks, Shipping/Receiving	14.80	Packers and Packagers, Hand	10.08
Computer Programmers	n/a	Physical Therapists	30.00
Computer Support Specialists	26.04	Postal Service Mail Carriers	21.85
Computer Systems Analysts	37.06	Real Estate Brokers	38.04
Cooks, Restaurant	11.70	Retail Salespersons	13.05
Dentists	n/a	Sales Reps., Exc. Tech./Scientific	29.26
Electrical Engineers	36.09	Sales Reps., Tech./Scientific	35.04
Electricians	26.68	Secretaries, Exc. Legal/Med./Exec.	16.18
Financial Managers	50.99	Security Guards	13.55
First-Line Supervisors/Mgrs., Sales	22.77	Surgeons	87.88
Food Preparation Workers	10.71	Teacher Assistants	12.60
General and Operations Managers	62.86	Teachers, Elementary School	21.70
Hairdressers/Cosmetologists	13.61	Teachers, Secondary School	22.50
Internists	78.35	Telemarketers	13.95
Janitors and Cleaners	12.44	Truck Drivers, Heavy/Tractor-Trailer	18.91
Landscaping/Groundskeeping Workers	13.27	Truck Drivers, Light/Delivery Svcs.	14.32
Lawyers	48.51	Waiters and Waitresses	10.78

Note: Wage data is for May 2005 and covers the Seattle-Bellevue-Everett, WA Metropolitan Division - see Appendix B for areas included. Hourly wages for elementary/secondary school teachers and teacher assistants were calculated by the editors from annual wage data assuming a 40 hour work week; n/a not available.
Source: Bureau of Labor Statistics, May 2005 Metro Area Occupational Employment and Wage Estimates

RESIDENTIAL REAL ESTATE

Building Permits

Area	Single-Family			Multi-Family			Total		
	2005	2006[p]	Pct. Chg.	2005	2006[p]	Pct. Chg.	2005	2006[p]	Pct. Chg.
City	533	482	-9.6	3,185	6,149	93.1	3,718	6,631	78.3
U.S.	1,682,000	1,380,000	-18.0	473,300	457,300	-3.4	2,155,300	1,837,300	-14.8

Note: (p) preliminary; figures represent new, privately-owned housing units authorized (unadjusted data); All permit data are based on estimates with imputation; U.S. figures are based on the new 20,000-place series.
Source: U.S. Census Bureau, Manufacturing, Mining, and Construction Statistics

Homeownership and Housing Vacancies

Area	Homeownership Rate[2] (%)			Rental Vacancy Rate[3] (%)			Homeowner Vacancy Rate[4] (%)		
	2004	2005	2006	2004	2005	2006	2004	2005	2006
MSA[1]	n/a	64.5	63.7	n/a	6.9	5.6	n/a	1.0	0.9
U.S.	69.0	68.9	68.8	10.2	9.8	9.7	1.7	1.9	2.4

Note: Comparable 2004 data was not available due to changes in metropolitan area definitions; (1) Metropolitan Statistical Area - see Appendix B for areas included; (2) The proportion of households that are owners; (3) The proportion of the rental inventory that is vacant for rent; (4) The proportion of the homeowner inventory that is vacant for sale; n/a not available
Source: U.S. Census Bureau, Housing Vacancies and Homeownership Annual Statistics: 2006

TAXES

State Corporate Income Tax Rates

State	Rate (%)	Number of Brackets	Low Bracket (Under $)	High Bracket (Over $)
Washington	None	na	na	na

Note: Tax rates as of December 31, 2006; na not applicable; Gross receipts tax called Business & Operations (B&O) Tax.
Source: Tax Foundation, www.taxfoundation.org

State Individual Income Tax Rates

State	Federal Deductibility	Marginal Rate (%)	Number of Brackets	Low Bracket (Under $)	High Bracket (Over $)
Washington	No	None	na	na	na

Note: Tax rates as of December 31, 2006; Brackets apply to single taxpayers and married people filing separately; na not applicable
Source: Tax Foundation, www.taxfoundation.org

Various State and Local Tax Rates

State and Local Sales and Use (%)	State Sales and Use (%)	Gasoline ($/gal.)	Cigarette ($/pack)	Spirits ($/gal.)	Table Wine ($/gal.)	Beer ($/gal.)
8.9	6.5	0.34 (p)	2.03	21.30 (b)	0.88	0.26

Note: Tax rates as of December 31, 2006; (b) States where the state government controls all sales. Excise tax rate is calculated using methodology designed by the Distilled Spirits Council of the United States (DISCUS); (p) Was $.28 per gallon. Will increase to $.36 per gallon July 1, 2007, $.375 July 1, 2008.
Source: Tax Foundation, www.taxfoundation.org; The Sales Tax Clearinghouse, www.thestc.com

State Tax Burdens

Area	Combined State and Local Tax Burden		Combined Federal, State and Local Tax Burden	
	Percent	Rank	Percent	Rank
Washington	10.9	13	33.7	4
U.S. Average	10.6	-	31.6	-

Note: Figures are for 2006 and measure taxes as a percentage of income
Source: Tax Foundation, www.taxfoundation.org

Internal Revenue Service Tax Audits

IRS District	Percent of Returns Audited				
	1996	1997	1998	1999	2000
Pacific Northwest	0.63	0.51	0.37	0.24	0.15
U.S.	0.66	0.61	0.46	0.31	0.20

Note: Figures cover IRS district audits of federal income tax returns filed by individuals. Geographic data on district audits after the year 2000 are being withheld by the IRS. TRAC is challenging this policy.
Source: Syracuse University, Transactional Records Access Clearinghouse (TRAC), "Odds of IRS District Tax Audit 2000"

COMMERCIAL REAL ESTATE

Office Market

Market Area	Inventory (sq. ft.)	Vacant (sq. ft.)	Vac. Rate (%)	Under Constr. (sq. ft.)	Asking Rent ($/sf)	
					Class A	Class B
Seattle	83,070,751	8,341,020	10.0	3,027,368	28.50	21.81

Source: Grubb & Ellis, Office Markets Trends, 4th Quarter 2006

Industrial Market

Market Area	Inventory (sq. ft.)	Vacant (sq. ft.)	Vac. Rate (%)	Under Constr. (sq. ft.)	Asking Rent ($/sf)	
					WH/Dist	R&D/Flex
Seattle	155,456,409	10,373,348	6.7	4,546,453	5.76	11.88

Source: Grubb & Ellis, Industrial Markets Trends, 4th Quarter 2006

COMMERCIAL UTILITIES

Typical Monthly Electric Bills

Area	Commercial Service ($/month)		Industrial Service ($/month)	
	40 kW demand 1,500 kWh	100 kW demand 20,000 kWh	1,500 kW demand 400,000 kWh	20,000 kW demand 10,000,000 kWh
City	88	1,237	22,527	531,750

Note: Based on rates in effect January 1, 2006
Source: Memphis Light, Gas and Water, 2006 Utility Bill Comparisons for Selected U.S. Cities

TRANSPORTATION

Means of Transportation to Work

Area	Car/Truck/Van		Public Transportation			Bicycle	Walked	Other Means	Worked at Home
	Drove Alone	Car-pooled	Bus	Subway	Railroad				
City	56.5	11.2	17.3	0.0	0.0	1.9	7.4	1.1	4.6
MSA[1]	70.4	12.6	7.8	0.0	0.0	0.7	3.2	0.9	4.4
U.S.	75.7	12.2	2.5	1.5	0.5	0.4	2.9	1.0	3.3

Note: Figures are percentages and cover workers 16 years of age and older;
(1) Metropolitan Statistical Area - see Appendix A for areas included
Source: Census 2000, Summary File 3

Travel Time to Work

Area	Less Than 15 Minutes	15 to 29 Minutes	30 to 44 Minutes	45 to 59 Minutes	60 Minutes or More
City	21.9	42.7	23.7	6.6	5.1
MSA[1]	22.1	36.9	23.9	9.2	7.9
U.S.	29.4	36.1	19.1	7.4	8.0

Note: Figures are percentages and include workers 16 years old and over; (1) Metropolitan Statistical Area - see Appendix A for areas included
Source: Census 2000, Summary File 3

Travel Time Index

Area	1982	1993	2002	2003
Urban Area[1]	1.07	1.35	1.36	1.38
Average[2]	1.12	1.28	1.37	1.37

Note: Travel Time Index - The ratio of travel time in the peak period to the travel time at free-flow conditions. A value of 1.35 indicates a 20-minute free-flow trip takes 27 minutes in the peak. Free-flow speeds (60 mph on freeways and 35 mph on principal arterials) are used as the comparison threshold; (1) Covers the Seattle, WA urban area; (2) average of 85 urban areas
Source: Texas Transportation Institute, The 2005 Urban Mobility Report, May 2005

Public Transportation

Agency name:	King County Department of Transportation (KC Metro)
Vehicle type:	Bus
Average fleet age in years:	5.6
No. operated in max. service:	1,176
Vehicle type:	Trolleybus
Average fleet age in years:	8.2
No. operated in max. service:	159
Vehicle type:	Demand response
Average fleet age in years:	4.8
No. operated in max. service:	471
Vehicle type:	Vanpool
Average fleet age in years:	3.4
No. operated in max. service:	746
Vehicle type:	Light rail
Average fleet age in years:	0.0
No. operated in max. service:	3

Source: Federal Transit Administration, National Transit Database, 2005

Air Transportation

Airport name and code:	Seattle-Tacoma International (SEA)
Domestic service (2006)	
Passenger airlines[1]:	31
Passenger enplanements:	13,560,817
Freight carriers[2]:	30
Freight (lbs.):	238,810,454
International service (2005)	
Passenger airlines[1]:	22
Passenger enplanements:	1,113,722
Freight carriers[2]:	22
Freight (lbs.):	88,323,996

Note: (1) Includes all major, minor and commuter airlines that carried at least one passenger during the year; (2) Includes all airlines and freight carriers that transported at least one pound of freight during the year
Source: Bureau of Transportation Statistics, The Intermodal Transportation Database, Air Carriers: T-100 International Market, 2004; Bureau of Transportation Statistics, The Intermodal Transportation Database, Air Carriers: T-100 Domestic Market, 2005

Other Transportation Statistics

Interstate highways:	I-50; I-90
Amtrak service:	Yes
Major waterways/ports:	Puget Sound; Port of Seattle

Source: Editor & Publisher Market Guide, 2006; Amtrak.com; Rand McNally 2006 Road Atlas

BUSINESSES

Major Business Headquarters

Company Name	2006 Rankings	
	Fortune[1]	Forbes[2]
Amazon.com	272	-
Nordstrom	293	-
SSA Marine	-	223
Starbucks	338	-
Washington Mutual	99	-

Note: (1) Fortune 500 - companies that produce a 10-K are ranked 1 to 500 based on 2005 revenue; (2) Forbes Largest Private Companies - all private companies with at least $1 billion in annual revenue are ranked 1 to 394; companies listed are located in the city; dashes indicate no ranking
Source: Fortune, April 17, 2006; Forbes, November 9, 2006

Best Companies to Work For

Adobe Systems; Nordstrom (HQ); PCL Construction; Perkins Coie (HQ); Recreational Equipment (REI); Starbucks Coffee (HQ), headquartered in Seattle, are among the "100 Best Companies to Work For." Criteria: More than 105,000 employees from 446 companies responded to a 57-question survey created by the Great Place to Work Institute. Two-thirds of a company's score is based on the survey, which covers topics such as attitudes towards management, job satisfaction, and camaraderie. The remaining third of the score comes from each company's responses to the Institute's Culture Audit, which includes detailed questions about demographic makeup, pay and benefits programs, and open-ended questions about the company's people-management philosophy, internal communications, opportunities, compensation practices, diversity programs, etc. Any company that is at least seven years old and has a minimum of 1,000 U.S. employees is eligible. The top three U.S. locations are shown for companies with more than one location. *Fortune, "100 Best Companies to Work for 2007," January 22, 2007*

Nordstrom; Washington Mutual, headquartered in Seattle, are among the "50 Best Companies for Minorities." Criteria: 1,200 of the largest U.S employers were surveyed. Those companies were analyzed on information such as the number of minorities in the workforce and on the board, and the rate at which minority employees are hired (and fired). *Fortune, "50 Best Companies for Minorities," June 28, 2004*

Fast-Growing Businesses

According to *Inc.*, Seattle is home to three of America's 500 fastest-growing private companies: **Specialty Bottle; ThePlatform; WhitePages.com**. Criteria: must be an independent, privately-held, U.S. corporation, proprietorship or partnership; net sales of at least $600,000 in FY2002; four-year operating/sales history; holding companies, regulated banks, and utilities were excluded. *Inc., "America's 500 Fastest-Growing Private Companies," September 2006*

Seattle is home to two of *Business Week's* "Hot Growth Companies:" **Blue Nile; aQuantive**. To qualify, a company must have annual sales of more than $50 million and less than $1.5 billion, a current market value greater than $25 million, a current stock price of at least $5, and be actively traded. Banks, insurers, real estate firms, and utilities are excluded. So are companies with declines in current financial results or in stock price, as well as companies where other developments raise questions about future performance. Companies were selected based on three-year results in sales growth, earnings growth, and return on invested capital. *Business Week, June 5, 2006*

According to *Business 2.0*, Seattle is home to two of America's 100 fastest-growing technology companies: **F5 Networks; aQuantive**. The 100 Fastest-Growing Technology Companies (B2 100) is a yearly ranking published by Business 2.0 magazine of businesses whose inventiveness and quick reflexes are helping them to set the pace for the economy. To find the B2 100, Zacks Investment Research of Chicago ranked 2,000 publicly traded companies using a rigorous combination of four financial criteria: growth in revenue, profit, and operating cash flow during the past three years; and the 12-month stock market return as of March 31, 2006. *Business 2.0, "100 Fastest-Growing Tech Companies 2006," June 2006*

According to Deloitte & Touche LLP, Seattle is home to four of North America's 500 fastest-growing high-technology companies: **CapitalStream; Posera; WhitePages.com; aQuantive**. Companies are ranked by percentage growth in revenue over a five-year period. Criteria for inclusion: company must be headquartered within North America; company must own proprietary intellectual property or proprietary technology that contributes to a significant portion of the company's operating revenue or devotes a significant proportion of revenues to research and development of technology; company must have been in business for a minumum of five years with 2001 operating revenues of at least $50,000 USD or $75,000 CD and 2005 operating revenues of at least $5 million USD/CD. *Deloitte & Touche LLP, 2006 Technology Fast 500*

Women-Owned Businesses: 1997 and 2002

Year	All Firms		Firms with Paid Employees			
	Firms	Sales ($000)	Firms	Sales ($000)	Employees	Payroll ($000)
1997	18,116	2,954,557	3,560	2,533,705	25,024	683,626
2002	19,945	3,106,401	3,271	2,670,842	21,387	635,805

Note: Figures cover firms located in the city; Women-owned business are defined as firms in which women own 51% or more of the stock or equity of the company; (a) Withheld to avoid disclosing data for individual companies; (b) Withheld because estimate did not meet publication standards; n/a not available
Source: 1997 Economic Census, Survey of Minority- and Women-Owned Business Enterprises; 2002 Economic Census, Survey of Business Owners (released February 9, 2006)

HOTELS

Hotels/Motels

Area	Hotels/Motels	Average Minimum Rates ($)		
		Tourist	First-Class	Deluxe
City	114	79	111	211

Source: OAG Travel Planner Online, Spring 2006

The Seattle metro area is home to four of the top 187 hotels in the U.S. according to *Travel & Leisure*: **Inn at the Market** (#51); **Bellevue Club Hotel** (#67); **Fairmont Olympic Hotel** (#150); **Alexis Hotel** (#179). Criteria: service; location; rooms; food; and value. *Travel & Leisure, "The T+L 500, 2007"*

EVENT SITES

Stadiums, Arenas, and Auditoriums

Name	Capacity
HEC Edmundson Pavilion	10,000
Safeco Field	47,116
Seattle Center	21,100

Source: www.officialtravelguide.com; www.eventective.com; original research

Convention Centers

Name	Overall Space (sq. ft.)	Exhibit Space (sq. ft.)	Meeting Space (sq. ft.)	Meeting Rooms
Seattle Center Exhibition Hall	n/a	n/a	34,000	n/a
Washington State Convention & Trade Center	n/a	45,000	205,700	62

Note: n/a not available
Source: www.officialtravelguide.com; www.eventective.com; original research

Hotels/Conference Centers

Name	Guest Rooms	Exhibit Space (sq. ft.)	Meeting Space (sq. ft.)
Seattle Sheraton Hotel & Towers	840	n/a	40,000
The Westin Seattle	925	n/a	37,760

Note: n/a not available
Source: www.officialtravelguide.com; www.eventective.com; original research

Living Environment

COST OF LIVING

Cost of Living Index

Year	Composite Index	Groceries	Housing	Utilities	Trans-portation	Health Care	Misc. Goods/ Services
2004	120.6	112.4	132.2	110.7	115.6	144.2	114.7
2005	117.0	110.0	132.7	105.3	110.4	121.6	111.2
2006	115.8	109.6	135.0	99.7	109.2	120.2	108.8

Note: U.S. = 100
Source: The Council for Community and Economic Research (formerly ACCRA), Cost of Living Index, 2004, 2005 and 2006 4-Quarter Averages

HOUSING

House Price Index (HPI)

Area	National Ranking[2]	Quarterly Change (%)	One-Year Change (%)	Five-Year Change (%)
MD[1]	18	1.52	14.50	64.62
U.S.[3]	-	1.12	5.87	55.21

Note: The HPI is a weighted repeat sales index. It measures average price changes in repeat sales or refinancings on the same properties. This information is obtained by reviewing repeat mortgage transactions on single-family properties whose mortgages have been purchased or securitized by Fannie Mae or Freddie Mac in January 1975; (1) Metropolitan Division - see Appendix B for areas included; (2) Rankings are based on annual percentage change for all metro areas containing at least 15,000 transactions over the last 10 years and ranges from 1 to 282; (3) figures based on a weighted division average; all figures are for the period ending December 31, 2006
Source: Office of Federal Housing Enterprise Oversight, House Price Index, March 1, 2007

House Price Valuations

Area	Q4 1999	Q4 2000	Q4 2001	Q4 2002	Q4 2003	Q4 2004	Q4 2005	Q4 2006
MSA[1]	-9.6	-2.7	2.0	6.2	10.0	-6.9	25.5	31.7

Note: Figures show the percentage of over- or under-valuation of single family homes relative to statistically normal house values (e.g. a value of 23.6 indicates that house values are 23.6% overvalued). Statistically normal house values are based on house prices, interest rates, household incomes, population densities, and any historical premiums or discounts metropolitan areas have exhibited over time; (1) Figures cover the Metropolitan Statistical Area - see Appendix B for areas included
Source: Global Insight/National City Corporation, House Prices in America, March 2007

Median Home Prices

Area	2004	2005	2006p	Percent Change 2005 to 2006
Metro Area[1]	284.6	316.8	361.2	14.0
U.S. Average	195.2	219.0	222.0	1.4

Note: Figures are median sales prices of existing single-family homes in thousands of dollars; (p) preliminary; n/a not available; (1) Covers the Seattle-Tacoma-Bellevue, WA Metropolitan Statistical Area - see Appendix B for areas included
Source: National Association of Realtors, Metropolitan Area Prices, 4th Quarter 2006

Housing: Year Structure Built

Area	1990 -2000	1980 -1989	1970 -1979	1960 -1969	1950 -1959	1940 -1949	Before 1940	Median Year
City	9.9	9.0	9.9	12.2	14.0	12.5	32.4	1954
MSA[1]	19.8	18.4	17.7	14.7	10.3	6.4	12.5	1973
U.S.	17.0	15.8	18.5	13.7	12.7	7.3	15.0	1971

Note: Figures are percentages; (1) Metropolitan Statistical Area - see Appendix A for areas included
Source: Census 2000, Summary File 3

Average New Home Price

Area	2004	2005	2006
City	328,253	366,755	407,594
U.S.	253,574	275,712	299,269

Note: Figures, in dollars, are based on a new home with 2,400 sq. ft. of living area on an 8,000 sq. ft. lot.
Source: The Council for Community and Economic Research (formerly ACCRA), Cost of Living Index, 2004, 2005 and 2006 4-Quarter Averages

Average Apartment Rent

Area	2004	2005	2006
City	1,054	1,062	1,055
U.S.	716	740	766

Note: Figures, in dollars per month, are based on an unfurnished two bedroom, 1-1/2 or 2 bath apartment, approximately 950 sq. ft. in size, excluding all utilities except water
Source: The Council for Community and Economic Research (formerly ACCRA), Cost of Living Index, 2004, 2005 and 2006 4-Quarter Averages

RESIDENTIAL UTILITIES

Average Residential Utility Costs

Area	All Electric ($/mth)	Part Electric ($/mth)	Other Energy ($/mth)	Phone ($/mth)
City	156.49	–	–	26.48
U.S.	136.00	76.53	90.52	25.87

Source: The Council for Community and Economic Research (formerly ACCRA), Cost of Living Index, 2006 4-Quarter Average

HEALTH

Average Health Care Costs

Area	Optometrist ($/visit)	Doctor ($/visit)	Dentist ($/visit)
City	104.93	91.36	93.85
U.S.	76.38	76.10	68.72

Note: Optometrist—based on a full vision eye exam for an established adult patient;
Doctor—based on a general practitioner's routine exam of an established patient;
Dentist—based on adult teeth cleaning and periodic oral exam.
Source: The Council for Community and Economic Research (formerly ACCRA), Cost of Living Index, 2006 4-Quarter Average

Mortality Rates

ICD-10 Sub-Chapter	ICD-10 Code	Age-Adjusted Death Rate per 100,000 population[1]	U.S. Age-Adjusted Death Rate per 100,000 population
Malignant neoplasms	C00-C97	165.4	185.8
Ischaemic heart diseases	I20-I25	108.9	150.2
Other forms of heart disease	I30-I51	31.7	50.8
Cerebrovascular diseases	I60-I69	50.7	50.0
Chronic lower respiratory diseases	J40-J47	32.1	41.1
Diabetes mellitus	E10-E14	20.3	24.5
Other degenerative diseases of the nervous system	G30-G31	34.2	22.3
Other external causes of accidental injury	W00-X59	22.9	21.2
Influenza and pneumonia	J10-J18	12.1	19.8
Hypertensive diseases	I10-I13	15.1	18.1

Note: ICD-10 = International Classification of Diseases 10th Revision; (1) Figures cover King County, WA
Source: Centers for Disease Control and Prevention, National Center for Health Statistics. Compressed Mortality File 1999-2004. CDC WONDER On-line Database, compiled from Compressed Mortality File 1999-2004 Series 20 No. 2J, 2007.

Health Risk Data

Item	Area[1] (%)	U.S. (%)
Adults who have been told they have high blood pressure	22.3	25.5
Adults who have been told they have high blood cholesterol	35.5	35.6
Adults who have been told they have diabetes[2]	6.3	7.3
Adults who have been told they have arthritis	23.3	27.0
Adults who have been told they currently have asthma	8.0	8.0
Adults who are current smokers	14.7	20.6

Note: (1) Figures cover the Metropolitan Division - see Appendix B for areas included; (2) Figures do not include pregnancy-related diabetes, pre-diabetes or borderline diabetes
Source: Centers for Disease Control and Prevention, Behaviorial Risk Factor Surveillance System, SMART: Selected Metropolitan/Micropolitan Area Trends, 2005

Distribution of Office-Based Physicians

Area	Total	Family/ General Practice	Specialties		
			Medical	Surgical	Other
CMSA[1] (number)	7,788	1,393	2,530	1,614	2,251
CMSA[1] (rate per 10,000 pop.)	21.6	3.9	7.0	4.5	6.2
Metro Average[2] (rate per 10,000 pop.)	19.4	2.1	7.5	4.5	5.3

Note: Data as of December 31, 2004; (1) Seattle-Tacoma-Bremerton, WA Consolidated Metropolitan Statistical Area includes the following counties: Island; King; Kitsap; Pierce; Snohomish; Thurston; (2) Average of the 79 unique MSAs and CMSAs in this book
Source: American Medical Association, Physician Characteristics & Distribution in the U.S., 2006

Hospitals

Seattle has the following hospitals: 6 general medical and surgical; 1 psychiatric; 1 alcoholism and other chemical dependency; 1 cancer; 2 long-term acute care; 1 other specialty; 1 children's general.
AHA Guide to the Healthcare Field 2007

According to *U.S. News,* the Seattle metro area is home to four of the best hospitals in the U.S.: **Children's Hospital and Regional Medical Center; Harborview Medical Center; University of Washington Medical Center; Virginia Mason Medical Center;** *U.S. News Online, "America's Best Hospitals 2006"*

EDUCATION

Public School District Statistics

District Name	Schls	Pupils	Pupil/ Teacher Ratio	Minority Pupils[1] (%)	Free Lunch Eligible[2] (%)	IEP[3] (%)
Highline Sch Dist 401	44	17,645	19.0	58.5	42.9	12.1
Seattle School Dist 1	111	46,746	18.1	59.0	33.8	12.5

Note: Table includes regular local school districts with 2,000 or more students; (1) Percentage of students that are not white, non-Hispanic; (2) Percentage of students that are eligible for the free lunch program; (3) Percentage of students that have an Individualized Education Program.
Source: U.S. Department of Education, National Center for Education Statistics, Common Core of Data, Local Education Agency (School District) Universe Survey: School Year 2004-2005; U.S. Department of Education, National Center for Education Statistics, Common Core of Data, Public Elementary/Secondary School Universe Survey: School Year 2004-2005

Top Public High Schools

High School Name	Index[1]	Rank[1]	Subsidized Lunch (%)[2]	E&E (%)[3]
Garfield	1.799	469	22.0	n/a

Note: (1) Public schools are ranked according to a ratio that is the number of Advanced Placement and/or International Baccalaureate tests taken by all students at a school in 2005 divided by the number of graduating seniors. All of the schools on the list have an index of at least 1.000; they are in the top five percent of public schools measured this way. The rankings range from 1 to 1,236; (2) Percentage of students receiving federally subsidized meals; (3) E & E stands for equity and excellence percentage: the portion of all graduating seniors at a school that had at least one passing grade on one AP or IB test; (*) Gave just IB tests; (**) Gave both IB and AP tests. AP and IB participation are indicators of a school's efforts to get students to excel and prepare for college; n/a not available
Source: Newsweek Online, May 23, 2006

Educational Quality

School District	Education Quotient[1]	Graduate Outcome[2]	Community Index[3]	Resource Index[4]	Rating[5]
Seattle SD 1	73	69	82	62	Blue

Note: Scores are national percentile rankings and range from 1 (worst) to 99 (best); (1) Combination of the Graduate Outcome, Community and Resource Indexes weighted to reflect the greater importance of the Graduate Outcome and Resource Index; (2) Based on graduation rates and college board scores (SAT/ACT); (3) Based on the surrounding community's level of affluence and adult education; (4) Based on teacher salaries, per-pupil expenditures and student-teacher ratios; (5) School districts receive one of five rankings: Gold Medal (top 16 percent of districts evaluated); Blue Ribbon (top third); Green Light (average); Yellow Light (bottom 25 percent); Red Light (bottom 10 percent).
Source: Expansion Management, "2007 Education Quotient," January 2007

Highest Level of Education

Area	Less than H.S.	H.S. Diploma	Some College, No Deg.	Associate Degree	Bachelors Degree	Masters Degree	Profess. School Degree	Doctorate Degree
City	10.8	15.3	20.6	6.5	29.8	10.8	3.9	2.3
MSA[1]	10.8	22.9	25.9	8.0	21.9	7.1	2.3	1.2
U.S.	19.4	28.4	21.2	6.4	15.7	5.9	2.0	1.0

Note: Figures are 2006 estimated percentages and cover persons age 25 and over; (1) Metropolitan Statistical Area - see Appendix B for areas included
Source: Claritas, Inc.

Educational Attainment by Race

Area	High School Graduate (%)					Bachelor's Degree (%)				
	Total	White	Black	Asian	Hisp.[2]	Total	White	Black	Asian	Hisp.[2]
City	89.5	93.9	77.2	75.7	70.5	47.2	53.3	20.1	37.0	26.1
MSA[1]	90.1	92.3	82.4	82.2	67.8	35.9	37.0	21.1	40.9	19.0
U.S.	80.4	83.6	72.3	80.4	52.4	24.4	26.1	14.3	44.1	10.4

Note: Figures shown cover persons 25 years old and over; (1) Metropolitan Statistical Area - see Appendix A for areas included; (2) people of Hispanic origin can be of any race
Source: Census 2000, Summary File 3

School Enrollment by Type

Area	Grades KG to 8				Grades 9 to 12			
	Public		Private		Public		Private	
	Enrollment	%	Enrollment	%	Enrollment	%	Enrollment	%
City	34,022	78.1	9,538	21.9	16,241	80.5	3,925	19.5
MSA[1]	260,622	88.3	34,672	11.7	116,866	91.1	11,446	8.9
U.S.	33,526,011	88.7	4,285,121	11.3	14,848,628	90.6	1,532,323	9.4

Note: Figures shown cover persons 3 years old and over; (1) Metropolitan Statistical Area - see Appendix A for areas included
Source: Census 2000, Summary File 3

School Enrollment by Race

Area	Grades KG to 8 (%)				Grades 9 to 12 (%)			
	White	Black	Asian	Hisp.[1]	White	Black	Asian	Hisp.[1]
City	52.9	14.5	16.5	8.2	50.5	16.7	17.5	7.8
MSA[2]	73.2	5.5	9.2	6.6	73.1	5.4	10.5	5.8
U.S.	68.5	15.5	3.3	16.8	68.8	15.5	3.8	15.7

Note: Figures shown cover persons 3 years old and over; (1) people of Hispanic origin can be of any race; (2) Metropolitan Statistical Area - see Appendix A for areas included
Source: Census 2000, Summary File 3

Average Salaries of Public School Teachers

District	2004-05		2005-06		Percent Change 2004-05 to 2005-06
	Dollars	Rank[1]	Dollars	Rank[1]	
WASHINGTON	45,718	20	46,326	22	1.33
U.S. Average	47,674	-	49,109	-	3.01

Note: (1) State rank ranges from 1 to 51.
Source: National Education Association, Rankings & Estimates: Rankings of the States 2005 and Estimates of School Statistics 2006, November 2006

Higher Education

Four-Year Colleges			Two-Year Colleges			Medical Schools[1]	Law Schools[2]	Voc/ Tech[3]
Public	Private Non-profit	Private For-profit	Public	Private Non-profit	Private For-profit			
1	4	5	3	1	2	1	2	6

Note: Figures cover institutions located within the city limits; (1) includes schools accredited by the Liaison Committee on Medical Education and the American Osteopathic Association; (2) includes American Bar Association-accredited law schools; (3) includes all schools with programs that are less than 2 years
Source: National Center for Education Statistics, The Integrated Postsecondary Education System (IPEDS) Peer Analysis System, 2006; www.usnews.com, America's Best Graduate Schools 2008, Medical School Directory; www.usnews.com, America's Best Graduate Schools 2008, Law School Directory

PRESIDENTIAL ELECTION

2004 Presidential Election Results

Area	Bush	Kerry	Nader	Other
King County	33.6	64.9	0.7	0.8
U.S.	50.7	48.3	0.4	0.6

Note: Results are percentages and may not add to 100% due to rounding
Source: Dave Leip's Atlas of U.S. Presidential Elections, www.uselectionatlas.org

MAJOR EMPLOYERS

Major Employers

Company Name	Industry	Type of Site
Alaska Airlines	General warehousing and storage	Branch
Bailey-Boushay House	Offices and clinics of medical doctors	Headquarters
Childrens Health Care System	Specialty hospitals, except psychiatric	Single
Harborview Medical Center	General medical and surgical hospitals	Single
Microsoft	Prepackaged software	Headquarters
Neurological Surgery	Colleges and universities	Branch
R U I One Corp	Eating places	Single
SNC Lavalin Thermal Power	Heavy construction, nec	Headquarters
Swedish Med Center/First Hl	General medical and surgical hospitals	Headquarters
TCI West Inc	Cable and other pay television services	Single
UPS	Air courier services	Branch
University of Washington Press	Colleges and universities	Headquarters
Washington University of Inc	Colleges and universities	Branch
Weyerhaeuser Company	General warehousing and storage	Branch
Weyerhaeuser Company	Lumber, plywood, and millwork	Branch

Note: Companies shown are located within the metropolitan area and have 2,700 or more employees; nec = not elsewhere classified.
Source: www.zapdata.com, January 2007

PUBLIC SAFETY

Crime Rate

Area	All Crimes	Violent Crimes				Property Crimes		
		Murder	Forcible Rape	Robbery	Aggrav. Assault	Burglary	Larceny -Theft	Motor Vehicle Theft
City	8,214.6	4.3	23.8	277.4	403.8	1,167.3	4,686.9	1,651.0
Suburbs[1]	5,211.6	2.8	42.1	99.4	194.2	911.7	2,964.4	996.9
Metro[2]	5,753.5	3.1	38.8	131.5	232.0	957.8	3,275.3	1,114.9
U.S.	3,899.0	5.6	31.7	140.7	291.1	726.7	2,286.3	416.7

Note: Figures are crimes per 100,000 population; (1) All areas within the metro area that are located outside the city limits; (2) Metropolitan Statistical Area - see Appendix B for areas included
Source: FBI Uniform Crime Reports, 2005

Hate Crimes

Area	Number of Quarters Reported	Bias Motivation				
		Race	Religion	Sexual Orientation	Ethnicity	Disability
City	4	12	1	5	0	0

Source: Federal Bureau of Investigation, Hate Crime Statistics 2005

RECREATION

Culture

Dance[1]	Theatre[1]	Instrumental Music[1]	Vocal Music[1]	Series/ Festivals	Museums	Zoos
5	11	10	3	13	17	1

Note: (1) number of professional perfoming groups
Source: The Grey House Performing Arts Directory, 2007; Official Museum Directory, 2007

Professional Sports Teams

Major League Baseball	National Basketball Association	National Football League	National Hockey League	Major League Soccer	Women's National Basketball Association
1	1	1	0	0	1

Note: Includes teams located in the Seattle-Bellevue metro area.
Source: www.sportsvenues.com, Listing of Venues by State/Province and City, 2006

MEDIA

Newspapers

Name	Target Audience	Frequency	Circulation
Ballard Tribune	General	Non-Daily	18,000
Beacon Hill News & South District Journal	General	Non-Daily	18,200
Capitol Hill Times	General	Non-Daily	16,000
The Catholic Northwest Progress	Catholic/Religious	Non-Daily	15,516
Facts	Black/General	Non-Daily	80,000
Hispanic News	Hispanic	Non-Daily	10,000
Jet City Maven Newspaper	General	Non-Daily	18,000
Northwest Asian Weekly	Asian	Non-Daily	10,000
Portland Medium	General	Non-Daily	16,000
Real Change: Seattle's Homeless Newspaper	General	Non-Daily	15,000
Seattle Chinese Post	Asian/General	Non-Daily	15,000
Seattle Medium	Black	Non-Daily	37,500
Seattle Post-Intelligencer	n/a	Daily	145,964
The Seattle Times	n/a	Daily	231,051
Seattle Weekly	Alternative	Non-Daily	120,000
The Skanner	General	Non-Daily	22,000
Tacoma True Citizen	Black/General	Non-Daily	16,000
West Seattle Herald	General	Non-Daily	30,000
White Center News	General	Non-Daily	28,000

Note: Includes newspapers whose offices are located in the city and whose circulations are 10,000 or more; n/a not available
Source: BurrellesLuce, MediaContacts Online, January 2006

Television Stations

Name	Ch.	Network(s)	Type	Ownership
KOMO	4	ABC	Commercial	Fisher Broadcasting Inc.
KING	5	NBC	Commercial	Belo Corporation
KIRO	7	CBS	Commercial	Cox Enterprises Inc.
KCTS	9	PBS	Public	KCTS
KSTW	11	UPN	Commercial	Paramount Communications Inc.
KBTC	12	PBS	Public	State Board for Community and Technical Colleges
KVOS	12	n/a	Commercial	Clear Channel Communications Inc.
KCPQ	13	Fox	Commercial	Tribune Broadcasting Company
KONG	16	n/a	Commercial	Zeus Corporation
KTBW	20	n/a	Non-comm.	Trinity Broadcasting Network
KTWB	22	WBN	Commercial	Dudley Broadcast Management
KBCB	24	n/a	Commercial	World Television of Washington
KCKA	28	PBS	Public	State Board for Community and Technical Colleges
KWPX	33	Pax	Commercial	Paxson Communications Corporation

Note: Stations included cover the Seattle-Tacoma DMA (Designated Market Area)
BurrellesLuce, MediaContacts Online, January 2006

Major AM Radio Stations

Call Letters	Freq. (kHz)	Station Type	Target Audience	Station Format	Music Format
KARI	550	n/a	Religious	News/Sports/Talk	n/a
KPQ	560	Commercial	General	News/Talk	n/a
KVI	570	Commercial	General	Talk	n/a
KAPS	660	n/a	General	Music/News	n/a
KIRO	710	Commercial	General	News/Talk	n/a
KNWX	770	n/a	General	News/Talk	n/a
KGMI	790	Commercial	General	News/Talk	n/a
KGNW	820	Commercial	General/Religious	News/Talk	n/a
KMTT	850	Commercial	General	Music	A.O. Rock
KHHO	850	n/a	General/Men	Music/News/Sports/Talk	n/a
KIXI	880	n/a	General	Music/News	n/a
KJR	950	n/a	General	Music/Sports/Talk	n/a
KOMO	1000	Commercial	General	News/Talk	n/a
KMAS	1030	Commercial	General	Music/News	Adult Contemp.
KYCW	1090	n/a	General	Music	n/a
KKNW	1150	n/a	General	News/Sports	n/a
KPUG	1170	Commercial	General	Sports/Talk	n/a
KLAY	1180	Commercial	General	News/Sports/Talk	n/a
KBSG	1210	Commercial	General	Music	Oldies
KKDZ	1250	n/a	Children	Music	n/a
KKOL	1300	Commercial	General	News/Talk	n/a
KMPS	1300	Commercial	General	Music/News/Sports	Country
KXRO	1320	Commercial	General	Talk	n/a
KKMO	1360	Commercial	General/Hispanic	Music/Talk	Latin
KRKO	1380	n/a	General	News/Sports/Talk	n/a
KITI	1420	Commercial	General	Music/News	Oldies
KBRC	1430	n/a	General	Music/News	n/a
KELA	1470	Commercial	General	News/Sports/Talk	n/a
KXPA	1540	n/a	Ethnic/Hispanic	Ed/Music/News/Talk	n/a
KRPI	1550	n/a	Religious	Educational/Music/News	n/a
KZIZ	1560	Commercial	General	Music	Urban Contemp.
KLFE	1590	Commercial	General/Religious	Music/Talk	Gospel
KYIZ	1620	Commercial	General	Music	Urban Contemp.

Note: Stations included cover the Seattle-Tacoma DMA (Designated Market Area); n/a not available
Source: BurrellesLuce, MediaContacts Online, January 2006

Major FM Radio Stations

Call Letters	Freq. (mHz)	Station Type	Target Audience	Station Format	Music Format
KPLU	88.5	College	General	Music/News	n/a
KVTI	90.9	College	Young Adult	Music/News/Sports	n/a
KLSY	92.5	n/a	General	Music/News	n/a
KISM	92.9	Commercial	General	Music/News	Classic Rock
KUBE	93.3	n/a	General	Music/Talk	n/a
KMPS	94.1	n/a	General	Music	n/a
KUOW	94.9	College	General	Educational/News	n/a
KJR	95.7	n/a	General	n/a	n/a
KXXO	96.1	n/a	General	Music/News	n/a
KBSG	97.3	n/a	General	Music/News	n/a
KING	98.1	Commercial	General	Music	Classical
KISW	99.9	Commercial	General	Music/News/Talk	Classic Rock
KQBZ	100.7	Commercial	General	Talk	n/a
KPLZ	101.5	n/a	General	Music/News	n/a
KMNT	102.9	Commercial	General	Music/News/Sports	Country
KMTT	103.7	n/a	General	Music	n/a
KAFE	104.3	Commercial	General	Music/News	Soft Rock
KCMS	105.3	Commercial	General/Religious	Music	Christian
KBKS	106.1	n/a	General/Women	Music/News/Talk	n/a
KWPZ	106.5	n/a	Religious	Music/Talk	n/a
KRWM	106.9	n/a	General	Music	n/a
KNDD	107.7	Commercial	General	Music/News/Talk	Modern Rock

Note: Stations included cover the Seattle-Tacoma DMA (Designated Market Area); n/a not available
BurrellesLuce, MediaContacts Online, January 2006

CLIMATE

Average and Extreme Temperatures

Temperature	Jan	Feb	Mar	Apr	May	Jun	Jul	Aug	Sep	Oct	Nov	Dec	Yr.
Extreme High (°F)	64	70	75	85	93	96	98	99	98	89	74	63	99
Average High (°F)	44	48	52	57	64	69	75	74	69	59	50	45	59
Average Temp. (°F)	39	43	45	49	55	61	65	65	60	52	45	41	52
Average Low (°F)	34	36	38	41	46	51	54	55	51	45	39	36	44
Extreme Low (°F)	0	1	11	29	28	38	43	44	35	28	6	6	0

Note: Figures cover the years 1948-1990
Source: National Climatic Data Center, International Station Meteorological Climate Summary, 9/96

Average Precipitation/Snowfall/Humidity

Precip./Humidity	Jan	Feb	Mar	Apr	May	Jun	Jul	Aug	Sep	Oct	Nov	Dec	Yr.
Avg. Precip. (in.)	5.7	4.2	3.7	2.4	1.7	1.4	0.8	1.1	1.9	3.5	5.9	5.9	38.4
Avg. Snowfall (in.)	5	2	1	Tr	Tr	0	0	0	0	Tr	1	3	13
Avg. Rel. Hum. 7am (%)	83	83	84	83	80	79	79	84	87	88	85	85	83
Avg. Rel. Hum. 4pm (%)	76	69	63	57	54	54	49	51	57	68	76	79	63

Note: Figures cover the years 1948-1990; Tr = Trace amounts (<0.05 in. of rain; <0.5 in. of snow)
Source: National Climatic Data Center, International Station Meteorological Climate Summary, 9/96

Weather Conditions

Temperature			Daytime Sky			Precipitation		
5°F & below	32°F & below	90°F & above	Clear	Partly cloudy	Cloudy	0.01 inch or more precip.	0.1 inch or more snow/ice	Thunder-storms
< 1	38	3	57	121	187	157	8	8

Note: Figures are average number of days per year and cover the years 1948-1990
Source: National Climatic Data Center, International Station Meteorological Climate Summary, 9/96

HAZARDOUS WASTE

Superfund Sites

Seattle has four hazardous waste sites on the EPA's Superfund Final National Priorities List: **Harbor Island (Lead)**; **Lockheed Shipyard No. 2**; **Lower Duwamish Waterway**; **Pacific**

Sound Resources. *U.S. Environmental Protection Agency, Final National Priorities List, March 20, 2007*

AIR & WATER QUALITY

Air Quality Index

Area	Percent of Days when Air Quality was...[2]				AQI Statistics	
	Good	Moderate	Unhealthy for Sensitive Groups	Unhealthy	Maximum	Median
MSA[1]	67.9	30.1	1.9	0.0	144	40

Note: The Air Quality Index (AQI) is an index for reporting daily air quality. EPA calculates the AQI for five major air pollutants regulated by the Clean Air Act: ground-level ozone, particle pollution (also known as particulate matter), carbon monoxide, sulfur dioxide, and nitrogen dioxide. The AQI runs from 0 to 500. The higher the AQI value, the greater the level of air pollution and the greater the health concern. There are six AQI categories: "Good" The AQI is between 0 and 50. Air quality is considered satisfactory; "Moderate" The AQI is between 51 and 100. Air quality is acceptable; "Unhealthy for Sensitive Groups" When AQI values are between 101 and 150, members of sensitive groups may experience health effects; "Unhealthy" When AQI values are between 151 and 200 everyone may begin to experience health effects; "Very Unhealthy" AQI values between 201 and 300 trigger a health alert; "Hazardous" AQI values over 300 trigger health warnings of emergency conditions; (1) Metropolitan Statistical Area - see Appendix A for areas included; (2) Based on 365 days with AQI data in 2005.
Source: U.S. Environmental Protection Agency, Air Quality Index Report, 2005

Air Quality Index Pollutants

Area	Percent of Days when AQI Pollutant was...[2]					
	Carbon Monoxide	Nitrogen Dioxide	Ozone	Sulfur Dioxide	Particulate Matter 2.5	Particulate Matter 10
MSA[1]	0.3	0.0	9.9	0.0	89.6	0.3

Note: The Air Quality Index (AQI) is an index for reporting daily air quality. EPA calculates the AQI for five major air pollutants regulated by the Clean Air Act: ground-level ozone, particle pollution (also known as particulate matter), carbon monoxide, sulfur dioxide, and nitrogen dioxide. The AQI runs from 0 to 500. The higher the AQI value, the greater the level of air pollution and the greater the health concern; (1) Metropolitan Statistical Area - see Appendix A for areas included; (2) Based on 365 days with AQI data in 2005.
Source: U.S. Environmental Protection Agency, Air Quality Index Report, 2005

Number of Days with Air Quality Index Values Greater than 100

Area	Trend Sites (9)								All Sites (63)
	1998	1999	2000	2001	2002	2003	2004	2005	2005
MSA[1]	3	6	7	6	6	2	1	1	1

Note: An AQI value greater than 100 indicates that air quality would have been in the unhealthful range on that day. Data from exceptional events are not included. These counts are presented in two ways. First, the counts are based on sites having an adequate record of monitoring data during the trend period (trend sites). These counts represent the relative change in the number of days with AQI values greater than 100. In the last column, the counts are based on all sites with data in the most recent year (because it is possible for a site to have data in the most recent year but not enough data to be a trend site); (1) Metropolitan Statistical Area - see Appendix A for areas included; n/a not available.
Source: U.S. Environmental Protection Agency, Air Trends Fact Book 2005

Maximum Pollutant Concentrations

	Particulate Matter 10 (ug/m^3)	Particulate Matter 2.5 (ug/m^3)	Ozone 1-hour (ppm)	Carbon Monoxide (ppm)	Sulfur Dioxide (ppm)	Nitrogen Dioxide (ppm)	Lead (ug/m^3)
MSA[1] Level	70	37	0.085	4	0.012	n/a	n/a
NAAQS[2]	150	65	0.125	9	0.140	0.053	1.50
Met NAAQS[2]	Yes	Yes	Yes	Yes	Yes	n/a	n/a

Note: Data from exceptional events are not included; (1) Metropolitan Statistical Area - see Appendix A for areas included; (2) National Ambient Air Quality Standards; n/a not available
Units: ppm = parts per million; ug/m^3 = micrograms per cubic meter
Source: U.S. Environmental Protection Agency, Air Trends Fact Book 2005

Watershed Health

The U.S. Environmental Protection Agency monitors the health of the aquatic resources for the nation's 2,000+ watersheds. **The Puget Sound watershed serves the Seattle area and received an overall Index of Watershed Indicators (IWI) score of 5 (more serious**

problems - low vulnerability). The IWI score is based on seven condition and nine vulnerability indicators. The overall IWI score ranges from 1 (best health) to 6 (worst health). The Condition Indicators include: designated use attainment, fish and wildlife consumption advisories, source water condition, contaminated sediments, ambient water quality, and wetlands loss index. The Vulnerability Indicators include: aquatic species at risk, conventional and toxic loads over permitted limits, urban and agricultural runoff potential, population change, hydrologic modification, estuarine pollution susceptibility, and air deposition. *Note: The IWI is no longer being updated by the U.S. EPA. Source: U.S. Environmental Protection Agency, Index of Watershed Indicators, October 26, 2001*

Drinking Water

Water System Name	Pop. Served	Primary Water Source Type	Number of Violations in 2006[a]		
			Health Based	Significant Monitoring	Monitoring
Seattle Public Utilities	629,000	Surface	None	None	None

Note: (a) Based on violation data from January 1, 2006 to December 31, 2006
Source: U.S. Environmental Protection Agency, Office of Ground Water and Drinking Water, Safe Drinking Water Information System (data extracted April 12, 2007)

Seattle tap water is alkaline, very soft.
Editor & Publisher Market Guide, 2005

Thousand Oaks, California

Background

Thousand Oaks, named for the many oak trees that line area hills, was created in 1964 as part of a master city planned by the Janss Corporation. The new city grew from a total plan that incorporates controlled growth and a balanced mix of residential areas, modern shopping centers, schools, business and industrial centers, parks and open spaces.

The area's first recorded European history dates back to 1542, when explorer Juan Rodriguez Cabrillo discovered Alta, California, and explored several local harbors. He placed his country's flag at Point Mugu and claimed the land for the King of Spain. Thereafter, the region remained undisturbed for two and a half centuries until Spanish explorers and missionaries arrived. In the early 1800's, a Spanish governor granted over 48,000 acres of land to two loyal soldiers. One of the grants included the area that became known as the Conejo Valley, (valley of the rabbits), within which Thousand Oaks was later established. For the next half-century, vaqueros roamed the terrain and tended great herds of cattle. In the late 1800s, the valley began to be parceled into ranchos. In the early 1900s, the Janss family, developers of several Southern California subdivisions, purchased 10,000 acres of Conejo farmland. Field crops, orchards, chicken, hog, and dairy farms dotted the landscape when the first local highway made it possible for motorists to escape Los Angeles to see the scenic countryside.

Today the city supports an active "slow growth" city council initiative that encourages protecting the town's oak trees and open land. More than 14,000 acres have been preserved, containing more than 75 miles of trails.

The Thousand Oaks economy centers on a small range of businesses focusing on biotechnology, electronics, and financing. Amgen and Baxter Healthcare offer many high-tech jobs, while Countrywide and Verizon Wireless manage regional offices. Other employers include General Dynamics, Jafra Cosmetics, and the Rockwell Science Center. Thousand Oaks is also home to many entrepreneurs and welcomes small business to the area. As a suburb, many residents also commute to neighboring Los Angeles and Westlake Village, where the regional headquarters of many large businesses, such as General Motors, are located. Commuters are served by a new regional transportation center that offers bus and shuttle lines to Los Angeles, Oxnard, Ventura, Simi Valley, and Santa Barbara.

Residents of Thousand Oaks enjoy a Mediterranean climate - 12 miles inland from the Pacific Ocean — with average temperatures between 65 and 75 degrees during the summer and 53 to 69 degrees in the winter. Rain is nearly nonexistent from May through August, and like most of Southern California, sunshine prevails year round.

Rankings

General Rankings

- Oxnard was ranked #147 out of 331 metro areas in *Cities Ranked & Rated*. Criteria: cost of living; climate; crime; transportation; economy and jobs; education; arts and culture; health and healthcare; leisure. *Cities Ranked & Rated, 1st Edition, 2004*

Business/Finance Rankings

- Intel, in partnership with Sperling's BestPlaces, ranked the 80 "Best Cities for Teleworking" in America. The Oxnard metro area ranked #5 among mid-sized metro areas. The study identifies cities that hold the greatest potential for teleworking based on a host of factors including typical commuting times, fuel prices, availability of broadband Internet access and percentage of the population in telework friendly jobs. The study also factored in extreme climate and natural hazards. *Intel, "Best Cities for Teleworking," March 30, 2006*

- The Oxnard metro area appeared on the Milken Institute "2005 Best Performing Cities" index. Rank: #38 out of 200 large metro areas. Criteria: job growth; wage and salary growth; high-tech output growth. *Milken Institute, "2005 Best Performing Cities," February 2006*

- The Oxnard metro area was selected as one of "The Best Cities for Doing Business in America." *Inc.* magazine measured employment growth in 393 regions using the following criteria: recent growth trend; mid-term growth; long-term trend; and current year growth. The Oxnard metro area ranked #52 among mid-sized metro areas and #221 overall. *Inc., May 2006*

- *Forbes* ranked the 200 most populous metro areas in the U.S. in terms of the "Best Places for Business and Careers." The Oxnard metro area was ranked #96. Criteria: business costs (labor, energy, tax and office space expenses); living costs (housing, transportation, food and other household expenditures); education levels of the work force; job growth; income growth; migration trends; crime rates; and culture/leisure. *Forbes, April 23, 2007*

- *Fortune* ranked the 100 largest metro areas in the U.S. in terms of projected median home price change in 2006. The Oxnard metro area ranked #89. *Fortune, "The Top 100: Is the Party Over?" December 26, 2005*

Health/Environment Rankings

- *Business Week* identified the 15 metro areas that saw the steepest declines in ground-level ozone pollution between 1990 and 2005. The Oxnard metro area ranked #15. *Business Week, "America's Most Cleaned-Up Metro Areas," March 23, 2007*

- The Oxnard metro area appeared in *Country Home's* "2007 Best Green Places Report". The area ranked #90. Criteria included: air and watershed quality; miles of mass transit; green power; number of farmer's markets, organic producers and groceries. *Country Home, "2007 Best Green Places Report," April 2007*

- Sperling's BestPlaces ranked 331 metro areas and identified the most and least stressful U.S. cities. The Oxnard metro area ranked #80 out of the 100 largest metro areas (#1 = most stressful). Criteria: divorce rate; unemployment rate; violent and property crime; suicide rate; commute time; mental health; alcohol consumption; cloudy days. *www.BestPlaces.net, January 9, 2004*

Women/Minorities Rankings

- Oxnard was ranked #6 out of 100 metro areas in *SELF Magazine's* ranking of "America's Best Places for Women." A panel of experts came up with nearly 40 criteria including: drinking and smoking rates; depression; unemployment; parks; crime; disease; healthcare insurance coverage; air quality; and commute times. *SELF Magazine, "America's Best Places for Women 2006," December 2006*

■ *Ladies Home Journal* ranked America's 200 largest cities based on the qualities women surveyed care about most. Thousand Oaks ranked #10 out of 143 in the smaller city category (population under 300,000). Criteria: crime; lifestyle; education; jobs; health; child care; politics; and the economy. *Ladies Home Journal Online, "The Best Cities for Women 2002"*

Seniors/Retirement Rankings

■ A.G. Edwards ranked America's 500 top-performing communities based on their residents' personal savings and investing behavior. The Oxnard metro area ranked #20 with an index score of 113.98 (national average = 100.00). A dozen statistical factors were measured including: participation in retirement savings plans; personal debt levels; and home ownership. *A.G. Edwards, "2006 Nest Egg Index", September 6, 2006*

Safety Rankings

■ Allstate ranked the 200 largest cities in America in terms of driver safety. Thousand Oaks ranked #100. In addition, drivers were 8.6% more likely to have had an accident compared to the national average. Allstate researchers analyzed internal Property Damage reported claims over a two-year period (from January 2003 to December 2004) to ensure the findings would not be affected by external influences such as weather or road construction. A weighted average of the two-year numbers determined the annual percentages. The report defines an auto crash as any collision resulting in a property damage claim. *Allstate, "Allstate America's Best Drivers Report 2006," May 24, 2006*

■ Thousand Oaks was identified as one of the safest cities in America by Morgan Quitno. All 371 cities with populations over 75,000 that reported crime rates in 2005 for murder, rape, robbery, aggravated assault, burglary, and motor vehicle thefts were ranked. The city ranked #11 out of the top 25. *www.morganquitno.com, 13th Annual America's Safest (and Most Dangerous) Cities Awards*

■ Thousand Oaks was identified as one of the safest mid-size cities in America by Morgan Quitno. All 213 cities with populations of 100,000 to 499,999 that reported crime rates in 2005 for murder, rape, robbery, aggravated assault, burglary, and motor vehicle thefts were ranked. The city ranked #5 out of the top 10. *www.morganquitno.com, 13th Annual America's Safest (and Most Dangerous) Cities Awards*

■ *Ladies Home Journal* ranked America's 200 largest cities in terms of safety. Thousand Oaks ranked #9 out of 200. Criteria: violent crimes; crimes against property; and rape. *Ladies Home Journal Online, "The Best Cities for Women 2002"*

Sports/Recreation Rankings

■ *Golf Digest* ranked 330 metro areas in the U.S. in terms of golf. The Oxnard metro area was ranked #168. Criteria: access to golf; weather; value of golf; and quality of golf. *Golf Digest, "Metro Golf Rankings," August 2005*

Dating/Romance Rankings

■ Sperling's BestPlaces in partnership with AXE Deodorant Bodyspray ranked 80 metro areas and identified "America's Best (and Worst) Cities for Dating." The Oxnard metro area ranked #48. Criteria: percentage of singles ages 18-24; population density; dating venues per capita. *AXE Deodorant Bodyspray, "America's Best (and Worst) Cities for Dating," May, 2004*

Business Environment

CITY FINANCES

City Government Finances

Component	2003-2004 ($000)	2003-2004 ($ per capita)
Total Revenues	139,002	1,133
Total Expenditures	143,382	1,169
Debt Outstanding	109,662	894
Cash and Securities	210,117	1,712

Source: U.S Census Bureau, Government Finances 2003-2004

City Government Revenue by Source

Source	2003-2004 ($000)	2003-2004 ($ per capita)
General Revenue		
From Federal Government	2,645	22
From State Government	10,085	82
From Local Governments	0	0
Taxes		
Property	24,898	203
Sales	38,798	316
Personal Income	0	0
License	0	0
Charges	29,297	239
Liquor Store	0	0
Utility	13,703	112
Employee Retirement	0	0
Other	19,576	160

Source: U.S Census Bureau, Government Finances 2003-2004

City Government Expenditures by Function

Function	2003-2004 ($000)	2003-2004 ($ per capita)	2003-2004 (%)
General Expenditures			
Airports	0	0	0.0
Corrections	165	1	0.1
Education	0	0	0.0
Fire Protection	0	0	0.0
Governmental Administration	12,867	105	9.0
Health	650	5	0.5
Highways	18,298	149	12.8
Hospitals	0	0	0.0
Housing and Community Development	10,797	88	7.5
Interest on General Debt	6,919	56	4.8
Libraries	8,498	69	5.9
Parking	0	0	0.0
Parks and Recreation	7,178	59	5.0
Police Protection	17,264	141	12.0
Public Welfare	0	0	0.0
Sewerage	30,114	245	21.0
Solid Waste Management	1,109	9	0.8
Liquor Store	0	0	0.0
Utility	16,829	137	11.7
Employee Retirement	0	0	0.0
Other	12,694	103	8.9

Source: U.S Census Bureau, Government Finances 2003-2004

Municipal Bond Ratings

Area	Moody's
City	n/a

Source: Mergent Bond Record, January 2007 (unless noted otherwise)

DEMOGRAPHICS

Population Growth

Area	1990 Census	2000 Census	2006 Estimate	2011 Projection	Population Growth (%) 1990-2000	Population Growth (%) 2000-2011
City	104,661	117,005	127,283	135,790	11.8	16.1
MSA[1]	669,016	753,197	811,349	861,071	12.6	14.3
U.S.	248,709,873	281,421,906	298,021,266	312,383,955	13.2	11.0

Note: (1) Metropolitan Statistical Area - see Appendix B for areas included
Source: Claritas, Inc.

Number of Households and Average Household Size

Area	2006 Estimate	2006 Average Household Size
City	45,819	2.78
MSA[1]	261,600	3.10
U.S.	112,267,302	2.65

Note: (1) Metropolitan Statistical Area - see Appendix B for areas included
Source: Claritas, Inc.

Race and Ethnicity

Area	White Alone[2]	Black Alone[2]	Asian Alone[2]	Other Race Alone[2]	Hispanic[3]
City	83.3	1.1	7.0	8.7	14.6
MSA[1]	67.5	1.9	6.1	24.5	36.1
U.S.	73.3	12.4	4.2	10.1	14.5

Note: Figures are 2006 estimates; (1) Metropolitan Statistical Area - see Appendix B for areas included
(2) Alone is defined as not being in combination with one or more other races; (3) May be of any race.
Source: Claritas, Inc.

Segregation

City Index[2]	City Rank[3]	MSA[1] Index[2]	MSA[1] Rank[4]
0.0	0	0.0	0

Note: Figures are based on an analysis of Census 2000 data; (1) Metropolitan Statistical Area - see Appendix A
for areas included; (2) White/Black Dissimilarity Index—the most commonly used measure of segregation
between two groups, reflecting their relative distributions across neighborhoods within a city or metropolitan
area. It can range in value from 0, indicating complete integration, to 100, indicating complete segregation; (3)
Ranges from 1 (most segregated) to 100 (least segregated) and includes all the cities in this book; (4) Ranges
from 1 (most segregated) to 318 (least segregated) and includes 318 metropolitan areas.
Source: www.CensusScope.org

Ancestry

Area	German	Irish[2]	English	American	Italian	Polish	French[3]	Scottish
City	17.3	13.4	13.8	5.0	7.9	4.1	3.4	2.9
MSA[1]	13.0	9.9	9.9	4.1	5.1	2.3	2.8	2.0
U.S.	15.2	10.9	8.7	7.3	5.6	3.2	3.0	1.7

Note: Figures include multiple ancestry (e.g. if a person reported being Irish and Italian, they were included in
both columns); (1) Metropolitan Statistical Area - see Appendix A for areas included; (2) Includes Celtic; (3)
Includes Alsatian but excludes Basque
Source: Census 2000, Summary File 3

Foreign-Born Population

Area	Any Foreign Country	Percent of Population Born in Europe	Asia	Africa	Oceania[2]	Canada	Mexico	Latin America[3]
City	15.6	3.2	4.6	0.3	0.1	0.9	4.2	2.2
MSA[1]	20.7	1.8	4.1	0.2	0.1	0.5	12.6	1.4
U.S.	11.1	1.7	2.9	0.3	0.1	0.3	3.3	2.5

Note: (1) Metropolitan Statistical Area - see Appendix A for areas included; (2) Includes Australia, New
Zealand subregion, Melanesia, Micronesia, Polynesia, and Oceania n.e.c; (3) Includes Central America
(excluding Mexico), South America, and the Caribbean.
Source: Census 2000, Summary File 3

Marriage Status

Area	Never Married	Now Married (excluding Separated)	Separated	Widowed	Divorced
City	22.9	61.2	1.3	5.2	9.4
MSA[1]	25.9	57.5	2.0	5.1	9.5
U.S.	27.1	54.4	2.2	6.6	9.7

Note: Figures are percentages and cover the population 15 years of age and older;
(1) Metropolitan Statistical Area - see Appendix A for areas included
Source: Census 2000, Summary File 3

Age Distribution

Area	Percent of Population						
	Under Age 5	Age 5 to 17	Age 18 to 34	Age 35 to 49	Age 50 to 64	Age 65 to 79	80 Years and Over
City	6.5	19.2	19.2	26.0	18.1	7.9	3.0
MSA[1]	7.4	20.9	22.7	24.6	14.3	7.4	2.6
U.S.	6.8	18.9	23.7	23.5	14.8	9.2	3.2

Note: (1) Metropolitan Statistical Area - see Appendix A for areas included
Source: Census 2000, Summary File 3

Male/Female Ratio

Area	Males	Females	Males per 100 Females
City	62,658	64,625	97.0
MSA[1]	405,622	405,727	100.0
U.S.	146,712,712	151,308,554	97.0

Note: Figures are 2006 estimates; (1) Metropolitan Statistical Area -
see Appendix B for areas included
Source: Claritas, Inc.

Religion

Area	Catholic	Southern Baptist	United Methodist	ELCA[1]	LDS[2]	Presbyterian Church USA	Jewish Est.	Muslim Est.
County	29.3	0.8	0.9	1.1	2.1	0.9	2.0	0.3
U.S.	22.0	7.1	3.7	1.8	1.5	1.1	2.2	0.6

Note: Figures are the number of adherents as a percentage of the total population; Adherents are defined as all
members, including full members, their children and the estimated number of other participants who are not
considered members (e.g. the baptized, those not confirmed, those regularly attending services, etc.);
(1) Evangelical Lutheran Church in America; (2) The Church of Jesus Christ of Latter Day Saints
Source: Reprinted with permission from Religious Congregations and Membership in the United States 2000
(Nashville, Glenmary Research Center, 2002) Copyright Association of Statisticians of American Religious
Bodies. All rights reserved.

ECONOMY

Gross Metropolitan Product

Area	2002	2003	2004	2005	2005 Rank[2]
MSA[1]	27.0	28.7	30.9	32.8	63

Note: Figures are in billions of dollars; (1) Oxnard-Thousand Oaks-Ventura, CA Metropolitan Statistical Area -
see Appendix A for areas included; (2) Rank ranges from 1 to 361
Source: The U.S. Conference of Mayors, "U.S. Metro Economies: GMP - The Engines of America's Growth,"
January 2007

Economic Growth

Area	1995 GMP	2005 GMP	Average Annual Growth Rate	Growth Rate Rank[2]
MSA[1]	17.7	32.8	6.4	84

Note: Figures are in billions of dollars; GMP = Gross Metropolitan Product; (1) Oxnard-Thousand Oaks-Ventura, CA Metropolitan Statistical Area - see Appendix A for areas included; (2) Rank ranges from 1 to 361
Source: The U.S. Conference of Mayors, "U.S. Metro Economies: GMP - The Engines of America's Growth," January 2007

INCOME

Per Capita/Median/Average Income

Area	Per Capita ($)	Median Household ($)	Average Household ($)
City	40,034	87,895	110,625
MSA[1]	28,627	68,800	87,832
U.S.	25,129	48,775	65,849

Note: Figures are 2006 estimates; (1) Metropolitan Statistical Area - see Appendix B for areas included
Source: Claritas, Inc.

Household Income Distribution

Area	Percent of Households Earning							
	Under $15,000	$15,000 -24,999	$25,000 -34,999	$35,000 -49,999	$50,000 -74,999	$75,000 -99,000	$100,000 -149,999	$150,000 and up
City	4.9	5.2	5.6	10.2	16.4	14.8	22.5	20.3
MSA[1]	7.3	7.2	7.8	13.1	19.5	15.0	18.0	12.2
U.S.	13.3	11.0	11.3	15.7	19.5	11.8	11.0	6.4

Note: Figures are 2006 estimates; (1) Metropolitan Statistical Area - see Appendix B for areas included
Source: Claritas, Inc.

Poverty Rates by Age

Area	All Ages	Under 5 Years Old	5 to 17 Years Old	18 to 64 Years Old	65 Years and Over
City	5.0	0.4	1.0	3.0	0.6
MSA[1]	9.2	1.0	2.5	5.2	0.6
U.S.	12.4	1.2	3.0	6.9	1.2

Note: Figures are percent of population with income in 1999 below poverty level and only include population for whom poverty status is determined; (1) Metropolitan Statistical Area - see Appendix A for areas included
Source: Census 2000, Summary File 3

Personal Bankruptcy Filing Rate

Area	2003	2004	2005
Ventura County	2.97	2.70	3.86
U.S.	5.57	5.31	6.88

Note: Numbers are per 1,000 population and include Chapter 7 and Chapter 13 filings
Source: Federal Deposit Insurance Corporation (FDIC), Regional Economic Conditions (RECON), 3/24/2006

EMPLOYMENT

Labor Force and Employment

Area	Civilian Labor Force			Workers Employed		
	Dec. 2005	Dec. 2006	% Chg.	Dec. 2005	Dec. 2006	% Chg.
City	70,267	71,074	1.1	67,992	68,743	1.1
MSA[1]	421,312	426,207	1.2	403,477	407,935	1.1
U.S.	149,874,000	152,571,000	1.8	142,918,000	146,081,000	2.2

Note: Data is not seasonally adjusted and covers workers 16 years of age and older;
(1) Metropolitan Statistical Area - see Appendix B for areas included
Source: Bureau of Labor Statistics, http://stats.bls.gov

Unemployment Rate

Area	2006											
	Jan.	Feb.	Mar.	Apr.	May	Jun.	Jul.	Aug.	Sep.	Oct.	Nov.	Dec.
City	3.5	3.4	3.1	2.9	2.9	3.4	3.6	3.5	3.4	3.0	3.4	3.3
MSA[1]	4.6	4.4	4.0	3.8	3.8	4.4	4.7	4.6	4.4	4.0	4.4	4.3
U.S.	5.1	5.1	4.8	4.5	4.4	4.8	5.0	4.6	4.4	4.1	4.3	4.3

Note: Data is not seasonally adjusted and covers workers 16 years of age and older; All figures are percentages; (1) Metropolitan Statistical Area - see Appendix B for areas included
Source: Bureau of Labor Statistics, http://stats.bls.gov

Employment by Occupation

Occupation Classification	City (%)	MSA[1] (%)	U.S. (%)
Sales and Office	28.0	27.3	26.7
Professional and Related	27.3	20.9	20.2
Service	11.5	13.4	14.9
Production, Transportation, and Material Moving	6.4	11.5	14.6
Management, Business, and Financial	21.2	15.6	13.5
Construction, Extraction, and Maintenance	5.4	8.2	9.4
Farming, Forestry, and Fishing	0.1	3.1	0.7

Note: Figures cover employed civilians 16 years of age and older;
(1) Metropolitan Statistical Area - see Appendix A for areas included
Source: Census 2000, Summary File 3

Employment by Industry

Sector	MSA[1]		U.S.
	Number of Employees	Percent of Total	Percent of Total
Government	43,000	14.2	16.3
Education and Health Services	29,600	9.8	13.2
Professional and Business Services	40,300	13.3	12.9
Retail Trade	39,400	13.0	11.5
Manufacturing	38,000	12.6	10.2
Leisure and Hospitality	30,200	10.0	9.5
Financial Activities	25,000	8.3	6.1
Construction	20,500	6.8	5.5
Wholesale Trade	12,600	4.2	4.3
Other Services	10,300	3.4	3.9
Transportation and Utilities	6,400	2.1	3.7
Information	6,000	2.0	2.2
Natural Resources and Mining	1,100	0.4	0.5

Note: Figures cover non-farm employment as of December 2006 and are not seasonally adjusted;
(1) Metropolitan Statistical Area - see Appendix B for areas included
Source: Bureau of Labor Statistics, http://stats.bls.gov

Occupations with Greatest Projected Employment Growth: 2002 - 2012

Occupation[1]	2002 Employment	2012 Projected Employment	Numeric Employment Change	Percent Employment Change
Retail Salespersons	435,400	513,200	77,800	17.9
Postsecondary Teachers	154,500	217,700	63,200	40.9
Combined Food Preparation and Serving Workers, Including Fast Food	215,100	277,300	62,200	28.9
Cashiers	358,800	420,700	61,900	17.3
Registered Nurses	201,600	258,400	56,800	28.2
Waiters and Waitresses	214,000	264,900	50,900	23.8
Customer Service Representatives	197,500	244,900	47,400	24.0
Office Clerks, General	400,300	446,500	46,200	11.5
General and Operations Managers	224,000	267,000	43,000	19.2
Teacher Assistants	179,600	222,300	42,700	23.8

Note: Projections cover California; (1) Sorted by numeric employment change
Source: www.projectionscentral.com, State Occupational Projections, 2002-2012 Long-Term Projections

Fastest Growing Occupations: 2002 - 2012

Occupation[1]	2002 Employment	2012 Projected Employment	Numeric Employment Change	Percent Employment Change
Physical Therapist Aides	4,200	6,800	2,600	61.9
Dental Hygienists	16,600	26,200	9,600	57.8
Dental Assistants	42,700	67,100	24,400	57.1
Tapers	9,200	14,400	5,200	56.5
Drywall and Ceiling Tile Installers	26,800	41,800	15,000	56.0
Tile and Marble Setters	8,600	13,400	4,800	55.8
Network Systems and Data Communications Analysts	20,300	31,600	11,300	55.7
Physical Therapist Assistants	3,900	6,000	2,100	53.8
Fitness Trainers and Aerobics Instructors	24,000	35,700	11,700	48.8
Self-Enrichment Education Teachers	24,200	35,800	11,600	47.9

Note: Projections cover California; (1) Sorted by percent employment change and excludes occupations with numeric employment change less than 1500
Source: www.projectionscentral.com, State Occupational Projections, 2002-2012 Long-Term Projections

Average Wages

Occupation	$/Hr.	Occupation	$/Hr.
Accountants and Auditors	27.64	Maids and Housekeeping Cleaners	9.08
Automotive Mechanics	17.83	Maintenance and Repair Workers	16.02
Bookkeepers	16.30	Marketing Managers	58.08
Carpenters	21.04	Nuclear Medicine Technologists	n/a
Cashiers	9.81	Nurses, Licensed Practical	19.36
Clerks, General Office	12.50	Nurses, Registered	30.84
Clerks, Receptionists/Information	11.56	Nursing Aides/Orderlies/Attendants	11.58
Clerks, Shipping/Receiving	12.62	Packers and Packagers, Hand	8.68
Computer Programmers	35.00	Physical Therapists	32.77
Computer Support Specialists	20.95	Postal Service Mail Carriers	21.79
Computer Systems Analysts	38.92	Real Estate Brokers	40.37
Cooks, Restaurant	9.96	Retail Salespersons	11.62
Dentists	n/a	Sales Reps., Exc. Tech./Scientific	30.57
Electrical Engineers	40.66	Sales Reps., Tech./Scientific	40.08
Electricians	26.36	Secretaries, Exc. Legal/Med./Exec.	17.57
Financial Managers	49.76	Security Guards	n/a
First-Line Supervisors/Mgrs., Sales	18.20	Surgeons	86.85
Food Preparation Workers	8.21	Teacher Assistants	11.70
General and Operations Managers	51.90	Teachers, Elementary School	25.50
Hairdressers/Cosmetologists	8.68	Teachers, Secondary School	28.30
Internists	91.63	Telemarketers	n/a
Janitors and Cleaners	11.84	Truck Drivers, Heavy/Tractor-Trailer	17.62
Landscaping/Groundskeeping Workers	10.91	Truck Drivers, Light/Delivery Svcs.	12.76
Lawyers	62.13	Waiters and Waitresses	8.17

Note: Wage data is for May 2005 and covers the Oxnard-Thousand Oaks-Ventura, CA Metropolitan Statistics Area - see Appendix B for areas included. Hourly wages for elementary/secondary school teachers and teacher assistants were calculated by the editors from annual wage data assuming a 40 hour work week; n/a not available.
Source: Bureau of Labor Statistics, May 2005 Metro Area Occupational Employment and Wage Estimates

RESIDENTIAL REAL ESTATE

Building Permits

Area	Single-Family			Multi-Family			Total		
	2005	2006p	Pct. Chg.	2005	2006p	Pct. Chg.	2005	2006p	Pct. Chg.
City	61	64	4.9	462	131	-71.6	523	195	-62.7
U.S.	1,682,000	1,380,000	-18.0	473,300	457,300	-3.4	2,155,300	1,837,300	-14.8

Note: (p) preliminary; figures represent new, privately-owned housing units authorized (unadjusted data); All permit data are based on estimates with imputation; U.S. figures are based on the new 20,000-place series.
Source: U.S. Census Bureau, Manufacturing, Mining, and Construction Statistics

Homeownership and Housing Vacancies

Area	Homeownership Rate[2] (%)			Rental Vacancy Rate[3] (%)			Homeowner Vacancy Rate[4] (%)		
	2004	2005	2006	2004	2005	2006	2004	2005	2006
MSA[1]	n/a	73.4	69.8	n/a	4.3	4.1	n/a	0.4	1.8
U.S.	69.0	68.9	68.8	10.2	9.8	9.7	1.7	1.9	2.4

*Note: Comparable 2004 data was not available due to changes in metropolitan area definitions; (1)
Metropolitan Statistical Area - see Appendix B for areas included; (2) The proportion of households that are
owners; (3) The proportion of the rental inventory that is vacant for rent; (4) The proportion of the homeowner
inventory that is vacant for sale; n/a not available*
Source: U.S. Census Bureau, Housing Vacancies and Homeownership Annual Statistics: 2006

TAXES

State Corporate Income Tax Rates

State	Rate (%)	Number of Brackets	Low Bracket (Under $)	High Bracket (Over $)
California	8.84	1	na	na

*Note: Tax rates as of December 31, 2006; na not applicable; 10.84% on financial institutions. Minimum tax is
$800. The tax rate on S-Corporations is 1.5% (3.5% for financial S-Corporations).*
Source: Tax Foundation, www.taxfoundation.org

State Individual Income Tax Rates

State	Federal Deductibility	Marginal Rate (%)	Number of Brackets	Low Bracket (Under $)	High Bracket (Over $)
California	No	1.0-10.3 (p)(r)	7	0	1,000,000

*Note: Tax rates as of December 31, 2006; Brackets apply to single taxpayers and married people filing
separately; na not applicable; (p) California's $1,000,000 bracket not doubled for married taxpayers; (r)
Indexed for Inflation.*
Source: Tax Foundation, www.taxfoundation.org

Various State and Local Tax Rates

State and Local Sales and Use (%)	State Sales and Use (%)	Gasoline ($/gal.)	Cigarette ($/pack)	Spirits ($/gal.)	Table Wine ($/gal.)	Beer ($/gal.)
7.25	6.25	0.192 (m)	0.87	3.3	0.20	0.20

*Note: Tax rates as of December 31, 2006; (m) Additional cents per gallon taxes added this year that were not
included in previous years' tables.*
Source: Tax Foundation, www.taxfoundation.org; The Sales Tax Clearinghouse, www.thestc.com

State Tax Burdens

Area	Combined State and Local Tax Burden		Combined Federal, State and Local Tax Burden	
	Percent	Rank	Percent	Rank
California	10.9	15	32.7	9
U.S. Average	10.6	-	31.6	-

Note: Figures are for 2006 and measure taxes as a percentage of income
Source: Tax Foundation, www.taxfoundation.org

Internal Revenue Service Tax Audits

IRS District	Percent of Returns Audited				
	1996	1997	1998	1999	2000
	0.00	0.00	0.00	0.00	0.00
U.S.	0.66	0.61	0.46	0.31	0.20

*Note: Figures cover IRS district audits of federal income tax returns filed by individuals. Geographic data on
district audits after the year 2000 are being withheld by the IRS. TRAC is challenging this policy.*
*Source: Syracuse University, Transactional Records Access Clearinghouse (TRAC), "Odds of IRS District Tax
Audit 2000"*

COMMERCIAL
UTILITIES

Typical Monthly Electric Bills

Area	Commercial Service ($/month)		Industrial Service ($/month)	
	3 kW demand 1,000 kWh	40 kW demand 14,000 kWh	1,000 kW demand 200,000 kWh	50,000 kW demand 15,000,000 kWh
City	215	2,636	60,545	2,448,677
Average[1]	123	1,413	22,000	1,306,315

Note: Based on total rates in effect July 1, 2006; (1) average based on 196 utilities
Source: Edison Electric Institute, Typical Bills and Average Rates Report, Summer 2006

TRANSPORTATION

Means of Transportation to Work

Area	Car/Truck/Van		Public Transportation			Bicycle	Walked	Other Means	Worked at Home
	Drove Alone	Car-pooled	Bus	Subway	Railroad				
City	80.6	9.5	0.4	0.0	0.2	0.5	2.1	0.8	5.9
MSA[1]	75.9	15.1	0.7	0.0	0.2	0.7	2.1	1.0	4.2
U.S.	75.7	12.2	2.5	1.5	0.5	0.4	2.9	1.0	3.3

Note: Figures are percentages and cover workers 16 years of age and older;
(1) Metropolitan Statistical Area - see Appendix A for areas included
Source: Census 2000, Summary File 3

Travel Time to Work

Area	Less Than 15 Minutes	15 to 29 Minutes	30 to 44 Minutes	45 to 59 Minutes	60 Minutes or More
City	33.9	32.4	15.0	7.0	11.6
MSA[1]	30.2	36.2	18.4	6.8	8.4
U.S.	29.4	36.1	19.1	7.4	8.0

Note: Figures are percentages and include workers 16 years old and over; (1) Metropolitan Statistical Area -
see Appendix A for areas included
Source: Census 2000, Summary File 3

Travel Time Index

Area	1982	1993	2002	2003
Urban Area[1]	1.04	1.10	1.21	1.23
Average[2]	1.12	1.28	1.37	1.37

Note: Travel Time Index - The ratio of travel time in the peak period to the travel time at
free-flow conditions. A value of 1.35 indicates a 20-minute free-flow trip takes 27 minutes
in the peak. Free-flow speeds (60 mph on freeways and 35 mph on principal arterials)
are used as the comparison threshold; (1) Covers the Oxnard-Ventura, CA urban area;
(2) average of 85 urban areas
Source: Texas Transportation Institute, The 2005 Urban Mobility Report, May 2005

Public Transportation

Agency name:	Thousand Oaks Transit (TOT)
Vehicle type:	Bus
Average fleet age in years:	5.9
No. operated in max. service:	6
Vehicle type:	Demand response
Average fleet age in years:	2.4
No. operated in max. service:	12

Source: Federal Transit Administration, National Transit Database, 2005

Air Transportation

Airport name and code:	Los Angeles International (LAX)
Domestic service (2006)	
Passenger airlines[1]:	34
Passenger enplanements:	21,339,036
Freight carriers[2]:	43
Freight (lbs.):	941,663,753
International service (2005)	
Passenger airlines[1]:	63
Passenger enplanements:	8,133,442
Freight carriers[2]:	74
Freight (lbs.):	807,999,284

Note: (1) Includes all major, minor and commuter airlines that carried at least one passenger during the year; (2) Includes all airlines and freight carriers that transported at least one pound of freight during the year
Source: Bureau of Transportation Statistics, The Intermodal Transportation Database, Air Carriers: T-100 International Market, 2004; Bureau of Transportation Statistics, The Intermodal Transportation Database, Air Carriers: T-100 Domestic Market, 2005

Other Transportation Statistics

Interstate highways:	SR-101 with access to: I-5; I-405; I-210
Amtrak service:	No
Major waterways/ports:	Near Pacific Ocean

Source: Editor & Publisher Market Guide, 2006; Amtrak.com; Rand McNally 2006 Road Atlas

BUSINESSES

Major Business Headquarters

Company Name	2006 Rankings	
	Fortune[1]	Forbes[2]
No companies listed	-	-

Note: (1) Fortune 500 - companies that produce a 10-K are ranked 1 to 500 based on 2005 revenue; (2) Forbes Largest Private Companies - all private companies with at least $1 billion in annual revenue are ranked 1 to 394; companies listed are located in the city; dashes indicate no ranking
Source: Fortune, April 17, 2006; Forbes, November 9, 2006

Best Companies to Work For

Amgen (HQ), headquartered in Thousand Oaks, is among the "100 Best Companies to Work For." Criteria: More than 105,000 employees from 446 companies responded to a 57-question survey created by the Great Place to Work Institute. Two-thirds of a company's score is based on the survey, which covers topics such as attitudes towards management, job satisfaction, and camaraderie. The remaining third of the score comes from each company's responses to the Institute's Culture Audit, which includes detailed questions about demographic makeup, pay and benefits programs, and open-ended questions about the company's people-management philosophy, internal communications, opportunities, compensation practices, diversity programs, etc. Any company that is at least seven years old and has a minimum of 1,000 U.S. employees is eligible. The top three U.S. locations are shown for companies with more than one location. *Fortune, "100 Best Companies to Work for 2007," January 22, 2007*

Fast-Growing Businesses

According to *Business 2.0*, Thousand Oaks is home to one of America's 100 fastest-growing technology companies: **Amgen**. The 100 Fastest-Growing Technology Companies (B2 100) is a yearly ranking published by Business 2.0 magazine of businesses whose inventiveness and quick reflexes are helping them to set the pace for the economy. To find the B2 100, Zacks Investment Research of Chicago ranked 2,000 publicly traded companies using a rigorous combination of four financial criteria: growth in revenue, profit, and operating cash flow during the past three years; and the 12-month stock market return as of March 31, 2006. *Business 2.0, "100 Fastest-Growing Tech Companies 2006," June 2006*

According to Deloitte & Touche LLP, Thousand Oaks is home to one of North America's 500 fastest-growing high-technology companies: **Amgen**. Companies are ranked by percentage growth in revenue over a five-year period. Criteria for inclusion: company must be headquartered within North America; company must own proprietary intellectual property or proprietary technology that contributes to a significant portion of the company's operating revenue or devotes a significant proportion of revenues to research and development of technology; company must have been in business for a minumum of five years with 2001 operating revenues of at least $50,000 USD or $75,000 CD and 2005 operating revenues of at least $5 million USD/CD. *Deloitte & Touche LLP, 2006 Technology Fast 500*

Women-Owned Businesses: 1997 and 2002

Year	All Firms		Firms with Paid Employees			
	Firms	Sales ($000)	Firms	Sales ($000)	Employees	Payroll ($000)
1997	4,850	394,119	506	288,906	1,994	42,536
2002	3,972	521,165	447	359,736	2,081	66,562

Note: Figures cover firms located in the city; Women-owned business are defined as firms in which women own 51% or more of the stock or equity of the company; (a) Withheld to avoid disclosing data for individual companies; (b) Withheld because estimate did not meet publication standards; n/a not available
Source: 1997 Economic Census, Survey of Minority- and Women-Owned Business Enterprises; 2002 Economic Census, Survey of Business Owners (released February 9, 2006)

Minority Business Opportunity

One of the 500 largest Hispanic-owned companies in the U.S. are located in Thousand Oaks. *Hispanic Business, "Hispanic Business 500," June 2006*

HOTELS

Hotels/Motels

Area	Hotels/Motels	Average Minimum Rates ($)		
		Tourist	First-Class	Deluxe
City	10	69	96	n/a

Note: n/a not available
Source: OAG Travel Planner Online, Spring 2006

EVENT SITES

Stadiums, Arenas, and Auditoriums

Name	Capacity
Fred Kavli Theatre for the Performing Arts	1,800

Source: www.officialtravelguide.com; www.eventective.com; original research

Hotels/Conference Centers

Name	Guest Rooms	Exhibit Space (sq. ft.)	Meeting Space (sq. ft.)
Best Western Thousand Oaks Inn	106	n/a	2,368

Note: n/a not available
Source: www.officialtravelguide.com; www.eventective.com; original research

Living Environment

COST OF LIVING

Cost of Living Index

Year	Composite Index	Groceries	Housing	Utilities	Trans-portation	Health Care	Misc. Goods/ Services
2004	n/a	n/a	n/a	n/a	n/a	n/a	n/a
2005	n/a	n/a	n/a	n/a	n/a	n/a	n/a
2006	n/a	n/a	n/a	n/a	n/a	n/a	n/a

Note: U.S. = 100; n/a not available
Source: The Council for Community and Economic Research (formerly ACCRA), Cost of Living Index, 2004, 2005 and 2006 4-Quarter Averages

HOUSING

House Price Index (HPI)

Area	National Ranking[2]	Quarterly Change (%)	One-Year Change (%)	Five-Year Change (%)
MSA[1]	192	-0.80	3.04	107.93
U.S.[3]	-	1.12	5.87	55.21

Note: The HPI is a weighted repeat sales index. It measures average price changes in repeat sales or refinancings on the same properties. This information is obtained by reviewing repeat mortgage transactions on single-family properties whose mortgages have been purchased or securitized by Fannie Mae or Freddie Mac in January 1975; (1) Metropolitan Statistical Area - see Appendix B for areas included; (2) Rankings are based on annual percentage change for all metro areas containing at least 15,000 transactions over the last 10 years and ranges from 1 to 282; (3) figures based on a weighted division average; all figures are for the period ending December 31, 2006
Source: Office of Federal Housing Enterprise Oversight, House Price Index, March 1, 2007

House Price Valuations

Area	Q4 1999	Q4 2000	Q4 2001	Q4 2002	Q4 2003	Q4 2004	Q4 2005	Q4 2006
MSA[1]	-16.8	-13.7	-7.3	4.4	17.4	32.4	44.4	40.9

Note: Figures show the percentage of over- or under-valuation of single family homes relative to statistically normal house values (e.g. a value of 23.6 indicates that house values are 23.6% overvalued). Statistically normal house values are based on house prices, interest rates, household incomes, population densities, and any historical premiums or discounts metropolitan areas have exhibited over time; (1) Figures cover the Metropolitan Statistical Area - see Appendix B for areas included
Source: Global Insight/National City Corporation, House Prices in America, March 2007

Median Home Prices

Area	2004	2005	2006p	Percent Change 2005 to 2006
Metro Area[1]	n/a	n/a	n/a	n/a
U.S. Average	195.2	219.0	222.0	1.4

Note: Figures are median sales prices of existing single-family homes in thousands of dollars; (p) preliminary; n/a not available; (1) Covers the Oxnard-Thousand Oaks-Ventura, CA Metropolitan Statistical Area - see Appendix B for areas included
Source: National Association of Realtors, Metropolitan Area Prices, 4th Quarter 2006

Housing: Year Structure Built

Area	1990 -2000	1980 -1989	1970 -1979	1960 -1969	1950 -1959	1940 -1949	Before 1940	Median Year
City	14.7	20.0	37.1	22.9	4.4	0.6	0.4	1976
MSA[1]	12.9	19.6	26.8	23.1	10.1	3.5	4.0	1973
U.S.	17.0	15.8	18.5	13.7	12.7	7.3	15.0	1971

Note: Figures are percentages; (1) Metropolitan Statistical Area - see Appendix A for areas included
Source: Census 2000, Summary File 3

Average New Home Price

Area	2004	2005	2006
City	n/a	n/a	n/a
U.S.	253,574	275,712	299,269

Note: n/a not available
Source: The Council for Community and Economic Research (formerly ACCRA), Cost of Living Index, 2004, 2005 and 2006 4-Quarter Averages

Average Apartment Rent

Area	2004	2005	2006
City	n/a	n/a	n/a
U.S.	716	740	766

Note: n/a not available
Source: The Council for Community and Economic Research (formerly ACCRA), Cost of Living Index, 2004, 2005 and 2006 4-Quarter Averages

RESIDENTIAL UTILITIES

Average Residential Utility Costs

Area	All Electric ($/mth)	Part Electric ($/mth)	Other Energy ($/mth)	Phone ($/mth)
City	n/a	n/a	n/a	n/a
U.S.	136.00	76.53	90.52	25.87

Note: n/a not available
Source: The Council for Community and Economic Research (formerly ACCRA), Cost of Living Index, 2006 4-Quarter Average

HEALTH

Average Health Care Costs

Area	Optometrist ($/visit)	Doctor ($/visit)	Dentist ($/visit)
City	n/a	n/a	n/a
U.S.	76.38	76.10	68.72

Note: n/a not available
Source: The Council for Community and Economic Research (formerly ACCRA), Cost of Living Index, 2006 4-Quarter Average

Mortality Rates

ICD-10 Sub-Chapter	ICD-10 Code	Age-Adjusted Death Rate per 100,000 population[1]	U.S. Age-Adjusted Death Rate per 100,000 population
Malignant neoplasms	C00-C97	154.3	185.8
Ischaemic heart diseases	I20-I25	142.8	150.2
Other forms of heart disease	I30-I51	30.5	50.8
Cerebrovascular diseases	I60-I69	46.0	50.0
Chronic lower respiratory diseases	J40-J47	37.5	41.1
Diabetes mellitus	E10-E14	19.6	24.5
Other degenerative diseases of the nervous system	G30-G31	19.3	22.3
Other external causes of accidental injury	W00-X59	17.2	21.2
Influenza and pneumonia	J10-J18	18.6	19.8
Hypertensive diseases	I10-I13	16.5	18.1

Note: ICD-10 = International Classification of Diseases 10th Revision; (1) Figures cover Ventura County, CA
Source: Centers for Disease Control and Prevention, National Center for Health Statistics. Compressed Mortality File 1999-2004. CDC WONDER On-line Database, compiled from Compressed Mortality File 1999-2004 Series 20 No. 2J, 2007.

Health Risk Data

Item	Area[1] (%)	U.S. (%)
Adults who have been told they have high blood pressure	n/a	25.5
Adults who have been told they have high blood cholesterol	n/a	35.6
Adults who have been told they have diabetes[2]	n/a	7.3
Adults who have been told they have arthritis	n/a	27.0
Adults who have been told they currently have asthma	n/a	8.0
Adults who are current smokers	n/a	20.6

Note: (1) Figures cover the Metropolitan Statistical Area - see Appendix B for areas included; n/a not available;
(2) Figures do not include pregnancy-related diabetes, pre-diabetes or borderline diabetes
Source: Centers for Disease Control and Prevention, Behaviorial Risk Factor Surveillance System, SMART:
Selected Metropolitan/Micropolitan Area Trends, 2005

Distribution of Office-Based Physicians

Area	Total	Family/ General Practice	Specialties Medical	Specialties Surgical	Specialties Other
CMSA[1] (number)	28,914	3,817	10,675	6,649	7,773
CMSA[1] (rate per 10,000 pop.)	17.1	2.3	6.3	3.9	4.6
Metro Average[2] (rate per 10,000 pop.)	19.4	2.1	7.5	4.5	5.3

Note: Data as of December 31, 2004; (1) Los Angeles-Riverside-Orange, CA Consolidated Metropolitan
Statistical Area includes the following counties: Los Angeles; Orange; Riverside; San Bernardino; Ventura;
(2) Average of the 79 unique MSAs and CMSAs in this book
Source: American Medical Association, Physician Characteristics & Distribution in the U.S., 2006

Hospitals

Thousand Oaks has the following hospitals: 1 general medical and surgical; 1 surgical.
AHA Guide to the Healthcare Field 2007

EDUCATION

Public School District Statistics

District Name	Schls	Pupils	Pupil/ Teacher Ratio	Minority Pupils[1] (%)	Free Lunch Eligible[2] (%)	IEP[3] (%)
Conejo Valley Unified	29	22,383	22.3	29.6	9.3	9.6

Note: Table includes regular local school districts with 2,000 or more students; (1) Percentage of students that
are not white, non-Hispanic; (2) Percentage of students that are eligible for the free lunch program;
(3) Percentage of students that have an Individualized Education Program.
Source: U.S. Department of Education, National Center for Education Statistics, Common Core of Data, Local
Education Agency (School District) Universe Survey: School Year 2004-2005; U.S. Department of Education,
National Center for Education Statistics, Common Core of Data, Public Elementary/Secondary School Universe
Survey: School Year 2004-2005

Top Public High Schools

High School Name	Index[1]	Rank[1]	Subsidized Lunch (%)[2]	E&E (%)[3]
Thousand Oaks	1.334	869	8.5	20.0

Note: (1) Public schools are ranked according to a ratio that is the number of Advanced Placement and/or
International Baccalaureate tests taken by all students at a school in 2005 divided by the number of graduating
seniors. All of the schools on the list have an index of at least 1.000; they are in the top five percent of public
schools measured this way. The rankings range from 1 to 1,236; (2) Percentage of students receiving federally
subsidized meals; (3) E & E stands for equity and excellence percentage: the portion of all graduating seniors
at a school that had at least one passing grade on one AP or IB test; (*) Gave just IB tests; (**) Gave both IB
and AP tests. AP and IB participation are indicators of a school's efforts to get students to excel and prepare for
college.
Source: Newsweek Online, May 23, 2006

Educational Quality

School District	Education Quotient[1]	Graduate Outcome[2]	Community Index[3]	Resource Index[4]	Rating[5]
Conejo Valley Unified	78	81	87	31	Blue

Note: Scores are national percentile rankings and range from 1 (worst) to 99 (best); (1) Combination of the Graduate Outcome, Community and Resource Indexes weighted to reflect the greater importance of the Graduate Outcome and Resource Index; (2) Based on graduation rates and college board scores (SAT/ACT); (3) Based on the surrounding community's level of affluence and adult education; (4) Based on teacher salaries, per-pupil expenditures and student-teacher ratios; (5) School districts receive one of five rankings: Gold Medal (top 16 percent of districts evaluated); Blue Ribbon (top third); Green Light (average); Yellow Light (bottom 25 percent); Red Light (bottom 10 percent).
Source: Expansion Management, "2007 Education Quotient," January 2007

Highest Level of Education

Area	Less than H.S.	H.S. Diploma	Some College, No Deg.	Associate Degree	Bachelors Degree	Masters Degree	Profess. School Degree	Doctorate Degree
City	8.7	15.5	25.8	7.9	26.5	10.1	3.2	2.4
MSA[1]	20.5	19.6	25.4	7.8	17.2	6.0	2.3	1.1
U.S.	19.4	28.4	21.2	6.4	15.7	5.9	2.0	1.0

Note: Figures are 2006 estimated percentages and cover persons age 25 and over; (1) Metropolitan Statistical Area - see Appendix B for areas included
Source: Claritas, Inc.

Educational Attainment by Race

Area	High School Graduate (%)					Bachelor's Degree (%)				
	Total	White	Black	Asian	Hisp.[2]	Total	White	Black	Asian	Hisp.[2]
City	91.4	93.1	89.5	94.1	61.7	42.2	41.7	50.3	72.5	15.0
MSA[1]	80.1	86.9	88.4	87.8	47.6	26.9	29.9	27.1	47.3	7.6
U.S.	80.4	83.6	72.3	80.4	52.4	24.4	26.1	14.3	44.1	10.4

Note: Figures shown cover persons 25 years old and over; (1) Metropolitan Statistical Area - see Appendix A for areas included; (2) people of Hispanic origin can be of any race
Source: Census 2000, Summary File 3

School Enrollment by Type

Area	Grades KG to 8				Grades 9 to 12			
	Public		Private		Public		Private	
	Enrollment	%	Enrollment	%	Enrollment	%	Enrollment	%
City	13,888	86.4	2,179	13.6	6,214	93.1	461	6.9
MSA[1]	100,814	89.0	12,408	11.0	46,013	93.3	3,285	6.7
U.S.	33,526,011	88.7	4,285,121	11.3	14,848,628	90.6	1,532,323	9.4

Note: Figures shown cover persons 3 years old and over; (1) Metropolitan Statistical Area - see Appendix A for areas included
Source: Census 2000, Summary File 3

School Enrollment by Race

Area	Grades KG to 8 (%)				Grades 9 to 12 (%)			
	White	Black	Asian	Hisp.[1]	White	Black	Asian	Hisp.[1]
City	82.4	1.3	5.1	16.4	80.8	2.2	5.1	14.1
MSA[2]	63.9	2.0	4.0	42.5	61.6	2.2	5.2	42.2
U.S.	68.5	15.5	3.3	16.8	68.8	15.5	3.8	15.7

Note: Figures shown cover persons 3 years old and over; (1) people of Hispanic origin can be of any race; (2) Metropolitan Statistical Area - see Appendix A for areas included
Source: Census 2000, Summary File 3

Average Salaries of Public School Teachers

District	2004-05 Dollars	2004-05 Rank[1]	2005-06 Dollars	2005-06 Rank[1]	Percent Change 2004-05 to 2005-06
CALIFORNIA	57,876	2	59,345	3	2.54
U.S. Average	47,674	-	49,109	-	3.01

Note: (1) State rank ranges from 1 to 51.
Source: National Education Association, Rankings & Estimates: Rankings of the States 2005 and Estimates of School Statistics 2006, November 2006

Higher Education

Four-Year Colleges			Two-Year Colleges			Medical Schools[1]	Law Schools[2]	Voc/ Tech[3]
Public	Private Non-profit	Private For-profit	Public	Private Non-profit	Private For-profit			
0	0	0	0	0	0	0	0	0

Note: Figures cover institutions located within the city limits; (1) includes schools accredited by the Liaison Committee on Medical Education and the American Osteopathic Association; (2) includes American Bar Association-accredited law schools; (3) includes all schools with programs that are less than 2 years
Source: National Center for Education Statistics, The Integrated Postsecondary Education System (IPEDS) Peer Analysis System, 2006; www.usnews.com, America's Best Graduate Schools 2008, Medical School Directory; www.usnews.com, America's Best Graduate Schools 2008, Law School Directory

PRESIDENTIAL ELECTION

2004 Presidential Election Results

Area	Bush	Kerry	Nader	Other
Ventura County	51.2	47.5	0.1	1.2
U.S.	50.7	48.3	0.4	0.6

Note: Results are percentages and may not add to 100% due to rounding
Source: Dave Leip's Atlas of U.S. Presidential Elections, www.uselectionatlas.org

MAJOR EMPLOYERS

Major Employers

Company Name	Industry	Type of Site
Amgen Inc	Biological products, except diagnostic	Headquarters
Weathersfield Elementary School	Elementary and secondary schools	Single
Baxter Biotech	Drugs, proprietaries, and sundries	Branch
Verizon	Engineering services	Branch
Community Memorial Hospital	General medical and surgical hospitals	Headquarters
Medical Center	Individual and family services	Branch
County of Ventura	Executive offices	Headquarters
Sheriffs Office	Police protection	Branch
Ventura County Medical Center	Administration of public health programs	Branch
Central Purchasing LLC	Hardware stores	Branch
Camarillo State Hospital	Psychiatric hospitals	Branch
Harbor Freight Tools	Catalog and mail-order houses	Headquarters
Technicolor Thomson Group	Household audio and video equipment	Branch
Kavlico Corporation	Process control instruments	Branch
Slashpoint Share Drive	Current-carrying wiring devices	Single

Note: Companies shown are located within the metropolitan area and have 1,000 or more employees; nec = not elsewhere classified.
Source: www.zapdata.com, January 2007

PUBLIC SAFETY

Crime Rate

Area	All Crimes	Violent Crimes				Property Crimes		
		Murder	Forcible Rape	Robbery	Aggrav. Assault	Burglary	Larceny -Theft	Motor Vehicle Theft
City	1,555.4	1.6	10.3	44.5	81.8	301.1	1,024.0	92.1
Suburbs[1]	2,488.8	4.4	19.6	99.4	158.5	501.2	1,429.2	276.5
Metro[2]	2,342.5	4.0	18.2	90.8	146.5	469.9	1,365.6	247.6
U.S.	3,899.0	5.6	31.7	140.7	291.1	726.7	2,286.3	416.7

Note: Figures are crimes per 100,000 population; (1) All areas within the metro area that are located outside the city limits; (2) Metropolitan Statistical Area - see Appendix B for areas included
Source: FBI Uniform Crime Reports, 2005

Hate Crimes

Area	Number of Quarters Reported	Bias Motivation				
		Race	Religion	Sexual Orientation	Ethnicity	Disability
City	4	2	2	2	1	0

Source: Federal Bureau of Investigation, Hate Crime Statistics 2005

RECREATION

Culture

Dance[1]	Theatre[1]	Instrumental Music[1]	Vocal Music[1]	Series/ Festivals	Museums	Zoos
0	0	2	0	3	2	0

Note: (1) number of professional perfoming groups
Source: The Grey House Performing Arts Directory, 2007; Official Museum Directory, 2007

Professional Sports Teams

Major League Baseball	National Basketball Association	National Football League	National Hockey League	Major League Soccer	Women's National Basketball Association
2	2	0	2	2	1

Note: Includes teams located in the Los Angeles-Anaheim metro area.
Source: www.sportsvenues.com, Listing of Venues by State/Province and City, 2006

MEDIA

Newspapers

Name	Target Audience	Frequency	Circulation

No newspapers listed.

Note: Includes newspapers whose offices are located in the city and whose circulations are 500 or more
Source: BurrellesLuce, MediaContacts Online, January 2006

Television Stations

Name	Ch.	Network(s)	Type	Ownership
KCBS	2	CBS	Commercial	CBS
KNBC	4	NBC	Commercial	General Electric Corporation
KTLA	5	WBN	Commercial	Tribune Broadcasting Company
KABC	7	ABC	Commercial	ABC Inc.
KCAL	9	CBS	Commercial	Viacom International Inc.
KTTV	11	Fox	Commercial	Fox Television Stations Inc.
KCOP	13	UPN	Commercial	Fox Television Stations Inc.
KSCI	18	n/a	Commercial	International Media Group
KWHY	22	Telemundo	Commercial	Telemundo Group Inc.
KVCR	24	PBS	Public	San Bernardino Community College District
KCET	28	PBS	Public	Community Television of Southern California
KPXN	30	Pax	Commercial	Paxson Communications Corporation
KVMD	31	APT	Commercial	n/a
KNET	38	n/a	Commercial	Venture Technology Group LLC.
KFTR	46	n/a	Commercial	Univision Communications Inc.
KOCE	50	PBS	Public	Coast Community College District
KVEA	52	Telemundo	Commercial	Telemundo Group Inc.
KDOC	56	n/a	Commercial	Golden Orange Broadcasting Company Inc.
KJLA	57	n/a	Commercial	Costa de Oro Television
KLCS	58	PBS	Public	Los Angeles Unified School District
KRCA	62	n/a	Commercial	Liberman Broadcasting
KADY	63	UPN	Commercial	Biltmore Broadcasting
KHIZ	64	n/a	Commercial	Sunbelt Broadcasting Company
KNLA	68	UPN	Non-comm.	Venture Technology Group LLC.

Note: Stations included cover the Los Angeles DMA (Designated Market Area)
BurrellesLuce, MediaContacts Online, January 2006

Major AM Radio Stations

Call Letters	Freq. (kHz)	Station Type	Target Audience	Station Format	Music Format
KLAC	570	Commercial	General	Sports/Talk	n/a
KAVL	610	Commercial	General	News/Sports/Talk	n/a
KFI	640	n/a	General	Music/News/Talk	n/a
KIRN	670	Commercial	Ethnic	Music/News/Talk	International
KDIS	710	Commercial	Children	Music/News	Top 40
KBRT	740	n/a	General/Religious	Talk	n/a
KABC	790	n/a	General	Music/News/Talk	n/a
KRLA	870	n/a	General	Talk	n/a
KOXR	910	n/a	Hispanic	News/Sports/Talk	n/a
KKHJ	930	Commercial	General/Hispanic	Music	Latin
KIXW	960	n/a	Hispanic	Talk	n/a
KFWB	980	Commercial	General	News/Sports	n/a
KTNQ	1020	n/a	Hispanic	News/Sports	n/a
KNX	1070	Commercial	General	News/Sports	n/a
KSPN	1110	Public	General	Music/Sports	Classical
KXTA	1150	Commercial	General	Sports/Talk	n/a
KXMX	1190	n/a	Hispanic	Music/Talk	n/a
KSUR	1260	n/a	General	Music	n/a
KKDD	1290	Commercial	Children	Educational/Music	Easy Listening
KAZN	1300	Commercial	Asian	Ed/Music/News/Sports/Talk	Easy Listening
KWKW	1330	n/a	Hispanic	Sports/Talk	n/a
KWRM	1370	Commercial	Hispanic	Ed/Music/News/Sports	Latin
KLTX	1390	Commercial	Christian/Gen/Hisp	Music/Talk	Latin
KCAL	1410	n/a	General/Hispanic	Music	n/a
KTYM	1460	Commercial	Black/General/Rel	Music/Talk	Gospel
KUTY	1470	Commercial	General/Hispanic	Music/News/Sports	Latin
KWIZ	1480	n/a	Asian	Music/News/Talk	n/a
KMZT	1510	n/a	General	Music	n/a
KVTA	1520	n/a	Hispanic	n/a	n/a
KHPY	1530	Commercial	General	Music	Oldies
KMPC	1540	Commercial	General/Men	Sports/Talk	n/a
KPRO	1570	Commercial	General/Religious	Music/Talk	Gospel
KMNY	1600	Commercial	Asian	Educational/News/Talk	n/a

Note: Stations included cover the Los Angeles DMA (Designated Market Area); n/a not available
Source: BurrellesLuce, MediaContacts Online, January 2006

Major FM Radio Stations

Call Letters	Freq. (mHz)	Station Type	Target Audience	Station Format	Music Format
KPFK	90.7	Non-Comm	General/Hispanic	Educational/Music	World Music
KCBS	93.1	Commercial	General	Music/News/Talk	Classic Rock
KFRG	95.1	n/a	General	Music/News/Talk	n/a
KLOS	95.5	n/a	General	Music/News/Talk	n/a
KXOL	96.3	n/a	General/Hispanic	n/a	n/a
KLSX	97.1	Commercial	General	Music/Sports/Talk	Classical
KSSE	97.5	Commercial	General/Hispanic	Music	Top 40
KLAX	97.9	n/a	General/Hispanic	Music/News/Talk	n/a
KYSR	98.7	n/a	General	Music/Talk	n/a
KKBT	100.3	Commercial	Black	Music/News/Talk	Urban Contemp.
KRTH	101.1	n/a	General	Music/News	n/a
KBIG	104.3	Commercial	General	Music	Adult Contemp.
KCAQ	104.7	n/a	General	Music	n/a
KPWR	105.9	n/a	General	Music/News/Talk	n/a

Note: Stations included cover the Los Angeles DMA (Designated Market Area); n/a not available
BurrellesLuce, MediaContacts Online, January 2006

CLIMATE

Average and Extreme Temperatures

Temperature	Jan	Feb	Mar	Apr	May	Jun	Jul	Aug	Sep	Oct	Nov	Dec	Yr.
Extreme High (°F)	88	92	95	102	97	104	97	98	110	106	101	94	110
Average High (°F)	65	66	65	67	69	72	75	76	76	74	71	66	70
Average Temp. (°F)	56	57	58	60	63	66	69	70	70	67	62	57	63
Average Low (°F)	47	49	50	53	56	59	63	64	63	59	52	48	55
Extreme Low (°F)	27	34	37	43	45	48	52	51	47	43	38	32	27

Note: Figures cover the years 1947-1990
Source: National Climatic Data Center, International Station Meteorological Climate Summary, 9/96

Average Precipitation/Snowfall/Humidity

Precip./Humidity	Jan	Feb	Mar	Apr	May	Jun	Jul	Aug	Sep	Oct	Nov	Dec	Yr.
Avg. Precip. (in.)	2.6	2.3	1.8	0.8	0.1	Tr	Tr	0.1	0.2	0.3	1.5	1.5	11.3
Avg. Snowfall (in.)	Tr	0	0	0	0	0	0	0	0	0	0	0	Tr
Avg. Rel. Hum. 7am (%)	69	72	76	76	77	80	80	81	80	76	69	67	75
Avg. Rel. Hum. 4pm (%)	60	62	64	64	66	67	67	68	67	66	61	60	64

Note: Figures cover the years 1947-1990; Tr = Trace amounts (<0.05 in. of rain; <0.5 in. of snow)
Source: National Climatic Data Center, International Station Meteorological Climate Summary, 9/96

Weather Conditions

Temperature			Daytime Sky			Precipitation		
10°F & below	32°F & below	90°F & above	Clear	Partly cloudy	Cloudy	0.01 inch or more precip.	0.1 inch or more snow/ice	Thunder-storms
0	< 1	5	131	125	109	34	0	1

Note: Figures are average number of days per year and cover the years 1947-1990
Source: National Climatic Data Center, International Station Meteorological Climate Summary, 9/96

HAZARDOUS WASTE

Superfund Sites

Thousand Oaks has no sites on the EPA's Superfund Final National Priorities List.
U.S. Environmental Protection Agency, Final National Priorities List, March 20, 2007

AIR & WATER QUALITY

Air Quality Index

Area	Percent of Days when Air Quality was...[2]				AQI Statistics	
	Good	Moderate	Unhealthy for Sensitive Groups	Unhealthy	Maximum	Median
MSA[1]	54.2	42.2	3.6	0.0	140	49

Note: The Air Quality Index (AQI) is an index for reporting daily air quality. EPA calculates the AQI for five major air pollutants regulated by the Clean Air Act: ground-level ozone, particle pollution (also known as particulate matter), carbon monoxide, sulfur dioxide, and nitrogen dioxide. The AQI runs from 0 to 500. The higher the AQI value, the greater the level of air pollution and the greater the health concern. There are six AQI categories: "Good" The AQI is between 0 and 50. Air quality is considered satisfactory; "Moderate" The AQI is between 51 and 100. Air quality is acceptable; "Unhealthy for Sensitive Groups" When AQI values are between 101 and 150, members of sensitive groups may experience health effects; "Unhealthy" When AQI values are between 151 and 200 everyone may begin to experience health effects; "Very Unhealthy" AQI values between 201 and 300 trigger a health alert; "Hazardous" AQI values over 300 trigger health warnings of emergency conditions; (1) Metropolitan Statistical Area - see Appendix A for areas included; (2) Based on 365 days with AQI data in 2005.
Source: U.S. Environmental Protection Agency, Air Quality Index Report, 2005

Air Quality Index Pollutants

Area	Percent of Days when AQI Pollutant was...[2]					
	Carbon Monoxide	Nitrogen Dioxide	Ozone	Sulfur Dioxide	Particulate Matter 2.5	Particulate Matter 10
MSA[1]	0.0	0.0	59.5	0.0	40.3	0.3

Note: The Air Quality Index (AQI) is an index for reporting daily air quality. EPA calculates the AQI for five major air pollutants regulated by the Clean Air Act: ground-level ozone, particle pollution (also known as particulate matter), carbon monoxide, sulfur dioxide, and nitrogen dioxide. The AQI runs from 0 to 500. The higher the AQI value, the greater the level of air pollution and the greater the health concern; (1) Metropolitan Statistical Area - see Appendix A for areas included; (2) Based on 365 days with AQI data in 2005.
Source: U.S. Environmental Protection Agency, Air Quality Index Report, 2005

Number of Days with Air Quality Index Values Greater than 100

Area	Trend Sites (16)								All Sites (38)
	1998	1999	2000	2001	2002	2003	2004	2005	2005
MSA[1]	29	24	31	24	10	22	13	11	12

Note: An AQI value greater than 100 indicates that air quality would have been in the unhealthful range on that day. Data from exceptional events are not included. These counts are presented in two ways. First, the counts are based on sites having an adequate record of monitoring data during the trend period (trend sites). These counts represent the relative change in the number of days with AQI values greater than 100. In the last column, the counts are based on all sites with data in the most recent year (because it is possible for a site to have data in the most recent year but not enough data to be a trend site); (1) Metropolitan Statistical Area - see Appendix A for areas included; n/a not available.
Source: U.S. Environmental Protection Agency, Air Trends Fact Book 2005

Maximum Pollutant Concentrations

	Particulate Matter 10 (ug/m^3)	Particulate Matter 2.5 (ug/m^3)	Ozone 1-hour (ppm)	Carbon Monoxide (ppm)	Sulfur Dioxide (ppm)	Nitrogen Dioxide (ppm)	Lead (ug/m^3)
MSA[1] Level	49	26	0.112	n/a	n/a	0.015	n/a
NAAQS[2]	150	65	0.125	9	0.140	0.053	1.50
Met NAAQS[2]	Yes	Yes	Yes	n/a	n/a	Yes	n/a

Note: Data from exceptional events are not included; (1) Metropolitan Statistical Area - see Appendix A for areas included; (2) National Ambient Air Quality Standards; n/a not available
Units: ppm = parts per million; ug/m^3 = micrograms per cubic meter
Source: U.S. Environmental Protection Agency, Air Trends Fact Book 2005

Watershed Health

The U.S. Environmental Protection Agency monitors the health of the aquatic resources for the nation's 2,000+ watersheds. **The Calleguas watershed serves the Thousand Oaks area and received an overall Index of Watershed Indicators (IWI) score of n/a (insufficient data).** The IWI score is based on seven condition and nine vulnerability indicators. The overall IWI score ranges from 1 (best health) to 6 (worst health). The Condition Indicators include: designated use attainment, fish and wildlife consumption advisories, source water condition, contaminated sediments, ambient water quality, and wetlands loss index. The Vulnerability Indicators include: aquatic species at risk, conventional and toxic loads over permitted limits, urban and agricultural runoff potential, population change, hydrologic modification, estuarine pollution susceptibility, and air deposition. *Note: The IWI is no longer being updated by the U.S. EPA. Source: U.S. Environmental Protection Agency, Index of Watershed Indicators, October 26, 2001*

Drinking Water

Water System Name	Pop. Served	Primary Water Source Type	Number of Violations in 2006[a]		
			Health Based	Significant Monitoring	Monitoring
Thousand Oaks Water Dept.	50,000	Purchased surface	None	None	None

Note: (a) Based on violation data from January 1, 2006 to December 31, 2006
Source: U.S. Environmental Protection Agency, Office of Ground Water and Drinking Water, Safe Drinking Water Information System (data extracted April 12, 2007)

Thousand Oaks tap water is not available.
Editor & Publisher Market Guide, 2005

Tucson, Arizona

Background

Tucson lies in a high desert valley which was once the floor of an ancient inland sea. Its name derives from the Papago tribes' term for the ancient settlement, Stukshon, which in Spanish is Tuquison. It is believed that the Spanish Jesuit Eusebio Francesco Kino, who established the San Xavier Mission, was the first European to visit the area in 1700. Spanish prospectors who came after Father Kino were driven out by the native tribes trying to protect their territory.

Tucson came under Mexican jurisdiction in 1821, when Mexico was no longer ruled by Spain. In 1853 Mexico sold the area to the U.S. and soon after, overland stage service from San Antonio was instituted.

The Civil War interrupted travel along this route to California. After the war, Tucson continued as a supply and distribution point, first for the army and then for miners. From 1867 to 1877, it was the capital of the territory.

Tucson grew slowly until World War II when it became more industrialized. Today, the city is both an industrial center and a health resort. Aircraft and missile manufacturing, as well as electronics research comprise Tucson's chief economic components. Tourism and retailing continue to dominate industry in the city, which, despite its increased industrialization, has not lost touch with its Native American and Mexican roots.

The city is currently engaged in the Livable Tucson Vision Program to improve the public transport system, promote safer neighborhoods, reduce poverty, establish more parks and recreational spaces within the city, and protect the natural desert environment.

Tucson has also instituted a Workforce Development program to attain a more productive, competitive edge in the twenty-first century economic environment. Reflecting this goal are budget allocations for neighborhood youth employment and quality job training. Also included in the city's fiscal budget are funds for business loans, downtown revitalization, and historical preservation.

Recreation in Tucson revolves around the breathtaking natural beauty of it surroundings. Its attractions include the Arizona-Sonoran Desert Museum — 21 acres of wild desert inhabited by over 300 animal species and 1,300 types of plants — and Kitt Peak Observatory, crowning a 6,882-foot mountain, where visitors can take advantage of 19 optical telescopes and two radio telescopes, along with exhibits and tours. Saguaro National Park is a 91,000-acre park featuring one of the world's largest saguaro, or tall cactus, stands. Mount Lemmon, over 9,000 feet high, offers hiking, camping, picnicking, and skiing. The Biosphere 2 was located nearby, where eight people attempted to live for two years in its glass-enclosed, airtight environment. The area is now slated to be redeveloped for a planned community.

Tucson is the only U.S. city to provide a Spring Training venue for three major league baseball teams: the Arizona Diamondbacks, the Chicago White Sox, and the Colorado Rockies. Tucson Electric Park, a state-of-the-art stadium, is home to the Sidewinders and White Sox. The city is a major golf area, with bountiful golf courses enhanced by spectacular scenery.

The college scene in Tucson includes the University of Arizona, one of the top research universities in the U.S., with 37,000 national and international students; and Pima Community College, serving 72,000 students on six campuses with occupational and special interest courses.

Nightlife in Tucson abounds with music of all kinds-blues, jazz, country, folk, Latino, and reggae. Dine on Cajun food in a casual atmosphere at the French Quarter restaurant, or try the tortilla soup at the Eclectic Cafe. Whatever your taste — Japanese, Southwestern, or Italian — Tucson is sure to accommodate.

The region is known for its nearly perfect climate. Surrounded by four mountain ranges, Tucson has much sunshine, dry air, and rich desert vegetation.

Rankings

General Rankings

■ Tucson was ranked #70 out of 331 metro areas in *Cities Ranked & Rated*. Criteria: cost of living; climate; crime; transportation; economy and jobs; education; arts and culture; health and healthcare; leisure. *Cities Ranked & Rated, 1st Edition, 2004*

■ The Tucson metro area was selected as one of "America's Best Places to Live and Work" by *Employment Review*. The area ranked #16 out of 20. Criteria: unemployment rate; projected job growth; cost of living; and industry specific data. *Employment Review, www.bestjobsusa.com, 2003*

■ The Tucson area was selected as one of "60 Cheap Places to Live" in the U.S. The area appeared in the "Steroid Cities" (fast-growing, business-friendly metro areas) category. *Forbes.com, August 20, 2004*

Business/Finance Rankings

■ Tucson was selected as one of the best places to start and grow a company by *Entrepreneur* and the National Policy Research Council. The Tucson metro area ranked #5 out of 63 mid-size metro areas. Criteria: business formation and growth (firms started four to 14 years ago that still employ at least 5 people and experienced rapid growth over the last four years). *Entrepreneur/National Policy Research Council, "Hot Cities for Entrepreneurs," September 2006*

■ Intel, in partnership with Sperling's BestPlaces, ranked the 80 "Best Cities for Teleworking" in America. The Tucson metro area ranked #24 among mid-sized metro areas. The study identifies cities that hold the greatest potential for teleworking based on a host of factors including typical commuting times, fuel prices, availability of broadband Internet access and percentage of the population in telework friendly jobs. The study also factored in extreme climate and natural hazards. *Intel, "Best Cities for Teleworking," March 30, 2006*

■ The Tucson metro area appeared on the Milken Institute "2005 Best Performing Cities" index. Rank: #14 out of 200 large metro areas. Criteria: job growth; wage and salary growth; high-tech output growth. *Milken Institute, "2005 Best Performing Cities," February 2006*

■ The Tucson metro area was selected as one of "The Best Cities for Doing Business in America." *Inc.* magazine measured employment growth in 393 regions using the following criteria: recent growth trend; mid-term growth; long-term trend; and current year growth. The Tucson metro area ranked #13 among mid-sized metro areas and #60 overall. *Inc., May 2006*

■ Tucson was identified as one of the 100 "Most Unwired Cities" in the U.S. The area ranked #69 out of the 100 largest metro areas in the U.S. Criteria: number of public and commercial wireless access points (hotspots); airports with wireless Internet access; broadband availability; local wireless networks; and wireless email devices. *Intel, "Most Unwired Cities Survey," June 7, 2005*

■ *Forbes* ranked the 200 most populous metro areas in the U.S. in terms of the "Best Places for Business and Careers." The Tucson metro area was ranked #85. Criteria: business costs (labor, energy, tax and office space expenses); living costs (housing, transportation, food and other household expenditures); education levels of the work force; job growth; income growth; migration trends; crime rates; and culture/leisure. *Forbes, April 23, 2007*

■ Tucson was selected as a 2006 Digital Cities Survey winner. The city ranked #3 in the large city (250,000 or more population) category. The survey examined and assessed how city governments are utilizing information technology to operate and deliver quality service to their customers and citizens. Survey questions focused on implementation and adoption of online service delivery; planning and governance; and the infrastructure and architecture that make the transformation to digital government possible. *Center for Digital Government, "2006 Digital Cities Survey"*

■ *Fortune* ranked the 100 largest metro areas in the U.S. in terms of projected median home price change in 2006. The Tucson metro area ranked #61. *Fortune, "The Top 100: Is the Party Over?" December 26, 2005*

Health/Environment Rankings

■ The Tucson metro area appeared in *Country Home's* "2007 Best Green Places Report". The area ranked #55. Criteria included: air and watershed quality; miles of mass transit; green power; number of farmer's markets, organic producers and groceries. *Country Home, "2007 Best Green Places Report," April 2007*

■ The American Podiatric Medical Association and *Prevention* magazine ranked America's 100 most populated cities based on fitness-walker friendliness. The best cities have safe streets, beautiful places to walk, mild weather and good air quality. Tucson ranked #86. *Prevention, "The Best Walking Cities of 2007," April 2007; American Podiatric Medical Association, "2007 Best Fitness-Walking Cities"*

■ Tucson was selected as one of the 25 fittest cities in America by *Men's Fitness Online*. It ranked #4 out of America's 50 largest cities. Criteria: gyms/sporting goods; nutrition; exercise/sports; overweight/sedentary; junk food; alcohol; smoking; television; air and water quality; climate; geography; commute time; parks/open space; recreation facilities; health care; motivation; civic legislation and leadership. *Men's Fitness Online, America's Fittest/Fattest Cities 2006*

■ Tucson was identified as a "2007 Asthma Capital." The area ranked #81 out of the nation's 100 largest metropolitan areas. Twelve factors were used to identify the most challenging places to live for people with asthma: estimated prevalence; self-reported prevalence; crude death rate for asthma; annual pollen score; annual air quality; public smoking laws; number of board-certified asthma specialists; school inhaler access laws; rescue medication use; controller medication use; uninsured rate; poverty rate. *Asthma and Allergy Foundation of America, "2007 Asthma Capitals"*

■ Tucson was identified as a "Spring Allergy Capital." The area ranked #5 out of 100. Three groups of factors were used to identify the most severe cities for people with allergies during the spring season: annual pollen levels; medicine utilization; access to board-certified allergists. *Asthma and Allergy Foundation of America, "2007 Spring Allergy Capital Rankings"*

■ Tucson was identified as a "Fall Allergy Capital." The area ranked #28 out of 100. Three groups of factors were used to identify the most severe cities for people with allergies during the fall season: annual pollen levels; medicine utilization; access to board-certified allergists. *Asthma and Allergy Foundation of America, "2006 Fall Allergy Capital Rankings"*

■ Tucson was selected as one of "America's Healthiest Cities" by *Natural Health* magazine. The city was ranked #30 out of the 50 largest urban areas in the U.S. Twenty-six criteria in the following four categories were examined: whether the city boasts natural offerings; how well the city promotes its residents' physical health; whether the city offers a healthy environment; how well the city fosters a sense of community. *Natural Health, April 2003*

■ *Men's Health* ranked the nation's largest 100 cities in terms of the *Best (and Worst) Cities for Men*. Tucson was ranked #60. Criteria: 24 statistical parameters of long life in the categories of health, quality of life, and fitness. *Men's Health, January/February 2007*

■ *Men's Health* ranked 100 U.S. cities in terms of the quality of their tap water. Tucson was ranked #63 and received a grade of C. Criteria: levels of total coliform bacteria, arsenic, lead, total trihalomethanes (linked to cancer), and halo-acetic acids, plus the number of EPA water-system violations from 1995 to 2005. *Men's Health, March 2007*

■ GlaxoSmithKline, in partnership with Sperling's BestPlaces, analyzed the nation's 100 largest metro areas and identified 25 asthma "hot spots" where high prevalence makes the condition a key issue and environmental triggers and other factors can make living with asthma a particular challenge. The Tucson metro area ranked #1 with #1 being the most challenging place to live. Criteria: asthma prevalence; asthma mortality; pollen scores; number of asthma specialists per capita; ratio of prescriptions for rescue medications to prescriptions for controller medications (an indicator of proper asthma treatment); air pollution; smoking laws; climate; and prevalence of tobacco use. *GlaxoSmithKline, "Asthma Hot Spots," October 29, 2002*

- Ortho-McNeil Neurologics, in partnership with Sperling's BestPlaces, analyzed 110 metro areas and identified those U.S. cities with the highest prevalence of factors that are most commonly associated with migraine headaches. The Tucson metro area ranked #64. Criteria: number of migraine-related drug prescriptions per capita; lifestyle factors that can contribute to migraines; environmental factors that can trigger migraines; and consumption of migraine-triggering foods. *Ortho-McNeil Neurologics, "America's Migraine Hot Spots," March 14, 2006*

- Sperling's BestPlaces ranked 331 metro areas and identified the most and least stressful U.S. cities. The Tucson metro area ranked #30 out of the 100 largest metro areas (#1 = most stressful). Criteria: divorce rate; unemployment rate; violent and property crime; suicide rate; commute time; mental health; alcohol consumption; cloudy days. *www.BestPlaces.net, January 9, 2004*

- Tucson was highlighted as one of the top 25 cleanest metro areas for long-term particle pollution (PM 2.5) in the U.S. The area ranked #5. *American Lung Association, State of the Air 2006*

Women/Minorities Rankings

- Tucson was ranked #42 out of 100 metro areas in *SELF Magazine's* ranking of "America's Best Places for Women." A panel of experts came up with nearly 40 criteria including: drinking and smoking rates; depression; unemployment; parks; crime; disease; healthcare insurance coverage; air quality; and commute times. *SELF Magazine, "America's Best Places for Women 2006," December 2006*

- *Ladies Home Journal* ranked America's 200 largest cities based on the qualities women surveyed care about most. Tucson ranked #14 out of 57 in the big city category (population over 300,000). Criteria: crime; lifestyle; education; jobs; health; child care; politics; and the economy. *Ladies Home Journal Online, "The Best Cities for Women 2002"*

- Tucson was profiled in the book *50 Fabulous Gay-Friendly Places to Live*. Criteria: an active gay community; positive gay health programs; youth outreach; gay-friendly politics; gay-owned and gay-friendly businesses; employment opportunities; fun nightlife; cultural opportunities; recreational opportunities; housing options. *50 Fabulous Gay-Friendly Places to Live, 2005*

- Tucson was selected as one of the "Top 10 Cities for Hispanics to Live In." The city was ranked #7. The cities were selected based on data from the following sources: U.S. Census; *Forbes*; *Fortune*; *Money*; local newspapers; natives and residents; www.bestplaces.net; www.findyourspot.com. *Hispanic Magazine, July/August 2004*

Seniors/Retirement Rankings

- Tucson was profiled in the book *Where to Retire: America's Best and Most Affordable Places*. Cities were selected based on personal visits by the author and interviews with local residents coupled with statistics from various government agencies. *Where to Retire: America's Best and Most Affordable Places, 2006*

- Tucson was identified as one of the "100 Most Popular Places to Retire" by *Where to Retire* magazine. The city ranked #9. Criteria: net retirees received from 1995-2000 (derived by subtracting all outbound retirees from inbound retirees for the county or county group - includes interstate moves only). *Where to Retire, "100 Most Popular Places to Retire," January/February 2007*

- Tucson was profiled in the book *Retire in Style: 60 Outstanding Places Across the USA and Canada*. Criteria: landscape; climate; quality of life; cost of living; transportation; retail services; health care; community services; cultural and educational activities; recreational activities; work and volunteer activities; crime rates and public safety. *Retire in Style: 60 Outstanding Places Across the USA and Canada, 2005*

- Tucson was selected as one of the best places to retire by *Retirement Places Rated*. Criteria: cost of living; climate; personal safety; services; economy. The city was ranked #6 out of 200. *Retirement Places Rated, 6th Edition, 2004*

■ A.G. Edwards ranked America's 500 top-performing communities based on their residents' personal savings and investing behavior. The Tucson metro area ranked #491 with an index score of 94.70 (national average = 100.00). A dozen statistical factors were measured including: participation in retirement savings plans; personal debt levels; and home ownership. *A.G. Edwards, "2006 Nest Egg Index", September 6, 2006*

Children/Family Rankings

■ *Zero Population Growth* ranked 100 cities in terms of children's health, safety, and economic well-being. Tucson was ranked #49 out of 80 Large Cities (remainder of the 100 largest cities in the U.S.) and was given a grade of B. Criteria: total population and population growth; percent of population under 18 years of age; percent of births to teens; infant mortality rate; percent of eligible women not receiving Title X services; contraceptive equity indicator; percent of children without health insurance; percent of city residents over age 25 with a high-school diploma; ration of PopEd (Population Connection's Education Program) teachers trained; sexuality education indicator; proficiency in reading and math; percent of kids living in poverty; percent growth in urbanized land; violent crime rate; recycling. *Population Connection, Kid Friendly Cities: Report Card 2004*

■ *Fit Pregnancy* magazine ranked the 50 best U.S. cities in which to have a baby. Tucson was ranked #25. Criteria: fertility services; maternal and infant health risk; access to hospitals and doctors; safety; affordability; stroller friendliness; and birthing options. *Fit Pregnancy, February/March, 2006*

Safety Rankings

■ Allstate ranked the 200 largest cities in America in terms of driver safety. Tucson ranked #63. In addition, drivers were 0.2% more likely to have had an accident compared to the national average. Allstate researchers analyzed internal Property Damage reported claims over a two-year period (from January 2003 to December 2004) to ensure the findings would not be affected by external influences such as weather or road construction. A weighted average of the two-year numbers determined the annual percentages. The report defines an auto crash as any collision resulting in a property damage claim. *Allstate, "Allstate America's Best Drivers Report 2006," May 24, 2006*

■ *Ladies Home Journal* ranked America's 200 largest cities in terms of safety. Tucson ranked #154 out of 200. Criteria: violent crimes; crimes against property; and rape. *Ladies Home Journal Online, "The Best Cities for Women 2002"*

Sports/Recreation Rankings

■ The Tucson metro area appeared on *The Sporting News* list of the "Best Sports Cities 2006". The area ranked #63 out of 99 cities in North America. To be included in the rankings, a city must have at least one of the following: NCAA Division I basketball team; Class A minor league baseball team; training camp for a major league or NFL team; NASCAR Nextel Cup race; NCAA Division I-A bowl game; PGA Tour tournament; Triple Crown horse race. Once a city qualifies, a 12-month snapshot is taken of the sports atmosphere, putting a heavy premium on regular-season won-lost records; playoff berths, bowl appearances and tournament bids; championships; applicable power ratings; quality of competition; overall fan fervor; sports atmosphere and fan knowledge; abundance of teams (quality over quantity); stadium/arena quality; ticket availability and prices; franchise ownership; and the marquee appeal of athletes. *SportingNews.com, "Best Sports Cities 2006," August 1, 2006*

■ Tucson was selected as one of "10 Great Biking Cities." Editors at the Washington Post asked Adventure Cycling Association, a non-profit bike organization in Montana, and *Bicycling* magazine for their suggestions on the most bike-friendly cities in the country. *Washington Post, October 1, 2006*

■ Tucson was chosen as one of America's best cities for bicycling. The city ranked #2 in the mid-sized city category (population 200,000 to 500,000). Criteria: cycling-friendly statistics (number of bike lanes and routes, number of bike racks, city bike projects completed and planned; bike culture (number of bike commuters, popular clubs, cool cycling events, renowned bike shops); climate/geography (the quality of roads and trails for riding, and how frequently mother nature lets riders enjoy them). *Bicycling, March 2006*

■ *Golf Digest* ranked 330 metro areas in the U.S. in terms of golf. The Tucson metro area was ranked #216. Criteria: access to golf; weather; value of golf; and quality of golf. *Golf Digest, "Metro Golf Rankings," August 2005*

Dating/Romance Rankings

■ The Tucson metro area was selected as one of the "Best Cities for Relocating Singles" by Worldwide ERC and Primacy Relocation. The area ranked #74 out of the 100 largest metro areas in the U.S. Areas were selected based on the following criteria: Population Criteria (local percentage and growth trends of unmarried residents aged 25-34; male-female ratios; the number of newcomers to the area; diversity and density); Economic Criteria (job growth vs. unemployment rates; apartment rental costs; fee and occupancy rates for temporary housing and mini-storage; higher education costs, including in-state and out-of-state tuition requirements; vehicle tax rates and quality of service from utility providers); Quality-of-Life Criteria (level of per capita volunteering; quality and quantity of collegiate and professional sports with fun, fan-friendly venues; number of Starbucks and other coffee shops; quality or popularity of restaurants, nightspots, health clubs, and online dating; moderate climates with sustainable water supplies). *Worldwide ERC and Primacy Relocation, "2006 Best Cities for Relocating Singles," October 11, 2006*

■ Sperling's BestPlaces in partnership with AXE Deodorant Bodyspray ranked 80 metro areas and identified "America's Best (and Worst) Cities for Dating." The Tucson metro area ranked #29. Criteria: percentage of singles ages 18-24; population density; dating venues per capita. *AXE Deodorant Bodyspray, "America's Best (and Worst) Cities for Dating," May, 2004*

Culture/Performing Arts Rankings

■ Scarborough Research, a leading market research firm, identified the top local markets for rock concert attendance. The Tucson DMA (Designated Market Area) ranked in the top 25 with 15% of consumers, 18 years old and over, reporting that they have attended a rock concert during the past year. *Scarborough Research, Scarborough USA+ 2003 Release 2*

Miscellaneous Rankings

■ Tucson was determined to be one of America's smartest cities. The city ranked #27 in the large city category (200,000+ adults 25 years and older). Criteria: the editors rated the collective brainpower of U.S communities based on the educational attainment of its residents. *American City Business Journals, www.bizjournals.com, June 12, 2006*

■ Tucson was identified as one of North America's most accommodating cities for travelers with pets. The city was ranked #10. Criteria: number of AAA Approved and Diamond rated pet-friendly hotels. *AAA, Traveling with your Pet: The AAA PetBook, 2006*

■ Tucson was selected as one of the "Top 100 Sweatiest Summer Cities". The city was ranked #24. The ranking was based on the average male/female height/weight, average high temperature, and average relative humidity levels for 2002 in each of the cities during June, July and August. The sweat level was analyzed based on the assumption that the individual was walking for one hour. *Procter & Gamble, Old Spice, June 18, 2003*

■ Tucson appeared on ApartmentRatings.com "Top Cities for Renters List 2006". The area ranked #94 out of 138. Criteria: renter satisfaction; affordability; and vacancy. *ApartmentRatings.com, "Top Cities for Renters List 2006"*

■ Sperling's BestPlaces in partnership with Pep Boys ranked 77 metro areas and identified "America's Most Drivable Cities." The Tucson metro area ranked #18. Criteria: climate; road roughness; urban mobility; gas prices. *Pep Boys, "America's Most Drivable Cities," April 9, 2003*

■ Tucson was selected as one of "America's Most Literate Cities." The city ranked #36 out of the 70 largest U.S. cities. Criteria: number of booksellers; library resources; Internet resources; educational attainment; periodical publishing resources; newspaper circulation. *Central Connecticut State University, "America's Most Literate Cities 2006"*

Business Environment

CITY FINANCES

City Government Finances

Component	2003-2004 ($000)	2003-2004 ($ per capita)
Total Revenues	846,900	1,683
Total Expenditures	807,215	1,604
Debt Outstanding	1,057,305	2,101
Cash and Securities	776,413	1,543

Source: U.S Census Bureau, Government Finances 2003-2004

City Government Revenue by Source

Source	2003-2004 ($000)	2003-2004 ($ per capita)
General Revenue		
From Federal Government	75,140	149
From State Government	146,402	291
From Local Governments	12,285	24
Taxes		
Property	48,385	96
Sales	207,945	413
Personal Income	0	0
License	0	0
Charges	95,762	190
Liquor Store	0	0
Utility	118,390	235
Employee Retirement	88,183	175
Other	54,408	108

Source: U.S Census Bureau, Government Finances 2003-2004

City Government Expenditures by Function

Function	2003-2004 ($000)	2003-2004 ($ per capita)	2003-2004 (%)
General Expenditures			
Airports	57,238	114	7.1
Corrections	0	0	0.0
Education	0	0	0.0
Fire Protection	46,396	92	5.7
Governmental Administration	58,469	116	7.2
Health	0	0	0.0
Highways	48,127	96	6.0
Hospitals	0	0	0.0
Housing and Community Development	56,269	112	7.0
Interest on General Debt	43,085	86	5.3
Libraries	18,578	37	2.3
Parking	0	0	0.0
Parks and Recreation	59,738	119	7.4
Police Protection	110,782	220	13.7
Public Welfare	0	0	0.0
Sewerage	0	0	0.0
Solid Waste Management	28,466	57	3.5
Liquor Store	0	0	0.0
Utility	187,634	373	23.2
Employee Retirement	31,872	63	3.9
Other	60,561	120	7.5

Source: U.S Census Bureau, Government Finances 2003-2004

Municipal Bond Ratings

Area	Moody's
City	Aaa

Source: Mergent Bond Record, January 2007 (unless noted otherwise)

DEMOGRAPHICS

Population Growth

Area	1990 Census	2000 Census	2006 Estimate	2011 Projection	Population Growth (%) 1990-2000	Population Growth (%) 2000-2011
City	417,942	486,699	523,861	563,293	16.5	15.7
MSA[1]	666,880	843,746	938,260	1,028,841	26.5	21.9
U.S.	248,709,873	281,421,906	298,021,266	312,383,955	13.2	11.0

Note: (1) Metropolitan Statistical Area - see Appendix B for areas included
Source: Claritas, Inc.

Number of Households and Average Household Size

Area	2006 Estimate	2006 Average Household Size
City	208,565	2.51
MSA[1]	371,240	2.53
U.S.	112,267,302	2.65

Note: (1) Metropolitan Statistical Area - see Appendix B for areas included
Source: Claritas, Inc.

Race and Ethnicity

Area	White Alone[2]	Black Alone[2]	Asian Alone[2]	Other Race Alone[2]	Hispanic[3]
City	67.2	4.5	2.7	25.6	39.6
MSA[1]	72.9	3.1	2.3	21.7	32.4
U.S.	73.3	12.4	4.2	10.1	14.5

Note: Figures are 2006 estimates; (1) Metropolitan Statistical Area - see Appendix B for areas included
(2) Alone is defined as not being in combination with one or more other races; (3) May be of any race.
Source: Claritas, Inc.

Segregation

City		MSA[1]	
Index[2]	Rank[3]	Index[2]	Rank[4]
35.0	93	44.2	277

Note: Figures are based on an analysis of Census 2000 data; (1) Metropolitan Statistical Area - see Appendix A
for areas included; (2) White/Black Dissimilarity Index—the most commonly used measure of segregation
between two groups, reflecting their relative distributions across neighborhoods within a city or metropolitan
area. It can range in value from 0, indicating complete integration, to 100, indicating complete segregation; (3)
Ranges from 1 (most segregated) to 100 (least segregated) and includes all the cities in this book; (4) Ranges
from 1 (most segregated) to 318 (least segregated) and includes 318 metropolitan areas.
Source: www.CensusScope.org

Ancestry

Area	German	Irish[2]	English	American	Italian	Polish	French[3]	Scottish
City	14.4	9.7	8.3	3.7	4.0	2.3	2.7	1.9
MSA[1]	16.2	10.6	10.3	4.1	4.4	2.5	3.1	2.3
U.S.	15.2	10.9	8.7	7.3	5.6	3.2	3.0	1.7

Note: Figures include multiple ancestry (e.g. if a person reported being Irish and Italian, they were included in
both columns); (1) Metropolitan Statistical Area - see Appendix A for areas included; (2) Includes Celtic; (3)
Includes Alsatian but excludes Basque
Source: Census 2000, Summary File 3

Foreign-Born Population

Area	Percent of Population Born in Any Foreign Country	Europe	Asia	Africa	Oceania[2]	Canada	Mexico	Latin America[3]
City	14.3	1.4	2.0	0.2	0.1	0.3	9.6	0.7
MSA[1]	11.9	1.5	1.7	0.2	0.1	0.5	7.4	0.6
U.S.	11.1	1.7	2.9	0.3	0.1	0.3	3.3	2.5

Note: (1) Metropolitan Statistical Area - see Appendix A for areas included; (2) Includes Australia, New
Zealand subregion, Melanesia, Micronesia, Polynesia, and Oceania n.e.c; (3) Includes Central America
(excluding Mexico), South America, and the Caribbean.
Source: Census 2000, Summary File 3

Marriage Status

Area	Never Married	Now Married (excluding Separated)	Separated	Widowed	Divorced
City	33.0	45.3	2.0	6.5	13.2
MSA[1]	27.8	52.0	1.6	6.6	12.0
U.S.	27.1	54.4	2.2	6.6	9.7

Note: Figures are percentages and cover the population 15 years of age and older;
(1) Metropolitan Statistical Area - see Appendix A for areas included
Source: Census 2000, Summary File 3

Age Distribution

Area	Percent of Population						
	Under Age 5	Age 5 to 17	Age 18 to 34	Age 35 to 49	Age 50 to 64	Age 65 to 79	80 Years and Over
City	7.1	17.3	29.4	21.7	12.5	8.7	3.3
MSA[1]	6.5	18.0	24.2	22.3	14.8	10.6	3.6
U.S.	6.8	18.9	23.7	23.5	14.8	9.2	3.2

Note: (1) Metropolitan Statistical Area - see Appendix A for areas included
Source: Census 2000, Summary File 3

Male/Female Ratio

Area	Males	Females	Males per 100 Females
City	257,383	266,478	96.6
MSA[1]	459,507	478,753	96.0
U.S.	146,712,712	151,308,554	97.0

Note: Figures are 2006 estimates; (1) Metropolitan Statistical Area -
see Appendix B for areas included
Source: Claritas, Inc.

Religion

Area	Catholic	Southern Baptist	United Methodist	ELCA[1]	LDS[2]	Presbyterian Church USA	Jewish Est.	Muslim Est.
County	26.7	2.7	1.1	1.3	2.0	1.1	2.4	0.1
U.S.	22.0	7.1	3.7	1.8	1.5	1.1	2.2	0.6

Note: Figures are the number of adherents as a percentage of the total population; Adherents are defined as all
members, including full members, their children and the estimated number of other participants who are not
considered members (e.g. the baptized, those not confirmed, those regularly attending services, etc.);
(1) Evangelical Lutheran Church in America; (2) The Church of Jesus Christ of Latter Day Saints
Source: Reprinted with permission from Religious Congregations and Membership in the United States 2000
(Nashville, Glenmary Research Center, 2002) Copyright Association of Statisticians of American Religious
Bodies. All rights reserved.

ECONOMY

Gross Metropolitan Product

Area	2002	2003	2004	2005	2005 Rank[2]
MSA[1]	25.7	27.1	28.7	31.1	67

Note: Figures are in billions of dollars; (1) Tucson, AZ Metropolitan Statistical Area - see Appendix A for areas
included; (2) Rank ranges from 1 to 361
Source: The U.S. Conference of Mayors, "U.S. Metro Economies: GMP - The Engines of America's Growth,"
January 2007

Economic Growth

Area	1995 GMP	2005 GMP	Average Annual Growth Rate	Growth Rate Rank[2]
MSA[1]	17.7	31.1	5.8	134

Note: Figures are in billions of dollars; GMP = Gross Metropolitan Product; (1) Tucson, AZ Metropolitan
Statistical Area - see Appendix A for areas included; (2) Rank ranges from 1 to 361
Source: The U.S. Conference of Mayors, "U.S. Metro Economies: GMP - The Engines of America's Growth,"
January 2007

INCOME

Per Capita/Median/Average Income

Area	Per Capita ($)	Median Household ($)	Average Household ($)
City	18,652	35,155	45,908
MSA[1]	23,261	43,083	58,109
U.S.	25,129	48,775	65,849

Note: Figures are 2006 estimates; (1) Metropolitan Statistical Area - see Appendix B for areas included
Source: Claritas, Inc.

Household Income Distribution

Area	Percent of Households Earning							
	Under $15,000	$15,000 -24,999	$25,000 -34,999	$35,000 -49,999	$50,000 -74,999	$75,000 -99,000	$100,000 -149,999	$150,000 and up
City	18.8	15.7	15.3	17.8	16.8	7.7	5.6	2.3
MSA[1]	14.6	13.0	13.2	17.1	18.7	10.0	8.7	4.7
U.S.	13.3	11.0	11.3	15.7	19.5	11.8	11.0	6.4

Note: Figures are 2006 estimates; (1) Metropolitan Statistical Area - see Appendix B for areas included
Source: Claritas, Inc.

Poverty Rates by Age

Area	All Ages	Under 5 Years Old	5 to 17 Years Old	18 to 64 Years Old	65 Years and Over
City	18.4	1.9	4.1	11.1	1.3
MSA[1]	14.7	1.4	3.5	8.6	1.2
U.S.	12.4	1.2	3.0	6.9	1.2

Note: Figures are percent of population with income in 1999 below poverty level and only include population
for whom poverty status is determined; (1) Metropolitan Statistical Area - see Appendix A for areas included
Source: Census 2000, Summary File 3

Personal Bankruptcy Filing Rate

Area	2003	2004	2005
Pima County	5.14	4.75	6.24
U.S.	5.57	5.31	6.88

Note: Numbers are per 1,000 population and include Chapter 7 and Chapter 13 filings
Source: Federal Deposit Insurance Corporation (FDIC), Regional Economic Conditions (RECON), 3/24/2006

EMPLOYMENT

Labor Force and Employment

Area	Civilian Labor Force			Workers Employed		
	Dec. 2005	Dec. 2006	% Chg.	Dec. 2005	Dec. 2006	% Chg.
City	256,757	268,293	4.5	244,879	257,222	5.0
MSA[1]	441,211	461,264	4.5	422,728	444,036	5.0
U.S.	149,874,000	152,571,000	1.8	142,918,000	146,081,000	2.2

Note: Data is not seasonally adjusted and covers workers 16 years of age and older;
(1) Metropolitan Statistical Area - see Appendix B for areas included
Source: Bureau of Labor Statistics, http://stats.bls.gov

Unemployment Rate

Area	2006											
	Jan.	Feb.	Mar.	Apr.	May	Jun.	Jul.	Aug.	Sep.	Oct.	Nov.	Dec.
City	5.6	4.9	4.4	4.5	4.1	5.1	5.3	4.0	4.3	4.3	4.2	4.1
MSA[1]	5.1	4.4	4.0	4.0	3.7	4.6	4.8	3.6	3.9	3.9	3.8	3.7
U.S.	5.1	5.1	4.8	4.5	4.4	4.8	5.0	4.6	4.4	4.1	4.3	4.3

Note: Data is not seasonally adjusted and covers workers 16 years of age and older; All figures are
percentages; (1) Metropolitan Statistical Area - see Appendix B for areas included
Source: Bureau of Labor Statistics, http://stats.bls.gov

Employment by Occupation

Occupation Classification	City (%)	MSA[1] (%)	U.S. (%)
Sales and Office	28.2	27.1	26.7
Professional and Related	21.9	23.0	20.2
Service	19.1	17.6	14.9
Production, Transportation, and Material Moving	9.6	9.4	14.6
Management, Business, and Financial	10.1	11.9	13.5
Construction, Extraction, and Maintenance	10.9	10.7	9.4
Farming, Forestry, and Fishing	0.2	0.2	0.7

Note: Figures cover employed civilians 16 years of age and older;
(1) Metropolitan Statistical Area - see Appendix A for areas included
Source: Census 2000, Summary File 3

Employment by Industry

Sector	MSA[1] Number of Employees	MSA[1] Percent of Total	U.S. Percent of Total
Government	80,200	20.5	16.3
Education and Health Services	54,300	13.9	13.2
Professional and Business Services	50,800	13.0	12.9
Retail Trade	45,900	11.7	11.5
Manufacturing	27,900	7.1	10.2
Leisure and Hospitality	42,000	10.7	9.5
Financial Activities	17,800	4.6	6.1
Construction	28,700	7.3	5.5
Wholesale Trade	9,600	2.5	4.3
Other Services	16,200	4.1	3.9
Transportation and Utilities	9,300	2.4	3.7
Information	6,600	1.7	2.2
Natural Resources and Mining	1,700	0.4	0.5

Note: Figures cover non-farm employment as of December 2006 and are not seasonally adjusted;
(1) Metropolitan Statistical Area - see Appendix B for areas included
Source: Bureau of Labor Statistics, http://stats.bls.gov

Occupations with Greatest Projected Employment Growth: 2002 - 2012

Occupation[1]	2002 Employment	2012 Projected Employment	Numeric Employment Change	Percent Employment Change
Cashiers	63,550	85,240	21,690	34.1
Registered Nurses	34,190	54,330	20,140	58.9
Combined Food Preparation and Serving Workers, Including Fast Food	48,950	63,360	14,410	29.4
Retail Salespersons	67,560	81,370	13,810	20.4
Customer Service Representatives	45,870	59,210	13,340	29.1
Carpenters	33,870	44,580	10,710	31.6
Landscaping and Groundskeeping Workers	30,700	39,990	9,290	30.3
Nursing Aides, Orderlies, and Attendants	18,390	27,620	9,230	50.2
Postsecondary Teachers	29,790	38,960	9,170	30.8
Medical Assistants	10,950	19,540	8,590	78.4

Note: Projections cover Arizona; (1) Sorted by numeric employment change
Source: www.projectionscentral.com, State Occupational Projections, 2002-2012 Long-Term Projections

Fastest Growing Occupations: 2002 - 2012

Occupation[1]	2002 Employment	2012 Projected Employment	Numeric Employment Change	Percent Employment Change
Emergency Medical Technicians and Paramedics	1,540	3,220	1,680	109.1
Medical Assistants	10,950	19,540	8,590	78.4
Physician Assistants	2,110	3,740	1,630	77.3
Medical Records and Health Information Technicians	3,000	5,190	2,190	73.0
Respiratory Therapy Technicians	680	1,170	490	72.1
Dental Hygienists	1,680	2,880	1,200	71.4
Respiratory Therapists	1,380	2,350	970	70.3
Dental Assistants	5,280	8,980	3,700	70.1
Home Health Aides	10,390	17,560	7,170	69.0
Physical Therapist Aides	1,490	2,450	960	64.4

Note: Projections cover Arizona; (1) Sorted by percent employment change and excludes occupations with numeric employment change less than 300
Source: www.projectionscentral.com, State Occupational Projections, 2002-2012 Long-Term Projections

Average Wages

Occupation	$/Hr.	Occupation	$/Hr.
Accountants and Auditors	24.24	Maids and Housekeeping Cleaners	8.09
Automotive Mechanics	17.88	Maintenance and Repair Workers	12.75
Bookkeepers	13.58	Marketing Managers	30.00
Carpenters	14.83	Nuclear Medicine Technologists	21.64
Cashiers	8.94	Nurses, Licensed Practical	18.16
Clerks, General Office	11.75	Nurses, Registered	26.29
Clerks, Receptionists/Information	10.30	Nursing Aides/Orderlies/Attendants	10.22
Clerks, Shipping/Receiving	11.36	Packers and Packagers, Hand	7.62
Computer Programmers	27.11	Physical Therapists	31.08
Computer Support Specialists	21.58	Postal Service Mail Carriers	21.82
Computer Systems Analysts	28.38	Real Estate Brokers	n/a
Cooks, Restaurant	8.61	Retail Salespersons	12.15
Dentists	n/a	Sales Reps., Exc. Tech./Scientific	25.27
Electrical Engineers	n/a	Sales Reps., Tech./Scientific	24.51
Electricians	17.71	Secretaries, Exc. Legal/Med./Exec.	12.49
Financial Managers	36.57	Security Guards	9.39
First-Line Supervisors/Mgrs., Sales	18.44	Surgeons	n/a
Food Preparation Workers	8.74	Teacher Assistants	10.30
General and Operations Managers	40.61	Teachers, Elementary School	19.80
Hairdressers/Cosmetologists	10.19	Teachers, Secondary School	19.00
Internists	74.05	Telemarketers	9.53
Janitors and Cleaners	9.23	Truck Drivers, Heavy/Tractor-Trailer	17.63
Landscaping/Groundskeeping Workers	9.67	Truck Drivers, Light/Delivery Svcs.	13.34
Lawyers	42.32	Waiters and Waitresses	6.30

Note: Wage data is for May 2005 and covers the Tucson, AZ Metropolitan Statistics Area - see Appendix B for areas included. Hourly wages for elementary/secondary school teachers and teacher assistants were calculated by the editors from annual wage data assuming a 40 hour work week; n/a not available.
Source: Bureau of Labor Statistics, May 2005 Metro Area Occupational Employment and Wage Estimates

RESIDENTIAL REAL ESTATE

Building Permits

Area	Single-Family			Multi-Family			Total		
	2005	2006p	Pct. Chg.	2005	2006p	Pct. Chg.	2005	2006p	Pct. Chg.
City	2,421	1,723	-28.8	370	475	28.4	2,791	2,198	-21.2
U.S.	1,682,000	1,380,000	-18.0	473,300	457,300	-3.4	2,155,300	1,837,300	-14.8

Note: (p) preliminary; figures represent new, privately-owned housing units authorized (unadjusted data); All permit data are based on estimates with imputation; U.S. figures are based on the new 20,000-place series.
Source: U.S. Census Bureau, Manufacturing, Mining, and Construction Statistics

Homeownership and Housing Vacancies

Area	Homeownership Rate[2] (%)			Rental Vacancy Rate[3] (%)			Homeowner Vacancy Rate[4] (%)		
	2004	2005	2006	2004	2005	2006	2004	2005	2006
MSA[1]	n/a	66.1	67.5	n/a	9.7	7.1	n/a	1.5	1.9
U.S.	69.0	68.9	68.8	10.2	9.8	9.7	1.7	1.9	2.4

Note: Comparable 2004 data was not available due to changes in metropolitan area definitions; (1) Metropolitan Statistical Area - see Appendix B for areas included; (2) The proportion of households that are owners; (3) The proportion of the rental inventory that is vacant for rent; (4) The proportion of the homeowner inventory that is vacant for sale; n/a not available
Source: U.S. Census Bureau, Housing Vacancies and Homeownership Annual Statistics: 2006

TAXES

State Corporate Income Tax Rates

State	Rate (%)	Number of Brackets	Low Bracket (Under $)	High Bracket (Over $)
Arizona	6.968	1	na	na

Note: Tax rates as of December 31, 2006; na not applicable; Minimum tax is $50.
Source: Tax Foundation, www.taxfoundation.org

State Individual Income Tax Rates

State	Federal Deductibility	Marginal Rate (%)	Number of Brackets	Low Bracket (Under $)	High Bracket (Over $)
Arizona	No	2.87-5.04	5	0	150,000

Note: Tax rates as of December 31, 2006; Brackets apply to single taxpayers and married people filing separately; na not applicable
Source: Tax Foundation, www.taxfoundation.org

Various State and Local Tax Rates

State and Local Sales and Use (%)	State Sales and Use (%)	Gasoline ($/gal.)	Cigarette ($/pack)	Spirits ($/gal.)	Table Wine ($/gal.)	Beer ($/gal.)
8.1	5.6	0.19 (m)	2	3	0.84	0.16

Note: Tax rates as of December 31, 2006; (m) Additional cents per gallon taxes added this year that were not included in previous years' tables.
Source: Tax Foundation, www.taxfoundation.org; The Sales Tax Clearinghouse, www.thestc.com

State Tax Burdens

Area	Combined State and Local Tax Burden		Combined Federal, State and Local Tax Burden	
	Percent	Rank	Percent	Rank
Arizona	10.1	32	29.9	29
U.S. Average	10.6	-	31.6	-

Note: Figures are for 2006 and measure taxes as a percentage of income
Source: Tax Foundation, www.taxfoundation.org

Internal Revenue Service Tax Audits

IRS District	Percent of Returns Audited				
	1996	1997	1998	1999	2000
Southwest	0.80	0.81	0.61	0.36	0.29
U.S.	0.66	0.61	0.46	0.31	0.20

Note: Figures cover IRS district audits of federal income tax returns filed by individuals. Geographic data on district audits after the year 2000 are being withheld by the IRS. TRAC is challenging this policy.
Source: Syracuse University, Transactional Records Access Clearinghouse (TRAC), "Odds of IRS District Tax Audit 2000"

**COMMERCIAL
UTILITIES**

Typical Monthly Electric Bills

Area	Commercial Service ($/month)		Industrial Service ($/month)	
	3 kW demand 1,000 kWh	40 kW demand 14,000 kWh	1,000 kW demand 200,000 kWh	50,000 kW demand 15,000,000 kWh
City	120	1,456	19,170	1,188,515
Average[1]	123	1,413	22,000	1,306,315

Note: Based on total rates in effect July 1, 2006; (1) average based on 196 utilities
Source: Edison Electric Institute, Typical Bills and Average Rates Report, Summer 2006

TRANSPORTATION

Means of Transportation to Work

Area	Car/Truck/Van		Public Transportation			Bicycle	Walked	Other Means	Worked at Home
	Drove Alone	Car-pooled	Bus	Subway	Railroad				
City	71.0	15.7	3.4	0.0	0.0	2.2	3.4	1.5	2.9
MSA[1]	73.8	14.7	2.4	0.0	0.0	1.4	2.6	1.4	3.6
U.S.	75.7	12.2	2.5	1.5	0.5	0.4	2.9	1.0	3.3

Note: Figures are percentages and cover workers 16 years of age and older;
(1) Metropolitan Statistical Area - see Appendix A for areas included
Source: Census 2000, Summary File 3

Travel Time to Work

Area	Less Than 15 Minutes	15 to 29 Minutes	30 to 44 Minutes	45 to 59 Minutes	60 Minutes or More
City	30.2	45.5	16.9	3.4	4.0
MSA[1]	25.8	42.4	21.5	5.6	4.7
U.S.	29.4	36.1	19.1	7.4	8.0

Note: Figures are percentages and include workers 16 years old and over; (1) Metropolitan Statistical Area -
see Appendix A for areas included
Source: Census 2000, Summary File 3

Travel Time Index

Area	1982	1993	2002	2003
Urban Area[1]	1.06	1.14	1.28	1.31
Average[2]	1.12	1.28	1.37	1.37

Note: Travel Time Index - The ratio of travel time in the peak period to the travel time at
free-flow conditions. A value of 1.35 indicates a 20-minute free-flow trip takes 27 minutes
in the peak. Free-flow speeds (60 mph on freeways and 35 mph on principal arterials)
are used as the comparison threshold; (1) Covers the Tucson, AZ urban area;
(2) average of 85 urban areas
Source: Texas Transportation Institute, The 2005 Urban Mobility Report, May 2005

Public Transportation

Agency name:	City of Tucson (COT)
Vehicle type:	Bus
Average fleet age in years:	10.0
No. operated in max. service:	155
Vehicle type:	Demand response
Average fleet age in years:	2.4
No. operated in max. service:	94

Source: Federal Transit Administration, National Transit Database, 2005

Air Transportation

Airport name and code:	Tucson International (TUS)
Domestic service (2006)	
Passenger airlines[1]:	21
Passenger enplanements:	2,064,595
Freight carriers[2]:	18
Freight (lbs.):	31,258,547
International service (2005)	
Passenger airlines[1]:	9
Passenger enplanements:	37,791
Freight carriers[2]:	4
Freight (lbs.):	229,047

*Note: (1) Includes all major, minor and commuter airlines that carried at least one passenger during the year;
(2) Includes all airlines and freight carriers that transported at least one pound of freight during the year
Source: Bureau of Transportation Statistics, The Intermodal Transportation Database, Air Carriers: T-100
International Market, 2004; Bureau of Transportation Statistics, The Intermodal Transportation Database, Air
Carriers: T-100 Domestic Market, 2005*

Other Transportation Statistics

Interstate highways:	I-10; I-19
Amtrak service:	Yes
Major waterways/ports:	None

Source: Editor & Publisher Market Guide, 2006; Amtrak.com; Rand McNally 2006 Road Atlas

BUSINESSES

Major Business Headquarters

Company Name	2006 Rankings	
	Fortune[1]	Forbes[2]
No companies listed	-	-

*Note: (1) Fortune 500 - companies that produce a 10-K are ranked 1 to 500 based on 2005 revenue; (2) Forbes
Largest Private Companies - all private companies with at least $1 billion in annual revenue are ranked 1 to
394; companies listed are located in the city; dashes indicate no ranking
Source: Fortune, April 17, 2006; Forbes, November 9, 2006*

Best Companies to Work For

Intuit, headquartered in Tucson, is among the "100 Best Companies to Work For." Criteria:
More than 105,000 employees from 446 companies responded to a 57-question survey created
by the Great Place to Work Institute. Two-thirds of a company's score is based on the survey,
which covers topics such as attitudes towards management, job satisfaction, and camaraderie.
The remaining third of the score comes from each company's responses to the Institute's
Culture Audit, which includes detailed questions about demographic makeup, pay and
benefits programs, and open-ended questions about the company's people-management
philosophy, internal communications, opportunities, compensation practices, diversity
programs, etc. Any company that is at least seven years old and has a minimum of 1,000 U.S.
employees is eligible. The top three U.S. locations are shown for companies with more than
one location. *Fortune, "100 Best Companies to Work for 2007," January 22, 2007*

Carondelet Health Network, headquartered in Tucson, is among the "50 Best Employers for
Workers Over 50." Criteria: recruiting practices; opportunities for training, education, and
career development; workplace accommodations; alternative work options, such as flexible
scheduling, job sharing, and phased retirement; employee health and pension benefits; and
retiree benefits. Any employer with at least 50 employees based in the U.S. is eligible. This
includes for-profit companies, not-for-profit organizations, and government employers.
AARP, "AARP Best Employers for Workers Over 50," 2006

Fast-Growing Businesses

Tucson is home to two of *Business Week's* "Hot Growth Companies:" **Providence Service;
Ventana Medical Systems**. To qualify, a company must have annual sales of more than $50
million and less than $1.5 billion, a current market value greater than $25 million, a current
stock price of at least $5, and be actively traded. Banks, insurers, real estate firms, and utilities
are excluded. So are companies with declines in current financial results or in stock price, as
well as companies where other developments raise questions about future performance.
Companies were selected based on three-year results in sales growth, earnings growth, and
return on invested capital. *Business Week, June 5, 2006*

According to *Business 2.0*, Tucson is home to one of America's 100 fastest-growing technology companies: **Ventana Medical Systems**. The 100 Fastest-Growing Technology Companies (B2 100) is a yearly ranking published by Business 2.0 magazine of businesses whose inventiveness and quick reflexes are helping them to set the pace for the economy. To find the B2 100, Zacks Investment Research of Chicago ranked 2,000 publicly traded companies using a rigorous combination of four financial criteria: growth in revenue, profit, and operating cash flow during the past three years; and the 12-month stock market return as of March 31, 2006. *Business 2.0, "100 Fastest-Growing Tech Companies 2006," June 2006*

Women-Owned Businesses: 1997 and 2002

Year	All Firms		Firms with Paid Employees			
	Firms	Sales ($000)	Firms	Sales ($000)	Employees	Payroll ($000)
1997	9,535	1,019,305	1,992	896,956	12,848	258,192
2002	11,568	1,341,401	1,642	1,126,464	14,648	337,516

Note: Figures cover firms located in the city; Women-owned business are defined as firms in which women own 51% or more of the stock or equity of the company; (a) Withheld to avoid disclosing data for individual companies; (b) Withheld because estimate did not meet publication standards; n/a not available
Source: 1997 Economic Census, Survey of Minority- and Women-Owned Business Enterprises; 2002 Economic Census, Survey of Business Owners (released February 9, 2006)

Minority Business Opportunity

Four of the 500 largest Hispanic-owned companies in the U.S. are located in Tucson. *Hispanic Business, "Hispanic Business 500," June 2006*

HOTELS

Hotels/Motels

Area	Hotels/Motels	Average Minimum Rates ($)		
		Tourist	First-Class	Deluxe
City	109	55	89	205

Source: OAG Travel Planner Online, Spring 2006

The Tucson metro area is home to one of the top 187 hotels in the U.S. according to *Travel & Leisure*: **Lodge at Ventana Canyon** (#158). Criteria: service; location; rooms; food; and value. *Travel & Leisure, "The T+L 500, 2007"*

EVENT SITES

Convention Centers

Name	Overall Space (sq. ft.)	Exhibit Space (sq. ft.)	Meeting Space (sq. ft.)	Meeting Rooms
Tucson Convention Center	205,000	10,640	147,690	12

Source: www.officialtravelguide.com; www.eventective.com; original research

Hotels/Conference Centers

Name	Guest Rooms	Exhibit Space (sq. ft.)	Meeting Space (sq. ft.)
Doubletree Hotel at Reid Park	295	13,000	22,000
Hilton El Conquistador Resort and Country Club	428	36,000	50,000
Loews Ventana Canyon Resort	398	29,503	21,424
The Westin La Paloma	487	18,000	42,000

Source: www.officialtravelguide.com; www.eventective.com; original research

Living Environment

COST OF LIVING

Cost of Living Index

Year	Composite Index	Groceries	Housing	Utilities	Trans- portation	Health Care	Misc. Goods/ Services
2004	95.9	107.4	84.4	96.5	106.8	103.2	97.8
2005	96.6	99.9	87.9	96.0	105.2	100.2	100.1
2006	98.8	99.5	95.7	91.7	103.4	101.4	101.5

Note: U.S. = 100
Source: The Council for Community and Economic Research (formerly ACCRA), Cost of Living Index, 2004, 2005 and 2006 4-Quarter Averages

HOUSING

House Price Index (HPI)

Area	National Ranking[2]	Quarterly Change (%)	One-Year Change (%)	Five-Year Change (%)
MSA[1]	66	1.14	8.60	84.91
U.S.[3]	-	1.12	5.87	55.21

Note: The HPI is a weighted repeat sales index. It measures average price changes in repeat sales or refinancings on the same properties. This information is obtained by reviewing repeat mortgage transactions on single-family properties whose mortgages have been purchased or securitized by Fannie Mae or Freddie Mac in January 1975; (1) Metropolitan Statistical Area - see Appendix B for areas included; (2) Rankings are based on annual percentage change for all metro areas containing at least 15,000 transactions over the last 10 years and ranges from 1 to 282; (3) figures based on a weighted division average; all figures are for the period ending December 31, 2006
Source: Office of Federal Housing Enterprise Oversight, House Price Index, March 1, 2007

House Price Valuations

Area	Q4 1999	Q4 2000	Q4 2001	Q4 2002	Q4 2003	Q4 2004	Q4 2005	Q4 2006
MSA[1]	-6.0	-5.9	-2.4	1.8	6.9	12.0	33.8	34.9

Note: Figures show the percentage of over- or under-valuation of single family homes relative to statistically normal house values (e.g. a value of 23.6 indicates that house values are 23.6% overvalued). Statistically normal house values are based on house prices, interest rates, household incomes, population densities, and any historical premiums or discounts metropolitan areas have exhibited over time; (1) Figures cover the Metropolitan Statistical Area - see Appendix B for areas included
Source: Global Insight/National City Corporation, House Prices in America, March 2007

Median Home Prices

Area	2004	2005	2006p	Percent Change 2005 to 2006
Metro Area[1]	177.3	231.6	244.9	5.7
U.S. Average	195.2	219.0	222.0	1.4

Note: Figures are median sales prices of existing single-family homes in thousands of dollars; (p) preliminary; n/a not available; (1) Covers the Tucson, AZ Metropolitan Statistical Area - see Appendix B for areas included
Source: National Association of Realtors, Metropolitan Area Prices, 4th Quarter 2006

Housing: Year Structure Built

Area	1990 -2000	1980 -1989	1970 -1979	1960 -1969	1950 -1959	1940 -1949	Before 1940	Median Year
City	15.6	19.1	25.4	14.4	15.5	5.7	4.3	1974
MSA[1]	23.2	22.4	25.6	11.7	10.4	3.7	3.0	1978
U.S.	17.0	15.8	18.5	13.7	12.7	7.3	15.0	1971

Note: Figures are percentages; (1) Metropolitan Statistical Area - see Appendix A for areas included
Source: Census 2000, Summary File 3

Average New Home Price

Area	2004	2005	2006
City	204,788	234,532	284,536
U.S.	253,574	275,712	299,269

Note: Figures, in dollars, are based on a new home with 2,400 sq. ft. of living area on an 8,000 sq. ft. lot.
Source: The Council for Community and Economic Research (formerly ACCRA), Cost of Living Index, 2004, 2005 and 2006 4-Quarter Averages

Average Apartment Rent

Area	2004	2005	2006
City	730	748	780
U.S.	716	740	766

Note: Figures, in dollars per month, are based on an unfurnished two bedroom, 1-1/2 or 2 bath apartment, approximately 950 sq. ft. in size, excluding all utilities except water
Source: The Council for Community and Economic Research (formerly ACCRA), Cost of Living Index, 2004, 2005 and 2006 4-Quarter Averages

RESIDENTIAL UTILITIES

Average Residential Utility Costs

Area	All Electric ($/mth)	Part Electric ($/mth)	Other Energy ($/mth)	Phone ($/mth)
City	–	92.06	58.94	22.26
U.S.	136.00	76.53	90.52	25.87

Source: The Council for Community and Economic Research (formerly ACCRA), Cost of Living Index, 2006 4-Quarter Average

HEALTH

Average Health Care Costs

Area	Optometrist ($/visit)	Doctor ($/visit)	Dentist ($/visit)
City	72.57	73.67	77.25
U.S.	76.38	76.10	68.72

Note: Optometrist—based on a full vision eye exam for an established adult patient;
Doctor—based on a general practitioner's routine exam of an established patient;
Dentist—based on adult teeth cleaning and periodic oral exam.
Source: The Council for Community and Economic Research (formerly ACCRA), Cost of Living Index, 2006 4-Quarter Average

Mortality Rates

ICD-10 Sub-Chapter	ICD-10 Code	Age-Adjusted Death Rate per 100,000 population[1]	U.S. Age-Adjusted Death Rate per 100,000 population
Malignant neoplasms	C00-C97	167.7	185.8
Ischaemic heart diseases	I20-I25	119.8	150.2
Other forms of heart disease	I30-I51	51.7	50.8
Cerebrovascular diseases	I60-I69	47.0	50.0
Chronic lower respiratory diseases	J40-J47	42.5	41.1
Diabetes mellitus	E10-E14	21.1	24.5
Other degenerative diseases of the nervous system	G30-G31	22.9	22.3
Other external causes of accidental injury	W00-X59	30.8	21.2
Influenza and pneumonia	J10-J18	21.0	19.8
Hypertensive diseases	I10-I13	12.8	18.1

Note: ICD-10 = International Classification of Diseases 10th Revision; (1) Figures cover Pima County, AZ
Source: Centers for Disease Control and Prevention, National Center for Health Statistics. Compressed Mortality File 1999-2004. CDC WONDER On-line Database, compiled from Compressed Mortality File 1999-2004 Series 20 No. 2J, 2007.

Health Risk Data

Item	Area[1] (%)	U.S. (%)
Adults who have been told they have high blood pressure	22.6	25.5
Adults who have been told they have high blood cholesterol	35.1	35.6
Adults who have been told they have diabetes[2]	7.5	7.3
Adults who have been told they have arthritis	24.0	27.0
Adults who have been told they currently have asthma	7.3	8.0
Adults who are current smokers	20.2	20.6

Note: (1) Figures cover the Metropolitan Statistical Area - see Appendix B for areas included; (2) Figures do not include pregnancy-related diabetes, pre-diabetes or borderline diabetes
Source: Centers for Disease Control and Prevention, Behaviorial Risk Factor Surveillance System, SMART: Selected Metropolitan/Micropolitan Area Trends, 2005

Distribution of Office-Based Physicians

Area	Total	Family/ General Practice	Specialties		
			Medical	Surgical	Other
MSA[1] (number)	1,788	200	612	395	581
MSA[1] (rate per 10,000 pop.)	20.4	2.3	7.0	4.5	6.6
Metro Average[2] (rate per 10,000 pop.)	19.4	2.1	7.5	4.5	5.3

Note: Data as of December 31, 2004; (1) Metropolitan Statistical Area - see Appendix A for areas included;
(2) Average of the 79 unique MSAs and CMSAs in this book
Source: American Medical Association, Physician Characteristics & Distribution in the U.S., 2006

Hospitals

Tucson has the following hospitals: 9 general medical and surgical; 2 rehabilitation; 1 alcoholism and other chemical dependency; 2 long-term acute care.
AHA Guide to the Healthcare Field 2007

According to *U.S. News,* the Tucson metro area is home to one of the best hospitals in the U.S.: **University Medical Center**; *U.S. News Online, "America's Best Hospitals 2006"*

EDUCATION

Public School District Statistics

District Name	Schls	Pupils	Pupil/ Teacher Ratio	Minority Pupils[1] (%)	Free Lunch Eligible[2] (%)	IEP[3] (%)
Amphitheater Unified District	20	16,703	17.6	41.5	36.0	23.4
Catalina Foothills Unified District	8	5,029	17.3	22.7	6.0	14.8
Flowing Wells Unified District	10	5,954	19.8	49.2	48.7	18.7
Sunnyside Unified District	22	16,524	18.4	93.8	82.4	19.2
Tucson Unified District	123	61,204	19.6	65.4	53.2	21.4

Note: Table includes regular local school districts with 2,000 or more students; (1) Percentage of students that are not white, non-Hispanic; (2) Percentage of students that are eligible for the free lunch program; (3) Percentage of students that have an Individualized Education Program.
Source: U.S. Department of Education, National Center for Education Statistics, Common Core of Data, Local Education Agency (School District) Universe Survey: School Year 2004-2005; U.S. Department of Education, National Center for Education Statistics, Common Core of Data, Public Elementary/Secondary School Universe Survey: School Year 2004-2005

Top Public High Schools

High School Name	Index[1]	Rank[1]	Subsidized Lunch (%)[2]	E&E (%)[3]
BASIS Charter	9.909	3	n/a	100.0
Catalina Foothills	1.269	949	0.0	33.1

Note: (1) Public schools are ranked according to a ratio that is the number of Advanced Placement and/or International Baccalaureate tests taken by all students at a school in 2005 divided by the number of graduating seniors. All of the schools on the list have an index of at least 1.000; they are in the top five percent of public schools measured this way. The rankings range from 1 to 1,236; (2) Percentage of students receiving federally subsidized meals; (3) E & E stands for equity and excellence percentage: the portion of all graduating seniors at a school that had at least one passing grade on one AP or IB test; (*) Gave just IB tests; (**) Gave both IB and AP tests. AP and IB participation are indicators of a school's efforts to get students to excel and prepare for college.
Source: Newsweek Online, May 23, 2006

Educational Quality

School District	Education Quotient[1]	Graduate Outcome[2]	Community Index[3]	Resource Index[4]	Rating[5]
Tucson Unified	59	65	40	20	Green

Note: Scores are national percentile rankings and range from 1 (worst) to 99 (best); (1) Combination of the Graduate Outcome, Community and Resource Indexes weighted to reflect the greater importance of the Graduate Outcome and Resource Index; (2) Based on graduation rates and college board scores (SAT/ACT); (3) Based on the surrounding community's level of affluence and adult education; (4) Based on teacher salaries, per-pupil expenditures and student-teacher ratios; (5) School districts receive one of five rankings: Gold Medal (top 16 percent of districts evaluated); Blue Ribbon (top third); Green Light (average); Yellow Light (bottom 25 percent); Red Light (bottom 10 percent).
Source: Expansion Management, "2007 Education Quotient," January 2007

Highest Level of Education

Area	Less than H.S.	H.S. Diploma	Some College, No Deg.	Associate Degree	Bachelors Degree	Masters Degree	Profess. School Degree	Doctorate Degree
City	19.3	23.9	27.0	6.7	14.0	6.4	1.5	1.3
MSA[1]	16.2	23.2	26.9	6.8	16.0	7.3	2.0	1.6
U.S.	19.4	28.4	21.2	6.4	15.7	5.9	2.0	1.0

Note: Figures are 2006 estimated percentages and cover persons age 25 and over; (1) Metropolitan Statistical Area - see Appendix B for areas included
Source: Claritas, Inc.

Educational Attainment by Race

Area	High School Graduate (%)					Bachelor's Degree (%)				
	Total	White	Black	Asian	Hisp.[2]	Total	White	Black	Asian	Hisp.[2]
City	80.4	84.6	80.8	77.0	60.5	22.9	25.9	14.7	40.0	9.8
MSA[1]	83.4	87.1	81.9	80.5	62.8	26.7	29.7	16.8	43.3	10.9
U.S.	80.4	83.6	72.3	80.4	52.4	24.4	26.1	14.3	44.1	10.4

Note: Figures shown cover persons 25 years old and over; (1) Metropolitan Statistical Area - see Appendix A for areas included; (2) people of Hispanic origin can be of any race
Source: Census 2000, Summary File 3

School Enrollment by Type

Area	Grades KG to 8				Grades 9 to 12			
	Public		Private		Public		Private	
	Enrollment	%	Enrollment	%	Enrollment	%	Enrollment	%
City	55,793	91.9	4,904	8.1	22,977	91.9	2,035	8.1
MSA[1]	98,857	91.6	9,092	8.4	42,008	91.8	3,736	8.2
U.S.	33,526,011	88.7	4,285,121	11.3	14,848,628	90.6	1,532,323	9.4

Note: Figures shown cover persons 3 years old and over; (1) Metropolitan Statistical Area - see Appendix A for areas included
Source: Census 2000, Summary File 3

School Enrollment by Race

Area	Grades KG to 8 (%)				Grades 9 to 12 (%)			
	White	Black	Asian	Hisp.[1]	White	Black	Asian	Hisp.[1]
City	59.4	5.2	1.6	51.2	58.9	5.5	1.7	51.4
MSA[2]	65.5	3.4	1.5	42.8	65.7	3.6	1.9	40.6
U.S.	68.5	15.5	3.3	16.8	68.8	15.5	3.8	15.7

Note: Figures shown cover persons 3 years old and over; (1) people of Hispanic origin can be of any race; (2) Metropolitan Statistical Area - see Appendix A for areas included
Source: Census 2000, Summary File 3

Average Salaries of Public School Teachers

District	2004-05		2005-06		Percent Change 2004-05 to 2005-06
	Dollars	Rank[1]	Dollars	Rank[1]	
ARIZONA	42,905	27	44,672	25	4.12
U.S. Average	47,674	-	49,109	-	3.01

Note: (1) State rank ranges from 1 to 51.
Source: National Education Association, Rankings & Estimates: Rankings of the States 2005 and Estimates of School Statistics 2006, November 2006

Higher Education

Four-Year Colleges			Two-Year Colleges			Medical Schools[1]	Law Schools[2]	Voc/ Tech[3]
Public	Private Non-profit	Private For-profit	Public	Private Non-profit	Private For-profit			
1	1	6	1	0	1	1	1	8

Note: Figures cover institutions located within the city limits; (1) includes schools accredited by the Liaison Committee on Medical Education and the American Osteopathic Association; (2) includes American Bar Association-accredited law schools; (3) includes all schools with programs that are less than 2 years
Source: National Center for Education Statistics, The Integrated Postsecondary Education System (IPEDS) Peer Analysis System, 2006; www.usnews.com, America's Best Graduate Schools 2008, Medical School Directory; www.usnews.com, America's Best Graduate Schools 2008, Law School Directory

PRESIDENTIAL ELECTION

2004 Presidential Election Results

Area	Bush	Kerry	Nader	Other
Pima County	46.6	52.6	0.1	0.7
U.S.	50.7	48.3	0.4	0.6

Note: Results are percentages and may not add to 100% due to rounding
Source: Dave Leip's Atlas of U.S. Presidential Elections, www.uselectionatlas.org

MAJOR EMPLOYERS

Major Employers

Company Name	Industry	Type of Site
12th Air Force Command	National security	Branch
ASPC-Tucson	Correctional institutions	Branch
American Airlines Inc	Job training and related services	Branch
Bombardier Aviation Service	Aircraft	Branch
Desert Diamond Casino 1	Amusement and recreation, nec	Single
Hospital Administration	Colleges and universities	Branch
IBM	Commercial physical research	Branch
Missile Systems Site	Guided missiles and space vehicles	Headquarters
Radiology Training	Specialty hospitals, except psychiatric	Branch
Saint Josephs Care Hospital	General medical and surgical hospitals	Branch
Southern AZ VAHC	Administration of veterans' affairs	Branch
TMC Healthcare	Management services	Headquarters
Texas Instruments	Semiconductors and related devices	Headquarters
Tucson Medical Center	General medical and surgical hospitals	Headquarters
US Post Office	U.S. Postal Service	Branch
University Medical Center Corp	General medical and surgical hospitals	Headquarters

Note: Companies shown are located within the metropolitan area and have 1,000 or more employees; nec = not elsewhere classified.
Source: www.zapdata.com, January 2007

PUBLIC SAFETY

Crime Rate

Area	All Crimes	Violent Crimes				Property Crimes		
		Murder	Forcible Rape	Robbery	Aggrav. Assault	Burglary	Larceny -Theft	Motor Vehicle Theft
City	6,865.1	10.4	71.4	318.3	553.4	968.9	3,709.9	1,232.8
Suburbs[1]	4,602.2	5.6	24.5	67.8	158.1	722.2	3,153.4	470.5
Metro[2]	5,879.6	8.3	51.0	209.2	381.3	861.5	3,467.5	900.8
U.S.	3,899.0	5.6	31.7	140.7	291.1	726.7	2,286.3	416.7

Note: Figures are crimes per 100,000 population; (1) All areas within the metro area that are located outside the city limits; (2) Metropolitan Statistical Area - see Appendix B for areas included
Source: FBI Uniform Crime Reports, 2005

Hate Crimes

| Area | Number of Quarters Reported | Bias Motivation | | | | |
		Race	Religion	Sexual Orientation	Ethnicity	Disability
City	4	8	8	6	5	0

Source: Federal Bureau of Investigation, Hate Crime Statistics 2005

RECREATION

Culture

Dance[1]	Theatre[1]	Instrumental Music[1]	Vocal Music[1]	Series/ Festivals	Museums	Zoos
0	2	9	3	5	18	1

Note: (1) number of professional perfoming groups
Source: The Grey House Performing Arts Directory, 2007; Official Museum Directory, 2007

Professional Sports Teams

Major League Baseball	National Basketball Association	National Football League	National Hockey League	Major League Soccer	Women's National Basketball Association
0	0	0	0	0	0

Note: Includes teams located in the Tucson metro area.
Source: www.sportsvenues.com, Listing of Venues by State/Province and City, 2006

MEDIA

Newspapers

Name	Target Audience	Frequency	Circulation
The Arizona Daily Star	n/a	Daily	103,028
Arizona Jewish Post	Jewish	Non-Daily	8,000
The Daily Territorial	n/a	Daily	1,000
The Desert Airman	General	Non-Daily	10,500
The DesertLeaf	General	Non-Daily	53,000
Inside Tucson Business	General	Non-Daily	8,427
Northwest Explorer Newspaper	General	Non-Daily	35,000
Today	General	Non-Daily	49,700
Tucson Citizen	n/a	Daily	35,453
Tucson Weekly	Alternative/General	Non-Daily	46,044
The Weekly Observer	Gay/Lesbian	Non-Daily	5,000

Note: Includes newspapers whose offices are located in the city and whose circulations are 1,000 or more; n/a not available
Source: BurrellesLuce, MediaContacts Online, January 2006

Television Stations

Name	Ch.	Network(s)	Type	Ownership
KVOA	4	NBC	Commercial	Evening Post Publishing
KUAT	6	PBS	Public	Arizona Board of Regents
KGUN	9	ABC	Commercial	Lee Enterprises Inc.
KMSB	11	Fox	Commercial	Belo Corporation
KOLD	13	CBS	Commercial	Raycom Media Inc.
KTTU	18	UPN	Commercial	Belo Corporation
KUAS	27	PBS	Public	Arizona Board of Regents
KHRR	40	Telemundo	Commercial	Television Apogeo de Tucson
KWBA	58	WBN	Commercial	Cascades Broadcasting Inc.

Note: Stations included cover the Tucson DMA (Designated Market Area)
BurrellesLuce, MediaContacts Online, January 2006

Major AM Radio Stations

Call Letters	Freq. (kHz)	Station Type	Target Audience	Station Format	Music Format
KSAZ	580	Commercial	General	Music/News	International
KNST	790	Commercial	General	Talk	n/a
KFLT	830	Non-Comm	General/Religious	Educational/Music	Christian
KAPR	930	Commercial	General	Music	Classic Rock
KGMS	940	Commercial	Christian/General	Educational	n/a
KTKT	990	Commercial	General	News/Talk	n/a
KEVT	1030	n/a	Hispanic/Religious	Music	n/a
KGVY	1080	Commercial	General	Music/News	Oldies
KQTL	1210	Commercial	General/Hispanic	Music/Talk	Latin
KHIL	1250	Commercial	General	Music	Country
KCUB	1290	Commercial	General	Sports	n/a
KJLL	1330	Commercial	General	News/Talk	n/a
KTUC	1400	Commercial	General	Music/News	Adult Standards
KTAN	1420	Commercial	General	News/Sports/Talk	n/a
KTZR	1450	n/a	Hispanic	Music/News/Sports	n/a
KDAP	1450	Commercial	General/Hisp/Rel	Music	Christian
KNXN	1470	n/a	Hispanic	Talk	n/a
KFFN	1490	Commercial	General	Talk	n/a
KUAZ	1550	College	General	Music/News	Jazz
KXEW	1600	n/a	Hispanic/Native Amer	Music	n/a

Note: Stations included cover the Tucson DMA (Designated Market Area); n/a not available
Source: BurrellesLuce, MediaContacts Online, January 2006

Major FM Radio Stations

Call Letters	Freq. (mHz)	Station Type	Target Audience	Station Format	Music Format
KUAZ	89.1	College	General	Music	Jazz
KRMB	90.1	Non-Comm	General/Hispanic	Music/News	Christian
KUAT	90.5	College	General	Music	Classical
KXCI	91.3	Non-Comm	General	Music/News	Blues
KRMC	91.7	Non-Comm	Hispanic	Educational/Music	Latin
KFMA	92.1	Commercial	General	Music	A.O. Rock
KWCD	92.3	Commercial	General	Music/Talk	Country
KWMT	92.9	Commercial	General	Music	Contemp. Country
KRQQ	93.7	Commercial	General	Music/News	Top 40
KMXZ	94.9	Commercial	General	Music/Talk	Soft Rock
KLPX	96.1	Commercial	General	Music	A.O. Rock
KWFM	97.1	Commercial	General	Music	Oldies
KSZR	97.5	n/a	General	Music/News/Sports/Talk	n/a
KOHT	98.3	Commercial	Hispanic	Music/News	Latin
KZNO	98.3	Commercial	General/Hisp/Rel	Music/Sports	Latin
KIIM	99.5	Commercial	General	Music	Contemp. Country
KZMK	100.9	Commercial	General	Music	Adult Contemp.
KKYZ	101.7	Commercial	General	Music/News	Oldies
KCMT	101.9	Commercial	General/Hispanic	Music	Latin
KNOG	102.7	n/a	Hispanic/Religious	Ed/Music/News/Talk	n/a
KZPT	104.1	Commercial	General/Women	Music/Talk	Adult Contemp.
KWCX	104.9	Commercial	General	Music/News	Adult Contemp.
KZLZ	105.3	Commercial	General/Hispanic	Music/Sports	Latin
KGMG	106.3	Commercial	General	Music/News/Talk	Oldies
KHYT	107.5	Commercial	General	Music/News	Classic Rock

Note: Stations included cover the Tucson DMA (Designated Market Area); n/a not available
BurrellesLuce, MediaContacts Online, January 2006

CLIMATE

Average and Extreme Temperatures

Temperature	Jan	Feb	Mar	Apr	May	Jun	Jul	Aug	Sep	Oct	Nov	Dec	Yr.
Extreme High (°F)	87	92	99	104	107	117	114	108	107	101	90	84	117
Average High (°F)	64	68	73	81	89	99	99	96	94	84	73	65	82
Average Temp. (°F)	51	54	59	66	74	84	86	84	81	71	59	52	69
Average Low (°F)	38	40	44	51	58	68	74	72	67	57	45	39	55
Extreme Low (°F)	16	20	20	33	38	47	62	61	44	26	24	16	16

Note: Figures cover the years 1946-1990
Source: National Climatic Data Center, International Station Meteorological Climate Summary, 9/96

Average Precipitation/Snowfall/Humidity

Precip./Humidity	Jan	Feb	Mar	Apr	May	Jun	Jul	Aug	Sep	Oct	Nov	Dec	Yr.
Avg. Precip. (in.)	0.9	0.7	0.7	0.3	0.1	0.2	2.5	2.2	1.4	0.9	0.6	0.9	11.6
Avg. Snowfall (in.)	Tr	Tr	Tr	Tr	0	0	0	0	0	0	Tr	Tr	2
Avg. Rel. Hum. 5am (%)	62	58	52	41	34	32	58	65	55	52	54	61	52
Avg. Rel. Hum. 5pm (%)	31	26	22	16	13	13	29	32	26	24	27	33	24

Note: Figures cover the years 1946-1990; Tr = Trace amounts (<0.05 in. of rain; <0.5 in. of snow)
Source: National Climatic Data Center, International Station Meteorological Climate Summary, 9/96

Weather Conditions

Temperature			Daytime Sky			Precipitation		
10°F & below	32°F & below	90°F & above	Clear	Partly cloudy	Cloudy	0.01 inch or more precip.	0.1 inch or more snow/ice	Thunderstorms
0	18	140	177	119	69	54	2	42

Note: Figures are average number of days per year and cover the years 1946-1990
Source: National Climatic Data Center, International Station Meteorological Climate Summary, 9/96

HAZARDOUS WASTE

Superfund Sites

Tucson has one hazardous waste site on the EPA's Superfund Final National Priorities List: **Tucson International Airport Area**. *U.S. Environmental Protection Agency, Final National Priorities List, March 20, 2007*

AIR & WATER QUALITY

Air Quality Index

Area	Percent of Days when Air Quality was...[2]				AQI Statistics	
	Good	Moderate	Unhealthy for Sensitive Groups	Unhealthy	Maximum	Median
MSA[1]	75.6	24.1	0.3	0.0	106	44

Note: The Air Quality Index (AQI) is an index for reporting daily air quality. EPA calculates the AQI for five major air pollutants regulated by the Clean Air Act: ground-level ozone, particle pollution (also known as particulate matter), carbon monoxide, sulfur dioxide, and nitrogen dioxide. The AQI runs from 0 to 500. The higher the AQI value, the greater the level of air pollution and the greater the health concern. There are six AQI categories: "Good" The AQI is between 0 and 50. Air quality is considered satisfactory; "Moderate" The AQI is between 51 and 100. Air quality is acceptable; "Unhealthy for Sensitive Groups" When AQI values are between 101 and 150, members of sensitive groups may experience health effects; "Unhealthy" When AQI values are between 151 and 200 everyone may begin to experience health effects; "Very Unhealthy" AQI values between 201 and 300 trigger a health alert; "Hazardous" AQI values over 300 trigger health warnings of emergency conditions; (1) Metropolitan Statistical Area - see Appendix A for areas included; (2) Based on 365 days with AQI data in 2005.
Source: U.S. Environmental Protection Agency, Air Quality Index Report, 2005

Air Quality Index Pollutants

Area	Percent of Days when AQI Pollutant was...[2]					
	Carbon Monoxide	Nitrogen Dioxide	Ozone	Sulfur Dioxide	Particulate Matter 2.5	Particulate Matter 10
MSA[1]	0.0	0.0	66.3	0.0	17.0	16.7

Note: The Air Quality Index (AQI) is an index for reporting daily air quality. EPA calculates the AQI for five major air pollutants regulated by the Clean Air Act: ground-level ozone, particle pollution (also known as particulate matter), carbon monoxide, sulfur dioxide, and nitrogen dioxide. The AQI runs from 0 to 500. The higher the AQI value, the greater the level of air pollution and the greater the health concern; (1) Metropolitan Statistical Area - see Appendix A for areas included; (2) Based on 365 days with AQI data in 2005.
Source: U.S. Environmental Protection Agency, Air Quality Index Report, 2005

Number of Days with Air Quality Index Values Greater than 100

Area	Trend Sites (20)								All Sites (52)
	1998	1999	2000	2001	2002	2003	2004	2005	2005
MSA[1]	0	7	0	0	3	1	0	2	2

Note: An AQI value greater than 100 indicates that air quality would have been in the unhealthful range on that day. Data from exceptional events are not included. These counts are presented in two ways. First, the counts are based on sites having an adequate record of monitoring data during the trend period (trend sites). These counts represent the relative change in the number of days with AQI values greater than 100. In the last column, the counts are based on all sites with data in the most recent year (because it is possible for a site to have data in the most recent year but not enough data to be a trend site); (1) Metropolitan Statistical Area - see Appendix A for areas included; n/a not available.
Source: U.S. Environmental Protection Agency, Air Trends Fact Book 2005

Maximum Pollutant Concentrations

	Particulate Matter 10 (ug/m³)	Particulate Matter 2.5 (ug/m³)	Ozone 1-hour (ppm)	Carbon Monoxide (ppm)	Sulfur Dioxide (ppm)	Nitrogen Dioxide (ppm)	Lead (ug/m³)
MSA[1] Level	88	14	0.091	2	0.003	0.015	n/a
NAAQS[2]	150	65	0.125	9	0.140	0.053	1.50
Met NAAQS[2]	Yes	Yes	Yes	Yes	Yes	Yes	n/a

Note: Data from exceptional events are not included; (1) Metropolitan Statistical Area - see Appendix A for areas included; (2) National Ambient Air Quality Standards; n/a not available
Units: ppm = parts per million; ug/m³ = micrograms per cubic meter
Source: U.S. Environmental Protection Agency, Air Trends Fact Book 2005

Watershed Health

The U.S. Environmental Protection Agency monitors the health of the aquatic resources for the nation's 2,000+ watersheds. **The Upper Santa Cruz watershed serves the Tucson area and received an overall Index of Watershed Indicators (IWI) score of 3 (less serious problems - low vulnerability).** The IWI score is based on seven condition and nine vulnerability indicators. The overall IWI score ranges from 1 (best health) to 6 (worst health). The Condition Indicators include: designated use attainment, fish and wildlife consumption advisories, source water condition, contaminated sediments, ambient water quality, and wetlands loss index. The Vulnerability Indicators include: aquatic species at risk, conventional and toxic loads over permitted limits, urban and agricultural runoff potential, population change, hydrologic modification, estuarine pollution susceptibility, and air deposition. *Note: The IWI is no longer being updated by the U.S. EPA. Source: U.S. Environmental Protection Agency, Index of Watershed Indicators, October 26, 2001*

Drinking Water

Water System Name	Pop. Served	Primary Water Source Type	Number of Violations in 2006[a]		
			Health Based	Significant Monitoring	Monitoring
City of Tucson	675,000	Ground	None	None	None

Note: (a) Based on violation data from January 1, 2006 to December 31, 2006
Source: U.S. Environmental Protection Agency, Office of Ground Water and Drinking Water, Safe Drinking Water Information System (data extracted April 12, 2007)

Tucson tap water is alkaline and very hard from South Side Reservoir No. 1 and alkaline, soft and not fluoridated from North Side Reservoir No. 3.
Editor & Publisher Market Guide, 2005

Appendix A: Historical Metropolitan Area Definitions

Metropolitan Statistical Areas (MSA) and New England County Metropolitan Areas (NECMA)
These historical metropolitan area definitions were in effect from June 30, 1993 to June 5, 2003

Albuquerque, NM MSA
Bernalillo, Sandoval, and Valencia Counties

Alexandria, VA
See Washington, DC-MD-VA-WV MSA

Anchorage, AK MSA
Anchorage Borough

Ann Arbor, MI MSA
Lenawee, Livingston and Washtenaw Counties

Athens, GA MSA
Clarke, Madison, and Oconee Counties

Atlanta, GA MSA
Barrow, Bartow, Carroll, Cherokee, Clayton, Cobb, Coweta, DeKalb, Douglas, Fayette, Forsyth, Fulton, Gwinnett, Henry, Newton, Paulding, Pickens, Rockdale, Spalding, and Walton Counties

Austin-San Marcos, TX MSA
Bastrop, Caldwell, Hays, Travis and Williamson Counties

Baltimore, MD MSA
Baltimore City; Anne Arundel, Baltimore, Carroll, Harford, Howard, and Queen Anne's Counties

Baton Rouge, LA MSA
Ascension, East Baton Rouge, Livingston, and West Baton Rouge Parish

Bellevue, WA
See Seattle-Bellevue-Everett, WA MSA

Birmingham, AL MSA
Blount, Jefferson, St. Clair, and Shelby Counties

Boise City, ID MSA
Ada and Canyon Counties

Boston, MA
Boston, MA-NH MSA
Parts of Bristol, Essex, Middlesex, Norfolk, Plymouth, and Worcester Counties, MA; and all of Suffolk County, MA; part of Rockingham County, NH
Boston-Worcester-Lawrence-Lowell-Brockton, MA-NH NECMA
Bristol, Essex, Middlesex, Norfolk, Plymouth, Suffolk, and Worcester Counties, MA;

Hillsborough, Rockingham, and Strafford Counties, NH

Boulder-Longmont, CO MSA
Boulder County

Buffalo-Niagara Falls, NY MSA
Erie and Niagara Counties

Cary, NC
See Raleigh-Durham-Chapel Hill, NC MSA

Cedar Rapids, IA MSA
Linn County

Charleston-North Charleston, SC MSA
Berkeley, Charleston, and Dorchester Counties

Charlotte-Gastonia-Rock Hill, NC-SC MSA
Cabarrus, Gaston, Lincoln, Mecklenburg, Rowan, and Union Counties, NC; York County, SC

Chattanooga, TN-GA MSA
Catoosa, Dade and Walker Counties, GA; Hamilton and Marion Counties, TN

Chicago, IL MSA
Cook, DeKalb, DuPage, Grundy, Kane, Kendall, Lake, McHenry and Will Counties

Cincinnati, OH-KY-IN MSA
Brown, Clermont, Hamilton, and Warren Counties, OH; Boone, Campbell, Gallatin, Grant, Kenton and Pendleton Counties, KY; Dearborn and Ohio Counties, IN

Cleveland, OH MSA
Ashtabula, Cuyahoga, Geauga, Lake, Lorain and Medina Counties

Colorado Springs, CO MSA
El Paso County

Columbia, SC MSA
Lexington and Richland Counties

Columbus, OH MSA
Delaware, Fairfield, Franklin, Licking, Madison, and Pickaway Counties

Dallas, TX MSA
Collin, Dallas, Denton, Ellis, Henderson, Hunt, Kaufman and Rockwall Counties

Denver, CO MSA
Adams, Arapahoe, Denver, Douglas, and Jefferson Counties

Des Moines, IA MSA
Dallas, Polk, and Warren Counties

Durham, NC
See Raleigh-Durham-Chapel Hill, NC MSA

Edison, NJ
See Middlesex-Somerset-Hunterdon, NJ MSA

El Paso, TX MSA
El Paso County

Eugene-Springfield, OR MSA
Lane County

Fort Collins-Loveland, CO MSA
Larimer County

Fort Lauderdale, FL MSA
Broward County

Fort Wayne, IN MSA
Adams, Allen, DeKalb, Huntington, Wells and Whitley Counties

Fort Worth-Arlington, TX MSA
Hood, Johnson, Parker and Tarrant Counties

Grand Rapids-Muskegon- Holland, MI MSA
Allegan, Kent, Muskegon and Ottawa Counties

Green Bay, WI MSA
Brown County

Greensboro–Winston-Salem–High Point, NC MSA
Alamance, Davidson, Davie, Forsyth, Guilford, Randolph, Stokes, and Yadkin Counties

Honolulu, HI MSA
Honolulu County

Houston, TX MSA
Chambers, Fort Bend, Harris, Liberty, Montgomery and Waller Counties

Huntsville, AL MSA
Limestone and Madison Counties

Indianapolis, IN MSA
Boone, Hamilton, Hancock, Hendricks, Johnson, Madison, Marion, Morgan, and Shelby Counties

Irvine, CA
See Orange County, CA MSA

Jacksonville, FL MSA
Clay, Duval, Nassau and St. Johns Counties

Kansas City, KS-MO MSA
Cass, Clay, Clinton, Jackson, Lafayette, Platte, and Ray Counties, MO; Johnson, Leavenworth, Miami, and Wyandotte Counties, KS

Knoxville, TN MSA
Anderson, Blount, Knox, Loudon, Sevier and Union Counties

Las Vegas, NV-AZ MSA
Clark and Nye Counties, NV; Mohave County, AZ

Lexington, KY MSA
Bourbon, Clark, Fayette, Jessamine, Madison, Scott and Woodford Counties

Lincoln, NE MSA
Lancaster County

Los Angeles-Long Beach, CA MSA
Los Angeles County

Louisville, KY-IN MSA
Bullitt, Jefferson, and Oldham Counties, KY; Clark, Floyd, Harrison, and Scott Counties, IN

Madison, WI MSA
Dane County

Manchester, NH
Manchester, NH MSA
Parts of Hillsborough, Merrimack and Rockingham Counties, NH
Boston-Worcester-Lawrence-Lowell-Brockton, MA-NH NECMA
Bristol, Essex, Middlesex, Norfolk, Plymouth, Suffolk, and Worcester Counties, MA; Hillsborough, Rockingham, and Strafford Counties, NH

Memphis, TN-AR-MS MSA
Fayette, Shelby, and Tipton Counties, TN; Crittenden County, AR; DeSoto County, MS

Miami, FL MSA
Miami-Dade County

Middlesex-Somerset-Hunterdon, NJ MSA
Hunterdon, Middlesex and Somerset Counties

Milwaukee-Waukesha, WI MSA
Milwaukee, Ozaukee, Washington, and Waukesha Counties

Minneapolis-St. Paul, MN-WI MSA
Anoka, Carver, Chisago, Dakota, Hennepin, Isanti, Ramsey, Scott, Sherburne, Washington, Wright and Pierce Counties, MN; St. Croix County, WI

Naperville, IL
See Chicago, IL MSA

Nashville, TN MSA
Cheatham, Davidson, Dickson, Robertson, Rutherford, Sumner, Williamson and Wilson Counties

New Orleans, LA MSA
Jefferson, Orleans, Plaquemines, St. Bernard, St. Charles, St. James, St. John the Baptist and St. Tammany Parishes

New York, NY MSA
Bronx, Kings, New York, Putnam, Queens, Richmond, Rockland, and Westchester Counties

Norfolk-Virginia Beach-Newport News, VA-NC MSA
Chesapeake, Hampton, Newport News, Norfolk, Poquoson, Portsmouth, Suffolk, Virginia Beach, and Williamsburg Cities, VA; Gloucester, Isle of Wright, James City, Mathews and York Counties, VA; Currituck County, NC

Oklahoma City, OK MSA
Canadian, Cleveland, Logan, McClain, Oklahoma and Pottawatomie Counties

Omaha, NE-IA MSA
Cass, Douglas, Sarpy, and Washington Counties, NE; Pottawattamie County, IA

Orange County, CA MSA
Orange County

Orlando, FL MSA
Lake, Orange, Osceola and Seminole Counties

Overland Park, KS
See Kansas City, KS-MO MSA

Philadelphia, PA-NJ MSA
Bucks, Chester, Delaware, Montgomery and Philadelphia Counties, PA; Burlington, Camden, Gloucester and Salem Counties, NJ

Phoenix-Mesa, AZ MSA
Maricopa and Pinal Counties

Pittsburgh, PA MSA
Allegheny, Beaver, Butler, Fayette, Washington and Westmoreland Counties

Plano, TX
See Dallas, TX MSA

Portland-Vancouver, OR-WA MSA
Clackamas, Columbia, Multnomah, Washington, and Yamhill Counties, OR; Clark County, WA

Providence, RI
Providence-Fall River-Warwick, RI-MA MSA
Parts of Newport and Washington Counties, RI; all of Bristol, Kent, and Providence Counties, RI; part of Bristol County, MA
Providence-Warwick-Pawtucket, RI NECMA
Bristol, Kent, Providence and Washington Counties

Provo-Orem, UT MSA
Utah County

Raleigh-Durham-Chapel Hill, NC MSA
Chatham, Durham, Franklin, Johnston, Orange, and Wake Counties

Reno, NV MSA
Washoe County

Richmond-Petersburg, VA MSA
Colonial Heights, Hopewell, Petersburg, and Richmond Cities; Charles City, Chesterfield, Dinwiddie, Goochland, Hanover, Henrico, New Kent, Powhatan, and Prince George Counties

Rochester, NY MSA
Genesee, Livingston, Monroe, Ontario, Orleans, and Wayne Counties

Sacramento, CA MSA
El Dorado, Placer, and Sacramento Counties

Saint Louis, MO-IL MSA
St. Louis and Sullivan Cities; Crawford (part), Franklin, Jefferson, Lincoln, St. Charles, St. Louis and Warren Counties, MO; Clinton, Jersey, Madison, Monroe, and St. Clair Counties, IL

Saint Paul, MN
See Minneapolis-St. Paul, MN-WI MSA

Salt Lake City-Ogden, UT MSA
Davis, Salt Lake, and Weber Counties

San Antonio, TX MSA
Bexar, Comal, Guadalupe and Wilson Counties

San Diego, CA MSA
San Diego County

San Francisco, CA MSA
Marin, San Francisco and San Mateo Counties

San Jose, CA MSA
Santa Clara County

Savannah, GA MSA
Bryan, Chatham, and Effingham Counties

Scottsdale, AZ
See Phoenix-Mesa, AZ MSA

Seattle-Bellevue-Everett, WA MSA
Island, King and Snohomish Counties

Sioux Falls, SD MSA
Lincoln and Minnehaha Counties

Springfield, MO MSA
Christian, Greene and Webster Counties

St. Petersburg, FL
See Tampa-St. Petersburg-Clearwater, FL MSA

Stamford, CT
Stamford-Norwalk, CT MSA
Part of Fairfield County
New Haven-Bridgeport-Stamford-Waterbury-Danbury, CT NECMA
Fairfield and New Haven Counties

Tampa-St. Petersburg- Clearwater, FL MSA
Hernando, Hillsborough, Pasco and Pinellas Counties

Thousand Oaks, CA
See Ventura, CA MSA

Tucson, AZ MSA
Pima County

Tulsa, OK MSA
Creek, Osage, Rogers, Tulsa, and Wagoner Counties

Ventura, CA MSA
Ventura County

Virginia Beach, VA
See Norfolk-Virginia Beach-Newport News, VA-NC MSA

Washington, DC-MD-VA-WV MSA
District of Columbia; Calvert, Charles, Frederick, Montgomery and Prince George Counties, MD; Alexandria, Fairfax, Falls Church, Fredericksburg, Manassas and Manassas Park cities; Arlington, Clarke, Culpeper, Fairfax, Fauquier, King George, Loudoun, Prince William, Spotsylvania, Stafford and Warren Counties, VA; Berkeley and Jefferson Counties, WV

Wichita, KS MSA
Butler, Harvey, and Sedgwick Counties

Appendix B: Current Metropolitan Area Definitions

Metropolitan Statistical Areas (MSA), Metropolitan Divisions (MD), New England City and Town Areas (NECTA), and New England City and Town Area Divisions (NECTA Division)
These current metropolitan area definitions went into effect June 6, 2003

Albuquerque, NM MSA
Bernalillo, Sandoval, Torrance, and Valencia Counties

Alexandria, VA
See Washington-Arlington-Alexandria, DC-VA-MD-WV MSA

Anchorage, AK MSA
Anchorage Municipality and Matanuska-Susitna Borough

Ann Arbor, MI MSA
Washtenaw County

Athens, GA MSA
Clarke, Madison, Oconee, and Oglethorpe Counties

Atlanta-Sandy Springs-Marietta, GA MSA
Barrow, Bartow, Butts, Carroll, Cherokee, Clayton, Cobb, Coweta, Dawson, DeKalb, Douglas, Fayette, Forsyth, Fulton, Gwinnett, Haralson, Heard, Henry, Jasper, Lamar, Meriwether, Newton, Paulding, Pickens, Pike, Rockdale, Spalding, and Walton Counties

Austin-Round Rock, TX MSA
Bastrop, Caldwell, Hays, Travis, and Williamson Counties

Baltimore-Towson, MD MSA
Baltimore city; Anne Arundel, Baltimore, Carroll, Harford, Howard, and Queen Anne's Counties

Baton Rouge, LA MSA
Ascension, East Baton Rouge, East Feliciana, Iberville, Livingston, Pointe Coupee, St. Helena, West Baton Rouge, and West Feliciana Parishes

Bellevue, WA
See Seattle-Tacoma-Bellevue, WA MSA

Birmingham-Hoover, AL MSA
Bibb, Blount, Chilton, Jefferson, Shelby, St. Clair, and Walker Counties

Boise City-Nampa, ID MSA
Ada, Boise, Canyon, Gem, and Owyhee Counties

Boston, MA
Boston-Cambridge-Quincy, MA-NH MSA
Essex, Middlesex, Norfolk, Plymouth, and Suffolk Counties, MA; Rockingham and Strafford Counties, NH
Boston-Quincy, MA MD
Norfolk, Plymouth, and Suffolk Counties
Boston-Cambridge-Quincy, MA-NH NECTA
Includes 155 cities and towns in Massachusetts and 38 cities and towns in New Hampshire
Boston-Cambridge-Quincy, MA NECTA Division
Includes 97 cities and towns in Massachusetts

Boulder, CO MSA
Boulder County

Bridgeport-Stamford-Norwalk, CT MSA
Fairfield County
Bridgeport-Stamford-Norwalk, CT NECTA
Includes 25 cities and towns in Connecticut

Buffalo-Niagara Falls, NY MSA
Erie and Niagara Counties

Cary, NC
See Raleigh-Cary, NC MSA

Cedar Rapids, IA MSA
Benton, Jones, and Linn Counties

Charleston-North Charleston, SC MSA
Berkeley, Charleston, and Dorchester Counties

Charlotte-Gastonia-Concord, NC-SC MSA
Anson, Cabarrus, Gaston, Mecklenburg, Union, and York Counties

Chattanooga, TN-GA MSA
Catoosa, Dade, and Walker Counties, GA; Hamilton, Marion, and Sequatchie Counties, TN

Chicago, IL
Chicago-Naperville-Joliet, IL-IN-WI MSA
Cook, DeKalb, DuPage, Grundy, Kane, Kendall, Lake, McHenry, and Will Counties, IL; Jasper, Lake, Newton, and Porter Counties, IN; Kenosha County, WI
Chicago-Naperville-Joliet, IL MD
Cook, DeKalb, DuPage, Grundy, Kane, Kendall, McHenry, and Will Counties

Cincinnati-Middletown, OH-KY-IN MSA
Dearborn, Franklin, and Ohio Counties, IN; Boone, Bracken, Campbell, Gallatin, Grant, Kenton, and Pendleton Counties, KY; Brown, Butler, Clermont, Hamilton, and Warren Counties, OH

Cleveland-Elyria-Mentor, OH MSA
Cuyahoga, Geauga, Lake, Lorain, and Medina Counties

Colorado Springs, CO MSA
El Paso and Teller Counties

Columbia, SC MSA
Calhoun, Fairfield, Kershaw, Lexington, Richland, and Saluda Counties

Columbus, OH MSA
Delaware, Fairfield, Franklin, Licking, Madison, Morrow, Pickaway, and Union Counties

Dallas, TX
Dallas-Fort Worth-Arlington, TX MSA
Collin, Dallas, Delta, Denton, Ellis, Hunt, Johnson, Kaufman, Parker, Rockwall, Tarrant, and Wise Counties
Dallas-Plano-Irving, TX MD
Collin, Dallas, Delta, Denton, Ellis, Hunt, Kaufman, and Rockwall Counties

Denver-Aurora, CO MSA
Adams, Arapahoe, Broomfield, Clear Creek, Denver, Douglas, Elbert, Gilpin, Jefferson, and Park Counties

Des Moines, IA MSA
Dallas, Guthrie, Madison, Polk, and Warren Counties

Durham, NC MSA
Chatham, Durham, Orange, and and Person Counties

Edison, NJ
Edison, NJ MD
Hunterdon, Middlesex and Somerset Counties
See also New York-Northern New Jersey-Long Island, NY-NJ-PA MSA

El Paso, TX MSA
El Paso County

Eugene-Springfield, OR MSA
Lane County

Fort Collins-Loveland, CO MSA
Larimer County

Fort Lauderdale, FL
Fort Lauderdale-Pompano Beach-Deerfield Beach, FL MD
Broward County
See also Miami-Fort Lauderdale-Miami Beach, FL MSA

Fort Wayne, IN MSA
Allen, Wells, and Whitley Counties

Fort Worth, TX
Fort Worth-Arlington, TX MD
Johnson, Parker, Tarrant, and Wise Counties
See also Dallas-Fort Worth-Arlington, TX MSA

Grand Rapids-Wyoming, MI MSA
Barry, Ionia, Kent, and Newaygo Counties

Green Bay, WI MSA
Brown, Kewaunee, and Oconto Counties

Greensboro-High Point, NC MSA
Guilford, Randolph, and Rockingham Counties

Honolulu, HI MSA
Honolulu County

Houston-Baytown-Sugar Land, TX MSA
Austin, Brazoria, Chambers, Fort Bend, Galveston, Harris, Liberty, Montgomery, San Jacinto, and Waller Counties

Huntsville, AL MSA
Limestone and Madison Counties

Indianapolis, IN MSA
Boone, Brown, Hamilton, Hancock, Hendricks, Johnson, Marion, Morgan, Putnam, and Shelby Counties

Irvine, CA
Santa Ana-Anaheim-Irvine, CA MD
Orange County
See also Los Angeles-Long Beach-Santa Ana, CA MSA

Jacksonville, FL MSA
Baker, Clay, Duval, Nassau, and St. Johns Counties

Kansas City, MO-KS MSA
Franklin, Johnson, Leavenworth, Linn, Miami, and Wyandotte Counties, KS; Bates, Caldwell,

Cass, Clay, Clinton, Jackson, Lafayette, Platte, and Ray Counties, MO

Knoxville, TN MSA
Anderson, Blount, Knox, Loudon, and Union Counties

Las Vegas-Paradise, NV MSA
Clark County

Lexington-Fayette, KY MSA
Bourbon, Clark, Fayette, Jessamine, Scott, and Woodford Counties

Lincoln, NE MSA
Lancaster and Seward Counties

Los Angeles, CA
Los Angeles-Long Beach-Santa Ana, CA MSA
Los Angeles and Orange Counties
Los Angeles-Long Beach-Glendale, CA MD
Los Angeles County
Santa Ana-Anaheim-Irvine, CA MD
Orange County

Louisville, KY-IN MSA
Clark, Floyd, Harrison, and Washington Counties, IN; Bullitt, Henry, Jefferson, Meade, Nelson, Oldham, Shelby, Spencer, and Trimble Counties, KY

Madison, WI MSA
Columbia, Dane, and Iowa Counties

Manchester-Nashua, NH MSA
Hillsborough County
Manchester, NH NECTA
Includes 9 cities and towns in New Hampshire

Memphis, TN-MS-AR MSA
Crittenden County, AR; DeSoto, Marshall, Tate, and Tunica Counties, MS; Fayette, Shelby, and Tipton Counties, TN

Miami, FL
Miami-Fort Lauderdale-Miami Beach, FL MSA
Broward, Miami-Dade, and Palm Beach Counties
Miami-Miami Beach-Kendall, FL MD
Miami-Dade County

Milwaukee-Waukesha-West Allis, WI MSA
Milwaukee, Ozaukee, Washington, and Waukesha Counties

Minneapolis-St. Paul-Bloomington, MN-WI MSA
Anoka, Carver, Chisago, Dakota, Hennepin, Isanti, Ramsey, Scott, Sherburne, Washington, and Wright Counties, MN; Pierce and St. Croix Counties, WI

Naperville, IL
See Chicago-Naperville-Joliet, IL-IN-WI MSA

Nashville-Davidson— Murfreesboro, TN MSA
Cannon, Cheatham, Davidson, Dickson, Hickman, Macon, Robertson, Rutherford, Smith, Sumner, Trousdale, Williamson, and Wilson Counties

New Orleans-Metairie-Kenner, LA MSA
Jefferson, Orleans, Plaquemines, St. Bernard, St. Charles, St. John the Baptist, and St. Tammany Parishes

New York, NY
New York-Northern New Jersey-Long Island, NY-NJ-PA MSA
Bergen, Essex, Hudson, Hunterdon, Middlesex, Monmouth, Morris, Ocean, Passaic, Somerset, Sussex, and Union Counties, NJ; Bronx, Kings, Nassau, New York, Putnam, Queens, Richmond, Rockland, Suffolk, and Westchester Counties, NY; Pike County, PA
New York-Wayne-White Plains, NY-NJ MD
Bergen, Hudson, and Passaic Counties, NJ; Bronx, Kings, New York, Putnam, Queens, Richmond, Rockland, and Westchester Counties, NY

Norfolk, VA
See Virginia Beach-Norfolk-Newport News, VA-NC MSA

Oklahoma City, OK MSA
Canadian, Cleveland, Grady, Lincoln, Logan, McClain, and Oklahoma Counties

Omaha-Council Bluffs, NE-IA MSA
Harrison, Mills, and Pottawattamie Counties, IA; Cass, Douglas, Sarpy, Saunders, and Washington Counties, NE

Orlando, FL MSA
Lake, Orange, Osceola, and Seminole Counties

Overland Park, KS
See Kansas City, MO-KS MSA

Oxnard-Thousand Oaks-Ventura, CA MSA
Ventura County

Philadelphia, PA
Philadelphia-Camden-Wilmington, PA-NJ-DE-MD MSA
New Castle County, DE; Cecil County, MD; Burlington, Camden, Gloucester, and Salem Counties, NJ; Bucks, Chester, Delaware, Montgomery, and Philadelphia Counties, PA

Philadelphia, PA MD
Bucks, Chester, Delaware, Montgomery, and Philadelphia Counties

Phoenix-Mesa-Scottsdale, AZ MSA
Maricopa and Pinal Counties

Pittsburgh, PA MSA
Allegheny, Armstrong, Beaver, Butler, Fayette, Washington, and Westmoreland Counties

Plano, TX
See Dallas-Fort Worth-Arlington, TX MSA

Portland-Vancouver-Beaverton, OR-WA MSA
Clackamas, Columbia, Multnomah, Washington, and Yamhill Counties, OR; Clark and Skamania Counties, WA

Providence-New Bedford-Fall River, RI-MA MSA
Bristol County, MA; Bristol, Kent, Newport, Providence, and Washington Counties, RI
Providence-Fall River-Warwick, RI-MA NECTA
Includes 12 cities and towns in Massachusetts and 37 cities and towns in Rhode Island

Provo-Orem, UT MSA
Juab and Utah Counties

Raleigh-Cary, NC MSA
Franklin, Johnston, and Wake Counties

Reno-Sparks, NV MSA
Storey and Washoe Counties

Richmond, VA MSA
Petersburg, Colonial Heights, Hopewell, and Richmond cities; Amelia, Caroline, Charles City, Chesterfield, Cumberland, Dinwiddie, Goochland, Hanover, Henrico, King William, King and Queen, Louisa, New Kent, Powhatan, Prince George, and Sussex Counties

Rochester, NY MSA
Livingston, Monroe, Ontario, Orleans, and Wayne Counties

Sacramento—Arden-Arcade—Roseville, CA MSA
El Dorado, Placer, Sacramento, and Yolo Counties

Saint Louis, MO-IL MSA
Bond, Calhoun, Clinton, Jersey, Macoupin, Madison, Monroe, and St. Clair Counties, IL; St. Louis city; Franklin, Jefferson, Lincoln, St. Charles, St. Louis, Warren, and Washington Counties, MO

Saint Paul, MN
See Minneapolis-St. Paul-Bloomington, MN-WI MSA

Saint Petersburg, FL
See Tampa-St. Petersburg-Clearwater, FL MSA

Salt Lake City, UT MSA
Salt Lake, Summit, and Tooele Counties

San Antonio, TX MSA
Atascosa, Bandera, Bexar, Comal, Guadalupe, Kendall, Medina, and Wilson Counties

San Diego-Carlsbad-San Marcos, CA MSA
San Diego County

San Francisco, CA
San Francisco-Oakland-Fremont, CA MSA
Alameda, Contra Costa, Marin, San Francisco, and San Mateo Counties
San Francisco-San Mateo-Redwood City, CA MD
Marin, San Francisco, and San Mateo Counties

San Jose-Sunnyvale-Santa Clara, CA MSA
San Benito and Santa Clara Counties

Savannah, GA MSA
Bryan, Chatham, and Effingham Counties

Scottsdale, AZ
See Phoenix-Mesa-Scottsdale, AZ MSA

Seattle, WA
Seattle-Tacoma-Bellevue, WA MSA
King, Pierce, and Snohomish Counties
Seattle-Bellevue-Everett, WA MD
King and Snohomish Counties

Sioux Falls, SD MSA
Lincoln, McCook, Minnehaha, and Turner Counties

Springfield, MO MSA
Christian, Dallas, Greene, Polk, and Webster Counties

Stamford, CT
See Bridgeport-Stamford-Norwalk, CT MSA

Tampa-St. Petersburg-Clearwater, FL MSA
Hernando, Hillsborough, Pasco, and Pinellas Counties

Thousand Oaks, CA
See Oxnard-Thousand Oaks-Ventura, CA MSA

Tucson, AZ MSA
Pima County

Tulsa, OK MSA
Creek, Okmulgee, Osage, Pawnee, Rogers, Tulsa, and Wagoner Counties

Virginia Beach-Norfolk-Newport News, VA-NC MSA
Currituck County, NC; Chesapeake, Hampton, Newport News, Norfolk, Poquoson, Portsmouth, Suffolk, Virginia Beach and Williamsburg cities, VA; Gloucester, Isle of Wight, James City, Mathews, Surry, and York Counties, VA

Washington, DC
Washington-Arlington-Alexandria, DC-VA-MD-WV MSA
District of Columbia; Calvert, Charles, Frederick, Montgomery, and Prince George's Counties, MD; Alexandria, Fairfax, Falls Church, Fredericksburg, Manassas Park, and Manassas cities, VA; Arlington, Clarke, Fairfax, Fauquier, Loudoun, Prince William, Spotsylvania, Stafford, and Warren Counties, VA; Jefferson County, WV
Washington-Arlington-Alexandria, DC-VA-MD-WV MD
District of Columbia; Calvert, Charles, and Prince George's Counties, MD; Alexandria, Fairfax, Falls Church, Fredericksburg, Manassas Park, and Manassas cities, VA; Arlington, Clarke, Fairfax, Fauquier, Loudoun, Prince William, Spotsylvania, Stafford, and Warren Counties, VA; Jefferson County, WV

Wichita, KS MSA
Butler, Harvey, Sedgwick, and Sumner Counties

Appendix C: Counties

Albuquerque, NM
Bernalillo County

Alexandria, VA
Alexandria City

Anchorage, AK
Anchorage County

Ann Arbor, MI
Washtenaw County

Athens, GA
Clarke County

Atlanta, GA
Fulton County

Austin, TX
Travis County

Baltimore, MD
Baltimore City

Baton Rouge, LA
East Baton Rouge Parish

Bellevue, WA
King County

Birmingham, AL
Jefferson County

Boise City, ID
Ada County

Boston, MA
Suffolk County

Boulder, CO
Boulder County

Buffalo, NY
Erie County

Cary, NC
Wake County

Cedar Rapids, IA
Linn County

Charleston, SC
Charleston County

Charlotte, NC
Mecklenburg County

Chattanooga, TN
Hamilton County

Chicago, IL
Cook County

Cincinnati, OH
Hamilton County

Cleveland, OH
Cuyahoga County

Colorado Springs, CO
El Paso County

Columbia, SC
Richland County

Columbus, OH
Franklin County

Dallas, TX
Dallas County

Denver, CO
Denver County

Des Moines, IA
Polk County

Durham, NC
Durham County

Edison, NJ
Middlesex County

El Paso, TX
El Paso County

Eugene, OR
Lane County

Fort Collins, CO
Larimer County

Fort Lauderdale, FL
Broward County

Fort Wayne, IN
Allen County

Fort Worth, TX
Tarrant County

Grand Rapids, MI
Kent County

Green Bay, WI
Brown County

Greensboro, NC
Guilford County

Honolulu, HI
Honolulu County

Houston, TX
Harris County

Huntsville, AL
Madison County

Indianapolis, IN
Marion County

Irvine, CA
Orange County

Jacksonville, FL
Duval County

Kansas City, MO
Jackson County

Knoxville, TN
Knox County

Las Vegas, NV
Clark County

Lexington, KY
Fayette County

Lincoln, NE
Lancaster County

Los Angeles, CA
Los Angeles County

Louisville, KY
Jefferson County

Madison, WI
Dane County

Manchester, NH
Hillsborough County

Memphis, TN
Shelby County

Miami, FL
Dade County

Milwaukee, WI
Milwaukee County

Minneapolis, MN
Hennepin County

Naperville, IL
DuPage County

Nashville, TN
Davidson County

New York, NY
New York County

Norfolk, VA
Norfolk City

Oklahoma City, OK
Oklahoma County

Omaha, NE
Douglas County

Orlando, FL
Orange County

Overland Park, KS
Johnson County

Philadelphia, PA
Philadelphia County

Phoenix, AZ
Maricopa County

Pittsburgh, PA
Allegheny County

Plano, TX
Collin County

Portland, OR
Multnomah County

Providence, RI
Providence County

Provo, UT
Utah County

Raleigh, NC
Wake County

Reno, NV
Washoe County

Richmond, VA
Richmond City

Rochester, NY
Monroe County

Sacramento, CA
Sacramento County

Saint Louis, MO
Saint Louis City

Saint Paul, MN
Ramsey County

Saint Petersburg, FL
Pinellas County

Salt Lake City, UT
Salt Lake County

San Antonio, TX
Bexar County

San Diego, CA
San Diego County

San Francisco, CA
San Francisco County

San Jose, CA
Santa Clara County

Savannah, GA
Chatham County

Scottsdale, AZ
Maricopa County

Seattle, WA
King County

Sioux Falls, SD
Minnehaha County

Springfield, MO
Greene County

Stamford, CT
Fairfield County

Tampa, FL
Hillsborough County

Thousand Oaks, CA
Ventura County

Tucson, AZ
Pima County

Tulsa, OK
Tulsa County

Virginia Beach, VA
Virginia Beach City

Washington, DC
District of Columbia

Wichita, KS
Sedgwick County

Note: in cases where a city's population is split over multiple counties, data in this book reflects the county where the majority of the population resides.

Appendix D: Chambers of Commerce

Albuquerque, NM

Albuquerque Chamber of Commerce
P.O. Box 25100
Albuquerque, NM 87125
Phone: (505) 764-3700
Fax: (505) 764-3714

Albuquerque Economic Development Dept
851 University Blvd SE
Suite 203
Albuquerque, NM 87106
Phone. (505) 246-6200
Fax: (505) 246-6219

Alexandria, VA

Alexandria Chamber of Commerce
801 North Fairfax Street
Suite 402
Alexandria, VA 22314
Phone: (703) 549-1000
Fax: (703) 739-3805

Anchorage, AK

Anchorage Chamber of Commerce
441 West 5th Avenue
Suite 300
Anchorage, AK 99501
Phone: (907) 272-2401
Fax: (907) 272-4117

Ann Arbor, MI

Ann Arbor Area Chamber of Commerce
425 South Main
Suite 103
Ann Arbor, MI 48104
Phone: (734) 665-4433
Fax: (734) 665-4191

Athens, GA

Athens Area Chamber of Commerce
246 W. Hancock Ave.
Athens, GA 30601
Phone: (706) 549-0095
Fax: (706) 549-5636

Atlanta, GA

Metro Atlanta Chamber of Commerce
PO Box 1740
Atlanta, GA 30303
Phone: (404) 586-8430
Fax: (404) 586-8464

Austin, TX

Greater Austin Chamber of Commerce
210 Barton Springs Road
Suite 400
Austin, TX 78704
Phone: (512) 322-5615
Fax: (512) 478-6389

Baltimore, MD

Baltimore City Chamber of Commerce
3 West Baltimore Street
Baltimore, MD 21201
Phone: (410) 837-7101
Fax: (410) 837-7104

City of Baltimore Development Corporation
36 South Charles Street
Suite 1600
Baltimore, MD 21201
Phone: (410) 837-9305
Fax: (410) 837-6363

Baton Rouge, LA

Baton Rouge Chamber of Commerce
PO Box 3217
Baton Rouge, LA70821
Phone: (225) 381-7150
Fax: (225) 336-4306

Economic Development Corporation
1051 North 3rd Street
Room 156
Baton Rouge, LA 70802
Phone: (225) 342-5388
Fax: (225) 342-5389

Bellevue, WA

Bellevue Chamber of Commerce
10500 8th Street Northeast
Suite 212
Bellevue, WA 98004
Phone: (425) 454-2464
Fax: (425) 462-4660

Birmingham, AL

Birmingham Area Chamber of Commerce
505 North 20th Street
Suite 200
Birmingham, AL 35203
Phone: (205) 324-2100
Fax: (205) 324-2314

Boise City, ID

Boise Metro Chamber of Commerce
250 S 5th Street
Suite 800
Boise City, ID 83702
Phone: (208) 472-5200
Fax: (208) 472-5201

Boston, MA

Greater Boston Chamber of Commerce
75 State Street
Boston, MA 02109
Phone: (617) 227-4500
Fax: (617) 227-7505

Boulder, CO

Boulder Chamber of Commerce
P.O. Box 73
Boulder, CO 80306
Phone: (303) 442-1044
Fax: (303) 938-8837

Buffalo, NY

Buffalo-Niagara Partnership
665 Main Street
Suite 200
Buffalo, NY 14203
Phone: (716) 852-7100
Fax: (716) 852-2761

Cary, NC

Cary Chamber of Commerce
307 North Academy Street
P.O. Box 4351
Cary, NC 27519
Phone: (919) 467-1016
Fax: (919) 469-2375

Cedar Rapids, IA

Cedar Rapids Chamber of Commerce &
Department of Economic Development
424 First Avenue NE
Cedar Rapids, IA 52401
Phone: (319) 398-5317
Fax: (319) 398-5228

Charleston, SC

Central Midlands Council of Government
Research Data Center
236 Stoneridge Drive
Columbia, SC 29210
Phone: (803) 376-5390
Fax: (803) 376-5394

Charlotte, NC

Charlotte Chamber of Commerce
P.O. Box 32785
Charlotte, NC 28232
Phone: (704) 378-1300
Fax: (704) 374-1903

Charlotte Regional Partnership
1001 Morehead Square Drive
Suite 200
Charlotte, NC 28203
Phone: (704) 347-8942
Fax: (704) 347-8981

Chattanooga, TN

Chattanooga Chamber of Commerce
811 Broad Street #100
Chattanooga, TN 37402
Phone: (423) 763-4342
Fax: (423) 267-7242

Community Development Department
100 East 11th Street
Room 104, City Hall Annex
Chattanooga, TN 37402
Phone: (423) 757-5133
Fax: (423) 425-6447

Chicago, IL

Chicagoland Chamber of Commerce
330 North Wabash
Suite2800
Chicago, IL 60611
Phone: (312) 494-6700
Fax: (312) 494-0196

City of Chicago
Department of Planning and Development
City Hall, Room 1000
121 North La Salle Street
Chicago, IL 60602
Phone: (312) 744-4190
Fax: (312) 744-2271

Cincinnati, OH

Greater Cincinnati
Chamber of Commerce
Suite 300
441 Vine Street
Cincinnati, OH 45202
Phone: (513) 579-3100
Fax: (513) 579-3101

Cleveland, OH

Cleveland Department of Economic
Development
601 Lakeside Avenue
Room 210
Cleveland, OH 44114-1015
Phone: (216) 664-2406
Fax: (216) 664-3681

Greater Cleveland Growth Association
200 Tower City Center
Cleveland, OH 44113
Phone: (216) 621-3300
Fax: (216) 621-6013

Colorado Springs, CO

Greater Colorado Springs Chamber of
Commerce
2 North Cascade Avenue
Suite 110
Colorado Springs, CO 80903
Phone: (719) 635-1551
Fax: (719) 635-1571

Greater Colorado Springs Economic
Development Corp
90 South Cascade Avenue
Suite 1050
Colorado Springs, CO 80903
Phone: (719) 471-8183
Fax: (719) 471-9733

Columbia, SC

City of Columbia Office of Economic
Development
1201 Main Street
Suite 250
Columbia, SC 29201
Phone: (803) 734-2700
Fax: (803) 734-2702

Columbia Chamber of Commerce
PO Box 1360
Columbia, SC 29202
Phone: (803) 733-1110
Fax: (803) 733-1125

Columbus, OH

Greater Columbus Chamber
37 North High Street
Columbus, OH 43215
Phone: (614) 221-1321
Fax: (614) 221-1408

Dallas, TX

City of Dallas
Economic Development Department
1500 Marilla Street
Room 5C South
Dallas, TX 75201
Phone: (214) 670-1685
Fax: (214) 670-0158

Greater Dallas Chamber of Commerce
700 North Pearl Street
Suite1200
Dallas, TX 75201
Phone: (214) 746-6600
Fax: (214) 746-6799

Denver, CO

Denver Metro Chamber of Commerce
1445 Market Street
Denver, CO 80202
Phone: (303) 534-8500
Fax: (303) 534-2145

Downtown Denver Partnership
511 16th Street
Suite 200
Denver, CO 80202
Phone: (303) 534-6161
Fax: (303) 534-2803

Des Moines, IA

Greater Des Moines Partnership
700 Locust Street
Suite 100
Des Moines, IA 50309
Phone: (515) 286-4950
Fax: (515) 286-4974

Durham, NC

Durham Chamber of Commerce
300 West Morgan Street
Suite1400
Durham, NC 27701
Phone: (919) 682-2133
Fax: (919) 688-8351

Edison, NJ

Edison Chamber of Commerce
336 Raritan Center Parkway
Campus Plaza 6
Edison, NJ 08837
Phone: (732) 738-9482
Fax: (732) 738-9485

El Paso, TX

City of El Paso Department
of Economic Development
2 Civic Center Plaza
El Paso, TX 79901
Phone: (915) 533-4284
Fax: (915) 541-1316

Greater El Paso Chamber of Commerce
10 Civic Center Plaza
El Paso, TX 79901
Phone: (915) 534-0593
Fax: (915) 534-0513

Eugene, OR

Eugene Area Chamber of Commerce
1401 Williamette Street
Eugene, OR 97401
Phone: (541) 484-1314
Fax: (541) 484-4942

Fort Collins, CO

Fort Collins Chamber of Commerce
225 South Meldrum
Fort Collins, CO 80521
Phone: (970) 482-3746
Fax: (970) 482-3774

Fort Lauderdale, FL

Fort Lauderdale Chamber of Commerce
512 NE 3rd Avenue
Fort Lauderdale, FL 33301
Phone: (954) 462-6000
Fax: (954) 527-8766

Fort Wayne, IN

City of Fort Wayne
Economic Development
City-County Building
Room 800
1 Main Street
Fort Wayne, IN 46802
Phone: (260) 427-1127
Fax: (260) 427-1375

Greater Fort Wayne Chamber of Commerce
826 Ewing Street
Fort Wayne, IN 46802
Phone: (260) 424-1435
Fax: (260) 426-7232

Fort Worth, TX

City of Fort Worth
Economic Development
City Hall
900 Monroe Street
Suite 301
Fort Worth, TX 76102
Phone: (817) 392-6103
Fax: (817) 392-2431

Fort Worth Chamber of Commerce
777 Taylor Street
Suite 900
Fort Worth, TX 76102-4997
Phone: (817) 336-2491
Fax: (817) 877-4034

Grand Rapids, MI

Grand Rapids Area
Chamber of Commerce
111 Pearl Street NW
Grand Rapids, MI 49503
Phone: (616) 771-0300
Fax: (616) 771-0318

Green Bay, WI

Economic Development
100 North Jefferson
Room 202
Green Bay, WI 54301
Phone: (920) 448-3397
Fax: (920) 448-3063

Green Bay Area Chamber of Commerce
400 South Washington Street
Green Bay, WI 54301
Phone: (920) 437-8704
Fax: (920) 437-1024

Greensboro, NC

Greensboro Area Chamber of Commerce
P.O. Box 3246
Greensboro, NC 27402
Phone: (336) 275-8675
Fax: (336) 275-9299

Honolulu, HI

Honolulu Chamber of Commerce
1132 Bishop Street
Suite 402
Honolulu, HI 96813
Phone: (808) 545-4300
Fax: (808) 545-4369

Houston, TX

Greater Houston Partnership
1200 Smith Street
Suite 700
Houston, TX 77002-4309
Phone: (713) 844-3600
Fax: (713) 844-0200

Huntsville, AL

Tennessee Valley Authority Economic
Development Corp.
Economic Development
P.O. Box 292409
Nashville, TN 37229-2409
Phone: 615-232-6225

Chamber of Commerce of Huntsville/Madison
County
PO Box 408
Huntsville, AL 35804
Phone: (256) 535-2000
Fax: (256) 535-2015

Indianapolis, IN

Greater Indianapolis
Chamber of Commerce
111 Monument Circle
Suite 1950
Indianapolis, IN 46204
Phone: (317) 464-2200
Fax: (317) 464-2217

The Indy Partnership
111 Monument Circle
Suite 1800
Indianapolis, IN 46204
Phone: (317) 236-6262
Fax: (317) 236-4332

Irvine, CA

Irvine Chamber of Commerce
2485 Mccabe Way
Suite 150
Irvine, CA 92614-6254
Phone: (949) 660-9112
Fax: (949) 660-0829

Irvine Economic Development
P.O. Box 19575
Irvine, CA 92623-9575
Phone: (949) 724-6000
Fax: (949) 724-6440

Jacksonville, FL

Jacksonville Chamber of Commerce
3 Independent Drive
Jacksonville, FL 32202
Phone: (904) 366-6686
Fax: (904) 366-6696

Kansas City, MO

Greater Kansas City
Chamber of Commerce
911 Main Street
2600 Commerce Tower
Kansas City, MO 64105
Phone: (816) 221-2424
Fax: (816) 221-7440

Kansas City Area Development Council
911 Main Street
Suite 2600
Kansas City, MO 64105
Phone: (816) 221-2121
Fax: (816) 842-2865

Knoxville, TN

Knoxville Area Chamber Partnership
17 Market Square
Suite 201
Knoxville, TN 37902-2021
Phone: (865) 637-4550
Fax: (865) 523-2071

Las Vegas, NV

Las Vegas Chamber of Commerce
3720 Howard Hughes Parkway
Las Vegas, NV 89109-0937
Phone: (702) 735-1616
Fax: (702) 735-2011

Las Vegas Office of Business Development
400 Stewart Avenue
Second Floor
Las Vegas, NV 89101
Phone: (702) 229-6551
Fax: (702) 385-3128

Lexington, KY

City of Lexington
Mayor's Office of Economic Development
200 East Main Street
Lexington, KY 40507
Phone: (859) 258-3131
Fax: (859) 258-3128

Greater Lexington Chamber of Commerce
330 East Main Street
Suite 100
Lexington, KY 40507
Phone: (859) 254-4447
Fax: (859) 233-3304

Lincoln, NE

Lincoln Chamber of Commerce
1135 M Street
Lincoln, NE 68508
Phone: (402) 436-2350
Fax: (402) 436-2360

Los Angeles, CA

Los Angeles County Economic Development
Corporation
444 South Flower Street
34th Floor
Los Angeles, CA 90071
Phone: (213) 622-4300
Fax: (213) 622-7100

Los Angeles Area Chamber of Commerce
350 South Bixel Street
Los Angeles, CA 90017
Phone: (213) 580-7500
Fax: (213) 580-7511

Louisville, KY

Louisville Chamber of Commerce
614 West Main Street
Louisville, KY 40202
Phone: (502) 625-0000
Fax: (502) 625-0010

Madison, WI

Greater Madison Chamber of Commerce
P.O. Box 71
Madison, WI 53701-0071
Phone: (608) 256-8348
Fax: (608) 256-0333

Manchester, NH

Greater Manchester
Chamber of Commerce
889 Elm Street
Manchester, NH 03101
Phone: (603) 666-6600
Fax: (603) 626-0910

Manchester Economic
Development Office
1 City Hall Plaza
Manchester, NH 03101
Phone: (603) 624-6505
Fax: (603) 624-6308

Memphis, TN

Memphis Regional Chamber
22 North Front Street
2nd Floor
Memphis, TN 38103
Phone: (901) 543-3500
Fax: (901) 543-3510

Miami, FL

Greater Miami Chamber of Commerce
Renaissance Hotel
1601 Biscayne Boulevard
Miami, FL 33132-1260
Phone: (305) 350-7700
Fax: (305) 374-6902

The Beacon Council
80 Southwest 8th Street
Suite 2400
Miami, FL 33130
Phone: (305) 579-1300
Fax: (305) 375-0271

Milwaukee, WI

City of Milwaukee
Department of City Development
Economic Development Department
809 North Broadway
P.O. Box 324
Milwaukee, WI 53202
Phone: (414) 286-5900
Fax: (414) 286-5778

Metropolitan Milwaukee
Association of Commerce
756 North Milwaukee Street
Milwaukee, WI 53202
Phone: (414) 287-4100

Minneapolis, MN

Minneapolis City Planning Department
350 South 5th Street
Room 210
Minneapolis, MN 55415
Phone: (612) 673-2597
Fax: (612) 673-2728

Minneapolis Community
Development Agency
Crown Roller Mill
105 5th Avenue South
Suite 200
Minneapolis, MN 55401
Phone: (612) 673-5095
Fax: (612) 673-5100

Minneapolis Regional
Chamber of Commerce
81 South 9th Street
Suite 200
Minneapolis, MN 55402
Phone: (612) 370-9100
Fax: (612) 370-9195

Naperville, IL

Naperville Area Chamber of Commerce
55 S Main Street
Suite 351
Naperville, IL 60540
Phone: (630) 355-4141
Fax: (630) 355-8335

Nashville, TN

Nashville Area Chamber of Commerce
211 Commerce Street
Suite 100
Nashville, TN 37201
Phone: (615) 743-3010
Fax: (615) 256-0393

New York, NY

New York City Economic
Development Corporation
110 William Street
New York, NY 10038
Phone: (212) (212) 312-3600
Fax: (212) 312-3909

New York City Partnership and
Chamber of Commerce
One Battery Park Plaza
New York, NY 10004
Phone: (212) 493-7400
Fax: (212) 344-3344

Norfolk, VA

Department of Development
500 East Main Street
Norfolk, VA 23510
Phone: (757) 664-4338
Fax: (757) 664-4315

Hampton Roads Chamber of Commerce
420 Bank Street
Norfolk, VA 23510
Phone: (757) 622-2313
Fax: (757) 622-5563

Oklahoma City, OK

Greater Oklahoma City Chamber of
Commerce
123 Park Avenue
Oklahoma City, OK 73102
Phone: (405) 297-8900
Fax: (405) 297-8916

Omaha, NE

Omaha Chamber of Commerce
1301 Harney Street
Omaha, NE 68102
Phone: (402) 346-5000
Fax: (402) 346-7050

Orlando, FL

Metro Orlando Economic Development
Commission of Mid-Florida
301 East Pine Street
Suite 900
Orlando, FL 32801
Phone: (407) 422-7159
Fax: (407) 425.6428

Orlando Regional Chamber of Commerce
75 South Ivanhoe Boulevard
Orlando, FL 32804
Phone: (407) 425-1234
Fax: (407) 839-5020

Overland Park, KS

Overland Park Chamber of Commerce
9001 West 110th Street
Suite 150
Overland Park, KS 66210
Phone: (913) 491-3600
Fax: (913) 491-0393

Philadelphia, PA

Greater Philadelphia Chamber of Commerce
200 South Broad Street
Philadelphia, PA 19102
Phone: (215) 545-1234
Fax: (215) 790-3600

Phoenix, AZ

City of Phoenix
Community and Economic Development
Department 200
West Washington
20th Floor
Phoenix, AZ 85003-1611
Phone: (602) 262-5040
Fax: (602) 495-5097

Greater Phoenix Chamber of Commerce
201 North Central Avenue
27th Floor
Phoenix, AZ 85073
Phone: (602) 254-5521
Fax: (602) 495-8913

Greater Phoenix Economic Council
2 North Central Avenue
Suite 2500
Phoenix, AZ 85004
Phone: (602) 256-7700
Fax: (602) 256-7744

Pittsburgh, PA

Allegheny County Industrial Development
Authority
425 6th Avenue
Suite 800
Pittsburgh, PA 15219
Phone: (412) 350-1000
Fax: (412) 642-2217

Greater Pittsburgh
Chamber of Commerce
425 6th Avenue
12th Floor
Pittsburgh, PA 15219
Phone: (412) 392-4500
Fax: (412) 392-4520

Plano, TX

Plano Chamber of Commerce
1200 East 15th Street
Plano, TX 75074
Phone: (972) 424-7547
Fax: (972) 422-5182

Plano Economic Development Board
4800 Preston Park Boulevard
Suite A-100
Plano, TX 75093
Phone: (972) 985-3700
Fax: (972) 985-3703

Portland, OR

Portland Business Alliance
520 SW Yamhill
Suite 1000
Portland, OR 97204
Phone: (503) 224-8684
Fax: (503) 323-9186

Providence, RI

Greater Providence
Chamber of Commerce
30 Exchange Terrace
Fourth Floor
Providence, RI 02903
Phone: (401) 521-5000
Fax: (401) 351-2090

Rhode Island Economic
Development Corporation
1 West Exchange Street
Providence, RI 02903
Phone: (401) 222-2601
Fax: (401) 222-2102

Provo, UT

Provo-Orem Chamber of Commerce
51 South University Avenue
Suite 215
Provo, UT 84601
Phone: (801) 851-2555
Fax: (801) 851-2557

Raleigh, NC

Greater Raleigh Chamber of Commerce
800 South Salisbury Street
Raleigh, NC 27601-2978
Phone: (919) 664-7000
Fax: (919) 664-7099

Reno, NV

Greater Reno-Sparks Chamber of Commerce
1 East First Street
16th Floor
Reno, NV 89505
Phone: (775) 337-3030
Fax: (775) 337-3038

Richmond, VA

Greater Richmond Chamber of Commerce
P.O. Box 12280
Richmond, VA 23241-2280
Phone: (804) 648-1234
Fax: (804) 783-9366

Greater Richmond Partnership
901 East Byrd Street
Suite 801
Richmond, VA 23219-4070
Phone: (804) 643-3227
Fax: (804) 343-7167

Rochester, NY

Rochester Business Alliance
150 State Street
Rochester, NY 14614
Phone: (585) 244.1800
Fax: (585) 263-3679

Rochester Economic Development Department
City of Rochester
30 Church Street
Room 005A
Rochester, NY 14614
Phone: (585)428-6808
Fax: (585) 428-6042

Sacramento, CA

Sacramento Chamber of Commerce
917 7th Street
Sacramento, CA 95814
Phone: (916) 552-6808
Fax: (916) 443-2672

Saint Louis, MO

St. Louis Regional Chamber &
Growth Association
One Metropolitan Square
Suite 1300
Saint Louis, MO 63102
Phone: (314) 231-5555
Fax:(314) 206-3222

Saint Paul, MN

Department of Trade and Economic
Development
500 Metro Square
121 7th Place East
Saint Paul, MN 55101
Phone: (651) 297-1291
Fax: (651) 284-0088

Saint Paul Area Chamber of Commerce
401 North Robert Street
Suite 150
Saint Paul, MN 55101
Phone: (651) 223-5000
Fax: (651) 223-5119

Saint Petersburg, FL

Saint Petersburg Area Chamber of Commerce
100 2nd Avenue North
Suite 150
Saint Petersburg, FL 33701
Phone: (727) 821-4069
Fax: (727) 895-6326

Salt Lake City, UT

Office of Business and Economic
Development
2001 South State Street
Suite N4300
SLC, UT 84109-3050
Phone: 801 468-2280
Fax: 801 468-2196

Salt Lake Area Chamber of Commerce
175 East 400 South
Suite 600
Salt Lake City, UT 84111
Phone: (801) 364-3631
Fax: (801) 328-5098

San Antonio, TX

The Greater San Antonio
Chamber of Commerce
602 E. Commerce Street
San Antonio, TX 78205
Phone: (210) 229-2100
Fax: (210) 229-1600

San Antonio Economic Development
Department
P.O. Box 839966
San Antonio, TX 78283-3966
Phone: (210) 207-8080
Fax: (210) 207-8151

San Diego, CA

San Diego Economic Development
Corporation
401 B Street
Suite 1100
San Diego, CA 92101
Phone: (619) 234-8484
Fax: (619) 234-1935

San Diego Regional Chamber of Commerce
402 West Broadway
Suite 1000
San Diego, CA 92101-3585
Phone: (619) 544-1300
Fax: (619) 744-7481

San Francisco, CA

San Francisco Chamber of Commerce
235 Montgomery Street
12th Floor
San Francisco, CA 94104
Phone: (415) 392-4520
Fax: (415) 392-0485

San Jose, CA

Office of Economic Development
60 South Market Street
Suite 470
San Jose, CA 95113
Phone: (408) 277-5880
Fax: (408) 277-3615

San Jose-Silicone Valley Chamber of
Commerce
310 South First Street
San Jose, CA 95113
Phone: (408) 291-5250
Fax: (408) 286-5019

Savannah, GA

Economic Development Authority
P.O. Box 128
Savannah, GA 31402
Phone: (912) 447-8450
Fax: (912) 447-8455

Savannah Chamber of Commerce
101 E. Bay Street
Savannah, GA 31402
Phone: (912) 644-6400
Fax: (912) 644-6499

Scottsdale, AZ

City of Scottsdale Economic Vitality
7447 East Indian School Road
Suite 200
Scottsdale, AZ 85251
Phone: (480) 312-7989
Fax: (480) 312-2672

Scottsdale Convention & Visitors Bureau
4343 N Scottsdale Road
Suite 170
Scottsdale, AZ 85251-4498
Phone: (480) 421-1004
Fax: (480) 421-9733

Seattle, WA

Greater Seattle Chamber of Commerce
1301 Fifth Avenue
Suite 2500
Seattle, WA 98101
Phone: (206) 389-7200
Fax: (206) 389-7288

Sioux Falls, SD

Sioux Falls Area Chamber of Commerce
200 North Phillips
Suite 102
Sioux Falls, SD 57104
Phone: (605) 336-1620
Fax: (605) 336-6499

Sioux Falls Development Foundation
200 North Phillips Avenue
Sioux Falls, SD 57104
Phone: (605) 339-0103
Fax: (605) 339-0055

Springfield, MO

City of Springfield
Department of Planning & Development
840 Booneville
Springfield, MO 65802
Phone: (417) 864-1000
Fax: (417) 864-1882

Springfield Area Chamber of Commerce
P.O. Box 1687
Springfield, MO 65801-1687
Phone: (417) 862-5567
Fax: (417) 862-1611

Stamford, CT

Stamford Chamber of Commerce
733 Summer Street
Stamford, CT 06901
Phone: (203) 359-4761
Fax: (203) 363-5069

Tampa, FL

Greater Tampa Chamber of Commerce
P.O. Box 420
Tampa, FL 33601-0420
Phone: (813) 276-9401
Fax: (813) 229-7855

Thousand Oaks, CA

Thousand Oaks-Westlake Village
Regional Chamber of Commerce
600 Hampshire Road
Suite #200
Westlake Village, CA 91361
Phone: (805) 370-0035
Fax: (805) 370-1083

Tucson, AZ

Tucson Metropolitan Chamber of Commerce
465 West St. Mary's Road
Tucson, AZ 85701
Phone: (520) 792-1212
Fax: (520) 882-5704

Tulsa, OK

Tulsa Metro Chamber
2 West 2nd Street
Williams Tower 2
Suite 150
Tulsa, OK 74103
Phone: (918) 585-1201
Fax: (918) 585-8016

Virginia Beach, VA

Hampton Roads Chamber of Commerce
420 Bank Street
Norfolk, VA 23510
Phone: (757) 622-2312
Fax: (757) 622-5563

Washington, DC

District of Columbia Chamber of Commerce
1213 K Street NW
Washington, DC 20005
Phone: (202) 347-7201
Fax: (202) 638-6762

District of Columbia Office of Planning
and Economic Development
J.A. Wilson Building
1350 Pennsylvania Avenue NW
Suite 317
Washington, DC 20004
Phone: (202) 727-6365
Fax: (202) 727-6703

Wichita, KS

City of Wichita
Economic Development Department
City Hall, 12th Floor
455 North Main Street
Wichita, KS 67202
Phone: (316) 268-4524
Fax: (316) 268-4656

Wichita Chamber of Commerce
350 West Douglas
Wichita, KS 67202
Phone: (316) 265-7771
Fax: (316) 265-7502

Appendix E: State Departments of Labor

Alabama

Commissioner
Alabama Department of Labor
P.O. Box 303500
Montgomery, AL 36130-3500
Phone: 334-242-3460
Fax: 334-240-3417

Director
Department of Industrial Relations
Industrial Relations Bldg.
649 Monroe Street, Room 204
Montgomery, AL 36131
Phone: 334-242-8990
Fax: 334-242-3960
Internet: www.dir.state.al.us

Alaska

Commissioner
Department of Labor and Workforce
Development
P.O. Box 21149
Juneau, AK 99801-1149
Phone: 907-465-2700
Fax: 907-465-2784
Internet: www.labor.state.ak.us

Arizona

Chairman
Industrial Commission
P.O. Box 19070
Phoenix, AZ 85005-9070
Phone: 602-542-4411
Fax: 602-542-7889

Director
State Labor Department
P.O. Box 19070
Phoenix, AZ 85005-9070
Phone: 602-542-4515
Fax: 602-542-8097
Internet: www.ica.state.az.us

California

Director
Department of Industrial Relations
455 Golden Gate Ave.,
10th Floor
San Francisco, CA 94102
Phone: 415-703-5050
Fax: 415-703-5059

State Labor Commissioner
Division of Labor Standards Enforcement
Department of Industrial Relations
455 Golden Gate Ave.,
9th Floor
San Francisco, CA 94102
Phone: 415-703-4810
Fax: 415-703-4807
Internet: www.dir.ca.gov

Colorado

Executive Director
Department of Labor and Employment
1515 Arapahoe Street, Tower 2, Suite 400
Denver, CO 80202-2117
Phone: 303-318-8000
Fax: 303-318-8048

Director
Labor Standards Office
1515 Arapahoe Street, Suite 375
Denver, CO 80202-2117
Phone: 303-318-8468
Fax: 303-318-8400
Internet: http://www.coworkforce.com

Connecticut

Commissioner
Labor Department
200 Folly Brook Boulevard
Wethersfield, CT 06109-1114
Phone: 860-263-6505
Fax: 860-263-6529
Internet: www.ctdol.state.ct.us

District of Columbia

Director
Department of Employment Services
Employment Security Building
54 New York Ave., NE, Suite 3007
Washington, D.C. 20002
Phone: 202-671-1900
Fax: 202-673-6993
Internet: does.ci.washington.dc.us

Florida

Secretary
Department of Business and Professional
Regulation
1940 N. Monroe St.
Tallahassee, FL 32399-0750
Phone: 850-488-3131
Fax: 850-487-1044
Internet: http://www.state.fl.us/dbpr/ or
http://www.MyFlorida.com
(Farm labor and child labor)

Director
Agency for Workforce Innovation
Caldwell Bldg., Suite 100
107 East Madison St.
Tallahassee, FL 32399-4120
Phone: 850-245-7105
Fax: 850-921-3223
Internet: http://www.floridajobs.org/ or
http://www.MyFlorida.com
(Employment related services)

Georgia

Commissioner
Department of Labor
Sussex Place - Room 600
148 International Blvd., N.E.
Atlanta, GA 30303
Phone: 404-656-3011
Fax: 404-656-2683
Internet: www.dol.state.ga.us

Hawaii

Director
Department of Labor and Industrial Relations
830 Punchbowl Street, Room 321
Honolulu, HI 96813
Phone: 808-586-8865/8844
Fax: 808-586-9099
Internet: hawaii.gov/labor

Idaho

Director
Department of Labor
317 W. Main Street
Boise, ID 83735-0001
Phone: 208-332-3579
Fax: 208-334-6430
Internet: www.labor.state.id.us

Illinois

Director
Department of Labor
160 N. LaSalle Street
13th Floor, Suite C-1300
Chicago, IL 60601
Phone: 312-793-1808
Fax: 312-793-5257
Internet: www.state.il.us/agency/idol

Indiana

Commissioner
Department of Labor
Indiana Government Center South
402 West Washington Street
Room W195
Indianapolis, IN 46204-2739
Phone: 317-232-2378
Fax: 317-233-5381
Internet: www.state.in.us/labor or
www.in.gov/labor/childlabor/safety.html

Iowa

Director
Iowa Workforce Development
1000 East Grand Avenue
Des Moines, IA 50319-0209
Phone: 515-281-5365
Fax: 515-281-4698

Labor Commissioner
Division of Labor Services
1000 East Grand Avenue
Des Moines, IA 50319
Phone: 515-281-3447
Fax: 515-281-4698
Internet: www.iowaworkforce.org/labor

Kansas

Secretary
Department of Human Resources
401 S.W. Topeka Boulevard
Topeka, KS 66603-3182
Phone: 785-296-7474
Fax: 785-368-6294
Internet: www2.hr.state.ks.us

Kentucky

Commissioner
Kentucky Department of Labor
1047 U.S. Hwy. 127 South, Suite 4
Frankfort, KY 40601-4381
Phone: 502-564-3070
Fax: 502-564-5387
Internet: labor.ky.gov

Louisiana

Secretary
Department of Labor
P.O. Box 94094
Baton Rouge, LA 70804-9094
Phone: 225-342-3011
Fax: 225-342-3778
Internet: www.ldol.state.la.us

Maryland

Secretary
Department of Labor, Licensing and
Regulation
500 N. Calvert Street, Suite 401
Baltimore, MD 21202
Phone: 410-230-6020 ext. 1393
Fax: 410-333-0853

Ass't Secretary
Department of Labor, Division of Workforce
Development.
1100 Eutaw St. - 6th Floor
Baltimore, MD 21201
Phone: 410-767-2999
Fax: 410-767-2986
Internet: www.dllr.state.md.us

Massachusetts

Director
Department of Labor & Work Force
Development
1 Ashburton Place, Rm 2112
Boston, MA 02108
Phone: 617-727-6573
Fax: 617-727-1090
Internet: www.mass.gov/dlwd or
www.state.ma.us

Michigan

Director
Department of Labor and Economic Growth
P.O. Box 30004
Lansing, MI 48909
Phone: 517-373-3034
Fax: 517-373-2129
Internet: www.michigan.gov/cis

Minnesota

Commissioner
Department of Labor and Industry
443 Lafayette Road
St. Paul, MN 55155
Phone: 651-284-5010
Fax: 651-284-5721
Internet: www.doli.state.mn.us

Missouri

Chairman
Labor and Industrial Relations Commission
P.O. Box 599
3315 W. Truman Boulevard
Jefferson City, MO 65102-0599
Phone: 573-751-2461
Fax: 573-751-7806

Members of the Commission
Labor and Industrial Relations Commission
P.O. Box 599
Jefferson City, MO 65102-0599
Phone: 573-751-2461
Fax: 573-751-7806

Director
Department of Labor & Industrial Relations
P.O. Box 504
Jefferson City, MO 65102-0504
Phone: 573-751-9691
Fax: 573-751-4135
Internet: www.dolir.mo.gov

Nebraska

Commissioner
Department of Labor
550 South 16th Street
Box 94600
Lincoln, NE 68509-4600
Phone: 402-471-3405
Fax: 402-471-2318
Internet: www.dol.state.ne.us/

Nevada

Commissioner
Office of the Nevada Labor Commissioner
Department of Business and Industry
555 E. Washington Avenue Suite 4100
Las Vegas, NV 89101-1050
Phone: 702-486-2650
Fax: 702-486-2660
Internet: www.LaborCommissioner.com or
http://dbi.state.nv.us

New Hampshire

Commissioner
Department of Labor
95 Pleasant Street
Concord, NH 03301
Phone: 603-271-3171
Fax: 603-271-6852
Internet: www.labor.state.nh.us

New Jersey

Department of Labor & Workforce
Development
John Fitch Plaza
13th Floor, Suite D
P.O. Box 110
Trenton, NJ 08625-0110
Phone: (609) 292-2323
Fax: (609) 633-9271
Internet: www.state.nj.us/labor

New Mexico

Secretary
Department of Labor
P.O. Box 1928
401 Broadway, N.E.
Albuquerque, NM 87103-1928
Phone: 505-841-8409
Fax: 505-841-8491
Internet:
www3.state.nm.us/dol/dol_home.html

New York

Commissioner
Department of Labor
State Campus, Building 12, Room 500
Albany, NY 12240-0003
Phone: 518-457-2741
Fax: 518-457-6908
-or-
345 Hudson Street
New York, NY 10014-0675
Phone: 212-352-6000
Internet: www.labor.state.ny.us

North Carolina

Commissioner
Department of Labor
4 West Edenton Street
Raleigh, NC 27601-1092
Phone: 919-733-0359
Fax: 919-733-0223
Internet: www.nclabor.com

Ohio

Director
Department of Commerce
77 South High St., 23rd floor
Columbus, OH 43215
Phone: 614-644-7047
Fax: 614-644-8292

Superintendant
Division of Labor and Worker Safety
50 West Broad St., 28th floor
Columbus, OH 43215
Phone: 614-644-2239
Fax: 614-728-8639-5650
Internet:
http://www.state.oh.us/ohio/agency.htm

Ohio Department of Job & Family Services
Office of Unemployment Compensation
Deputy Director
4300 Kimberly Parkway, Floor 4
Columbus, Ohio 43232
Phone: 614-995-7066
Fax: 614-466-6873
Internet: http://jfs.ohio.gov/ouc

Oklahoma

Commissioner
Department of Labor
4001 N. Lincoln Blvd.
Oklahoma City, OK 73105-5212
Phone: 405-528-1500, ext. 200
Fax: 405-528-5751
Internet: www.state.ok.us/~okdol

Oregon

Commissioner
Bureau of Labor and Industries
800 NE Oregon Street #32
Portland, OR 97232
Phone: 503-731-4070
Fax: 503-731-4103
Internet: www.boli.state.or.us

Pennsylvania

Secretary
Department of Labor and Industry
1700 Labor and Industry Building
7th and Forster Streets
Harrisburg, PA 17120
Phone: 717-787-5279
Fax: 717-787-8826
Internet: www.dli.state.pa.us

Rhode Island

Director
Department of Labor and Training
1511 Pontiac Avenue
Cranston, RI 02920
Phone: 401-462-8870
Fax: 401-462-8872
Internet: www.det.state.ri.us

South Carolina

Director
Dept. of Labor, Licensing & Regulations
Synergy Center - Kingstree Building
110 Center View Drive
P.O.Box 11329
Columbia, SC 29211-1329
Phone: 803-896-4300
Fax: 803-896-4393
Internet: www.llr.state.sc.us

South Dakota

Secretary
Department of Labor
700 Governors Drive
Pierre, SD 57501-2291
Phone: 605-773-3101
Fax: 605-773-4211
Internet: www.state.sd.us/dol/dol.htm

Tennessee

Commissioner
Department of Labor
Andrew Johnson Tower
710 James Robertson Pky.
8th Floor
Nashville, TN 37243-0655
Phone: 615-741-6642
Fax: 615-741-5078
Internet:www.state.tn.us/labor-wfd/

Texas

Executive Director
Texas Workforce Commission
101 East 15th Street, Rm 618
Austin, TX 78778
Phone: 512-463-0735
Fax: 512-475-2321

Commissioner Representing Labor
Texas Workforce Commission
101 East 15th Street, Rm 674
Austin, TX 78778
Phone: 512-463-2829
Fax: 512-475-2152
Internet: www.twc.state.tx.us

Utah

Commissioner
Utah Labor Commission
P.O. Box 146610
Salt Lake City, UT 84114-6610
Phone: 801-530-6880
Fax: 801-530-6804
Internet: www.labor.state.ut.us

Virginia

Commissioner
Dept. of Labor and Industry
Powers-Taylor Building
13 S. 13th St.
Richmond, VA 23219
Phone: 804-786-2377
Fax: 804-371-6524
Internet: www.dli.state.va.us

Washington

Director
Department of Labor & Industries
P.O. Box 44001
Olympia, WA 98504-4001
Phone: 360-902-4203
Fax: 360-902-4202
Internet: www.lni.wa.gov

Wisconsin

Secretary
Department of Workforce Development
201 East Washington Avenue, # A400
P.O. Box 7946
Madison, WI 53707-7946
Phone: 608-267-9692
Fax: 608-266-1784
Internet: www.dwd.state.wi.us

Appendix F:
Comparative Statistics

Population Growth: City

City	1990 Census	2000 Census	2006 Estimate	2006 Projection	Population Growth (%) 1990-2000	Population Growth (%) 2000-2011
Albuquerque	388,375	448,607	496,349	538,474	15.5	20.0
Alexandria	111,526	128,283	132,028	138,174	15.0	7.7
Anchorage	226,338	260,283	280,215	299,649	15.0	15.1
Ann Arbor	111,018	114,024	113,479	113,798	2.7	-0.2
Athens	86,561	100,266	103,825	107,339	15.8	7.1
Atlanta	394,092	416,474	419,483	422,907	5.7	1.5
Austin	499,053	656,562	689,258	724,669	31.6	10.4
Baltimore	736,014	651,154	632,002	618,008	-11.5	-5.1
Baton Rouge	223,299	227,818	221,874	218,588	2.0	-4.1
Bellevue	99,057	109,569	115,750	121,418	10.6	10.8
Birmingham	266,532	242,820	229,659	220,145	-8.9	-9.3
Boise City	144,317	185,787	190,621	196,868	28.7	6.0
Boston	574,283	589,141	559,205	531,782	2.6	-9.7
Boulder	87,737	94,673	92,593	91,744	7.9	-3.1
Buffalo	328,123	292,648	279,734	269,323	-10.8	-8.0
Cary	49,835	94,536	105,879	115,796	89.7	22.5
Cedar Rapids	110,829	120,758	121,142	121,816	9.0	0.9
Charleston	96,102	96,650	103,214	109,218	0.6	13.0
Charlotte	428,283	540,828	587,815	630,833	26.3	16.6
Chattanooga	152,695	155,554	154,090	153,690	1.9	-1.2
Chicago	2,783,726	2,896,016	2,848,075	2,810,383	4.0	-3.0
Cincinnati	363,974	331,285	308,590	290,671	-9.0	-12.3
Cleveland	505,333	478,403	453,176	432,735	-5.3	-9.5
Colorado Spgs.	283,798	360,890	370,258	378,756	27.2	5.0
Columbia	115,475	116,278	116,242	117,032	0.7	0.6
Columbus	648,656	711,470	731,326	746,932	9.7	5.0
Dallas	1,006,971	1,188,580	1,222,260	1,260,039	18.0	6.0
Denver	467,153	554,636	559,136	564,246	18.7	1.7
Des Moines	193,569	198,682	193,063	189,855	2.6	-4.4
Durham	151,737	187,035	204,204	218,675	23.3	16.9
Edison	88,680	97,687	101,075	104,070	10.2	6.5
El Paso	515,541	563,662	603,937	639,691	9.3	13.5
Eugene	118,073	137,893	144,090	149,543	16.8	8.4
Ft. Collins	89,555	118,652	127,205	133,641	32.5	12.6
Ft. Lauderdale	149,908	152,397	163,944	173,480	1.7	13.8
Ft. Wayne	205,671	205,727	203,369	202,483	0.0	-1.6
Ft. Worth	448,311	534,694	613,878	682,293	19.3	27.6
Grand Rapids	189,145	197,800	194,341	192,191	4.6	-2.8
Green Bay	96,466	102,313	100,007	98,966	6.1	-3.3
Greensboro	193,389	223,891	232,377	240,494	15.8	7.4
Honolulu	376,465	371,657	379,336	387,662	-1.3	4.3
Houston	1,697,610	1,953,631	2,027,393	2,107,075	15.1	7.9
Huntsville	161,842	158,216	164,347	169,982	-2.2	7.4
Indianapolis	730,993	781,870	784,844	788,055	7.0	0.8
Irvine	111,754	143,072	189,775	225,209	28.0	57.4
Jacksonville	635,221	735,617	801,934	867,665	15.8	18.0
Kansas City	434,967	441,545	446,344	451,668	1.5	2.3
Knoxville	173,288	173,890	176,626	179,784	0.3	3.4
Las Vegas	261,374	478,434	557,484	636,036	83.0	32.9
Lexington	225,366	260,512	268,470	275,509	15.6	5.8
Lincoln	193,629	225,581	238,857	249,757	16.5	10.7
Los Angeles	3,487,671	3,694,820	3,910,145	4,110,733	5.9	11.3
Louisville	269,160	256,231	245,308	237,980	-4.8	-7.1
Madison	193,451	208,054	220,669	231,276	7.5	11.2
Manchester	99,567	107,006	110,153	113,082	7.5	5.7

Table continued on next page.

City	1990 Census	2000 Census	2006 Estimate	2006 Projection	Population Growth (%)	
					1990-2000	2000-2011
Memphis	660,536	650,100	637,526	631,057	-1.6	-2.9
Miami	358,843	362,470	386,127	408,593	1.0	12.7
Milwaukee	628,095	596,974	581,168	570,791	-5.0	-4.4
Minneapolis	368,383	382,618	376,248	374,541	3.9	-2.1
Naperville	90,506	128,358	145,038	158,558	41.8	23.5
Nashville	488,364	545,524	549,040	553,995	11.7	1.6
New York	7,322,552	8,008,278	8,119,187	8,194,265	9.4	2.3
Norfolk	261,229	234,403	236,466	237,485	-10.3	1.3
Oklahoma City	445,065	506,132	536,284	561,124	13.7	10.9
Omaha	371,972	390,007	395,404	402,593	4.8	3.2
Orlando	161,172	185,951	207,702	229,467	15.4	23.4
Overland Park	111,803	149,080	166,051	179,924	33.3	20.7
Philadelphia	1,585,577	1,517,550	1,457,955	1,413,189	-4.3	-6.9
Phoenix	989,873	1,321,045	1,425,284	1,537,377	33.5	16.4
Pittsburgh	369,785	334,563	319,271	307,504	-9.5	-8.1
Plano	128,507	222,030	251,883	280,486	72.8	26.3
Portland	485,833	529,121	541,219	557,910	8.9	5.4
Providence	160,734	173,618	180,664	186,624	8.0	7.5
Provo	87,148	105,166	109,959	114,999	20.7	9.3
Raleigh	226,841	276,093	326,148	368,287	21.7	33.4
Reno	139,950	180,480	204,313	226,382	29.0	25.4
Richmond	202,783	197,790	190,982	186,313	-2.5	-5.8
Rochester	231,642	219,773	210,578	203,585	-5.1	-7.4
Sacramento	368,923	407,018	468,468	515,264	10.3	26.6
St. Louis	396,685	348,189	340,122	332,765	-12.2	-4.4
St. Paul	272,235	287,151	278,326	274,246	5.5	-4.5
St. Petersburg	238,846	248,232	250,579	255,172	3.9	2.8
Salt Lake City	159,796	181,743	177,325	175,202	13.7	-3.6
San Antonio	997,258	1,144,646	1,250,996	1,340,329	14.8	17.1
San Diego	1,111,048	1,223,400	1,294,273	1,369,292	10.1	11.9
San Francisco	723,959	776,733	750,596	746,548	7.3	-3.9
San Jose	784,324	894,943	915,192	938,342	14.1	4.8
Savannah	138,038	131,510	128,197	126,760	-4.7	-3.6
Scottsdale	130,300	202,705	223,930	245,298	55.6	21.0
Seattle	516,262	563,374	578,033	594,270	9.1	5.5
Sioux Falls	102,262	123,975	137,905	149,655	21.2	20.7
Springfield	142,557	151,580	149,816	149,435	6.3	-1.4
Stamford	108,087	117,083	120,825	123,907	8.3	5.8
Tampa	279,960	303,447	328,825	353,813	8.4	16.6
Thousand Oaks	104,661	117,005	127,283	135,790	11.8	16.1
Tucson	417,942	486,699	523,861	563,293	16.5	15.7
Tulsa	367,241	393,049	379,948	370,248	7.0	-5.8
Virginia Beach	393,069	425,257	440,908	452,071	8.2	6.3
Washington	606,900	572,059	546,363	530,783	-5.7	-7.2
Wichita	313,693	344,284	345,850	347,372	9.8	0.9
U.S.	248,709,873	281,421,906	298,021,266	312,383,955	13.2	11.0

Source: Claritas, Inc.

Population Growth: Metro Area

Metro Area	1990 Census	2000 Census	2006 Estimate	2011 Projection	Population Growth (%) 1990-2000	Population Growth (%) 2000-2011
Albuquerque	599,416	729,649	801,836	865,893	21.7	18.7
Alexandria	4,122,914	4,796,183	5,269,444	5,685,999	16.3	18.6
Anchorage	266,021	319,605	355,824	387,974	20.1	21.4
Ann Arbor	282,937	322,895	344,413	361,981	14.1	12.1
Athens	136,025	166,079	176,797	186,544	22.1	12.3
Atlanta	3,069,411	4,247,981	4,862,409	5,381,977	38.4	26.7
Austin	846,217	1,249,763	1,466,301	1,653,071	47.7	32.3
Baltimore	2,382,172	2,552,994	2,667,970	2,766,356	7.2	8.4
Baton Rouge	623,853	705,973	738,158	766,883	13.2	8.6
Bellevue	2,559,164	3,043,878	3,226,674	3,397,122	18.9	11.6
Birmingham	956,894	1,052,238	1,093,755	1,130,850	10.0	7.5
Boise City	319,596	464,840	544,754	612,275	45.4	31.7
Boston	4,133,895	4,391,344	4,424,623	4,439,570	6.2	1.1
Boulder	208,898	269,758	282,726	294,207	29.1	9.1
Buffalo	1,189,288	1,170,111	1,149,986	1,134,016	-1.6	-3.1
Cary	541,081	797,071	954,438	1,086,265	47.3	36.3
Cedar Rapids	210,640	237,230	247,005	255,223	12.6	7.6
Charleston	506,875	549,033	597,679	641,209	8.3	16.8
Charlotte	1,024,331	1,330,448	1,525,254	1,690,741	29.9	27.1
Chattanooga	433,166	476,531	494,513	510,886	10.0	7.2
Chicago	8,182,076	9,098,316	9,486,011	9,808,520	11.2	7.8
Cincinnati	1,844,917	2,009,632	2,074,785	2,129,253	8.9	6.0
Cleveland	2,102,219	2,148,143	2,133,762	2,122,866	2.2	-1.2
Colorado Spgs.	409,482	537,484	584,959	622,060	31.3	15.7
Columbia	548,325	647,158	691,656	730,942	18.0	12.9
Columbus	1,405,176	1,612,694	1,720,106	1,807,254	14.8	12.1
Dallas	3,989,294	5,161,544	5,888,054	6,519,110	29.4	26.3
Denver	1,666,935	2,179,296	2,375,424	2,534,563	30.7	16.3
Des Moines	416,346	481,394	522,995	558,168	15.6	15.9
Durham	344,646	426,493	459,936	490,467	23.7	15.0
Edison	16,845,992	18,323,002	18,811,585	19,193,362	8.8	4.8
El Paso	591,610	679,622	728,243	771,806	14.9	13.6
Eugene	282,912	322,959	336,438	348,705	14.2	8.0
Ft. Collins	186,136	251,494	272,172	288,180	35.1	14.6
Ft. Lauderdale	4,056,100	5,007,564	5,453,527	5,841,440	23.5	16.7
Ft. Wayne	354,435	390,156	405,903	419,146	10.1	7.4
Ft. Worth	3,989,294	5,161,544	5,888,054	6,519,110	29.4	26.3
Grand Rapids	645,914	740,482	775,786	804,232	14.6	8.6
Green Bay	243,698	282,599	300,307	315,453	16.0	11.6
Greensboro	540,257	643,430	676,090	705,130	19.1	9.6
Honolulu	836,231	876,156	909,408	940,689	4.8	7.4
Houston	3,767,335	4,715,407	5,329,525	5,850,510	25.2	24.1
Huntsville	293,047	342,376	369,472	392,185	16.8	14.5
Indianapolis	1,294,217	1,525,104	1,653,822	1,760,996	17.8	15.5
Irvine	11,273,720	12,365,627	13,155,105	13,873,953	9.7	12.2
Jacksonville	925,213	1,122,750	1,270,515	1,405,524	21.4	25.2
Kansas City	1,636,528	1,836,038	1,954,765	2,052,488	12.2	11.8
Knoxville	534,919	616,079	657,935	693,813	15.2	12.6
Las Vegas	741,459	1,375,765	1,752,385	2,083,252	85.5	51.4
Lexington	348,428	408,326	430,691	450,071	17.2	10.2
Lincoln	229,091	266,787	281,798	294,166	16.5	10.3
Los Angeles	11,273,720	12,365,627	13,155,105	13,873,953	9.7	12.2
Louisville	1,055,973	1,161,975	1,215,634	1,262,451	10.0	8.6
Madison	432,323	501,774	539,548	570,103	16.1	13.6
Manchester	336,073	380,841	403,939	422,869	13.3	11.0

Table continued on next page.

Metro Area	1990 Census	2000 Census	2006 Estimate	2011 Projection	Population Growth (%) 1990-2000	Population Growth (%) 2000-2011
Memphis	1,067,263	1,205,204	1,267,324	1,322,167	12.9	9.7
Miami	4,056,100	5,007,564	5,453,527	5,841,440	23.5	16.7
Milwaukee	1,432,149	1,500,741	1,518,612	1,534,398	4.8	2.2
Minneapolis	2,538,834	2,968,806	3,175,226	3,353,914	16.9	13.0
Naperville	8,182,076	9,098,316	9,486,011	9,808,520	11.2	7.8
Nashville	1,048,218	1,311,789	1,427,210	1,527,075	25.1	16.4
New York	16,845,992	18,323,002	18,811,585	19,193,362	8.8	4.8
Norfolk	1,449,389	1,576,370	1,655,652	1,716,580	8.8	8.9
Oklahoma City	971,042	1,095,421	1,161,740	1,217,895	12.8	11.2
Omaha	685,797	767,041	818,349	862,791	11.8	12.5
Orlando	1,224,852	1,644,561	1,958,637	2,242,511	34.3	36.4
Overland Park	1,636,528	1,836,038	1,954,765	2,052,488	12.2	11.8
Philadelphia	5,435,470	5,687,147	5,844,055	5,982,700	4.6	5.2
Phoenix	2,238,480	3,251,876	3,865,907	4,394,608	45.3	35.1
Pittsburgh	2,468,289	2,431,087	2,392,480	2,363,183	-1.5	-2.8
Plano	3,989,294	5,161,544	5,888,054	6,519,110	29.4	26.3
Portland	1,523,741	1,927,881	2,104,306	2,251,340	26.5	16.8
Providence	1,509,789	1,582,997	1,642,000	1,688,649	4.8	6.7
Provo	269,407	376,774	454,396	515,085	39.9	36.7
Raleigh	541,081	797,071	954,438	1,086,265	47.3	36.3
Reno	257,193	342,885	399,472	449,914	33.3	31.2
Richmond	949,244	1,096,957	1,175,013	1,242,759	15.6	13.3
Rochester	1,002,410	1,037,831	1,043,061	1,047,363	3.5	0.9
Sacramento	1,481,126	1,796,857	2,068,151	2,280,011	21.3	26.9
St. Louis	2,582,013	2,700,011	2,786,623	2,859,997	4.6	5.9
St. Paul	2,538,834	2,968,806	3,175,226	3,353,914	16.9	13.0
St. Petersburg	2,067,959	2,395,997	2,649,132	2,869,003	15.9	19.7
Salt Lake City	768,075	968,858	1,033,776	1,086,733	26.1	12.2
San Antonio	1,407,745	1,711,703	1,900,421	2,059,440	21.6	20.3
San Diego	2,498,016	2,813,833	2,996,862	3,182,742	12.6	13.1
San Francisco	3,686,592	4,123,740	4,184,673	4,270,050	11.9	3.5
San Jose	1,534,280	1,735,819	1,759,428	1,792,371	13.1	3.3
Savannah	258,060	293,000	317,871	340,125	13.5	16.1
Scottsdale	2,238,480	3,251,876	3,865,907	4,394,608	45.3	35.1
Seattle	2,559,164	3,043,878	3,226,674	3,397,122	18.9	11.6
Sioux Falls	153,500	187,093	209,324	228,132	21.9	21.9
Springfield	298,818	368,374	399,687	426,666	23.3	15.8
Stamford	827,645	882,567	909,943	932,975	6.6	5.7
Tampa	2,067,959	2,395,997	2,649,132	2,869,003	15.9	19.7
Thousand Oaks	669,016	753,197	811,349	861,071	12.6	14.3
Tucson	666,880	843,746	938,260	1,028,841	26.5	21.9
Tulsa	761,019	859,532	887,429	909,644	12.9	5.8
Virginia Beach	1,449,389	1,576,370	1,655,652	1,716,580	8.8	8.9
Washington	4,122,914	4,796,183	5,269,444	5,685,999	16.3	18.6
Wichita	511,111	571,166	588,984	603,312	11.7	5.6
U.S.	248,709,873	281,421,906	298,021,266	312,383,955	13.2	11.0

Note: Figures cover the Metropolitan Statistical Area (MSA) - see Appendix B for areas included
Source: Claritas, Inc.

Number of Households and Average Household Size: City

City	2006 Estimate	2006 Average Household Size
Albuquerque	204,602	2.43
Alexandria	63,775	2.07
Anchorage	102,096	2.74
Ann Arbor	46,601	2.44
Athens	40,938	2.54
Atlanta	170,316	2.46
Austin	278,341	2.48
Baltimore	256,508	2.46
Baton Rouge	87,691	2.53
Bellevue	49,309	2.35
Birmingham	94,759	2.42
Boise City	77,356	2.46
Boston	229,204	2.44
Boulder	38,924	2.38
Buffalo	118,085	2.37
Cary	38,190	2.77
Cedar Rapids	50,552	2.40
Charleston	44,910	2.30
Charlotte	235,324	2.50
Chattanooga	65,504	2.35
Chicago	1,042,014	2.73
Cincinnati	140,494	2.20
Cleveland	181,965	2.49
Colorado Spgs.	145,963	2.54
Columbia	43,276	2.69
Columbus	314,555	2.32
Dallas	459,445	2.66
Denver	236,917	2.36
Des Moines	78,629	2.46
Durham	81,979	2.49
Edison	36,374	2.78
El Paso	196,953	3.07
Eugene	61,501	2.34
Ft. Collins	49,388	2.58
Ft. Lauderdale	74,147	2.21
Ft. Wayne	83,780	2.43
Ft. Worth	223,150	2.75
Grand Rapids	72,469	2.68
Green Bay	41,394	2.42
Greensboro	96,308	2.41
Honolulu	145,319	2.61
Houston	740,774	2.74
Huntsville	71,135	2.31
Indianapolis	324,743	2.42
Irvine	66,776	2.84
Jacksonville	311,757	2.57
Kansas City	188,115	2.37
Knoxville	79,610	2.22
Las Vegas	202,372	2.75
Lexington	113,564	2.36
Lincoln	96,894	2.47
Los Angeles	1,342,430	2.91
Louisville	108,502	2.26
Madison	96,587	2.28
Manchester	45,964	2.40

Table continued on next page.

City	2006 Estimate	2006 Average Household Size
Memphis	247,763	2.57
Miami	143,465	2.69
Milwaukee	227,911	2.55
Minneapolis	159,837	2.35
Naperville	49,313	2.94
Nashville	230,716	2.38
New York	3,045,115	2.67
Norfolk	85,387	2.77
Oklahoma City	217,574	2.46
Omaha	160,920	2.46
Orlando	91,193	2.28
Overland Park	66,406	2.50
Philadelphia	572,210	2.55
Phoenix	500,680	2.85
Pittsburgh	139,331	2.29
Plano	95,374	2.64
Portland	228,778	2.37
Providence	64,298	2.81
Provo	31,498	3.49
Raleigh	133,185	2.45
Reno	83,036	2.46
Richmond	81,939	2.33
Rochester	85,572	2.46
Sacramento	176,122	2.66
St. Louis	144,699	2.35
St. Paul	107,976	2.58
St. Petersburg	110,573	2.27
Salt Lake City	69,884	2.54
San Antonio	447,215	2.80
San Diego	477,188	2.71
San Francisco	318,072	2.36
San Jose	280,122	3.27
Savannah	50,134	2.56
Scottsdale	100,800	2.22
Seattle	265,973	2.17
Sioux Falls	55,558	2.48
Springfield	65,433	2.29
Stamford	46,842	2.58
Tampa	135,052	2.43
Thousand Oaks	45,819	2.78
Tucson	208,565	2.51
Tulsa	160,926	2.36
Virginia Beach	162,877	2.71
Washington	241,391	2.26
Wichita	140,069	2.47
U.S.	112,267,302	2.65

Source: Claritas, Inc.

Number of Households and Average Household Size: Metro Area

City	2006 Estimate	2006 Average Household Size
Albuquerque	312,869	2.56
Alexandria	1,980,700	2.66
Anchorage	128,706	2.76
Ann Arbor	136,329	2.53
Athens	67,905	2.60
Atlanta	1,764,419	2.76
Austin	547,566	2.68
Baltimore	1,032,049	2.59
Baton Rouge	273,195	2.70
Bellevue	1,270,402	2.54
Birmingham	435,309	2.51
Boise City	198,867	2.74
Boston	1,710,643	2.59
Boulder	111,423	2.54
Buffalo	467,152	2.46
Cary	366,297	2.61
Cedar Rapids	99,184	2.49
Charleston	233,822	2.56
Charlotte	588,716	2.59
Chattanooga	199,120	2.48
Chicago	3,416,814	2.78
Cincinnati	815,238	2.55
Cleveland	858,735	2.48
Colorado Spgs.	218,358	2.68
Columbia	268,576	2.58
Columbus	687,355	2.50
Dallas	2,129,558	2.76
Denver	919,327	2.58
Des Moines	206,729	2.53
Durham	182,474	2.52
Edison	6,842,970	2.75
El Paso	227,382	3.20
Eugene	137,577	2.45
Ft. Collins	105,909	2.57
Ft. Lauderdale	2,055,392	2.65
Ft. Wayne	159,056	2.55
Ft. Worth	2,129,558	2.76
Grand Rapids	287,639	2.70
Green Bay	118,083	2.54
Greensboro	270,747	2.50
Honolulu	300,924	3.02
Houston	1,859,937	2.87
Huntsville	148,012	2.50
Indianapolis	649,127	2.55
Irvine	4,284,258	3.07
Jacksonville	493,066	2.58
Kansas City	769,215	2.54
Knoxville	274,743	2.39
Las Vegas	643,950	2.72
Lexington	175,695	2.45
Lincoln	112,412	2.51
Los Angeles	4,284,258	3.07
Louisville	491,551	2.47
Madison	222,214	2.43
Manchester	154,626	2.61

Table continued on next page.

City	2006 Estimate	2006 Average Household Size
Memphis	477,162	2.66
Miami	2,055,392	2.65
Milwaukee	605,939	2.51
Minneapolis	1,220,672	2.60
Naperville	3,416,814	2.78
Nashville	558,628	2.55
New York	6,842,970	2.75
Norfolk	616,984	2.68
Oklahoma City	459,900	2.53
Omaha	317,413	2.58
Orlando	743,424	2.63
Overland Park	769,215	2.54
Philadelphia	2,216,456	2.64
Phoenix	1,408,131	2.75
Pittsburgh	994,864	2.40
Plano	2,129,558	2.76
Portland	812,600	2.59
Providence	644,745	2.55
Provo	124,826	3.64
Raleigh	366,297	2.61
Reno	153,697	2.60
Richmond	459,198	2.56
Rochester	403,990	2.58
Sacramento	763,086	2.71
St. Louis	1,095,803	2.54
St. Paul	1,220,672	2.60
St. Petersburg	1,114,110	2.38
Salt Lake City	338,691	3.05
San Antonio	672,793	2.82
San Diego	1,055,563	2.84
San Francisco	1,555,486	2.69
San Jose	581,696	3.02
Savannah	120,949	2.63
Scottsdale	1,408,131	2.75
Seattle	1,270,402	2.54
Sioux Falls	81,456	2.57
Springfield	159,536	2.51
Stamford	333,909	2.73
Tampa	1,114,110	2.38
Thousand Oaks	261,600	3.10
Tucson	371,240	2.53
Tulsa	348,809	2.54
Virginia Beach	616,984	2.68
Washington	1,980,700	2.66
Wichita	227,927	2.58
U.S.	112,267,302	2.65

Note: Figures cover the Metropolitan Statistical Area (MSA) - see Appendix B for areas included
Source: Claritas, Inc.

Race and Ethnicity: City

City	White alone[2]	Black alone[2]	Asian alone[2]	Other Race alone[2]	Hispanic[3]
Albuquerque	69.3	3.2	2.4	25.1	42.7
Alexandria	63.3	20.2	4.6	11.9	14.3
Anchorage	69.2	5.9	6.5	18.4	7.2
Ann Arbor	71.9	7.9	15.1	5.1	3.7
Athens	63.4	26.9	3.4	6.3	8.9
Atlanta	35.2	57.7	2.6	4.5	5.9
Austin	62.4	8.8	5.6	23.1	35.0
Baltimore	30.4	65.0	1.8	2.9	2.3
Baton Rouge	42.2	52.8	3.0	2.0	2.1
Bellevue	69.0	2.0	21.7	7.3	6.7
Birmingham	20.5	76.5	0.9	2.1	2.3
Boise City	90.5	1.0	2.4	6.1	5.7
Boston	53.1	24.4	8.1	14.3	16.7
Boulder	86.6	1.3	4.5	7.5	10.2
Buffalo	52.0	38.8	1.8	7.5	8.4
Cary	78.6	6.2	10.7	4.5	5.4
Cedar Rapids	90.4	4.2	2.0	3.3	1.9
Charleston	65.3	31.0	1.5	2.2	2.0
Charlotte	53.3	34.9	4.0	7.7	10.6
Chattanooga	57.6	37.0	1.9	3.5	2.9
Chicago	40.8	36.1	4.6	18.4	28.7
Cincinnati	49.8	45.4	1.7	3.1	1.7
Cleveland	38.5	52.8	1.6	7.1	8.3
Colorado Spgs.	79.1	6.4	3.1	11.4	13.9
Columbia	48.2	46.1	2.0	3.7	3.4
Columbus	63.9	26.7	4.0	5.4	3.7
Dallas	48.6	24.3	3.0	24.2	42.8
Denver	64.0	10.3	3.1	22.7	35.4
Des Moines	79.2	8.4	4.0	8.4	9.4
Durham	44.5	41.4	4.4	9.8	12.6
Edison	50.1	7.4	37.0	5.4	8.0
El Paso	72.8	2.8	1.1	23.2	79.8
Eugene	86.2	1.4	4.5	8.0	6.0
Ft. Collins	87.9	1.3	2.8	8.0	10.0
Ft. Lauderdale	61.4	30.1	1.2	7.3	11.3
Ft. Wayne	72.3	18.5	1.9	7.3	7.7
Ft. Worth	57.4	19.9	2.9	19.8	34.6
Grand Rapids	63.6	21.2	1.7	13.5	17.1
Green Bay	81.4	2.2	4.1	12.2	11.1
Greensboro	51.7	39.4	3.3	5.6	6.1
Honolulu	19.1	2.0	56.3	22.6	4.7
Houston	47.5	24.5	5.5	22.5	42.6
Huntsville	62.3	31.6	2.4	3.6	2.4
Indianapolis	66.1	27.0	1.4	5.5	6.1
Irvine	53.9	1.3	36.9	7.9	7.4
Jacksonville	61.1	31.0	3.3	4.6	5.5
Kansas City	59.1	31.2	2.1	7.6	8.9
Knoxville	78.0	16.8	1.9	3.4	2.3
Las Vegas	65.5	10.9	5.6	18.0	29.0
Lexington	79.4	13.6	3.0	4.0	5.0
Lincoln	87.8	3.2	3.5	5.5	4.6
Los Angeles	46.1	10.1	10.4	33.4	49.5
Louisville	59.8	35.1	1.7	3.3	2.6
Madison	81.0	6.1	7.3	5.6	5.4
Manchester	88.6	2.8	3.5	5.0	6.6

Table continued on next page.

City	White alone[2]	Black alone[2]	Asian alone[2]	Other Race alone[2]	Hispanic[3]
Memphis	29.2	65.7	1.7	3.4	4.0
Miami	68.4	20.0	0.7	10.9	67.5
Milwaukee	45.2	39.8	3.3	11.8	14.8
Minneapolis	60.7	19.5	6.6	13.2	10.9
Naperville	79.6	3.9	13.6	2.8	4.3
Nashville	62.4	28.3	2.8	6.5	7.0
New York	43.5	25.6	10.9	20.0	27.9
Norfolk	47.6	43.9	3.0	5.5	4.3
Oklahoma City	66.0	15.4	3.9	14.7	13.1
Omaha	75.5	13.7	2.2	8.6	10.5
Orlando	56.9	27.9	3.3	11.9	21.8
Overland Park	87.3	3.6	5.3	3.8	4.8
Philadelphia	41.8	44.3	5.1	8.7	10.1
Phoenix	66.4	5.2	2.2	26.2	40.8
Pittsburgh	65.6	28.0	3.4	3.0	1.6
Plano	68.4	7.3	15.5	8.7	13.0
Portland	76.1	6.4	6.8	10.6	8.8
Providence	48.6	15.1	6.1	30.2	37.5
Provo	86.2	0.4	2.0	11.3	14.0
Raleigh	59.2	29.1	4.1	7.5	10.0
Reno	74.3	2.6	5.9	17.2	23.2
Richmond	38.3	56.2	1.3	4.1	3.6
Rochester	44.0	41.4	2.6	12.0	14.0
Sacramento	45.2	14.5	18.2	22.0	24.5
St. Louis	43.7	50.9	2.0	3.3	2.4
St. Paul	62.3	14.0	13.3	10.5	9.4
St. Petersburg	67.7	24.6	3.3	4.4	5.5
Salt Lake City	76.9	2.0	3.8	17.4	23.8
San Antonio	66.9	6.5	1.7	24.9	61.1
San Diego	58.9	6.7	14.7	19.6	27.8
San Francisco	48.4	7.1	33.1	11.4	14.0
San Jose	43.0	3.2	30.9	22.9	31.1
Savannah	35.8	59.3	1.8	3.1	2.6
Scottsdale	90.2	1.6	2.5	5.8	8.5
Seattle	68.6	7.9	14.5	9.1	6.3
Sioux Falls	89.9	2.1	1.3	6.7	3.7
Springfield	90.6	3.6	1.5	4.3	2.9
Stamford	67.1	14.2	6.4	12.4	21.3
Tampa	61.6	26.9	2.8	8.8	22.2
Thousand Oaks	83.3	1.1	7.0	8.7	14.6
Tucson	67.2	4.5	2.7	25.6	39.6
Tulsa	67.2	16.4	1.9	14.5	10.3
Virginia Beach	69.1	19.8	5.3	5.7	4.9
Washington	33.7	55.9	3.0	7.3	8.7
Wichita	72.5	11.7	4.5	11.2	12.0
U.S.	73.3	12.4	4.2	10.1	14.5

Note: Figures are 2006 estimates; (2) Alone is defined as not being in combination with one or more other races;
(3) May be of any race
Source: Claritas, Inc.

Race and Ethnicity: Metro Area

Metro Area	White alone[2]	Black alone[2]	Asian alone[2]	Other Race alone[2]	Hispanic[3]
Albuquerque	68.1	2.6	1.7	27.6	43.3
Alexandria	57.2	25.9	8.0	8.8	11.2
Anchorage	72.9	4.9	5.3	16.9	6.3
Ann Arbor	75.4	12.1	7.9	4.6	3.1
Athens	72.9	19.9	2.4	4.7	6.4
Atlanta	59.8	30.2	3.9	6.1	8.7
Austin	70.3	7.5	4.2	17.9	29.4
Baltimore	65.2	28.2	3.4	3.1	2.7
Baton Rouge	62.0	34.7	1.5	1.8	2.1
Bellevue	75.5	5.2	10.0	9.3	6.6
Birmingham	68.7	28.2	0.9	2.2	2.6
Boise City	88.4	0.7	1.4	9.5	10.5
Boston	81.0	6.3	5.7	7.1	7.6
Boulder	86.2	1.0	3.8	9.1	12.9
Buffalo	82.9	12.1	1.6	3.4	3.2
Cary	70.2	20.1	3.5	6.3	7.9
Cedar Rapids	93.8	2.5	1.3	2.4	1.4
Charleston	65.2	29.9	1.5	3.4	3.0
Charlotte	68.8	23.3	2.5	5.5	7.6
Chattanooga	82.3	14.1	1.2	2.4	1.9
Chicago	65.3	18.1	4.9	11.7	18.9
Cincinnati	84.7	11.7	1.5	2.1	1.5
Cleveland	75.0	19.6	1.7	3.7	3.8
Colorado Spgs.	80.4	6.1	2.6	10.9	12.6
Columbia	61.9	33.6	1.4	3.1	3.2
Columbus	79.6	14.0	2.8	3.6	2.5
Dallas	66.0	14.0	4.5	15.5	25.9
Denver	77.5	5.4	3.3	13.8	21.9
Des Moines	89.0	3.8	2.4	4.8	5.2
Durham	61.2	27.6	3.9	7.3	9.1
Edison	59.7	17.7	8.6	13.9	21.0
El Paso	73.5	2.7	1.0	22.8	81.4
Eugene	89.2	0.9	2.5	7.5	5.6
Ft. Collins	90.1	0.8	1.8	7.3	9.5
Ft. Lauderdale	70.0	19.7	2.0	8.4	37.9
Ft. Wayne	83.8	9.9	1.5	4.7	4.7
Ft. Worth	66.0	14.0	4.5	15.5	25.9
Grand Rapids	84.0	7.7	1.7	6.6	7.6
Green Bay	90.8	1.4	1.9	5.9	4.7
Greensboro	68.8	24.0	2.2	5.0	6.1
Honolulu	20.5	2.9	46.5	30.1	7.2
Houston	60.6	16.4	5.5	17.5	32.4
Huntsville	73.2	21.4	1.8	3.6	2.5
Indianapolis	80.1	14.5	1.6	3.8	4.0
Irvine	50.5	7.4	13.4	28.6	43.8
Jacksonville	70.9	22.4	2.7	4.1	4.9
Kansas City	80.2	12.2	1.9	5.7	6.5
Knoxville	90.0	6.4	1.3	2.3	1.7
Las Vegas	67.6	9.5	6.5	16.5	26.1
Lexington	84.2	10.3	2.1	3.4	4.0
Lincoln	89.2	2.8	3.1	4.9	4.1
Los Angeles	50.5	7.4	13.4	28.6	43.8
Louisville	82.8	13.2	1.2	2.8	2.3
Madison	88.4	3.7	3.8	4.1	4.0
Manchester	92.0	1.6	2.8	3.6	4.3

Table continued on next page.

Metro Area	White alone[2]	Black alone[2]	Asian alone[2]	Other Race alone[2]	Hispanic[3]
Memphis	50.3	45.2	1.6	2.9	3.1
Miami	70.0	19.7	2.0	8.4	37.9
Milwaukee	75.0	16.4	2.5	6.2	7.7
Minneapolis	83.7	6.1	4.8	5.4	4.3
Naperville	65.3	18.1	4.9	11.7	18.9
Nashville	78.7	15.1	1.9	4.3	4.7
New York	59.7	17.7	8.6	13.9	21.0
Norfolk	61.1	31.4	3.0	4.5	3.6
Oklahoma City	74.4	10.7	2.8	12.1	8.6
Omaha	84.6	7.7	1.8	5.9	6.9
Orlando	71.2	14.9	3.3	10.7	21.1
Overland Park	80.2	12.2	1.9	5.7	6.5
Philadelphia	70.5	20.4	4.0	5.0	5.9
Phoenix	73.8	3.9	2.4	19.9	29.3
Pittsburgh	89.0	8.2	1.3	1.5	0.9
Plano	66.0	14.0	4.5	15.5	25.9
Portland	82.4	2.7	5.2	9.7	9.4
Providence	84.8	4.2	2.3	8.7	8.7
Provo	91.3	0.3	1.2	7.3	8.5
Raleigh	70.2	20.1	3.5	6.3	7.9
Reno	77.6	2.2	4.8	15.4	20.0
Richmond	63.9	30.3	2.4	3.4	3.1
Rochester	82.4	11.1	2.2	4.3	4.9
Sacramento	66.5	7.2	10.5	15.9	17.5
St. Louis	77.9	18.1	1.7	2.3	1.9
St. Paul	83.7	6.1	4.8	5.4	4.3
St. Petersburg	80.4	11.1	2.4	6.2	13.2
Salt Lake City	84.6	1.2	2.7	11.5	14.5
San Antonio	70.6	6.1	1.5	21.8	52.5
San Diego	64.2	5.1	9.9	20.8	29.6
San Francisco	53.9	8.8	21.6	15.7	19.5
San Jose	49.5	2.5	29.0	19.0	25.7
Savannah	60.6	34.6	1.8	3.0	2.7
Scottsdale	73.8	3.9	2.4	19.9	29.3
Seattle	75.5	5.2	10.0	9.3	6.6
Sioux Falls	92.5	1.5	1.0	5.0	2.7
Springfield	94.3	1.7	0.9	3.1	2.0
Stamford	77.4	10.1	3.9	8.6	14.1
Tampa	80.4	11.1	2.4	6.2	13.2
Thousand Oaks	67.5	1.9	6.1	24.5	36.1
Tucson	72.9	3.1	2.3	21.7	32.4
Tulsa	74.7	8.8	1.3	15.2	6.3
Virginia Beach	61.1	31.4	3.0	4.5	3.6
Washington	57.2	25.9	8.0	8.8	11.2
Wichita	80.8	7.5	3.1	8.6	8.8
U.S.	73.3	12.4	4.2	10.1	14.5

Note: Figures are 2006 estimates and cover the Metropolitan Statistical Area (MSA) - see Appendix B for areas included
(2) Alone is defined as not being in combination with one or more other races; (3) May be of any race
Source: Claritas, Inc.

Age Distribution: City

Area	Percent of Population						
	Under Age 5	Age 5 to 17	Age 18 to 34	Age 35 to 49	Age 50 to 64	Age 65 to 79	80 Years and Over
Albuquerque	6.9	17.5	25.4	23.9	14.4	8.7	3.2
Alexandria	6.2	10.5	34.3	25.4	14.6	6.2	2.7
Anchorage	7.6	21.5	24.9	27.2	13.5	4.3	1.0
Ann Arbor	5.1	11.5	45.2	19.2	11.1	5.8	2.1
Athens	5.3	12.4	47.6	16.2	10.4	5.8	2.1
Atlanta	6.4	15.9	32.8	22.3	12.7	7.0	2.9
Austin	7.1	15.4	37.5	22.9	10.5	4.9	1.7
Baltimore	6.4	18.3	25.2	22.6	14.2	9.8	3.4
Baton Rouge	6.8	17.6	31.1	20.2	12.8	8.5	3.0
Bellevue	5.6	15.5	23.4	24.6	17.4	10.2	3.3
Birmingham	6.8	18.3	25.9	22.6	12.9	9.9	3.7
Boise City	7.0	18.2	27.8	23.9	13.0	6.9	3.2
Boston	5.4	14.3	37.2	20.8	11.8	7.5	2.9
Boulder	3.9	10.7	45.5	20.4	11.5	5.3	2.6
Buffalo	7.1	19.2	25.4	22.1	12.6	9.8	3.7
Cary	8.1	21.0	23.3	29.9	12.3	4.1	1.2
Cedar Rapids	6.9	17.5	25.6	22.7	14.2	9.3	3.8
Charleston	5.6	14.4	32.1	20.4	13.8	9.6	4.1
Charlotte	7.1	17.6	29.4	24.3	12.9	6.6	2.1
Chattanooga	5.9	16.4	24.8	21.9	15.7	11.2	4.1
Chicago	7.5	18.6	29.4	21.5	12.6	7.7	2.6
Cincinnati	7.2	17.3	29.6	21.6	12.0	8.7	3.7
Cleveland	8.1	20.4	24.5	22.1	12.4	9.3	3.3
Colorado Spgs.	7.5	19.0	25.6	24.9	13.5	7.1	2.5
Columbia	5.4	14.7	39.3	19.5	10.8	7.4	2.8
Columbus	7.4	16.7	33.5	22.0	11.5	6.6	2.2
Dallas	8.3	18.2	31.5	22.0	11.4	6.3	2.3
Denver	6.7	15.1	31.2	22.9	12.9	8.1	3.2
Des Moines	7.6	17.0	27.1	22.4	13.5	8.8	3.6
Durham	7.1	15.8	34.1	22.2	11.5	6.7	2.7
Edison	6.3	16.4	24.6	25.3	15.5	8.9	2.9
El Paso	8.3	22.6	24.1	21.6	12.7	8.5	2.2
Eugene	5.3	15.3	31.9	21.6	13.8	8.2	3.9
Ft. Collins	6.0	15.3	39.0	21.6	10.2	5.5	2.3
Ft. Lauderdale	5.1	14.1	22.6	26.1	16.7	11.1	4.3
Ft. Wayne	7.9	19.2	26.1	21.6	12.9	8.7	3.7
Ft. Worth	8.4	19.7	28.1	22.4	11.8	7.0	2.6
Grand Rapids	8.1	18.9	29.9	21.0	10.5	7.7	3.9
Green Bay	7.2	18.2	27.3	23.0	12.5	7.9	3.8
Greensboro	6.2	16.1	30.5	21.9	13.4	8.8	3.1
Honolulu	5.0	14.1	23.3	23.1	16.5	13.0	5.0
Houston	8.2	19.2	29.2	22.7	12.4	6.4	1.9
Huntsville	6.1	17.0	23.9	23.2	16.6	10.3	3.0
Indianapolis	7.4	18.2	26.7	23.6	13.1	8.2	2.8
Irvine	5.6	17.8	29.2	25.7	14.5	5.4	1.8
Jacksonville	7.3	19.4	25.1	24.2	13.8	7.8	2.4
Kansas City	7.1	18.2	26.0	23.4	13.6	8.7	3.0
Knoxville	5.8	13.8	32.4	20.4	13.2	10.3	4.1
Las Vegas	7.6	18.1	25.1	22.7	15.0	9.5	2.0
Lexington	6.2	15.1	31.6	23.5	13.7	7.4	2.6
Lincoln	6.7	16.3	32.1	22.0	12.5	7.6	2.9
Los Angeles	7.6	18.9	29.1	22.7	12.1	7.2	2.5
Louisville	6.6	17.1	24.8	23.3	13.6	10.4	4.3
Madison	5.1	12.4	39.4	21.3	12.5	6.7	2.6

Table continued on next page.

Area	Percent of Population						
	Under Age 5	Age 5 to 17	Age 18 to 34	Age 35 to 49	Age 50 to 64	Age 65 to 79	80 Years and Over
Manchester	6.8	17.0	26.2	23.5	13.6	9.0	4.0
Memphis	7.7	20.1	26.4	22.1	12.7	8.1	2.8
Miami	5.9	15.8	23.6	22.3	15.3	12.4	4.6
Milwaukee	7.9	20.8	27.8	21.0	11.7	7.9	3.0
Minneapolis	6.4	15.5	35.0	23.1	10.9	5.9	3.1
Naperville	8.3	23.7	19.2	29.4	13.1	4.6	1.7
Nashville	6.6	15.5	29.6	23.8	13.6	8.1	2.9
New York	6.7	17.5	26.8	22.9	14.4	8.6	3.1
Norfolk	7.1	16.9	33.6	20.5	11.0	8.1	2.8
Oklahoma City	7.3	18.2	25.6	23.0	14.4	8.6	2.9
Omaha	7.2	18.4	26.4	22.6	13.6	8.6	3.2
Orlando	6.5	15.5	31.2	23.3	12.1	8.3	3.1
Overland Park	7.1	18.5	21.7	26.1	15.0	8.2	3.3
Philadelphia	6.4	18.8	25.7	21.3	13.7	10.2	3.9
Phoenix	8.6	20.3	28.0	22.9	12.2	6.1	1.9
Pittsburgh	5.3	14.5	29.2	20.8	13.7	11.7	4.8
Plano	8.2	20.3	22.7	29.5	14.5	3.7	1.1
Portland	6.0	15.0	28.5	24.9	14.0	8.0	3.6
Providence	6.9	19.1	34.2	18.7	10.5	7.2	3.3
Provo	8.6	13.5	56.5	10.0	5.7	4.0	1.7
Raleigh	6.3	14.5	36.6	22.6	11.7	6.2	2.1
Reno	6.7	16.5	27.3	23.3	14.9	8.6	2.7
Richmond	6.3	15.6	29.7	22.1	12.9	9.5	3.9
Rochester	7.8	20.3	28.5	21.5	12.0	6.6	3.3
Sacramento	7.0	20.2	25.6	22.8	13.0	8.2	3.2
St. Louis	6.7	19.0	26.0	22.3	12.3	9.6	4.1
St. Paul	7.5	19.5	29.2	22.2	11.1	6.9	3.5
St. Petersburg	5.6	15.9	21.1	24.5	15.4	12.1	5.4
Salt Lake City	7.8	15.6	35.0	20.4	10.1	7.4	3.7
San Antonio	8.0	20.4	26.1	22.3	12.7	7.9	2.5
San Diego	6.7	17.2	30.0	23.3	12.4	7.8	2.6
San Francisco	4.0	10.4	32.1	25.0	14.6	10.0	3.8
San Jose	7.6	18.8	27.8	24.5	13.3	6.3	1.8
Savannah	7.0	18.6	27.7	20.1	13.2	9.4	4.0
Scottsdale	5.0	14.2	20.9	23.6	19.4	13.0	3.9
Seattle	4.6	10.9	33.5	25.1	13.8	8.1	4.0
Sioux Falls	7.3	17.9	27.8	23.3	12.7	7.9	3.1
Springfield	5.9	14.0	31.8	20.1	13.2	10.3	4.7
Stamford	6.7	15.3	24.7	24.6	14.8	10.0	3.9
Tampa	6.7	17.9	25.8	23.4	13.6	9.1	3.4
Thousand Oaks	6.5	19.2	19.2	26.0	18.1	7.9	3.0
Tucson	7.1	17.3	29.4	21.7	12.5	8.7	3.3
Tulsa	7.2	17.4	25.9	22.6	14.1	9.4	3.5
Virginia Beach	7.1	20.3	26.2	25.2	12.8	6.6	1.8
Washington	5.7	14.3	30.5	22.4	14.9	9.0	3.2
Wichita	7.9	19.1	25.0	23.0	13.1	8.8	3.1
U.S.	6.8	18.9	23.7	23.5	14.8	9.2	3.2

Source: Census 2000, Summary File 3

Age Distribution: Metro Area

Metro Area	Percent of Population						
	Under Age 5	Age 5 to 17	Age 18 to 34	Age 35 to 49	Age 50 to 64	Age 65 to 79	80 Years and Over
Albuquerque	7.0	19.2	23.6	24.3	14.6	8.4	2.8
Alexandria	6.9	18.3	24.6	25.8	15.3	6.8	2.2
Anchorage	7.6	21.5	24.9	27.2	13.5	4.3	1.0
Ann Arbor	6.5	18.0	27.7	24.4	14.6	6.7	2.2
Athens	5.9	15.5	38.3	19.4	12.3	6.3	2.3
Atlanta	7.5	19.1	27.0	25.4	13.5	5.8	1.8
Austin	7.4	17.9	31.5	24.4	11.7	5.4	1.8
Baltimore	6.5	18.8	22.3	24.9	15.5	9.0	3.0
Baton Rouge	7.2	20.0	26.9	22.9	13.6	7.3	2.2
Bellevue	6.3	17.4	25.2	26.1	14.7	7.4	2.9
Birmingham	6.7	18.4	23.5	23.7	15.0	9.5	3.2
Boise City	8.1	20.2	25.8	23.1	13.1	6.9	2.8
Boston	6.2	16.2	25.2	24.4	14.9	9.4	3.7
Boulder	6.0	16.8	29.5	26.0	13.8	5.7	2.1
Buffalo	6.0	18.3	20.9	23.5	15.3	11.6	4.3
Cary	6.9	17.3	29.0	24.9	13.3	6.5	2.1
Cedar Rapids	6.9	18.3	24.3	23.3	14.9	8.8	3.4
Charleston	6.7	19.0	25.6	23.6	14.8	8.0	2.4
Charlotte	7.1	18.3	25.7	24.4	14.5	7.8	2.4
Chattanooga	6.1	17.6	22.8	23.3	16.7	10.2	3.3
Chicago	7.4	19.4	24.9	23.6	13.9	7.9	2.8
Cincinnati	7.1	19.5	23.1	24.1	14.3	8.9	3.0
Cleveland	6.6	18.8	20.9	23.8	15.4	10.6	3.9
Colorado Spgs.	7.5	19.9	25.5	25.0	13.3	6.6	2.0
Columbia	6.5	18.5	26.5	24.2	14.5	7.6	2.3
Columbus	7.1	18.3	26.7	23.9	14.0	7.7	2.4
Dallas	8.1	19.9	27.3	24.4	12.7	5.8	1.8
Denver	7.1	18.6	25.6	25.6	14.1	6.8	2.2
Des Moines	7.5	18.4	24.6	23.9	14.4	8.1	3.0
Durham	6.9	17.3	29.0	24.9	13.3	6.5	2.1
Edison	6.7	17.6	22.8	26.1	15.0	8.9	2.9
El Paso	8.6	23.3	24.8	21.4	12.1	7.8	2.0
Eugene	5.7	17.1	24.9	22.9	16.1	9.7	3.6
Ft. Collins	6.0	17.6	28.5	24.4	13.9	7.1	2.5
Ft. Lauderdale	6.3	17.2	21.3	24.8	14.4	10.7	5.4
Ft. Wayne	7.5	20.3	22.8	23.2	14.2	8.6	3.4
Ft. Worth	7.7	20.2	25.2	24.6	13.5	6.7	2.0
Grand Rapids	7.5	20.8	24.2	23.6	13.1	7.8	3.0
Green Bay	6.9	19.1	25.2	24.5	13.6	7.5	3.2
Greensboro	6.6	17.4	24.3	23.6	15.6	9.5	3.0
Honolulu	6.4	17.3	24.8	23.1	14.9	10.2	3.3
Houston	8.1	21.1	26.0	24.6	12.9	5.8	1.6
Huntsville	6.8	18.6	23.1	25.0	15.6	8.6	2.3
Indianapolis	7.4	19.1	24.0	24.3	14.2	8.1	2.8
Irvine	7.5	19.4	25.6	24.0	13.7	7.3	2.5
Jacksonville	6.8	19.3	23.3	24.6	15.0	8.5	2.6
Kansas City	7.2	19.3	23.0	24.5	14.6	8.4	3.0
Knoxville	6.0	16.6	23.8	23.5	16.7	10.2	3.3
Las Vegas	7.3	17.9	24.2	22.7	16.1	9.7	2.1
Lexington	6.4	16.3	29.7	23.3	14.2	7.6	2.6
Lincoln	6.6	16.9	30.5	22.5	13.0	7.6	2.8
Los Angeles	7.7	20.3	26.7	23.0	12.6	7.3	2.4
Louisville	6.7	18.0	22.7	24.5	15.5	9.5	3.1
Madison	6.0	16.5	30.3	24.3	13.6	6.7	2.7

Table continued on next page.

Metro Area	Percent of Population						
	Under Age 5	Age 5 to 17	Age 18 to 34	Age 35 to 49	Age 50 to 64	Age 65 to 79	80 Years and Over
Manchester	6.8	19.0	23.2	25.8	14.3	7.9	3.1
Memphis	7.6	20.7	24.1	23.7	13.9	7.6	2.4
Miami	6.4	18.3	23.9	23.2	14.9	9.9	3.4
Milwaukee	6.9	19.5	22.8	23.9	14.3	9.1	3.4
Minneapolis	7.1	19.6	24.5	25.5	13.7	6.9	2.7
Naperville	7.4	19.4	24.9	23.6	13.9	7.9	2.8
Nashville	6.9	17.9	25.9	24.8	14.5	7.6	2.5
New York	6.7	17.6	25.9	23.2	14.7	8.8	3.2
Norfolk	6.9	19.4	25.7	24.2	13.6	7.9	2.4
Oklahoma City	6.9	18.6	25.4	23.1	14.6	8.5	2.8
Omaha	7.3	19.8	24.6	23.7	13.9	7.9	2.8
Orlando	6.5	18.2	24.4	24.2	14.4	9.5	2.9
Overland Park	7.2	19.3	23.0	24.5	14.6	8.4	3.0
Philadelphia	6.4	18.9	22.2	23.9	14.9	10.0	3.6
Phoenix	7.7	19.0	25.8	22.0	13.5	9.0	3.0
Pittsburgh	5.5	16.7	20.2	23.7	16.1	12.9	4.9
Plano	8.1	19.9	27.3	24.4	12.7	5.8	1.8
Portland	7.0	18.4	24.8	24.7	14.7	7.4	3.0
Providence	6.0	17.8	23.2	23.5	14.9	10.4	4.3
Provo	10.9	23.0	36.0	15.4	8.2	4.8	1.7
Raleigh	6.9	17.3	29.0	24.9	13.3	6.5	2.1
Reno	6.8	18.0	24.1	24.8	15.9	8.3	2.3
Richmond	6.5	18.7	23.2	25.3	15.1	8.5	2.8
Rochester	6.2	19.4	22.1	24.0	15.4	9.1	3.8
Sacramento	6.9	20.3	22.4	24.4	14.4	8.7	2.9
St. Louis	6.7	19.6	22.0	24.2	14.7	9.5	3.4
St. Paul	7.1	19.6	24.5	25.5	13.7	6.9	2.7
St. Petersburg	5.7	16.1	20.1	22.8	16.1	13.9	5.4
Salt Lake City	9.1	22.2	28.1	20.9	11.4	6.2	2.1
San Antonio	7.7	20.6	24.8	22.9	13.4	8.1	2.6
San Diego	7.0	18.6	26.9	23.5	12.8	8.3	2.9
San Francisco	5.1	13.5	26.7	25.6	15.8	9.6	3.6
San Jose	7.0	17.7	26.9	25.0	13.9	7.2	2.3
Savannah	6.8	19.3	24.7	22.9	14.4	8.9	3.0
Scottsdale	7.7	19.0	25.8	22.0	13.5	9.0	3.0
Seattle	6.3	17.4	25.2	26.1	14.7	7.4	2.9
Sioux Falls	7.4	19.2	25.6	24.0	12.9	7.8	3.1
Springfield	6.5	17.3	26.2	22.4	14.7	9.3	3.6
Stamford	7.2	17.7	19.1	26.0	16.3	10.0	3.7
Tampa	5.7	16.1	20.1	22.8	16.1	13.9	5.4
Thousand Oaks	7.4	20.9	22.7	24.6	14.3	7.4	2.6
Tucson	6.5	18.0	24.2	22.3	14.8	10.6	3.6
Tulsa	7.1	19.5	23.1	23.5	15.1	8.9	2.9
Virginia Beach	6.9	19.4	25.7	24.2	13.6	7.9	2.4
Washington	6.9	18.3	24.6	25.8	15.3	6.8	2.2
Wichita	7.6	20.4	23.0	23.7	13.4	8.8	3.0
U.S.	6.8	18.9	23.7	23.5	14.8	9.2	3.2

Note: Figures cover the Metropolitan Statistical Area (MSA) - see Appendix A for areas included
Source: Census 2000, Summary File 3

Segregation

Area	City		MSA[1]	
	Index[2]	Rank[3]	Index[2]	Rank[4]
Albuquerque	39.5	86	40.0	301
Alexandria	46.0	72	66.2	88
Anchorage	41.4	82	41.4	295
Ann Arbor	38.7	87	67.5	76
Athens	53.5	65	55.0	200
Atlanta	83.5	3	68.8	67
Austin	60.9	46	57.1	179
Baltimore	75.2	12	71.8	44
Baton Rouge	75.1	13	73.1	33
Bellevue	33.5	95	57.9	172
Birmingham	66.3	31	77.4	15
Boise City	32.9	96	37.1	310
Boston	75.8	10	68.8	68
Boulder	34.2	94	36.7	312
Buffalo	73.9	15	80.4	8
Cary	0.0	0	0.0	0
Cedar Rapids	45.9	73	51.8	219
Charleston	63.8	34	54.1	205
Charlotte	61.1	44	61.1	135
Chattanooga	66.9	30	73.1	34
Chicago	87.3	1	83.6	5
Cincinnati	63.0	39	78.0	14
Cleveland	79.4	8	79.7	9
Colorado Spgs.	46.1	71	46.5	261
Columbia	63.8	35	58.9	160
Columbus	61.0	45	66.9	78
Dallas	71.5	19	64.4	110
Denver	67.4	29	66.2	86
Des Moines	55.3	62	61.0	137
Durham	57.8	56	52.7	214
Edison	0.0	0	0.0	0
El Paso	39.5	85	41.1	296
Eugene	25.5	100	37.9	308
Ft. Collins	37.0	90	42.5	286
Ft. Lauderdale	80.5	6	64.8	101
Ft. Wayne	68.8	24	75.4	26
Ft. Worth	62.5	40	64.5	106
Grand Rapids	58.6	53	71.9	41
Green Bay	38.5	88	53.1	211
Greensboro	62.3	41	64.5	108
Honolulu	49.4	69	44.0	281
Houston	75.5	11	71.8	45
Huntsville	67.9	27	60.5	141
Indianapolis	67.4	28	75.5	24
Irvine	37.3	89	43.8	282
Jacksonville	55.8	61	59.3	154
Kansas City	70.7	22	72.7	37
Knoxville	59.6	49	63.2	119
Las Vegas	42.4	78	47.4	254
Lexington	50.2	68	51.7	220
Lincoln	44.3	75	46.6	260
Los Angeles	74.0	14	70.5	53
Louisville	73.8	16	68.6	69
Madison	43.3	77	53.0	213
Manchester	40.8	83	68.8	68

Table continued on next page.

Area	City Index[2]	City Rank[3]	MSA[1] Index[2]	MSA Rank[4]
Memphis	68.6	25	72.2	40
Miami	80.3	7	75.8	22
Milwaukee	71.4	20	84.4	3
Minneapolis	61.3	43	64.5	107
Naperville	35.6	92	83.6	5
Nashville	57.6	57	61.7	128
New York	85.3	2	84.3	4
Norfolk	57.5	58	53.0	212
Oklahoma City	59.0	52	60.5	142
Omaha	70.2	23	69.8	57
Orlando	71.8	18	60.0	146
Overland Park	30.9	97	72.7	37
Philadelphia	80.6	5	76.9	18
Phoenix	54.4	63	49.1	244
Pittsburgh	71.3	21	72.5	38
Plano	28.2	99	64.4	110
Portland	57.0	59	55.8	189
Providence	50.8	67	65.5	95
Provo	36.9	91	46.0	263
Raleigh	56.2	60	52.7	214
Reno	41.6	79	44.1	279
Richmond	68.3	26	62.9	122
Rochester	58.0	55	71.1	50
Sacramento	49.1	70	59.6	150
St. Louis	72.4	17	78.0	13
St. Paul	52.6	66	64.5	107
St. Petersburg	76.7	9	68.4	72
Salt Lake City	44.7	74	47.8	252
San Antonio	53.5	64	55.5	191
San Diego	63.6	36	58.2	171
San Francisco	62.2	42	65.6	94
San Jose	44.0	76	45.9	264
Savannah	60.3	48	64.6	103
Scottsdale	28.8	98	49.1	244
Seattle	64.2	33	57.9	172
Sioux Falls	40.1	84	48.2	249
Springfield	41.4	80	55.0	201
Stamford	63.4	37	71.1	51
Tampa	65.4	32	68.4	72
Thousand Oaks	0.0	0	0.0	0
Tucson	35.0	93	44.2	277
Tulsa	60.3	47	64.1	113
Virginia Beach	41.4	81	53.0	212
Washington	81.5	4	66.2	88
Wichita	59.4	51	63.4	117

Note: Figures are based on an analysis of Census 2000 data; (1) Metropolitan Statistical Area - see Appendix A for areas included; (2) White/Black Dissimilarity Index—the most commonly used measure of segregation between two groups, reflecting their relative distributions across neighborhoods within a city or metropolitan area. It can range in value from 0, indicating complete integration, to 100, indicating complete segregation; (3) Ranges from 1 (most segregated) to 100 (least segregated) and includes all the cities in this book; (4) Ranges from 1 (most segregated) to 318 (least segregated) and includes 318 metropolitan areas.
Source: www.CensusScope.org

Religion

City	County	Catholic	Southern Baptist	United Meth-odist	ELCA[1]	LDS[2]	Presby-terian Church USA	Jewish Est.	Muslim Est.
Albuquerque	Bernalillo	34.4	4.0	2.0	1.4	1.5	0.9	1.4	0.3
Alexandria	Alexandria City	18.8	3.9	3.0	0.0	0.6	3.6	4.2	3.0
Anchorage	Anchorage	8.8	4.6	0.9	1.8	3.2	0.8	0.9	0.5
Ann Arbor	Washtenaw	12.9	0.7	2.2	1.7	0.5	1.4	2.2	1.5
Athens	Clarke	4.9	12.8	7.0	0.4	0.5	2.5	0.4	0.3
Atlanta	Fulton	8.8	10.0	9.2	0.8	0.3	3.7	8.1	2.7
Austin	Travis	20.4	9.5	2.7	1.5	0.6	1.3	1.7	0.4
Baltimore	Baltimore City	12.5	0.8	2.7	1.8	0.1	1.5	8.7	1.6
Baton Rouge	East Baton Rouge	23.2	13.7	5.7	0.2	0.4	1.0	0.2	0.4
Bellevue	King	16.2	0.7	1.1	2.0	2.3	1.6	1.9	0.5
Birmingham	Jefferson	6.7	29.7	8.0	0.2	0.3	1.5	0.8	0.3
Boise City	Ada	12.3	1.0	2.0	1.0	15.2	0.7	0.3	0.1
Boston	Suffolk	45.0	0.6	0.2	0.1	0.1	0.1	3.6	2.0
Boulder	Boulder	20.2	1.0	1.8	3.0	1.6	1.8	4.5	1.4
Buffalo	Erie	57.3	0.2	2.0	2.0	0.2	1.3	2.1	0.6
Cary	Wake	9.5	12.6	7.4	0.9	0.6	2.7	1.0	0.5
Cedar Rapids	Linn	23.3	0.6	7.5	5.7	0.7	2.9	0.2	1.2
Charleston	Charleston	7.7	11.6	5.7	1.9	0.5	3.9	1.6	0.7
Charlotte	Mecklenburg	8.5	10.8	6.7	1.2	0.5	6.0	1.2	1.1
Chattanooga	Hamilton	3.2	21.6	8.0	0.3	0.2	1.3	0.5	0.7
Chicago	Cook	39.9	1.2	0.8	1.2	0.2	0.7	4.4	1.8
Cincinnati	Hamilton	26.8	1.8	3.6	0.7	0.4	2.3	2.7	0.1
Cleveland	Cuyahoga	34.9	0.3	2.2	1.4	0.2	1.1	5.7	1.5
Colorado Spgs.	El Paso	11.3	4.0	2.0	1.6	2.2	1.7	0.3	0.1
Columbia	Richland	4.0	13.5	7.0	2.7	0.3	3.1	0.9	0.4
Columbus	Franklin	13.7	2.1	4.1	2.8	0.4	1.5	1.5	0.6
Dallas	Dallas	21.7	12.7	4.8	0.5	0.5	1.3	1.7	1.0
Denver	Denver	28.7	1.3	1.6	0.9	0.6	1.1	6.9	1.1
Des Moines	Polk	15.5	0.2	5.3	6.3	0.5	1.9	0.6	0.3
Durham	Durham	4.4	12.8	5.6	0.8	0.8	2.0	1.8	0.9
Edison	Middlesex	45.7	0.1	0.8	0.6	0.2	1.0	6.0	0.9
El Paso	El Paso	51.5	3.6	1.3	0.2	0.8	0.4	0.7	0.1
Eugene	Lane	4.8	1.3	1.0	1.3	2.6	0.5	1.0	0.2
Ft. Collins	Larimer	12.8	0.9	2.1	2.1	2.5	1.8	0.4	0.5
Ft. Lauderdale	Broward	21.1	3.6	1.2	0.3	0.3	0.4	13.1	0.4
Ft. Wayne	Allen	17.4	1.1	4.5	3.8	0.3	1.0	0.3	0.2
Ft. Worth	Tarrant	11.5	18.7	6.8	0.6	0.8	0.8	0.4	1.0
Grand Rapids	Kent	20.0	0.1	1.8	1.3	0.4	0.8	0.3	1.2
Green Bay	Brown	52.4	0.3	2.0	6.2	0.3	0.7	0.2	0.0
Greensboro	Guilford	5.1	12.8	10.5	1.1	0.4	3.9	0.6	0.9
Honolulu	Honolulu	17.6	1.9	0.8	0.3	3.3	0.0	0.7	0.1
Houston	Harris	18.2	14.3	5.0	0.5	0.7	1.1	1.1	1.4
Huntsville	Madison	5.8	22.4	7.7	0.7	0.8	1.6	0.3	0.4
Indianapolis	Marion	12.7	1.7	3.7	0.7	0.3	1.8	1.2	0.3
Irvine	Orange	27.4	1.2	0.6	0.8	1.7	0.9	2.1	1.4
Jacksonville	Duval	8.3	18.4	3.7	0.5	0.7	1.7	0.8	0.3
Kansas City	Jackson	15.5	11.5	4.2	0.4	0.9	1.8	1.1	1.0
Knoxville	Knox	4.0	31.5	8.4	0.7	0.4	2.6	0.5	0.9
Las Vegas	Clark	17.2	1.9	0.4	0.6	6.0	0.3	5.5	0.1
Lexington	Fayette	10.0	14.1	6.1	0.5	0.7	1.8	0.8	0.4
Lincoln	Lancaster	10.5	0.9	6.3	5.1	0.9	2.3	0.3	0.5
Los Angeles	Los Angeles	40.0	1.2	0.6	0.3	1.0	0.6	5.9	1.0
Louisville	Jefferson	22.6	15.6	2.9	0.5	0.4	1.5	1.3	0.3
Madison	Dane	28.0	0.1	2.0	11.6	0.3	1.0	1.1	0.3

Table continued on next page.

City	County	Catholic	Southern Baptist	United Meth-odist	ELCA[1]	LDS[2]	Presby-terian Church USA	Jewish Est.	Muslim Est.
Manchester	Hillsborough	45.5	0.2	1.0	0.4	0.5	0.4	1.6	0.0
Memphis	Shelby	5.7	16.9	5.4	0.2	0.3	1.2	1.0	0.4
Miami	Dade	24.1	3.6	0.8	0.3	0.3	0.2	5.5	0.3
Milwaukee	Milwaukee	27.8	1.0	1.0	3.0	0.2	0.5	1.8	0.3
Minneapolis	Hennepin	23.4	0.2	2.1	13.7	0.4	1.6	2.8	0.7
Naperville	DuPage	38.7	0.2	2.2	3.0	0.3	1.1	0.2	1.7
Nashville	Davidson	0.0	0.0	0.0	0.0	0.0	0.0	0.0	0.0
New York	New York	36.7	0.1	0.8	0.3	0.3	0.7	20.5	2.4
Norfolk	Norfolk City	4.7	10.5	3.3	0.7	0.3	2.2	3.2	0.4
Oklahoma City	Oklahoma	6.5	26.4	9.4	0.6	0.7	1.3	0.4	0.4
Omaha	Douglas	27.7	1.7	2.8	5.4	1.0	2.3	1.4	0.4
Orlando	Orange	13.3	8.2	3.3	0.6	0.6	1.7	1.2	0.2
Overland Park	Johnson	21.3	3.1	4.5	1.8	0.8	3.5	2.7	0.0
Philadelphia	Philadelphia	32.4	1.2	1.3	1.0	0.1	0.7	5.7	2.8
Phoenix	Maricopa	17.3	2.5	1.1	1.7	5.0	0.6	2.0	0.3
Pittsburgh	Allegheny	49.4	0.2	3.7	2.5	0.2	4.7	2.7	0.6
Plano	Collin	18.3	16.0	6.1	0.6	1.3	0.7	1.4	1.2
Portland	Multnomah	22.7	0.7	0.9	1.2	1.6	1.6	2.9	0.6
Providence	Providence	52.1	0.0	0.6	0.3	0.2	0.1	1.7	0.3
Provo	Utah	1.0	0.1	0.0	0.0	88.1	0.1	0.0	0.0
Raleigh	Wake	9.5	12.6	7.4	0.9	0.6	2.7	1.0	0.5
Reno	Washoe	16.2	1.1	0.8	0.6	3.5	0.5	0.6	0.2
Richmond	Richmond City	5.1	12.5	5.8	0.3	0.0	0.4	7.6	0.4
Rochester	Monroe	35.7	0.1	2.0	1.4	0.4	1.9	3.1	0.6
Sacramento	Sacramento	18.3	1.7	0.6	0.7	2.5	0.9	1.4	0.5
St. Louis	Saint Louis City	20.3	4.4	1.4	1.4	0.1	0.8	1.3	1.2
St. Paul	Ramsey	31.2	0.1	1.6	12.2	0.4	1.2	1.6	0.5
St. Petersburg	Pinellas	12.2	3.9	4.4	0.9	0.2	1.3	2.6	0.5
Salt Lake City	Salt Lake	6.0	0.6	0.5	0.4	56.0	0.4	0.5	0.4
San Antonio	Bexar	41.2	8.6	3.0	1.0	0.7	0.8	0.8	0.2
San Diego	San Diego	29.5	1.0	0.7	0.6	1.6	0.9	2.5	0.3
San Francisco	San Francisco	23.3	0.4	1.7	0.2	0.2	0.5	6.4	2.9
San Jose	Santa Clara	28.7	1.0	0.9	0.6	1.2	0.6	3.2	1.1
Savannah	Chatham	9.0	14.9	6.7	1.5	0.3	1.4	1.3	0.3
Scottsdale	Maricopa	17.3	2.5	1.1	1.7	5.0	0.6	2.0	0.3
Seattle	King	16.2	0.7	1.1	2.0	2.3	1.6	1.9	0.5
Sioux Falls	Minnehaha	22.4	0.4	4.1	21.2	0.6	1.6	0.1	0.0
Springfield	Greene	6.0	21.7	5.4	0.5	0.9	1.9	0.1	0.3
Stamford	Fairfield	49.2	0.2	1.7	0.8	0.3	0.7	4.4	1.7
Tampa	Hillsborough	16.6	10.3	3.3	0.7	0.4	1.0	2.0	0.5
Thousand Oaks	Ventura	29.3	0.8	0.9	1.1	2.1	0.9	2.0	0.3
Tucson	Pima	26.7	2.7	1.1	1.3	2.0	1.1	2.4	0.1
Tulsa	Tulsa	7.3	19.5	11.7	0.6	0.8	1.8	0.5	0.4
Virginia Beach	Virginia Beach City	9.6	4.7	4.6	0.5	0.5	1.4	1.8	0.0
Washington	District of Columbia	28.0	6.8	2.7	0.7	0.1	1.5	4.5	10.6
Wichita	Sedgwick	13.8	7.0	6.0	0.7	0.8	1.6	0.3	0.4
U.S.		22.0	7.1	3.7	1.8	1.5	1.1	2.2	0.6

Note: Figures shown are the number of adherents as a percentage of the total population; Adherents are defined as all members, including full members, their children and the estimated number of other participants who are not considered members (e.g. the baptized, those not confirmed, those not eligible for communion, those regularly attending services, etc.); (1) Evangelical Lutheran Church in America; (2) The Church of Jesus Christ of Latter Day Saints

Ancestry: City

Area	German	Irish[1]	English	American	Italian	Polish	French[2]	Scottish
Albuquerque	12.6	9.2	9.0	4.1	3.7	1.7	2.6	2.2
Alexandria	11.2	11.4	10.5	3.0	4.6	2.4	2.2	2.5
Anchorage	17.6	11.6	10.0	6.0	3.2	2.3	3.4	2.7
Ann Arbor	19.8	11.1	11.8	2.6	4.7	6.4	3.6	3.3
Athens	9.4	8.9	10.4	6.4	2.4	1.6	2.3	2.7
Atlanta	4.5	4.5	5.9	3.0	1.6	0.8	1.2	1.6
Austin	12.9	8.4	8.8	4.3	2.5	1.4	2.7	2.3
Baltimore	7.4	6.0	3.2	2.5	2.8	2.8	0.7	0.7
Baton Rouge	6.2	5.7	6.3	4.2	3.9	0.5	8.9	1.1
Bellevue	15.8	10.3	12.8	3.4	3.3	2.1	3.5	3.1
Birmingham	2.3	2.8	3.2	3.9	0.8	0.3	0.6	0.8
Boise City	20.6	12.5	17.2	7.1	3.1	1.5	3.6	3.9
Boston	4.1	15.8	4.5	3.3	8.3	2.3	1.9	1.2
Boulder	20.9	13.9	15.1	2.9	5.6	3.7	3.3	4.2
Buffalo	13.6	12.2	4.0	1.6	11.7	11.7	1.8	0.9
Cary	17.3	12.3	14.3	7.4	6.5	3.6	3.0	3.2
Cedar Rapids	35.5	17.1	9.4	5.5	1.9	1.5	2.9	1.9
Charleston	10.7	9.2	10.9	6.2	3.2	1.6	2.8	3.3
Charlotte	10.1	7.8	8.5	6.7	3.3	1.5	1.8	2.4
Chattanooga	6.4	7.5	7.9	12.3	1.1	0.5	1.5	1.9
Chicago	6.5	6.6	2.0	1.3	3.5	7.3	0.8	0.5
Cincinnati	19.9	10.4	5.4	4.8	3.3	1.1	1.7	1.2
Cleveland	9.2	8.2	2.8	2.7	4.6	4.8	0.9	0.5
Colorado Spgs.	22.0	12.5	12.4	5.5	4.6	2.5	3.4	2.9
Columbia	8.3	6.2	7.7	5.2	2.1	0.9	1.9	2.2
Columbus	19.4	11.7	7.9	7.2	5.0	2.0	1.9	1.7
Dallas	6.1	5.0	5.8	4.1	1.4	0.8	1.5	1.2
Denver	13.8	9.6	8.3	3.4	3.5	2.0	2.5	2.0
Des Moines	21.5	12.7	9.3	6.8	3.9	0.9	2.4	1.6
Durham	7.2	5.7	8.1	5.0	2.1	1.3	1.3	1.8
Edison	8.7	11.1	3.5	2.4	14.8	7.4	0.9	0.8
El Paso	4.6	2.9	2.8	2.7	1.2	0.5	1.0	0.6
Eugene	20.3	13.1	14.8	4.8	3.7	2.0	4.1	3.8
Ft. Collins	28.7	14.2	14.2	4.0	5.4	2.9	4.1	3.6
Ft. Lauderdale	10.4	10.3	8.2	5.9	7.6	2.9	2.7	1.8
Ft. Wayne	27.5	10.5	7.6	7.0	2.3	2.0	3.8	1.7
Ft. Worth	7.4	6.2	6.5	6.5	1.4	0.8	1.8	1.5
Grand Rapids	13.8	8.6	6.9	3.0	2.1	7.8	2.6	1.2
Green Bay	35.0	9.4	4.6	3.6	1.7	9.8	6.0	0.7
Greensboro	8.8	6.5	9.8	7.3	2.6	1.2	1.7	2.3
Honolulu	4.6	3.4	3.8	1.2	1.5	0.7	1.3	0.9
Houston	6.1	4.3	5.0	3.7	1.6	1.0	1.9	1.0
Huntsville	9.0	8.2	10.8	11.5	1.8	1.1	1.9	2.1
Indianapolis	16.6	10.2	7.7	9.3	2.2	1.4	2.0	1.7
Irvine	11.6	8.2	10.3	3.2	4.7	2.4	2.4	2.1
Jacksonville	9.6	9.0	8.5	9.3	3.5	1.4	2.2	1.8
Kansas City	15.4	10.4	8.1	5.8	3.6	1.4	2.1	1.5
Knoxville	10.0	9.9	10.2	13.3	1.9	0.9	1.7	2.5
Las Vegas	12.2	9.8	8.4	4.5	6.7	2.5	2.8	1.7
Lexington	13.5	12.0	12.4	11.7	2.6	1.3	2.0	2.4
Lincoln	39.8	12.7	11.0	3.9	1.8	2.4	2.8	1.6
Los Angeles	4.5	3.8	3.5	2.6	2.6	1.5	1.3	0.8
Louisville	15.2	11.2	7.8	8.7	1.7	0.7	1.7	1.4
Madison	35.9	14.6	9.8	2.7	3.8	5.4	3.1	1.8
Manchester	6.3	18.1	10.0	4.8	6.2	4.8	18.0	2.9
Memphis	4.2	4.9	5.2	4.5	1.6	0.5	1.1	1.2

Table continued on next page.

Area	German	Irish[1]	English	American	Italian	Polish	French[2]	Scottish
Miami	1.2	1.0	1.1	3.1	1.4	0.4	0.8	0.3
Milwaukee	20.9	6.3	2.6	1.9	2.9	9.6	2.0	0.5
Minneapolis	21.5	10.1	6.1	1.6	2.2	4.1	3.3	1.7
Naperville	27.0	18.5	9.9	2.5	10.6	10.9	2.8	1.7
Nashville	8.8	8.9	9.0	10.9	1.9	0.9	1.8	2.0
New York	3.2	5.3	1.6	3.0	8.7	2.7	0.7	0.4
Norfolk	8.6	8.1	6.9	5.2	3.5	1.6	2.0	1.7
Oklahoma City	11.7	9.2	8.5	9.0	1.4	0.8	2.2	1.6
Omaha	28.7	16.0	8.5	3.5	4.8	4.7	2.5	1.3
Orlando	9.8	8.7	7.9	6.7	4.6	1.8	2.3	1.7
Overland Park	27.7	16.1	14.4	5.5	4.1	2.9	3.5	3.0
Philadelphia	8.1	13.6	2.9	1.8	9.2	4.3	0.7	0.5
Phoenix	13.7	9.4	8.0	4.0	4.4	2.4	2.4	1.6
Pittsburgh	19.7	15.8	4.6	2.2	11.8	8.4	1.4	1.3
Plano	16.3	10.8	11.9	6.8	4.1	2.5	3.0	2.6
Portland	18.8	12.2	11.7	3.8	3.7	1.9	3.5	3.2
Providence	3.4	9.7	4.9	2.5	13.8	2.4	3.8	1.0
Provo	11.5	4.7	30.4	4.6	2.4	0.6	2.3	4.9
Raleigh	10.0	8.4	11.9	6.2	3.5	1.9	2.1	2.9
Reno	15.9	12.7	11.4	4.5	6.6	1.7	3.5	2.6
Richmond	6.1	5.4	8.5	3.8	1.9	0.9	1.3	2.0
Rochester	10.9	9.6	5.8	2.2	10.0	2.7	2.1	1.2
Sacramento	8.4	6.8	6.3	3.1	3.8	0.8	2.1	1.3
St. Louis	14.5	8.6	3.9	3.1	3.6	1.5	2.4	0.7
St. Paul	25.5	12.8	5.3	1.8	3.2	3.8	3.8	1.2
St. Petersburg	14.7	12.4	11.1	5.7	6.8	3.0	3.8	2.5
Salt Lake City	10.8	6.7	20.9	4.3	2.8	1.0	2.4	4.3
San Antonio	9.0	5.2	5.0	3.2	1.9	1.3	1.8	1.0
San Diego	10.8	8.7	8.0	3.2	4.6	2.1	2.4	1.8
San Francisco	7.7	8.9	6.1	1.6	5.0	1.8	2.3	1.8
San Jose	7.6	6.1	5.6	1.9	4.8	1.2	1.8	1.2
Savannah	5.2	5.9	5.9	5.1	1.6	0.8	1.3	1.9
Scottsdale	20.6	14.1	13.4	4.5	8.5	4.4	3.7	2.9
Seattle	15.2	11.9	11.3	2.5	3.9	2.2	3.3	3.5
Sioux Falls	40.7	12.1	6.6	3.4	1.0	1.6	3.2	0.9
Springfield	18.7	12.8	10.9	11.4	2.3	1.3	3.1	2.1
Stamford	6.6	10.5	5.2	3.0	17.0	5.6	1.7	1.1
Tampa	9.2	8.4	7.7	6.2	5.6	1.7	2.4	1.8
Thousand Oaks	17.3	13.4	13.8	5.0	7.9	4.1	3.4	2.9
Tucson	14.4	9.7	8.3	3.7	4.0	2.3	2.7	1.9
Tulsa	13.2	10.4	10.1	8.0	1.8	1.0	2.7	2.0
Virginia Beach	13.7	12.4	11.8	7.3	5.6	2.5	2.9	2.6
Washington	4.8	4.9	4.4	1.7	2.2	1.4	1.2	1.1
Wichita	20.7	9.8	9.8	8.5	1.7	1.1	2.8	1.7
U.S.	15.2	10.9	8.7	7.3	5.6	3.2	3.0	1.7

Note: Figures include multiple ancestry (e.g. if a person reported being Irish and Italian, they were included in both columns); (1) Includes Celtic; (2) Includes Alsatian but excludes Basque
Source: Census 2000, Summary File 3

Ancestry: Metro Area

Metro Area	German	Irish[1]	English	American	Italian	Polish	French[2]	Scottish
Albuquerque	11.8	8.5	8.5	4.3	3.5	1.6	2.4	1.9
Alexandria	12.0	10.5	9.2	5.4	4.4	2.4	2.0	2.0
Anchorage	17.6	11.6	10.0	6.0	3.2	2.3	3.4	2.7
Ann Arbor	23.9	12.8	12.7	5.3	4.5	7.5	4.6	3.1
Athens	8.8	9.1	10.4	11.8	2.3	1.3	2.2	2.5
Atlanta	8.3	8.5	8.8	10.4	2.7	1.4	1.8	2.0
Austin	15.3	9.3	9.7	5.3	2.5	1.5	2.9	2.4
Baltimore	18.7	13.4	9.2	5.1	6.2	4.8	1.9	1.7
Baton Rouge	7.1	7.8	6.6	8.9	4.7	0.5	13.0	1.1
Bellevue	17.6	11.5	12.3	4.3	3.6	2.0	3.6	3.3
Birmingham	6.0	7.7	9.0	12.8	1.9	0.6	1.5	2.0
Boise City	19.3	11.1	16.0	7.7	2.8	1.2	3.1	3.4
Boston	5.9	24.3	10.9	3.9	15.4	3.5	4.7	2.6
Boulder	24.1	13.9	14.9	4.0	5.3	3.4	3.5	3.9
Buffalo	26.8	16.6	8.5	2.5	16.2	17.9	3.1	1.7
Cary	10.4	8.6	11.8	9.9	3.5	1.8	2.1	2.7
Cedar Rapids	36.8	16.7	10.1	5.8	1.8	1.4	2.9	1.8
Charleston	10.7	9.0	9.5	9.4	3.1	1.3	2.7	2.4
Charlotte	11.7	8.1	8.4	12.4	2.7	1.3	1.7	2.2
Chattanooga	8.0	9.8	9.6	18.7	1.3	0.6	1.6	2.0
Chicago	16.1	12.1	4.9	2.4	7.2	10.1	1.7	1.0
Cincinnati	30.6	14.4	9.5	9.8	3.8	1.3	2.5	1.6
Cleveland	20.1	13.8	8.1	4.0	9.6	8.3	1.7	1.6
Colorado Spgs.	22.4	12.4	12.0	5.9	4.5	2.5	3.4	2.8
Columbia	11.2	7.7	8.5	10.7	2.1	1.0	1.8	2.0
Columbus	23.4	13.1	10.0	9.3	5.0	2.2	2.2	2.0
Dallas	10.0	8.1	8.2	7.8	2.1	1.2	2.1	1.7
Denver	21.3	12.5	11.5	4.5	4.9	2.5	3.4	2.5
Des Moines	27.5	13.7	11.0	7.0	3.2	1.2	2.6	1.8
Durham	10.4	8.6	11.8	9.9	3.5	1.8	2.1	2.7
Edison	12.8	15.0	5.7	2.9	17.2	9.8	1.5	1.3
El Paso	4.2	2.7	2.5	2.6	1.1	0.5	0.9	0.5
Eugene	20.8	12.8	14.3	6.2	3.4	1.8	4.1	3.5
Ft. Collins	29.7	14.0	14.4	4.9	4.5	2.6	3.9	3.2
Ft. Lauderdale	9.1	9.0	5.7	6.5	9.5	3.7	2.2	1.2
Ft. Wayne	31.5	9.7	8.1	9.2	2.0	1.9	3.8	1.6
Ft. Worth	11.4	9.2	9.1	9.7	2.0	1.2	2.4	1.9
Grand Rapids	19.7	10.1	9.8	5.0	2.5	6.7	3.9	1.6
Green Bay	38.4	10.4	4.5	3.7	2.2	11.0	6.4	0.8
Greensboro	10.5	7.0	9.7	14.8	2.0	1.0	1.5	2.0
Honolulu	5.3	4.0	3.8	1.4	1.7	0.8	1.3	0.9
Houston	9.2	6.6	6.6	5.9	2.2	1.4	2.6	1.3
Huntsville	9.0	9.3	10.1	15.8	1.7	1.0	1.9	2.0
Indianapolis	20.0	11.2	9.8	12.1	2.2	1.6	2.2	2.0
Irvine	11.7	8.7	8.9	3.5	4.7	1.9	2.6	1.9
Jacksonville	11.0	10.5	10.2	10.3	4.1	1.8	2.7	2.1
Kansas City	21.8	13.2	11.2	8.1	3.2	1.7	2.8	2.0
Knoxville	11.2	10.9	11.4	17.4	1.8	1.0	2.0	2.5
Las Vegas	13.4	10.5	9.3	5.0	6.6	2.6	3.0	1.7
Lexington	12.4	11.5	12.5	16.0	2.1	1.1	1.9	2.2
Lincoln	40.6	12.5	11.0	4.0	1.7	2.3	2.7	1.6
Los Angeles	5.8	4.6	4.4	2.5	2.8	1.3	1.5	1.0
Louisville	19.4	12.9	9.9	13.2	2.1	1.0	2.3	1.7
Madison	40.4	14.3	9.7	3.1	3.3	5.0	3.3	1.7
Manchester	7.8	19.8	12.7	5.2	8.1	5.0	16.3	3.0
Memphis	6.3	7.5	7.2	8.6	2.2	0.7	1.6	1.5

Table continued on next page.

Metro Area	German	Irish[1]	English	American	Italian	Polish	French[2]	Scottish
Miami	2.6	2.3	2.0	4.0	2.3	1.0	1.0	0.4
Milwaukee	37.7	10.0	5.1	2.7	4.4	12.7	3.1	0.9
Minneapolis	34.4	12.8	6.8	2.7	2.8	5.0	4.4	1.4
Naperville	16.1	12.1	4.9	2.4	7.2	10.1	1.7	1.0
Nashville	9.8	10.2	10.4	15.4	2.1	1.1	2.1	2.2
New York	3.9	6.7	2.0	3.1	10.4	2.9	0.8	0.5
Norfolk	10.8	9.5	10.5	8.1	4.0	1.9	2.3	2.1
Oklahoma City	13.4	10.3	9.4	10.2	1.6	1.0	2.5	1.8
Omaha	32.3	16.3	9.6	4.2	4.5	4.5	2.8	1.4
Orlando	13.2	10.9	10.1	7.7	6.0	2.5	2.9	2.1
Overland Park	21.8	13.2	11.2	8.1	3.2	1.7	2.8	2.0
Philadelphia	17.1	20.6	8.3	3.2	14.4	5.7	1.6	1.4
Phoenix	16.2	10.5	10.3	4.6	4.9	2.7	2.9	1.9
Pittsburgh	26.5	17.1	8.5	3.8	15.2	8.9	1.8	1.9
Plano	10.0	8.1	8.2	7.8	2.1	1.2	2.1	1.7
Portland	20.8	11.8	12.7	5.5	3.5	1.8	3.7	3.1
Providence	4.6	17.6	11.7	3.0	16.9	4.1	11.9	1.8
Provo	10.8	4.7	33.5	6.9	2.1	0.5	2.2	4.8
Raleigh	10.4	8.6	11.8	9.9	3.5	1.8	2.1	2.7
Reno	17.1	13.8	12.6	4.6	6.8	1.9	3.9	2.6
Richmond	10.1	8.6	12.3	10.5	3.2	1.4	2.0	2.2
Rochester	22.4	16.7	13.9	4.4	16.7	5.4	3.5	2.2
Sacramento	14.4	10.7	10.7	4.6	5.4	1.4	3.3	2.2
St. Louis	29.6	13.9	8.5	6.2	4.5	2.6	4.4	1.3
St. Paul	34.4	12.8	6.8	2.7	2.8	5.0	4.4	1.4
St. Petersburg	15.6	13.1	11.3	7.5	8.3	3.4	3.6	2.3
Salt Lake City	12.0	6.2	27.4	6.4	2.8	0.8	2.3	4.3
San Antonio	11.7	6.2	5.9	3.8	2.0	1.7	2.0	1.2
San Diego	12.6	9.6	9.0	3.8	4.7	2.0	2.8	2.0
San Francisco	9.7	10.1	7.8	2.1	6.8	1.9	2.7	2.1
San Jose	9.2	7.1	7.2	2.3	5.2	1.5	2.2	1.6
Savannah	8.6	8.6	8.3	10.5	2.2	1.1	1.9	2.3
Scottsdale	16.2	10.5	10.3	4.6	4.9	2.7	2.9	1.9
Seattle	17.6	11.5	12.3	4.3	3.6	2.0	3.6	3.3
Sioux Falls	42.3	11.7	6.5	3.5	1.0	1.5	3.1	0.9
Springfield	19.0	12.3	11.5	13.8	2.2	1.2	3.1	1.9
Stamford	10.1	15.4	10.4	3.9	17.3	5.3	2.5	2.3
Tampa	15.6	13.1	11.3	7.5	8.3	3.4	3.6	2.3
Thousand Oaks	13.0	9.9	9.9	4.1	5.1	2.3	2.8	2.0
Tucson	16.2	10.6	10.3	4.1	4.4	2.5	3.1	2.3
Tulsa	13.6	11.1	9.4	10.3	1.7	0.9	2.6	1.8
Virginia Beach	10.8	9.5	10.5	8.1	4.0	1.9	2.3	2.1
Washington	12.0	10.5	9.2	5.4	4.4	2.4	2.0	2.0
Wichita	23.5	10.2	10.2	9.3	1.7	1.1	3.0	1.8
U.S.	15.2	10.9	8.7	7.3	5.6	3.2	3.0	1.7

Note: Figures cover the Metropolitan Statistical Area (MSA) - see Appendix A for areas included; Figures include multiple ancestry (e.g. if a person reported being Irish and Italian, they were included in both columns); (1) Includes Celtic; (2) Includes Alsatian but excludes Basque
Source: Census 2000, Summary File 3

Foreign-Born Population: City

City	Percent of Population Born in:							
	Any Foreign Country	Europe	Asia	Africa	Oceania[1]	Canada	Mexico	Latin America[2]
Albuquerque	8.9	1.1	1.6	0.1	0.1	0.3	4.9	0.8
Alexandria	25.4	2.2	6.3	6.0	0.1	0.4	0.9	9.7
Anchorage	8.2	1.6	4.1	0.1	0.2	0.5	0.6	1.1
Ann Arbor	16.6	3.7	9.6	0.8	0.1	0.9	0.3	1.2
Athens	8.5	0.8	2.5	0.6	0.1	0.3	2.9	1.4
Atlanta	6.6	0.9	1.4	0.7	0.0	0.2	2.1	1.1
Austin	16.6	1.1	3.8	0.3	0.1	0.3	9.4	1.6
Baltimore	4.6	1.1	1.2	0.6	0.0	0.1	0.2	1.4
Baton Rouge	4.4	0.7	2.2	0.4	0.0	0.1	0.2	0.8
Bellevue	24.5	5.3	13.6	0.6	0.3	1.6	2.2	0.9
Birmingham	2.1	0.3	0.6	0.2	0.0	0.1	0.7	0.3
Boise City	4.8	2.0	1.4	0.1	0.0	0.3	0.7	0.2
Boston	25.8	4.5	6.2	2.3	0.1	0.4	0.3	12.0
Boulder	11.5	2.8	3.3	0.4	0.2	0.6	3.5	0.7
Buffalo	4.4	1.6	1.3	0.4	0.0	0.3	0.1	0.7
Cary	14.0	2.8	6.5	1.1	0.1	0.8	1.8	1.0
Cedar Rapids	3.3	0.7	1.7	0.2	0.0	0.1	0.4	0.2
Charleston	3.6	1.4	1.1	0.2	0.0	0.2	0.2	0.4
Charlotte	11.0	1.4	2.9	0.9	0.1	0.3	3.1	2.5
Chattanooga	3.4	0.6	1.5	0.1	0.0	0.1	0.5	0.6
Chicago	21.7	5.0	3.9	0.4	0.0	0.1	10.1	2.1
Cincinnati	3.8	1.2	1.3	0.5	0.0	0.1	0.2	0.5
Cleveland	4.5	1.8	1.3	0.2	0.0	0.1	0.1	0.9
Colorado Spgs.	7.0	2.1	2.2	0.1	0.1	0.4	1.5	0.6
Columbia	4.1	0.9	1.5	0.2	0.0	0.2	0.6	0.7
Columbus	6.7	1.0	3.1	1.3	0.0	0.2	0.6	0.5
Dallas	24.4	0.9	2.6	0.9	0.0	0.2	17.6	2.3
Denver	17.4	1.8	2.3	0.6	0.1	0.3	11.4	0.9
Des Moines	7.9	1.6	2.6	0.5	0.0	0.1	2.3	0.7
Durham	12.0	1.0	2.9	1.0	0.1	0.4	4.8	1.9
Edison	33.1	4.9	22.8	1.5	0.0	0.3	0.4	3.4
El Paso	26.1	1.0	1.0	0.1	0.0	0.1	23.4	0.5
Eugene	6.6	1.3	2.7	0.2	0.1	0.7	1.2	0.4
Ft. Collins	5.3	1.4	1.9	0.3	0.1	0.3	1.0	0.4
Ft. Lauderdale	21.7	3.8	1.3	0.4	0.1	1.1	0.5	14.5
Ft. Wayne	5.0	1.0	1.4	0.2	0.0	0.2	1.7	0.5
Ft. Worth	16.3	0.8	2.2	0.2	0.1	0.1	12.0	0.9
Grand Rapids	10.5	1.7	1.6	0.4	0.0	0.4	4.6	1.9
Green Bay	6.8	0.4	2.2	0.0	0.0	0.1	3.7	0.4
Greensboro	8.1	1.1	2.2	1.3	0.0	0.3	2.2	0.9
Honolulu	25.3	1.1	21.7	0.1	1.5	0.3	0.1	0.4
Houston	26.4	1.2	4.7	0.9	0.1	0.2	14.0	5.4
Huntsville	4.9	1.3	1.7	0.4	0.0	0.3	0.5	0.8
Indianapolis	4.6	0.8	1.2	0.3	0.0	0.1	1.6	0.6
Irvine	32.1	3.1	24.3	1.1	0.2	0.9	1.1	1.3
Jacksonville	5.9	1.5	2.4	0.2	0.0	0.2	0.2	1.5
Kansas City	5.8	0.7	1.7	0.5	0.0	0.1	2.0	0.8
Knoxville	3.0	0.9	1.2	0.1	0.0	0.1	0.4	0.3
Las Vegas	18.9	1.9	3.6	0.2	0.1	0.6	10.0	2.6
Lexington	5.9	1.1	2.2	0.3	0.0	0.2	1.7	0.5
Lincoln	5.9	1.2	3.0	0.3	0.1	0.1	0.8	0.5
Los Angeles	40.9	2.7	10.2	0.6	0.1	0.4	16.9	10.1
Louisville	3.8	1.0	1.3	0.3	0.0	0.1	0.2	0.9
Madison	9.1	1.4	4.7	0.5	0.1	0.3	1.3	0.8

Table continued on next page.

City	Percent of Population Born in:							
	Any Foreign Country	Europe	Asia	Africa	Oceania[1]	Canada	Mexico	Latin America[2]
Manchester	9.4	2.9	2.2	0.5	0.0	1.8	0.5	1.5
Memphis	4.0	0.4	1.4	0.3	0.0	0.1	1.5	0.4
Miami	59.5	1.2	0.6	0.1	0.0	0.1	0.6	56.8
Milwaukee	7.7	1.3	2.0	0.2	0.0	0.1	3.5	0.6
Minneapolis	14.5	1.4	4.5	3.3	0.1	0.3	3.5	1.4
Naperville	11.7	2.6	6.9	0.2	0.1	0.7	0.6	0.6
Nashville	7.1	0.9	2.3	0.8	0.0	0.2	1.9	1.0
New York	35.9	7.0	8.6	1.2	0.1	0.2	1.5	17.3
Norfolk	5.0	0.9	2.5	0.3	0.0	0.1	0.2	1.0
Oklahoma City	8.5	0.5	3.0	0.3	0.0	0.1	4.0	0.6
Omaha	6.6	0.9	1.6	0.4	0.0	0.1	2.9	0.7
Orlando	14.4	1.4	2.4	0.5	0.0	0.5	0.6	8.9
Overland Park	7.4	1.5	3.6	0.2	0.1	0.3	1.0	0.8
Philadelphia	9.0	2.7	3.5	0.6	0.0	0.1	0.2	1.9
Phoenix	19.5	1.6	1.7	0.2	0.1	0.4	14.4	1.1
Pittsburgh	5.6	2.2	2.4	0.3	0.1	0.2	0.1	0.5
Plano	17.1	2.1	8.4	0.6	0.1	0.8	3.7	1.4
Portland	13.0	3.3	5.0	0.5	0.3	0.6	2.5	0.9
Providence	25.3	3.0	4.5	1.8	0.1	0.3	0.6	15.0
Provo	9.6	0.9	1.5	0.2	0.3	0.7	3.8	2.2
Raleigh	11.7	1.4	3.2	1.3	0.0	0.5	3.6	1.8
Reno	17.3	1.6	4.2	0.2	0.3	0.5	8.3	2.2
Richmond	3.9	0.7	1.0	0.3	0.0	0.1	0.4	1.4
Rochester	7.3	2.1	2.1	0.5	0.0	0.3	0.1	2.2
Sacramento	20.3	2.0	9.9	0.3	1.0	0.2	6.0	0.9
St. Louis	5.6	2.5	1.9	0.4	0.0	0.1	0.5	0.3
St. Paul	14.3	1.1	8.1	1.6	0.1	0.2	2.1	1.1
St. Petersburg	9.1	3.3	2.3	0.2	0.1	0.7	0.2	2.3
Salt Lake City	18.3	3.1	3.0	0.7	1.0	0.4	8.5	1.7
San Antonio	11.7	0.7	1.4	0.1	0.0	0.2	8.5	0.8
San Diego	25.7	2.4	10.5	0.8	0.2	0.5	10.1	1.2
San Francisco	36.8	5.1	22.6	0.4	0.4	0.5	3.0	4.9
San Jose	36.9	2.5	20.4	0.6	0.2	0.4	11.1	1.7
Savannah	3.9	0.9	1.3	0.2	0.1	0.2	0.6	0.7
Scottsdale	9.5	2.9	2.1	0.3	0.1	1.4	2.2	0.6
Seattle	16.9	2.7	9.4	1.3	0.3	0.9	1.4	0.8
Sioux Falls	4.6	1.4	1.1	1.1	0.0	0.1	0.5	0.4
Springfield	2.4	0.6	0.9	0.2	0.1	0.1	0.4	0.2
Stamford	29.6	8.1	4.2	0.4	0.1	0.4	0.7	15.8
Tampa	12.2	1.3	1.9	0.2	0.0	0.3	1.3	7.1
Thousand Oaks	15.6	3.2	4.6	0.3	0.1	0.9	4.2	2.2
Tucson	14.3	1.4	2.0	0.2	0.1	0.3	9.6	0.7
Tulsa	6.5	0.7	1.7	0.2	0.0	0.2	3.1	0.7
Virginia Beach	6.7	1.5	3.6	0.2	0.0	0.2	0.2	0.9
Washington	12.9	2.3	2.2	1.6	0.1	0.2	0.4	6.1
Wichita	8.1	0.6	3.2	0.3	0.1	0.2	3.4	0.5
U.S.	11.1	1.7	2.9	0.3	0.1	0.3	3.3	2.5

Note: (1) Includes Australia, New Zealand subregion, Melanesia, Micronesia, Polynesia, and Oceania n.e.c.; (2) Includes Central America (excluding Mexico), South America, and the Caribbean.
Source: Census 2000, Summary File 3

Foreign-Born Population: Metro Area

Metro Area	Any Foreign Country	Europe	Asia	Africa	Oceania[1]	Canada	Mexico	Latin America[2]
				Percent of Population Born in:				
Albuquerque	7.9	1.0	1.2	0.1	0.0	0.3	4.7	0.6
Alexandria	16.9	2.1	6.1	1.9	0.1	0.2	0.7	5.9
Anchorage	8.2	1.6	4.1	0.1	0.2	0.5	0.6	1.1
Ann Arbor	6.8	1.8	3.2	0.3	0.0	0.7	0.3	0.6
Athens	6.6	0.7	1.9	0.4	0.1	0.3	2.3	1.0
Atlanta	10.3	1.3	2.8	0.9	0.0	0.2	2.9	2.1
Austin	12.2	1.0	2.9	0.3	0.0	0.2	6.7	1.1
Baltimore	5.7	1.5	2.2	0.5	0.0	0.2	0.2	1.1
Baton Rouge	3.0	0.5	1.3	0.2	0.0	0.1	0.3	0.6
Bellevue	13.8	2.8	6.9	0.7	0.2	1.0	1.5	0.6
Birmingham	2.3	0.4	0.7	0.1	0.0	0.1	0.7	0.3
Boise City	5.6	1.3	1.0	0.1	0.0	0.3	2.6	0.3
Boston	14.9	4.3	4.2	0.9	0.1	0.7	0.2	4.7
Boulder	9.4	2.1	2.5	0.2	0.1	0.5	3.5	0.5
Buffalo	4.4	2.0	1.1	0.2	0.0	0.7	0.0	0.4
Cary	9.2	1.2	2.5	0.7	0.1	0.4	3.2	1.3
Cedar Rapids	2.6	0.6	1.3	0.1	0.0	0.1	0.3	0.1
Charleston	3.3	1.0	1.0	0.1	0.1	0.2	0.6	0.4
Charlotte	6.7	0.9	1.5	0.4	0.0	0.2	2.3	1.4
Chattanooga	2.4	0.6	0.9	0.1	0.0	0.1	0.3	0.4
Chicago	17.2	4.4	3.9	0.3	0.0	0.2	7.1	1.3
Cincinnati	2.6	0.8	1.0	0.2	0.0	0.1	0.2	0.2
Cleveland	5.1	2.8	1.4	0.2	0.0	0.2	0.2	0.4
Colorado Spgs.	6.4	2.1	2.0	0.1	0.1	0.4	1.3	0.5
Columbia	3.5	0.9	1.2	0.1	0.0	0.2	0.6	0.6
Columbus	4.6	0.9	2.1	0.7	0.0	0.2	0.4	0.3
Dallas	16.8	0.9	3.4	0.6	0.0	0.3	9.8	1.8
Denver	11.1	1.7	2.3	0.4	0.1	0.4	5.5	0.7
Des Moines	5.3	1.3	1.7	0.3	0.0	0.1	1.3	0.6
Durham	9.2	1.2	2.5	0.7	0.1	0.4	3.2	1.3
Edison	20.8	4.4	8.9	1.1	0.0	0.2	1.1	5.1
El Paso	27.4	0.9	0.9	0.1	0.0	0.1	25.0	0.5
Eugene	4.9	1.1	1.6	0.1	0.1	0.5	1.3	0.3
Ft. Collins	4.3	1.0	1.2	0.1	0.0	0.3	1.3	0.3
Ft. Lauderdale	25.3	3.6	1.9	0.4	0.0	1.3	0.7	17.5
Ft. Wayne	3.0	0.7	0.8	0.1	0.0	0.2	0.8	0.3
Ft. Worth	11.4	0.8	2.6	0.4	0.1	0.2	6.5	0.8
Grand Rapids	5.2	1.1	1.3	0.1	0.0	0.3	1.7	0.6
Green Bay	3.9	0.4	1.4	0.0	0.0	0.1	1.8	0.3
Greensboro	5.7	0.7	1.1	0.3	0.0	0.2	2.8	0.7
Honolulu	19.2	0.8	16.4	0.1	1.2	0.3	0.2	0.4
Houston	20.5	1.1	4.3	0.6	0.0	0.2	10.4	3.8
Huntsville	3.5	0.8	1.3	0.2	0.0	0.2	0.5	0.5
Indianapolis	3.4	0.7	1.0	0.2	0.0	0.1	1.0	0.4
Irvine	29.9	2.0	10.9	0.4	0.2	0.6	13.7	2.1
Jacksonville	5.4	1.5	2.0	0.2	0.0	0.3	0.2	1.3
Kansas City	4.5	0.7	1.4	0.2	0.0	0.2	1.5	0.5
Knoxville	2.1	0.6	0.8	0.1	0.0	0.1	0.3	0.2
Las Vegas	16.5	1.7	3.8	0.3	0.1	0.6	7.9	2.2
Lexington	4.0	0.7	1.4	0.2	0.0	0.2	1.2	0.3
Lincoln	5.4	1.2	2.7	0.3	0.1	0.1	0.7	0.4
Los Angeles	36.2	2.0	10.7	0.5	0.1	0.4	16.0	6.5
Louisville	2.7	0.8	1.0	0.2	0.0	0.1	0.3	0.4
Madison	6.3	1.1	2.8	0.3	0.0	0.3	1.2	0.6

Table continued on next page.

Metro Area	Percent of Population Born in:							
	Any Foreign Country	Europe	Asia	Africa	Oceania[1]	Canada	Mexico	Latin America[2]
Manchester	6.6	2.0	1.4	0.4	0.0	1.6	0.3	0.9
Memphis	3.3	0.5	1.2	0.2	0.0	0.1	1.0	0.3
Miami	50.9	2.0	1.3	0.2	0.0	0.2	0.9	46.3
Milwaukee	5.4	1.6	1.5	0.2	0.0	0.1	1.6	0.4
Minneapolis	7.1	1.1	3.0	1.0	0.0	0.3	1.0	0.6
Naperville	17.2	4.4	3.9	0.3	0.0	0.2	7.1	1.3
Nashville	4.7	0.7	1.5	0.4	0.0	0.2	1.3	0.6
New York	33.7	6.8	7.9	1.1	0.1	0.2	1.5	16.1
Norfolk	4.5	1.1	2.1	0.2	0.0	0.2	0.1	0.7
Oklahoma City	5.7	0.5	2.2	0.3	0.0	0.1	2.2	0.4
Omaha	4.8	0.8	1.3	0.3	0.0	0.1	1.8	0.5
Orlando	12.0	1.6	2.2	0.4	0.0	0.5	1.0	6.3
Overland Park	4.5	0.7	1.4	0.2	0.0	0.2	1.5	0.5
Philadelphia	7.0	2.3	2.8	0.4	0.0	0.2	0.3	1.1
Phoenix	14.1	1.5	1.8	0.2	0.1	0.6	9.2	0.8
Pittsburgh	2.6	1.3	0.9	0.1	0.0	0.1	0.0	0.2
Plano	16.8	0.9	3.4	0.6	0.0	0.3	9.8	1.8
Portland	10.9	2.5	3.6	0.2	0.2	0.6	3.1	0.6
Providence	12.0	4.8	1.9	1.0	0.0	0.4	0.2	3.6
Provo	6.3	0.7	0.9	0.1	0.2	0.6	2.5	1.4
Raleigh	9.2	1.2	2.5	0.7	0.1	0.4	3.2	1.3
Reno	14.1	1.4	3.4	0.1	0.3	0.5	6.7	1.7
Richmond	4.5	1.0	1.7	0.3	0.0	0.2	0.3	1.0
Rochester	5.7	2.4	1.7	0.2	0.0	0.5	0.1	0.9
Sacramento	13.9	2.7	5.9	0.2	0.4	0.4	3.6	0.7
St. Louis	3.1	1.1	1.2	0.2	0.0	0.1	0.3	0.2
St. Paul	7.1	1.1	3.0	1.0	0.0	0.3	1.0	0.6
St. Petersburg	9.8	2.6	1.7	0.2	0.0	0.8	1.1	3.3
Salt Lake City	8.6	1.5	1.7	0.2	0.4	0.3	3.5	1.1
San Antonio	10.2	0.8	1.3	0.1	0.0	0.2	7.1	0.7
San Diego	21.6	2.0	7.0	0.4	0.1	0.5	10.4	1.0
San Francisco	32.1	4.6	16.6	0.4	0.7	0.6	4.7	4.6
San Jose	34.1	3.4	19.5	0.5	0.2	0.6	8.3	1.5
Savannah	3.5	0.8	1.3	0.2	0.0	0.2	0.4	0.6
Scottsdale	14.1	1.5	1.8	0.2	0.1	0.6	9.2	0.8
Seattle	13.8	2.8	6.9	0.7	0.2	1.0	1.5	0.6
Sioux Falls	3.7	1.1	0.9	0.8	0.0	0.1	0.4	0.3
Springfield	1.6	0.5	0.6	0.1	0.0	0.1	0.2	0.1
Stamford	20.4	6.5	3.4	0.4	0.1	0.6	0.8	8.6
Tampa	9.8	2.6	1.7	0.2	0.0	0.8	1.1	3.3
Thousand Oaks	20.7	1.8	4.1	0.2	0.1	0.5	12.6	1.4
Tucson	11.9	1.5	1.7	0.2	0.1	0.5	7.4	0.6
Tulsa	4.1	0.6	1.1	0.1	0.0	0.2	1.7	0.4
Virginia Beach	4.5	1.1	2.1	0.2	0.0	0.2	0.1	0.7
Washington	16.9	2.1	6.1	1.9	0.1	0.2	0.7	5.9
Wichita	5.9	0.5	2.3	0.2	0.0	0.2	2.4	0.3
U.S.	11.1	1.7	2.9	0.3	0.1	0.3	3.3	2.5

Note: Figures cover the Metropolitan Statistical Area - see Appendix A for areas included; (1) Includes Australia, New Zealand subregion, Melanesia, Micronesia, Polynesia, and Oceania n.e.c.; (2) Includes Central America (excluding Mexico), South America, and the Caribbean.
Source: Census 2000, Summary File 3

Marriage Status: City

Area	Never Married	Now Married (excluding Separated)	Separated	Widowed	Divorced
Albuquerque	30.2	48.7	1.7	5.7	13.7
Alexandria	39.0	43.1	2.8	4.6	10.5
Anchorage	28.4	53.7	2.1	3.2	12.5
Ann Arbor	50.3	38.5	0.9	3.2	7.1
Athens	48.4	37.6	1.9	4.5	7.6
Atlanta	45.5	31.4	4.1	7.7	11.3
Austin	39.4	43.9	2.0	3.7	11.0
Baltimore	42.5	32.0	5.6	9.3	10.5
Baton Rouge	39.3	40.6	2.8	7.2	10.1
Bellevue	25.3	58.5	1.0	5.1	10.1
Birmingham	35.2	38.0	4.0	9.5	13.3
Boise City	27.0	53.3	1.1	4.9	13.6
Boston	50.5	33.6	3.0	5.7	7.1
Boulder	49.1	37.5	1.1	3.5	8.8
Buffalo	40.0	36.2	4.3	9.1	10.4
Cary	23.5	65.7	1.5	2.5	6.7
Cedar Rapids	27.6	53.9	1.2	6.4	10.8
Charleston	40.2	40.0	3.2	7.9	8.8
Charlotte	32.7	49.6	3.0	5.2	9.4
Chattanooga	28.3	46.1	2.6	9.4	13.6
Chicago	40.9	39.9	3.4	7.0	8.8
Cincinnati	42.4	34.3	3.6	7.6	12.1
Cleveland	38.9	34.9	3.3	9.0	13.9
Colorado Spgs.	25.0	56.5	1.9	4.9	11.8
Columbia	41.6	40.5	3.3	6.5	8.2
Columbus	38.3	41.8	2.2	5.4	12.4
Dallas	34.4	45.8	3.5	5.4	10.8
Denver	35.9	43.2	2.3	5.8	12.7
Des Moines	28.2	51.0	1.7	6.5	12.7
Durham	37.4	44.4	3.1	5.9	9.1
Edison	25.5	61.3	1.4	5.8	6.0
El Paso	26.8	54.3	3.2	6.1	9.7
Eugene	36.2	44.8	1.5	5.6	12.0
Ft. Collins	40.3	46.1	0.9	3.9	8.9
Ft. Lauderdale	35.3	40.0	3.3	7.3	14.0
Ft. Wayne	30.3	47.6	1.9	7.3	12.9
Ft. Worth	28.5	50.8	3.1	5.9	11.8
Grand Rapids	36.7	44.2	1.8	6.6	10.6
Green Bay	31.3	49.4	1.4	6.3	11.6
Greensboro	34.3	46.2	3.0	6.6	9.8
Honolulu	31.6	49.7	1.7	7.2	9.7
Houston	32.2	48.9	3.6	5.4	10.0
Huntsville	26.5	52.4	2.4	6.7	12.0
Indianapolis	31.8	46.6	2.1	6.4	13.1
Irvine	33.3	53.2	1.2	3.6	8.7
Jacksonville	26.5	50.9	3.0	6.3	13.3
Kansas City	32.5	45.1	2.7	6.6	13.1
Knoxville	34.6	41.6	2.2	8.4	13.3
Las Vegas	25.7	52.1	2.7	5.6	13.9
Lexington	32.2	49.4	2.0	5.5	11.0
Lincoln	33.4	50.6	1.1	5.1	9.8
Los Angeles	37.1	45.5	3.5	5.4	8.4
Louisville	35.2	38.5	3.1	8.9	14.3
Madison	44.3	41.7	1.1	3.8	9.1

Table continued on next page.

Area	Never Married	Now Married (excluding Separated)	Separated	Widowed	Divorced
Manchester	31.0	47.7	1.8	7.0	12.4
Memphis	36.1	39.2	4.8	7.9	12.0
Miami	32.2	42.0	4.7	8.3	12.8
Milwaukee	41.4	38.3	2.7	6.6	11.1
Minneapolis	46.2	35.9	2.0	5.1	10.7
Naperville	22.2	67.7	0.7	3.5	6.0
Nashville	32.6	45.5	2.3	6.4	13.2
New York	37.6	43.4	4.3	7.0	7.7
Norfolk	37.0	40.6	5.3	6.8	10.3
Oklahoma City	26.4	51.3	2.4	6.4	13.6
Omaha	31.6	48.6	1.7	6.4	11.7
Orlando	35.8	40.5	3.7	6.1	13.8
Overland Park	23.1	61.2	0.9	5.6	9.3
Philadelphia	40.8	36.8	4.4	9.4	8.6
Phoenix	29.9	51.0	2.4	4.8	11.9
Pittsburgh	40.3	38.4	2.7	9.6	9.1
Plano	21.1	66.5	1.3	2.7	8.4
Portland	34.6	44.1	2.0	5.9	13.3
Providence	46.3	35.1	3.6	6.0	9.0
Provo	47.2	45.9	0.6	2.4	3.9
Raleigh	37.5	46.0	2.9	4.4	9.2
Reno	29.1	46.6	2.5	5.9	15.9
Richmond	40.9	34.7	4.2	8.6	11.5
Rochester	43.7	32.6	5.6	7.0	11.1
Sacramento	33.4	44.5	3.1	6.8	12.2
St. Louis	41.5	32.7	4.4	9.2	12.3
St. Paul	39.7	41.9	2.0	5.8	10.6
St. Petersburg	27.8	45.5	2.8	9.0	14.9
Salt Lake City	34.7	46.9	1.9	5.7	10.8
San Antonio	28.7	50.5	3.0	6.0	11.8
San Diego	35.0	47.5	2.4	4.9	10.2
San Francisco	44.8	38.6	1.9	6.1	8.6
San Jose	31.2	54.0	2.0	4.4	8.4
Savannah	35.6	40.2	3.5	8.8	11.9
Scottsdale	23.7	56.0	1.3	6.6	12.5
Seattle	41.8	39.9	1.6	5.4	11.4
Sioux Falls	30.0	52.5	1.3	5.8	10.4
Springfield	31.4	46.0	1.8	7.1	13.7
Stamford	30.5	52.3	1.9	7.0	8.1
Tampa	31.0	43.8	3.6	7.6	14.0
Thousand Oaks	22.9	61.2	1.3	5.2	9.4
Tucson	33.0	45.3	2.0	6.5	13.2
Tulsa	27.2	50.3	2.1	6.7	13.7
Virginia Beach	25.5	57.1	3.2	4.7	9.5
Washington	48.4	29.9	4.2	7.8	9.7
Wichita	25.5	53.6	1.7	6.4	12.8
U.S.	27.1	54.4	2.2	6.6	9.7

Note: Figures cover population 15 years of age and older
Source: Census 2000, Summary File 3

Marriage Status: Metro Area

Metro Area	Never Married	Now Married (excluding Separated)	Separated	Widowed	Divorced
Albuquerque	28.6	51.5	1.6	5.6	12.6
Alexandria	30.9	52.7	2.8	5.1	8.5
Anchorage	28.4	53.7	2.1	3.2	12.5
Ann Arbor	31.3	54.5	0.9	4.5	8.7
Athens	39.2	46.0	1.7	5.1	8.0
Atlanta	29.1	53.8	2.1	4.8	10.2
Austin	32.2	51.7	1.8	3.8	10.4
Baltimore	29.4	50.9	3.3	7.1	9.1
Baton Rouge	30.8	51.1	2.2	6.0	10.0
Bellevue	29.2	53.2	1.5	4.8	11.3
Birmingham	25.1	54.5	2.1	7.6	10.8
Boise City	23.4	58.9	1.2	4.7	11.7
Boston	33.4	50.6	1.8	6.6	7.5
Boulder	32.9	52.1	1.2	3.7	10.1
Buffalo	28.4	52.1	2.2	8.6	8.7
Cary	30.0	54.2	2.5	4.9	8.4
Cedar Rapids	26.1	57.0	1.1	5.9	10.1
Charleston	29.5	51.6	3.3	6.3	9.3
Charlotte	25.5	57.0	2.7	5.8	8.9
Chattanooga	22.0	57.0	1.7	7.7	11.7
Chicago	31.2	52.1	2.0	6.4	8.3
Cincinnati	27.1	54.2	1.8	6.7	10.3
Cleveland	27.8	51.9	1.7	8.0	10.7
Colorado Spgs.	24.6	58.2	1.8	4.4	10.9
Columbia	28.7	53.3	2.9	5.9	9.3
Columbus	29.6	52.1	1.7	5.5	11.1
Dallas	27.2	55.6	2.5	4.6	10.1
Denver	27.8	54.2	1.7	4.6	11.7
Des Moines	25.0	57.6	1.3	5.5	10.7
Durham	30.0	54.2	2.5	4.9	8.4
Edison	26.3	58.8	1.6	6.2	7.0
El Paso	26.8	55.3	3.1	5.7	9.1
Eugene	28.1	52.2	1.6	5.9	12.1
Ft. Collins	30.3	55.0	1.0	4.2	9.6
Ft. Lauderdale	25.9	51.3	2.6	8.4	11.8
Ft. Wayne	24.6	57.3	1.3	6.3	10.4
Ft. Worth	24.3	57.5	2.3	4.9	11.0
Grand Rapids	27.2	56.8	1.2	5.4	9.4
Green Bay	27.7	56.5	1.1	5.5	9.3
Greensboro	24.3	56.6	2.9	6.7	9.5
Honolulu	30.7	53.4	1.6	5.9	8.4
Houston	27.4	55.6	2.8	4.8	9.5
Huntsville	22.6	58.7	1.9	5.9	10.9
Indianapolis	25.8	55.0	1.6	6.0	11.6
Irvine	28.4	55.4	2.1	5.1	9.1
Jacksonville	24.4	54.1	2.5	6.2	12.6
Kansas City	25.1	55.6	1.8	6.0	11.4
Knoxville	22.7	57.5	1.5	7.0	11.4
Las Vegas	24.7	53.3	2.5	5.8	13.7
Lexington	28.6	53.2	1.9	5.6	10.7
Lincoln	32.1	52.4	1.0	5.0	9.5
Los Angeles	34.1	48.8	3.1	5.5	8.5
Louisville	25.4	53.5	1.9	7.0	12.2
Madison	34.8	51.0	1.1	4.0	9.1

Table continued on next page.

Metro Area	Never Married	Now Married (excluding Separated)	Separated	Widowed	Divorced
Manchester	27.0	55.1	1.4	5.9	10.5
Memphis	29.8	49.1	3.6	6.7	10.7
Miami	28.7	49.2	3.6	6.9	11.5
Milwaukee	30.4	52.3	1.5	6.5	9.3
Minneapolis	29.7	55.1	1.1	4.8	9.2
Naperville	31.2	52.1	2.0	6.4	8.3
Nashville	26.3	54.8	1.8	5.6	11.5
New York	36.2	45.3	4.0	7.0	7.6
Norfolk	27.1	53.5	3.9	6.1	9.4
Oklahoma City	25.2	54.4	1.8	6.2	12.4
Omaha	27.6	54.8	1.4	5.7	10.5
Orlando	26.6	54.0	2.4	6.0	11.0
Overland Park	25.1	55.6	1.8	6.0	11.4
Philadelphia	30.6	51.3	2.7	7.6	7.8
Phoenix	26.5	55.0	1.9	5.6	11.0
Pittsburgh	26.2	54.5	1.9	9.2	8.3
Plano	27.2	55.6	2.5	4.6	10.1
Portland	26.8	54.6	1.7	5.3	11.6
Providence	29.2	52.0	1.9	7.7	9.2
Provo	32.6	58.6	0.8	3.0	4.9
Raleigh	30.0	54.2	2.5	4.9	8.4
Reno	25.7	52.1	1.9	5.4	14.9
Richmond	27.5	53.2	3.0	6.6	9.8
Rochester	28.8	52.6	2.8	6.9	8.9
Sacramento	26.8	53.1	2.4	5.9	11.8
St. Louis	27.3	53.3	1.9	7.1	10.3
St. Paul	29.7	55.1	1.1	4.8	9.2
St. Petersburg	22.6	53.7	2.3	8.9	12.5
Salt Lake City	27.6	57.6	1.4	4.1	9.3
San Antonio	26.9	53.6	2.6	5.9	11.1
San Diego	30.2	52.0	2.3	5.3	10.2
San Francisco	35.8	47.1	1.8	6.1	9.3
San Jose	30.2	54.8	1.8	4.7	8.5
Savannah	27.7	51.8	2.4	7.0	11.1
Scottsdale	26.5	55.0	1.9	5.6	11.0
Seattle	29.2	53.2	1.5	4.8	11.3
Sioux Falls	27.5	56.4	1.1	5.5	9.5
Springfield	24.2	56.8	1.5	6.1	11.5
Stamford	25.7	58.6	1.5	6.5	7.7
Tampa	22.6	53.7	2.3	8.9	12.5
Thousand Oaks	25.9	57.5	2.0	5.1	9.5
Tucson	27.8	52.0	1.6	6.6	12.0
Tulsa	22.7	57.5	1.7	6.1	12.1
Virginia Beach	27.1	53.5	3.9	6.1	9.4
Washington	30.9	52.7	2.8	5.1	8.5
Wichita	23.5	57.6	1.4	6.1	11.5
U.S.	27.1	54.4	2.2	6.6	9.7

*Note: Figures cover population 15 years of age and older in the Metropolitan Statistical Area -
see Appendix A for areas included*
Source: Census 2000, Summary File 3

Male/Female Ratio: City

City	Males	Females	Males per 100 Females
Albuquerque	241,413	254,936	94.7
Alexandria	63,978	68,050	94.0
Anchorage	142,084	138,131	102.9
Ann Arbor	56,131	57,348	97.9
Athens	50,781	53,044	95.7
Atlanta	210,088	209,395	100.3
Austin	354,481	334,777	105.9
Baltimore	295,456	336,546	87.8
Baton Rouge	106,105	115,769	91.7
Bellevue	57,289	58,461	98.0
Birmingham	106,960	122,699	87.2
Boise City	94,960	95,661	99.3
Boston	270,233	288,972	93.5
Boulder	47,872	44,721	107.0
Buffalo	132,413	147,321	89.9
Cary	52,822	53,057	99.6
Cedar Rapids	59,245	61,897	95.7
Charleston	49,320	53,894	91.5
Charlotte	289,525	298,290	97.1
Chattanooga	73,292	80,798	90.7
Chicago	1,389,316	1,458,759	95.2
Cincinnati	146,668	161,922	90.6
Cleveland	215,605	237,571	90.8
Colorado Spgs.	182,715	187,543	97.4
Columbia	57,506	58,736	97.9
Columbus	356,702	374,624	95.2
Dallas	621,753	600,507	103.5
Denver	282,997	276,139	102.5
Des Moines	94,014	99,049	94.9
Durham	98,590	105,614	93.3
Edison	49,763	51,312	97.0
El Paso	286,929	317,008	90.5
Eugene	70,589	73,501	96.0
Ft. Collins	63,877	63,328	100.9
Ft. Lauderdale	86,043	77,901	110.5
Ft. Wayne	98,945	104,424	94.8
Ft. Worth	304,995	308,883	98.7
Grand Rapids	95,763	98,578	97.1
Green Bay	49,535	50,472	98.1
Greensboro	110,313	122,064	90.4
Honolulu	184,264	195,072	94.5
Houston	1,017,202	1,010,191	100.7
Huntsville	79,453	84,894	93.6
Indianapolis	381,520	403,324	94.6
Irvine	92,347	97,428	94.8
Jacksonville	389,750	412,184	94.6
Kansas City	216,870	229,474	94.5
Knoxville	84,546	92,080	91.8
Las Vegas	283,237	274,247	103.3
Lexington	132,133	136,337	96.9
Lincoln	119,133	119,724	99.5
Los Angeles	1,950,821	1,959,324	99.6
Louisville	116,832	128,476	90.9
Madison	108,714	111,955	97.1
Manchester	54,327	55,826	97.3

Table continued on next page.

City	Males	Females	Males per 100 Females
Memphis	302,981	334,545	90.6
Miami	192,191	193,936	99.1
Milwaukee	279,368	301,800	92.6
Minneapolis	189,737	186,511	101.7
Naperville	71,129	73,909	96.2
Nashville	267,000	282,040	94.7
New York	3,868,024	4,251,163	91.0
Norfolk	123,564	112,902	109.4
Oklahoma City	264,004	272,280	97.0
Omaha	193,682	201,722	96.0
Orlando	101,510	106,192	95.6
Overland Park	81,176	84,875	95.6
Philadelphia	680,128	777,827	87.4
Phoenix	727,168	698,116	104.2
Pittsburgh	153,087	166,184	92.1
Plano	126,103	125,780	100.3
Portland	268,271	272,948	98.3
Providence	87,009	93,655	92.9
Provo	52,988	56,971	93.0
Raleigh	162,420	163,728	99.2
Reno	104,406	99,907	104.5
Richmond	89,596	101,386	88.4
Rochester	101,357	109,221	92.8
Sacramento	228,538	239,930	95.3
St. Louis	160,858	179,264	89.7
St. Paul	135,219	143,107	94.5
St. Petersburg	120,435	130,144	92.5
Salt Lake City	90,322	87,003	103.8
San Antonio	607,158	643,838	94.3
San Diego	652,780	641,493	101.8
San Francisco	381,372	369,224	103.3
San Jose	466,156	449,036	103.8
Savannah	61,259	66,938	91.5
Scottsdale	108,626	115,304	94.2
Seattle	289,945	288,088	100.6
Sioux Falls	68,367	69,538	98.3
Springfield	72,473	77,343	93.7
Stamford	58,926	61,899	95.2
Tampa	161,625	167,200	96.7
Thousand Oaks	62,658	64,625	97.0
Tucson	257,383	266,478	96.6
Tulsa	185,332	194,616	95.2
Virginia Beach	217,837	223,071	97.7
Washington	258,989	287,374	90.1
Wichita	171,303	174,547	98.1
U.S.	146,712,712	151,308,554	97.0

Note: Figures are 2006 estimates
Source: Claritas, Inc.

Male/Female Ratio: Metro Area

Metro Area	Males	Females	Males per 100 Females
Albuquerque	393,455	408,381	96.3
Alexandria	2,574,062	2,695,382	95.5
Anchorage	181,327	174,497	103.9
Ann Arbor	171,240	173,173	98.9
Athens	86,817	89,980	96.5
Atlanta	2,413,961	2,448,448	98.6
Austin	744,028	722,273	103.0
Baltimore	1,286,964	1,381,006	93.2
Baton Rouge	362,468	375,690	96.5
Bellevue	1,609,994	1,616,680	99.6
Birmingham	528,148	565,607	93.4
Boise City	273,723	271,031	101.0
Boston	2,148,711	2,275,912	94.4
Boulder	142,943	139,783	102.3
Buffalo	552,843	597,143	92.6
Cary	475,805	478,633	99.4
Cedar Rapids	122,289	124,716	98.1
Charleston	293,365	304,314	96.4
Charlotte	750,923	774,331	97.0
Chattanooga	239,403	255,110	93.8
Chicago	4,656,140	4,829,871	96.4
Cincinnati	1,012,350	1,062,435	95.3
Cleveland	1,024,809	1,108,953	92.4
Colorado Spgs.	292,912	292,047	100.3
Columbia	335,612	356,044	94.3
Columbus	846,352	873,754	96.9
Dallas	2,949,456	2,938,598	100.4
Denver	1,191,679	1,183,745	100.7
Des Moines	255,775	267,220	95.7
Durham	222,127	237,809	93.4
Edison	9,074,311	9,737,274	93.2
El Paso	350,656	377,587	92.9
Eugene	165,412	171,026	96.7
Ft. Collins	135,858	136,314	99.7
Ft. Lauderdale	2,644,547	2,808,980	94.1
Ft. Wayne	199,515	206,388	96.7
Ft. Worth	2,949,456	2,938,598	100.4
Grand Rapids	387,046	388,740	99.6
Green Bay	149,965	150,342	99.7
Greensboro	327,848	348,242	94.1
Honolulu	452,910	456,498	99.2
Houston	2,662,628	2,666,897	99.8
Huntsville	182,133	187,339	97.2
Indianapolis	812,185	841,637	96.5
Irvine	6,518,886	6,636,219	98.2
Jacksonville	621,510	649,005	95.8
Kansas City	959,629	995,136	96.4
Knoxville	319,937	337,998	94.7
Las Vegas	889,679	862,706	103.1
Lexington	211,450	219,241	96.4
Lincoln	141,081	140,717	100.3
Los Angeles	6,518,886	6,636,219	98.2
Louisville	592,482	623,152	95.1
Madison	267,616	271,932	98.4
Manchester	200,034	203,905	98.1

Table continued on next page.

Metro Area	Males	Females	Males per 100 Females
Memphis	611,824	655,500	93.3
Miami	2,644,547	2,808,980	94.1
Milwaukee	739,255	779,357	94.9
Minneapolis	1,571,791	1,603,435	98.0
Naperville	4,656,140	4,829,871	96.4
Nashville	702,945	724,265	97.1
New York	9,074,311	9,737,274	93.2
Norfolk	818,538	837,114	97.8
Oklahoma City	573,327	588,413	97.4
Omaha	403,492	414,857	97.3
Orlando	967,617	991,020	97.6
Overland Park	959,629	995,136	96.4
Philadelphia	2,820,211	3,023,844	93.3
Phoenix	1,946,170	1,919,737	101.4
Pittsburgh	1,147,017	1,245,463	92.1
Plano	2,949,456	2,938,598	100.4
Portland	1,047,771	1,056,535	99.2
Providence	792,555	849,445	93.3
Provo	225,398	228,998	98.4
Raleigh	475,805	478,633	99.4
Reno	202,304	197,168	102.6
Richmond	570,624	604,389	94.4
Rochester	508,026	535,035	95.0
Sacramento	1,016,122	1,052,029	96.6
St. Louis	1,347,631	1,438,992	93.7
St. Paul	1,571,791	1,603,435	98.0
St. Petersburg	1,285,018	1,364,114	94.2
Salt Lake City	522,851	510,925	102.3
San Antonio	930,307	970,114	95.9
San Diego	1,506,333	1,490,529	101.1
San Francisco	2,072,695	2,111,978	98.1
San Jose	894,153	865,275	103.3
Savannah	155,076	162,795	95.3
Scottsdale	1,946,170	1,919,737	101.4
Seattle	1,609,994	1,616,680	99.6
Sioux Falls	104,309	105,015	99.3
Springfield	195,485	204,202	95.7
Stamford	441,865	468,078	94.4
Tampa	1,285,018	1,364,114	94.2
Thousand Oaks	405,622	405,727	100.0
Tucson	459,507	478,753	96.0
Tulsa	435,902	451,527	96.5
Virginia Beach	818,538	837,114	97.8
Washington	2,574,062	2,695,382	95.5
Wichita	292,526	296,458	98.7
U.S.	146,712,712	151,308,554	97.0

Note: Figures are 2006 estimates and cover the Metropolitan Statistical Area (MSA) - see Appendix B for areas included
Source: Claritas, Inc.

Gross Metropolitan Product

MSA[1]	2002	2003	2004	2005	2005 Rank[2]
Albuquerque	24.7	27.0	29.9	32.3	65
Alexandria	238.6	256.3	280.1	300.4	4
Anchorage	15.3	16.4	18.8	20.5	91
Ann Arbor	14.7	15.1	15.4	16.0	114
Athens	5.5	5.8	6.1	6.5	228
Atlanta	178.4	184.0	197.1	212.4	10
Austin	52.0	54.3	59.7	66.2	38
Baltimore	101.4	105.9	113.7	121.6	18
Baton Rouge	23.6	25.7	28.4	31.5	66
Bellevue	138.9	142.3	149.0	158.0	13
Birmingham	33.2	34.7	37.2	39.9	54
Boise City	14.5	15.3	17.3	19.2	97
Boston	210.9	218.1	230.5	241.1	8
Boulder	13.3	13.5	14.2	15.2	122
Buffalo	51.4	53.1	56.6	59.1	41
Cary	31.2	32.8	35.3	38.4	55
Cedar Rapids	8.9	9.3	9.7	10.2	170
Charleston	17.0	17.9	19.1	20.6	90
Charlotte	60.6	63.1	66.1	71.3	35
Chattanooga	17.3	18.2	19.4	20.5	92
Chicago	365.9	381.9	399.9	422.0	3
Cincinnati	71.1	74.5	78.9	82.4	28
Cleveland	77.5	80.3	84.5	87.3	25
Colorado Spgs.	22.0	22.7	24.2	26.1	76
Columbia	22.3	23.3	24.4	26.3	74
Columbus	63.8	66.5	70.2	73.1	34
Dallas	229.2	238.6	260.0	284.5	5
Denver	98.7	102.4	108.5	116.4	19
Des Moines	19.4	20.9	21.7	23.1	83
Durham	19.3	19.4	20.5	21.8	88
Edison	820.9	847.1	902.4	952.6	1
El Paso	21.0	22.0	23.7	25.5	78
Eugene	10.3	10.6	11.9	12.8	148
Fort Collins	9.7	10.2	10.9	11.8	155
Fort Lauderdale	162.4	171.8	187.0	206.1	11
Fort Wayne	15.0	15.8	16.4	17.2	110
Fort Worth	229.2	238.6	260.0	284.5	5
Grand Rapids	31.5	32.3	32.8	34.0	57
Green Bay	11.0	11.6	12.4	12.9	145
Greensboro	28.4	29.4	30.5	32.6	64
Honolulu	33.0	35.1	38.0	40.9	53
Houston	191.9	204.0	221.2	244.4	7
Huntsville	11.9	12.8	13.9	15.0	124
Indianapolis	58.6	62.4	66.1	69.1	36
Irvine	502.1	528.0	567.6	604.8	2
Jacksonville	42.6	45.4	49.3	54.2	43
Kansas City	66.9	69.7	73.9	78.6	31
Knoxville	21.9	23.3	25.1	26.5	73
Las Vegas	56.1	61.8	69.5	78.8	29
Lexington	15.3	15.9	16.7	17.7	109
Lincoln	10.1	10.6	11.0	11.6	156
Los Angeles	502.1	528.0	567.6	604.8	2
Louisville	39.8	41.4	43.6	45.7	50
Madison	20.9	21.9	23.5	24.9	80
Manchester	15.3	16.1	17.3	18.3	102
Memphis	42.5	45.0	47.5	50.3	46

Table continued on next page.

MSA[1]	2002	2003	2004	2005	2005 Rank[2]
Miami	162.4	171.8	187.0	206.1	11
Milwaukee	56.9	58.6	61.3	63.7	39
Minneapolis	128.6	135.8	145.2	151.9	15
Naperville	365.9	381.9	399.9	422.0	3
Nashville	48.8	51.8	56.3	60.3	40
New York	820.9	847.1	902.4	952.6	1
Norfolk	64.7	68.7	73.8	78.6	30
Oklahoma City	34.0	36.4	39.6	43.1	51
Omaha	28.5	30.5	31.7	33.5	60
Orlando	61.8	66.6	74.2	83.8	27
Overland Park	66.9	69.7	73.9	78.6	31
Philadelphia	227.1	236.5	250.3	264.8	6
Phoenix	120.3	128.0	136.2	153.2	14
Pittsburgh	84.7	87.6	91.9	96.2	22
Plano	229.2	238.6	260.0	284.5	5
Portland	70.3	72.1	80.0	85.7	26
Providence	56.4	60.0	63.8	66.6	37
Provo	9.9	10.5	11.6	12.9	146
Raleigh	31.2	32.8	35.3	38.4	55
Reno	15.4	16.6	18.2	19.9	94
Richmond	46.5	49.0	52.8	56.8	42
Rochester	46.7	48.1	51.1	53.5	44
Sacramento	73.5	78.8	85.3	91.6	24
Saint Louis	95.3	99.1	103.4	108.9	21
Saint Paul	128.6	135.8	145.2	151.9	15
Saint Petersburg	85.6	90.6	99.8	110.5	20
Salt Lake City	38.2	39.5	42.2	46.4	48
San Antonio	61.2	64.6	69.7	76.2	32
San Diego	117.0	124.4	134.5	143.4	16
San Francisco	186.1	190.8	201.5	213.5	9
San Jose	82.6	82.8	87.6	93.6	23
Savannah	10.4	10.8	12.0	13.0	144
Scottsdale	120.3	128.0	136.2	153.2	14
Seattle	138.9	142.3	149.0	158.0	13
Sioux Falls	8.9	9.0	9.6	10.4	169
Springfield	12.3	13.0	13.8	14.7	127
Stamford	44.5	45.9	48.8	52.0	45
Tampa	85.6	90.6	99.8	110.5	20
Thousand Oaks	27.0	28.7	30.9	32.8	63
Tucson	25.7	27.1	28.7	31.1	67
Tulsa	26.8	28.3	30.1	32.9	62
Virginia Beach	64.7	68.7	73.8	78.6	30
Washington	238.6	256.3	280.1	300.4	4
Wichita	19.4	19.5	20.7	22.1	87

Note: Figures are in billions of dollars; (1) Metropolitan Statistical Area - see Appendix A for areas included;
(2) Rank ranges from 1 to 318
Source: The U.S. Conference of Mayors, "U.S. Metro Economies: GMP - The Engines of America's Growth," January 2007

Per Capita/Median/Average Income: City

City	Per Capita ($)	Median Household ($)	Average Household ($)
Albuquerque	24,791	45,256	59,413
Alexandria	44,899	66,637	91,537
Anchorage	29,398	64,048	79,341
Ann Arbor	30,761	51,453	73,454
Athens	19,633	32,335	48,644
Atlanta	30,628	42,890	73,903
Austin	27,082	47,803	66,168
Baltimore	19,972	34,445	48,456
Baton Rouge	21,550	34,579	53,789
Bellevue	39,205	68,015	91,588
Birmingham	17,876	30,789	42,036
Boise City	26,058	48,200	63,296
Boston	27,600	46,322	65,906
Boulder	30,468	49,778	70,967
Buffalo	16,588	27,112	38,378
Cary	39,644	90,728	109,619
Cedar Rapids	25,115	47,946	59,368
Charleston	26,649	41,151	60,322
Charlotte	30,680	53,488	75,923
Chattanooga	22,620	37,116	52,287
Chicago	23,052	44,434	62,252
Cincinnati	23,195	33,606	49,832
Cleveland	15,950	29,208	38,974
Colorado Spgs.	26,683	52,833	67,021
Columbia	22,220	35,522	55,572
Columbus	24,377	44,931	56,160
Dallas	24,582	42,835	64,647
Denver	28,939	48,282	67,586
Des Moines	22,114	43,015	53,371
Durham	25,453	47,109	62,515
Edison	35,302	79,003	97,149
El Paso	17,098	38,131	51,960
Eugene	23,884	39,922	55,135
Ft. Collins	27,199	54,018	69,027
Ft. Lauderdale	31,908	44,671	69,472
Ft. Wayne	20,471	39,763	48,986
Ft. Worth	21,323	42,883	57,405
Grand Rapids	19,504	41,206	50,939
Green Bay	22,505	43,946	53,550
Greensboro	25,759	43,912	61,224
Honolulu	27,514	49,419	70,534
Houston	22,350	41,359	60,462
Huntsville	28,159	46,346	64,367
Indianapolis	25,358	46,103	60,576
Irvine	38,301	85,125	107,885
Jacksonville	23,806	46,492	60,516
Kansas City	23,946	43,167	56,278
Knoxville	20,825	31,529	44,892
Las Vegas	23,819	48,879	64,687
Lexington	27,475	46,138	63,875
Lincoln	24,625	47,008	59,626
Los Angeles	22,274	41,076	63,909
Louisville	21,473	33,584	47,617
Madison	27,944	48,933	62,625
Manchester	23,937	45,406	56,351

Table continued on next page.

City	Per Capita ($)	Median Household ($)	Average Household ($)
Memphis	20,166	36,748	51,081
Miami	17,574	27,236	45,878
Milwaukee	18,575	36,929	46,648
Minneapolis	26,356	44,239	60,746
Naperville	40,763	98,781	119,263
Nashville	26,332	46,247	61,768
New York	24,796	43,542	65,347
Norfolk	20,465	38,004	51,293
Oklahoma City	22,677	41,344	55,236
Omaha	24,562	45,003	59,687
Orlando	23,728	40,178	53,463
Overland Park	37,007	70,062	91,878
Philadelphia	19,469	35,662	48,583
Phoenix	22,355	45,862	62,924
Pittsburgh	21,557	32,599	47,772
Plano	40,806	82,329	107,508
Portland	26,832	47,046	62,627
Providence	17,006	29,898	46,253
Provo	15,179	38,674	51,756
Raleigh	28,099	52,066	67,834
Reno	25,135	46,125	61,031
Richmond	24,124	37,007	54,762
Rochester	16,105	28,483	38,727
Sacramento	21,721	43,480	57,010
St. Louis	19,054	32,217	44,111
St. Paul	23,693	45,439	59,628
St. Petersburg	24,505	40,427	54,655
Salt Lake City	24,535	43,564	61,491
San Antonio	20,491	42,529	56,459
San Diego	27,624	53,762	73,544
San Francisco	40,769	67,024	94,966
San Jose	30,046	78,207	97,407
Savannah	18,769	32,470	46,496
Scottsdale	44,519	65,783	98,337
Seattle	33,136	50,252	70,554
Sioux Falls	25,176	48,292	61,763
Springfield	20,618	33,321	45,804
Stamford	37,629	66,179	96,131
Tampa	24,838	39,862	59,485
Thousand Oaks	40,034	87,895	110,625
Tucson	18,652	35,155	45,908
Tulsa	24,794	40,301	57,939
Virginia Beach	26,503	56,881	70,926
Washington	34,568	48,347	76,464
Wichita	23,555	45,162	57,587
U.S.	25,129	48,775	65,849

Note: Figures are 2006 estimates
Source: Claritas, Inc.

Per Capita/Median/Average Income: Metro Area

Metro Area	Per Capita ($)	Median Household ($)	Average Household ($)
Albuquerque	24,037	46,123	60,958
Alexandria	35,817	73,796	94,539
Anchorage	28,496	63,018	77,607
Ann Arbor	32,098	60,579	79,766
Athens	21,278	39,115	54,573
Atlanta	28,183	59,599	76,961
Austin	27,648	56,305	73,316
Baltimore	29,426	58,910	75,207
Baton Rouge	21,820	44,057	58,108
Bellevue	29,569	58,417	74,194
Birmingham	24,953	45,563	62,140
Boise City	23,024	48,281	62,235
Boston	33,072	64,020	84,572
Boulder	34,342	65,719	86,342
Buffalo	23,549	44,165	57,243
Cary	29,181	59,712	75,493
Cedar Rapids	25,392	50,894	62,272
Charleston	24,155	46,414	60,910
Charlotte	28,045	54,710	72,121
Chattanooga	23,254	43,409	57,151
Chicago	28,128	59,125	77,427
Cincinnati	27,215	52,800	68,684
Cleveland	26,128	48,501	64,279
Colorado Spgs.	26,471	56,186	69,927
Columbia	23,990	46,785	60,742
Columbus	27,529	53,097	68,317
Dallas	27,046	55,541	74,178
Denver	30,901	61,786	79,304
Des Moines	27,308	54,076	68,299
Durham	26,875	49,027	66,909
Edison	29,637	57,277	80,690
El Paso	15,892	36,455	50,080
Eugene	22,815	42,403	55,209
Ft. Collins	29,196	59,509	74,306
Ft. Lauderdale	25,337	46,201	66,563
Ft. Wayne	24,097	48,161	60,963
Ft. Worth	27,046	55,541	74,178
Grand Rapids	24,154	51,148	64,349
Green Bay	25,491	53,368	64,072
Greensboro	24,430	45,423	60,383
Honolulu	25,565	59,606	75,432
Houston	25,035	51,814	71,215
Huntsville	26,381	50,219	65,312
Indianapolis	27,599	53,857	69,577
Irvine	24,259	51,573	73,593
Jacksonville	25,572	49,491	65,230
Kansas City	27,180	53,658	68,423
Knoxville	24,868	43,762	58,901
Las Vegas	24,531	51,001	66,118
Lexington	26,168	47,162	63,227
Lincoln	25,046	48,801	61,746
Los Angeles	24,259	51,573	73,593
Louisville	25,731	48,116	63,050
Madison	29,704	57,730	71,260
Manchester	29,340	61,386	75,872

Table continued on next page.

Metro Area	Per Capita ($)	Median Household ($)	Average Household ($)
Memphis	23,803	46,572	62,660
Miami	25,337	46,201	66,563
Milwaukee	27,398	53,126	67,998
Minneapolis	31,071	64,080	80,009
Naperville	28,128	59,125	77,427
Nashville	26,580	51,051	67,252
New York	29,637	57,277	80,690
Norfolk	24,473	50,530	63,788
Oklahoma City	23,002	43,668	57,342
Omaha	25,893	52,308	66,207
Orlando	24,265	47,663	63,398
Overland Park	27,180	53,658	68,423
Philadelphia	28,647	56,750	74,477
Phoenix	25,352	52,008	68,998
Pittsburgh	24,558	43,325	58,205
Plano	27,046	55,541	74,178
Portland	26,897	54,266	69,014
Providence	25,503	49,520	64,059
Provo	18,489	53,785	66,823
Raleigh	29,181	59,712	75,493
Reno	27,321	53,466	70,291
Richmond	27,522	54,217	69,436
Rochester	24,637	48,913	62,636
Sacramento	26,098	54,161	69,937
St. Louis	26,387	51,168	66,412
St. Paul	31,071	64,080	80,009
St. Petersburg	25,340	44,025	59,566
Salt Lake City	24,295	58,289	73,468
San Antonio	21,825	45,937	60,772
San Diego	26,918	55,945	74,929
San Francisco	36,175	70,806	96,333
San Jose	35,989	83,053	107,853
Savannah	24,290	45,921	62,842
Scottsdale	25,352	52,008	68,998
Seattle	29,569	58,417	74,194
Sioux Falls	24,712	51,145	62,828
Springfield	21,363	40,021	52,595
Stamford	41,121	72,785	111,193
Tampa	25,340	44,025	59,566
Thousand Oaks	28,627	68,800	87,832
Tucson	23,261	43,083	58,109
Tulsa	23,091	44,024	58,241
Virginia Beach	24,473	50,530	63,788
Washington	35,817	73,796	94,539
Wichita	23,797	48,776	60,852
U.S.	25,129	48,775	65,849

Note: Figures are 2006 estimates and cover the Metropolitan Statistical Area (MSA) - see Appendix B for areas included
Source: Claritas, Inc.

Household Income Distribution: City

City	Percent of Households Earning							
	Under $15,000	$15,000 -24,999	$25,000 -34,999	$35,000 -49,999	$50,000 -74,999	$75,000 -99,000	$100,000 -149,999	$150,000 and up
Albuquerque	13.8	12.2	12.5	16.8	19.0	10.9	10.1	4.7
Alexandria	7.3	6.0	8.0	15.2	20.3	13.9	15.6	13.7
Anchorage	6.7	7.8	9.6	14.1	21.1	15.2	16.5	9.1
Ann Arbor	14.5	10.2	9.5	14.9	17.0	11.7	12.9	9.4
Athens	26.9	14.3	12.0	14.2	14.9	6.9	6.7	4.2
Atlanta	20.7	11.7	10.7	13.1	14.4	9.0	9.8	10.6
Austin	13.4	10.7	12.1	16.3	19.0	11.1	10.5	7.0
Baltimore	24.0	14.0	12.7	15.9	15.7	8.1	6.3	3.4
Baton Rouge	23.7	14.5	12.3	14.1	14.1	8.4	7.7	5.2
Bellevue	7.1	6.4	8.0	13.9	20.2	14.6	16.4	13.4
Birmingham	26.2	15.8	13.9	16.4	14.7	6.4	4.5	2.1
Boise City	10.3	11.9	12.3	17.6	20.7	11.9	10.0	5.3
Boston	19.3	10.1	10.1	13.9	17.1	11.0	11.2	7.3
Boulder	14.8	10.5	10.6	14.3	17.0	11.0	12.9	8.9
Buffalo	29.6	17.5	13.8	14.3	13.2	6.0	3.8	1.8
Cary	3.0	4.3	5.3	9.9	17.3	16.3	24.1	19.8
Cedar Rapids	10.9	11.2	12.6	17.8	23.2	12.4	8.4	3.6
Charleston	20.3	11.8	11.8	14.9	16.5	9.3	9.1	6.3
Charlotte	10.1	9.2	11.5	16.3	19.9	12.1	11.6	9.1
Chattanooga	20.2	14.4	13.2	16.2	16.7	8.6	6.3	4.4
Chicago	18.1	11.1	11.0	15.6	18.0	10.3	9.7	6.3
Cincinnati	23.7	14.6	13.7	15.3	14.7	7.6	6.3	4.1
Cleveland	27.8	16.2	14.3	15.7	14.5	6.1	3.9	1.5
Colorado Spgs.	9.5	9.9	11.8	16.3	21.7	13.0	11.8	5.9
Columbia	22.4	14.4	12.7	15.7	14.9	7.2	6.8	5.9
Columbus	14.4	11.4	12.7	17.4	20.6	11.3	8.8	3.4
Dallas	14.7	12.5	13.7	17.5	16.9	9.0	8.4	7.3
Denver	13.1	10.4	11.8	16.6	19.1	11.0	10.8	7.2
Des Moines	13.7	12.5	14.0	18.4	21.6	10.1	7.1	2.7
Durham	14.9	10.7	11.6	15.8	19.3	11.6	10.5	5.6
Edison	6.0	5.6	5.9	10.9	19.0	16.8	20.8	15.1
El Paso	18.8	14.3	13.5	16.3	17.6	8.7	7.3	3.5
Eugene	18.9	13.1	12.6	16.6	17.5	8.9	7.8	4.7
Ft. Collins	11.6	10.5	10.1	14.7	19.5	13.2	13.9	6.6
Ft. Lauderdale	16.0	12.2	11.9	15.3	17.4	9.2	9.1	8.9
Ft. Wayne	14.9	14.5	14.5	19.4	19.7	9.0	5.9	2.1
Ft. Worth	15.1	12.8	13.0	17.5	18.4	10.2	8.5	4.5
Grand Rapids	15.9	13.2	13.3	18.4	19.7	10.3	6.6	2.6
Green Bay	13.4	12.9	13.0	18.0	22.4	10.4	7.1	2.9
Greensboro	13.5	12.5	13.7	17.4	19.0	9.7	8.3	5.9
Honolulu	13.7	10.0	11.2	15.8	17.6	11.1	12.0	8.7
Houston	16.5	13.0	13.4	16.8	16.6	8.9	8.5	6.3
Huntsville	15.2	12.0	11.7	14.8	17.9	10.9	10.8	6.8
Indianapolis	12.7	11.8	12.6	17.4	19.9	11.2	9.6	4.8
Irvine	7.8	4.9	5.2	9.3	16.8	14.9	21.0	20.2
Jacksonville	13.2	11.1	12.4	17.4	20.6	11.3	9.4	4.6
Kansas City	15.6	12.0	13.1	17.0	19.4	10.4	8.7	3.9
Knoxville	24.8	16.1	14.0	15.8	14.5	6.7	5.1	3.0
Las Vegas	11.7	11.0	12.0	16.6	20.2	12.1	11.0	5.5
Lexington	14.6	12.1	12.0	15.2	18.6	11.1	10.2	6.2
Lincoln	11.5	11.8	12.6	17.6	21.0	11.9	9.4	4.1
Los Angeles	18.9	13.1	12.1	14.7	15.6	9.1	9.0	7.5
Louisville	23.2	14.9	13.8	16.0	15.6	7.2	6.0	3.3
Madison	13.2	10.0	10.9	17.0	20.6	12.3	10.8	5.1

Table continued on next page.

City	Percent of Households Earning							
	Under $15,000	$15,000 -24,999	$25,000 -34,999	$35,000 -49,999	$50,000 -74,999	$75,000 -99,000	$100,000 -149,999	$150,000 and up
Manchester	13.3	11.8	12.4	17.9	21.6	11.7	8.0	3.2
Memphis	20.2	14.0	13.8	17.0	17.0	8.0	6.2	3.8
Miami	31.2	16.0	12.6	13.2	11.9	5.8	5.2	4.2
Milwaukee	19.4	14.4	14.0	17.7	18.0	8.7	5.8	2.0
Minneapolis	15.2	12.0	12.6	16.7	18.3	10.4	9.5	5.4
Naperville	3.3	3.8	4.7	7.6	15.5	16.0	25.8	23.4
Nashville	13.6	10.9	12.5	17.3	20.0	10.8	9.6	5.3
New York	20.9	10.8	10.3	14.0	16.4	10.0	9.9	7.7
Norfolk	18.4	13.9	14.2	17.4	18.1	8.1	6.2	3.7
Oklahoma City	16.0	13.5	13.4	16.9	18.3	9.8	8.2	3.9
Omaha	12.9	12.2	13.1	17.6	19.5	10.9	9.1	4.6
Orlando	14.8	13.6	14.8	19.5	18.1	8.9	6.5	3.8
Overland Park	5.0	6.1	8.4	14.0	20.6	15.1	17.3	13.6
Philadelphia	23.5	13.5	12.3	15.6	16.3	8.7	7.0	3.0
Phoenix	12.5	12.0	12.9	17.5	19.1	10.6	9.6	5.9
Pittsburgh	24.4	15.7	13.1	15.0	15.0	7.4	5.8	3.7
Plano	4.4	4.7	6.7	11.6	18.2	15.1	21.1	18.3
Portland	13.6	11.1	11.8	16.8	19.9	11.3	10.0	5.5
Providence	28.7	15.2	12.3	14.0	13.9	6.9	5.4	3.6
Provo	14.1	16.0	15.1	19.5	16.7	8.2	7.1	3.3
Raleigh	10.4	9.6	11.6	16.7	20.3	12.6	12.3	6.5
Reno	12.7	11.9	12.8	17.0	20.2	11.2	9.3	4.9
Richmond	20.5	13.8	13.5	15.8	16.2	8.1	7.1	5.0
Rochester	27.9	17.3	13.9	15.5	13.9	6.2	3.7	1.7
Sacramento	16.4	12.2	11.9	16.7	18.8	10.3	9.2	4.5
St. Louis	24.5	15.6	13.7	15.8	15.3	7.1	5.4	2.5
St. Paul	14.2	11.6	12.7	16.7	19.7	10.9	9.5	4.8
St. Petersburg	15.6	13.7	14.4	17.3	18.1	9.2	7.6	4.0
Salt Lake City	15.2	12.9	12.7	16.0	18.5	9.9	8.8	5.9
San Antonio	15.6	12.9	13.0	17.0	18.8	9.8	8.7	4.3
San Diego	11.8	10.2	10.6	14.7	18.5	12.4	13.2	8.7
San Francisco	12.4	7.5	7.3	11.6	16.5	12.4	16.2	16.1
San Jose	7.0	5.8	6.4	10.8	18.1	15.3	20.3	16.3
Savannah	23.9	15.7	13.9	15.1	15.5	7.6	5.3	2.9
Scottsdale	7.8	7.9	8.9	13.5	18.6	11.9	14.8	16.4
Seattle	13.1	10.0	11.0	15.7	18.6	11.9	11.7	8.0
Sioux Falls	10.1	10.8	13.1	18.1	22.4	11.2	9.5	4.9
Springfield	19.1	17.8	15.7	18.9	14.5	6.4	4.7	2.9
Stamford	10.6	7.8	7.9	12.4	17.4	12.8	15.0	16.1
Tampa	18.5	13.2	13.0	16.5	16.7	8.4	7.4	6.3
Thousand Oaks	4.9	5.2	5.6	10.2	16.4	14.8	22.5	20.3
Tucson	18.8	15.7	15.3	17.8	16.8	7.7	5.6	2.3
Tulsa	15.9	14.3	13.7	17.1	16.9	8.8	7.8	5.4
Virginia Beach	6.4	7.8	11.1	18.1	24.1	14.3	12.2	6.0
Washington	17.8	9.3	10.2	14.3	16.0	10.0	11.4	11.0
Wichita	13.1	12.3	12.9	17.3	20.7	11.2	8.7	3.8
U.S.	13.3	11.0	11.3	15.7	19.5	11.8	11.0	6.4

Note: Figures are 2006 estimates
Source: Claritas, Inc.

Household Income Distribution: Metro Area

Metro Area	Percent of Households Earning							
	Under $15,000	$15,000 -24,999	$25,000 -34,999	$35,000 -49,999	$50,000 -74,999	$75,000 -99,000	$100,000 -149,999	$150,000 and up
Albuquerque	13.3	12.0	12.2	16.8	19.5	11.0	10.2	5.0
Alexandria	6.8	5.5	7.0	12.4	19.2	15.5	19.1	14.4
Anchorage	7.4	8.1	9.5	14.1	21.1	15.2	16.2	8.5
Ann Arbor	10.9	8.5	9.2	13.8	18.2	13.4	15.8	10.2
Athens	20.9	13.1	11.8	15.3	17.0	8.9	8.2	4.7
Atlanta	9.1	8.0	9.6	15.2	21.2	14.1	14.1	8.7
Austin	10.5	8.8	10.2	15.3	20.3	13.5	13.2	8.1
Baltimore	10.9	8.6	9.4	14.1	19.8	14.0	14.8	8.4
Baton Rouge	17.2	12.2	11.4	15.2	18.1	11.4	10.0	4.4
Bellevue	9.3	8.4	9.9	15.2	21.1	14.4	14.0	7.6
Birmingham	15.8	11.4	11.6	15.9	18.6	10.9	9.9	5.8
Boise City	10.4	11.4	12.5	17.6	21.0	12.1	10.1	4.7
Boston	10.9	7.9	8.2	12.5	18.6	14.0	16.2	11.6
Boulder	9.2	7.5	8.4	13.2	18.6	13.8	16.8	12.4
Buffalo	15.7	12.9	12.1	15.4	19.1	11.2	9.6	4.1
Cary	9.3	8.2	9.7	14.8	20.5	14.1	14.9	8.5
Cedar Rapids	9.7	10.5	11.7	17.4	23.1	13.5	10.3	3.9
Charleston	14.5	11.2	11.9	16.3	19.9	11.4	9.9	4.9
Charlotte	10.2	9.0	10.8	16.0	21.1	13.1	12.3	7.5
Chattanooga	15.4	12.4	12.7	17.0	19.9	10.2	8.1	4.4
Chicago	10.7	8.5	9.3	14.3	20.0	13.9	14.3	9.1
Cincinnati	11.6	10.0	10.7	15.5	20.4	13.0	12.3	6.6
Cleveland	13.2	11.0	11.4	15.9	19.9	12.1	10.7	5.7
Colorado Spgs.	8.3	8.9	11.1	16.1	22.5	13.6	13.0	6.4
Columbia	13.6	11.4	11.9	16.8	20.2	11.7	9.7	4.7
Columbus	11.0	9.5	10.9	16.0	20.7	13.2	12.4	6.3
Dallas	9.9	9.1	10.7	15.8	19.9	13.0	13.1	8.4
Denver	7.9	7.5	9.5	15.1	21.1	14.6	15.2	9.1
Des Moines	9.3	9.5	11.2	16.3	22.1	13.8	11.9	5.8
Durham	14.1	10.4	11.2	15.3	19.3	11.5	10.9	7.2
Edison	14.3	8.9	8.9	12.9	17.2	12.3	14.1	11.5
El Paso	19.1	15.3	14.0	16.5	16.9	8.2	6.8	3.2
Eugene	15.8	12.9	12.6	17.6	19.6	9.9	7.7	3.9
Ft. Collins	8.8	8.9	9.7	14.5	21.4	14.3	15.0	7.5
Ft. Lauderdale	14.9	11.7	11.7	15.6	18.1	10.6	10.2	7.2
Ft. Wayne	10.8	11.4	12.3	17.7	21.7	12.3	9.8	4.1
Ft. Worth	9.9	9.1	10.7	15.8	19.9	13.0	13.1	8.4
Grand Rapids	10.2	10.5	11.4	16.9	22.3	13.1	10.7	4.9
Green Bay	9.4	10.1	11.1	16.3	23.7	14.2	11.0	4.3
Greensboro	13.4	11.7	12.7	17.5	20.1	10.6	8.9	5.1
Honolulu	10.0	8.3	9.7	14.5	19.5	13.9	15.4	8.6
Houston	12.2	10.1	11.0	15.4	18.5	12.0	12.7	8.1
Huntsville	12.9	10.9	11.0	15.0	19.2	12.5	12.4	6.0
Indianapolis	10.0	10.0	10.9	15.9	20.8	13.3	12.5	6.6
Irvine	13.3	10.5	10.5	14.5	17.8	11.7	12.4	9.2
Jacksonville	11.6	10.5	11.8	16.7	21.0	12.1	10.7	5.7
Kansas City	10.2	9.4	11.1	16.2	21.3	13.4	12.2	6.2
Knoxville	15.8	12.3	12.5	16.1	18.8	10.4	9.2	4.9
Las Vegas	10.3	10.2	11.5	17.1	21.3	12.7	11.2	5.6
Lexington	14.0	11.8	11.7	15.5	19.2	11.7	10.5	5.6
Lincoln	11.0	11.2	12.2	17.0	21.6	12.5	10.1	4.5
Los Angeles	13.3	10.5	10.5	14.5	17.8	11.7	12.4	9.2
Louisville	13.2	11.0	11.8	16.0	20.4	11.7	10.5	5.4
Madison	9.2	8.5	9.9	15.6	22.1	14.9	13.5	6.3

Table continued on next page.

Metro Area	Percent of Households Earning							
	Under $15,000	$15,000 -24,999	$25,000 -34,999	$35,000 -49,999	$50,000 -74,999	$75,000 -99,000	$100,000 -149,999	$150,000 and up
Manchester	8.4	8.2	9.1	14.3	21.9	15.2	14.9	8.0
Memphis	15.4	11.1	11.5	15.7	19.1	11.5	10.2	5.6
Miami	14.9	11.7	11.7	15.6	18.1	10.6	10.2	7.2
Milwaukee	11.1	10.1	10.6	15.6	20.8	13.5	12.2	6.1
Minneapolis	7.4	7.5	8.9	14.2	21.4	15.8	16.1	8.7
Naperville	10.7	8.5	9.3	14.3	20.0	13.9	14.3	9.1
Nashville	11.8	9.9	11.2	16.3	21.1	12.3	11.2	6.3
New York	14.3	8.9	8.9	12.9	17.2	12.3	14.1	11.5
Norfolk	11.0	10.0	11.6	16.9	21.8	12.8	11.1	4.9
Oklahoma City	14.5	12.6	12.9	17.1	19.4	10.5	8.8	4.1
Omaha	9.9	10.2	11.6	16.4	21.7	13.3	11.7	5.3
Orlando	11.0	11.3	12.6	17.9	20.6	11.2	9.9	5.4
Overland Park	10.2	9.4	11.1	16.2	21.3	13.4	12.2	6.2
Philadelphia	12.0	9.1	9.6	14.1	19.1	13.3	14.1	8.6
Phoenix	10.2	10.2	11.4	16.5	20.6	12.5	11.9	6.8
Pittsburgh	15.2	13.3	12.6	16.0	18.8	10.6	8.9	4.6
Plano	9.9	9.1	10.7	15.8	19.9	13.0	13.1	8.4
Portland	9.8	9.4	10.7	16.4	21.6	13.4	12.3	6.4
Providence	14.9	11.1	10.1	14.4	19.5	12.6	11.8	5.6
Provo	8.0	9.7	11.1	17.7	23.0	13.2	12.0	5.3
Raleigh	9.3	8.2	9.7	14.8	20.5	14.1	14.9	8.5
Reno	9.9	9.7	11.4	16.0	21.1	13.0	12.1	6.7
Richmond	10.4	9.3	10.9	15.8	20.9	13.5	12.6	6.5
Rochester	12.7	11.3	11.2	15.9	20.3	12.6	11.0	5.0
Sacramento	11.1	9.7	10.3	15.5	20.0	13.0	13.3	7.0
St. Louis	11.7	10.3	11.1	15.9	20.6	12.8	11.5	6.0
St. Paul	7.4	7.5	8.9	14.2	21.4	15.8	16.1	8.7
St. Petersburg	13.2	12.8	13.5	17.3	19.2	10.1	8.7	5.0
Salt Lake City	7.9	8.4	10.0	16.2	22.8	14.2	13.6	7.0
San Antonio	13.8	11.8	12.2	16.8	19.7	10.8	9.8	5.1
San Diego	10.2	9.7	10.5	15.0	19.4	12.9	13.7	8.7
San Francisco	9.2	6.9	7.3	11.9	17.6	13.9	17.5	15.7
San Jose	6.6	5.4	6.1	10.2	17.1	14.7	20.2	19.8
Savannah	15.6	11.6	11.9	14.9	18.7	11.5	10.0	5.7
Scottsdale	10.2	10.2	11.4	16.5	20.6	12.5	11.9	6.8
Seattle	9.3	8.4	9.9	15.2	21.1	14.4	14.0	7.6
Sioux Falls	9.3	9.9	12.2	17.5	24.0	12.6	10.0	4.5
Springfield	14.9	14.5	14.5	18.4	18.9	8.9	6.6	3.4
Stamford	8.9	7.1	7.5	11.4	16.5	12.7	15.8	20.1
Tampa	13.2	12.8	13.5	17.3	19.2	10.1	8.7	5.0
Thousand Oaks	7.3	7.2	7.8	13.1	19.5	15.0	18.0	12.2
Tucson	14.6	13.0	13.2	17.1	18.7	10.0	8.7	4.7
Tulsa	14.2	12.8	12.8	17.0	19.3	10.7	8.9	4.4
Virginia Beach	11.0	10.0	11.6	16.9	21.8	12.8	11.1	4.9
Washington	6.8	5.5	7.0	12.4	19.2	15.5	19.1	14.4
Wichita	11.4	11.0	12.0	17.0	21.8	12.7	10.1	4.0
U.S.	13.3	11.0	11.3	15.7	19.5	11.8	11.0	6.4

Note: Figures are 2006 estimates and cover the Metropolitan Statistical Area (MSA) - see Appendix B for areas included
Source: Claritas, Inc.

Poverty Rates by Age: City

City	All Ages	Under 5 Years Old	5 to 17 Years Old	18 to 64 Years Old	65 Years and Over
Albuquerque	13.5	1.4	3.0	8.2	1.0
Alexandria	8.9	0.8	1.6	5.8	0.7
Anchorage	7.3	0.8	1.9	4.3	0.3
Ann Arbor	16.6	0.5	1.0	14.7	0.4
Athens	28.6	1.6	3.2	22.7	1.1
Atlanta	24.4	2.7	6.4	13.2	2.1
Austin	14.4	1.3	2.6	10.0	0.6
Baltimore	22.9	2.3	5.5	12.8	2.4
Baton Rouge	24.0	2.5	5.5	14.3	1.6
Bellevue	5.7	0.3	1.0	3.6	0.8
Birmingham	24.7	2.6	6.4	13.3	2.4
Boise City	8.4	0.9	1.7	5.3	0.6
Boston	19.5	1.4	3.9	12.4	1.9
Boulder	17.4	0.6	1.2	15.1	0.5
Buffalo	26.6	3.2	7.1	14.4	1.8
Cary	3.4	0.2	0.6	2.4	0.2
Cedar Rapids	7.5	0.8	1.5	4.4	0.9
Charleston	19.1	1.6	3.5	12.1	1.9
Charlotte	10.6	1.0	2.5	6.3	0.8
Chattanooga	17.9	1.8	4.4	9.6	2.1
Chicago	19.6	2.2	5.3	10.6	1.6
Cincinnati	21.9	2.6	5.5	12.0	1.8
Cleveland	26.3	3.4	7.5	13.3	2.1
Colorado Spgs.	8.7	0.9	2.1	5.0	0.7
Columbia	22.1	2.1	4.9	13.0	2.0
Columbus	14.8	1.5	3.1	9.2	0.9
Dallas	17.8	2.2	4.6	9.9	1.1
Denver	14.3	1.4	3.1	8.7	1.1
Des Moines	11.4	1.4	2.5	6.5	0.9
Durham	15.0	1.6	3.0	9.1	1.2
Edison	4.8	0.3	0.9	2.9	0.7
El Paso	22.2	2.6	6.7	11.1	1.9
Eugene	17.1	1.1	2.1	13.0	0.9
Ft. Collins	14.0	0.7	1.2	11.6	0.5
Ft. Lauderdale	17.7	1.6	4.1	10.3	1.7
Ft. Wayne	12.5	1.7	3.2	6.7	0.9
Ft. Worth	15.9	2.0	4.2	8.6	1.1
Grand Rapids	15.7	1.7	3.9	9.0	1.1
Green Bay	10.5	1.1	2.3	6.1	1.0
Greensboro	12.3	1.2	2.5	7.3	1.2
Honolulu	11.8	0.8	2.1	7.3	1.5
Houston	19.2	2.3	5.0	10.8	1.2
Huntsville	12.8	1.4	3.0	7.2	1.2
Indianapolis	11.9	1.4	2.9	6.7	0.9
Irvine	9.1	0.4	1.2	7.1	0.4
Jacksonville	12.2	1.3	3.2	6.4	1.2
Kansas City	14.3	1.6	3.6	7.9	1.2
Knoxville	20.8	1.9	3.5	13.7	1.7
Las Vegas	11.9	1.3	2.8	6.9	0.9
Lexington	12.9	1.1	2.2	8.8	0.9
Lincoln	10.1	0.9	1.8	6.8	0.6
Los Angeles	22.1	2.4	5.7	12.8	1.2
Louisville	21.6	2.6	5.5	11.6	1.9
Madison	15.0	0.7	1.4	12.5	0.4
Manchester	10.6	1.2	2.3	5.6	1.5

Table continued on next page.

City	All Ages	Under 5 Years Old	5 to 17 Years Old	18 to 64 Years Old	65 Years and Over
Memphis	20.6	2.7	5.8	10.4	1.6
Miami	28.5	2.2	6.2	15.0	5.0
Milwaukee	21.3	2.7	6.5	11.0	1.2
Minneapolis	16.9	1.6	4.0	10.4	0.9
Naperville	2.2	0.2	0.6	1.2	0.3
Nashville	13.3	1.5	3.0	7.6	1.2
New York	21.2	2.0	5.3	11.9	2.0
Norfolk	19.4	2.2	5.2	10.5	1.5
Oklahoma City	16.0	2.0	4.1	9.0	1.0
Omaha	11.3	1.2	2.9	6.4	0.8
Orlando	15.9	2.0	4.1	8.5	1.3
Overland Park	3.2	0.3	0.6	2.0	0.4
Philadelphia	22.9	2.1	5.9	12.5	2.4
Phoenix	15.8	2.1	4.1	8.8	0.8
Pittsburgh	20.4	1.8	4.0	12.3	2.2
Plano	4.3	0.4	1.0	2.5	0.4
Portland	13.1	1.0	2.4	8.4	1.2
Providence	29.1	3.1	8.2	15.8	2.0
Provo	26.8	1.5	2.0	23.0	0.3
Raleigh	11.5	1.0	2.1	7.6	0.8
Reno	12.6	1.5	2.4	7.8	0.8
Richmond	21.4	2.2	5.3	11.8	2.1
Rochester	25.9	3.1	7.7	13.6	1.4
Sacramento	20.0	2.1	6.0	10.9	1.0
St. Louis	24.6	2.6	6.9	12.7	2.3
St. Paul	15.6	1.7	4.8	8.1	1.0
St. Petersburg	13.3	1.1	3.1	7.2	1.8
Salt Lake City	15.3	1.5	3.0	9.9	0.9
San Antonio	17.3	2.2	4.9	8.8	1.4
San Diego	14.6	1.4	3.5	8.9	0.8
San Francisco	11.3	0.5	1.5	7.9	1.4
San Jose	8.8	0.8	2.1	5.4	0.6
Savannah	21.8	2.4	5.8	11.5	2.1
Scottsdale	5.8	0.3	0.8	3.7	1.0
Seattle	11.8	0.6	1.7	8.3	1.2
Sioux Falls	8.4	1.0	1.7	4.9	0.8
Springfield	15.9	1.4	2.6	10.7	1.2
Stamford	7.9	0.6	1.3	4.7	1.3
Tampa	18.1	1.9	4.8	9.4	1.9
Thousand Oaks	5.0	0.4	1.0	3.0	0.6
Tucson	18.4	1.9	4.1	11.1	1.3
Tulsa	14.1	1.8	3.4	7.9	1.0
Virginia Beach	6.5	0.7	1.8	3.7	0.4
Washington	20.2	1.9	4.6	11.7	2.0
Wichita	11.2	1.3	2.7	6.3	0.9
U.S.	12.4	1.2	3.0	6.9	1.2

Note: Figures are percent of population with income in 1999 below poverty level and only include population for whom poverty status is determined
Source: Census 2000, Summary File 3

Poverty Rates by Age: Metro Area

MSA[1]	All Ages	Under 5 Years Old	5 to 17 Years Old	18 to 64 Years Old	65 Years and Over
Albuquerque	13.8	1.5	3.4	7.9	1.0
Alexandria	7.4	0.7	1.7	4.4	0.7
Anchorage	7.3	0.8	1.9	4.3	0.3
Ann Arbor	8.2	0.6	1.2	5.8	0.6
Athens	21.4	1.4	2.8	16.1	1.2
Atlanta	9.4	1.0	2.3	5.4	0.7
Austin	11.1	1.0	2.1	7.4	0.6
Baltimore	9.8	0.9	2.3	5.5	1.1
Baton Rouge	16.2	1.6	3.9	9.5	1.2
Bellevue	7.9	0.6	1.6	5.0	0.7
Birmingham	13.1	1.3	3.2	7.1	1.6
Boise City	9.0	1.1	2.2	5.0	0.7
Boston	8.6	0.6	1.7	5.1	1.1
Boulder	9.5	0.6	1.3	7.1	0.5
Buffalo	11.9	1.3	2.9	6.5	1.2
Cary	10.2	1.0	1.9	6.4	1.0
Cedar Rapids	6.5	0.7	1.4	3.7	0.8
Charleston	14.0	1.4	3.6	7.7	1.3
Charlotte	9.3	0.9	2.2	5.3	1.0
Chattanooga	11.9	1.1	2.8	6.4	1.5
Chicago	10.5	1.1	2.7	5.8	0.9
Cincinnati	9.7	1.1	2.4	5.2	0.9
Cleveland	10.8	1.2	2.8	5.6	1.2
Colorado Spgs.	8.0	0.9	2.0	4.5	0.6
Columbia	11.7	1.1	2.7	6.8	1.1
Columbus	10.1	1.1	2.2	6.0	0.8
Dallas	11.1	1.3	2.8	6.3	0.7
Denver	8.1	0.8	1.8	4.8	0.6
Des Moines	7.5	0.9	1.6	4.3	0.7
Durham	10.2	1.0	1.9	6.4	1.0
Edison	5.4	0.4	1.1	3.3	0.6
El Paso	23.8	2.8	7.4	11.8	1.8
Eugene	14.4	1.2	2.6	9.6	1.0
Ft. Collins	9.2	0.5	1.2	7.1	0.4
Ft. Lauderdale	11.5	1.0	2.7	6.2	1.6
Ft. Wayne	8.2	1.0	2.1	4.3	0.8
Ft. Worth	10.3	1.2	2.6	5.7	0.8
Grand Rapids	8.4	0.9	2.0	4.8	0.7
Green Bay	6.9	0.7	1.5	3.9	0.8
Greensboro	10.4	1.1	2.3	5.7	1.4
Honolulu	9.9	0.9	2.2	5.8	1.0
Houston	13.9	1.6	3.7	7.7	0.9
Huntsville	10.9	1.2	2.6	5.9	1.2
Indianapolis	8.6	0.9	2.0	4.8	0.8
Irvine	10.3	1.0	2.6	6.1	0.6
Jacksonville	10.7	1.1	2.8	5.7	1.1
Kansas City	8.5	0.9	2.1	4.7	0.8
Knoxville	12.0	1.1	2.4	7.3	1.3
Las Vegas	11.1	1.2	2.6	6.4	0.9
Lexington	12.6	1.2	2.3	8.0	1.1
Lincoln	9.5	0.8	1.8	6.3	0.6
Los Angeles	17.9	1.9	4.9	10.1	1.0
Louisville	10.9	1.3	2.7	5.9	1.0
Madison	9.4	0.5	1.2	7.3	0.4
Manchester	7.1	0.7	1.5	3.7	1.1

Table continued on next page.

MSA[1]	All Ages	Under 5 Years Old	5 to 17 Years Old	18 to 64 Years Old	65 Years and Over
Memphis	15.3	1.9	4.3	7.7	1.3
Miami	18.0	1.5	4.3	9.7	2.5
Milwaukee	10.6	1.3	3.0	5.5	0.8
Minneapolis	6.7	0.6	1.7	3.8	0.6
Naperville	10.5	1.1	2.7	5.8	0.9
Nashville	10.1	1.1	2.3	5.7	1.0
New York	19.5	1.8	4.9	10.9	1.9
Norfolk	10.6	1.2	2.9	5.7	0.9
Oklahoma City	13.5	1.5	3.3	7.8	0.9
Omaha	8.4	0.9	2.2	4.7	0.7
Orlando	10.7	1.0	2.6	6.1	1.0
Overland Park	8.5	0.9	2.1	4.7	0.8
Philadelphia	11.1	1.0	2.8	6.1	1.3
Phoenix	12.0	1.4	3.0	6.7	0.9
Pittsburgh	10.8	0.9	2.4	5.9	1.6
Plano	11.1	1.3	2.8	6.3	0.7
Portland	9.5	0.9	2.0	5.7	0.7
Providence	11.8	1.1	2.9	6.2	1.6
Provo	12.0	1.1	1.9	8.6	0.3
Raleigh	10.2	1.0	1.9	6.4	1.0
Reno	10.0	1.1	2.1	6.1	0.6
Richmond	9.3	0.9	2.3	5.1	0.9
Rochester	10.3	1.0	2.7	5.7	0.9
Sacramento	12.2	1.2	3.5	6.8	0.7
St. Louis	9.9	1.0	2.7	5.2	1.0
St. Paul	6.7	0.6	1.7	3.8	0.6
St. Petersburg	11.2	1.0	2.5	6.0	1.6
Salt Lake City	7.7	1.0	1.9	4.4	0.4
San Antonio	15.1	1.8	4.3	7.7	1.2
San Diego	12.4	1.2	3.2	7.3	0.8
San Francisco	8.4	0.5	1.3	5.7	1.0
San Jose	7.5	0.6	1.6	4.7	0.6
Savannah	14.5	1.5	3.8	7.8	1.4
Scottsdale	12.0	1.4	3.0	6.7	0.9
Seattle	7.9	0.6	1.6	5.0	0.7
Sioux Falls	7.1	0.8	1.5	4.0	0.8
Springfield	11.8	1.1	2.5	7.2	1.0
Stamford	5.7	0.4	1.1	3.3	0.8
Tampa	11.2	1.0	2.5	6.0	1.6
Thousand Oaks	9.2	1.0	2.5	5.2	0.6
Tucson	14.7	1.4	3.5	8.6	1.2
Tulsa	11.4	1.3	2.8	6.2	1.1
Virginia Beach	10.6	1.2	2.9	5.7	0.9
Washington	7.4	0.7	1.7	4.4	0.7
Wichita	9.1	1.1	2.2	5.0	0.8
U.S.	12.4	1.2	3.0	6.9	1.2

Note: Figures are percent of population with income in 1999 below poverty level and only include population for whom poverty status is determined; (1) Metropolitan Statistical Area - see Appendix A for areas included
Source: Census 2000, Summary File 3

Personal Bankruptcy Filing Rate

City	Area Covered	2003	2004	2005
Albuquerque	Bernalillo County	5.59	5.27	6.71
Alexandria	City of Alexandria	3.01	2.91	3.58
Anchorage	Anchorage Borough	2.59	2.88	3.92
Ann Arbor	Washtenaw County	3.67	3.75	6.15
Athens	Clarke County	4.63	4.69	4.62
Atlanta	Fulton County	6.27	5.88	6.87
Austin	Travis County	3.82	3.70	5.33
Baltimore	City of Baltimore	9.90	8.87	11.13
Baton Rouge	East Baton Rouge Parish	5.73	6.10	7.79
Bellevue	King County	4.88	4.69	6.13
Birmingham	Jefferson County	13.86	14.09	16.92
Boise City	Ada County	7.51	7.18	8.93
Boston	Suffolk County	2.52	2.58	3.68
Boulder	Boulder County	3.66	3.92	6.09
Buffalo	Erie County	6.21	6.25	9.12
Cary	Wake County	4.38	4.22	5.76
Cedar Rapids	Linn County	4.17	4.42	6.84
Charleston	Charleston County	2.88	2.85	2.69
Charlotte	Mecklenburg County	3.57	3.47	5.07
Chattanooga	Hamilton County	10.30	9.92	9.63
Chicago	Cook County	7.11	6.40	8.57
Cincinnati	Hamilton County	7.02	7.06	10.59
Cleveland	Cuyahoga County	9.39	8.98	15.13
Colorado Spgs.	El Paso County	6.63	6.49	9.80
Columbia	Richland County	4.83	4.46	4.39
Columbus	Franklin County	9.28	9.52	13.78
Dallas	Dallas County	4.64	4.83	5.80
Denver	Denver County	5.52	6.15	9.76
Des Moines	Polk County	5.26	5.49	7.64
Durham	Durham County	5.65	4.99	5.00
Edison	Middlesex County	3.26	3.23	4.29
El Paso	El Paso County	4.65	4.36	4.25
Eugene	Lane County	7.09	6.43	8.61
Fort Collins	Larimer County	5.12	5.80	8.13
Fort Lauderdale	Broward County	5.43	4.49	5.86
Fort Wayne	Allen County	8.20	8.43	12.77
Fort Worth	Tarrant County	6.14	6.46	8.04
Grand Rapids	Kent County	4.69	4.75	6.72
Green Bay	Brown County	4.45	4.34	7.39
Greensboro	Guilford County	4.71	4.14	4.87
Honolulu	Honolulu County	3.04	2.43	3.45
Houston	Harris County	3.66	3.82	5.23
Huntsville	Madison County	6.74	7.16	8.96
Indianapolis	Marion County	12.77	12.06	16.82
Irvine	Orange County	3.10	2.56	3.90
Jacksonville	Duval County	7.25	6.93	8.04
Kansas City	Jackson County	7.88	7.99	11.50
Knoxville	Knox County	6.72	6.52	8.17
Las Vegas	Clark County	9.97	7.71	10.70
Lexington	Fayette County	5.17	4.84	7.22
Lincoln	Lancaster County	4.85	4.93	6.80
Los Angeles	Los Angeles County	4.26	3.41	4.90
Louisville	Jefferson County	9.20	8.46	11.90
Madison	Dane County	3.79	3.45	4.81
Manchester	Hillsborough County	3.27	3.61	4.34
Memphis	Shelby County	20.87	19.67	21.67

Table continued on next page.

City	Area Covered	2003	2004	2005
Miami	Miami-Dade County	n/a	n/a	n/a
Milwaukee	Milwaukee County	8.93	8.87	11.78
Minneapolis	Hennepin County	4.43	3.45	5.27
Naperville	DuPage County	3.64	3.54	4.94
Nashville	Davidson County	9.45	9.24	9.28
New York	Bronx County	4.24	4.80	6.65
New York	Kings County	3.22	3.43	4.95
New York	New York County	2.91	3.15	5.11
New York	Queens County	3.54	3.67	5.10
New York	Richmond County	2.83	2.78	4.21
Norfolk	City of Norfolk	7.86	7.00	7.76
Oklahoma City	Oklahoma County	9.41	9.36	14.48
Omaha	Douglas County	6.06	6.31	8.33
Orlando	Orange County	5.87	5.26	6.49
Overland Park	Johnson County	4.39	4.70	7.17
Philadelphia	Philadelphia County	6.76	6.10	6.53
Phoenix	Maricopa County	6.18	6.03	7.24
Pittsburgh	Allegheny County	5.47	6.03	8.50
Plano	Collin County	6.22	5.58	7.93
Portland	Multnomah County	6.85	6.80	9.36
Providence	Providence County	4.58	4.15	5.86
Provo	Utah County	6.64	5.98	6.35
Raleigh	Wake County	4.38	4.22	5.76
Reno	Washoe County	6.96	6.08	7.62
Richmond	City of Richmond	10.18	10.82	12.81
Rochester	Monroe County	4.29	4.64	6.43
Sacramento	Sacramento County	4.54	4.12	5.99
Saint Louis	City of Saint Louis	9.54	11.64	13.12
Saint Paul	Ramsey County	4.29	3.27	4.92
Saint Petersburg	Pinellas County	6.22	5.66	7.07
Salt Lake City	Salt Lake County	11.25	10.60	10.89
San Antonio	Bexar County	3.82	3.67	4.37
San Diego	San Diego County	3.79	3.55	4.98
San Francisco	San Francisco County	2.73	2.55	4.05
San Jose	Santa Clara County	2.99	2.92	3.57
Savannah	Chatham County	11.16	10.21	9.22
Scottsdale	Maricopa County	6.18	6.03	7.24
Seattle	King County	4.88	4.69	6.13
Sioux Falls	Minnehaha County	5.74	5.36	8.46
Springfield	Greene County	5.68	5.96	8.47
Stamford	Fairfield County	2.28	1.85	2.80
Tampa	Hillsborough County	6.37	5.92	7.12
Thousand Oaks	Ventura County	2.97	2.70	3.86
Tucson	Pima County	5.14	4.75	6.24
Tulsa	Tulsa County	7.96	7.96	11.79
Virginia Beach	City of Virginia Beach	7.48	6.29	6.53
Washington	District of Columbia	n/a	n/a	n/a
Wichita	Sedgwick County	6.97	7.21	10.43
U.S.	U.S.	5.57	5.31	6.88

Note: Numbers are per 1,000 population and include Chapter 7 and Chapter 13 filings; n/a not available
Source: Federal Deposit Insurance Corporation (FDIC),
Regional Economic Conditions (RECON), 3/24/2006

Building Permits

City	Single-Family			Multi-Family			Total		
	2005	2006ᵖ	Pct. Chg.	2005	2006ᵖ	Pct. Chg.	2005	2006ᵖ	Pct. Chg.
Albuquerque	4,764	3,414	-28.3	314	660	110.2	5,078	4,074	-19.8
Alexandria	195	131	-32.8	822	523	-36.4	1,017	654	-35.7
Anchorage	668	550	-17.7	998	812	-18.6	1,666	1,362	-18.2
Ann Arbor	261	193	-26.1	59	64	8.5	320	257	-19.7
Athens	772	463	-40.0	235	472	100.9	1,007	935	-7.1
Atlanta	1,564	1,842	17.8	6,410	8,937	39.4	7,974	10,779	35.2
Austin	4,569	4,343	-4.9	4,225	5,277	24.9	8,794	9,620	9.4
Baltimore	643	353	-45.1	613	349	-43.1	1,256	702	-44.1
Baton Rouge	554	257	-53.6	360	919	155.3	914	1,176	28.7
Bellevue	171	238	39.2	367	805	119.3	538	1,043	93.9
Birmingham	220	303	37.7	445	980	120.2	665	1,283	92.9
Boise City	955	588	-38.4	354	584	65.0	1,309	1,172	-10.5
Boston	97	94	-3.1	1,059	2,325	119.5	1,156	2,419	109.3
Boulder	77	55	-28.6	107	124	15.9	184	179	-2.7
Buffalo	97	13	-86.6	13	20	53.8	110	33	-70.0
Cary	1,456	1,982	36.1	235	1,004	327.2	1,691	2,986	76.6
Cedar Rapids	351	356	1.4	390	133	-65.9	741	489	-34.0
Charleston	1,176	890	-24.3	1,011	575	-43.1	2,187	1,465	-33.0
Charlotte[1]	8,473	9,287	9.6	2,355	4,389	86.4	10,828	13,676	26.3
Chattanooga	711	668	-6.0	151	264	74.8	862	932	8.1
Chicago	1,507	1,415	-6.1	9,252	12,668	36.9	10,759	14,083	30.9
Cincinnati	190	193	1.6	426	699	64.1	616	892	44.8
Cleveland	345	253	-26.7	98	94	-4.1	443	347	-21.7
Colorado Spgs.[1]	6,250	4,129	-33.9	532	295	-44.5	6,782	4,424	-34.8
Columbia	597	667	11.7	59	387	555.9	656	1,054	60.7
Columbus	2,360	1,208	-48.8	2,224	1,283	-42.3	4,584	2,491	-45.7
Dallas	3,353	3,168	-5.5	2,436	3,563	46.3	5,789	6,731	16.3
Denver	2,029	1,808	-10.9	1,135	1,967	73.3	3,164	3,775	19.3
Des Moines	453	287	-36.6	325	454	39.7	778	741	-4.8
Durham	2,176	2,002	-8.0	162	879	442.6	2,338	2,881	23.2
Edison	95	19	-80.0	42	319	659.5	137	338	146.7
El Paso	3,252	2,903	-10.7	996	263	-73.6	4,248	3,166	-25.5
Eugene	756	528	-30.2	571	203	-64.4	1,327	731	-44.9
Fort Collins	732	466	-36.3	380	295	-22.4	1,112	761	-31.6
Fort Lauderdale	424	289	-31.8	626	1,021	63.1	1,050	1,310	24.8
Fort Wayne	331	231	-30.2	254	185	-27.2	585	416	-28.9
Fort Worth	10,046	8,948	-10.9	2,411	2,560	6.2	12,457	11,508	-7.6
Grand Rapids	170	127	-25.3	148	156	5.4	318	283	-11.0
Green Bay	166	79	-52.4	88	96	9.1	254	175	-31.1
Greensboro	1,867	1,640	-12.2	387	1,494	286.0	2,254	3,134	39.0
Honolulu[1]	2,079	1,727	-16.9	1,909	879	-54.0	3,988	2,606	-34.7
Houston	7,194	7,503	4.3	4,600	9,988	117.1	11,794	17,491	48.3
Huntsville	992	1,375	38.6	0	316	-	992	1,691	70.5
Indianapolis	2,760	1,947	-29.5	1,517	746	-50.8	4,277	2,693	-37.0
Irvine	1,164	593	-49.1	1,691	2,922	72.8	2,855	3,515	23.1
Jacksonville	8,175	6,291	-23.0	5,003	3,521	-29.6	13,178	9,812	-25.5
Kansas City	2,267	1,328	-41.4	1,098	1,887	71.9	3,365	3,215	-4.5
Knoxville	808	644	-20.3	297	395	33.0	1,105	1,039	-6.0
Las Vegas	4,271	2,998	-29.8	2,287	2,204	-3.6	6,558	5,202	-20.7
Lexington	2,399	1,521	-36.6	364	559	53.6	2,763	2,080	-24.7
Lincoln	1,232	958	-22.2	221	217	-1.8	1,453	1,175	-19.1
Los Angeles	2,482	2,421	-2.5	6,723	12,027	78.9	9,205	14,448	57.0
Louisville[1]	2,041	1,445	-29.2	359	622	73.3	2,400	2,067	-13.9
Madison	628	429	-31.7	1,394	961	-31.1	2,022	1,390	-31.3

Table continued on next page.

City	Single-Family			Multi-Family			Total		
	2005	2006ᵖ	Pct. Chg.	2005	2006ᵖ	Pct. Chg.	2005	2006ᵖ	Pct. Chg.
Manchester	251	150	-40.2	85	64	-24.7	336	214	-36.3
Memphis[1]	4,769	4,085	-14.3	947	1,154	21.9	5,716	5,239	-8.3
Miami	107	133	24.3	10,607	7,837	-26.1	10,714	7,970	-25.6
Milwaukee	204	174	-14.7	580	473	-18.4	784	647	-17.5
Minneapolis	198	218	10.1	1,308	1,539	17.7	1,506	1,757	16.7
Naperville	407	364	-10.6	158	230	45.6	565	594	5.1
Nashville	3,681	3,959	7.6	1,201	1,039	-13.5	4,882	4,998	2.4
New York	1,300	914	-29.7	30,299	30,013	-0.9	31,599	30,927	-2.1
Norfolk	526	375	-28.7	657	216	-67.1	1,183	591	-50.0
Oklahoma City	4,066	3,540	-12.9	209	197	-5.7	4,275	3,737	-12.6
Omaha	2,870	1,879	-34.5	592	1,023	72.8	3,462	2,902	-16.2
Orlando	1,865	1,563	-16.2	3,577	2,790	-22.0	5,442	4,353	-20.0
Overland Park	602	499	-17.1	342	599	75.1	944	1,098	16.3
Philadelphia	383	448	17.0	2,123	1,716	-19.2	2,506	2,164	-13.6
Phoenix	12,391	9,025	-27.2	2,752	2,244	-18.5	15,143	11,269	-25.6
Pittsburgh	65	123	89.2	0	6	-	65	129	98.5
Plano	803	867	8.0	606	2,032	235.3	1,409	2,899	105.7
Portland	981	1,256	28.0	2,755	2,295	-16.7	3,736	3,551	-5.0
Providence	44	80	81.8	44	268	509.1	88	348	295.5
Provo	260	286	10.0	104	275	164.4	364	561	54.1
Raleigh	4,410	3,464	-21.5	259	2,702	943.2	4,669	6,166	32.1
Reno	2,885	1,497	-48.1	1,025	273	-73.4	3,910	1,770	-54.7
Richmond	525	483	-8.0	229	246	7.4	754	729	-3.3
Rochester	65	75	15.4	0	0	-	65	75	15.4
Sacramento	1,856	1,785	-3.8	1,236	1,749	41.5	3,092	3,534	14.3
Saint Louis	360	249	-30.8	505	375	-25.7	865	624	-27.9
Saint Paul	139	140	0.7	285	403	41.4	424	543	28.1
Saint Petersburg	925	496	-46.4	335	164	-51.0	1,260	660	-47.6
Salt Lake City	96	117	21.9	830	191	-77.0	926	308	-66.7
San Antonio	8,266	7,266	-12.1	6,910	5,209	-24.6	15,176	12,475	-17.8
San Diego	1,059	815	-23.0	3,880	1,693	-56.4	4,939	2,508	-49.2
San Francisco	51	95	86.3	2,487	2,303	-7.4	2,538	2,398	-5.5
San Jose	805	602	-25.2	1,970	2,373	20.5	2,775	2,975	7.2
Savannah	178	337	89.3	77	411	433.8	255	748	193.3
Scottsdale	1,282	909	-29.1	226	559	147.3	1,508	1,468	-2.7
Seattle	533	482	-9.6	3,185	6,149	93.1	3,718	6,631	78.3
Sioux Falls	1,152	1,093	-5.1	318	460	44.7	1,470	1,553	5.6
Springfield	443	412	-7.0	665	880	32.3	1,108	1,292	16.6
Stamford	206	185	-10.2	52	62	19.2	258	247	-4.3
Tampa	2,144	1,940	-9.5	2,555	985	-61.4	4,699	2,925	-37.8
Thousand Oaks	61	64	4.9	462	131	-71.6	523	195	-62.7
Tucson	2,421	1,723	-28.8	370	475	28.4	2,791	2,198	-21.2
Tulsa	717	699	-2.5	394	2	-99.5	1,111	701	-36.9
Virginia Beach	894	681	-23.8	1,209	906	-25.1	2,103	1,587	-24.5
Washington	125	126	0.8	2,735	1,979	-27.6	2,860	2,105	-26.4
Wichita	1,625	1,545	-4.9	256	613	139.5	1,881	2,158	14.7
U.S.	1,682,000	1,380,000	-18.0	473,300	457,300	-3.4	2,155,300	1,837,300	-14.8

Note: (p) Preliminary; Figures represent new, privately-owned housing units authorized (unadjusted data); All permit data are based on estimates with imputation; U.S. figures are based on the new 20,000-place series. Figures cover the city except where noted; (1) County level data
Source: U.S. Census Bureau, Manufacturing, Mining, and Construction Statistics

Homeownership and Housing Vacancies

MSA[1]	Homeownership Rate[2] (%)			Rental Vacancy Rate[3] (%)			Homeowner Vacancy Rate[4] (%)		
	2004	2005	2006	2004	2005	2006	2004	2005	2006
Albuquerque	n/a	n/a	n/a	n/a	n/a	n/a	n/a	n/a	n/a
Alexandria	n/a	68.4	68.9	n/a	7.1	8.4	n/a	1.3	2.1
Anchorage	n/a	n/a	n/a	n/a	n/a	n/a	n/a	n/a	n/a
Ann Arbor	n/a	n/a	n/a	n/a	n/a	n/a	n/a	n/a	n/a
Atlanta	n/a	66.4	67.9	n/a	15.3	12.3	n/a	3.4	3.8
Austin	n/a	63.9	66.7	n/a	9.4	7.2	n/a	2.4	1.5
Baltimore	n/a	70.6	72.9	n/a	10.3	11.7	n/a	1.5	2.4
Baton Rouge	n/a	71.0	65.0	n/a	15.9	7.2	n/a	2.3	0.9
Bellevue	n/a	64.5	63.7	n/a	6.9	5.6	n/a	1.0	0.9
Birmingham	n/a	75.1	76.1	n/a	13.8	17.2	n/a	1.6	2.9
Boise City	n/a	n/a	n/a	n/a	n/a	n/a	n/a	n/a	n/a
Boston	n/a	63.0	64.7	n/a	5.1	5.3	n/a	1.2	2.0
Boulder	n/a	n/a	n/a	n/a	n/a	n/a	n/a	n/a	n/a
Buffalo	n/a	66.3	66.3	n/a	10.5	13.1	n/a	1.4	1.5
Cary	n/a	71.4	71.1	n/a	10.7	9.0	n/a	2.3	1.6
Cedar Rapids	n/a	n/a	n/a	n/a	n/a	n/a	n/a	n/a	n/a
Charleston	n/a	n/a	n/a	n/a	n/a	n/a	n/a	n/a	n/a
Charlotte	n/a	65.8	66.1	n/a	11.1	13.5	n/a	2.3	2.9
Chattanooga	n/a	n/a	n/a	n/a	n/a	n/a	n/a	n/a	n/a
Chicago	n/a	70.0	69.6	n/a	13.1	13.0	n/a	1.9	2.3
Cincinnati	n/a	68.4	65.5	n/a	12.7	12.3	n/a	2.3	3.2
Cleveland	n/a	74.4	76.9	n/a	18.3	13.5	n/a	3.4	4.1
Colorado Spgs.	n/a	n/a	n/a	n/a	n/a	n/a	n/a	n/a	n/a
Columbia	n/a	76.3	72.2	n/a	7.5	8.9	n/a	2.8	2.8
Columbus	n/a	68.9	65.8	n/a	13.8	13.1	n/a	3.0	3.4
Dallas	n/a	62.3	60.7	n/a	13.6	11.7	n/a	2.2	2.3
Denver	n/a	70.7	70.0	n/a	12.0	11.1	n/a	2.7	3.7
Des Moines	n/a	n/a	n/a	n/a	n/a	n/a	n/a	n/a	n/a
Durham	n/a	n/a	n/a	n/a	n/a	n/a	n/a	n/a	n/a
Edison	n/a	54.6	53.6	n/a	5.0	5.4	n/a	1.9	1.8
El Paso	n/a	72.6	65.0	n/a	6.8	5.5	n/a	0.5	0.3
Eugene	n/a	n/a	n/a	n/a	n/a	n/a	n/a	n/a	n/a
Fort Collins	n/a	n/a	n/a	n/a	n/a	n/a	n/a	n/a	n/a
Fort Lauderdale	n/a	69.2	67.4	n/a	7.3	7.3	n/a	2.3	3.4
Fort Wayne	n/a	n/a	n/a	n/a	n/a	n/a	n/a	n/a	n/a
Fort Worth	n/a	62.3	60.7	n/a	13.6	11.7	n/a	2.2	2.3
Grand Rapids	n/a	72.6	76.5	n/a	11.2	11.4	n/a	3.4	2.9
Green Bay	n/a	n/a	n/a	n/a	n/a	n/a	n/a	n/a	n/a
Greensboro	n/a	66.3	62.2	n/a	10.5	7.5	n/a	2.8	2.4
Honolulu	n/a	58.0	58.4	n/a	3.9	3.9	n/a	0.6	0.8
Houston	n/a	61.7	63.5	n/a	15.4	16.8	n/a	3.5	2.8
Huntsville	n/a	n/a	n/a	n/a	n/a	n/a	n/a	n/a	n/a
Indianapolis	n/a	77.1	79.0	n/a	15.7	19.4	n/a	3.7	3.5
Irvine	n/a	54.6	54.4	n/a	4.4	4.0	n/a	0.9	1.2
Jacksonville	n/a	67.9	70.0	n/a	10.2	12.5	n/a	3.3	4.9
Kansas City	n/a	71.3	69.5	n/a	15.6	14.1	n/a	2.6	4.1
Knoxville	n/a	n/a	n/a	n/a	n/a	n/a	n/a	n/a	n/a
Las Vegas	n/a	61.4	63.3	n/a	9.0	9.6	n/a	3.8	2.8
Lexington	n/a	n/a	n/a	n/a	n/a	n/a	n/a	n/a	n/a
Lincoln	n/a	n/a	n/a	n/a	n/a	n/a	n/a	n/a	n/a
Los Angeles	n/a	54.6	54.4	n/a	4.4	4.0	n/a	0.9	1.2
Louisville	n/a	62.9	66.4	n/a	9.3	9.9	n/a	2.9	3.0
Madison	n/a	n/a	n/a	n/a	n/a	n/a	n/a	n/a	n/a
Manchester	n/a	n/a	n/a	n/a	n/a	n/a	n/a	n/a	n/a

Table continued on next page.

MSA[1]	Homeownership Rate[2] (%)			Rental Vacancy Rate[3] (%)			Homeowner Vacancy Rate[4] (%)		
	2004	2005	2006	2004	2005	2006	2004	2005	2006
Memphis	n/a	64.8	61.6	n/a	10.2	9.5	n/a	1.9	1.9
Miami	n/a	69.2	67.4	n/a	7.3	7.3	n/a	2.3	3.4
Milwaukee	n/a	65.7	65.2	n/a	11.6	7.8	n/a	1.3	1.1
Minneapolis	n/a	74.9	73.4	n/a	10.6	8.4	n/a	1.7	2.6
Naperville	n/a	70.0	69.6	n/a	13.1	13.0	n/a	1.9	2.3
Nashville	n/a	73.0	72.4	n/a	14.6	10.5	n/a	1.9	1.5
New Orleans	n/a	71.2	70.3	n/a	9.0	8.6	n/a	2.2	2.6
New York	n/a	54.6	53.6	n/a	5.0	5.4	n/a	1.9	1.8
Norfolk	n/a	68.0	68.3	n/a	7.4	7.7	n/a	0.6	1.2
Oklahoma City	n/a	72.9	71.8	n/a	13.5	10.9	n/a	2.5	2.5
Omaha	n/a	69.7	68.1	n/a	8.5	11.3	n/a	1.5	2.8
Orlando	n/a	70.5	71.1	n/a	10.3	6.9	n/a	2.0	5.2
Overland Park	n/a	71.3	69.5	n/a	15.6	14.1	n/a	2.6	4.1
Philadelphia	n/a	73.5	73.1	n/a	11.6	11.6	n/a	1.7	1.7
Phoenix	n/a	71.2	72.5	n/a	11.2	9.1	n/a	1.0	3.1
Pittsburgh	n/a	73.1	72.2	n/a	10.0	13.4	n/a	2.1	2.3
Plano	n/a	62.3	60.7	n/a	13.6	11.7	n/a	2.2	2.3
Portland	n/a	68.3	66.0	n/a	9.7	7.1	n/a	1.6	1.7
Providence	n/a	63.1	65.5	n/a	7.0	8.6	n/a	1.4	1.8
Provo	n/a	n/a	n/a	n/a	n/a	n/a	n/a	n/a	n/a
Raleigh	n/a	71.4	71.1	n/a	10.7	9.0	n/a	2.3	1.6
Reno	n/a	n/a	n/a	n/a	n/a	n/a	n/a	n/a	n/a
Richmond	n/a	69.7	68.9	n/a	12.3	13.8	n/a	1.0	1.0
Rochester	n/a	74.9	73.4	n/a	7.3	6.0	n/a	1.3	1.0
Sacramento	n/a	64.1	64.2	n/a	8.5	12.7	n/a	1.2	3.3
Saint Louis	n/a	74.4	72.8	n/a	15.5	12.6	n/a	2.1	2.2
Saint Paul	n/a	74.9	73.4	n/a	10.6	8.4	n/a	1.7	2.6
Saint Petersburg	n/a	71.7	71.6	n/a	9.4	7.8	n/a	1.8	3.5
Salt Lake City	n/a	68.8	69.6	n/a	7.0	4.7	n/a	1.5	2.7
San Antonio	n/a	66.0	62.6	n/a	15.4	14.1	n/a	1.7	2.4
San Diego	n/a	60.5	61.2	n/a	6.3	7.3	n/a	2.1	2.8
San Francisco	n/a	57.8	59.4	n/a	8.0	6.9	n/a	1.6	2.4
San Jose	n/a	59.2	59.4	n/a	6.7	6.0	n/a	1.5	1.6
Savannah	n/a	n/a	n/a	n/a	n/a	n/a	n/a	n/a	n/a
Scottsdale	n/a	71.2	72.5	n/a	11.2	9.1	n/a	1.0	3.1
Seattle	n/a	64.5	63.7	n/a	6.9	5.6	n/a	1.0	0.9
Sioux Falls	n/a	n/a	n/a	n/a	n/a	n/a	n/a	n/a	n/a
Springfield	n/a	n/a	n/a	n/a	n/a	n/a	n/a	n/a	n/a
Stamford	n/a	68.2	70.4	n/a	5.6	6.0	n/a	1.3	4.3
Tampa	n/a	71.7	71.6	n/a	9.4	7.8	n/a	1.8	3.5
Thousand Oaks	n/a	73.4	69.8	n/a	4.3	4.1	n/a	0.4	1.8
Tucson	n/a	66.1	67.5	n/a	9.7	7.1	n/a	1.5	1.9
Tulsa	n/a	71.7	67.9	n/a	16.3	14.5	n/a	3.3	1.9
Virginia Beach	n/a	68.0	68.3	n/a	7.4	7.7	n/a	0.6	1.2
Washington	n/a	68.4	68.9	n/a	7.1	8.4	n/a	1.3	2.1
Wichita	n/a	n/a	n/a	n/a	n/a	n/a	n/a	n/a	n/a
U.S.	69.0	68.9	68.8	10.2	9.8	9.7	1.7	1.9	2.4

Note: Comparable 2004 data was not available due to changes in metropolitan area definitions; (1) Metropolitan Statistical Area - see Appendix B for areas included; (2) The proportion of households that are owners; (3) The proportion of the rental inventory that is vacant for rent; (4) The proportion of the homeowner inventory that is vacant for sale; n/a not available
Source: U.S. Census Bureau, Housing Vacancies and Homeownership Annual Statistics: 2006

Employment by Industry

Metro Area[1]	(A)	(B)	(C)	(D)	(E)	(F)	(G)	(H)	(I)	(J)	(K)	(L)	(M)
Albuquerque	20.3	12.2	16.1	11.6	6.1	9.6	4.8	n/a	3.4	3.1	2.7	2.3	n/a
Alexandria[2]	22.9	10.4	22.6	9.1	1.8	8.3	4.8	n/a	2.2	6.0	2.4	3.4	n/a
Anchorage	20.7	13.7	10.6	12.8	1.2	10.3	6.1	6.1	3.1	3.8	7.0	3.0	1.5
Ann Arbor	34.0	11.6	13.4	9.1	9.7	6.8	2.9	n/a	2.9	3.2	1.9	1.8	n/a
Athens	27.2	n/a	7.9	11.9	n/a	9.7	n/a	n/a	n/a	n/a	n/a	n/a	n/a
Atlanta	13.3	10.1	16.6	11.4	7.2	9.3	6.8	5.7	6.5	4.0	5.3	3.7	0.1
Austin	21.0	10.1	13.7	10.9	8.0	10.2	6.0	n/a	5.3	3.8	1.7	3.0	n/a
Baltimore	17.0	16.7	14.5	11.5	5.5	8.5	6.3	n/a	4.3	4.2	3.5	1.6	n/a
Baton Rouge	20.2	12.1	11.9	11.4	7.0	8.9	5.2	10.5	3.6	3.9	3.5	1.5	0.4
Bellevue[2]	13.9	10.4	14.4	10.6	11.3	9.1	6.2	6.4	5.0	3.5	3.6	5.6	0.1
Birmingham	15.6	11.8	12.8	12.2	8.3	8.4	7.4	6.5	5.9	4.4	3.8	2.3	0.5
Boise City	15.3	11.6	14.3	12.7	11.5	8.6	5.4	n/a	4.3	2.8	2.8	1.6	n/a
Boston[4]	11.7	20.6	17.9	9.2	6.3	8.5	9.1	3.7	3.8	3.6	2.4	3.2	<0.1
Boulder	18.4	11.1	18.1	10.5	11.1	10.0	4.5	n/a	3.4	3.0	1.0	5.3	n/a
Buffalo	17.5	15.9	12.3	11.8	11.0	8.5	6.4	n/a	4.2	4.1	3.2	1.6	n/a
Cary	18.2	9.6	16.9	11.8	6.6	8.9	5.2	n/a	4.3	4.7	2.5	3.5	n/a
Cedar Rapids	11.7	12.1	8.8	12.4	15.8	8.4	7.3	n/a	4.0	4.0	6.1	3.7	n/a
Charleston	19.0	10.5	13.0	13.8	7.1	11.8	4.6	n/a	2.8	4.4	4.0	1.8	n/a
Charlotte	12.8	8.8	14.9	11.3	9.9	8.9	9.4	n/a	5.6	4.5	4.4	2.6	n/a
Chattanooga	14.3	10.2	11.1	11.4	14.3	8.7	7.6	n/a	3.6	4.3	8.4	1.5	n/a
Chicago[2]	12.2	12.9	16.9	10.4	10.0	8.5	7.8	4.5	5.5	4.4	4.8	2.1	<0.1
Cincinnati	12.8	13.3	15.1	10.9	11.6	9.8	6.3	n/a	5.7	4.1	4.0	1.5	n/a
Cleveland	13.0	16.2	13.0	10.5	13.4	8.7	7.2	n/a	5.3	4.1	3.2	1.7	n/a
Colorado Spgs.	17.3	10.0	15.4	11.9	6.8	11.7	7.0	n/a	2.3	5.6	2.1	3.1	n/a
Columbia	22.3	11.0	12.3	10.7	8.4	8.2	7.5	n/a	4.7	4.0	3.2	1.7	n/a
Columbus	16.7	11.6	15.3	11.8	8.2	9.3	7.8	n/a	4.0	3.9	5.0	2.0	n/a
Dallas[2]	12.3	10.3	15.9	10.7	9.8	9.1	9.0	n/a	6.2	3.6	3.7	3.7	n/a
Denver	13.8	10.1	16.5	10.7	5.9	10.2	8.2	n/a	5.4	3.8	4.2	3.8	n/a
Des Moines	12.8	11.7	10.9	12.2	6.4	9.2	15.3	n/a	5.7	3.9	3.4	3.0	n/a
Durham	18.2	9.6	16.9	11.8	6.6	8.9	5.2	n/a	4.3	4.7	2.5	3.5	n/a
Edison[2]	14.7	13.0	16.4	13.0	7.3	7.4	6.2	n/a	5.7	4.7	3.7	3.0	n/a
El Paso	23.4	11.9	11.1	13.3	8.0	9.7	4.0	n/a	3.9	2.9	5.1	1.8	n/a
Eugene	18.7	12.7	11.1	13.0	12.8	9.0	5.4	5.1	3.8	3.3	2.2	2.4	0.5
Fort Collins	20.8	10.7	13.0	13.2	9.1	11.3	4.5	n/a	2.3	3.5	2.0	1.9	n/a
Fort Lauderdale[2]	13.2	11.3	16.1	13.4	3.9	9.9	8.5	7.6	6.0	4.3	3.0	2.5	n/a
Fort Wayne	10.0	16.1	9.7	11.0	17.5	8.7	5.4	n/a	6.0	3.6	5.0	1.6	n/a
Fort Worth[2]	13.9	11.2	11.4	12.0	11.5	9.6	5.7	n/a	4.7	3.9	7.3	1.9	n/a
Grand Rapids	9.6	14.5	14.0	10.9	18.6	8.4	5.7	n/a	5.6	4.1	2.7	1.4	n/a
Green Bay	12.8	12.8	9.1	10.4	17.4	9.3	7.1	n/a	4.0	4.3	6.7	1.5	n/a
Greensboro	12.1	12.4	12.3	10.9	17.0	8.5	6.0	n/a	5.2	3.8	4.7	1.8	n/a
Honolulu	21.4	12.3	14.0	10.6	2.5	13.6	5.0	n/a	3.1	4.5	5.5	2.0	n/a
Houston	14.3	11.0	14.5	10.7	9.1	8.8	5.6	7.4	5.3	3.9	4.9	1.4	3.2
Huntsville	20.5	7.5	20.8	11.4	16.0	8.0	3.0	n/a	2.9	3.6	1.5	1.2	n/a
Indianapolis	12.9	12.4	13.4	11.1	11.0	9.8	7.0	5.6	5.2	3.9	5.8	1.8	0.1
Irvine[2]	10.4	9.3	18.1	10.9	11.9	11.0	9.0	7.0	5.4	3.1	1.9	2.0	<0.1
Jacksonville	11.9	11.9	15.4	12.3	5.1	9.9	9.5	7.9	4.6	4.3	5.3	1.8	<0.1
Kansas City	14.7	11.5	14.3	11.4	8.3	9.3	7.4	n/a	4.9	4.0	4.7	4.1	n/a
Knoxville	15.9	12.2	11.7	13.7	11.5	10.4	5.2	n/a	4.7	4.2	3.4	1.8	n/a
Las Vegas	10.4	6.6	12.5	11.0	3.0	29.1	5.5	11.5	2.6	2.8	3.8	1.2	<0.1
Lexington	18.1	12.2	12.6	11.7	13.8	10.0	4.4	n/a	3.7	3.8	3.1	1.9	n/a
Lincoln	22.0	14.0	10.8	10.6	8.7	9.2	7.2	n/a	2.3	4.3	4.6	1.6	n/a
Los Angeles[2]	14.4	11.9	14.6	10.8	11.0	9.4	6.0	3.7	5.5	3.5	4.1	5.1	0.1
Louisville	12.9	12.4	11.9	10.8	12.8	9.2	6.7	n/a	4.8	4.5	7.0	1.7	n/a
Madison	23.5	9.9	10.3	12.5	9.3	8.1	7.9	n/a	3.6	5.0	2.5	2.6	n/a
Manchester[3]	11.3	16.4	12.5	13.3	9.5	8.5	8.4	n/a	4.8	4.0	n/a	3.3	n/a
Memphis	13.8	11.8	13.2	11.8	8.1	11.0	5.1	n/a	5.9	3.8	10.1	1.2	n/a

Table continued on next page.

Metro Area[1]	(A)	(B)	(C)	(D)	(E)	(F)	(G)	(H)	(I)	(J)	(K)	(L)	(M)
Miami[2]	14.5	13.2	14.7	12.3	4.5	9.7	7.1	5.2	7.0	3.9	5.8	2.1	<0.1
Milwaukee	11.0	16.2	13.1	10.1	15.5	8.1	6.7	4.0	4.8	4.8	3.7	2.1	0.1
Minneapolis	13.6	13.4	14.5	10.9	11.3	8.8	8.0	n/a	4.9	4.3	3.7	2.2	n/a
Naperville[2]	12.2	12.9	16.9	10.4	10.0	8.5	7.8	4.5	5.5	4.4	4.8	2.1	<0.1
Nashville	13.0	13.7	13.4	11.8	11.1	9.9	6.0	n/a	4.9	4.0	4.2	2.6	n/a
New York[2]	14.9	18.2	15.1	9.2	4.0	7.5	11.0	n/a	4.7	4.2	3.6	4.0	n/a
Norfolk	19.9	11.4	13.3	12.5	7.5	10.5	5.3	n/a	3.2	4.4	3.5	2.0	n/a
Oklahoma City	19.9	12.6	12.6	11.4	6.6	9.8	6.1	4.7	4.0	4.9	2.8	2.4	2.4
Omaha	13.2	14.3	13.5	11.9	7.2	9.0	8.2	n/a	3.9	3.6	6.7	2.8	n/a
Orlando	10.7	9.9	17.8	11.6	4.0	17.4	6.1	7.9	4.2	4.9	2.8	2.6	<0.1
Overland Park	14.7	11.5	14.3	11.4	8.3	9.3	7.4	n/a	4.9	4.0	4.7	4.1	n/a
Philadelphia[2]	11.4	20.8	15.2	10.9	8.1	7.6	7.6	n/a	4.5	4.4	3.2	2.1	n/a
Phoenix	12.4	10.2	17.1	12.4	7.1	9.5	8.1	9.7	4.6	3.8	3.3	1.6	0.1
Pittsburgh	11.4	19.9	12.9	11.9	8.7	9.0	5.9	4.7	4.3	4.8	4.1	2.0	0.4
Plano[2]	12.3	10.3	15.9	10.7	9.8	9.1	9.0	n/a	6.2	3.6	3.7	3.7	n/a
Portland	13.7	12.3	13.1	11.1	12.3	9.1	6.8	6.2	5.6	3.5	3.7	2.3	0.2
Providence[3]	12.7	19.2	10.8	12.2	11.3	9.8	6.7	4.9	3.6	4.4	2.2	1.9	0.1
Provo	13.5	21.4	12.2	12.8	10.3	7.2	3.5	n/a	2.5	2.2	1.2	4.3	n/a
Raleigh	18.2	9.6	16.9	11.8	6.6	8.9	5.2	n/a	4.3	4.7	2.5	3.5	n/a
Reno	13.0	8.9	13.6	11.1	6.4	17.4	4.7	10.0	4.8	3.2	5.5	1.2	0.2
Richmond	18.1	11.7	15.2	11.0	7.1	7.6	7.5	n/a	4.4	5.0	3.2	1.8	n/a
Rochester	16.1	20.0	11.7	11.2	14.5	7.3	4.2	3.3	3.6	3.6	2.1	2.1	0.1
Sacramento	25.5	10.2	11.8	11.5	5.4	9.5	7.2	7.6	3.2	3.2	2.7	2.2	0.1
Salt Lake City	14.7	9.1	16.1	11.3	8.8	9.1	8.0	n/a	4.7	3.0	4.8	3.0	n/a
San Antonio	18.1	13.9	12.8	11.8	6.1	11.1	7.9	5.8	3.5	3.5	2.7	2.5	0.4
San Diego	16.9	9.6	16.5	11.7	7.8	12.0	6.2	6.8	3.4	3.8	2.2	2.8	<0.1
San Francisco[2]	13.5	10.8	19.9	10.3	4.5	12.4	9.2	4.4	2.7	3.9	4.4	4.0	<0.1
San Jose	10.7	11.4	18.6	9.8	18.8	8.4	4.1	5.3	4.3	2.8	1.5	4.4	<0.1
Savannah	13.7	13.2	12.0	12.1	9.2	12.5	4.1	n/a	4.3	5.1	6.3	1.2	n/a
Scottsdale	12.4	10.2	17.1	12.4	7.1	9.5	8.1	9.7	4.6	3.8	3.3	1.6	0.1
Seattle[2]	13.9	10.4	14.4	10.6	11.3	9.1	6.2	6.4	5.0	3.5	3.6	5.6	0.1
Sioux Falls	9.1	17.9	7.7	13.1	10.0	9.4	12.3	n/a	5.1	3.6	3.9	2.3	n/a
Springfield	12.9	17.4	9.5	13.3	9.0	9.4	6.2	n/a	5.3	4.3	5.3	2.2	n/a
Saint Louis	12.6	15.0	14.3	11.2	10.2	10.1	5.8	n/a	4.5	4.3	3.6	2.2	n/a
Saint Paul	13.6	13.4	14.5	10.9	11.3	8.8	8.0	n/a	4.9	4.3	3.7	2.2	n/a
Saint Petersburg	11.4	12.0	23.1	11.8	5.7	9.0	7.8	6.7	4.0	3.7	2.3	2.5	<0.1
Stamford[3]	11.3	14.5	16.9	12.5	9.7	7.8	10.5	n/a	3.5	4.0	2.7	2.7	n/a
Tampa	11.4	12.0	23.1	11.8	5.7	9.0	7.8	6.7	4.0	3.7	2.3	2.5	<0.1
Thousand Oaks	14.2	9.8	13.3	13.0	12.6	10.0	8.3	6.8	4.2	3.4	2.1	2.0	0.4
Tucson	20.5	13.9	13.0	11.7	7.1	10.7	4.6	7.3	2.5	4.1	2.4	1.7	0.4
Tulsa	12.4	13.2	14.4	10.8	11.7	8.2	6.0	5.1	4.3	5.1	5.1	2.2	1.5
Virginia Beach	19.9	11.4	13.3	12.5	7.5	10.5	5.3	n/a	3.2	4.4	3.5	2.0	n/a
Washington[2]	22.9	10.4	22.6	9.1	1.8	8.3	4.8	n/a	2.2	6.0	2.4	3.4	n/a
Wichita	13.9	13.8	9.6	10.7	21.4	9.0	3.8	n/a	3.8	3.8	2.8	2.0	n/a
U.S.	16.3	13.2	12.9	11.5	10.2	9.5	6.1	5.5	4.3	3.9	3.7	2.2	0.5

Note: All figures are percentages covering non-farm employment as of December 2006 and are not seasonally adjusted; (1) Figures cover the Metropolitan Statistical Area (MSA) except where noted. See Appendix B for areas included; (2) Metropolitan Division; (3) New England City and Town Area; (4) New England City and Town Area Division; (A) Government; (B) Education and Health Services; (C) Professional and Business Services; (D) Retail Trade; (E) Manufacturing; (F) Leisure and Hospitality; (G) Finance Activities; (H) Construction; (I) Wholesale Trade; (J) Other Services; (K) Transportation and Utilities; (L) Information; (M) Natural Resources and Mining; n/a not available
Source: Bureau of Labor Statistics, http://stats.bls.gov

Labor Force, Employment and Job Growth: City

City	Civilian Labor Force			Workers Employed		
	Dec. 2005	Dec. 2006	% Chg.	Dec. 2005	Dec. 2006	% Chg.
Albuquerque	263,806	264,742	0.4	253,830	257,181	1.3
Alexandria	83,809	86,258	2.9	81,861	84,396	3.1
Anchorage	152,431	158,071	3.7	144,666	150,116	3.8
Ann Arbor	66,993	67,081	0.1	64,276	63,958	-0.5
Athens	60,081	61,955	3.1	57,700	59,720	3.5
Atlanta	204,375	210,278	2.9	192,382	199,410	3.7
Austin	408,576	421,924	3.3	392,636	408,464	4.0
Baltimore	276,075	283,174	2.6	259,221	266,073	2.6
Baton Rouge	112,360	108,036	-3.8	105,342	104,051	-1.2
Bellevue	65,962	67,287	2.0	63,594	65,143	2.4
Birmingham	105,122	107,985	2.7	100,642	103,800	3.1
Boise City	122,534	125,796	2.7	119,395	122,691	2.8
Boston	289,979	291,761	0.6	276,273	277,169	0.3
Boulder	55,968	57,954	3.5	53,520	55,784	4.2
Buffalo	124,297	122,903	-1.1	116,946	116,555	-0.3
Cary	57,638	60,363	4.7	55,969	58,840	5.1
Cedar Rapids	70,440	70,934	0.7	67,413	68,335	1.4
Charleston	53,029	54,272	2.3	50,234	51,583	2.7
Charlotte	332,843	341,826	2.7	319,195	328,456	2.9
Chattanooga	74,509	76,837	3.1	70,625	73,710	4.4
Chicago	1,303,486	1,349,003	3.5	1,222,567	1,291,243	5.6
Cincinnati	157,670	160,739	1.9	148,463	151,689	2.2
Cleveland	189,041	190,441	0.7	175,416	177,143	1.0
Colorado Spgs.	206,633	213,846	3.5	197,086	204,983	4.0
Columbia	53,177	55,118	3.7	49,370	51,166	3.6
Columbus	411,757	417,434	1.4	391,895	398,653	1.7
Dallas	609,424	624,945	2.5	576,772	596,831	3.5
Denver	307,294	315,019	2.5	290,786	300,390	3.3
Des Moines	109,308	112,549	3.0	104,132	108,249	4.0
Durham	109,731	113,335	3.3	105,694	109,371	3.5
Edison	55,702	56,234	1.0	53,922	54,696	1.4
El Paso	252,254	260,238	3.2	237,829	245,674	3.3
Eugene	77,688	79,681	2.6	74,134	76,252	2.9
Fort Collins	78,780	81,103	2.9	75,070	77,873	3.7
Fort Lauderdale	92,072	95,815	4.1	89,402	93,270	4.3
Fort Wayne	113,008	114,909	1.7	106,934	109,214	2.1
Fort Worth	297,213	304,146	2.3	283,235	291,291	2.8
Grand Rapids	105,374	105,806	0.4	97,896	97,502	-0.4
Green Bay	58,638	59,144	0.9	54,661	55,345	1.3
Greensboro	126,207	127,479	1.0	120,514	121,912	1.2
Honolulu	453,851	464,522	2.4	443,437	457,288	3.1
Houston	1,010,182	1,033,676	2.3	950,893	989,412	4.1
Huntsville	88,968	92,651	4.1	86,563	90,304	4.3
Indianapolis	420,917	427,918	1.7	398,612	408,387	2.5
Irvine	84,898	85,560	0.8	82,908	83,559	0.8
Jacksonville	396,887	412,108	3.8	384,617	398,614	3.6
Kansas City	235,844	239,619	1.6	220,783	225,339	2.1
Knoxville	92,400	96,099	4.0	87,198	91,714	5.2
Las Vegas	274,701	296,422	7.9	264,892	283,721	7.1
Lexington	149,827	153,687	2.6	142,823	148,131	3.7
Lincoln	141,990	142,736	0.5	137,267	139,582	1.7
Los Angeles	1,900,522	1,886,424	-0.7	1,794,288	1,798,788	0.3
Louisville	358,706	364,824	1.7	336,361	347,463	3.3
Madison	142,256	146,276	2.8	138,579	142,159	2.6
Manchester	62,835	64,189	2.2	60,501	61,875	2.3

Table continued on next page.

City	Civilian Labor Force			Workers Employed		
	Dec. 2005	Dec. 2006	% Chg.	Dec. 2005	Dec. 2006	% Chg.
Memphis	308,001	320,055	3.9	288,779	302,352	4.7
Miami	157,784	166,349	5.4	151,726	160,170	5.6
Milwaukee	266,855	271,892	1.9	249,451	254,266	1.9
Minneapolis	222,137	223,308	0.5	213,880	214,798	0.4
Naperville	74,217	77,388	4.3	71,425	75,437	5.6
Nashville	311,103	327,692	5.3	298,076	315,854	6.0
New York	3,796,112	3,807,580	0.3	3,589,048	3,653,927	1.8
Norfolk	100,107	102,253	2.1	95,535	98,222	2.8
Oklahoma City	268,984	269,707	0.3	257,536	259,167	0.6
Omaha	227,109	225,590	-0.7	216,524	219,050	1.2
Orlando	121,146	127,019	4.8	117,886	123,642	4.9
Overland Park	94,408	94,777	0.4	90,803	91,351	0.6
Philadelphia	628,851	634,198	0.9	591,509	597,378	1.0
Phoenix	805,650	837,762	4.0	770,833	805,427	4.5
Pittsburgh	154,512	154,708	0.1	147,640	148,349	0.5
Plano	143,520	147,736	2.9	137,957	142,755	3.5
Portland	295,816	302,337	2.2	280,606	287,513	2.5
Providence	80,372	80,686	0.4	75,668	76,226	0.7
Provo	63,382	65,520	3.4	61,165	64,038	4.7
Raleigh	190,358	199,806	5.0	184,110	193,559	5.1
Reno	108,392	115,919	6.9	104,634	111,352	6.4
Richmond	97,546	98,614	1.1	92,895	94,517	1.7
Rochester	94,775	94,798	0.0	89,395	90,035	0.7
Sacramento	213,136	216,594	1.6	202,773	205,391	1.3
Salt Lake City	107,103	109,813	2.5	102,630	106,870	4.1
San Antonio	596,234	613,360	2.9	570,886	591,114	3.5
San Diego	677,288	681,145	0.6	652,670	655,815	0.5
San Francisco	422,324	427,973	1.3	404,691	411,536	1.7
San Jose	429,206	434,007	1.1	407,861	413,837	1.5
Savannah	64,676	67,576	4.5	61,773	64,646	4.7
Scottsdale	135,767	141,434	4.2	132,104	138,032	4.5
Seattle	353,519	360,482	2.0	338,552	346,799	2.4
Sioux Falls	80,348	84,520	5.2	77,673	82,240	5.9
Springfield	86,126	88,472	2.7	82,595	85,237	3.2
Saint Louis	159,369	160,482	0.7	148,171	150,256	1.4
Saint Paul	149,991	150,570	0.4	143,850	144,467	0.4
Saint Petersburg	132,352	137,205	3.7	128,591	133,502	3.8
Stamford	65,326	67,019	2.6	63,055	64,988	3.1
Tampa	161,704	167,888	3.8	157,110	163,110	3.8
Thousand Oaks	70,267	71,074	1.1	67,992	68,743	1.1
Tucson	256,757	268,293	4.5	244,879	257,222	5.0
Tulsa	210,999	213,405	1.1	202,138	205,149	1.5
Virginia Beach	223,671	229,583	2.6	217,264	223,376	2.8
Washington	292,049	293,377	0.5	275,382	275,188	-0.1
Wichita	184,910	187,705	1.5	175,433	179,038	2.1
U.S.	149,874,000	152,571,000	1.8	142,918,000	146,081,000	2.2

Note: Data is not seasonally adjusted and covers workers 16 years of age and older
Source: Bureau of Labor Statistics, http://stats.bls.gov

Labor Force, Employment and Job Growth: Metro Area

Metro Area	Civilian Labor Force			Workers Employed		
	Dec. 2005	Dec. 2006	% Chg.	Dec. 2005	Dec. 2006	% Chg.
Albuquerque	406,138	407,809	0.4	389,781	394,927	1.3
Alexandria[2]	2,259,235	2,319,951	2.7	2,193,342	2,251,724	2.7
Anchorage	188,635	195,636	3.7	178,092	184,802	3.8
Ann Arbor	194,745	194,922	0.1	187,355	186,427	-0.5
Athens	100,630	103,734	3.1	96,790	100,178	3.5
Atlanta	2,625,587	2,702,498	2.9	2,497,934	2,589,178	3.7
Austin	814,072	841,099	3.3	782,684	814,237	4.0
Baltimore	1,376,817	1,414,030	2.7	1,325,659	1,360,702	2.6
Baton Rouge	363,362	351,996	-3.1	344,107	339,892	-1.2
Bellevue[2]	1,384,455	1,408,918	1.8	1,323,572	1,350,252	2.0
Birmingham	539,456	555,422	3.0	523,134	539,553	3.1
Boise City	289,945	297,751	2.7	282,087	289,875	2.8
Boston[4]	1,472,543	1,482,564	0.7	1,414,723	1,419,314	0.3
Boulder	168,778	174,907	3.6	162,302	169,166	4.2
Buffalo	587,588	581,856	-1.0	557,466	555,603	-0.3
Cary	512,248	537,863	5.0	494,249	519,614	5.1
Cedar Rapids	140,907	141,698	0.6	134,260	136,096	1.4
Charleston	293,928	301,098	2.4	278,862	286,349	2.7
Charlotte	805,649	826,323	2.6	768,147	788,406	2.6
Chattanooga	253,359	261,131	3.1	242,357	251,324	3.7
Chicago[2]	3,990,819	4,118,762	3.2	3,782,316	3,961,464	4.7
Cincinnati	1,103,333	1,127,826	2.2	1,047,047	1,073,828	2.6
Cleveland	1,080,973	1,085,284	0.4	1,024,864	1,028,278	0.3
Colorado Spgs.	300,108	310,498	3.5	285,915	297,371	4.0
Columbia	359,286	371,714	3.5	339,602	351,960	3.6
Columbus	930,529	943,913	1.4	886,238	901,519	1.7
Dallas[2]	2,053,774	2,110,452	2.8	1,958,444	2,026,554	3.5
Denver	1,315,904	1,350,723	2.6	1,255,309	1,296,771	3.3
Des Moines	302,282	311,679	3.1	289,879	301,341	4.0
Durham	512,248	537,863	5.0	494,249	519,614	5.1
Edison[2]	1,183,800	1,194,852	0.9	1,137,288	1,153,608	1.4
El Paso	293,971	303,152	3.1	275,773	284,870	3.3
Eugene	174,812	179,531	2.7	165,559	170,288	2.9
Fort Collins	165,256	170,299	3.1	158,492	164,409	3.7
Fort Lauderdale[2]	965,943	1,006,008	4.1	938,031	978,624	4.3
Fort Wayne	213,334	216,989	1.7	202,671	206,993	2.1
Fort Worth[2]	1,012,188	1,035,993	2.4	967,456	994,963	2.8
Grand Rapids	415,880	416,492	0.1	393,922	392,339	-0.4
Green Bay	171,135	173,071	1.1	163,391	165,436	1.3
Greensboro	361,986	366,570	1.3	344,787	348,787	1.2
Honolulu	453,851	464,522	2.4	443,437	457,288	3.1
Houston	2,668,786	2,744,357	2.8	2,531,875	2,634,434	4.1
Huntsville	197,641	205,906	4.2	192,374	200,689	4.3
Indianapolis	876,529	891,990	1.8	835,149	855,630	2.5
Irvine[2]	1,610,610	1,623,137	0.8	1,559,722	1,571,968	0.8
Jacksonville	630,727	654,853	3.8	611,960	634,231	3.6
Kansas City	1,031,964	1,043,814	1.1	980,953	995,207	1.5
Knoxville	341,336	356,607	4.5	327,703	344,677	5.2
Las Vegas	875,790	945,220	7.9	845,466	905,562	7.1
Lexington	232,996	239,044	2.6	221,910	230,158	3.7
Lincoln	166,014	167,511	0.9	160,655	163,364	1.7
Los Angeles[2]	4,895,787	4,873,751	-0.5	4,652,703	4,670,475	0.4
Louisville	618,408	628,377	1.6	581,077	598,905	3.1
Madison	335,693	345,028	2.8	325,612	334,024	2.6
Manchester[3]	107,481	109,909	2.3	104,006	106,369	2.3

Table continued on next page.

Metro Area	Civilian Labor Force			Workers Employed		
	Dec. 2005	Dec. 2006	% Chg.	Dec. 2005	Dec. 2006	% Chg.
Memphis	605,916	623,968	3.0	570,482	591,847	3.7
Miami[2]	1,146,208	1,175,253	2.5	1,102,568	1,134,618	2.9
Milwaukee	783,904	799,566	2.0	748,386	762,831	1.9
Minneapolis	1,856,983	1,870,572	0.7	1,789,895	1,799,006	0.5
Naperville[2]	3,990,819	4,118,762	3.2	3,782,316	3,961,464	4.7
Nashville	754,669	795,224	5.4	724,547	767,760	6.0
New York[2]	5,468,734	5,430,536	-0.7	5,186,731	5,220,453	0.7
Norfolk	798,874	818,131	2.4	771,208	792,965	2.8
Oklahoma City	591,375	593,527	0.4	568,717	572,321	0.6
Omaha	445,163	447,982	0.6	427,288	433,906	1.5
Orlando	1,023,738	1,074,583	5.0	995,264	1,043,862	4.9
Overland Park	1,031,964	1,043,814	1.1	980,953	995,207	1.5
Philadelphia[2]	1,940,215	1,957,209	0.9	1,858,686	1,877,129	1.0
Phoenix	1,952,929	2,032,289	4.1	1,880,490	1,964,883	4.5
Pittsburgh	1,209,981	1,212,447	0.2	1,155,529	1,161,077	0.5
Plano[2]	2,053,774	2,110,452	2.8	1,958,444	2,026,554	3.5
Portland	1,109,417	1,130,606	1.9	1,055,669	1,077,585	2.1
Providence[3]	710,870	714,923	0.6	675,103	678,975	0.6
Provo	209,912	217,254	3.5	203,273	212,819	4.7
Raleigh	512,248	537,863	5.0	494,249	519,614	5.1
Reno	212,680	227,537	7.0	205,431	218,620	6.4
Richmond	621,392	629,562	1.3	601,420	611,916	1.7
Rochester	527,177	527,394	0.0	503,046	506,651	0.7
Sacramento	1,032,494	1,048,457	1.5	990,211	1,002,996	1.3
Salt Lake City	566,884	582,605	2.8	546,818	569,410	4.1
San Antonio	902,868	929,522	3.0	864,134	894,753	3.5
San Diego	1,517,188	1,525,826	0.6	1,462,017	1,469,060	0.5
San Francisco[2]	919,312	932,195	1.4	884,278	899,235	1.7
San Jose	847,575	857,267	1.1	809,031	820,886	1.5
Savannah	168,662	176,011	4.4	162,041	169,577	4.7
Scottsdale	1,952,929	2,032,289	4.1	1,880,490	1,964,883	4.5
Seattle[2]	1,384,455	1,408,918	1.8	1,323,572	1,350,252	2.0
Sioux Falls	120,967	123,935	2.5	117,228	120,630	2.9
Springfield	216,252	222,556	2.9	208,427	215,094	3.2
Saint Louis	1,459,524	1,476,843	1.2	1,388,598	1,409,613	1.5
Saint Paul	1,856,983	1,870,572	0.7	1,789,895	1,799,006	0.5
Saint Petersburg	1,301,903	1,352,600	3.9	1,263,753	1,312,014	3.8
Stamford[3]	460,325	471,748	2.5	442,755	456,330	3.1
Tampa	1,301,903	1,352,600	3.9	1,263,753	1,312,014	3.8
Thousand Oaks	421,312	426,207	1.2	403,477	407,935	1.1
Tucson	441,211	461,264	4.5	422,728	444,036	5.0
Tulsa	458,021	463,336	1.2	440,356	446,913	1.5
Virginia Beach	798,874	818,131	2.4	771,208	792,965	2.8
Washington[2]	2,259,235	2,319,951	2.7	2,193,342	2,251,724	2.7
Wichita	305,367	310,113	1.6	291,076	297,057	2.1
U.S.	149,874,000	152,571,000	1.8	142,918,000	146,081,000	2.2

Note: Data is not seasonally adjusted and covers workers 16 years of age and older; (1) Figures cover the Metropolitan Statistical Area (MSA) except where noted. See Appendix B for areas included; (2) Metropolitan Division; (3) New England City and Town Area; (4) New England City and Town Area Division
Source: Bureau of Labor Statistics, http://stats.bls.gov

Unemployment Rate: City

City	2006											
	Jan.	Feb.	Mar.	Apr.	May	Jun.	Jul.	Aug.	Sep.	Oct.	Nov.	Dec.
Albuquerque	4.1	4.1	3.2	3.5	3.4	4.1	4.2	3.7	3.7	3.7	3.5	2.9
Alexandria	2.5	2.5	2.4	2.4	2.3	2.6	2.5	2.5	2.5	2.2	2.2	2.2
Anchorage	5.8	6.2	5.9	5.9	5.6	5.6	5.4	4.8	5.2	4.5	4.6	5.0
Ann Arbor	4.5	4.8	5.0	4.5	4.3	4.7	5.3	4.9	4.9	4.4	4.4	4.7
Athens	4.1	4.3	3.9	3.5	4.1	4.6	4.3	3.9	3.9	3.9	3.6	3.6
Atlanta	6.1	6.1	5.3	5.0	5.6	6.4	6.3	5.8	5.5	5.6	5.1	5.2
Austin	4.4	4.3	4.1	3.9	4.0	4.5	4.4	4.2	3.9	3.8	3.7	3.2
Baltimore	6.8	6.4	6.0	6.0	6.4	7.0	7.8	7.2	6.6	6.3	6.4	6.0
Baton Rouge	5.8	4.3	4.4	4.1	4.7	5.6	3.5	3.8	3.7	4.0	4.1	3.7
Bellevue	3.4	3.8	3.4	3.2	3.8	3.7	3.4	3.3	3.8	3.4	3.7	3.2
Birmingham	5.3	5.2	4.2	4.1	3.9	5.2	5.4	5.0	4.1	3.9	3.8	3.9
Boise City	3.4	3.3	3.2	3.0	2.7	3.0	2.9	2.7	2.6	2.4	2.7	2.5
Boston	5.3	5.4	5.4	5.1	5.3	5.9	5.6	5.5	5.7	4.7	5.0	5.0
Boulder	5.1	4.5	4.5	4.1	4.2	4.7	4.7	4.7	4.2	4.1	3.9	3.7
Buffalo	6.3	6.5	6.3	6.6	6.3	6.3	7.2	6.5	6.1	5.7	5.5	5.2
Cary	2.9	3.1	2.8	2.5	2.9	2.9	3.0	2.7	2.4	2.4	2.8	2.5
Cedar Rapids	4.5	4.6	3.9	3.6	3.0	3.5	3.3	3.1	3.0	3.1	3.1	3.7
Charleston	5.2	5.6	5.2	5.1	4.8	6.0	5.3	5.8	5.5	5.6	5.2	5.0
Charlotte	4.2	4.4	4.0	3.6	4.1	4.3	4.6	4.5	4.0	4.0	4.1	3.9
Chattanooga	5.8	5.6	5.0	4.9	4.8	5.9	5.8	5.7	4.3	4.1	4.4	4.1
Chicago	6.4	6.0	5.9	5.7	5.0	5.5	5.5	5.2	5.0	4.3	4.4	4.3
Cincinnati	6.0	6.2	5.4	5.9	5.4	6.0	6.3	5.9	5.4	5.4	5.8	5.6
Cleveland	7.7	7.3	6.7	6.4	6.1	6.9	7.1	7.4	6.7	6.1	6.7	7.0
Colorado Spgs.	5.2	4.8	4.8	4.3	4.4	5.0	4.9	5.0	4.5	4.4	4.3	4.1
Columbia	7.1	7.5	7.4	7.0	7.1	8.4	7.6	8.0	7.7	7.7	7.2	7.2
Columbus	5.0	5.2	4.6	4.9	4.5	4.8	5.1	5.0	4.6	4.3	4.6	4.5
Dallas	5.9	5.7	5.4	5.3	5.5	6.0	6.0	5.7	5.3	5.2	5.1	4.5
Denver	6.2	5.6	5.5	4.9	5.0	5.5	5.5	5.5	5.1	4.9	4.7	4.6
Des Moines	5.0	5.3	4.4	3.8	3.2	3.6	3.4	3.4	3.4	3.3	3.4	3.8
Durham	3.7	3.9	3.5	3.2	3.7	3.8	4.1	3.8	3.6	3.4	3.8	3.5
Edison	3.7	3.7	3.5	4.0	3.8	3.9	4.6	4.2	3.8	3.1	3.4	2.7
El Paso	6.3	6.4	6.2	6.3	6.5	7.1	7.0	6.6	6.3	6.3	6.3	5.6
Eugene	5.2	5.9	5.5	5.1	4.8	5.2	5.3	5.0	4.6	4.2	4.5	4.3
Fort Collins	5.5	4.9	4.9	4.3	4.3	4.8	4.8	4.7	4.2	4.1	3.9	4.0
Fort Lauderdale	3.1	3.0	2.8	2.7	2.8	3.1	3.2	3.2	3.1	2.7	2.9	2.7
Fort Wayne	5.3	6.3	5.6	5.2	5.5	5.4	5.9	5.5	5.0	4.9	4.8	5.0
Fort Worth	5.1	5.1	5.0	4.9	5.0	5.6	5.6	5.2	4.8	4.8	4.7	4.2
Grand Rapids	7.4	8.2	8.4	7.7	7.0	7.7	9.0	8.1	8.2	7.3	7.6	7.8
Green Bay	7.4	7.9	7.7	7.3	6.7	7.0	6.7	5.9	5.8	5.7	6.2	6.4
Greensboro	4.5	5.0	4.4	4.2	4.5	4.9	5.1	4.7	4.3	4.2	4.6	4.4
Honolulu	2.2	2.2	2.4	2.7	2.7	3.6	3.2	2.7	2.6	1.9	2.2	1.6
Houston	6.4	6.0	5.5	5.3	5.4	6.0	5.9	5.5	5.1	5.0	4.9	4.3
Huntsville	3.5	3.5	2.8	2.6	2.6	3.4	3.5	3.2	2.7	2.6	2.5	2.5
Indianapolis	5.1	5.6	5.2	5.0	4.7	5.3	5.4	5.3	4.9	4.7	4.5	4.6
Irvine	2.6	2.6	2.5	2.4	2.4	2.8	2.8	2.6	2.5	2.3	2.5	2.3
Jacksonville	3.4	3.3	3.1	2.9	3.2	3.9	4.1	3.8	3.6	3.2	3.5	3.3
Kansas City	6.4	6.6	6.2	5.7	5.3	6.3	6.2	6.3	6.9	7.0	6.2	6.0
Knoxville	6.2	6.1	5.8	5.7	5.4	6.4	6.4	6.2	4.5	4.4	5.0	4.6
Las Vegas	4.1	4.0	3.8	4.1	3.7	4.5	4.7	4.2	4.2	4.1	4.2	4.3
Lexington	4.9	5.3	4.9	4.5	4.2	4.9	4.8	4.3	3.6	3.6	4.0	3.6
Lincoln	3.9	3.8	3.2	3.2	3.0	2.9	3.1	2.9	2.6	2.5	2.6	2.2
Los Angeles	6.0	6.1	5.3	5.0	5.4	5.2	5.6	5.6	5.3	4.7	4.5	4.6
Louisville	6.8	6.9	6.3	5.9	5.6	5.9	6.0	5.5	5.3	5.2	5.2	4.8
Madison	2.9	3.3	3.2	3.2	3.2	3.7	3.4	3.0	3.0	2.9	2.9	2.8
Manchester	4.4	4.6	4.5	3.9	3.7	3.6	3.9	3.7	3.3	3.3	3.6	3.6

Table continued on next page.

City	2006											
	Jan.	Feb.	Mar.	Apr.	May	Jun.	Jul.	Aug.	Sep.	Oct.	Nov.	Dec.
Memphis	6.7	6.7	6.8	6.5	6.3	7.7	7.7	7.6	5.7	5.4	6.0	5.5
Miami	3.7	3.8	4.1	3.8	3.8	4.1	4.3	4.7	4.9	4.5	4.0	3.7
Milwaukee	7.1	7.8	7.5	7.4	7.1	7.8	8.0	7.1	6.7	6.4	6.7	6.5
Minneapolis	4.3	4.2	4.2	3.8	3.4	4.0	4.1	3.8	4.1	3.7	3.7	3.8
Naperville	3.8	3.6	3.5	3.6	3.2	3.7	3.6	3.4	3.1	2.6	2.7	2.5
Nashville	4.4	4.4	4.4	4.4	4.2	4.9	4.8	5.0	3.7	3.7	4.1	3.6
New York	5.6	5.6	5.3	5.0	4.7	4.8	5.6	4.8	4.4	4.3	4.3	4.0
Norfolk	5.0	4.9	4.8	4.8	4.4	5.0	5.1	4.9	4.8	4.1	4.3	3.9
Oklahoma City	4.8	4.4	4.6	3.9	4.4	4.3	4.0	4.2	4.0	3.8	3.9	3.9
Omaha	5.3	5.5	4.3	4.2	4.0	4.1	4.3	3.9	3.6	3.4	3.2	2.9
Orlando	2.9	2.9	2.7	2.5	2.6	2.9	3.1	3.2	2.9	2.6	2.9	2.7
Overland Park	4.4	4.6	4.4	3.8	4.1	4.6	4.5	4.6	3.8	4.0	4.0	3.6
Philadelphia	6.4	6.7	6.6	5.9	6.5	6.6	6.7	6.7	6.3	5.9	6.3	5.8
Phoenix	5.2	4.6	4.1	4.2	3.8	4.6	4.8	3.6	3.9	3.9	3.9	3.9
Pittsburgh	5.0	5.3	5.1	4.6	5.1	5.2	5.2	5.2	4.5	4.3	4.5	4.1
Plano	4.3	4.3	4.2	4.1	4.2	4.5	4.5	4.3	4.0	3.9	3.8	3.4
Portland	5.6	6.1	5.9	5.6	5.5	5.6	5.4	5.2	5.0	4.6	5.0	4.9
Providence	6.8	6.9	6.9	6.6	6.8	7.3	7.7	7.2	5.8	5.5	5.7	5.5
Provo	4.3	4.3	3.7	3.5	3.5	3.5	3.7	3.6	2.7	2.4	2.5	2.3
Raleigh	3.3	3.6	3.2	2.9	3.3	3.5	3.7	3.4	3.1	3.0	3.3	3.1
Reno	4.5	4.2	4.2	4.2	3.7	4.1	4.4	3.8	3.8	3.7	3.8	3.9
Richmond	4.9	5.0	4.9	4.8	4.4	4.8	4.9	4.9	5.0	4.3	4.5	4.2
Rochester	6.0	6.2	6.1	6.1	6.0	5.9	6.6	6.1	5.8	5.2	5.3	5.0
Sacramento	5.6	5.7	5.5	5.4	5.1	5.7	5.8	5.4	5.2	4.9	5.2	5.2
Salt Lake City	4.8	5.0	4.3	4.1	4.0	4.0	4.1	4.1	3.2	2.8	2.9	2.7
San Antonio	4.8	4.7	4.6	4.4	4.5	5.3	5.2	4.8	4.4	4.3	4.2	3.6
San Diego	4.0	4.1	3.8	3.7	3.6	4.2	4.3	4.1	3.9	3.6	3.9	3.7
San Francisco	4.7	4.7	4.4	4.2	4.1	4.6	4.7	4.5	4.1	3.8	4.0	3.8
San Jose	5.5	5.6	5.3	5.0	4.9	5.5	5.6	5.3	5.0	4.6	5.0	4.6
Savannah	4.6	4.7	4.1	4.2	4.6	5.5	5.4	4.8	4.6	4.7	4.2	4.3
Scottsdale	3.3	2.9	2.6	2.6	2.4	2.9	3.0	2.2	2.4	2.5	2.4	2.4
Seattle	4.0	4.3	3.9	3.6	4.2	4.1	3.9	3.8	4.2	3.8	4.2	3.8
Sioux Falls	3.4	3.5	3.4	2.5	2.5	2.5	2.6	2.4	2.4	2.4	2.5	2.7
Springfield	4.4	4.7	4.3	3.7	3.8	4.6	4.1	4.2	4.3	4.5	4.2	3.7
Saint Louis	7.0	7.2	6.8	6.5	6.2	7.5	7.1	7.6	7.1	7.1	7.0	6.4
Saint Paul	4.9	4.8	4.7	4.3	3.7	4.3	4.3	4.0	4.4	3.9	4.0	4.1
Saint Petersburg	3.1	3.1	2.9	2.7	2.9	3.2	3.4	3.3	3.1	2.7	3.0	2.7
Stamford	4.1	4.1	3.9	3.1	3.2	3.6	3.8	3.6	3.6	3.1	3.4	3.0
Tampa	3.1	3.0	2.8	2.7	2.9	3.2	3.4	3.3	3.1	2.9	3.1	2.8
Thousand Oaks	3.5	3.4	3.1	2.9	2.9	3.4	3.6	3.5	3.4	3.0	3.4	3.3
Tucson	5.6	4.9	4.4	4.5	4.1	5.1	5.3	4.0	4.3	4.3	4.2	4.1
Tulsa	4.7	4.3	4.5	3.9	4.4	4.3	4.0	4.2	4.1	3.9	3.9	3.9
Virginia Beach	3.2	3.2	3.1	3.1	2.8	3.2	3.2	3.1	3.4	3.0	2.9	2.7
Washington	5.4	5.5	5.5	5.2	5.7	5.8	6.3	6.1	6.0	5.6	5.7	6.2
Wichita	5.9	5.8	5.8	5.2	4.9	5.4	5.7	5.5	4.8	4.9	4.7	4.6
U.S.	5.1	5.1	4.8	4.5	4.4	4.8	5.0	4.6	4.4	4.1	4.3	4.3

Note: Data is not seasonally adjusted and covers workers 16 years of age and older; All figures are percentages
Source: Bureau of Labor Statistics, http://stats.bls.gov

Unemployment Rate: Metro Area

Metro Area[1]	2006											
	Jan.	Feb.	Mar.	Apr.	May	Jun.	Jul.	Aug.	Sep.	Oct.	Nov.	Dec.
Albuquerque	4.6	4.5	3.5	3.8	3.7	4.4	4.6	4.0	4.0	4.0	3.8	3.2
Alexandria[2]	3.1	3.0	3.0	3.0	3.0	3.3	3.5	3.3	3.1	2.9	3.0	2.9
Anchorage	6.4	6.8	6.5	6.3	5.9	5.8	5.7	5.0	5.4	4.8	5.0	5.5
Ann Arbor	4.2	4.5	4.7	4.2	4.0	4.4	5.0	4.6	4.6	4.1	4.2	4.4
Athens	3.8	4.0	3.6	3.3	3.8	4.2	4.0	3.6	3.6	3.6	3.4	3.4
Atlanta	4.9	5.1	4.4	4.2	4.6	5.0	4.9	4.5	4.4	4.5	4.2	4.2
Austin	4.3	4.2	4.1	3.9	4.0	4.4	4.4	4.2	3.8	3.7	3.7	3.2
Baltimore	4.3	4.0	3.8	3.7	4.0	4.4	5.0	4.4	4.0	3.9	4.1	3.8
Baton Rouge	5.0	3.8	4.0	3.7	4.4	5.3	3.3	3.5	3.4	3.6	3.8	3.4
Bellevue[2]	4.3	4.7	4.5	4.0	4.4	4.4	4.1	4.0	4.4	4.1	4.5	4.2
Birmingham	3.8	3.8	3.1	2.9	2.9	3.8	3.9	3.6	3.0	2.9	2.8	2.9
Boise City	3.6	3.5	3.3	3.0	2.6	2.9	2.9	2.6	2.5	2.3	2.8	2.6
Boston[4]	4.5	4.7	4.6	4.2	4.4	4.8	4.4	4.3	4.7	3.8	4.2	4.3
Boulder	4.4	4.0	4.0	3.6	3.7	4.2	4.1	4.1	3.7	3.6	3.4	3.3
Buffalo	5.6	5.9	5.6	5.4	4.9	4.9	5.5	4.9	4.7	4.3	4.5	4.5
Cary	3.5	3.8	3.4	3.1	3.4	3.6	3.8	3.5	3.3	3.3	3.6	3.4
Cedar Rapids	5.0	5.2	4.3	3.7	3.1	3.6	3.5	3.4	3.2	3.2	3.3	4.0
Charleston	5.1	5.4	5.1	4.9	4.7	5.8	5.1	5.6	5.4	5.5	5.2	4.9
Charlotte	4.6	5.0	4.5	4.1	4.6	4.8	4.9	4.8	4.5	4.5	4.8	4.6
Chattanooga	4.7	4.8	4.5	4.4	4.4	5.1	5.0	4.9	3.8	4.0	4.1	3.8
Chicago[2]	5.3	5.0	4.9	4.6	4.2	4.7	4.7	4.4	4.1	3.5	3.7	3.8
Cincinnati	5.6	5.7	5.2	5.3	4.9	5.2	5.5	5.2	4.7	4.4	4.8	4.8
Cleveland	5.7	5.8	5.3	5.0	5.0	5.6	5.7	5.6	5.3	4.8	5.1	5.3
Colorado Spgs.	5.4	4.9	4.9	4.4	4.5	5.1	5.1	5.1	4.6	4.5	4.3	4.2
Columbia	5.5	5.8	5.5	5.3	5.3	6.2	5.5	5.9	5.8	5.8	5.5	5.3
Columbus	5.1	5.3	4.6	4.8	4.4	4.6	5.0	4.8	4.4	4.2	4.4	4.5
Dallas[2]	5.1	5.0	4.8	4.7	4.8	5.3	5.3	5.0	4.6	4.5	4.5	4.0
Denver	5.3	4.8	4.8	4.4	4.4	4.9	4.8	4.8	4.4	4.2	4.1	4.0
Des Moines	4.4	4.6	3.8	3.2	2.8	3.2	3.0	2.9	2.9	2.9	2.9	3.3
Durham	3.5	3.8	3.4	3.1	3.4	3.6	3.8	3.5	3.3	3.3	3.6	3.4
Edison[2]	4.6	4.8	4.4	4.6	4.4	4.5	5.0	4.6	4.5	3.6	3.8	3.5
El Paso	6.8	6.9	6.7	6.8	6.9	7.6	7.5	7.1	6.8	6.8	6.7	6.0
Eugene	6.0	6.6	6.2	5.7	5.4	5.6	5.8	5.5	5.1	4.7	5.1	5.1
Fort Collins	4.8	4.3	4.3	3.8	3.8	4.1	4.2	4.1	3.6	3.6	3.4	3.5
Fort Lauderdale[2]	3.1	3.0	2.8	2.7	2.8	3.1	3.3	3.2	3.1	2.8	3.0	2.7
Fort Wayne	5.0	6.2	5.2	4.7	5.3	4.9	5.5	5.0	4.6	4.5	4.5	4.6
Fort Worth[2]	4.9	4.8	4.7	4.6	4.7	5.2	5.3	4.9	4.5	4.5	4.4	4.0
Grand Rapids	5.6	6.2	6.4	5.8	5.2	5.7	6.8	5.9	6.0	5.3	5.6	5.8
Green Bay	5.0	5.6	5.5	5.1	4.6	4.9	4.7	4.1	4.0	3.9	4.2	4.4
Greensboro	4.8	5.1	4.5	4.2	4.7	4.9	5.3	5.0	4.7	4.6	5.1	4.9
Honolulu	2.2	2.2	2.4	2.7	2.7	3.6	3.2	2.7	2.6	1.9	2.2	1.6
Houston	5.6	5.3	5.0	4.9	5.0	5.6	5.5	5.1	4.7	4.5	4.5	4.0
Huntsville	3.4	3.4	2.7	2.5	2.5	3.3	3.4	3.0	2.5	2.5	2.3	2.5
Indianapolis	4.7	5.0	4.7	4.3	4.3	4.6	4.8	4.6	4.3	4.1	4.0	4.1
Irvine[2]	3.5	3.6	3.4	3.2	3.2	3.7	3.8	3.6	3.4	3.1	3.4	3.2
Jacksonville	3.2	3.1	3.0	2.8	3.0	3.6	3.8	3.6	3.4	3.1	3.4	3.1
Kansas City	5.3	5.5	5.1	4.5	4.4	5.2	5.1	5.1	5.1	5.3	4.8	4.7
Knoxville	4.4	4.3	4.2	4.2	3.9	4.7	4.5	4.4	3.2	3.3	3.8	3.3
Las Vegas	3.9	3.8	3.7	4.0	3.6	4.3	4.6	4.1	4.0	4.0	4.0	4.2
Lexington	5.2	5.5	5.1	4.6	4.3	5.0	4.9	4.3	3.7	3.6	4.0	3.7
Lincoln	3.7	3.5	3.2	3.1	2.9	2.8	3.1	2.8	2.5	2.4	2.5	2.5
Los Angeles[2]	5.2	5.2	4.7	4.5	4.6	4.7	5.3	5.1	4.7	4.2	4.2	4.2
Louisville	6.5	6.6	6.1	5.6	5.3	5.7	5.9	5.4	5.3	5.3	5.2	4.7
Madison	3.4	3.9	3.7	3.5	3.3	3.6	3.4	3.0	3.0	2.9	3.1	3.2
Manchester[3]	3.8	3.9	3.8	3.4	3.2	3.3	3.5	3.4	3.1	3.0	3.2	3.2

Table continued on next page.

Metro Area[1]	2006											
	Jan.	Feb.	Mar.	Apr.	May	Jun.	Jul.	Aug.	Sep.	Oct.	Nov.	Dec.
Memphis	6.1	6.0	6.0	5.8	5.7	6.7	6.6	6.4	5.2	5.0	5.6	5.1
Miami[2]	3.6	3.7	3.7	3.6	3.5	3.9	4.1	4.2	4.0	3.8	3.5	3.5
Milwaukee	5.0	5.6	5.4	5.2	5.0	5.5	5.5	4.8	4.7	4.5	4.7	4.6
Minneapolis	4.4	4.4	4.3	3.8	3.1	3.5	3.5	3.3	3.6	3.3	3.5	3.8
Naperville[2]	5.3	5.0	4.9	4.6	4.2	4.7	4.7	4.4	4.1	3.5	3.7	3.8
Nashville	4.4	4.3	4.3	4.3	4.1	4.8	4.7	4.7	3.5	3.5	3.9	3.5
New York[2]	5.5	5.4	5.2	5.0	4.6	4.8	5.7	5.0	4.5	4.0	4.2	3.9
Norfolk	3.8	3.8	3.6	3.5	3.2	3.7	3.7	3.6	3.8	3.3	3.3	3.1
Oklahoma City	4.3	3.9	4.1	3.5	3.9	4.0	3.7	3.8	3.7	3.5	3.6	3.6
Omaha	4.6	4.4	4.0	3.7	3.4	3.5	3.7	3.3	3.0	2.9	3.0	3.1
Orlando	3.0	2.9	2.8	2.6	2.8	3.1	3.2	3.2	3.1	2.8	3.1	2.9
Overland Park	5.3	5.5	5.1	4.5	4.4	5.2	5.1	5.1	5.1	5.3	4.8	4.7
Philadelphia[2]	4.7	5.1	4.8	4.3	4.8	4.9	5.0	4.9	4.4	4.2	4.4	4.1
Phoenix	4.5	3.9	3.5	3.6	3.3	3.9	4.1	3.1	3.3	3.4	3.3	3.3
Pittsburgh	5.2	5.6	5.3	4.5	4.9	5.1	5.1	4.9	4.2	3.9	4.4	4.2
Plano[2]	5.1	5.0	4.8	4.7	4.8	5.3	5.3	5.0	4.6	4.5	4.5	4.0
Portland	5.3	6.0	5.6	5.2	5.0	5.3	5.3	5.2	4.8	4.4	4.7	4.7
Providence[3]	6.1	6.3	6.2	5.5	5.3	5.5	5.8	5.6	4.9	4.5	4.7	5.0
Provo	3.9	3.9	3.3	3.2	3.1	3.1	3.3	3.3	2.4	2.1	2.2	2.0
Raleigh	3.5	3.8	3.4	3.1	3.4	3.6	3.8	3.5	3.3	3.3	3.6	3.4
Reno	4.5	4.1	4.1	4.1	3.6	4.0	4.2	3.7	3.7	3.6	3.7	3.9
Richmond	3.4	3.4	3.3	3.3	3.0	3.4	3.4	3.4	3.3	2.8	3.0	2.8
Rochester	5.0	5.1	5.0	4.7	4.5	4.5	4.9	4.4	4.3	3.8	4.0	3.9
Sacramento	4.7	4.8	4.7	4.6	4.2	4.7	4.7	4.4	4.2	3.9	4.3	4.3
Salt Lake City	4.1	4.2	3.6	3.5	3.4	3.4	3.4	3.5	2.7	2.4	2.5	2.3
San Antonio	4.8	4.7	4.6	4.4	4.6	5.3	5.3	4.8	4.4	4.4	4.3	3.7
San Diego	4.0	4.1	3.9	3.7	3.7	4.2	4.3	4.1	3.9	3.6	3.9	3.7
San Francisco[2]	4.3	4.3	4.1	3.9	3.8	4.3	4.3	4.1	3.8	3.5	3.7	3.5
San Jose	5.1	5.1	4.8	4.6	4.4	5.0	5.0	4.7	4.5	4.2	4.5	4.2
Savannah	4.0	4.1	3.6	3.5	3.9	4.6	4.5	4.1	3.9	3.9	3.6	3.7
Scottsdale	4.5	3.9	3.5	3.6	3.3	3.9	4.1	3.1	3.3	3.4	3.3	3.3
Seattle[2]	4.3	4.7	4.5	4.0	4.4	4.4	4.1	4.0	4.4	4.1	4.5	4.2
Sioux Falls	3.3	3.4	3.3	2.4	2.5	2.5	2.5	2.3	2.4	2.5	2.5	2.7
Springfield	4.0	4.2	3.8	3.3	3.3	4.0	3.6	3.7	3.7	3.9	3.7	3.4
Saint Louis	5.5	5.6	5.3	4.8	4.6	5.3	5.1	5.3	4.8	4.9	4.8	4.6
Saint Paul	4.4	4.4	4.3	3.8	3.1	3.5	3.5	3.3	3.6	3.3	3.5	3.8
Saint Petersburg	3.2	3.2	2.9	2.7	3.0	3.3	3.4	3.4	3.2	3.0	3.3	3.0
Stamford[3]	4.6	4.6	4.3	3.5	3.6	4.0	4.3	4.1	4.1	3.4	3.7	3.3
Tampa	3.2	3.2	2.9	2.7	3.0	3.3	3.4	3.4	3.2	3.0	3.3	3.0
Thousand Oaks	4.6	4.4	4.0	3.8	3.8	4.4	4.7	4.6	4.4	4.0	4.4	4.3
Tucson	5.1	4.4	4.0	4.0	3.7	4.6	4.8	3.6	3.9	3.9	3.8	3.7
Tulsa	4.3	4.0	4.0	3.5	4.0	3.9	3.6	3.8	3.7	3.5	3.5	3.5
Virginia Beach	3.8	3.8	3.6	3.5	3.2	3.7	3.7	3.6	3.8	3.3	3.3	3.1
Washington[2]	3.1	3.0	3.0	3.0	3.0	3.3	3.5	3.3	3.1	2.9	3.0	2.9
Wichita	5.4	5.2	5.3	4.7	4.4	5.0	5.3	5.1	4.4	4.4	4.2	4.2
U.S.	5.1	5.1	4.8	4.5	4.4	4.8	5.0	4.6	4.4	4.1	4.3	4.3

Note: Data is not seasonally adjusted and covers workers 16 years of age and older; All figures are percentages; (1) Figures cover the Metropolitan Statistical Area (MSA) except where noted. See Appendix B for areas included; (2) Metropolitan Division; (3) New England City and Town Area; (4) New England City and Town Area Division
Source: Bureau of Labor Statistics, http://stats.bls.gov

Average Hourly Wages: Occupations A - C

MSA[1]	Accountants/ Auditors	Automotive Mechanics	Book- keepers	Carpenters	Cashiers	Clerks, Gen. Office	Clerks, Recep./Info.
Albuquerque	25.39	16.21	13.86	13.70	8.30	10.55	10.16
Alexandria	32.21	21.05	17.83	19.84	9.03	14.67	12.51
Anchorage	27.26	21.40	17.65	25.35	10.49	14.65	13.25
Ann Arbor	26.82	21.73	15.73	21.48	9.75	12.18	12.56
Athens	26.58	17.82	13.03	16.15	7.36	8.91	10.20
Atlanta	26.20	17.99	14.82	15.94	8.18	11.73	11.88
Austin	25.03	18.98	14.26	16.01	8.35	11.01	11.83
Baltimore	28.52	16.44	16.40	17.34	8.79	12.87	11.85
Baton Rouge	21.51	14.53	13.21	15.76	7.10	9.18	9.38
Bellevue	29.34	21.00	16.35	23.96	11.43	13.73	12.41
Birmingham	27.30	15.84	14.44	14.47	7.44	10.53	10.20
Boise City	21.05	16.24	13.06	14.41	8.52	11.32	10.63
Boston	29.70	20.86	18.25	24.64	9.26	14.90	12.70
Boulder	29.90	19.91	16.31	17.87	10.25	13.77	12.32
Buffalo	28.94	14.50	13.98	18.85	7.75	10.94	11.02
Cary	26.47	17.50	14.75	17.35	8.05	11.87	11.00
Cedar Rapids	26.70	16.31	14.37	18.01	7.75	11.55	10.68
Charleston	23.37	15.91	13.26	15.55	7.38	10.81	10.27
Charlotte	27.55	19.53	14.70	15.53	8.07	11.84	11.51
Chattanooga	22.54	14.09	13.75	14.79	7.43	10.65	10.39
Chicago	31.83	18.43	15.79	25.30	8.63	12.53	11.87
Cincinnati	27.64	17.63	14.90	18.00	8.32	11.30	10.60
Cleveland	26.07	16.72	14.56	18.41	7.90	11.39	10.87
Colorado Spgs.	25.20	17.11	14.54	18.25	9.07	12.18	11.25
Columbia	23.00	17.10	13.54	14.67	7.29	10.96	10.91
Columbus	27.38	18.07	15.61	16.57	8.34	11.70	10.64
Dallas	29.46	17.18	15.31	14.23	8.15	12.14	11.88
Denver	28.98	18.16	16.46	18.63	9.85	13.86	12.70
Des Moines	26.49	16.74	15.27	17.95	8.29	11.99	11.53
Durham	26.25	21.83	15.28	13.97	8.12	13.07	10.85
Edison	34.30	18.01	16.84	25.49	8.74	12.85	11.76
El Paso	24.63	13.46	11.91	10.09	6.98	9.22	8.57
Eugene	26.49	16.99	14.02	18.34	9.54	12.04	11.88
Fort Collins	26.84	20.59	15.45	15.95	8.85	11.98	11.56
Fort Lauderdale	26.20	16.23	14.26	15.91	8.19	11.04	10.89
Fort Wayne	26.70	18.19	14.12	17.26	7.59	10.86	10.39
Fort Worth	26.49	15.65	14.67	13.12	8.07	10.86	10.65
Grand Rapids	24.44	17.55	14.29	17.26	8.40	12.08	12.09
Green Bay	25.72	15.67	13.74	18.01	8.10	11.58	11.15
Greensboro	26.59	17.39	14.23	14.64	7.29	11.35	11.17
Honolulu	23.89	17.90	15.14	25.59	8.78	11.39	11.26
Houston	28.90	16.26	15.05	14.26	7.79	11.28	11.23
Huntsville	24.79	14.27	13.12	13.80	7.92	10.46	9.72
Indianapolis	27.22	18.92	15.45	17.76	8.11	11.90	11.33
Irvine	29.68	18.99	17.10	22.19	9.67	13.14	12.24
Jacksonville	25.70	15.51	14.24	14.19	8.05	11.07	9.84
Kansas City	25.94	17.22	14.39	20.20	8.32	11.76	11.55
Knoxville	25.45	15.87	14.90	13.92	7.67	11.60	10.29
Las Vegas	25.42	18.43	14.40	19.87	9.19	11.68	11.45
Lexington	22.79	15.33	13.46	15.94	8.29	12.00	10.42
Lincoln	25.33	16.27	13.59	15.85	7.66	11.55	9.97
Los Angeles	29.07	18.97	16.17	21.85	9.61	12.32	11.69
Louisville	26.34	15.41	13.88	16.55	7.74	11.11	10.56
Madison	27.16	16.82	14.92	19.92	8.39	12.04	11.72
Manchester	23.33	18.62	16.08	19.36	8.66	13.38	11.99

Table continued on next page.

MSA[1]	Accountants/ Auditors	Automotive Mechanics	Book- keepers	Carpenters	Cashiers	Clerks, Gen. Office	Clerks, Recep./Info.
Memphis	23.26	16.31	15.13	16.32	7.96	11.90	10.50
Miami	30.05	15.85	14.49	14.60	7.91	10.83	9.78
Milwaukee	29.95	17.89	15.22	21.69	8.21	11.62	11.55
Minneapolis	27.71	17.91	16.25	22.35	8.94	13.09	12.29
Naperville	31.83	18.43	15.79	25.30	8.63	12.53	11.87
Nashville	22.81	16.20	14.04	14.05	8.36	12.30	11.27
New York	34.88	17.78	17.56	24.72	8.96	13.09	13.07
Norfolk	24.39	16.73	13.70	16.73	7.41	11.60	9.57
Oklahoma City	22.69	14.82	14.04	14.13	7.53	10.53	9.96
Omaha	27.11	17.41	14.07	15.91	8.36	11.21	11.28
Orlando	25.70	18.18	13.69	14.52	8.13	11.26	10.04
Overland Park	25.94	17.22	14.39	20.20	8.32	11.76	11.55
Philadelphia	31.50	17.39	15.92	20.24	8.36	13.17	12.07
Phoenix	24.71	18.71	14.70	16.41	9.12	12.50	11.15
Pittsburgh	27.51	15.43	13.57	18.02	7.21	10.83	9.31
Plano	29.46	17.18	15.31	14.23	8.15	12.14	11.88
Portland	27.34	16.46	15.79	19.86	10.07	13.04	12.14
Providence	30.50	16.93	15.78	18.58	8.73	11.92	11.59
Provo	24.01	17.77	13.31	14.81	7.74	9.99	9.68
Raleigh	26.47	17.50	14.75	17.35	8.05	11.87	11.00
Reno	24.29	18.67	14.27	20.62	8.85	11.67	11.71
Richmond	28.16	18.87	15.23	16.65	8.01	13.12	10.53
Rochester	28.00	15.53	14.62	16.69	7.70	11.70	10.63
Sacramento	27.79	18.02	16.56	22.56	10.09	13.59	11.87
Salt Lake City	24.19	17.09	14.01	15.06	8.65	11.25	10.90
San Antonio	24.66	16.66	13.29	13.52	7.68	10.44	9.39
San Diego	27.79	20.53	16.39	20.90	9.69	12.14	11.49
San Francisco	32.01	24.36	18.99	24.70	10.98	14.08	14.25
San Jose	33.71	22.52	18.76	26.73	10.70	15.59	14.82
Savannah	23.52	14.73	14.04	14.88	7.51	10.18	9.74
Scottsdale	24.71	18.71	14.70	16.41	9.12	12.50	11.15
Seattle	29.34	21.00	16.35	23.96	11.43	13.73	12.41
Sioux Falls	23.28	15.60	12.06	13.20	7.79	9.25	9.98
Springfield	22.50	15.47	12.53	13.98	7.67	9.76	9.31
Saint Louis	29.20	17.88	14.71	23.06	8.66	12.09	10.65
Saint Paul	27.71	17.91	16.25	22.35	8.94	13.09	12.29
Saint Petersburg	27.44	17.17	13.67	14.94	7.94	10.83	10.52
Stamford	34.89	20.77	18.47	23.26	9.44	14.37	13.76
Tampa	27.44	17.17	13.67	14.94	7.94	10.83	10.52
Thousand Oaks	27.64	17.83	16.30	21.04	9.81	12.50	11.56
Tucson	24.24	17.88	13.58	14.83	8.94	11.75	10.30
Tulsa	23.29	15.19	14.19	13.98	7.64	10.89	10.04
Virginia Beach	24.39	16.73	13.70	16.73	7.41	11.60	9.57
Washington	32.21	21.05	17.83	19.84	9.03	14.67	12.51
Wichita	25.12	16.09	13.32	16.34	7.70	10.48	10.12

Notes: Wage data is for May 2005 and covers the Metropolitan Statistical Area - see Appendix A for areas included; n/a not available
Source: Bureau of Labor Statistics, May 2005 Metro Area Occupational Employment and Wage Estimates

Average Hourly Wages: Occupations C - E

MSA[1]	Clerks, Ship./Rec.	Computer Programmers	Computer Support Specialists	Computer Systems Analysts	Cooks, Restaurant	Dentists	Electrical Engineers
Albuquerque	11.77	29.67	18.85	29.59	8.50	n/a	38.35
Alexandria	14.12	33.26	23.40	37.99	11.15	n/a	39.33
Anchorage	16.57	29.75	22.38	35.30	13.01	n/a	41.78
Ann Arbor	13.56	30.81	19.80	32.30	10.72	n/a	34.76
Athens	11.67	26.02	n/a	26.07	9.16	n/a	32.64
Atlanta	13.07	35.68	20.83	36.09	10.18	n/a	36.03
Austin	12.01	35.93	19.70	31.26	8.91	n/a	44.70
Baltimore	13.56	32.09	20.87	34.89	10.64	n/a	34.09
Baton Rouge	12.13	23.76	21.97	26.61	8.64	n/a	32.91
Bellevue	14.80	n/a	26.04	37.06	11.70	n/a	36.09
Birmingham	12.33	30.61	17.90	28.81	8.93	n/a	36.57
Boise City	11.74	28.22	19.12	30.18	8.79	n/a	n/a
Boston	15.17	39.50	26.87	35.54	12.28	n/a	41.75
Boulder	13.76	37.61	25.72	n/a	9.87	n/a	42.90
Buffalo	12.15	27.86	15.23	28.74	9.55	n/a	30.41
Cary	12.31	33.96	20.59	33.20	9.76	n/a	33.00
Cedar Rapids	15.94	24.82	19.92	30.59	9.95	n/a	n/a
Charleston	14.33	26.39	19.31	30.33	8.89	n/a	32.28
Charlotte	12.79	34.67	21.11	35.30	9.72	n/a	n/a
Chattanooga	12.27	25.14	18.38	30.48	8.78	n/a	34.57
Chicago	13.36	31.42	22.80	36.26	9.44	n/a	34.71
Cincinnati	13.66	28.35	20.48	32.39	9.86	n/a	30.87
Cleveland	13.60	29.87	19.87	32.35	9.67	n/a	35.23
Colorado Spgs.	12.02	29.22	19.84	33.13	10.01	n/a	40.00
Columbia	11.83	23.57	20.49	27.80	8.58	n/a	33.55
Columbus	13.32	30.38	21.12	33.28	10.21	n/a	31.25
Dallas	12.04	35.97	22.18	35.86	8.48	n/a	39.94
Denver	13.39	37.26	24.61	35.01	10.00	n/a	36.52
Des Moines	12.95	28.03	20.11	30.60	9.81	n/a	30.77
Durham	13.01	32.08	n/a	37.33	9.35	n/a	31.49
Edison	13.94	39.54	23.68	37.21	10.83	n/a	37.48
El Paso	9.81	24.21	17.33	29.48	7.60	n/a	32.15
Eugene	11.95	27.30	17.61	28.49	9.29	n/a	36.13
Fort Collins	12.15	30.27	20.61	36.15	9.81	n/a	29.31
Fort Lauderdale	11.93	30.29	18.22	27.55	10.60	n/a	34.05
Fort Wayne	12.44	27.12	17.98	28.98	9.49	n/a	34.67
Fort Worth	12.52	35.54	19.91	36.90	8.88	n/a	36.29
Grand Rapids	13.95	26.66	19.59	30.40	9.16	n/a	28.01
Green Bay	12.80	28.45	19.97	27.29	10.08	n/a	33.25
Greensboro	12.53	28.16	19.55	33.27	8.65	n/a	38.99
Honolulu	13.28	26.88	18.32	33.13	10.96	n/a	36.54
Houston	12.39	39.13	20.72	33.08	8.09	n/a	42.80
Huntsville	11.09	38.05	17.94	34.47	8.97	n/a	35.88
Indianapolis	12.65	28.43	18.50	32.04	10.00	n/a	29.91
Irvine	12.97	34.87	22.63	36.36	10.42	n/a	37.65
Jacksonville	13.02	36.66	17.89	31.27	10.06	n/a	35.28
Kansas City	13.68	30.94	21.33	33.94	10.17	n/a	35.12
Knoxville	10.96	24.53	19.62	27.15	9.20	n/a	32.22
Las Vegas	13.91	30.23	16.64	34.63	12.60	n/a	37.71
Lexington	12.38	28.63	16.24	29.39	9.05	n/a	32.36
Lincoln	11.72	26.24	18.27	26.40	9.60	n/a	32.05
Los Angeles	12.37	34.18	20.95	33.42	10.33	n/a	39.22
Louisville	12.71	29.16	19.68	32.30	9.33	n/a	35.25
Madison	13.06	27.52	18.92	29.49	10.00	n/a	29.59
Manchester	14.11	20.11	21.33	30.79	11.94	n/a	33.22

Table continued on next page.

MSA[1]	Clerks, Ship./Rec.	Computer Program- mers	Computer Support Specialists	Computer Systems Analysts	Cooks, Restaurant	Dentists	Electrical Engineers
Memphis	12.06	30.41	20.88	30.06	9.32	n/a	30.71
Miami	11.30	29.39	18.75	29.40	10.59	n/a	35.14
Milwaukee	13.20	30.57	19.30	32.15	9.91	n/a	35.87
Minneapolis	14.43	32.88	22.50	33.02	10.62	n/a	37.42
Naperville	13.36	31.42	22.80	36.26	9.44	n/a	34.71
Nashville	12.07	28.99	19.81	29.57	10.38	n/a	34.54
New York	13.29	35.98	25.67	37.61	12.85	n/a	39.23
Norfolk	12.34	24.79	20.56	33.15	9.11	n/a	35.66
Oklahoma City	12.63	26.06	17.07	30.99	8.13	n/a	33.58
Omaha	12.69	31.19	18.61	31.51	9.86	n/a	36.47
Orlando	11.17	34.53	18.02	30.03	10.51	n/a	34.06
Overland Park	13.68	30.94	21.33	33.94	10.17	n/a	35.12
Philadelphia	14.17	30.51	21.45	33.79	10.78	n/a	36.89
Phoenix	10.44	29.39	21.41	31.83	9.95	n/a	36.74
Pittsburgh	12.32	28.68	18.92	29.52	9.36	n/a	33.82
Plano	12.04	35.97	22.18	35.86	8.48	n/a	39.94
Portland	13.89	30.37	21.40	33.41	10.51	n/a	40.71
Providence	13.44	29.86	18.79	32.92	11.23	n/a	36.75
Provo	10.69	27.33	17.91	26.55	9.15	n/a	26.96
Raleigh	12.31	33.96	20.59	33.20	9.76	n/a	33.00
Reno	12.88	29.62	16.84	29.24	10.45	n/a	33.16
Richmond	13.40	37.29	21.47	33.69	9.53	n/a	32.20
Rochester	12.30	28.75	20.13	32.55	10.05	n/a	35.02
Sacramento	12.91	30.79	24.59	31.88	10.78	n/a	36.11
Salt Lake City	12.34	32.86	18.29	31.26	10.24	n/a	37.56
San Antonio	11.68	27.53	19.42	30.97	8.68	n/a	34.90
San Diego	12.80	36.67	21.53	34.88	10.24	n/a	41.15
San Francisco	14.79	41.65	28.99	39.38	12.10	n/a	43.32
San Jose	14.87	43.69	29.72	41.11	10.55	n/a	45.35
Savannah	13.69	24.59	20.78	32.54	8.42	n/a	33.11
Scottsdale	10.44	29.39	21.41	31.83	9.95	n/a	36.74
Seattle	14.80	n/a	26.04	37.06	11.70	n/a	36.09
Sioux Falls	11.97	20.73	15.49	28.64	8.98	n/a	31.10
Springfield	11.20	21.65	17.89	24.40	8.18	n/a	32.36
Saint Louis	13.05	31.20	18.74	33.02	9.84	n/a	32.53
Saint Paul	14.43	32.88	22.50	33.02	10.62	n/a	37.42
Saint Petersburg	12.67	27.97	17.67	31.33	10.23	n/a	34.38
Stamford	14.81	39.72	27.57	38.42	13.99	n/a	38.01
Tampa	12.67	27.97	17.67	31.33	10.23	n/a	34.38
Thousand Oaks	12.62	35.00	20.95	38.92	9.96	n/a	40.66
Tucson	11.36	27.11	21.58	28.38	8.61	n/a	n/a
Tulsa	12.08	27.62	14.41	31.09	8.72	n/a	31.11
Virginia Beach	12.34	24.79	20.56	33.15	9.11	n/a	35.66
Washington	14.12	33.26	23.40	37.99	11.15	n/a	39.33
Wichita	12.38	25.76	18.04	28.80	8.71	n/a	30.70

Notes: Wage data is for May 2005 and covers the Metropolitan Statistical Area - see Appendix A for areas included; n/a not available
Source: Bureau of Labor Statistics, May 2005 Metro Area Occupational Employment and Wage Estimates

Average Hourly Wages: Occupations E - I

MSA[1]	Electricians	Financial Managers	First-Line Supervisors/ Mgrs., Sales	Food Preparation Workers	General/ Oper. Mgrs.	Hairdressers/ Cosmetologists	Internists
Albuquerque	17.99	35.60	15.57	7.74	42.39	9.43	86.54
Alexandria	23.27	49.32	19.61	9.37	54.98	15.49	80.43
Anchorage	28.36	37.77	17.86	10.30	35.26	12.63	81.91
Ann Arbor	29.95	47.28	18.92	10.42	47.30	14.67	n/a
Athens	19.55	37.19	14.20	8.29	33.46	10.71	68.12
Atlanta	19.48	45.74	16.94	8.54	43.74	11.57	76.46
Austin	17.34	46.20	17.62	9.10	44.94	14.73	n/a
Baltimore	20.14	42.71	19.10	9.24	47.77	11.23	60.32
Baton Rouge	18.46	31.75	16.63	6.55	38.89	12.11	n/a
Bellevue	26.68	50.99	22.77	10.71	62.86	13.61	78.35
Birmingham	18.50	39.59	16.65	7.89	45.28	16.54	84.28
Boise City	19.66	33.51	18.16	8.22	29.85	9.05	n/a
Boston	27.90	57.02	19.47	9.79	53.12	14.16	70.49
Boulder	22.46	55.55	20.30	9.16	49.90	12.23	88.90
Buffalo	23.27	46.96	17.64	8.22	47.52	10.30	82.00
Cary	14.37	39.88	17.06	8.40	50.97	10.55	74.55
Cedar Rapids	24.85	46.95	16.66	8.34	43.85	10.56	n/a
Charleston	17.90	34.87	17.05	7.88	36.71	13.35	n/a
Charlotte	18.00	46.80	16.57	8.28	50.31	15.44	82.65
Chattanooga	20.26	36.15	15.53	7.68	40.97	14.46	79.00
Chicago	28.25	47.66	19.80	8.85	47.55	11.08	70.17
Cincinnati	20.32	45.44	18.08	8.84	45.25	10.38	79.37
Cleveland	25.46	48.48	18.69	8.08	48.49	12.50	65.13
Colorado Spgs.	20.47	50.19	19.34	9.06	42.69	12.38	n/a
Columbia	17.55	36.60	17.71	10.81	37.25	13.22	79.67
Columbus	19.83	44.68	18.61	8.79	47.02	11.06	81.34
Dallas	17.81	46.62	19.18	8.20	52.08	11.76	86.36
Denver	21.54	48.31	19.82	9.18	51.71	12.84	81.84
Des Moines	22.19	45.28	19.42	8.39	44.46	11.91	85.07
Durham	17.56	44.07	16.69	8.83	50.86	14.47	n/a
Edison	25.95	58.81	22.17	8.80	64.44	11.39	80.00
El Paso	13.85	35.14	15.20	7.16	37.00	8.15	n/a
Eugene	23.30	42.52	17.40	9.07	42.73	n/a	n/a
Fort Collins	19.62	44.65	18.50	8.87	39.10	11.69	85.01
Fort Lauderdale	18.21	48.37	21.56	8.94	49.27	10.81	75.51
Fort Wayne	23.04	40.75	17.46	8.20	42.73	9.04	n/a
Fort Worth	17.69	41.15	18.18	8.08	45.14	14.96	90.56
Grand Rapids	21.66	38.21	18.90	8.58	41.92	9.87	71.82
Green Bay	21.91	53.74	18.04	9.17	47.94	11.19	n/a
Greensboro	16.67	41.17	17.03	7.84	47.27	10.78	83.71
Honolulu	28.49	42.84	17.97	9.70	46.33	12.36	87.82
Houston	19.42	50.34	19.23	7.43	49.72	11.97	59.11
Huntsville	19.04	38.63	15.56	8.06	43.60	8.29	80.69
Indianapolis	24.31	46.69	19.37	8.64	47.54	10.46	63.24
Irvine	21.33	52.95	18.67	8.80	54.14	9.83	83.84
Jacksonville	17.47	44.16	19.91	9.02	49.89	11.76	91.25
Kansas City	24.40	43.32	18.89	8.42	46.51	11.79	72.46
Knoxville	19.80	32.52	17.33	8.48	39.30	11.41	66.65
Las Vegas	23.57	42.23	17.72	10.70	52.77	11.55	86.54
Lexington	18.11	35.67	16.49	9.06	37.23	13.17	55.62
Lincoln	18.84	36.16	16.44	8.09	40.83	11.15	80.98
Los Angeles	23.80	50.04	18.64	8.72	52.97	12.76	77.11
Louisville	19.88	40.50	16.78	8.88	37.91	10.27	61.60
Madison	22.78	48.05	19.51	9.26	46.38	12.82	83.29
Manchester	18.78	36.96	18.78	9.35	42.31	10.80	n/a

Table continued on next page.

MSA[1]	Electricians	Financial Managers	First-Line Supervisors/ Mgrs., Sales	Food Preparation Workers	General/ Oper. Mgrs.	Hairdressers/ Cosmetologists	Internists
Memphis	18.49	35.99	16.92	8.30	42.33	16.35	n/a
Miami	17.75	48.34	22.72	8.44	52.19	11.19	77.42
Milwaukee	23.91	52.33	19.62	8.63	51.16	11.05	89.38
Minneapolis	29.96	52.93	17.37	9.98	51.02	14.05	73.55
Naperville	28.25	47.66	19.80	8.85	47.55	11.08	70.17
Nashville	18.35	33.76	18.44	8.82	37.37	13.17	74.09
New York	31.34	66.00	21.51	10.41	63.76	12.64	76.44
Norfolk	17.86	44.18	18.65	8.13	51.82	9.54	88.45
Oklahoma City	16.21	34.56	16.04	7.10	35.14	10.55	91.45
Omaha	19.58	44.15	19.97	8.16	45.02	12.93	71.28
Orlando	15.84	44.97	20.16	8.66	45.10	10.52	66.58
Overland Park	24.40	43.32	18.89	8.42	46.51	11.79	72.46
Philadelphia	29.44	52.26	21.16	8.65	51.81	10.66	n/a
Phoenix	17.32	41.31	18.04	9.61	42.41	11.75	84.23
Pittsburgh	23.53	42.26	19.35	8.31	44.86	8.28	85.16
Plano	17.81	46.62	19.18	8.20	52.08	11.76	86.36
Portland	27.95	47.39	19.54	9.89	47.48	11.98	79.19
Providence	23.24	41.43	18.04	9.35	45.16	11.66	85.07
Provo	14.95	36.20	16.73	7.53	37.95	10.89	91.57
Raleigh	14.37	39.88	17.06	8.40	50.97	10.55	74.55
Reno	21.08	41.40	19.32	9.51	48.75	10.52	89.86
Richmond	20.58	54.22	18.33	8.78	50.53	12.39	78.00
Rochester	22.38	45.71	17.63	7.85	47.89	10.50	90.18
Sacramento	21.80	42.58	18.64	9.29	48.36	10.37	64.31
Salt Lake City	18.57	39.35	17.50	7.83	42.78	10.39	n/a
San Antonio	16.20	46.17	17.34	7.74	41.68	10.86	92.12
San Diego	22.92	45.29	18.48	8.27	52.85	11.99	59.63
San Francisco	32.98	57.88	19.64	10.16	56.87	16.07	76.80
San Jose	30.70	60.64	20.75	9.67	60.83	11.21	58.26
Savannah	16.82	37.29	16.75	7.81	35.50	8.49	91.98
Scottsdale	17.32	41.31	18.04	9.61	42.41	11.75	84.23
Seattle	26.68	50.99	22.77	10.71	62.86	13.61	78.35
Sioux Falls	16.92	42.25	18.05	8.03	47.09	11.18	91.13
Springfield	15.51	41.14	20.53	7.92	42.39	9.42	n/a
Saint Louis	26.89	46.13	20.19	8.31	46.65	11.13	77.54
Saint Paul	29.96	52.93	17.37	9.98	51.02	14.05	73.55
Saint Petersburg	15.49	41.76	20.23	8.79	46.12	10.94	86.64
Stamford	23.53	63.91	23.27	10.55	67.49	14.71	67.36
Tampa	15.49	41.76	20.23	8.79	46.12	10.94	86.64
Thousand Oaks	26.36	49.76	18.20	8.21	51.90	8.68	91.63
Tucson	17.71	36.57	18.44	8.74	40.61	10.19	74.05
Tulsa	17.79	36.03	15.45	7.20	36.74	11.37	85.61
Virginia Beach	17.86	44.18	18.65	8.13	51.82	9.54	88.45
Washington	23.27	49.32	19.61	9.37	54.98	15.49	80.43
Wichita	21.21	38.42	17.39	7.75	37.26	9.84	71.39

Notes: Wage data is for May 2005 and covers the Metropolitan Statistical Area - see Appendix A for areas included; n/a not available
Source: Bureau of Labor Statistics, May 2005 Metro Area Occupational Employment and Wage Estimates

Average Hourly Wages: Occupations J - N

MSA[1]	Janitors/ Cleaners	Landscapers	Lawyers	Maids/ House- keepers	Main- tenance Repairers	Marketing Managers	Nuclear Medicine Technologists
Albuquerque	8.95	8.15	48.70	6.95	13.54	36.03	n/a
Alexandria	10.14	11.05	63.26	10.09	17.47	48.88	28.93
Anchorage	12.34	11.89	47.22	10.20	18.73	34.48	n/a
Ann Arbor	12.39	11.55	45.73	10.01	19.10	37.89	30.08
Athens	8.50	9.91	40.35	8.18	14.60	39.70	n/a
Atlanta	9.53	10.57	56.97	8.19	16.04	45.58	28.11
Austin	9.31	9.11	47.17	8.21	13.52	49.61	28.98
Baltimore	9.21	11.12	53.92	9.68	15.63	45.51	34.02
Baton Rouge	7.91	9.28	43.31	6.97	13.95	32.45	25.95
Bellevue	12.44	13.27	48.51	9.81	18.74	60.40	33.41
Birmingham	8.49	10.08	51.91	7.29	15.14	37.67	25.45
Boise City	9.36	10.69	48.19	7.54	14.40	41.32	22.45
Boston	12.45	13.04	61.80	10.81	18.90	57.32	32.57
Boulder	11.64	11.51	n/a	8.84	16.43	48.97	29.91
Buffalo	10.35	11.88	49.69	8.38	16.27	38.98	26.52
Cary	8.73	10.69	39.36	8.10	15.68	45.52	29.71
Cedar Rapids	10.02	11.05	41.71	8.23	17.35	42.73	n/a
Charleston	7.85	9.18	48.78	7.67	15.44	32.17	26.91
Charlotte	9.45	10.08	47.79	8.02	17.15	46.09	29.23
Chattanooga	8.73	9.61	56.59	7.30	15.45	29.44	n/a
Chicago	10.56	11.29	61.65	8.92	19.03	45.28	31.29
Cincinnati	10.64	10.88	51.45	9.31	16.35	46.61	28.21
Cleveland	10.67	11.07	50.76	8.94	16.21	47.40	27.76
Colorado Spgs.	11.35	10.66	40.70	9.00	15.62	45.94	27.79
Columbia	8.68	9.27	44.53	7.85	14.97	32.87	25.70
Columbus	11.01	10.68	45.92	8.61	16.17	45.43	28.59
Dallas	8.86	9.95	60.32	8.30	14.52	47.14	29.47
Denver	10.07	11.58	51.51	9.17	16.31	43.67	28.77
Des Moines	9.81	11.32	51.42	8.67	15.03	42.20	28.94
Durham	9.02	10.15	41.61	7.58	16.28	51.58	28.39
Edison	11.16	12.28	54.49	9.09	17.51	58.78	33.94
El Paso	7.81	8.22	48.11	6.36	10.70	34.01	31.88
Eugene	10.80	11.01	51.19	8.59	15.82	35.48	n/a
Fort Collins	10.21	12.45	37.33	9.06	15.26	33.58	n/a
Fort Lauderdale	8.96	9.96	55.99	8.91	13.71	49.82	30.11
Fort Wayne	11.24	10.54	39.31	7.81	15.60	39.92	23.38
Fort Worth	8.99	9.65	45.91	7.41	14.88	45.87	27.90
Grand Rapids	11.02	11.03	44.23	9.05	17.35	35.79	26.28
Green Bay	9.73	8.97	55.17	8.82	16.36	48.84	n/a
Greensboro	8.96	9.62	55.36	8.83	15.95	46.52	n/a
Honolulu	9.98	11.76	44.92	11.95	16.70	39.44	n/a
Houston	8.16	8.45	58.12	7.10	14.40	51.72	29.04
Huntsville	8.16	9.33	52.35	7.48	15.92	42.06	n/a
Indianapolis	9.54	10.43	41.53	8.15	15.68	41.94	28.36
Irvine	10.61	10.47	64.36	8.51	15.90	54.37	33.79
Jacksonville	9.07	10.06	45.93	8.10	15.08	44.13	30.05
Kansas City	10.13	11.06	48.70	8.39	16.46	43.90	28.15
Knoxville	9.24	9.86	42.89	7.82	14.92	36.71	25.81
Las Vegas	10.82	11.47	52.69	11.02	17.73	43.15	28.89
Lexington	9.31	9.50	45.66	7.75	17.26	35.00	24.55
Lincoln	9.28	11.16	38.19	7.90	14.49	41.11	n/a
Los Angeles	10.53	12.23	64.38	9.26	16.91	52.80	32.04
Louisville	9.11	11.11	45.65	8.46	15.22	43.04	24.42
Madison	11.04	12.21	42.41	9.06	16.20	41.92	28.62
Manchester	10.61	12.83	50.95	9.43	16.33	39.89	n/a

Table continued on next page.

MSA[1]	Janitors/ Cleaners	Landscapers	Lawyers	Maids/ House- keepers	Main- tenance Repairers	Marketing Managers	Nuclear Medicine Technologists
Memphis	8.79	10.72	45.60	7.61	16.25	47.33	27.90
Miami	8.73	9.58	51.92	7.72	12.74	49.94	30.10
Milwaukee	10.30	11.42	52.40	8.67	17.55	53.59	31.42
Minneapolis	10.90	12.69	56.21	9.88	18.75	56.33	30.32
Naperville	10.56	11.29	61.65	8.92	19.03	45.28	31.29
Nashville	9.95	10.34	46.84	7.83	15.77	34.45	28.34
New York	12.38	13.08	62.51	14.10	16.99	65.66	31.89
Norfolk	8.55	9.76	54.94	7.52	14.46	36.54	25.82
Oklahoma City	8.92	9.07	45.00	7.31	13.71	33.74	29.31
Omaha	9.88	11.04	51.14	8.64	15.14	45.08	n/a
Orlando	8.85	9.77	50.68	8.49	13.46	49.03	28.17
Overland Park	10.13	11.06	48.70	8.39	16.46	43.90	28.15
Philadelphia	10.98	11.78	49.23	9.58	16.75	49.12	29.97
Phoenix	8.71	9.52	47.56	8.07	14.95	39.27	27.21
Pittsburgh	10.09	10.18	52.09	8.49	15.27	47.18	23.09
Plano	8.86	9.95	60.32	8.30	14.52	47.14	29.47
Portland	10.72	11.39	44.80	8.99	17.04	43.80	31.99
Providence	11.43	12.21	41.66	9.97	15.95	39.76	31.42
Provo	10.51	9.32	50.69	7.69	15.02	42.12	n/a
Raleigh	8.73	10.69	39.36	8.10	15.68	45.52	29.71
Reno	9.59	11.30	56.08	8.45	15.96	42.37	n/a
Richmond	8.48	10.49	52.82	8.23	15.35	53.28	25.99
Rochester	9.95	11.18	43.10	8.52	14.95	52.19	26.53
Sacramento	11.12	10.67	48.15	9.34	17.14	46.33	38.25
Salt Lake City	9.27	10.35	53.41	8.69	15.79	40.30	24.29
San Antonio	8.46	8.90	48.89	7.33	12.44	42.85	27.47
San Diego	10.25	10.99	53.55	8.76	16.67	53.93	35.36
San Francisco	11.98	15.47	64.24	12.53	20.97	61.07	39.17
San Jose	11.59	13.86	73.85	11.05	20.45	66.92	38.80
Savannah	8.91	9.34	50.30	7.02	13.35	33.65	n/a
Scottsdale	8.71	9.52	47.56	8.07	14.95	39.27	27.21
Seattle	12.44	13.27	48.51	9.81	18.74	60.40	33.41
Sioux Falls	9.15	9.59	36.79	8.33	12.29	40.06	23.10
Springfield	9.15	10.55	42.01	7.83	13.55	40.32	n/a
Saint Louis	9.67	11.41	57.05	8.82	17.07	44.77	26.15
Saint Paul	10.90	12.69	56.21	9.88	18.75	56.33	30.32
Saint Petersburg	8.95	9.97	51.24	7.92	13.36	42.03	27.89
Stamford	11.71	13.70	55.82	10.79	19.14	62.46	31.84
Tampa	8.95	9.97	51.24	7.92	13.36	42.03	27.89
Thousand Oaks	11.84	10.91	62.13	9.08	16.02	58.08	n/a
Tucson	9.23	9.67	42.32	8.09	12.75	30.00	21.64
Tulsa	8.42	9.32	48.11	7.44	15.10	43.87	26.60
Virginia Beach	8.55	9.76	54.94	7.52	14.46	36.54	25.82
Washington	10.14	11.05	63.26	10.09	17.47	48.88	28.93
Wichita	9.49	9.19	42.81	7.44	14.32	37.73	27.95

Notes: Wage data is for May 2005 and covers the Metropolitan Statistical Area - see Appendix A for areas included; n/a not available
Source: Bureau of Labor Statistics, May 2005 Metro Area Occupational Employment and Wage Estimates

Average Hourly Wages: Occupations N - R

MSA[1]	Nurses, Licensed Practical	Nurses, Registered	Nursing Aides/ Orderlies/ Attendants	Packers/ Packagers	Physical Therapists	Postal Mail Carriers	R.E. Brokers
Albuquerque	18.28	27.03	10.13	8.70	26.91	21.79	n/a
Alexandria	20.52	29.90	12.15	9.57	32.75	21.89	34.17
Anchorage	20.01	30.34	n/a	11.03	36.88	22.55	n/a
Ann Arbor	20.03	29.16	12.21	11.26	30.12	21.07	32.56
Athens	16.46	n/a	9.20	9.72	27.47	20.66	28.91
Atlanta	16.32	25.66	10.13	9.01	31.31	20.77	42.43
Austin	17.89	25.94	10.42	7.95	28.28	21.27	45.88
Baltimore	21.98	33.70	12.48	10.33	31.40	21.54	41.57
Baton Rouge	15.55	23.19	7.85	6.92	33.72	20.68	35.43
Bellevue	20.88	32.89	12.72	10.08	30.00	21.85	38.04
Birmingham	14.59	24.00	8.99	7.33	30.22	20.40	n/a
Boise City	16.57	24.38	9.34	8.04	32.16	20.96	n/a
Boston	22.92	33.87	13.12	10.21	30.06	22.28	35.69
Boulder	19.29	27.81	11.63	9.18	26.98	21.64	n/a
Buffalo	15.90	25.58	10.73	9.99	25.78	21.99	39.46
Cary	17.07	24.74	10.58	9.56	30.81	20.69	17.16
Cedar Rapids	16.36	21.33	10.88	8.77	26.13	21.70	n/a
Charleston	15.71	24.67	8.72	7.87	26.48	20.41	n/a
Charlotte	17.64	26.32	10.12	9.35	30.94	20.62	25.50
Chattanooga	16.17	23.12	9.67	9.04	30.92	21.08	n/a
Chicago	18.39	27.58	10.40	9.29	31.71	22.23	33.66
Cincinnati	18.40	26.50	11.27	8.87	32.55	21.56	27.69
Cleveland	18.62	26.90	10.69	9.78	30.52	22.60	21.99
Colorado Spgs.	17.32	25.54	10.84	9.13	31.36	21.42	22.28
Columbia	16.14	25.10	9.45	7.87	29.75	20.89	34.24
Columbus	18.97	26.12	11.10	9.34	29.77	21.15	n/a
Dallas	18.43	27.26	9.70	8.76	37.52	21.35	43.27
Denver	19.02	28.35	12.63	9.08	27.64	21.76	30.46
Des Moines	17.11	22.99	11.62	8.55	29.44	21.88	22.77
Durham	18.23	27.03	10.81	9.41	29.79	21.18	15.93
Edison	22.35	29.89	12.21	8.72	34.17	22.10	42.47
El Paso	18.37	25.92	9.18	6.56	38.00	22.32	n/a
Eugene	17.33	n/a	11.14	9.32	31.49	22.14	n/a
Fort Collins	18.36	25.21	11.08	8.54	25.37	21.29	30.71
Fort Lauderdale	18.21	26.95	9.85	9.53	30.00	22.75	n/a
Fort Wayne	16.44	23.17	10.75	7.50	26.01	21.54	33.28
Fort Worth	18.42	26.84	9.58	8.70	31.01	21.14	62.64
Grand Rapids	17.64	25.10	10.91	8.64	30.36	20.89	n/a
Green Bay	16.73	27.09	11.26	8.62	31.34	20.78	23.12
Greensboro	17.11	24.04	9.86	9.37	34.77	20.97	16.18
Honolulu	18.60	31.84	12.11	8.81	31.14	23.16	38.26
Houston	18.10	28.23	9.44	7.93	32.72	21.84	34.36
Huntsville	15.10	23.61	8.63	8.26	28.67	20.65	n/a
Indianapolis	17.98	25.65	11.12	10.23	31.71	21.18	n/a
Irvine	21.07	32.98	10.77	8.89	33.40	22.56	n/a
Jacksonville	18.26	24.32	10.02	7.79	30.88	21.33	n/a
Kansas City	16.64	25.65	11.06	9.03	27.68	21.45	33.02
Knoxville	14.24	22.08	9.33	9.74	31.63	20.67	n/a
Las Vegas	18.49	28.59	11.96	8.54	34.38	21.74	n/a
Lexington	17.25	24.57	10.07	9.20	31.16	21.44	n/a
Lincoln	16.53	23.92	11.00	9.17	29.91	21.51	n/a
Los Angeles	20.09	32.53	10.47	8.61	32.19	22.72	44.55
Louisville	17.27	26.07	11.13	9.64	29.07	21.10	n/a
Madison	18.60	27.66	12.36	11.36	27.76	20.91	21.77
Manchester	20.30	26.25	12.89	n/a	28.46	22.33	25.58

Table continued on next page.

MSA[1]	Nurses, Licensed Practical	Nurses, Registered	Nursing Aides/ Orderlies/ Attendants	Packers/ Packagers	Physical Therapists	Postal Mail Carriers	R.E. Brokers
Memphis	15.99	25.15	9.71	9.23	32.38	21.42	n/a
Miami	17.38	27.44	10.01	8.41	33.08	22.82	n/a
Milwaukee	19.11	27.23	11.56	10.18	30.41	21.88	33.66
Minneapolis	18.31	30.01	12.88	10.30	26.72	21.55	45.63
Naperville	18.39	27.58	10.40	9.29	31.71	22.23	33.66
Nashville	16.66	27.68	10.23	8.80	29.92	20.73	25.78
New York	20.67	33.72	14.20	8.89	37.58	22.12	43.19
Norfolk	16.17	24.98	9.43	8.54	31.74	21.99	49.97
Oklahoma City	16.24	23.05	9.27	8.17	30.90	21.23	n/a
Omaha	17.04	24.92	11.63	9.05	27.72	21.45	n/a
Orlando	16.85	24.39	9.76	8.68	27.83	21.68	47.94
Overland Park	16.64	25.65	11.06	9.03	27.68	21.45	33.02
Philadelphia	21.73	28.77	11.94	10.01	32.67	22.50	36.49
Phoenix	18.89	27.38	10.73	7.90	30.04	21.55	43.89
Pittsburgh	16.60	24.65	10.65	9.94	30.02	21.86	29.05
Plano	18.43	27.26	9.70	8.76	37.52	21.35	43.27
Portland	20.12	30.09	11.59	9.56	31.51	21.77	n/a
Providence	20.80	28.06	12.20	9.51	29.58	22.13	n/a
Provo	15.16	25.43	8.64	7.85	28.87	21.15	55.71
Raleigh	17.07	24.74	10.58	9.56	30.81	20.69	17.16
Reno	20.36	29.46	12.06	10.28	31.92	21.90	n/a
Richmond	17.20	26.25	10.53	8.45	34.48	20.76	27.67
Rochester	16.70	23.61	10.84	10.08	27.08	21.61	n/a
Sacramento	21.17	33.16	12.64	9.88	37.87	20.97	33.02
Salt Lake City	16.88	26.06	10.05	7.78	29.10	21.64	29.53
San Antonio	16.22	25.35	9.28	7.97	32.45	21.09	42.23
San Diego	19.26	31.92	11.37	8.69	32.95	22.27	n/a
San Francisco	25.05	38.64	15.48	8.98	35.03	22.65	72.33
San Jose	24.84	42.28	15.55	9.93	36.78	22.07	n/a
Savannah	14.48	24.19	8.37	8.14	30.05	20.53	n/a
Scottsdale	18.89	27.38	10.73	7.90	30.04	21.55	43.89
Seattle	20.88	32.89	12.72	10.08	30.00	21.85	38.04
Sioux Falls	14.39	24.27	10.43	8.95	28.21	20.92	n/a
Springfield	13.55	n/a	8.86	8.72	31.86	20.47	n/a
Saint Louis	16.90	24.46	10.21	10.74	26.52	21.71	39.86
Saint Paul	18.31	30.01	12.88	10.30	26.72	21.55	45.63
Saint Petersburg	17.02	25.46	10.46	8.42	33.57	21.43	33.10
Stamford	23.78	28.69	12.98	9.74	35.76	22.46	38.56
Tampa	17.02	25.46	10.46	8.42	33.57	21.43	33.10
Thousand Oaks	19.36	30.84	11.58	8.68	32.77	21.79	40.37
Tucson	18.16	26.29	10.22	7.62	31.08	21.82	n/a
Tulsa	15.17	22.79	9.38	8.37	30.09	21.27	n/a
Virginia Beach	16.17	24.98	9.43	8.54	31.74	21.99	49.97
Washington	20.52	29.90	12.15	9.57	32.75	21.89	34.17
Wichita	15.77	20.71	10.19	9.26	28.25	21.49	21.56

Notes: Wage data is for May 2005 and covers the Metropolitan Statistical Area - see Appendix A for areas included; n/a not available
Source: Bureau of Labor Statistics, May 2005 Metro Area Occupational Employment and Wage Estimates

Average Hourly Wages: Occupations R - T

MSA[1]	Retail Salespersons	Sales Reps., Except Tech./Scien.	Sales Reps., Tech./Scien.	Secretaries, Exc. Leg./ Med./Exec.	Security Guards	Surgeons	Teacher Assistants
Albuquerque	10.75	20.29	29.20	12.62	10.57	84.95	8.00
Alexandria	11.28	28.25	38.55	18.19	12.83	71.19	11.80
Anchorage	12.86	22.63	29.37	16.58	12.17	n/a	n/a
Ann Arbor	10.67	30.83	39.82	15.81	n/a	88.38	11.60
Athens	9.97	27.11	n/a	11.70	8.67	92.08	7.70
Atlanta	11.15	27.49	39.80	13.12	10.71	84.60	8.20
Austin	10.84	25.59	27.55	12.92	10.59	90.43	10.40
Baltimore	10.74	27.72	30.58	14.72	11.46	82.70	10.50
Baton Rouge	9.96	23.46	31.08	11.63	11.13	83.40	7.30
Bellevue	13.05	29.26	35.04	16.18	13.55	87.88	12.60
Birmingham	10.98	24.73	31.11	12.49	8.79	91.95	7.50
Boise City	11.68	20.33	22.88	10.70	10.77	93.76	7.90
Boston	11.64	32.14	39.08	17.46	11.99	80.78	11.90
Boulder	12.91	31.90	43.28	15.21	13.03	n/a	11.10
Buffalo	10.13	24.98	36.09	12.77	9.20	n/a	10.50
Cary	10.63	27.34	31.33	13.54	10.95	n/a	9.40
Cedar Rapids	11.52	24.74	29.72	12.78	10.59	n/a	9.60
Charleston	10.95	22.55	23.72	12.48	10.72	n/a	8.10
Charlotte	11.28	24.24	30.88	13.07	11.26	93.82	9.10
Chattanooga	11.39	23.35	28.70	11.65	n/a	80.09	8.30
Chicago	11.30	29.01	31.78	13.88	11.55	73.72	10.10
Cincinnati	10.69	29.86	33.62	13.61	10.67	93.46	10.10
Cleveland	11.47	29.42	31.88	13.89	10.60	87.71	11.90
Colorado Spgs.	12.50	23.84	34.51	14.75	11.74	91.63	10.40
Columbia	11.65	24.89	25.69	12.03	10.85	90.55	7.60
Columbus	10.98	29.36	30.45	14.06	11.28	88.89	11.70
Dallas	11.32	28.05	37.01	12.78	11.42	92.06	9.10
Denver	11.95	27.86	34.36	15.11	12.32	82.67	11.40
Des Moines	11.18	24.55	32.79	13.51	11.88	83.87	8.10
Durham	10.26	21.55	35.49	14.17	10.71	90.06	9.30
Edison	11.84	32.08	38.84	16.21	11.00	87.66	10.50
El Paso	8.81	22.73	19.29	10.66	8.77	n/a	9.30
Eugene	12.12	22.19	30.49	13.40	10.24	n/a	11.30
Fort Collins	10.72	27.86	31.20	14.61	10.33	n/a	10.80
Fort Lauderdale	13.03	26.20	32.02	12.65	9.55	80.46	n/a
Fort Wayne	10.74	22.81	24.98	12.46	9.10	93.05	9.30
Fort Worth	11.20	26.60	30.99	11.83	11.53	92.80	7.70
Grand Rapids	11.29	27.43	26.90	13.29	10.37	83.09	11.80
Green Bay	12.63	29.72	30.01	13.22	10.39	n/a	11.70
Greensboro	11.26	24.84	29.36	12.58	9.47	n/a	9.30
Honolulu	10.57	20.29	29.03	15.28	10.05	n/a	9.60
Houston	11.16	26.62	34.42	12.31	10.70	76.35	8.20
Huntsville	10.00	27.95	25.70	12.53	9.36	n/a	6.50
Indianapolis	11.15	27.76	34.27	13.48	10.61	92.78	10.40
Irvine	12.12	30.12	35.34	15.95	10.50	78.92	13.90
Jacksonville	11.42	23.20	24.47	12.70	9.05	83.08	n/a
Kansas City	11.41	28.78	35.80	13.12	13.02	90.65	8.70
Knoxville	10.78	23.53	30.87	11.24	8.69	86.16	8.80
Las Vegas	11.82	26.49	37.54	14.63	11.09	92.53	11.40
Lexington	10.66	24.27	35.39	12.02	9.79	n/a	n/a
Lincoln	11.47	22.35	25.00	12.14	11.65	n/a	10.00
Los Angeles	11.91	25.59	32.45	15.49	10.74	80.56	12.80
Louisville	10.40	25.49	34.71	11.98	10.28	92.81	9.70
Madison	11.15	26.36	30.02	13.97	9.24	n/a	11.90
Manchester	11.14	25.39	37.00	13.69	11.56	n/a	10.70

Table continued on next page.

MSA[1]	Retail Salespersons	Sales Reps., Except Tech./Scien.	Sales Reps., Tech./Scien.	Secretaries, Exc. Leg./ Med./Exec.	Security Guards	Surgeons	Teacher Assistants
Memphis	11.09	28.89	35.60	12.93	9.06	n/a	8.10
Miami	11.76	22.47	32.25	12.41	9.16	68.33	n/a
Milwaukee	11.50	30.19	34.95	13.93	11.65	88.75	12.50
Minneapolis	11.06	30.85	38.69	16.30	12.65	92.32	10.70
Naperville	11.30	29.01	31.78	13.88	11.55	73.72	10.10
Nashville	11.25	30.03	30.15	12.33	10.30	89.43	9.00
New York	11.77	32.67	39.05	15.84	11.62	85.96	11.10
Norfolk	10.14	25.48	33.07	14.29	10.43	n/a	10.00
Oklahoma City	10.78	23.49	24.45	11.36	11.43	n/a	7.60
Omaha	11.41	24.56	30.88	13.23	11.99	87.81	9.30
Orlando	11.41	24.82	28.87	12.04	9.85	90.36	9.60
Overland Park	11.41	28.78	35.80	13.12	13.02	90.65	8.70
Philadelphia	11.38	28.36	35.62	14.64	10.13	64.86	9.40
Phoenix	11.77	22.88	25.55	12.69	10.33	78.30	9.60
Pittsburgh	10.37	26.80	32.52	12.07	9.92	91.35	9.40
Plano	11.32	28.05	37.01	12.78	11.42	92.06	9.10
Portland	12.39	26.87	34.11	14.41	11.09	63.57	12.10
Providence	11.04	26.55	31.09	14.97	11.51	92.44	11.80
Provo	10.21	22.27	27.46	11.31	11.81	n/a	9.80
Raleigh	10.63	27.34	31.33	13.54	10.95	n/a	9.40
Reno	11.84	24.26	35.56	14.54	10.56	n/a	n/a
Richmond	11.06	28.54	31.59	14.78	13.00	92.92	10.40
Rochester	11.47	26.97	32.61	12.76	11.49	91.04	9.10
Sacramento	11.67	26.58	30.99	14.79	10.17	72.51	11.10
Salt Lake City	11.44	25.12	32.91	12.93	11.53	n/a	8.90
San Antonio	9.89	23.47	40.83	11.73	9.64	89.60	8.70
San Diego	11.93	28.88	36.22	15.37	10.57	83.08	12.20
San Francisco	12.71	32.32	36.86	18.45	12.49	70.48	15.00
San Jose	13.34	34.28	42.51	17.73	13.33	69.44	13.80
Savannah	10.63	23.09	27.73	11.91	9.50	87.65	n/a
Scottsdale	11.77	22.88	25.55	12.69	10.33	78.30	9.60
Seattle	13.05	29.26	35.04	16.18	13.55	87.88	12.60
Sioux Falls	10.35	21.99	29.51	10.71	11.01	85.13	n/a
Springfield	11.48	22.95	26.32	11.46	9.62	n/a	7.30
Saint Louis	11.77	29.20	34.63	13.73	11.34	86.57	9.20
Saint Paul	11.06	30.85	38.69	16.30	12.65	92.32	10.70
Saint Petersburg	11.75	25.03	30.59	12.11	9.57	93.52	9.10
Stamford	13.28	41.42	43.38	17.79	11.73	84.54	n/a
Tampa	11.75	25.03	30.59	12.11	9.57	93.52	9.10
Thousand Oaks	11.62	30.57	40.08	17.57	n/a	86.85	11.70
Tucson	12.15	25.27	24.51	12.49	9.39	n/a	10.30
Tulsa	10.39	25.63	27.99	10.95	10.94	93.25	7.70
Virginia Beach	10.14	25.48	33.07	14.29	10.43	n/a	10.00
Washington	11.28	28.25	38.55	18.19	12.83	71.19	11.80
Wichita	11.03	24.82	28.03	12.10	12.11	n/a	9.80

Notes: Wage data is for May 2005 and covers the Metropolitan Statistical Area - see Appendix A for areas included; hourly wages for teacher assistants were calculated by the editors from annual wage data assuming a 40 hour work week; n/a not available
Source: Bureau of Labor Statistics, May 2005 Metro Area Occupational Employment and Wage Estimates

Average Hourly Wages: Occupations T - Z

MSA[1]	Teachers, Elementary School	Teachers, Secondary School	Tele-marketers	Truck Driv., Heavy/ Trac. Trail.	Truck Drivers, Light	Waiters/ Waitresses
Albuquerque	17.80	21.10	12.57	17.53	12.54	6.66
Alexandria	27.70	30.90	13.72	17.55	13.53	8.31
Anchorage	n/a	n/a	8.33	20.61	14.52	10.53
Ann Arbor	n/a	n/a	11.94	20.30	16.26	7.90
Athens	n/a	21.80	n/a	15.54	10.73	7.12
Atlanta	22.40	23.40	11.78	18.12	13.62	6.72
Austin	20.60	21.10	10.56	15.08	13.89	6.65
Baltimore	23.20	22.70	11.35	17.72	12.46	7.24
Baton Rouge	18.10	18.70	15.09	14.93	12.28	6.80
Bellevue	21.70	22.50	13.95	18.91	14.32	10.78
Birmingham	18.50	19.50	8.27	16.45	12.90	6.73
Boise City	n/a	n/a	9.42	14.22	11.02	6.57
Boston	27.40	26.80	15.57	19.54	15.09	11.01
Boulder	23.40	24.00	13.16	16.71	12.99	8.28
Buffalo	23.90	26.50	12.56	16.64	11.75	8.38
Cary	18.80	19.80	11.34	15.91	13.63	8.02
Cedar Rapids	16.60	16.50	10.00	12.69	12.35	7.15
Charleston	19.60	19.80	9.37	15.43	12.17	6.49
Charlotte	18.40	19.00	11.96	17.86	13.85	7.35
Chattanooga	19.50	21.00	10.67	15.60	12.57	6.46
Chicago	24.90	29.00	12.45	20.01	15.56	8.22
Cincinnati	22.00	23.40	11.20	17.67	12.93	7.22
Cleveland	25.50	25.10	11.95	19.21	14.33	7.29
Colorado Spgs.	19.30	19.10	n/a	17.15	12.61	7.29
Columbia	19.20	20.40	8.43	17.39	13.42	6.35
Columbus	23.80	23.00	8.56	17.92	14.03	6.75
Dallas	21.40	22.00	11.89	18.70	12.22	7.28
Denver	22.50	23.30	11.66	18.47	14.12	8.32
Des Moines	17.80	18.60	10.83	17.53	14.11	7.44
Durham	18.40	19.80	13.52	15.62	13.19	8.77
Edison	26.10	26.60	13.43	18.93	15.08	8.82
El Paso	20.50	20.40	n/a	14.73	12.39	6.56
Eugene	22.00	21.30	9.25	14.63	12.98	8.88
Fort Collins	22.10	21.60	10.57	20.05	12.09	7.38
Fort Lauderdale	n/a	n/a	12.14	15.55	12.81	7.84
Fort Wayne	21.50	21.50	13.15	19.06	15.38	7.05
Fort Worth	20.80	22.30	10.03	16.84	12.87	6.92
Grand Rapids	n/a	n/a	10.03	17.69	15.06	6.73
Green Bay	23.40	22.00	n/a	19.14	11.53	7.25
Greensboro	17.80	18.80	12.02	17.14	14.73	6.96
Honolulu	20.40	22.50	n/a	18.05	12.80	10.25
Houston	21.50	22.60	10.56	16.25	13.24	7.26
Huntsville	19.50	21.30	n/a	16.25	13.43	6.13
Indianapolis	20.60	21.50	11.03	18.86	12.93	7.00
Irvine	26.70	30.80	13.36	18.16	12.31	8.25
Jacksonville	18.30	n/a	11.93	18.20	15.41	7.37
Kansas City	18.60	18.80	10.97	18.71	12.38	6.92
Knoxville	18.50	n/a	11.53	15.63	12.15	6.84
Las Vegas	16.90	19.40	10.29	18.22	13.49	8.48
Lexington	19.60	20.40	n/a	17.51	13.23	6.54
Lincoln	19.80	19.90	10.28	n/a	11.83	6.68
Los Angeles	24.70	27.40	12.12	17.08	12.62	8.34
Louisville	19.90	20.40	11.90	15.93	13.45	6.73
Madison	20.60	21.00	9.79	18.34	12.91	8.44
Manchester	22.00	n/a	n/a	17.99	14.96	8.54

Table continued on next page.

MSA[1]	Teachers, Elementary School	Teachers, Secondary School	Tele-marketers	Truck Driv., Heavy/ Trac. Trail.	Truck Drivers, Light	Waiters/ Waitresses
Memphis	21.30	21.90	8.86	17.24	12.55	6.82
Miami	n/a	n/a	10.76	16.14	13.41	8.52
Milwaukee	24.10	25.20	13.93	18.18	12.28	7.68
Minneapolis	22.40	22.30	12.26	18.97	13.93	8.47
Naperville	24.90	29.00	12.45	20.01	15.56	8.22
Nashville	19.40	20.80	10.97	17.52	11.68	7.10
New York	36.00	38.50	14.42	19.84	15.42	11.62
Norfolk	24.60	25.20	9.62	15.36	10.04	7.80
Oklahoma City	16.20	17.30	8.01	15.91	11.54	6.68
Omaha	21.10	20.40	10.34	n/a	14.32	7.44
Orlando	19.40	20.30	10.05	15.51	14.29	8.36
Overland Park	18.60	18.80	10.97	18.71	12.38	6.92
Philadelphia	24.30	26.50	13.65	18.42	13.89	7.75
Phoenix	16.00	18.80	10.14	18.29	13.12	7.79
Pittsburgh	25.00	22.10	12.36	16.27	11.67	7.28
Plano	21.40	22.00	11.89	18.70	12.22	7.28
Portland	22.30	22.90	10.88	17.39	13.66	9.90
Providence	25.90	26.10	11.32	17.99	13.64	8.98
Provo	17.30	19.20	11.86	17.28	11.15	7.55
Raleigh	18.80	19.80	11.34	15.91	13.63	8.02
Reno	n/a	n/a	11.09	19.19	15.07	6.93
Richmond	23.90	24.10	n/a	17.51	11.31	7.96
Rochester	24.30	28.00	9.88	15.65	12.50	8.69
Sacramento	24.90	25.70	13.12	18.09	13.19	7.99
Salt Lake City	20.20	20.30	8.28	18.74	12.51	8.53
San Antonio	21.20	22.30	9.07	14.57	11.12	6.86
San Diego	28.80	27.90	12.92	18.31	12.66	8.40
San Francisco	26.30	29.00	14.63	19.82	15.06	9.04
San Jose	25.70	29.30	13.63	20.21	14.52	8.18
Savannah	n/a	21.40	n/a	16.80	12.07	6.46
Scottsdale	16.00	18.80	10.14	18.29	13.12	7.79
Seattle	21.70	22.50	13.95	18.91	14.32	10.78
Sioux Falls	n/a	n/a	9.52	15.80	11.91	6.61
Springfield	16.60	18.40	9.71	19.01	13.20	6.37
Saint Louis	20.80	22.10	11.80	18.04	13.74	7.70
Saint Paul	22.40	22.30	12.26	18.97	13.93	8.47
Saint Petersburg	21.40	22.50	10.69	15.27	11.30	8.00
Stamford	27.30	28.50	12.54	19.14	13.32	9.75
Tampa	21.40	22.50	10.69	15.27	11.30	8.00
Thousand Oaks	25.50	28.30	n/a	17.62	12.76	8.17
Tucson	19.80	19.00	9.53	17.63	13.34	6.30
Tulsa	16.70	17.70	10.02	16.85	10.97	6.97
Virginia Beach	24.60	25.20	9.62	15.36	10.04	7.80
Washington	27.70	30.90	13.72	17.55	13.53	8.31
Wichita	18.30	18.50	9.61	15.83	10.71	7.11

Notes: Wage data is for May 2005 and covers the Metropolitan Statistical Area - see Appendix A for areas included; hourly wages for elementary and secondary school teachers were calculated by the editors from annual wage data assuming a 40 hour work week; n/a not available

Source: Bureau of Labor Statistics, May 2005 Metro Area Occupational Employment and Wage Estimates

Means of Transportation to Work: City

City	Car/Truck/Van		Public Transportation			Bicycle	Walked	Other Means	Worked at Home
	Drove Alone	Car-pooled	Bus	Subway	Railroad				
Albuquerque	77.7	12.5	1.6	0.0	0.0	1.1	2.7	0.7	3.6
Alexandria	62.8	13.2	6.4	9.3	0.1	0.5	3.0	1.2	3.5
Anchorage	74.4	14.6	1.8	0.0	0.0	0.5	2.7	2.3	3.7
Ann Arbor	62.6	7.9	6.3	0.0	0.0	2.3	15.8	0.7	4.4
Athens	75.0	14.4	2.2	0.0	0.0	0.9	4.3	0.8	2.3
Atlanta	64.0	12.4	11.5	3.0	0.2	0.3	3.5	1.3	3.8
Austin	73.6	13.9	4.3	0.0	0.0	0.9	2.5	1.3	3.4
Baltimore	54.7	15.2	16.2	1.4	0.8	0.3	7.1	1.9	2.3
Baton Rouge	77.6	12.4	2.2	0.0	0.0	0.8	3.8	0.8	2.4
Bellevue	74.0	10.6	6.6	0.0	0.0	0.4	2.6	0.6	5.1
Birmingham	76.9	15.8	2.4	0.0	0.0	0.1	2.4	1.1	1.2
Boise City	79.9	10.3	1.1	0.0	0.0	1.7	2.3	0.8	4.0
Boston	41.5	9.2	12.2	16.3	1.0	1.0	13.0	3.4	2.4
Boulder	59.8	8.7	8.3	0.0	0.0	6.9	9.0	0.8	6.5
Buffalo	65.4	14.4	11.3	0.6	0.0	0.4	5.3	0.9	1.7
Cary	84.2	8.9	0.2	0.0	0.0	0.1	0.8	0.8	4.9
Cedar Rapids	82.3	10.7	1.1	0.0	0.0	0.4	2.5	0.7	2.3
Charleston	73.5	11.6	2.7	0.0	0.0	1.2	6.6	1.6	2.7
Charlotte	77.8	13.4	3.0	0.0	0.0	0.1	1.5	1.0	3.2
Chattanooga	79.5	13.3	1.6	0.0	0.0	0.2	2.2	1.2	2.1
Chicago	50.1	14.5	13.7	9.7	1.7	0.5	5.7	1.8	2.4
Cincinnati	69.5	11.4	9.8	0.0	0.0	0.2	5.5	1.0	2.6
Cleveland	67.8	13.5	11.1	0.5	0.1	0.2	4.0	1.1	1.6
Colorado Spgs.	79.6	11.7	1.0	0.0	0.0	0.5	2.5	0.9	3.8
Columbia	65.4	11.3	3.7	0.0	0.0	0.4	13.4	3.1	2.7
Columbus	79.0	10.8	3.8	0.0	0.0	0.3	3.2	0.6	2.3
Dallas	70.8	17.8	5.0	0.2	0.2	0.1	1.9	1.2	2.8
Denver	68.3	13.5	8.0	0.1	0.1	1.0	4.3	1.1	3.7
Des Moines	78.9	12.5	2.3	0.0	0.0	0.2	2.9	0.7	2.3
Durham	72.7	17.0	3.3	0.0	0.0	0.4	3.1	0.8	2.7
Edison	74.6	10.2	0.8	0.4	9.5	0.1	2.0	0.6	1.8
El Paso	76.5	15.8	2.2	0.0	0.0	0.1	2.0	1.1	2.2
Eugene	66.8	11.2	4.8	0.0	0.0	5.5	6.1	0.8	4.7
Ft. Collins	75.3	10.2	1.4	0.0	0.0	4.4	3.6	0.6	4.3
Ft. Lauderdale	75.2	11.3	4.4	0.0	0.2	1.1	2.4	1.7	3.8
Ft. Wayne	81.8	12.2	1.1	0.0	0.0	0.2	2.1	0.6	2.0
Ft. Worth	77.0	16.7	1.3	0.0	0.0	0.1	1.7	1.0	2.1
Grand Rapids	76.5	12.8	2.1	0.0	0.0	0.4	4.0	1.4	2.7
Green Bay	82.9	10.3	1.3	0.0	0.0	0.4	2.8	0.5	1.8
Greensboro	79.3	12.8	1.3	0.0	0.0	0.3	2.4	1.2	2.7
Honolulu	57.7	18.1	11.3	0.0	0.0	1.2	6.6	2.0	3.1
Houston	71.8	15.9	5.7	0.0	0.0	0.5	2.3	1.4	2.3
Huntsville	83.8	11.2	0.3	0.0	0.0	0.2	1.5	0.7	2.4
Indianapolis	80.0	12.3	2.3	0.0	0.0	0.2	2.0	0.7	2.5
Irvine	79.2	8.2	0.5	0.0	0.1	1.1	4.8	0.7	5.4
Jacksonville	79.2	13.4	1.7	0.0	0.0	0.4	1.8	1.5	1.9
Kansas City	78.7	11.8	3.6	0.0	0.0	0.1	2.3	0.8	2.6
Knoxville	80.5	10.5	1.3	0.0	0.0	0.3	4.2	0.8	2.3
Las Vegas	73.8	15.1	4.7	0.0	0.0	0.4	2.2	1.5	2.4
Lexington	79.9	11.2	1.2	0.0	0.0	0.6	4.0	0.6	2.5
Lincoln	80.7	10.1	1.2	0.0	0.0	1.0	3.4	0.8	2.9
Los Angeles	65.7	14.7	9.7	0.2	0.1	0.6	3.6	1.2	4.1
Louisville	73.5	12.6	6.7	0.0	0.0	0.4	4.1	0.8	1.8
Madison	65.7	9.6	6.9	0.0	0.0	3.2	10.7	0.8	3.1

Table continued on next page.

City	Car/Truck/Van		Public Transportation			Bicycle	Walked	Other Means	Worked at Home
	Drove Alone	Car-pooled	Bus	Subway	Railroad				
Manchester	81.0	11.9	1.1	0.0	0.0	0.2	2.9	0.7	2.2
Memphis	76.6	15.7	2.8	0.0	0.0	0.1	1.9	1.1	1.7
Miami	64.5	16.3	10.0	0.7	0.3	0.6	3.7	1.9	2.1
Milwaukee	68.8	13.6	10.0	0.0	0.0	0.3	4.7	0.8	1.7
Minneapolis	61.6	11.3	14.4	0.0	0.0	1.9	6.6	0.8	3.4
Naperville	78.6	4.9	0.1	0.1	8.7	0.1	1.4	0.6	5.6
Nashville	78.5	13.5	1.7	0.0	0.0	0.1	2.4	0.8	3.0
New York	24.9	8.0	11.4	37.6	1.6	0.5	10.4	2.8	2.9
Norfolk	66.8	14.2	4.2	0.0	0.0	0.5	6.8	3.7	3.8
Oklahoma City	80.4	13.1	0.7	0.0	0.0	0.1	1.6	1.3	2.7
Omaha	81.3	11.1	1.8	0.0	0.0	0.1	2.4	0.7	2.6
Orlando	78.9	11.2	3.9	0.0	0.0	0.6	1.9	1.3	2.2
Overland Park	86.8	6.5	0.4	0.0	0.0	0.1	0.7	0.5	5.1
Philadelphia	49.2	12.8	17.4	4.8	2.3	0.9	9.1	1.6	1.9
Phoenix	71.7	17.4	3.0	0.0	0.0	0.9	2.2	1.5	3.3
Pittsburgh	54.8	11.4	19.7	0.2	0.0	0.4	9.8	1.3	2.4
Plano	83.1	8.9	1.0	0.0	0.0	0.1	1.2	0.9	4.7
Portland	63.7	11.9	11.3	0.4	0.2	1.8	5.2	1.3	4.3
Providence	60.5	15.4	5.9	0.1	1.0	1.0	12.2	1.3	2.5
Provo	63.2	15.5	1.7	0.0	0.0	1.9	12.8	0.6	4.1
Raleigh	78.7	11.5	2.0	0.0	0.0	0.3	2.9	1.3	3.3
Reno	72.6	14.3	4.1	0.0	0.0	0.9	4.4	1.2	2.4
Richmond	70.6	12.6	8.1	0.0	0.0	1.1	4.4	0.9	2.3
Rochester	69.6	12.1	7.7	0.0	0.0	0.5	6.5	1.2	2.3
Sacramento	71.0	16.3	3.8	0.1	0.1	1.4	2.8	1.5	2.9
St. Louis	68.9	13.6	9.9	0.3	0.1	0.3	4.0	1.1	1.7
St. Paul	69.2	12.4	8.5	0.0	0.0	0.7	5.4	0.9	3.0
St. Petersburg	78.1	11.8	2.5	0.0	0.0	0.9	2.2	1.4	3.1
Salt Lake City	69.3	13.9	5.9	0.0	0.1	1.5	4.9	1.1	3.2
San Antonio	75.6	15.2	3.7	0.0	0.0	0.2	2.2	1.0	2.2
San Diego	74.0	12.2	3.8	0.0	0.0	0.7	3.6	1.5	4.0
San Francisco	40.5	10.8	21.4	6.0	0.6	2.0	9.4	4.8	4.6
San Jose	76.4	14.1	3.3	0.1	0.4	0.6	1.4	1.3	2.5
Savannah	70.8	15.3	4.5	0.0	0.0	1.1	4.3	1.6	2.4
Scottsdale	80.3	7.6	0.9	0.0	0.0	0.8	1.7	1.5	7.1
Seattle	56.5	11.2	17.3	0.0	0.0	1.9	7.4	1.1	4.6
Sioux Falls	84.3	9.2	0.7	0.0	0.0	0.2	2.3	0.6	2.7
Springfield	80.1	11.0	1.0	0.0	0.0	0.6	3.6	1.1	2.6
Stamford	70.1	10.6	4.6	0.1	5.7	0.2	3.7	1.2	3.8
Tampa	76.6	13.7	2.6	0.0	0.0	0.9	2.3	1.3	2.6
Thousand Oaks	80.6	9.5	0.4	0.0	0.2	0.5	2.1	0.8	5.9
Tucson	71.0	15.7	3.4	0.0	0.0	2.2	3.4	1.5	2.9
Tulsa	79.4	13.1	1.1	0.0	0.0	0.2	2.2	1.0	3.1
Virginia Beach	82.0	10.8	0.7	0.0	0.0	0.3	2.0	1.4	2.8
Washington	38.4	11.0	14.6	17.4	0.2	1.2	11.8	1.6	3.8
Wichita	84.4	10.2	0.7	0.0	0.0	0.2	1.4	0.8	2.3
U.S.	75.7	12.2	2.5	1.5	0.5	0.4	2.9	1.0	3.3

Note: Figures shown are percentages and cover workers 16 years of age and older
Source: Census 2000, Summary File 3

Means of Transportation to Work: Metro Area

MSA[1]	Car/Truck/Van		Public Transportation			Bicycle	Walked	Other Means	Worked at Home
	Drove Alone	Car-pooled	Bus	Subway	Railroad				
Albuquerque	77.7	13.3	1.2	0.0	0.0	0.8	2.3	0.9	3.9
Alexandria	67.8	13.4	4.0	6.5	0.4	0.3	3.0	0.9	3.7
Anchorage	74.4	14.6	1.8	0.0	0.0	0.5	2.7	2.3	3.7
Ann Arbor	80.1	8.5	1.8	0.0	0.0	0.6	4.9	0.6	3.4
Athens	77.2	14.1	1.5	0.0	0.0	0.6	3.2	0.8	2.6
Atlanta	77.0	13.6	2.4	1.0	0.1	0.1	1.3	1.1	3.5
Austin	76.5	13.7	2.5	0.0	0.0	0.6	2.1	1.1	3.6
Baltimore	75.5	11.5	4.3	0.9	0.6	0.2	2.9	1.0	3.2
Baton Rouge	82.0	11.7	1.0	0.0	0.0	0.3	2.0	0.8	2.2
Bellevue	70.4	12.6	7.8	0.0	0.0	0.7	3.2	0.9	4.4
Birmingham	83.5	11.7	0.7	0.0	0.0	0.1	1.2	0.7	2.2
Boise City	79.9	11.4	0.6	0.0	0.0	1.0	2.2	0.8	4.1
Boston	68.2	8.2	4.1	6.5	2.1	0.5	5.3	1.6	3.4
Boulder	70.8	10.4	4.8	0.0	0.0	2.8	4.1	0.7	6.4
Buffalo	81.7	9.4	3.1	0.2	0.0	0.2	2.7	0.6	2.1
Cary	78.5	12.9	1.5	0.0	0.0	0.4	2.3	0.9	3.5
Cedar Rapids	82.3	10.3	0.9	0.0	0.0	0.3	2.6	0.6	2.9
Charleston	78.1	13.0	1.1	0.0	0.0	0.5	3.5	1.6	2.2
Charlotte	80.9	12.9	1.3	0.0	0.0	0.1	1.2	0.8	2.8
Chattanooga	82.7	12.2	0.6	0.0	0.0	0.1	1.5	0.8	2.1
Chicago	69.3	11.0	5.0	3.6	3.5	0.3	3.2	1.1	3.0
Cincinnati	80.8	10.2	3.2	0.0	0.0	0.1	2.2	0.7	2.8
Cleveland	81.3	9.0	3.5	0.3	0.1	0.2	2.2	0.8	2.7
Colorado Spgs.	78.0	12.0	0.8	0.0	0.0	0.4	3.7	0.9	4.0
Columbia	79.3	11.9	1.1	0.0	0.0	0.1	3.7	1.3	2.5
Columbus	82.0	9.6	2.2	0.0	0.0	0.2	2.4	0.6	3.0
Dallas	77.6	14.3	2.1	0.1	0.1	0.1	1.5	1.0	3.1
Denver	76.1	11.6	4.4	0.1	0.0	0.4	2.1	0.8	4.5
Des Moines	81.8	10.7	1.5	0.0	0.0	0.2	2.1	0.5	3.3
Durham	78.5	12.9	1.5	0.0	0.0	0.4	2.3	0.9	3.5
Edison	77.2	9.9	2.7	0.2	3.6	0.2	2.4	0.9	2.9
El Paso	75.9	16.2	2.2	0.0	0.0	0.1	2.2	1.3	2.1
Eugene	71.6	12.2	3.2	0.0	0.0	3.0	4.2	0.6	5.1
Ft. Collins	77.4	11.0	0.8	0.0	0.0	2.4	2.7	0.6	5.1
Ft. Lauderdale	80.0	12.0	1.9	0.0	0.1	0.5	1.3	1.1	2.9
Ft. Wayne	83.6	10.4	0.5	0.0	0.0	0.2	1.8	0.6	2.8
Ft. Worth	81.2	13.3	0.4	0.0	0.0	0.1	1.4	0.9	2.7
Grand Rapids	84.0	9.2	0.7	0.0	0.0	0.2	2.1	0.7	3.1
Green Bay	84.7	8.4	0.8	0.0	0.0	0.2	2.8	0.5	2.5
Greensboro	81.2	13.1	0.7	0.0	0.0	0.1	1.6	0.9	2.4
Honolulu	61.4	19.4	8.1	0.0	0.0	0.9	5.6	1.7	2.9
Houston	76.6	14.4	3.4	0.0	0.0	0.3	1.6	1.2	2.5
Huntsville	83.9	11.5	0.2	0.0	0.0	0.1	1.3	0.7	2.3
Indianapolis	82.8	10.5	1.2	0.0	0.0	0.2	1.7	0.7	2.9
Irvine	76.5	13.3	2.5	0.0	0.2	0.8	2.0	0.9	3.7
Jacksonville	80.3	12.6	1.3	0.0	0.0	0.5	1.7	1.4	2.3
Kansas City	82.8	10.4	1.2	0.0	0.0	0.1	1.4	0.7	3.4
Knoxville	84.2	10.0	0.4	0.0	0.0	0.1	1.9	0.6	2.7
Las Vegas	74.5	15.0	3.9	0.0	0.0	0.5	2.4	1.3	2.3
Lexington	79.8	11.9	0.7	0.0	0.0	0.4	3.9	0.6	2.7
Lincoln	80.6	10.2	1.1	0.0	0.0	0.9	3.2	0.7	3.2
Los Angeles	70.4	15.1	6.1	0.2	0.2	0.6	2.9	1.1	3.5
Louisville	82.0	10.9	2.1	0.0	0.0	0.2	1.7	0.7	2.4
Madison	74.1	9.5	4.0	0.0	0.0	1.7	6.2	0.6	3.8

Table continued on next page.

| MSA[1] | Car/Truck/Van | | Public Transportation | | | Bicycle | Walked | Other Means | Worked at Home |
	Drove Alone	Car-pooled	Bus	Subway	Railroad				
Manchester	82.5	10.2	0.8	0.0	0.0	0.2	2.4	0.8	3.0
Memphis	80.9	13.0	1.6	0.0	0.0	0.1	1.3	0.9	2.2
Miami	73.8	14.6	4.3	0.6	0.2	0.5	2.2	1.2	2.7
Milwaukee	79.7	9.9	4.1	0.0	0.0	0.2	2.9	0.6	2.6
Minneapolis	78.3	10.0	4.4	0.0	0.0	0.4	2.4	0.6	3.8
Naperville	69.3	11.0	5.0	3.6	3.5	0.3	3.2	1.1	3.0
Nashville	80.7	12.8	0.9	0.0	0.0	0.1	1.5	0.8	3.2
New York	31.4	8.3	10.4	31.8	3.0	0.4	9.3	2.5	3.0
Norfolk	78.9	12.1	1.7	0.0	0.0	0.3	2.7	1.6	2.7
Oklahoma City	81.8	12.0	0.5	0.0	0.0	0.2	1.7	1.0	2.8
Omaha	82.9	10.5	1.1	0.0	0.0	0.1	1.9	0.6	2.9
Orlando	80.6	12.1	1.6	0.0	0.0	0.4	1.3	1.2	2.9
Overland Park	82.8	10.4	1.2	0.0	0.0	0.1	1.4	0.7	3.4
Philadelphia	72.3	10.1	5.5	1.8	2.1	0.3	4.1	0.9	2.9
Phoenix	74.6	15.3	1.8	0.0	0.0	0.9	2.1	1.4	3.7
Pittsburgh	77.4	9.7	5.6	0.1	0.0	0.1	3.6	1.0	2.4
Plano	77.6	14.3	2.1	0.1	0.1	0.1	1.5	1.0	3.1
Portland	73.1	11.5	5.3	0.4	0.2	0.8	3.0	1.1	4.6
Providence	80.7	10.6	1.7	0.0	0.6	0.2	3.3	0.8	2.1
Provo	72.5	14.9	1.3	0.0	0.0	0.8	4.9	0.5	5.0
Raleigh	78.5	12.9	1.5	0.0	0.0	0.4	2.3	0.9	3.5
Reno	75.3	13.8	3.0	0.0	0.0	0.7	3.2	1.2	2.9
Richmond	82.0	10.4	1.9	0.0	0.0	0.3	1.9	0.8	2.6
Rochester	81.8	9.1	1.9	0.0	0.0	0.2	3.5	0.6	2.9
Sacramento	76.2	13.6	2.0	0.1	0.2	0.7	2.0	1.2	4.1
St. Louis	82.6	9.9	2.1	0.2	0.0	0.1	1.6	0.7	2.8
St. Paul	78.3	10.0	4.4	0.0	0.0	0.4	2.4	0.6	3.8
St. Petersburg	79.7	12.4	1.2	0.0	0.0	0.6	1.7	1.2	3.1
Salt Lake City	77.2	13.1	2.5	0.1	0.2	0.4	1.8	0.9	3.8
San Antonio	76.2	14.7	2.8	0.0	0.0	0.1	2.4	1.2	2.6
San Diego	73.9	13.0	2.9	0.0	0.2	0.6	3.4	1.6	4.4
San Francisco	56.5	11.6	12.3	3.7	0.9	1.4	5.6	3.1	4.8
San Jose	77.3	12.2	2.6	0.1	0.6	1.2	1.8	1.0	3.1
Savannah	77.8	13.4	2.3	0.0	0.0	0.5	2.4	1.1	2.4
Scottsdale	74.6	15.3	1.8	0.0	0.0	0.9	2.1	1.4	3.7
Seattle	70.4	12.6	7.8	0.0	0.0	0.7	3.2	0.9	4.4
Sioux Falls	83.7	9.3	0.6	0.0	0.0	0.2	2.3	0.6	3.4
Springfield	81.8	10.8	0.5	0.0	0.0	0.3	2.1	0.9	3.6
Stamford	69.1	8.4	2.6	0.2	9.9	0.1	2.9	0.9	5.9
Tampa	79.7	12.4	1.2	0.0	0.0	0.6	1.7	1.2	3.1
Thousand Oaks	75.9	15.1	0.7	0.0	0.2	0.7	2.1	1.0	4.2
Tucson	73.8	14.7	2.4	0.0	0.0	1.4	2.6	1.4	3.6
Tulsa	81.1	12.6	0.6	0.0	0.0	0.1	1.6	0.8	3.1
Virginia Beach	78.9	12.1	1.7	0.0	0.0	0.3	2.7	1.6	2.7
Washington	67.8	13.4	4.0	6.5	0.4	0.3	3.0	0.9	3.7
Wichita	84.6	9.7	0.5	0.0	0.0	0.2	1.6	0.7	2.7
U.S.	75.7	12.2	2.5	1.5	0.5	0.4	2.9	1.0	3.3

Note: Figures shown are percentages and cover workers 16 years of age and older; (1) Metropolitan Statistical Area - see Appendix A for areas included
Source: Census 2000, Summary File 3

Travel Time to Work: City

City	Less Than 15 Minutes	15 to 29 Minutes	30 to 44 Minutes	45 to 59 Minutes	60 Minutes or More
Albuquerque	29.4	50.5	14.3	2.5	3.3
Alexandria	16.0	34.4	27.7	13.9	7.9
Anchorage	36.4	46.7	11.2	2.3	3.4
Ann Arbor	44.1	35.8	11.0	5.6	3.5
Athens	46.0	38.5	7.2	3.3	5.0
Atlanta	22.3	40.2	20.9	6.7	10.0
Austin	27.0	45.2	19.1	4.5	4.2
Baltimore	17.9	38.9	22.8	8.0	12.4
Baton Rouge	32.7	46.4	13.6	3.2	4.1
Bellevue	28.8	44.5	20.2	3.8	2.7
Birmingham	23.7	48.1	19.8	3.7	4.6
Boise City	38.4	48.2	9.3	1.6	2.4
Boston	17.6	34.7	28.6	10.7	8.3
Boulder	45.5	35.1	10.1	4.8	4.5
Buffalo	32.2	46.4	13.4	3.5	4.6
Cary	23.7	47.6	21.5	4.1	3.1
Cedar Rapids	49.2	39.3	7.2	1.8	2.4
Charleston	34.8	44.1	14.7	3.2	3.2
Charlotte	22.3	42.7	23.6	6.4	5.0
Chattanooga	33.4	48.0	13.1	2.4	3.2
Chicago	13.2	27.9	28.3	14.7	16.0
Cincinnati	26.0	46.5	18.3	4.7	4.6
Cleveland	22.0	45.0	20.7	5.6	6.7
Colorado Spgs.	31.4	48.0	13.7	2.8	4.1
Columbia	45.1	39.6	9.8	2.0	3.5
Columbus	26.1	49.1	17.7	3.6	3.4
Dallas	20.3	39.7	25.4	7.8	6.8
Denver	24.6	41.8	22.0	6.1	5.5
Des Moines	38.9	47.7	9.4	2.0	2.0
Durham	30.9	46.3	15.7	3.9	3.2
Edison	21.6	31.8	19.4	9.6	17.6
El Paso	25.4	47.9	19.5	3.7	3.4
Eugene	48.2	40.4	6.4	1.8	3.2
Ft. Collins	45.6	38.9	7.8	2.8	4.9
Ft. Lauderdale	29.7	38.5	19.7	5.8	6.4
Ft. Wayne	32.7	48.9	12.3	2.7	3.3
Ft. Worth	24.6	42.7	19.9	6.5	6.2
Grand Rapids	36.1	47.1	10.7	2.7	3.3
Green Bay	45.4	42.9	6.4	2.5	2.8
Greensboro	34.3	45.6	13.3	2.8	3.9
Honolulu	26.2	42.2	21.6	5.4	4.6
Houston	20.8	37.3	26.1	8.3	7.5
Huntsville	38.0	47.4	10.4	1.9	2.3
Indianapolis	25.8	47.6	18.8	3.8	4.0
Irvine	29.9	44.5	14.1	5.0	6.5
Jacksonville	21.2	43.7	24.1	6.4	4.6
Kansas City	27.7	46.8	18.8	3.4	3.3
Knoxville	33.2	46.8	13.8	3.2	3.1
Las Vegas	19.7	45.9	24.5	4.6	5.3
Lexington	34.2	48.0	12.2	2.8	2.8
Lincoln	43.9	45.0	6.3	1.7	3.1
Los Angeles	18.9	35.6	25.7	9.3	10.6
Louisville	32.6	48.8	12.4	2.5	3.7
Madison	39.0	45.7	10.3	2.3	2.7
Manchester	39.2	37.2	13.0	4.0	6.6

Table continued on next page.

City	Less Than 15 Minutes	15 to 29 Minutes	30 to 44 Minutes	45 to 59 Minutes	60 Minutes or More
Memphis	24.0	48.2	20.0	3.9	3.9
Miami	20.0	38.9	24.8	6.6	9.6
Milwaukee	27.8	46.2	17.0	4.4	4.6
Minneapolis	26.1	50.0	17.0	3.3	3.7
Naperville	21.3	29.8	19.0	11.8	17.9
Nashville	24.2	46.1	21.1	4.6	3.9
New York	11.6	22.9	25.3	15.7	24.5
Norfolk	31.3	44.4	16.6	3.6	4.2
Oklahoma City	30.0	49.2	15.1	2.5	3.2
Omaha	36.0	50.3	9.9	1.4	2.5
Orlando	21.7	43.7	23.6	5.9	5.1
Overland Park	34.2	46.2	15.1	2.4	2.0
Philadelphia	17.2	32.2	26.2	11.7	12.7
Phoenix	22.5	38.4	25.1	7.9	6.1
Pittsburgh	27.1	43.5	19.6	5.1	4.8
Plano	21.1	36.0	25.3	10.4	7.2
Portland	25.5	45.6	19.2	4.9	4.8
Providence	40.6	38.7	11.6	3.8	5.3
Provo	55.7	32.3	5.6	3.1	3.3
Raleigh	29.2	44.5	18.1	4.3	3.9
Reno	41.4	45.8	7.0	2.4	3.4
Richmond	28.7	47.6	15.1	3.7	4.8
Rochester	36.7	46.3	10.6	2.3	4.0
Sacramento	27.5	45.6	17.3	4.4	5.3
St. Louis	25.0	43.8	19.4	5.7	6.1
St. Paul	30.0	46.8	16.0	3.9	3.2
St. Petersburg	30.8	41.1	17.9	5.7	4.5
Salt Lake City	38.1	43.7	12.2	2.8	3.2
San Antonio	23.2	46.0	21.7	4.5	4.5
San Diego	25.1	46.2	19.8	4.4	4.6
San Francisco	14.9	35.0	27.4	11.3	11.4
San Jose	16.8	39.9	26.4	9.3	7.5
Savannah	34.2	41.9	15.3	4.0	4.6
Scottsdale	26.9	39.4	22.6	7.1	4.1
Seattle	21.9	42.7	23.7	6.6	5.1
Sioux Falls	48.1	45.1	3.4	0.9	2.5
Springfield	45.3	43.2	7.2	1.7	2.7
Stamford	33.9	39.2	13.1	3.7	10.0
Tampa	30.1	41.6	18.5	4.9	4.9
Thousand Oaks	33.9	32.4	15.0	7.0	11.6
Tucson	30.2	45.5	16.9	3.4	4.0
Tulsa	36.1	49.5	9.8	1.8	2.8
Virginia Beach	23.1	46.6	21.5	5.0	3.8
Washington	15.7	36.6	28.5	10.0	9.2
Wichita	35.7	51.4	9.3	1.4	2.3
U.S.	29.4	36.1	19.1	7.4	8.0

Note: Figures are percentages and include workers 16 years old and over
Source: Census 2000, Summary File 3

Travel Time to Work: Metro Area

MSA[1]	Less Than 15 Minutes	15 to 29 Minutes	30 to 44 Minutes	45 to 59 Minutes	60 Minutes or More
Albuquerque	26.9	45.1	18.4	5.3	4.3
Alexandria	16.3	30.3	25.7	13.7	14.0
Anchorage	36.4	46.7	11.2	2.3	3.4
Ann Arbor	29.7	35.1	19.3	9.3	6.5
Athens	37.6	41.7	10.9	4.0	5.8
Atlanta	18.3	32.4	25.1	12.4	11.8
Austin	24.5	38.6	22.5	8.3	6.1
Baltimore	19.9	35.5	23.8	10.1	10.6
Baton Rouge	24.9	41.2	21.2	7.0	5.7
Bellevue	22.1	36.9	23.9	9.2	7.9
Birmingham	21.4	40.4	24.4	8.1	5.6
Boise City	33.1	45.9	15.3	3.1	2.7
Boston	23.3	31.4	24.3	11.0	10.1
Boulder	34.2	37.9	16.4	6.2	5.2
Buffalo	32.5	43.8	16.8	3.7	3.2
Cary	24.7	40.4	22.3	7.4	5.2
Cedar Rapids	43.6	42.0	9.9	2.1	2.5
Charleston	26.7	39.6	21.5	6.9	5.2
Charlotte	23.8	38.7	23.0	8.5	6.1
Chattanooga	25.4	44.3	20.6	5.6	4.1
Chicago	20.4	29.8	24.0	12.2	13.6
Cincinnati	24.9	41.4	22.0	6.8	4.8
Cleveland	26.3	40.5	21.8	6.7	4.7
Colorado Spgs.	30.4	44.9	16.0	3.9	4.8
Columbia	27.7	42.5	20.2	5.0	4.6
Columbus	26.6	44.1	19.6	5.5	4.2
Dallas	22.0	35.0	24.7	10.4	7.9
Denver	21.6	38.4	25.3	8.6	6.1
Des Moines	35.2	46.7	13.0	2.8	2.3
Durham	24.7	40.4	22.3	7.4	5.2
Edison	23.3	31.2	20.7	10.3	14.6
El Paso	25.7	45.9	20.5	4.3	3.5
Eugene	39.8	41.1	11.6	3.0	4.5
Ft. Collins	38.7	37.7	12.8	4.7	6.0
Ft. Lauderdale	20.9	36.5	26.0	9.5	7.1
Ft. Wayne	34.5	43.3	14.8	3.9	3.5
Ft. Worth	23.4	37.8	22.6	8.8	7.5
Grand Rapids	34.9	42.9	14.8	4.1	3.3
Green Bay	43.0	44.2	7.7	2.3	2.7
Greensboro	30.0	44.3	16.9	4.6	4.3
Honolulu	23.5	34.3	23.8	9.5	8.9
Houston	20.3	33.8	25.5	11.1	9.3
Huntsville	28.7	44.5	19.1	4.6	3.0
Indianapolis	27.0	40.8	21.6	6.1	4.4
Irvine	22.1	37.6	23.8	8.0	8.5
Jacksonville	22.2	38.8	24.4	8.7	5.9
Kansas City	28.0	41.9	20.6	5.8	3.7
Knoxville	26.6	43.0	21.0	5.5	3.9
Las Vegas	24.4	45.2	20.9	4.2	5.2
Lexington	35.1	40.6	15.7	4.8	3.8
Lincoln	41.7	45.4	7.9	1.9	3.1
Los Angeles	20.7	34.6	24.1	9.7	10.9
Louisville	26.3	46.0	19.8	4.2	3.6
Madison	35.1	45.2	14.0	2.7	3.0
Manchester	31.3	38.0	16.5	5.7	8.5

Table continued on next page.

MSA[1]	Less Than 15 Minutes	15 to 29 Minutes	30 to 44 Minutes	45 to 59 Minutes	60 Minutes or More
Memphis	22.9	43.4	23.2	6.1	4.4
Miami	17.4	34.2	27.2	10.9	10.3
Milwaukee	29.7	43.7	18.3	4.6	3.7
Minneapolis	26.4	41.4	21.3	6.7	4.2
Naperville	20.4	29.8	24.0	12.2	13.6
Nashville	23.9	38.6	23.0	8.8	5.7
New York	13.3	24.0	24.4	14.9	23.5
Norfolk	26.0	42.9	20.3	5.9	4.9
Oklahoma City	30.2	43.4	18.3	4.4	3.7
Omaha	33.9	48.4	12.9	2.2	2.5
Orlando	21.1	38.1	25.8	8.8	6.2
Overland Park	28.0	41.9	20.6	5.8	3.7
Philadelphia	23.7	33.2	22.6	10.4	10.0
Phoenix	23.8	37.0	24.1	8.8	6.3
Pittsburgh	28.3	36.4	20.2	8.3	6.9
Plano	22.0	35.0	24.7	10.4	7.9
Portland	26.3	40.0	21.1	7.0	5.5
Providence	32.2	39.9	16.3	5.4	6.2
Provo	45.0	35.9	10.7	4.2	4.2
Raleigh	24.7	40.4	22.3	7.4	5.2
Reno	35.2	49.2	9.5	2.7	3.3
Richmond	24.0	44.3	21.4	5.8	4.5
Rochester	33.6	42.7	15.6	4.6	3.6
Sacramento	25.2	39.3	21.7	6.9	6.8
St. Louis	24.9	37.9	23.1	8.4	5.6
St. Paul	26.4	41.4	21.3	6.7	4.2
St. Petersburg	26.4	37.8	21.3	8.1	6.5
Salt Lake City	29.2	43.6	18.0	4.8	4.4
San Antonio	23.9	43.2	22.2	5.7	5.0
San Diego	24.7	40.7	21.6	6.7	6.4
San Francisco	19.1	34.5	25.0	10.8	10.6
San Jose	21.1	40.8	23.4	7.9	6.8
Savannah	26.2	41.1	21.6	6.1	5.0
Scottsdale	23.8	37.0	24.1	8.8	6.3
Seattle	22.1	36.9	23.9	9.2	7.9
Sioux Falls	42.6	46.3	7.1	1.3	2.7
Springfield	33.5	43.7	15.5	3.7	3.6
Stamford	31.7	33.8	13.7	5.1	15.7
Tampa	26.4	37.8	21.3	8.1	6.5
Thousand Oaks	30.2	36.2	18.4	6.8	8.4
Tucson	25.8	42.4	21.5	5.6	4.7
Tulsa	30.7	44.9	16.6	4.3	3.5
Virginia Beach	26.0	42.9	20.3	5.9	4.9
Washington	16.3	30.3	25.7	13.7	14.0
Wichita	34.8	47.3	13.2	2.4	2.3
U.S.	29.4	36.1	19.1	7.4	8.0

Note: Figures are percentages and include workers 16 years old and over; (1) Metropolitan Statistical Area - see Appendix A for areas included
Source: Census 2000, Summary File 3

2004 Presidential Election Results

City	Area Covered	Bush	Kerry	Nader	Other
Albuquerque	Bernalillo County	47.3	51.5	0.6	0.6
Alexandria	Alexandria city	32.3	66.8	0.0	0.9
Anchorage	Anchorage - Region II	62.3	34.7	1.5	1.4
Ann Arbor	Washtenaw County	35.5	63.5	0.5	0.5
Athens	Clarke County	40.4	58.3	0.3	0.9
Atlanta	Fulton County	40.0	59.4	0.1	0.6
Austin	Travis County	42.0	56.0	0.4	1.6
Baltimore	Baltimore city	17.0	82.0	0.5	0.6
Baton Rouge	East Baton Rouge Parish	54.4	44.8	0.3	0.4
Bellevue	King County	33.6	64.9	0.7	0.8
Birmingham	Jefferson County	54.2	45.2	0.3	0.3
Boise City	Ada County	61.0	37.7	0.2	1.0
Boston	Suffolk County	22.8	75.9	0.2	1.1
Boulder	Boulder County	32.4	66.3	0.6	0.7
Buffalo	Erie County	41.4	56.4	1.9	0.2
Cary	Wake County	50.8	48.7	0.1	0.4
Cedar Rapids	Linn County	44.6	54.6	0.4	0.4
Charleston	Charleston County	51.6	46.8	0.4	1.2
Charlotte	Mecklenburg County	48.0	51.6	0.1	0.3
Chattanooga	Hamilton County	57.4	41.8	0.4	0.4
Chicago	Cook County	29.1	70.2	0.0	0.6
Cincinnati	Hamilton County	52.5	47.1	0.0	0.4
Cleveland	Cuyahoga County	32.9	66.6	0.0	0.5
Colorado Spgs.	El Paso County	66.7	32.1	0.5	0.6
Columbia	Richland County	42.0	57.0	0.3	0.6
Columbus	Franklin County	45.1	54.4	0.0	0.5
Dallas	Dallas County	50.3	49.0	0.1	0.6
Denver	Denver County	29.3	69.6	0.6	0.6
Des Moines	Polk County	47.3	51.9	0.3	0.5
Durham	Durham County	31.6	68.0	0.1	0.4
Edison	Middlesex County	42.8	56.3	0.6	0.3
El Paso	El Paso County	43.2	56.1	0.2	0.5
Eugene	Lane County	40.4	58.0	0.0	1.7
Fort Collins	Larimer County	51.8	46.6	0.7	0.9
Fort Lauderdale	Broward County	34.6	64.2	0.5	0.6
Fort Wayne	Allen County	63.3	36.0	0.1	0.6
Fort Worth	Tarrant County	62.4	37.0	0.1	0.5
Grand Rapids	Kent County	58.9	40.2	0.5	0.5
Green Bay	Brown County	54.5	44.6	0.5	0.4
Greensboro	Guilford County	49.3	50.2	0.1	0.4
Honolulu	Honolulu County	48.3	51.1	0.0	0.6
Houston	Harris County	54.8	44.6	0.2	0.5
Huntsville	Madison County	58.9	40.2	0.4	0.5
Indianapolis	Marion County	48.6	50.6	0.0	0.7
Irvine	Orange County	59.7	39.0	0.2	1.1
Jacksonville	Duval County	57.8	41.6	0.3	0.3
Kansas City	Jackson County	41.3	58.1	0.0	0.6
Knoxville	Knox County	62.1	37.0	0.4	0.5
Las Vegas	Clark County	46.8	51.7	0.6	1.0
Lexington	Fayette County	52.9	46.2	0.6	0.3
Lincoln	Lancaster County	56.0	42.4	0.8	0.8
Los Angeles	Los Angeles County	35.6	63.1	0.1	1.2
Louisville	Jefferson County	48.8	50.4	0.5	0.2
Madison	Dane County	33.0	66.0	0.5	0.5
Manchester	Hillsborough County	51.0	48.2	0.6	0.2
Memphis	Shelby County	41.9	57.5	0.3	0.3

Table continued on next page.

City	Area Covered	Bush	Kerry	Nader	Other
Miami	Miami-Dade County	46.6	52.9	0.3	0.2
Milwaukee	Milwaukee County	37.4	61.7	0.5	0.4
Minneapolis	Hennepin County	39.4	59.3	0.6	0.6
Naperville	Du Page County	54.4	44.8	0.2	0.7
Nashville	Davidson County	44.5	54.8	0.4	0.3
New York	New York City	24.1	75.0	0.8	0.2
Norfolk	Norfolk city	37.4	61.7	0.0	0.9
Oklahoma City	Oklahoma County	64.2	35.8	0.0	0.0
Omaha	Douglas County	58.3	40.2	0.7	0.7
Orlando	Orange County	49.6	49.8	0.3	0.3
Overland Park	Johnson County	61.1	37.8	0.5	0.5
Philadelphia	Philadelphia County	19.3	80.4	0.0	0.3
Phoenix	Maricopa County	57.0	42.3	0.1	0.6
Pittsburgh	Allegheny County	42.1	57.2	0.0	0.7
Plano	Collin County	71.2	28.1	0.1	0.6
Portland	Multnomah County	27.1	71.6	0.0	1.3
Providence	Providence County	35.6	62.6	1.0	0.8
Provo	Utah County	86.0	11.6	0.9	1.5
Raleigh	Wake County	50.8	48.7	0.1	0.4
Reno	Washoe County	51.3	47.0	0.6	1.1
Richmond	City of Richmond	29.1	70.2	0.0	0.7
Rochester	Monroe County	47.7	50.6	1.5	0.3
Sacramento	Sacramento County	49.3	49.5	0.2	1.0
Saint Louis	Saint Louis city	19.2	80.3	0.0	0.5
Saint Paul	Ramsey County	35.6	63.0	0.6	0.7
Saint Petersburg	Pinellas County	49.6	49.5	0.5	0.4
Salt Lake City	Salt Lake County	59.6	37.5	1.7	1.2
San Antonio	Bexar County	54.8	44.4	0.2	0.6
San Diego	San Diego County	52.5	46.4	0.1	1.0
San Francisco	San Francisco County	15.2	83.0	0.4	1.3
San Jose	Santa Clara County	34.6	63.9	0.2	1.2
Savannah	Chatham County	49.7	49.9	0.1	0.4
Scottsdale	Maricopa County	57.0	42.3	0.1	0.6
Seattle	King County	33.6	64.9	0.7	0.8
Sioux Falls	Minnehaha County	56.9	41.6	1.0	0.4
Springfield	Greene County	62.2	37.2	0.0	0.6
Stamford	Fairfield County	47.3	51.4	0.6	0.8
Tampa	Hillsborough County	53.0	46.2	0.4	0.3
Thousand oaks, CA	Ventura County	51.2	47.5	0.1	1.2
Tucson	Pima County	46.6	52.6	0.1	0.7
Tulsa	Tulsa County	64.4	35.6	0.0	0.0
Virginia Beach	City of Virginia Beach	59.1	40.2	0.0	0.7
Washington	District of Columbia	9.3	89.2	0.7	0.8
Wichita	Sedgwick County	62.1	36.5	0.8	0.6
U.S.	U.S.	50.7	48.3	0.4	0.6

Note: Results are percentages and may not add to 100% due to rounding
Source: Dave Leip's Atlas of U.S. Presidential Elections, www.uselectionatlas.org

House Price Index (HPI)

Metro Area[1]	National Ranking[3]	Quarterly Change (%)	One-Year Change (%)	Five-Year Change (%)
Albuquerque	19	1.69	14.46	55.12
Alexandria[2]	105	0.30	6.31	103.66
Anchorage	76	0.31	8.15	57.34
Ann Arbor	251	2.11	0.38	18.67
Athens	145	-0.19	4.96	28.02
Atlanta	160	1.56	4.28	23.67
Austin	54	1.47	9.12	21.52
Baltimore	55	0.99	9.11	97.64
Baton Rouge	43	1.19	10.18	34.77
Bellevue[2]	18	1.52	14.50	64.62
Birmingham	113	0.92	5.92	31.54
Boise City	5	1.02	17.94	67.66
Boston[2]	254	0.41	0.08	49.96
Boulder	223	0.14	1.68	15.17
Buffalo	159	2.41	4.29	29.20
Cary	93	1.85	7.38	22.21
Cedar Rapids	214	-0.21	2.03	17.02
Charleston	46	1.79	10.11	61.13
Charlotte	56	2.85	9.09	24.92
Chattanooga	137	0.34	5.27	30.70
Chicago[2]	106	0.86	6.30	49.28
Cincinnati	197	1.08	2.82	20.51
Cleveland	261	-0.22	-0.30	14.39
Colorado Spgs.	153	1.19	4.70	27.95
Columbia	103	2.94	6.36	29.19
Columbus	234	0.07	1.24	18.50
Dallas[2]	167	0.62	4.11	17.07
Denver	231	0.30	1.32	16.75
Des Moines	203	0.59	2.42	24.42
Durham	111	1.65	6.09	24.44
Edison[2]	161	-0.09	4.27	80.08
El Paso	6	1.59	16.52	47.71
Eugene	37	0.31	11.38	65.51
Fort Collins	240	-1.19	0.85	17.10
Fort Lauderdale[2]	92	-1.14	7.41	123.15
Fort Wayne	238	1.63	0.97	11.91
Fort Worth[2]	146	1.32	4.90	18.78
Grand Rapids	259	0.69	-0.18	16.77
Green Bay	211	1.67	2.18	24.36
Greensboro	173	-0.01	3.61	17.37
Honolulu	89	-2.04	7.49	101.08
Houston	99	1.16	6.73	25.48
Huntsville	81	0.66	7.90	28.00
Indianapolis	237	-0.12	0.98	14.22
Irvine[2]	124	-0.28	5.53	115.47
Jacksonville	26	1.75	12.68	82.62
Kansas City	180	1.66	3.46	25.35
Knoxville	70	1.25	8.45	36.41
Las Vegas	133	0.06	5.36	102.61
Lexington	162	0.17	4.24	28.08
Lincoln	212	-0.76	2.12	19.41
Los Angeles[2]	53	0.13	9.20	131.90
Louisville	179	0.40	3.47	22.13
Madison	166	0.79	4.12	39.14
Manchester	218	1.32	1.96	51.79

Table continued on next page.

Metro Area[1]	National Ranking[3]	Quarterly Change (%)	One-Year Change (%)	Five-Year Change (%)
Memphis	122	2.22	5.70	19.93
Miami[2]	13	1.86	15.30	134.62
Milwaukee	148	1.47	4.84	42.50
Minneapolis	217	0.77	1.96	42.07
Naperville[2]	106	0.86	6.30	49.28
Nashville	52	1.66	9.32	32.88
New York[2]	110	0.70	6.14	78.30
Norfolk	42	1.09	10.34	98.63
Oklahoma City	163	0.79	4.23	29.59
Omaha	210	0.09	2.25	20.44
Orlando	33	0.58	11.67	102.65
Overland Park	180	1.66	3.46	25.35
Philadelphia[2]	98	1.08	6.74	72.13
Phoenix	60	0.78	9.04	99.79
Pittsburgh	171	1.38	3.75	25.67
Plano[2]	167	0.62	4.11	17.07
Portland	22	1.51	13.45	66.86
Providence	204	0.51	2.39	76.31
Provo	3	4.18	19.92	38.59
Raleigh	93	1.85	7.38	22.21
Reno	265	-0.33	-0.84	96.03
Richmond	38	2.16	10.84	66.53
Rochester	241	-0.21	0.82	20.35
Sacramento	274	-1.20	-2.41	88.66
Saint Louis	154	1.20	4.68	37.67
Saint Paul	217	0.77	1.96	42.07
Saint Petersburg	36	1.64	11.42	98.64
Salt Lake City	4	3.34	19.76	48.98
San Antonio	84	1.29	7.71	34.96
San Diego	260	-0.90	-0.18	92.27
San Francisco[2]	213	-1.19	2.06	58.13
San Jose	164	0.14	4.19	56.73
Savannah	29	4.48	12.00	59.97
Scottsdale	60	0.78	9.04	99.79
Seattle[2]	18	1.52	14.50	64.62
Sioux Falls	194	0.18	2.99	24.63
Springfield	121	1.12	5.74	29.47
Stamford	209	-1.13	2.30	57.79
Tampa	36	1.64	11.42	98.64
Thousand Oaks	192	-0.80	3.04	107.93
Tucson	66	1.14	8.60	84.91
Tulsa	177	2.15	3.57	17.83
Virginia Beach	42	1.09	10.34	98.63
Washington[2]	105	0.30	6.31	103.66
Wichita	199	0.90	2.71	17.79
U.S.[4]	-	1.12	5.87	55.21

Note: The HPI is a weighted repeat sales index. It measures average price changes in repeat sales or refinancings on the same properties. This information is obtained by reviewing repeat mortgage transactions on single-family properties whose mortgages have been purchased or securitized by Fannie Mae or Freddie Mac in January 1975; (1) figures cover the Metropolitan Statistical Area (MSA) unless noted otherwise - see Appendix B for areas included; (2) Metropolitan Division - see Appendix B for areas included; (3) Rankings are based on annual percentage change, for all MSAs containing at least 15,000 transactions over the last 10 years and ranges from 1 to 275; (4) figures based on a weighted division average; all figures are for the period ended December 31, 2006; n/a not available
Source: Office of Federal Housing Enterprise Oversight, House Price Index, March 1, 2007

Housing: Year Structure Built: City

City	1990 -2000	1980 -1989	1970 -1979	1960 -1969	1950 -1959	1940 -1949	Before 1940	Median Year
Albuquerque	20.1	18.4	23.5	13.8	14.6	5.9	3.6	1975
Alexandria	11.0	11.9	22.0	18.7	13.4	12.6	10.4	1967
Anchorage	12.6	28.2	34.7	13.8	7.9	2.1	0.6	1977
Ann Arbor	9.3	10.4	19.9	23.1	14.1	6.4	16.8	1966
Athens	23.1	17.9	23.0	15.8	8.9	4.2	7.0	1976
Atlanta	11.2	9.2	13.8	20.6	17.8	10.7	16.8	1962
Austin	21.4	26.4	23.9	12.0	8.4	4.1	3.8	1979
Baltimore	2.7	4.5	7.7	11.3	18.9	18.0	36.8	1947
Baton Rouge	7.3	14.9	25.5	20.1	16.6	9.4	6.2	1969
Bellevue	17.2	18.9	25.7	23.6	11.8	1.5	1.2	1975
Birmingham	5.4	9.2	16.6	19.7	21.6	12.8	14.7	1960
Boise City	26.6	15.4	23.8	10.0	10.3	5.9	8.0	1977
Boston	3.4	5.8	8.3	9.9	9.7	9.5	53.5	1939
Boulder	12.3	16.9	26.7	21.3	11.7	2.8	8.3	1972
Buffalo	2.5	1.9	3.7	5.9	13.0	15.4	57.7	1939
Cary	54.1	24.9	13.8	4.5	1.5	0.4	0.8	1991
Cedar Rapids	14.8	7.8	17.3	16.1	15.7	6.2	22.1	1964
Charleston	16.3	17.3	15.9	14.7	10.3	7.6	17.9	1970
Charlotte	26.9	20.7	17.0	15.3	11.1	5.0	4.0	1979
Chattanooga	10.4	12.5	17.3	19.3	16.9	10.2	13.4	1965
Chicago	4.5	4.0	8.5	13.6	17.1	14.3	38.0	1948
Cincinnati	2.8	4.0	9.7	14.8	16.0	12.7	40.0	1948
Cleveland	2.5	1.9	5.3	9.0	15.2	16.9	49.3	1940
Colorado Spgs.	20.1	22.5	24.3	13.4	9.2	2.8	7.7	1977
Columbia	13.5	10.5	15.1	18.3	19.3	11.0	12.3	1964
Columbus	18.5	14.6	17.6	15.3	12.7	7.2	14.1	1970
Dallas	12.5	20.2	20.1	18.5	16.0	7.0	5.7	1971
Denver	7.5	8.9	16.3	14.3	18.6	9.9	24.5	1958
Des Moines	7.3	7.7	13.6	12.0	17.4	11.4	30.6	1955
Durham	24.9	20.4	16.6	13.9	10.9	6.5	6.7	1977
Edison	11.8	24.0	15.4	19.7	18.5	5.7	5.0	1971
El Paso	17.7	18.7	22.5	15.7	14.2	5.1	6.0	1974
Eugene	21.7	8.8	24.9	16.9	12.7	7.5	7.6	1972
Ft. Collins	30.4	20.2	25.0	10.2	5.2	2.3	6.6	1980
Ft. Lauderdale	4.6	6.9	24.9	29.0	25.1	6.2	3.2	1965
Ft. Wayne	7.6	10.0	17.6	19.4	15.7	9.5	20.1	1962
Ft. Worth	16.0	19.9	13.8	13.9	17.5	10.1	8.8	1970
Grand Rapids	6.4	7.0	8.6	12.6	16.6	12.3	36.5	1951
Green Bay	12.2	13.9	18.1	13.3	16.2	9.1	17.2	1966
Greensboro	20.7	17.9	18.4	16.1	13.4	6.4	7.1	1974
Honolulu	9.2	10.4	28.5	24.8	14.4	6.5	6.1	1969
Houston	11.1	17.8	27.8	18.6	13.4	6.1	5.2	1972
Huntsville	14.0	19.7	20.1	28.0	11.7	3.1	3.4	1972
Indianapolis	13.9	13.6	15.6	16.8	14.6	8.9	16.6	1966
Irvine	26.1	32.4	35.5	4.9	0.6	0.4	0.1	1983
Jacksonville	20.3	20.9	17.0	15.1	14.2	7.0	5.4	1975
Kansas City	10.2	9.9	13.7	16.2	17.1	10.3	22.6	1960
Knoxville	11.2	11.1	17.8	17.4	18.6	11.0	12.9	1964
Las Vegas	48.9	19.0	13.2	10.9	5.9	1.6	0.6	1989
Lexington	20.6	17.0	20.4	16.7	11.8	5.3	8.2	1974
Lincoln	20.0	12.8	19.2	12.9	14.4	4.9	15.9	1971
Los Angeles	6.2	11.1	15.0	17.5	20.5	13.0	16.7	1960
Louisville	4.5	4.1	9.2	14.1	19.2	15.9	32.9	1951
Madison	16.1	11.9	17.6	16.4	13.6	7.5	16.9	1967
Manchester	8.5	14.4	11.3	9.1	12.9	9.1	34.7	1955

Table continued on next page.

City	1990 -2000	1980 -1989	1970 -1979	1960 -1969	1950 -1959	1940 -1949	Before 1940	Median Year
Memphis	7.6	12.8	20.4	21.2	19.4	9.4	9.0	1966
Miami	7.7	11.3	19.0	17.9	19.2	14.2	10.6	1963
Milwaukee	2.8	3.9	10.0	13.8	22.8	13.1	33.6	1951
Minneapolis	2.5	6.2	9.5	9.4	11.9	9.6	51.0	1939
Naperville	36.1	32.1	16.9	6.5	4.1	0.9	3.3	1986
Nashville	16.0	19.2	19.7	16.8	13.7	6.8	7.8	1973
New York	4.1	4.9	8.6	15.2	15.8	15.3	36.0	1949
Norfolk	7.5	11.0	13.2	15.7	23.7	14.1	14.8	1959
Oklahoma City	12.4	18.9	19.7	16.4	15.0	8.3	9.3	1970
Omaha	9.2	9.8	19.2	18.2	14.0	7.6	21.9	1964
Orlando	23.5	22.4	17.7	12.2	13.7	5.3	5.1	1978
Overland Park	26.9	24.9	15.4	19.6	9.4	2.4	1.5	1981
Philadelphia	2.1	3.3	6.9	12.3	17.0	16.6	41.7	1945
Phoenix	20.0	22.9	25.1	13.4	12.5	3.6	2.5	1977
Pittsburgh	2.3	3.6	6.3	9.5	14.0	13.6	50.7	1939
Plano	47.2	27.6	19.7	4.2	0.7	0.3	0.2	1989
Portland	10.1	5.7	12.1	11.5	14.9	11.5	34.0	1953
Providence	4.8	6.6	9.7	8.8	11.5	11.6	47.0	1943
Provo	24.0	12.7	24.1	13.9	10.5	6.7	8.2	1974
Raleigh	26.3	26.6	17.6	12.9	7.7	4.1	4.9	1981
Reno	25.0	18.4	22.8	14.8	9.3	5.0	4.6	1977
Richmond	3.5	7.3	14.3	15.8	17.8	13.1	28.3	1955
Rochester	1.9	2.6	7.9	8.4	11.8	12.0	55.4	1939
Sacramento	9.0	18.4	18.4	15.2	15.5	10.6	13.0	1967
St. Louis	2.2	3.7	4.6	10.3	14.5	16.1	48.5	1941
St. Paul	2.2	6.5	10.8	11.1	14.9	9.4	45.1	1945
St. Petersburg	5.3	10.5	20.2	19.9	26.2	7.6	10.2	1963
Salt Lake City	7.3	7.6	13.6	11.1	15.2	13.4	31.7	1953
San Antonio	16.4	22.0	19.9	14.9	13.2	6.9	6.6	1974
San Diego	12.3	19.6	24.0	15.4	14.8	6.2	7.7	1972
San Francisco	4.1	4.9	7.0	9.4	11.4	13.2	49.9	1940
San Jose	12.3	14.8	28.5	23.6	11.9	3.8	5.2	1972
Savannah	6.9	12.6	17.0	16.3	19.5	11.4	16.4	1962
Scottsdale	37.7	23.8	19.1	12.4	6.1	0.4	0.3	1985
Seattle	9.9	9.0	9.9	12.2	14.0	12.5	32.4	1954
Sioux Falls	22.1	16.4	18.9	10.1	12.1	6.9	13.4	1974
Springfield	14.9	14.3	20.8	15.2	13.1	8.0	13.8	1970
Stamford	8.8	12.7	15.1	18.7	18.1	9.2	17.4	1963
Tampa	13.5	14.9	15.5	16.0	20.2	9.2	10.8	1966
Thousand Oaks	14.7	20.0	37.1	22.9	4.4	0.6	0.4	1976
Tucson	15.6	19.1	25.4	14.4	15.5	5.7	4.3	1974
Tulsa	8.9	16.3	21.9	17.2	17.8	8.4	9.5	1968
Virginia Beach	17.3	32.5	24.9	14.5	7.7	1.8	1.3	1980
Washington	2.6	5.0	8.7	15.3	17.0	16.8	34.6	1949
Wichita	15.1	13.8	14.3	10.6	22.5	11.6	12.0	1964
U.S.	17.0	15.8	18.5	13.7	12.7	7.3	15.0	1971

Note: Figures are percentages except for Median Year
Source: Census 2000, Summary File 3

Housing: Year Structure Built: Metro Area

MSA[1]	1990 -2000	1980 -1989	1970 -1979	1960 -1969	1950 -1959	1940 -1949	Before 1940	Median Year
Albuquerque	24.3	20.3	22.0	12.5	12.0	5.1	3.7	1978
Alexandria	18.2	18.9	18.1	16.1	11.9	7.2	9.6	1973
Anchorage	12.6	28.2	34.7	13.8	7.9	2.1	0.6	1977
Ann Arbor	22.3	11.9	20.0	13.6	11.1	5.6	15.5	1972
Athens	26.4	20.1	21.7	13.8	7.4	3.8	6.9	1978
Atlanta	30.8	24.6	18.0	12.0	7.1	3.2	4.2	1982
Austin	30.2	27.4	20.2	8.8	6.2	3.3	3.9	1983
Baltimore	15.2	14.9	15.6	13.3	15.0	9.9	16.0	1967
Baton Rouge	19.2	21.5	24.5	14.9	10.6	5.3	4.0	1976
Bellevue	19.8	18.4	17.7	14.7	10.3	6.4	12.5	1973
Birmingham	20.3	15.4	19.6	15.3	13.3	7.7	8.4	1973
Boise City	33.8	12.7	24.4	8.3	8.1	5.2	7.4	1979
Boston	7.0	9.3	11.6	11.8	13.2	8.5	38.6	1952
Boulder	24.6	17.7	26.4	14.4	7.7	2.5	6.9	1977
Buffalo	7.4	6.3	10.8	12.1	19.4	12.6	31.5	1953
Cary	33.2	22.9	16.6	10.9	7.2	3.9	5.4	1983
Cedar Rapids	18.4	8.3	17.9	15.6	13.7	5.4	20.7	1967
Charleston	22.0	23.9	21.3	14.0	8.4	4.7	5.9	1978
Charlotte	30.3	19.1	16.3	12.7	10.0	5.5	6.1	1980
Chattanooga	18.1	15.8	20.0	15.9	13.4	8.0	8.9	1972
Chicago	12.4	9.8	15.9	15.3	16.1	9.2	21.3	1962
Cincinnati	16.4	11.2	14.8	13.9	14.5	8.3	20.9	1965
Cleveland	9.2	6.9	13.5	15.1	19.5	11.3	24.6	1957
Colorado Spgs.	22.0	22.2	23.6	13.1	9.2	2.6	7.2	1978
Columbia	24.8	20.1	22.1	14.4	9.9	4.2	4.6	1978
Columbus	20.7	13.5	17.5	15.0	12.8	6.3	14.2	1971
Dallas	23.9	24.7	20.2	13.7	9.8	4.0	3.7	1979
Denver	19.4	18.0	23.7	13.2	12.4	4.4	9.0	1975
Des Moines	18.8	11.9	17.8	12.1	12.4	7.2	19.9	1969
Durham	33.2	22.9	16.6	10.9	7.2	3.9	5.4	1983
Edison	15.2	18.7	13.3	16.8	16.2	6.8	13.0	1968
El Paso	20.6	19.7	22.0	14.4	12.9	4.8	5.6	1976
Eugene	19.3	9.5	26.3	17.0	11.7	8.3	8.0	1972
Ft. Collins	29.5	17.7	26.9	10.3	5.2	2.6	8.0	1979
Ft. Lauderdale	19.5	21.2	29.8	17.2	9.5	1.7	1.0	1977
Ft. Wayne	16.8	11.6	16.3	14.2	12.0	7.1	22.1	1966
Ft. Worth	21.4	26.8	19.2	12.5	11.1	4.9	4.1	1979
Grand Rapids	20.1	13.7	15.7	12.2	12.7	7.9	17.6	1970
Green Bay	21.4	14.7	19.3	12.6	12.1	6.4	13.4	1973
Greensboro	23.3	17.8	18.1	14.3	12.3	6.3	7.8	1975
Honolulu	14.7	13.1	26.5	22.5	13.2	5.6	4.4	1972
Houston	19.8	23.0	26.6	13.6	9.4	4.3	3.4	1977
Huntsville	26.1	22.7	16.9	19.2	8.6	3.0	3.4	1979
Indianapolis	20.9	12.9	16.1	14.7	12.8	7.1	15.5	1970
Irvine	14.1	17.5	27.6	22.6	12.8	3.0	2.5	1973
Jacksonville	24.1	23.9	17.6	12.7	11.5	5.5	4.8	1979
Kansas City	17.2	15.0	18.1	15.5	14.1	7.1	12.9	1970
Knoxville	25.5	16.9	18.4	12.7	11.2	7.8	7.5	1976
Las Vegas	47.0	21.7	17.9	8.4	3.5	1.0	0.6	1989
Lexington	24.4	16.8	20.0	14.0	10.0	4.9	9.9	1976
Lincoln	20.4	12.6	19.6	12.7	13.5	4.7	16.4	1971
Los Angeles	6.9	12.3	15.6	17.8	22.3	12.2	12.9	1961
Louisville	16.6	10.3	18.6	16.6	15.6	8.4	13.8	1967
Madison	21.1	13.1	20.0	14.6	10.6	5.6	15.1	1972
Manchester	13.7	19.6	16.2	9.2	10.1	6.4	24.8	1969

Table continued on next page.

MSA[1]	1990 -2000	1980 -1989	1970 -1979	1960 -1969	1950 -1959	1940 -1949	Before 1940	Median Year
Memphis	21.3	16.3	20.1	16.1	13.2	6.6	6.4	1974
Miami	15.2	18.2	22.5	16.8	16.5	6.7	4.2	1973
Milwaukee	12.6	8.2	14.8	13.7	18.6	9.2	22.9	1960
Minneapolis	17.6	16.8	18.1	12.8	12.3	5.3	17.1	1971
Naperville	12.4	9.8	15.9	15.3	16.1	9.2	21.3	1962
Nashville	25.8	20.1	19.1	13.8	9.8	4.9	6.6	1978
New York	4.5	5.4	9.2	15.5	16.2	14.6	34.7	1950
Norfolk	18.4	22.1	18.9	15.2	12.5	6.4	6.4	1975
Oklahoma City	13.8	19.8	21.9	16.3	13.4	7.1	7.8	1972
Omaha	15.8	11.8	19.5	15.8	11.9	6.1	19.1	1968
Orlando	31.0	28.1	18.7	9.7	7.7	2.3	2.4	1983
Overland Park	17.2	15.0	18.1	15.5	14.1	7.1	12.9	1970
Philadelphia	9.4	10.0	13.0	13.9	17.3	11.1	25.3	1958
Phoenix	30.4	25.5	23.2	10.4	7.1	2.0	1.4	1982
Pittsburgh	7.8	7.5	12.7	12.3	17.2	11.9	30.5	1954
Plano	23.9	24.7	20.2	13.7	9.8	4.0	3.7	1979
Portland	24.6	13.0	20.9	11.3	9.1	6.5	14.7	1974
Providence	8.7	11.1	13.3	12.7	13.7	9.8	30.7	1957
Provo	33.9	12.7	22.8	9.1	8.4	5.4	7.8	1978
Raleigh	33.2	22.9	16.6	10.9	7.2	3.9	5.4	1983
Reno	27.3	20.6	25.0	13.0	7.3	3.5	3.3	1979
Richmond	18.6	19.7	19.2	13.8	12.2	6.5	10.0	1974
Rochester	9.6	10.4	14.8	14.7	12.6	7.2	30.8	1960
Sacramento	19.4	20.5	22.9	14.5	12.3	5.1	5.3	1976
St. Louis	14.0	13.4	15.6	16.0	15.2	8.8	17.0	1966
St. Paul	17.6	16.8	18.1	12.8	12.3	5.3	17.1	1971
St. Petersburg	17.2	25.9	25.4	13.6	11.0	3.3	3.5	1977
Salt Lake City	22.0	16.4	22.5	11.9	11.7	6.0	9.4	1975
San Antonio	20.1	22.5	20.1	13.6	11.3	6.1	6.2	1976
San Diego	13.9	21.9	26.3	15.0	12.9	4.9	5.1	1975
San Francisco	5.5	7.3	12.8	15.2	17.5	12.1	29.6	1955
San Jose	11.5	13.4	25.2	22.8	16.6	5.2	5.3	1970
Savannah	22.6	18.4	16.9	12.2	12.7	7.4	9.9	1975
Scottsdale	30.4	25.5	23.2	10.4	7.1	2.0	1.4	1982
Seattle	19.8	18.4	17.7	14.7	10.3	6.4	12.5	1973
Sioux Falls	23.0	14.7	19.0	9.7	10.8	6.3	16.4	1974
Springfield	25.8	16.7	20.0	11.9	8.9	5.5	11.2	1976
Stamford	7.4	11.4	12.9	17.1	20.2	9.2	21.9	1959
Tampa	17.2	25.9	25.4	13.6	11.0	3.3	3.5	1977
Thousand Oaks	12.9	19.6	26.8	23.1	10.1	3.5	4.0	1973
Tucson	23.2	22.4	25.6	11.7	10.4	3.7	3.0	1978
Tulsa	15.2	19.1	23.4	14.1	13.2	6.5	8.5	1973
Virginia Beach	18.4	22.1	18.9	15.2	12.5	6.4	6.4	1975
Washington	18.2	18.9	18.1	16.1	11.9	7.2	9.6	1973
Wichita	17.6	14.1	15.3	10.1	20.9	9.5	12.6	1967
U.S.	17.0	15.8	18.5	13.7	12.7	7.3	15.0	1971

Note: Figures are percentages; (1) Metropolitan Statistical Area - see Appendix A for areas included
Source: Census 2000, Summary File 3

Educational Quality

City	School District	Education Quotient[1]	Graduate Outcome[2]	Community Index[3]	Resource Index[4]	Rating[5]
Albuquerque	Albuquerque Public Schools	56	62	56	4	Green
Alexandria	Alexandria City Public Schools	n/a	n/a	n/a	n/a	n/a
Anchorage	Anchorage	48	52	73	17	Green
Ann Arbor	Ann Arbor Public Schools	87	83	91	75	Gold
Athens	Clarke County	n/a	n/a	n/a	n/a	n/a
Atlanta	Atlanta City	11	2	55	87	Yellow
Austin	Austin ISD	61	60	72	50	Green
Baltimore	Baltimore City Public Schools	7	3	13	75	Red
Baton Rouge	East Baton Rouge Parish	27	25	51	47	Green
Bellevue	Bellevue SD 405	81	81	91	49	Blue
Birmingham	Birmingham City	3	2	39	41	Red
Boise City	Boise Independent	64	67	68	32	Green
Boston	Boston	19	6	72	97	Yellow
Boulder	Boulder Valley RE 2	82	79	90	64	Blue
Buffalo	Buffalo City	8	2	20	79	Red
Cary	Wake County Schools	83	86	80	38	Gold
Cedar Rapids	Cedar Rapids Community	72	79	63	9	Blue
Charleston	Charleston County	29	23	61	67	Green
Charlotte	Charlotte-Mecklenburg Schools	33	32	74	37	Green
Chattanooga	Hamilton County	26	26	32	47	Green
Chicago	City of Chicago SD 299	12	3	43	89	Yellow
Cincinnati	Cincinnati City	15	6	40	88	Yellow
Cleveland	Cleveland Municipal	5	1	3	76	Red
Colorado Spgs.	Academy 20	71	68	92	57	Blue
Columbia	Richland County SD 02	48	42	78	62	Green
Columbus	Columbus City	10	6	31	70	Red
Dallas	Dallas ISD	11	9	32	54	Yellow
Denver	Denver County 1	9	4	42	67	Red
Des Moines	Des Moines Ind. Community	64	65	38	49	Green
Durham	Durham Public Schools	39	33	67	69	Green
Edison	Edison Township	96	93	86	96	Gold
El Paso	El Paso ISD	16	16	24	45	Yellow
Eugene	Eugene 04J	87	94	59	25	Gold
Fort Collins	Poudre R-1	53	48	68	66	Green
Fort Lauderdale	Broward County	n/a	n/a	n/a	n/a	n/a
Fort Wayne	Fort Wayne Community Schools	27	34	35	5	Green
Fort Worth	Fort Worth ISD	23	27	33	20	Yellow
Grand Rapids	Grand Rapids Public Schools	32	29	47	59	Green
Green Bay	Green Bay Area	91	91	61	78	Gold
Greensboro	Guilford County Schools	36	34	63	48	Green
Honolulu	Hawaii Dept. of Education	49	43	57	70	Green
Houston	Houston ISD	17	21	49	19	Yellow
Huntsville	Huntsville City	68	67	63	57	Blue
Indianapolis	Indianapolis Public Schools	8	3	24	71	Red
Irvine	Irvine Unified	90	96	91	32	Gold
Jacksonville	Duval County	13	17	45	14	Yellow
Kansas City	Kansas City 33	25	20	19	80	Yellow
Knoxville	Knox County	45	48	47	27	Green
Las Vegas	Clark County	24	31	35	2	Yellow
Lexington	Fayette County	74	69	74	74	Blue
Lincoln	Lincoln Public Schools	62	60	70	52	Green
Los Angeles	Los Angeles Unified	7	6	14	58	Red
Louisville	Jefferson County	29	22	56	72	Green
Madison	Madison Metropolitan	95	94	64	86	Gold
Manchester	Manchester	42	46	57	20	Green

Table continued on next page.

City	School District	Education Quotient[1]	Graduate Outcome[2]	Community Index[3]	Resource Index[4]	Rating[5]
Memphis	Memphis City	16	14	24	54	Yellow
Miami	Miami-Dade County	3	7	28	24	Red
Milwaukee	Milwaukee	18	16	21	60	Yellow
Minneapolis	Minneapolis	14	4	51	83	Yellow
Naperville	Naperville CUD 203	97	99	97	80	Gold
Nashville	Nashville-Davidson Co.	18	12	59	69	Yellow
New York	New York City Public Schools	11	3	55	79	Yellow
Norfolk	Norfolk City Public Schools	29	23	23	84	Green
Oklahoma City	Oklahoma City	1	4	14	2	Red
Omaha	Omaha Public Schools	41	41	36	46	Green
Orlando	Orange County	20	21	59	25	Yellow
Overland Park	Blue Valley	98	98	99	86	Gold
Philadelphia	Philadelphia City	17	11	38	74	Yellow
Phoenix	Deer Valley Unified	68	77	61	3	Blue
Pittsburgh	Pittsburgh	24	13	41	97	Yellow
Plano	Plano ISD	90	90	91	63	Gold
Portland	Portland 1J	72	72	70	48	Blue
Providence	Providence	8	3	17	76	Red
Provo	Provo	n/a	n/a	n/a	n/a	n/a
Raleigh	Wake County Schools	83	86	80	38	Gold
Reno	Washoe County	47	54	47	4	Green
Richmond	Richmond City Public Schools	27	19	26	91	Green
Rochester	Rochester City	15	10	23	68	Yellow
Sacramento	Sacramento City Unified	11	11	23	49	Yellow
Saint Louis	St. Louis City	6	1	11	81	Red
Saint Paul	Saint Paul	21	12	51	84	Yellow
Saint Petersburg	Pinellas County	58	60	52	31	Green
Salt Lake City	Granite	29	37	39	1	Green
San Antonio	Alamo Heights ISD	90	93	88	45	Gold
San Diego	San Diego Unified	26	22	55	61	Green
San Francisco	San Francisco Unified	36	34	60	49	Green
San Jose	San Jose Unified	57	53	67	57	Green
Savannah	Chatham County	12	8	30	61	Yellow
Scottsdale	Scottsdale Unified	85	94	86	7	Gold
Seattle	Seattle SD 1	73	69	82	62	Blue
Sioux Falls	Sioux Falls 49-5	61	68	67	5	Green
Springfield	Springfield R-XII	71	80	42	9	Blue
Stamford	Stamford	50	39	76	92	Green
Tampa	Hillsborough County	41	44	52	19	Green
Thousand Oaks	Conejo Valley Unified	78	81	87	31	Blue
Tucson	Tucson Unified	59	65	40	20	Green
Tulsa	Tulsa	14	21	37	3	Yellow
Virginia Beach	Virginia Beach City Pub Schl	63	56	71	82	Green
Washington	District of Columbia Pub Schls	24	13	64	94	Yellow
Wichita	Wichita	25	19	32	72	Yellow

Note: Scores are national percentile rankings and range from 1 (worst) to 99 (best); (1) Combination of the Graduate Outcome, Community and Resource Indexes weighted to reflect the greater importance of the Graduate Outcome and Resource Index; (2) Based on graduation rates and college board scores (SAT/ACT); (3) Based on the surrounding community's level of affluence and adult education; (4) Based on teacher salaries, per-pupil expenditures and student-teacher ratios; (5) School districts receive one of five rankings: Gold Medal (top 16 percent of districts evaluated); Blue Ribbon (top third); Green Light (average); Yellow Light (bottom 25 percent); Red Light (bottom 10 percent).
Source: Expansion Management, "2007 Education Quotient," January 2007

Highest Level of Education: City

Area	Less than H.S.	H.S. Diploma	Some College, No Deg.	Associate Degree	Bachelors Degree	Masters Degree	Profess. School Degree	Doctorate Degree
Albuquerque	13.9	24.1	24.4	6.0	18.4	9.0	2.3	1.9
Alexandria	13.5	12.7	15.5	4.4	29.5	15.8	6.1	2.5
Anchorage	9.6	24.2	29.3	7.9	18.7	7.0	2.3	0.9
Ann Arbor	4.4	8.7	13.4	3.9	30.2	23.6	6.5	9.4
Athens	19.4	21.9	15.7	3.8	20.6	10.7	2.2	5.8
Atlanta	23.2	22.1	16.3	3.7	21.1	8.6	3.7	1.5
Austin	16.5	16.9	21.0	5.0	25.9	9.8	2.7	2.2
Baltimore	31.2	28.0	17.7	3.5	10.7	5.7	2.1	1.1
Baton Rouge	19.5	23.3	22.5	2.6	19.2	8.0	2.7	2.2
Bellevue	5.7	12.7	20.7	6.9	34.6	13.2	3.8	2.4
Birmingham	23.8	27.3	23.8	5.7	12.4	4.5	1.7	0.8
Boise City	8.8	21.1	29.1	7.2	23.1	7.4	2.3	1.0
Boston	21.6	24.0	14.5	4.8	20.1	9.7	3.5	1.8
Boulder	5.4	8.9	15.5	3.9	36.3	19.4	4.1	6.6
Buffalo	25.0	28.8	19.6	7.7	10.8	5.6	1.6	0.8
Cary	4.6	10.6	15.8	7.1	38.6	16.3	3.0	3.9
Cedar Rapids	9.6	29.1	23.7	8.7	21.4	5.3	1.6	0.5
Charleston	16.1	19.4	20.2	6.4	23.7	8.1	4.1	1.9
Charlotte	14.6	19.8	22.2	6.5	26.5	7.4	2.2	0.8
Chattanooga	21.8	26.8	23.5	5.6	14.4	5.0	1.9	0.9
Chicago	28.3	22.8	18.5	4.6	15.7	6.6	2.6	0.9
Cincinnati	23.1	25.7	18.9	5.4	16.5	6.8	2.3	1.4
Cleveland	31.0	33.1	20.0	4.3	7.7	2.6	1.0	0.4
Colorado Spgs.	8.6	21.5	26.3	9.2	21.9	9.5	1.8	1.1
Columbia	17.3	20.2	20.5	6.0	21.5	9.2	3.6	1.7
Columbus	15.5	26.9	22.0	5.7	20.5	6.2	1.9	1.2
Dallas	29.6	19.6	18.9	4.2	18.2	6.1	2.6	0.8
Denver	21.4	20.2	19.7	5.0	21.7	7.7	3.2	1.2
Des Moines	16.8	33.4	21.6	6.2	15.5	4.1	1.9	0.6
Durham	16.8	17.3	17.6	5.5	24.2	10.5	3.9	4.1
Edison	12.4	23.6	15.8	5.7	25.3	12.3	3.0	2.0
El Paso	30.6	22.4	23.0	5.3	12.4	4.0	1.8	0.5
Eugene	8.5	19.2	27.7	7.2	22.0	9.8	2.9	2.6
Ft. Collins	5.8	16.0	22.7	6.6	30.5	12.3	2.4	3.7
Ft. Lauderdale	21.0	24.4	20.5	6.2	17.4	6.0	3.6	0.8
Ft. Wayne	16.8	32.8	23.3	7.5	13.0	4.8	1.2	0.5
Ft. Worth	26.0	23.8	22.1	4.9	15.7	5.1	1.6	0.8
Grand Rapids	22.4	26.0	21.1	6.9	15.6	5.7	1.5	0.8
Green Bay	17.2	35.2	20.1	8.1	14.4	3.5	1.1	0.4
Greensboro	15.5	22.3	22.4	5.9	23.3	7.4	1.9	1.4
Honolulu	16.8	25.9	19.5	6.8	20.4	6.4	2.7	1.4
Houston	29.4	20.4	19.2	4.0	17.3	5.9	2.5	1.2
Huntsville	14.0	20.1	23.4	5.9	23.6	9.4	1.9	1.7
Indianapolis	18.4	29.3	21.1	5.6	16.9	5.6	2.2	1.0
Irvine	4.6	10.2	18.1	8.2	34.4	15.7	4.8	4.1
Jacksonville	17.3	29.4	24.2	7.5	14.9	4.4	1.7	0.6
Kansas City	17.2	27.6	23.7	5.4	17.4	5.9	2.1	0.7
Knoxville	21.2	27.9	20.9	4.9	15.4	6.2	2.0	1.5
Las Vegas	20.4	28.7	25.8	5.8	12.6	4.1	2.1	0.6
Lexington	13.5	21.8	21.4	6.5	21.8	9.1	3.5	2.3
Lincoln	9.5	24.2	24.1	8.5	22.5	6.8	2.4	2.1
Los Angeles	33.8	17.4	18.3	5.3	16.3	5.2	2.7	1.0
Louisville	23.8	28.8	21.1	4.8	12.6	5.7	2.3	0.8
Madison	7.3	17.6	18.5	7.6	27.8	13.1	3.8	4.2
Manchester	19.3	30.5	19.9	8.0	15.3	5.1	1.6	0.3

Table continued on next page.

Area	Less than H.S.	H.S. Diploma	Some College, No Deg.	Associate Degree	Bachelors Degree	Masters Degree	Profess. School Degree	Doctorate Degree
Memphis	23.0	27.6	23.0	4.8	13.6	5.1	2.0	0.9
Miami	46.9	19.7	12.5	4.2	8.7	3.6	3.3	1.0
Milwaukee	25.1	30.0	20.6	5.7	12.5	4.2	1.3	0.7
Minneapolis	15.3	20.7	21.2	5.5	24.1	8.4	3.0	1.7
Naperville	3.7	11.5	17.8	6.2	37.2	17.8	3.3	2.6
Nashville	18.3	24.6	21.7	5.0	20.3	6.6	2.3	1.3
New York	27.9	24.5	15.2	5.2	15.7	7.5	2.9	1.1
Norfolk	21.5	29.6	24.5	4.9	11.9	5.1	1.6	0.9
Oklahoma City	18.0	25.9	26.1	5.4	16.4	5.4	2.1	0.7
Omaha	13.7	26.8	24.5	5.8	20.1	5.7	2.4	1.0
Orlando	17.4	24.3	21.4	8.5	20.1	5.7	2.1	0.6
Overland Park	3.9	14.0	22.2	5.8	36.2	12.7	3.7	1.5
Philadelphia	28.8	33.1	15.5	4.4	10.5	4.7	2.0	1.0
Phoenix	23.6	22.8	24.4	6.6	15.1	4.9	1.9	0.6
Pittsburgh	18.6	32.3	16.1	6.1	14.0	7.5	3.0	2.4
Plano	5.8	11.9	22.0	6.1	36.5	14.1	2.2	1.5
Portland	14.5	22.5	25.0	5.8	21.1	7.2	2.8	1.2
Providence	35.3	23.4	13.7	4.6	12.5	6.3	2.5	1.7
Provo	10.1	14.2	30.4	9.1	25.1	6.3	1.6	3.1
Raleigh	11.4	16.1	20.6	7.0	30.6	9.7	2.5	2.0
Reno	17.3	23.7	27.3	6.8	16.6	5.3	2.0	1.0
Richmond	24.9	23.6	19.0	3.3	18.5	6.8	2.7	1.2
Rochester	26.7	28.5	16.5	7.7	12.3	5.8	1.4	0.9
Sacramento	22.6	21.5	24.0	8.0	15.4	5.1	2.6	0.8
St. Louis	28.4	27.4	20.4	4.4	11.6	5.2	1.6	0.9
St. Paul	16.2	25.6	20.4	5.6	20.1	7.2	3.1	1.8
St. Petersburg	17.9	27.8	23.2	8.0	15.1	5.0	2.3	0.8
Salt Lake City	16.6	19.6	22.7	6.1	20.8	8.0	3.7	2.6
San Antonio	23.7	23.7	23.7	5.9	14.5	5.6	2.0	0.8
San Diego	17.1	16.8	23.2	7.5	22.0	8.0	3.2	2.2
San Francisco	19.0	14.0	16.9	5.6	28.4	10.1	4.5	1.7
San Jose	22.3	18.2	20.8	7.7	20.6	7.7	1.5	1.3
Savannah	23.5	28.2	23.2	4.7	13.6	4.5	1.6	0.7
Scottsdale	6.2	16.1	26.2	6.6	29.8	9.7	3.9	1.5
Seattle	10.8	15.3	20.6	6.5	29.8	10.8	3.9	2.3
Sioux Falls	11.0	28.3	23.9	8.0	20.9	5.1	2.1	0.7
Springfield	17.1	30.4	24.7	4.6	15.3	5.0	2.0	0.9
Stamford	18.6	24.7	13.5	4.7	22.1	11.5	3.6	1.3
Tampa	22.2	24.8	19.3	7.0	17.1	5.7	3.0	0.8
Thousand Oaks	8.7	15.5	25.8	7.9	26.5	10.1	3.2	2.4
Tucson	19.3	23.9	27.0	6.7	14.0	6.4	1.5	1.3
Tulsa	15.4	25.1	24.4	6.4	19.3	5.7	2.7	0.9
Virginia Beach	9.5	25.9	29.0	7.6	19.1	6.3	1.9	0.6
Washington	22.4	20.5	15.3	2.8	18.1	11.9	6.0	3.0
Wichita	15.6	28.1	25.1	5.0	17.8	5.7	1.9	0.8
U.S.	19.4	28.4	21.2	6.4	15.7	5.9	2.0	1.0

Figures are 2006 estimates and cover persons age 25 and over; (1) Metropolitan Statistical Area - see Appendix B for areas included Source: Claritas, Inc.

Highest Level of Education: Metro Area

Area	Less than H.S.	H.S. Diploma	Some College, No Deg.	Associate Degree	Bachelors Degree	Masters Degree	Profess. School Degree	Doctorate Degree
Albuquerque	15.9	25.9	23.9	6.1	16.5	7.9	2.2	1.6
Alexandria	12.8	20.4	19.4	5.1	23.5	12.4	3.9	2.4
Anchorage	10.1	25.7	29.4	8.1	17.4	6.5	2.0	0.8
Ann Arbor	8.4	17.1	20.4	6.1	24.5	15.0	3.8	4.7
Athens	20.7	27.0	16.2	4.0	17.6	8.5	2.0	4.1
Atlanta	16.6	25.3	21.9	5.7	20.7	6.8	2.1	0.9
Austin	15.0	20.0	23.0	5.6	24.3	8.2	2.2	1.7
Baltimore	17.6	27.0	20.3	5.5	17.7	8.1	2.6	1.4
Baton Rouge	20.2	32.5	21.6	2.8	14.9	5.2	1.7	1.1
Bellevue	10.8	22.9	25.9	8.0	21.9	7.1	2.3	1.2
Birmingham	20.8	28.8	21.6	5.5	15.2	5.2	2.0	0.8
Boise City	13.9	26.0	27.8	6.9	17.7	5.3	1.7	0.7
Boston	13.5	26.0	16.8	7.1	21.4	10.4	2.9	2.0
Boulder	7.4	14.8	19.4	5.7	31.4	14.2	3.2	4.0
Buffalo	16.8	31.1	18.9	9.6	13.9	6.9	1.9	0.9
Cary	13.5	20.9	20.1	7.6	25.9	8.4	1.9	1.7
Cedar Rapids	9.9	32.5	23.0	9.2	18.8	4.7	1.4	0.4
Charleston	18.3	26.7	22.3	7.1	16.7	5.8	2.1	1.0
Charlotte	18.1	24.6	21.8	6.9	20.6	5.7	1.6	0.6
Chattanooga	23.2	29.8	21.8	5.6	13.0	4.3	1.5	0.7
Chicago	18.7	25.4	21.2	5.7	18.4	7.3	2.3	1.0
Cincinnati	17.3	32.0	19.7	6.1	16.2	6.1	1.7	0.9
Cleveland	16.8	31.8	21.6	5.8	15.3	5.6	2.3	0.8
Colorado Spgs.	8.2	22.5	27.4	9.6	20.6	9.1	1.5	1.1
Columbia	17.5	27.4	20.8	7.5	17.7	6.3	1.8	1.0
Columbus	13.8	30.6	21.0	5.8	19.5	6.1	2.0	1.1
Dallas	19.2	22.3	23.5	5.7	20.3	6.4	1.7	0.8
Denver	13.2	21.8	23.8	6.8	23.2	7.8	2.3	1.0
Des Moines	10.9	30.4	22.0	7.5	20.8	5.2	2.4	0.7
Durham	16.8	20.6	16.9	5.9	21.6	10.3	3.7	4.2
Edison	21.4	26.4	16.5	5.6	17.7	8.2	3.0	1.2
El Paso	33.8	22.5	21.9	5.1	11.2	3.6	1.6	0.5
Eugene	12.4	25.7	28.9	7.3	15.7	6.6	1.9	1.5
Ft. Collins	7.5	20.9	24.3	7.2	25.6	10.0	2.0	2.6
Ft. Lauderdale	23.4	25.3	20.1	6.9	14.9	5.3	3.3	0.9
Ft. Wayne	14.1	34.2	22.5	7.9	14.1	5.2	1.5	0.5
Ft. Worth	19.2	22.3	23.5	5.7	20.3	6.4	1.7	0.8
Grand Rapids	15.6	30.9	23.2	7.5	15.5	5.3	1.6	0.5
Green Bay	14.4	37.2	19.7	8.6	15.0	3.7	1.2	0.3
Greensboro	21.5	28.3	20.4	6.0	16.8	4.9	1.4	0.7
Honolulu	15.2	27.7	21.3	7.9	19.0	5.8	2.1	1.0
Houston	23.0	22.8	22.2	5.1	18.1	5.7	2.0	1.0
Huntsville	16.3	23.7	22.5	5.9	21.0	8.1	1.3	1.2
Indianapolis	15.1	31.2	20.2	6.0	18.3	6.2	2.0	0.9
Irvine	28.2	18.5	20.6	6.6	17.0	5.6	2.4	1.0
Jacksonville	16.1	29.2	24.0	7.6	15.6	4.9	1.9	0.6
Kansas City	12.9	28.4	23.9	5.9	19.3	6.8	2.1	0.7
Knoxville	19.6	29.6	20.4	5.4	15.7	6.0	1.9	1.4
Las Vegas	18.9	29.3	27.2	5.9	12.4	4.0	1.7	0.6
Lexington	16.3	26.3	20.9	6.2	18.2	7.7	2.7	1.8
Lincoln	9.4	25.2	23.9	8.9	21.7	6.5	2.3	2.0
Los Angeles	28.2	18.5	20.6	6.6	17.0	5.6	2.4	1.0
Louisville	18.8	32.4	21.7	5.8	13.2	5.6	1.9	0.6
Madison	8.5	24.6	20.4	8.8	23.3	9.1	2.8	2.6
Manchester	13.0	27.4	20.4	9.1	20.1	7.6	1.6	0.8

Table continued on next page.

Area	Less than H.S.	H.S. Diploma	Some College, No Deg.	Associate Degree	Bachelors Degree	Masters Degree	Profess. School Degree	Doctorate Degree
Memphis	20.3	28.0	23.8	5.3	14.8	5.1	1.9	0.8
Miami	23.4	25.3	20.1	6.9	14.9	5.3	3.3	0.9
Milwaukee	15.3	29.1	21.7	6.9	18.4	5.9	2.0	0.8
Minneapolis	9.3	25.6	24.3	7.7	23.1	6.6	2.3	1.1
Naperville	18.7	25.4	21.2	5.7	18.4	7.3	2.3	1.0
Nashville	19.2	28.7	21.0	5.0	17.7	5.5	1.9	0.9
New York	21.4	26.4	16.5	5.6	17.7	8.2	3.0	1.2
Norfolk	15.2	27.7	26.3	6.9	15.5	6.1	1.6	0.7
Oklahoma City	16.0	27.9	26.1	5.3	16.3	5.6	1.9	0.9
Omaha	11.7	28.5	24.9	6.8	19.5	5.7	2.0	0.8
Orlando	17.0	27.5	22.7	8.0	17.2	5.1	1.8	0.7
Overland Park	12.9	28.4	23.9	5.9	19.3	6.8	2.1	0.7
Philadelphia	17.3	31.4	17.5	5.8	17.4	6.8	2.5	1.3
Phoenix	17.9	23.4	26.6	7.1	16.7	5.8	1.8	0.8
Pittsburgh	15.0	38.0	16.4	7.0	15.0	5.7	2.0	1.0
Plano	19.2	22.3	23.5	5.7	20.3	6.4	1.7	0.8
Portland	12.7	23.9	27.7	7.0	19.2	6.5	2.1	0.9
Providence	23.8	28.4	17.1	7.1	15.0	6.0	1.7	0.8
Provo	8.8	19.5	30.7	9.8	21.6	6.3	1.6	1.8
Raleigh	13.5	20.9	20.1	7.6	25.9	8.4	1.9	1.7
Reno	15.6	25.2	28.2	7.2	15.9	5.0	1.9	0.9
Richmond	18.3	27.1	21.7	5.2	18.6	6.3	2.0	0.9
Rochester	15.5	28.6	18.1	10.0	16.6	8.3	1.8	1.1
Sacramento	15.2	22.1	27.0	8.8	17.8	5.7	2.3	1.0
St. Louis	16.7	29.1	23.2	6.2	15.8	6.3	1.8	0.8
St. Paul	9.3	25.6	24.3	7.7	23.1	6.6	2.3	1.1
St. Petersburg	18.2	29.8	22.3	7.4	14.7	4.8	2.0	0.7
Salt Lake City	12.7	24.2	28.1	7.6	18.5	5.7	2.1	1.1
San Antonio	21.9	25.1	24.0	6.0	14.7	5.6	1.9	0.7
San Diego	17.3	19.6	25.5	7.6	19.0	6.8	2.6	1.5
San Francisco	16.1	17.6	21.3	6.8	24.0	9.1	3.3	1.9
San Jose	17.4	16.2	19.9	7.4	23.4	11.2	2.2	2.4
Savannah	19.6	29.3	22.7	5.3	15.6	4.9	1.9	0.9
Scottsdale	17.9	23.4	26.6	7.1	16.7	5.8	1.8	0.8
Seattle	10.8	22.9	25.9	8.0	21.9	7.1	2.3	1.2
Sioux Falls	11.4	30.7	23.8	8.1	19.3	4.4	1.8	0.5
Springfield	16.7	33.0	24.1	4.6	14.5	4.5	1.8	0.8
Stamford	16.1	23.7	15.4	5.6	22.7	11.9	3.4	1.1
Tampa	18.2	29.8	22.3	7.4	14.7	4.8	2.0	0.7
Thousand Oaks	20.5	19.6	25.4	7.8	17.2	6.0	2.3	1.1
Tucson	16.2	23.2	26.9	6.8	16.0	7.3	2.0	1.6
Tulsa	16.5	29.8	24.1	7.0	15.7	4.6	1.7	0.6
Virginia Beach	15.2	27.7	26.3	6.9	15.5	6.1	1.6	0.7
Washington	12.8	20.4	19.4	5.1	23.5	12.4	3.9	2.4
Wichita	14.2	29.7	25.7	5.5	17.1	5.5	1.7	0.7
U.S.	19.4	28.4	21.2	6.4	15.7	5.9	2.0	1.0

Note: Figures cover persons age 25 and over; Figures are 2006 estimates and cover the Metropolitan Statistical Area (MSA) - see Appendix B for areas included
Source: Claritas, Inc.

School Enrollment by Race: City

City	Grades KG to 8 (%)				Grades 9 to 12 (%)			
	White	Black	Asian	Hisp.[1]	White	Black	Asian	Hisp.[1]
Albuquerque	63.7	3.5	1.8	49.7	64.3	3.8	2.0	47.7
Alexandria	42.0	33.4	3.8	25.1	41.3	33.9	4.8	22.8
Anchorage	64.7	6.7	5.2	7.1	65.9	7.7	6.9	7.1
Ann Arbor	69.2	13.9	10.3	2.5	73.8	14.2	7.4	3.6
Athens	37.2	51.4	3.8	8.2	40.3	51.4	1.9	7.0
Atlanta	15.6	80.4	1.1	3.7	13.5	82.6	1.1	3.1
Austin	54.5	13.6	3.5	42.7	55.5	14.5	3.1	39.1
Baltimore	19.9	76.5	0.8	1.6	17.6	78.5	1.0	1.6
Baton Rouge	29.5	66.4	1.9	1.8	33.2	62.2	3.0	1.0
Bellevue	67.4	2.5	17.8	6.3	65.5	2.3	20.8	6.6
Birmingham	8.9	89.3	0.3	1.2	9.5	88.5	0.4	1.1
Boise City	90.6	0.9	1.4	6.0	90.5	1.2	1.8	4.3
Boston	30.2	41.7	6.7	24.2	28.9	42.2	7.7	21.4
Boulder	83.8	1.5	3.1	12.6	85.4	1.5	3.3	10.4
Buffalo	38.9	49.5	0.6	11.6	42.1	48.3	1.2	11.1
Cary	81.3	6.3	7.9	4.2	81.6	7.6	6.9	3.3
Cedar Rapids	87.6	5.3	1.9	2.7	88.2	5.1	2.7	1.8
Charleston	43.6	52.9	1.6	1.3	47.2	50.6	0.8	0.9
Charlotte	48.0	42.7	3.3	6.5	47.0	43.7	4.0	5.4
Chattanooga	43.3	51.4	1.5	2.3	42.8	52.5	2.2	1.0
Chicago	29.0	46.0	3.0	34.4	28.9	46.0	3.6	31.8
Cincinnati	34.8	61.3	0.6	1.0	35.8	59.7	0.6	1.3
Cleveland	30.2	61.3	0.8	9.2	29.6	61.8	0.9	8.8
Colorado Spgs.	76.6	7.4	2.1	14.6	75.7	8.3	3.4	14.1
Columbia	30.5	64.3	0.9	2.7	30.6	65.9	0.6	2.7
Columbus	56.5	34.6	2.5	2.7	55.9	35.3	2.9	2.8
Dallas	38.8	31.5	2.0	46.8	36.8	34.6	2.6	41.8
Denver	47.5	16.5	2.1	49.0	48.7	16.8	3.5	45.0
Des Moines	74.1	11.8	3.8	8.5	76.8	10.3	4.4	7.5
Durham	31.2	59.1	2.2	7.1	35.2	57.9	2.3	4.5
Edison	55.2	8.4	30.7	8.4	56.5	10.6	28.5	6.7
El Paso	71.0	3.1	0.8	83.3	71.2	3.0	1.1	82.1
Eugene	83.8	1.7	2.8	8.7	85.5	1.6	2.9	5.6
Ft. Collins	87.4	1.0	1.9	10.0	88.5	1.2	1.3	11.0
Ft. Lauderdale	40.8	50.4	1.0	8.8	35.5	52.6	1.5	10.2
Ft. Wayne	65.5	24.6	1.4	6.4	66.6	25.1	2.3	5.9
Ft. Worth	51.1	23.2	2.3	39.7	47.8	27.5	2.8	35.1
Grand Rapids	51.3	31.1	1.8	17.1	54.0	29.9	2.6	16.3
Green Bay	76.5	2.5	8.4	9.6	79.2	1.2	8.3	7.6
Greensboro	44.4	46.4	3.6	4.8	48.4	43.3	4.1	3.4
Honolulu	12.2	1.7	46.0	7.2	10.7	1.8	54.7	5.4
Houston	41.3	29.3	3.9	46.6	40.3	29.7	5.3	43.3
Huntsville	55.6	37.8	1.2	2.8	57.1	34.8	2.7	3.1
Indianapolis	59.7	33.7	0.9	3.8	60.6	34.3	1.1	4.0
Irvine	60.3	1.4	27.3	8.6	60.0	1.3	27.9	9.1
Jacksonville	54.5	38.4	2.3	4.5	54.0	38.8	2.9	4.9
Kansas City	47.9	41.9	1.6	8.9	45.8	44.0	2.7	6.8
Knoxville	68.2	26.4	1.0	2.0	66.5	28.6	1.6	1.0
Las Vegas	62.3	13.1	3.4	32.3	63.0	13.3	4.5	29.8
Lexington	74.7	18.7	1.8	4.0	74.3	19.4	1.7	3.2
Lincoln	84.0	4.5	3.7	5.0	85.3	4.0	4.2	5.7
Los Angeles	39.1	11.7	6.5	62.8	36.8	11.9	8.0	61.5
Louisville	48.0	46.4	1.3	1.9	50.7	43.9	1.3	1.5
Madison	71.1	12.6	7.4	6.1	73.9	11.4	7.1	5.1
Manchester	88.0	4.2	1.8	6.6	87.9	4.6	2.1	5.9

Table continued on next page.

City	Grades KG to 8 (%)				Grades 9 to 12 (%)			
	White	Black	Asian	Hisp.[1]	White	Black	Asian	Hisp.[1]
Memphis	20.0	76.1	1.1	2.6	21.6	74.8	1.1	2.1
Miami	56.2	32.0	0.3	54.1	52.1	33.2	0.4	57.2
Milwaukee	28.9	53.7	3.8	15.5	32.5	51.2	3.3	14.1
Minneapolis	38.2	31.9	12.0	10.0	38.2	33.9	12.3	8.9
Naperville	84.1	2.9	9.7	3.6	86.1	3.0	8.1	4.9
Nashville	52.8	38.8	2.2	4.9	52.6	39.8	2.4	4.2
New York	33.8	32.8	8.6	34.7	32.5	33.5	9.7	33.5
Norfolk	33.9	58.2	2.3	3.0	35.3	56.6	2.5	3.3
Oklahoma City	56.4	20.5	3.5	15.4	58.9	21.5	4.1	11.5
Omaha	69.6	19.2	1.4	10.1	72.5	18.4	1.7	6.8
Orlando	44.2	42.9	1.6	21.3	44.0	40.0	2.8	21.8
Overland Park	89.8	2.8	3.1	4.4	90.4	2.0	4.0	3.9
Philadelphia	31.4	54.1	3.7	12.3	33.2	52.7	4.5	10.6
Phoenix	62.9	5.8	1.6	45.6	64.9	6.2	2.1	40.5
Pittsburgh	50.1	44.7	1.2	1.3	55.1	39.1	1.0	1.4
Plano	75.6	5.6	11.0	11.1	77.2	5.9	9.7	10.7
Portland	68.0	9.7	7.1	9.9	68.3	11.0	8.0	8.0
Providence	36.6	20.1	7.0	43.8	33.4	19.0	8.7	44.4
Provo	83.7	0.7	0.8	18.1	90.3	0.2	1.1	11.9
Raleigh	51.6	38.0	3.2	7.2	54.1	36.1	3.6	6.6
Reno	69.5	2.4	4.7	29.5	68.0	3.3	6.0	28.9
Richmond	17.0	79.2	0.4	2.4	14.1	82.4	1.0	1.9
Rochester	27.6	53.4	1.4	19.3	27.2	53.6	2.4	17.5
Sacramento	32.7	21.1	19.3	28.5	34.1	18.5	23.4	24.6
St. Louis	26.6	68.0	1.5	2.0	29.1	65.3	1.8	1.9
St. Paul	44.1	17.0	24.4	10.2	47.2	15.5	24.4	10.2
St. Petersburg	56.1	35.5	3.1	4.7	53.9	36.0	4.9	4.8
Salt Lake City	68.8	3.2	3.0	29.5	72.1	3.9	3.2	22.0
San Antonio	62.1	6.8	1.1	67.9	63.3	7.3	1.3	67.0
San Diego	47.8	10.3	13.2	38.5	45.8	9.9	15.9	36.8
San Francisco	28.6	12.6	38.9	21.5	26.9	11.3	40.8	23.6
San Jose	41.2	3.4	25.1	39.9	39.4	3.4	27.0	39.0
Savannah	21.4	74.6	1.3	2.2	21.6	74.5	1.8	1.3
Scottsdale	89.0	1.2	1.9	10.3	89.1	1.6	2.7	9.3
Seattle	52.9	14.5	16.5	8.2	50.5	16.7	17.5	7.8
Sioux Falls	87.8	2.1	1.5	3.7	89.8	3.6	1.4	2.4
Springfield	88.8	3.9	1.3	3.4	86.5	4.1	2.9	1.8
Stamford	58.5	23.3	4.1	20.5	54.6	27.0	3.6	23.1
Tampa	49.9	37.9	1.4	21.2	49.2	38.2	2.5	20.5
Thousand Oaks	82.4	1.3	5.1	16.4	80.8	2.2	5.1	14.1
Tucson	59.4	5.2	1.6	51.2	58.9	5.5	1.7	51.4
Tulsa	58.5	22.2	1.5	9.1	60.5	22.6	2.9	7.4
Virginia Beach	64.5	24.6	4.0	5.2	65.9	22.5	5.7	5.0
Washington	13.0	78.3	1.1	8.9	12.6	77.7	1.8	9.9
Wichita	65.9	15.5	3.9	13.9	66.9	16.3	4.9	11.5
U.S.	68.5	15.5	3.3	16.8	68.8	15.5	3.8	15.7

Note: Figures shown cover persons 3 years old and over; (1) people of Hispanic origin can be of any race;
Source: Census 2000, Summary File 3

School Enrollment by Race: Metro Area

MSA[1]	Grades KG to 8 (%)				Grades 9 to 12 (%)			
	White	Black	Asian	Hisp.[2]	White	Black	Asian	Hisp.[2]
Albuquerque	61.5	2.6	1.2	50.4	62.9	2.5	1.5	49.0
Alexandria	54.3	30.4	5.8	9.9	53.1	30.9	6.6	10.2
Anchorage	64.7	6.7	5.2	7.1	65.9	7.7	6.9	7.1
Ann Arbor	84.0	8.3	2.6	3.5	85.5	8.1	2.3	4.0
Athens	60.5	31.0	2.9	5.9	60.5	33.1	1.5	5.5
Atlanta	56.5	35.2	3.0	6.2	56.3	35.5	3.6	5.3
Austin	66.6	9.5	2.7	34.2	67.3	10.3	2.5	31.0
Baltimore	61.1	32.7	2.4	2.3	60.1	33.3	3.0	2.3
Baton Rouge	56.8	40.0	1.2	1.8	58.4	38.0	1.9	1.6
Bellevue	73.2	5.5	9.2	6.6	73.1	5.4	10.5	5.8
Birmingham	60.1	37.1	0.6	2.0	59.8	38.0	0.6	1.3
Boise City	87.2	0.6	0.9	12.0	87.9	0.8	1.2	10.6
Boston	76.8	10.0	4.6	8.7	75.2	11.1	4.9	8.7
Boulder	85.0	0.7	3.0	15.5	87.0	0.8	2.6	12.7
Buffalo	77.2	16.4	0.9	4.5	79.7	14.7	1.5	4.0
Cary	63.0	28.2	2.6	6.1	64.9	27.9	2.6	4.7
Cedar Rapids	90.7	3.5	1.4	2.1	92.2	3.2	1.8	1.3
Charleston	54.5	40.7	1.0	2.6	53.4	42.0	1.5	2.5
Charlotte	67.2	26.1	1.8	5.0	67.2	27.1	2.2	3.8
Chattanooga	77.2	19.3	0.9	1.8	77.6	18.9	1.4	1.3
Chicago	58.6	23.4	3.9	22.2	58.7	23.2	4.6	20.2
Cincinnati	79.8	16.8	0.9	1.2	81.5	15.6	0.9	1.1
Cleveland	69.8	24.2	1.1	4.9	72.1	22.3	1.3	4.3
Colorado Spgs.	77.2	7.0	1.7	14.0	77.5	7.4	2.9	13.4
Columbia	56.0	40.0	1.0	2.7	54.2	41.6	1.4	2.2
Columbus	76.5	17.1	2.0	2.1	77.3	16.8	1.9	2.0
Dallas	60.7	18.0	3.6	28.9	61.2	18.7	4.0	25.8
Denver	73.1	6.9	2.7	24.9	74.5	6.6	3.4	21.9
Des Moines	86.3	5.3	2.2	5.5	87.0	5.0	2.5	4.7
Durham	63.0	28.2	2.6	6.1	64.9	27.9	2.6	4.7
Edison	70.1	9.4	11.4	13.9	68.2	10.9	10.7	14.7
El Paso	72.4	2.8	0.7	85.0	71.9	2.8	1.0	83.9
Eugene	87.2	1.1	1.6	7.4	89.2	0.8	1.7	5.1
Ft. Collins	89.5	0.7	1.3	10.4	90.4	0.6	1.5	10.5
Ft. Lauderdale	59.2	30.1	2.2	19.3	55.9	32.4	2.4	19.4
Ft. Wayne	84.1	10.1	1.0	3.8	84.1	10.6	1.3	3.3
Ft. Worth	69.1	12.9	2.8	23.7	69.0	14.1	3.6	19.9
Grand Rapids	80.5	9.8	1.9	8.5	82.7	8.9	2.3	7.3
Green Bay	86.5	1.5	4.3	5.0	87.8	1.4	4.4	3.5
Greensboro	67.9	25.4	1.4	5.8	69.5	24.5	1.8	4.7
Honolulu	14.7	2.2	34.3	10.2	11.5	1.6	41.7	9.4
Houston	56.0	19.6	4.3	36.5	56.0	19.8	5.4	32.8
Huntsville	70.7	23.3	1.3	2.8	68.7	25.2	1.6	2.8
Indianapolis	77.4	17.7	1.0	2.6	77.7	18.0	1.1	2.7
Irvine	58.6	1.6	11.8	42.5	56.2	1.9	14.8	38.8
Jacksonville	64.6	29.0	1.9	4.4	64.2	28.7	2.5	5.0
Kansas City	75.5	16.1	1.3	6.4	75.6	16.7	1.9	5.5
Knoxville	88.4	8.0	0.9	1.3	88.5	8.2	1.0	1.1
Las Vegas	66.2	10.5	3.6	29.2	67.1	10.0	4.8	25.8
Lexington	83.1	11.8	1.4	2.6	82.8	12.4	1.3	2.0
Lincoln	85.6	4.0	3.3	4.4	86.9	3.5	3.7	5.0
Los Angeles	41.8	10.5	9.1	57.7	39.8	10.3	11.2	55.9
Louisville	77.1	18.5	0.9	1.7	78.3	17.6	0.8	1.6
Madison	84.2	6.6	3.5	4.3	85.2	6.2	3.7	3.5
Manchester	92.8	2.3	1.5	3.5	92.9	2.5	1.4	3.6

Table continued on next page.

MSA[1]	Grades KG to 8 (%)				Grades 9 to 12 (%)			
	White	Black	Asian	Hisp.[2]	White	Black	Asian	Hisp.[2]
Memphis	43.1	53.1	1.2	2.2	44.0	52.4	1.3	1.9
Miami	62.1	27.4	1.1	49.4	57.8	29.7	1.2	52.5
Milwaukee	64.7	24.8	2.4	8.9	68.9	21.5	2.4	7.6
Minneapolis	79.3	7.7	6.0	4.4	80.8	7.1	6.3	3.8
Naperville	58.6	23.4	3.9	22.2	58.7	23.2	4.6	20.2
Nashville	74.7	19.8	1.4	3.3	74.4	20.7	1.5	2.6
New York	39.1	30.1	8.0	32.0	37.2	31.2	9.0	31.3
Norfolk	54.7	37.5	2.3	3.5	56.0	36.3	2.9	3.6
Oklahoma City	67.3	13.6	2.2	9.9	69.2	14.0	2.4	7.6
Omaha	80.5	11.0	1.2	7.2	82.0	10.7	1.4	5.6
Orlando	67.1	19.4	2.3	20.1	65.6	20.0	2.9	20.0
Overland Park	75.5	16.1	1.3	6.4	75.6	16.7	1.9	5.5
Philadelphia	65.6	24.9	3.1	7.0	64.8	25.6	3.7	6.4
Phoenix	68.7	4.4	1.7	35.6	70.9	4.6	2.0	31.5
Pittsburgh	84.8	11.9	1.0	0.9	87.2	9.9	0.9	1.0
Plano	60.7	18.0	3.6	28.9	61.2	18.7	4.0	25.8
Portland	80.1	3.1	4.4	9.9	81.9	3.4	4.8	7.7
Providence	79.3	5.8	2.7	12.8	79.8	5.6	3.6	11.5
Provo	91.8	0.5	0.6	7.5	93.6	0.2	0.6	6.1
Raleigh	63.0	28.2	2.6	6.1	64.9	27.9	2.6	4.7
Reno	74.2	2.0	3.8	25.1	74.0	3.0	4.4	22.4
Richmond	58.3	36.1	1.7	2.7	57.9	36.4	2.4	2.3
Rochester	76.9	14.5	1.7	6.7	79.0	13.5	2.3	5.3
Sacramento	61.7	9.9	9.5	19.4	63.2	9.0	11.1	17.1
St. Louis	71.8	24.1	1.1	1.8	73.7	22.5	1.3	1.8
St. Paul	79.3	7.7	6.0	4.4	80.8	7.1	6.3	3.8
St. Petersburg	73.7	16.6	2.0	14.0	74.3	15.8	2.8	13.6
Salt Lake City	85.4	1.1	1.7	12.7	87.1	1.0	2.1	10.6
San Antonio	65.0	6.8	1.1	60.4	66.3	7.4	1.3	58.9
San Diego	57.2	7.0	7.8	38.2	56.6	6.7	9.5	35.9
San Francisco	48.4	6.7	23.4	25.0	44.9	6.9	26.0	25.5
San Jose	47.3	2.6	24.3	32.8	45.3	3.1	25.2	33.5
Savannah	51.2	44.0	1.5	2.2	49.0	47.2	1.5	1.7
Scottsdale	68.7	4.4	1.7	35.6	70.9	4.6	2.0	31.5
Seattle	73.2	5.5	9.2	6.6	73.1	5.4	10.5	5.8
Sioux Falls	90.6	1.4	1.3	2.9	92.1	2.5	1.1	2.1
Springfield	93.3	1.7	0.7	2.1	91.7	2.2	1.4	1.9
Stamford	76.6	11.9	4.0	11.6	73.0	14.2	3.5	14.8
Tampa	73.7	16.6	2.0	14.0	74.3	15.8	2.8	13.6
Thousand Oaks	63.9	2.0	4.0	42.5	61.6	2.2	5.2	42.2
Tucson	65.5	3.4	1.5	42.8	65.7	3.6	1.9	40.6
Tulsa	68.0	11.5	1.2	6.0	69.6	11.3	1.8	5.2
Virginia Beach	54.7	37.5	2.3	3.5	56.0	36.3	2.9	3.6
Washington	54.3	30.4	5.8	9.9	53.1	30.9	6.6	10.2
Wichita	76.1	9.8	2.7	10.3	77.3	10.1	3.5	8.4
U.S.	68.5	15.5	3.3	16.8	68.8	15.5	3.8	15.7

Note: Figures shown cover persons 3 years old and over; (1) Metropolitan Statistical Area - see Appendix A for areas included; (2) people of Hispanic origin can be of any race
Source: Census 2000, Summary File 3

School Enrollment by Type: City

City	Grades KG to 8				Grades 9 to 12			
	Public		Private		Public		Private	
	Enrollment	%	Enrollment	%	Enrollment	%	Enrollment	%
Albuquerque	47,609	87.4	6,870	12.6	22,015	89.4	2,624	10.6
Alexandria	8,227	83.2	1,664	16.8	3,573	84.2	671	15.8
Anchorage	36,289	91.6	3,329	8.4	14,603	93.1	1,075	6.9
Ann Arbor	7,740	82.9	1,602	17.1	3,508	91.5	324	8.5
Athens	7,869	88.2	1,048	11.8	3,495	89.5	409	10.5
Atlanta	44,189	90.4	4,700	9.6	18,138	88.8	2,282	11.2
Austin	66,530	92.0	5,793	8.0	26,233	93.4	1,863	6.6
Baltimore	73,446	84.0	14,015	16.0	32,879	86.3	5,206	13.7
Baton Rouge	22,342	77.9	6,338	22.1	10,183	81.1	2,369	18.9
Bellevue	10,116	86.7	1,558	13.3	4,678	90.8	473	9.2
Birmingham	29,131	89.8	3,301	10.2	12,815	92.3	1,073	7.7
Boise City	21,529	90.8	2,176	9.2	9,656	92.2	819	7.8
Boston	50,589	79.9	12,717	20.1	25,077	85.3	4,321	14.7
Boulder	6,276	88.9	787	11.1	2,815	90.5	296	9.5
Buffalo	34,925	84.6	6,361	15.4	14,330	86.7	2,189	13.3
Cary	13,377	91.4	1,252	8.6	4,691	89.2	566	10.8
Cedar Rapids	13,027	85.2	2,266	14.8	5,715	93.5	397	6.5
Charleston	8,108	80.5	1,962	19.5	3,422	79.0	908	21.0
Charlotte	59,671	85.3	10,257	14.7	23,929	88.0	3,270	12.0
Chattanooga	15,709	84.9	2,790	15.1	6,176	85.0	1,091	15.0
Chicago	329,687	83.5	65,116	16.5	132,701	82.7	27,737	17.3
Cincinnati	33,493	79.5	8,653	20.5	12,622	80.6	3,043	19.4
Cleveland	61,753	83.8	11,908	16.2	22,670	84.3	4,212	15.7
Colorado Spgs.	43,127	89.7	4,978	10.3	18,240	90.6	1,898	9.4
Columbia	10,338	87.7	1,454	12.3	4,994	87.1	741	12.9
Columbus	76,928	88.3	10,154	11.7	28,639	88.2	3,833	11.8
Dallas	141,212	89.6	16,443	10.4	54,733	89.9	6,166	10.1
Denver	53,202	87.7	7,484	12.3	20,810	89.6	2,412	10.4
Des Moines	21,715	90.5	2,270	9.5	9,273	91.6	852	8.4
Durham	19,104	87.1	2,825	12.9	7,233	91.8	647	8.2
Edison	9,300	83.3	1,859	16.7	4,251	82.4	911	17.6
El Paso	86,000	93.3	6,128	6.7	39,565	94.1	2,469	5.9
Eugene	13,156	90.3	1,418	9.7	5,815	90.0	645	10.0
Ft. Collins	11,716	91.9	1,037	8.1	5,017	94.6	286	5.4
Ft. Lauderdale	12,934	82.4	2,769	17.6	6,278	84.6	1,141	15.4
Ft. Wayne	22,233	79.5	5,716	20.5	9,629	82.4	2,062	17.6
Ft. Worth	69,958	91.1	6,845	8.9	27,222	91.5	2,543	8.5
Grand Rapids	21,692	79.4	5,611	20.6	8,867	78.2	2,475	21.8
Green Bay	10,521	78.8	2,839	21.3	5,035	90.5	528	9.5
Greensboro	23,064	88.7	2,930	11.3	10,366	93.7	693	6.3
Honolulu	29,361	79.6	7,541	20.4	13,054	74.2	4,550	25.8
Houston	256,005	92.3	21,375	7.7	101,938	92.5	8,210	7.5
Huntsville	16,163	87.1	2,404	12.9	7,179	87.7	1,010	12.3
Indianapolis	83,767	82.2	18,091	17.8	34,219	86.1	5,520	13.9
Irvine	16,380	91.9	1,441	8.1	7,620	95.7	345	4.3
Jacksonville	88,145	85.4	15,094	14.6	35,819	86.6	5,563	13.4
Kansas City	49,028	85.0	8,649	15.0	20,065	85.3	3,465	14.7
Knoxville	15,184	88.4	1,990	11.6	6,409	89.2	776	10.8
Las Vegas	58,821	93.1	4,349	6.9	22,255	93.9	1,435	6.1
Lexington	24,534	85.4	4,202	14.6	9,857	86.3	1,563	13.7
Lincoln	20,876	82.5	4,438	17.5	10,055	85.9	1,653	14.1
Los Angeles	454,318	86.5	70,607	13.5	201,618	89.3	24,200	10.7
Louisville	27,065	84.1	5,098	15.9	11,516	84.9	2,042	15.1
Madison	15,810	87.7	2,221	12.3	8,024	93.3	580	6.7

Table continued on next page.

City	Grades KG to 8				Grades 9 to 12			
	Public		Private		Public		Private	
	Enrollment	%	Enrollment	%	Enrollment	%	Enrollment	%
Manchester	11,385	86.3	1,802	13.7	4,940	93.2	362	6.8
Memphis	85,881	90.2	9,354	9.8	35,249	89.5	4,154	10.5
Miami	38,677	92.7	3,053	7.3	21,451	92.1	1,842	7.9
Milwaukee	77,113	81.2	17,815	18.8	30,746	84.8	5,525	15.2
Minneapolis	37,584	86.5	5,872	13.5	15,840	89.4	1,875	10.6
Naperville	20,099	91.4	1,887	8.6	7,436	89.8	844	10.2
Nashville	50,605	83.9	9,685	16.1	21,680	83.5	4,271	16.5
New York	821,776	80.7	196,006	19.3	390,758	82.0	85,562	18.0
Norfolk	26,349	89.8	2,984	10.2	10,488	91.1	1,029	8.9
Oklahoma City	59,290	90.6	6,153	9.4	24,860	91.1	2,438	8.9
Omaha	40,515	79.6	10,359	20.4	17,898	82.5	3,800	17.5
Orlando	18,420	88.8	2,333	11.2	8,123	92.1	697	7.9
Overland Park	16,589	84.5	3,042	15.5	6,945	86.9	1,044	13.1
Philadelphia	153,896	76.1	48,216	23.9	75,971	78.8	20,421	21.2
Phoenix	180,398	93.3	12,894	6.7	68,750	92.8	5,365	7.2
Pittsburgh	26,858	78.3	7,436	21.7	12,690	80.6	3,050	19.4
Plano	28,544	88.8	3,606	11.2	11,760	93.6	799	6.4
Portland	48,210	87.7	6,772	12.3	21,811	89.2	2,630	10.8
Providence	21,820	87.6	3,080	12.4	8,725	89.8	989	10.2
Provo	9,048	96.1	366	3.9	4,330	93.4	304	6.6
Raleigh	26,402	88.9	3,313	11.1	9,915	89.5	1,168	10.5
Reno	20,254	94.4	1,201	5.6	8,597	92.7	679	7.3
Richmond	19,801	87.2	2,901	12.8	7,775	88.1	1,047	11.9
Rochester	30,274	87.9	4,160	12.1	10,807	88.7	1,375	11.3
Sacramento	54,640	92.1	4,702	7.9	23,025	91.2	2,210	8.8
St. Louis	38,345	80.1	9,537	19.9	15,889	82.1	3,470	17.9
St. Paul	34,035	83.9	6,535	16.1	15,176	86.3	2,399	13.7
St. Petersburg	23,502	83.5	4,648	16.5	10,943	89.8	1,239	10.2
Salt Lake City	18,258	90.9	1,820	9.1	7,946	91.4	743	8.6
San Antonio	153,162	90.8	15,589	9.2	66,419	92.3	5,523	7.7
San Diego	139,884	91.0	13,786	9.0	59,532	93.0	4,489	7.0
San Francisco	42,881	72.8	16,049	27.2	24,540	83.1	4,991	16.9
San Jose	106,741	88.9	13,294	11.1	49,044	91.1	4,769	8.9
Savannah	15,838	89.9	1,787	10.1	7,278	90.2	792	9.8
Scottsdale	17,720	87.3	2,589	12.7	7,609	92.4	629	7.6
Seattle	34,022	78.1	9,538	21.9	16,241	80.5	3,925	19.5
Sioux Falls	13,213	86.9	1,987	13.1	6,279	89.1	769	10.9
Springfield	13,701	92.2	1,155	7.8	5,634	91.5	525	8.5
Stamford	11,491	86.7	1,770	13.3	5,128	87.4	737	12.6
Tampa	34,437	87.0	5,154	13.0	14,603	90.2	1,585	9.8
Thousand Oaks	13,888	86.4	2,179	13.6	6,214	93.1	461	6.9
Tucson	55,793	91.9	4,904	8.1	22,977	91.9	2,035	8.1
Tulsa	42,689	85.8	7,070	14.2	16,642	85.1	2,912	14.9
Virginia Beach	55,674	90.5	5,847	9.5	23,625	92.9	1,817	7.1
Washington	52,899	85.5	8,975	14.5	22,303	83.6	4,391	16.4
Wichita	39,908	84.6	7,241	15.4	16,815	87.2	2,474	12.8
U.S.	33,526,011	88.7	4,285,121	11.3	14,848,628	90.6	1,532,323	9.4

Note: Figures shown cover persons 3 years old and over
Source: Census 2000, Summary File 3

School Enrollment by Type: Metro Area

MSA[1]	Grades KG to 8				Grades 9 to 12			
	Public		Private		Public		Private	
	Enrollment	%	Enrollment	%	Enrollment	%	Enrollment	%
Albuquerque	84,412	88.0	11,536	12.0	37,748	89.6	4,358	10.4
Alexandria	556,504	85.7	92,990	14.3	239,684	88.0	32,576	12.0
Anchorage	36,289	91.6	3,329	8.4	14,603	93.1	1,075	6.9
Ann Arbor	66,568	89.7	7,641	10.3	29,523	93.9	1,913	6.1
Athens	14,902	88.7	1,890	11.3	6,410	90.4	679	9.6
Atlanta	511,746	90.2	55,562	9.8	207,156	91.5	19,214	8.5
Austin	147,604	92.3	12,299	7.7	60,104	94.4	3,576	5.6
Baltimore	286,618	83.7	55,822	16.3	126,427	85.6	21,257	14.4
Baton Rouge	66,397	78.6	18,036	21.4	31,093	82.9	6,425	17.1
Bellevue	260,622	88.3	34,672	11.7	116,866	91.1	11,446	8.9
Birmingham	108,002	88.8	13,686	11.2	46,620	91.2	4,503	8.8
Boise City	55,566	91.3	5,311	8.7	24,072	92.7	1,882	7.3
Boston	347,941	87.2	51,024	12.8	147,396	85.5	25,007	14.5
Boulder	30,621	88.7	3,890	11.3	13,101	92.0	1,146	8.0
Buffalo	128,746	84.5	23,691	15.5	58,792	88.9	7,351	11.1
Cary	134,391	89.7	15,408	10.3	51,033	90.4	5,428	9.6
Cedar Rapids	21,662	86.5	3,372	13.5	9,839	93.7	663	6.3
Charleston	65,879	86.6	10,174	13.4	27,841	87.9	3,845	12.1
Charlotte	176,153	88.3	23,233	11.7	71,217	91.1	6,951	8.9
Chattanooga	50,400	86.5	7,842	13.5	19,835	83.3	3,969	16.7
Chicago	980,199	85.2	169,831	14.8	411,578	87.3	59,611	12.7
Cincinnati	180,810	79.1	47,767	20.9	77,135	80.6	18,574	19.4
Cleveland	248,070	81.7	55,751	18.3	109,279	86.0	17,810	14.0
Colorado Spgs.	65,944	90.7	6,787	9.3	27,884	91.4	2,632	8.6
Columbia	64,099	91.7	5,837	8.3	28,539	92.5	2,319	7.5
Columbus	178,054	88.0	24,285	12.0	73,403	89.9	8,275	10.1
Dallas	456,971	90.7	46,953	9.3	181,249	92.2	15,405	7.8
Denver	250,673	90.0	27,814	10.0	104,095	91.3	9,939	8.7
Des Moines	53,644	90.8	5,417	9.2	23,513	92.7	1,860	7.3
Durham	134,391	89.7	15,408	10.3	51,033	90.4	5,428	9.6
Edison	129,755	87.7	18,130	12.3	53,556	88.7	6,806	11.3
El Paso	107,817	94.1	6,804	5.9	49,887	94.5	2,915	5.5
Eugene	34,800	91.9	3,082	8.1	15,788	92.5	1,272	7.5
Ft. Collins	27,705	89.6	3,226	10.4	12,585	93.9	818	6.1
Ft. Lauderdale	175,895	86.9	26,604	13.1	77,084	87.7	10,767	12.3
Ft. Wayne	57,627	81.1	13,469	18.9	25,703	87.4	3,711	12.6
Ft. Worth	224,258	91.0	22,110	9.0	91,305	92.3	7,600	7.7
Grand Rapids	136,670	84.9	24,380	15.1	60,710	86.6	9,386	13.4
Green Bay	24,377	79.6	6,235	20.4	12,009	90.5	1,257	9.5
Greensboro	142,941	90.4	15,232	9.6	58,865	93.0	4,436	7.0
Honolulu	89,045	82.9	18,407	17.1	38,196	79.4	9,908	20.6
Houston	589,699	92.3	49,169	7.7	244,239	93.2	17,795	6.8
Huntsville	39,989	87.7	5,601	12.3	16,226	89.1	1,975	10.9
Indianapolis	187,223	86.2	29,909	13.8	76,997	89.2	9,345	10.8
Irvine	358,527	88.6	45,927	11.4	154,346	93.5	10,681	6.5
Jacksonville	131,666	86.5	20,471	13.5	55,375	88.2	7,379	11.8
Kansas City	212,067	87.5	30,212	12.5	90,420	89.1	11,050	10.9
Knoxville	72,586	90.0	8,074	10.0	31,473	91.8	2,809	8.2
Las Vegas	190,592	94.6	10,904	5.4	72,968	94.8	3,972	5.2
Lexington	48,932	86.9	7,363	13.1	20,298	89.2	2,451	10.8
Lincoln	24,001	83.0	4,912	17.0	11,765	86.3	1,865	13.7
Los Angeles	1,261,035	88.4	164,761	11.6	560,595	91.0	55,347	9.0
Louisville	104,712	80.1	25,959	19.9	47,494	83.5	9,408	16.5
Madison	44,489	89.8	5,034	10.2	20,659	94.4	1,235	5.6

Table continued on next page.

MSA[1]	Grades KG to 8				Grades 9 to 12			
	Public		Private		Public		Private	
	Enrollment	%	Enrollment	%	Enrollment	%	Enrollment	%
Manchester	23,694	87.1	3,521	12.9	9,986	91.3	949	8.7
Memphis	149,569	88.4	19,693	11.6	61,138	87.4	8,828	12.6
Miami	257,812	87.1	38,141	12.9	130,916	88.5	16,983	11.5
Milwaukee	168,628	79.3	43,942	20.7	79,263	87.0	11,852	13.0
Minneapolis	360,354	87.5	51,396	12.5	163,520	92.1	13,991	7.9
Naperville	980,199	85.2	169,831	14.8	411,578	87.3	59,611	12.7
Nashville	136,243	86.5	21,347	13.5	56,641	85.6	9,515	14.4
New York	965,235	80.8	229,009	19.2	450,178	81.9	99,330	18.1
Norfolk	196,408	89.6	22,702	10.4	83,827	92.7	6,565	7.3
Oklahoma City	129,199	91.2	12,443	8.8	57,617	92.5	4,701	7.5
Omaha	82,606	83.0	16,937	17.0	37,494	86.1	6,066	13.9
Orlando	186,352	87.2	27,385	12.8	83,562	92.0	7,301	8.0
Overland Park	212,067	87.5	30,212	12.5	90,420	89.1	11,050	10.9
Philadelphia	544,674	79.7	138,763	20.3	248,356	81.5	56,489	18.5
Phoenix	414,735	93.4	29,200	6.6	163,065	93.8	10,740	6.2
Pittsburgh	237,516	86.3	37,647	13.7	114,399	91.8	10,230	8.2
Plano	456,971	90.7	46,953	9.3	181,249	92.2	15,405	7.8
Portland	219,761	88.8	27,653	11.2	95,236	91.4	8,906	8.6
Providence	131,803	87.2	19,325	12.8	57,810	87.9	7,987	12.1
Provo	56,391	96.9	1,786	3.1	24,610	96.2	976	3.8
Raleigh	134,391	89.7	15,408	10.3	51,033	90.4	5,428	9.6
Reno	41,138	94.0	2,646	6.0	17,229	93.4	1,216	6.6
Richmond	120,997	91.0	12,001	9.0	50,424	91.5	4,709	8.5
Rochester	137,259	89.9	15,386	10.1	59,420	91.9	5,236	8.1
Sacramento	213,241	90.3	22,784	9.7	93,412	92.7	7,388	7.3
St. Louis	288,749	80.5	70,107	19.5	129,252	83.7	25,180	16.3
St. Paul	360,354	87.5	51,396	12.5	163,520	92.1	13,991	7.9
St. Petersburg	239,025	86.3	38,069	13.7	103,629	90.5	10,836	9.5
Salt Lake City	189,691	94.4	11,196	5.6	93,135	95.6	4,302	4.4
San Antonio	212,457	90.6	22,110	9.4	93,622	92.5	7,639	7.5
San Diego	345,699	90.9	34,480	9.1	149,710	93.8	9,945	6.2
San Francisco	132,872	78.0	37,427	22.0	64,080	83.2	12,973	16.8
San Jose	184,435	86.6	28,642	13.4	83,075	89.8	9,411	10.2
Savannah	35,191	85.9	5,780	14.1	14,841	85.9	2,431	14.1
Scottsdale	414,735	93.4	29,200	6.6	163,065	93.8	10,740	6.2
Seattle	260,622	88.3	34,672	11.7	116,866	91.1	11,446	8.9
Sioux Falls	20,204	88.6	2,600	11.4	9,568	91.6	879	8.4
Springfield	35,976	91.5	3,328	8.5	15,302	93.2	1,123	6.8
Stamford	39,768	84.9	7,049	15.1	14,756	83.9	2,827	16.1
Tampa	239,025	86.3	38,069	13.7	103,629	90.5	10,836	9.5
Thousand Oaks	100,814	89.0	12,408	11.0	46,013	93.3	3,285	6.7
Tucson	98,857	91.6	9,092	8.4	42,008	91.8	3,736	8.2
Tulsa	100,102	89.6	11,603	10.4	42,559	90.5	4,446	9.5
Virginia Beach	196,408	89.6	22,702	10.4	83,827	92.7	6,565	7.3
Washington	556,504	85.7	92,990	14.3	239,684	88.0	32,576	12.0
Wichita	67,343	85.4	11,552	14.6	29,490	89.3	3,529	10.7
U.S.	33,526,011	88.7	4,285,121	11.3	14,848,628	90.6	1,532,323	9.4

Note: Figures shown cover persons 3 years old and over; (1) Metropolitan Statistical Area - see Appendix A for areas included
Source: Census 2000, Summary File 3

Educational Attainment by Race: City

City	High School Graduate (%)					Bachelor's Degree (%)				
	Total	White	Black	Asian	Hisp.[1]	Total	White	Black	Asian	Hisp.[1]
Albuquerque	85.9	88.6	86.3	81.1	72.4	31.8	35.8	23.7	40.3	15.2
Alexandria	86.8	93.3	79.9	86.9	51.5	54.3	66.9	28.3	55.9	21.3
Anchorage	90.3	93.6	87.9	73.2	76.4	28.9	32.6	15.5	24.0	16.3
Ann Arbor	95.7	97.0	84.3	96.9	89.6	69.3	70.9	38.7	87.4	60.4
Athens	81.0	89.0	65.3	93.0	49.8	40.0	52.2	11.4	76.5	21.2
Atlanta	76.9	92.4	66.8	79.2	53.6	34.6	66.1	12.7	54.0	20.8
Austin	83.4	90.2	79.1	90.7	55.7	40.4	47.6	19.0	67.0	15.5
Baltimore	68.4	73.3	65.3	77.8	62.2	19.1	33.0	10.0	52.3	24.6
Baton Rouge	80.1	91.9	67.2	74.1	77.6	31.7	45.1	15.6	47.8	34.5
Bellevue	94.3	95.9	93.4	92.8	65.9	54.1	54.2	39.1	63.0	28.7
Birmingham	75.5	81.0	73.1	88.3	56.2	18.5	30.7	12.8	66.8	15.7
Boise City	91.1	91.8	85.4	81.8	76.5	33.6	33.9	30.8	45.2	18.2
Boston	78.9	86.2	73.0	64.3	57.3	35.6	46.8	15.6	37.0	15.3
Boulder	94.7	96.1	92.7	92.1	54.4	66.9	68.1	48.8	78.6	29.3
Buffalo	74.6	77.4	71.3	73.2	59.5	18.3	22.7	10.2	40.5	13.0
Cary	95.1	96.2	93.8	92.5	59.4	60.7	61.1	47.7	74.0	33.4
Cedar Rapids	90.1	90.6	78.7	89.9	72.9	28.4	28.4	12.2	53.4	23.2
Charleston	83.7	93.3	64.5	86.3	77.3	37.5	48.8	14.7	57.2	26.3
Charlotte	84.9	90.9	77.8	76.8	48.4	36.4	45.9	18.9	39.6	13.0
Chattanooga	77.6	81.7	69.9	86.7	58.9	21.5	27.0	9.3	51.1	16.3
Chicago	71.8	78.4	70.7	79.7	46.6	25.5	36.3	13.5	48.2	8.5
Cincinnati	76.7	82.7	67.2	89.3	76.0	26.6	36.5	10.0	69.2	39.0
Cleveland	69.0	72.3	66.5	72.8	54.2	11.4	15.6	6.5	42.2	7.8
Colorado Spgs.	90.9	92.4	90.4	83.2	72.9	33.6	36.0	19.2	38.7	14.1
Columbia	82.3	91.5	70.5	96.6	77.9	35.7	52.8	13.9	63.6	25.2
Columbus	83.8	86.1	77.7	84.9	67.7	29.0	32.5	14.3	59.2	19.3
Dallas	70.4	78.3	73.9	78.5	33.4	27.7	38.5	13.5	50.5	6.5
Denver	78.9	85.1	79.7	77.0	46.1	34.5	42.0	17.8	40.7	7.8
Des Moines	83.0	85.4	78.8	61.0	49.4	21.8	23.2	14.2	17.2	8.9
Durham	82.6	89.4	77.9	94.4	36.4	41.8	54.2	26.3	78.3	14.4
Edison	87.6	86.6	89.3	90.3	75.4	42.3	31.4	31.0	71.1	21.5
El Paso	68.6	69.6	89.6	83.4	59.9	18.3	20.0	21.7	42.7	12.0
Eugene	91.5	92.3	85.3	93.8	70.3	37.3	37.8	34.3	56.4	19.1
Ft. Collins	94.0	95.1	90.4	92.6	69.4	48.4	49.4	40.0	68.1	22.0
Ft. Lauderdale	79.0	88.9	50.3	72.9	68.3	27.9	35.4	5.2	30.3	22.7
Ft. Wayne	83.2	85.7	75.9	76.5	52.7	19.4	21.7	8.4	32.5	5.9
Ft. Worth	72.8	79.2	74.8	71.8	37.3	22.3	28.2	11.4	36.3	6.7
Grand Rapids	78.0	83.6	68.9	65.5	35.5	23.8	28.7	10.2	27.5	6.5
Green Bay	82.6	85.5	70.0	44.7	38.4	19.3	20.3	11.4	15.3	6.9
Greensboro	84.3	88.8	79.9	66.3	46.5	33.9	42.3	20.6	32.0	13.5
Honolulu	83.4	93.3	90.0	79.4	83.6	31.1	44.3	23.6	29.6	18.9
Houston	70.4	77.0	74.7	78.7	38.8	27.0	35.5	15.9	47.4	7.9
Huntsville	85.7	89.2	76.0	84.3	69.8	36.1	41.2	20.5	54.9	28.4
Indianapolis	81.3	83.8	74.9	85.8	54.1	25.4	28.9	13.3	57.8	13.9
Irvine	95.3	96.3	96.3	94.5	86.6	58.4	57.0	35.7	67.2	38.6
Jacksonville	82.3	85.4	74.2	81.5	79.0	21.1	23.7	13.2	34.7	21.9
Kansas City	82.5	87.3	74.5	72.8	58.3	25.7	31.9	11.9	36.7	10.8
Knoxville	78.4	79.4	73.3	88.1	69.6	24.6	26.0	13.5	63.2	26.4
Las Vegas	78.5	82.7	76.1	83.2	44.6	18.2	19.8	12.5	30.2	6.1
Lexington	85.8	87.5	76.2	91.6	54.5	35.6	38.3	14.5	68.0	14.6
Lincoln	90.2	91.8	81.3	67.6	64.3	33.3	34.2	17.7	35.8	19.5
Los Angeles	66.6	75.6	76.0	82.1	35.5	25.5	32.7	17.1	42.4	6.1
Louisville	76.1	78.9	69.2	74.4	53.8	21.3	26.5	8.2	43.7	15.5
Madison	92.4	94.1	77.5	86.8	72.0	48.2	49.3	20.0	67.1	34.1
Manchester	80.7	81.4	75.5	70.8	58.0	22.3	22.1	19.3	39.5	9.3

Table continued on next page.

City	High School Graduate (%)					Bachelor's Degree (%)				
	Total	White	Black	Asian	Hisp.[1]	Total	White	Black	Asian	Hisp.[1]
Memphis	76.4	86.1	69.8	75.8	46.1	20.9	32.9	11.3	49.5	12.6
Miami	52.7	54.4	49.6	81.4	47.2	16.2	19.5	6.5	44.6	13.4
Milwaukee	74.8	81.8	67.6	66.6	45.2	18.3	23.9	9.1	32.9	8.0
Minneapolis	85.0	90.7	75.0	63.1	48.7	37.4	44.7	14.0	32.2	13.3
Naperville	96.3	96.9	93.1	94.4	81.9	60.6	59.6	43.7	78.0	35.6
Nashville	81.1	84.2	75.1	80.9	53.2	29.7	32.9	20.1	49.9	14.3
New York	72.3	79.6	70.4	69.4	53.4	27.4	36.6	15.8	36.2	10.5
Norfolk	78.4	86.0	67.9	79.7	81.5	19.6	26.3	9.7	34.9	16.5
Oklahoma City	81.3	84.9	78.4	73.3	42.0	24.0	26.8	14.6	31.9	7.2
Omaha	86.0	89.0	76.2	88.0	46.2	28.7	31.4	11.4	57.5	9.9
Orlando	82.2	88.9	63.5	86.0	73.8	28.2	34.0	12.4	41.9	18.7
Overland Park	95.8	96.4	94.4	91.0	77.0	52.1	52.2	50.2	67.9	29.5
Philadelphia	71.2	76.1	68.4	62.9	49.5	17.9	23.7	10.3	32.7	9.2
Phoenix	76.6	82.5	77.5	80.1	43.1	22.7	26.1	15.2	42.1	6.1
Pittsburgh	81.3	83.0	75.2	92.0	76.7	26.2	29.1	12.2	76.6	40.3
Plano	93.9	95.7	92.8	94.3	63.3	53.3	53.0	46.1	72.6	24.7
Portland	85.7	88.8	78.4	68.5	59.5	32.6	35.5	15.3	26.7	14.5
Providence	65.8	72.0	67.6	59.5	45.3	24.4	31.8	15.0	29.0	6.6
Provo	89.4	92.1	75.4	88.5	62.4	35.7	37.3	25.4	51.7	15.5
Raleigh	88.5	93.6	81.0	87.7	45.0	44.9	53.7	24.2	60.7	13.6
Reno	82.4	86.4	82.6	83.7	42.6	25.0	26.9	15.2	34.6	6.6
Richmond	75.2	86.5	65.9	82.2	59.6	29.5	51.3	11.2	49.8	20.3
Rochester	73.0	80.4	64.8	68.5	53.4	20.1	28.5	8.2	33.5	8.2
Sacramento	77.3	84.1	80.6	65.6	57.2	23.9	29.6	13.6	25.6	10.3
St. Louis	71.3	77.7	64.7	66.8	61.8	19.1	28.1	8.8	33.2	16.6
St. Paul	83.8	89.2	79.1	52.6	56.7	32.0	37.0	16.3	17.2	12.9
St. Petersburg	81.9	85.8	67.8	67.0	77.2	22.8	26.0	10.1	24.7	20.2
Salt Lake City	83.4	87.7	76.5	77.2	47.5	34.9	38.0	16.2	45.5	9.4
San Antonio	75.1	77.9	82.1	82.3	61.8	21.6	25.0	17.0	41.4	10.5
San Diego	82.8	88.8	83.4	80.0	52.4	35.0	40.9	15.7	38.4	11.9
San Francisco	81.2	91.7	76.1	67.3	62.5	45.0	59.3	18.1	31.8	20.3
San Jose	78.3	84.8	88.0	79.7	52.1	31.6	33.9	28.0	40.7	8.9
Savannah	76.1	85.6	68.2	73.9	67.2	20.2	30.2	11.1	35.2	22.5
Scottsdale	93.5	94.3	92.6	92.6	69.8	44.1	44.6	41.6	58.1	21.3
Seattle	89.5	93.9	77.2	75.7	70.5	47.2	53.3	20.1	37.0	26.1
Sioux Falls	88.5	90.1	76.9	54.1	48.8	27.8	28.7	20.4	30.8	7.1
Springfield	82.8	83.2	83.2	80.0	68.8	23.0	23.4	12.4	40.7	16.5
Stamford	82.2	86.6	69.6	91.0	58.8	39.6	44.5	17.0	70.0	11.8
Tampa	77.1	81.5	65.9	79.5	60.8	25.4	30.8	9.9	38.8	14.7
Thousand Oaks	91.4	93.1	89.5	94.1	61.7	42.2	41.7	50.3	72.5	15.0
Tucson	80.4	84.6	80.8	77.0	60.5	22.9	25.9	14.7	40.0	9.8
Tulsa	84.4	87.1	79.4	77.7	48.3	28.3	31.9	14.2	40.3	9.6
Virginia Beach	90.4	92.0	85.9	84.2	87.2	28.1	30.4	18.1	33.4	19.1
Washington	77.8	94.4	70.4	81.9	47.8	39.1	77.3	17.5	58.2	24.8
Wichita	83.8	87.6	77.8	62.5	48.1	25.3	28.1	12.6	24.5	9.4
U.S.	80.4	83.6	72.3	80.4	52.4	24.4	26.1	14.3	44.1	10.4

Note: Figures shown cover persons 25 years old and over; (1) people of Hispanic origin can be of any race
Source: Census 2000, Summary File 3

Educational Attainment by Race: Metro Area

MSA[1]	High School Graduate (%)					Bachelor's Degree (%)				
	Total	White	Black	Asian	Hisp.[2]	Total	White	Black	Asian	Hisp.[2]
Albuquerque	83.9	87.3	85.3	81.1	70.4	28.4	32.8	22.5	39.4	13.2
Alexandria	86.7	91.1	81.3	85.4	57.7	41.8	49.2	24.1	53.9	21.0
Anchorage	90.3	93.6	87.9	73.2	76.4	28.9	32.6	15.5	24.0	16.3
Ann Arbor	90.1	90.7	83.0	94.1	75.4	36.9	36.4	24.1	80.5	28.9
Athens	80.1	84.9	64.7	91.3	50.4	34.1	39.8	11.0	72.6	20.0
Atlanta	84.0	86.8	81.0	80.0	51.7	32.0	36.1	21.9	46.4	16.1
Austin	84.8	89.7	80.0	88.5	58.6	36.7	41.1	20.1	62.2	14.7
Baltimore	81.9	85.1	72.9	84.4	75.1	29.2	33.0	16.1	53.2	28.7
Baton Rouge	81.9	87.1	69.6	75.9	77.9	24.9	27.9	16.4	50.0	30.0
Bellevue	90.1	92.3	82.4	82.2	67.8	35.9	37.0	21.1	40.9	19.0
Birmingham	80.6	83.2	74.2	87.6	57.9	24.7	28.3	14.6	65.5	17.3
Boise City	86.5	88.6	80.5	80.6	50.0	26.5	27.3	26.3	38.7	8.8
Boston	87.1	89.5	76.4	78.3	61.0	39.5	41.1	20.8	53.4	18.7
Boulder	92.8	94.6	91.5	90.1	57.6	52.4	53.8	45.0	65.2	18.2
Buffalo	83.0	84.7	70.7	83.9	61.9	23.2	24.3	11.1	63.4	15.6
Cary	85.4	89.4	76.6	91.6	43.0	38.9	43.7	22.2	70.0	15.3
Cedar Rapids	90.6	90.9	80.0	91.0	74.0	27.7	27.7	13.2	55.1	22.7
Charleston	81.3	87.4	67.3	79.3	67.5	25.0	30.9	10.7	38.0	16.5
Charlotte	80.5	83.0	74.7	76.4	48.6	26.5	29.1	16.5	37.8	11.9
Chattanooga	77.0	78.0	70.8	83.7	64.3	19.7	20.9	10.3	46.1	17.3
Chicago	81.0	85.8	74.3	86.9	47.8	30.1	34.1	15.6	57.5	8.9
Cincinnati	82.4	83.9	71.6	90.8	73.9	25.3	26.6	12.6	64.3	29.0
Cleveland	82.9	85.4	72.3	85.6	62.6	23.3	25.5	10.8	59.1	12.1
Colorado Spgs.	91.3	92.5	91.7	82.6	74.5	31.8	34.0	19.0	35.4	14.1
Columbia	84.3	87.6	77.2	84.6	70.2	29.2	34.1	17.3	50.7	21.1
Columbus	85.8	87.2	78.1	86.1	67.9	29.1	30.4	15.4	59.7	21.6
Dallas	79.4	84.4	78.9	83.4	41.5	30.0	34.0	18.5	52.2	8.7
Denver	86.4	89.6	83.6	79.8	55.9	34.2	37.3	21.0	40.6	10.6
Des Moines	88.6	90.1	80.3	67.9	54.6	28.7	29.7	16.3	28.7	11.7
Durham	85.4	89.4	76.6	91.6	43.0	38.9	43.7	22.2	70.0	15.3
Edison	86.5	87.6	83.3	91.3	61.9	37.4	35.0	27.2	71.5	13.3
El Paso	65.8	66.5	88.1	83.2	57.0	16.6	18.0	21.1	42.7	10.6
Eugene	87.5	88.2	84.5	88.0	64.8	25.5	25.6	29.2	49.4	15.8
Ft. Collins	92.3	93.3	91.7	89.9	66.2	39.5	40.2	39.4	62.0	17.4
Ft. Lauderdale	82.0	85.5	69.2	81.0	75.7	24.5	26.8	14.7	38.8	23.0
Ft. Wayne	85.3	86.5	76.6	77.9	58.5	19.4	20.0	9.8	39.3	7.9
Ft. Worth	81.0	84.9	80.2	72.4	46.6	25.1	27.3	16.8	36.3	9.2
Grand Rapids	84.6	86.8	72.6	69.9	50.8	22.9	24.3	9.7	31.2	8.3
Green Bay	86.3	88.0	64.7	52.0	42.1	22.5	23.1	7.7	21.3	7.3
Greensboro	78.6	80.4	75.8	70.3	37.9	22.9	24.5	16.7	36.0	8.7
Honolulu	84.8	93.5	93.0	80.8	84.3	27.9	39.6	20.9	28.2	15.1
Houston	75.9	81.4	77.5	80.1	43.6	27.2	31.4	18.4	47.7	8.5
Huntsville	83.3	84.9	76.4	85.1	68.7	30.9	32.8	21.8	53.4	22.4
Indianapolis	84.0	85.5	75.6	86.7	58.9	25.8	27.4	13.8	57.3	16.7
Irvine	79.5	86.0	88.1	81.2	45.1	30.8	33.4	27.6	41.4	8.5
Jacksonville	83.6	86.2	74.0	81.5	79.5	22.9	25.0	13.2	35.2	21.4
Kansas City	86.7	88.8	77.4	80.9	61.4	28.5	30.6	14.6	46.6	13.3
Knoxville	79.6	79.8	76.0	88.9	71.4	23.5	23.6	15.6	60.9	23.6
Las Vegas	79.2	82.2	78.5	81.5	47.9	16.4	17.2	11.9	27.2	6.4
Lexington	82.1	82.9	75.1	91.2	52.8	28.7	29.7	13.5	66.5	13.9
Lincoln	90.5	92.0	81.5	67.8	64.1	32.6	33.3	17.7	36.0	19.3
Los Angeles	69.9	77.0	79.3	82.4	42.1	24.9	29.3	17.8	42.9	6.8
Louisville	81.3	82.3	74.6	84.7	64.4	22.2	23.4	11.8	51.0	17.2
Madison	92.2	93.3	77.6	87.0	67.8	40.6	41.0	19.2	65.5	27.2
Manchester	84.8	85.3	79.1	73.4	64.4	27.0	27.0	23.3	42.3	11.8

Table continued on next page.

MSA[1]	High School Graduate (%)					Bachelor's Degree (%)				
	Total	White	Black	Asian	Hisp.[2]	Total	White	Black	Asian	Hisp.[2]
Memphis	79.8	87.1	69.6	78.7	52.4	22.7	29.2	12.1	48.4	14.1
Miami	67.9	69.4	63.3	80.5	61.2	21.7	24.3	11.5	45.1	18.1
Milwaukee	84.5	88.2	68.3	77.2	52.4	27.0	29.7	10.3	46.6	10.7
Minneapolis	90.6	92.5	79.9	70.9	61.5	33.3	34.4	19.1	36.3	16.7
Naperville	81.0	85.8	74.3	86.9	47.8	30.1	34.1	15.6	57.5	8.9
Nashville	81.4	83.2	74.4	81.1	54.5	26.9	28.2	18.9	46.1	14.2
New York	74.0	81.2	70.8	70.9	53.9	29.2	37.9	16.3	38.1	11.0
Norfolk	84.7	88.7	75.1	82.7	84.9	23.8	27.6	14.2	35.2	19.8
Oklahoma City	83.6	85.7	80.7	76.8	50.1	24.4	26.1	15.6	37.3	9.6
Omaha	88.0	89.9	78.2	85.8	53.7	28.0	29.3	13.5	51.1	11.6
Orlando	82.8	85.7	69.3	82.2	71.6	24.8	26.5	14.6	42.3	17.0
Overland Park	86.7	88.8	77.4	80.9	61.4	28.5	30.6	14.6	46.6	13.3
Philadelphia	82.2	85.7	71.9	77.2	55.5	27.7	31.1	12.8	46.7	12.8
Phoenix	81.9	86.3	81.6	84.9	49.3	25.1	27.3	19.4	46.6	7.8
Pittsburgh	85.1	85.5	78.2	90.5	80.7	23.8	24.2	12.8	70.8	31.6
Plano	79.4	84.4	78.9	83.4	41.5	30.0	34.0	18.5	52.2	8.7
Portland	87.2	89.4	80.4	79.1	53.7	28.8	29.6	18.0	38.3	11.8
Providence	76.0	77.8	70.5	68.3	50.2	23.6	24.5	16.8	35.4	8.5
Provo	90.9	92.2	78.7	91.5	62.8	31.5	32.1	25.7	48.7	16.2
Raleigh	85.4	89.4	76.6	91.6	43.0	38.9	43.7	22.2	70.0	15.3
Reno	83.9	87.3	84.2	83.2	45.9	23.7	25.2	16.7	34.2	6.9
Richmond	82.6	87.0	72.7	78.7	68.8	29.2	34.5	15.4	47.0	20.2
Rochester	84.4	87.0	65.1	80.3	57.7	27.1	28.7	10.6	52.6	12.2
Sacramento	85.0	88.7	83.1	73.8	63.6	25.9	27.8	16.2	31.6	12.3
St. Louis	83.4	85.5	73.4	84.0	74.3	25.3	27.3	13.0	55.2	24.0
St. Paul	90.6	92.5	79.9	70.9	61.5	33.3	34.4	19.1	36.3	16.7
St. Petersburg	81.5	83.1	71.0	78.4	65.8	21.7	22.4	13.0	39.2	16.2
Salt Lake City	87.5	89.9	83.0	78.2	56.5	26.5	27.6	19.5	34.8	9.4
San Antonio	77.3	80.2	83.2	81.4	62.3	22.4	25.5	18.0	38.4	10.6
San Diego	82.6	87.7	86.1	81.3	53.5	29.5	33.1	16.3	37.2	10.7
San Francisco	84.2	91.3	75.9	75.6	59.2	43.6	51.3	18.5	38.9	16.2
San Jose	83.4	88.4	88.6	84.8	55.1	40.5	42.5	29.7	51.3	11.0
Savannah	79.9	85.3	69.5	72.5	69.5	23.2	27.9	12.4	37.0	24.2
Scottsdale	81.9	86.3	81.6	84.9	49.3	25.1	27.3	19.4	46.6	7.8
Seattle	90.1	92.3	82.4	82.2	67.8	35.9	37.0	21.1	40.9	19.0
Sioux Falls	88.6	89.7	78.0	54.3	52.0	25.9	26.5	20.4	29.5	8.2
Springfield	84.0	84.3	82.2	80.5	71.0	22.4	22.6	13.9	40.9	15.1
Stamford	87.6	90.4	71.6	91.8	62.0	49.4	53.5	17.2	69.9	14.2
Tampa	81.5	83.1	71.0	78.4	65.8	21.7	22.4	13.0	39.2	16.2
Thousand Oaks	80.1	86.9	88.4	87.8	47.6	26.9	29.9	27.1	47.3	7.6
Tucson	83.4	87.1	81.9	80.5	62.8	26.7	29.7	16.8	43.3	10.9
Tulsa	83.7	85.2	79.2	77.8	54.2	23.2	25.0	14.8	37.4	11.8
Virginia Beach	84.7	88.7	75.1	82.7	84.9	23.8	27.6	14.2	35.2	19.8
Washington	86.7	91.1	81.3	85.4	57.7	41.8	49.2	24.1	53.9	21.0
Wichita	85.3	88.1	78.0	62.4	51.5	24.7	26.5	13.0	23.7	9.6
U.S.	80.4	83.6	72.3	80.4	52.4	24.4	26.1	14.3	44.1	10.4

Note: Figures shown cover persons 25 years old and over; (1) Metropolitan Statistical Area - see Appendix A for areas included; (2) people of Hispanic origin can be of any race
Source: Census 2000, Summary File 3

Cost of Living Index

Area	Composite	Groceries	Housing	Utilities	Transp.	Health	Misc.
Albuquerque	102.5	105.2	109.7	93.0	103.4	101.1	98.4
Alexandria[1]	141.7	109.9	221.4	117.7	109.6	112.3	109.2
Anchorage	119.1	125.7	126.0	93.0	102.6	133.5	121.8
Ann Arbor	n/a	n/a	n/a	n/a	n/a	n/a	n/a
Athens	n/a	n/a	n/a	n/a	n/a	n/a	n/a
Atlanta	97.6	96.5	95.7	87.8	106.3	102.8	99.3
Austin	96.1	92.7	87.5	90.1	99.4	100.3	104.6
Baltimore	119.4	105.7	152.8	117.0	110.2	105.8	102.7
Baton Rouge	95.9	99.6	92.1	105.0	98.6	101.0	93.6
Bellevue[2]	115.8	109.6	135.0	99.7	109.2	120.2	108.8
Birmingham[1]	96.1	104.5	82.7	109.8	103.6	101.1	96.9
Boise City	97.3	93.8	88.2	93.8	99.8	101.3	105.8
Boston	136.1	118.8	169.4	127.3	109.6	130.8	126.6
Boulder	n/a	n/a	n/a	n/a	n/a	n/a	n/a
Buffalo	104.2	116.2	93.1	132.1	104.9	98.7	101.0
Cary[15]	94.9	99.9	82.8	97.5	99.0	111.4	98.8
Cedar Rapids	92.8	89.7	79.0	104.3	96.7	106.7	98.9
Charleston[1]	98.8	101.6	95.2	94.5	99.0	112.4	100.1
Charlotte	91.8	97.0	77.3	79.4	100.3	110.2	100.5
Chattanooga	93.7	96.0	87.2	95.8	97.7	96.8	95.9
Chicago	114.7	112.0	133.5	110.4	111.1	109.7	103.4
Cincinnati	93.6	91.9	85.8	106.4	91.8	95.7	97.1
Cleveland	99.7	107.6	93.2	115.1	99.6	100.8	97.6
Colorado Springs	94.6	98.2	87.4	96.6	106.0	107.0	93.8
Columbia	93.5	96.7	84.7	100.2	90.6	108.3	96.7
Columbus	102.5	99.5	102.6	113.0	103.7	105.3	99.9
Dallas[1]	94.6	100.5	77.5	114.1	105.1	101.6	96.9
Denver[1]	101.9	104.7	107.1	99.7	96.5	104.8	98.6
Des Moines	92.6	88.1	88.8	101.5	92.3	90.6	95.1
Durham	91.4	99.6	77.9	90.3	100.0	99.3	96.2
Edison[5]	130.2	118.2	173.9	108.6	107.3	109.6	114.9
El Paso	91.8	106.3	74.8	98.6	98.8	99.9	95.1
Eugene	109.1	95.2	127.8	83.6	108.1	114.5	106.4
Fort Collins	103.4	111.1	105.5	81.4	99.3	105.4	106.0
Fort Lauderdale	117.0	103.0	154.8	97.5	106.8	112.2	100.9
Fort Wayne[3]	91.3	93.9	83.1	104.1	96.7	90.2	91.8
Fort Worth	88.9	92.6	77.6	95.9	99.5	93.2	91.0
Grand Rapids	103.4	107.4	95.2	123.7	103.8	98.3	103.1
Green Bay	94.6	89.5	89.5	102.9	102.1	96.2	95.7
Greensboro[4]	90.4	98.9	77.7	84.4	94.5	104.3	96.5
Honolulu	161.3	154.4	248.5	116.3	118.1	110.3	125.3
Houston[1]	89.4	83.4	73.0	108.0	100.4	99.8	95.1
Huntsville	91.6	93.9	78.9	83.9	102.6	90.4	100.3
Indianapolis	95.9	97.7	96.2	97.6	103.1	95.6	92.4
Irvine[6]	155.3	130.9	258.5	106.7	113.3	115.7	112.2
Jacksonville	96.3	98.0	90.1	89.7	105.9	99.2	99.5
Kansas City[1]	94.8	93.0	88.2	94.9	98.4	95.8	99.6
Knoxville	88.1	87.9	79.4	89.2	88.0	90.2	94.7
Las Vegas	109.2	99.4	130.0	112.1	105.1	105.7	96.9
Lexington[1]	95.8	99.8	88.1	104.1	94.1	99.2	98.2
Lincoln	n/a	n/a	n/a	n/a	n/a	n/a	n/a
Los Angeles[1]	155.6	131.3	265.8	102.6	111.8	114.7	108.6
Louisville	96.8	94.8	86.2	97.2	110.7	98.5	101.7
Madison	n/a	n/a	n/a	n/a	n/a	n/a	n/a
Manchester	n/a	n/a	n/a	n/a	n/a	n/a	n/a
Memphis	93.4	93.8	85.2	85.2	97.7	98.8	100.2

Table continued on next page.

Area	Composite	Groceries	Housing	Utilities	Transp.	Health	Misc.
Miami[7]	115.0	102.2	141.8	98.5	108.4	115.5	104.7
Milwaukee[1]	100.4	98.9	105.2	96.4	102.2	102.1	97.7
Minneapolis	n/a	n/a	n/a	n/a	n/a	n/a	n/a
Naperville[8]	101.1	107.5	102.6	98.5	103.3	102.6	97.5
Nashville[9]	93.8	99.2	82.6	94.6	93.6	92.4	100.7
New York[10]	204.2	142.3	377.9	145.2	114.2	129.5	139.4
Norfolk[11]	104.9	98.2	114.1	116.1	100.2	100.8	98.7
Oklahoma City	90.9	87.5	80.9	95.2	96.9	97.7	96.4
Omaha	88.9	87.6	80.2	92.2	100.7	95.0	91.4
Orlando	104.2	99.3	107.5	100.3	106.5	95.0	104.8
Overland Park[1]	94.8	93.0	88.2	94.9	98.4	95.8	99.6
Philadelphia	124.9	124.5	146.7	115.6	108.3	114.3	116.0
Phoenix	101.4	98.9	104.8	91.6	103.2	101.3	101.9
Pittsburgh	95.1	97.2	92.1	102.4	98.1	89.2	94.4
Plano	98.6	96.3	84.2	103.0	105.3	106.5	107.0
Portland[1]	116.8	116.6	125.4	114.3	106.0	112.8	114.2
Providence	124.6	117.1	145.1	118.4	104.1	113.6	119.8
Provo[12]	n/a	n/a	n/a	n/a	n/a	n/a	n/a
Raleigh	94.9	99.9	82.8	97.5	99.0	111.4	98.8
Reno[13]	109.7	110.8	119.2	95.3	102.8	114.8	107.1
Richmond	108.1	98.5	116.8	103.9	108.9	103.3	106.1
Rochester	101.5	97.2	91.7	110.5	114.8	95.4	105.1
Sacramento	122.8	121.9	163.7	94.8	105.5	113.6	104.4
Saint Louis[1]	96.2	105.1	92.4	100.8	95.2	95.0	94.9
Saint Paul	n/a	n/a	n/a	n/a	n/a	n/a	n/a
Saint Petersburg[14]	99.9	101.1	103.0	100.1	102.2	91.9	97.0
Salt Lake City	99.2	104.1	95.5	91.4	97.8	94.2	103.5
San Antonio	92.1	81.3	84.9	87.1	92.3	101.0	102.3
San Diego	147.1	116.7	230.4	98.2	113.3	119.4	118.5
San Francisco	171.2	143.6	284.5	90.9	114.5	124.4	135.4
San Jose	156.8	144.6	253.5	101.9	111.4	118.9	117.0
Savannah	101.4	95.1	93.4	118.9	99.5	102.4	105.6
Scottsdale[16]	101.4	98.9	104.8	91.6	103.2	101.3	101.9
Seattle	115.8	109.6	135.0	99.7	109.2	120.2	108.8
Sioux Falls	91.8	91.8	76.2	114.0	91.6	89.0	98.4
Springfield	92.2	96.7	78.2	91.9	95.3	91.7	101.1
Stamford	148.9	118.1	232.8	121.8	111.2	116.5	115.6
Tampa	98.5	100.1	96.3	95.3	104.5	95.5	99.3
Thousand Oaks	n/a	n/a	n/a	n/a	n/a	n/a	n/a
Tucson	98.8	99.5	95.7	91.7	103.4	101.4	101.5
Tulsa	90.4	90.2	74.8	92.1	101.7	96.6	98.5
Virginia Beach[11]	104.9	98.2	114.1	116.1	100.2	100.8	98.7
Washington[1]	141.7	109.9	221.4	117.7	109.6	112.3	109.2
Wichita	94.2	86.2	86.8	104.8	96.4	93.3	99.6
U.S.	100.0	100.0	100.0	100.0	100.0	100.0	100.0

Note: (1) Metropolitan Statistical Area (MSA) - see Appendix B for areas included; (2) Seattle (data for Bellevue was not available); (3) Fort Wayne-Allen County; (4) Winston-Salem (data for Greensboro was not available); (5) Middlesex-Monmouth area; (6) Orange County; (7) Miami-Dade County; (8) Joliet/Will County, IL (located within the Chicago MSA); (9) Nashville-Franklin; (10) Manhattan; (11) Hampton Roads/SE Virginia area; (12) Provo-Orem; (13) Reno-Sparks; (14) St. Petersburg-Clearwater; (15) Raleigh (data for Cary was not available); (16) Phoenix (data for Scottsdale was not available)
Source: The Council for Community and Economic Research (formerly ACCRA), Cost of Living Index, 2006 4-Quarter Average

Average New Home Prices and Apartment Rent

Area	Home Price ($)	Rent ($/month)
Albuquerque	332,293	774
Alexandria[1]	671,289	1,720
Anchorage	371,296	998
Ann Arbor	n/a	n/a
Athens	n/a	n/a
Atlanta	287,801	761
Austin	234,965	989
Baltimore	467,061	1,146
Baton Rouge	266,935	787
Bellevue[2]	407,594	1,055
Birmingham[1]	239,384	711
Boise City	257,334	764
Boston	501,098	1,360
Boulder	n/a	n/a
Buffalo	270,144	777
Cary[15]	247,528	654
Cedar Rapids	239,193	610
Charleston[1]	280,658	828
Charlotte	222,754	719
Chattanooga	264,856	651
Chicago	360,316	1,488
Cincinnati	249,560	747
Cleveland	265,815	892
Colorado Springs	257,833	706
Columbia	242,386	788
Columbus	312,443	762
Dallas[1]	219,381	759
Denver[1]	331,381	742
Des Moines	276,681	594
Durham	228,488	689
Edison[5]	534,842	1,258
El Paso	214,042	679
Eugene	396,167	768
Fort Collins	318,828	756
Fort Lauderdale	480,056	1,065
Fort Wayne[3]	246,200	657
Fort Worth	215,598	802
Grand Rapids	280,149	770
Green Bay	269,989	607
Greensboro[4]	232,877	621
Honolulu	747,077	1,933
Houston[1]	205,139	784
Huntsville	233,591	646
Indianapolis	281,860	770
Irvine[6]	809,450	1,508
Jacksonville	262,629	762
Kansas City[1]	262,713	732
Knoxville	239,570	599
Las Vegas	400,837	867
Lexington[1]	261,874	712
Lincoln	n/a	n/a
Los Angeles[1]	833,405	1,619
Louisville	242,572	824
Madison	n/a	n/a
Manchester	n/a	n/a

Table continued on next page.

Area	Home Price ($)	Rent ($/month)
Memphis	238,359	854
Miami[7]	424,703	1,126
Milwaukee[1]	317,945	764
Minneapolis	n/a	n/a
Naperville[8]	284,214	1,015
Nashville[9]	240,492	674
New York[10]	1,093,560	3,442
Norfolk[11]	338,238	908
Oklahoma City	232,059	713
Omaha	239,553	649
Orlando	324,793	816
Overland Park[1]	262,713	732
Philadelphia	425,611	1,264
Phoenix	318,810	751
Pittsburgh	277,702	631
Plano	231,187	893
Portland[1]	389,049	862
Providence	433,955	1,113
Provo[12]	n/a	n/a
Raleigh	247,528	654
Reno[13]	369,178	749
Richmond	346,463	919
Rochester	265,407	718
Sacramento	508,892	934
Saint Louis[1]	271,207	790
Saint Paul	n/a	n/a
Saint Petersburg[14]	306,068	841
Salt Lake City	287,756	723
San Antonio	226,086	1,004
San Diego	712,092	1,595
San Francisco	871,443	1,995
San Jose	817,688	1,216
Savannah	285,885	699
Scottsdale[16]	318,810	751
Seattle	407,594	1,055
Sioux Falls	223,685	656
Springfield	233,417	606
Stamford	698,417	1,857
Tampa	278,753	851
Thousand Oaks	n/a	n/a
Tucson	284,536	780
Tulsa	224,354	571
Virginia Beach[11]	338,238	908
Washington[1]	671,289	1,720
Wichita	264,309	614
U.S.	299,269	766

Note: Home prices are based on a new home with 2,400 sq. ft. of living area on an 8,000 sq. ft. lot; Rents are based on an unfurnished two bedroom, 1-1/2 or 2 bath apartment, approximately 950 sq. ft., excluding utilities except water; n/a not available;
(1) Metropolitan Statistical Area (MSA) - see Appendix B for areas included; All figures are 2006 4-quarter averages; (2) Seattle (data for Bellevue was not available); (3) Fort Wayne-Allen County; (4) Winston-Salem (data for Greensboro was not available); (5) Middlesex-Monmouth area; (6) Orange County; (7) Miami-Dade County; (8) Joliet/Will County, IL (located within the Chicago MSA); (9) Nashville-Franklin; (10) Manhattan; (11) Hampton Roads/SE Virginia area; (12) Provo-Orem; (13) Reno-Sparks; (14) St. Petersburg-Clearwater; (15) Raleigh (data for Cary was not available); (16) Phoenix (data for Scottsdale was not available)
Source: The Council for Community and Economic Research (formerly ACCRA), Cost of Living Index, 2006 4-Quarter Average

Average Residential Utility Costs

Area	All Electric ($/mth)	Part Electric ($/mth)	Other Energy ($/mth)	Phone ($/mth)
Albuquerque	–	55.76	87.40	25.18
Alexandria[1]	–	69.08	113.78	31.41
Anchorage	–	64.53	86.94	23.04
Ann Arbor	n/a	n/a	n/a	n/a
Athens	n/a	n/a	n/a	n/a
Atlanta	126.25	–	–	25.99
Austin	–	91.37	57.96	21.67
Baltimore	–	87.07	78.47	35.36
Baton Rouge	147.32	–	–	32.16
Bellevue[2]	156.49	–	–	26.48
Birmingham[1]	–	75.39	91.16	30.31
Boise City	–	48.10	89.77	27.01
Boston	–	82.91	118.62	33.01
Boulder	n/a	n/a	n/a	n/a
Buffalo	–	107.95	119.77	29.92
Cary[15]	135.97	–	–	29.98
Cedar Rapids	–	99.20	94.86	19.67
Charleston[1]	156.42	–	–	22.73
Charlotte	118.99	–	–	22.31
Chattanooga	–	54.10	107.93	22.17
Chicago	–	59.10	113.53	29.15
Cincinnati	–	76.40	90.71	27.90
Cleveland	–	66.50	145.96	22.14
Colorado Springs	–	55.40	80.70	29.35
Columbia	155.60	–	–	26.76
Columbus	–	70.81	116.44	27.17
Dallas[1]	–	107.07	50.72	34.22
Denver[1]	–	82.67	78.83	24.94
Des Moines	–	65.79	104.58	23.87
Durham	124.13	–	–	28.18
Edison[5]	–	82.45	83.14	29.75
El Paso	–	80.35	63.80	28.60
Eugene	121.83	–	–	24.38
Fort Collins	–	35.57	78.30	25.04
Fort Lauderdale	162.31	–	–	23.25
Fort Wayne[3]	–	49.55	113.53	27.43
Fort Worth	–	107.96	43.59	24.95
Grand Rapids	–	59.76	158.66	26.28
Green Bay	–	67.51	118.83	20.66
Greensboro[4]	120.09	–	–	25.34
Honolulu	208.87	–	–	23.83
Houston[1]	–	145.23	49.64	21.89
Huntsville	109.03	–	–	27.85
Indianapolis	–	61.14	112.78	20.33
Irvine[6]	–	102.95	65.09	28.11
Jacksonville	127.32	–	–	26.99
Kansas City[1]	–	56.74	108.38	20.81
Knoxville	–	58.16	85.49	22.52
Las Vegas	–	112.35	58.02	30.84
Lexington[1]	–	44.08	102.68	31.75
Lincoln	n/a	n/a	n/a	n/a
Los Angeles[1]	–	101.56	60.89	26.41
Louisville	–	50.84	93.31	27.67
Madison	n/a	n/a	n/a	n/a
Manchester	n/a	n/a	n/a	n/a

Table continued on next page.

Area	All Electric ($/mth)	Part Electric ($/mth)	Other Energy ($/mth)	Phone ($/mth)
Memphis	–	65.81	73.30	20.99
Miami[7]	164.99	–	–	23.25
Milwaukee[1]	–	67.23	107.07	19.67
Minneapolis	n/a	n/a	n/a	n/a
Naperville[8]	–	58.76	91.02	27.11
Nashville[9]	–	64.41	74.37	27.27
New York[10]	–	139.96	108.26	32.93
Norfolk[11]	–	84.75	91.69	32.00
Oklahoma City	–	80.92	75.86	23.14
Omaha	–	56.85	87.86	24.19
Orlando	149.56	–	–	28.35
Overland Park[1]	–	56.74	108.38	20.81
Philadelphia	–	55.44	106.13	35.43
Phoenix	149.46	–	–	22.62
Pittsburgh	–	71.17	105.34	22.90
Plano	–	108.52	36.95	31.20
Portland[1]	–	90.15	89.10	30.08
Providence	–	80.37	101.22	32.20
Provo[12]	n/a	n/a	n/a	n/a
Raleigh	135.97	–	–	29.98
Reno[13]	–	77.85	91.10	20.06
Richmond	152.65	–	–	29.95
Rochester	–	69.80	132.95	21.75
Sacramento	–	147.59	29.75	17.91
Saint Louis[1]	–	61.08	91.46	27.92
Saint Paul	n/a	n/a	n/a	n/a
Saint Petersburg[14]	166.47	–	–	23.88
Salt Lake City	–	50.02	76.47	28.35
San Antonio	–	89.19	55.79	20.77
San Diego	–	83.75	73.45	25.22
San Francisco	–	72.80	63.66	25.44
San Jose	–	108.52	62.30	23.96
Savannah	199.91	–	–	28.12
Scottsdale[16]	149.46	–	–	22.62
Seattle	156.49	–	–	26.48
Sioux Falls	–	66.26	100.29	33.32
Springfield	–	50.45	86.76	25.90
Stamford	–	110.56	112.77	24.07
Tampa	151.42	–	–	24.56
Thousand Oaks	n/a	n/a	n/a	n/a
Tucson	–	92.06	58.94	22.26
Tulsa	–	72.26	76.29	23.18
Virginia Beach[11]	–	84.75	91.69	32.00
Washington[1]	–	69.08	113.78	31.41
Wichita	–	63.25	101.89	27.57
U.S.	136.00	76.53	90.52	25.87

Note: (1) Metropolitan Statistical Area (MSA) - see Appendix B for areas included; (2) Seattle (data for Bellevue was not available);
(3) Fort Wayne-Allen County; (4) Winston-Salem (data for Greensboro was not available); (5) Middlesex-Monmouth area;
(6) Orange County; (7) Miami-Dade County; (8) Joliet/Will County, IL (located within the Chicago MSA); (9) Nashville-Franklin;
(10) Manhattan; (11) Hampton Roads/SE Virginia area; (12) Provo-Orem; (13) Reno-Sparks; (14) St. Petersburg-Clearwater;
(15) Raleigh (data for Cary was not available); (16) Phoenix (data for Scottsdale was not available)
Source: The Council for Community and Economic Research (formerly ACCRA), Cost of Living Index, 2006 4-Quarter Average

Average Health Care Costs

Area	Optometrist ($/visit)	Doctor ($/visit)	Dentist ($/visit)
Albuquerque	78.56	82.28	66.93
Alexandria[1]	73.09	95.65	82.91
Anchorage	112.10	111.25	108.39
Ann Arbor	n/a	n/a	n/a
Athens	n/a	n/a	n/a
Atlanta	56.37	82.19	73.76
Austin	80.78	66.48	72.30
Baltimore	59.84	81.48	77.81
Baton Rouge	102.09	86.17	64.96
Bellevue[2]	104.93	91.36	93.85
Birmingham[1]	93.44	61.55	76.41
Boise City	76.32	78.34	72.63
Boston	82.92	113.64	104.73
Boulder	n/a	n/a	n/a
Buffalo	49.20	58.11	73.16
Cary[15]	79.68	72.18	87.74
Cedar Rapids	71.98	74.65	86.40
Charleston[1]	78.95	72.81	93.06
Charlotte	84.60	87.04	81.78
Chattanooga	81.13	87.55	53.95
Chicago	82.39	81.47	83.61
Cincinnati	81.66	66.04	65.06
Cleveland	84.06	74.19	68.65
Colorado Springs	86.03	83.13	77.98
Columbia	69.67	73.97	85.94
Columbus	88.47	67.98	81.63
Dallas[1]	71.80	73.76	72.56
Denver[1]	77.98	85.77	75.42
Des Moines	70.61	74.22	58.57
Durham	72.16	84.30	65.56
Edison[5]	80.04	67.42	87.36
El Paso	66.78	75.24	68.50
Eugene	107.71	105.56	77.61
Fort Collins	86.45	78.44	72.95
Fort Lauderdale	77.84	84.28	84.68
Fort Wayne[3]	70.61	63.45	59.01
Fort Worth	54.67	65.39	65.90
Grand Rapids	71.38	70.45	67.77
Green Bay	49.91	90.35	63.37
Greensboro[4]	74.65	82.49	74.33
Honolulu	84.22	83.93	71.06
Houston[1]	79.65	80.54	67.44
Huntsville	87.11	59.30	56.79
Indianapolis	79.00	69.89	63.00
Irvine[6]	86.49	99.29	79.35
Jacksonville	54.54	68.89	73.84
Kansas City[1]	76.57	73.28	63.21
Knoxville	72.34	71.25	56.90
Las Vegas	85.93	88.83	73.50
Lexington[1]	81.27	67.25	71.02
Lincoln	n/a	n/a	n/a
Los Angeles[1]	82.74	97.67	80.22
Louisville	81.70	72.32	64.50
Madison	n/a	n/a	n/a
Manchester	n/a	n/a	n/a

Table continued on next page.

Area	Optometrist ($/visit)	Doctor ($/visit)	Dentist ($/visit)
Memphis	66.34	69.43	69.56
Miami[7]	66.06	99.35	85.51
Milwaukee[1]	42.61	86.74	74.91
Minneapolis	n/a	n/a	n/a
Naperville[8]	70.03	83.31	72.37
Nashville[9]	85.46	67.53	60.00
New York[10]	77.37	106.63	101.22
Norfolk[11]	66.74	71.78	76.14
Oklahoma City	79.03	73.47	66.20
Omaha	70.58	82.36	59.54
Orlando	58.45	66.27	67.90
Overland Park[1]	76.57	73.28	63.21
Philadelphia	86.44	87.57	85.50
Phoenix	94.16	72.47	71.68
Pittsburgh	52.75	64.29	52.80
Plano	74.88	93.64	75.47
Portland[1]	84.34	88.30	81.12
Providence	80.46	100.10	77.71
Provo[12]	n/a	n/a	n/a
Raleigh	79.68	72.18	87.74
Reno[13]	87.50	82.06	93.88
Richmond	82.73	66.77	75.15
Rochester	54.18	72.82	62.08
Sacramento	108.09	85.51	79.87
Saint Louis[1]	58.73	74.00	67.10
Saint Paul	n/a	n/a	n/a
Saint Petersburg[14]	62.09	65.08	63.94
Salt Lake City	73.29	78.79	58.52
San Antonio	80.70	71.81	77.25
San Diego	103.80	85.43	92.87
San Francisco	105.09	103.96	86.58
San Jose	102.58	108.66	81.01
Savannah	74.78	75.57	72.45
Scottsdale[16]	94.16	72.47	71.68
Seattle	104.93	91.36	93.85
Sioux Falls	75.06	64.13	57.56
Springfield	60.64	73.31	59.54
Stamford	95.64	91.37	87.21
Tampa	60.81	65.49	68.99
Thousand Oaks	n/a	n/a	n/a
Tucson	72.57	73.67	77.25
Tulsa	66.68	82.38	65.01
Virginia Beach[11]	66.74	71.78	76.14
Washington[1]	73.09	95.65	82.91
Wichita	91.47	68.70	58.28
U.S.	76.38	76.10	68.72

Note: Optometrist—based on a full vision eye exam for an established adult patient; Doctor - based on a general practitioner's routine exam of an established patient; Dentist - based on adult teeth cleaning and periodic oral exam; n/a not available; (1) Metropolitan Statistical Area (MSA) - see Appendix B for areas included; (2) Seattle (data for Bellevue was not available); (3) Fort Wayne-Allen County; (4) Winston-Salem (data for Greensboro was not available); (5) Middlesex-Monmouth area; (6) Orange County; (7) Miami-Dade County; (8) Joliet/Will County, IL (located within the Chicago MSA); (9) Nashville-Franklin; (10) Manhattan; (11) Hampton Roads/SE Virginia area; (12) Provo-Orem; (13) Reno-Sparks; (14) St. Petersburg-Clearwater; (15) Raleigh (data for Cary was not available); (16) Phoenix (data for Scottsdale was not available)
Source: The Council for Community and Economic Research (formerly ACCRA), Cost of Living Index, 2006 4-Quarter Average

Distribution of Office-Based Physicians

MSA[1]	Total	Family/ General Practice	Specialties		
			Medical	Surgical	Other
Albuquerque	20.4	2.9	7.3	4.0	6.2
Alexandria[20]	22.5	1.8	9.4	5.1	6.2
Anchorage	25.0	4.4	6.8	6.7	7.1
Ann Arbor[9]	17.6	1.8	7.3	3.9	4.6
Athens	17.1	1.3	5.5	5.4	4.9
Atlanta	17.7	1.6	6.8	4.5	4.8
Austin	17.9	2.8	5.7	4.3	5.2
Baltimore[20]	22.5	1.8	9.4	5.1	6.2
Baton Rouge	18.2	2.5	6.3	4.9	4.5
Bellevue[19]	21.6	3.9	7.0	4.5	6.2
Birmingham	22.8	1.8	9.0	6.2	5.8
Boise City	19.2	3.6	5.2	5.7	4.7
Boston[3]	29.0	2.0	12.6	6.0	8.4
Boulder[8]	18.7	2.6	6.7	4.0	5.4
Buffalo	17.6	1.8	7.0	4.6	4.3
Cary	23.7	2.6	9.1	5.1	6.9
Cedar Rapids	16.3	4.2	3.9	3.7	4.6
Charleston	26.6	3.1	8.7	6.8	7.9
Charlotte	18.0	2.4	6.6	4.6	4.4
Chattanooga	18.0	2.0	6.5	4.8	4.6
Chicago[4]	18.5	2.1	7.5	4.0	4.9
Cincinnati[5]	14.5	1.8	5.5	3.2	3.9
Cleveland[6]	17.9	1.7	7.2	4.1	4.8
Colorado Springs	17.1	2.0	5.0	4.6	5.5
Columbia	22.1	2.9	7.5	5.5	6.2
Columbus	18.6	2.9	6.2	4.2	5.2
Dallas[7]	15.1	1.9	5.2	3.8	4.2
Denver[8]	18.7	2.6	6.7	4.0	5.4
Des Moines	14.3	1.8	4.6	3.9	3.9
Durham	23.7	2.6	9.1	5.1	6.9
Edison[14]	22.2	1.1	10.2	5.1	5.9
El Paso	11.6	1.2	4.2	3.2	3.0
Eugene	20.9	4.2	6.4	4.6	5.7
Fort Collins	19.0	5.0	4.8	4.6	4.6
Fort Lauderdale[12]	15.7	1.9	6.4	3.7	3.7
Fort Wayne	14.0	2.0	4.2	3.8	4.0
Fort Worth[7]	15.1	1.9	5.2	3.8	4.2
Grand Rapids	11.8	2.1	3.7	2.8	3.3
Green Bay	22.1	2.9	7.0	6.1	6.2
Greensboro	17.0	2.3	6.1	4.3	4.3
Honolulu	24.5	2.3	9.9	5.6	6.7
Houston[10]	17.1	2.2	6.3	4.0	4.7
Huntsville	19.0	3.5	5.6	5.0	4.8
Indianapolis	21.6	3.0	7.4	4.9	6.4
Irvine[11]	17.1	2.3	6.3	3.9	4.6
Jacksonville	20.6	3.0	7.3	4.6	5.7
Kansas City	11.8	1.5	4.4	2.9	3.1
Knoxville	24.6	3.5	8.9	6.0	6.3
Las Vegas	14.8	1.8	5.7	3.3	4.0
Lexington	21.8	2.0	7.9	5.3	6.6
Lincoln	20.7	3.6	6.7	5.1	5.2
Los Angeles[11]	17.1	2.3	6.3	3.9	4.6
Louisville	23.2	2.6	8.3	5.7	6.6
Madison	29.2	5.0	10.1	5.5	8.6
Manchester[3]	29.0	2.0	12.6	6.0	8.4

Table continued on next page.

MSA[1]	Total	Family/ General Practice	Specialties		
			Medical	Surgical	Other
Memphis	18.9	1.8	7.7	4.7	4.7
Miami[12]	15.7	1.9	6.4	3.7	3.7
Milwaukee[13]	22.6	2.8	7.9	4.9	7.1
Minneapolis	16.7	3.3	5.7	3.6	4.2
Naperville[4]	18.5	2.1	7.5	4.0	4.9
Nashville	23.2	2.0	8.5	6.1	6.7
New York[14]	22.2	1.1	10.2	5.1	5.9
Norfolk	13.9	2.1	5.0	3.6	3.2
Oklahoma City	18.2	2.5	6.0	4.3	5.4
Omaha	20.7	3.3	6.7	5.3	5.4
Orlando	17.3	2.4	6.5	4.1	4.4
Overland Park	11.8	1.5	4.4	2.9	3.1
Philadelphia[15]	19.2	1.7	7.7	4.3	5.5
Phoenix	16.7	2.1	5.8	4.0	4.7
Pittsburgh	20.2	2.3	7.6	4.6	5.7
Plano[7]	15.1	1.9	5.2	3.8	4.2
Portland[16]	18.6	2.5	6.6	4.3	5.2
Providence	17.0	1.3	7.5	4.2	4.1
Provo	11.6	2.3	3.3	3.0	3.0
Raleigh	23.7	2.6	9.1	5.1	6.9
Reno	21.7	2.9	6.0	5.9	6.9
Richmond	19.5	2.5	7.2	4.8	5.0
Rochester	17.5	1.5	8.0	3.8	4.2
Sacramento[17]	19.5	2.9	6.8	4.4	5.4
Saint Louis	17.5	1.3	7.2	4.3	4.7
Saint Paul	16.7	3.3	5.7	3.6	4.2
Saint Petersburg	17.5	1.9	7.1	4.0	4.6
Salt Lake City	14.8	1.9	4.9	3.6	4.4
San Antonio	19.4	2.8	6.4	4.5	5.7
San Diego	21.0	2.8	7.2	4.9	6.2
San Francisco[18]	24.5	2.5	9.7	5.3	7.1
San Jose[18]	24.5	2.5	9.7	5.3	7.1
Savannah	18.7	2.0	6.6	5.3	4.7
Scottsdale	16.7	2.1	5.8	4.0	4.7
Seattle[19]	21.6	3.9	7.0	4.5	6.2
Sioux Falls	28.9	4.5	9.8	7.1	7.6
Springfield	19.5	2.4	6.5	5.0	5.7
Stamford[14]	22.2	1.1	10.2	5.1	5.9
Tampa	17.5	1.9	7.1	4.0	4.6
Thousand Oaks[11]	17.1	2.3	6.3	3.9	4.6
Tucson	20.4	2.3	7.0	4.5	6.6
Tulsa	15.0	2.1	5.4	3.7	3.9
Virginia Beach	13.9	2.1	5.0	3.6	3.2
Washington[20]	22.5	1.8	9.4	5.1	6.2
Wichita	16.3	3.5	4.7	3.9	4.1
Metro Average[2]	19.4	2.1	7.5	4.5	5.3

Note: Data as of December 31, 2004; Figures are rates per 10,000 population; (1) Figures cover the Metropolitan Statistical Area unless otherwise noted - see Appendix A for areas included; (2) Average of the 79 unique MSAs and CMSAs in this book; (3) Boston-Worcester-Lawrence, MA-NH-ME-CT CMSA; (4) Chicago-Gary-Kenosha, IL-IN-WI CMSA; (5) Cincinnati-Hamilton, OH-KY-IN CMSA; (6) Cleveland-Akron, OH CMSA; (7) Dallas-Fort Worth, TX CMSA; (8) Denver-Boulder-Greeley, CO CMSA; (9) Detroit-Ann Arbor-Flint, MI CMSA; (10) Houston-Galveston-Brazoria, TX CMSA; (11) Los Angeles-Riverside-Orange, CA CMSA; (12) Miami-Fort Lauderdale, FL CMSA; (13) Milwaukee-Racine, WI CMSA; (14) New York-Northern New Jersey-Long Island, NY-NJ-CT-PA CMSA; (15) Philadelphia-Wilmington-Atlantic City, PA-NJ-DE-MD CMSA; (16) Portland-Salem, OR-WA CMSA; (17) Sacramento-Yolo, CA CMSA; (18) San Francisco-Oakland-San Jose, CA CMSA; (19) Seattle-Tacoma-Bremerton, WA CMSA; (20) Washington-Baltimore, DC-MD-VA-WV CMSA; CMSA - Consolidated Metropolitan Statistical Area Source: American Medical Association, Physician Characteristics & Distribution in the U.S., 2006

Crime Rate: City

City	All Crimes	Violent Crimes				Property Crimes		
		Murder	Forcible Rape	Robbery	Aggrav. Assault	Burglary	Larceny -Theft	Motor Vehicle Theft
Albuquerque	7,115.9	10.8	58.1	234.4	648.6	1,170.7	4,219.7	773.7
Alexandria	2,916.4	2.3	16.9	153.0	183.0	226.1	1,976.1	359.1
Anchorage	4,851.7	5.8	81.1	139.1	509.6	645.8	2,987.2	483.1
Ann Arbor	3,287.9	0.0	32.6	89.7	192.7	755.8	2,007.7	209.4
Athens	5,627.7	4.7	38.8	127.7	166.5	990.3	3,958.3	341.4
Atlanta	8,965.2	20.9	51.8	664.3	937.8	1,543.7	4,410.1	1,336.5
Austin	6,502.1	3.8	45.0	170.6	270.3	1,051.2	4,593.7	367.7
Baltimore	6,939.5	42.0	25.3	609.9	1,077.4	1,144.6	3,071.5	969.0
Baton Rouge	7,606.7	21.8	37.0	442.3	700.7	1,755.1	3,986.4	663.3
Bellevue	4,082.0	1.7	24.5	41.4	77.6	502.1	2,956.2	478.5
Birmingham	9,537.4	44.3	102.7	609.2	714.1	2,103.0	5,099.5	864.6
Boise City	4,221.3	2.6	61.5	44.1	275.4	696.4	2,885.5	255.9
Boston	5,758.4	12.9	47.2	466.7	790.9	798.3	2,811.4	831.1
Boulder	4,108.1	0.0	44.9	36.4	149.8	589.5	3,018.0	269.6
Buffalo	7,296.2	19.8	65.0	588.5	717.0	1,496.8	3,561.6	847.6
Cary	2,036.0	0.0	12.6	48.6	68.0	419.6	1,387.1	100.0
Cedar Rapids	5,548.6	0.8	36.7	98.6	203.8	869.6	4,093.0	246.1
Charleston	5,417.3	9.4	46.1	272.8	615.2	761.9	3,258.5	453.4
Charlotte	8,052.0	12.6	47.7	538.9	572.4	1,887.8	3,944.3	1,048.3
Chattanooga	9,176.9	14.7	74.1	282.5	749.6	1,399.5	5,984.8	671.7
Chicago	n/a	15.6	n/a	555.6	624.4	881.0	2,901.5	782.9
Cincinnati	8,315.2	25.1	100.2	737.8	321.4	1,727.7	4,463.7	939.3
Cleveland	7,618.2	23.8	104.2	815.7	454.6	1,873.7	2,864.6	1,481.9
Colorado Spgs.	5,717.5	3.2	67.0	117.2	291.1	981.6	3,782.3	475.1
Columbia	7,626.9	12.7	47.5	323.1	728.5	1,129.7	4,675.6	709.9
Columbus	8,250.0	14.0	70.9	517.2	234.7	1,999.6	4,343.8	1,069.8
Dallas	8,484.4	16.4	45.7	559.4	632.6	1,817.7	4,252.2	1,160.4
Denver	6,800.8	10.5	58.1	253.7	473.5	1,303.7	3,280.1	1,421.3
Des Moines	7,702.5	2.6	56.4	150.7	419.8	1,348.1	5,148.8	576.1
Durham	6,589.6	17.1	43.4	305.7	354.0	1,539.4	3,873.6	456.4
Edison	2,677.3	0.0	6.0	70.7	153.4	468.3	1,708.8	270.0
El Paso	3,703.5	2.3	49.0	74.4	308.6	357.4	2,479.9	431.8
Eugene	7,078.3	3.5	37.4	82.3	103.8	1,109.1	4,593.6	1,148.6
Fort Collins	3,787.9	1.6	91.7	44.3	205.9	593.5	2,516.2	334.8
Fort Lauderdale	7,557.7	8.9	39.8	440.3	404.1	1,518.2	4,494.5	651.8
Fort Wayne	5,197.7	11.3	38.1	170.0	112.4	1,012.4	3,555.0	298.3
Fort Worth	6,706.8	9.8	50.7	224.9	353.8	1,416.0	4,045.7	605.8
Grand Rapids	6,005.9	4.1	33.8	345.2	621.7	1,043.7	3,610.3	347.2
Green Bay	3,372.1	4.9	57.1	70.9	354.3	595.5	2,066.0	223.4
Greensboro	6,925.0	12.7	36.1	334.3	441.4	1,679.7	3,907.5	513.2
Honolulu	n/a	n/a	n/a	n/a	n/a	n/a	n/a	n/a
Houston	7,059.2	16.3	42.6	544.0	569.6	1,346.3	3,542.8	997.6
Huntsville	7,710.1	13.3	53.3	302.8	369.4	1,481.1	4,831.5	658.8
Indianapolis	7,250.9	13.5	65.8	409.1	504.7	1,443.0	3,691.2	1,123.6
Irvine	1,880.8	1.1	9.5	23.4	50.1	395.0	1,231.7	169.9
Jacksonville	6,302.0	11.4	23.8	283.3	511.4	1,131.5	3,719.9	620.7
Kansas City	9,233.4	28.1	65.9	446.5	918.7	1,658.6	4,823.0	1,292.7
Knoxville	7,106.0	13.9	55.0	302.8	588.4	1,372.9	4,094.7	678.4
Las Vegas	5,581.9	11.3	48.1	272.6	411.6	1,121.0	2,160.8	1,556.5
Lexington	4,395.0	5.6	54.8	214.5	275.6	810.1	2,756.6	277.9
Lincoln	5,917.7	1.7	47.1	94.7	430.4	796.3	4,370.0	177.5
Los Angeles	3,850.4	12.6	28.5	356.4	423.0	583.6	1,704.2	741.9
Louisville	5,024.9	8.8	33.5	292.1	290.2	1,145.7	2,749.6	505.0

Table continued on next page.

City	All Crimes	Violent Crimes				Property Crimes		
		Murder	Forcible Rape	Robbery	Aggrav. Assault	Burglary	Larceny -Theft	Motor Vehicle Theft
Madison	3,873.2	0.9	36.1	148.6	193.3	654.4	2,566.2	273.7
Manchester	3,472.2	3.6	66.3	127.1	82.6	628.9	2,332.4	231.4
Memphis	10,222.4	20.2	58.9	657.4	1,123.4	2,333.5	4,806.0	1,223.0
Miami	7,585.7	13.9	16.0	520.0	1,029.9	1,384.8	3,587.5	1,033.8
Milwaukee	6,619.3	20.6	26.9	499.1	478.1	779.2	3,684.7	1,130.6
Minneapolis	7,411.8	12.5	106.8	686.7	648.2	1,471.0	3,451.7	1,034.9
Naperville	n/a	2.1	n/a	17.8	32.0	206.2	1,498.7	52.6
Nashville	8,037.2	17.1	60.3	438.0	1,095.6	1,157.6	4,649.6	619.0
New York	2,675.5	6.6	17.4	304.6	344.4	286.0	1,489.9	226.5
Norfolk	6,176.6	24.5	38.1	367.2	333.2	733.2	4,208.2	472.1
Oklahoma City	8,780.1	10.2	67.3	224.4	551.6	1,678.6	5,385.7	862.3
Omaha	5,916.4	7.5	48.3	165.5	343.3	767.7	3,658.8	925.2
Orlando	10,474.6	10.5	78.5	572.5	1,146.0	1,846.0	5,789.6	1,031.4
Overland Park	3,094.8	1.2	18.4	38.6	244.4	298.9	2,242.2	251.1
Philadelphia	5,569.1	25.6	69.5	683.6	688.4	744.1	2,582.6	775.3
Phoenix	7,094.0	15.0	36.4	289.0	388.8	1,108.6	3,583.0	1,673.3
Pittsburgh	5,747.9	19.0	35.4	488.8	480.1	912.4	3,125.0	687.2
Plano	3,767.5	0.8	21.6	47.7	218.9	547.2	2,695.2	236.1
Portland	7,680.2	3.7	60.1	210.4	439.7	1,132.7	4,773.2	1,060.3
Providence	5,823.8	11.3	59.8	239.0	370.4	1,034.4	2,832.7	1,276.3
Provo	3,379.2	2.9	53.4	16.5	103.9	653.5	2,347.0	202.0
Raleigh	4,390.2	6.0	26.5	229.5	355.6	915.4	2,553.6	303.5
Reno	6,108.5	3.9	53.7	205.6	478.1	935.8	3,686.0	745.3
Richmond	7,826.6	43.0	41.0	612.5	524.9	1,295.1	4,182.9	1,127.2
Rochester	7,426.3	24.9	47.0	482.2	373.6	1,296.1	4,147.8	1,054.6
Sacramento	6,854.3	11.4	37.2	441.2	661.4	1,277.1	2,912.4	1,513.5
Saint Louis	13,458.8	37.9	79.8	856.9	1,430.9	2,084.7	6,614.4	2,354.3
Saint Paul	5,789.9	8.6	78.9	279.2	509.9	1,250.1	2,784.8	878.4
Saint Petersburg	7,954.1	11.8	39.7	376.5	1,117.7	1,387.4	4,081.1	939.9
Salt Lake City	9,284.7	5.4	39.0	225.9	424.6	1,176.4	6,287.3	1,126.1
San Antonio	7,082.2	6.8	47.2	171.4	411.8	1,143.2	4,826.5	475.3
San Diego	4,151.7	4.0	29.6	146.4	339.1	586.6	1,934.8	1,111.3
San Francisco	5,373.1	12.8	23.0	410.9	352.3	828.6	2,654.5	1,091.1
San Jose	2,901.8	2.9	28.9	97.1	254.7	444.7	1,468.8	604.8
Savannah	6,115.1	14.0	38.9	329.6	268.3	1,184.5	3,559.7	720.1
Scottsdale	3,574.6	1.7	22.2	54.5	124.3	815.0	2,050.7	506.2
Seattle	8,214.6	4.3	23.8	277.4	403.8	1,167.3	4,686.9	1,651.0
Sioux Falls	3,442.8	2.9	105.4	51.6	183.9	495.7	2,364.3	239.1
Springfield	8,963.1	3.3	56.0	133.6	394.3	1,158.0	6,622.7	595.1
Stamford	2,278.8	0.8	14.9	130.3	148.6	354.5	1,444.5	185.1
Tampa	7,591.3	6.1	63.8	352.5	1,008.1	1,493.5	3,818.4	848.8
Thousand Oaks	1,555.4	1.6	10.3	44.5	81.8	301.1	1,024.0	92.1
Tucson	6,865.1	10.4	71.4	318.3	553.4	968.9	3,709.9	1,232.8
Tulsa	7,806.1	15.0	78.4	283.6	915.6	1,705.9	3,842.3	965.3
Virginia Beach	3,243.8	4.5	21.5	139.3	90.0	495.7	2,324.1	168.7
Washington	5,979.1	35.4	30.0	636.1	700.1	648.7	2,572.5	1,356.4
Wichita	6,873.5	8.1	65.4	175.8	558.7	1,103.4	4,464.3	497.8
U.S.	3,899.0	5.6	31.7	140.7	291.1	726.7	2,286.3	416.7

Note: Figures are crimes per 100,000 population; n/a not available
Source: FBI Uniform Crime Reports 2005

Crime Rate: Suburbs

Suburbs[1]	All Crimes	Violent Crimes				Property Crimes		
		Murder	Forcible Rape	Robbery	Aggrav. Assault	Burglary	Larceny -Theft	Motor Vehicle Theft
Albuquerque	3,533.2	7.0	30.6	62.1	555.3	979.3	1,458.2	440.7
Alexandria	3,820.3	10.4	21.5	259.0	261.9	390.7	2,133.0	743.9
Anchorage	8,198.5	0.0	25.8	83.8	966.8	638.1	5,910.4	573.6
Ann Arbor	3,362.2	3.5	47.8	75.7	232.1	643.0	2,050.9	309.1
Athens	2,745.2	0.0	6.9	24.7	164.8	384.5	1,985.8	178.5
Atlanta	4,181.3	5.5	19.3	150.1	201.5	877.6	2,390.9	536.5
Austin	2,593.5	2.2	25.7	27.6	156.9	533.5	1,725.6	122.0
Baltimore	3,467.7	3.4	19.0	156.9	366.4	531.6	2,104.6	285.7
Baton Rouge	4,481.4	7.5	27.5	82.3	387.5	723.4	2,995.0	258.2
Bellevue	5,817.6	3.1	39.3	135.0	238.0	975.3	3,287.5	1,139.3
Birmingham	n/a	n/a	n/a	n/a	n/a	n/a	n/a	n/a
Boise City	n/a	n/a	n/a	n/a	n/a	n/a	n/a	n/a
Boston	2,148.2	1.5	20.4	68.4	169.9	393.6	1,282.3	212.0
Boulder	n/a	n/a	n/a	n/a	n/a	n/a	n/a	n/a
Buffalo	2,306.0	1.1	17.9	69.4	143.5	379.7	1,585.4	109.0
Cary	3,400.1	3.7	21.9	120.0	210.4	823.0	2,002.1	219.0
Cedar Rapids	1,260.3	0.0	16.3	3.3	103.4	279.2	786.4	71.6
Charleston	5,198.6	6.2	49.9	185.3	580.4	932.7	2,925.9	518.3
Charlotte	4,323.9	4.0	29.0	104.8	424.7	912.2	2,554.0	295.3
Chattanooga	3,390.6	2.3	20.0	29.6	293.0	671.1	2,096.9	277.7
Chicago	n/a	n/a	n/a	n/a	n/a	n/a	n/a	n/a
Cincinnati	3,274.5	2.1	34.0	76.2	107.6	560.4	2,285.8	208.4
Cleveland	n/a	n/a	n/a	n/a	n/a	n/a	n/a	n/a
Colorado Spgs.	2,559.7	2.4	31.5	17.2	424.8	465.3	1,407.8	210.7
Columbia	4,144.9	6.0	39.9	103.7	496.5	736.2	2,459.6	302.9
Columbus	3,009.4	0.9	31.3	59.0	50.9	667.8	2,037.6	161.8
Dallas	3,825.8	3.1	25.3	68.5	185.7	720.5	2,489.1	333.6
Denver	4,305.8	3.2	41.8	81.9	207.1	653.8	2,688.7	629.4
Des Moines	2,575.2	0.3	15.4	12.5	122.3	460.7	1,827.8	136.1
Durham	3,696.7	5.1	15.0	77.7	220.0	844.9	2,363.6	170.3
Edison	2,019.4	1.2	10.8	59.7	98.1	329.8	1,396.1	123.6
El Paso	2,572.0	3.3	34.1	23.6	223.5	378.8	1,712.0	196.7
Eugene	4,744.6	1.6	26.7	37.1	197.5	1,022.7	2,730.5	728.5
Fort Collins	2,764.3	2.1	32.7	18.1	97.3	420.5	2,035.2	158.5
Fort Lauderdale	3,899.1	3.0	29.1	161.8	365.3	667.7	2,296.1	376.1
Fort Wayne	1,502.1	1.1	12.5	23.9	66.9	293.3	986.7	117.6
Fort Worth	4,529.9	3.7	33.8	94.6	258.1	827.1	2,965.6	347.1
Grand Rapids	2,741.7	0.7	55.2	36.8	164.3	558.0	1,784.8	141.9
Green Bay	2,106.2	2.6	13.3	1.0	31.7	351.7	1,613.2	92.7
Greensboro	4,127.3	5.4	14.7	88.2	189.5	1,158.3	2,427.3	243.9
Honolulu	n/a	n/a	n/a	n/a	n/a	n/a	n/a	n/a
Houston	3,582.2	4.4	31.5	108.3	276.1	787.3	2,075.5	299.1
Huntsville	3,355.0	5.0	25.1	75.2	176.4	811.9	2,032.9	228.5
Indianapolis	2,436.0	1.7	14.6	39.4	115.1	391.9	1,715.0	158.3
Irvine	2,728.5	2.6	14.9	95.8	183.0	448.8	1,531.7	451.6
Jacksonville	3,432.8	2.8	27.5	58.8	499.8	644.0	1,987.8	212.1
Kansas City	4,105.7	4.3	30.7	72.1	253.6	616.7	2,670.4	457.9
Knoxville	3,219.5	3.0	20.0	39.2	239.5	751.5	1,929.2	237.1
Las Vegas	4,402.9	7.0	25.4	136.1	299.8	924.9	2,043.7	966.0
Lexington	3,250.0	0.0	20.7	39.5	96.0	575.5	2,350.1	168.2
Lincoln	2,423.6	0.0	37.8	7.1	47.2	465.4	1,785.8	80.3
Los Angeles	3,317.7	9.5	20.9	210.3	323.3	591.4	1,479.1	683.2
Louisville	2,704.0	1.7	17.4	59.3	108.1	547.9	1,760.6	209.0

Table continued on next page.

Suburbs[1]	All Crimes	Violent Crimes				Property Crimes		
		Murder	Forcible Rape	Robbery	Aggrav. Assault	Burglary	Larceny -Theft	Motor Vehicle Theft
Madison	2,507.0	0.0	17.6	28.1	78.0	316.6	1,982.0	84.7
Manchester	1,705.1	1.0	16.8	20.6	67.9	249.0	1,257.6	92.3
Memphis	3,862.0	6.5	29.5	78.3	310.9	920.6	2,191.3	324.9
Miami	5,992.5	5.8	35.3	264.5	570.5	996.3	3,466.5	653.6
Milwaukee	2,326.5	1.1	16.2	38.4	47.3	316.7	1,784.3	122.4
Minneapolis	n/a	n/a	n/a	n/a	n/a	n/a	n/a	n/a
Naperville	n/a	n/a	n/a	n/a	n/a	n/a	n/a	n/a
Nashville	3,066.6	2.2	34.7	45.8	343.4	525.8	1,911.0	203.6
New York	2,225.9	3.4	9.6	154.0	174.5	342.1	1,310.9	231.5
Norfolk	3,811.2	7.0	28.9	162.0	222.8	581.9	2,561.1	247.3
Oklahoma City	3,391.6	1.6	31.1	41.4	183.7	725.3	2,159.9	248.5
Omaha	3,244.9	0.5	33.0	34.8	222.6	568.7	2,070.7	314.6
Orlando	4,472.4	4.8	37.9	162.4	493.8	995.7	2,361.1	416.7
Overland Park	5,493.6	10.6	40.7	169.7	422.4	909.1	3,253.4	687.7
Philadelphia	2,166.5	3.3	15.4	77.0	169.6	281.8	1,465.7	153.7
Phoenix	4,918.9	4.4	31.6	84.9	258.7	967.0	2,809.4	762.9
Pittsburgh	2,323.6	2.6	16.1	62.5	173.7	365.2	1,551.9	151.7
Plano	5,410.4	7.8	32.5	236.4	335.0	1,104.7	3,073.2	620.9
Portland	3,708.7	2.3	37.3	50.6	102.5	569.1	2,516.1	430.9
Providence	n/a	n/a	n/a	n/a	n/a	n/a	n/a	n/a
Provo	3,128.2	0.6	25.4	10.8	52.9	513.2	2,363.0	162.4
Raleigh	2,615.2	1.8	17.7	46.8	105.2	702.2	1,589.8	151.6
Reno	3,068.1	3.1	34.2	61.2	212.0	688.9	1,697.1	371.7
Richmond	n/a	5.4	19.0	85.0	133.4	480.0	2,148.7	n/a
Rochester	2,250.9	1.1	15.9	32.2	75.2	344.9	1,681.9	99.9
Sacramento	3,988.7	4.6	24.4	103.3	269.3	807.4	2,024.4	755.3
Saint Louis	2,872.3	3.2	11.2	58.7	207.3	401.5	1,974.3	216.2
Saint Paul	n/a	n/a	n/a	n/a	n/a	n/a	n/a	n/a
Saint Petersburg	4,588.8	3.5	41.4	126.6	493.5	906.6	2,622.3	394.9
Salt Lake City	4,840.4	2.8	46.9	43.5	162.1	671.0	3,465.6	448.6
San Antonio	3,418.7	3.3	31.5	36.8	197.5	704.8	2,287.4	157.3
San Diego	3,493.4	2.8	26.1	123.8	278.9	607.7	1,762.6	691.6
San Francisco	3,009.8	3.5	22.3	93.1	195.1	516.2	1,799.5	380.1
San Jose	3,031.3	2.1	18.0	54.2	169.0	512.9	1,963.9	311.1
Savannah	3,714.8	2.8	14.2	86.1	342.5	693.6	2,351.3	224.3
Scottsdale	5,887.1	8.9	34.1	169.7	320.1	1,034.1	3,171.6	1,148.7
Seattle	5,211.6	2.8	42.1	99.4	194.2	911.7	2,964.4	996.9
Sioux Falls	927.5	3.0	20.9	4.5	64.1	265.4	501.0	68.6
Springfield	2,161.5	1.7	9.5	9.5	189.9	421.6	1,403.0	126.3
Stamford	2,571.9	3.9	15.8	114.5	151.0	387.6	1,597.2	301.9
Tampa	4,532.4	4.0	38.1	122.0	489.0	876.1	2,612.9	390.4
Thousand Oaks	2,488.8	4.4	19.6	99.4	158.5	501.2	1,429.2	276.5
Tucson	4,602.2	5.6	24.5	67.8	158.1	722.2	3,153.4	470.5
Tulsa	2,593.3	2.8	20.3	25.5	197.2	588.0	1,530.6	228.7
Virginia Beach	4,485.7	11.4	33.5	210.8	293.1	643.3	2,973.0	320.5
Washington	3,445.9	6.1	20.0	195.5	189.8	343.8	2,057.8	632.8
Wichita	2,935.0	1.3	29.2	9.2	171.9	620.1	1,978.9	124.4
U.S.	3,899.0	5.6	31.7	140.7	291.1	726.7	2,286.3	416.7

Note: Figures are crimes per 100,000 population; n/a not available; (1) All areas within the metro area that are located outside the city limits
Source: FBI Uniform Crime Reports 2005

Crime Rate: Metro Area

Metro Area[1]	All Crimes	Violent Crimes				Property Crimes		
		Murder	Forcible Rape	Robbery	Aggrav. Assault	Burglary	Larceny -Theft	Motor Vehicle Theft
Albuquerque	5,753.3	9.3	47.6	168.9	613.1	1,097.9	3,169.4	647.0
Alexandria[2]	3,791.2	10.1	21.4	255.6	259.3	385.4	2,128.0	731.5
Anchorage	5,029.8	5.5	78.2	136.1	533.9	645.4	3,142.7	488.0
Ann Arbor	3,337.3	2.4	42.7	80.4	218.9	680.8	2,036.4	275.7
Athens	4,452.1	2.8	25.8	85.7	165.8	743.2	3,153.8	275.0
Atlanta	4,607.2	6.9	22.2	195.9	267.1	936.9	2,570.6	607.7
Austin	4,480.5	2.9	35.0	96.6	211.6	783.4	3,110.2	240.6
Baltimore	4,304.7	12.7	20.5	266.1	537.8	679.4	2,337.7	450.5
Baton Rouge	5,442.5	11.9	30.4	193.0	483.8	1,040.7	3,299.9	382.7
Bellevue	5,753.5	3.1	38.8	131.5	232.0	957.8	3,275.3	1,114.9
Birmingham	n/a	n/a	n/a	n/a	n/a	n/a	n/a	n/a
Boise City	n/a	n/a	n/a	n/a	n/a	n/a	n/a	n/a
Boston[2]	3,283.3	5.1	28.8	193.7	365.2	520.9	1,763.0	406.6
Boulder	n/a	n/a	n/a	n/a	n/a	n/a	n/a	n/a
Buffalo	3,528.8	5.7	29.4	196.6	284.0	653.4	2,069.7	290.0
Cary	3,249.1	3.3	20.9	112.1	194.6	778.4	1,934.0	205.8
Cedar Rapids	3,403.3	0.4	26.5	50.9	153.5	574.3	2,438.8	158.8
Charleston	5,237.9	6.8	49.2	201.1	586.6	902.0	2,985.7	506.6
Charlotte	6,008.3	7.9	37.4	300.9	491.4	1,353.0	3,182.2	635.5
Chattanooga	5,212.0	6.2	37.0	109.2	436.7	900.4	3,320.7	401.7
Chicago[2]	n/a	n/a	n/a	n/a	n/a	n/a	n/a	n/a
Cincinnati	4,042.8	5.6	44.1	177.1	140.2	738.3	2,617.7	319.8
Cleveland	n/a	n/a	n/a	n/a	n/a	n/a	n/a	n/a
Colorado Spgs.	4,583.8	2.9	54.3	81.3	339.1	796.3	2,929.8	380.2
Columbia	4,741.1	7.1	41.2	141.3	536.2	803.6	2,839.0	372.6
Columbus	5,267.9	6.6	48.4	256.5	130.1	1,241.8	3,031.5	553.1
Dallas[2]	5,304.7	7.3	31.8	224.3	327.5	1,068.8	3,048.8	596.1
Denver	4,902.0	5.0	45.7	123.0	270.7	809.1	2,830.0	818.6
Des Moines	4,521.5	1.2	30.9	65.0	235.2	797.6	3,088.5	303.1
Durham	4,990.0	10.5	27.7	179.6	279.9	1,155.4	3,038.7	298.2
Edison[2]	2,048.1	1.1	10.6	60.2	100.5	335.9	1,409.8	130.0
El Paso	3,511.5	2.5	46.5	65.8	294.1	361.0	2,349.6	391.9
Eugene	5,748.8	2.4	31.3	56.6	157.2	1,059.9	3,532.2	909.3
Fort Collins	3,247.6	1.8	60.5	30.4	148.6	502.2	2,262.3	241.7
Fort Lauderdale[2]	4,242.2	3.5	30.1	187.9	368.9	747.5	2,502.2	401.9
Fort Wayne	3,518.2	6.7	26.5	103.6	91.8	685.6	2,387.8	216.2
Fort Worth[2]	5,225.8	5.6	39.2	136.3	288.7	1,015.4	3,310.9	429.8
Grand Rapids	3,571.5	1.6	49.7	115.2	280.5	681.5	2,248.9	194.1
Green Bay	2,539.3	3.4	28.3	24.9	142.1	435.1	1,768.1	137.4
Greensboro	5,097.7	8.0	22.1	173.6	276.9	1,339.1	2,940.7	337.3
Honolulu	4,947.9	1.7	25.8	92.6	162.9	683.4	3,233.4	748.2
Houston	4,933.0	9.1	35.8	277.6	390.2	1,004.5	2,645.5	570.5
Huntsville	5,327.3	8.8	37.8	178.2	263.8	1,115.0	3,300.3	423.4
Indianapolis	4,799.2	7.5	39.7	220.8	306.3	907.8	2,685.0	632.1
Irvine[2]	2,677.9	2.5	14.6	91.5	175.0	445.6	1,513.8	434.8
Jacksonville	5,253.8	8.3	25.1	201.3	507.2	953.4	3,087.1	471.4
Kansas City	5,291.4	9.8	38.8	158.6	407.4	857.6	3,168.2	650.9
Knoxville	4,289.2	6.0	29.7	111.8	335.5	922.5	2,525.2	358.6
Las Vegas	5,288.0	10.3	42.4	238.6	383.7	1,072.1	2,131.6	1,409.3
Lexington	3,968.2	3.5	42.1	149.2	208.7	722.6	2,605.1	237.0
Lincoln	5,389.5	1.4	45.7	81.4	372.4	746.3	3,979.4	162.8
Los Angeles[2]	3,523.8	10.7	23.8	266.8	361.9	588.4	1,566.2	705.9
Louisville	3,901.8	5.4	25.7	179.5	202.1	856.4	2,271.0	361.8

Table continued on next page.

Metro Area[1]	All Crimes	Violent Crimes				Property Crimes		
		Murder	Forcible Rape	Robbery	Aggrav. Assault	Burglary	Larceny -Theft	Motor Vehicle Theft
Madison	3,073.0	0.4	25.3	78.0	125.8	456.6	2,224.0	163.0
Manchester	2,189.8	1.7	30.4	49.8	71.9	353.2	1,552.4	130.4
Memphis	7,282.7	13.9	45.3	389.8	747.9	1,680.4	3,597.5	807.9
Miami[2]	6,248.5	7.1	32.2	305.6	644.3	1,058.7	3,485.9	714.7
Milwaukee	3,979.4	8.6	20.4	215.8	213.2	494.8	2,516.1	510.6
Minneapolis	n/a	n/a	n/a	n/a	n/a	n/a	n/a	n/a
Naperville[2]	n/a	n/a	n/a	n/a	n/a	n/a	n/a	n/a
Nashville	5,029.5	8.1	44.8	200.7	640.5	775.3	2,992.5	367.7
New York[2]	2,544.0	5.7	15.1	260.6	294.7	302.4	1,437.6	227.9
Norfolk	4,153.3	9.5	30.3	191.7	238.8	603.8	2,799.4	279.9
Oklahoma City	5,878.1	5.6	47.8	125.8	353.5	1,165.2	3,648.4	531.8
Omaha	4,606.1	4.1	40.8	101.4	284.1	670.1	2,879.9	625.7
Orlando	5,135.4	5.4	42.4	207.7	565.9	1,089.6	2,739.8	484.6
Overland Park	5,291.4	9.8	38.8	158.6	407.4	857.6	3,168.2	650.9
Philadelphia[2]	3,454.9	11.7	35.9	306.7	366.0	456.9	1,888.6	389.1
Phoenix	5,749.1	8.4	33.4	162.8	308.4	1,021.0	3,104.6	1,110.4
Pittsburgh	2,794.3	4.8	18.7	121.1	215.8	440.4	1,768.1	225.3
Plano[2]	5,304.7	7.3	31.8	224.3	327.5	1,068.8	3,048.8	596.1
Portland	4,734.9	2.6	43.2	91.9	189.6	714.7	3,099.4	593.5
Providence	n/a	n/a	n/a	n/a	n/a	n/a	n/a	n/a
Provo	3,188.9	1.2	32.1	12.2	65.2	547.1	2,359.1	172.0
Raleigh	3,249.1	3.3	20.9	112.1	194.6	778.4	1,934.0	205.8
Reno	4,633.5	3.5	44.3	135.5	349.0	816.0	2,721.1	564.0
Richmond	n/a	11.7	22.6	172.9	198.7	615.9	2,487.9	n/a
Rochester	3,306.7	5.9	22.2	124.0	136.1	538.9	2,185.0	294.6
Sacramento	4,634.3	6.1	27.2	179.4	357.6	913.3	2,224.5	926.1
Saint Louis	4,187.7	7.5	19.7	157.9	359.4	610.6	2,550.8	481.9
Saint Paul	n/a	n/a	n/a	n/a	n/a	n/a	n/a	n/a
Saint Petersburg	4,912.7	4.3	41.3	150.7	553.5	952.9	2,762.7	447.4
Salt Lake City	5,619.5	3.2	45.5	75.5	208.1	759.6	3,960.2	567.3
San Antonio	5,861.5	5.7	42.0	126.6	340.3	997.1	3,980.4	369.4
San Diego	3,777.2	3.3	27.6	133.5	304.8	598.6	1,836.8	872.5
San Francisco[2]	4,050.8	7.6	22.6	233.1	264.3	653.8	2,176.1	693.3
San Jose	2,964.1	2.5	23.7	76.5	213.5	477.5	1,706.7	463.7
Savannah	5,320.5	10.3	30.7	249.0	292.9	1,022.0	3,159.7	556.0
Scottsdale	5,749.1	8.4	33.4	162.8	308.4	1,021.0	3,104.6	1,110.4
Seattle	5,753.5	3.1	38.8	131.5	232.0	957.8	3,275.3	1,114.9
Sioux Falls	2,618.6	2.9	77.7	36.2	144.6	420.2	1,753.7	183.2
Springfield	4,783.2	2.3	27.4	57.3	268.7	705.4	3,414.9	307.0
Stamford	2,532.1	3.5	15.7	116.6	150.7	383.1	1,576.4	286.0
Tampa	4,912.7	4.3	41.3	150.7	553.5	952.9	2,762.7	447.4
Thousand Oaks	2,342.5	4.0	18.2	90.8	146.5	469.9	1,365.6	247.6
Tucson	5,879.6	8.3	51.0	209.2	381.3	861.5	3,467.5	900.8
Tulsa	4,861.9	8.1	45.6	137.9	509.9	1,074.6	2,536.7	549.3
Virginia Beach	4,153.3	9.5	30.3	191.7	238.8	603.8	2,799.4	279.9
Washington[2]	3,791.2	10.1	21.4	255.6	259.3	385.4	2,128.0	731.5
Wichita	5,331.5	5.5	51.3	110.5	407.3	914.2	3,491.3	351.6
U.S.	3,899.0	5.6	31.7	140.7	291.1	726.7	2,286.3	416.7

Note: Figures are crimes per 100,000 population; n/a not available; (1) Figures cover the Metropolitan Statistical Area except where noted. See Appendix B for areas included; (2) Metropolitan Division
Source: FBI Uniform Crime Reports 2005

Temperature & Precipitation: Yearly Averages and Extremes

City	Extreme Low (°F)	Average Low (°F)	Average Temp. (°F)	Average High (°F)	Extreme High (°F)	Average Precip. (in.)	Average Snow (in.)
Albuquerque	-17	43	57	70	105	8.5	11
Alexandria	-5	49	58	67	104	39.5	18
Anchorage	-34	29	36	43	85	15.7	71
Ann Arbor	-21	39	49	58	104	32.4	41
Athens[1]	-8	52	62	72	105	49.8	2
Atlanta	-8	52	62	72	105	49.8	2
Austin	-2	58	69	79	109	31.1	1
Baltimore	-7	45	56	65	105	41.2	21
Baton Rouge	8	57	68	78	103	58.5	Trace
Bellevue	0	44	52	59	99	38.4	13
Birmingham	-6	51	63	74	106	53.5	2
Boise City	-25	39	51	63	111	11.8	22
Boston	-12	44	52	59	102	42.9	41
Boulder	-25	37	51	64	103	15.5	63
Buffalo	-20	40	48	56	99	38.1	90
Cary	-9	48	60	71	105	42.0	8
Cedar Rapids	-34	36	47	57	105	34.4	33
Charleston	6	55	66	76	104	52.1	1
Charlotte	-5	50	61	71	104	42.8	6
Chattanooga	-10	49	60	71	106	53.3	4
Chicago	-27	40	49	59	104	35.4	39
Cincinnati	-25	44	54	64	103	40.9	23
Cleveland	-19	41	50	59	104	37.1	55
Colorado Spgs.	-24	36	49	62	99	17.0	48
Columbia	-1	51	64	75	107	48.3	2
Columbus	-19	42	52	62	104	37.9	28
Dallas	-2	56	67	77	112	33.9	3
Denver	-25	37	51	64	103	15.5	63
Des Moines	-24	40	50	60	108	31.8	33
Durham	-9	48	60	71	105	42.0	8
Edison	-2	47	55	62	104	47.0	23
El Paso	-8	50	64	78	114	8.6	6
Eugene	-12	42	53	63	108	47.3	7
Fort Collins[2]	-25	37	51	64	103	15.5	63
Fort Lauderdale[3]	30	69	76	83	98	57.1	0
Fort Wayne	-22	40	50	60	106	35.9	33
Fort Worth	-1	55	66	76	113	32.3	3
Grand Rapids	-22	38	48	57	102	34.7	73
Green Bay	-31	34	44	54	99	28.3	46
Greensboro	-8	47	58	69	103	42.5	10
Honolulu	52	70	77	84	94	22.4	0
Houston	7	58	69	79	107	46.9	Trace
Huntsville	-11	50	61	71	104	56.8	4
Indianapolis	-23	42	53	62	104	40.2	25
Irvine	25	53	64	75	112	11.9	Trace
Jacksonville	7	58	69	79	103	52.0	0
Kansas City	-23	44	54	64	109	38.1	21
Knoxville	-24	48	59	69	103	46.7	13
Las Vegas	8	53	67	80	116	4.0	1
Lexington	-21	45	55	65	103	45.1	17
Lincoln	-33	39	51	62	108	29.1	27
Los Angeles	27	55	63	70	110	11.3	Trace
Louisville	-20	46	57	67	105	43.9	17
Madison	-37	35	46	57	104	31.1	42
Manchester	-33	34	46	57	102	36.9	63

Table continued on next page.

City	Extreme Low (°F)	Average Low (°F)	Average Temp. (°F)	Average High (°F)	Extreme High (°F)	Average Precip. (in.)	Average Snow (in.)
Memphis	0	52	65	77	107	54.8	1
Miami	30	69	76	83	98	57.1	0
Milwaukee	-26	38	47	55	103	32.0	49
Minneapolis	-34	35	45	54	105	27.1	52
Naperville	-27	40	49	59	104	35.4	39
Nashville	-17	49	60	70	107	47.4	11
New York	-2	47	55	62	104	47.0	23
Norfolk	-3	51	60	68	104	45.0	8
Oklahoma City	-8	49	60	71	110	32.8	10
Omaha	-23	40	51	62	110	30.1	29
Orlando	19	62	72	82	100	47.7	Trace
Overland Park	-23	44	54	64	109	38.1	21
Philadelphia	-7	45	55	64	104	41.4	22
Phoenix	17	59	72	86	122	7.3	Trace
Pittsburgh	-18	41	51	60	103	37.1	43
Plano	-2	56	67	77	112	33.9	3
Portland	-3	45	54	62	107	37.5	7
Providence	-13	42	51	60	104	45.3	35
Provo	-22	40	52	64	107	15.6	63
Raleigh	-9	48	60	71	105	42.0	8
Reno	-16	33	50	67	105	7.2	24
Richmond	-8	48	58	69	105	43.0	13
Rochester	-19	39	48	57	100	31.8	92
Sacramento	18	48	61	73	115	17.3	Trace
Saint Louis	-18	46	56	66	115	36.8	20
Saint Paul	-34	35	45	54	105	27.1	52
Saint Petersburg	18	63	73	82	99	46.7	Trace
Salt Lake City	-22	40	52	64	107	15.6	63
San Antonio	0	58	69	80	108	29.6	1
San Diego	29	57	64	71	111	9.5	Trace
San Francisco	24	49	57	65	106	19.3	Trace
San Jose	21	50	59	68	105	13.5	Trace
Savannah	3	56	67	77	105	50.3	Trace
Scottsdale	17	59	72	86	122	7.3	Trace
Seattle	0	44	52	59	99	38.4	13
Sioux Falls	-36	35	46	57	110	24.6	38
Springfield	-17	45	56	67	113	42.0	18
Stamford	-7	44	52	60	103	41.4	25
Tampa	18	63	73	82	99	46.7	Trace
Thousand Oaks	27	55	63	70	110	11.3	Trace
Tucson	16	55	69	82	117	11.6	2
Tulsa	-8	50	61	71	112	38.9	10
Virginia Beach	-3	51	60	69	104	44.8	8
Washington	-5	49	58	67	104	39.5	18
Wichita	-21	45	57	68	113	29.3	17

Note: (1) Data is for Atlanta, which is located 65 miles west of Athens; (2) Data is for Denver, which is located 60 miles south of Fort Collins; (3) Data is for Miami, which is located 22 miles south of Fort Lauderdale
Source: National Climatic Data Center, International Station Meteorological Climate Summary, 9/96

Weather Conditions

City	Temperature			Daytime Sky			Precipitation		
	10°F & below	32°F & below	90°F & above	Clear	Partly cloudy	Cloudy	.01 inch or more precip.	1.0 inch or more snow/ice	Thunder-storms
Albuquerque	4	114	65	140	161	64	60	9	38
Alexandria	2	71	34	84	144	137	112	9	30
Anchorage	n/a	194	n/a	50	115	200	113	49	2
Ann Arbor	n/a	136	12	74	134	157	135	38	32
Athens[1]	1	49	38	98	147	120	116	3	48
Atlanta	1	49	38	98	147	120	116	3	48
Austin	<1	20	111	105	148	112	83	1	41
Baltimore	6	97	31	91	143	131	113	13	27
Baton Rouge	<1	21	86	99	150	116	113	<1	73
Bellevue	n/a	38	3	57	121	187	157	8	8
Birmingham	1	57	59	91	161	113	119	1	57
Boise City	n/a	124	45	106	133	126	91	22	14
Boston	n/a	97	12	88	127	150	253	48	18
Boulder	24	155	33	99	177	89	90	38	39
Buffalo	n/a	131	4	47	144	174	169	65	30
Cary	n/a	n/a	39	98	143	124	110	3	42
Cedar Rapids	n/a	156	16	89	132	144	109	28	42
Charleston	<1	33	53	89	162	114	114	1	59
Charlotte	1	65	44	98	142	125	113	3	41
Chattanooga	2	73	48	88	141	136	120	3	55
Chicago	n/a	132	17	83	136	146	125	31	38
Cincinnati	14	107	23	80	126	159	127	25	39
Cleveland	n/a	123	12	63	127	175	157	48	34
Colorado Spgs.	21	161	18	108	157	100	98	33	49
Columbia	<1	58	77	97	149	119	110	1	53
Columbus	n/a	118	19	72	137	156	136	29	40
Dallas	1	34	102	108	160	97	78	2	49
Denver	24	155	33	99	177	89	90	38	39
Des Moines	n/a	137	26	99	129	137	106	25	46
Durham	n/a	n/a	39	98	143	124	110	3	42
Edison	n/a	n/a	18	85	166	114	120	11	20
El Paso	1	59	106	147	164	54	49	3	35
Eugene	n/a	n/a	15	75	115	175	136	4	3
Fort Collins[2]	24	155	33	99	177	89	90	38	39
Fort Lauderdale[3]	n/a	n/a	55	48	263	54	128	0	74
Fort Wayne	n/a	131	16	75	140	150	131	31	39
Fort Worth	1	40	100	123	136	106	79	3	47
Grand Rapids	n/a	146	11	67	119	179	142	57	34
Green Bay	n/a	163	7	86	125	154	120	40	33
Greensboro	3	85	32	94	143	128	113	5	43
Honolulu	n/a	n/a	23	25	286	54	98	0	7
Houston	n/a	n/a	96	83	168	114	101	1	62
Huntsville	2	66	49	70	118	177	116	2	54
Indianapolis	19	119	19	83	128	154	127	24	43
Irvine	0	2	18	95	192	78	41	0	4
Jacksonville	<1	16	83	86	181	98	114	1	65
Kansas City	22	110	39	112	134	119	103	17	51
Knoxville	3	73	33	85	142	138	125	8	47
Las Vegas	<1	37	134	185	132	48	27	2	13
Lexington	11	96	22	86	136	143	129	17	44
Lincoln	n/a	145	40	108	135	122	94	19	46
Los Angeles	0	<1	5	131	125	109	34	0	1
Louisville	8	90	35	82	143	140	125	15	45
Madison	n/a	161	14	88	119	158	118	38	40

Table continued on next page.

City	Temperature			Daytime Sky			Precipitation		
	10°F & below	32°F & below	90°F & above	Clear	Partly cloudy	Cloudy	.01 inch or more precip.	1.0 inch or more snow/ice	Thunder-storms
Manchester	n/a	171	12	87	131	147	125	32	19
Memphis	1	53	86	101	152	112	104	2	59
Miami	n/a	n/a	55	48	263	54	128	0	74
Milwaukee	n/a	141	10	90	118	157	126	38	35
Minneapolis	n/a	156	16	93	125	147	113	41	37
Naperville	n/a	132	17	83	136	146	125	31	38
Nashville	5	76	51	98	135	132	119	8	54
New York	n/a	n/a	18	85	166	114	120	11	20
Norfolk	< 1	54	32	89	149	127	115	6	37
Oklahoma City	5	79	70	124	131	110	80	8	50
Omaha	n/a	139	35	100	142	123	97	20	46
Orlando	n/a	n/a	90	76	208	81	115	0	80
Overland Park	22	110	39	112	134	119	103	17	51
Philadelphia	5	94	23	81	146	138	117	14	27
Phoenix	0	10	167	186	125	54	37	< 1	23
Pittsburgh	n/a	121	8	62	137	166	154	42	35
Plano	1	34	102	108	160	97	78	2	49
Portland	n/a	37	11	67	116	182	152	4	7
Providence	n/a	117	9	85	134	146	123	21	21
Provo	n/a	128	56	94	152	119	92	38	38
Raleigh	n/a	n/a	39	98	143	124	110	3	42
Reno	14	178	50	143	139	83	50	17	14
Richmond	3	79	41	90	147	128	115	7	43
Rochester	n/a	135	11	58	137	170	157	65	27
Sacramento	0	21	73	175	111	79	58	< 1	2
Saint Louis	13	100	43	97	138	130	109	14	46
Saint Paul	n/a	156	16	93	125	147	113	41	37
Saint Petersburg	n/a	n/a	85	81	204	80	107	< 1	87
Salt Lake City	n/a	128	56	94	152	119	92	38	38
San Antonio	n/a	n/a	112	97	153	115	81	1	36
San Diego	0	< 1	4	115	126	124	40	0	5
San Francisco	0	6	4	136	130	99	63	< 1	5
San Jose	0	5	5	106	180	79	57	< 1	6
Savannah	< 1	29	70	97	155	113	111	< 1	63
Scottsdale	0	10	167	186	125	54	37	< 1	23
Seattle	n/a	38	3	57	121	187	157	8	8
Sioux Falls	n/a	n/a	n/a	95	136	134	n/a	n/a	n/a
Springfield	12	102	42	113	119	133	109	14	55
Stamford	n/a	n/a	7	80	146	139	118	17	22
Tampa	n/a	n/a	85	81	204	80	107	< 1	87
Thousand Oaks	0	< 1	5	131	125	109	34	0	1
Tucson	0	18	140	177	119	69	54	2	42
Tulsa	6	78	74	117	141	107	88	8	50
Virginia Beach	< 1	53	33	89	149	127	115	5	38
Washington	2	71	34	84	144	137	112	9	30
Wichita	13	110	63	117	132	116	87	13	54

Note: Figures are average number of days per year; (1) Data is for Atlanta, which is located 65 miles west of Athens; (2) Data is for Denver, which is located 60 miles south of Fort Collins; (3) Data is for Miami, which is located 22 miles south of Fort Lauderdale
Source: National Climatic Data Center, International Station Meteorological Climate Summary, 9/96

Watershed Health

City	Watershed	Index of Watershed Indicators Score (IWI definition)
Albuquerque	Rio Grande-Albuquerque	3 (less serious problems - low vulnerability)
Alexandria	Middle Potomac-Anacostia-Occoquan	4 (less serious problems - high vulnerability)
Anchorage	Anchorage	n/a (insufficient data)
Ann Arbor	Huron	5 (more serious problems - low vulnerability)
Athens	Upper Oconee	n/a (insufficient data)
Atlanta	Upper Ocmulgee	3 (less serious problems - low vulnerability)
Austin	Austin-Travis Lakes	3 (less serious problems - low vulnerability)
Baltimore	Gunpowder-Patapsco	4 (less serious problems - high vulnerability)
Baton Rouge	Amite	6 (more serious problems - high vulnerability)
Bellevue	Puget Sound	5 (more serious problems - low vulnerability)
Birmingham	Locust	3 (less serious problems - low vulnerability)
Boise City	Lower Boise	5 (more serious problems - low vulnerability)
Boston	Charles	6 (more serious problems - high vulnerability)
Buffalo	Buffalo-Eighteenmile	1 (better quality - low vulnerability)
Cary	Upper Neuse	n/a (insufficient data)
Cedar Rapids	Lower Cedar	1 (better quality - low vulnerability)
Charlotte	Lower Catawba	4 (less serious problems - high vulnerability)
Chattanooga	Middle Tennessee-Chickamauga	3 (less serious problems - low vulnerability)
Chicago	Chicago	5 (more serious problems - low vulnerability)
Cincinnati	Middle Ohio-Laughery	6 (more serious problems - high vulnerability)
Cleveland	Cuyahoga	5 (more serious problems - low vulnerability)
Colorado Springs	Fountain	1 (better quality - low vulnerability)
Columbia	Congaree	3 (less serious problems - low vulnerability)
Columbus	Upper Scioto	4 (less serious problems - high vulnerability)
Dallas	Upper Trinity	5 (more serious problems - low vulnerability)
Denver	Middle South Platte-Cherry Creek	1 (better quality - low vulnerability)
Des Moines	Middle Des Moines	3 (less serious problems - low vulnerability)
Durham	Upper Neuse	2 (better quality - high vulnerability)
Edison	Raritan	n/a (insufficient data)
El Paso	Rio Grande-Fort Quitman	1 (better quality - low vulnerability)
Eugene	Upper Willamette	3 (less serious problems - low vulnerability)
Fort Collins	Cache La Poudre	1 (better quality - low vulnerability)
Fort Lauderdale	Everglades	4 (less serious problems - high vulnerability)
Fort Wayne	St. Joseph	6 (more serious problems - high vulnerability)
Fort Worth	Lower West Fork Trinity	1 (better quality - low vulnerability)
Grand Rapids	Lower Grand	5 (more serious problems - low vulnerability)
Green Bay	Lower Fox	6 (more serious problems - high vulnerability)
Greensboro	Haw	2 (better quality - high vulnerability)
Honolulu	Oahu	3 (less serious problems - low vulnerability)
Houston	Buffalo-San Jacinto	5 (more serious problems - low vulnerability)
Huntsville	Wheeler Lake	6 (more serious problems - high vulnerability)
Indianapolis	Upper White	6 (more serious problems - high vulnerability)
Irvine	Newport Bay	5 (more serious problems - low vulnerability)
Jackson	Middle Pearl-Strong	4 (less serious problems - high vulnerability)
Jacksonville	Lower St. Johns	6 (more serious problems - high vulnerability)
Kansas City	Lower Missouri-Crooked	6 (more serious problems - high vulnerability)
Knoxville	Watts Bar Lake	5 (more serious problems - low vulnerability)
Las Vegas	Las Vegas Wash	3 (less serious problems - low vulnerability)
Lexington	Lower Kentucky	4 (less serious problems - high vulnerability)
Lincoln	Salt	3 (less serious problems - low vulnerability)
Los Angeles	Los Angeles	3 (less serious problems - low vulnerability)
Louisville	Silver-Little Kentucky	6 (more serious problems - high vulnerability)
Madison	Upper Rock	4 (less serious problems - high vulnerability)
Manchester	Merrimack	6 (more serious problems - high vulnerability)
Memphis	Lower Mississippi-Memphis	1 (better quality - low vulnerability)
Miami	Everglades	4 (less serious problems - high vulnerability)

Table continued on next page.

City	Watershed	Index of Watershed Indicators Score (IWI definition)
Milwaukee	Milwaukee	5 (more serious problems - low vulnerability)
Minneapolis	Twin Cities	6 (more serious problems - high vulnerability)
Naperville	Des Plaines	5 (more serious problems - low vulnerability)
Nashville	Lower Cumberland-Sycamore	3 (less serious problems - low vulnerability)
New York	Lower Hudson	2 (better quality - high vulnerability)
Norfolk	Lynnhaven-Poquoson	3 (less serious problems - low vulnerability)
Oakland	San Francisco Bay	2 (better quality - high vulnerability)
Oklahoma City	Lower North Canadian	3 (less serious problems - low vulnerability)
Omaha	Big Papillion-Mosquito	1 (better quality - low vulnerability)
Orlando	Kissimmee	3 (less serious problems - low vulnerability)
Overland Park	Lower Missouri-Crooked	6 (more serious problems - high vulnerability)
Philadelphia	Schuylkill	6 (more serious problems - high vulnerability)
Phoenix	Lower Salt	2 (better quality - high vulnerability)
Pittsburgh	Lower Allegheny	3 (less serious problems - low vulnerability)
Plano	Upper Trinity	5 (more serious problems - low vulnerability)
Portland	Lower Willamette	5 (more serious problems - low vulnerability)
Providence	Narragansett	4 (less serious problems - high vulnerability)
Provo	Provo	3 (less serious problems - low vulnerability)
Raleigh	Upper Neuse	2 (better quality - high vulnerability)
Reno	Truckee	3 (less serious problems - low vulnerability)
Richmond	Middle James-Willis	n/a (insufficient data)
Rochester	Lower Genesee	3 (less serious problems - low vulnerability)
Sacramento	Lower Sacramento	3 (less serious problems - low vulnerability)
Saint Louis	Cahokia-Joachim	5 (more serious problems - low vulnerability)
Saint Paul	Twin Cities	6 (more serious problems - high vulnerability)
Saint Petersburg	Tampa	4 (less serious problems - high vulnerability)
Salt Lake City	Jordan	3 (less serious problems - low vulnerability)
San Antonio	Upper San Antonio	3 (less serious problems - low vulnerability)
San Diego	San Diego	2 (better quality - high vulnerability)
San Francisco	San Francisco Bay	2 (better quality - high vulnerability)
San Jose	Coyote	5 (more serious problems - low vulnerability)
Savannah	Lower Savannah	5 (more serious problems - low vulnerability)
Scottsdale	Lower Salt	2 (better quality - high vulnerability)
Seattle	Puget Sound	5 (more serious problems - low vulnerability)
Sioux Falls	Lower Big Sioux	5 (more serious problems - low vulnerability)
Springfield	James	1 (better quality - low vulnerability)
Stamford	Saugatuck	5 (more serious problems - low vulnerability)
Tampa	Hillsborough	6 (more serious problems - high vulnerability)
Thousand Oaks	Calleguas	n/a (insufficient data)
Tucson	Upper Santa Cruz	3 (less serious problems - low vulnerability)
Tulsa	Polecat-Snake	3 (less serious problems - low vulnerability)
Virginia Beach	Lynnhaven-Poquoson	3 (less serious problems - low vulnerability)
Washington	Middle Potomac-Anacostia-Occoquan	4 (less serious problems - high vulnerability)
Wichita	Little Arkansas	3 (less serious problems - low vulnerability)

Note: Watersheds are holding areas for the nation's drinking water supply. The Index of Watershed Indicators (IWI) score is based on seven condition and nine vulnerability indicators. The overall IWI score ranges from 1 (best health) to 6 (worst health).
Source: U.S. Environmental Protection Agency, Index of Watershed Indicators, October 26, 2001

Tap Water Characteristics

City	Tap Water
Albuquerque	Alkaline, hard and fluoridated
Alexandria	Slightly alkaline and medium soft
Anchorage	Neutral, hard and fluoridated
Ann Arbor	Alkaline, soft and fluoridated
Athens	Alkaline, very soft and fluoridated
Atlanta	Neutral, soft
Austin	Alkaline, soft and fluoridated
Baltimore	Alkaline, very soft and fluoridated
Baton Rouge	Neutral, very soft and not fluoridated
Bellevue	Soft
Birmingham	Alkaline, soft
Boise City	Alkaline, soft
Boston	The Metropolitan Water District (combined sources, Quabbin Reservoir and Wachusett Reservoir) supplies municipal Boston and the ABC City Zone. Water is soft and slightly acid.
Boulder	Neutral, very soft and fluoridated
Buffalo	Alkaline, hard and fluoridated
Cary	Not available
Cedar Rapids	Alkaline, hard and fluoridated
Charleston	Alkaline, very soft and fluoridated
Charlotte	Alkaline, very soft and fluoridated
Chattanooga	Slightly alkaline, moderately hard and fluoridated
Chicago	Alkaline (Lake Michigan) and fluoridated
Cincinnati	Alkaline, hard and fluoridated
Cleveland	Alkaline, hard and fluoridated
Colorado Springs	From watershed on Pikes Peak and Continental Divide. It's pure, filtered and fluoridated
Columbia	Alkaline, very soft and fluoridated
Columbus	Slightly alkaline, moderately hard
Dallas	Moderately hard and fluoridated
Denver	Alkaline, 53% of supply hard, 47% of supply soft; West Slope, fluoridated. East Slope, not fluoridated
Des Moines	Alkaline, soft and fluoridated
Durham	Alkaline, soft and fluoridated
Edison	Not available
El Paso	Soft and fluoridated
Eugene	Neutral, very soft
Fort Collins	Alkaline, very soft
Fort Lauderdale	Alkaline, very soft and fluoridated
Fort Wayne	Alkaline, soft and fluoridated
Fort Worth	Alkaline, hard and fluoridated
Grand Rapids	Alkaline, hard and fluoridated
Green Bay	From Lake Michigan. It's alkaline, hard and fluoridated
Greensboro	Alkaline, soft
Honolulu	Alkaline, soft and not fluoridated
Houston	Alkaline, hard
Huntsville	Neutral, hard and fluoridated
Indianapolis	Alkaline, hard and fluoridated. Three separate systems with separate sources and purification plants
Irvine	Not available
Jacksonville	Alkaline, very hard and naturally fluoridated
Kansas City	Neutral, soft and fluoridated
Knoxville	Alkaline, hard and fluoridated
Las Vegas	Alkaline, hard
Lexington	Alkaline, medium and fluoridated
Lincoln	Alkaline, hard and fluoridated
Los Angeles	Hardness ranges from 4.2-15.1 gpg. The alkalinity also varies, ranging from 5.4-8.6 gpg. The Owens River Aqueduct accounts for approximately 70% of the water supply and is slightly alkaline and moderately soft with 4.2 gpg total hardness.
Louisville	Fluoridated
Madison	Alkaline, hard and fluoridated

Table continued on next page.

City	Tap Water
Manchester	Slightly acid and very soft
Memphis	Neutral, hardness 46ppm and fluoridated
Miami	Alkaline, soft and fluoridated
Milwaukee	Alkaline, medium hard and fluoridated
Minneapolis	Alkaline, soft and fluoridated. Water is hard in the suburbs.
Naperville	Alkaline (Lake Michigan) and fluoridated
Nashville	Alkaline, soft
New York	There are three major sources: the Catskills & Delaware subsytems (neutral, soft, average pH 7.0) and Croton subsystem (alkaline, moderately hard, average pH 7.1). All three supplies are fluoridated and chlorinated.
Norfolk	Low alkalinity, slightly soft and fluoridated
Oklahoma City	Alkaline, soft and fluoridated
Omaha	Moderately alkaline, moderately soft, fluoridated
Orlando	Alkaline, hard and fluoridated
Overland Park	Neutral, soft and fluoridated
Philadelphia	Slightly acid, moderately hard (Schuykill River), moderately soft (Delaware River); fluoridated
Phoenix	Alkaline, approximately 11 grains of hardness per gallon and fluoridated
Pittsburgh	Alkaline, soft 9 months, hard 3 months (June, July, August); fluoridated
Plano	Alkaline, soft and fluoridated
Portland	Neutral, very soft and not fluoridated
Providence	Alkaline and very soft
Provo	Alkaline and hard
Raleigh	Neutral, soft and fluoridated
Reno	Alkaline, very soft and not fluoridated
Richmond	Alkaline, soft and fluoridated
Rochester	Neutral, soft
Sacramento	Varies, soft to hard and not fluoridated
Saint Louis	Alkaline, moderately hard and fluoridated
Saint Paul	Alkaline, soft and fluoridated
Saint Petersburg	Slightly alkaline, hard and not fluoridated
Salt Lake City	Alkaline, hard and not fluoridated
San Antonio	Not fluoridated and has moderate mineral content, chiefly sodium bicarbonate
San Diego	Hard and not fluoridated
San Francisco	Alkaline, very soft and fluoridated
San Jose	Alkaline, very hard and not fluoridated
Savannah	Alkaline, hard and fluoridated
Scottsdale	Alkaline and hard
Seattle	Alkaline, very soft
Sioux Falls	Alkaline, hard and fluoridated
Springfield	Alkaline, hard and fluoridated
Stamford	Slightly acid, moderately soft and fluoridated
Tampa	Alkaline, moderately hard and not fluoridated
Thousand Oaks	Not available
Tucson	Alkaline and very hard from South Side Reservoir No. 1 and alkaline, soft and not fluoridated from North Side Reservoir No. 3
Tulsa	Alkaline, soft and fluoridated
Virginia Beach	Low alkalinity, slightly soft and fluoridated
Washington	Slightly alkaline and medium soft
Wichita	Soft

Source: Editor & Publisher Market Guide 2005

Air Quality Index

Area (Days[1])	Percent of Days when Air Quality was...				AQI Statistics	
	Good	Moderate	Unhealthy for Sensitive Groups	Unhealthy	Maximum	Median
Albuquerque (365)	32.1	61.9	4.7	1.4	169	59
Alexandria (365)	48.2	45.8	6.0	0.0	140	51
Anchorage (302)	90.4	9.3	0.3	0.0	131	20
Ann Arbor (360)	41.9	51.7	6.4	0.0	149	54
Athens (364)	64.6	34.3	1.1	0.0	141	44
Atlanta (365)	40.0	54.5	4.9	0.5	174	55
Austin (365)	78.6	20.5	0.8	0.0	109	38
Baltimore (365)	42.5	50.7	5.8	1.1	172	54
Baton Rouge (365)	54.2	41.6	4.1	0.0	145	48
Bellevue (365)	67.9	30.1	1.9	0.0	144	40
Birmingham (365)	23.8	67.1	9.0	0.0	145	65
Boise City (365)	76.7	21.4	1.9	0.0	138	38
Boston (365)	57.5	39.2	3.3	0.0	147	47
Boulder (365)	88.8	11.2	0.0	0.0	100	38
Buffalo (365)	60.8	35.3	3.8	0.0	147	43
Cary (365)	52.3	45.5	2.2	0.0	135	48
Cedar Rapids (365)	69.3	29.6	1.1	0.0	119	40
Charleston (365)	63.6	34.8	1.6	0.0	120	44
Charlotte (365)	46.8	48.2	4.7	0.3	166	52
Chattanooga (365)	42.7	54.5	2.7	0.0	137	53
Chicago (365)	37.3	56.4	5.8	0.5	172	57
Cincinnati (365)	46.0	47.9	5.5	0.5	172	53
Cleveland (365)	44.7	48.5	6.3	0.5	185	54
Colorado Spgs. (365)	90.1	9.6	0.3	0.0	104	38
Columbia (365)	47.7	49.0	3.3	0.0	129	52
Columbus (365)	33.7	59.5	6.3	0.5	154	59
Dallas (365)	57.5	33.7	8.5	0.3	159	47
Denver (365)	54.0	44.7	1.4	0.0	116	49
Des Moines (365)	73.7	25.2	1.1	0.0	119	38
Durham (365)	52.3	45.5	2.2	0.0	135	48
Edison (365)	71.5	24.4	4.1	0.0	140	40
El Paso (365)	41.9	53.7	4.1	0.3	160	54
Eugene (365)	69.9	23.6	6.3	0.3	155	36
Fort Collins (365)	90.4	9.6	0.0	0.0	100	39
Fort Lauderdale (358)	90.8	9.2	0.0	0.0	95	31
Fort Wayne (365)	62.2	34.5	3.3	0.0	116	43
Fort Worth (365)	57.5	35.1	6.6	0.8	182	45
Grand Rapids (365)	23.3	65.2	10.1	1.4	172	67
Green Bay (364)	72.3	25.0	2.7	0.0	135	33
Greensboro (365)	44.4	53.2	2.5	0.0	124	54
Honolulu (365)	98.6	0.8	0.3	0.3	164	20
Houston (364)	38.2	49.2	10.7	1.9	197	56
Huntsville (365)	58.1	39.5	2.5	0.0	133	46
Indianapolis (365)	43.8	49.6	6.6	0.0	146	54
Irvine (365)	66.0	31.5	2.5	0.0	129	44
Jacksonville (365)	69.3	28.8	1.6	0.3	176	43
Kansas City (365)	44.4	49.3	5.8	0.5	177	53
Knoxville (365)	33.7	60.8	5.5	0.0	119	58
Las Vegas (365)	46.8	49.9	2.7	0.5	181	52
Lexington (365)	75.6	23.6	0.8	0.0	108	38
Lincoln (363)	93.4	6.6	0.0	0.0	91	26
Los Angeles (365)	32.9	45.8	17.0	4.4	207	62
Louisville (365)	9.0	80.3	10.4	0.3	152	72
Madison (260)	76.5	22.7	0.8	0.0	107	38

Table continued on next page.

Area (Days[1])	Percent of Days when Air Quality was...				AQI Statistics	
	Good	Moderate	Unhealthy for Sensitive Groups	Unhealthy	Maximum	Median
Manchester (365)	82.2	17.8	0.0	0.0	100	31
Memphis (365)	43.6	50.1	6.0	0.3	156	54
Miami (365)	77.3	22.7	0.0	0.0	77	41
Milwaukee (365)	25.5	66.6	7.4	0.5	164	62
Minneapolis (365)	62.5	35.9	1.4	0.3	155	44
Naperville (365)	37.3	56.4	5.8	0.5	172	57
Nashville (365)	48.5	47.7	3.8	0.0	140	52
New York (365)	42.5	52.3	4.7	0.5	192	54
Norfolk (365)	68.2	31.5	0.3	0.0	104	42
Oklahoma City (365)	75.1	23.8	1.1	0.0	124	41
Omaha (365)	55.9	43.6	0.5	0.0	123	47
Orlando (365)	76.2	22.2	1.6	0.0	138	39
Overland Park (365)	44.4	49.3	5.8	0.5	177	53
Philadelphia (365)	36.2	56.2	7.7	0.0	150	58
Phoenix (365)	21.6	68.5	9.9	0.0	140	67
Pittsburgh (365)	33.7	52.9	10.4	3.0	171	59
Plano (365)	57.5	33.7	8.5	0.3	159	47
Portland (365)	75.1	23.0	1.9	0.0	150	34
Providence (365)	71.0	26.6	2.5	0.0	127	38
Provo (365)	77.8	20.5	1.4	0.3	169	38
Raleigh (365)	52.3	45.5	2.2	0.0	135	48
Reno (365)	63.3	35.6	1.1	0.0	146	46
Richmond (365)	63.0	35.3	1.4	0.3	151	43
Rochester (365)	74.8	24.7	0.5	0.0	104	35
Sacramento (365)	22.2	62.7	12.1	3.0	182	61
Saint Louis (365)	12.9	72.3	14.0	0.8	164	72
Saint Paul (365)	62.5	35.9	1.4	0.3	155	44
Saint Petersburg (365)	64.7	34.0	1.4	0.0	118	45
Salt Lake City (365)	58.4	32.9	8.5	0.3	159	46
San Antonio (365)	77.3	21.6	1.1	0.0	116	40
San Diego (365)	53.4	44.1	2.5	0.0	111	49
San Francisco (365)	85.8	13.4	0.8	0.0	107	30
San Jose (365)	81.9	15.9	2.2	0.0	129	36
Savannah (365)	62.7	36.4	0.8	0.0	121	43
Scottsdale (365)	21.6	68.5	9.9	0.0	140	67
Seattle (365)	67.9	30.1	1.9	0.0	144	40
Sioux Falls (365)	91.0	9.0	0.0	0.0	79	31
Springfield (365)	83.8	16.2	0.0	0.0	97	34
Stamford (365)	83.8	12.9	3.0	0.3	164	31
Tampa (365)	64.7	34.0	1.4	0.0	118	45
Thousand Oaks (365)	54.2	42.2	3.6	0.0	140	49
Tucson (365)	75.6	24.1	0.3	0.0	106	44
Tulsa (365)	67.9	30.4	1.6	0.0	129	42
Virginia Beach (365)	68.2	31.5	0.3	0.0	104	42
Washington (365)	48.2	45.8	6.0	0.0	140	51
Wichita (365)	85.2	14.5	0.3	0.0	104	35

Note: The Air Quality Index (AQI) is an index for reporting daily air quality. EPA calculates the AQI for five major air pollutants regulated by the Clean Air Act: ground-level ozone, particle pollution (also known as particulate matter), carbon monoxide, sulfur dioxide, and nitrogen dioxide. The AQI runs from 0 to 500. The higher the AQI value, the greater the level of air pollution and the greater the health concern. There are six AQI categories: "Good" The AQI is between 0 and 50. Air quality is considered satisfactory; "Moderate" The AQI is between 51 and 100. Air quality is acceptable; "Unhealthy for Sensitive Groups" When AQI values are between 101 and 150, members of sensitive groups may experience health effects; "Unhealthy" When AQI values are between 151 and 200 everyone may begin to experience health effects; "Very Unhealthy" AQI values between 201 and 300 trigger a health alert; "Hazardous" AQI values over 300 trigger health warnings of emergency conditions; Figures cover the Metropolitan Statistical Area - see Appendix A for areas included; (1) Number of days with AQI data in 2005.
Source: U.S. Environmental Protection Agency, Air Quality Index Report, 2005

Air Quality Index Pollutants

Area (Days[1])	Percent of Days when AQI Pollutant was...					
	Carbon Monoxide	Nitrogen Dioxide	Ozone	Sulfur Dioxide	Particulate Matter 2.5	Particulate Matter 10
Albuquerque (365)	0.0	0.0	12.1	0.0	44.4	43.6
Alexandria (365)	0.5	0.0	39.7	0.0	58.1	1.6
Anchorage (302)	42.7	0.0	0.0	0.0	20.9	36.4
Ann Arbor (360)	0.0	0.0	8.3	0.0	91.7	0.0
Athens (364)	0.0	0.0	23.4	0.0	76.6	0.0
Atlanta (365)	0.0	0.0	23.0	0.0	76.7	0.3
Austin (365)	0.0	0.0	54.8	0.0	45.2	0.0
Baltimore (365)	0.0	0.0	19.5	0.0	80.3	0.3
Baton Rouge (365)	0.0	0.0	39.5	0.8	58.4	1.4
Bellevue (365)	0.3	0.0	9.9	0.0	89.6	0.3
Birmingham (365)	10.7	0.0	6.6	0.0	65.8	17.0
Boise City (365)	4.1	0.0	33.4	0.0	52.3	10.1
Boston (365)	0.0	0.0	25.5	0.8	73.4	0.3
Boulder (365)	0.8	0.0	81.6	0.0	17.3	0.3
Buffalo (365)	0.0	0.0	31.0	0.5	68.5	0.0
Cary (365)	0.0	0.0	29.3	0.0	70.7	0.0
Cedar Rapids (365)	0.0	0.0	34.0	6.0	60.0	0.0
Charleston (365)	0.0	0.0	20.8	0.0	78.9	0.3
Charlotte (365)	0.0	0.0	29.6	0.0	70.1	0.3
Chattanooga (365)	0.0	0.0	11.8	0.0	88.2	0.0
Chicago (365)	0.0	0.0	16.7	0.0	80.0	3.3
Cincinnati (365)	0.0	0.0	26.0	1.6	72.3	0.0
Cleveland (365)	0.8	0.0	27.1	6.6	53.4	12.1
Colorado Spgs. (365)	1.6	0.0	91.0	0.0	4.7	2.7
Columbia (365)	0.0	0.0	18.6	0.0	62.2	19.2
Columbus (365)	0.0	0.0	15.6	0.0	83.0	1.4
Dallas (365)	0.0	0.0	52.9	0.3	45.5	1.4
Denver (365)	0.0	0.0	45.5	0.0	34.8	19.7
Des Moines (365)	0.8	0.0	35.3	0.0	59.7	4.1
Durham (365)	0.0	0.0	29.3	0.0	70.7	0.0
Edison (365)	0.0	0.0	57.8	0.0	42.2	0.0
El Paso (365)	0.3	0.0	26.8	0.0	40.8	32.1
Eugene (365)	0.3	0.0	36.2	0.0	63.0	0.5
Fort Collins (365)	0.3	0.0	95.1	0.0	3.8	0.8
Fort Lauderdale (358)	1.1	0.0	42.7	0.0	55.0	1.1
Fort Wayne (365)	1.6	0.0	25.8	0.0	71.5	1.1
Fort Worth (365)	0.0	0.0	55.9	0.0	43.8	0.3
Grand Rapids (365)	0.0	0.0	8.2	0.0	91.8	0.0
Green Bay (364)	0.0	0.0	30.2	8.0	61.8	0.0
Greensboro (365)	0.0	0.0	14.2	0.5	85.2	0.0
Honolulu (365)	1.1	0.0	44.4	0.0	17.5	37.0
Houston (364)	0.0	0.0	36.5	0.0	55.2	8.2
Huntsville (365)	0.0	0.0	18.1	0.0	81.9	0.0
Indianapolis (365)	0.0	0.0	21.4	0.8	77.5	0.3
Irvine (365)	1.9	0.0	49.3	0.0	48.5	0.3
Jacksonville (365)	0.0	0.0	24.7	0.8	70.1	4.4
Kansas City (365)	0.0	0.0	29.0	2.7	67.1	1.1
Knoxville (365)	0.0	0.0	31.2	7.7	55.3	5.8
Las Vegas (365)	0.3	0.0	54.8	0.0	20.8	24.1
Lexington (365)	0.0	0.0	46.8	20.0	33.2	0.0
Lincoln (363)	28.9	0.0	50.7	0.0	20.4	0.0
Los Angeles (365)	1.6	0.0	51.5	0.0	45.2	1.6
Louisville (365)	0.0	0.0	7.1	0.0	92.6	0.3
Madison (260)	0.0	0.0	64.2	0.0	35.8	0.0

Area (Days[1])	Percent of Days when AQI Pollutant was...					
	Carbon Monoxide	Nitrogen Dioxide	Ozone	Sulfur Dioxide	Particulate Matter 2.5	Particulate Matter 10
Manchester (365)	1.1	0.0	34.8	2.7	60.3	1.1
Memphis (365)	0.0	0.0	27.7	1.1	70.4	0.8
Miami (365)	0.5	0.0	26.0	0.0	73.4	0.0
Milwaukee (365)	0.3	0.0	9.6	0.0	90.1	0.0
Minneapolis (365)	0.0	0.0	31.0	0.0	67.1	1.9
Naperville (365)	0.0	0.0	16.7	0.0	80.0	3.3
Nashville (365)	0.3	0.0	20.8	0.0	78.9	0.0
New York (365)	0.0	0.0	17.5	0.0	82.5	0.0
Norfolk (365)	0.8	0.0	34.0	2.2	63.0	0.0
Oklahoma City (365)	0.0	0.0	64.4	0.0	35.1	0.5
Omaha (365)	0.0	0.0	13.7	2.7	48.5	35.1
Orlando (365)	0.3	0.0	44.7	0.0	55.1	0.0
Overland Park (365)	0.0	0.0	29.0	2.7	67.1	1.1
Philadelphia (365)	0.0	0.0	29.6	0.3	69.0	1.1
Phoenix (365)	0.8	0.0	36.7	0.0	2.2	60.3
Pittsburgh (365)	0.0	0.0	17.5	5.5	73.7	3.3
Plano (365)	0.0	0.0	52.9	0.3	45.5	1.4
Portland (365)	1.4	0.0	32.1	0.0	65.8	0.8
Providence (365)	0.3	0.0	32.9	2.5	64.1	0.3
Provo (365)	6.8	0.0	36.2	0.0	43.6	13.4
Raleigh (365)	0.0	0.0	29.3	0.0	70.7	0.0
Reno (365)	0.3	0.0	48.2	0.0	5.5	46.0
Richmond (365)	0.8	0.0	34.5	2.2	62.5	0.0
Rochester (365)	0.0	0.0	34.0	0.0	66.0	0.0
Sacramento (365)	0.0	0.0	33.7	0.0	65.8	0.5
Saint Louis (365)	0.0	0.0	15.3	1.6	58.1	24.9
Saint Paul (365)	0.0	0.0	31.0	0.0	67.1	1.9
Saint Petersburg (365)	0.0	0.0	30.4	1.4	62.7	5.5
Salt Lake City (365)	5.2	0.0	33.2	0.0	46.3	15.3
San Antonio (365)	0.0	0.0	59.5	0.0	38.9	1.6
San Diego (365)	1.1	0.0	59.5	0.0	34.2	5.2
San Francisco (365)	0.3	0.0	54.0	0.0	45.8	0.0
San Jose (365)	0.0	0.0	65.8	0.0	33.2	1.1
Savannah (365)	0.0	0.0	15.6	2.5	80.5	1.4
Scottsdale (365)	0.8	0.0	36.7	0.0	2.2	60.3
Seattle (365)	0.3	0.0	9.9	0.0	89.6	0.3
Sioux Falls (365)	0.0	0.0	75.9	0.0	18.6	5.5
Springfield (365)	13.7	0.0	48.2	15.6	22.5	0.0
Stamford (365)	28.5	0.0	44.4	4.9	21.9	0.3
Tampa (365)	0.0	0.0	30.4	1.4	62.7	5.5
Thousand Oaks (365)	0.0	0.0	59.5	0.0	40.3	0.3
Tucson (365)	0.0	0.0	66.3	0.0	17.0	16.7
Tulsa (365)	0.0	0.0	56.4	1.1	41.9	0.5
Virginia Beach (365)	0.8	0.0	34.0	2.2	63.0	0.0
Washington (365)	0.5	0.0	39.7	0.0	58.1	1.6
Wichita (365)	2.2	0.0	60.5	0.0	16.4	20.8

Note: The Air Quality Index (AQI) is an index for reporting daily air quality. EPA calculates the AQI for five major air pollutants regulated by the Clean Air Act: ground-level ozone, particle pollution (also known as particulate matter), carbon monoxide, sulfur dioxide, and nitrogen dioxide. The AQI runs from 0 to 500. The higher the AQI value, the greater the level of air pollution and the greater the health concern; Figures cover the Metropolitan Statistical Area - see Appendix A for areas included; (1) Number of days with AQI data in 2005.
Source: U.S. Environmental Protection Agency, Air Quality Index Report, 2005

Number of Days with Air Quality Index Values Greater than 100

Area (# trend sites)	1998	1999	2000	2001	2002	2003	2004	2005
Albuquerque (18)	0	1	0	1	4	2	2	0
Alexandria (42)	46	42	22	28	34	13	10	19
Atlanta (19)	50	73	39	24	20	12	11	11
Austin (1)	5	8	6	0	5	3	2	1
Baltimore (20)	51	41	23	33	42	20	16	27
Baton Rouge (12)	14	17	29	5	5	15	11	12
Bellevue (9)	3	6	7	6	6	2	1	1
Birmingham (21)	23	51	49	36	17	10	13	31
Boston (10)	0	3	0	3	7	6	1	1
Buffalo (10)	13	8	5	13	22	8	0	9
Cary (6)	21	27	8	4	18	5	1	5
Charleston (12)	3	5	7	0	3	0	1	4
Charlotte (10)	47	34	22	14	27	4	5	12
Chicago (46)	10	19	13	33	23	10	9	23
Cincinnati (17)	13	18	15	15	31	10	4	14
Cleveland (27)	20	36	21	29	30	17	18	25
Columbus (7)	17	24	12	14	21	9	1	8
Dallas (7)	24	16	20	14	7	5	9	10
Denver (23)	7	3	2	8	7	16	0	1
Durham (6)	21	27	8	4	18	5	1	5
Edison (4)	21	23	9	14	21	9	6	12
El Paso (14)	6	5	3	5	10	6	1	2
Fort Lauderdale (13)	1	4	3	3	3	0	0	0
Fort Worth (7)	17	19	17	17	23	25	11	22
Grand Rapids (13)	19	23	7	18	24	12	4	21
Greensboro (10)	25	22	14	11	24	4	2	2
Honolulu (11)	0	2	2	2	2	2	2	3
Houston (22)	38	51	42	27	21	31	22	28
Indianapolis (26)	19	23	8	14	24	11	1	18
Irvine (8)	5	4	5	6	4	5	3	0
Jacksonville (14)	3	2	1	3	0	0	0	3
Kansas City (16)	14	3	10	6	7	11	0	10
Knoxville (18)	54	63	34	21	43	14	3	14
Las Vegas (9)	0	0	0	1	2	3	1	2
Los Angeles (52)	49	54	63	81	81	88	65	45
Louisville (17)	29	47	15	18	28	12	3	17
Memphis (13)	27	35	28	15	17	9	2	12
Miami (15)	8	7	2	1	1	1	3	1
Milwaukee (17)	10	18	5	21	11	9	6	17
Minneapolis (17)	1	0	4	6	1	1	0	2
Naperville (46)	10	19	13	33	23	10	9	23
Nashville (17)	30	36	19	7	16	7	1	9
New York (15)	14	22	19	21	26	14	6	15
Norfolk (12)	15	17	5	7	15	4	2	1
Oklahoma City (10)	7	4	7	2	3	3	0	2
Omaha (13)	5	5	2	2	0	2	1	1
Orlando (14)	11	4	3	4	1	0	0	5
Overland Park (16)	14	3	10	6	7	11	0	10
Philadelphia (43)	37	32	21	35	35	20	14	26
Phoenix (25)	14	9	11	7	8	8	1	4
Pittsburgh (44)	39	40	32	55	50	37	39	48
Plano (7)	24	16	20	14	7	5	9	10
Portland (14)	3	5	7	3	6	0	3	4
Providence (6)	0	3	0	1	3	3	0	1
Raleigh (6)	21	27	8	4	18	5	1	5
Richmond (10)	22	21	5	12	21	3	1	6

Area (# trend sites)	1998	1999	2000	2001	2002	2003	2004	2005
Rochester (6)	4	9	1	5	13	3	0	0
Sacramento (21)	27	56	41	46	57	35	26	39
Saint Louis (43)	23	31	20	20	34	13	2	29
Saint Paul (17)	1	0	4	6	1	1	0	2
Saint Petersburg (24)	11	10	8	4	0	5	0	4
Salt Lake City (13)	12	13	20	27	33	10	37	26
San Antonio (2)	6	9	0	0	17	4	4	3
San Diego (29)	32	33	31	30	20	20	16	7
San Francisco (11)	0	2	3	5	1	0	0	0
San Jose (5)	5	17	20	12	9	6	2	6
Scottsdale (25)	14	9	11	7	8	8	1	4
Seattle (9)	3	6	7	6	6	2	1	1
Tampa (24)	11	10	8	4	0	5	0	4
Thousand Oaks (16)	29	24	31	24	10	22	13	11
Tucson (20)	0	7	0	0	3	1	0	2
Tulsa (8)	7	13	10	6	5	7	0	4
Virginia Beach (12)	15	17	5	7	15	4	2	1
Washington (42)	46	42	22	28	34	13	10	19

Note: An AQI value greater than 100 indicates that air quality would have been in the unhealthful range on that day; (1) Metropolitan Statistical Area - see Appendix A for areas included; n/a not available.
Source: U.S. Environmental Protection Agency, Air Trends Fact Book 2005

Maximum Pollutant Concentrations

	Particulate Matter 10 (ug/m³)	Particulate Matter 2.5 (ug/m³)	Ozone 1-hour (ppm)	Carbon Monoxide (ppm)	Sulfur Dioxide (ppm)	Nitrogen Dioxide (ppm)	Lead (ug/m³)
Albuquerque	162	19	0.093	3	n/a	0.016	n/a
Alexandria	72	38	0.113	3	0.020	0.024	n/a
Anchorage	145	18	n/a	5	n/a	n/a	n/a
Ann Arbor	n/a	52	0.101	n/a	n/a	n/a	0.01
Athens	n/a	33	0.098	n/a	n/a	n/a	n/a
Atlanta	60	37	0.124	2	0.019	0.017	0.10
Austin	33	n/a	0.095	1	n/a	0.004	n/a
Baltimore	60	42	0.130	3	0.019	0.022	n/a
Baton Rouge	72	n/a	0.129	2	0.038	0.016	n/a
Bellevue	70	37	0.085	4	0.012	n/a	n/a
Birmingham	179	50	0.109	9	0.014	n/a	0.03
Boise City	94	44	0.099	3	n/a	n/a	n/a
Boston	58	37	0.115	2	0.040	0.023	0.02
Boulder	38	18	0.094	2	n/a	n/a	n/a
Buffalo	n/a	43	0.111	2	0.035	0.019	n/a
Cary	56	30	0.103	2	n/a	n/a	n/a
Cedar Rapids	51	35	0.083	1	0.042	n/a	n/a
Charleston	48	33	0.085	1	0.012	0.010	0.00
Charlotte	51	34	0.131	2	0.014	0.015	0.00
Chattanooga	45	37	0.103	n/a	n/a	n/a	n/a
Chicago	88	52	0.113	3	0.029	0.030	0.04
Cincinnati	59	51	0.115	2	0.036	0.021	n/a
Cleveland	115	51	0.129	3	0.077	0.022	0.15 (a)
Colorado Spgs.	74	17	0.098	3	n/a	n/a	0.09
Columbia	128	37	0.113	2	0.017	0.012	0.01
Columbus	85	45	0.106	2	0.028	n/a	0.01 (b)
Dallas	54	27	0.120	3	0.027	0.017	0.7 (c)
Denver	97	27	0.103	3	0.009	0.028	0.56
Des Moines	72	34	0.082	2	n/a	0.011	n/a
Durham	56	30	0.103	2	n/a	n/a	n/a
Edison	n/a	34	0.125	2	0.021	0.018	0.16 (h)
El Paso	208	41	0.125	5	0.008	0.017	0.02
Eugene	74	58	0.088	3	n/a	n/a	n/a
Fort Collins	46	16	0.102	2	n/a	n/a	n/a
Fort Lauderdale	59	n/a	0.089	3	0.009	0.008	n/a
Fort Wayne	92	38	0.095	2	n/a	n/a	n/a
Fort Worth	43	26	0.134	3	n/a	0.014	n/a
Grand Rapids	58	45	0.123	2	0.010	0.015	0.01
Green Bay	n/a	44	0.099	n/a	0.014	n/a	n/a
Greensboro	58	35	0.101	3	0.019	0.011	n/a
Honolulu	99	11	0.055	2	0.008	0.005	0.00
Houston	137	29	0.156	3	0.027	0.019	0.01
Huntsville	52	40	0.086	n/a	n/a	n/a	n/a
Indianapolis	58	46	0.101	2	0.035	0.015	0.03 (d)
Irvine	54	42	0.107	3	0.007	0.025	n/a
Jacksonville	204	27	0.092	2	0.035	0.013	n/a
Kansas City	77	35	0.130	3	0.059	0.018	n/a
Knoxville	96	34	0.103	n/a	0.089	n/a	0.01
Las Vegas	142	29	0.116	5	0.008	0.020	n/a
Lexington	47	36	0.095	n/a	0.014	0.012	n/a
Lincoln	n/a	28	0.067	3	n/a	n/a	n/a
Los Angeles	79	53	0.171	6	0.010	0.031	0.02
Louisville	72	46	0.115	3	0.031	0.017	n/a
Madison	n/a	40	0.086	n/a	n/a	n/a	0.01

	Particulate Matter 10 (ug/m³)	Particulate Matter 2.5 (ug/m³)	Ozone 1-hour (ppm)	Carbon Monoxide (ppm)	Sulfur Dioxide (ppm)	Nitrogen Dioxide (ppm)	Lead (ug/m³)
Manchester	47	27	0.089	2	0.021	0.011	n/a
Memphis	60	43	0.130	3	0.037	n/a	n/a
Miami	56	20	0.087	3	0.001	0.014	n/a
Milwaukee	69	42	0.129	5	0.012	0.017	n/a
Minneapolis	63	32	0.103	3	0.025	0.012	0.1 (e)
Naperville	88	52	0.113	3	0.029	0.030	0.04
Nashville	56	41	0.101	3	0.013	0.018	n/a
New York	n/a	40	0.123	2	0.042	0.037	0.03
Norfolk	37	30	0.094	2	0.013	n/a	n/a
Oklahoma City	48	30	0.109	2	0.004	0.012	n/a
Omaha	123	30	0.079	3	0.049	n/a	n/a
Orlando	58	26	0.114	3	0.003	0.009	n/a
Overland Park	77	35	0.130	3	0.059	0.018	n/a
Philadelphia	78	40	0.128	3	0.029	0.026	0.04
Phoenix	200	41	0.115	5	0.007	0.032	n/a
Pittsburgh	142	70	0.106	2	0.067	0.022	0.15
Plano	54	27	0.120	3	0.027	0.017	0.7 (c)
Portland	54	26	0.091	5	0.006	n/a	n/a
Providence	54	32	0.112	3	0.023	0.017	n/a
Provo	77	37	0.114	3	n/a	0.021	n/a
Raleigh	56	30	0.103	2	n/a	n/a	n/a
Reno	142	41	0.081	3	n/a	n/a	n/a
Richmond	n/a	32	0.107	2	0.016	0.016	n/a
Rochester	n/a	n/a	0.090	2	0.014	n/a	n/a
Sacramento	67	49	0.129	4	0.002	0.016	n/a
St. Louis	196	45	0.127	3	0.068	0.017	1.93 (f)
St. Paul	63	32	0.103	3	0.025	0.012	0.1 (e)
St. Petersburg	78	26	0.110	3	0.033	0.008	1.12 (g)
Salt Lake City	123	44	0.121	5	0.012	0.024	0.08
San Antonio	72	n/a	0.107	3	n/a	0.017	n/a
San Diego	154	30	0.106	4	0.013	0.024	n/a
San Francisco	70	33	0.075	3	0.006	0.016	n/a
San Jose	67	40	0.104	3	n/a	0.019	n/a
Savannah	62	31	0.083	n/a	0.040	n/a	0.00
Scottsdale	200	41	0.115	5	0.007	0.032	n/a
Seattle	70	37	0.085	4	0.012	n/a	n/a
Sioux Falls	48	26	0.076	n/a	0.006	0.006	n/a
Springfield	44	34	0.091	3	0.029	0.012	n/a
Stamford	36	35	0.124	3	0.019	0.015	n/a
Tampa	78	26	0.110	3	0.033	0.008	1.12 (g)
Thousand Oaks	49	26	0.112	n/a	n/a	0.015	n/a
Tucson	88	14	0.091	2	0.003	0.015	n/a
Tulsa	59	35	0.114	1	0.029	0.011	n/a
Virginia Beach	37	30	0.094	2	0.013	n/a	n/a
Washington	72	38	0.113	3	0.020	0.024	n/a
Wichita	55	31	0.084	5	n/a	0.011	n/a
NAAQS[2]	150	65	0.125	9	0.140	0.053	1.50

Note: (1) Metropolitan Statistical Area - see Appendix A for areas included; (2) National Ambient Air Quality Standard; n/a not available; (a) Localized impact from an industrial source in Cleveland. Concentration from highest nonpoint source site is 0.04 ug/m³ in Cleveland (b) Localized impact from an industrial source in Columbus (c) Localized impact from an industrial source in Dallas. Concentration from highest nonpoint source site is 0.21 ug/m³ in Collin County (d) Localized impact from an industrial source in Indianapolis (e) Localized impact from an industrial source in Eagan, MN. Concentration from highest nonpoint source site is 0.02 ug/m³ in Minneapolis (f) Localized impact from an industrial source in Herculaneum, MO. Concentration from highest nonpoint source site is 1.12 ug/m³ in St. Clair County (g) Localized impact from an industrial source in Tampa. Concentration from highest nonpoint source site in metro area is 0.01 ug/m³ in Pinellas County; (h) Localized impact from an industrial source in New Brunswick NJ; ppm = parts per million; ug/m³ = micrograms per cubic meter
Source: U.S. Environmental Protection Agency, Air Trends Fact Book 2005